REA's Test Prep Books Are The Best!

(a sample of the <u>hundreds of letters</u> REA receives each year)

" Using this book with the companion book, *The Best Test Preparation for the CLEP General Exams*, saved me from sitting in the classroom for a whole semester. Provides sample tests, study tips — everything you need to be successful. "

Student, Port Orchard, WA

" My students report your chapters of review as the most valuable single resource they used for review and preparation. "

Teacher, American Fork, UT

" Your book was such a better value and was so much more complete than anything your competition has produced (and I have them all!) "

Teacher, Virginia Beach, VA

" Compared to the other books that my fellow students had, your book was the most useful in helping me get a great score. "

Student, North Hollywood, CA

" Your book was responsible for my success on the exam, which helped me get into the college of my choice... I will look for REA the next time I need help. "

Student, Chesterfield, MO

" Just a short note to say thanks for the great support your book gave me in helping me pass the test... I'm on my way to a B.S. degree because of you! "

Student, Orlando, FL

(more on next page)

(continued from front page)

" I just wanted to thank you for helping me get a great score
on the AP U.S. History exam... Thank you for making great test preps! "

Student, Los Angeles, CA

" Your Fundamentals of Engineering Exam book was the absolute best
preparation I could have had for the exam, and it is one of the major
reasons I did so well and passed the FE on my first try. "

Student, Sweetwater, TN

" I used your book to prepare for the test and found that the advice and the
sample tests were highly relevant... Without using any other material, I earned
very high scores and will be going to the graduate school of my choice. "

Student, New Orleans, LA

" What I found in your book was a wealth of information sufficient to shore up
my basic skills in math and verbal... The section on analytical ability was
excellent. The practice tests were challenging and the answer explanations most
helpful. It certainly is the Best Test Prep for the GRE! "

Student, Pullman, WA

" I really appreciate the help from your excellent book. Please keep up
the great work. "

Student, Albuquerque, NM

" I am writing to thank you for your test preparation... your book helped me
immeasurably and I have nothing but praise for your GRE preparation."

Student, Benton Harbor, MI

(more on back page)

The Best REVIEW for the CLEP
GENERAL EXAMS

Jane Adas, Ph.D.
Lecturer
Rutgers University, New Brunswick, NJ

Michael V. Angrosino, Ph.D.
Professor of Anthropology
University of South Florida, Tampa, FL

Jennifer Carpignano
Performing Arts Consultant
Scotch Plains, NJ

Anita C. Danker, M.A., M.Ed.
Social Studies Instructor
Hopkinton Jr./Sr. High School, Hopkinton, MA

Anita Price Davis, Ed.D.
Chair, Education Department
Converse College, Spartanburg, SC

Robyn A. Goldstein Fuchs
Adjunct Assistant Professor
New York University, New York, NY

Linda Leal, Ph.D.
Associate Professor of Psychology
Eastern Illinois University, Charleston, IL

Elizabeth M. Powell, M.S.
Science Writer
Edison, NJ

Robert S. Rycroft, Ph.D.
Chair, Economics Department
Mary Washington College, Fredericksburg, VA

Michael Sporer
Meteorologist
Edison, NJ

Gregory Suriano, M.A.
Art History Consultant
Union, NJ

Michael Wagner
Mathematics Consultant
Boonton, NJ

Research & Education Association
61 Ethel Road West
Piscataway, New Jersey 08854

The Best Review for the
CLEP GENERAL EXAMINATIONS

Library of Congress Catalog Card Number 98-65433

International Standard Book Number 0-87891-900-7

Research & Education Association
61 Ethel Road West
Piscataway, New Jersey 08854

REA supports the effort to conserve and
protect environmental resources by
printing on recycled papers.

ABOUT RESEARCH & EDUCATION ASSOCIATION

Research & Education Association (REA) is an organization of educators, scientists, and engineers specializing in various academic fields. Founded in 1959 with the purpose of disseminating the most recently developed scientific information to groups in industry, government, high schools, and universities, REA has since become a successful and highly respected publisher of study aids, test preps, handbooks, and reference works.

REA's Test Preparation series includes study guides for all academic levels in almost all disciplines. Research & Education Association publishes test preps for students who have not yet completed high school, as well as high school students preparing to enter college. Students from countries around the world seeking to attend college in the United States will find the assistance they need in REA's publications. For college students seeking advanced degrees, REA publishes test preps for many major graduate school admission examinations in a wide variety of disciplines, including engineering, law, and medicine. Students at every level, in every field, with every ambition can find what they are looking for among REA's publications.

While most test preparation books present practice tests that bear little resemblance to the actual exams, REA's series presents tests that accurately depict the official exams in both degree of difficulty and types of questions. REA's practice tests are always based upon the most recently administered exams, and include every type of question that can be expected on the actual exams.

REA's publications and educational materials are highly regarded and continually receive an unprecedented amount of praise from professionals, instructors, librarians, parents, and students. Our authors are as diverse as the fields represented in the books we publish. They are well-known in their respective disciplines and serve on the faculties of prestigious high schools, colleges, and universities throughout the United States and Canada.

ACKNOWLEDGMENTS

In addition to our authors, we would like to thank Dr. Max Fogiel, President, for his overall guidance, which brought this book to completion; Larry B. Kling, Quality Control Manager of Books in Print, for directing production of this revised edition; Nicole Mimnaugh, New Book Development Manager, for coordinating development of the book; Kristin Massaro, Editorial Assistant, for assisting with revisions; Eric Boime, Amanda Goble, Gary Land, Ph.D., and Miriam Perkoff, M.M. (in Performance), for their editorial contributions; Wende Solano for typesetting the first edition, Michael Cote and Lynda Polk for composing revisions; and Jeff LoBalbo, Senior Graphic Designer, for designing the cover.

CONTENTS

Chapter 4

Chapter 5

Chapter 6

CLEP GENERAL INDEPENDENT STUDY SCHEDULE

This study schedule will help you become thoroughly prepared for the CLEP General Examinations. It is intended to enable you to chart your progress in preparation for one General Exam at a time. Ideally, it should be used in conjunction with REA's *The Best Test Preparation for the CLEP General Examinations*, which is sold separately. While our study schedule is designed for a six-week study cycle, it can be shortened by compressing each two-week period into one. Be sure to set aside enough time—at least two hours a day—to study.

Week	Activity
1–2	Read and study Chapter 1, which will introduce you to the CLEP General Exams. Then take Practice Test 1 of the exam of your choice in REA's *The Best Test Preparation for the CLEP General Examinations* to determine your strengths and weaknesses. Score each section by using the score chart found in Chapter 1 of the *Test Preparation* book. You can then determine the areas in which you need to strengthen your skills.
3–4	Carefully read and study the subject review in this book that corresponds to the test for which you are preparing.
5	Take Practice Test 2 in the *Test Preparation* book. After scoring your exam, carefully review the detailed explanations for all the items you answered incorrectly. If there are any types of questions—or particular subjects—that seem difficult, review those areas by re-reading the appropriate section of this book.
6	Take Practice Test 3 in the *Test Preparation* book, and after scoring your exam, carefully review all incorrect answer explanations. If there are any types of questions—or particular subjects—that seem difficult, review those areas by re-reading the appropriate section of this book.

Repeat these steps for each General Exam for which you are preparing. Good luck on the CLEP General Examinations!

CHAPTER 1

ABOUT THE CLEP GENERAL EXAMINATIONS

Chapter 1

ABOUT THE CLEP GENERAL EXAMINATIONS

ABOUT THIS BOOK

This book provides you with an accurate and complete review for the five CLEP General Examinations. Inside you will find reviews for each of the following subjects: English Composition, Humanities, Mathematics, Natural Sciences, and Social Sciences and History—all based on the official CLEP exams. You will also find drill questions that will help you prepare for the actual exam. For each drill, you will find an answer key with detailed explanations designed to help you better understand the test material.

ABOUT THE EXAMS
WHO TAKES THE CLEP GENERAL EXAMINATIONS AND WHAT ARE THEY USED FOR?

CLEP (College-Level Examination Program) examinations are usually taken by people who have acquired knowledge outside the classroom and wish to bypass certain college courses and earn college credit. The CLEP Program is designed to reward students for learning—no matter where or how that knowledge was acquired. The CLEP is the most widely accepted credit-by-examination program in the country.

Although most CLEP examinees are adults returning to college, many graduating high school seniors, enrolled college students, and international students also take the exams to earn college credit or to demonstrate their ability to perform at the college level. There are no prerequisites, such as age or educational status, for taking CLEP examinations. However, you must meet any specific requirements of the particular institution from which you wish to receive CLEP credit.

There are two categories of CLEP examinations:

1. **CLEP General Examinations**, which are five separate tests that cover material usually taken as requirements during the first two years of college. CLEP General Examinations are available for English Composition (with or without essay), Humanities, Mathematics, Natural Sciences, and Social Sciences and History.

2. **CLEP Subject Examinations**, which include material usually covered in an undergraduate course with a similar title.

WHO ADMINISTERS THE EXAMS?

The CLEP is developed by the College Board, administered by the Educational Testing Service (ETS), and involves the assistance of educators throughout the country. The test development process is designed and implemented to ensure that the content and difficulty level of the tests are appropriate.

WHEN AND WHERE ARE THE EXAMS GIVEN?

The CLEP General Examinations are administered each month throughout the year at more than 1,200 test centers in the United States and can be arranged for candidates abroad on request. To find out the test center nearest you and to register for the exam, you must obtain a copy of the free booklets *CLEP Colleges* and *CLEP Information for Candidates and Registration Form*, which are available at most colleges where CLEP credit is granted, or by contacting:

CLEP
P.O. Box 6601
Princeton, NJ 08541-6601
Phone: (609) 771-7865
Website: www.collegeboard.org

HOW TO USE THIS BOOK
WHAT DO I STUDY FIRST?

Read over this introduction and the suggestions for test-taking. Choose the review(s) that correspond with the exam(s) you are taking. Use the drill questions provided throughout the reviews to determine your area(s) of weakness, and then go back and focus your study on those specific problems. Studying the subject reviews thoroughly will reinforce the basic skills you will need to do well on the exam. This book produces the best results when used in conjunction with REA's *The Best Test Preparation for the CLEP General Examinations* (sold separately), which provides every type of question that you can expect to appear on the exam.

To best utilize your study time, follow our Independent Study Schedule in the front of this book. This schedule is designed to guide you through one of the CLEP General Examinations at a time. You should repeat the schedule for each exam you are taking. The schedule is based on a six-week program, but can be condensed to three weeks if necessary by collapsing each two-week period into one.

WHEN SHOULD I START STUDYING?

It is never too early to start studying for the CLEP General Examinations. The earlier you begin, the more time you will have to sharpen your skills. Do not procrastinate! Cramming is *not* an effective way to study, since it does not allow you the time needed to learn the test material. The sooner you learn the format of the exam, the more time you will have to familiarize yourself with it.

FORMAT OF THE CLEP GENERAL EXAMINATIONS

The five CLEP General Examinations cover material taught in classes most students take as requirements in the first two years of college.

There are two versions of the **English Composition** exam. The first version has 100 multiple-choice questions, each with five possible answer choices, to be answered in two separately timed 45-minute sections. The second version has one section with 55 multiple-choice questions, each with five possible answer choices, and a second section with one essay. The student has 45 minutes to complete each of these two sections.

The approximate breakdown of topics is as follows:

All-Multiple-Choice Version:

Section I (55%)

Sentence boundaries

Economy and clarity of expression

Concord/Agreement: subject-verb; verb tense; pronoun reference, shift, number

Active/passive voice

Diction and idiom

Syntax: parallelism, coordination, subordination, dangling modifiers

Sentence variety

Types of Questions in Section I:

Identifying Sentence Errors — This type of question requires the examinee to identify wording that violates the standard rules of grammar.

Improving Sentences — This type of question requires the examinee to choose the phrase, clause, or sentence that best conveys the intended meaning of a sentence.

Revising Work in Progress — This type of question asks the examinee to identify ways to improve an early draft of an essay.

Section II (45%)

Main idea, thesis

Organization of ideas in paragraph or essay

Relevance of evidence, sufficiency of detail, levels of specificity

Audience and purpose (effect on style, tone, language, or argument)

Logic of argument (inductive, deductive reasoning)

Coherence within and between paragraphs

Rhetorical emphasis, effect

Sustaining tense or point of view

Sentence joining, sentence variety

Types of Questions in Section II:

Identifying Sentence Errors — This type of question requires the examinee to identify wording that violates the standard rules of grammar.

Restructuring Sentences — This type of question asks the examinee to reword a given sentence in order to change emphasis or improve clarity. The correct answer must be chosen from five options of the phrase that will likely appear in the new sentence.

Revising Work in Progress — This type of question asks the examinee to identify ways to improve an early draft of an essay.

Analyzing Writing — This type of question requires the examinee to answer questions about each passage and about the strategies used by the author of each passage.

Multiple-Choice-with-Essay Version:

Section I (50%)

Contains all the subjects listed in the all-multiple-choice version

Types of Questions in Section I:

Identifying Sentence Errors — This type of question asks the examinee to identify wording that violates the standard rules of grammar.

Improving Sentences — This type of question requires the examinee to choose the phrase, clause, or sentence that best conveys the intended meaning of a sentence.

Revising Work in Progress — This type of question asks the examinee to identify ways to improve an early draft of an essay.

Section II (50%)

The Essay: The examinee is expected to present a point of view in response to a topic and to support it with a logical argument and appropriate evidence.

In the **Humanities** exam there are 150 multiple-choice questions, each with five possible answer choices, to be answered in two separately timed 45-minute sections.

The approximate breakdown of topics is as follows:

Fine Arts (50%)

25%   Visual arts (painting, sculpture, etc.)

15%	Music
5%	Performing arts (film, dance, etc.)
5%	Architecture

Literature (50%)

5-10%	Drama
15-20%	Poetry
10-15%	Fiction
5-10%	Nonfiction
5%	Philosophy

In the **Mathematics** exam there are approximately 65 multiple-choice questions, each with five possible answer choices, to be answered in two separately timed 45-minute sections.

The approximate breakdown of topics is as follows:

10%	Sets
10%	Logic
30%	Real Number Systems
20%	Functions and Their Graphs
15%	Probability and Statistics
15%	Miscellaneous Topics

In the **Natural Sciences** exam there are 120 multiple-choice questions, each with five possible answer choices, to be answered in two separately timed 45-minute sections.

The approximate breakdown of topics is as follows:

Biological Science (50%)

10%	Origin and evolution of life
10%	Cell organization, cell division, chemical nature of the gene, bioenergetics, biosynthesis
20%	Structure, function, and development in organisms; patterns of heredity

| 10% | Concepts of population biology with emphasis on ecology |

Physical Science (50%)

7%	Atomic structure and properties, elementary particles, nuclear reactions
10%	Chemical elements, compounds, and reactions; molecular structure and bonding
12%	Heat, thermodynamics, and states of matter; classical mechanics; relativity
4%	Electricity and magnetism, waves, light and sound
7%	The universe: galaxies, stars, the solar system
10%	The Earth: atmosphere, hydrosphere, structure, properties, surface features, geological processes, history

In the **Social Sciences and History** exam there are 130 multiple-choice questions, each with five possible answer choices, to be answered in two separately timed 45-minute sections.

The approximate breakdown of topics is as follows:

History (40%)

17%	United States history
15%	Western civilization
8%	World civilization

Social Sciences (60%)

13%	Government/Political Science
11%	Sociology
10%	Economics
10%	Psychology
10%	Geography
6%	Anthropology

ABOUT OUR REVIEWS

There are five reviews in this book, one for each of the CLEP General Examinations. The reviews are designed to further students' understanding of the test material. Each review contains a description of what to expect on the examination and a thorough review of the major topics found on the exams.

The English composition review is broken down into two areas—English language skills and writing skills. The humanities review is broken down into five areas—literature, visual arts and architecture, philosophy, music, and performing arts. The mathematics review is broken down into seven areas—arithmetic, algebra, geometry and trigonometry, sets and logic, real and complex numbers, functions, and probability and statistics. The natural sciences review is broken down into seven areas—biology, chemistry, physics, earth science, geology, astronomy, and meteorology. The social sciences review is broken down into eight areas—political science, sociology, economics, psychology, geography, anthropology, western and world civilization, and United States history.

SCORING THE CLEP GENERAL EXAMINATIONS

The CLEP General Examinations are scored on a scale of 200 to 800. This does not apply, however, to the English Composition with Essay Questions Exam. The essays on this exam are scored on a scale of 2 to 8. There is a drill question in the writing skills section of the English Composition review that asks you to write an essay on a given topic. To score your essay, we suggest you give it to two English teachers or professors to grade. Refer to the completed essays in the detailed explanations of answers section of the review for scoring criteria. The completed essays will show you what the judges will be looking for, and the essay score from the English teachers will help you judge your progress.

WHEN WILL I RECEIVE MY SCORE REPORT AND WHAT WILL IT LOOK LIKE?

Your score report will arrive about three weeks after you take the test. Your scores are reported only to you, unless you ask to have them sent elsewhere. If you want your scores reported to a college or other institution, you must fill in the correct code number on your answer sheet at the time you take the examination. Since your scores are kept on file for 20 years, you may also request transcripts from ETS at a later date.

STUDYING FOR THE CLEP GENERAL EXAMINATIONS

It is very important for you to choose the time and place for studying that works best for you. Some students may set aside a certain number of hours every morning, while others may choose to study at night before going to sleep. Other students may study during the day while waiting on a line, or even while eating lunch. Only you can determine when and where your study time will be most effective. But be consistent and use your time wisely. Work out a study routine and stick to it!

Set aside extra time for the more difficult subjects. You can determine what subject areas require the most study time. Look at your grades: those courses with the lowest grades probably need the most study. You will need some way to measure your preparedness, either with problems from books or with a review book that has sample test questions like the ones on the CLEP General Examinations. This book contains sample problems in each section which can be used before, during, or after you review the material to measure your understanding of the subject matter. For example, if you are a wizard in geometry, and you are taking the CLEP General Examination in Mathematics, select a few drill questions to see how well you can solve the problems. If you do well on these initial problems, then momentum has been established. You still may want to perform a cursory review of the material, since there is always something to learn.

If you do poorly on a section, do not develop a negative attitude—it only means you need to further review the material. You should carefully study the reviews that cover your areas of difficulty, as this will build your skills in those areas. A negative attitude could prove to be your biggest stumbling block. It is important that you get a good start and that you are positive as you review and study the material.

TEST-TAKING TIPS

Although you may not be familiar with standardized tests such as the CLEP General Examinations, there are many ways to acquaint yourself with this type of examination and help alleviate your test-taking anxieties. Listed below are ways to help you become accustomed to the CLEP, some of which may be applied to other standardized tests as well.

Use the process of elimination. Go through each answer for a question and eliminate as many of the answer choices as possible. By eliminating just two answer choices, you give yourself a better chance of getting the item correct, since there will only be three choices left from which to choose your answer.

Work quickly and steadily. You will have only 45 minutes to work on each section, so work quickly and steadily to avoid focusing on any one question too long. Taking the drills in this book will help you learn to budget your time.

Learn the directions and format for each section of the test. Familiarizing yourself with the directions and format of the exam will save you valuable time on the day of the actual test.

Be sure that the answer oval you are marking corresponds to the number of the question in the test booklet. Since the exam is graded by machine, marking one wrong answer can throw off your answer key and your score. Be extremely careful when filling in your answer sheet.

Should I guess? If you do not know the answer to a question, try to eliminate answers that you know are wrong and then pick the best answer from the ones that are left. However, if you do guess, guess wisely since you will be penalized for a wrong answer. You will not, however, be penalized for not answering a question. If you cannot eliminate any answers **do not** guess! But by eliminating three answer choices, you give yourself a fifty-fifty chance of answering correctly, since there will only be two answer choices left.

THE DAY OF THE EXAM
BEFORE THE EXAM

On the day of the test, you should wake up early (after a decent night's rest, it is hoped) and have a good breakfast. Make sure to dress comfortably, so that you are not distracted by being too hot or too cold while taking the test. Also plan to arrive at the test center early. This will allow you to collect your thoughts and relax before the test, and will also spare you the anxiety that comes with being late. As an added incentive to make sure you arrive early, keep in mind that NO ONE WILL BE ALLOWED INTO THE TEST SESSION AFTER THE TEST HAS BEGUN.

Before you leave for the test center, make sure that you have your admission form and another form of identification, which must contain a recent photograph, your name, and signature (i.e., driver's license, student identification card, or current alien registration card). You will not be admitted to the test center if you do not have proper identification.

YOU MUST ALSO BRING SEVERAL SHARPENED NO. 2 PENCILS WITH ERASERS, AS NONE WILL BE PROVIDED AT THE TEST CENTER.

If you would like, you may wear a watch to the test center; it must be noiseless, however. No dictionaries, textbooks, notebooks, briefcases, or packages will be permitted, and drinking, smoking, and eating are prohibited.

DURING THE EXAM

Once you enter the test center, follow all of the rules and instructions given by the test supervisor. If you do not, you risk being dismissed from the test and having your scores canceled.

When all of the test materials have been passed out, the test supervisor will give you directions for filling out your answer sheet. You must fill out this sheet carefully since this information will be printed on your score report. Fill in your name exactly as it appears on your identification documents and admission ticket, unless otherwise instructed.

AFTER THE EXAM

Once your test materials have been collected, you will be dismissed. Then, go home and relax—you deserve it!

CHAPTER 2
ENGLISH COMPOSITION REVIEW

Chapter 2

ENGLISH COMPOSITION REVIEW

The following English Composition Review is divided into three sections, as follows:

    I.   **Description of the CLEP General Examination in English Composition**

    II.   **English Language Skills Review**

    III.   **Writing Skills Review**

By thoroughly studying this course review, you will be well-prepared for the material on the CLEP General Examination in English Composition.

I. DESCRIPTION OF THE CLEP GENERAL EXAMINATION IN ENGLISH COMPOSITION

The CLEP General Examination in English Composition measures the writing skills most first-year college students need. There are two versions of this examination. The first version consists of two sections of multiple-choice questions, each 45 minutes in length. Section I contains 55 questions, and Section II has 45 questions. The other version of the CLEP English Composition also consists of two 45-minute sections. Again, Section I contains 55 multiple-choice questions, but Section II consists of a single essay question. Both versions of the CLEP English Composition exam measure competence at the sentence level and in understanding context.

Testing on the Sentence Level   55% all-multiple-choice exam
30% multiple-choice and essay version

To measure skills at the sentence level (an understanding of logic, structure, and grammar), these tests use three main types of questions: 1) identifying sentence errors; 2) improving sentences; and 3) restructuring sentences.

Testing Skills in Context   45% all multiple-choice exam
20% multiple-choice and essay version

To measure writing skills in context, the examinations use two main types of questions: 1) revising work in progress and 2) analyzing writing.

TYPES OF QUESTIONS AND EXAMPLES
IDENTIFYING SENTENCE ERRORS

These sentences evaluate your ability to recognize correct grammar, usage, diction, and idioms. There will not be more than one error in any sentence, and some sentences will be correct. If there is an error, it is in a section that has been underlined and lettered. Assume that any section that is not underlined is correct.

● **EXAMPLE**

1. <u>Mrs. Jones and her</u> worked <u>diligently to complete</u> the <u>baling of the</u>
        A   **B**   **C**

    <u>hay</u> before the torrential rains began. <u>No Error</u>.
    C   **D**   **E**

The answer is (A); since a pronoun is part of the compound subject of the sentence, the nominative case (she) is correct—not the objective case (her). (B) is correct as it appears; since the adverb diligently occurs outside the infinitive to complete, there is no split infinitive. There is no error in (C); of the hay is a prepositional phrase used to modify the gerund baling. Since the adverbial clause before the torrential rains began is correct as written, (D) is not the proper choice. Since there is an error in the sentence, the examinee should not select answer choice (E); the sentence is not correct as it appears.

IMPROVING SENTENCES

These questions will ask you to evaluate the correctness and effectiveness of expression at the sentence level. To answer these questions correctly, you will need to consider every element of a well-constructed sentence.

Either a section of the sentence or the entire sentence has been underlined. Five versions of the underlined sentence or section of the sentence follow the original version. (A) repeats the original; the other four choices are different. You should select the choice that best maintains the meaning of the original sentence. Your answer should create a clear and precise sentence.

- **EXAMPLE**

1.   Keeping the boat afloat, the storm was exhausting to the only passenger of the small craft.

   (A)   , the storm was exhausting to the only passenger of the small craft.

   (B)   , the small craft was not easily kept afloat by the passenger.

   (C)   , the only passenger of the small craft was finding during the storm that he was becoming exhausted.

   (D)   , the small craft was difficult to keep afloat.

   (E)   , during the storm was exhausting to the only passenger of the small craft.

(E) is the best answer; it gives the main sense of the sentence in few words and is grammatically correct. (A) is not a good choice; it contains storm as the subject, which makes the introductory phrase a misplaced modifier or a dangling participle. (B) is likewise a poor choice since it, too, contains an introductory participle which does not modify that which it precedes.

(C) changes the meaning of the sentence somewhat; the passenger, for instance, might be a woman and not a <u>he</u>. (D) contains a misplaced modifier, or dangling participle.

REVISING WORK IN PROGRESS

These questions ask the student to read a selection from a draft of a student essay. The sentences are numbered for easy reference. Some of the sentences need changes. You must read each passage and answer the questions that follow it. Some questions will ask you to make changes at the sentence level; any such changes should be made following the rules of standard written English. Other questions will ask you about the passage as a whole. Still other questions will ask you to consider organization, purpose, and effectiveness of the passage. Select the best answer to each question.

● **EXAMPLE**

(1) Jim Trelease is the author of *The Read Aloud Handbook*. (2) It was on the *New York Times'* bestseller list for 17 weeks. (3) Trelease reports that one of the best kept secrets today is the importance of reading aloud to children. (4) Trelease says that even children who can read by themselves need to hear others read to them. (5) Trelease lists three items necessary for producing good readers; a book for each child, a bathroom with reading materials, and visiting a furniture store in order to buy a bedside lamp. (6) My aunt bought such a lamp for me. (7) Trelease advocates 15 minutes of reading per day.

1. Which of the following is the best way to revise sentences (1) and (2) so that the two sentences are combined?

    Jim Trelease is the author of *The Read Aloud Handbook*. It was on the *New York Times'* bestseller list for 17 weeks.

    (A) of *The Read Aloud Handbook*, it was on the

    (B) of *The Read Aloud Handbook*, which was on the

    (C) Since Jim Trelease is the author of *The Read Aloud Handbook*, it was

    (D) Because he was on the *New York Times'* bestseller list for 17 weeks, Jim Trelease

    (E) Being the author of *The Read Aloud Handbook*, Jim Trelease

The correct answer is (B) since the sentence is grammatically correct and expresses the meaning correctly. (A) is not a good choice since the given sentence is a run-on sentence. (C), (D), and (E) are not logically correct. The book was not on the bestseller list "Since" (C) or "Because" (D) Jim Trelease was the author; the rewritten sentences suggest this cause and effect. Even though (E) is grammatically correct, the meaning of the original sentence is changed somewhat; the author's main point is not that Jim Trelease was on the list because he was the author of the *Handbook*; the author's point is that Jim Trelease wrote a book which was on the list for 17 weeks and that the book has certain main points.

RESTRUCTURING SENTENCES

These questions test a writer's ability to choose effective revisions among the many options available in a sentence. Each question will present a sentence and ask you to revise it according to the directions that follow each sentence. Some directions will require you to change only part of the original sentence; others ask you to revise the entire sentence. You will be required to omit and add certain words to construct an acceptable revision, but you must keep the meaning of your revised sentence as close to the original sentence as possible. Your revision should follow the rules of standard written English and be clear and concise.

Look at the five answer choices presented for the appropriate word or phrase that you need for your revised sentence. If you have thought of a revised sentence and none of the answer choices reflect that revision, rewrite the original sentence again so that it does include wording presented in the answer choices.

● **EXAMPLE**

1. Past winners of the Great Transatlantic Derby, including Ray Robby, Steven Jones, and Grace Hasbro, were present for the award ceremony.

   Change <u>were present for</u> to <u>attend</u>.

   (A) Hasbro, were able to   (D) Hasbro, could

   (B) Hasbro, come to   (E) Hasbro, might have

   (C) Hasbro, were

The correct answer is (A); since these revisions are grammatically correct and keep the meaning of the original sentence. Answer choices (B) and

(C) are incorrect because they are not grammatically sound and do not make any sense. (D), while grammatically correct, changes the meaning of the original sentence; the original states that the past winners were present for the awards ceremony, it does not emphasize that the past winners were able to attend. Finally, choice (E) is also incorrect because it changes the meaning of the original sentence; the original states that the past winners were present at the ceremony, not that they did not attend but could have, as choice (E) implies.

ANALYZING WRITING

For this type of question there are several passages that consist of numbered sentences. Since these selections are parts of longer works, the passages may not provide a complete discussion of the topic presented. Several questions that test your awareness of the characteristics of good writing follow the paragraph(s).

● **EXAMPLE**

(1) A generation has now passed away since Wordsworth was laid with the family in the churchyard at Grasmere. (2) Perhaps it is hardly yet time to take a perfectly impartial measure of his value as a poet. (3) To do this is especially hard for those who are old enough to remember the last shot which the foe was sullenly firing in that long war of critics which began when he published his manifesto as Pretender, and which came to a pause rather than end when they flung up their caps with the rest at his final coronation.

1.   The function of sentence (1) is

   (A)   to establish the basis for the comparisons that will follow in the paragraph.

   (B)   to demonstrate the writer's authority on the subject he discusses in the paragraph.

   (C)   to describe the idea which the author contradicts for the rest of the paragraph.

   (D)   to provide the time, place, and subject for the rest of the paragraph.

   (E)   to show the author's mild distaste for Artists and Moralists.

(D) is the best answer; the first sentence gives the time (about a century ago), the general place (the churchyard at Grasmere), and the subject

(Wordsworth). The main subject of the sentence is not to give comparisons, so (A) is not a good choice. The most important function of the first sentence is not to demonstrate the writer's authority (B), although the writer does seem knowledgeable. Since the author does not contradict an idea for the rest of the paragraph, (C) is not the best answer. The writer does not seem to show a distaste for Artists and Moralists, so (E) is not the best choice.

THE ESSAY

For Section II of the Essay Version of the CLEP English Composition Exam, you have 45 minutes to prepare and write an essay on the topic presented. Take a few minutes to read the topic and organize your thoughts before starting to write. Be sure to express your thoughts clearly and in a manner that will be of interest to the reader. Be as specific as possible, and include supporting examples if appropriate. Your essay is scored on the quality of your writing, not the quantity. Note: *You must write on the topic assigned. An essay on any other topic is unacceptable.*

● EXAMPLE

When Thomas Jefferson wrote *The Declaration of Independence* he claimed that "we hold these truths to be self-evident, that all men are created equal, that they are endowed by their Creator with certain unalienable rights, that among these are life, liberty and the pursuit of happiness." Write an essay stating support of or opposition to the argument that Jefferson was describing all human beings when he wrote "all men are created equal." Be sure to use examples from Colonial life and philosophers who were contemporaries of Jefferson.

II. ENGLISH LANGUAGE SKILLS REVIEW

The requirements for informal spoken English are much more relaxed than the rigid rules for "standard written English." While slang, colloquialisms, and other informal expressions are acceptable and sometimes very appropriate in casual speech, they are inappropriate in academic and business writing. More often than not, writers, especially student writers, do not make a distinction between the two: they use the same words, grammar, and sentence structure from their everyday speech in their college papers, albeit unsuccessfully.

The CLEP General Examination in English Composition does not require you to know grammatical terms such as *gerund*, *subject complement*, or *dependent clause*, although general familiarity with such terms may be helpful to you in determining whether a sentence or part of a sentence is correct or incorrect. You should watch for errors in grammar, spelling, punctuation, capitalization, sentence structure, and word choice. Remember: this is a test of written language skills; therefore, your responses should be based on what you know to be correct for written work, not what you know to be appropriate for a casual conversation. For instance, in informal speech, you might say "Who are you going to choose?" But in formal academic writing, you would write "Whom are you going to choose?" Your choices, then, should be dictated by requirements for *written*, not *conversational* English.

WORD CHOICE SKILLS
CONNOTATIVE AND DENOTATIVE MEANINGS

The denotative meaning of a word is its *literal,* dictionary definition: what the word denotes or "means." The connotative meaning of a word is what the word connotes or "suggests"; it is a meaning apart from what the word literally means. A writer should choose a word based on the tone and context of the sentence; this ensures that a word bears the appropriate connotation while still conveying some exactness in denotation. For example, a gift might be described as "cheap," but the directness of this word has a negative connotation—something cheap is something of little or no value. The word "inexpensive" has a more positive connotation, though "cheap" is a synonym for "inexpensive." Questions of this type require you to make a decision regarding the appropriateness of words and phrases for the context of a sentence.

WORDINESS AND CONCISENESS

Effective writing is concise. Wordiness, on the other hand, decreases the clarity of expression by cluttering sentences with unnecessary words.

Wordiness questions test your ability to detect redundancies (unnecessary repetitions), circumlocution (failure to get to the point), and padding with loose synonyms. Wordiness questions require you to choose sentences that use as few words as possible to convey a message clearly, economically, and effectively.

Notice the difference in impact between the first and second sentences in the following pairs:

INCORRECT: The medical exam that he gave me was entirely complete.

CORRECT: The medical exam he gave me was complete.

INCORRECT: Larry asked his friend John, who was a good, old friend, if he would join him and go along with him to see the foreign film made in Japan.

CORRECT: Larry asked his good, old friend John if he would join him in seeing the Japanese film.

INCORRECT: I was absolutely, totally happy with the present that my parents gave to me at 7 a.m. on the morning of my birthday.

CORRECT: I was happy with the present my parents gave me on the morning of my birthday.

☞ Drill: Word Choice Skills

DIRECTIONS: Choose the correct option.

---

1. His <u>principal</u> reasons for resigning were his <u>principles</u> of right and wrong.

    (A) principal . . . principals   (C) principle . . . principles

    (B) principle . . . principals   (D) No change is necessary.

2. The book tells about Alzheimer's disease—how it <u>affects</u> the patient and what <u>effect</u> it has on the patient's family.

    (A) effects ... affect
    (C) effects ... effects

    (B) affects ... affect
    (D) No change is necessary.

3. The <u>amount</u> of homeless children we can help depends on the <u>number</u> of available shelters.

    (A) number ... number
    (C) number ... amount

    (B) amount ... amount
    (D) No change is necessary.

4. All students are <u>suppose to</u> pass the test before <u>achieving</u> upper-division status.

    (A) suppose to ... acheiving

    (B) suppose to ... being acheived

    (C) supposed to ... achieving

    (D) No change is necessary.

5. The reason he <u>succeeded</u> is <u>because</u> he worked hard.

    (A) succeeded ... that
    (C) succede ... because of

    (B) seceded ... that
    (D) No change is necessary.

DIRECTIONS: Select the sentence that clearly and effectively states the idea and has no structural errors.

---

6. (A) South of Richmond, the two roads converge together to form a single highway.

    (B) South of Richmond, the two roads converge together to form an interstate highway.

    (C) South of Richmond, the two roads converge to form an interstate highway.

    (D) South of Richmond, the two roads converge to form a single interstate highway.

7. (A) The student depended on his parents for financial support.

    (B) The student lacked the ways and means to pay for his room and board, so he depended on his parents for this kind of money and support.

    (C) The student lacked the ways and means or the wherewithal to support himself, so his parents provided him with the financial support he needed.

    (D) The student lacked the means to pay for his room and board, so he depended on his parents for financial support.

8. (A) Vincent van Gogh and Paul Gauguin were close personal friends and companions who enjoyed each other's company and frequently worked together on their artwork.

    (B) Vincent van Gogh and Paul Gauguin were friends who frequently painted together.

    (C) Vincent van Gogh was a close personal friend of Paul Gauguin's, and the two of them often worked together on their artwork because they enjoyed each other's company.

    (D) Vincent van Gogh, a close personal friend of Paul Gauguin's, often worked with him on their artwork.

9. (A) A college education often involves putting away childish thoughts, which are characteristic of youngsters, and concentrating on the future, which lies ahead.

    (B) A college education involves putting away childish thoughts, which are characteristic of youngsters, and concentrating on the future.

    (C) A college education involves putting away childish thoughts and concentrating on the future.

    (D) A college education involves putting away childish thoughts and concentrating on the future which lies ahead.

10. (A) I had the occasion to visit an Oriental pagoda while I was a tourist on vacation and visiting in Kyoto, Japan.

    (B) I visited a Japanese pagoda in Kyoto.

    (C) I had occasion to visit a pagoda when I was vacationing in Kyoto, Japan.

    (D) On my vacation, I visited a Japanese pagoda in Kyoto.

SENTENCE STRUCTURE SKILLS
PARALLELISM

Parallel structure is used to express matching ideas. It refers to the grammatical balance of a series of any of the following:

Phrases:

The squirrel ran *along the fence*, *up the tree*, and *into his burrow* with a mouthful of acorns.

Adjectives:

The job market is flooded with *very talented*, *highly motivated*, and *well-educated* young people.

Nouns:

You will need a *notebook*, *pencil*, and *dictionary* for the test.

Clauses:

The children were told to decide *which toy they would keep* and *which toy they would give away*.

Verbs:

The farmer *plowed*, *planted*, and *harvested* his corn in record time.

Verbals:

Reading, *writing*, and *calculating* are fundamental skills that all of us should possess.

Correlative conjunctions:

Either you will do your homework *or* you will fail.

Repetition of structural signals:

(such as articles, auxiliaries, prepositions, and conjunctions)

> INCORRECT: I have quit my job, enrolled in school, and am looking for a reliable baby-sitter.

> CORRECT: I *have quit* my job, *have enrolled* in school, and *am looking* for a reliable baby-sitter.

Note: Repetition of prepositions is considered formal and is not necessary.

> You can travel *by car, by plane, or by train;* it's all up to you.

OR

> You can travel *by car, plane, or train;* it's all up to you.

When a sentence contains items in a series, check for both punctuation and sentence balance. When you check for punctuation, make sure the commas are used correctly. When you check for parallelism, make sure that the conjunctions connect similar grammatical constructions, such as all adjectives or all clauses.

MISPLACED AND DANGLING MODIFIERS

A misplaced modifier is one that is in the wrong place in the sentence. Misplaced modifiers come in all forms—words, phrases, and clauses. Sentences containing misplaced modifiers are often very comical: *Mom made me eat the spinach instead of my brother.* Misplaced modifiers, like the one in this sentence, are usually too far away from the word or words they modify. This sentence should read: *Mom made me, instead of my brother, eat the spinach.*

Modifiers like *only*, *nearly*, and *almost* should be placed next to the word they modify and not in front of some other word, especially a verb, that they are not intended to modify.

A modifier is misplaced if it appears to modify the wrong part of the sentence or if we cannot be certain what part of the sentence the writer intended it to modify. To correct a misplaced modifier, move the modifier next to the word it describes.

> INCORRECT: She served hamburgers to the men on paper plates.

> CORRECT: She served hamburgers on paper plates to the men.

Split infinitives also result in misplaced modifiers. Infinitives consist of the marker *to* plus the plain form of the verb. The two parts of the infinitive make up a grammatical unit that should not be split. Splitting an infinitive is placing an adverb between the *to* and the verb.

> INCORRECT: The weather service expects temperatures to not rise.

> CORRECT: The weather service expects temperatures not to rise.

Sometimes a split infinitive may be natural and preferable, though it may still bother some readers.

> EX: Several U.S. industries expect *to* more than *triple* their use of robots within the next decade.

A squinting modifier is one that may refer to either a preceding or a following word, leaving the reader uncertain about what it is intended to modify. Correct a squinting modifier by moving it next to the word it is intended to modify.

> INCORRECT: Snipers who often fired on the soldiers escaped capture.
>
> CORRECT: Snipers who fired on the soldiers often escaped capture.
>
> OR Snipers who fired on the soldiers escaped capture often.

A dangling modifier is a modifier or verb in search of a subject: the modifying phrase (usually an *-ing* word group, an *-ed* or *-en* word group, or a *to + a verb* word group—participle phrase or infinitive phrase respectively) either appears to modify the wrong word or has nothing to modify. It is literally dangling at the beginning or the end of a sentence. The sentences often look and sound correct: *To be a student government officer, your grades must be above average.* (However, the verbal modifier has nothing to describe. Who is *to be a student government officer*? Your grades?) Questions of this type require you to determine whether a modifier has a headword or whether it is dangling at the beginning or the end of the sentence.

To correct a dangling modifier, reword the sentence by either: 1) changing the modifying phrase to a clause with a subject, or 2) changing the subject of the sentence to the word that should be modified. The following are examples of a dangling gerund, a dangling infinitive, and a dangling participle:

> INCORRECT: Shortly after leaving home, the accident occurred.
>
> Who is <u>leaving home</u>, the accident?
>
> CORRECT: Shortly after we left home, the accident occurred.

> INCORRECT: To get up on time, a great effort was needed.
>
> <u>To get up</u> needs a subject.
>
> CORRECT: To get up on time, I made a great effort.

FRAGMENTS

A fragment is an incomplete construction which may or may not have a subject and a verb. Specifically, a fragment is a group of words pretending to be a sentence. Not all fragments appear as separate sentences, however. Often, fragments are separated by semicolons.

INCORRECT: Traffic was stalled for ten miles on the freeway. Because repairs were being made on potholes.

CORRECT: Traffic was stalled for ten miles on the freeway because repairs were being made on potholes.

INCORRECT: It was a funny story; one that I had never heard before.

CORRECT: It was a funny story, one that I had never heard before.

RUN-ON/FUSED SENTENCES

A run-on/fused sentence is not necessarily a long sentence or a sentence that the reader considers too long; in fact, a run-on may be two short sentences: *Dry ice does not melt it evaporates.* A run-on results when the writer fuses or runs together two separate sentences without any correct mark of punctuation separating them.

INCORRECT: Knowing how to use a dictionary is no problem each dictionary has a section in the front of the book telling how to use it.

CORRECT: Knowing how to use a dictionary is no problem. Each dictionary has a section in the front of the book telling how to use it.

Even if one or both of the fused sentences contains internal punctuation, the sentence is still a run-on.

INCORRECT: Bob bought dress shoes, a suit, and a nice shirt he needed them for his sister's wedding.

CORRECT: Bob bought dress shoes, a suit, and a nice shirt. He needed them for his sister's wedding.

COMMA SPLICES

A comma splice is the unjustifiable use of only a comma to combine what really is two separate sentences.

INCORRECT: One common error in writing is incorrect spelling, the other is the occasional use of faulty diction.

CORRECT: One common error in writing is incorrect spelling; the other is the occasional use of faulty diction.

Both run-on sentences and comma splices may be corrected in one of the following ways:

RUN-ON: Neal won the award he had the highest score.

COMMA SPLICE: Neal won the award, he had the highest score.

Separate the sentences with a period:

Neal won the award. He had the highest score.

Separate the sentences with a comma and a coordinating conjunction *(and, but, or, nor, for, yet, so)*:

Neal won the award for he had the highest score.

Separate the sentences with a semicolon:

Neal won the award; he had the highest score.

Separate the sentences with a subordinating conjunction such as *although, because, since, if*:

Neal won the award because he had the highest score.

SUBORDINATION, COORDINATION, AND PREDICATION

Suppose, for the sake of clarity, you wanted to combine the information in these two sentences to create one statement:

I studied a foreign language. I found English quite easy.

How you decide to combine this information should be determined by the relationship you'd like to show between the two facts. *I studied a foreign language, and I found English quite easy* seems rather illogical. The **coordination** of the two ideas (connecting them with the coordinating conjunction *and*) is ineffective. Using **subordination** instead (connecting the sentences with a subordinating conjunction) clearly shows the degree of relative importance between the expressed ideas:

After I studied a foreign language, I found English quite easy.

When using a conjunction, be sure that the sentence parts you are joining are in agreement.

INCORRECT: She loved him dearly but not his dog.

CORRECT: She loved him dearly but she did not love his dog.

A common mistake that is made is to forget that each member of the pair must be followed by the same kind of construction.

> INCORRECT: They complimented them both for their bravery and they thanked them for their kindness.

> CORRECT: They both complimented them for their bravery and thanked them for their kindness.

While refers to time and should not be used as a substitute for *although, and,* or *but.*

> INCORRECT: While I'm usually interested in Fellini movies, I'd rather not go tonight.

> CORRECT: Although I'm usually interested in Fellini movies, I'd rather not go tonight.

Where refers to place and should not be used as a substitute for *that.*

> INCORRECT: We read in the paper where they are making great strides in DNA research.

> CORRECT: We read in the paper that they are making great strides in DNA research.

After words like *reason* and *explanation,* use *that,* not *because.*

> INCORRECT: His explanation for his tardiness was because his alarm did not go off.

> CORRECT: His explanation for his tardiness was that his alarm did not go off.

☞ Drill: Sentence Structure Skills

> **DIRECTIONS:** Choose the sentence that expresses the thought most clearly and that has no error in structure.

1.　(A)　Many gases are invisible, odorless, and they have no taste.

　　(B)　Many gases are invisible, odorless, and have no taste.

　　(C)　Many gases are invisible, odorless, and tasteless.

　　(D)　Many gases are invisible and odorless and have no taste.

2.　(A)　Everyone agreed that she had neither the voice or the skill to be a speaker.

(B) Everyone agreed that she had neither the voice nor the skill to be a speaker.

(C) Everyone agreed that she had either the voice nor the skill to be a speaker.

(D) Everyone agreed that she had not the voice nor the skill to be a speaker.

3. (A) The mayor will be remembered because he kept his campaign promises and because of his refusal to accept political favors.

(B) The mayor will be remembered because he kept his campaign promises and because he refused to accept political favors.

(C) The mayor will be remembered because of his refusal to accept political favors and he kept his campaign promises.

(D) The mayor will be remembered because of his refusal to accept political favors and that he kept his campaign promises.

4. (A) While taking a shower, the doorbell rang.

(B) While I was taking a shower, the doorbell rang.

(C) While taking a shower, someone rang the doorbell.

(D) The doorbell rang, while taking a shower.

5. (A) He swung the bat, while the runner stole second base.

(B) The runner stole second base while he swung the bat.

(C) While he was swinging the bat, the runner stole second base.

(D) The runner was stealing second base while he was swinging at the bat.

DIRECTIONS: Choose the correct option.

---

6. Nothing grows as well in Mississippi as <u>cotton. Cotton</u> being the state's principal crop.

(A) cotton, cotton   (C) cotton cotton

(B) cotton; cotton   (D) No change is necessary.

7. It was a heartwrenching <u>movie; one</u> that I had never seen before.

   (A) movie and   (C) movie. One

   (B) movie, one   (D) No change is necessary.

8. Traffic was stalled for three miles on the <u>bridge. Because</u> repairs were being made.

   (A) bridge because   (C) bridge, because

   (B) bridge; because   (D) No change is necessary.

9. The ability to write complete sentences comes with <u>practice writing</u> run-on sentences seems to occur naturally.

   (A) practice, writing   (C) practice and

   (B) practice. Writing   (D) No change is necessary.

10. Even though she had taken French classes, she could not understand native French <u>speakers they</u> all spoke too fast.

    (A) speakers, they   (C) speaking

    (B) speakers. They   (D) No change is necessary.

VERBS

VERB FORMS

This section covers the principal parts of some irregular verbs including troublesome verbs like *lie* and *lay*. The use of regular verbs like *look* and *receive* poses no real problem to most writers since the past and past participle forms end in *-ed*; it is the irregular forms which pose the most serious problems—for example, *seen*, *written*, and *begun*.

VERB TENSES

Tense sequence indicates a logical time sequence.

Use present tense

in statements of universal truth:

> I learned that the sun *is* ninety-million miles from the earth.

in statements about the contents of literature and other published works:

> In this book, Sandy *becomes* a nun and *writes* a book on psychology.

Use past tense

in statements concerning writing or publication of a book:

He *wrote* his first book in 1949, and it *was published* in 1952.

Use present perfect tense

for an action that began in the past but continues into the future:

I *have lived* here all my life.

Use past perfect tense

for an earlier action that is mentioned in a later action:

Cindy ate the apple that she *had picked*.

(First she picked it, then she ate it.)

Use future perfect tense

for an action that will have been completed at a specific future time:

By May, I *shall have* graduated.

Use a present participle

for action that occurs at the same time as the verb:

Speeding down the interstate, I saw a cop's flashing lights.

Use a perfect participle

for action that occurred before the main verb:

Having read the directions, I started the test.

Use the subjunctive mood

to express a wish or state a condition contrary to fact:

If it were not raining, we could have a picnic.

in *that* clauses after verbs like *request, recommend, suggest, ask, require*, and *insist*; and after such expressions as *it is important* and *it is necessary*:

It is necessary that all papers *be* submitted on time.

SUBJECT-VERB AGREEMENT

Agreement is the grammatical correspondence between the subject and the verb of a sentence: *I do, we do, they do, he, she, it does.*

Every English verb has five forms, two of which are the bare form (plural) and the *-s* form (singular). Simply put, singular verb forms end in *-s;* plural forms do not.

Study these rules governing subject-verb agreement:

A verb must agree with its subject, not with any additive phrase in the sentence such as a prepositional or verbal phrase. Ignore such phrases.

> Your *copy* of the rules *is* on the desk.

> Ms. Craig's *record* of community service and outstanding teaching *qualifies* her for promotion.

In an inverted sentence beginning with a prepositional phrase, the verb still agrees with its subject.

> At the end of the summer *come* the best *sales.*

> Under the house *are* some old Mason *jars.*

Prepositional phrases beginning with compound prepositions such as *along with, together with, in addition to,* and *as well as* should be ignored, for they do not affect subject-verb agreement.

> *Gladys Knight,* as well as the Pips, *is* riding the midnight train to Georgia.

A verb must agree with its subject, not its subject complement.

> *Taxes are* a problem.

> A *problem is* taxes.

> His main *source* of pleasure *is* food and women.

> *Food and women are* his main sources of pleasure.

When a sentence begins with an expletive such as *there, here,* or *it,* the verb agrees with the subject, not the expletive.

> Surely, there *are* several *alumni* who would be interested in forming a group.

> There *are* 50 *students* in my English class.

> There *is* a horrifying *study* on child abuse in *Psychology Today.*

Indefinite pronouns such as *each, either, one, everyone, everybody,* and *everything* are singular.

> *Somebody* in Detroit *loves* me.

> *Does either* [one] of you have a pencil?

> *Neither* of my brothers *has* a car.

Indefinite pronouns such as *several, few, both,* and *many* are plural.

> *Both* of my sorority sisters *have* decided to live off campus.

> *Few seek* the enlightenment of transcendental meditation.

Indefinite pronouns such as *all, some, most,* and *none* may be singular or plural depending on their referents.

> *Some* of the food *is* cold.

> *Some* of the vegetables *are* cold.

> I can think of some retorts, but *none seem* appropriate.

> *None* of the children *is* as sweet as Sally.

Fractions such as *one-half* and *one-third* may be singular or plural depending on the referent.

> *Half* of the mail *has* been delivered.

> *Half* of the letters *have* been read.

Subjects joined by *and* take a plural verb unless the subjects are thought to be one item or unit.

> *Jim* and *Tammy were* televangelists.

> *Guns and Roses is* my favorite group.

In cases when the subjects are joined by *or, nor, either...or,* or *neither... nor,* the verb must agree with the subject closer to it.

> Either the teacher or the *students are* responsible.

> Neither the students nor the *teacher is* responsible.

Relative pronouns, such as *who, which,* or *that,* which refer to plural antecedents require plural verbs. However, when the relative pronoun refers to a singular subject, the pronoun takes a singular verb.

> She is one of the girls *who cheer* on Friday nights.

> She is the only cheerleader *who has* a broken leg.

Subjects preceded by *every, each,* and *many a* are singular.

> *Every* man, woman, and child *was* given a life preserver.

> *Each* undergraduate *is* required to pass a proficiency exam.

> *Many a* tear *has* to fall before one matures.

A collective noun, such as *audience, faculty, jury,* etc., requires a singular verb when the group is regarded as a whole, and a plural verb when the members of the group are regarded as individuals.

The *jury has* made its decision.

The *faculty are* preparing their grade rosters.

Subjects preceded by *the number of* or *the percentage of* are singular, while subjects preceded by *a number of* or *a percentage of* are plural.

The number of vacationers in Florida *increases* every year.

A number of vacationers *are* young couples.

Titles of books, companies, name brands, and groups are singular or plural depending on their meaning.

Great Expectations is my favorite novel.

The *Rolling Stones are* performing in the Super Dome.

Certain nouns of Latin and Greek origin have unusual singular and plural forms.

Singular	Plural
criterion	criteria
alumnus	alumni
datum	data
medium	media

The *data are* available for inspection.

The only *criterion* for membership *is* a high GPA.

Some nouns such as *deer*, *shrimp*, and *sheep* have the same spellings for both their singular and plural forms. In these cases, the meaning of the sentence will determine whether they are singular or plural.

Deer are beautiful animals.

The spotted *deer is* licking the sugar cube.

Some nouns like *scissors*, *jeans*, and *wages* have plural forms but no singular counterparts. These nouns almost always take plural verbs.

The *scissors are* on the table.

My new *jeans fit* me like a glove.

Words used as examples, not as grammatical parts of the sentence, require singular verbs.

Can't is the contraction for "cannot."

Cats is the plural form of "cat."

Mathematical expressions of subtraction and division require singular verbs, while expressions of addition and multiplication take either singular or plural verbs.

> Ten *divided* by two *equals* five.
>
> Five *times* two *equals* ten.
>
> OR   Five *times* two *equal* ten.

Nouns expressing time, distance, weight, and measurement are singular when they refer to a unit and plural when they refer to separate items.

> Fifty yards *is* a short distance.
>
> Ten years *have* passed since I finished college.

Expressions of quantity are usually plural.

> Nine out of ten dentists *recommend* that their patients floss.

Some nouns ending in *-ics,* such as *economics* and *ethics*, take singular verbs when they refer to principles or a field of study; however, when they refer to individual practices, they usually take plural verbs.

> Ethics *is* being taught in the spring.
>
> His unusual business *ethics are* what got him into trouble.

Some nouns like *measles*, *news*, and *calculus* appear to be plural but are actually singular in number. These nouns require singular verbs.

> Measles *is* a very contagious disease.
>
> Calculus *requires* great skill in algebra.

A verbal noun (infinitive or gerund) serving as a subject is treated as singular, even if the object of the verbal phrase is plural.

> *Hiding* your mistakes *does* not make them go away.
>
> *To run* five miles *is* my goal.

A noun phrase or clause acting as the subject of a sentence requires a singular verb.

> *What I need* is to be loved.
>
> *Whether there is any connection between them* is unknown.

Clauses beginning with *what* may be singular or plural depending on the meaning, that is, whether *what* means "the thing" or "the things."

> What I *want* for Christmas is a new *motorcycle*.
>
> What *matters* are Clinton's *ideas*.

A plural subject followed by a singular appositive requires a plural verb; similarly, a singular subject followed by a plural appositive requires a singular verb.

When the girls throw a party, *they* each bring a *gift*.

The *board*, all ten members, *is* meeting today.

☞ Drill: Verbs

> **DIRECTIONS:** Choose the correct option.

1. If you <u>had been concerned</u> about Marilyn, you <u>would have went</u> to greater lengths to ensure her safety.

    (A) had been concern . . . would have gone

    (B) was concerned . . . would have gone

    (C) had been concerned . . . would have gone

    (D) No change is necessary.

2. Susan <u>laid</u> in bed too long and missed her class.

    (A) lays   (C) lied

    (B) lay   (D) No change is necessary.

3. The Great Wall of China <u>is</u> fifteen hundred miles long; it <u>was built</u> in the third century B.C.

    (A) was . . . was built   (C) has been . . . was built

    (B) is . . . is built   (D) No change is necessary.

4. Joe stated that the class <u>began</u> at 10:30 a.m.

    (A) begins   (C) was beginning

    (B) had begun   (D) No change is necessary.

5. The ceiling of the Sistine Chapel <u>was</u> painted by Michelangelo; it <u>depicted</u> scenes from the Creation in the Old Testament.

    (A) was . . . depicts   (C) has been . . . depicting

    (B) is . . . depicts   (D) No change is necessary.

6. After Christmas <u>comes</u> the best sales.

   (A) has come   (C) is coming

   (B) come   (D) No change is necessary.

7. The bakery's specialty <u>are</u> wedding cakes.

   (A) is   (C) be

   (B) were   (D) No change is necessary.

8. Every man, woman, and child <u>were given</u> a life preserver.

   (A) have been given   (C) was given

   (B) had gave   (D) No change is necessary.

9. Hiding your mistakes <u>don't</u> make them go away.

   (A) doesn't   (C) have not

   (B) do not   (D) No change is necessary.

10. The Board of Regents <u>has recommended</u> a tuition increase.

   (A) have recommended   (C) had recommended

   (B) has recommend   (D) No change is necessary.

PRONOUNS
PRONOUN CASE

Pronoun case questions test your knowledge of the use of nominative and objective case pronouns:

Nominative Case	Objective Case
I	me
he	him
she	her
we	us
they	them
who	whom

This review section answers the most frequently asked grammar questions: when to use *I* and when to use *me*; when to use *who* and when to use *whom.* Some writers avoid *whom* altogether, and instead of distinguishing between *I* and *me,* many writers incorrectly use *myself.*

Use the nominative case (subject pronouns)

for the subject of a sentence:

We students studied until early morning for the final.

Alan and *I* "burned the midnight oil," too.

for pronouns in apposition to the subject:

Only two students, Alex and *I,* were asked to report on the meeting.

for the predicate nominative/subject complement:

The actors nominated for the award were *she* and *I.*

for the subject of an elliptical clause:

Molly is more experienced than *he.*

for the subject of a subordinate clause:

Robert is the driver *who* reported the accident.

for the complement of an infinitive with no expressed subject:

I would not want to be *he.*

Use the objective case (object pronouns)

for the direct object of a sentence:

Mary invited *us* to her party.

for the object of a preposition:

The books that were torn belonged to *her.*

Just between you and *me,* I'm bored.

for the indirect object of a sentence:

Walter gave a dozen red roses to *her.*

for the appositive of a direct object:

The committee elected two delegates, Barbara and *me.*

for the object of an infinitive:

The young boy wanted to help *us* paint the fence.

for the object of a gerund:

Enlisting *him* was surprisingly easy.

for the object of a past participle:

> Having called the other students and *us*, the secretary went home for the day.

for a pronoun that precedes an infinitive (the subject of an infinitive):

> The supervisor told *him* to work late.

for the complement of an infinitive with an expressed subject:

> The fans thought the best player to be *him*.

for the object of an elliptical clause:

> Bill tackled Joe harder than *me*.

for the object of a verb in apposition:

> Charles invited two extra people, Carmen and *me*, to the party.

When a conjunction connects two pronouns or a pronoun and a noun, remove the "and" and the other pronoun or noun to determine what the correct pronoun form should be:

> Mom gave ~~Tom and~~ myself a piece of cake.
>
> Mom gave ~~Tom and~~ I a piece of cake
>
> Mom gave ~~Tom and~~ me a piece of cake.

Removal of these words reveals what the correct pronoun should be:

> Mom gave *me* a piece of cake.

The only pronouns that are acceptable after *between* and other prepositions are: *me, her, him, them,* and *whom.* When deciding between *who* and *whom,* try substituting *he* for *who* and *him* for *whom;* then follow these easy transformation steps:

1. Isolate the *who* clause or the *whom* clause:

   > whom we can trust

2. Invert the word order, if necessary. Place the words in the clause in the natural order of an English sentence, subject followed by the verb:

   > we can trust whom

3. Read the final form with the *he* or *him* inserted:

   > We can trust ~~whom~~ him.

When a pronoun follows a comparative conjunction like *than* or *as,* complete the elliptical construction to help you determine which pronoun is correct.

EX: She has more credit hours than me [do].

She has more credit hours than I [do].

PRONOUN-ANTECEDENT AGREEMENT

These kinds of questions test your knowledge of using an appropriate pronoun to agree with its antecedent in number (singular or plural form) and gender (masculine, feminine, or neuter). An antecedent is a noun or pronoun to which another noun or pronoun refers.

Here are the two basic rules for pronoun reference-antecedent agreement:

1. Every pronoun must have a conspicuous antecedent.

2. Every pronoun must agree with its antecedent in number, gender, and person.

When an antecedent is one of dual gender like *student*, *singer*, *artist*, *person*, *citizen*, etc., use *his* or *her*. Some careful writers change the antecedent to a plural noun to avoid using the sexist, singular masculine pronoun his:

INCORRECT: Everyone hopes that he will win the lottery.

CORRECT: Most people hope that they will win the lottery.

Ordinarily, the relative pronoun *who* is used to refer to people, *which* to refer to things and places, *where* to refer to places, and *that* to refer to places or things. The distinction between *that* and *which* is a grammatical distinction (see the section on Word Choice Skills).

Many writers prefer to use *that* to refer to collective nouns.

EX: A family *that* traces its lineage is usually proud of its roots.

Many writers, especially students, are not sure when to use the reflexive case pronoun and when to use the possessive case pronoun. The rules governing the usage of the reflexive case and the possessive case are quite simple.

Use the possessive case

before a noun in a sentence:

Our friend moved during the semester break.

My dog has fleas, but *her* dog doesn't.

before a gerund in a sentence:

>*Her* running helps to relieve stress.
>
>*His* driving terrified her.

as a noun in a sentence:

>*Mine* was the last test graded that day.

to indicate possession:

>Karen never allows anyone else to drive *her* car.
>
>Brad thought the book was *his,* but it was someone else's.

Use the reflexive case

as a direct object to rename the subject:

>I kicked *myself.*

as an indirect object to rename the subject:

>Henry bought *himself* a tie.

as an object of a prepositional phrase:

>Tom and Lillie baked the pie for *themselves.*

as a predicate pronoun:

>She hasn't been *herself* lately.

Do not use the reflexive in place of the nominative pronoun:

>INCORRECT: Both Randy and *myself* plan to go.
>
>CORRECT: Both Randy and *I* plan to go.

>INCORRECT: *Yourself* will take on the challenges of college.
>
>CORRECT: *You* will take on the challenges of college.

>INCORRECT: Either James or *yourself* will paint the mural.
>
>CORRECT: Either James or *you* will paint the mural.

Watch out for careless use of the pronoun form:

>INCORRECT: George *hisself* told me it was true.
>
>CORRECT: George *himself* told me it was true.

>INCORRECT: They washed the car *theirselves.*
>
>CORRECT: They washed the car *themselves.*

Notice that reflexive pronouns are not set off by commas:

INCORRECT: Mary, *herself*, gave him the diploma.

CORRECT: Mary *herself* gave him the diploma.

INCORRECT: I will do it, *myself*.

CORRECT: I will do it *myself*.

PRONOUN REFERENCE

Pronoun reference questions require you to determine whether the antecedent is conspicuously written in the sentence or whether it is remote, implied, ambiguous, or vague, none of which results in clear writing. Make sure that every italicized pronoun has a conspicuous antecedent and that one pronoun substitutes only for another noun or pronoun, not for an idea or a sentence.

Pronoun reference problems occur

when a pronoun refers to either of two antecedents:

INCORRECT: Joanna told Tim that *she* was getting fat.

CORRECT: Joanna told Tim, "I'm getting fat."

when a pronoun refers to a remote antecedent:

INCORRECT: A strange car followed us closely, and *he* kept blinking his lights at us.

CORRECT: A strange car followed us closely, and its driver kept blinking his lights at us.

when *this*, *that*, and *which* refer to the general idea of the preceding clause or sentence rather than the preceding word:

INCORRECT: The students could not understand the pronoun reference handout, which annoyed them very much.

CORRECT: The students could not understand the pronoun reference handout, a fact which annoyed them very much.

OR   The students were annoyed because they could not understand the pronoun reference handout.

when a pronoun refers to an unexpressed but implied noun:

INCORRECT: My husband wants me to knit a blanket, but I'm not interested in it.

CORRECT: My husband wants me to knit a blanket, but I'm not interested in knitting.

when *it* is used as something other than an expletive to postpone a subject:

INCORRECT: It says in today's paper that the newest shipment of cars from Detroit, Michigan, seems to include outright imitations of European models.

CORRECT: Today's paper says that the newest shipment of cars from Detroit, Michigan, seems to include outright imitations of European models.

———————

INCORRECT: The football game was canceled because it was bad weather.

CORRECT: The football game was canceled because the weather was bad.

when *they* or *it* is used to refer to something or someone indefinitely, and there is no definite antecedent:

INCORRECT: At the job placement office, they told me to stop wearing ripped jeans to my interviews.

CORRECT: At the job placement office, I was told to stop wearing ripped jeans to my interviews.

when the pronoun does not agree with its antecedent in number, gender, or person:

INCORRECT: Any graduate student, if they are interested, may attend the lecture.

CORRECT: Any graduate student, if he or she is interested, may attend the lecture.

OR All graduate students, if they are interested, may attend the lecture.

———————

INCORRECT: Many Americans are concerned that the overuse of slang and colloquialisms is corrupting the language.

CORRECT: Many Americans are concerned that the overuse of slang and colloquialisms is corrupting their language.

———————

INCORRECT: The Board of Regents will not make a decision about tuition increase until their March meeting.

CORRECT: The Board of Regents will not make a decision about tuition increase until its March meeting.

when a noun or pronoun has no expressed antecedent:

INCORRECT: In the president's address to the union, he promised no more taxes.

CORRECT: In his address to the union, the president promised no more taxes.

☞ Drill: Pronouns

> **DIRECTIONS:** Choose the correct option.

1. My friend and <u>myself</u> bought tickets for *Cats*.

   (A) I

   (B) me

   (C) us

   (D) No change is necessary.

2. Alcohol and tobacco are harmful to <u>whomever</u> consumes them.

   (A) whom

   (B) who

   (C) whoever

   (D) No change is necessary.

3. Everyone is wondering <u>whom</u> her successor will be.

   (A) who

   (B) whose

   (C) who'll

   (D) No change is necessary.

4. Rosa Lee's parents discovered that it was <u>her who</u> wrecked the family car.

   (A) she who

   (B) she whom

   (C) her whom

   (D) No change is necessary.

5. A student <u>who</u> wishes to protest <u>his or her</u> grades must file a formal grievance in the Dean's office.

   (A) that . . . their

   (B) which . . . his

   (C) whom . . . their

   (D) No change is necessary.

6. One of the best things about working for this company is that <u>they pay</u> big bonuses.

   (A) it pays   (C) they paid

   (B) they always pay   (D) No change is necessary.

7. Every car owner should be sure that <u>their</u> automobile insurance is adequate.

   (A) your   (C) its

   (B) his or her   (D) No change is necessary.

8. My mother wants me to become a teacher, but I'm not interested in <u>it</u>.

   (A) this   (C) that

   (B) teaching   (D) No change is necessary.

9. Since I had not paid my electric bill, <u>they</u> sent me a delinquent notice.

   (A) the power company   (C) it

   (B) he   (D) No change is necessary.

10. Margaret seldom wrote to her sister when <u>she</u> was away at college.

   (A) who   (C) her sister

   (B) her   (D) No change is necessary.

ADJECTIVES AND ADVERBS

CORRECT USAGE

Adjectives are words that modify nouns or pronouns by defining, describing, limiting, or qualifying those nouns or pronouns.

Adverbs are words that modify verbs, adjectives, or other adverbs and that express such ideas as time, place, manner, cause, and degree. Use adjectives as subject complements with linking verbs; use adverbs with action verbs.

EX:	The old man's speech was *eloquent*.	ADJECTIVE
	Mr. Brown speaks *eloquently*.	ADVERB
	Please be *careful*.	ADJECTIVE
	Please drive *carefully*.	ADVERB

Good or well

Good is an adjective; its use as an adverb is colloquial and nonstandard.

> INCORRECT: He plays *good*.
>
> CORRECT: He looks *good* to be an octogenarian.
>
> The quiche tastes very *good*.

Well may be either an adverb or an adjective. As an adjective, *well* means "in good health."

> CORRECT: He plays *well*.   ADVERB
>
> My mother is not *well*.   ADJECTIVE

Bad or badly

Bad is an adjective used after sense verbs such as *look, smell, taste, feel*, or *sound*, or after linking verbs (*is, am, are, was, were*).

> INCORRECT: I feel *badly* about the delay.
>
> CORRECT: I feel *bad* about the delay.

Badly is an adverb used after all other verbs.

> INCORRECT: It doesn't hurt very *bad*
>
> CORRECT: It doesn't hurt very *badly*.

Real or really

Real is an adjective; its use as an adverb is colloquial and nonstandard. It means "genuine."

> INCORRECT: He writes *real* well.
>
> CORRECT: This is *real* leather.

Really is an adverb meaning "very."

> INCORRECT: This is *really* diamond.
>
> CORRECT: Have a *really* nice day.

> EX: This is *real* amethyst.   ADJECTIVE
>
> This is *really* difficult.   ADVERB
>
> This is a *real* crisis   ADJECTIVE
>
> This is *really* important.   ADVERB

Sort of and kind of

Sort of and *kind of* are often misused in written English by writers who actually mean *rather* or *somewhat*.

> INCORRECT: Jan was *kind of* saddened by the results of the test.

> CORRECT: Jan was *somewhat* saddened by the results of the test.

FAULTY COMPARISONS

Sentences containing a faulty comparison often sound correct because their problem is not one of grammar but of logic. Read these sentences closely to make sure that like things are being compared, that the comparisons are complete, and that the comparisons are logical.

When comparing two persons or things, use the comparative, not the superlative form, of an adjective or an adverb. Use the superlative form for comparison of more than two persons or things. Use *any*, *other*, or *else* when comparing one thing or person with a group of which it/he or she is a part.

Most one- and two-syllable words form their comparative and superlative degrees with *-er* and *-est* suffixes. Adjectives and adverbs of more than two syllables form their comparative and superlative degrees with the addition of *more* and *most*.

Positive	Comparative	Superlative
good	better	best
old	older	oldest
friendly	friendlier	friendliest
lonely	lonelier	loneliest
talented	more talented	most talented
beautiful	more beautiful	most beautiful

A double comparison occurs when the degree of the modifier is changed incorrectly by adding both *-er* and *more* or *-est* and *most* to the adjective or adverb.

> INCORRECT: He is the *most nicest* brother.

> CORRECT: He is the *nicest* brother.

> INCORRECT: She is the *more meaner* of the sisters.

> CORRECT: She is the *meaner* sister.

Illogical comparisons occur when there is an implied comparison between two things that are not actually being compared or that cannot be logically compared.

INCORRECT: The interest at a loan company is higher *than* a bank.

CORRECT: The interest at a loan company is higher *than* that *at* a bank.

OR The interest at a loan company is higher *than at* a bank.

Ambiguous comparisons occur when elliptical words (those omitted) create for the reader more than one interpretation of the sentence.

INCORRECT: I like Mary better than you. (than you *what?*)

CORRECT: I like Mary better than I like you.

OR I like Mary better than you do.

Incomplete comparisons occur when the basis of the comparison (the two categories being compared) is not explicitly stated.

INCORRECT: Skywriting is *more* spectacular.

CORRECT: Skywriting is *more* spectacular *than* billboard advertising.

Do not omit the words *other, any,* or *else* when comparing one thing or person with a group of which it/he or she is a part.

INCORRECT: Joan writes better *than any* student in her class.

CORRECT: Joan writes better *than any other* student in her class.

Do not omit the second *as* of *as . . . as* when making a point of equal or superior comparison.

INCORRECT: The University of West Florida is *as large* or larger than the University of North Florida.

CORRECT: The University of West Florida is *as large as* or larger than the University of Northern Florida.

Do not omit the first category of the comparison, even if the two categories are the same.

INCORRECT: This is one of the best, if not the best, college in the country.

CORRECT: This is one of the best colleges in the country, if not the best.

The problem with the incorrect sentence is that *one of the best* requires the plural word *colleges*, not *college*.

☞ Drill: Adjectives and Adverbs

> **Directions:** Choose the correct option.

1. Although the band performed <u>badly</u>, I feel <u>real bad</u> about missing the concert.

    (A) badly . . . real badly   (C) badly . . . very bad

    (B) bad . . . badly   (D) No change is necessary.

2. These reports are <u>relative simple</u> to prepare.

    (A) relatively simple   (C) relatively simply

    (B) relative simply   (D) No change is necessary.

3. He did <u>very well</u> on the test although his writing skills are not <u>good</u>.

    (A) real well . . . good   (C) good . . . great

    (B) very good . . . good   (D) No change is necessary.

4. Shake the medicine bottle <u>good</u> before you open it.

    (A) very good   (C) well

    (B) real good   (D) No change is necessary.

5. Though she speaks <u>fluently</u>, she writes <u>poorly</u> because she doesn't observe <u>closely</u> or think <u>clear</u>.

    (A) fluently, poorly, closely, clearly

    (B) fluent, poor, close, clear

    (C) fluently, poor, closely, clear

    (D) No change is necessary.

> **DIRECTIONS:** Select the sentence that clearly and effectively states the idea and has no structural errors.

6. (A) Los Angeles is larger than any city in California.

    (B) Los Angeles is larger than all the cities in California.

(C)   Los Angeles is larger than any other city in California.

(D)   Los Angeles is larger than the cities in California.

7.   (A)   Art history is as interesting as, if not more interesting than, music appreciation.

(B)   Art history is as interesting, if not more interesting than, music appreciation.

(C)   Art history is as interesting as, if not more interesting, music appreciation.

(D)   Art history is as interesting as, if not more interesting as, music appreciation.

8.   (A)   The baseball team here is as good as any other university.

(B)   The baseball team here is as good as all the other universities.

(C)   The baseball team here is as good as any other university's.

(D)   The baseball team here is as good as the other universities.

9.   (A)   I like him better than you.

(B)   I like him better than I like you.

(C)   I like him better.

(D)   I like him more than you.

10.   (A)   You are the most stingiest person I know.

(B)   You are the most stingier person I know.

(C)   You are the stingiest person I know.

(D)   You are the more stingiest person I know.

PUNCTUATION
COMMAS

Commas should be placed according to standard rules of punctuation for purpose, clarity, and effect. The proper use of commas is explained in the following rules and examples:

In a series:

When more than one adjective describes a noun, use a comma to separate and emphasize each adjective. The comma takes the place of the word *and* in the series.

> the long, dark passageway
>
> another confusing, sleepless night
>
> an elaborate, complex, brilliant plan
>
> the old, grey, crumpled hat

Some adjective-noun combinations are thought of as one word. In these cases, the adjective in front of the adjective-noun combination needs no comma. If you inserted *and* between the adjective-noun combination, it would not make sense.

> a stately oak tree
>
> an exceptional wine glass
>
> my worst report card
>
> a china dinner plate

The comma is also used to separate words, phrases, and whole ideas (clauses); it still takes the place of *and* when used this way.

> an apple, a pear, a fig, and a banana
>
> a lovely lady, an elegant dress, and many admirers
>
> She lowered the shade, closed the curtain, turned off the light, and went to bed.

The only question that exists about the use of commas in a series is whether or not one should be used before the final item. It is standard usage to do so, although many newspapers and magazines have stopped using the final comma. Occasionally, the omission of the comma can be confusing.

> INCORRECT: He got on his horse, tracked a rabbit and a deer and rode on to Canton.
>
> We planned the trip with Mary and Harold, Susan, Dick and Joan, Gregory and Jean and Charles.

With a long introductory phrase:

Usually if a phrase of more than five or six words or a dependent clause precedes the subject at the beginning of a sentence, a comma is used to set it off.

After last night's fiasco at the disco, she couldn't bear the thought of looking at him again.

Whenever I try to talk about politics, my wife leaves the room.

Provided you have said nothing, they will never guess who you are.

It is not necessary to use a comma with a short sentence.

In January she will go to Switzerland.

After I rest I'll feel better.

During the day no one is home.

If an introductory phrase includes a verb form that is being used as another part of speech (a *verbal*), it must be followed by a comma.

INCORRECT: When eating Mary never looked up from her plate.

CORRECT: When eating, Mary never looked up from her plate.

INCORRECT: Because of her desire to follow her faith in James wavered.

CORRECT: Because of her desire to follow, her faith in James wavered.

INCORRECT: Having decided to leave Mary James wrote her a letter.

CORRECT: Having decided to leave Mary, James wrote her a letter.

To separate sentences with two main ideas:

To understand this use of the comma, you need to be able to recognize compound sentences. When a sentence contains more than two subjects and verbs (clauses), and the two clauses are joined by a conjunction (*and, but, or, nor, for, yet*), use a comma before the conjunction to show that another clause is coming.

I thought I knew the poem by heart, but he showed me three lines I had forgotten.

Are we really interested in helping the children, or are we more concerned with protecting our good names?

He is supposed to leave tomorrow, but he is not ready to go.

Jim knows you are disappointed, and he has known it for a long time.

If the two parts of the sentence are short and closely related, it is not necessary to use a comma.

He threw the ball and the dog ran after it.

Jane played the piano and Michael danced.

Be careful not to confuse a sentence that has a compound verb and a single subject with a compound sentence. If the subject is the same for both verbs, there is no need for a comma.

INCORRECT: Charles sent some flowers, and wrote a long letter explaining why he had not been able to attend.

CORRECT: Charles sent some flowers and wrote a long letter explaining why he had not been able to attend.

INCORRECT: Last Thursday we went to the concert with Julia, and afterwards dined at an old Italian restaurant.

CORRECT: Last Thursday we went to the concert with Julia and afterwards dined at an old Italian restaurant.

INCORRECT: For the third time, the teacher explained that the literacy level for high school students was much lower than it had been in previous years, and, this time, wrote the statistics on the board for everyone to see.

CORRECT: For the third time, the teacher explained that the literacy level for high school students was much lower than it had been in previous years and this time wrote the statistics on the board for everyone to see.

In general, words and phrases that stop the flow of the sentence or are unnecessary for the main idea are set off by commas.

Abbreviations after names:

Did you invite John Paul, Jr., and his sister?

Martha Harris, Ph.D., will be the speaker tonight.

Interjections (an exclamation without added grammatical connection):

Oh, I'm so glad to see you.

I tried so hard, alas, to do it.

Hey, let me out of here.

Direct address:

Roy, won't you open the door for the dog?

I can't understand, Mother, what you are trying to say.

May I ask, Mr. President, why you called us together?

Hey, lady, watch out for that car!

Tag questions:

I'm really hungry, aren't you?

Jerry looks like his father, doesn't he?

Geographical names and addresses:

The concert will be held in Chicago, Illinois, on August 12.

The letter was addressed to Mrs. Marion Heartwell, 1881 Pine Lane, Palo Alto, California 95824.

(Note: No comma is needed before the ZIP code, because it is already clearly set off from the state name.)

Transitional words and phrases:

On the other hand, I hope he gets better.

In addition, the phone rang constantly this afternoon.

I'm, nevertheless, going to the beach on Sunday.

You'll find, therefore, that no one is more loyal than I am.

Parenthetical words and phrases:

You will become, I believe, a great statesman.

We know, of course, that this is the only thing to do.

In fact, I planted corn last summer.

The Mannes affair was, to put it mildly, a surprise.

Unusual word order:

The dress, new and crisp, hung in the closet.

Intently, she stared out the window.

With nonrestrictive elements:

Parts of a sentence that modify other parts are sometimes essential to the meaning of the sentence and sometimes not. When a modifying word or group of words is not vital to the meaning of the sentence, it is set off by commas. Since it does not restrict the meaning of the words it modifies, it is called "nonrestrictive." Modifiers that are essential to the meaning of the sentence are called "restrictive" and are not set off by commas.

ESSENTIAL:	The girl *who wrote the story* is my sister.
NONESSENTIAL:	My sister, *the girl who wrote the story*, has always loved to write.

ESSENTIAL:	John Milton's famous poem *Paradise Lost* tells a remarkable story.
NONESSENTIAL:	Dante's greatest work, *The Divine Comedy*, marked the beginning of the Renaissance.

ESSENTIAL:	The cup *that is on the piano* is the one I want.
NONESSENTIAL:	The cup, *which my brother gave me last year*, is on the piano.

ESSENTIAL:	The people *who arrived late* were not seated.
NONESSENTIAL:	George, *who arrived late*, was not seated.

To set off direct quotations:

Most direct quotes or quoted materials are set off from the rest of the sentence by commas.

"Please read your part more loudly," the director insisted.

"I won't know what to do," said Michael, "if you leave me."

The teacher said sternly, "I will not dismiss this class until I have silence."

Who was it who said "Do not ask for whom the bell tolls; it tolls for thee"?

Note: Commas always go inside the closing quotation mark, even if the comma is not part of the material being quoted.

Be careful not to set off indirect quotes or quotes that are used as subjects or complements.

"To be or not to be" is the famous beginning of a soliloquy in Shakespeare's *Hamlet*. (subject)

She said she would never come back. (indirect quote)

Back then my favorite poem was "Evangeline." (complement)

To set off contrasting elements:

> Her intelligence, not her beauty, got her the job.

> Your plan will take you a little further from, rather than closer to, your destination.

> It was a reasonable, though not appealing, idea.

> He wanted glory, but found happiness instead.

In dates:

Both forms of the date are acceptable.

> She will arrive on April 6, 1998.

> He left on 5 December 1980.

> In January 1967, he handed in his resignation.

> On October 22, 1992, Frank and Julie were married.

Usually, when a subordinate clause is at the end of a sentence, no comma is necessary preceding the clause. However, when a subordinate clause introduces a sentence, a comma should be used after the clause. Some common subordinating conjunctions are:

after	although	as
as if	because	before
even though	if	inasmuch as
so that	though	till
unless	until	when
whenever	while	since

SEMICOLONS

Questions testing semicolon usage require you to be able to distinguish between the semicolon and the comma, and the semicolon and the colon. This review section covers the basic uses of the semicolon: to separate independent clauses not joined by a coordinating conjunction, to separate independent clauses separated by a conjunctive adverb, and to separate items in a series with internal commas. It is important to be consistent; if you use a semicolon between *any* of the items in the series, you must use semicolons to separate *all* of the items in the series.

Usually, a comma follows the conjunctive adverb. Note also that a period can be used to separate two sentences joined by a conjunctive adverb. Some common conjunctive adverbs are:

accordingly	besides	consequentially
finally	furthermore	however
indeed	in fact	moreover
nevertheless	next	nonetheless
now	on the other hand	otherwise
perhaps	still	therefore

Then is also used as a conjunctive adverb, but it is not usually followed by a comma.

Use the semicolon

To separate independent clauses which are not joined by a coordinating conjunction:

> I understand how to use commas; the semicolon I have not yet mastered.

To separate two independent clauses connected by a conjunctive adverb:

> He took great care with his work; *therefore*, he was very successful.

To combine two independent clauses connected by a coordinating conjunction if either or both of the clauses contain other internal punctuation:

> Success in college, some maintain, requires intelligence, industry, and perseverance; *but* others, fewer in number, assert that only personality is important.

To separate items in a series when each item has internal punctuation:

> I bought an old, dilapidated chair; an antique table which was in beautiful condition; and a new, ugly, blue and white rug.

> Call our customer service line for assistance: Arizona, 1-800-555-6020; New Mexico, 1-800-555-5050; California, 1-800-555-3140; or Nevada, 1-800-555-3214.

Do not use the semicolon

To separate a dependent and an independent clause:

> INCORRECT: You should not make such statements; even though they are correct.

> CORRECT: You should not make such statements even though they are correct.

To separate an appositive phrase or clause from a sentence:

INCORRECT: His immediate aim in life is centered around two things; becoming an engineer and learning to fly an airplane.

CORRECT: His immediate aim in life is centered around two things: becoming an engineer and learning to fly an airplane.

To precede an explanation or summary of the first clause:

(Note: Although the sentence below is punctuated correctly, the use of the semicolon provides a miscue, suggesting that the second clause is merely an extension, not an explanation, of the first clause. The colon provides a better clue.)

WEAK: The first week of camping was wonderful; we lived in cabins instead of tents.

BETTER: The first week of camping was wonderful: we lived in cabins instead of tents.

To substitute for a comma:

INCORRECT: My roommate also likes sports; particularly football, basketball, and baseball.

CORRECT: My roommate also likes sports, particularly football, basketball, and baseball.

To set off other types of phrases or clauses from a sentence:

INCORRECT: Being of a cynical mind; I should ask for a recount of the ballots.

CORRECT: Being of a cynical mind, I should ask for a recount of the ballots.

INCORRECT: The next meeting of the club has been postponed two weeks; inasmuch as both the president and vice-president are out of town.

CORRECT: The next meeting of the club has been postponed two weeks, inasmuch as both the president and vice-president are out of town.

Note: The semicolon is not a terminal mark of punctuation; therefore, it should not be followed by a capital letter unless the first word in the second clause ordinarily requires capitalization.

COLONS

While it is true that a colon is used to precede a list, one must also make sure that a complete sentence precedes the colon. The colon signals the reader that a list, explanation, or restatement of the preceding will follow. It is like an arrow, indicating that something is to follow. The difference between the colon and the semicolon and between the colon and the period is that the colon is an introductory mark, not a terminal mark. Look at the following examples:

> The Constitution provides for a separation of powers among the three branches of government.

> **government.** The period signals a new sentence.

> **government;** The semicolon signals an interrelated sentence.

> **government,** The comma signals a coordinating conjunction followed by another independent clause.

> **government:** The colon signals a list.

> The Constitution provides for a separation of powers among the three branches of *government*: executive, legislative, and judicial.

Ensuring that a complete sentence precedes a colon means following these rules:

Use the colon to introduce a list (one item may constitute a list):

> I hate this one course: English.

> Three plays by William Shakespeare will be presented in repertory this summer at the University of Michigan: *Hamlet, Macbeth,* and *Othello.*

To introduce a list preceded by *as follows* or *the following*:

> The reasons he cited for his success are as follows: integrity, honesty, industry, and a pleasant disposition.

To separate two independent clauses, when the second clause is a restatement or explanation of the first:

> All of my high school teachers said one thing in particular: college is going to be difficult.

To introduce a word or word group which is a restatement, explanation, or summary of the first sentence:

> These two things he loved: an honest man and a beautiful woman.

To introduce a formal appositive:

> I am positive there is one appeal which you can't overlook: money.

To separate the introductory words from a quotation which follows, if the quotation is formal, long, or paragraphed separately:

> The actor then stated: "I would rather be able to adequately play the part of Hamlet than to perform a miraculous operation, deliver a great lecture, or build a magnificent skyscraper."

The colon should only be used after statements that are grammatically complete.

Do *not* use a colon after a verb:

> INCORRECT: My favorite holidays are: Christmas, New Year's, and Halloween.
>
> CORRECT: My favorite holidays are Christmas, New Year's, and Halloween.

Do *not* use a colon after a preposition:

> INCORRECT: I enjoy different ethnic foods such as: Greek, Chinese, and Italian.
>
> CORRECT: I enjoy different ethnic foods such as Greek, Chinese, and Italian.

Do *not* use a colon interchangeably with the dash:

> INCORRECT: Mathematics, German, English: These gave me the greatest difficulty of all my studies.
>
> CORRECT: Mathematics, German, English—these gave me the greatest difficulty of all my studies.

Information preceding the colon should be a complete sentence regardless of the explanatory information following the clause.

Do *not* use the colon before the words *for example, namely, that is,* or *for instance* even though these words may be introducing a list.

> INCORRECT: We agreed to it: namely, to give him a surprise party.
>
> CORRECT: There are a number of well-known American women writers, including the following: Nikki Giovanni, Phillis Wheatley, Emily Dickinson, and Maya Angelou.

Colon usage questions test your knowledge of the colon preceding a list, restatement, or explanation. These questions also require you to be able to distinguish between the colon and the period, the colon and the comma, and the colon and the semicolon.

APOSTROPHES

Apostrophe questions require you to know when an apostrophe has been used appropriately to make a noun possessive, not plural. Remember the following rules when considering how to show possession.

Add *'s* to singular nouns and indefinite pronouns:

Tiffany's flowers	a dog's bark
everybody's computer	at the owner's expense
today's paper	

Add *'s* to singular nouns ending in s, unless this distorts the pronunciation:

Delores's paper	the boss's pen
Dr. Yots' class	for righteousness' sake
Dr. Evans's office OR Dr. Evans' office	

Add *an apostrophe* to plural nouns ending in s or es:

two cents' worth	ladies' night
thirteen years' experience	two weeks' pay

Add *'s* to plural nouns not ending in s:

men's room	children's toys

Add *'s* to the last word in compound words or groups:

brother-in-law's car	someone else's paper

Add *'s* to the last name when indicating joint ownership:

Joe and Edna's home	Julie and Kathy's party
women and children's clinic	

Add *'s* to both names if you intend to show ownership by each person:

Joe's and Edna's trucks	Julie's and Kathy's pies
Ted's and Jane's marriage vows	

Possessive pronouns change their forms *without* the addition of an apostrophe:

her, his, hers	your, yours
their, theirs	it, its

Use the possessive form of a noun preceding a gerund:

His driving annoys me.   My bowling a strike irritated him.

Do you mind our stopping by?   We appreciate your coming.

So long as no confusion will result, add *s* alone to numbers, symbols, and letters to show that they are plural:

TVs   VCRs

the 1800s   the returning POWs

When confusion could result from the addition of *s* alone, add *'s* to words and initials to show that they are plural:

no if's, and's, or but's   the do's and don't's of dating

three A's   M.A.'s and Ph.D.'s

QUOTATION MARKS AND ITALICS

These kinds of questions test your knowledge of the proper use of quotation marks with other marks of punctuation, with titles, and with dialogue. These kinds of questions also test your knowledge of the correct use of italics and underlining with titles and words used as sample words (for example, *the word <u>is</u> is a common verb*).

The most common use of double quotation marks (") is to set off quoted words, phrases, and sentences.

> "If everybody minded their own business," said the Duchess in a hoarse growl, "the world would go round a great deal faster than it does."
>
> "Then you would say what you mean," the March Hare went on.
>
> "I do," Alice hastily replied: "at least—at least I mean what I say—that's the same thing, you know."
>
> —from Lewis Carroll's *Alice in Wonderland*

Single quotation marks are used to set off quoted material within a quote.

> "Shall I bring 'Rime of the Ancient Mariner' along with us?" she asked her brother.
>
> Mrs. Green said, "The doctor told me, 'Go immediately to bed when you get home!'"
>
> "If she said that to me," Katherine insisted, "I would tell her, 'I never intend to speak to you again! Goodbye, Susan!'"

When writing dialogue, begin a new paragraph each time the speaker changes.

"Do you know what time it is?" asked Jane.

"Can't you see I'm busy?" snapped Mary.

"It's easy to see that you're in a bad mood today!" replied Jane.

Use quotation marks to enclose words used as words (sometimes italics are used for this purpose).

"Judgment" has always been a difficult word for me to spell.

Do you know what "abstruse" means?

"Horse and buggy" and "bread and butter" can be used either as adjectives or as nouns.

If slang is used within more formal writing, the slang words or phrases should be set off with quotation marks.

Harrison's decision to leave the conference and to "stick his neck out" by flying to Jamaica was applauded by the rest of the conference attendees.

When words are meant to have an unusual or specific significance to the reader, for instance ironic or humorous, they are sometimes placed in quotation marks.

For years, men did not allow women to buy real estate in order to "protect" them from unscrupulous dealers.

The "conversation" resulted in one black eye and a broken nose.

To set off titles of TV shows, poems, stories, and book chapters, use quotation marks. (Book, motion picture, newspaper, and magazine titles are underlined when handwritten and italicized when printed.)

The article "Moving South in the Southern Rain," by Jergen Smith in the *Southern News*, attracted the attention of our editor.

The assignment is "Childhood Development," Chapter 18 of *Human Behavior.*

My favorite essay by Montaigne is "On Silence."

"Happy Days" led the TV ratings for years, didn't it?

You will find Keats' "Ode on a Grecian Urn" in Chapter 3, "The Romantic Era," in Lastly's *Selections from Great English Poets.*

Errors to avoid:

Be sure to remember that quotation marks always come in pairs. Do not make the mistake of using only one set.

INCORRECT: "You'll never convince me to move to the city, said Thurman. I consider it an insane asylum."

CORRECT: "You'll never convince me to move to the city," said Thurman. "I consider it an insane asylum."

INCORRECT: "Idleness and pride tax with a heavier hand than kings and parliaments," Benjamin Franklin is supposed to have said. If we can get rid of the former, we may easily bear the latter."

CORRECT: "Idleness and pride tax with a heavier hand than kings and parliaments," Benjamin Franklin is supposed to have said. "If we can get rid of the former, we may easily bear the latter."

When a quote consists of several sentences, do not put the quotation marks at the beginning and end of each sentence; put them at the beginning and end of the entire quotation.

INCORRECT: "It was during his student days in Bonn that Beethoven fastened upon Schiller's poem." "The heady sense of liberation in the verses must have appealed to him." "They appealed to every German." —John Burke

CORRECT: "It was during his student days in Bonn that Beethoven fastened upon Schiller's poem. The heady sense of liberation in the verses must have appealed to him. They appealed to every German." —John Burke

Instead of setting off a long quote with quotation marks, if it is longer than five or six lines you may want to indent and single space it. If you do indent, do not use quotation marks.

In his *First Inaugural Address,* Abraham Lincoln appeals to the war-torn American people:

We are not enemies, but friends. We must not be enemies. Though passion may have strained, it must not break our bonds of affection. The mystic chords of memory, stretching from every battlefield and patriot grave to every living heart and hearthstone all over this broad land, will yet swell the chorus of the Union when again touched, as surely they will be, by the better angels of our nature.

Be careful not to use quotation marks with indirect quotations.

INCORRECT: Mary wondered "if she would get over it."

CORRECT: Mary wondered if she would get over it.

INCORRECT: The nurse asked "how long it had been since we had visited the doctor's office."

CORRECT: The nurse asked how long it had been since we had visited the doctor's office.

When you quote several paragraphs, it is not sufficient to place quotation marks at the beginning and end of the entire quote. Place quotation marks at the *beginning of each paragraph,* but only at the *end of the last paragraph.* Here is an abbreviated quotation for an example:

"Here begins an odyssey through the world of classical mythology, starting with the creation of the world . . .

"It is true that themes similar to the classical may be found in any corpus of mythology . . . Even technology is not immune to the influence of Greece and Rome . . .

"We need hardly mention the extent to which painters and sculptors . . . have used and adapted classical mythology to illustrate the past, to reveal the human body, to express romantic or antiromantic ideals, or to symbolize any particular point of view."

Commas and periods are *always* placed inside the quotation marks, even if they are not actually part of the quote.

INCORRECT: "Life always gets colder near the summit", Nietzsche is purported to have said, "—the cold increases, responsibility grows".

CORRECT: "Life always gets colder near the summit," Nietzsche is purported to have said, "—the cold increases, responsibility grows."

INCORRECT: "Get down here right away", John cried. "You'll miss the sunset if you don't."

CORRECT: "Get down here right away," John cried. "You'll miss the sunset if you don't."

INCORRECT: "If my dog could talk", Mary mused, "I'll bet he would say, 'Take me for a walk right this minute'".

CORRECT: "If my dog could talk," Mary mused, "I'll bet he would say, 'Take me for a walk right this minute.'"

Other marks of punctuation, such as question marks, exclamation points, colons, and semicolons, go inside the quotation marks if they are part of the quoted material. If they are not part of the quotation, however, they go outside the quotation marks. Be careful to distinguish between the placement of the comma and period, which always go inside the quotation marks, and that of other marks of punctuation.

> INCORRECT: "I'll always love you"! he exclaimed happily.
>
> CORRECT: "I'll always love you!" he exclaimed happily.

> INCORRECT: Did you hear her say, "He'll be there early?"
>
> CORRECT: Did you hear her say, "He'll be there early"?

> INCORRECT: She called down the stairs, "When are you going"?
>
> CORRECT: She called down the stairs, "When are you going?"

> INCORRECT: "Let me out"! he cried. "Don't you have any pity"?
>
> CORRECT: "Let me out!" he cried. "Don't you have any pity?"

Remember to use only one mark of punctuation at the end of a sentence ending with a quotation mark.

> INCORRECT: She thought out loud, "Will I ever finish this paper in time for that class?".
>
> CORRECT: She thought out loud, "Will I ever finish this paper in time for that class?"

> INCORRECT: "Not the same thing a bit!", said the Hatter. "Why, you might just as well say that 'I see what I eat' is the same thing as 'I eat what I see'!".
>
> CORRECT: "Not the same thing a bit!" said the Hatter. "Why, you might just as well say that 'I see what I eat' is the same thing as 'I eat what I see'!"

☞ Drill: Punctuation

> **Directions:** Choose the correct option.

1. Indianola, <u>Mississippi, where B.B. King and my father grew up,</u> has a population of less than 50,000 people.

(A)   Mississippi where, B.B. King and my father grew up,

(B)   Mississippi where B.B. King and my father grew up,

(C)   Mississippi; where B.B. King and my father grew up,

(D)   No change is necessary.

2.   John Steinbeck's best known novel, *The Grapes of Wrath,* is the story of the <u>Joads and Oklahoma family</u> who were driven from their dustbowl farm and forced to become migrant workers in California.

(A)   Joads, an Oklahoma family

(B)   Joads, an Oklahoma family,

(C)   Joads; an Oklahoma family

(D)   No change is necessary.

3.   All students who are interested in student teaching next <u>semester, must submit an application to the Teacher Education Office.</u>

(A)   semester must submit an application to the Teacher Education Office.

(B)   semester, must submit an application, to the Teacher Education Office.

(C)   semester: must submit an application to the Teacher Education Office.

(D)   No change is necessary.

4.   Whenever you travel by <u>car, or plane, you</u> must wear a seatbelt.

(A)   car or plane you   (C)   car or plane, you

(B)   car, or plane you   (D)   No change is necessary.

5.   Wearing a seatbelt is not just a good <u>idea, it's</u> the law.

(A)   idea; it's   (C)   idea. It's

(B)   idea it's   (D)   No change is necessary.

6.   Senators and representatives can be reelected <u>indefinitely; a</u> president can serve only two terms.

(A)   indefinitely but a   (C)   indefinitely a

(B)   indefinitely, a   (D)   No change is necessary.

7. Students must pay a penalty for overdue library <u>books, however, there</u> is a grace period.

   (A) books; however, there   (C) books: however, there

   (B) books however, there   (D) No change is necessary.

8. Among the states that seceded from the Union to join the Confederacy in 1860-1861 <u>were</u>: Mississippi, Florida, and Alabama.

   (A) were   (C) were.

   (B) were;   (D) No change is necessary.

9. The art exhibit displayed works by many famous <u>artists such as:</u> Dali, Picasso, and Michelangelo.

   (A) artists such as;   (C) artists. Such as

   (B) artists such as   (D) No change is necessary.

10. The National Shakespeare Company will perform <u>the following plays:</u> *Othello, Macbeth, Hamlet,* and *As You Like It.*

    (A) the following plays,   (C) the following plays

    (B) the following plays;   (D) No change is necessary.

CAPITALIZATION

When a word is capitalized, it calls attention to itself. This attention should be for a good reason. There are standard uses for capital letters. In general, capitalize (1) all proper nouns, (2) the first word of a sentence, and (3) the first word of a direct quotation.

WHAT SHOULD BE CAPITALIZED

Names of ships, aircraft, spacecraft, and trains:

Apollo 13	DC-10	Sputnik 11
Mariner IV	HMS Bounty	Boeing 767

Names of divine beings:

God	Allah	Buddha
Jehovah	Jupiter	Holy Ghost
Venus	Shiva	

Geological periods:

Neolithic age	late Pleistocene times	Cenozoic era
Ice Age		

Names of astronomical bodies:

Mercury	The Milky Way	Ursa Major
Big Dipper	Halley's comet	North Star

Personifications:

Reliable Nature brought her promised Spring.

Bring on Melancholy in his sad might.

She believed that Love was the answer to all her problems.

Historical periods:

the Middle Ages	World War I
Reign of Terror	Great Depression
Christian Era	Roaring Twenties
Age of Louis XIV	Renaissance

Organizations, associations, and institutions:

Girl Scouts	North Atlantic Treaty Organization
Kiwanis Club	League of Women Voters
New York Yankees	Unitarian Church
Smithsonian Institution	Common Market
Library of Congress	Franklin Glen High School
New York Philharmonic	Harvard University

Government and judicial groups:

United States Court of Appeals	U.S. Senate
Committee on Foreign Affairs	British Parliament
Georgetown City Council	Peace Corps
Arkansas Supreme Court	U.S. Census Bureau
U.S. House of Representatives	Department of State

A general term that accompanies a specific name is capitalized only if it follows the specific name. If it stands alone, comes before the specific name, or is used on second reference, it is lowercased:

Washington State	the state of Washington
Senator Dixon	the senator from Illinois
Central Park	the park

Golden Gate Bridge	the bridge
President Clinton	the president of the United States
Pope John XXIII	the pope
Queen Elizabeth I	the queen of England
Tropic of Capricorn	the tropics
Monroe Doctrine	the doctrine of expansion
the Mississippi River	the river
Easter Day	the day
Treaty of Versailles	the treaty
Webster's Dictionary	the dictionary
Equatorial Current	the equator

Use a capital to start a sentence:

> Our car would not start.
>
> When will you leave? I need to know right away.
>
> Never!
>
> Let me in! Please!

When a sentence appears within a sentence, start it with a capital letter:

> We had only one concern: When would we eat?
>
> My sister said, "I'll find the Monopoly game."
>
> He answered, "We can only stay a few minutes."

The most important words of titles are capitalized. Those words not capitalized are conjunctions (*and*, *or*, *but*) and short prepositions (*of*, *on*, *by*, *for*). The first and last word of a title must always be capitalized:

A Man for All Seasons	*Crime and Punishment*
Of Mice and Men	*Rise of the West*
Strange Life of Ivan Osokin	"Sonata in G Minor"
"Let Me In"	"Ode to Billy Joe"
"Rubaiyat of Omar Khayyam"	
"All in the Family"	

Capitalize newspaper and magazine titles:

U.S. News & World Report	*National Geographic*
the *New York Times*	the *Washington Post*

Capitalize radio and TV network abbreviations or station call letters:

ABC	NBC	CNN
WNEW	WBOP	HBO

Capitalize regions:

| the South | the Northeast | BUT: | the south of France |
| the West | Eastern Europe | | the east side of town |

Capitalize specific military units:

| the U.S. Army | the 7th Fleet |
| the German Navy | the 1st Infantry Division |

Capitalize political groups and philosophies:

Democracy	Marxist	Whig
Existentialism	Communism	Nazism
Federalist	Transcendentalism	

But: Do not capitalize systems of government or individual adherents to a philosophy:

| democracy | communism |
| fascist | agnostic |

Do not capitalize compass directions or seasons:

west	south	spring
east	winter	autumn
north	summer	

☞ Drill: Capitalization

> **DIRECTIONS:** Choose the correct option.

---

1. Mexico is the southernmost country in <u>North America</u>. It borders the United States on the north; it is bordered on the <u>south</u> by Belize and Guatemala.

    (A) north America . . . South

    (B) North America . . . South

    (C) North america . . . south

    (D) No change is necessary.

2. (A) Until 1989, Tom Landry was the only Coach the Dallas cowboys ever had.

    (B) Until 1989, Tom Landry was the only coach the Dallas Cowboys ever had.

    (C) Until 1989, Tom Landry was the only Coach the Dallas Cowboys ever had.

    (D) Until 1989, Tom Landry was the only Coach the Dallas Cowboys ever had.

3. The <u>Northern Hemisphere</u> is the half of the <u>earth</u> that lies north of the <u>Equator.</u>

    (A) Northern hemisphere . . . earth . . . equator

    (B) Northern hemisphere . . . Earth . . . Equator

    (C) Northern Hemisphere . . . earth . . . equator

    (D) No change is necessary.

4. (A) My favorite works by Ernest Hemingway are "The Snows of Kilamanjaro," *The Sun Also Rises,* and *For Whom the Bell Tolls.*

    (B) My favorite works by Ernest Hemingway are "The Snows Of Kilamanjaro," *The Sun Also Rises,* and *For Whom The Bell Tolls.*

    (C) My favorite works by Ernest Hemingway are "The Snows of Kilamanjaro," *The Sun also Rises,* and *For whom the Bell Tolls.*

    (D) My favorite works by Ernest Hemingway are "The Snows Of Kilamanjaro," *The Sun Also Rises,* and *For Whom the Bell Tolls.*

5. Aphrodite (<u>Venus in Roman Mythology</u>) was the <u>Greek</u> goddess of love.

    (A) Venus in Roman mythology . . . greek

    (B) venus in roman mythology . . . Greek

    (C) Venus in Roman mythology . . . Greek

    (D) No change is necessary.

6. The Koran is considered by Muslims to be the holy word.

   (A) koran . . . muslims   (C) Koran . . . muslims

   (B) koran . . . Muslims   (D) No change is necessary.

7. (A) The freshman curriculum at the community college includes english, a foreign language, Algebra I, and history.

   (B) The freshman curriculum at the community college includes English, a foreign language, Algebra I, and history.

   (C) The Freshman curriculum at the Community College includes English, a foreign language, Algebra I, and History.

   (D) The freshman curriculum at the community college includes english, a foreign language, algebra I, and history.

8. At the spring graduation ceremonies, the university awarded over 2,000 bachelor's degrees.

   (A) Spring . . . Bachelor's   (C) Spring . . . bachelor's

   (B) spring . . . Bachelor's   (D) No change is necessary.

9. The fall of the Berlin wall was an important symbol of the collapse of Communism.

   (A) berlin Wall . . . communism

   (B) Berlin Wall . . . communism

   (C) berlin wall . . . Communism

   (D) No change is necessary.

10. A photograph of mars was printed in the *New York Times*.

    (A) Mars . . . *The New York Times*

    (B) mars . . . *The New York times*

    (C) mars . . . *The New York Times*

    (D) No change is necessary.

SPELLING

Spelling questions test your ability to recognize misspelled words. This section reviews spelling tips and rules to help you spot incorrect spellings. Problems such as the distinction between *to* and *too* and *lead* and *led* are covered under the Word Choice Skills section of this review.

- Remember, *i* before *e* except after *c*, or when sounded as "a" as in *neighbor* and *weigh*.

- There are only three words in the English language that end in *-ceed*:

  proceed, succeed, exceed

- There are several words that end in *-cede*:

  secede, recede, concede, precede

- There is only one word in the English language that ends in *-sede*:

  supersede

Many people learn to read English phonetically; that is, by sounding out the letters of the words. However, many English words are not pronounced the way they are spelled, and those who try to spell English words phonetically often make spelling *errors*. It is better to memorize the correct spelling of English words rather than relying on phonetics to spell correctly.

FREQUENTLY MISSPELLED WORDS

The following list of words are frequently misspelled words. Study the spelling of each word by having a friend or teacher drill you on the words. Then mark down the words that you misspelled and study those select ones again. (The words appear in their most popular spellings.)

a lot	accompanied	acquaintance
ability	accomplish	acquainted
absence	accumulation	acquire
absent	accuse	across
abundance	accustomed	address
accept	ache	addressed
acceptable	achieve	adequate
accident	achievement	advantage
accommodate	acknowledge	advantageous

advertise
advertisement
advice
advisable
advise
advisor
aerial
affect
affectionate
again
against
aggravate
aggressive
agree
aisle
all right
almost
already
although
altogether
always
amateur
American
among
amount
analysis
analyze
angel
angle
annual
another
answer
antiseptic
anxious
apologize
apparatus
apparent
appear
appearance
appetite
application
apply

appreciate
appreciation
approach
appropriate
approval
approve
approximate
argue
arguing
argument
arouse
arrange
arrangement
article
artificial
ascend
assistance
assistant
associate
association
attempt
attendance
attention
audience
August
author
automobile
autumn
auxiliary
available
avenue
awful
awkward
bachelor
balance
balloon
bargain
basic
beautiful
because
become
before

beginning
being
believe
benefit
benefited
between
bicycle
board
bored
borrow
bottle
bottom
boundary
brake
breadth
breath
breathe
brilliant
building
bulletin
bureau
burial
buried
bury
bushes
business
cafeteria
calculator
calendar
campaign
capital
capitol
captain
career
careful
careless
carriage
carrying
category
ceiling
cemetery
cereal

certain
changeable
characteristic
charity
chief
choose
chose
cigarette
circumstance
citizen
clothes
clothing
coarse
coffee
collect
college
column
comedy
comfortable
commitment
committed
committee
communicate
company
comparative
compel
competent
competition
compliment
conceal
conceit
conceivable
conceive
concentration
conception
condition
conference
confident
congratulate
conquer
conscience
conscientious

conscious
consequence
consequently
considerable
consistency
consistent
continual
continuous
controlled
controversy
convenience
convenient
conversation
corporal
corroborate
council
counsel
counselor
courage
courageous
course
courteous
courtesy
criticism
criticize
crystal
curiosity
cylinder
daily
daughter
daybreak
death
deceive
December
deception
decide
decision
decisive
deed
definite
delicious
dependent

deposit
derelict
descend
descent
describe
description
desert
desirable
despair
desperate
dessert
destruction
determine
develop
development
device
dictator
died
difference
different
dilemma
dinner
direction
disappear
disappoint
disappointment
disapproval
disapprove
disastrous
discipline
discover
discriminate
disease
dissatisfied
dissection
dissipate
distance
distinction
division
doctor
dollar
doubt

dozen
earnest
easy
ecstasy
ecstatic
education
effect
efficiency
efficient
eight
either
eligibility
eligible
eliminate
embarrass
embarrassment
emergency
emphasis
emphasize
enclosure
encouraging
endeavor
engineer
English
enormous
enough
entrance
envelope
environment
equipment
equipped
especially
essential
evening
evident
exaggerate
exaggeration
examine
exceed
excellent
except
exceptional

exercise
exhausted
exhaustion
exhilaration
existence
exorbitant
expense
experience
experiment
explanation
extreme
facility
factory
familiar
fascinate
fascinating
fatigue
February
financial
financier
flourish
forcibly
forehead
foreign
formal
former
fortunate
fourteen
fourth
frequent
friend
frightening
fundamental
further
gallon
garden
gardener
general
genius
government
governor
grammar

grateful
great
grievance
grievous
grocery
guarantee
guess
guidance
half
hammer
handkerchief
happiness
healthy
heard
heavy
height
heroes
heroine
hideous
himself
hoarse
holiday
hopeless
hospital
humorous
hurried
hurrying
ignorance
imaginary
imbecile
imitation
immediately
immigrant
incidental
increase
independence
independent
indispensable
inevitable
influence
influential
initiate

innocence
inoculate
inquiry
insistent
instead
instinct
integrity
intellectual
intelligence
intercede
interest
interfere
interference
interpreted
interrupt
invitation
irrelevant
irresistible
irritable
island
its
it's
itself
January
jealous
journal
judgment
kindergarten
kitchen
knew
knock
know
knowledge
labor
laboratory
laid
language
later
latter
laugh
leisure
length

lesson
library
license
light
lightning
likelihood
likely
literal
literature
livelihood
loaf
loneliness
loose
lose
losing
loyal
loyalty
magazine
maintenance
maneuver
marriage
married
marry
match
material
mathematics
measure
medicine
million
miniature
minimum
miracle
miscellaneous
mischief
mischievous
misspelled
mistake
momentous
monkey
monotonous
moral
morale

mortgage
mountain
mournful
muscle
mysterious
mystery
narrative
natural
necessary
needle
negligence
neighbor
neither
newspaper
newsstand
niece
noticeable
o'clock
obedient
obstacle
occasion
occasional
occur
occurred
occurrence
ocean
offer
often
omission
omit
once
operate
opinion
opportune
opportunity
optimist
optimistic
origin
original
oscillate
ought
ounce

overcoat	pocket	promise
paid	poison	pronounce
pamphlet	policeman	pronunciation
panicky	political	propeller
parallel	population	prophet
parallelism	portrayal	prospect
particular	positive	psychology
partner	possess	pursue
pastime	possession	pursuit
patience	possessive	quality
peace	possible	quantity
peaceable	post office	quarreling
pear	potatoes	quart
peculiar	practical	quarter
pencil	prairie	quiet
people	precede	quite
perceive	preceding	raise
perception	precise	realistic
perfect	predictable	realize
perform	prefer	reason
performance	preference	rebellion
perhaps	preferential	recede
period	preferred	receipt
permanence	prejudice	receive
permanent	preparation	recipe
perpendicular	prepare	recognize
perseverance	prescription	recommend
persevere	presence	recuperate
persistent	president	referred
personal	prevalent	rehearsal
personality	primitive	reign
personnel	principal	relevant
persuade	principle	relieve
persuasion	privilege	remedy
pertain	probably	renovate
picture	procedure	repeat
piece	proceed	repetition
plain	produce	representative
playwright	professional	requirements
pleasant	professor	resemblance
please	profitable	resistance
pleasure	prominent	resource

respectability	solemn	tenement
responsibility	sophomore	therefore
restaurant	soul	thorough
rhythm	source	through
rhythmical	souvenir	title
ridiculous	special	together
right	specified	tomorrow
role	specimen	tongue
roll	speech	toward
roommate	stationary	tragedy
sandwich	stationery	transferred
Saturday	statue	treasury
scarcely	stockings	tremendous
scene	stomach	tries
schedule	straight	truly
science	strength	twelfth
scientific	strenuous	twelve
scissors	stretch	tyranny
season	striking	undoubtedly
secretary	studying	United States
seize	substantial	university
seminar	succeed	unnecessary
sense	successful	unusual
separate	sudden	useful
service	superintendent	usual
several	suppress	vacuum
severely	surely	valley
shepherd	surprise	valuable
sheriff	suspense	variety
shining	sweat	vegetable
shoulder	sweet	vein
shriek	syllable	vengeance
siege	symmetrical	versatile
sight	sympathy	vicinity
signal	synonym	vicious
significance	technical	view
significant	telegram	village
similar	telephone	villain
similarity	temperament	visitor
sincerely	temperature	voice
site	tenant	volume
soldier	tendency	waist

weak	weigh	whole
wear	weird	wholly
weather	whether	whose
Wednesday	which	wretched
week	while	

☞ Drill: Spelling

> **DIRECTIONS:** Identify the misspelled word in each set.

1. (A) probly   (C) acquaintance

   (B) accommodate   (D) among

2. (A) auxiliary   (C) beginning

   (B) atheletic   (D) awkward

3. (A) environment   (C) Febuary

   (B) existence   (D) daybreak

4. (A) ocassion   (C) omitted

   (B) occurrence   (D) fundamental

5. (A) perspiration   (C) priviledge

   (B) referring   (D) kindergarten

> **DIRECTIONS:** Choose the correct option.

6. <u>Preceding</u> the <u>business</u> session, lunch will be served in a <u>separate</u> room.

   (A) preceeding . . . business . . . seperate

   (B) proceeding . . . bussiness . . . seperate

   (C) proceeding . . . business . . . seperite

   (D) No change is necessary.

7. Monte <u>inadvertently</u> left <u>several</u> of his <u>libary</u> books in the cafeteria.

   (A) inadverdently . . . serveral . . . libery

   (B) inadvertently . . . several . . . library

   (C) inadvertentely . . . several . . . librery

   (D) No change is necessary.

8. Sam wished he had more <u>liesure</u> time so he could <u>persue</u> his favorite hobbies.

   (A) leisure . . . pursue   (B) Liesure . . . pursue

   (C) leisure . . . persue   (D) No change is necessary.

9. One of my <u>favrite charecters</u> in <u>litrature</u> is Bilbo from *The Hobbit*.

   (A) favrite . . . characters . . . literature

   (B) favorite . . . characters . . . literature

   (C) favourite . . . characters . . . literature

   (D) No change is necessary.

10. Even <u>tho</u> Joe was badly hurt in the <u>accidant</u>, the company said they were not <u>lible</u> for damages.

    (A) though . . . accidant . . . libel

    (B) though . . . accident . . . liable

    (C) though . . . acident . . . liable

    (D) No change is necessary.

ENGLISH LANGUAGE SKILLS REVIEW

ANSWER KEY

Drill: Word Choice Skills

1.	(D)	4.	(C)	7.	(A)	9.	(C)
2.	(D)	5.	(A)	8.	(B)	10.	(B)
3.	(A)	6.	(C)				

Drill: Sentence Structure Skills

1.	(C)	4.	(B)	7.	(B)	9.	(B)
2.	(B)	5.	(A)	8.	(C)	10.	(B)
3.	(B)	6.	(A)				

Drill: Verbs

1.	(C)	4.	(A)	7.	(A)	9.	(A)
2.	(D)	5.	(A)	8.	(C)	10.	(D)
3.	(D)	6.	(B)				

Drill: Pronouns

1.	(A)	4.	(A)	7.	(B)	9.	(A)
2.	(C)	5.	(D)	8.	(B)	10.	(C)
3.	(A)	6.	(A)				

Drill: Adjectives and Adverbs

1.	(C)	4.	(C)	7.	(A)	9.	(B)
2.	(A)	5.	(A)	8.	(C)	10.	(C)
3.	(D)	6.	(C)				

Drill: Punctuation

1.	(D)	4.	(C)	7.	(A)	9.	(B)
2.	(A)	5.	(A)	8.	(A)	10.	(D)
3.	(A)	6.	(D)				

Drill: Capitalization

1.	(D)	4.	(A)	7.	(B)	9.	(B)
2.	(B)	5.	(C)	8.	(D)	10.	(A)
3.	(C)	6.	(D)				

Drill: Spelling

1.	(A)	4.	(A)	7.	(B)	9.	(B)
2.	(B)	5.	(C)	8.	(A)	10.	(B)
3.	(C)	6.	(D)				

DETAILED EXPLANATIONS OF ANSWERS

Drill: Word Choice Skills

1. **(D)** Choice (D) is correct. No change is necessary. *Principal* as an adjective means "most important." *Principle* is a noun meaning "axiom" or "rule of conduct."

2. **(D)** Choice (D) is correct. No change is necessary. *Affect* is a verb meaning "to influence" or "to change." *Effect* is a noun meaning "result."

3. **(A)** Choice (A) is correct. Use *amount* with noncountable, mass nouns (*amount* of food, help, money); use *number* with countable, plural nouns (*number* of children, classes, bills).

4. **(C)** Choice (C) is correct. *Supposed to* and *used to* should be spelled with a final *d*. *Achieving* follows the standard spelling rule—*i* before *e*.

5. **(A)** Choice (A) is correct. Use *that*, not *because*, to introduce clauses after the word *reason*. Choices (B) and (C) contain incorrect spellings of "succeeded."

6. **(C)** Choice (C) is correct. *Converge together* is redundant, and *single* is not needed to convey the meaning of *a highway*.

7. **(A)** Choice (A) is correct. It is economical and concise. The other choices contain unnecessary repetition.

8. **(B)** Choice (B) is correct. Choices (A) and (C) pad the sentences with loose synonyms that are redundant. Choice (D), although a short sentence, does not convey the meaning as clearly as choice (B).

9. **(C)** Choice (C) is correct. The other choices all contain unnecessary repetition.

10. **(B)** Choice (B) is correct. Choices (A) and (C) contain circumlocution; they fail to get to the point. Choice (D) does not express the meaning of the sentence as concisely as choice (B).

Drill: Sentence Structure Skills

1. **(C)** Choice (C) is correct. Each response contains items in a series. In choices (A), (B), and (D), the word group after the conjunction is not an adjective like the first words in the series. Choice (C) contains three adjectives.

2. **(B)** Choice (B) is correct. Choices (A) and (C) combine conjunctions incorrectly. Choice (D) incorrectly uses the adverb *not*.

3. **(B)** Choice (B) is correct. Choices (A) and (C) appear to be parallel because the conjunction *and* connects two word groups that both begin with *because*, but the structures on both sides of the conjunction are very different. Choice (D) has the same structural problem as both (A) and (C), and it uses the conjunctions *that* unnecessarily. *Because he kept his campaign promises* is a clause; *because of his refusal to accept political favors* is a prepositional phrase. Choice (B) connects two dependent clauses.

4. **(B)** Choice (B) is correct. Choices (A), (C), and (D) contain the elliptical clause *While . . . taking a shower*. It appears that the missing subject in the elliptical clause is the same as that in the independent clause—the *doorbell* in choice (A) and *someone* in choice (C), neither of which is a logical subject for the verbal *taking a shower*. Choice (B) removes the elliptical clause and provides the logical subject.

5. **(A)** Choice (A) is correct. Who swung the bat? Choices (B), (C), and (D) imply that it is the runner who swung the bat. Only choice (A) makes it clear that as *he* swung the bat, someone else (the *runner*) stole second base.

6. **(A)** Choice (A) is correct. The punctuation in the original sentence and in choice (B) creates a fragment. *Cotton being the state's principal crop* is not an independent thought because it lacks a complete verb—*being* is not a complete verb.

7. **(B)** Choice (B) is correct. The punctuation in the original sentence and in choice (A) creates a fragment. Both the semicolon and the period should be used to separate two independent clauses. The word group *one that I have never seen before* does not express a complete thought and therefore is not an independent clause.

8.   **(C)**   Choice (C) is correct. The dependent clause *because repairs were being made* in choices (B) and (C) is punctuated as if it were a sentence. The result is a fragment.

9.   **(B)**   Choice (B) is correct. Choices (A) and (C) do not separate the complete thoughts in the independent clauses with the correct punctuation.

10.   **(B)**   Choice (B) is correct. Choices (A) and (C) do not separate the independent clauses with the correct punctuation.

Drill: Verbs

1.   **(C)**   Choice (C) is correct. The past participle form of each verb is required because of the auxiliaries (helping verbs) *had been* (concerned) and *would have* (gone).

2.   **(D)**   Choice (D) is correct. The forms of the irregular verb meaning *to rest* are *lie (rest), lies (rests), lay (rested),* and *has lain (has rested).* The forms of the verb meaning *to put* are *lay (put), lays (puts), laying (putting), laid (put),* and *have laid (have put).*

3.   **(D)**   Choice (D) is correct. The present tense is used for universal truths and the past tense is used for historical truths.

4.   **(A)**   Choice (A) is correct. The present tense is used for customary happenings. Choice (B), *had begun,* is not a standard verb form. Choice (C), *was beginning,* indicates that 10:30 a.m. is not the regular class time.

5.   **(A)**   Choice (A) is correct. The past tense is used for historical statements, and the present tense is used for statements about works of art.

6.   **(B)**   Choice (B) is correct. The subject of the sentence is the plural noun *sales,* not the singular noun *Christmas,* which is the object of the prepositional phrase.

7.   **(A)**   Choice (A) is correct. The subject *specialty* is singular.

8.   **(C)**   Choice (C) is correct. Subjects preceded by *every* are considered singular and therefore require a singular verb form.

9.   **(A)**   Choice (A) is correct. The subject of the sentence is the gerund *hiding,* not the object of the gerund phrase *mistakes. Hiding* is singular; therefore, the singular verb form *does* should be used.

10. **(D)** Choice (D) is correct. Though the form of the subject *Board of Regents* is plural, it is singular in meaning.

Drill: Pronouns

1. **(A)** Choice (A) is correct. Do not use the reflexive pronoun *myself* as a substitute for *I*.

2. **(C)** Choice (C) is correct. In the clause *whoever consumes them*, *whoever* is the subject. *Whomever* is the objective case pronoun and should be used only as the object of a sentence, never as the subject.

3. **(A)** Choice (A) is correct. Use the nominative case pronoun *who* as the subject complement after the verb *is*.

4. **(A)** Choice (A) is correct. In this sentence use the nominative case/subject pronouns *she who* as the subject complement after the *be* verb *was*.

5. **(D)** Choice (D) is correct. *Student* is an indefinite, genderless noun that requires a singular personal pronoun. While *his* is a singular personal pronoun, a genderless noun includes both the masculine and feminine forms and requires *his or her* as the singular personal pronoun.

6. **(A)** Choice (A) is correct. The antecedent *company* is singular, requiring the singular pronoun *it*, not the plural *they*.

7. **(B)** Choice (B) is correct. Choice (A) contains a person shift: *Your* is a second person pronoun, and *his* and *her* are third person pronouns. The original sentence uses the third person plural pronoun *their* to refer to the singular antecedent *every car owner*. Choice (B) correctly provides the masculine and feminine forms *his or her* required by the indefinite, genderless *every car owner*.

8. **(B)** Choice (B) is correct. The implied antecedent is *teaching*. Choices (A) and (C) each contain a pronoun with no antecedent. Neither *it* nor *this* are suitable substitutions for *teacher*.

9. **(A)** Choice (A) is correct. The pronoun *they* in the original sentence has no conspicuous antecedent. Since the doer of the action is obviously unknown (and therefore genderless), choice (B), *he*, is not the correct choice.

10. **(C)** Choice (C) is correct. The original sentence is ambiguous: the pronoun *she* has two possible antecedents; we don't know whether it is Margaret or her sister who is away at college.

Drill: Adjectives and Adverbs

1. **(C)** Choice (C) is correct. *Bad* is an adjective; *badly* is an adverb. *Real* is an adjective meaning *genuine* (*a real problem, real leather*). To qualify an adverb of degree to express how bad, how excited, how boring, etc., choose *very*.

2. **(A)** Choice (A) is correct. Use an adverb as a qualifier for an adjective. *How simple? Relatively simple.*

3. **(D)** Choice (D) is correct. *Good* is an adjective; *well* is both an adjective and an adverb. As an adjective, *well* refers to health; it means "not ill."

4. **(C)** Choice (C) is correct. All the other choices use *good* incorrectly as an adverb. *Shake* is an action verb that requires an adverb, not an adjective.

5. **(A)** Choice (A) is correct. The action verbs *speaks, writes, observe,* and *think* each require adverbs as modifiers.

6. **(C)** Choice (C) is correct. The comparisons in choices (A), (B), and (D) are illogical: these sentences suggest that Los Angeles is not in California because it *is larger than any city in California.*

7. **(A)** Choice (A) is correct. Do not omit the second *as* of the correlative pair *as . . . as* when making a point of equal or superior comparison, as in choice (B). Choice (C) omits *than* from "if not more interesting [than]". Choice (D) incorrectly uses *as* instead of *than*.

8. **(C)** Choice (C) is correct. Choice (A) illogically compares *baseball team* to a *university*, and choices (B) and (D) illogically compare *baseball team* to *all the other universities*. Choice (C) logically compares the baseball team here to the one at any other university, as implied by the possessive ending on university—*university's.*

9. **(B)** Choice (B) is correct. Choices (A), (C), and (D) are ambiguous; because these sentences are too elliptical, the reader does not know where to place the missing information.

10. **(C)**   Choice (C) is correct. Choice (A) is redundant; there is no need to use *most* with *stingiest*. Choice (B) incorrectly combines the superlative word *most* with the comparative form *stingier*. Choice (D) incorrectly combines the comparative word *more* with the superlative form *stingiest*.

Drill: Punctuation

1. **(D)**   Choice (D) is correct. Nonrestrictive clauses, like other nonrestrictive elements, should be set off from the rest of the sentence with commas.

2. **(A)**   Choice (A) is correct. Use a comma to separate a nonrestrictive appositive from the word it modifies. "An Oklahoma family" is a nonrestrictive appositive.

3. **(A)**   Choice (A) is correct. Do not use unnecessary commas to separate a subject and verb from their complement. Both choices (B) and (C) use superfluous punctuation.

4. **(C)**   Choice (C) is correct. Do not separate two items in a compound with commas. The original sentence incorrectly separates "car or plane." Choice (A) omits the comma after the introductory clause.

5. **(A)**   Choice (A) is correct. Use a semicolon to separate two independent clauses/sentences that are not joined by a coordinating conjunction, especially when the ideas in the sentences are interrelated.

6. **(D)**   Choice (D) is correct. Use a semicolon to separate two sentences not joined by a coordinating conjunction.

7. **(A)**   Choice (A) is correct. Use a semicolon to separate two sentences joined by a conjunctive adverb.

8. **(A)**   Choice (A) is correct. Do not use a colon after a verb or a preposition. Remember that a complete sentence must precede a colon.

9. **(B)**   Choice (B) is correct. Do not use a colon after a preposition, and do not use a colon to separate a preposition from its objects.

10. **(D)**   Choice (D) is correct. Use a colon preceding a list that is introduced by words such as *the following* and *as follows*.

Drill: Capitalization

1. **(D)** Choice (D) is correct. *North America*, like other proper names, is capitalized. *North, south, east,* and *west* are only capitalized when they refer to geographic regions (*the Southwest, Eastern Europe);* as compass directions, they are not capitalized.

2. **(B)** Choice (B) is correct. Although persons' names are capitalized, a person's title is not (*coach*, not *Coach*). Capitalize the complete name of a team, school, river, etc. (Dallas Cowboys). *The*, whether it is part of the official title or not, is never capitalized when it appears in text.

3. **(C)** Choice (C) is correct. Capitalize all geographic units, and capitalize *earth* only when it is mentioned with other planets. *Equator* is not capitalized.

4. **(A)** Choice (A) is correct. Capitalize the first word in a title and all other words in a title except articles, prepositions with fewer than five letters, and conjunctions.

5. **(C)** Choice (C) is correct. Capitalize proper adjectives (proper nouns used as adjectives): *Greek* goddess, *Roman* mythology.

6. **(D)** Choice (D) is correct. Capitalize all religious groups, books, and names referring to religious deities.

7. **(B)** Choice (B) is correct. Do not capitalize courses unless they are languages (English) or course titles followed by a number (Algebra I).

8. **(D)** Choice (D) is correct. Do not capitalize seasons unless they accompany the name of an event such as *Spring Break.* Do not capitalize types of degrees (*bachelor's degrees*); capitalize only the name of the degree (*Bachelor of Arts degree*).

9. **(B)** Choice (B) is correct. As a landmark, *Berlin Wall* is capitalized; however, do not capitalize systems of government or individual adherents to a philosophy, such as *communism*.

10. **(A)** Choice (A) is correct. The names of planets, as well as the complete names of newspapers and other periodicals, are capitalized.

Drill: Spelling

1.   **(A)**   The correct spelling of choice (A) is "probably."

2.   **(B)**   The correct spelling is "athletic."

3.   **(C)**   Choice (C) should be spelled "February."

4.   **(A)**   The correct spelling of this word is "occasion."

5.   **(C)**   Choice (C) should be spelled "privilege."

6.   **(D)**   Choice (D) is the best response. *Business* has only three -*s's*. *Separate* has an -*e* at the beginning and the end, not in the middle.

7.   **(B)**   Choice (B) is the best response. *Library* has two *r's*.

8.   **(A)**   Choice (A) is the best response. *Leisure* is one of the few English words that does not follow the *i* before *e* except after *c* rule. *Pursue* has two *u's* and only one *e*.

9.   **(B)**   Choice (B) is the best response. "Favorite," "characters," and "literature" are commonly mispronounced, and when someone who mispronounces them tries to spell them phonetically, he or she often misspells them.

10.   **(B)**   Choice (B) is the best response. Advertisements often misspell words to catch the consumer's eye (*lite* for light, *tho* for though, etc.), and these misspellings are becoming more common in student writing. "Accident" and "liable" are examples of words that are not pronounced the way they are spelled.

III. WRITING SKILLS REVIEW

RECOGNIZING THE WRITER'S PURPOSE AND INTENDED AUDIENCE

Now that you know what you are being tested for in this exam, you should know what characteristics of prose passages or essays guide the reader to clear understanding. Listed below are some guidelines to help you become more alert to reading cues in writing that you may need to understand a given passage.

ANALYZING A PASSAGE FOR PURPOSE AND AUDIENCE

Read the whole passage through once. On your first pass look for the following key items to comprehend the overall purpose of the passage and the audience it serves.

DETERMINE WHAT ESSAY STRATEGY THE WRITER USES: EXPLAIN, INFORM, OR PERSUADE

All writing is organized to achieve a particular purpose, either implied or stated; all of an essay's organizational strategies may be used to argue. Writers use **seven basic** strategies to organize information and ideas in essays to help prove their point (thesis, or **T**) and achieve a particular purpose (to inform, explain, or persuade). All of the seven strategies might be useful in persuading a reader to see the issue the writer's way.

To prove a thesis, writers may

1. show how a *process* or a procedure does or should work step by step in time;

2. *compare or contrast* two or more things or ideas to show important differences or similarities;

3. *identify a problem* and then explain how to solve it;

4. *analyze* into its components, or *classify* by its types or categories an idea or thing to show how it is put together or how it works or how it is designed;

5. *explain* why something happens to produce a particular result or set of results;

6. *describe* the particular individual characteristics, beauty and features of a place, person(s), time, or idea;

7. *define* what a thing is or what an idea means.

In a given essay, one pattern tends to dominate the discussion, depending on the object or idea in question. (For example, I might *describe* and *explain* in order to *define* the varied meanings of "love".)

CONSIDER IMPLICATIONS AND INFERENCES

Writers sometimes *imply* things that would be a logical extension of what they actually say. For example, it would be unreasonable to suggest that the writer in the passage below is implying that he wants a liberated feminist career woman for his spouse. It doesn't logically fit the examples (**E**'s) he offers in his paragraph. These examples don't support that idea.

(**E**) I want a wife who will wash my clothes and iron my shirts. (**E**) I want a wife who will clean the house and do the dishes. (**E**) I want a wife who will change the babies' diapers and cook my meals. (**E**) I want a wife who will do the shopping and greet me with my favorite cocktail when I come home tired from work.

It is obvious that the writer wants a wife. Now, whatever you may think of the writer (never let your emotions cloud your feelings and get in the way of what was said), he is making a point about *what kind* of wife he wants. Notice that the paragraph is nothing but (**E**'s) examples. All of the sentences show, or exemplify, characteristics of the "wife" this guy wants — but no one of them brings us to a firm conclusion. So, this writer *implies* in the paragraph, without actually stating, the kind of wife he wants. Yet we still get a pretty clear picture or idea of her:

[The writer] wants a traditional housekeeper wife. (**T**) This would probably be close to the **T** sentence of this writer's paragraph or passage if he had not implied it, but had stated it instead. Some of you may have been *feeling* that what he wants is a slave, not a wife — but be careful: that's what you may feel, not what the writer is implying. Don't confuse your feelings with the writer's facts or illustrations.

These tests will often require you to understand and recognize what a reader can *infer* from the passage once you have read it. Actually, implications and inferences are very similar; the only difference is who is making them: Writers imply, readers infer. For example, in this case, the reader could *infer* that the writer is a male who wants a conventional wife. He probably likes football, too. Probably — that's an **inference:** a reader's probable and reasonable conclusion or interpretation of an idea based upon what the writer has written. For example, it would be unreasonable to infer the writer was a woman — women generally have husbands, not wives.

DETERMINE THE NATURE OF THE AUDIENCE

If you ask a series of questions about a given passage, you can determine the nature of the audience. As you read, keep in mind the writer's purpose as you understand it. Using the questions below, develop through your answers a mental picture of the audience (besides yourself) reading this passage.

1. What does the writer intend the readers of this passage to take away with them? The writer's point of view? Information?

2. How old are the readers?

3. What is their level of education?

4. What attitudes, prejudices, opinions, fears, experience, and concerns might the audience for this passage have?

Considerations of audience will directly affect the tone of a passage, and thus determine what level of usage or meaning is appropriate in a given paragraph or section of an essay. For example, if I am writing to a 13-year-old, should I write: "Please peruse with comprehension the tome offered," or "Please be sure to read and study what is in this book." The latter sentence, with its simple vocabulary, is the appropriate choice.

RECOGNIZING EFFECTIVE ORGANIZATION: UNITY, FOCUS, AND DEVELOPMENT

LOOK FOR KEY SECTIONS (T) AND (t)

In reading a particular passage, you want to identify what portions or sections of a whole essay you confront. Depending upon which section of an essay is offered, you may decide whether you are reading the writer's main point (or thesis), purpose, or evidence. You will also need to know or recognize what sort of logic the writer is using, such as cause/effect, or problem/solution, and so on.

KEY SECTIONS TO RECOGNIZE

Introduction: The introductory paragraph usually shows the writer's point of view, or thesis (**T**), about an issue and introduces that position with some lead-in or general data to support the thesis. The thesis of an essay is the writer's stated or implied position on a particular issue or idea;

the writer's thesis (**T**) is the writer's stand on the subject under discussion. Identify the writer's purpose and point of view.

● **EXAMPLE**

Find the main idea by reading the following passage and then answer the question.

Passage A (from *National Geographic*, 1917)

The eruption of Mount Katmai in June, 1912, was one of the most tremendous volcanic explosions ever recorded. A mass of ash and pumice whose volume has been estimated at nearly five cubic miles was thrown into the air. In
5 its fall this material buried an area as large as the state of Connecticut to a depth varying from 10 inches to over 10 feet, while small amounts of ash fell as much as 900 miles away.

10 Great quantities of very fine dust were thrown into the higher regions of the atmosphere and were quickly distributed over the whole world, so as to have a profound effect on the weather, being responsible for the notoriously cold, wet summer of that year.

The comparative magnitude of the eruption can be bet-
15 ter realized if one should imagine a similar eruption of Vesuvius. Such an eruption would bury Naples under 15 feet of ash; Rome would be covered nearly a foot deep; the sound would be heard at Paris; dust from the crater would fall in Brussels and Berlin, and the fumes would be notice-
20 able far beyond Christiania, Norway.

Fortunately, the volcano is situated in a country so sparsely inhabited that the damage caused by the eruption was insignificant—very much less than in many relatively small eruptions in populous districts, such as that of
25 Vesuvius, which destroyed Pompeii and Herculaneum. Indeed, so remote and little known is the volcano that there were not any witnesses near enough to see the eruption, and it was not until the National Geographic Society's expeditions explored the district that it was settled definitely which
30 of several nearby volcanoes was really the seat of the disturbance.

The most important settlement in the devastated district
is Kodiak, which, although a hundred miles from the volcano, was buried nearly a foot deep in ash. This ashy blan-
35   ket transformed the "Green Kodiak" of other days into a
gray desert of sand, whose redemption and revegetation
seemed utterly hopeless. When I first visited it, a year later,
it presented an appearance barren and desolate. It seemed to
every one there that it must be many years before it could
40   recover its original condition.

Which statement below most accurately describes the main idea of
this passage?

(A)   Volcanic explosions are the most destructive events in nature.

(B)   The eruption of Mount Katmai was one of the largest volcanic
explosions on record.

(C)   Mount Katmai is so remotely located that no one witnessed its
eruption.

(D)   The most important settlement in the area of Mount Katmai is
Kodiak.

The passage makes a statement like choice (B) right at the beginning.
But is it the main idea? The passage describes the size and extent of the
explosion, tries to help us appreciate its magnitude by describing what a
similar eruption of Vesuvius would do to the cities of Europe, explains
that this tremendous explosion caused little damage because of its remoteness, and describes its effects on a settlement named Kodiak.

Everything in the passage seems related to the idea that the eruption of
Mount Katmai was one of the greatest volcanic explosions ever. It may be
true that volcanic explosions are the most destructive in nature, but no-
where in the passage does the author make this claim or compare volcanic
eruptions with other destructive natural events such as earthquakes and
hurricanes. Choice (A), therefore, cannot be right. The passage does state
that Mount Katmai is so remote that no one witnessed the eruption. But
how can this be the main idea? The first three paragraphs focus not on the
remoteness of the volcano but on the great size of the eruption. The point
about the volcano's remote location is made only to explain why such a
terrific explosion caused such little damage. Choice (C), therefore, cannot
be right. The fact that Kodiak is the most important settlement in the area
of Mount Katmai is used to illustrate the size and power of Mount Katmai's
eruption. Even though the village is 100 miles away from the mountain, it

was still covered by a layer of ash 12 inches deep. Again, the author's main point is that the eruption was one of the most tremendous on record. Therefore, choice (D) cannot be right. Choice (B) is the best answer.

Development: Three middle paragraphs (or more) which prove the writer's position from different angles, using evidence from real-life experience and knowledge. Evidence may take the form of facts, examples, statistics, illustrations, opinions, or analogies. For our purposes, we will call all such evidence **examples** (**E**)'s.

In addition, each paragraph within the development section will have a stated or implied main point (*t*) used to support the thesis (**T**) of the whole passage. The main point (*t*) of a paragraph in the development section will be used to support the essay's whole thesis (**T**). For example, my thesis might be, "Dogs are better than cats." Having said that, I might write a whole paragraph with supporting examples to show a main point (*t*) in support of that idea. The main point (*t*) of the paragraph that needs support, then, might be as follows:

First of all, dogs are more loyal than cats. (*t*)

The evidence (**E**) that I summon to support that point (*t*) which, in turn, supports my overall thesis (**T**), would therefore have to be either facts, statistics, expert testimony, or anecdotal knowledge that showed that dogs were indeed more loyal than cats. For example: "The A.S.P.C.A. reports that 99 out of 100 dogs cannot adjust to new owners after the death of their original masters, while only two out of 100 cats cannot adjust in the same situation." (**E**)

- **EXAMPLE**

Answer the following question based on the earlier passage about Mount Katmai

The example that Naples would be buried in 15 feet of ash is used to illustrate

(A) the enormous size of the eruption of Mount Katmai.

(B) the folly of building cities and towns in the vicinity of a volcano.

(C) the tremendous power of Mount Vesuvius.

(D) the fact that ancient volcanic eruptions are much like modern ones.

The sentence preceding the example about Naples reads, "The comparative magnitude of the eruption can be better realized if one should imagine a similar eruption of Vesuvius." The author is trying to help us appreciate the enormous devastation that Mount Katmai *could have* caused if it were not so remote from population centers. Choice (A), therefore, must be correct.

It may very well be foolish to build near a volcano, but the author's focus here is not on the proximity of Naples to Vesuvius. It is on the spectacular power of Mount Katmai's eruption. Choice (B), therefore, is incorrect.

The author asks us to imagine what would happen if Vesuvius erupted with an explosion the size of Mount Katmai's. The actual power of Vesuvius is beside the point, making (C) incorrect. Choice (D) is incorrect because the passage says nothing about the similarity of ancient and modern eruptions.

Conclusion: The last paragraph, or two, usually (but not always) sums up the writer's position (**T**) and may add some final reminder of what the issue was, some speculation, or some call to action that the writer suggests.

Depending on the author's purpose, he or she will organize information and ideas according to a particular pattern or arrangement. If, for example, his or her purpose is to describe the differences between a horse and a donkey, the author would most likely choose the organizational pattern called *contrast*. The second critical reading skill tested on the CLEP is the ability to identify the organizational pattern of a passage.

Fortunately, there are not very many different ways in which authors normally develop their material. Here is a list of types of patterns you may be asked to identify, along with the purposes for which each pattern is used. Study the list to familiarize yourself with the different patterns. Then try to answer the question about a sample passage.

Organizational Pattern	Purpose
(1) time order	to narrate events in chronological order
(2) location order	to describe a scene or object in an orderly way (e.g., top to bottom)
(3) comparison	to call attention to the *similarities* between two things, people, or events
(4) contrast	to call attention to the *differences* between two things, people, or events

Organizational Pattern	Purpose
(5) summary	to sum up in brief what has already been said at greater length
(6) definition	to clarify the meaning of a word or term by defining it precisely
(7) classification	to divide up a subject into different categories or classes
(8) addition	to develop a subject simply by making one point after another
(9) simple listing	to make a list of items, qualities, characteristics, etc.
(10) cause and effect	to demonstrate how an event came about due to certain conditions or causes
(11) statement and clarification	to explain more fully and clearly what is said at the beginning of the passage
(12) generalization and example	to support a general statement by giving one or more specific examples that illustrate its truth

CHECK FOR LOGIC

Make sure the evidence proves the writer's point and not something else.

Be careful about conclusions. The writer may not have proven his point. An essay is essentially a syllogism that proves something by induction or deduction. Induction is that sort of reasoning which arrives at a general conclusion based on the relationship among the particular elements of a thing or idea. Deduction reasons from the general to the particular. For example, I may assert that all frogs croak before they jump, and then go on to find supporting evidence in frog ponds around the world. If I never find a frog that doesn't croak, I may assume that my deduction is correct.

Sometimes, however, the premises of an argument are false or unprovable. For example,

Premise One:	Harry Jones has a beard.
Premise Two:	All goats have beards.
Conclusion:	Therefore, Harry is a goat.

The conclusion may be correct based on the premises, but the premises are unrelated. What about the fact that Harry may be a human being and that goats are not human beings? Because there is insufficient information, you should not conclude that Harry is a goat.

Here are typical fallacies that some writers fall into:

Either/Or: The writer assumes only two opposing possibilities apply. "Either we abolish cars, or the environment is doomed." Other factors may contribute to destroying the environment.

Oversimplification: "Only motivated athletes become champions." Maybe not; unfortunately, sometimes athletes with enhancing steroids become champions, too.

Begging the Question: The writer assumes as proven something which needs to be proven: "Faithful dogs never leave their masters." Dogs, however, may sometimes prove unfaithful.

Ignoring the Issue: An argument against the truth of a person's argument shifts from what the writer observed to how the testimony is no good because it is about a disgusting or repulsive topic.

Arguing Against a Person, Not an Idea: The writer argues that somebody's idea has no merit because s/he is immoral or personally stupid. "John can't prove anything about dogs being faithful; he can't even understand basic mathematics." One has nothing to do with the other.

Non Sequitur: Leaping to a wrong conclusion: "John is tall; he must know a lot about basketball."

Drawing the Wrong Conclusion from a Sequence: "He trained and then read and then trained some more and therefore won the match." Perhaps something else besides this sequence of events led to his winning the match.

Fallacy	Definition	Example
circular thinking	Merely repeating in other words the thing you are trying to prove or argue	"The poor need our help because they are so destitute." ("Poor" and "destitute" mean the same thing.)
ad hominem (against the person)	Attacking one's opponent rather than his or her arguments	"What do *you* know about child care reform? You've been divorced twice!"
faulty analogy	Comparing two situations that are quite different in some ways	"Unemployment's up, the stock market is falling—we're in for another Depression."
hasty generalization	Drawing a conclusion based on too few cases	"That's the third cat I've seen. This town is full of cats."
begging the question	*Assuming* that part of your argument is true rather than providing evidence	"Since the grading system is unfair, we need to change it." (But *is* it unfair? That needs to be argued.)
non sequitur (it doesn't follow)	Drawing a conclusion which is not logically connected to the preceding statements	"She was an Olympic athlete, so I'm sure she'll be a great Secretary of Labor."
either/or (false dilemma)	Reducing an issue to only two alternatives when others exist	"America—love it or leave it." (It is possible to be critical of one's government without wanting to leave the country.)

Fallacy	Definition	Example
post hoc, ergo propter hoc (after this, therefore because of this)	Assuming that because one event followed another, the first must have caused the second	"You're sneezing! I knew you'd catch a cold at that concert last night."
red herring	Introducing an irrelevant issue to distract attention from the real issue	"Before we go and elect this woman mayor, I'd like to remind you that our last female mayor resigned in disgrace."
ad populum (to the people)	Playing upon expected emotional responses of readers to certain words, phrases, or concepts	"To keep this great country of ours second to none, we need to vote for higher tariffs on imports."

● **EXAMPLE**

Find the best answer.

1.   "The French are rude. I know three different people who have been to France, and they all talk about how rude the French are."

Is the argument in the above quotation valid or invalid?

(A) Valid   (B) Invalid

2.   "Every Swiss citizen has access to health care. If their system works there, it will work in the U.S., too."

Which of the following fallacies does the above argument use?

(A) Ad hominem (to the man)   (C) Faulty analogy

(B) Circular thinking   (D) Bandwagon

ANSWER

1.   **(B)**   The argument is invalid, (B). It is a hasty generalization based on too few cases.

2.   **(C)**   The statement uses a faulty analogy, (C), assuming that the U.S. is the same as Switzerland, but there are many differences which could make the Swiss system unworkable in the U.S.

DISTINGUISHING BETWEEN FACT AND OPINION

Critical readers do not accept everything they read as true. They realize that many kinds of writing are mixtures of objective facts and the author's opinions, and critical readers are able to tell which is which. A few questions on the CLEP, therefore, will ask you to indicate whether a particular statement is a statement of fact or a statement of opinion.

In answering these questions, keep in mind that a "statement of fact" must be proved or provable by objective means—for example, the means may be checking the date of Washington's birth in an encyclopedia, finding the spelling of "abacus" in a dictionary, or discovering the winner of the 1967 World Series in an almanac. If a statement cannot be verified or disproved by "looking it up," then it must be a statement of opinion.

Even if an author's opinion or view seems to be obviously true, it is still a statement of opinion. You may agree strongly, for example, that "Americans spend too much time watching TV." But that is still an opinion—a personal view that cannot be proved or disproved by "looking it up."

On the other hand, a "statement of fact" may be made in error and still remain a "statement of fact." For example, an author might mistakenly write, "Bill Clinton is our 52nd president." That is a "statement of fact" even though it is not true. (Clinton is the 42nd president of the United States.) What makes it a "statement of fact" is that it can be verified or disproved by looking it up, by checking the facts.

● EXAMPLE

Determine whether the following statements are statements of fact or statements of opinion.

1. The statement that "The United States made a mistake in selling wheat to Russia" is a statement of

    (A) fact.

    (B) opinion.

2. The statement, "The day after the sale of wheat to Russia, the stock market rose 50 points" is a statement of

    (A) fact.

    (B) opinion.

3.   The statement, "The best seasoning to use with Italian dishes is oregano" is a statement of

(A)   fact.   (B)   opinion.

Question 1 gives us a statement of opinion: people might disagree as to whether or not the sale was a mistake. Question 2 is a statement of fact: we could check its accuracy by looking up the date of the sale and the stock market reports for that day and the following day. Question 3 is a statement of opinion: even if 99.99% of all people in the world agree that oregano is "the best" seasoning, it is still a statement of opinion, a matter of taste.

DETECTING BIAS

Closely related to the ability to distinguish between fact and opinion is the ability to detect an author's bias. Bias is a predisposition in favor of or against someone or something: it is a liking for or a dislike of a person or thing. "Prejudice" is close in meaning to "bias," but "prejudice" is a more negative word; it implies a lack of reasonableness, an irrational prejudgment, and it is usually a dislike of a certain group or race.

By contrast, bias is simply a person's feeling for or against something. While it is important to recognize an author's bias, we should not condemn the writer for having a bias. Most readers enjoy learning how an author feels about the subject matter. Bias makes writing more human. Without it, most writing would be too dry.

How do you detect bias in a passage or statement? Watch for these tell-tale signs:

(1)   The author assumes the truth of something that she or he does not try to argue or defend: "It goes without saying that German cars are the best designed in the world."

(2)   The author uses very emotional language in making a point: "They should collect every handgun in the country and dump them all in the ocean."

(3)   The author exaggerates: "Television has ruined this great country!"

(4)   The author stereotypes: "French waiters must go to a special school to learn rudeness."

(5)   The author resorts to name-calling: "Those illiterate, foul-mouthed, bare-chested fans ruined the game for me."

On the CLEP you may be asked to identify which subject the author shows bias in favor of or against. You also may be given four statements and be asked which one shows bias.

● **EXAMPLE**

Read the following passage and see if you can spot the biased statement.

Passage B (from Henry Adams, *History of the United States of America during the Administration of Thomas Jefferson,* 1884-1885)

That Americans should not have been liked was natural; but that they should not have been understood was more significant by far. After the downfall of the French republic they had no right to expect a kind word from Europe, and
5 during the next twenty years they rarely received one. The liberal movement of Europe was cowed, and no one dared express democratic sympathies until the Napoleonic tempest had passed. With this attitude Americans had no right to find fault, for Europe cared less to injure them than to
10 protect herself. Nevertheless, observant readers could not but feel surprised that none of the numerous Europeans who then wrote and spoke about America seemed to study the subject seriously. The ordinary traveler was apt to be little more reflective than a bee or an ant, but some of these
15 critics possessed powers far from ordinary; yet Talleyrand alone showed that had he but seen America a few years later than he did, he might have suggested some sufficient reason for apparent contradictions that perplexed him in the national character.

The author shows bias when he says

(A) "during the next twenty years they rarely received one." (line 5)

(B) "Europe cared less to injure them than to protect herself." (lines 9–10)

(C) "The ordinary traveler was apt to be little more reflective than a bee or an ant." (lines 13–14)

(D) "he might have suggested some sufficient reason for apparent contradictions that perplexed him in the national character." (lines 17–20)

Choice (C) says that "the ordinary traveler" was no more thoughtful or "reflective" than bees or ants. This definitely shows bias against ordinary travelers as a group by stereotyping them. Choice (A) seems to be based on historical fact; it is therefore not biased. Choice (B) says that Europe was most concerned with protecting herself, which is a reasonable statement. Choice (D) speculates about what Talleyrand might have said if he had visited America a few years later. It is complimentary of Talleyrand's intelligence, but certainly not nearly as biased as choice (C).

DRAWING LOGICAL INFERENCES AND CONCLUSIONS

The last critical reading comprehension skill is the ability to determine what an author implies—that is, what an author does not say directly but what we can reasonably assume the author believes based on what he has said. When we say what an author implies, we are drawing inferences. Closely related to an inference is a conclusion: based on your reading, what might you reasonably conclude about the subject or about the author's attitudes or beliefs?

In answering questions about inferences and conclusions, make sure that an answer choice is a statement that can be inferred or concluded on the basis of the given passage. Some answer choices may sound true by themselves, but that does not mean they are implied in the passage. Also, be sure that the statement you choose is not actually in the passage itself; if it is, then it cannot be an inference or a conclusion since it is directly stated.

● **EXAMPLE**

Read the following passage and answer the question.

> "From that moment on, my life changed. My heart grew cold. Whenever someone happened to look at me, I turned aside. If an acquaintance called to me on the street, I pretended not to notice. When the phone rang, I did not answer."

From this passage, you could infer that

(A) the author's life changed.

(B) the author was more sociable before "that moment."

(C) the author was never a very nice person.

(D) the author had no friends.

Since the author's life changed, and since the author behaved unsociably after the change, we may infer that the author was more sociable before the change. Choice (B) seems correct, but consider the others. It is true that the author's life changed, (A), but the author states that directly. We cannot infer what is directly stated. We do not have enough evidence to assume that the author was never "nice," (C). In fact, the passage seems to imply that before the change, he or she was more friendly. We cannot conclude that the author had no friends, (D). Someone calls to him on the street, and someone telephones. In any case, there is no way of knowing about the author's friends or lack of friends.

IDENTIFYING RELATIONSHIPS WITHIN SENTENCES

The skill tested here is very similar to the second critical comprehension skill, identifying organizational patterns, since both skills involve seeing logical relationships. The only difference is that earlier you were asked to spot relationships within a whole passage, whereas here you are asked to see relationships within a simple sentence.

The kinds of relationships within a sentence are also similar to the kinds of organizational patterns in a whole passage which we saw earlier. For example, a passage may be organized according to the principle of contrast, such as the author enumerating the differences between a horse and a donkey. And a single sentence in that passage may also contain a relationship of contrast: "The horse makes a high-pitched neigh, *but* the donkey emits a loud, harsh sound called a bray." In this sentence the connecting word "but" tips us off to the kind of relationship between the two parts of the sentence: "but" signals a contrast between the preceding statement and the following one.

What kinds of relationships might you be asked to identify within sentences? Here is a list of the most common ones, along with the connecting words and phrases that signal the relationship.

Kind of Relationship	Connecting Words
addition	and, in addition, moreover, furthermore
contrast	but, however, on the other hand, by contrast, nevertheless, yet, although
comparison	similarly, likewise, just as
cause and effect	thus, so, hence, because, as a result, since, consequently, therefore

The CLEP General Examination in English Composition may ask you to identify relationships between sentences in two different ways. One way is to correct sentences which omit the connecting words. Another way is to examine a sentence and identify, from four choices, the kind of relationship that exists between two parts of a sentence. An example of each type of question follows.

● **EXAMPLE**

The following passage has some words deleted. For each blank, choose the word or phrase that best completes the passage.

Passage C (from Sarah Orne Jewett, "A White Heron," 1886)

> The woods were already filled with shadows one June evening, just before eight o'clock, _____ (1) _____ a bright sunset still glimmered faintly among the trunks of the trees. A little girl was driving home her cow, a plodding, dilatory, provoking creature in her behavior, _____ (2) _____ a valued companion for all that. They were going away from whatever light there was, and striking deep into the woods, but their feet were familiar with the path, _____ (3) _____ it was no matter whether their eyes could see it or not.

1. The most appropriate word for blank (1) would be

    (A) therefore.   (C) similarly.

    (B) though.   (D) so.

2. The most appropriate word for blank (2) would be

    (A) but.   (C) for.

    (B) and.   (D) thus.

3. The most appropriate word for blank (3) would be

    (A) but.   (C) nevertheless.

    (B) since.   (D) and.

4. Read the following sentence and then select the word or phrase that best describes the relationship between the first part of the sentence ("Hard work...rewarded") and the second part ("irresponsibility ...dismissal").

"Hard work and diligence will be rewarded; irresponsibility, on the other hand, will lead to dismissal."

(A) Addition   (C) Contrast

(B) Comparison   (D) Cause and effect

ANSWER:

1. **(B)** The correct choice is (B) "though." The first part of the sentence emphasizes the shadows in the woods; the second part mentions "a bright sunset." So the relationship is one of *contrast*, which is best expressed by the word "though."

2. **(A)** The correct choice is (A) "but." Before the blank, the cow is called a "plodding, dilatory, provoking creature" (all negative qualities). After the blank, the cow is called a "valued companion." Again, the relationship is one of contrast, expressed by the word "but."

3. **(D)** The correct choice is (D) "and." Before the blank, the paragraph states that the travelers' feet are familiar with the path. Following the blank is the statement that it did not matter that they could not see. Since these ideas are similar, the best connecting word is "and."

4. **(C)** The correct choice is (C) "contrast." The contrast between "hard work and diligence" in the first part of the sentence and "irresponsibility" in the second part is signaled by the phrase "on the other hand."

IDENTIFYING RELATIONSHIPS BETWEEN SENTENCES

The only difference between this skill and the previous one is that here you will be asked to identify relationships *between* sentences instead of relationships within a single sentence. Some of the relationships are the same as within a sentence: addition, comparison, contrast, and cause and effect. Other possibilities are statement and clarification, generalization and example, and summary.

● **EXAMPLE**

Read the following passage and then answer the question.

Passage D (from Mark Twain, *Life on the Mississippi*, 1875)

When I was a boy, there was but one permanent ambition among my comrades in our village on the west bank of

the Mississippi River. That was, to be a steamboatman. We
had transient ambitions of other sorts, but they were only
5   transient. When a circus came and went, it left us all burning to become clowns; the first negro minstrel show that
ever came to our section left us all suffering to try that kind
of life; now and then we had a hope that, if we lived and
were good, God would permit us to be pirates. These ambi-
10 tions faded out, each in its turn; but the ambition to be a
steamboatman always remained.

1.   What is the relationship between the second sentence ("That was…")
     and the first sentence ("When I was a boy…")?

   (A)   Statement and clarification

   (B)   Contrast

   (C)   Cause and effect

   (D)   Addition

2.   What is the relationship between the third sentence ("We had tran-
     sient ambitions…") and the second sentence ("That was…")?

   (A)   Statement and clarification

   (B)   Contrast

   (C)   Cause and effect

   (D)   Addition

ANSWER

1.   **(A)**   The second sentence tells us specifically that the boys wanted
to be steamboatmen. This explains what the author meant in the first sentence by "one permanent ambition." Therefore, the correct answer is (A).

2.   **(B)**   The third sentence mentions other "transient" (passing) ambitions, but these are in contrast to the "permanent" ambition to be a
steamboatman, making (B) the correct answer.

TRANSITIONS

As you review the passage a second time, look for and circle transitions that reveal the connections among the writer's ideas. Transitions
show how the writer is reasoning to get to the point — perhaps it is a

cause/effect pattern or a problem/solution discussion in which the writer provides the solution. S/he may use transitions either at the beginnings of paragraphs or to show connections among ideas within a single paragraph.

Here are some typical transitional words and phrases:

Linking similar ideas
For explanation, analogy, and accruing factual evidence or opinions for a point of view.

again	for example	likewise
also	for instance	moreover
and	further	nor
another	furthermore	of course
besides	in addition	similarly
equally important	in like manner	too

Linking dissimilar/contradictory ideas
To show comparison or contrast among similar or opposing notions.

although	however	otherwise
and yet	in spite of	provided that
as if	instead	still
but	nevertheless	yet
conversely	on the contrary	
even if	on the other hand	

Indicating cause, purpose, result
To show the solutions to a problem or the outcome of a certain series of causes. Causes may be immediate or remote: The immediate cause for my spilling the glass of water was that I knocked it over with my hand. The remote cause might be that I was trying to put on my hat, and in the process I lost my focus on the glass of water in line with my sweeping hand, which was going for my hat across the table.

as for	for this reason	then
as a result	hence	therefore
because	so	thus
consequently	since	

Indicating time or position

Used in process and procedure explanations or chronological narratives to show a sequence in time or place.

above	before	meanwhile
across	beyond	next
afterward	eventually	presently
around	finally	second
at once	first	thereafter
at the present time	here	thereupon

Indicating an example or summary

Used to point to supporting evidence or explanatory material and to complete an idea within a paragraph or within a whole essay.

as a result	in any event	in short
as I have said	in brief	on the whole
for example	in conclusion	to sum up
for instance	in fact	
in any case	in other words	

To prepare yourself for the questions you will encounter on this section of the CLEP General Examination in English Composition, test yourself with this grammar Diagnostic. After you have completed the test, check your answers against the Diagnostic Answer Key at the end of the test to determine your areas of weakness. As you will see, the Diagnostic Answer Key includes detailed explanations to all of the answers. At the end of each explanation is a section reference in brackets [. . .] that refers to the English Language Skills Review which precedes the test. If you get a particular item wrong, the section reference in brackets will be an area in which you need further review.

☞ Drill: Diagnostic

DIRECTIONS: Rewrite the following items so that they follow the rules of correct standard written English.

1. About the television.

    Rewrite:

2. I like television and I think people should watch it television is good because it is so real I think many people would die without it.

    Rewrite:

3. In my opinion, I believe that in order to be able to understand this issue many hours and a lot of time must be devoted to comprehending what the message is that the writer is trying to communicate with ideas due to the fact that s/he is so involved with them.

    Rewrite:

4. Since the car was so old, it was difficult for the mechanic to find the correct parts.

    Rewrite:

5. While waiting for the check, the doorbell rang in the living room.

    Rewrite:

6.   I like eating fish and to go to the shore.

Rewrite:

7.   I bought a computer and some word processing software which was quick and inexpensive.

Rewrite:

8.   We cannot reimburse you for moving boats over 14 feet.

Rewrite:

9.   We could of been contenders in the contest, but the sweep of events make us losers in the end.

Rewrite:

10. This book is more better than yours, but John's is the worse of all three that we read.

Rewrite:

11. Each employee should take his paycheck to the counter. This is the first one you will see.

Rewrite:

12. The doctor was ready and but he could not operate until dawn.

    Rewrite:

13. After the ball was over Scarlet went back to her plantation.

    Rewrite:

14. Captain Kirk Admiral of the Starfleet was also the Captain of the *Enterprise*.

    Rewrite:

15. The dog ate the bones and Richard punished him.

    Rewrite:

16. I like inland woodland ducks, however, I prefer the silent white swans.

    Rewrite:

17. The woman said she had never worked with a "gopher".

    Rewrite:

18. The stores in Brooklyn had been terminated; the Harley Skull Gang had torched, or set fire, to them as an act of political revenge. Head Skull John Harley said, We were only protecting our own turf, as we call it.

Rewrite:

19. The boys couldnt find a way to get to the childrens pool over at the Jones house without the Harley boys gang knowing about it.

Rewrite:

20. the article about france, entitled "come to the heart of europe now" was cited by senator smith whom i had known as a Professor in sociology 101.

Rewrite:

FIVE WRITING STEPS

If you choose the version of the CLEP English Composition with an essay section, you will have 45 minutes to write your essay. You might allocate your time for the five writing steps in this manner:

1. Prewriting, Planning: 4 minutes

2. Rough Draft: 15 minutes

3. Organizing, Checking evidence, Checking "flow," and Paragraphing: 15 minutes.

4. Polishing, Editing: 4–7 minutes

5. Proofreading: 2–4 minutes

If you have more time or less time, adjust this schedule proportionately. Practice this with someone timing you.

PREWRITING/PLANNING TIME

Read the essay question and decide on your purpose. Do you want to persuade your reader? Would you rather explain something?

Sample: "Television is bad for people."

Do you agree or disagree with this statement? Decide. Take a stand. Don't be noncommittal. Write down the statement of your position.

Sample: I agree that television is bad for people.

or

Television is an excellent learning tool and is good for most people.

This is your thesis statement.

CONSIDER YOUR AUDIENCE

The writer's responsibility is to write clearly, honestly, and cleanly for the reader's sake. Essays would be pointless without an audience. Why write an essay if no one wants or needs to read it? Why add evidence, organize your ideas, or correct bad grammar? The reason to do any of these things is that someone out there needs to understand what you mean or say. What would the audience need to know in order to believe you or to come over to your position? Imagine someone you know (visualize her or him) listening to you declare your position or opinion and then saying, "Oh yeah? Prove it!"

In writing your essay, make sure to answer the following questions:

What evidence do you need to prove your idea to this skeptic?

What would s/he disagree with you about?

What does s/he share with you as common knowledge?

What does s/he need to be told by you?

CONTROL YOUR POINT OF VIEW

We may write essays from one of three points of view, depending upon the essay's audience. The points of view below are discussed from Informal to Formal.

1. Subjective/Personal Point of View:

   "*I think*

   "*I believe* . . . cars are more trouble than they are worth."

   "*I feel*

2. Second Person (We . . . You; I . . . You): "If *you* own a car, *you* soon find out that it is more trouble than it is worth."

3. Third Person Point of View: (focuses on the idea, not what "I" think of it): "*Cars* are more trouble than *they* are worth."

Stick with one or another; don't switch your "point of view" in the middle. Any one is acceptable.

CONSIDER YOUR SUPPORT

Next, during prewriting, jot down a few phrases that show ideas and examples that support your point of view. Do this quickly on a separate piece of paper for about *four minutes*. Don't try to outline, simply *list things* that you think might be important to discuss. After you have listed several, pick at least three to five things you want or need to discuss, and number them in the order of importance that is relevant to proving your point.

WRITE YOUR ROUGH DRAFT

Spend about *15 minutes* writing your *rough draft*. Looking over at your prewriting list, write down what you think is useful to prove your point in the order you think best to convince the reader. Be sure to *use real evidence* from your life experience or knowledge to support what you say. You do not have to draw evidence from books; your own life is equally appropriate.

For example, don't write, "Cars are more trouble to fix than bicycles" and then not show evidence for your idea. Give *examples* of what you mean: "*For example*, my father's Buick needs two hundred parts to make one brake work, but my bicycle only has four pieces that make up the brakes, and I can replace those myself." Write naturally and quickly. Don't worry too much at this point about paragraphing, spelling, punctuation — just write down what you think or want to say in the order determined on your list.

GRAMMAR

Correct use of grammar is also a very important element in writing a good essay. Therefore, you should make sure to correctly employ all of the rules of standard written English. If you feel that your grammar skills are not up to par, go back and restudy our English Language Skills Review, which appears earlier in this chapter.

PROVIDING EVIDENCE IN YOUR ESSAY

You may call on one or all four of the following kinds of evidence to support the thesis of your essay. Identify which kind(s) of evidence you can use to prove the points of your essay. In test situations, most essayists use anecdotal evidence or analogy to explain, describe, or prove a thesis. But if you know salient facts or statistics, don't hesitate to call upon them.

1.   **Hard data** (facts, statistics, scientific evidence, research) — documented evidence that has been verified to be true.

2.   **Anecdotal evidence** — stories from the writer's own experience and knowledge that illustrate a particular point or idea.

3.   **Expert opinions** — assertions, usually by authorities on the matter under discussion.

4.   **Analogies** — show a resemblance between one phenomenon and another.

ORGANIZING AND REVIEWING THE PARAGRAPHS

The unit of work for revising is the paragraph. After you have written what you wanted to say based on your prewriting list, spend about *15 minutes* revising your draft by looking to see if you need to indent for paragraphs anywhere. If you do, make a little proofreader's mark (¶) to indicate to the reader that you think a paragraph should start here. Check to see if you want to add anything that would make your point of view more convincing. Be sure to supply useful transitions to keep up the flow and maintain the focus of your ideas. If you don't have room on the paper, or if your new paragraph shows up out of order, add that paragraph and indicate with a number or some other mark where you want it to go. Check to *make sure* that you gave examples or illustrations for your statements. In the examples below, two paragraphs are offered: one without concrete evidence and one with evidence for its idea. Study each. Note the topic sentence (**T**) and how that sentence is or is not supported with evidence.

PARAGRAPHING WITH NO EVIDENCE

(**T**) Television is bad for people. *Watching television takes time away from other things.* Programs on television are often stupid and depict crimes that people later copy. Television takes time away from loved ones, and it often becomes addictive. So, television is bad for people because it is no good.

Comment: In this example, the author has not give any concrete evidence for any of the good ideas presented. S/he just declares them to be so. Any one of the sentences above might make a good opening sentence for a whole paragraph. Take the second sentence for example:

Watching television takes time away from other things. (first piece of evidence) For example, all those hours people spend sitting in front of the tube, they could be working on building a chair or fixing the roof. *(second piece of evidence)* Maybe the laundry needs to be done, but because people watch television, they may end up not having time to do it. Then Monday comes around again and they have no socks to wear to work — all because they couldn't stand to miss that episode of "All in the Family." *(third piece of evidence)* Someone could be writing a letter to a friend in Boston who hasn't been heard from or written to for months. *(fourth piece of evidence)* Or maybe someone misses the opportunity to take in a beautiful day in the park because s/he had to see a game show. They'll repeat a game show, but this beautiful day only comes around once. Watching television definitely keeps people from getting things done.

The primary evidence the author uses here is that of probable illustrations taken from life experience, largely anecdotal. Always *supply evidence.* Three examples or illustrations of your idea per paragraph is a useful number. Four is OK, but stop there. Don't go on and on about a single point. You don't have time. In order for a typical test essay to be fully developed, it should have about five paragraphs, organized in the following manner:

Introduction: A paragraph which shows your point of view (thesis) about an issue and introduces your position with three general ideas which support your thesis.

Development: Three middle paragraphs which prove your position from different angles, using evidence from real life and knowledge. Each paragraph of the middle should support each of the three ideas you started out with in Paragraph 1.

Conclusion: The last paragraph, which sums up your position and adds one final reminder of what the issue was, perhaps points to a solution:

So, television takes away from the quality of life and is therefore bad for human beings. We should be watching the sun, the sky, the birds, and each other, not the "boob tube."

Write a paragraph using this sentence as your focus:

"Television takes valuable time away from our loved ones."

POLISHING AND EDITING YOUR ESSAY

If the unit of work for revising is the paragraph, the unit of work for editing is the sentence. In *the last four to seven minutes*, check your paper for mistakes in editing. To help you in this task, follow our checklist.

Polishing Checklist

- Are all your sentences *really* sentences, or have you written some fragments or run-on sentences?

- Are you using your vocabulary correctly?

- Have you used some word which seems colloquial or informal?

- Did you leave out punctuation anywhere? Did you capitalize correctly? Did you check for commas, periods, and quotation marks?

Proofreading

In *the last two to four minutes*, read your paper word for word, first forward and then backward, reading from the end to the beginning. Doing so can help you find errors that you may have missed by having read forwards only.

Now, try your hand at applying these techniques by completing the following drill.

☞ Drill: Writing Your Essay

> **DIRECTIONS:** Write an essay on the following topic.

Many scholars note the decline of interest in literature written before the twentieth century. A diminishing number of students pursue studies in Classical, Medieval, and even Renaissance literature. In an essay written to an English teacher, argue whether you feel that the trend of studying modern versus past literature is commendable or contemptible. Reflect on modern culture and the effects of literature upon it. Discuss the advantages/disadvantages of a study that excludes or minimizes the literature of earlier periods. Finally, draw upon your own exposure to and attitude toward modern and past literatures, respectively.

WRITING SKILLS REVIEW

DETAILED EXPLANATIONS OF ANSWERS

Drill: Diagnostic

1. This is a fragment; it has no subject or verb to complete it so you will have to choose your own subject and verb. In fact, it is merely a prepositional phrase. Notice that it has no action in it. Notice that the television, though a noun, is not doing anything. Correction: John knows nothing about television. [See Fragments—Sentence Structure Skills.]

2. This is a run-on sentence. It has many subject and verb units not correctly separated by punctuation. Correction: I like television, and I think people should watch it. Television is good because it is so real. I think many people would die without it. [See Run-On/Fused Sentences—Sentence Structure Skills.]

3. This is a wordy sentence. Rewrite this as one or two short sentences that convey the same idea. Correction: Readers must spend time to understand this issue since the writer is so involved with the ideas.

4. Though this sentence is correct grammatically, it is longer than necessary. The problems here are wordiness and effective usage. A better version of this sentence would read: "Since the car was so old, the mechanic had difficulty finding the right parts."

5. This is an example of a dangling modifier. Reading this sentence, one would think that the doorbell works for a living, i.e., who was really waiting for the check? Correction: While *I* was waiting for the check, the doorbell rang in the living room. [See Misplaced and Dangling Modifiers—Sentence Structure Skills.]

6. This sentence does not link up the phrases that begin "eating…," and "to go…" They are not parallel. Correction: I like eat*ing* fish and go*ing* to the shore. [See Parallelism—Sentence Structure Skills.]

7.   This sentence suggests that either the computer or the software is quick and inexpensive. Which is it? The reader can't be sure because s/he can't tell which word the phrase that begins with "which" refers to. Correction: I bought a computer, which was quick and inexpensive, and some word processing software. [See Phrases; Clauses—Sentence Structure Skills.]

8.   This sentence is confusing because the meaning of "14 feet" seems ambiguous. Does the writer mean 14-foot long boats? Surely moving boats over 14 feet is not a costly proposition. Correction: For boats over 14 feet long, we cannot reimburse you for moving expenses. [See Connotative and Denotative Meanings—Word Choice Skills.]

9.   This sentence has two major flaws: (1) "could of" should be "could have." "Of" is never part of a verb; (2) in the second half, "make" should be "makes" to agree with the real subject, "sweep." The trouble is the writer probably thought "events" was the subject during the writing of the sentence. Correction: We could have been contenders in the contest, but the sweep of events makes us losers in the end. [See Subject-Verb Agreement—Verbs.]

10.   Here the writer uses two comparative forms (better/more) where only the one, "better," is appropriate. In English, comparative adjectives have three forms: relative, comparative, and superlative. To compare items that have relative degrees of "goodness" we may say that a single item (say a cookie) is good. But if we have two of the item and we compare them in terms of "good," then one is "better" than the other. If I decide to compare three or more, then I must describe one among them as "the best."

The sentence above also has an error in the use of "worse." The writer should have used the superlative form "worst." Know the comparatives of Standard English, especially the irregular ones. Below, for example, you might expect the comparative version of "worse" to be "worser." [See Faulty Comparisons—Adjectives and Adverbs.]

relative	comparative	superlative
worse	worse	worst

Correction: This book is better than yours, but John's is the worst of all three that we read.

11. The mistake is with the word "This." What does it refer to — the counter or the paycheck? Make sure you know your pronouns are clear. [See Pronoun Reference—Pronouns.]

12. Conjunctions (and, but, so, or, nor, for, if, yet) join together units of syntax which would be independent sentences without them. Use only one to join together two independent thoughts or sentence units. Also, make sure that if you have written two independent sentences joined by a conjunction that you punctuate the place of joining (the conjunction of the two ideas) with a comma just before you begin the clause with the conjunction. In this case, the writer should have said "The doctor was ready, *but* he could not operate until dawn." [See Correlative Conjunctions—Sentence Structure Skills.]

13. This sentence is incorrectly punctuated. There should be a comma after "over" and before "Scarlet." Any sentence that has words, phrases, or dependent clauses coming before the main independent subject and verb unit should have a comma separating that word, phrase, or dependent clause from the main event. Thus: *In the beginning,* John could not work alone. [See Commas—Punctuations.]

14. Put a pair of commas around words, phrases, or clauses enclosed in an independent sentence unit. Thus above, "Admiral of the Starfleet" should be set off with a pair (not one) of commas on either side of it. The same thing would be true if I inserted in the same place in the main sentence something like "who happened to be Admiral of the Starfleet," or simply, "however," [See Commas—Punctuations.]

15. The dog ate the bones, *and* Richard punished him. Notice that on either side of the unit (, and) is a word group, or clause, that without the conjunction could be a sentence that could stand by itself. [See Commas—Punctuations.]

16. This sentence is incorrectly punctuated with commas. It is actually two sentences on either side of the "however." Consequently, a semicolon [;] could be placed after "ducks." You might also use (.) or if you replace "however," you could use (, but). [See Commas; Semi-Colons—Punctuations.]

17. All quotation marks, no matter how much is being quoted in a given sentence, are placed outside the punctuation associated with them. In this case, it ought to be "gopher." If the sentence demanded a comma after "gopher," it would appear as just shown.

The only exception is a semicolon. If something is placed in quotes in the first part of a sentence using a semicolon, the quotation mark stays inside the semicolon punctuation. Thus: The dog was "smart"; however, George hated him anyway. [See Quotation Marks; Semi-Colons—Punctuations.]

18.   When words are used in a special sense by the writer or speaker, not that of a Standard English meaning for the context, then the writer must put quotation marks around the specially used word or phrase. Also, if a word is quoted inside another quote, it should be set off by a single quotation mark ('turf') rather than two. So, these sentences should be punctuated as follows:

The stores in Brooklyn had been "terminated"; the Harley Skull Gang had "torched," or set fire to, them as an act of "political" revenge. Head Skull John Harley said, "We were only protecting our own 'turf,' as we call it." [See Quotations Marks—Punctuations.]

19.   Apostrophes are the problem here. The sentence should read: "The boys couldn't find a way to get to the children's pool over at the Jones' house without the Harley boys' gang knowing about its whereabouts." [See Apostrophe—Punctuations.]

20.   Beware of faulty capitalization and weak mechanics. The sentence should read: *T*he article about *F*rance, entitled "*C*ome to the *H*eart of *E*urope *N*ow!" was cited by *S*enator *S*mith, whom *I* had known as a professor in *S*ociology 101. [See Capitalization—Sentence Structure Skills.]

Drill: Writing Your Essay

ESSAY WITH A SCORE OF 8, 7, OR 6

The Literature of the Past

The direction of modern literary scholarship points toward an alarming conclusion. The depreciation of the literary study of bygone periods is a sign of two disturbing trends. First, scholars are avoiding more difficult study in preference to what seems light or facile. Furthermore, the neglect of the literature of former eras is a denial of the contribution that past authors have made toward modern literature. This is not to suggest that all scholars who study modern literature do so because they are either intimidated by past literature or do not appreciate its value. However, the shrinking minority of past literary scholarship is a clear indication that intimidation and awe of past conventions are deterrents to many students of literature.

The dread associated with past literature reflects poorly upon our society. The attempts to simplify literature to accommodate simpler audiences has resulted in a form of literary deflation. The less society taxes its audience's minds, the less comprehensive those unexercised minds become. Information and ideas are now transmitted to the average man through the shallow medium of television programming. Modern students are evolving from this medium, and the gap separating them from the complexity of the classics is continuing to grow.

Once more, it is important to stress that this essay does not seek to diminish students of modern literature. The only demand this argument makes upon modern students is that they supplement their study with significant portions of the classics from which all subsequent literature has been derived, whether consciously or unconsciously. Failure to do so is an act akin to denying the importance of history itself. Like history, literature exists as an evolutionary process; modern literature can only have come into existence through the development of past literature.

Concerning the relative complexity of the classics to modern literature, the gap is not so great as one may think. Surely, one who glances at the works of Shakespeare or Milton without prior exposure will be daunted by them. However, a disciplined mind can overcome the comprehensive barriers erected over the past few centuries through persistence and perseverance.

Unfortunately, the ability to overcome the barriers to past literature may eventually become obsolete. The more frequently students select their courses of study through fear rather than interest, the wider the literary gap will become, until the pampered minds of all future readers will prove unequal to the task of reading the literature of our fathers. The more frequently students deny the usefulness of the literature antedating this century, the more frequently they deny their own literary heritage, the more probable it will become for modern literature's structure to crumble through lack of firm foundation.

FEATURES OF THE ESSAY SCORING 8, 7, OR 6
Appropriateness

The paper's topic and the writer's viewpoint are both well laid out in the first paragraph. The two trends described by the author in the topic paragraph are explored in deeper detail throughout the essay. The language and style fit the writer's audience. The style is formal, but possesses a personalized voice.

Unity and Focus

The essay follows the course presented in the topic paragraph, reemphasizing major points such as the writer's reluctance to condemn all modern scholars. This emphasis is not straight repetition, but carries different viewpoints and evidence for the writer's argument. The digression on television in the second paragraph neatly rounds off the writer's overall concern for cultural consequences of past literature's depreciation.

Development

The writer follows the suggestions of the writing assignment closely, structuring his essay around the reflections and discussions listed therein. Each paragraph bears an example to lend authority to the writer's argument. The second paragraph uses the theory of television's vegetative influence. The third paragraph utilizes the evolutionary equality of history. The fourth paragraph evokes names that the reader can relate to in terms of comprehensive difficulty.

Organization

Many transitional conventions are utilized. "Once more…"; "Concerning the relative complexity…"; "Unfortunately…" The examples throughout the paragraphs have a pointed direction. The conclusion paragraph rounds off the argument with a premonition of future calamity should its warning go unheeded.

Sentence Structure

The sentences are standardized and vary in form, although some passive constructions ("will be daunted," "the more probable it will become") may have been avoided. The repetition of "the more frequently" in the final paragraph is particularly effective and pointed.

Usage

Words are chosen to offer variety. "Past literature" is supplemented by "literary study of bygone days" and "the literature of former eras." Phrasing is consistent and standard, although the third sentence of the second paragraph ("The less society taxes…the less comprehensive…") is slightly awkward, though the repetition does achieve some effect.

Mechanical Conventions

Spelling and punctuation are mostly standard throughout the essay. The sentences in the final paragraph might be divided and shortened, although this might diminish their effect.

ESSAY WITH A SCORE OF 5

Modern Literature

It doesn't matter whether or not we read past literature. Past literature has been converted into what we now know as "modern literature." The elements of the past are therefore incorporated into the body of what we now have.

When we read a work of modern literature based upon the classics, such as Joyce's *Ulysses*, it doesn't matter whether or not we've read Homer's *Odyssey*. What matters is what Joyce made out of Homer's epic; not what Homer started out with.

When we see *West Side Story* in the movies, it doesn't matter whether or not we've read *Romeo and Juliet*: the end result is the same; therefore, we do not need to know the original source. I don't think it makes a difference whether or not we even recognize Tony and Maria as Romeo and Juliet. Tony and Maria are today's versions of Romeo and Juliet, and they match the culture that they are told in.

It has been said that all of the good plots have been used up by past ages, and that all we create now are variations of those plots. This statement is false. It is rather the case that these plots are universal variables that each age must interpret in its own unique way. I find it rather faseatious to study the interpretation of other cultures. We should be concerned only with our own.

Past literature is not necessary in a modern world that has reformed the mistakes of the past. Anything that hasn't carried over from the past is negligible: what was good for Shakespeare's audience may not be what we need. In conclusion, I would have to strongly conclude that the "trend of studying modern versus past literature" is commendable, and not contemptible.

FEATURES OF THE ESSAY SCORING 5 OR 4

Appropriateness

The main topic is not supplied directly within the work. Though the reader is aware of the conflict between modern and past literature, there is no sense of scholarly consensus as suggested by the writing assignment. The writer's somewhat informal style is unbalanced throughout the work by his uncertainty with his audience.

Unity and Focus

Though the writer knows the point he is trying to promote, his evidence is presented haphazardly and without a logical design. However, his rather abrupt conclusion is somewhat supported by his points.

Development

The essay does not follow a logical pattern; one premise does not meld comfortably into another. Though the premises loosely support the conclusion, they do not support each other.

Organization

Transitions are slight, if any. The repetition of "when we" opening two paragraphs is noticeable. Each point should have been further developed. The writer assumes his reader is quite familiar with *West Side Story* and its characters.

Sentence Structure

Most sentences follow standard sentence structure, although some are very irregular. The first sentence of paragraph three expresses two or three independent thoughts and should be separated accordingly. The final sentence of the fourth paragraph contains an unclear modifier: "own" should read either "own interpretation" or "own culture."

Usage

Most words are used in their proper context, and an attempt has been made to use some erudite words. "End result" is redundant; "end" should have been excluded. The declaration that "this statement is false" in the fourth paragraph is not supported by logical evidence. In this case, the writer should have asserted that this was his own opinion. However, in other cases it is recommended that the writer be bold with assertions. A degree of proof is all that is required to make those assertions. "In conclusion" is redundant with "conclude" in the final sentence of the essay. Contractions such as "we've" and "don't" should be written out in their long forms.

Mechanical Conventions

Most words are spelled properly, although "faseatious" should be spelt "facetious." The period in the second sentence of the first paragraph should lie within the quotation marks. The comma after "commendable" in the final paragraph should be eliminated because it does not introduce a new clause.

ESSAY WITH A SCORE OF 3 OR 2

Modern literature is no better than past literature, and vice-versa. It is interest that matters. If people aren't interested in the past, then so be it. A famous man once said "To each his own". I agree.

For example, you can see that books are getting easier and easier to understand. This is a good thing, because more knowledge may be comunicated this way. Comunication is what literature is all about: Some people comunicate with the past, and others with the present.

I communicate with the present. I'm not saying we all should. It's all up to your point of view. When a scholer chooses past over present, or vice-versa, that's his perogative. It doesn't make him better or worse than anybody else. We should all learn to accept each other's point of view.

When I read someone like Fitzgerald or Tolkien, I get a different feeling than Shakespeare. Shakespeare can inspire many people, but I just don't get that certain feeling from his plays. "The Hobbit," "The Great Gatsby," "Catcher in the Rye," and "Of Mice and Men." These are all great classics from this century. We should be proud of them. However, some people prefer "The Trojan War" and "Beowulf." Let them have it. Remember: "To each his own."

FEATURES OF THE ESSAY SCORING 3 OR 2
Appropriateness

The writer misconstrues the topic and writes about the relative worth of modern and past literature. The topic does not call for a judgment of period literatures; it calls for a study on the way in which they are studied. His personal style is too familiarized; it is unclear to whom the essay is addressed.

Unity and Focus

The writer seems to contradict his own points at times, favoring modern literature rather than treating the subject as objective as he had proposed. It is clear that the writer's train of thought shifted during the essay. This was covered up by ending with the catch phrase, "to each his own."

Development

The writer attempts to angle his argument in different ways by presenting such concepts as "communication" and "point of view." However, his thought processes are abrupt and underdeveloped.

Organization

There is neither direction nor logical flow in the essay. One point follows the next without any transition or connection. All three persons are used to prove his argument: the writer resorts to "I," "you," and "a famous man." It is clear there is no overall thesis guiding the essay.

Sentence Structure

Some sentences follow standard formation. Sentence three of the final paragraph is a fragment. The sentences are short and choppy, as is the thought they convey. Too many sentences are merely brief remarks on the preceding statements (e.g., "I agree"; "Let them have it"; etc.). These are not appropriate because they do not evoke new thought. The reference to Shakespeare in the first sentence of the final paragraph implies more than the writer intended. It should read: "than when I read Shakespeare."

Usage

Many words are repeated without any attempt to supply synonyms (e.g., "communication," "past"). Colloquial expressions are widespread, and should be avoided. *The Trojan War* is evidently an improper reference to Homer's *Iliad*.

Mechanical Conventions

There are many mechanical errors. Punctuation and spelling are inconsistent. "Comunication" and "comunicate" are spelt improperly in paragraph two, while "communicate" is spelt correctly in paragraph three. "Scholer" should be spelt "scholar." "Perogative" should be spelt "prerogative." In the fourth sentence of the first paragraph, the period should lie within the quotation marks as it does in the final sentence of the essay. The book titles in sentences three and six of the final paragraph should be underlined and not quoted.

▼

CHAPTER 3
HUMANITIES
REVIEW

Chapter 3

HUMANITIES REVIEW

The following Humanities Review is divided into six sections, as follows:

    I.   **Description of the CLEP General Examination in Humanities**

    II.   **Literature Review**

   III.   **Visual Arts and Architecture Review**

   IV.   **Philosophy Review**

    V.   **Music Review**

   VI.   **Performing Arts Review**

By thoroughly studying this course review, you will be well-prepared for the material on the CLEP General Examination in Humanities.

I. DESCRIPTION OF THE CLEP GENERAL EXAMINATION IN HUMANITIES

The CLEP Humanities examination consists of 150 multiple-choice questions, divided evenly into two 45-minute sections. It is designed to test your current knowledge of literature, music, philosophy, art, architecture, and the performing arts. The test is broad in its coverage, with questions concerning all periods, from classical to contemporary. You will be expected to demonstrate your understanding of the humanities through recall of specific information, understanding and application of concepts, and analyzing and interpreting works of art. A percent distribution of the topics covered on this exam follows:

Fine Arts	**50%**
Visual Arts (painting, sculpture)	25%
Music	15%
Performing Arts	5%
Architecture	5%
Literature	**50%**
Drama	5–10%
Poetry	15–20%
Fiction	10–15%
Nonfiction	5–10%
Philosophy	5%

Because the test is so broad in its coverage, it is unlikely that you will be knowledgeable about all the areas it covers. The questions will be taken from the entire history of Western art and culture as well as the Oriental and African cultures. Many of the questions will test your knowledge of terminology, genre and style; others will cross disciplines. Your knowledge of the basics of literature, philosophy, music, and the arts, and your ability to relate these basics to the general environment, will be tested.

You do not need to be a liberal arts student to answer these questions; most of them involve what is observable from the visual provided with each question. For the literature part, it will be helpful to brush up on literary terms, such as simile, onomatopoeia, metaphor, and irony. CLEP examinations are constructed so that average students who have met distribution requirements in this area can usually answer about one-half of the questions correctly.

TYPES OF QUESTIONS AND EXAMPLES

The sample questions that follow are provided to acquaint you with the types of test items that will appear on the General Examination in Humanities. There will be three basic types of questions on the Humanities exam: 1) questions that test your understanding and interpretation of literary and artistic works that the candidate will probably not have seen before 2) questions testing your knowledge of factual information (pieces of art, names, dates, etc...) and 3) questions testing your ability to recognize literary and artistic techniques, characteristics of certain artists and schools or periods. What follows are examples of the types of questions you will encounter on this test.

UNDERSTANDING AND INTERPRETING LITERARY PASSAGES AND ART WORK

The following lines are from a little-known poem by Elizabeth Barrett Browning. You are not expected to have previously read it. The question that accompanies the passage is designed to test your ability to analyze and interpret poetry.

> Grief taught to me this smile, she said
> And Wrong did teach this jesting bold
> These flowers were plucked from garden-bed
> While a death-chime was tolled.
> But in your bitter world, she said
> Face-joy's a costly mask to wear,
> 'Tis bought with pangs long nourished
> And rounded to despair
> Grief's earnest makes life's play, she said.

1.   In the context of the lines quoted above, the phrase "face-joy's a costly mask to wear" means

(A)   the mask had been expensive to buy.

(B)   a gay, smiling countenance was too difficult to maintain.

(C)   cynicism was being expressed.

(D)   the mask was required by the world.

(E)   this tragedy was to be the only one in her life.

The correct answer choice is (B). In this question you have been asked to demonstrate your understanding of poetic language dealing with grief. In addition, you needed to consider the meanings of the words or phrases used in the choices.

The idea of the mask is central to the meaning of the poem. The mask refers to a smiling face and the disguise of an extroverted, jesting personality. In this work, Browning says that Grief had taught her to jest-all to hide a broken heart. The correct answer is (B). The gay, smiling, carefree countenance was false; her true feelings were of grief and sorrow. (A) is incorrect; the poem refers to emotions and the effort to hide them behind a smile (C) is incorrect, cynicism is absent from the poem. (D) is also incorrect. Others did not require a smile and laughter, but it was self-imposed. (E) is incorrect; the last line alludes to "grief's earnest," indicating sorrows in the future. In her despair, she does not see life getting any better.

KNOWLEDGE OF FACTUAL INFORMATION

This type of question will test your knowledge of specific authors, dates, movements, and schools of art technique. The question that accompanies the following passage is designed to test your ability to link authors with nationality, style, dates, and content in order to identify the author of the passage.

> "I wish I was with the British. It would be so much
> simpler. Still I would probably have been killed.
> British ambulance drivers were killed sometimes. I
> knew I would not be killed. Not in this war. It had
> nothing to do with me."

2.   The preceding paragraph was written by

    (A)   John Milton.   (D)   Edmund Spenser.

    (B)   George Orwell.   (E)   Willa Cather.

    (C)   Ernest Hemingway.

The correct answer choice is (C). This question asks you to identify the author of a passage based on its content and style. Ernest Hemingway (C) is the author of the paragraph. Milton (A) and Spenser (D) were both poets. George Orwell (B) wrote futuristic novels. Willa Cather (E) wrote of pioneer days.

RECOGNITION OF TECHNIQUES AND CHARACTERISTICS OF CERTAIN WRITERS AND ARTISTS

The final type of test question you may encounter on this exam will ask you to relate a piece of work to a particular artist, style, and time frame.

3. During the period of 1940-1961 abstract art dominated the international art market, yet in the midst of this era, one American folk artist personified the primitive tradition. That American artist was

   (A)   Alexander Calder.   (D)   Grandma Moses.

   (B)   Robert Motherwell.   (E)   Jasper Johns.

   (C)   Ad Reinhardt.

The correct answer choice is (D). This question asks you to relate the work of an artist to a particular style and time frame. While all the American artists named worked during the 1940-1961 time period, Grandma Moses (D) was the folk artist who worked in the primitive tradition. Alexander Calder (A) created mobiles. Robert Motherwell (B) and Ad Reinhardt (C) were abstract expressionists. Jasper Johns (E) was part of the pop art movement popularized by Andy Warhol.

II. LITERATURE REVIEW

PROSE
GENERAL RULES AND IDEAS

Why do people write prose? Certainly such a question has a built-in counter: As opposed to writing what, poetry? One possible answer is that the person is a poor poet. The requirements and restrictions of the various genres make different demands upon a writer; most writers find their niche and stay there, secure in their private "comfort zone." Shakespeare did not write essays; Hemingway did not write poetry. If either did venture outside of his literary domain, the world took little note.

Students are sometimes confused as to what exactly is prose. Basically, prose is **not** poetry. **Prose** is what we write and speak most of the time in our everyday intercourse: unmetered, unrhymed language. Which is not to say that prose does not have its own rhythms—language, whether written or spoken, has cadence and balance. And certainly prose can have instances of rhyme or assonance, alliteration or onomatopoeia. Language is, after all, **phonic**.

Fiction and Non-fiction

Furthermore, prose may be either **fiction** or **non-fiction**. A novel (like a short story) is fiction; an autobiography is non-fiction. While a novel (or short story) may have autobiographical elements, an autobiography is presumed to be entirely factual. Essays are usually described in other terms: expository, argumentative, persuasive, critical, narrative. Essays may have elements of either fiction or non-fiction, but are generally classed as a separate subgenre.

Satire, properly speaking, is not a genre at all, but rather a **mode**, elements of which can be found in any category of literature—from poetry and drama to novels and essays. Satire is a manifestation of authorial attitude (tone) and purpose. Our discussion of satire will be limited to its use in prose.

But we have not addressed the initial question: "Why do people write prose?" The answer depends, in part, on the writer's intent. If he wishes to tell a rather long story, filled with many characters and subplots, interlaced with motifs, symbols, and themes, with time and space to develop interrelationships and to present descriptive passages, the writer generally chooses the novel as his medium. If he believes he can present his story more compactly and less complexly, he may choose the novella or the short story.

These subgenres require from the reader a different kind of involvement than does the essay. The essay, rather than presenting a story from which the reader may discern meaning through the skillful analysis of character, plot, symbol, and language, presents a relatively straightforward account of the writer's opinion(s) on an endless array of topics. Depending upon the type of essay, the reader may become informed (expository), provoked (argumentative), persuaded, enlightened (critical), or, in the case of the narrative essay, better acquainted with the writer who wishes to illustrate a point with his story, whether it is autobiographical or fictitious.

Encountering satire in prose selections demands that the reader be sensitive to the nuances of language and form, that he detect the double-edged sword of irony, and that he correctly assess both the writer's tone and his purpose.

Reading Prose

Readers of prose, like readers of poetry, seek aesthetic pleasure, entertainment, and knowledge, not necessarily in that order. Fiction offers worlds—real and imagined—in which characters and ideas, events and language, interact in ways familiar and unfamiliar. As readers, we take delight in the wisdom we fancy we have acquired from a novel or short story. Non-fiction offers viewpoints which we may find comforting or horrifying, amusing or sobering, presented by the author rather than by his once-removed persona. Thus, we are tempted to believe that somehow the truths presented in non-fiction are more "real" than the truths revealed by fiction. But we must resist! **Truth** is not "genre-specific."

Reading prose for the CLEP General Examination in English Composition is really no different from reading prose for your own purposes, except for the time constraints, of course! Becoming a competent reader is a result of practicing certain skills. Probably most important is acquiring a broad reading base. Read widely; read eclectically; read actively; read avidly. The idea is not that you might stumble onto a familiar prose selection on the CLEP and have an edge in writing about it; the idea is that your familiarity with many authors and works gives you a framework upon which to build your understanding of **whatever** prose selection you encounter on the CLEP General Examination in English Composition. So read, read, read!

READING NOVELS

Most literary handbooks will define a novel as an extended fictional prose narrative, derived from the Italian *novella*, meaning "tale, piece of news." The term "novelle," meaning short tales, was applied to works such as Boccaccio's *The Decameron*, a collection of stories which had an impact on later works such as Chaucer's *Canterbury Tales*. In most European countries, the word for **novel** is **roman**, short for **romance**, which was applied to longer verse narratives (Malory's *Morte d'Arthur*), which were later written in prose. Early romances were associated with "legendary, imaginative, and poetic material"—tales "of the long ago or the far away or the imaginatively improbable"; novels, on the other hand, were felt to be "bound by the facts of the actual world and the laws of probability" (*A Handbook to Literature*, C. Hugh Holman, p. 354).

The novel has, over some 600 years, developed into many special forms which are classified by subject matter: detective novel, psychological novel, historical novel, regional novel, picaresque novel, Gothic novel, stream-of-consciousness novel, epistolary novel, and so on. These terms, of course, are not exhaustive nor mutually exclusive. Furthermore, depending on the conventions of the author's time period, his style, and his outlook on life, his *mode* may be termed **realism**, **romanticism**, **impressionism**, **expressionism**, **naturalism**, or **neo-classicism** (Holman, p. 359).

Our earlier description of a novel ("...a rather long story, filled with many characters and subplots, interlaced with motifs, symbols, and themes, with time and space to develop interrelationships and to present descriptive passages") is satisfactory for our purposes here. The works generally included on the CLEP are those which have stood the test of time in significance, literary merit, and reader popularity. New works are incorporated into the canon which is a reflection of what works are being taught in literature classes. And teachers begin to teach those works which are included frequently among the questions. So the process is circular, but the standards remain high for inclusion.

Plots

Analyzing novels is a bit like asking the journalist's five questions: what? who? why? where? and how? The **what?** is the story, the narrative, the plot and subplots. Most students are familiar with Freytag's Pyramid, originally designed to describe the structure of a five-act drama but now widely used to analyze fiction as well. The stages generally specified are **introduction** or **exposition**, **complication**, **rising action**, **climax**, **falling action**, and **denouement** or **conclusion**. As the novel's events are charted, the "change which structures the story" should emerge. There are many events in a long narrative; but generally only one set of events comprises the "real" or "significant" story.

However, subplots often parallel or serve as counterpoints to the main plot line, serving to enhance the central story. Minor characters sometimes have essentially the same conflicts and goals as the major characters, but the consequences of the outcome seem less important. Sometimes the parallels involve reversals of characters and situations, creating similar yet distinct differences in the outcomes. Nevertheless, seeing the parallels makes understanding the major plot line less difficult.

Sometimes an author divides the novel into chapters—named or unnamed, perhaps just numbered. Or he might divide the novel into "books" or "parts," with chapters as subsections. Readers should take their cue from these divisions; the author must have had some reason for them. Take note of what happens in each larger section, as well as within the smaller chapters. Whose progress is being followed? What event or occurrence is being foreshadowed or prepared for? What causal or other relationships are there between sections and events? Some writers, such as Steinbeck in *The Grapes of Wrath*, use intercalary chapters, alternating between the "real" story (the Joads) and peripheral or parallel stories (the Okies and migrants in general). Look for the pattern of such organization; try to see the interrelationships of these alternating chapters.

Characters

Of course, plots cannot happen in isolation from characters, the **who?** element of a story. Not only are there major and minor characters to consider; we need to note whether the various characters are **static** or **dynamic**. Static characters do not change in significant ways—that is, in ways which relate to the story which is structuring the novel. A character may die, i.e., change from alive to dead, and still be static, unless his death is central to the narrative. For instance, in Golding's *Lord of the Flies*, the boy with the mulberry birthmark apparently dies in a fire early in the novel. Momentous as any person's death is, this boy's death is not what the novel is about. However, when Simon is killed, and later Piggy, the narrative is directly impacted because the reason for their deaths is central to the novel's theme regarding man's innate evil. A dynamic character may change only slightly in his attitudes, but those changes may be the very ones upon which the narrative rests. For instance, Siddhartha begins as a very pure and devout Hindu but is unfulfilled spiritually. He eventually does achieve spiritual contentment, but his change is more a matter of degree than of substance. He is not an evil man who attains salvation, nor a pious man who becomes corrupt. It is the process of his search, the stages in his pilgrimage, which structure the novel *Siddhartha*.

We describe major characters or "actors" in novels as **protagonists** or **antagonists**. Built into those two terms is the Greek word **agon**, meaning "struggle." The *protagonist* struggles **toward** or for someone or something; the *ant(i)*agonist struggles **against** someone or something. The possible conflicts are usually cited as man against himself, man against man, man against society, or man against nature. Sometimes more than one of these conflicts appears in a story, but usually one is dominant and is the structuring device.

A character can be referred to as **stock**, meaning that he exists because the plot demands it. For instance, a Western with a gunman who robs the bank will require a number of **stock** characters: the banker's lovely daughter, the tough but kindhearted barmaid, the cowardly white-shirted citizen who sells out the hero to save his own skin, and the young freckle-faced lad who shoots the bad guy from a second-story hotel window.

Or a character can be a **stereotype**, without individuating characteristics. For instance, a sheriff in a small Southern town; a football player who is all brawn; a librarian clucking over her prized books; the cruel commandant of a POW camp.

Characters often serve as **foils** for other characters, enabling us to see one or more of them better. A classic example is Tom Sawyer, the romantic foil for Huck Finn's realism. Or, in Lee's *To Kill a Mockingbird*, Scout as the naive observer of events which her brother Jem, four years older, comes to understand from the perspective of the adult world.

Sometimes characters are **allegorical**, standing for qualities or concepts rather than for actual personages. For instance, Jim Casey (initials "J. C.") in *The Grapes of Wrath* is often regarded as a Christ figure, pure and self-sacrificing in his aims for the migrant workers. Or Kamala, Siddhartha's teacher in the art of love, whose name comes from the tree whose bark is used as a purgative; she purges him of his ascetic ways on his road to self-hood and spiritual fulfillment.

Other characters are fully three-dimensional, "rounded," "mimetic" of humans in all their virtue, vice, hope, despair, strength, and weakness. This verisimilitude aids the author in creating characters who are credible and plausible, without being dully predictable and mundane.

Themes

The interplay of plot and characters determines in large part the **theme** of a work, the **why?** of the story. First of all, we must distinguish between a mere topic and a genuine theme or thesis; and then between a theme and contributing *motifs*. A **topic** is a phrase, such as "man's inhumanity to man"; or "the fickle nature of fate." A **theme**, however, turns a phrase into a statement: "Man's inhumanity to man is barely concealed by 'civilization.'" Or "Man is a helpless pawn, at the mercy of fickle fate." Many writers may deal with the same topic, such as the complex nature of true love; but their themes may vary widely, from "True love will always win out in the end," to "Not even true love can survive the cruel ironies of fate."

To illustrate the relationship between plot, character, and theme, let's examine two familiar fairy tales. In "The Ugly Duckling," the structuring story line is "Once upon a time there was an ugly duckling, who in turn became a beautiful swan." In this case, the duckling did nothing to merit either his ugliness nor his eventual transformation; but he did not curse fate. He only wept and waited, lonely and outcast. And when he became beautiful, he did not gloat; he eagerly joined the other members of his flock, who greatly admired him. The theme here essentially is: "Good things come to him who waits," or "Life is unfair—you don't get what you deserve, nor deserve what you get." What happens to the theme if the ugly duckling remains an ugly duckling: "Some guys just never get a break"?

Especially rewarding to examine for the interdependence of plot and theme is "Cinderella": "Once upon a time, a lovely, sweet-natured young girl was forced to labor for and serve her ugly and ungrateful stepmother and two stepsisters. But thanks to her fairy godmother, Cinderella and the Prince marry, and live happily ever after."

We could change events (plot elements) at any point, but let's take the penultimate scene where the Prince's men come to the door with the single glass slipper. Cinderella has been shut away so that she is not present when the other women in the house try on the slipper. Suppose that the stepmother or either of the two stepsisters tries on the slipper—and it fits! Cinderella is in the back room doing the laundry, and her family waltzes out the door to the palace and she doesn't even get an invitation to the wedding. And imagine the Prince's dismay when the ugly, one-slippered lady lifts her wedding veil for the consummating kiss! Theme: "There is no justice in the world, for those of low or high station" or "Virtue is not its own reward."

Or let's say that during the slipper-test scene, the stepsisters, step-mother, and finally Cinderella all try on the shoe, but to no avail. And then in sashays the fairy godmother, who gives them all a knowing smirk, puts out her slipper-sized foot and cackles hysterically, like the mechanical witch in the penny arcade. Theme: "You can't trust anybody these days" or, a favorite statement of theme, "Appearances can be deceiving." The link between plot and theme is very strong, indeed.

Motifs

Skilled writers often employ **motifs** to help unify their works. A motif is a detail or element of the story which is repeated throughout, and which may even become symbolic. Television shows are ready examples of the use of motifs. A medical show, with many scenes alternately set in the hospital waiting room and operating room, uses elements such as the pacing, anxious parent or loved one, the gradually filling ashtray, the large wall clock whose hands melt from one hour to another. And in the operating room, the half-masked surgeon whose brow is frequently mopped by the nurse; the gloved hand open-palmed to receive scalpel, sponge, and so on; the various oscilloscopes giving read-outs of the patient's very fragile condition; the expanding and collapsing bladder manifesting that the patient is indeed breathing; and, again, the wall clock, assuring us that this procedure is taking forever. These are all **motifs**, details which in concert help convince the reader that this story occurs in a hospital, and that the mood is pretty tense, that the medical team is doing all it can, and that Mom and Dad will be there when Junior or Sissy wakes up.

But motifs can become symbolic. The oscilloscope line quits blipping, levels out, and gives off the ominous hum. And the doctor's gloved hand sets down the scalpel and shuts off the oscilloscope. In the waiting room, Dad crushes the empty cigarette pack; Mom quits pacing and sinks into the sofa. The door to the waiting room swings shut silently behind the retreating doctor. All these elements signal "It's over, finished."

This example is very crude and mechanical, but motifs in the hands of a skillful writer are valuable devices. And in isolation, and often magnified, a single motif can become a controlling image with great significance. For instance, Emma Bovary's shoes signify her obsession with material things; and when her delicate slippers become soiled as she crosses the dewy grass to meet her lover, we sense the impurity of her act as well as its futility. Or when wise Piggy, in *Lord of the Flies,* is reduced to one lens in his specs, and finally to no specs at all, we see the loss of insight and wisdom on the island, and chaos follows.

Settings in Novels

Setting is the **where?** element of the story. But setting is also the **when** element: time of day, time of year, time period or year; it is the dramatic moment, the precise intersection of time and space when this story is being told. Setting is also the atmosphere: positive or negative ambiance, calm, chaotic, Gothic, Romantic. The question for the reader to answer is whether the setting is ultimately essential to the plot/theme, or whether it is incidental; i.e., could this story/theme have been told successfully in another time and/or place? For instance, could the theme in *Lord of the Flies* be made manifest if the boys were not on an island? Could they have been isolated in some other place? Does it matter whether the "war" which they are fleeing is WWII or WWIII or some other conflict, in terms of the theme?

Hopefully, the student will see that the four elements of plot, character, theme, and setting are intertwined and largely interdependent. A work must really be read as a whole, rather than dissected and analyzed in discrete segments.

Style

The final question, **how?**, relates to an author's style. Style involves language (word choice), syntax (word order, sentence type, and length), the balance between narration and dialogue, the choice of narrative voice (first person participant, third person with limited omniscience), use of descriptive passages, and other aspects of the actual words on the page which are basically irrelevant to the first four elements (plot, character, theme, and setting). Stylistic differences are fairly easy to spot among such diverse writers as Jane Austen, whose style is—to today's reader— very formal and mannered; Mark Twain, whose style is very casual and colloquial; William Faulkner, whose prose often spins on without punctuation or paragraphs far longer than the reader can hold either the thought or his breath; and Hemingway, whose dense but spare, pared-down style has earned the epithet, "Less is more."

READING SHORT STORIES

The modern short story differs from earlier short fiction, such as the parable, fable, and tale, in its emphasis on character development through scenes rather than summary: through *showing* rather than *telling*. Gaining popularity in the nineteenth century, the short story generally was realistic, presenting detailed accounts of the lives of middle-class personages. This tendency toward realism dictates that the plot be grounded in *probability*, with causality fully in operation. Furthermore, the characters are human with recognizable human motivations, both social and psychological. Setting—time and place—is realistic rather than fantastic. And, as Poe stipulated, the elements of plot, character, setting, style, point of view, and theme all work toward a single *unified* effect.

However, some modern writers have stretched these boundaries and have mixed in elements of nonrealism—such as the supernatural and the fantastic—sometimes switching back and forth between realism and nonrealism, confusing the reader who is expecting conventional fiction. Barth's "Lost in the Funhouse" and Allen's "The Kugelmass Episode" are two stories which are not, strictly speaking, *realistic*. However, if the reader will approach and accept this type of story on its own terms, he will be better able to understand and appreciate them fully.

Unlike the novel, which has time and space to develop characters and interrelationships, the short story must rely on flashes of insight and revelation to develop plot and characters. The "slice of life" in a short story is of necessity much narrower than that in a novel; the time span is much shorter, the focus much tighter. To attempt anything like the panoramic canvas available to the novelist would be to view fireworks through a soda straw: occasionally pretty, but ultimately not very satisfying or enlightening.

Point of View

The elements of the short story are those of the novel, discussed earlier. However, because of the compression of time and concentration of effect, probably the short story writer's most important decision is **point of view**. A narrator may be *objective*, presenting information without bias or comment. Hemingway frequently uses the objective *third-person* narrator, presenting scenes almost dramatically, i.e., with a great deal of dialogue and very little narrative, none of which directly reveals the thoughts or feelings of the characters. The third-person narrator may, however, be less objective in his presentation, directly revealing the thoughts and feelings, of one or more of the characters, as Chopin does in "The Story of an Hour." We say that such a narrator is fully or partially *omniscient*, depending on how complete his knowledge is of the characters' psychological and emotional makeup. The least objective narrator is the *first-person* narrator, who presents information from the perspective of a single character who is a participant in the action. Such a narrative choice allows the author to present the discrepancies between the writer's/reader's perceptions and those of the narrator.

One reason the choice of narrator, the point of view from which to tell the story, is immensely important in a short story is that the narrator reveals character and event in ways which affect our understanding of theme. For instance, in Faulkner's "A Rose for Emily," the unnamed narrator who seems to be a townsperson recounts the story out of chronological order, juxtaposing events whose causality and significance are uncertain. The narrator withholds information which would explain events being presented, letting the reader puzzle over Emily Grierson's motivations, a device common in detective fiction. In fact, the narrator presents contradictory information, making the reader alternately pity and resent the spinster. When we examine the imagery and conclude that Miss Emily and her house represent the decay and decadence of the Old South which resisted the invasion of "progress" from the North, we see the importance of setting and symbol in relation to theme.

Similarly, in Mansfield's "Bliss," the abundant description of setting creates the controlling image of the lovely pear tree. But this symbol of fecundity becomes ironic when Bertha Young belatedly feels sincere and overwhelming desire for her husband. The third-person narrator's omniscience is limited to Bertha's thoughts and feelings; otherwise we would have seen her husband's infidelity with Miss Fulton.

In O'Connor's "Good Country People," the narrator is broadly omniscient, but the reader is still taken by surprise at the cruelty of the Bible salesman who seduces Joy-Hulga. That he steals her artificial leg is perhaps poetic justice, since she (with her numerous degrees) had fully intended to seduce him ("just good country people"). The story's title, the characters' names—Hopewell, Freeman, Joy; the salesman's professed Christianity, the Bibles hollowed out to hold whiskey and condoms, add to the irony of Mrs. Freeman's final comment on the young man: "Some can't be that simple... I know I never could."

Examples of Initiation Stories

The *initiation story* frequently employs the first-person narrator. To demonstrate the subtle differences which can occur in stories which ostensibly have the same point of view and general theme, let's look at three: "A Christmas Memory" (Capote), "Araby" (Joyce), and "A & P" (Updike).

Early in "A Christmas Memory," Capote's narrator identifies himself:

> The person to whom she is speaking is myself. I am seven; she is sixty-something. We are cousins, very distant ones, and we have lived together—well, as long as I can remember. Other people inhabit the house, relatives; and though they have power over us, and frequently make us cry, we are not, on the whole, too much aware of them. We

are each other's best friend. She calls me Buddy, in memory of a boy who was formerly her best friend. The other Buddy died in the 1880s, when she was still a child. She is still a child.

Buddy and his cousin, who is called only "my friend," save their meager earnings throughout the year in order to make fruitcakes at Christmas to give mainly to "persons we've met maybe once, perhaps not at all... Like President Roosevelt.... Or Abner Packer, the driver of the six o'clock bus from Mobile, who exchanges waves with us everyday...." Their gifts to one another each year are always handmade, often duplicates of the year before, like the kites they present on what was to be their last Christmas together.

Away at boarding school, when Buddy receives word of his friend's death, it "merely confirms a piece of news some secret vein had already received, severing from me an irreplaceable part of myself, letting it loose like a kite on a broken string. That is why, walking across a school campus on this particular December morning, I keep searching the sky. As if I expected to see, rather like hearts, a lost pair of kites hurrying toward heaven."

Buddy's characterizations of his friend are also self-revelatory. He and she are peers, equals, despite their vast age difference. They are both totally unselfish, joying in the simple activities mandated by their economic circumstances. They are both "children."

The story is told in present tense, making the memories from the first paragraphs seem as "real" and immediate as those from many years later. And Buddy's responses from the early years ("Well, I'm disappointed. Who wouldn't be? With socks, a Sunday school shirt, some handkerchiefs, a hand-me-down sweater and a year's subscription to a religious magazine for children, *The Little Shepherd*. It makes me boil. It really does.") are as true to his seven-year-old's perspective, as are those when he, much older, has left home ("I have a new home too. But it doesn't count. Home is where my friend is, and there I never go.").

The youthful narrator in "A & P" also uses present tense, but not consistently, which gives his narrative a very colloquial, even unschooled flavor. Like Buddy, Sammy identifies himself in the opening paragraph: "In walks these three girls in nothing but bathing suits. I'm in the third checkout slot, with my back to the door, so I don't see them until they're over by the bread." And later, "Stokesie's married, with two babies chalked up on his fuselage already, but as far as I can tell that's the only difference. He's twenty-two, and I was nineteen this April." The girls incur the wrath of the store manager, who scolds them for their inappropriate dress. And Sammy, in his adolescent idealism, quits on the spot; although he realizes that he does not want to "do this" to his parents, he tells us "… it seems to me that once you begin a gesture it's fatal not to go through with it." But his *beau geste* is ill-spent: "I look around for my girls, but they're gone, of course…. I could see Lengel in my place in the slot, checking the sheep through. His face was dark gray and his back stiff, as if he'd just had an injection of iron, and my stomach kind of fell as I felt how hard the world was going to be to me hereafter."

Like Buddy, Sammy tells his story from a perch not too distant from the events he recounts. Both narrators still feel the immediacy of their rites of passage very strongly. Buddy, however, reveals himself to be a more admirable character, perhaps because his story occurs mainly when he is seven—children tend not to be reckless in the way that Sammy is. Sammy was performing for an audience, doing things he knew would cause pain to himself and his family, for the sake of those three girls who never gave him the slightest encouragement and whom he would probably never even see again.

In "Araby," the unnamed narrator tells of a boyhood crush he had on the older sister of one of his chums: "I thought little of the future. I did not know whether I would ever speak to her or not or, if I spoke to her, how I could tell her of my confused adoration. But my body was like a harp and her words and gestures were like fingers running upon the wires." She asks the boy if he is going to Araby, a "splendid bazaar," and reveals that she cannot. He promises to go himself and bring her something. But his uncle's late homecoming delays the boy's excursion until the bazaar is nearly closed for the night, and he is unable to find an appropriate gift. Forlornly, "I turned away slowly and walked down the middle of the bazaar…. Gazing up into the darkness I saw myself as a creature driven and derided by vanity; and my eyes burned with anguish and anger." This narrator is recounting his story from much further away than either Buddy or Sammy tells his own. The narrator of "Araby" has the perspective of an adult, looking back at a very important event in his boyhood. His "voice" reflects wisdom born of experience. The incident was very painful then; but its memory, while poignant, is no longer devastating. Like Sammy, this narrator sees the dichotomy between his adolescent idealism and the mundane reality of "romance." However, the difference is in the narrator's ability to turn the light on himself; Sammy is still so close to the incident that he very likely would whip off his checker's apron again if the girls returned to the A & P. The "Araby" narrator has "mellowed" and can see the futility—and the necessity—of adolescent love.

READING ESSAYS
Categories of Essays

Essays fall into four rough categories: **speculative**, **argumentative**, **narrative**, and **expository**. Depending on the writer's purpose, his essay will fit more or less into one or these groupings.

The **speculative** essay is so named because, as its Latin root suggests, it *looks* at ideas; explores them rather than explains them. While the speculative essay may be said to be *meditative*, it often makes one or more points. But the thesis may not be as obvious or clear-cut as that in an expository or argumentative essay. The writer deals with ideas in an associative manner, playing with ideas in a looser structure than he would in an expository or argumentative essay. This "flow" may even produce *intercalary* paragraphs, which present alternately a narrative of sorts and thoughtful responses to the events being recounted, as in White's "The Ring of Time."

The purposes of the **argumentative** essay, on the other hand, are always clear: to present a point and provide evidence, which may be factual or anecdotal, and to support it. The structure is usually very formal, as in a debate, with counterpositions and counterarguments. Whatever the organizational pattern, the writer's intent in an argumentative essay is to persuade his reader of the validity of some claim, as Bacon does in "Of Love."

Narrative and **expository** essays have elements of both the speculative and argumentative modes. The narrative essay may recount an incident or a series of incidents and is almost always autobiographical, in order to make a point, as in Orwell's "Shooting an Elephant." The informality of the storytelling makes the narrative essay less insistent than the argumentative essay, but more directed than the speculative essay.

Students are probably most familiar with the **expository** essay, the primary purpose of which is to explain and clarify ideas. While the expository essay may have narrative elements, that aspect is minor and subservient to that of explanation. Furthermore, while nearly all essays have some element of persuasion, argumentation is incidental in the expository essay. In any event, the four categories—speculative, argumentative, narrative, and expository—are neither exhaustive nor mutually exclusive.

Elements of Essays

As non-fiction, essays have a different set of elements from novels and short stories: **voice**, **style**, **structure**, and **thought**.

Voice in non-fiction is similar to the narrator's tone in fiction; but the major difference is in who is "speaking." In fiction, the author is not the speaker—the **narrator** is the speaker. Students sometimes have difficulty with this distinction, but it is necessary if we are to preserve the integrity of the fictive "story." In an essay, however, the author speaks directly to the reader, even if he is presenting ideas which he may not actually espouse personally—as in a satire. This directness creates the writer's **tone**, his attitude toward his subject.

Style in non-fiction derives from the same elements as style in fiction: word choice, syntax, balance between dialogue and narration, voice, use of description—those things specifically related to words on the page. Generally speaking, an argumentative essay will be written in a more formal style than will a narrative essay, and a meditative essay will be less formal than an expository essay. But such generalizations are only descriptive, not prescriptive.

Structure and **thought**, the final elements of essays, are so intertwined as to be inextricable. We must be aware that to change the structure of an essay will alter its meaning. For instance, in White's "The Ring of Time," to abandon the *intercalary* paragraph organization, separating the paragraphs which narrate the scenes with the young circus rider from those which reflect on the circularity and linearity of time, would alter our understanding of the essay's thesis. Writers signal structural shifts with alterations in focus, as well as with visual clues (spacing), verbal clues— (*but, therefore, however*), or shifts in the kind of information being presented (personal, scientific, etc.).

Thought is perhaps the single element which most distinguishes non-fiction from fiction. The essayist chooses his form not to tell a story but to present an idea. Whether he chooses the speculative, narrative, argumentative, or expository format, the essayist has something on his mind that he wants to convey to his readers. And it is this idea which we are after when we analyze his essay.

Example of the Structure of an Essay

Often anthologized is Orwell's "Shooting an Elephant," a narrative essay recounting the writer's (presumably) experience in Burma as an officer of the British law that ruled the poverty-ridden people of a small town. Orwell begins with two paragraphs which explain that, as a white, European authority figure, he was subjected to taunts and abuse by the natives. Ironically, he sympathized with the Burmese and harbored fairly strong anti-British feelings regarding the imperialists as the oppressors rather than the saviors. He tells us that he felt caught, trapped between his position of authority which he himself resented and the hatred of those he was required to oversee.

The body of the essay—some 11 paragraphs—relates the incident with an otherwise tame elephant gone "must" which had brought chaos and destruction to the village. Only occasionally does Orwell interrupt the narrative to reveal his reactions directly, but his descriptions of the Burmese are sympathetically drawn. The language is heavily connotative, revealing the helplessness of the villagers against both the elephant and the miserable circumstances of their lives.

Orwell recounts how, having sent for an elephant gun, he found that he was compelled to shoot the animal, even though its destruction was by now unwarranted and even ill-advised, given the value of the elephant to the village. But the people expected it, demanded it; the white man realized that he did not have dominion over these people of color after all. They were in charge, not he.

To make matters worse, Orwell bungles the "murder" of the beast, which takes half an hour to die in great agony. And in the aftermath of discussions of the rightness or wrongness of his action, Orwell wonders if anyone realizes he killed the elephant only to save face. It is the final sentence of the final paragraph which directly reveals the author's feelings, although he has made numerous indirect references to them throughout the essay. Coupled with the opening paragraphs, this conclusion presents British imperialism of the period in a very negative light: "the unable doing the unnecessary to the ungrateful."

Having discovered Orwell's main idea, we must look at the other elements (voice, style, structure) to see *how* he communicates it to the reader. The voice of the first-person narrative is fairly formal, yet remarkably candid, using connotation to color our perception of the events. Orwell's narrative has many complex sentences, with vivid descriptive phrases in series, drawing our eye along the landscape and through the crowds as he ponders his next move. Structurally, the essay first presents a premise about British imperialism, then moves to a gripping account of the officer's reluctant shooting of the elephant; and ends with an admission of his own culpability as an agent of the institution he detests. Orwell frequently signals shifts between his role as officer and his responses as a humane personage with *but*, or with dashes to set off his responses to the events he is recounting.

READING SATIRE

Satire is a *mode* which may be employed by writers of various genres: poetry, drama, fiction, non-fiction. It is more a perspective than a product.

Satire mainly exposes and ridicules, derides and denounces vice, folly, evil, stupidity, as these qualities manifest themselves in persons, groups of persons, ideas, institutions, customs, or beliefs. While the satirist has many techniques at his disposal, there are basically only two types of satire: gentle or harsh, depending on the author's intent, his audience, and his methods.

Role of Satire

The terms *romanticism*, *realism*, and *naturalism* can help us understand the role of *satire*. Romanticism sees the world idealistically, as perfectible if not perfect. Realism sees the world as it is, with healthy doses of both good and bad. Naturalism sees the world as imperfect, with evil often triumphing over good. The satirist is closer to the naturalist than he is to the romantic or realist, for both the satirist and the naturalist focus on what is wrong with the world, intending to expose the foibles of man and his society. The difference between them lies in their techniques. The naturalist is very direct and does not necessarily employ humor; the satirist is more subtle, and does.

For instance, people plagued with overpopulation and starvation is not, on first glance, material for humor. Many works have treated such conditions with sensitivity, bringing attention to the plight of the world's unfortunate. Steinbeck's *Grapes of Wrath* is such a work. However, Swift's "A Modest Proposal" takes essentially the same circumstances and holds them up for our amused examination. How does the satirist make an unfunny topic humorous? And why would he do so?

Techniques of Satire

The satirist's techniques—his weapons—include **irony**, **parody**, **reversal** or **inversion**, **hyperbole**, **understatement**, **sarcasm**, **wit**, and **invective**. By exaggerating characteristics, by saying the opposite of what he means, by using his cleverness to make cutting or even cruel remarks at the expense of his subject, the writer of satire can call the reader's attention to those things he believes are repulsive, despicable, or destructive.

Whether he uses more harsh (Juvenalian) or more gentle (Horatian) satire depends upon the writer's attitude and intent. Is he merely flaunting his clever intellect, playing with words for our amusement or to inflate his own sense of superiority? Is he probing the psychological motivations for the foolish or destructive actions of some person(s)? Is he determined to waken an unenlightened or apathetic audience, moving its members to thought or action? Are the flaws which the satirist is pointing out truly destructive or evil, or are they the faults we would all recognize in ourselves if we glanced in the mirror, not admirable but not really harmful to ourselves or society? Is the author amused, sympathetic, objective, irritated, scornful, bitter, pessimistic, mocking? The reader needs to identify the satirist's purpose and tone. Its subtlety sometimes makes satire a difficult mode to detect and to understand.

Irony

Irony is perhaps the satirist's most powerful weapon. The basis of irony is inversion or reversal, doing or saying the opposite or the unexpected. Shakespeare's famous sonnet beginning "My mistress' eyes are nothing like the sun..." is an ironic tribute to the speaker's beloved, who, he finally declares is "as rare/As any she belied with false compare." At the same time, Shakespeare is poking fun at the sonnet form as it was used by his contemporaries—himself included—to extol the virtues of their ladies. By selecting a woman who, by his own description, is physically unattractive in every way imaginable, and using the conventions of the love sonnet to present her many flaws, he has inverted the sonnet tradition. And then by asserting that she compares favorably with any of the other ladies whose poet-lovers have lied about their virtues, he presents us with the unexpected twist. Thus, he satirizes both the love sonnet form and its subject by using irony.

Poetic Satires

Other notable poetic satires include Koch's "Variations on a Theme by William Carlos Williams," in which he parodies Williams' "This Is Just to Say." Koch focuses on the simplicity and directness of Williams' imagery and makes the form and ideas seem foolish and trivial. In "Boom!," Nemerov takes issue with a pastor's assertion that modern technology has resulted in a concomitant rise in religious activities and spiritual values. Nemerov catalogues the instant, disposable, and extravagant aspects of Americans' lifestyles, which result in "pray as you go... pilgrims" for whom religion is another convenience, commercial rather than spiritual.

Satire in Drama

Satire in drama is also common; Wilde's "The Importance of Being Earnest" is wonderfully funny in its constant word play (notably on the name *Ernest*) and its relentless ridiculing of the superficiality which Wilde saw as characteristic of British gentry. Barrie's "The Admirable Chrichton" has a similar theme, with the added assertion that it is the "lower" or servant class which is truly superior—again, the ironic reversal so common in satire. Both of these plays are mild in their ridicule; the authors do not expect or desire any change in society or in the viewer. The satire is gentle; the satirists are amused, or perhaps bemused at the society whose foibles they expose.

Satire in Classic Novels

Classic novels which employ satire include Swift's *Gulliver's Travels* and Voltaire's *Candide*, both of which fairly vigorously attack aspects of the religions, governments, and prevailing intellectual beliefs of their respective societies. A modern novel which uses satire is Heller's *Catch-22*, which is basically an attack on war and the government's bureaucratic bungling of men and material, specifically in WWII. But by extension, Heller is also viewing with contempt the unmotivated, illogical, capricious behavior of all institutions which operate by that basic law: "catch-22." Like Swift and Voltaire, Heller is angry. And although his work, like the other two, has humor, wit, exaggeration, and irony, his purpose is more than intellectual entertainment for his readers. Heller hopes for reform.

Heller's attack is frontal, his assault direct. Swift had to couch his tale in a fantastic setting with imaginary creatures in order to present his views with impunity. The audience, as well as the times, also affect the satirist's work. If the audience is hostile, the writer must veil his theme; if the audience is indifferent, he must jolt them with bitter and reviling language if he desires change. If he does not fear reprisals, the satirist may take any tone he pleases.

We can see satire in operation in two adaptations of the biblical story of King Solomon, who settled the dispute between two mothers regarding an infant: Cut the baby in two and divide it between you, he told them. The rightful mother protested and was promptly awarded the child. The story is meant to attest to the King's wisdom and understanding of parental love, in this case.

However, Twain's Huck Finn has some difficulty persuading runaway slave Jim that Solomon was wise. Jim insists that Solomon, having fathered "'bout five million chillen," was "waseful.... *He* as soon chop a chile in two as a cat. Dey's plenty mo'. A chile er two, mo' er less, warn't no consekens to Solermun, dad fetch him!" Twain is ridiculing not only Jim's ingenuousness, as he does throughout the novel; he is also deflating time-honored beliefs about the Bible and its traditional heroes, as he earlier does with the account of Moses and the "bulrushers." While Twain's tone is fairly mild, his intent shows through as serious; Twain was disgusted with traditional Christianity and its hypocritical followers, as we see later in *Huck Finn* when young Buck Grangerford is murdered in the feud with the Shepherdsons: "I wished I hadn't ever come ashore that night to see such things."

A second satiric variation on the Solomon theme appears in Asprin's *Myth Adventures*, in the volume *Hit or Myth*. Skeebe, the narrator, realizes that he, as king pro-tem, must render a decision regarding the ownership of a cat. Hoping to inspire them to compromise, he decrees that they divide the cat between them: "Instead they thanked me for my wisdom, shook hands, and left smiling, presumably to carve up their cat." He concludes that many of the citizens of this realm "don't have both oars in the water," a conclusion very like Huck's: "I never see such a nigger. If he got a notion in his head once, there warn't no getting it out again." The citizens' unthinking acceptance of the infallibility of authority is as laughable as Jim's out-of-hand rejection of Solomon's wisdom because no wise man would "want to live in the mids' er sich a blim-blammin' all de time" as would prevail in the harem with the King's "million wives."

POETRY

Opening a book to study for an examination is perhaps the worst occasion on which to read poetry, or about poetry, because above all, poetry should be enjoyed; it is definitely "reading for pleasure." This last phrase seems to have developed recently to describe the reading we do other than for information or for study. Perhaps you personally would not choose poetry as pleasure reading because of the bad name poetry has received over the years. Some students regard the "old" poetry such as Donne's or Shelley's as effete (for "wimps" and "nerds" only, in current language), or modern poetry as too difficult or weird. It is hard to imagine that poetry was the "current language" for students growing up in the Elizabethan or Romantic eras. Whereas in our world information can be retrieved in a nanosecond, in those worlds time was plentiful to sit down, clear the mind, and let poetry take over. Very often the meaning of a poem does not come across in a nanosecond and for the modern student this proves very frustrating. Sometimes it takes years for a poem to take on meaning—the reader simply knows that the poem sounds good and it provokes an emotional response that cannot be explained. With time, more emotional experience, more reading of similar experiences, more life, the reader comes to a meaning of that poem that satisfies for the time being. In a few more years that poem may take on a whole new meaning.

READING POETRY FOR AN EXAMINATION

This is all very well for reading for pleasure, but you are now called upon, in your present experience, to learn poetry for an important examination. Perhaps the first step in the learning process is to answer the question, "Why do people write poetry?" An easy answer is that they wish to convey an experience, an emotion, an insight, or an observation in a startling or satisfying way, one that remains in the memory for years. But why not use a straightforward sentence or paragraph? Why wrap up that valuable insight in fancy words, rhyme, paradox, meter, allusion, symbolism, and all the other seeming mumbo-jumbo that explicators of poetry use? Why not just come right out and say it like "normal people" do? An easy answer to these questions is that poetry is not a vehicle for conveying meaning alone. Gerard Manley Hopkins, one of the great innovators of rhythm in poetry, claimed that poetry should be "heard for its own sake and interest even over and above its interest or meaning." Poetry provides intellectual stimulus of course. One of the best ways of studying a poem is to consider it a jigsaw puzzle presented to you whole, an integral work of art, which can be taken apart piece by piece (word by word), analyzed scientifically, labelled, and put back together again into a whole, and then the meaning is complete. But people write poetry to convey more than meaning.

MEANINGS IN POETRY

T. S. Eliot maintained that the meaning of the poem existed purely to distract us "while the poem did its work." One interpretation of a poem's "work" is that it changes us in some way. We see the world in a new way because of the way the poet has seen it and told us about it. Maybe one of the reasons people write poetry is to encourage us to *see* things in the first place. Simple things like daffodils take on a whole new aspect when we read the way Wordsworth saw them. Why did Wordsworth write that poem? His sister had written an excellent account of the scene in her journal. Wordsworth not only evokes nature as we have never seen it before, alive, joyous, exuberant, he shows nature's healing powers, its restorative quality as the scene flashes "upon that inward eye/Which is the bliss of solitude." Bent over your books studying, how many times has a similar quality of nature's power in the memory come to you? Maybe for you a summer beach scene rather than daffodils by the lake is more meaningful, but the poet captures a moment that we have all experienced. The poet's magic is to make that moment new again.

If poets enhance our power of sight they also awaken the other senses as powerfully. We can hear Emily Dickinson's snake in the repeated "s" sound of the lines:

His notice sudden is—
The Grass divides as with a Comb—
A spotted shaft is seen—

and because of the very present sense of sound, we experience the indrawn gasp of breath of fear when the snake appears. We can touch the little chimneysweep's hair "that curled like a lamb's back" in William Blake's poetry, and because of that tactile sense we are even more shocked to read that the child's hair is all shaved off so that the soot will not spoil its whiteness. We can smell the poison gas as Wilfred Owen's soldiers fumble with their gas masks; we can taste the blood gurgling in the poisoned lungs.

Poets write, then, to awaken the senses. They have crucial ideas but the words they use are often more important than the meaning. More important still than ideas and sense awakening is the poet's appeal to the emotions. And it is precisely this area that disturbs a number of students. Our modern society tends to block out emotions—we need reviews to tell us if we enjoyed a film or a critic's praise to see if a play or novel is worth our time. We hesitate to laugh at something in case it is not the "in" thing to do. We certainly do not cry—at least in front of others. Poets write to overcome that blocking (very often it is their own blocking of emotion they seek to alleviate), but that is not to say that poetry immediately sets us laughing, crying, loving, or hating. The important fact about the emotional release in poetry is that poets help us explore our own emotions, sometimes by shocking us, sometimes by drawing attention to balance and pattern, and sometimes by cautioning us to move carefully in this inner world.

Poets tell us nothing really new. They tell us old truths about human emotions that we begin to restructure anew, to reread our experiences in light of theirs, to reevaluate our world view. Whereas a car manual helps us understand the workings of a particular vehicle, a poem helps us understand the inner workings of human beings. Poets frequently write to help their emotional life—the writing then becomes cathartic, purging or cleansing the inner life, feeding that part of us that separates us from the animal. Many poets might paraphrase Byron, who claimed that he had to write or go mad. Writer and reader of poetry enter into a collusion, each helping the other to find significance in the human world, to find safety in a seemingly alien world.

REASONS FOR READING POETRY

This last point brings any reader of poetry to ask the next question: Why read poetry? One might contend that a good drama, novel, or short story might provide the same emotional experience. But a poem is much more accessible. Apart from the fact that poems are shorter than other genres, there is a unique directness to them which hinges purely on language. Poets can say in one or two lines what may take novelists and playwrights entire works to express. For example, Keats' lines—

Beauty is truth, truth beauty,—that is all
Ye know on earth, and all ye need to know—

studied, pondered, and opened to each reader's interpretations, linger in the memory with more emphasis than George Eliot's *Middlemarch*, or Ibsen's *The Wild Duck*, which endeavor to make the same point.

In your reading of poems remember that poetry is perhaps the oldest art and yet surrounds us without our even realizing it. Listeners thrilled to Homer's poetry; tribes chanted invocations to their gods; today we listen to pop-song lyrics and find ourselves, sometimes despite ourselves, repeating certain rhythmic lines. Advertisements we chuckle over or say we hate have a way of repeating themselves as we use the catchy phrase or snappy repetition. Both lyricists and advertisers cleverly use language, playing on the reader's/listener's/watcher's ability to pick up on a repeated sound or engaging rhythm or inner rhyme. Think of a time as a child when you thoroughly enjoyed poetry: nursery rhymes, ball-game rhythms, jump-rope patterns. Probably you had no idea of the meaning of the words ("Little Miss Muffet sat on a tuffet..." a tuffet?!) but you responded to the sound, the pattern. As adults we read poetry for that sense of sound and pattern. With more experience at reading poetry there is an added sense of pleasure as techniques are recognized: alliteration, onomatopoeia; forms of poetry become obvious—the sonnet, the rondelle. Even greater enjoyment comes from watching a poet's development, tracing themes and ideas, analyzing maturity in growth of imagery, use of rhythm.

To the novice reader of poetry, a poem can speak to the reader at a particular time and become an experience in itself. A freshman's experience after her mother's death exemplifies this. Shortly after the death, the student found Elizabeth Jennings' poem "Happy Families." Using the familiar names of the cards, Mrs. Beef and Master Bun, the poet describes how strangers try to help the family carry on their lives normally although one of the "happy family" is "missing." The card game continues although no one wants it to. At the end the players go back to their individual rooms and give way to their individual grief. The student described the relief at knowing that someone else had obviously experienced her situation where everyone in the family was putting up a front, strangers were being very kind, and a general emptiness prevailed because of that one missing family member. The poem satisfied. The student saw death through another's eyes; the experience was almost the same, yet helped the reader to re-evaluate, to view a universal human response to grief as well as encourage her to deal with her own.

On reading a poem the brain works on several different levels: it responds to the sounds; it responds to the words themselves and their connotations; it responds to the emotions; it responds to the insights or learning of the world being revealed. For such a process poetry is a very good training ground—a boot camp—for learning how to read literature in general. All the other genres have elements of poetry within them. Learn to read poetry well and you will be a more accomplished reader, even of car manuals! Perhaps the best response to reading poetry comes from a poet herself, Emily Dickinson, who claimed that reading a book of poetry made her feel "as if the top of [her] head were taken off!"

Before such a process happens to you, here are some tips for reading poetry before and during the examination.

TIPS FOR PREPARATION

1) Make a list of poets and poems you remember; analyze poems you liked, disliked, loved, hated, and were indifferent to. Find the poems. Reread them and for each one analyze your *feelings*, first of all, about the poetry itself. Have your feelings changed? Now what do you like or hate? Then paraphrase the *meaning* of each poem. Notice how the "magic" goes from the poem, i.e., "To Daffodils"—the poet sees many daffodils by the side of a lake and then thinks how the sight of them later comforts him.

2) Choose a poem at random from an anthology or one mentioned in this introduction. Read it a couple of times, preferably aloud, because the speaking voice will automatically grasp the rhythm and that will help the meaning. Do not become bogged down in individual word connotation or the meaning of the poem—let the poetry do its "work" on you; absorb the poem as a whole jigsaw puzzle.

3) Now take the puzzle apart. Look carefully at the title. Sometimes a straightforward title helps you focus. Sometimes a playful title helps you get an angle on the meaning. "Happy Families," of course, is an ironic title because the family playing the card game of that name is not happy.

4) Look carefully at the punctuation. Does the sense of a line carry from one to another? Does a particular mark of punctuation strike you as odd? Ask why that mark was used.

5) Look carefully at the words. Try to find the meaning of words with which you are not familiar within the context. Familiar words may be used differently: ask why that particular use. Having tapped into your memory bank of vocabulary and you are still at a loss, go to a dictionary. Once you have the *denotation* of the word, start wondering about the *connotation*. Put yourself in the poet's position and think why that word was used.

6) Look carefully at all the techniques being used. You will gain these as you progress through this section and through the test preparation. As soon as you come across a new idea—"caesura" perhaps—learn the word, see how it applies to poetry, where it is used. Be on the lookout for it in other poetry. Ask yourself questions such as why the poet used alliteration here; why the rhythm changes there; why the poet uses a sonnet form and which sonnet form is in use. Forcing yourself to ask the WHY questions, and answering them, will train the brain to read more perceptively. Poetry is not accidental; poets are deliberate people; they do things for specific reasons. Your task under a learning situation is to discover WHY.

7) Look carefully at the speaker. Is the poet using another persona? Who is that persona? What is revealed about the speaker? Why use that particular voice?

8) Start putting all the pieces of the puzzle together. The rhythm helps the meaning. The word choice helps the imagery. The imagery adds to the meaning. Paraphrase the meaning. Ask yourself simple questions: What is the poet saying? How can I relate to what is being said? What does this poem mean to me? What does this poem contribute to human experience?

9) Find time to read about the great names in poetry. Locate people within time areas and analyze what those times entailed. For example, the Elizabethans saw a contest between secular love and love of God. The Romantics (Wordsworth, Coleridge, Keats, Shelley, Byron) loved nature and saw God within nature. The Victorians (Tennyson, Blake) saw nature as a threat to mankind and God, being replaced by the profit cash-nexus of the Industrial Age. The moderns (T. S. Eliot, Pound, Yeats) see God as dead and man as hollow, unwanted, and unsafe in an alien world. The Post-Moderns see life as "an accident," a comic/cosmic joke, fragmented, purposeless—often their topics will be political: apartheid, abortion, unjust imprisonment.

10) Write a poem of your own. Choose a particular style; use the sonnet form; parody a famous poem; express yourself in free verse on a crucial, personal aspect of your life. Then analyze your own poetry with the above ideas.

TIPS FOR TEST-TAKING

You will have established a routine for reading poetry, but now you are under pressure, must work quickly, and will have no access to a dictionary. You cannot read aloud but you can do the following:

1) Internalize the reading—hear the reading in your head. Read through the poem two or three times following the absorbing procedure.

2) If the title and poet are supplied, analyze the title as before and determine the era of the poetry. Often this pushes you toward the meaning.

3) Look carefully at the questions which should enable you to "tap into" your learning process. Answer the ones that are immediately clear to you: form, technique, language perhaps.

4) Go back for another reading for those questions that challenge you—theme or meaning perhaps—analyze the speaker or the voice at work—paraphrase the meaning—ask the simple question "What is the poet saying?"

5) If a question asks you about a specific line, metaphor, opening, or closing lines, highlight or underline them to force your awareness of each crucial word. Internalize another reading emphasizing the highlighted area—analyze again the options you have for your answers.

6) Do not waste time on an answer that eludes you. Move onto another section and let the poetry do its "work." Very often the brain will continue working on the problem on another level of consciousness. When you go back to the difficult question, it may well become clear.

7) If you still are not sure of the answer, choose the option that you *think* is the closest to correct.

VERSE AND METER
Verse

As children reading or learning poetry in school, we referred to each section of a poem as a verse. We complained we had ten verses to learn for homework. In fact the word **verse** strictly refers to a line of poetry, perhaps from the original Latin word "versus": a row or a line, and the notion of turning, "vertere," to turn or move to a new idea. In modern use we refer to poetry often as "verse" with the connotation of rhyme, rhythm, and meter; but we still recognize verse because of the positioning of lines on the page, the breaking of lines that distinguish verse from prose.

The verses we learned for homework are in fact known as **stanzas**: a grouping of lines with a metrical order and often a repeated rhyme which we know as the **rhyme scheme**. Such a scheme is shown by letters to show the repeating sounds. Byron's "Stanzas" will help you recall the word, see the use of a definite rhyme, and how to mark it:

"Stanzas"

(When a man hath no freedom to fight for at home)

When a man hath no freedom to fight for at home,	*a*
Let him combat for that of his neighbors;	*b*
Let him think of the glories of Greece and of Rome,	*a*
And get knocked on the head for his labors.	*b*
To do good to mankind is the chivalrous plan,	*c*
And is always as nobly requited;	*d*
Then battle for freedom wherever you can,	*c*
And, if not shot or hanged, you'll get knighted.	*d*

The rhyme scheme is simple: *abab* and your first question should be "Why such a simple, almost sing-song rhyme?" The simplicity reinforces the **tone** of the poem: sarcastic, cryptic, cynical. There is almost a sneer behind the words "And get knocked on the head for his labors." It is as if the poet sets out to give a lecture or at least a homily along the lines of: "Neither a lender nor a borrower be," but then undercuts the seriousness. The **irony** of the poem rests in the fact that Byron joined a freedom fighting group in Greece and died, not gloriously, but of a fever. We shall return to this poem for further discussion.

Forms of Rhymes

Certain types of rhyme are worth learning. The most common is the **end rhyme**, which has the rhyming word at the end of the line, bringing the line to a definite stop but setting up for a rhyming word in another line later on, as in "Stanzas": home... Rome, a perfect rhyme. **Internal rhyme** includes at least one rhyming word within the line, often for the purpose of speeding the rhythm or making it linger. Look at the effect of Byron's internal rhymes mixed with half-rhymes: "combat... for that"; "Can/And... hanged" slowing the rhythm, making the reader dwell on the harsh long "a" sound, prolonging the sneer which almost becomes a snarl of anger. **Slant rhyme**, sometimes referred to as half, off, near, or approximate rhyme, often jolts a reader who expects a perfect rhyme; poets thus use such a rhyme to express disappointment or a deliberate let-down. **Masculine rhyme** uses one-syllable words or stresses the final syllable of polysyllabic words, giving the feeling of strength and impact. **Feminine rhyme** uses a rhyme of two or more syllables, the stress not falling upon the last syllable, giving a feeling of softness and lightness, one can see that these terms for rhyme were written in a less enlightened age! The terms themselves for the rhymes are less important than realizing or at least appreciating the effects of the rhymes.

If the lines from "Stanzas" had been unrhymed and varying in metrical pattern, the verse would have been termed **free**, or to use the French term, *"Vers libre,"* not to be confused with **blank verse**, which is also unrhymed but has a strict rhythm. The Elizabethan poets Wyatt and Surrey introduced blank verse, which Shakespeare uses to such good effect in his plays, and later, Milton in the great English epic *Paradise Lost*. Free verse has become associated with "modern" poetry, often adding to its so-called obscurity because without rhyme and rhythm, poets often resort to complicated syntactical patterns, repeated phrases, awkward cadences, and parallelism. Robert Frost preferred not to use it because, as he put it, "Writing free verse is like playing tennis with the net down," suggesting that free verse is easier than rhymed and metrical. However, if you have ever tried writing such verse, you will know the problems. (Perhaps a good exercise after you learn about meter is to write some "free" verse.) T. S. Eliot, who uses the form most effectively in "The Journey of the Magi," claimed that no *"vers"* is *"libre"* for the poet who wanted to do a good job.

Meter

Such a claim for the artistry and hard work behind a poem introduces perhaps the most difficult of the skills for a poet to practice and a reader to learn: meter. This time the Greeks provide the meaning of the word from *"metron,"* meaning measure. **Meter** simply means the pattern or measure of stressed or accented words within a line of verse. When studying meter a student should note where stresses fall on syllables—that is why reading aloud is so important, because it catches the natural rhythm of the speaking voice—and if an absence of stressed syllables occurs there is always an explanation why. We "expect" stressed and unstressed syllables because that is what we use in everyday speech. We may stress one syllable over another for a certain effect, often using the definite article "THE well known author..." or the preposition "Get OUT of here!" Usually, however, we use a rising and falling rhythm, known as **iambic rhythm**. A line of poetry that alternates stressed and unstressed syllables is said to have

iambic meter. A line of poetry with ten syllables of rising and falling stresses is known as **iambic pentameter**, best used by Shakespeare and Milton in their blank verse. The basic measuring unit in a line of poetry is called a **foot**. An **iambic foot** has one unstressed syllable followed by a stressed marked by u. Pentameter means "five-measure." Therefore, **iambic pentameter** has five groups of two syllables, or ten beats, to the line. Read aloud the second and fourth, sixth and eighth lines of "Stanzas," tapping the beat on your desk or your palm, and the ten beat becomes obvious. Read again with the stresses unstressed and stressed (or soft and loud, short or long, depending on what terminology works for you) and the iambic foot becomes clear.

Tapping out the other alternate lines in this poem you will not find ten beats but twelve. The term for this line is **hexameter**, or six feet, rather than five. Other line-length names worth learning are:

monometer	one foot	**dimeter**	two feet
trimeter	three feet	**tetrameter**	four feet
heptameter	seven feet	**octameter**	eight feet

Other foot names worth learning are:

the **anapest** marked u u /, the most famous anapestic line being:

> u u /   u u   / u   u / u   u /

"Twas the night before Christmas, when all through the house…"

the **trochee**, marked / u, the most memorable trochaic line being:

> / u   / u / u   / u

"Double double toil and trouble…"

and the **dactyl** marked / u u, the most often quoted dactylic line being:

> / u u / u u

"Take her up tenderly…"

Accentual Meter

Old English poetry employs a meter known as **accentual meter**, with four stresses to the line without attention to the unstressed syllables. Contemporary poets tend not to use it, but one of the greatest innovators in rhythm and meter, Gerard Manley Hopkins, used it as the "base line" for his counterpointed "Sprung Rhythm." Living in the nineteenth century, Hopkins produced poetry that even today strikes the reader as "modern," in that the rhymes and rhythms often jar the ear, providing stressed syllables where we expect unstressed and vice versa. The rhythm was measured by feet of from one to four syllables, and any number of unstressed syllables. Underneath the rhythm we hear the "regular" rhythm we are used to in speech, and an intriguing counterpoint develops. One stanza from "The Caged Skylark" will show the method at work:

> As a dare-gale skylark scanted in a dull cage
> Man's mounting spirit in his bone-house, mean house, dwells—
> That bird beyond the remembering his free fells;
> This in drudgery, day-labouring-out life's age.

The stress on "That" and "This" works particularly well to draw attention to the two captives: the skylark and Man. The accentual meter in the second line reinforces the wretchedness of the human condition. No reader could possibly read that line quickly, nor fail to put the full length of the syllable on "dwells." The dash further stresses the length and the low pitch of the last word.

If at first the terms for meter are new and strange, remember that what is most important is not that you mindlessly memorize the terminology but are able to recognize the meter and analyze why the poet has used it in the particular context of the poem. For example, Shakespeare did not want the lyrical fall and rise of the iamb for his witches around the cauldron, so he employs the much more unusual trochee to suggest the gloom and mystery of the heath in "Macbeth." Many poets will "mix and match" their meter and your task as a student of poetry is to analyze why. Perhaps the poet sets up the regular greeting card meter, rising and falling rhythm, regular end-stopped rhyme. If the poet abruptly changes that pattern, there is a reason. If the poet subtly moves from a disruptive meter into a smooth one, then analyze what is going on in the meaning. If the poet is doing "a good job" as T. S. Eliot suggested, then the rhyme, rhythm, and meter should all work together in harmony to make the poem an integral whole. Answer the test essay questions to practice the points in this section and the integrity of a poem as a single unit will become clearer.

FIGURATIVE LANGUAGE AND POETIC DEVICES

It will start becoming ever more obvious that a poem is not created from mere inspiration. No doubt the initial movement for a poem has something of divine intervention: the ancients talked of being visited by the Muse of Poetry; James Joyce coined the word "epiphany" for the clear moment of power of conception in literature, but then the poet sets to working at the expression to make it the best it can be.

Perhaps what most distinguishes poetry from any other genre is the use of figurative language—figures of speech—used through the ages to convey the poet's own particular world-view in a unique way. Words have **connotation** and **denotation**, **figurative** and **literal** meanings. We can look in the dictionary for denotation and literal meaning, but figurative language works its own peculiar magic, tapping into shared experiences within the psyche. A simple example involves the word "home." If we free-associated for awhile among a group of 20 students, we would find a number of connotations for the word, depending on the way home was for us in our experiences: comforting, scary, lonely, dark, creepy, safety, haven, hell…. However, the denotation is quite straightforward: a house or apartment or dwelling that provides shelter for an individual or family. Poets include in their skill various figures of speech to "plug into" the reader's experiences, to prompt the reader to say "I would have never thought of it in those terms but now I see!"

Metaphors and Similes

The most important of these skills is perhaps the **metaphor**, which compares two unlike things, feelings, or objects, and the **simile**. Metaphors are more difficult to find than **similes**, which also compare two dissimilar things but always use the words "as if" (for a clause) or "like" (for a word or phrase). Metaphors suggest the comparison; the meaning is implicit. An easy way to distinguish between the two is the simple example of the camel. **Metaphor**: the camel is the ship of the desert. **Simile**: a camel is like a ship in the desert. Both conjure up the camel's almost sliding across the desert, storing up its water as a ship must do for survival for its passengers, and the notion of the vastness of the desert parallels the sea. The metaphor somehow crystallizes the image. Metaphors can be *extended* so that an entire poem consists of a metaphor, or unfortunately they can be *mixed*. The latter rarely happens in poetry unless the poet is deliberately playing with his readers and provoking humor.

Start thinking of how many times you use similes in your own writing or speech. The secret is, as Isaac Babel once said, that similes must be "as precise as a slide rule and as natural as the smell of dill." The precision and naturalness coming together perfectly often set up an equation of comparison. A student once wrote "I felt torn apart by my loyalty to my mother and grandmother, like the turkey wishbone at Thanksgiving." We have all experienced divided loyalties. Using the graphic wishbone-tearing idea, something we have all done or have seen done at Thanksgiving lets us more easily relate to the student's experience. Another student wrote of his friends waiting for the gym class to begin "like so many captive gazelles." Again, the visual point of comparison is important but also the sense of freedom in the idea of gazelle, the speed, the grace; juxtaposing that freedom with the word "captive" is a master stroke that makes a simile striking.

The same student went on to an *extended simile* to state precisely and naturally his feelings upon going into a fistfight: "I was like the kid whose parents were killed by the crooked sheriff, waiting for high noon and the showdown that would pit a scared kid with his father's rusty old pistol against the gleaming steel of a matched pair, nestled in the black folds of the sheriff's holsters. I knew there was no way out. Surrounded by friends, I marched out into the brilliant sun, heading for the back fields of the playground, desperately trying to polish the rusty old gun." Although this student was writing in prose, his use of figurative language is poetic. He plugs into readers' movie experience with the central idea of the show-down at high noon, an **allusion** that involves the reader on the same plane as the writer. The notion of the black holster extends the allusion of the old cowboy films where the "baddies" wore black hats and rode black horses. The use of the word "nestled" provokes some interesting connota-tions of something soft and sweet like a kitten nestling into something. But then the gun is an implement of destruction and death; maybe "nestles" takes on the connotation of how a snake might curl in the sun at the base of a tree. The metaphor then ends with the child going out into the sun. The "rusty gun" in context of the essay was in fact the outmoded ideas and morals his father and old books had inculcated in him. All in all a very clever use of figurative language in prose. If the same concept had been pursued in poetry, the metaphor would have moved more speedily, more subtly—a poet cannot waste words—and of course would have employed line breaks, rhythm, and meter.

Personification

Personification is a much easier area than metaphor to detect in po-etry. Usually the object that is being personified—referred to as a human with the personal pronoun sometimes, or possessing human attributes—is capitalized, as in this stanza from Thomas Gray's "Ode on a Distant Pros-pect of Eton College":

> Ambition this shall tempt to rise,
> Then whirl the wretch from high,
> To bitter Scorn a sacrifice,
> And grinning Infamy.
> The stings of Falsehood those shall try,
> And hard Unkindness' altered eye,

> That mocks the tear it forced to flow;
> And keen Remorse with blood defiled,
> And moody Madness laughing wild
> Amid severest woe.

As the poet watches the young Eton boys, he envisions what the years have to offer them, and the qualities he sees he gives human status. Thus, Ambition is not only capable of tempting, an amoral act, but also of "whirling," a physical act. Scorn is bitter, Infamy grinning, and so on. Coleridge employs a more visual personification in "The Ancient Mariner," for the sun whom he describes as:

> ...the Sun (was) flecked with bars
> (Heaven's Mother send us grace!)
> As if through a dungeon-grate he peered
> With broad and burning face.

More so than with Gray's more formal personification, Coleridge's supplies an image that is precise—we can see the prisoner behind the bars, and what's more this particular prisoner has a broad and burning face... of course because he is the sun! The personification brings us that flash of recognition when we can say "Yes, I see that!"

Image

The word **image** brings us to another important aspect of figurative language. Not a figure of speech in itself, the image plays a large role in poetry because the reader is expected to **imagine** what the poet is evoking, through the senses. The image can be **literal**, wherein the reader has little adjustment to make to see or touch or taste the image; a **figurative image** demands more from readers, almost as if they have to be inside the poet's imagination to understand the image. Very often this is where students of poetry, modern poetry particularly, find the greatest problems because the poetry of **imagism**, a term coined by Ezra Pound, is often intensely personal, delving into the mind of the poet for the comparison and connection with past memories that many readers cannot possibly share. Such an image is referred to as *free*, open to many interpretations. This concept suits the post-modern poet who feels that life is fragmented, open to multi-interpretations—there is no fixed order. Poets of the Elizabethan and Romantic eras saw the world as whole, steady, *fixed*, exactly the word used for their type of images. Readers of this poetry usually share the same response to the imagery. For example, the second stanza of Keats' "Ode to a Nightingale" sets up the taste imagery of a

> draught of vintage that hath been
> Cooled a long age in the deep-delvéd earth,
> Tasting of Flora and the country green,
> Dance, and Provençal song, and sunburnt mirth!
> O for a beaker of the warm South,
> Full of the true, the blushful Hippocrene,
> With beaded bubbles winking at the brim,
> And purple-stainéd mouth;

Even though Flora and Hippocrene are not names we are readily familiar with, the image of the cool wine, the taste, the look, the feeling evoked
of the South and warmth, all come rushing into our minds as we enter the
poet's imagination and find images in common.

Blake's imagery in "London" works in a similar way but as readers we
have to probe a little harder, especially for the last line of the last stanza:

> But, most thro' midnight streets I hear
> How the youthful Harlot's curse
> Blasts the new-born Infant's tear,
> And blights with plagues the Marriage hearse.

Notice how the "Marriage hearse" immediately sets up a double image.
Marriage we associate with happiness and joy; hearse we associate with
death and sorrow. The image is troubling. We go back to the previous lines.
The harlot curses her newborn—the curse of venereal disease. She also
foresees that the child ultimately will wed and carry the disease into marriage. Does marriage then becomes death? The image is intriguing and open
to interpretation.

Symbol

Image in figurative language inevitably leads to **symbol**. When an object, an image, or a feeling takes on a larger meaning outside of itself, then a
poet is employing a symbol, something which stands for something greater.
Because mankind has used symbols for so long, many have become **stock** or
conventional: the rose standing for love; the flag standing for patriotism,
love of one's country (thus the controversy over flag-burning today); the
color yellow standing for corruption (hence Gatsby's Daisy Buchanan—the
white-dressed virginal lady with the center core of carelessness); the bird for
freedom; the sea for eternity; the cross for suffering and sacrifice. If you are
not versed in the Christian tradition, it might be useful to read its symbols
because the older poetry dwells on the church and the trials of loving God
and loving Woman—the latter also has become a symbol deteriorating over
the ages from Eve to the Madonna to Whore.

If the symbol is not conventional then it may carry with it many interpretations, depending on the reader's insight. Some students "get carried away" with symbolism, seeing more in the words than the poets do! If the poet is "doing a good job," the poetry will steer you in the "right" direction of symbolism. Sometimes we are unable to say what "stands for" what, but simply that the symbol evokes a mood; it suggests an idea to you that is difficult to explain. The best way to approach symbolism is to understand a literal meaning first and then shift the focus, as with a different camera lens, and see if the poet is saying something even more meaningful. Blake again supplies an interesting example. In his poem "The Chimney Sweeper" he describes the young child's dream of being locked up in "coffins of black." Literally of course coffins are brown wood, the color of mourning is black. Shift the focus then to the young child chimney sweeper, so young he can barely lisp the street cry "Sweep" so it comes out "'weep! 'weep! 'weep! 'weep!" (a symbolic line in itself). Your reading of the Industrial Age's cruelty to children who were exploited as cheap, plentiful, and an expendable labor force will perhaps have taught you that children were used as chimney brushes—literally thrust up the thin black chimneys of Victorian houses and factories, where very often they became trapped, suffocated, sometimes burned to death if fires were set by unknowing owners. Now the black coffins stand for the black-with-soot chimneys the little children had to sweep, chimneys which sometimes became their coffins. The realization of the symbol brings a certain horror to the poem. In the dream an Angel releases the children who then run down "a green plain leaping, laughing.../And wash in a river, and shine in the sun." The action is of course symbolic in that in real life the children's movements were restricted, living in monstrous cities where green plains would be enjoyed only by the rich, and totally limited by the size of the chimneys. They were always black with soot. They rarely saw the sun, never mind shone in it! Again, the symbolism adds something to the poem. In many students there have been reactions of tears and anger when they *see* the symbolism behind such simple lines.

Allusion

The idea of reading about the Industrial Age brings us to an important part of figurative language, briefly mentioned before: **allusion**. Poets tap into previous areas of experience to relate their insights, to draw their readers into shared experiences. Remember how the student writer alluded to old cowboy movies, the classic "high noon." Poets will refer to history, myth, other older poems, plays, music, heroes, famous people. Allusion is becoming more and more difficult for the modern student because reading is becoming more and more a lost art. Core courses in schools have become hotbeds of controversy about what students should know. Fortunately, modern poets are shifting their allusions so that contemporary readers can appreciate and join in with their background of knowledge. However, be aware that for the examination in poetry it will be useful to have a working knowledge of the traditional canon of literature. Think of areas of history that were landmarks: the burning of Carthage; Hannibal's elephants; Caesar's greatness; Alexander the Great; the First World War and its carnage of young men; the Second World War and the Holocaust. Think of the great Greek and Roman myths: the giving of fire to the world; the entrance of sin into the world; the labyrinth; the names associated with certain myths (Daedalus, Hercules, the Medusa). You may never have a question on the areas you read but your background for well-rounded college study will already be formulated.

Alliteration: the repetition of consonants at the beginning of words that are next to each other or close by. The Hopkins stanza quoted earlier provides some fine examples: "skylark scanted"; "Man's mounting… mean house"; "free fells"; "drudgery, day-labouring-out life's age." Always try to understand the reason for the alliteration. Does it speed or slow the rhythm? Is it there for emphasis? What does the poet want you to focus on?

Apostrophe: the direct address of someone or something that is not present. Many odes begin this way. Keats' "Ode on a Grecian Urn" for example: "Thou still unravished bride of quietness," and "Ode to Psyche": "O Goddess! hear these tuneless numbers."

Assonance: the repetition of vowel sounds usually internally rather than initially. "Her goodly eyes like sapphires shining bright." Here the poet, Spenser, wants the entire focus on the blue eyes, the crispness, and the light.

Bathos: deliberate anticlimax to make a definite point or draw attention to a falseness. The most famous example is from Pope's "Rape of the Lock": "Here thou, great Anna! whom three realms obey, /Dost sometimes counsel take—and sometimes tea."

The humor in the bathos is the fact that Anna is the Queen of England—she holds meetings in the room Pope describes but also indulges in the venerable English custom of afternoon tea. The fact that tea should rhyme with obey doubles the humor as the elongated vowel of the upper-class laconic English social group is also mocked.

Caesura: the pause, marked by punctuation (/) or not within the line. Sometimes the caesura (sometimes spelled cesura) comes at an unexpected point in the rhythm and gives the reader pause for thought.

Conceits: very elaborate comparisons between unlikely objects. The metaphysical poets such as John Donne were criticized for "yoking" together outrageous terms, describing lovers in terms of instruments, or death in terms of battle.

Consonance: similar to slant rhyme—the repetition of consonant sounds without the vowel sound repeated. Hopkins again frequently uses this as in "Pied Beauty": "All things counter, original, spare, strange;... adazzle, dim."

Diction: the word for word choice. Is the poet using formal or informal language? Does the poetry hinge on slang or a dialect? If so what is the purpose? Are the words "highfalutin" or low-brow? As always, the diction needs examining and questions like these answering.

Enjambment: the running-on of one line of poetry into another. Usually the end of lines are rhymed so there is an end-stop. In more modern poetry, without rhyme, poets often use run-on lines to give a speedier flow, the sound of the speaking voice or a conversational tone.

Hyperbole: is an obvious and intentional exaggeration. Donne's instruction to the woman he is trying to seduce not to kill the flea, by contrasting her reluctance with "a marriage" of blood within a flea, reinforces the hyperbole used throughout the poem:

> Oh stay, three lives in one flea spare,
> Where we almost, yea, more than married are.

This couplet is also a good example of an unexpected caesura for emphasis at the second pause.

Irony: plays an important role in voice or tone, inferring a discrepancy between what is said and what is meant. A famous example is Shelley's "Ozymandias," which tells of the great ruler who thought that he and his name would last forever, but the traveller describes the huge statue in ruins with the inscription speaking truer than the ruler intended: "My name is Ozymandias, king of kings: /Look on my works, ye Mighty, and despair!"

Metonymy: a figure of speech in which a term is used to evoke or stand for a related idea. Example: "The pen is mightier than the sword." Pen and sword are metonymical designations for (the artful use of) words and (engagement in) physical battle.

Onomatopoeia: a device in which the word captures the sound. In many poems the words are those in general use: the whiz of fireworks; the crashing of waves on the shore; the booming of water in an underground seacave.

Oxymoron: a rhetorical device of epigrammatic form in which incongruous or contradictory terms are conjoined. Examples: "painful pleasure," "sweet sorrow."

Paradox: a situation, action, or statement that appears to be contradictory but that nevertheless holds true.

Pun: a play on words often for humorous or sarcastic effect. The Elizabethans were very fond of them; many of Shakespeare's comedies come from punning. Much of Donne's sexual taunting involves the use of the pun.

Sarcasm: when verbal irony is too harsh, it moves into the sarcastic realm. It is the "lowest form of wit" of course but can be used to good effect in the tone of a poem. Browning's dramatic monologues make excellent use of the device.

Synecdoche: when a part of an object is used to represent the entire thing or vice versa. When we ask someone to give us a hand, we would be horrified if they cut off their hand; what we want is the person's help, from all of the body!

Syntax: the ordering of words into a particular pattern. If a poet shifts words from the usual word order, you know you are dealing with an older style of poetry (Shakespeare, Milton) or a poet who wants to shift emphasis onto a particular word.

Tone: the voice or attitude of the speaker. Remember that the voice need not be that of the poet's. He or she may be adopting a particular tone for a purpose. Your task is to analyze if the tone is angry, sad, conversational, abrupt, wheedling, cynical, affected, satiric, etc. Is the poet including you in a cozy way by using "you," or is he accusing "you" of what he is criticizing? Is the poet keeping you at a distance with coldness and third person pronouns. If so, why? The most intriguing of voices is Browning's in his **dramatic monologues**: poems that address another person who remains silent. Browning brought this type of poetry to an art. Think of all the variations of voices and attitudes and be prepared to meet them in poetry.

TYPES OF POETRY

Having begun to grasp that poetry contains a great deal more than what initially meets the eye, you should now start thinking about the various types of poetry. Of course, when reading for pleasure, it is not vital to recognize that the poem in hand is a sonnet or a villanelle, but for the exam you may well be asked to determine what sort of poem is under scrutiny. Knowing the form of poem may dictate certain areas of rhyme or meter and may enhance the meaning.

Form

The pattern or design of a poem is known as **form**, and even the strangest, most experimental poetry will have some type of form to it. Allen Ginsberg's "A Supermarket in California" caused a stir because it didn't read like poetry, but on the page there is a certain form to it. Some poets even try to match the shape of the poem to the subject. Find in anthologies John Hollander's "Swan and Shadow" and Dorthi Charles' "Concrete Cat." Such visual poems are not just fun to look at and read but the form adds to the subject and helps the reader appreciate the poet's world view. **Closed form** will be immediately recognizable because lines can be counted and shape determined. The poet must keep to the recognized form, in number of lines, rhyme scheme, and/or meter. **Open form** developed from "vers libre," which name some poets objected to as it suggested that there was little skill or craft behind the poem, simply creativity, as the name suggests, gives a freedom of pattern to the poet.

Sonnets

The most easily recognized closed form of poetry is the **sonnet**, sometimes referred to as a **fixed form**. The sonnet always has 14 lines, but there are two types of sonnets, the Petrarchan (or Italian, and the Shakespearean (or English). The word sonnet in fact comes from the Italian word "sonnetto" meaning a "little song." Petrarch, the fourteenth century Italian poet, took the form to its peak with his sonnets to his loved one, Laura. This woman died before he could even declare his love, and such poignant, unrequited love became the theme for many Elizabethan sonnets. As a young man might telephone a young woman for a date in today's society, the Elizabethan would send a sonnet. The Petrarchan sonnet is organized into two groups: eight lines and six—the **octave** and the **sestet**. Usually the rhyme scheme is abbaabba-cdecde, but the sestet can vary in its pattern. The octave may set up a problem or a proposition, and then the answer or resolution follows in the sestet after a turn or a shift. The Shakespearean sonnet organizes the lines into three groups of four lines: **quatrains** and a **couplet** (two rhyming lines). The rhyming scheme is always abab cdcd efef gg, and the turn or shift can happen at one of three places or leave the resolution or a "twist in the tail" at the end.

Couplets

The couplet, mentioned earlier, leads us to a closed form of poetry that is very useful for the poet. It is a two-line stanza that usually rhymes with an end rhyme. If the couplet is firmly end-stopped and written in iambic pentameter, it is known as an **heroic couplet**, after the use was made of it in the English translations of the great classical or heroic epics such as *The Iliad* and *The Odyssey*. Alexander Pope became a master of the heroic couplet, sometimes varying to the 12-syllable line from the old French poetry on Alexander the Great. The line became known as the **Alexandrine**. Pope gained fame first as a translator of the epics and then went on to write **mock-heroic** poems like "The Rape of the Lock," written totally in heroic couplets which never become monotonous, as a succession of regularly stepped-out couplets can, because he varied the place of the caesura and masterfully employed enjambment.

Epics

Rarely in an exam will you be presented with an **epic** because part of the definition of the word is vastness of size and range. You may, however, be confronted with an excerpt and will need to recognize the structure. The translation will usually be in couplets and the meter regular with equal line lengths, because originally these poems were sung aloud or chanted to the beat of drums. Because of their oral quality, repetition plays an important part, so that if the bard, or singer, forgot the line, the audience, who had heard the stories many times before, could help him out. The subject deals with great deeds of heroes: Odysseus (Ulysses), Hector, and Aeneus, their adventures and their trials; the theme will be of human grief or pride, divided loyalties—but all "writ large." The one great English epic, *Paradise Lost*, is written by Milton and deals with the story of Adam and Eve and the Fall. Adam thus becomes the great hero. The huge battle scenes of *The Iliad* are emulated in the War of the Heavens when Satan and his crew are expelled into Hell; the divided loyalties occur when Adam must choose between obedience to God and love for his wife.

Ballads

On much simpler lines are the **ballads**, sometimes the earliest poems we learn as children. Folk or popular ballads were first sung as early as the fifteenth century and then handed down through generations until finally written down. Usually the ballads are anonymous and simple in theme, having been composed by working folk who originally could not read or write. The stories—a ballad is a story in a song—revolve around love and hate and lust and murder, often rejected lovers, knights, and the supernatural. As with the epic, and for the same reason, repetition plays a strong part in the ballad and often a repeated refrain holds the entire poem together. The form gave rise to the **ballad stanza**, four lines rhyming *abcb* with lines 1 and 3 having eight syllables and lines 2 and 4 having six. Poets who later wrote what are known as **literary ballads** kept the same pattern. Read Coleridge's "Rime of the Ancient Mariner" and all the elements of the ballad come together as he reconstructs the old folk story but writes it in a very closed form.

Lyrics

The earlier poetry dealt with narrative. The "father of English poetry," Geoffrey Chaucer, told stories within a story for the great *Canterbury Tales*. The Elizabethans turned to love and the humanistic battle between love of the world and love of God. Wordsworth and Coleridge marked a turning point by not only using "the language of men" in poetry but also by moving away from the narrative poem to the **lyric**. The word comes again from the Greek, meaning a story told with the poet playing upon a lyre. Wordsworth moves from story to emotion, often "emotion recollected in tranquillity" as we saw in "Daffodils." Although sometimes a listener is inferred, very often the poet seems to be musing aloud.

Part of the lyric "family" is the **elegy**, a lament for someone's death or the passing of a love or concept. The most famous is Thomas Gray's "Elegy Written in a Country Churchyard," which mourns not only the passing of individuals but of a past age and the wasted potential within every human being, no matter how humble. Often **ode** and elegy become synonymous, but an ode, also part of the lyric family, is usually longer, dealing with more profound areas of human life than simply death. Keats' odes are perhaps the most famous and most beloved in English poetry.

Specialized Types of Poetry

More specialized types of poetry need mentioning so that you may recognize and be able to explicate how the structure of the poem enhances the meaning or theme. For example the **villanelle**: a courtly love poem structure from medieval times, built on five three-line stanzas known as **tercets**, with the rhyme scheme aba, followed by a four-line stanza, and a **quatrain** which ends the poem abaa. As if this were not pattern and order enough, the poem's first line appears again as the last line of the 2nd and

4th tercets; *and* the third line appears again in the last line of the 3rd and 5th tercets; *and* these two lines appear again as rhyming lines at the end of the poem! The most famous and arguably the best villanelle, as some of the older ones can be so stiff in their pattern that the meaning is inconsequential, is Dylan Thomas' "Do not go gentle into that good night." The poem stands on its own with a magisterial meaning of mankind raging against death, but when one appreciates the structure also, the rage is even more emphatic because it is so controlled. A poem well worth finding for "reading for pleasure." In James Joyce's *A Portrait of the Artist as a Young Man*, writing a villanelle on an empty cigarette packet turns the young boy, Stephen Dedalus, dreaming of being an artist, into a poet, a "real" artist.

Said to be the most difficult of all closed forms is the **sestina**, also French, sung by medieval troubadours, a "song of sixes." The poet presents six six-line stanzas, with six end-words in a certain order, then repeats those six repeated words in any order in a closing tercet. Find Elizabeth Bishop's "Sestina" or W.H. Auden's "Hearing of Harvests Rotting in the Valleys" and the idea of six images running through the poet's head and being skillfully repeated comes across very clearly. You might even try working out a sestina for yourself.

Perhaps at this stage an **epigram** might be more to your liking and time scale because it is short, even abrupt, a little cynical and always to the point. The cynical Alexander Pope mastered the epigram, as did Oscar Wilde centuries later. Perhaps at some stage we have all written **doggerel**, rhyming poetry that becomes horribly distorted to fit the rhymes, not through skill but the opposite. In contrast, **limericks** are very skilled: five lines using the anapest meter with the rhyme scheme: aabba. Unfortunately, they can deteriorate into types such as "There was a young lady from....," but in artful hands such as Shakespeare's (see Ophelia's mad song in *Hamlet*: "And will he not come again?") and Edward Lear's, limericks display fine poetry. Finally, if you are trying to learn all the different types of closed-form poetry, you might try an **aubade**—originally a song or piece of music sung or played at dawn—a poem written to the dawn or about lovers at dawn—the very time when poetic creation is extremely high!

Although the name might suggest open-form, **blank verse** is in fact closed-form poetry. As we saw earlier, lines written in blank verse are unrhymed and in iambic pentameter. Open-form poets can arrange words on the page in any order, not confined by any rhyme pattern or meter. Often it seems as if words have spilled onto the page at random with a direct address to the readers, as if the poets are cornering them in their room, or simply chatting over the kitchen table. The lines break at any point—the dash darts in and out—the poets are talking to the audience with all the "natural" breaks that the speaking voice will demonstrate. Open-form poets can employ rhyme, but sometimes it seems as if the rhyme has slipped into the poem quite easily—there is no wrenching of the word "to make it rhyme." Very often there is more internal rhyme as poets play with words, often giving the sensation they are thinking aloud. Open-form poetry is usually thought of as "modern," at least post-World War I, but the use of space on the page, the direct address of the voice, and the use of the dash clearly marks Emily Dickinson as an open-form poet, but she lived from 1830–1886.

DRAMA AND THEATER

The Glass Menagerie by Tennessee Williams begins when one of its four characters, Tom, steps into the downstage light and addresses the audience directly as though he were the chorus from a much earlier play. "I have tricks in my pocket, I have things up my sleeve," says Tom. "But I am the opposite of a stage magician. He gives you illusion that has the appearance of truth. I give you truth in the pleasant disguise of illusion."

To sit among the audience and watch a skillful production of *The Glass Menagerie* is to visit Tom's paradoxical world of theater, a magic place in which known imposters and stagecraft trickery create a spectacle which we know is illusion but somehow recognize as truth. Theater, as a performed event, combines the talents and skills of numerous artists and craftspersons, but before the spectacle must come the playwright's work, the pages of words designating what the audience sees and hears. These words, the written script separate from the theatrical performance of them, is what we call *drama*, and the words give the spectacle its significance because without them the illusion has neither frame nor content. Truth requires boundaries and substance. When Shakespeare's Hamlet advises actors just before their performance, he places careful emphasis on the importance of the words, cautioning the players to speak them "trippingly on the tongue." If all actions are not suited to the words, Hamlet adds, the performance will fail because the collaborative purpose combining the dramatist's literary art and the actors' performing art "is to hold as 'twere the mirror up to Nature."

COMPARISON OF DRAMA TO PROSE AND POETRY

Although drama is literature written to be performed, it closely resembles the other genres. In fact, both poetry and prose also can be performed; but as captivating as these public readings sometimes are, only performed drama best creates the immediate living "illusion as truth" Tom promises. Like fiction and narrative poetry, drama tells a tale—that is, it has plot, characters, and setting—but the author's voice is distant, heard only through the stage directions and perhaps some supplementary notes. With rare exceptions, dialogue dominates the script. Some drama is poetry, such as the works of Shakespeare and Molière, and all plays resemble poems as abstractions because both forms are highly condensed, figurative expressions. Even in Henrik Ibsen's social realism, the dramatic action is metaphorical.

A scene set inside a house, for instance, requires a room with only three walls. No audience complains, just as no movie audience feels betrayed by film characters' appearing ridiculously large. Without a thought, audiences employ what Samuel Taylor Coleridge called "a willing suspension of disbelief"; in other words, they know that the images before them are not real but rather representations, reflections in the mirror of which Hamlet speaks, not the real world ("Nature").

A play contains conflict which can be enacted immediately on the stage without any alterations in the written word. **Enacted** means performed by an actor or actors free to use the entire stage and such theatrical devices as sets, costumes, makeup, special lighting, and props for support. This differs from the oral interpretation of prose or poetry. No matter how animated, the public reader is not acting. This is the primary distinction between drama and other literary forms. Their most obvious similarity is that any form of literature is a linguistic expression. There is, however, one other feature shared by all kinds of narratives: the pulsating energy which pushes the action along is generated by human imperfection. We speak of tragic characters as having "flaws," but the same is true about comic characters as well. Indeed, nothing is more boring either on a stage or in a written text than a consistently flawless personality, because such characters can never be congruent with the real people of our everyday experiences. The most fundamental human truth is human frailty.

Although it can be argued that a play, like a musical composition, must be performed to be realized, the script's linguistic foundation always gives the work potential as a literary experience. Moreover, there is never a "definitive" interpretation. The script, in a sense, remains unfinished because it never stops inviting new variations, and among those invited to participate are individual readers whose imaginations should not be discounted. For example, when *Death of a Salesman* was originally produced, Lee J. Cobb played Willy Loman. Aside from the character's age, Dustin Hoffman's Willy in a revival 40 years later bore hardly any physical resemblance to Cobb's. Yet both portrayals "worked." The same could be said about the Willys created by the minds of the play's countless readers. Quite capable of composing its own visions and sounds, the human imagination is the original mirror, the place where all human truths evolve from perceived data.

Mimesis

Hamlet's mirror and Tom's truthful illusions are figures of speech echoing drama's earliest great critic, Aristotle, who believed art should create a **mimesis**, the Greek word for "imitation." For centuries this "mimetic theory" has asserted that a successful imitation is one which reproduces natural objects and actions in as realistic portrayal as possible. Later, this notion of imitation adopted what has been called the "expressive theory," a variation allowing the artist a freer, more individual stylized approach. A drama by Ibsen, for example, attempts to capture experience as unadorned raw sense, the way it normally appears to be. This is realistic imitation. As twentieth century drama moved toward examinations of people's inner consciousness as universal representations of some greater human predicament, new expressive styles emerged. The diversity in the works of Eugene O'Neill, Samuel Beckett, and Harold Pinter illustrate how dramatists' imitations can disrupt our sense of the familiar as their plays become more personally expressive. But the theater of Aristotle's time was hardly "realistic" in today's objective sense. Instead, it was highly stylized and full of conventions derived from theater's ritualistic origins. The same is true of medieval morality plays and the rigid formality of Japanese Kabuki theater, yet these differ greatly from each other and from ancient Greek and Roman dramas. In other words, imitating "what's out there" requires only that the form be consistent with itself, and any form is permissible.

PLOT STRUCTURE
Exposition

As with other narrative types, a play's **plot** is its sequence of events, its organized collection of incidents. At one time it was thought that all the actions within a play should be contained within a single 24-hour period. Few lengthy plays have plots which cover only the period of time enacted on the stage. Most plays condense and edit time much as novels do. Decades can be reduced to two hours. Included in the plot is the **exposition**, the revealing of whatever information we need in order to understand the impending conflict. This exposed material should provide us with a sense of place and time (**setting**), the central participants, important prior incidents, and the play's overall mood. In some plays such as Shakespeare's, the exposition comes quickly. Notice, for instance, the opening scenes in *Macbeth, Hamlet*, and *Romeo and Juliet*: not one presents us with a central character, yet each—with its witches or king's ghost or street brawl— clearly establishes an essential tension heralding the main conflict to come. These initial expositions attack the audience immediately and are followed by subsequent events in chronological order. Sophocles' *Oedipus Rex* works somewhat differently, presenting the central character late in the myth from which the play is taken. The exposition must establish what has come previously, even for an audience familiar with the story, before the plot can advance. Like Shakespeare, Sophocles must start his exposition at the beginning, but he takes a longer (though not tedious) time revealing the essential facts. Arthur Miller, in his *Death of a Salesman,* continuously interrupts the central action with dislocated expositions from earlier times as though the past were always in the present. He carefully establishes character, place, mood, and conflict throughout the earliest scenes; however, whatever present he places on stage is always caught in a tension between the audience's anticipation of the future and its suspicions of the past. The plots in plays like *Oedipus Rex* and *Death of a Salesman* tend not to attack us head-on but rather to surround us and gradually close in, the circle made tighter by each deliberately released clue to a mysterious past.

Complication and Crisis

Conflict requires two opposing forces. We see, for instance, how King Lear's irresponsible abdication and conceited anger are countered by Goneril and Regan's duplicity and lusts for power. We also see how Creon's excessive means for restoring order in Thebes is met by Antigone's allegiance to personal conscience. Fairly soon in a play we must experience some incident that incites the fundamental conflict when placed against some previously presented incident or situation. In most plays the conflict's abrasive conditions continuously chafe and even lacerate each other. The play's tempo might provide some interruptions or variations in the pace; nevertheless, conflicts generate the actions which make the characters' worlds worse before they can get better. Any plot featuring only repetitious altercations, however, would soon become tiresome. Potentially, anything can happen in a conflict. The **complication** is whatever presents an element capable of altering the action's direction. Perhaps some new information is discovered or a previously conceived scheme fails, creating a reversal of what had been expected. The plot is not a series of similar events but rather a compilation of related events leading to a culmination, a **crisis**.

Resolution

In retrospect we should be able to accept a drama's progression of actions leading to the crisis as inevitable. After the crisis comes the **resolution** (or **denouement**), which gives the play its concluding boundary. This does not mean that the play should offer us solutions for whatever human issues it raises. Rather, the playwright's obligation is to make the experience he presents to us seem filled within its own perimeters. George Bernard Shaw felt he had met this obligation when he ended *Pygmalion* with his two principal characters, Higgins and Eliza, utterly incapable of voicing any romantic affection for each other; and the resolution in Ibsen's *A Doll's House* outraged audiences a hundred years ago and still disturbs some people today, even though it concludes the play with believable consequences.

Terms such as **exposition**, **complication**, **crisis**, and **resolution**, though helpful in identifying the conflict's currents and directions, at best only artificially define how a plot is molded. If the play provides unity in its revelations, these seams are barely noticeable. Moreover, any successful creative composition clearly shows that the artist accomplished much more than merely plugging components together to create a finished work. There are no rules which all playwrights must follow, except the central precept that the play's unified assortment of actions be complete and contained within itself. *Antigone*, for instance, depicts the third phase of Sophocles' *Oedipus* trilogy, although it was actually written and performed before *Oedipus Rex* and *Oedipus at Colonus*. And although a modern reader might require some background information before starting, *Antigone* gives a cohesive dramatic impact independent from the other two plays.

CHARACTER
Examples of Characters from Hamlet

Essential to the plot's success are the characters who participate in it. Midpoint in *Hamlet* when Elsinore Castle is visited by the traveling theater company, the prince joyously welcomes the players, but his mood quickly returns to bitter depression shortly after he asks one actor to recite a dramatic passage in which the speaker recalls the fall of Troy and particularly Queen Hecuba's response to her husband's brutal murder. The player, caught by the speech's emotional power, becomes distraught and cannot finish. Left alone on stage, Hamlet compares the theatrical world created by the player with Hamlet's "real" world and asks: "What's Hecuba to him, or he to Hecuba,/That he should weep for her!" Under ordinary circumstances Hamlet's anxiety would not overshadow his Renaissance sensibilities, because he knows well that fictional characters always possess the potential to move us. As though by instinct, we know the same. We read narratives and go to the theater precisely because we want to be shocked, delighted, thrilled, saddened, titillated, or invigorated by "a dream of passion." Even though some characters are more complex and interesting than others, they come in countless types as the playwright's delegates to our imaginations and as the imitations of reality seeking our response.

Examples of Characters from Antigone

Antigone begins with two characters, Antigone and Ismene, on stage. They initiate the exposition through their individual reactions to a previous event, King Creon's edict following the battle in which Thebes defeated an invading army. Creon has proclaimed Eteocles and the others who recently died defending Thebes as heroes worthy of the highest burial honors; in addition, Creon has forbidden anyone, on penalty of death, from burying Poloneices and the others who fell attacking the city. Since Antigone, Ismene, Polyneices, and Eteocles are the children of Oedipus and Iocaste, the late king and queen, conflict over Creon's law seems imminent. These first two characters establish this inevitability. They also reveal much about themselves as individuals.

ANTIGONE:… now you must prove what you are:
A true sister, or a traitor to your family.

ISMENE: Antigone, are you mad! What could I possibly do?

ANTIGONE: You must decide whether you will help me or not.

ISMENE: I do not understand you. Help you in what?

ANTIGONE: Ismene, I am going to bury him. Will you come?

ISMENE: Bury him! You have just said the new law forbids it.

ANTIGONE: He is my brother. And he is your brother, too.

ISMENE: But think of the danger! Think what Creon will do!

ANTIGONE: Creon is not strong enough to stand in my way.

ISMENE: Ah sister!
Oedipus died, everyone hating him
For what his own search brought to light, his eyes
Ripped out by his own hand; and Iocaste died,
His mother and wife at once: she twisted the cords
That strangled her life; and our two brothers died,
Each killed by the other's sword. And we are left:
But oh, Antigone,

Think how much more terrible than these
Our own death would be if we should go against Creon
And do what he has forbidden! We are only women,
We cannot fight with men, Antigone!
The law is strong, we must give in to the law
In this thing, and in worse. I beg the Dead
To forgive me, but I am helpless: I must yield
To those in authority. And I think it is dangerous business
To be always meddling.

ANTIGONE: If that is what you think,
I should not want you, even if you asked to come.
You have made your choice, you can be what you want to be.
But I will bury him; and if I must die,
I say that this crime is holy: I shall lie down
With him in death, and I shall be as dear
To him as he to me.
It is the dead,
Not the living, who make the longest demands:
We die for ever...
You may do as you like,
Since apparently, the laws of the gods mean nothing to you.

ISMENE: They mean a great deal to me; but I have no strength
To break laws that were made for the public good.

ANTIGONE: That must be your excuse, I suppose. But as for me,
I will bury the brother I love.

ISMENE: Antigone, I am so afraid for you!

ANTIGONE: You need not be:
You have yourself to consider, after all.

ISMENE: But no one must hear of this, you must tell no one!
I will keep it a secret, I promise!

ANTIGONE: Oh tell it! Tell everyone!
Think how they'll hate you when it all comes out
If they learn that you knew about it all the time!

ISMENE: So fiery! You should be cold with fear.

ANTIGONE: Perhaps. But I am doing only what I must.

ISMENE: But can you do it? I say that you cannot.

ANTIGONE: Very well: when my strength gives out, I shall do no more.

ISMENE: Impossible things should not be tried at all.

ANTIGONE: Go away, Ismene:
I shall be hating you soon, and the dead will too,
For your words are hateful. Leave me my foolish plan:
I am not afraid of the danger; if it means death,
It will not be the worst of deaths—death without honor.

ISMENE: Go then, if you feel that you must.
You are unwise,
But a loyal friend to those who love you.

[Exit into the palace. ANTIGONE goes off...]

READING THE PLAY

All we know about Antigone and Ismene in this scene comes from what they say; therefore, we read their spoken words carefully. However, we must also remain attentive to dramatic characters, propensity for not revealing all they know and feel about a given issue, and often characters do not recognize all the implications in what they say. We might be helped by what one says about the other, yet these observations are not necessarily accurate or sincere. Even though the previous scene contains fewer ambiguities than some others in dramatic literature, we would be oversimplifying to say the conflict here is between one character who is "right" and another who is "wrong." Antigone comes out challenging, determined and unafraid, whereas Ismene immediately reacts fearfully. Antigone brims with the self-assured power of righteousness while Ismene expresses vulnerability. Yet Antigone's boast that "Creon is not strong enough to stand in my way" suggests a rash temperament. We might admire her courage, but we question her judgment. Meanwhile, Ismene can evoke our sympathies with her burden of family woes, at least until she confesses her helplessness and begs the Dead to forgive her, at which point we realize her objections stem from cowardice and not conscience.

Although we might remain unsettled by Antigone's single-mindedness, we soon find ourselves sharing her disdain for Ismene's trepidation, particularly when Ismene rationalizes her position as the more responsible and labels unauthorized intervention in royal decisions as "meddling" against the "public good." Soon, as we realize the issue here demands moral conscience, we measure Ismene far short of what is required. Quickly, though, Ismene is partly redeemed by her obvious concern for Antigone's well-being: "I am so afraid for you." Unaffected, Antigone retorts with sarcasm and threats, but her demeanor never becomes so impetuously caustic that we dismiss her as a conceited adolescent. In fact, we are touched by her integrity and devotion, seeing no pretensions when she says: "I am not afraid of the danger: if it means death,/It will not be the worst of deaths—death without honor." Ismene's intimation that loyalty and love are unwise counters Antigone's idealism enough to make us suspect that the stark, cruel world of human imperfection will not tolerate Antigone's solitary rebellion, no matter how selfless her motivation. At the same time we wonder how long Ismene could remain neutral if Antigone were to clash with Creon.

What immediately strikes us about Antigone and Ismene is that each possesses a sense of self, a conscious awareness about her existence and her connection with forces greater than herself. This is why we can identify with them. It may not always feel reassuring, yet we too can define our existence by saying "I am, and I am not alone." As social creatures, a condition about which they have had no choice, both Antigone and Ismene have senses of self which are touched by their identification with others: each belongs to a family, and each belongs to a civil state. Indeed, much of the play's conflict focuses on which identification should be stronger. Another connection influences them as well—the unbreakable tie to truth. This truth, or ultimate reality, will vary from play to play, and not all characters ever realize it is there, and few will define it the same way. Still, the universe which characters inhabit has definition, even if the resolution suggests a great human absurdity in our insufficient capacity to grasp this definition or, worse, asserts the only definition is the absence of an ultimate reality. With Antigone, we see how her sense of self cannot be severed from its bonds to family obligations and certain moral principles.

Theme

Characters with a sense of self and an identity framed by social connections and unmitigated truths dwell in all good narratives. As readers we wander within these connecting perimeters, following the plot and sensing a commentary about life in general. This commentary, the **theme,** places us within the mirror's image along with the characters and their actions. We look and see ourselves. The characters' universe is ours, the playwright would have us believe, for a while at least. If his art succeeds, we do believe him. But reading literary art is no passive experience; it requires active work. And since playwrights seldom help us decide *how* characters say what they do or interrupt to explain *why* they say what they do, what personal voice he gives through stage directions deserves special attention, because playwrights never tell as much as novelists; instead they show. Our reading should focus on the tone of the dialogue as much as on the information in what is said. Prior to the nineteenth century, dramatists relied heavily on poetic diction to define their characters. Later playwrights provided stage directions which detail stage activities and modify dialogue. Modern writers usually give precise descriptions for the set and costume design and even prescribe particular background music. But no matter when a play was written or what its expressive style is, our role as readers and audience is to make judgments about characters in action, just as we make judgments about Antigone and Ismene the first time we see them. We should strive to be "fooled" by the truthful illusion by activating our sensitivities to human imperfections and the potential conflicts such flaws can generate. And, finally, as we peer into the playwright's mirror, we seek among the populated reflections shadows of ourselves.

Types of Plays

When Polonius presents the traveling players to Hamlet, he reads from the theater company's license, which identifies them as

> The best actors in the world, either for tragedy, comedy, history, pastoral, pastoral-comical, historical-pastoral, tragical-historical, tragical-comical-historical-pastoral, scene individable or poem unlimited…

Shakespeare's sense of humor runs through this speech which sounds like a parody of the license granted Shakespeare's own company by James I, authorizing "the Arte and faculty of playing Comedies, Tragedies, histories, Enterludes, moralls, pastoralls, Stageplaies and Such others..." for the king's subjects and himself. The joke is on those who think all plays somehow can be categorized according to preconceived definitions, as though playwrights follow literary recipes. The notion is not entirely ridiculous, to be sure, since audiences and readers can easily tell a serious play from a humorous one, and a play labeled "tragedy" or "comedy" will generate certain valid expectations from us all, regardless of whether we have read a word by Aristotle or any other literary critic. Still, if beginning playwrights had to choose between writing according to some rigid strictures designating the likes of a "tragical-comical-historical-pastoral" or writing a play unrestricted by such rules (a "poem unlimited"), they would probably choose the latter.

Thought

All plays contain thought—its accumulated themes, arguments, and overall meaning of the action—together with a mood or tone, and we tend to categorize dramatic thought into three clusters: the serious, the comic, and the seriocomic. These distinctions echo the primitive rites from which theater evolved, religious observances usually tied to seasonal cycles. In the course of a year numerous situations could arise which would initiate dramatic, communal prayers of supplication or thanksgiving. Indeed, for humanity to see its fate held by the will of a god is to see the intricate unity of flesh and spirit, a paradox ripe for representation as dramatic conflict. And if winter's chill brings the pangs of tragedy and summer's warmth the delight of comedy, the year becomes a metaphor for the overall human condition, which contains both. Thus, in our attempts to interpret life's complexities, it is tempting to place the art forms representing it in precise, fixed designations. From this can come critical practices which ascertain how well a work imitates life by how well it adheres to its designated form. Of course, such a critical system's rigidity would limit the range of possible human experiences expressed on stage to a narrow few, but then the range could be made elastic enough to provide for possible variations and combinations. Like the old Ptolemaic theories which held that the Earth was the center of the Solar System, these precepts could work for a while. After a few centuries, though, it would become clear that there is a better way of explaining what a play's form should be—not so much fixed as organic. In other words, we should think of a play as similar to a plant's growing and taking shape according to its own design. This analogy works well because the plant is not a mechanical device constructed from a predetermined plan, yet every plant is a species and as such contains qualities which identify it with others. So just as Shakespeare could ridicule overly precise definitions for dramatic art, he could still write dramas which he clearly identified as tragedies, comedies, or histories, even though he would freely mix two or more of these together in the same play. For the purpose of understanding some of the different perspectives available to the playwright's examining eye, we will look at plays from different periods which follow the three main designations Shakespeare used, followed by a fourth which is indicative of modern American drama. A knowledge of *The Importance of Being Earnest*, *Othello*, *A Man for All Seasons*, and *Death of a Salesman* will be helpful.

COMEDY

Forms of Comedy

The primary aim of comedy is to amuse us with a happy ending, although comedies can vary according to the attitudes they project, which can be broadly identified as either **high** or **low**, terms having nothing to do with an evaluation of the play's merit. Generally, the amusement found in comedy comes from an eventual victory over threats or ill fortune. Much of the dialogue and plot development might be laughable, yet a play need not be funny to be comic. **Farce** is low comedy intended to make us laugh by means of a series of exaggerated, unlikely situations that depend less on plot and character than on gross absurdities, sight gags, and coarse dialogue. The "higher" a comedy goes, the more natural the characters seem and the less boisterous their behavior. The plots become more sustained, and the dialogue shows more weighty thought. As with all dramas, comedies are about things that go wrong. Accordingly, comedies create deviations from accepted normalcy, presenting incongruities which we might or might not see as harmless. If these incongruities make us judgmental about the involved characters and events, the play takes on the features of **satire**, a rather high comic form implying that humanity and human institutions are in need of reform. If the action triggers our sympathy for the characters, we feel even less protected from the incongruities as the play tilts more in the direction of **tragi-comedy**. In other words, the action determines a figurative distance between the audience and the play. Such factors as characters' personalities and the plot's predictability influence this distance. The farther away we sit, the more protected we feel and usually the funnier the play becomes. Closer proximity to believability in the script draws us nearer to the conflict, making us feel more involved in the action and less safe in its presence. It is a rare play that can freely manipulate its audience back and forth along this plane and still maintain its unity. Shakespeare's *The Merchant of Venice* is one example.

Example of a Comedy

A more consistent play is Oscar Wilde's *The Importance of Being Earnest*, which opened in 1895. In the following scene, Lady Bracknell questions Jack Worthing, who has just announced that Lady Bracknell's daughter, Gwendolyn, has agreed to marry him. Being satisfied with Jack's answers concerning his income and finding his upper-class idleness and careless ignorance about world affairs an asset, she queries him about his family background. In grave tones, the embarrassed Jack reveals his mysterious lineage. His late guardian, Thomas Cardew—"an old gentleman of a very charitable and kindly disposition"—had found the baby Jack in an abandoned handbag.

LADY BRACKNELL: A hand-bag?

JACK (very seriously): Yes, Lady Bracknell. I was in a hand-bag—a somewhat large, black leather hand-bag, with handles to it—an ordinary hand-bag in fact.

LADY BRACKNELL: In what locality did this Mr. James, or Thomas, Cardew come across this ordinary hand-bag?

JACK: In the cloak-room at Victoria Station. It was given him in mistake for his own.

LADY BRACKNELL: The cloak-room at Victoria Station?

JACK: Yes. The Brighton line.

LADY BRACKNELL: The line is immaterial, Mr. Worthing. I confess I feel somewhat bewildered by what you have just told me. To be born, or at any rate bred, in a hand-bag, whether it had handles or not, seems to me to display a contempt for the ordinary decencies of family life that reminds one of the worst excesses of the French Revolution. And I presume you know what that unfortunate movement led to? As for the particular locality in which the hand-bag was found, a cloak-room at a railway station might serve to conceal a social indiscretion—has probably, indeed, been used for that purpose before now—but it could hardly be regarded as an assured basis for recognized position in good society.

JACK: May I ask you then what would you advise me to do? I need hardly say I would do anything in the world to ensure Gwendolyn's happiness.

LADY BRACKNELL: I would strongly advise you, Mr. Worthing, to try and acquire some relations as soon as possible, and to make a definite effort to produce at any rate one parent, of either sex, before the season is over.

JACK: Well, I don't see how I could possibly manage to do that. I can produce the hand-bag at any moment. It is in my dressing-room at home. I really think that should satisfy you, Lady Bracknell.

LADY BRACKNELL: Me, sir! What has it to do with me? You can hardly imagine that I and Lord Bracknell would dream of allowing our only daughter—a girl brought up with the utmost care—to marry into a cloak-room, and form an alliance with a parcel. Good morning, Mr. Worthing!

(LADY BRACKNELL sweeps out in majestic indignation.)

This dialogue between Lady Bracknell and Jack is typical of what runs throughout the entire play. It is full of exaggerations, in both the situation being discussed and the manner in which the characters, particularly Lady Bracknell, express their reactions to the situation. Under other circumstances a foundling would not be the focus of a comedy, but we are relieved from any concern for the child since the adult Jack is obviously secure, healthy, and, with one exception, carefree. Moreover, we laugh when Lady Bracknell exaggerates Jack's heritage by comparing it with the excesses of the French Revolution. On the other hand, at the core of their discussion is the deeply ingrained and oppressive notion of English class consciousness, a mentality so flawed it almost begs to be satirized. Could there be more there than light, witty entertainment?

TRAGEDY
Terms

The term "tragedy" when used to define a play has historically meant something very precise, not simply a drama which ends with unfortunate consequences. This definition originated with Aristotle, who insisted that the play be an imitation of complex actions which should arouse an emotional response combining fear and pity. Aristotle believed that only a certain kind of plot could generate such a powerful reaction. Comedy, as we have seen, shows us a progression from adversity to prosperity. Tragedy must show the reverse; moreover, this progression must be experienced by a certain kind of character, says Aristotle, someone whom we can designate as the **tragic hero**. This central figure must be basically good and noble: "good" because we will not be aroused to fear and pity over the misfortunes of a villain, and "noble" both by social position and moral stature because the fall to misfortune would not otherwise be great enough for tragic impact. These virtues do not make the tragic hero perfect, however, for he must also possess **hamartia**—a tragic flaw—the frailty which leads him to make an error in judgment which initiates the reversal in his fortunes, causing his death or the death of others or both. These dire consequences become the hero's **catastrophe**. The most common tragic flaw is **hubris**, an excessive pride that adversely influences the protagonist's judgment.

Often the catastrophic consequences involve an entire nation because the tragic hero's social rank carries great responsibilities. Witnessing these events produces the emotional reaction Aristotle believed the audience should experience, the **catharsis**. Although tragedy must arouse our pity for the tragic hero as he endures his catastrophe and must frighten us as we witness the consequences of a flawed behavior which anyone could exhibit, there must also be a purgation, "a cleansing," of these emotions which should leave the audience feeling not depressed but relieved and almost elated. The assumption is that while the tragic hero endures a crushing reversal somehow he is not thoroughly defeated as he gains new stature though suffering and the knowledge that comes with suffering.

Classical tragedy insists that the universe is ordered. If truth or universal law is ignored, the results are devastating, causing the audience to react emotionally; simultaneously, the tragic results prove the existence of truth, thereby reassuring our faith that existence is sensible.

Example of a Tragedy

Sophocles' plays give us some of the clearest examples of Aristotle's definition of tragedy. Shakespeare's tragedies are more varied and more modern in their complexities. *Othello* is one of Shakespeare's most innovative and troublesome extensions of tragedy's boundaries. The title character commands the Venetian army and soon becomes acting governor of Cypress. He is also a Moor, a dark-skinned African whose secret marriage to the beautiful Desdemona has infuriated her father, a wealthy and influential Venetian, whose anger reveals a racist element in Venice which Othello tries to ignore. Iago hates Othello for granting a promotion to Cassio which Iago believes should rightfully be his. With unrelenting determination and malicious deception, Iago attempts to persuade Othello that Desdemona has committed adultery with Cassio. The following excerpt catches Iago in the early stages of his successful manipulation:

IAGO: In Venice they [wives] do let heaven see pranks
They dare not show their husbands; their best conscience
Is not to leave 't undone, but keep 't unknown.

OTHELLO: Dost thou say so?

IAGO: She did deceive her father, marrying you;
And when she seem'd to shake and fear your looks,
She lov'd them most.

OTHELLO: And so she did.

IAGO: Why, go to, then;
She that so young could give out such a seeming,
To see her father's eyes up close as oak,
He thought 'twas witchcraft; but I am much to blame;
I humbly do beseech you of your pardon
For too much loving you.

OTHELLO: I am bound to thee forever.

IAGO: I see, this hath a little dash'd your spirits.

OTHELLO: Not a jot, not a jot.

IAGO: I' faith, I fear it has.
I hope you will consider what is spoke
Comes from my love. But I do see you're mov'd;
I am to pray you not to strain my speech
To grosser issues nor to larger reach
Than to suspicion.

OTHELLO: I will not.

IAGO: Should you do so, my lord,
My speech should fall into such vile success
As my thoughts aim not at. Cassio's my worthy friend—
My lord, I see you're mov'd.

OTHELLO: No, not much mov'd:
I do not think but Desdemona's honest.

IAGO: Long live she so! and long live you to think so!

OTHELLO: And yet, how nature erring from itself,—

IAGO: Ay, there's the point: as, to be bold with you,
Not to affect many proposed matches
Of her own clime, complexion, and degree,
Whereto, we see, in all things nature tends;
Foh! one may smell in such, a will most rank,
Foul disproportion, thoughts unnatural.
But pardon me; I do not in position
Distinctly speak of her, though I may fear
Her will, recoiling to her better judgment,
May fall to match you with her country forms
And happily repent.

OTHELLO: Farewell, farewell:
If more thou dost perceive, let me know more;
Set on thy wife to observe. Leave me, Iago.

IAGO: My lord, I take my leave. (Going)

OTHELLO: Why did I marry? This honest creature, doubtless,
Sees and knows more, much more, than he unfolds.

Notice that Iago speaks much more than Othello. This is typical of their conversations, as though Iago were the superior of the two. Dramatically, for Iago's machinations to compel our interests we must perceive in Othello tragic proportions, both in his strengths and weaknesses; otherwise, *Othello* would slip into a malevolent tale about a rogue and his dupe. Much of the tension in this scene emanates from Othello's reluctance either to accept Iago's innuendos immediately or to dismiss them. This confusion places him on the rack of doubt, a torture made more severe because he questions his own desirability as a husband. Consequently, since Iago is not the "honest creature" he appears to be and Othello is unwilling to confront openly his own self-doubts, Iago becomes the dominant personality—a situation which a flawless Othello would never tolerate.

HISTORY

The playwright's raw data can spring from any source. A passion play, for instance, is a dramatic adaptation of the Crucifixion as told in the gospels. A history play is a dramatic perspective of some event or series of events identified with recognized historical figures. Television docudramas are the most recent examples. Among the earliest histories were the chronicle plays which flourished during Shakespeare's time and often relied on *Chronicles* by Raphael Holinshed, first published in 1577. Holinshed's volumes and similar books by others glorified English history and were very popular throughout the Tudor period, especially following the defeat of the Spanish Armada. Similarly, Shakespeare's *Henry V* and *Henry VIII* emphasize national and religious chauvinism in their treatments of kings who, from a more objective historical perspective appear less than nobly motivated. These plays resemble romantic comedies with each one's protagonist defeating some adversary and establishing national harmony through royal marriage. *King Lear* and *Macbeth*, on the other hand, movingly demonstrate Shakespeare's skill at turning historical figures into tragic heroes.

Example of a History Play

Ever since the sixteenth century history plays have seldom risen above the level of patriotic whitewash and political propaganda. Of course there are notable exceptions to this trend: Robert Bolt's *A Man for All Seasons* is one. The title character, Sir Thomas More, is beheaded at the play's conclusion, following his refusal to condone Henry VIII's break from the Roman Catholic Church and the king's establishment of the Church of England with the monarch as its head. Henry wants More to condone these actions because the Pope will not grant Henry a divorce from Queen Catherine so that he can marry Anne Boleyn, who the king believes will bear him the male heir he desperately wants. The central issue for us is not whether More's theology is valid but whether any person of conscience can act freely in a world dominated by others far less principled. In Henry's only scene he arrives at Sir Thomas' house hoping his Lord Chancellor will not disappoint him:

[music in background]

HENRY: Son after son she's borne me, Thomas, all dead at birth, or dead within a month; I never saw the hand of God so clear in anything... I have a daughter, she's a good child, a well-set child—But I have no son. (He flares up) It is my bounden duty to put away the Queen, and all the Popes back to St. Peter shall not come between me and my duty! How is it that you cannot see? Everybody else does.

MORE: (Eagerly) Then why does Your Grace need my poor support?

HENRY: Because you are honest. What's more to the purpose, you're known to be honest... There are those like Norfolk who follow me because I wear the crown, and there are those like Master Cromwell who follow me because they are jackals with sharp teeth and I am their lion, and there is a mass that follow me because it follows anything that moves— and there is you.

MORE: I am sick to think how much I must displease Your Grace.

HENRY: No, Thomas, I respect your sincerity. Respect? Oh, man, it's water in the desert... How did you like our music? That air they played, it had a certain—well, tell me what you thought of it.

MORE: (Relieved at this turn; smiling) Could it have been Your Grace's own?

HENRY: (Smiles back) Discovered! Now I'll never know your true opinion. And that's irksome, Thomas, for we artists, though we love praise, yet we love truth better.

MORE: (Mildly) Then I will tell Your Grace truly what I thought of it.

HENRY: (A little disconcerted) Speak then.

MORE: To me it seemed—delightful.

HENRY: Thomas—I chose the right man for Chancellor.

MORE: I must in fairness add that my taste in music is reputably deplorable.

(From *A Man for All Seasons* by Robert Bolt. Copyright © 1960, 1962 by Robert Bolt. Reprinted by permission of Random House Inc.)

To what extent Henry and More discussed the king's divorce and its subsequent events nobody knows, let alone what was actually said, although we can be certain they spoke an English distinctively different from the language in the play. Bolt's imagination, funneled through the dramatist's obligation to tell an interesting story, presides over the historical data and dictates the play's projections of More, Henry, and the other participants. Thus, we do not have "history"; instead, we have a dramatic perception of history shaped, altered, and adorned by Robert Bolt, writing about sixteenth century figures from a 1960 vantage point. But as the scene above shows, the characters' personalities are not simple reductions of what historical giants should be. Henry struts a royal self-assurance noticeably colored by vanity and frustration; yet although he lacks More's wit and intelligence, the king clearly is no fool. Likewise, as troubled as More is by the controversy before him, he projects a formidable power of his own. *A Man for All Seasons* succeeds dramatically because Bolt provides only enough historical verisimilitude to present a context for the characters' development while he allows the resultant thematic implications to touch all times, all seasons. When we read any history play, we should search for similar implications; otherwise, the work can never become more than a theatrical précis with a narrow, didactic focus.

MODERN DRAMA
Forms of Modern Drama

From the 1870s to the present, the theater has participated in the artistic movements reflecting accumulated theories of science, social science, and philosophy which attempt to define reality and the means we use to discern it. First caught in a pendulum of opposing views, modern drama eventually synthesized these perspectives into new forms, familiar in some ways and boldly original in others. Henrik Ibsen's plays began the modern era with their emphasis on **realism**, a seeking of truth through direct observation using the five senses. As objectively depicted, contemporary life received a closer scrutiny than ever before, showing everyday people in everyday situations. Before Ibsen, theatrical sets were limited, with rare exceptions, to castles and country estates. After Ibsen the farmhouse and city tenement were suitable for the stage. Ibsen's work influenced many others, and from realism came two main variations. The first, **naturalism**, strove to push realism towards a direct transformation of life on stage, a "slice of life" showing how the scientific principles of heredity and environment have shaped society, especially in depicting the plights of the lower classes. The second variation, **expressionism**, moved in a different direction and actually denied realism's premise that the real world could be objectively perceived; instead—influenced by Sigmund Freud's theories about human behavior's hidden, subconscious motivations and by other modernist trends in the arts, such as James Joyce's fiction and Picasso's paintings—expressionism imitated a disconnected dream-like world filled with psychological images at odds with the tangible world surrounding it. While naturalism attempts to imitate life directly, expressionism is abstract and often relies on symbols.

A modern play can employ any number of elements found in the spectrum between these extremes as well as suggest divergent philosophical views about whether humanity has the power to change its condition or whether any of its ideas about the universe are verifiable. Moreover, no work of art is necessarily confined within a particular school of thought. It is quite possible that seemingly incongruent forms can appear in the same play and work well. *The Glass Menagerie*, *A Man for All Seasons*, and *Death of a Salesman* feature characters and dialogue indicative of realistic drama, but the sets described in the stage directions are expressionistic, offering either framed outlines of places or distorted representations. Conventions from classical drama are also available to the playwright. As previously noted, Tom acts as a Greek chorus as well as an important character in his play; the same is true of the Common Man, whose identity changes from scene to scene. Playwrights Eugene Ionesco and Harold Pinter have created characters speaking and behaving in extraordinary ways while occupying sets which are typically realistic. In short, anything is possible in modern drama, a quality which is wholly compatible with the diversity and unpredictability of twentieth century human experiences.

Example of a Modern Drama

In a sense all good drama is modern. No label about a play's origin or form can adequately describe its content. Establishing the people, places, and thought within the play is crucial to our understanding. For the characters to interest us, we must perceive the issues that affect their lives, and eventually we will discover why the characters' personalities and backgrounds, together with their social situations, inevitably converge with these issues and create conflicts. We must also stay aware of drama's kinship with lyric poetry's subjective mood and tone, a quality dominating all plays regardless of the form. *Death of a Salesman* challenges the classical definitions of tragedy by giving us a modern American, Willy Loman, who is indeed a "low man," a person of little social importance and limited moral fiber. His delusionary values have brought him at age 64 to failure and despair, yet more than ever he clings to his dreams and painted memories for solace and hope. Late one night, after Willy has returned from an aborted sales trip, his rambling conversation with his wife Linda returns to the topic which haunts him the most, his son Biff.

WILLY: Biff is a lazy bum!

LINDA: They're sleeping. Get something to eat. Go on down.

WILLY: Why did he come home? I would like to know what brought him home.

LINDA: I don't know. I think he's still lost, Willy. I think he's very lost.

WILLY: Biff Loman is lost. In the greatest country in the world a young man with such—personal attractiveness, gets lost. And such a hard worker. There's one thing about Biff—he's not lazy.

LINDA: Never.

WILLY (with pity and resolve): I'll see him in the morning; I'll have a nice talk with him. I'll get him a job selling. He could be big in no time. My God! Remember how they used to follow him around in high school? When he smiled at one of them their faces lit up. When he walked down the street... (He loses himself in reminiscences.)

LINDA (trying to bring him out of it): Willy, dear, I got a new kind of American-type cheese today. It's whipped.

WILLY: Why do you get American cheese when you know I like Swiss?

LINDA: I just thought you'd like a change—

WILLY: I don't want change! I want Swiss cheese. Why am I always being contradicted?

LINDA (with a covering laugh): I just thought it would be a surprise.

WILLY: Why don't you open a window in here, for God's sake?

LINDA (with infinite patience): They're all open dear.

WILLY: The way they boxed us in here. Bricks and windows, windows and bricks.

LINDA: We should have bought the land next door.

WILLY: The street is lined with cars. There's not a breath of fresh air in the neighborhood. The grass don't grow any more, you can't raise a carrot in the backyard. They should've had a law against apartment houses. Remember those two beautiful elms out there? When I and Biff hung the swing between them?

LINDA: Yeah, like a million miles from the city.

WILLY: They should've arrested the builder for cutting those down. They massacred the neighborhood. (Lost) More and more I think of those days, Linda. This time of year it was lilac and wisteria. And then the peonies would come out, and the daffodils. What fragrance in this room!

LINDA: Well, after all, people had to move somewhere.

WILLY: No, there's more people now.

LINDA: I don't think there's more people. I think—

WILLY: There's more people! That's what's ruining this country! Population is getting out of control. The competition is maddening! Smell the stink from that apartment house! And another on the other side... How can they whip cheese?

In Arthur Miller's stage directions for *Death of a Salesman*, the Loman house is outlined by simple framing with various floors represented by short elevated platforms. Outside the house the towering shapes of the city angle inward presenting the crowded oppressiveness Willy complains about. First performed in 1949, the play continues to make a powerful commentary on modern American life. We see Willy as more desperate than angry about his condition, which he defines in ways as contradictory as his assessments of Biff. In his suffocating world so nebulously delineated, Willy gropes for peace while hiding from truth; and although his woes are uniquely American in some ways, they touch broader, more universal human problems as well.

IMPORTANT LITERARY FIGURES AND THEIR MAJOR WORKS

ANCIENT GREECE AND ROME

Homer
(ca. ninth century B.C.)
Odyssey, Iliad
   —Products of a non-literate culture. First works of Western literature.

Sappho
(ca. 612 B.C.—?)
Verse fragments
   —Early Greek poetry.

Aeschylus
(525 B.C.–456 B.C.)
Oresteia (Agamemnon, Chophori, and *Eumenides)*
   —Responsible for the origin and development of Greek drama; introduced second speaking character and concept of conflict.

Sophocles
(496 B.C.–406 B.C.)
Oedipus Tyrannus, Antigone, Electra
   —Added third speaking character and moved Greek drama further from religious commentary to more basic human interaction.

Euripides
(485 B.C.–405 B.C.)
The Trojan Women, Helen, The Bacchae
   —Chiefly responsible for introducing the technique of *deus ex machina.*

Aristophanes
(450 B.C.–385 B.C.)
Lysistrata, The Clouds, The Birds
   —Considered the father of Greek comedy.

Plato
(428 B.C.–399 B.C.)
Republic, Apology, Symposium
   —Father of Western philosophy.

Aristotle
(384 B.C.–322 B.C.)
The Poetics
   —Introduced and popularized the concept of literary criticism.

Virgil
(70 B.C.–19 B.C.)
The Aeneid
   —(Publius Vegilius Maro) Popularized the pastoral poem and the concept of civic virtue.

Ovid
(43 B.C.–18 A.D.)
Metamorphoses, Love's Remedy
   —(Publius Ovidius Naso) Brought erotic verse to popularity.

THE MIDDLE AGES AND THE RENAISSANCE

Dante Alighieri
(1265–1321)
Divine Comedy (The Inferno, Purgatorio, Paridiso)
   —Considered to have founded modern European literature; perfected "terza rima" (rhyme in threes).

Giovanni Boccaccio
(1313–1375)
The Decameron
   —Introduced the use of the vernacular in classically focused literature.

Francesco Petrarch
(1304–1374)
The Canzoniere
   —His works provided the basis for love poetry and popularized the theme of humanism.

Geoffrey Chaucer
(1340–1400)
The Canterbury Tales, Troilus and Criseyde
   —Chiefly responsible for bringing literature to the middle class.

Nicolo Machiavelli
(1469–1527)
The Prince, La Madrigola
   —*The Prince* outlined a governmental structure based on the self-interest of the ruler. Such rule is still called Machiavellian.

François Rabelais
(1494–1553)
Gargantua, Pantagruel
   —Introduced satiric narrative.

Miguel de Cervantes Saavedra
(1547–1616)
Don Quixote
   —Wrote the first modern novel.

Edmund Spenser
(1552–1599)
The Faerie Queen, Amoretti
   —Popularized the use of allegory.

Francis Bacon

(1561–1626)

Essays, *The New Atlantis*
—Founder of the inductive method of modern science and philosophical writings about science.

Christopher Marlowe

(1564–1593)

The Tragedy of Doctor Faustus, Edward the Second
—Author of first real historical drama and first English tragedy.

William Shakespeare

(1564–1616)

Hamlet, King Lear, Macbeth, Romeo and Juliet, Twelfth Night, Richard III, Julius Caesar, Much Ado About Nothing, Sonnets
—Considered the greatest English poet and dramatist.

Ben Jonson

(1573–1637)

Every Man in His Humour
—English playwright.

John Milton

(1608–1674)

Paradise Lost, Paradise Regained
—Puritan poet noted for allegorical religious epics.

THE NEOCLASSICAL PERIOD

Molière (Jean-Baptiste Poquelin)

(1622–1673)

Don Juan, Tartuffe, The Misanthrope
—Perfected literary conversation and introduced everyday speech to theater.

John Dryden

(1631–1700)

Alexander's Feast, Heroic Stanzas
—Influential in establishing the heroic couplet.

Jean Racine
(1639–1699)
Andromaque, Bernice & Phaedre
  —Renowned for lyric poetry based on Greek and Roman literature.

THE ENLIGHTENMENT

Jonathan Swift
(1667–1745)
Gulliver's Travels, Tale of a Tub
  —Noted for his direct style, clear, sharp prose, and critical wit.

Joseph Addison
(1672–1719)
The Tattler, The Spectator, Cato
  —Outstanding poet, critic, and playwright whose numerous essays
  marked political free thinking of his time.

Alexander Pope
(1688–1744)
The Dunciad, The Rape of the Lock
  —Classicist and wit who formulated rules for poetry and satirized British social circles.

Voltaire (François-Marie Arouet)
(1694–1778)
Candide, Zadig
  —Progressive philosopher and free thinker best known for synthesizing
  French and English critical theory.

Benjamin Franklin
(1706–1790)
Poor Richard's Almanac, Observations on the Increase of Mankind,
numerous essays and state papers
  —Scientist, educator, abolitionist, philosopher, economist, political
  theorist, and statesman who defined the colonial New World in his
  writings; principal figure of the American Enlightenment.

Jean Jacques Rousseau
(1712–1778)
Social Contract
  —Libertine whose focused prose inspired the French Revolution.

William Blake

(1757–1827)

Songs of Innocence, Songs of Experience

—Visual artist and poet who defied neoclassical convention.

THE ROMANTICS AND TRANSCENDENTALISTS

William Wordsworth

(1770–1850)

The Prelude, Lyrical Ballads

—Romantic poet who broke with neoclassical theory in much of his nature poetry.

Jane Austen

(1775–1817)

Sense and Sensibility, Pride and Prejudice

—Principally known for novels of manners and middle-class English society.

Samuel Taylor Coleridge

(1772–1834)

Rime of the Ancient Mariner

—Foremost literary critic of the romantic period.

George Gordon Lord Byron

(1788–1824)

Don Juan

—Major figure in Romantic movement and inspiration for the Byronic hero.

Percy Bysshe Shelley

(1792–1822)

Adonais

—Romantic poet who mastered metaphor and metrical form.

John Keats

(1795–1821)

Hyperion, Ode on a Grecian Urn

—Most versatile of the Romantics.

Mary Shelley
(1797–1851)
Frankenstein, The Last Man
 —Romantic novelist whose liberal social and political views underscore
 her work.

Nathaniel Hawthorne
(1804–1864)
The Scarlet Letter, House of the Seven Gables
 —American transcendentalist

Elizabeth Barrett Browning
(1806–1861)
Sonnets from the Portuguese, Aurora Leigh
 —English poet.

Edgar Allan Poe
(1809–1849)
Fall of the House of Usher, Tell Tale Heart, The Raven
 —American transcendentalist who dealt with macabre issues of insanity
 and horror.

Harriet Beecher Stowe
(1811–1896)
Uncle Tom's Cabin
 —American novelist, wrote the most important novel of the abolitionist
 movement.

Robert Browning
(1812–1889)
Bells and Pomegranates
 —English poet.

Charles Dickens
(1812–1870)
Great Expectations, Oliver Twist
 —English novelist.

Charlotte Brontë
(1816–1855)
Jane Eyre
 —Victorian novelist.

Emily Brontë
(1816–1848)
Wuthering Heights
—Victorian novelist.

Henry David Thoreau
(1818–1848)
Walden
—American Transcendentalist and social theorist.

George Eliot (Mary Ann Evans)
(1819–1880)
Mill on the Floss, Middlemarch
—English author.

Herman Melville
(1819–1891)
Moby-Dick, Billy Budd
—American transcendentalist.

Walt Whitman
(1819–1892)
Leaves of Grass
—American poet.

Fyodor Dostoyevsky
(1821–1881)
Crime and Punishment, Notes from the Underground
—Russian novelist.

Gustave Flaubert
(1821–1880)
Madame Bovary
—French novelist.

Charles Baudelaire
(1821–1867)
Flowers of Evil (Les Fleurs du Mal)
—French Symbolist poet.

Henrik Ibsen

(1828–1906)

A Doll's House

   —Norwegian playwright and forerunner of the Expressionist movement.

Leo Nikolayevich Tolstoy

(1828–1910)

War and Peace, Anna Karenina

   —Major Russian novelist.

Emily Dickinson

(1830–1886)

Because I Could Not Stop for Death

   —American poet.

Christina Rossetti

(1830–1894)

Goblin Market

   —English poet

Mark Twain (Samuel Clemens)

(1835–1910)

Huckleberry Finn, Tom Sawyer

   —American novelist, essayist and satirist

Oscar Wilde

(1854–1900)

The Importance of Being Earnest, The Picture of Dorian Gray

   —English novelist, dramatist, and social critic.

George Bernard Shaw

(1856–1950)

Arms and the Man, Saint Joan

   —Irish-born British author and playwright

Joseph Conrad

(1857–1924)

Heart of Darkness, Lord Jim

   —Ukranian born of Polish parents, major English post-colonialist novelist.

William Butler Yeats
(1865–1939)
The Wind Among the Reeds, The Winding Stair
  —Irish poet and dramatist.

Robert Frost
(1874–1963)
Birches, The Road Not Taken
  —Major American poet.

Gertrude Stein
(1874–1946)
3 Lives
  —American modernist author.

Upton Sinclair
(1878–1968)
The Jungle
  —American novelist and social critic, characterized as a "muckraker."

James Joyce
(1882–1941)
Portrait of the Artist as a Young Man, Ulysses
  —Premier Modernist novelist of Ireland, pioneered stream of consciousness, and non-linear narratives.

Virginia Woolf
(1882–1941)
A Room of One's Own, To the Lighthouse
  —Modernist novelist and early feminist.

Franz Kafka
(1883–1924)
Metamorphosis, The Castle
  —Major Existentialist novelist.

Ezra Pound
(1885–1972)
The Cantos
  —American poet.

D. H. Lawrence
(1885–1930)
Lady Chatterly's Lover, The Rainbow
   —English novelist.

Sinclair Lewis
(1885–1951)
Babbitt, Elmer Gantry
   —American novelist and social critic.

Eugene O'Neill
(1888–1953)
Anna Christie, The Hairy Ape
   —Major American dramatist.

T. S. Eliot
(1888–1965)
The Waste Land
   —Modernist poet and theorist.

Henry Miller
(1891–1980)
The Tropic of Cancer, The Tropic of Capricorn
   —Controversial American novelist.

e.e. cummings
(1894–1962)
Tulips and Chimneys
   —Known for non-traditional forms of poetry.

William Faulkner
(1897–1962)
The Sound and the Fury, Absalom! Absalom!
   —Major author of the American South.

Vladimir Nabokov
(1899–1977)
Lolita, Invitation to a Beheading
   —Russian novelist.

Ernest Hemingway
(1899–1961)
The Old Man and the Sea, A Farewell to Arms
　—Known for lean prose and ardently masculine themes and characters.

Zora Neale Hurston
(1901–1960)
Their Eyes Were Watching God, Tell My Horse
　—American novelist and folklorist.

John Steinbeck
(1902–1968)
Grapes of Wrath, Cannery Row
　—American novelist whose major theme was the life of the American
　　worker.

Langston Hughes
(1902–1967)
Collected Works
　—Harlem Renaissance poet.

Samuel Beckett
(1906–1989)
Waiting for Godot, Happy Days
　—Irish-born French playwright and novelist. Themes include existen-
　　tialism and absurdity.

Elizabeth Bishop
(1911–1979)
Collected Works
　—American poet.

Tennessee Williams
(1911–1983)
A Streetcar Named Desire, The Glass Menagerie
　—American playwright.

Arthur Miller
(1915–　)
Death of a Salesman, The Crucible
　—American playwright.

Aleksandr Isayevitch Solzhenitsyn
(1918–)
The Gulag Archipelago
    —Major Russian novelist and social critic.

Jack Kerouac
(1922–1969)
On the Road, Dharma Bums
    —American Beat poet and novelist.

Nadine Gordimer
(1923–)
A Sport of Nature
    —South African novelist.

James Baldwin
(1924–1987)
The Fire Next Time
    —American poet and novelist.

Allen Ginsberg
(1926–1997)
Howl
    —American Beat poet.

Adrienne Rich
(1929–)
Aunt Jennifer's Tigers
    —American poet.

Toni Morrison
(1931–)
The Bluest Eye, Song of Solomon, Beloved
    —American novelist.

V.S. Naipaul
(1932–)
Enigma of Arrival, House for Mr. Biswas
    —Post-colonialist novelist, born in Trinidad of Indian parents, raised in
    England.

Sylvia Plath
(1932–1963)
Ariel, The Bell Jar
 —American poet and novelist.

Thomas Pynchon
(1937–   )
Vineland, Gravity's Rainbow, The Crying of Lot 49
 —Reclusive American novelist.

Alice Walker
(1944–   )
The Color Purple, Possessing the Secrets of Joy
 —American novelist.

Salman Rushdie
(1947–   )
The Satanic Verses, Shame
 —Known for death sentence placed upon him by Ayatollah Khomeini owing to what Khomeini and fellow Islamic fundamentalists viewed as blasphemy in *The Satanic Verses*.

LITERARY TERMS

allegory—Poetry or prose in which abstract ideas are represented by individual characters, events, or objects.

alliteration—Rapid repetition of consonants in a given line of poetry or prose.

allusion—Reference to one literary work in another.

anachronism—A chronological displacement in which a relationship between events or objects is historically impossible.

anapest—A metrical foot with two unstressed syllables followed by a stressed syllable.

antagonist—The character in a literary work that goes against the actions of the hero.

anti-hero—The protagonist of a literary work who does not possess heroic qualities.

apostrophe—Direct address to someone or something not present.

assonance—Rapid repetition of vowels in a given line of poetry or prose.

ballad—A poem, often intended to be sung, that tells a story.

bathos—A sudden shift from the lofty to the commonplace.

bildungsroman—A coming-of-age story, usually autobiographical.

blank verse—Unrhymed poetry usually written in iambic pentameter.

caesura—A deliberate pause in a line of poetry.

canto—Analogous to a chapter in a novel, it is a division in a poem.

climax—The peak of action in a literary work.

conceits—Elaborate comparisons between unlike objects.

consonance—Repetition of consonant sounds with unlike vowels—similar to alliteration.

couplet—A pair or rhyming lines of poetry in the same meter.

dactyl—A metrical foot comprised of one stressed syllable followed by two unstressed syllables.

denouement—The action following the climax in a literary work.

diction—Word choice or syntax.

doggerel—Crudely written poetry, in which words are often mangled to fit a rhyme scheme.

elegy—A poem lamenting the passage of something.

enjambment—In poetry, the continuation of a phrase or sentence onto the following line.

epistolary—Refers to a novel or story told in the form of letters.

fable—A story used to illustrate a moral lesson.

foot—A group of syllables that make up a metered unit of verse.

haiku—A Japanese poetical form, having three lines and 17 syllables, five in the first line, seven in the second, and five in the third.

hubris—In tragic drama, the excessive pride that leads to the fall of a hero.

hyperbole—Exaggeration for effect.

iamb—A foot containing two syllables, a short then a long (in quantitative meter).

irony—A deliberate discrepancy between literal meaning and intended meaning.

malapropism—Often used for humorous effect, it is the substitution of a word for one that sounds similar but has radically different meaning.

metaphor—A form of comparison in which something is said to be something else, often an unlikely pairing.

meter—The combination of stressed and unstressed syllables that creates the rhythm of a poem.

metonymy—A figure of speech in which a term is used to evoke or stand for an associated idea.

motif—The recurrence of a word or theme in a novel or poem.

onomatopoeia—A word whose sound suggests its meaning; for example, "crash."

oxymoron—Two contradictory words used together to create deeper meaning; for example, sweet sorrow.

paradox—A seemingly contradictory phrase, which proves to be true upon comparison.

pathos—An appeal that evokes pity or sympathy.

scansion—The annotation of the meter of a poem.

simile—Means of comparison using either "like" or "as."

sonnet—A verse form consisting of 14 lines arranged in an octet (eight lines) and a sextet (six lines), usually ending in a couplet; in common English form, arranged in three quatrains followed by a couplet.

spondee—A metrical foot comprised of two stressed syllables.

synecdoche—The use of part of a thing to represent the whole; for example, "wheels" for a car.

tone—Attitude of the speaker, setting the mood for a given passage.

trochee—A metrical foot composed of a stressed syllable followed by an unstressed syllable.

villanelle—A verse form consisting of five tercets and a quatrain, the first and third lines of the tercet recur alternately as the last lines of the other tercets and together as the last lines of the quatrain.

☞ Drill: Literature

1. Though often considered a work for children, this nineteenth century classic continues to amuse and amaze adults interested in puzzles, poems, and hidden meanings.

   (A) *The Cat in the Hat Comes Back*

   (B) *Lord of the Rings*

   (C) *Alice in Wonderland*

   (D) *Gulliver's Travels*

2. Which of the following presents a series of entertaining monologues and bawdy tales told by individuals with a common purpose?

   (A) *The Canterbury Tales*

   (B) *The Martian Chronicles*

(C) *Tales from the Twilight Zone*

(D) *The Complete Works of Edgar Allan Poe*

3. Which of the following is generally recognized as the most accurate literary representation of American soldiers in battle?

   (A) Heller's *Catch-22*

   (B) Remarque's *All's Quiet on the Western Front*

   (C) Mailer's *The Naked and the Dead*

   (D) Crane's *Red Badge of Courage*

4. In which of the following works does the author deal with his or her blindness?

   (A) Dickinson's "My Life Closed Twice Before Its Close"

   (B) Malory's *Morte D'Arthur*

   (C) Milton's "When I Consider How My Light Is Spent"

   (D) Asimov's *Nightfall*

5. Which of the following can be seen as a fable in which the main characters represent political personages engaged in the conflict of political systems?

   (A) *Gulliver's Travels*   (C) *1984*

   (B) *The Time Machine*   (D) *Animal Farm*

6. Which of the following presents a fascinating survey of English life at the time of William the Conqueror?

   (A) *Edwin Drood*   (C) *Twickenam Garden*

   (B) *The Battle of Malden*   (D) *The Domesday Book*

7. Many of Shakespeare's works are based on which of the following philosophical and literary constructs?

   (A) The Platonic Ideal

   (B) The Great Chain of Being

   (C) The Duality of Man

   (D) Man's Inhumanity to Man

8. Which of the following was written by Charles Dodgson under a pen name?

   (A) *Tom Sawyer*

   (B) *The Heart of Darkness*

   (C) *Alice in Wonderland*

   (D) *Locksley Hall*

9. Which of the following poets is known for dramatic monologues such as "Andrea del Sarto"?

   (A) Alfred Tennyson

   (B) Robert Browning

   (C) S. T. Coleridge

   (D) P. B. Shelley

10. Which of the following American novelists was known for his love of deep sea fishing and bullfighting?

    (A) Norman Mailer

    (B) Theodore Dreiser

    (C) John Steinbeck

    (D) Ernest Hemingway

11. Which of the following novels revolved around the bureaucratic aspects of the pursuit of war?

    (A) Steinbeck's *Grapes of Wrath*

    (B) Heller's *Catch-22*

    (C) Remarque's *All Quiet on the Western Front*

    (D) Mailer's *The Naked and the Dead*

12. John Donne is considered one of the

    (A) decadents.

    (B) beat poets.

    (C) metaphysicals.

    (D) restoration poets.

13. Considered one of the greatest expressions of Existentialism, this play by Beckett involves only two characters.

    (A) *The American Dream*

    (B) *The Zoo Story*

    (C) *The Fantasticks*

    (D) *Waiting for Godot*

14. Which of the following modern novels portrays a New England prep school as America is about to go to war?

    (A) *The Catcher in the Rye*

    (B) *A Separate Peace*

    (C) *Being There*

    (D) *Goodbye, Mr. Chips*

15. Which famous ship is the subject of a novel about World War II mutiny?

    (A) HMS *Bounty*   (C) USS *Caine*

    (B) USS *Nautilus*   (D) *Golden Hinde*

16. Which nineteenth century novel ends with a hanging at sea?

    (A) Melville's *Billy Budd*

    (B) Capote's *In Cold Blood*

    (C) Clark's *The Oxbow Incident*

    (D) Bierce's *An Incident at Owl Creek Bridge*

17. Some of Shakespeare's sonnets are presumed to be written to someone critics call

    (A) Lady Ruffles.   (C) Lady Jane.

    (B) Dark Lady.   (D) Lady Juliet.

Question 18 refers to the following verse:

> The Silkworm and the Spider Houses make,
> All their materials from their Bowels take…
> Yet they are Curious, built with Art and Care,
> Like Lovers, who build Castles in the Air,
> Which ev'ry puff of Wind is apt to break,
> As imaginations, when Reason's weak.

18. The poem is written in

    (A) iambic pentameter.

    (B) iambic pentameter and rhyming couplets.

    (C) iambic pentameter and concrete language.

    (D) feminine rhyme.

19. What are the rules for a villanelle?

    (A) A fixed form of 14 lines with a concluding couplet

    (B) Six stanzas of six lines each

    (C) A free-form poem of five tercets

    (D) A fixed form with five tercets and a quatrain

20. An aubade is a poem that greets:

(A)   the moon.   (C)   nightfall.

(B)   the sun.   (D)   the dawn.

LITERATURE REVIEW

ANSWER KEY

Drill: Literature

1.	(C)	6.	(D)	11.	(B)	16.	(A)
2.	(A)	7.	(B)	12.	(C)	17.	(B)
3.	(D)	8.	(C)	13.	(D)	18.	(A)
4.	(C)	9.	(B)	14.	(B)	19.	(D)
5.	(D)	10.	(D)	15.	(C)	20.	(D)

DETAILED EXPLANATIONS OF ANSWERS

Drill: Literature

1.   **(C)**   Lewis Carroll's *Alice in Wonderland*, written in the 1870s, has long been considered a children's book—though critics have spoken about it for years as a work of intricate imagination and always in need of revised analysis (as in the new work *The Annotated Alice*). Some have considered it a compendium of playful games—reversed poems, anagrams, riddles, and gibberish rhymes. Others see in the book drug references, psychological allegories, and a fantastic map of the unconscious.

Each possible answer has been considered at some time a children's book, although *Gulliver's Travels* (D) is a political satire. Seuss's *The Cat in the Hat* (A) is of course very popular with adults, but only insofar as it provides fun tongue-twisters and the like; the storyline clearly is aimed at the younger set. Tolkien's work (B) may have been interpreted well by animators, but is certainly too difficult to be considered children's material.

2.   **(A)**   The key to this answer is the word "bawdy." Many students who have only a cursory knowledge of Chaucer's "Canterbury Tales" (A), do not realize that many of his stories ("The Wife of Bath's Tale," for example) are risqué, and, if written in modern English instead of Middle, and if composed by a writer of less importance, would probably be avoided by many high schools, and even some colleges. Chaucer's unifying premise is that the monologues and stories within stories are being told by travelers on a pilgrimage to the church of Canterbury. Poe (D) is certainly horrifying, but not bawdy. The same may be said about Rod Serling's wonderful stories (C). Bradbury's *Martian Chronicles* (B) is certainly a collection in which the stories have a singular purpose (describing the colonization of Mars by Earthmen), but, again, "bawdy" does not apply.

3.   **(D)**   This question may pose some difficulties, as all the choices are well-known war novels. The operative phrase here is "generally recognized," and for this, the student must be aware of the particular strength of Crane's *Red Badge of Courage* (D) as well as the recognized critical viewpoint that perhaps no other war story so accurately portrays the heat of battle. This point is always emphasized when *Red Badge* is taught, for two reasons. Crane was a Realist writer who believed that his works

should record sound, sight, and sensation as much as any painter would. Secondly, Crane was a newspaper reporter who was born after the Civil War (the subject of *Red Badge*), and who never witnessed battle until after the book was published! Even so, veterans of the Civil War and other wars since regularly cite *Red Badge* for its accuracy.

Catch-22 (A) discusses the dizzying aspects of bureaucratized war; *All Quiet* (B) is certainly vivid in its portrayal of German soldiers during World War I. Mailer's *The Naked and the Dead* (C) has enjoyed great popularity by veterans of World War II, but is not recognized for the attention to the universality of emotions that suffuse all soldiers in battle.

4.   **(C)**   Though all of the choices here deal with different ways to experience darkness, this question requires specific biographical knowledge of John Milton (C). His famous short poem which speaks of "this dark world" and his desire in remaining years to serve "my Maker" contains the famous line: "They also serve who only stand and wait." While the title of Asimov's science fiction classic work (D) is tantalizing, *Nightfall* deals with darkness of a different kind: an eclipse. Malory's work (B), as its title indicates, deals with the death of the legendary King Arthur. The American poet Dickinson (A) is generally considered to be speaking about a lost love.

5.   **(D)**   Orwell's *Animal Farm* is perhaps the most artful of his works, because it combines fable with political commentary. Swift's *Travels* (A) does the same, but without a consistent representation of political systems in conflict, as in *Animal Farm,* in which Marxist-Leninism, Monarchy, and Western Democracy play out their conflict according to Orwell's interpretation of history from the Russian Revolution to World War II. Orwell's other great work, *1984* (C), is a more straightforward explication of the dangers of totalitarianism. H. G. Wells' work (B) offers intriguing possibilities: there are animal-like characters, and political systems in conflict, but one would be hard put to construe this novel as a fable.

6.   **(D)**   *The Domesday Book*, commissioned by William the Conqueror, which surveyed manor farms throughout England around the year 1086 A.D., presents the most accurate picture we have today of the early feudal society that William governed. Population estimates, lists of individuals and their trades, and a general mapping of the main cities, marketplaces, and monasteries create a vivid picture. Donne's poem (C) was written in the 1600s. *Edwin Drood* (A) was Dickens' unfinished

novel. *The Battle of Malden* (B) would be an interesting choice, but that it speaks of a specific Viking invasion of Britain in 991 A.D.

7. **(B)**   Shakespeare respected a fundamental Elizabethan world construct: The Great Chain of Being. The Chain conjectured a world in which all the creatures of the Earth—including man—were set forth in increasing importance and decreasing distance to the angels and to God. Mankind was closest to the angels, but within our species was further ordering: kings, for example, were of a higher order than regular workmen, with lesser royalty somewhere in-between. Shakespeare's writings have regularly been seen to respect this order. Revolution is punished. Rash and irrational acts result in equally brutal retribution.

Platonism (A) holds that the real world is but a shadow of the ideal. Duality (C)—the existence of good and evil in the same individual—is not a keynote Shakespearean characterization, and Man's Inhumanity to Man (D) is a rather modern concept—far different in perspective from Shakespearean justice where those who disrupt the proper order of things get all the bad things they deserve.

8. **(C)**   Lewis Carroll was the pen name of Charles Dodgson, the Oxford Don who wrote *Alice in Wonderland* for Alice Liddle ("Little Alice"), the daughter of a friend. It has been suggested that a pen name was a must for an Oxford mathematician with an academic reputation to uphold. The novel *Tom Sawyer* (A) was written by an author under the pen name Mark Twain. Tennyson's poetic work (D) was authored without the use of a pseudonym. Joseph Conrad (author of *Heart of Darkness*) is an anglicization of Jozef Konrad Korteniowski.

9. **(B)**   Robert Browning is known for his dramatic monologues, in which the poem takes the form of a speech by the subject—and in so doing, elucidates the personality of the individual. "Andrea del Sarto" is perhaps one of Browning's most famous poems in this form—a form which Browning is credited with developing. Tennyson (A), Shelley (D), and Coleridge (C) did not employ this technique.

10. **(D)**   Ernest Hemingway was a very active sportsman, and was considered to personify "machismo" in both his personal and literary life. *The Old Man and the Sea*, for example, was based on his experience deep sea fishing off the coast of Cuba. Later research has tended to contradict this once popular conception of the author. Mailer (A) has also pursued sports like boxing, but not deep sea fishing or bullfighting. Dreiser (B) and Steinbeck (C) are not known as sportsmen, nor do they concentrate upon

sport in their writing.

11. **(B)** Heller's famous novel about American bomber pilots flying out of Sicily during World War II is based on a fundamental but changing principal of the battle group Catch-22. Briefly put, in order to be pulled off combat duty, a soldier would have to be crazy, but, of course, anyone who wanted to be removed could surely not be crazy, because the business of war is crazy. Remarque's novel (C) is about trench warfare during World War I; Mailer's (D) is about jungle warfare during World War II. Steinbeck's novel (A) has nothing to do with war, though its title might indicate that it does.

12. **(C)** John Donne is considered the leader of the Metaphysical poets of the seventeenth century, which include Crashaw and Crowley. The Decadents (A) were writers at the end of the last century; the Beats (B) were Greenwich Village poets of the 1950s; Restoration poets (D), like Dryden, are of the period after 1660.

13. **(D)** Beckett's play uses the conversation of two "bums" as they wait for Godot. Beckett's own beliefs (he and Sartre are considered fraternal Existentialists) and the content and interpretation of the play indicate Existentialist influence. Albee's plays—(A) and (B)—do not involve only two characters. *The Fantasticks* (C) is not Existentialist.

14. **(B)** John Knowles' autobiographical work depicts the Devon School (actually St. Paul's in New Hampshire) just before and during the early stages of World War II. The impending war came to profoundly affect life "inside" the prep school, as teachers were called up, and then students began to help the war effort by volunteering in town. Salinger's work (A) took place at a Pennsylvania prep school in the late 1940s, and there are no references to war. (D) *Goodbye, Mr. Chips* is a famous story about an English prep school. Kosinski's work (C) is not relevant here.

15. **(C)** *The Caine Mutiny* is based on a real incident that took place on an American minesweeper in the South Pacific during World War II. The tyrannical Captain Queeg is replaced by his first officers for incompetence during battle. One of the most famous mutinies in the British navy occurred on the *Bounty* (A). Drake's ship (D) of the 1500s and the first atomic submarine (B) were never objects of mutiny.

16. **(A)** All of the novels but one presented here involve a hanging, but only *Billy Budd* involves a hanging at sea. Billy, a foretopman aboard the HMS *Indomitable*, is sentenced to death for inadvertently killing John

Claggart, the evil master at arms. (B) Capote's work involves the hanging of a murderer in the 1950s, Clark's (C) a hanging in the Wild West, and Bierce's (D) an impromptu execution during the Civil War.

17. **(B)**   About one-third of Shakespeare's 108 known sonnets are written to someone who has come to be known as the "Dark Lady of the Sonnets." The themes of these poems are many, but consistent: love that endures through time; love of an older man for a younger woman; testimonials to beauty that endures even after death. There has been some discussion as to whether these poems are simply formulaic: that Shakespeare had no specific person in mind. Many of Shakespeare's sonnets are addressed to a young boy. The other possibilities here are simply incorrect, although Lady Juliet (D) is clearly meant to trip up the reader with a specific reference. (C) is a reference to a Yeats poem, and (A) is an invention.

18. **(A)**   Through your review you will now be familiar with all the various terms for meter and rhyme; note that iambic pentameter is the form favored by Shakespeare and Milton, easily recognized by the ten beat, stressed/unstressed syllabic line. (B) is incorrect because the poem is not entirely composed of rhyming couplets. Concrete language (C) is present early in the poem, but it moves to abstract language after line 3 for the contrast. Although some of the rhymes are feminine, the opening couplet is masculine, so (D) is incorrect.

19. **(D)**   You may not be familiar with this term so work your way through what you do know—pull in other works you have read: Stephen Dedalus in *Portrait of the Artist as a Young Man* demonstrates his skill as a young budding poet by writing a villanelle in a few minutes on the back of a cigarette packet! Choices (A), (B), and (C) do not meet the requirements of a villanelle, so they are incorrect choices.

20. **(D)**   Learn the various poetry forms from glossaries in anthologies—they may not cover all the terms but then you can distinguish and eliminate all those you do know that do not fit the definition. If the poem had greeted (A) the moon, (B) the sun, or (C) nightfall, then it would not be an aubade. Thus, all of these choices are incorrect.

III. VISUAL ARTS AND ARCHITECTURE REVIEW

CLASSICAL PERIOD

More than 20,000 years before the start of recorded history, humans were creating art. In an effort to master their environment, Paleolithic artists painted graceful and realistic animals on the walls of caves (Paleolithic sites of Lascaux in France and Altimira in Spain) and carved stone statuettes of females, symbols of fecundity (the "Venus" figures of Willendorf, Lespugue, and Lausell, named for their European discovery sites). Neolithic people erected megalithic structures (Stonehenge in England) of huge stones to create an environment for religious ritual and the sophisticated measurement and tracking of celestial bodies.

With the rise of the great cities, stable agricultural communities, trade, political systems, and organized religion, art and architecture became the powerful tools of kings, priests, and commerce. An obsession with the afterlife caused the ancient Egyptians to build lavish tombs, especially for their pharaohs, or god-kings. These tombs appeared first in the form of pyramids, like the Great Pyramid of Khufu at Giza (c. 2500 B.C.), and later as mortuary temples built into the sides of cliffs, like that for Queen Hatshepsut at Dier El-Bahri (c. 1500 B.C.). The Egyptians also constructed magnificent temples at Karnak and Luxor, which are characterized by massive stone columns and heavy walls organized along a central axis. The monuments and carvings of the Mesopotamian kingdom of the Assyrians (about 1500–612 B.C.) recorded in powerful visual terms the warrior-kings' victories over rival nations and in the hunt. An extraordinary example of these stylized and meticulously decorative relief carvings (sculptural images only slightly raised from their stone surfaces) and the nearly naturalistic depiction of animals are the Lion-Hunting Reliefs of the palace of King Assurbanipal (Ninevah, c. 645–640 B.C.). Their exciting energy provides a striking contrast to the stately repose of most Egyptian art.

The classical period of architecture and art begins with, and is best represented by, the civilization of the ancient Greeks; the city-state of Athens being the most dominant. The accomplishments of Athenian architecture, drama, philosophy, government, science, and sculpture laid the foundation for all of western European culture. The Greeks of the classical period were fascinated by physical beauty: their Olympian gods were fashioned in the human image, and a universe of perfection, guided by a master plan, was re-created in their idealized and gracefully proportioned sculptures, architecture, and paintings.

The amazing innovations of classical Greek art had their origins in earlier "Greek" civilizations—the Minoans of Crete and the people of mainland Mycenae. The Minoans flourished about 2500–1400 B.C. Their palace at Knossos is known for the lively, sinuous forms of their characteristic wall paintings, revealing a people enamored of acrobatics, leisure, and the beauty of the sea. The Minoans produced increasingly sophisticated terracotta and bronze figurines and painted vases. Both Crete and Mycenae were sources for many of the heroic tales of the ancient Greeks. For example, in the mazelike complex of the palace at Knossos, frescoes of bull-leaping games can be found, suggesting a basis for the Greek legend of the battle of Theseus with the Minotaur in the labyrinth. The Mycenaeans on mainland Greece were more warlike, but they traded with the Minoans, whose culture they adapted after the destruction of Crete by a natural disaster about 1450 B.C. The Mycenaeans produced beautiful work in gold, such as face masks, and artistically adopted the Minoans' ritual animal, the bull, but with a more aggressive character. Much of their best ornamentation was reserved for weapons. The culture of the Mycenaeans was destroyed about 1100 B.C. Only after three more centuries was a revitalized mainland-Greek culture able to spread trade (and settle colonies) throughout the Mediterranean, and organize into a system of city-states.

The earliest period of Greek city-state civilization, the Archaic, boasted exemplary art in the form of vase paintings, whose simple, precise, linear decoration evolved from the earlier, geometric style of the ninth and eighth centuries B.C.—zigzag, meandering, and triangular designs—to include, by the end of the eighth century, lively animals and humans. By the sixth century the dominant method of painting black figures as silhouettes on vases gave way to red figures with drawn-in details on a black background; pictured were heroes, athletes, feasts, weddings, and genre scenes. Contact with Egyptian culture in the mid-seventh century encouraged development of marble statuary in Greece: *The Lady of Auxerre* prefigures the standard forms of Greek *kourai* and *kouroi* (life-sized draped female and nude male figures), and in its stylized pose resembles Egyptian statues. The emphasis on nakedness in the *kouros* led quickly to the virtuosic treatment of naturalistic representation. The *Kouros of Anavysos* (Attica, 540–515 B.C.) retains the static Egyptian pose but already displays great subtlety in muscular modeling. The famous *Kritios Boy* (c. 490–480 B.C.) marks the apogee of Archaic sculpture, with an elegance and naturalism of form and relatively relaxed pose that befitted a culture increasingly dedicated to exalting beauty. It epitomizes the elements that were to characterize the spirit of ancient Greek art: respect for and re-creation of visual reality; a love of beauty in itself; and the application of rules and formulas to achieve representations of ideal beauty. The philosopher Plato's emphasis on the existence, in the spiritual realm or mind of God, of ideal forms for everything on earth was the basis of much artistic creativity in both art and architecture.

The Greek temple developed as a columnar structure, with sculptures on the pediments (triangular space just below the roof) and relief sculpture (usually of narrative action) on the rectangular panels of the friezes (metopes) that banded the buildings above the columns. The most perfect example of classical proportions is found in the great Greek temples on the Athenian Acropolis. In the Parthenon (fifth century B.C.), the architect Ictinus created a structure that represented the striving for perfection and ideal beauty in Athenian culture; refinement and perfect proportions are achieved by subtle curvatures in the relation of vertical elements and the tapering of the Doric columns. The style and elements of the Parthenon and other Greek buildings (such as the Erechtheon and the Temple of Athene Nike, also on the Acropolis) provided the forms—from the three major classical orders of columns (Doric, Ionic, and Corinthian) to pediments and sculptural friezes (relief sculptures in realistic narratives)—for two millennia of Western architecture.

The turning point for Greek sculpture came with the preeminence of Athens, after that city's victory over the Persians in the early fifth century. The classical period of the next hundred years boasted the great tragic playwrights Euripedes, Aeschylus, and Sophocles, the historians Thucydides and Herodotus, and the moral philosophers Plato and Aristotle. Pericles established Athenian democracy and built a massive complex on the Acropolis, including the Parthenon (447–432 B.C.). Under the direction of the sculptor Phydias (d. 432 B.C.) there were created ninety-two figures in high relief on the metopes, in mythological combat scenes; sculptural figures on the pediments are characterized by fluid movement and dynamic drapery. Many Greek sculptures are known through Roman marble copies, notably Myron's *Diskobolos* (c. 400 B.C.), a masterpiece of ideal grace and potential action.

In the fourth century the Greek city-states warred upon one another, and Macedonia prevailed, first under Philip II, then under his son Alexander, who by 323 B.C. had expanded the Greek empire to include Persia. The art of this period is characterized by greater naturalism, a wider variety of poses and of emotional display, and the intricate play of drapery. Praxiteles

(*Hermes and the Infant Dionysus,* c. 350–330 B.C.) was skilled in portraying the human body in a rhythmic curve; he produced the first free-standing lifesize female nude, *The Cnidian Aphrodite* (known from a marble copy; originally c. 350–330 B.C.). Scopus was known for his naturalistic portraiture, notably the statues on the tomb of Mausolos at Halicarnassus (c. 353 B.C.).

During the Hellenistic period (323–31 B.C.), Greek culture spread throughout the Mediterranean. Art was characterized by new freedoms, insistent naturalism, more genre subjects (not merely heroic figures, but old women, sportsmen, etc.), less symmetry, and emphasis on technical virtuosity and the depiction of movement. Examples are the Altar of Zeus at Pergamum (180–150 B.C.), especially the *Battle of the Gods and Giants* frieze—a tour-de-force of light and shade, whirling movement, and expressive musculature and gestures. One of the most famous of Hellenistic sculptures is also from Pergamum: *The Dying Gaul* (c. 200 B.C.), an ultranaturalistic genre piece, with its shaggy hair and palpable agony. Few examples of Greek painting survive, but notable painters were Apelles and Nikias in the fourth century B.C. Many works, however, survive in later mosaic copies, such as the Alexander painting by Philoxenos (about 300 B.C.), found at Pompeii in a mosaic copy (90 B.C.): it depicts Alexander the Great's dramatic meeting with the Persian king Darius in battle—and brilliantly conveys depth, light, and shade.

The Romans adopted much of the art and architectural forms of ancient Greece. The culture of Rome excelled in engineering and building, whose purpose it was to efficiently organize a vast empire and to provide an aesthetic environment for private and public use. The Romans built temples, roads, bath complexes, civic buildings, palaces, and aqueducts.

The cult of individual prestige and power was of major significance in Roman culture, and thus many of the statues were personalized and realistic. Greek ideal beauty was replaced by monuments and portraiture exalting specific personalities. The decoration of homes and public places by paintings and mosaics reflects the importance of a leisure-oriented "consumer" lifestyle. The paintings of Pompeii and Herculaneum (both towns victims of the Mt. Vesuvius eruption in 79 A.D.) reveal the Roman mastery of realistic form and modeling, of inspired decorative elements, and attempts at convincing spatial relationships. Roman architecture's strides emanated from the value placed on engineering and include innovations important for later centuries. The first-century development of the dome—a major engineering and artistic contribution to world architecture—for public buildings was important for the Renaissance and later periods, when the writings of the great Roman architect Vitruvius (first century B.C.) were widely studied. The Roman basilica (an oblong building ending in a semicircular apse) was the basis for church architecture during the early Christian and medieval periods (300–1300).

Roman culture dates from the time of the mythical founding of Rome by Romulus and Remus in 753 B.C. Roman territory gradually expanded to include the Etruscan, or native Italian, culture in the fourth century, the Greek colonies in southern Italy in the third, and continuous expansion throughout the Mediterranean world until the height of Roman power in 100 A.D. under the emperor Trajan. Roman art was heavily influenced by the Greeks, especially after the sack of Syracuse in 212 B.C., when Greek artistic treasures—including the artists themselves—began pouring into Rome. While Greek forms were adopted, Greek ideas of beauty and perfection were not: Roman art served to provide luxury, as status symbols, and to enhance social position. Portraiture became very important, and the Romans eagerly adopted the innovation of the portrait bust from the Etruscans. Significant early busts are the *Capitoline Brutus* (third century B.C.) and *Pompey* (c. 50 B.C.), the earliest realistic likeness of a major Roman historical figure. In the Augustan age (first century A.D.), Greek prototypes were readopted to portray an idealized emperor. One of the most famous sculptures of the Roman empire is the *Laocoon* (first century A.D.), usually attributed to three Greek artists from Rhodes (Agessander, Athenodorus, and Polydorus): in this masterful, energetic, and dynamic composition (in the Hellenistic style of Pergamum), serpents sent by Apollo slay Laocoon and his sons. Examples of Roman painting fortunately still exist, due to their preservation by the hardened volcanic ashes of the destroyed southern towns of Pompeii and Herculaneum. The decorative paintings at Pompeii, such as those at the House of the Vettii (before 79 A.D.), depict realistically modeled humans in convincing landscapes, portraits of real characters, and the Roman fondness for trompe l'oeil — painting intended to fool the eye into believing one is seeing real three-dimensional objects, architectural details, or natural vistas.

The major Roman artistic statements were related to monumental architecture and sculpture. The Arch of Titus (c. 81 A.D.) describes the emperor's triumph and the spoils of Jerusalem in deep relief sculpture, a narrative of real events with lively poses. Trajan's Column (98–117 A.D.) is unlike any previous carved record: its story of Trajan's campaigns against the Dacians winds unbroken for more than 650 feet up the shaft of the 125-foot-high marble column; in low relief, like most ancient sculpture it was originally heightened with color. In the golden age of the empire, the emperor Hadrian (reigned 117–138 A.D.), an admirer of Greek culture, built extensively. His villa at Tivoli is a magnificent complex of baths, temples, gardens, and pavilions, and he commissioned the rebuilding of the greatest achievement of Roman architecture, the Pantheon in Rome. The relatively plain exterior of this temple "of all the gods" belies the astonishing technical accomplishment and interior decorative details. Inside, the wall of the main circular section of the building is characterized by rectangular niches and apses, small tabernacles, and a wealth of variously colored marble panels. A massive concrete dome is broken by a central oculus, or hole, that lets in an ever-moving shaft of light. Another imperial monument, to the emperor Marcus Aurelius, is the best surviving equestrian statue from antiquity, and the inspiration for the revival of the form in Renaissance Italy by Donatello.

The late classical era overlaps the early Christian period. Beginning with the monuments in the age of Constantine—the first Roman emperor to embrace Christianity—a new emphasis can be seen, more on spiritual meaning and symbolism, less on the realistic depiction of the world and personal accomplishments. The commanding bust of Constantine (c. 313 A.D.) is a large (eight feet high) head expressive of personality and majesty, but its huge eyes already represent the medieval Christian concept of "windows of the soul" to express inner being. In the Arch of Constantine, celebrating the emperor's victory over Maxentius in 312, there is little attempt at a cohesive style or realism, with many sculptural elements from other architecture physically incorporated. Already the familiar medieval large heads and squat figures are apparent. Similar de-emphasis of the real world and a burgeoning Christian iconography (salvation of souls, divine intervention, miracles) can be found in the art of the Catacombs, underground burial chambers outside Rome (200-400 A.D.); the image of Apollo was adopted to represent Christ in a small wall painting, *The Good Shepherd,* in the Catacomb of Priscilla.

MEDIEVAL AND RENAISSANCE PERIODS

During the Middle Ages, the Romans' cultural and artistic legacy lived on in the Byzantine empire, whose capital was the magnificent city of Constantinople (modern Istanbul, in Turkey). This empire lasted for a thousand years after the fall of the western Roman empire. Perhaps the greatest of the Byzantine emperors was Justinian (527–565 A.D.), who reaffirmed the empire and made Ravenna, a northeast Italian city on the Adriatic coast, the government center of the West. In Ravenna the important surviving art in the Byzantine style is at its finest. There, the seventh-century church of San Vitale echoes the mosaic mastery of the eastern

Roman, or Byzantine, empire in Constantinople: its grandiose apse mosaics of glittering gold and sparkling color include walls depicting Emperor Justinian and Empress Theodora. The Byzantine style was meant to convey a supernatural, otherworldly effect. The most important church in Constantinople was Hagia Sophia, designed by the architects Isidorus and Anthemius—a magical, soaring structure with a beautiful dome, commissioned along with many other buildings by the Emperor Justinian in the mid-sixth century.

During the Dark Ages (about fifth to eighth centuries), Celtic artists of Ireland, Scotland, and northern Britain, especially in the monasteries, kept Western art alive in stone carvings and crosses with interlace patterns, and in magnificent illuminated manuscripts, whose design was influenced by Celtic metalwork. Among these manuscripts are the Book of Durrow (680), the Lindisfarne Gospels (c. 690), and the Book of Kells (c. 800—the most sophisticated and flamboyant, with four hundred decorative initial letters). The end of the Dark Ages was officially marked by the coronation of the Frankish king Charlemagne as Holy Roman Emperor by the pope on Christmas Day 800. Charlemagne, whose capital was at Achen (Aix-la-Chapelle), aspired to create an empire that rivaled the Roman empire as well as reviving classical culture and learning. He acquired ancient Roman sculptures, established schools, gathered around him the scholars Alcuin and Theodulf, and commissioned illuminated manuscripts. Some of the finest of the early ninth-century manuscripts are the Utrecht Psalter, the Ebbo Gospels, and the Lorsch Gospels. The empire lapsed after Charlemagne but was revived by Otto the Great (after his 955 victory over the Hungarians). This period is marked by a revival of early Christian, Carolingian, and Byzantine art (Echternach Gospels, bronze doors at Hildesheim).

The Romanesque style of art and architecture was preeminent in the eleventh and twelfth centuries. A great expansion of building and sculpture occurred: it was the era of the First Crusade, Europe was more secure and settled, and there were more professional artisans, who traveled all over Europe. By then many local styles, including the decorative arts of the Byzantines, the Near East, and the German and Celtic tribes, were contributing to European culture. Common features of Romanesque churches are round arches, vaulted ceilings, and heavy walls that are profusely decorated—primarily with symbolic figures of Christianity, the realism of which for its creators had become less and less important and was, instead, subordinate to the message. Examples of the style are the abbey church in Cluny, France; Worms Cathedral (St. Peter's) in Germany; and Durham Cathedral in England. Sculpture, usually relief in stone, was an integral part of church architecture on portals (doorways) and capitals (column crowns). In France, prominent sculptural areas were around the door jambs and the semicircular area above the door, the tympanum. Romanesque sculpture grew out of the church almost organically, and was decoratively sophisticated. Examples are the tympanums at Sainte Foy in Conques and the Abbey of Moissac near Toulouse (the *Apocalypse*). The Great Tympanum depicting *Christ in Majesty* and the *Last Judgment* at St. Lazare (Autun Cathedral) is the work of Gislebertus, who signed his name. It is marked by an overall unity of design and an inventive use of narrative detail; it contains biblical scenes, allegories, and imagery from the mystery plays. One of the finest free-standing Romanesque sculptural works is the brass baptismal font of Renier de Huy, a work whose figures display realistic proportions and classical influence, thus pointing the way to the innovations of the Gothic and early Renaissance styles.

Gothic art flourished in Europe from the twelfth through the fifteenth centuries and was primarily a French and northern European style. The cathedrals in this style are some of the purest expressions of an age: they combine a continued search for engineering and structural improvement with features that convey a relentless verticality, a reach toward heaven, and the unbridled adoration of God. Soaring and airy, these cathedrals were constructed using such elements as flying buttresses and pointed arches and vaults, and are decorated by a profusion of sculptures and stained-glass windows that were, for the worshippers, visual encyclopedias of Christian teachings and stories. The first major Gothic church was Abbot Suger's Church of St. Denis, outside Paris (begun 1137–1144). The finest example of the Gothic use of stained glass is the decoration of Sainte Chapelle (c. 1245) in Paris, whose walls of stained glass create a jewel-like flood of heavenly light. Gothic art emphasized greater spirituality, as well as greater humanity and tenderness, than previous Christian art; its most important religious figure is the Virgin Mary. The style in sculpture displays grace and realism, and figures are often elongated to match the skyward-stretching form of the architecture. Rheims Cathedral, one of the masterpieces of the northern Gothic style, boasts some two thousand sculptures (c. 1230-1240). Other important Gothic cathedrals are Chartres, Beauvais, Bourges, and Amiens in France, and in England, Salisbury and Wells.

The work of Nicholas of Verdun at the end of the twelfth century reveals a classical style; the awakening of the spirit of humanism in Gothic art led to a new interest in the natural world and a revival of the classical tradition. The thirteenth and fourteenth centuries were a vital and exciting period that came to be considered both Gothic and proto-Renaissance. In northern Europe, life itself became more festive, the artisan and merchant classes achieved some status—among richer courts, tales of knights, and the great romances—all of which inspired the colorful and realistic paintings of the sumptuous books of hours (the Limbourg Brothers: *Les Tres Riches Heures du Duc de Berri,* 1413–1416).

The Italian school of this period—from 1250 onward—provides the first glimmers of the Renaissance—in a new naturalism, plus an emphasis on wall decoration in fresco and the painting of altarpieces (panels—the forerunners of the easel paintings). The Florentine painter Cimabue (active 1272–1302) produced tempera paintings that signaled a clear movement toward the naturalistic treatment of human figures (*San Trinita Madonna*). Duccio (active 1278–1318) of Sienna painted the *Rucellai Madonna,* in which Mary is portrayed as a real human in real space, shown from the side. And Duccio's *Virgin in Majesty* (from the *Maesta* altarpiece, 1308–1311, for Siena Cathedral) has figures of even greater solidity, clearly inhabiting realistic space. Giotto (c. 1267–1337) was famed and successful in his lifetime; his work is often regarded as the beginning of Renaissance art in Florence. He is known for his ability to depict physical beings, dramatic and realistic details and gestures, human reactions, and real spatial arrangements. His *Ognissanti Madonna* shows real people beneath the drapery, as well as delicacy and grace and convincing spatial relationships. His Arena Chapel paintings in Padua depict the life story of the Virgin and Christ in a series of independent but continuous-narrative pictures, full of drama and psychological nuance. Giotto's other works include *The Life of St. Francis* paintings in the Bardi Chapel, Santa Croce, Florence (1316–1320) and *The Life of St. John the Baptist* in the Peruzzi Chapel. In the fourteenth century, Sienese painters were among the leaders in innovation in the new realism: Simone Martini (1285–1344 ; *The Annunciation*) and Ambrogio Lorenzetti (active first half of the fourteenth century; *The Presentation in the Temple* and *The Allegory of Good Government* and other frescoes in the Palazzo Publico in Sienna).

Lines were often blurred between the Gothic and the early Renaissance in sculpture. In Pisa, innovations were made in the thirteenth and fourteenth centuries by Nicola Pisano (active 1258–1284) and his son Giovanni. Nicola created the marble pulpit for the Baptistry at Pisa (he signed and dated it); based on classical models, it has crowded figures, multiple poses, and realistic movement. His pulpit for Sienna Cathedral is marked by even more animated movement. Giovanni's Pisa Cathedral pulpit (1302–1310) contains a naked female figure and merges Gothic and classical influences.

In fifteenth-century Florence, first among all the newly rich and independent Italian cities, wealthy patrons, merchants, and nobles consciously revived classical art and philosophy, set humankind at the center of life, and made celebrations of civic pride of the highest importance. The technical discovery of proportion was used in architecture and art, and the great artists of the Renaissance often combined talents in all fields. Architecture, in the hands of Filippo Brunelleschi and Leon Battista Alberti, revived the Greco-Roman elements and took a scientific, ordered approach, one similarly expressed in painting with the emphasis on the calculated composition of figures in space known as perspective. Brunelleschi (1377–1440?) invented single-vanishing-point perspective, and the dome he designed for Florence Cathedral (added 1420–36) was a symbol of both technical and classical rebirth. Alberti (1404–1472) was an important early Renaissance architect (Palazzo Rucellai, Florence, 1446–55) and wrote on the mathematics of perspective in *On Painting* (1435). Michelozzo (1396–1472) designed the first great Renaissance palace, the Palazzo Medici in Florence. In Rome, Donato Bramante (1444–1514) designed—in addition to ambitious plans for rebuilding St. Peter's—a structure for the spot where St. Peter was crucified, the Tempietto (San Pietro in Montorio, 1502). It is the first Renaissance building created in imitation of a circular Roman temple and is vaulted by a hemispherical dome and encircled by classical columns. Andrea Palladio (1508–1580), the writer of the most influential treatise on architecture for centuries *(The Four Books of Architecture)*, created in the Villa Rotonda in Vincenza (begun 1567–69) a perfect unity of geometric forms: four temple fronts face the four compass points and surround an inner cube of rooms; the central dome provides a symbol of unity.

The sculptor Lorenzo Ghiberti won the 1401 competition for the bronze doors of the Florence Baptistry—his relief-sculpted panels boast graceful, realistic, classical figures. Other important sculptors were Nanni di Banco and Jacopo della Quercia. The greatest of the early Renaissance sculptors, however, was Ghiberti's pupil Donatello (1386–1466), whose work was not only classically inspired and realistic, but highly theatrical and full of psychological undertones. *St. George* is a lifesize marble statue of a handsome hero, full of earthly life and potential power. His *David,* one of the most famous Renaissance bronze sculptures, marks the revival of the classical free-standing nude male—sinuous in form, in an elegant, almost impish pose. His *Gattamelata* (1443–48) revived the free-standing equestrian statue, based on the ancient Marcus Aurelius statue in Rome.

The first great painter of the Renaissance was Masaccio (1401–c.1428). In the *Holy Trinity* fresco for the Church of Santa Maria Novella in Florence, he used perspective based on Brunelleschi's ideas; there is a clear light source that unifies the whole, plus classical details, such as the Corinthian pilasters framing Ionic columns. In the *Tribute Money* (fresco for the Brancacci Chapel in Santa Maria Carmine in Florence) real characters in expressive poses inhabit a realistic landscape (based on the hills east of Florence), all united by Brunelleschian perspective. Other important early Renaissance painters were Paolo Uccello, who was obsessed by perspective (*The Battle of San Romano,* c. 1455); Fra Angelico (c. 1395–1455), whose work was colorful and calmly sweet (*The Deposition; The Annunciation*); Fra Filippo Lippi (1406–1469; *The Madonna and Child with Two Angels);* and Piero della Francesca (c. 1416–1492; *The Flagellation of Christ; The Resurrection* [with its foreshortened sleeping soldiers]). More than any other painter, Botticelli (c.1445–1510) epitomized the spirit of the early Renaissance. A favorite of the Medicis, his work is intensely religious and allegorical and insistent on recalling the images of classical antiquity. He painted many Madonnas (which since the nineteenth century have been admired for their sweet countenances), as well as humanist allegories of classical inspiration: *The Birth of Venus* (the ultimate symbolic depiction of the period's rebirth) and *Primavera* (a visual celebration of spring). Other notable artists of this period were Andrea Mantegna (known for his bold experiments in perspective), who worked in Mantua (Ducal Palace paintings), and Giovanni Bellini of Venice (*St. Francis in Ecstasy*).

The three pillars of the High Renaissance of the early sixteenth century are Leonardo da Vinci, Michelangelo, and Raphael. Leonardo's intellectual curiosity led him to make scientific deductions (and sketch out inventions such as flying machines) based on observed reality; these he recorded in his famous Notebooks. In addition to *The Last Supper* (1495–98) and the *Mona Lisa* (1503), he painted *The Virgin of the Rocks* (1483–85), which epitomizes his artistic approach: strange and metaphysical, suffused with mysterious light, the picture uses the technique of sfumato, a smoky-shadowy way of modeling form.

Michelangelo, too, excelled in many fields: he was a poet, painter, sculptor, and architect. In addition to his architectural designs of the Medici Chapel in San Lorenzo and the Laurentian Library, he redesigned St. Peter's in Rome, adding an enormous dome and completing the work previously planned by Bramante and Raphael. His sculptures (*David; Moses;* the Tomb of Giuliano de' Medici), which are powerful and heroic, seek to portray bodily perfection, and convey a perfect synthesis of the human and the divine—the epitome of the Neoplatonic philosophy of the Renaissance (that is, the body expresses the spirit). The Sistine Chapel frescoes in the Vatican in Rome are his masterpieces: in painting a complex system of dynamic figures full of raw human power and divine spirit, Michelangelo created some of the world's most unforgettable artistic images (*The Creation of Adam; The Creation of Eve;* the Sybils; the Prophets; *The Creation of the World*, all on the ceiling [1508–12], as well as *The Last Judgment,* on the wall [1534–41]). For centuries the paintings of Raphael (1483–1520) have been the measure of artistic perfection. Raphael's Madonnas are both spiritual ideals and clear personalities, set against a serene landscape, and represent perfect compositional balance (*The Madonna and Child with St. John* [c.1506] and *The Sistine Madonna* [1512]). In *The School of Athens* at the Stanza della Segnatura in the Vatican (1509–11), Raphael combines, in a massive composition of figures and architecture, elements of major Renaissance paintings—obvious perspective, classically inspired architecture, portraits of ancient philosophers, and even likenesses of Leonardo, Michelangelo, and himself. His *Transfiguration,* with its dramatic lighting, mixture of heavenly and earthly spheres, and floating figures in clouds, crowns the Renaissance ideal of art and is a blueprint for the pictorial elements used in Baroque art.

Venetian and northern Italian painters worked in highly personal styles, leading toward the style called Baroque. The Mannerists of the first half of the sixteenth century produced work full of exaggerations: floating angels, the confusion of illusion and reality, contorted and elongated figures, awkward spatial relationships, and strange lighting effects. The great Mannerists were Parmagianino (*The Madonna with the Long Neck*), Pontormo (*The Deposition*), and Bronzino (*Venus, Cupid, Folly, and Time*). Giulio Romano painted the fantastic Sala dei Giganti in Mantua's Palazzo del Te, a structure he designed with typical Mannerist wildness: amidst classical perfection in form, massive stones jut out like monstrous ruins. In Parma, Correggio created pre-Baroque art full of drama and mysterious light, and incorporated floating angels (*The Adoration of the Shepherds*). Among the great Venetians were Bellini (the San Zaccaria Altarpiece) and Giorgione (an innovator in "mood painting": of pastoral classical worlds, a favorite subject of the Baroque and later Rococo artists; *The Tempest; Venus*). The giant among the Venetians is Titian (active c. 1500–1576), whose brilliant color and dynamic brushwork made him one of the most admired artists of his time and made his name synonymous with great art through the succeeding centuries. There are plenty of floating clouds and cherubs in Titian's paintings, and the importance of the female nude is evident in *The Rape of Europa, Sacred and Profane Love,* and *The Venus of Urbino* (significant because this female nude is not associated with a classical/mythological theme). Among his religious masterpieces are *The Assumption of the Virgin* and the *Pesary Madonna.* Drawing ever closer to the Baroque spirit were two other Venetians: Veronese, who specialized in vast pageants unfolding in a single, grand painting (*The Feast in the House of Levi*), and Tintoretto, whose unique canvases team with vibrant life and dramatic incident, from the intimate *Susanna and the Elders* (c. 1557) to the astonishing, turbulent, glowing scene of *The Last Supper* (1592–94).

The northern European Renaissance also displayed a renewed interest in the visible world, and works by Albrecht Dürer, Lucas Cranach, Matthias Grünewald, and Albrecht Altdorfer reveal an emphasis on the symbolism of minutely observed details and an accurate realism based on observation of reality rather than on prescribed rules. This unique northern emphasis can be seen as far back as the fifteenth century. Northern art, particularly in the Netherlands (later Flanders and Holland) and Germany, pursued a parallel course to that in Italy from the Gothic period to the Baroque era— but with a clear difference: the reawakening to the material world was less intellectual and less based on classical models than in the south. Rather, it was a realism based on the tastes of a rising wealthy merchant and middle class, delighting in their everyday lives. This joyous visual naturalism was marked by jewel-like color in painting. In sculpture, Claus Sluter (d. 1406) carved the Well of Moses, an innovative masterpiece of realism and human characterization. Jan van Eyck (c. 1385–1441) exemplified the continuous northern insistence on the symbolism of objects, on a naturalism so precious in its details and observation of reality that all paintings, whether portraits or religious scenes, seem to have real-life bourgeois persons and their possessions as subjects. Among van Eyck's vibrantly colored masterpieces are the *Madonna with Chancellor Rolin* (c. 1435) and *The Arnolfini Marriage* (1434). Other important Flemish painters of the fifteenth century were Rogier van der Weyden (*The Last Judgment* [c. 1450] and *Portrait of a Young Woman* [c. 1440]); Hugo van der Goes (the Portinari Altarpiece) and Hans Memling (c. 1430–1494). In the work of Hieronymus Bosch (active 1470–1516), the symbolism of the north is taken to its most extreme in his bizarre and highly personal mystical masterwork, *The Garden of Earthly Delights* (c. 1505–10).

In Germany the Renaissance produced many outstanding painters: Dürer, Grünewald, and Altdorfer, as well as Lucas Cranach, Hans Holbein, and Pieter Bruegel. By far the greatest of these was Albrecht Dürer (1471–1528), in many ways equal to Michelangelo in stature and innovation. Dürer traveled extensively and was influenced by the art of the Venetians; his scientific curiosity about the natural world was nearly equal to Leonardo's. Dürer lavished the same meticulous attention on lowly subjects (*The Piece of Turf; Hare*) that he did on major paintings (*The Four Apostles; The Adoration of the Trinity*). Dürer's fame spread throughout Europe because of his prolific and groundbreaking work in the area of printmaking (*The Great Passion* and *The Apocalypse* series; *Adam and Eve; Melancolia I*); as a virtuoso in the art of the woodcut (multiple copies printed from a raised surface) and metal engraving (multiple copies printed from an incised surface), Dürer has never been surpassed. The masterpiece of Grünewald (c. 1475–1528) is the Isenheim Altarpiece of 1515; Lucas Cranach the Elder (1472–1553) painted several portraits of Martin Luther, as well as *Adam and Eve* (1526); Albrecht Altdorfer depicted majestic landscapes, full of power and mystery, that dwarf the people in them (*St. George and the Dragon; The Battle of Alexander and Darius on the Issus*). One of the finest painters of the sixteenth century was Hans Holbein the Younger (1497–1543), who continued the northern emphasis on symbolic detail and highly finished realism, particularly in the area of portraiture. When he moved to London he became court painter to Henry VIII (*The Ambassadors* of 1553; *Sir Thomas More;* portraits of the king), and he is also known for his woodcut series *The Dance of Death*. The Flemish artist Pieter Bruegel specialized in robust depictions of peasants and ordinary people at work and play (*The Hunters in the Snow; The Peasant Wedding; The Corn Harvest*), often in landscape vistas viewed from a height.

THE SEVENTEENTH AND EIGHTEENTH CENTURIES

Presaged by the works of the Venetian artist Tintoretto (the radiating *Last Supper*) and El Greco in Spain (the visionary *Toledo; The Immaculate Conception*), the Baroque period of the seventeenth century produced artists who added heightened drama to the forms of Renaissance art. Bernini (1598–1680) was the giant of the style in Italy and enjoyed papal patronage, working in sculpture and architecture to create some of the most dynamic and personal statements of art. His architectural triumph was the design for the Piazza of St. Peter's in Rome, which united the various buildings of two centuries in two colonnaded galleries resembling outstretched arms. Bernini's sculpture is equally innovative and startling: his *David* is not an elegant, noble youth, but a powerful, angry warrior in motion; *St. Peter's Chair* is a complex sculpture of bronze, marble, stained glass, and stucco that grows out of the architecture of the church, incorporates the light of the oval stained glass, and overlaps the surrounding pilasters and walls with protruding shafts of bronze light-rays, clouds, and cherubs. *The Vision of the Ecstasy of St. Teresa* (Cornaro Chapel, Santa Maria della Vittoria in Rome) is a mesmerizing portrayal of mystical ecstasy, from the bronze shafts of heavenly light to the agitated and quirky folds of the saint's garment. Bernini's rival was Francesco Borromini, the other great Italian architect of the Baroque; his masterpieces in Rome include the Oratorio di San Filippo Neri, with its marriage of curved and triangular pediments, and Sant'Ivo della Sapienza, with its plan based on two interlocking equilateral triangles forming a six-pointed star with a single domed center.

In France, Baroque splendor was carried to its grandest at Versailles, a complex supervised by Charles Le Brun. Vast terraces, water gardens, fountains, and the gallery of mirrors were all calculated to equate Louis XIV, the Sun King, with the god Apollo. In England, however, the seventeenth century marked the beginning of a new classicism, particularly through the influential writings of Palladio. The designs of Inigo Jones (1573–1652) were sober, grand, classical (the Banqueting House and Queen's Chapel in London). Christopher Wren (1632–1723) rebuilt much of London after the fire of 1666 in a new style of Baroque energy, classical elements, and even a touch of Gothic. The Palladian/classical "revival" in architecture—neoclassicism—continued throughout the eighteenth and early nineteenth centuries. Examples in England are William Kent's Mereworth Castle (1723); Lord Burlington's Chiswick House (1720–25); and Robert Adam's Syon House in Isleworth (1762–69), with its interior of green marble and gilt copies of famous ancient classical statues. In America, the author of the Declaration of Independence and third U.S. president, Thomas Jefferson, designed his Monticello estate in Virginia according to Palladian principles.

In painting, the most significant proponent of the Italian Baroque was Caravaggio (1571–1610), whose models were ordinary people, and whose use of contrasting shadow and light was revolutionary and made for works of bold drama (*The Calling of Saint Matthew; The Conversion of Saint Paul*). The Flemish masters Peter Paul Rubens (1577–1640; *Marie de Medici Lands at Marseilles; The Raising of the Cross; The Descent from the Cross*) and Jacob Jordaens portrayed figures in constant motion, draperies of agitated angles, and effects of lighting and shadow that amplified emotional impact and mystery. In this spirit followed such painters of court life and middle-class portraiture as Velazquez (1599–1660; *The Infanta Margarita; The Maids of Honor*) in Spain; Anthony Van Dyck (*Charles I Hunting*) in England; and in Holland, Frans Hals (1581–1666; *The Laughing Cavalier*) and Rembrandt van Rijn. Rembrandt (1601–1669), one of the greatest artists of all time, used expressive brushwork and mysterious light contrasts to enliven religious and genre painting and portraiture, particularly of groups. Rembrandt's influence has remained consistently potent throughout the centuries, since his art appears to impart universal truths, and sections of his compositions glow with a mysterious inner light (*The Night Watch; The Descent from the Cross; The Anatomy Lesson of Dr. Tulp;* many self-portraits). Rembrandt also set the standard for perfection in the art of etching (printing from a metal plate with incised lines that have been etched away by acid; *Christ Healing the Sick*).

The art of the early eighteenth century is often called Rococo. Painters like Jean Antoine Watteau (*Embarkation for Cythera*, 1717), Giambattista Tiepolo (frescoes of the Wurzberg Residenz), François Boucher (*Diana Bathing,* 1742), and Jean Honoré Fragonard (*Women Bathing,* 1777), often creating decorative wall and ceiling schemes, turned the agitated drama of the Baroque into light, pastel-toned, swirling compositions that seem placed in an idyllic land of a golden age. Rococo style in architecture is marked by a profusion of elegant and fantastic decorative elements, often employing representations of shells, scrolls, and leaves. The influence of Versailles, with its mirrors radiating light and theatricality, is seen in the stucco fantasies covering Rococo interiors like living organisms, the relentless vegetation often supported by floating cherubs (the Zimmermann brothers, Church of Die Wies, Bavaria). The major Rococo palaces are the Residenz at Wurzburg by Balthasar Neumann, and the Munich Residenz, Amalienburg Pavilon, and Residenz Theater, all designed by François Cuvillies in the 1730s.

In the seventeenth and eighteenth centuries, European artists also responded to middle-class life and everyday objects to create genre paintings: Jan Vermeer (1632–1675; *The Artist's Studio; The Head of a Girl*); Adriaen van Ostade; Jean Baptiste Chardin (1699–1779; *The House of Cards; Saying Grace*). Jean Baptiste Greuze in France (*The Broken Pitcher*) and William Hogarth (*The Rake's Progress* and *Marriage ala Mode* series) in England endowed their everyday subjects with a wealth of narrative detail that aimed to impart a specific moral message. Such narrative art combined in the late eighteenth and early nineteenth centuries with romantic literature—Goethe, Byron, Shelley, Scott, Wordsworth, and others—and political events to produce works with a political point of view or a story to tell, in a variety of styles. Jacques Louis David (1748–1825) used a severe classical sculptural style (Neoclassicism) in his paintings to revive antique art and ennoble images of the French Revolution and Napoleon's empire (*The Death of Marat; The Oath of the Horatii; Napoleon in His Study*). The spiritual godfather of Neoclassicism is Nicholas Poussin (1593–1665), whose paintings of the seventeenth century are perfectly balanced, severe, idealized, and sculptural models of pristine classicism (*The Holy Family on the Steps; The Poet's Inspiration*). Neoclassical sculpture in the late eighteenth century revived the aloof severity and perfection of form of ancient art. Leading sculptors were Jean Antoine Houdon (*Voltaire; George Washington*), Antonio Canova (*Pauline Borghese as Venus Victrix*), and Bertal Thorvaldsen (*Hebe*). In England, the draughtsman and engraver John Flaxman produced engraved outline illustrations reminiscent of Greek vase paintings for illustrations to the *Illiad;* his work was the basis for the enduring style of Wedgwood pottery.

THE NINETEENTH CENTURY

In the late eighteenth century, with the rise of democracy and republics, the revolutions in France and America, and the discovery of the preserved Roman city of Pompeii, there occurred a full-blown revival of Greek and Roman design. Important architectural examples are the Bank of England by John Soane, Canova's Temple of Possagno—which combines elements of both the Parthenon and the Pantheon—and the Virginia State Capitol in Richmond, designed by Thomas Jefferson to resemble a Roman temple. Another revival stressed the Gothic style, championed by architect Augustus Pugin and writer John Ruskin—inspiring numerous Victorian Gothic buildings in England (Charles Barry's Houses of Parliament in London, 1840–65) and America (Richard Upjohn's Trinity Church in New York).

Political and other national events were important subjects for the romantic-realist painters of the early nineteenth century. The Spanish painter Francisco de Goya commented powerfully on political events in his painting *May 3, 1808*. In France, Eugene Delacroix (1798–1863; *The Death of Sardanapalus; Liberty Leading the People*) and Theodore Gericault (1791–1824; *The Raft of the Medusa*) imbued subjects from literature, the Bible, exotic lands, and current events with dramatic, heroic intensity. The grandeur and transcendence of nature, the emotional reaction to inner dreams, and metaphysical truths of romanticism are seen in the work of such mystical artists as England's William Blake (a master of innovative printmaking), Henry Fuseli, and John Martin, and America's Thomas Cole. Caspar David Friedrich in Germany and the English Pre-Raphaelites (William Holman Hunt, John Everett Millais, Dante Gabriel Rossetti, Ford Madox Ford, Arthur Hughes, and others) endowed their keenly observed, minutely detailed works with a romantic spirit of poetic yearning and literary references, and accurately re-created the natural world in brilliantly colored landscapes.

In the first half of the nineteenth century, landscape painting in England reached a zenith with the works with John Constable (1776–1837; *The White Horse; The Haywain*) and Joseph Mallord William Turner (1775–1851; *The Slave Ship; Snowstorm: Hannibal Crossing the Alps*). Turner's awe-inspiring landscapes, revolutionary in their lighting effects achieved through bold, expressive brushwork, form a bridge between the spirit of romanticism and the expressionistic brushwork and realism of the Barbizon School in France, whose chief painters were Charles Daubigny and Jean Baptiste Camille Corot. Beginning with Barbizon, the French painters of the nineteenth century concentrated more and more on the reporter-like depiction of everyday life and the natural environment in a free, painterly (gestural brushwork) style. The realist pioneers Gustave Courbet (*The Stone Breakers; A Burial at Ormans*), Jean Francois Millet (*The Sower; The Angelus*), and Honoré Daumier (*The Third-Class Carriage*)—renowned as a political caricaturist, Daumier's chief medium was the lithograph—paved the way for the stylistic and subject innovations of the Impressionists.

In Impressionism, traditional means of composing a picture—academic methods of figure modeling, of color relations, and accurate and exact rendering of people and objects—were rejected in favor of an art that emphasized quickly observed and sketched moments from life, the relation of shapes and forms and colors, the effects of light, and the act of painting itself. Beginning with Edouard Manet (*Le Déjeuner sur l'Herbe; Olympia*) in the 1860s, French artists continually blurred the boundaries of realism and abstraction. The great Impressionist painters concentrated on landscapes and scenes of everyday life. Claude Monet (1840–1926) painted *Ladies in the Garden, Gare St. Lazare* (a steam-drenched train station), and multiple views of haystacks and Rouen Cathedral in varying daylight conditions. Auguste Renoir (1841–1919) painted people from contemporary life as well as robust female nudes (*Umbrellas; The Luncheon Party; The Bathers*). Like Manet and many other French artists, Edgar Degas (1834–1917) was influenced by the compositional techniques of Japanese prints; he delighted in achieving spontaneity by depicting his subjects from unusual angles and with figures seemingly arbitrarily cut off at the edge. Degas specialized in scenes of Parisian life and horses, nudes, and dancers (*The Glass of Absinthe; Ballet Rehearsal*). Other important Impressionist painters are Camille Pissarro, Alfred Sisley, Frederic Bazille, and Mary Cassatt—an American whose domestic interiors were greatly influenced by the flatness and coloring of Japanese prints. Auguste Rodin (1840–1917; *The Burghers of Calais; The Thinker; Honoré de Balzac*) produced powerful sculptures with the freedom of Impressionist style, and Degas also depicted his favored ballet dancers in bronze.

By the 1880s pure Impressionism gave way to the more experimental arrangements of form and color of the Postimpressionists—Japanese prints held much allure for Paul Gauguin (1848–1903), who arbitrarily placed almost garish colors in compositions where design and shape took precedence over any sense of perspective or proportion (*Vision after the Serman* [*Jacob Wrestling with the Angel*]; and two works inspired by his stay in Tahiti: *Nevermore* and the woodcut *Noa Noa*). Vincent Van Gogh (1853–1890) was the exception that seems to have become a rule: the misunderstood, struggling, emotionally disturbed genius whose art was only recognized after his death. Van Gogh adopted Gauguin's harsh and unusual color schemes that were unrelated to the reality of a scene, and painted with an innovative, personal, expressive brushwork of thick swirling lines— which paved the way for twentieth-century expressionism (*The Night Café; Sunflowers; Starry Night*). Georges Seurat (1859–1891) produced noble and serene compositions in a style called pointillism, which allowed the viewer to visually mix the colors of a painting that had been applied in minute individual dots (*La Grande Jatte; The Circus*). Henri de Toulouse-Lautrec, more than any other French artist, concentrated on themes of night life and entertainment and employed thick outlines and the flatness of shapes and color of Japanese prints, especially in his many color lithographic posters. Paul Cézanne, considered by many to be the father of modern art, used the lessons of Impressionism to make the subjectivity of the artist paramount. He bent his subjects' shapes and contours away from realistic proportions and relationships, and assigned colors based on harmonious balance in the picture. Cézanne (1839–1906; numerous self-portraits; *The Great Bathers; Still Life with Onions*) was able to break apart and re-form reality, and make the act of painting itself significant, and in so doing he was able to usher in the achievements of twentieth-century Cubism and abstract art.

Other important groups in the last two decades of the nineteenth century that distorted reality and pursued sinewy forms or abstract patterning were the Nabis (Pierre Bonnard and Edouard Vuillard); the art nouveau artists (Toulouse-Lautrec, Aubrey Beardsley [illustrations for *Le Morte d'Arthur* and *Salome*], and Gustav Klimt [*The Kiss*]), the early expressionists (James Ensor [*The Entry of Christ into Brussels*] and Edvard Munch [*The Scream*]), and the Symbolists (Gustave Moreau, Odilon Redon, Puvis de Chavannes, and Edward Burne-Jones).

The most significant innovations in nineteenth-century architecture were related to technical accomplishment; the possibility of construction on a large scale in metal, iron, and glass allowed for revolutionary skeletal structures. The Crystal Palace, built for London's Great Exhibition in 1851 by Joseph Paxton, was 1600 feet long, and basically a glass building. A famous metal monument of no apparent purpose other than to symbolize another world's fair (in Paris in 1889) was Gustave Eiffel's tower. English railway stations had similar designs, using metal and glass vaulted roofs (John Dobson's Central Railway Station, Newcastle-upon-Tyne). And in America, the steel-skeleton structure dictated no-nonsense, stripped-down, functional city buildings by Daniel H. Burnham and John W. Root (Reliance Building, Chicago, 1890-1894) and Louis Sullivan (Wainwright Building, St. Louis, 1890-1891). The curves and vegetal ornamentation of the art nouveau style were employed in the buildings of Hector Guimard, Victor Horta, and Antonio Gaudi.

THE TWENTIETH CENTURY

Architecture in the twentieth century announced a clean break with the past, building upon the technical and structural innovations of such nineteenth-century masters as Joseph Paxton and Louis Sullivan. Frank Lloyd Wright (1867–1959) was perhaps the new century's greatest innovator, who transformed both commercial and residential architecture into structures that perfectly matched their surroundings, broke with the decorative language of the past, and offered functionalism in working and living spaces. Such private residences as the Robie house (1909) in Illinois and Fallingwater (the Kaufman house) in Pennsylvania brilliantly and innovatively mingle interior and exterior space. In the 1920s, the Bauhaus school of design in Dessau, Germany, championed abstract art, geometric design, machine-age elements, and restricted ornament. The director was the important architect Walter Gropius, whose design for the Bauhaus school building featured glass facades—pure line and geometric shapes. In Berlin in the 1920s Miës van der Rohe abandoned the ornamental vocabulary of the past for glass and steel skyscrapers and concrete office blocks. In America, Miës van der Rohe's apartment buildings on Chicago's Lake Shore Drive are rectangular blocks (1948–51), and his Seagram building in New York (1954—58) is perhaps the most famous example of the trend of skyscraper glass rectangles. This American glass-box aesthetic is also seen in Wright's Johnson Wax building (1936–39) in Racine, Wisconsin; the Lever Brothers and Pepsi-Cola buildings in New York by the firm of Skidmore, Owings, and Merrill; the presidential Palace of the Alvorada in Brasilia (1958) by Oscar Neimeyer; and Le Corbusier's United Nations design. This style of technology-driven, unadorned, stripped-to-essentials architecture in the industrialized nations since the 1930s has been called International Style or simply modernism. In the last twenty years, the austerity of modernism has been redirected into a more decorative and humanistic style, often termed postmodernism, which incorporates cultural influences, imaginative decorative touches, and historical architectural elements into designs appropriate to modern technology and uses. Among the architects working in the style are Robert Venturi and Michael Graves.

Sculpture and painting, from the beginning of the twentieth century, built upon the rejection of realistic proportions and naturalistic depiction, substituting a breakup of forms and a play of shape and color such as employed by Gauguin, Van Gogh, Cezanne, the Nabis, and others. The new freer form of art centered around the personality of the artist and celebrated personal style and the manipulation of two-dimensional pictorial elements. In the late nineteenth and early twentieth centuries this evolved in a number of directions. Some artists turned inward to explore mystical, symbolic, and psychological truths: Symbolists, expressionists, and exponents of art nouveau, such as Odilon Redon, Jan Toorop, Edvard Munch, James Ensor, and Gustav Klimt. The German Expressionists portrayed disturbing psychological truths through highly personal styles and disjointed compositions, and they frequently worked in woodcut. These German artists banded together from 1905 to 1913 in a group called Die Brucke; their aims were unabashedly revolutionary, and their work was often meant to shock. Die Brucke's members were Ernst Kirchner, Karl Schmidt-Ruttluff, Erich Heckel, Otto Mueller, Max Pechstein, and Emil Nolde—all of whose compositions emphasized distortion, angular and contorted figures, sometimes screaming color, and outrageous themes. In the face of the horrors of World War I, shock value and humor were the artistic weapons of choice for the Dada artists (Francis Picabia, Man Ray, Hans Arp, Kurt Schwitters, Marcel Duchamp, Max Ernst), whose "antiart" or "nonart" works often assembled any materials available ("found objects"), from newspaper clippings and photographs to bicycle wheels (Marcel Duchamp's *Ready-made,* 1913, a wooden stool with a bicycle wheel attached).

Among the artists who pursued formal innovations were Henri Matisse, Pablo Picasso, Georges Braque, and Juan Gris. Matisse (1869–1954) was the leading figure of the Fauves (dubbed "wild beasts" because of their relentlessly unreal use of color). Matisse's most important works reduced a picture to its essentials—flat color and line (*The Dance; Le Luxe II*). Other Fauves were Andre Derain, Georges Braque, Maurice Vlaminck, and peripherally, Georges Rouault, whose art was distinctly religious. The most revolutionary and far-reaching art movement of the twentieth century was Cubism—which, by its blatant visual decomposition and reassemblage of observed reality, seemed the most direct call for the total destruction of realistic depiction and for abstraction. The greatest Cubist artist and one of the most important figures in the history of art was Pablo Picasso (1881–1973; *Les Demoiselles d'Avignon; Three Musicians; Ma Jolie*). His use of African and Oceanic tribal art, and his emphasis on taking objects apart and reassembling them—thus showing a subject's multiplicity of aspects and dissolving time and space—led to similar experiments by Georges Braque, Juan Gris, Fernand Léger, Marcel Duchamp (*Nude Descending a Staircase,* 1912), the sculptors Alexander Archipenko and Jacques Lipchitz, and the Italian Futurist Umberto Boccioni (*Unique Forms of Continuity in Space,* sculpture, 1913, and *The City Rises,* painting, 1911).

In the first decades of the twentieth century, pure abstraction, with little or no relation to the outside world, was approached in the more emotional, expressionistic, and color-oriented paintings of Wassily Kandinsky (with Franz Marc, a proponent of the Blue Rider school), Robert Delauney, and Paul Klee. More cerebral arrangements of abstract geometrical shapes and colors were the mark of Kasimir Malevich (his Suprematist compositions), Piet Mondrian, and the Bauhaus School of Design in Germany (Klee, Kandinsky, Joseph Albers, Walter Gropius, Laszlo Moholy-Nagy; where Marcel Breuer originated the first tubular steel chair, a standard of mid-century "modern" furniture design). The Bauhaus's simplified and usually geometric-oriented aesthetic influenced architecture, industrial and commercial design, sculpture, and the graphic arts for half a century. In architecture can be seen the most obvious results of this new tradition, the simplified, sleek structures of Miës van der Rohe, Walter Gropius, Le Corbusier, and Frank Lloyd Wright.

Inspired by the psychoanalytic writings of Sigmund Freud and Carl Jung, the subconscious and the metaphysical became another important element in art, especially in the work of the Surrealist artists Salvador Dali (*The Persistence of Memory*), Giorgio de Chirico, Max Ernst, René Magritte, Juan Miro, and Yves Tanguy. Important sculptors who manipulated abstract shapes and/or were influenced by tribal arts in the twentieth century include Constantin Brancusi (*The Kiss,* 1910), Henry Moore (influenced by American Pre-Columbian art; *Mother and Child, 1924; Reclining Figure,* 1929), Hans Arp, and Alberto Giacometti. Alexander Calder created floating assemblies called mobiles, and Louise Nevelson made constructions and wall sculptures from scraps of everyday objects.

Obsession with self and with abstraction also led to the major American art movement after World War II, Abstract Expressionism, whose chief exponents were Clyfford Still, Jackson Pollock ("drip"paintings), William De Kooning, Franz Kline, and Robert Motherwell. Other Americans took this movement into the area of color-field painting, a cooler, more reserved formalism of simple shapes and experimental color relationships: Mark Rothko, Barnett Newman, Joseph Albers, and Ad Reinhardt.

Other important trends in American art in the twentieth century were reflective of a democratic and consumer society. The muralists and social realists during the first half of the century created art that was dynamically realistic—representative of a youthful and vigorous America—and whose subjects were accessible to the average person. John Sloan, George Bellows (*Stag at Sharkey's,* 1909), Edward Hopper (the new life in the lonely city, noble, quiet, stark: *The Automat, 1927; Nighthawks,* 1942), Thomas Hart Benton, Grant Wood, and John Stuart Curry were among those who celebrated the American scene in paintings, and frequently in murals for public buildings and through widely available fine prints. The great Mexican muralists, who usually concentrated on political themes—Diego Rivera, José Clemente Orozco, and David Siqueiros—brought their work to the public both in Mexico and in the United States.

The icons of American popular culture found their way, in the movement known as Pop art, into canvases by Andy Warhol (the multiplied silk-screened images of Campbell Soup cans and Marilyn Monroe), Robert Indiana, Larry Rivers, Jasper Johns (use of the American flag), Roy Lichtenstein (enlarged comic book panels), and Robert Rauschenberg. Other developments during the last thirty years include: Kinetic art (works that move or produce an illusion of movement) and Op art (manipulation of abstract color and repetitive patterns to play tricks on the eye [Victor Vasarely; Bridget Riley]); Minimal art (the work reduced to essentials) and Conceptual art (the idea itself, rather than the technical accomplishment); and the actual movement of, or covering of, land and monuments on a massive scale (Christo: *The Arco della Pace Wrapped,* 1970; *Running Fence,* 1972–76, a nylon fence along the hills in northern California). Super- or Photorealism is the style of the sculptor Duane Hanson and the painters Chuck Close, Richard Estes, and Philip Pearlstein.

☞ Drill: Visual Arts and Architecture

1. Pop artists used recognizable imagery from the mass media such as commercial products, comics, and celebrities because

    (A) they wanted to criticize the superficiality and consumerism of American culture.

    (B) they wanted to celebrate the images of their time.

    (C) they wanted to take advantage of new techniques and materials to present new products.

    (D) None of the above.

2. The Minimalists sought to

    (A) reduce shape and form to its simplest, purest state.

    (B) remove all evidence of the human hand's part in the construction of their work.

    (C) imitate industrial production in the slickness and coldness of their work.

    (D) All of the above.

3. Andy Warhol, the first artist to truly make use of the mass media, worked in each of the following media *except*

   (A) television.   (C) sculpture.

   (B) film.   (D) All of the above.

4. Warhol often repeated the same image many times within a single painting because

   (A) he was imitating the way the media saturates us with an image.

   (B) he wanted to show how we become numb to an image after seeing it so many times.

   (C) it was easy.

   (D) All of the above.

5. Which of the following is NOT considered by artists to be a technique of forming clay "by hand"?

   (A) Throwing   (C) Slab building

   (B) Coiling   (D) Modeling

6. "Form Follows Function" is an expression coined by

   (A) Frank Lloyd Wright.   (C) Le Corbusier.

   (B) Louis Sullivan.   (D) Miës van der Rohe.

7. Which of the following architects were founding members of the Bauhaus School of architecture?

   (A) Walter Gropius and Ludwig Miës van der Rohe

   (B) I.M. Pei and Robert Venturi

   (C) Theo van Doesburg and Le Corbusier

   (D) Benjamin Latrobe and Louis Sullivan

8. The Ionic Order of Greek architecture is characterized primarily by

   (A) cushion-shaped capitals.   (C) bell-shaped capitals.

   (B) volute-shaped capitals.   (D) fluted columns.

9. Giacomo della Porta's design for the facade of the Church of II Gesu in Rome dates from which of the following periods of art history?

   (A) Early Christian   (C) Northern Renaissance

   (B) Romanesque   (D) Baroque

10. The central vertical supporting pillar of Romanesque and Gothic portals is called a

(A) lintel.

(C) column.

(B) jamb.

(D) trumeau.

11. The twentieth-century movement in architecture which immediately succeeded the International Style, and which was defined largely by the writings of Robert Venturi, is

(A) Modernismo.

(C) Constructivism.

(B) Post-Modernism.

(D) Romanticism.

12. The staircase in the Hotel van Eetvelde, designed by Victor Horta in 1895, illustrates which one of the following art historical styles?

(A) Art Nouveau

(C) Neo-Classicism

(B) Post-Modernism

(D) Post-Impressionism

13. The earliest-known example of town planning in the history of architecture is

(A) Forum of Caesar, Rome.

(C) Acropolis, Athens.

(B) Stonehenge, England.

(D) Catal Huyuk, Turkey.

14. The dome of Florence Cathedral was built in the fifteenth century, according to which of the following architect's designs?

(A) Leonardo da Vinci

(C) Leon Battista Alberti

(B) Filippo Brunelleschi

(D) Giuliano da Sangallo

15. Supports used in post-and-lintel architecture that are carved in imitation of female figures are called

(A) sirens.

(C) atlantes.

(B) caryatids.

(D) Corinthian columns.

16. The central dome of St. Mark's in Venice rests on curved triangular supports called

(A) squinches.

(C) corbelled arches.

(B) pendentives.

(D) fan vaults.

17. Reinforced concrete, also known as ferroconcrete, is defined as concrete that is

    (A) covered with brick facing.

    (B) combined with stone masonry blocks.

    (C) embedded with iron rods or mesh.

    (D) mixed with a water repellant.

18. The plan of Charlemagne's Palace Chapel at Aachen is often compared to that of which of the following buildings?

    (A) Hagia Sophia, Istanbul

    (B) The Pantheon, Rome

    (C) Sant'Apollinare in Classe, Ravenna

    (D) San Vitale, Ravenna

VISUAL ARTS AND ARCHITECTURE REVIEW

ANSWER KEY

Drill: Visual Arts and Architecture

1.	(D)	6.	(B)	11.	(B)	16.	(B)
2.	(D)	7.	(A)	12.	(A)	17.	(C)
3.	(D)	8.	(B)	13.	(D)	18.	(D)
4.	(D)	9.	(D)	14.	(B)		
5.	(A)	10.	(D)	15.	(B)		

DETAILED EXPLANATIONS OF ANSWERS

Drill: Visual Arts and Architecture

1. **(D)** Pop artists wanted neither to criticize nor celebrate American culture, but simply to take pieces of it and show it back to the society which produced it, to put a mirror up to society. (A) is incorrect. This is too simplistic a reading of pop art and there is no evidence to show this intent. (B) is incorrect. This is also too simplistic a reading of pop art. There is no evidence to show this intent over any other. (C) is incorrect because the pop artists employed already-established techniques such as silk screening and lithograph for their works.

2. **(D)** Choices (A), (B), and (C) are all goals of minimalism.

3. **(D)** The correct answer is (D), all of the above. (A) is incorrect because Warhol had a short-lived TV show on MTV called *Andy Warhol's Fifteen Minutes*. (B) is incorrect because Warhol made many films including the experimental *Sleep*, an eight-hour-long shot of a man sleeping. (C) is incorrect because Warhol worked in sculpture from the 1960s onward. His most famous pieces are the *Brillo Boxes* from the early part of that decade.

4. **(D)** Choices (A), (B), and (C) are all true according to statements which Warhol himself made.

5. **(A)** Coiling, slab building, and modeling are all methods of forming clay strictly by hand. "Throwing" clay involves the use of a potter's wheel, and thus is not technically considered a method of hand-forming clay.

6. **(B)** Louis Sullivan, an architect best known for his late nineteenth century skyscrapers, promoted the idea that a building's form should follow its function. His slogan "form follows function" became one of the Great Truths for modern architects of the twentieth century, among them Gropius and Miës van der Rohe.

7. **(A)** Walter Gropius and Ludwig Miës van der Rohe helped found the Bauhaus School in Germany in the 1920s but later moved to the

United States, where they exerted profound influence on twentieth-century American architecture. I.M. Pei and Robert Venturi (B) were active as architects in the later twentieth century (especially in the 1970s), well after the founding of the Bauhaus. Theo van Doesburg and Le Corbusier (C) were architectural contemporaries of the Bauhaus founders, but were not themselves involved in the school. Benjamin Latrobe and Louis Sullivan (D) were architects working in the nineteenth century, thus pre-dating the founding of the Bauhaus. Inigo Jones, the first of the great English architects, precedes the Bauhaus, having lived and worked in the seventeenth century.

8.   **(B)**   Volute-shaped capitals, whose circular spiral motifs, or volutes, are carved on the corners of the capitals at the tops of each column, are the distinguishing characteristic of the Ionic order. Cushion-shaped capitals (A) characterize the Doric order of Greek architecture; and bell-shaped capitals (C), usually adorned with acanthus tendrils, identify the Corinthian order. Fluted columns (D) appear in all Greek architectural orders and are not used as criteria to identify the individual order.

9.   **(D)**   The two-storied facade, the levels of which are unified by the large flanking scrolls; the paired columns; and the pedimented windows and niches were widely imitated in the Baroque period to varying degrees on other buildings. The dramatic effect of the building's overtly anti-classical design was typical of Baroque-era architecture. Early Christian (A) and Romanesque (B) churches were designed with much simpler, more austere facades; and there are no comparable facades in the architecture of the (C) Northern Renaissance.

10.   **(D)**   Trumeau, which is often in imitation of human or animal forms. A lintel (A) is the horizontal beam that rests upon the (B) jambs (frames) of a doorway. A column (C) refers to any simple cylindrical support; however, simple columns were not used as central supports in such doorways.

11.   **(B)**   Post-Modernism was the period of architectural history that was formulated in the 1970s. The definition of Post-Modern architecture is complex, and the phrase is rejected by many modern architectural historians; loosely defined, it refers to contemporary architecture that seeks to challenge and re-examine traditional methods of architectural expression. Modernismo (A) refers to the Spanish version of Art Nouveau. (C) Constructivism is a term used to define the works (both sculptural and architectural) of a group of early twentieth century Russian artists. Ro-

manticism (D) is a nineteenth-century movement in architecture, in which architects sought to imitate architectural styles of past eras, including those of classical Greece and Rome and medieval Europe.

12. **(A)** Art Nouveau is distinguished by the use of such curvilinear, decorative details of interior design. Post-Modernism (B) is a later period in the history of architecture, and is not defined by such decorative elements. Neo-Classicism (C), a nineteenth-century era of architecture, is characterized by the use of classical Greek and Roman architectural details, which are more austere in nature Post Impressionism (D) is a movement in painting, which has no equivalent in the history of architectural design.

13. **(D)** Catal Huyuk, Turkey, which dates from ca. 6000 B.C., revealed upon excavation multiple dwelling units and structures apparently designed for worship, indicating that the complex was designed for the dwelling of a large number of persons. The Forum of Caesar, Rome (A) dates from the first century B.C. Stonehenge, England (B) dates from c. 2000 B.C. and is not believed to have served as living space. The Periclean Acropolis, Athens (C) dates from the fifth century B.C.

14. **(B)** Filippo Brunelleschi, whose dome (built 1420–1436) was unprecedented in design. To span the 140-foot space, Brunelleschi designed his dome with an avoid profile (to reduce the thrust at the dome's base), and with a double shell and 24 ribs to lighten the weight yet provide the dome with sufficient stability. Leonardo da Vinci (A) is not known to have designed a comparable dome, nor has any such construction been attributed to him. Leone Battista Alberti (C) was much influenced by Brunelleschi, but had no part in the design of the dome of Florence Cathedral, nor did Giuliano da Sangallo (D), who succeeded Brunelleschi as an architect.

15. **(B)** The correct choice is (B) Caryatids. Sirens (A) are female *characters* from Greek mythology, not an architectural form. Atlantes (C) are supports in post-and-lintel architecture which are carved in imitation of *male* figures; they are the counterparts of caryatids. Corinthian columns (D) are an order of Greek architecture, and are distinguished by bell-shaped capitals carved with acanthus tendrils.

16. **(B)** The correct choice is (B) Pendentives. Squinches (A) are also utilized to support domes, but these are block-like members laid across the corners of a structural unit to support a dome of similar structure. Cor-

belled arches (C) are arches formed by stepping stones outward from a base until the stones meet at midpoint. Fan vaults (D) are elaborate groin vaults, with tracery defining their wedge-shaped forms.

17. **(C)** Embedded with iron rods or mesh, as indicated by the term *"ferro*concrete." Concrete that is (A) covered with brick facing or (B) used with stone masonry blocks, is simply concrete that is combined with other building materials. Concrete mixed with a water repellant (D) is referred to as an *ad*mixture.

18. **(D)** San Vitale, Ravenna, which is also a centrally-planned building with central nave and encircling ambulatory. It is commonly believed that Charlemagne either visited Ravenna and viewed the plan of San Vitale, or that he was made familiar with its plan through architects at his court. Hagia Sophia in Istanbul (A), the Pantheon in Rome (B), and the Orthodox Baptistery in Ravenna are all centrally-planned buildings, but in size, interior elevation, and division of interior space, they are not comparable to Charlemagne's Palace Chapel. The church of Sant'Apollinare in Classe in Ravenna is not centrally-planned, but designed along a longitudinal axis.

IV. PHILOSOPHY REVIEW

ANCIENT PHILOSOPHERS

All of the Greek philosophers before Socrates were known as the pre-Socratics. Pythagoras was a sixth century B.C. pre-Socratic philosopher and mathematician. Pythagoras, who made many scientific and mathematical discoveries, believed in the transmigration of souls.

Thales, a sixth and fifth century B.C. pre-Socratic philosopher, is sometimes called "the father of Western philosophy." Thales held that the first principle, or substance, that everything in the universe is made out of is water.

Parmenides was a pre-Socratic philosopher in the fifth and fourth century B.C.. He denied the existence of time, plurality, and motion. He is considered the founder of metaphysics.

Heraclitus, in the fourth century B.C., was a pre-Socratic philosopher. Heraclitus was said to have believed that everything is in a continuous state of flux. He was opposed to the idea of a single ultimate reality.

Zeno was a pre-Socratic philosopher in the fourth century B.C. and a disciple of Parmenides. He was famous for a set of paradoxes, which are intended to show that plurality and motion do not really exist.

Socrates was an Athenian fourth century B.C. philosopher. He supposedly wrote down none of his views, because he believed writing distorted ideas. His ideas have survived only through the writings of his followers, most notably Plato. It is unclear to what extent the views attributed to Socrates' character in Plato's dialogues were the views of the actual historical Socrates.

Atomism is the belief that matter consists of atoms. Both Leucippus, a fourth century B.C. Greek philosopher, and Democritus, a fourth and third century B.C. Greek philosopher, were atomists. They both concluded atoms are different-shaped bits of matter.

Plato, who lived from 427 to 347 B.C., was a Greek philosopher. Plato wrote dialogues, many of which contain Socrates as the main character. These dialogues provided the starting point for many later developments in various areas, for example: ethics, the study of morals; epistemology, the study of knowledge; and metaphysics, the study of reality. Plato's best known theory is the theory of Forms (or Ideas). According to this theory, the objects of knowledge are universals, such as The Good and The Just. Because specific things in this world, such as a just person, are mere reflections of the Forms, they can only be the objects of opinion.

Aristotle, who lived in the third century B.C., was an extremely influential Greek philosopher. Aristotle, who criticized Plato's theory of Forms, was the first to systematize logic. The medieval study and development of Aristotle's philosophy is known as Aristotelianism.

PHILOSOPHERS OF THE FIRST MILLENIUM

Neoplatonism was the dominant philosophy in Europe from 250 through 1250 A.D.. Begun by Plotinus, a third century A.D. philosopher, Neoplatonism is a combination of Plato's ideas with those of other philosophers, such as Aristotle and Pythagoras. Another Neoplatonist was Augustine, a fourth and fifth century bishop and philosopher. Augustine had a profound effect on medieval religious thought.

St. Anslem, an eleventh century philosopher, was an Italian monk who became archibishop of Canterbury. He founded Scholasticism. Anselm was best known for his ontological argument for the existence of God.

St. Thomas Aquinas, a thirteenth century philosopher, was best known for his "Five Ways," five proofs of the existence of God. The philosophy of Aquinas and his followers is called Thomism. He is considered the greatest thinker of the Scholastic School. His ideas were made the official Catholic philosophy in 1879.

Ockham was a fourteenth century English philosopher and cleric. He was famous for the dictum "Do not multiply entities beyond necessity."

Hobbes (1588–1679) was a British materialist. One of his famous works is *Leviathan* in which he argues that men are selfish by nature. Because of this belief, Hobbes felt that a powerful absolute ruler is necessary.

Rationalism is the view that knowledge of the external world can be derived from reason alone, without recourse to experience. Notable rationalists include Descartes, Leibniz, and Spinoza. Descartes (1596–1650) was an extremely influential French philosopher and mathematician. He held a view of the relation between the mind and body which has come to be known as Cartesian dualism. In this view, the mind and body are two distinct, though interactive, entities. Descartes is famous for the statement "*cogito ergo sum*," or "I think therefore I am."

Two other well known Rationalists were Gottfried Wilhelm von Leibniz and Benedict Spinoza. Leibniz (1646–1716) was a German philosopher who argued, in his *Theodicy*, that this is the best of all possible worlds. He is considered one of the greatest minds of all times. Spinoza (1632–1677), a Dutch-born philosopher, is best known for his *Tractacus Theologico-Politicus*. He felt mind and body are aspects of a single substance, which he called God or Nature.

Blaise Pascal (1623–1662) was a French philosopher, mathematician, and theologian. He is most famous for an argument called "Pascal's Wager," which provides prudent reasons for believing in God. His work, *Pensées* (Thoughts), published after his death, argues that reason is by itself insufficient for man's spiritual needs and cannot bring man to God.

Empiricism is the view that all knowledge is derived from experience. Three well-known empiricists are Locke, Berkeley, and Hume. John Locke (1632–1704) was an English philosopher. In his *Essay Concerning Human Understanding*, Locke attempted to present an empiricist account of the origins, nature, and limits of human reason. Berkeley (1685–1753), another empiricist, was an Irish philosopher and an idealist. Idealism is the view that the so-called "external world" is actually a creation of the mind (another well-known idealist is Hegel). Finally, David Hume (1711–1776) was a Scots philosopher. An empiricist, Hume drew attention to the problem of induction.

Jean Jacques Rousseau (1712–1778) was a German born political philosopher and a philosopher of education. His major work was *The Social Contract* (1762). Rousseau emphasized man's natural goodness.

Adam Smith (1723–1790) was a Scots philosopher and political economist. He wrote *The Wealth of Nations*. Smith has had an enormous impact on economics into the present day.

Immanuel Kant (1724–1804) was a German idealist philosopher. He was most famous for the categorical imperative—"Act only on that maxim which you can at the same time will to become a universal law"—as a test of moral principles. Kant is also well known for his epistemological work, including his ideas of the Noumenon and Phenomenon.

Jeremy Bentham (1748–1832) was a British philosopher and a lawyer. He was one of the founders of utilitarianism. He was a powerful reformer of the British legal, judicial, and prison system.

Georg Wilhelm Friedrich Hegel (1770–1831), a German idealist philosopher, is famous for his theory of the dialectic. According to the theory, a dialectic is a process of argument which proceeds from a thesis and its antithesis to a synthesis of the two. His idealistic system of metaphysics was highly influential.

James Mill (1773–1836) was a Scots philosopher and economist. Mill was also the father of the better-known philosopher J.S. Mill. J.S. Mill (1806–1873), son of James Mill, was an English empiricist philosopher. J.S. Mill is best known both for his *System of Logic* and for his ethical writings, including *Utilitarianism* and *On Liberty*.

Arthur Schopenhauer (1788–1860), a German philosopher, was a Kantian best known for *The World as Will and Idea*. Schopenhauer believed that only art and contemplation could offer escape from determinism and pessimism. Schopenhauer had a strong influence on Freud, Nietzsche, Proust, Tolstoy, and Thomas Mann.

Søren Kierkegaard (1813–1855), a Danish philosopher, was probably the first existentialist. Existentialism is the view that the subject of philosophy is *being*, which cannot be made the subject of objective inquiry but can only be investigated by reflection on one's own existence. Sartre is another notable existentialist.

Karl Marx (1818–1883), author of *Das Kapital*, was a German social theorist. Engels (1820–1895), Marx's collaborator, was a dialectical materialist. Dialectical materialism is the metaphysical doctrine originally propounded by Engels. According to the doctrine, matter, rather than the mind, is primary. Matter, also, is governed by dialectical laws in this view. Dialectical materialism is included in Marxism, the body of doctrines originally held by Marx and Engels.

Brentano (1838–1917) was a German philosopher and psychologist who is remembered for his "doctrine of intentionality."

Charles Peirce (1839–1914), an American philosopher, was the founder of pragmatism. As used by Peirce, pragmatism was originally a theory of meaning. Later, William James (1842–1910), an American (empiricist) philosopher and psychologist, used pragmatism as a theory of truth according to which "ideas become true just so far as they help us get into satisfactory relations with other parts of our experience."

Friedrich Wilhelm Nietzsche (1844–1900), a German philosopher, is best known for introducing the concept of the *Übermensch,* or the Overman. As a moralist, he rejected Christian values.

Bradley (1846–1924) was an English philosopher. An idealist, Bradley wrote *Appearance and Reality*.

Frege (1848–1925) was a German philosopher and mathematician. Frege is considered the founding father of modern logic, philosophy of mathematics, and philosophy of language.

Edmund Husserl (1859–1938), a German philosopher, developed phenomenology. Phenomenology is a method of inquiry which begins with the scrupulous inspection of one's own conscious thought processes. Husserl's goal was to create a completely accurate description of consciousness and conscious experience.

John Dewey (1859–1952) was an American pragmatist philosopher and educational theorist. Dewey developed the views of William James and Charles Peirce into his own version of pragmatism. He emphasized the importance of inquiry into acquiring knowledge. George Santayana (1863–1952) was an American Platonist philosopher, novelist, and poet. Santayana was a student of James. He attempted to reconcile Platonism and materialism.

Bertrand Russell (1872–1970) was a British philosopher. Along with Whitehead, he was the author of the extremely influential *Principia Mathematica*. Russell, in such seminal papers as "On Denoting" and "The Principles of Logical Atomism," argued that the structure of the world can be revealed by the proper analysis of language.

G.E. Moore (1873–1958), a British philosopher, is best known for his *Principia Ethica*. Moore emphasized the common sense view of the reality of material objects.

Logical positivism, a radical empiricist position, is the doctrine that the meaning of a proposition consists in the method of its verification. Logical positivism is also known as "logical empiricism." A group of logical positivists, known as the Vienna Circle, centered around the University of Vienna in the 1920s and 1930s. Founded by Schlick (1882–1936), a logical positivist philosopher, the Vienna Circle also included Neurath (1882–1945), an Austrian logical positivist philosopher, and Carnap (1891–1970), a German logical positivist philosopher.

Ludwig Wittgenstein (1889–1951), a Viennese-born philosopher, has had an enormous influence on the later philosophy of language. *Tractatus Logico-Philosophicus*, his first and most famous work, was a defense of a picture theory of meaning. This work contains such often quoted aphorisms as "The world is everything that is the case."

Martin Heidegger (1889–1976), a German philosopher, is commonly regarded, despite his objections, as an existentialist. Heidegger studied with Husserl and was influenced by Kierkegaard. Heidegger's own philosophy emphasized the need to understand "being."

Alfred Tarski (1902–1993) was a logician and mathematician. He is famous for his definition of the concept of truth for formal logical languages, which has been used extensively by philosophers of language as a basis for theories of meaning for natural language.

Sir Karl Popper (1902–1994), a philosopher of science, wrote *The Logic of Scientific Discovery*. He is best known for his claim that falsifiability is the hallmark of science.

Jean-Paul Sartre (1905–1980) was a French philosopher. Sartre was a founder of Marxism and existentialism. Sartre believed man is condemned to be free and to bear the responsibility of making free choices.

Hempel (1905–   ) is a German empiricist philosopher of science. His theories of confirmation and explanation have been extremely influential. Goodman (1906–   ), an American philosopher, is a nominalist. Goodman wrote, most notably, *Fact Fiction and Forecast* and *Languages of Art*.

Merleau-Ponty (1908–1961) was a French philosopher who worked on ethics and problems of consciousness. Willard Van Orman Quine (1908–   ) is an American empiricist philosopher of language and a logician. Sir Alfred Jules Ayer (1910–1989), an English philosopher, is a logical positivist and member of the Vienna Circle. He wrote *Language, Truth and Logic*. Austin (1911–1960) was a British philosopher of language. He developed the speech act theory. Strawson (1919–   ), a British philosopher of language and a metaphysician, is best known for arguing, in "On Referring," that some meaningful sentences have no truth value. Rawls (1921–   ), an American political philosopher, is best known for *A Theory of Justice*. Noam Chomsky (1928–   ) is an influential American linguist and philosopher. Chomsky argues that there is an innate universal grammar. Davidson (1930–   ) is an American philosopher of language and the mind. He holds a theory of the mind called anomalous monism. Kripke (1941–   ) is an American philosopher of language, philosopher of the mind, and logician. His most influential work, "Naming and Necessity," launched the causal theory of reference. His theory, in part, deals with the distinction between a statement's sense and its reference.

☞ Drill: Philosophy

1. It is not surprising that Rationalists like Leibniz, Spinoza, and Hegel all accepted some version of the Coherence theory of truth because the main alternative, the Correspondence theory, places too much weight on

   (A) innate ideas.   (C) the relations among ideas.

   (B) experience.   (D) knowledge.

2. Benjamin Franklin, Thomas Jefferson, and George Washington all rejected theism, but were not atheists. This is because they were

   (A) deists.   (C) Christians.

   (B) skeptics.   (D) immoralists.

3. Sextus Empiricus was the codifier of Greek skepticism, a view that held we cannot give our firm assent to any

   (A) creed.   (C) belief.

   (B) dogma.   (D) moral code.

4. Jealousy and envy are often conflated or confused, but central cases of jealousy and envy differ in at least one important respect:

   (A) jealousy involves more than two people.

   (B) envy can be expressed.

   (C) jealousy involves a belief.

   (D) jealousy is sexual.

PHILOSOPHY REVIEW

ANSWER KEY

Drill: Philosophy

1. (B) 2. (A) 3. (C) 4. (A)

DETAILED EXPLANATIONS OF ANSWERS

Drill: Philosophy

1.　**(B)**　Choice (B) identifies the Correspondence theory with experience. Hence, the Correspondence theory is mainly identified with Empiricism, the main rival to Rationalism. Choice (A) cannot be correct because Empiricists do not accept a doctrine of innate ideas, nor do they think truth is a function of the relations among ideas (C). Both Empiricists and Rationalists are concerned with (D) knowledge. However, they approach these matters differently.

2.　**(A)**　The early Americans rejected theism but were not atheists because they believed in a God, but not the God of theism. Their God was a Creator but otherwise an "absentee God" of the sort proclaimed by Voltaire and other deists. Choice (B) is too vague, for it does not specify what the skepticism concerned. Choice (C) is incorrect because some Christians were theists while others were deists. None of the three was (D) an immoralist.

3.　**(C)**　The Skeptics differed from the dogmatists who believed that certain knowledge was possible but also differed from those who dogmatically asserted that knowledge is impossible. Sextus recommended suspending judgment about all beliefs, preferring to remain an open-minded inquirer. The correct answer is (C), since his skepticism was sweeping. All the other terms are too narrow to capture the scope of his view. One might suspend judgment about a (B) dogma, or (A) creed, or (D) moral code without suspending judgment about all beliefs. Sextus does not claim these are all false, but only that we are not in a position to know that they are true. He thus thinks other skeptics went too far in claiming falsehood.

4.　**(A)**　A person can envy his neighbor's good fortune, but jealousy involves more than two people since it typically involves a response to the belief that another person is paying too much attention to a third person. Thus, Tom may be jealous of Jane's attention to Fred, but not envious of Jane's attention to Fred. The other answers all mention a feature that is common to jealousy and envy, as various philosophies of emotion have shown. Both jealousy and envy involve belief (C), and envy may be sexual (D), since one might envy someone's sexual prowess.

V. MUSIC REVIEW

Music is the organization of sound in time. Because it exists only in time, what some people call the fourth dimension, rather than in three-dimensional space, music is one of the more elusive art forms. Given this abstract quality and the enormous variety of music that exists in the world, it is surprising to realize that there are only four ways that one sound can differ from another. Each individual tone has four properties that give it a particular character: duration, frequency, intensity, and timbre. Musicians make choices within each of these categories to create the effect they hope their music will have on its listeners.

Duration refers to how long a sound or a silence lasts and the rate at which one sound succeeds another. **Rhythm** is based on this fundamental property of sound and is essential to our perception of time. Rhythm is built into the natural world. There is rhythm in the movement of the stars, in the cycle of seasons, in the alternation of day and night, in our very heartbeats and breathing. If there were no rhythm, we would not be aware that time was happening.

Most of the music that we hear and all music to which we dance or march has a steady beat, a regular **pulse** that underlies the melody. Whereas the pulse is steady with an unchanging note value, melodic rhythm involves a variety of note values. If you sing any song and clap the pulse, you will notice that some of the beats have more than one melodic note to them and some melodic notes extend over several beats. For instance, in "Happy Birthday to You," both of the notes of "happy" occur on a single beat while "you" extends over two beats.

Tempo refers to the speed of the pulse. The designation for different tempi are in Italian. Thus, if the beats are in the range of our heartbeats, around 72 pulses a minute, the tempo is *moderato* (moderate). If the beats are faster than our heartbeats, the tempo is *vivace*, or if very much faster, it is *presto*. If the beats are slower than our heartbeats, the tempo is *lento* or *largo*. A fast tempo conveys a mood of energy and excitement; a slow tempo produces a more somber or thoughtful feeling.

As rhythm in nature involves repeated patterns, such as the tide moving in and out twice a day, so the beat in music is most often organized into patterns. Patterns are formed when some beats are regularly stronger than others. Music organized in this fashion is said to be **metric**. In order to have meter, there must be both a steady pulse and a pattern of accented and unaccented beats. Music that does not have a steady pulse (such as recitative in operas or some atonal music), or music that has a steady pulse but no accents at all (such as Gregorian chant) or has unpredictable accents that do not form a recognizable pattern (such as Stravinsky's *Rite of Spring*) is said to be **ametric**. Most of the music in the world, however, is metric.

In Western music, we have only two basic patterns. A strong beat followed by a weak beat (ONE two, ONE two) or a strong beat followed by three weak beats (ONE two three four) is said to be **duple meter.** This is a meter you can walk and march to; it has a left - right, left - right straight-ahead sort of feeling. Almost all popular music is duple. The other pattern is **triple**, with a strong beat followed by two weak ones (ONE two three, ONE two three). Triple meter has a more swaying, side-to-side feeling and is used for waltzing, skating, or skipping. Some triple-meter songs are "Happy Birthday to You," "The Star-Spangled Banner," and "My Country 'Tis of Thee."

In notated music, each occurrence of the pattern constitutes a **measure** or **bar** and is set off by vertical bar lines. The meter itself is denoted by a **time signature** placed at the beginning of the music. This consists of two numbers positioned vertically. The upper number indicates how many beats are in a measure and the lower number identifies which kind of note gets the beat. For example, if the time signature is ¾, there are three beats per bar and each bar will have the equivalent of three quarter notes.

Duple and triple refer to how beats are joined together. Beats can also be subdivided, that is, a single beat may carry several melodic notes. If the beat is subdivided into two or multiples of two, the meter is said to be **simple**. Duple simple meter is counted 1 & 2 & / 1 & 2 &, and triple simple meter is counted 1 & 2 & 3 & / 1 & 2 & 3 &. Sometimes, however, there are three melodic notes evenly spread over a single beat. In this case, the meter is said to be **compound**. "Row, row, row your boat" is in duple compound meter, counted 1 & a 2 & a / 1 & a 2 & a. This is evident in the words "merrily, merrily, merrily, merrily." Compound triple meter, counted 1 & a 2 & a 3 & a, also exists, but is less common. A beautiful example is J. S. Bach's "Jesu, Joy of Man's Desiring."

Sometimes there is a strong underlying meter, but the melodic accents come where you don't expect them — between the beats or on weak rather than strong beats, as in 1 & 2 **&**. This is called **syncopation** and is the means by which jazz conveys a feeling of swing.

Meter in much of the rest of the world is more complex than it is in even the most sophisticated Western music. In the music of India and the

Arab world for instance, the patterns might extend for over 20 beats, in contrast to our simple two- or three-beat patterns. In the music of Africa, many different patterns are heard simultaneously, creating a layering of patterns that produces a dense, highly complex meter.

Sound happens when something that is capable of vibrating, such as a taut string or a vocal chord, is set in motion by the movement of air. If the vibrations are irregular, the result is noise, such as the sound of wind in the trees, a car engine, or a cough. If the vibrations are regular, the result is a tone that has the property of pitch. Pitch refers to how high or low the ear perceives the tone to be. Frequency determines pitch and measures the number of regular vibrations per second. These are too fast to see; 440 vibrations per second produces the pitch to which instrumentalists tune, which is the note "A." The higher the frequency, the more vibrations per second and the higher the pitch; fewer vibrations per second produce a lower pitch.

When the number of vibrations is doubled or halved, the pitch that is produced is the same, but in a different register. That is to say, as pitches rise or descend, they repeat at a regular distance. Since 440 vibrations per second produce a note called "A," 220 will also produce an "A" but in a lower register; 880 will produce an "A" but in a higher register, and so on. An **interval** is the distance between two pitches. The interval from one pitch to its next repetition, for example from A220 to A440, is called an **octave.**

There are several ways of dividing up the octave into smaller intervals. In music of the Arab world and India, for example, the octave is divided into two dozen different pitches producing quarter-steps. In Western music, the octave is divided into only twelve intervals of equal size. These are called **half steps** and are the smallest intervals possible in Western music.

We name the pitches according to the alphabet, from A to G, at which point the pitches repeat. On a piano keyboard, pitch ascends as we move from left to right. Only the white keys are given alphabet names:

c d e f g a b c d e f g a b

Notice that the black keys are arranged in a pattern of alternating twos and threes. This asymmetrical arrangement helps in identifying the pitches. The white key between the pair of black keys is always D. The black keys are named according to their relationship to the white keys. When the black key is named in relationship to the white key on its left, it raises the pitch of that key a half step and is called a **sharp.** The symbol for a sharp is ♯. When the same black key is considered in relationship to the white key on its right, its pitch is a half step lower and is called a **flat**. The symbol for a flat is ♭. Thus the same pitch may have two different names, depending on the context. For example, C♯ is the same pitch as D♭.

On a keyboard, a half step is between adjacent keys, such as between a black key and its neighboring white key. There are also two places on the keyboard where half steps exist between two white keys that have no intervening black key: between E and F, and between B and C. A whole step consists of two half steps, for instance the distance from C to D, and from C♯ to D♯, and so on.

The arrangement of pitches within an octave is called a **scale**, which comes from the Italian *scala*, meaning ladder. Pitches are like the rungs of a ladder going from one level to the next. There are many different kinds of scales. A scale which contains all twelve half steps, that is, one that uses every key on the piano, is called a **chromatic** scale. A scale consisting only of whole steps is called a whole tone scale. Most scales, however, are a mixture of whole and half steps, and some have augmented 2nds, which is an interval of three half steps.

Almost all Western music is based on **diatonic** scales, that is, scales that use each letter name only once, and thus have seven different pitches. Not all scales are diatonic. A **pentatonic** scale has, as its name suggests, only five different pitches and therefore skips some letter names. Using only the black keys on the piano, you can produce a pentatonic scale. Much Japanese, Indonesian, Scottish, and folk music is based on pentatonic scales, as is the well-known hymn "Amazing Grace." A **blues scale** has six different pitches, but one letter name is repeated and two are skipped: G B♭ C C♯ D F G.

There are two forms of diatonic scales: **major** and **minor**. If you play a scale from one C to the next using only white notes, you will produce a major scale. It consists of half steps between the 3rd and 4th notes and between the 7th and 8th notes. All other steps are whole steps. As long as this arrangement is kept intact: 1 - 2 - 3 4 - 5 - 6 - 7 8, a major scale can be built from any note. A scale built on D would be spelled: D - E - F♯ G - A - B - C♯ D. One on F would be: F - G - A B♭ - C - D - E F. Notice that each letter name is used only once. In the scale on F, although A♯ would produce the same pitch as B♭, we have already used an A and may not skip the letter B.

The scale that a piece of music is built on is indicated in notated music by a **key signature** at the beginning of the music, just after the time signature. For example, in the scale built on D, the key signature would have two sharps, one on F and one on C. For the scale on F, the key signature would have one flat on B.

A diatonic scale in the **minor** mode is found on the white keys beginning on A. Here the half steps are between 2 and 3 and between 5 and 6 to produce the arrangement:

1 - 2 3 - 4 - 5 6 - 7 - 8. It may seem like a small detail, whether the third note of the scale is two whole steps or a whole step and a half step above the starting pitch, but the difference in effect is big. To most people, music using a major scale sounds bright and happy compared to music in a minor key, which sounds darker and sadder. Perhaps that is why most popular music is in a major mode.

The note on which a diatonic scale is built is called the **tonic**. Music that uses a diatonic scale is said to be **in the key of** the tonic note upon which the scale is built. Thus, music that uses the white notes beginning on C is said to be **in the key of** C major. Music that uses the scale beginning on C but with half-steps between 2 & 3 and 5 & 6 (C - D E♭ - F - G A♭ - B♭ - C) is said to be **in the key of** C minor. In both cases, C is the tonic, the home note, the goal of the music. Music that is in C major or C minor will not sound finished until it arrives on its tonic note of C. All the other notes of the diatonic scale are named in relation to this most important note. The note an interval of a 5th above the tonic (G in C major) is called the **dominant**. The one a 5th below the tonic (F in C major) is called the **subdominant**. The note between the tonic and the dominant (E in C major) is the **mediant**; that between the subdominant and the tonic is the **submediant**. The second step of the scale is the **supertonic**. And the note a half-step below the tonic in a major scale is called the **leading tone.** The notes can also be identified by solfege syllables:

Tonic	Supertonic	Mediant	Subdominant	Dominant	Mediant	Leading Tone	Tonic
Do	Re	Mi	Fa	Sol	La	Ti	Do

When three or more notes are sounded simultaneously, the result is a **chord**. The most prevalent chord is a **triad**. As the name suggests, a triad is a three-note chord comprised of alternating scale degrees. Examples are C - E - G; D - F - A; E - G - B, and so on. The tonic triad in C major is spelled C - E - G. C is the root of the triad; E is the third and G the fifth of the triad. From C to E are two whole steps, which is called the interval of a **major 3rd (M3rd)**. From E to G are a whole step and a half step, an interval of a **minor 3rd (m3rd)**. The distance from the root to the fifth is three and a half steps, the interval of a **perfect 5th (P5th)**. This is the definition of a major triad: M3rd on bottom; m3rd on top; P5th from root to fifth. There are four possible kinds of triads, depending on the arrangement of major and minor thirds:

Quality of triad	MAJOR	MINOR	DIMINISHED	AUGMENTED
Root to Third	Major	Minor	Minor	Major
Third to Fifth	Minor	Major	Minor	Major
Root to Fifth	Perfect	Perfect	Diminished	Augmented

Triads may be built on each step of the scale. Their position and quality are identified by roman numerals: upper case for major, lower case for minor, a small circle for diminished, and a plus sign (+) for augmented. For example, a tonic triad is indicated by the roman numeral I. In a major scale, the triads built on the first, fourth, and fifth steps of the scale are major, hence the upper-case roman numerals. The triads built on the second, third, and sixth steps of the scale are minor, hence the lower-case roman numerals. And that built on the seventh step is diminished:

	Tonic	Supertonic	Mediant	Subdominant	Dominant	Mediant	Leading Tone	Tonic
Major scale:	I	ii	iii	IV	V	vi	vii°	I
Minor scale:	i	ii°	III	iv	v	VI	VII	i

The most common triads are I, IV, and V. With only these three chords, many songs can be accompanied.

Chords are pitches that happen simultaneously, or vertically. Pitches that occur horizontally, that is, in succession over time, create melody. **Melody** is a succession of pitches in a particular rhythmic pattern. Melody is a broad term that includes music that we may not consider very melodic. Melodies we can remember easily are "tunes." Each of us has hundreds of tunes stored in our memories.

Melodic direction refers to the shape of the arrangement of pitches. A melody may be mostly ascending, mostly descending, may seem to curl around itself, or, as is most often the case, use a mixture of all three. **Range** refers to how far the highest note is from the lowest note in a given melody. The wider the range, the more energy the music seems to have.

Melodic motion is how a tune gets from one pitch to the next. If the melody moves by small steps, it is said to be using conjunct motion. If it moves by leaps, it is using disjunct motion. All of these factors together produce the mood of a melody. If a composer wants to portray happy excitement, she will probably use much disjunct motion that mostly ascends over a wide range. Gloomy disappointment would be portrayed by conjunct motion, limping downward within a very narrow range.

Melodies are organized according to the principle of repetition and contrast. If a melody has too much repetition, it is dull; too much contrast sounds chaotic and unmemorable. So a good melody has the right balance between the two. As an example, "Twinkle, twinkle, little star" is in four musical phrases. The second and fourth phrases are exactly like the first —repetition. The third is different—contrast. So the phrases of this simple tune could be diagrammed as: a a b a. Large symphonic movements are more complex and happen over a larger space of time, but are in musical forms organized according to this same principle.

Texture refers to how melodies are presented. If there is only a single melody with no accompaniment at all, the texture is monophonic. This is true even if many performers and singers are playing the same melody. For instance, the famous opening notes of Beethoven's fifth symphony, "ta ta ta dum," are monophonic. If two or more melodies are happening at the same time and seem to be of equal interest and to be competing for the listener's attention, as happens when people sing a round beginning at different times, the texture is polyphonic. If there is a single melody in the foreground with subsidiary melodies or chords accompanying it in the background, the texture is homophonic. The use of harmony to accompany melody is what sets Western music apart from other kinds of music. Most of the music in much of the non-Western world is monophonic, but in the West the most prevalent texture is homophony.

Intensity refers to how loud or soft a tone is. The musical term for this is **dynamics**. As with tempo markings, the names for dynamics are in Italian. Ranging from softest to loudest they are:

pianissimo	*piano*	*mezzopiano*	*mezzoforte*	*forte*	*fortissimo*
pp	p	mp	mf	f	ff

Dynamics are a big factor in contributing to the effect of a piece of music. The louder the music, the more extroverted and energetic; softer music is more intimate and tender. Music can also gradually go from loud to soft (*decrescendo*) or from soft to loud (*crescendo*). It can be in a *piano* dynamic and suddenly become loud (*subito forte*), or in a *forte* dynamic and suddenly get soft (*subito piano*).

Timbre refers to the source of the musical sound, which instrument or what kind of voice is producing the music. Timbre has to do with the physics of sound, specifically what overtones are present and in what proportions. The concept is difficult to explain, but easy to hear. It's why we can tell the difference between a trumpet and a flute or a piano and how we can recognize our friends' voices.

The earliest musical instrument was undoubtedly the human voice. Using our voices in a musical manner seems to be universal in the human community. Voices are classified partly according to their range and partly according to their tone color. The lowest male voice is a bass, the highest a tenor, and in between the two is the baritone. The comparable female voices are alto, soprano, and mezzosoprano.

Instruments are categorized according to two different systems. One method is based on how the sound is produced and is useful for many different kinds of music. Chordphones produce sound when a taut string or chord is set in motion, by either bowing, hammering, or plucking. Violins, pianos, harpsichords, and guitars are chordophones. Aerophones are instruments that confine a column of air that is set in motion by breath. They include flutes, trumpets, and whistles. Membranophones produce sound when a membrane that is stretched across a hollow cavity is struck. These are drums of all kinds. Idiophones are instruments that themselves vibrate when struck, such as bells, cymbals, and rattles.

The second method classifies instruments according to families in a symphony orchestra and is appropriate only for Western music. The string family includes violins, violas, cellos, and double basses. The wind family includes flutes, single-reed instruments like the clarinet, and double-reed instruments like the oboe and bassoon. The brass family comprises trumpets, French horns, trombones, and tubas. The percussion section includes all drums and anything that is struck, such as the xylophone.

Timbre is particularly important in the music of China. The Chinese have a large assortment of instruments that are classified according to the material of which they are made, such as silk, bamboo, brass, clay, wood, and so forth. Each timbre and each musical tone carries an extra-musical significance that is more important than any purely musical considerations. For example, a single tone may carry the connotation of autumn, water, and the north.

We have seen, in passing, that in different cultures, certain aspects of music are emphasized more than others. In Western music, harmony is treated in a sophisticated manner, while rhythm and melody remain relatively simple. In the music of Africa, rhythm is given a highly complex treatment, while harmony and melody are less developed. In the music of the Arab world and India, both melody and rhythm are more intricate, but there is little, if any, harmony. And in China, the emphasis is placed on subtleties of timbre.

WESTERN MUSIC

The history of Western music is divided into six periods, each with recognizably distinct characteristics: Medieval, Renaissance, Baroque, Classical, Romantic, and Twentieth Century. The pattern seemed to be that a musical style emerged, and, over a period of time, grew more and more intricate. There is then a reaction against that complexity, resulting in a new stylistic period.

The **MEDIEVAL** period begins with the earliest music in Europe for which any notated music survives and ends around the year 1450. Gradually during this period, musical notation was developed. It came about because monks in monasteries were required to learn an enormous body of chants that required some sort of *aide memoire*. At first only the direction of the melodic motion was indicated. Then, over time, a more precise method was devised for fixing pitches: noteheads were placed on ledger lines, which numbered anywhere from two to ten before finally settling into today's five-line staff. These fixed a relative, but not absolute, pitch. For that, a clef sign was needed to identify a single pitch from which the others could be derived. Clef signs therefore are designed to resemble letter names: the G-clef is our soprano clef; the F-clef our bass clef. There are also C-clefs, which are used by voices and violas. Finally, late in the period, a method was devised for indicating durations of notes, thus allowing rhythmic variety.

Paper was precious and expensive, and very few people could write words, let alone music. The only music that was notated was liturgical chant—that is, music that was performed as part of a religious service. Although this is the only music from the early part of this period that has come down to us, we can be sure that secular, popular music did, in fact, exist, but because it was not written down, we don't really know what it was like. We do know that there were nomadic poet-musicians known as troubadours and trouveres who sang songs of chivalric devotion and crusader feats as well as pilgrim songs, and that these were monophonic.

The liturgical music was called plainchant, or more commonly, albeit misleadingly, Gregorian chant. It was performed *a capella*—that is, voices only with no instrumental accompaniment or doubling, and was monophonic. Beginning around the tenth century, a stunning innovation took place. Perhaps emerging because boys and men sing at different octaves, or because some monks sang "out of tune," medieval polyphony gradually came about. At first the accompanying lines were mere drones, but little by little a second independent melodic line was achieved, and this eventually laid the foundation for the development of harmony.

By the twelfth century, Paris was the most important cultural center in Europe, and it is there that we have the first named composers. The cathedral of Notre Dame, then in the process of being built, had attached to it musicians who constituted the School of Notre Dame. **Leonin** (c. 1135–1201) composed the first complete annual cycle of chants for the mass in two parts. His successor **Perotin** (fl. 1190–c. 1225) did the same in four parts.

The fourteenth century was a turbulent period that saw the Hundred Years War, the Black Death, and great corruption in the church. Because of advances in musical notation, especially in the area of rhythm, music got enormously complex. Musicians of the time, as **Guillaume Machaut**, self-consciously called themselves *Ars Nova*, to set themselves apart from what they considered old-fashioned, conservative musical practices. In some secular music, as in the *Roman de Fauvel,* which was a cynical critique of both church and government, the voices simultaneously have different texts, often in different languages, and different melodic lines. Two or more of the voices would be quite active and independent of one another while one or more other voices would hold long drone notes. The inevitable reaction against an excess of complexity led to the next stylistic musical period.

The **RENAISSANCE** period in music begins around 1450 and extends to 1600. The word literally means "rebirth." It was a time of renewed confidence and a flowering of the arts influenced in part by the discovery of classical Greek philosophy. Renaissance musicians, inspired by the Greeks' belief in the power of music to shape one's soul and of words to express emotions and influence actions, had a great reverence for the importance of text when combined with music. In what was a new urge toward cohesion, all the voices have the same text set to the same music, although not sung at the same time, as the voices enter one after the other. Unlike *Ars Nova* polyphony, all the voices are of equal value; none is relegated to drone status. This new kind of texture, called **imitative polyphony,** is the most characteristic feature of Renaissance music.

As the church had reformed itself, there was a renewed emphasis on sacred compositions. Whereas Medieval composers had set mainly the Propers of the mass, those sections which change from day to day such as the Gradual and the Introit, Renaissance composers concentrated on the Ordinary of the mass, the Kyrie, Gloria, Credo, Sanctus and Benedictus, and Agnus Dei, that never vary from day to day. These, being sacred and for liturgical use, were in Latin, and were sung *a capella* in imitative polyphony. Free standing religious compositions, called **motets**, have the same characteristics as mass settings. Renaissance composers also wrote secular (non-religious) compositions called **madrigals.** They are similar to mass movements and motets, except they are in the vernacular—such as Italian or English—rather than Latin and tend to be in a livelier style.

Renaissance musical instruments were of two kinds: softer "indoor" instruments like the viol and lute, and louder "outdoor" ones like shawms, crumhorns, and sackbuts. The indoor instruments tended to be used for instrumental music that was modeled on vocal forms to create a textless imitative polyphony. Outdoor instruments were used for movement, such as processionals and dances, and were therefore more obviously metrical.

The most outstanding composer of the Renaissance period was **Josquin Desprez** (1440–1521). Martin Luther, the moving spirit behind the Reformation, said of Josquin that he was master of the notes, whereas the reverse was true for other composers. During the period of the Counter-Reformation, when the Catholic church was again trying to reform itself from within, the decision was taken at the Council of Trent to ban polyphony from church services. Legend has it that **Giovanni Palestrina** (c. 1525–1594) saved Catholic church music by demonstrating to the cardinals at the Council of Trent that music could be polyphonic and yet be clearly understood with his Pope Marcellus Mass. Music written for the Roman Catholic church has been conservative ever since.

Experimentation was, however, taking place in the area of secular vocal music. Composers like **Carlo Gesualdo** (c. 1561–1613) wrote madrigals that displayed daring harmonic dissonances, but had a precious, mannered approach to the text. Each separate word was given its own illustrative treatment, making nonsense of the text as a whole. The reaction to this practice not only ushered in a new stylistic period, but led to the creation of an entirely new musical genre.

The **BAROQUE** period begins around 1600 with the invention of **opera** and ends around 1750 with the death of Johann Sebastian Bach. In the last decade of the sixteenth century, a group of intellectuals in Italy called the "Florentine Camerata" once again looked back to classical Greece for inspiration to reform music. Whereas at the beginning of the Renaissance, it was Greek philosophy that influenced music, for the Florentine Camerata it was Greek drama. They conceived of the idea that drama could be sung throughout with the simplest of accompaniments, and thus **opera** was created.

This produced far-reaching changes in musical style. The Renaissance ideal sound was three to six equal voices with no instrumentai accompaniment. Each vocal line was conceived of horizontally, as a melodic line. In early opera, the ideal was a solo voice with a light instrumental accompaniment. The latter consisted of a bass line with a system of numbers over certain bass notes to indicate vertical harmony. A sustaining instrument such as a cello played the bass line while the harmony was improvised by a harpsichord or lute player. This was called **basso continuo** and is characteristic of almost all Baroque music. The Baroque ideal sound was a solo melodic line supported by a strong bass line with the space between the two filled in by harmony—in other words, a more vertical approach to musical organization. It was during this period that **functional tonal harmony** using major and minor diatonic scales was established.

Another difference in style between the Renaissance and Baroque has to do with rhythm. Except for instrumental music expressly written for the dance, Renaissance music is free-flowing and almost without accents, hence not quite metric. Baroque music, on the other hand, is strongly metrical. Baroque music, of all kinds and for whatever purpose, dances. Very often in Baroque music, once a rhythmical pattern is established, it persists throughout the entire piece or movement, reflecting an urge toward cohesion and unity.

The first great opera composer was **Claudio Monteverdi** (1567–1643), whose *Orfeo* is still performed today. But the most famous composer of Italian *opera seria* was a German who spent most of his creative life in London: **George Frideric Handel** (1685–1759). As the name suggests, *opera seria* deals with serious topics borrowed from Roman mythology or from ancient history. The elements of Italian opera are an instrumental overture, then alternating vocal recitative and arias. **Recitative** is like heightened speech and occurs in that part of the drama where action is carried forward. It is in prose with only basso continuo accompaniment. An **aria** is more akin to poetry and has a fuller orchestral accompaniment. When London audiences turned against Italian opera as an "irrational and exotic entertainment," Handel gave them unstaged opera in English using biblical stories as his subject matter and adding the new ingredient of the chorus: the **oratorio.** His *Messiah* is one of the most beloved musical works of all time.

An exact contemporary of Handel's whose music is the epitome of the High Baroque style is **Johann Sebastian Bach** (1685–1750). Bach never wrote an opera, but he wrote **cantatas** and The St. John and St. Matthew **passions** for the Lutheran church that, like Handel's oratorios, have all the characteristics of opera. Bach included in them the Lutheran chorale, a form of congregational hymn-singing introduced by Martin Luther.

During the Baroque period, instrumental music for the first time came to be as important as vocal music. This was the beginning of **absolute music**—that is, abstract instrumental music that is not dependent on words or movement for its form. Composers therefore had to look within the music itself, to the principles of repetition and contrast, to create musical forms. The rapidly developing tonal system also contributed to the creation of form, which essentially consists of establishing the tonic, moving away from the tonic, and returning to the tonic.

The most important of the new instruments was the violin, made popular by, among others, **Arcangelo Corelli** (1653–1713), who wrote exclusively for the violin in the genres of solo sonatas (one solo instrument plus continuo), and trio sonatas (two solo instruments plus continuo), and **Antonio Vivaldi** (1678–1741), who established the three-movement instrumental concerto (one or more solo instruments plus orchestra), as in his famous *The Four Seasons*, a set of four concerti with each one representing a season of the year.

Keyboard music was also important. The harpsichord was essential to almost all Baroque music as part of the *basso continuo*, but was also used extensively as a solo instrument. Bach, who was the greatest organist of his day, wrote **fugues** for organ and harpsichord as well as for vocal chorus. "Fugue" comes from the Italian *"fuga,"* meaning to chase. As in imitative polyphony, different voices sing the same melody at different times. In Renaissance imitative polyphony, however, each phrase is given its own music. In the Baroque fugue, a single musical idea, called the fugue subject, appears throughout, first in the tonic, then in other key areas, and finally in the tonic again. The repetition of the fugue subject provides unity; its appearance in different keys provides contrast.

The **CLASSICAL** period, dating from the death of J. S. Bach in 1750 until the 1820s, came about because of great changes taking place in society. The traditional sources of musical patronage, the aristocracy and the church, were losing ground to the emerging middle classes. Quality music was no longer limited to the privileged few. This period saw the proliferation of public concerts, which anybody could attend for the price of a ticket. Music publishing flourished, meaning the latest compositions were quickly available for the amateur music market. Composers therefore had to find ways of appealing to a broader public. They imbued their music with clarity, naturalness, and a pleasing variety, all hallmarks of the newly emerging Classical style.

The beginnings of the new style are found in what happened to opera late in the Baroque period. Italian *opera seria* comprised three acts. In the first half of the eighteenth century, a two-act *opera buffa* (comic opera) was often inserted between the acts to entertain the audience. In *opera seria*, the drama was less important than beautiful and bravura singing, and the characters were lofty historical figures. *Opera buffa* was about real people in everyday situations, such as problems between servants and their bourgeois masters. The emphasis was on fast-moving dramatic action, clever dialogue, and lightly accompanied and appealing arias. In time, *opera buffa* became so popular that it was detached from *opera seria* and became a genre in its own right, eventually eclipsing *opera seria* entirely. The best known examples are Mozart's *Marriage of Figaro, Don Giovanni,* and *Cosi fan tutte.*

Franz Josef Haydn (1732–1809) did much to develop two new classical instrumental genres and **Wolfgang Amadeus Mozart** (1756–1791) further perfected them. The **symphony**, a work for full orchestra, and the **string quartet** (two violins, viola, and cello) are generally in four movements. The first movement is usually in **sonata** form, which is more of a dynamic process than a form. It comprises three sections that correspond to three acts of a drama. In the **exposition,** a musical idea is presented in the tonic key. There is then a transition to a new key area and, usually, contrasting thematic ideas. There is thus tension between the two key areas. In the **development** section, the plot thickens as material presented in the exposition is broken apart, combined in new ways, and taken to more distant key areas. The denouement in the **recapitulation** is brought about by repeating the exposition, but this time keeping everything in the tonic—the home key—to provide a resolution. Sonata form was so fundamental to the classical approach that it influenced other forms as well.

The second movement of symphonies and quartets is often a slow movement. It might be in sonata form, or theme and variations, or ternary form. The latter has three parts diagrammed as A B A: the first is in the tonic, the middle section presents contrasting material in a different key, and the third is a repetition of the first. The third movement, paired dances that hark back to the Baroque suite, is also in ternary form, with the A sections being a minuet or scherzo and the contrasting B section a trio. The fourth movement is usually fast and may be in sonata form, theme and variations, or rondo-sonata. Rondo form, inherited from the Baroque period, is an extension of the ternary idea with several contrasting sections, each in a different key, alternating with the A section, which is always in the tonic, for example A B A C A D A. In rondo-sonata form, the D section is replaced by the B section, which is now resolved in the tonic.

The classical **concerto** for soloist and orchestra omits the fourth movement, but is otherwise organized in the same manner, as is the classical **piano sonata,** for which the number of movements is more variable. The *fortepiano* was invented around the middle of the eighteenth century. Because it was capable of producing a wide range of dynamics, the piano rapidly replaced the softer-voiced harpsichord as the keyboard instrument of choice for solos, concerti, and chamber music that was performed in ever larger public concert halls.

Unlike Haydn and Mozart, **Ludwig van Beethoven** (1770–1827) was born late enough to have been influenced by the French Revolution. His music is considered revolutionary, not because he overthrew existing practices, but because he expanded all the elements of the classical style and enlarged the range of expression. His nine symphonies, for example, are longer and for larger performing forces than Haydn's or Mozart's. His dynamic range is wider, his rhythm more propulsive, and his harmonic resources greatly extended.

Rather than reacting against the Classical style, composers of the **RO-MANTIC** period, which extends through the end of the nineteenth century, carried Beethoven's innovations even further to new levels of expressiveness. Where Classical composers aimed at clarity, Romantic composers sought ambiguity. Rhythm became more complex through the use of shifting meters and *rubato*, a surging forward or holding back of the pulse. Tonal harmony was obscured through the increasing use of *chromaticism*, which is the inclusion of notes that are foreign to the key, and through a tendency to defer a sense of resolution by seeming to evade arrival at the tonic. Phrases became longer and less clearly articulated. The symphony orchestra was enlarged and included a greater variety of wind and brass instruments.

Music during the Romantic period tended toward the grandiose, and audiences prized showy virtuosity. The pianist and composer **Franz Liszt** (1811–1886) and the violinist **Niccolo Paganini** (1782–1840) enjoyed the kind of adulation we associate with today's rock stars. **Program** music grew in importance during this period. Program music, in contrast to absolute music, is instrumental music that depends for its inspiration and its understanding on something external to music—a landscape, as in the

Hebrides Overture by **Felix Mendelssohn** (1809–1847); drama, as in the symphonic overture *Romeo and Juliet* by the Russian composer **Peter Ilyich Tchaikovsky** (1840–1893); nature, as in the piano character piece *Papillons* (butterflies) by **Robert Schumann** (1810–1856); or even the composer's autobiography, as in the *Symphonie Fantastique* by the French composer **Hector Berlioz** (1803–1869). One composer who resisted the trend was **Johannes Brahms** (1833–1897). His symphonies, concerti, and chamber music adhere to abstract musical principles.

In an age when bigger seemed to be better, it is surprising to find two new intimate genres. *Lieder*, which is German for art songs, is poetry set to music for a solo singer with piano accompaniment. **Franz Schubert** (1797–1828) wrote hundreds of *lieder,* including one written when he was only eighteen, his well-known setting of Goethe's ballad-poem *Der Erlkönig*. Like *lieder*, piano character pieces are one-movement miniatures that aim to set a mood in a brief space of time. Most Romantic composers wrote in many genres, but one, **Frederic Chopin** (1810–1849), wrote exclusively for the piano. His solo piano works include polonaises, études, and impromptus.

Opera during the nineteenth century was dominated by two composers. The Italian **Giuseppe Verdi** (1813–1901) wrote 28 operas, including some of the most beloved in the repertoire: *Rigoletto, La Traviata, Aida,* and *Otello*. His exact German contemporary, **Richard Wagner** (1813–1883), wrote his own *libretti* drawing on German mythic legends. His masterpiece, *Der Ring des Nibelungen*, is a cycle of four operas.

By the end of the nineteenth century, the romantics had stretched the elements of Western music so far that there was a reaction against what was viewed as emotional excess. Composers experimented with new techniques of composition and explored new directions for their music. Music of the **twentieth century** is therefore not distinguished by a single style. Instead we find several different approaches, none of which seem to have firmly caught hold. Most have in common an abandonment of tonality.

In the period preceding the first world war, contemporary movements in painting inspired three distinct musical styles. Impressionist painters, such as Monet, fragmented the visual into its elements of color and shape. **Impressionism** in music tried to do the same thing by careful attention to tone color and the manipulation of melodic fragments. An example is the three-movement orchestral work, *La Mer*, by the French composer **Claude Debussy** (1862–1918). **Expressionist** painters and composers were influenced by the work of Sigmund Freud on the irrational subconscious. They depict the outer world through a sort of deranged subjectivity. *Pierrot*

Lunaire is a song cycle for soprano and five instrumentalists by the German composer **Arnold Schönberg** (1874–1951) that depicts the increasing lunacy of "Pierrot." The soprano uses *sprechstimme*, a style of performing characterized by wide, angular, unpredictable intervals where the exact pitches of the notes are not indicated. **Primitivism** was influenced by the Spanish painter Pablo Picasso, who painted the sets for the ballet *Sacre du Printemps* depicting the fertility rites of early Slavic tribes with music by the Russian composer **Igor Stravinsky** (1882–1971). This music is characterized by powerful dissonances; *ostinatos* in which Stravinsky obsessively repeats fragments taken from Russian folk songs; and an enlarged percussion section that was given unprecedented prominence.

In the 1920s, Arnold **Schönberg** devised a new method for organizing atonal music. He called it the *twelve-tone* method or *serialism*, whereby the composer makes a pre-compositional decision about the order in which the twelve notes of the chromatic scale will be heard. This was called the *tone row*. Once the composer sets the tone row, the pitches may only come in that order, although the row may be inverted (turned upside down) or played retrograde (backwards). Other composers, such as the American **Milton Babbitt** (b. 1916), took this even further and "serialized" duration and dynamic level as well as pitch.

Diametrically opposed to such total control was **chance music**, which also had parallels in the other arts such as participatory theater and art events known as "happenings." The ultimate example of this is *4'33"* by the American composer **John Cage** (1912–1992), wherein the performers sit in silence for the entire piece, drawing attention to ambient sounds in the environment. With advances in technology, some composers experimented with computer-generated music, such as *poème électronique* of the French composer **Edgard Varèse** (1883–1965). **Minimalism**, a more recent movement, represents a return to tonality and meter, but with a minimum of musical ideas obsessively repeated, for example *Glassworks* by the American composer **Philip Glass** (b. 1937). Composers today find inspiration from music of the distant past, from other cultural traditions, and from other fields, such as jazz.

Many people consider **JAZZ** to be America's only original contribution to music. It originated in American black culture around the beginning of the twentieth century. Some of its roots are found in the **call and response** of "field hollers," work songs where a leader sings a line and the others respond sympathetically, a technique that is still heard in African folk songs; **blues** songs; **gospel** singing; and the **ragtime** piano style of black artists like **Scott Joplin** (1868–1917).

Jazz is more of a performer's than a composer's art since the music is improvised rather than read from a score or memorized. This means that the performers agree on a tune, key, tempo, and form, then, based on that, make up what they play as they go along in a spontaneous way. Syncopation—putting an accent where one doesn't expect it—is an important element in jazz. This happens at two levels: the rhythm section provides a steady "back-beat"(one TWO one TWO) over which the melody instruments move a fraction of a beat ahead or behind the pulse. When this happens, the music is said to swing.

In its brief history, jazz has gone through several styles. The earliest is **New Orleans** style, also called Dixieland. Small ensembles consisted of a rhythm section of drums, piano, and/or bass and two or more soloists on trumpet, saxophone, clarinet, trombone, or voice. **Louis Armstrong** (1900–1971) played trumpet and sang in a style called "scat," where the voice, singing syllables rather than words, is used as another instrument. During the Depression years of the early 1930s, solo piano came to the fore with **stride** and **boogie woogie**. In the late 1930s and early 1940s during World War II, **swing** or **big-band** jazz "crossed over" and became widely popular. Swing bands were large ensembles of ten to twenty performers playing under the direction of a leader from written-out arrangements called "charts," which left less room for improvisation. One of the greatest of the swing band leaders was the pianist and composer **Duke Ellington** (1899–1974).

After the war years, when the popularity of the big bands collapsed as the mass market turned to rock and roll, jazz performers returned to the emphasis on improvisation afforded by smaller ensembles. But they did so with a new virtuosity and more sophisticated, complex harmonies in a style called **bebop**. Some of the outstanding performers of bebop were the alto saxophonist **Charlie Parker** (1920–1955) and the trumpeter **Miles Davis** (1926–1991). Bebop has been succeeded by many different jazz styles, such as the more laid back cool jazz and free jazz (total improvisation), as well as a nostalgic return to the "classical" New Orleans style. As in art music, jazz musicians are currently looking to other fields, such as rap, Afro-Cuban music, and the music of other cultures, to produce a blended style called **fusion.**

☞ Drill: Music

1. Which of the following are examples of musical scales?

    I.   Chromatic   III. Blues

    II. Octatonic   IV. Raga

    (A) I only   (C) I and II

    (B) I and III   (D) All of the above.

2. Which of the following is an example of ametric music?

    (A) African drumming   (C) Jazz

    (B) Gregorian chant   (D) Rap music

3. A major diatonic scale has half-steps between

    (A) 1-2 and 5-6.   (C) 3-4 and 7-8.

    (B) 2-3 and 5-6.   (D) 4-5 and 7-8.

4. A major triad has

    (A) two major thirds.   (C) two minor thirds.

    (B) a minor third below a   (D) a minor third above a
         major third.   major third.

5. An important innovation during the Medieval period was

    I.   notation.   III. opera.

    II. serialism.   IV. polyphony.

    (A) I and IV   (C) I and II

    (B) I only   (D) I and III

6. An important characteristic of Renaissance music is:

    (A) compound meter.   (C) imitative polyphony.

    (B) *sprechstimme*.   (D) recitative.

7. Which of the following is an example of absolute music?

   (A) Bach's *St. John Passion* (C) Brahms' Piano Concerto #1

   (B) Beethoven's Symphony #6 (D) Tchaikovsky's *Swan Lake*

8. Swing, in jazz, has to do with

   (A) stop time. (C) 32-bar chorus.

   (B) improvisation. (D) rhythm.

9. J.S. Bach never wrote for which of the following instruments?

   I. Viola da gamba III. Fortepiano

   II. Clarinet IV. Oboe de caccia

   (A) I and III (C) II and III

   (B) III and IV (D) I and II

10. Which of the following does not belong with the others?

   (A) Mozart's *The Magic Flute* (C) Tchaikovsky's *The Nutcracker Suite*

   (B) Stravinsky's *Firebird* (D) Prokofiev's *Romeo and Juliet*

11. Which of the following contributed to the development of Rock and Roll in the 1950s?

   I. Economic prosperity III. Tin Pan Alley

   II. Country and Western IV. Rhythm and Blues

   (A) II and IV (C) I and II

   (B) II, III, and IV (D) All of the above.

12. Which of the following is not a genre typical of the Romantic period?

   (A) Tone poem (C) Symphonic overture

   (B) Concerto grosso (D) Song cycle

MUSIC REVIEW

ANSWER KEY

Drill: Music

1.	(D)	4.	(D)	7.	(C)	10.	(A)
2.	(B)	5.	(A)	8.	(D)	11.	(D)
3.	(C)	6.	(C)	9.	(C)	12.	(B)

DETAILED EXPLANATIONS OF ANSWERS

Drill: Music

1. **(D)** All are examples of scales. The chromatic scale is one that uses every note in the Western octave and consists only of half-steps. The octatonic scale is one devised by Igor Stravinsky and consists of alternating half and whole steps. The blues scale is a particular arrangement of pitches (it has two augmented 2nds, two half steps, and two whole steps) that gives the blues its distinctive sound. Raga refers to both the arrangement of pitches within the octave and to the musical form of classical Indian music.

2. **(B)** Metric music has both a steady pulse and a pattern of regular accents. Gregorian chant is ametric because, although it has a steady pulse, it has no accents. Rap music, which is essentially poetic, is strongly metric. In African drumming, several meters occur simultaneously, producing polymeters. Jazz exhibits rhythmic complexity in having a great deal of syncopation, but this occurs over and within a strong, underlying meter.

3. **(C)** A major scale has half-steps between the third and fourth notes and the seventh and eighth notes. (B) is where the half-steps occur in a diatonic minor scale. The other two arrangements are of medieval modes; (A) is the phrygian mode, beginning on the pitch E, and (D) is the lydian mode, beginning on F. The other medieval modes are dorian (half-steps between 2-3 and 6-7, beginning on D) and mixolydian (half-steps between 3-4 and 6-7, beginning on G).

4. **(D)** A major triad consists of a major third between the root and middle note and a minor third between the middle note and the upper note, producing a perfect fifth between the outer notes. If their position is reversed, with the minor third on the bottom, the result is a minor triad. If both thirds are major, the resulting fifth is augmented, and the triad is an augmented triad. If both thirds are minor, the fifth is diminished, and the triad is a diminished triad.

5. **(A)** Both the notation of music and the development of medieval polyphony had their beginnings before 1000 A.D. Opera was invented around 1600 and serialism, also called the twelve-tone method, in the 1920s.

6.   **(C)**   The Renaissance sound ideal was *a capella* voices singing the same text to the same melody but entering at different times—imitative polyphony. The rhythm was flexible, without strong accents and therefore not strongly metric. Recitative refers to those sections of baroque and classical operas that were written in heightened speech style with a minimum of instrumental accompaniment. *Sprechstimme* was a singing style developed by Arnold Schoenberg, wherein the direction of the melodic motion, but not exact pitches, is indicated.

7.   **(C)**   Absolute music is abstract instrumental music that is not based on extra-musical references, such as Brahms's two piano concertos. Most of Beethoven's symphonies are examples of absolute music, but the sixth is not. Beethoven entitled it *"Symphonie Pastorale"* and gave each of its five movements a descriptive heading. This particular symphony is thus an example of program music. Bach's two Passions are for voices as well as instruments. Tchaikovsky's *Swan Lake* is ballet music.

8.   **(D)**   Swing is the essential rhythmic component of jazz. Trumpeter Wynton Marsalis says jazz swings when the bass player is walking his instrument and the drummer is riding the cymbals. The rhythm section is then providing a steady beat over which the lead instruments are free to syncopate around the beat. Improvisation is equally essential to jazz. The performers embellish a given tune, adding notes and continuously varying the melody as they go along, making it up on the spot. The 32-bar chorus is one of several jazz forms. It consists of four phrases of which is each eight bars long: A A B A. The first phrase is repeated, probably in a varied style; the third phrase is a contrasting one called the bridge; the fourth phrase is again a repetition of the first. In the last two bars of the second and fourth phrases, the rhythm section falls silent to allow the lead performer to improvise freely. This is called stop-time.

9.   **(C)**   Bach wrote for both the viola da gamba and the oboe da caccia. The viola da gamba is a bowed, fretted, six-string instrument tuned like a guitar that was widely used during the Renaissance. Little is known of the oboe da caccia. The conjecture is that it was an alto oboe that had a curved shape like a hunting horn. The fortepiano, a keyboard instrument with a hammer action, was invented in 1709. Bach had the opportunity to try one out in the 1730s, but was unimpressed with it. In the following decades, rapid technological improvements gained the fortepiano broad favor. The clarinet, a single-reed woodwind instrument, was not invented until the mid-eighteenth century.

10. **(A)** Mozart's *The Magic Flute* is an opera, or more appropriately a *singspiel*, meaning it is in the German language with sung arias interspersed with spoken dialogue. The other three are all ballets.

11. **(D)** The postwar prosperity of the 1950s in America meant that, for the first time ever, enough young people had sufficient disposable income to constitute a separate, lucrative market for music. Tin Pan Alley, shorthand for the popular music consumer industry and so called because it was centered in a noisy street full of shops with player pianos in New York City, aimed for as broad an appeal as possible, including cross-generational. Tin Pan Alley composers ranged from hacks to George Gershwin. Rhythm and Blues came about with the southern migration of blacks to the cities. It is an urbanized version of the country blues, often more energetic and with an electric guitar. Muddy Waters and Son House were some of the great rhythm and blues singers. Country and Western was, in the beginning, southern, white, and rural. When Sam Phillips signed Elvis Presley because he was a white man who sounded like a black man, Phillips brought together the two strains of black and white popular music to create rock and roll.

12. **(B)** The concerto grosso is a baroque genre. It is a multi-movement work for two or more soloists. The passages for the soloists alternate with *tutti* sections where all the performers participate. The *tutti* passages are called *ritornelli* because they generally "return" to the opening theme while the *soli* passages usually contain contrasting material. Both the Tone Poem and the Symphonic Overture are one-movement orchestral works and are almost always examples of program music. Liszt was particularly associated with the former. His *Les Préludes* was inspired by the French Romantic poet Lamartine. An overture was historically used to introduce something—a drama, opera, or ballet. But the Romantic symphonic overture lost that function and is heard in concert as a free-standing work. An example is Brahms's *Academic Festival Overture*.

VI. PERFORMING ARTS REVIEW

THEATER REVIEW

ORIGINS OF THEATER

As long as humans have been capable of communication, they have probably employed some form of drama and performance. Cave paintings supply evidence for the early use of costumes and masks to bolster mimetic performances, which, either as magic or prayer, functioned to encourage the productivity of nature.

THEATER IN GREECE

In keeping with this tradition, the earliest Greek plays were probably ritualistic performances that might involve, for instance, a conflict between winter and summer, and that would include a combat, a death, and a resurrection. These simple plays may have evolved into the dithyramb, a frenzied and impassioned hymn performed by a chorus of 50 men costumed in goatskins. The purposes and concerns of the earliest plays were reflected in the first **dithyrambs**, which celebrated Dionysus, the god of the abundance of nature. Aristotle described the dithyramb as the forerunner of tragedy, and the gradual development from dithyramb to tragic drama began as spoken lines were inserted into the lyrics, causing the leader of the chorus to become a solo performer.

According to legend, the fundamental changes that brought these early performances to the level of drama were made by Thespis, a poet and actor from whose name we derive the word *thespian*. He is known as the founder of classical **tragedy**. He is credited with inventing a new breed of performer, the actor, who would engage the audience by impersonating one or more characters between the dances of a chorus. Thespis also came up with the notion of a prologue to the choral narrative. With the creation of the actor to tell the story, the reaction of the chorus assumed greater importance, for it served to offer commentatary on the struggles of the narrative's hero. Thespis is also credited with directing the emotional scope of Classical drama to concentrate on the hero's faults, on the obstacles facing the hero, and ultimately on the hero's death—i.e., the elements of tragedy.

Aeschylus, another actor and author of a trilogy of plays entitled the *Oresteia*, further refined the form and content of the Greek tragedy. Among the many improvements attributed to him is the addition of a second and third actor, which allowed for conflict between the characters. Conflict, requiring resolution, provoked a more developed sense of plot, and Aeschylus heightened this by providing a structure with which to organize the narrative episodes. He also introduced the concept of choice, providing the hero with a decision he or she must make, which frequently leads to his or her downfall.

By the fifth century B.C., the form of Greek tragedy had taken on a recurring structure. Most plays began with a prologue, spoken by a single actor in iambic verse, which described the events leading up to the action of the play. This was usually followed by the entrance of the chorus, a body of 15 people who chanted in anapestic meter to introduce the action and to create the desired mood in the audience. This was followed by a series of alternating **episodes** (scenes of action) and **stasima** (lyric songs sung by the chorus). The play was concluded by the **exodos**, during which the chorus continued to chant as the characters departed.

Aside from Aeschylus, there are only two other playwrights of this period from whom we have a substantial amount of work extant. Sophocles (496?–406 B.C.) is thought to have written nearly 125 plays, among them *Oedipus Tyrannus, Antigone*, and *Electra*. His plays deal with men and women whose flaws lead to suffering and destruction, but ultimately result in increased wisdom and divine retribution. Euripides (480?–406 B.C.) is the author of nineteen extant plays, including: *The Trojan Women, Medea*, and *The Bacchae*. Euripides is known for the dramatic realism of his plays, achieved by complex plots, increasingly natural speech, and the combination of good and evil found in all of his characters, be they human or divine.

Greek drama was a seasonal event, performed only at certain times of year during specific festivals. The plays were performed in competition with each other, as part of the festival. All dramatists were required, along with mastering the art of creating tragic trilogies, to perfect at least one comic form. Very few comedies survived, so little is known about the form of Classical Greek Comedy. It is thought that there were three forms of comedy—Old, Middle, and New. The Old Comic form probably employed three actors, contained burlesque, parody, and farce, and was wild and bawdy. Old Comedies always featured music, and frequently made use of fantastical subjects and settings. Old Comedy had a rigid structure similar to that of Classical Tragedy, combining lyrical, prosaic, and choral passages. Aristophanes (450–385 B.C.), as the only Old Comedian whose work survived intact, is considered the father of Greek comedy. His plays include *The Clouds* and *The Birds*.

Middle Comedy, the primary dramatic form between 400 and 338 B.C., was far less obscene than Old Comedy, and led to the much more refined and sophisticated New Comedy. New Comedies were usually comedies of manners designed for an educated leisure class. They involved a number of stock scenes and stock characters and followed a five-act structure. The only New Comedies that survive are those of Menander of Athens (c. 342–c. 292 B.C.), including *The Grouch*.

Greek tragic actors wore large masks that covered their whole faces and made them appear much taller than they actually were. Actors would wear several masks during a performance, to allow them to play a variety of roles. Characters might require a number of different masks to represent the changes that they undergo over the course of the play. The weight and size of the masks contributed to an emphasis on the study of movement, which tended to be slow, graceful, and stately, and to emphasize a number of standard gestures. The costumes for comedy were more colorful and fantastic than those for tragedy, and tended to exaggerate certain parts of the actors' bodies. Comedians, too, wore masks; however, comedic masks portrayed a larger variety of characters than the tragic masks.

THEATER IN CHINA

The first performances in China were recorded about 1500 B.C., during the Shang Dynasty. Dance, music, and ritual were important elements in Chinese life. Temples were associated with performers and records of a raised stage were found by archaeologists.

The Han Dynasty (206 B.C.–A.D. 221) actively encouraged the arts and founded the Imperial Office of Music in 104 B.C., which functioned to organize entertainment and to promote dance and music.

Chinese Shadow Puppets (c. 121 B.C.) were first used to materialize departed gods or souls, but later evolved into a source of entertainment.

Marionettes, puppets moved by string or hand, were created between A.D. 265 and A.D. 420. Many festivals and plays continued to spread through China around A.D. 610.

Emperor Hsuan Tsung established "The Pear Garden," a school for dancers, singers, and various court entertainers that stressed current forms of performance. Storytelling using puppets became a popular dramatic form from A.D. 960–A.D. 1279.

Historians in the 1920s uncovered the oldest surviving Chinese plays, *Chang Hsieh* and *The Doctor of Letters*, which consisted of a prologue and a main story.

Stage direction was practiced in Chinese theaters by the fourteenth century. The stage was usually stripped bare, with a door on either side for exits and entrances and an embroidered decorative wall hanging between the two doors as a backdrop. Both men and women performed in productions, and swords and fans were used as props during performances.

Drama began to emerge from the south. The southern plays tended to be long and formal, usually consisting of 50 or more acts, each of which had its own title. Theater in China was influenced by Western drama early in the twentieth century and gradually became less formal.

MEDIEVAL PERIOD

Medieval theater originally began as a springtime religious observance. It was a communal and public event that drew large audiences to celebrate the teachings of the Old and New Testaments of the Bible. Religious theater was restricted by such elements as the liturgy, church calendar, and ecclesiastical dress.

In England during the Middle Ages, pageant plays known as **cycles** were created using biblical and religious literature. The cycles were performed by a troupe of actors who traveled from town to town in wagons that also served as stages for performances. The double-decker wagon was narrow with two vertical levels that were utilized to demonstrate scenes of heaven and hell. Curtains concealed the wagon's undercarriage and served as the dressing area for the actors.

Morality plays were also performed during this time. They represented the conscience of the Middle Ages. After approximately 200 years, drama moved out of the church because the troupes were too restricted by the church's ruling.

Medieval producers made use of special effects such as trap doors in stages that were movable or fixed. The stages were set against buildings at outdoor festivals, and a stage wagon transported background scenery. This type of stage made special effects easy to perform.

The playwrights in the Medieval period wrote anonymously. Historians document that women never performed in medieval plays for two reasons. First, male-dominated, rigidly hierarchical groups like clergy, craftsmen, and merchants predominated. Secondly, it was believed that boys with trained voices could produce more volume than women.

Medieval audiences consisted of local and neighboring citizens. There was no fee charged to spectators of English cycle plays.

ELIZABETHAN THEATER IN ENGLAND

During the Elizabethan era in England, theater was used for the first time as a commercial enterprise. Philip Henslowe of London was the best-known theatrical manager. The stage became lavish with detailed scenery and colorful costumes. There were two basic types of costumes, contemporary and symbolic. Symbolic costumes were worn to distinguish the important characters from the ordinary people.

Theater companies acquired new plays by request from freelancers and from actor/playwrights. Notable playwrights of the Elizabethan era include Christopher Marlowe (1564–1593), author of a number of plays including *The Jew of Malta* and *Edward II,* and Ben Jonson (1573–1637), satirist, critic, and author of plays ranging from comedy and satire to court masques and tragedy, including *Every Man in His Humour* and *The Devil Is an Ass.* Ben Jonson said of his contemporary William Shakespeare that "He was not of an age but for all time!" It is certainly true that in his more than thirty tragedies, histories, and comedies, Shakespeare created enduring characters and addressed timeless questions that still resonate for us today. It would be impossible in a short space to describe Shakespeare's contribution to poetry, drama, and language.

THEATER IN ITALY

The Romans, borrowing architectural design from the Greeks, built amphitheaters of permanent stone. These theaters were built for a variety of entertainment, such as dancing, acrobatics, and gladiatorial events.

Italy's professional theater evolved from *commedia dell'arte* in the mid-1500s. *Commedia dell'arte* was a popular form of entertainment akin to street theater, designed to appeal to a mass audience. The plays, performed by a number of traveling troupes, were largely improvisational, though their plots were usually limited to the misadventures of a set of stock characters whose actions were commented on by a chorus of clowns or *zannis.* Many of the characters' names, personalities, and costumes are still familiar today—among them Harlequin, Pulcinella, Pantalone, Dottore, and Scaramuccia.

Throughout Europe in the late fifteenth century, audiences were entertained between the acts of larger comedies by short dramatic and musical works. In Italy, these became known as Intermezzi, and became more and more centered around spectacle. Eventually, dialogue was almost entirely phased out in favor of elaborate presentation. These works usually involved music, and as the entr'acte spectacles became longer and more important than the acts themselves, opera was born.

THEATER IN SEVENTEENTH-CENTURY FRANCE

French playwright/actor/director, Jean Baptiste Poquelin (1622–1673), also known as Molière, wrote and acted in *Tartuffe*, *The Misanthrope*, *The Doctor in Spite of Himself*, *The Miser*, and *The Imaginary Invalid*. Molière's comedies weigh follies of humanity against common good sense. Two other famous playwrights at this time were Pierre Corneille (1606–1684) and Jean Racine (1639–1699). Corneille's most successful play was entitled *The Cid*. Racine's most widely performed plays were *Phaedra* and *Iphigenie en Aulide*.

Costumes, hairstyles, and makeup on the French stage mirrored popular fashions on the street or at court. The audience in Parisian theaters varied from valets, soldiers, and pickpockets to nobility, gentlemen, and merchants. Respectable women usually did not attend the theater in the early 1600s. Women who did attend wore masks and sat in loges.

The first proscenium arch stage, which resembled a picture frame, was built in France in 1618 by Teatro Farnese. The proscenium was a wall with one large center opening that divided the theater-goers from the raised stage.

RESTORATION PERIOD

During the Restoration period in England (1642–1660), theater and acting were banned due to political upheavals at the command of Oliver Cromwell. Once theaters were reopened, Charles II (1630–1685) marked the start of the modern proscenium playhouse, and repertory companies flourished. Two official theatrical companies, the King's Company and the Duke's Company, were started at this time.

Popular playwrights of the Restoration period were John Dryden, Richard Steele, William Wycherley, William Congreve, George Farquhar, George Etherege, and Richard Brinsley Sheridan. The term "comedy of manners" describes the majority of the Restoration prose plays. They were witty in dialogue and revolved around sexual intrigue.

CONTEMPORARY THEATER

Many successful playwrights emerged from nineteenth-century Europe. Henrik Ibsen, Johann Wolfgang Goethe, and August Strindberg are a few among many popular writers. These playwrights introduced stage realism and naturalism. English naturalist Charles Darwin and French philosopher Auguste Comte were two major influences on the theater of realism. Contemporary theater emerged from this emphasis on naturalism and realism.

In Russia, Konstantin Stanislavsky (1863–1938) developed an acting technique that came to be called "The Method" on account of its broad impact on the schooling of Western actors. Stanislavsky's approach to actor-training was essentially psychological. Cheryl Crawford, Harold Clurman, Lee Strasberg, and Stella Adler taught acting technique using "**The Method**." In 1931 they formed the Group Theater in America, which consisted of actors and directors who provided actor-training workshops in New York City.

Playwright Eugene O'Neill brought to American drama a powerful insight into human passion and suffering. Other accomplished American playwrights of the twentieth century include Arthur Miller, Tennessee Williams, and Lillian Hellman. Their plays are produced on and off-Broadway. Experimental shows are generally produced in off-off Broadway theaters.

In Britain, the **Fringe theater** was considered equivalent to America's off-off Broadway theater. **Mobile theater** (the Fun Bus) and **avant-garde theater** brought the arts into urban communities and bridged the gap between nations and classes.

There were a number of significant off-off Broadway companies. La Mama theater, for example, provided a showcase for new playwrights. The Circle Repertory Company stressed the development of new plays by its own performing group. The Manhattan Theatre Club opened three theaters to assist playwrights through readings and productions. The New York Shakespeare Festival Public Theatre was founded by Joseph Papp in 1954. Papp's goal was to make theater more accessible. Papp established free summer performances at the Delacorte Theatre in Central Park, New York City.

In 1968, censorship of British theater was abolished. The rock musical *Hair,* which contained nudity and obscenity, was produced in London. Plays with homosexual themes, such as John Osborne's *A Patriot for Me,* were performed. Meanwhile, in the United States during the late 1960s, musicals like *Oh, Calcutta,* which included various scenes involving nudity, and *Che!,* which displayed explicit sexual acts, challenged theater audiences.

DANCE REVIEW
ORIGINS OF DANCE

Archaeologists have studied ancient drawings depicting dancing hunters costumed as animals wearing make-up and masks. Egyptian dance paintings were found that depict religious dancing in funeral processions. War dances, hunting dances, medicine dances, dances for health, and fertility dances were performed as a form of sympathetic magic or medicine. There were dances for death, birth, peace, and courtship.

The emergence of dance was evident in early Greek culture. Plato believed that dance was not solely an exercise for the body, but an art form given to us by the gods so we could please them. The Greeks themselves used dance accompanied by music in the intermezza of a performance event. Dance was a communal activity, enjoyed as entertainment and religious ritual.

For the Romans, dance was a vehicle for spectacle rather than for a classic dramatic presentation, and commonly included acrobatics. As Christian emperors became more powerful, the church became more controlling, and pagan rituals, spectacles, and gladiatorial combats were forbidden.

Dancing was incorporated in Christian services until the twelfth century at which time theologians decided that dancing was distracting and impious. In 1207, the Pope banned the clergy from wearing masks and dancing because theologians felt that these practices might cause the mind to wander from God. Later, music and acting were banned by the church.

FORMS OF DANCE

The first major ballet, entitled *The Ballet Comique de la Reine,* was choreographed by an Italian named Balthasar de Beaujoyeux (formerly Baldassari de Belgiojoso) in 1581. This event was commissioned by Catherine de' Medici in France, who was the daughter of one of the greatest families.

In France, Louis XIV, who was an accomplished dancer himself, and a great champion of ballet in particular, was known as a patron of the arts. His passion for dance favored court ballets. In 1661, he established a school which produced the best and most experienced dance masters. This school was called the Academie Royale de Danse.

The establishment of the five positions of the feet became the foundation of ballet technique. In the first position, legs are turned out away from the hips and heels and knees touch each other. The feet are to be out so as to form a straight line. Similar to first position, the legs remain turned out away from the hips during the second position, but the heels must be approximately 10 to 12 inches apart. During the third position, the heel of each foot is touching the middle of the other foot while one foot is placed directly in front of the other. The legs must be turned out away from the hips. In the fourth position, one foot is in front of the other with about eight inches separating the two feet. In the fifth position, the legs are turned out from the hips, and one foot is directly in front of the other. The heel of the front foot should also be placed at the joint to the toe of the rear foot. Correct weight and body balance, arm control, and attitude are essential in ballet.

Marius Petipa (1822–1910), often referred to as the father of classic ballet, transplanted the glory of the Romantic ballet from France to Russia. This was a turning point at the birth of a new era. Petipa reached success with one five-act ballet entitled *La Fille du Pharaon*. Petipa made Russia the leading country of ballet, and he raised the standard of dance technique with assistance from Swedish dancer Christian Johansson, Italian dancer Enrico Cecchetti, and Russian dancer Lev Ivanov. His other works include *La Bayadère* and *Sleeping Beauty*.

Isadora Duncan (1878–1927) contributed greatly to the creation of Modern Dance. She believed dancing was an expression of one's whole self, including body, mind, and soul. She wanted to be free of the control of ballet and desired to let the body rather than the mind dictate movement. She took off her ballet slippers and danced barefoot, wearing loose-fitting clothing so her body was not restricted. Her works were based on Greek art. Duncan founded schools in Berlin, Paris, and Moscow. In modern dance, there are no established patterns or steps. It requires the dancer to create his or her own, emanating from the natural movement of the body. Other contributors to modern dance were Agnes de Milles, Martha Graham, Ruth St. Denis, and Ted Shawn.

American dancer and choreographer Martha Graham's technique begins with the center of the body and follows contractions and releases of muscles when movement occurs. Ultimately, her technique is based on breath rhythms and is recognized for sharpness and preciseness.

Choreographer Doris Humphrey's movement technique was softer and more lyrical than Graham's. Humphrey's technique was created from natural observations of human movement. She examined rhythms of breath, weight shifts, motion, and successional flow.

The bridge between classical ballet and modern dance was connected under Agnes de Mille's direction. She stressed the understanding that dance is movement, and the body is its instrument. Choreographers worked with time, force, and space. De Mille believed that a personal exploration must be completed to understand and use the body.

Jazz dancing is a controlled style of dancing, though it is creative and allows free body movements. It is characterized by parallel feet, flat-footed steps, undulating torso, body isolation, and syncopated rhythms. Jazz became a popular form of dance in American musicals.

Ballet troupes and opera houses were established in America, among them the New York City Ballet, the Metropolitan Opera, Lincoln Center for the Performing Arts, and the American Ballet Theater. Edward Villella, Jacques d'Amboise, Arthur Mitchell, Diana Adams, Tanaquil Le Clerq, and Maria Tallchief became well-known dancers in New York City. In the 1950s, 18-year-old Darci Kistler became the youngest principal dancer in the City Ballet's history.

In the 1960s, Americans flocked to clubs and dance halls. Ballroom dancing, the foxtrot, the samba, and the salsa became popular. In the 1970s, choreographers added jazz to the most successful American musicals, such as *West Side Story*, *Fiddler on the Roof, 42nd Street, Chicago, A Chorus Line,* and *Evita.* A few famous choreographers and directors were Jerome Robbins, Gower Champion, Bob Fosse, Michael Bennett, and Harold Prince.

A form of dance known as body art became popular in the 1970s, which emerged from the general mood of most Americans, which at the time was irritated and angry. This form of dance was used to demonstrate at political rallies. The artists were costumed or appeared nude and performed in galleries and small performance spaces.

American dancing has gone through many styles. Popular dances of the 1930s were the Peabody and the foxtrot. In the 1940s, they danced the jitterbug. The 1950s brought about the stroll, the mashed potato, and the cha-cha. The salsa, the monkey, and the pony were created in the 1960s. In the 1970s, two new types of dances were born—the hustle and the boogie, which became American favorites. In the 1980s, head banging to heavy metal rock and roll music emerged and faded away. With each new decade, dance styles change and vibrant new forms emerge.

FILM REVIEW
ORIGIN OF FILM

The creation of film was the result of a centuries-old fascination with the control and capture of movement. There is no one moment of history and no one inventor who can be credited with the creation of cinema as we know it today. A series of inventions and ideas, from Plato's shadows on the cave wall to magic lanterns and zoetropes, by means of curiosity, ingenuity, and accident, by the turn of the twentieth century we could reproduce movement. This new invention, which hung somewhere between a science and an art, was to capture the international imagination as a means to entertain, to shock, and increasingly, to earn money.

Around 1889, Thomas Alva Edison and his assistant, W.K.L. Dickinson, combined a number of existing inventions to create the **kinetoscope**, the original motion picture machine. This machine was designed as a cabinet that held revolving spools of film. When a coin was inserted, an electric light was projected on the rear of the cabinet. To view the movie, one would look through a small peephole. The average film ran for one minute and was 50 feet in length. Edison usually filmed action or movement, such as an animal eating or a person dancing.

Edison believed that films were simply a passing fad. Consequently, he did not develop a way to project films on screen. This task was performed by the Lumière brothers, Louis and Auguste. The Lumière brothers developed their own camera, which also served as a developing machine and projector. The Lumières held the first public showing of motion pictures projected on a screen at the Grand Café in Paris. The Lumière brothers helped to develop the form cinema would take.

Edison soon abandoned kinetoscopes to form his own production company to make films for theaters. Edison founded the first motion picture studio, "The Black Maria," in West Orange, New Jersey. In the studio, **vaudeville** entertainers and celebrities performed for the camera. There were several actors who later gained fame in the early days of motion picture, among them Mme. Bertholdi, a contortionist; Annie Oakley; and Colonel William Cody, the original Buffalo Bill.

In 1895, the Lumière brothers produced their first experimental film entitled *L'Arroseur Arrosé*. Previously, the cinema had consisted of mainly newsreel footage, but narrative form quickly entered. The brothers understood the profit to be made from narrative films, so they perfected their experiment. The first two French production houses were established by Charles Pathé and Léon Gaumont. Their competitor was Georges Méliès.

The Lumière brothers wanted to catch nature in the act, but Méliès, who was fascinated with the art of illusion, was considered "the creator of cinematic spectacle." Méliès constructed the first cinema set building that was completely made of glass for daylight shooting purposes.

The first American motion picture theater, established on April 16, 1902, was called "The Electric." Because each show cost a nickel, movie theaters were nicknamed "**nickelodeons**." Meanwhile, in France, Méliès created a film entitled *Trip to the Moon*. In America, Edwin Porter made *The Great Train Robbery*, an early prototype for the classic American Western. As motion pictures prospered, American and French companies regularly employed actors, and more theaters and nickelodeons were built.

Vitagraph, Edison's motion picture company, began producing one-reel films of Shakespearean plays like *Richard III*, *Antony and Cleopatra*, *The Merchant of Venice*, and *Romeo and Juliet*. Edison's determination to exploit the cinema for residuals led to his attempt to force competing filmmakers out of business by bringing lawsuits against them for violation of patents. Several companies, particularly Biograph, managed to survive by inventing cameras that differed from those Edison had patented. In 1908, Edison brought these companies under control by forming the Motion Pictures Patents Company (MPPC), a group of ten firms based primarily in Chicago, New York, and New Jersey. The MPPC never succeeded in eliminating its competition. Many independent companies were formed throughout this period. D.W. Griffith, considered to be Biograph's most important director, formed his own company in 1913. The U.S. government brought a lawsuit against the MPPC in 1912, and in 1915 it was declared a monopoly.

In France, the first Theatre Pathé was built in 1901. It was later rebuilt to hold larger audiences. The progress of French cinema was becoming paralyzed at the time of World War I. France, Germany, and Russia became influenced by realism used in theater. Most Soviet silent films dealt with themes of conflict and revolution.

In the 1920s, America, which did not experience the post–World War I depression as strongly as European countries, became dominant in film production. Particularly in Hollywood, the star system controlled the medium, causing it to become superficial and commercial. After 1912, old nickelodeons were outdated and new theaters were rapidly being built.

German actor/director/writer/set and costume designer Erich von Stroheim brought eroticism, brutality, and cynicism to American cinema after 1920. Stroheim's first films were entitled *Blind Husbands*, *The Devil's Passkey*, and *Foolish Wives*.

THE HOLLYWOOD ERA

After 1910, film companies began moving to a small town outside of Los Angeles, California, known as Hollywood. Some film historians feel that the independent companies moved west to avoid the wrath of the MPPC. In addition, filming in Hollywood had many advantages—the climate permitted year-round shooting, and California provided a great number of locations, from mountains to ocean to desert. By the 1920s, large studios were being built.

The Academy of Motion Picture Arts and Sciences (AMPAS) was founded in 1927 by Louis B. Mayer and other film industry innovators, including Cecil B. DeMille, Douglas Fairbanks, and Mary Pickford. The purpose of the AMPAS was to raise the educational, cultural, and technical standards of American movies. The Academy of Motion Picture Arts and Sciences was pioneered by writers, actors, producers, and directors.

INTRODUCTION OF SOUND IN FILM

Sound was introduced in 1926 with the release of *Don Juan*, a film with an orchestral accompaniment, sound effects, and a series of vaudeville shorts. Warner Brothers, in an attempt to promote the concept of films with sound, released *The Jazz Singer* (1927), a part sound/part silent film that was a huge success. In the same year, Warner Brothers decided that all of its silent films would include musical accompaniment and announced plans to purchase one major theater in every large American city. In 1928, Walt Disney produced *Steamboat Willie*, his first musical cartoon, contributing to the sound film genre and introducing to the world the beloved character, Mickey Mouse. By 1930, most American theaters were wired for sound. Silent films became part of film history by the late 1930s.

INTRODUCTION OF COLOR

During the 1930s, color film became widely used for the first time. Although photographic color had been used in various forms since 1908, only a few films in the 1920s had **Technicolor** sequences, because the process was too expensive to use on a large-scale basis. However, by the mid-1930s, three-strip Technicolor proved to be economically feasible. After the release of the all-color feature-length film, *Becky Sharp,* in 1935, and the release of *The Trail of the Lonesome Pine* in 1936, film studios began using Technicolor extensively.

THE ACADEMY AWARDS

The main function of the AMPAS is the annual presentation of the Academy Awards, or "Oscars," for distinguished film achievement in the previous year. The first film to win an academy award was *Wings* in 1928. *Gone with the Wind* won the most academy awards in a single year in 1939, and featured Oscar winners Vivien Leigh (Best Actress) and Hattie McDaniel (Best Supporting Actress). *Gone with the Wind* also marked the first time a black actor or actress (McDaniel) won an academy award. Other Best Picture winners of the 1930s and 1940s included *Grand Hotel* (1932), *It Happened One Night* (1934), *You Can't Take It with You* (1938), *Mrs. Miniver* (1942), *Casablanca* (1943), *The Lost Weekend* (1945), and *All the King's Men* (1949). Best Actor winners of the 1930s and 1940s included Clark Gable, Spencer Tracy, James Stewart, Bing Crosby, Ray Milland, and Laurence Olivier. Best Actress winners of the 1930s and 1940s included Bette Davis, Katharine Hepburn, Ginger Rogers, Ingrid Bergman, Joan Crawford, and Olivia de Havilland.

TELEVISION, COLOR, AND FILM

Television affected box-office sales. Americans who owned television sets stayed home rather than go to the cinema and spend money. As a result, profits were not being generated. Hollywood fought back by exploiting the technological advantages which film possessed—the vast size of the images and the capacity to produce the images in color. As a result of the competition between television and films, Hollywood made a rapid conversion from black-and-white to color production between 1952 and 1955. In 1947, only 12 percent of American feature films were made in color. By 1954, the figure rose to over 50 percent.

The transition was made possible largely through a 1950 anti-trust decree which disassembled the Technicolor Corporation's monopoly on color cinematography and ordered it to release its basic patents to all producers. When this occurred, new color systems were developed quickly, aided by the war-time development of a new type of color film stock called "integral tripak." By 1952, the Eastman Kodak Corporation had developed the Eastmancolor system. Although the system has since come to be known by the trade names of the studios who pay to use it or the laboratories that process it, it was Kodak Eastmancolor that initiated and maintained the full-color age with dye-coupler printing. By 1975, even the Technicolor Corporation had changed to an Eastman-based process. Ninety-six percent of all American feature films by 1979 were being made in color.

FILM IN THE 1950s AND 1960s

Hollywood's mania for producing films on a large scale in the 1950s damaged the conventional dramatic film. First, the standard length of a feature film rose from 90 minutes to an average of three hours before settling at a more manageable two hours in the mid-1960s. Second, there was a tendency on behalf of the studios to package every A-class film as a dazzling, big-budget spectacle, whether or not this format suited the material of the film. From 1955 to 1965, most traditional American genres experienced an inflation of production values that destroyed their original forms and caused them to be recreated into new ones. These genres included **musicals**, **comedies**, **Westerns**, **science fiction**, **gangster** and **anti-communist** films.

The musical genre underwent a period of great change in the 1950s and 1960s. Hollywood abandoned original scripts in favor of successful stage plays. This tendency peaked with the release in 1965 of *The Sound of Music*, which grossed more money than any other film had before. Comedy suffered in the early 1950s due to a focus on production values rather than verbal or visual humor. By the 1960s, the genre shifted to big-budget sex comedies concerned with strategies of seduction (*Sex and the Single Girl*, 1965, *A Guide for the Married Man*, 1967), which reflected the sexual revolution of the decade, and to corporate comedies, which dealt with business fraud and government deceit in a humorous light. American comedy became increasingly sophisticated in the 1950s and 1960s.

The Western experienced major changes in attitude and theme in correspondence to changes in American society. The heroic, idealized epic westerns of John Ford and his imitators remained popular in the 1950s but were gradually replaced by the adult Western which concentrated on the psychological and moral conflicts of the hero in society. Furthermore, by the 1960s, the portrayal of the Native American changed from one of hostile savages to one of intelligent, gentle people who were murdered by the U.S. military.

Science fiction emerged as a distinct genre in the 1950s. The common theme in the science fiction films of the 1950s was some form of a world-threatening crisis, usually produced by nuclear war or alien invasion. Another popular theme was the arrival of a dangerous creature from another planet, as in *The Thing* (1951).

In the 1960s, low-budget monster films were replaced by medium-to-high budget science fiction films, including *The Time Machine* (1960) and *Planet of the Apes* (1967). Serious filmmakers, including Stanley Kubrick

(*2001: A Space Odyssey*, 1965), became interested in science fiction.

The gangster film re-emerged in the late 1940s after being replaced by domestic espionage films during the war. Two types of gangster films appeared in the 1950s—the caper film and the anti-communist film. The caper film concentrated on a plan to pull off a big heist, which could be either serious or humorous. The first caper film was John Huston's *The Asphalt Jungle* in 1950. The anti-communist film was a centered, original form that appeared only in the early 1950s. In these films, the criminal figure was a Communist spy and the syndicate was the international Communist conspiracy. However, the traditional concept of the gangster film was preserved. Although the anti-communist films appeared only in the 1950s, the theme of these movies can be seen in the James Bond espionage thrillers and imitations in the 1960s. These films replaced the gangster genre in the early 1960s by presenting criminal conspiracy on a worldwide scale and offering violence on the part of both the conspirators and the hero.

Academy Award-winning films in the 1950s and 1960s included *All About Eve* (1950), *From Here to Eternity* (1953), *The Bridge on the River Kwai* (1957), *Ben-Hur* (1959), *West Side Story* (1961), *My Fair Lady* (1965), *The Sound of Music* (1965), and *Midnight Cowboy* (1969). Best Actor winners in the 1950s and 1960s included Gary Cooper, William Holden, Yul Brynner, Charlton Heston, Rod Steiger, and John Wayne. Best Actress winners included Audrey Hepburn, Grace Kelly, Joanne Woodward, Susan Hayward, Anne Bancroft, Elizabeth Taylor, and Sophia Loren. In 1963, Sidney Poitier won an academy award for Best Actor for his performance in *Lilies of the Field*. Nineteen sixty-eight marked the occurrence of the first tie in the Best Actress category. Both Katharine Hepburn, for her performance in *The Lion in Winter*, and Barbra Streisand, for her performance in *Funny Girl*, shared the Oscar.

FILMS IN THE 1970s AND 1980s

The enormous success in 1970 of two conventional films, *Love Story* and *Airport*, restored Hollywood's faith in the big-budget feature. Production costs of American films were the largest in the industry's history. Between 1972 and 1977, the average production budget for a film increased by 178 percent. By the end of 1979, average production costs had nearly doubled the 1977 figure to reach the sum of $7.5 million per feature film. Profits were based on the film's success, so the financial risks of production multiplied. Consequently, fewer and fewer films were made every year, and there was a steady increase in the amount spent on advertising campaigns to ensure the success of the film. Often, the price for advertising would cost twice as much as the production cost of the film itself.

With fewer than 70 major films being produced each year, compared to 538 in 1937, there were serious questions about the creative spirit of the American cinema. However, the 1970s could be considered a renaissance of creative talent, as a result of many young directors who studied at American film schools, compared to the directors of the 1960s who were trained in television. Some of the directors of this renaissance were Francis Ford Coppola, George Lucas, Martin Scorsese, Steven Spielberg, and Brian DePalma. Coppola's epic of organized crime in the United States, *The Godfather Parts I, II,* and *III,* is one of the most significant American cinematic achievements of the 1970s. Lucas's *Star Wars* and Spielberg's *Jaws* (1975) and *Close Encounters of the Third Kind* (1977) were historically important for their use of dazzling special effects. DePalma directed some of the most stylish horror films of the 1970s, including *Carrie* (1976), while Scorsese directed *Taxi Driver* (1976). Not only were these films critically acclaimed, but they were financially successful. *Star Wars* grossed over $200 million, *Jaws* over $130 million, and *Close Encounters of the Third Kind*, over $83 million.

Some of the academy award winners for Best Picture in the 1970s were *The Godfather* (1972), *The Godfather II* (1974), *One Flew over the Cuckoo's Nest* (1975), *The Deer Hunter* (1978), and *Kramer vs. Kramer* (1979). Some of the Best Actress winners were Jane Fonda, Ellen Burstyn, Faye Dunaway, Diane Keaton, and Sally Field. Some of the Best Actor winners were Gene Hackman, Jack Lemmon, Jack Nicholson, Richard Dreyfuss, and Jon Voight. Two Best Actor winners, George C. Scott for his role in *Patton* in 1970, and Marlon Brando for his role in *The Godfather* in 1972, made history by refusing their awards.

FILM IN THE PRESENT

As in the 1950s with the invention of television, in the 1980s Hollywood was again faced with technological advances that would affect box office sales. **Cable television** services and **video cassette recorders** (VCRs) brought theatrical movies into the home for a monthly subscription or rental fee, transforming the entire system of film distribution. However, the speculation that movie theaters would become obsolete and that all films would one day be distributed through some form of home video technology remains a theory in the 1990s. People are still going to the movies in theaters and paying rising prices for tickets to experience the spectacle of the big screen. Directors like Allison Anders, Spike Lee, and Jim Jarmusch have produced innovative work and introduced new film techniques in the 1980s and 1990s.

Some of the Best Picture winners for the 1980s and 1990s were *Ordinary People* (1980), *Gandhi* (1982), *Amadeus* (1984), *Platoon* (1986), *Rainman* (1988), *Schindler's List* (1993), *Forrest Gump* (1994), and *Braveheart* (1995). Some of the Best Actor winners included Robert DeNiro, William Hurt, Michael Douglas, Paul Newman, Dustin Hoffman, Sir Anthony Hopkins, Tom Hanks, and Nicholas Cage. Some of the Best Actress winners included Sissy Spacek, Meryl Streep, Shirley MacLaine, Cher, Jody Foster, Jessica Tandy, Emma Thompson, Jessica Lange, and Susan Sarandon.

☞ Drill: Performing Arts

1. American choreographer Martha Graham often used sets designed by which of the following sculptors?

    (A) Henry Moore   (C) David Smith

    (B) Isamu Noguchi   (D) Louise Nevelson

2. Which of the following contemporary filmmakers sees a connection between Marxist politics and gender relations?

    (A) Werner Herzog   (C) John Ford

    (B) Woody Allen   (D) Lina Wertmuller

3. Igor Stravinsky's ballet *Petrouchka* drew heavily on which of the following influences?

    (A) Renaissance dance music

    (B) Russian folklore and tradition

    (C) Medieval mystery plays

    (D) Eighteenth-century Italian opera

4. Which of the following films was the work of the visionary German director Werner Herzog?

    (A) *Love and Anarchy*   (C) *Aguirre, The Wrath of God*

    (B) *Reds*   (D) *Love and Death*

5. Which film tells the story of a totalitarian society in which books are banned and burned?

(A) *A Clockwork Orange*   (C) *Fahrenheit-451*

(B) *1984*   (D) *Brazil*

6. Which of the following individuals would be out of place in the musical and theatrical circles of 1920s Paris?

(A) Stravinsky   (C) Nijinsky

(B) Satie   (D) Shostakovich

7. John Ford's 1939 epic Western *Stagecoach* featured which actor as the classic American male?

(A) Humphrey Bogart   (C) John Wayne

(B) Gary Cooper   (D) David Wayne

8. Which of the following directors is not associated with the French "New Wave" cinema?

(A) Abel Gance   (C) Alain Resnais

(B) Louis Malle   (D) Jean-Luc Godard

9. Composer Stephen Sondheim scored all of the following musicals except

(A) *Company.*

(B) *A Little Night Music.*

(C) *Sunday in the Park with George.*

(D) *Pippin.*

10. Which Wagner opera tells the story of a legendary, doomed love affair?

(A) *Parsifal*   (C) *Siegfried*

(B) *Tristan and Isolde*   (D) *Die Meistersinger*

11. Which of the following operas tells the tragic story of a young Japanese bride?

(A) *La Bohème*   (C) *Aida*

(B) *Tosca*   (D) *Madama Butterfly*

12. Which of the following best describes *opera buffa*?

   (A) Tragedy   (C) Melodrama

   (B) Serial   (D) Comedy

13. Which film established James Dean as an icon of American youth?

   (A) *East of Eden*   (C) *The Wild One*

   (B) *Rebel Without a Cause* (D) *Giant*

14. The popular Broadway show *West Side Story* was loosely based on the play

   (A) *Measure for Measure.*

   (B) *The Taming of the Shrew.*

   (C) *A Midsummer Night's Dream.*

   (D) *Romeo and Juliet.*

15. The controversial practice developed during the 1960s in which artists confronted or interacted with spectators, or used their own bodies as an artistic medium is called

   (A) pop art.   (C) video sculpture.

   (B) minimalism.   (D) performance art.

16. Which modern choreographer, based in New York City and featuring a company of young black, white, and Asian dancers, used dance as a means to explore and interpret the American black experience?

   (A) Paul Taylor   (C) Merce Cunningham

   (B) Alwin Nikolais   (D) Alvin Ailey

PERFORMING ARTS REVIEW

ANSWER KEY

Drill: Performing Arts

1.	(B)	5.	(C)	9.	(D)	13.	(B)
2.	(D)	6.	(D)	10.	(B)	14.	(D)
3.	(B)	7.	(C)	11.	(D)	15.	(D)
4.	(C)	8.	(A)	12.	(D)	16.	(D)

DETAILED EXPLANATIONS OF ANSWERS

Drill: Performing Arts

1. **(B)** Japanese-American sculptor Isamu Noguchi (1904–1988) collaborated with Martha Graham on such abstract ballet sets as *Frointeir* in 1935. Neither Henry Moore (A), David Smith (C), nor Louise Nevelson (D) are known for their theater designs.

2. **(D)** Italian director Lina Wertmuller, a student of Federico Fellini, often analyzes sex in terms of Marxist politics in works such as *Love and Anarchy* (1973) and *Swept Away* (1974). Werner Herzog (A) is the proponent of German visionary cinema, while Woody Allen (B) films modern urban comedies and dramas. John Ford (C) was an American director who often made westerns and adventure films.

3. **(B)** Stravinsky's *Petrouchka*, produced by Diaghilev's Ballet Russe in 1911 in Paris, draws its narrative from the story of a Russian country fair at which Petrouchka is one of the three dolls brought to life by a magician. Although Stravinsky was an eclectic composer with a strong religious strain, he drew neither from Renaissance dance (A), medieval mystery (C), nor Italian opera (D).

4. **(C)** Herzog's *Aguirre, The Wrath of God* (1972) tells the heavily symbolic tale of an obsessive Spanish conquistador's journey into the Amazonian jungle to find the mystical city El Dorado. *Love and Anarchy* (A) is a political film by the Italian Lina Wertmuller, while *Love and Death* (D) is a Woody Allen spoof of Tolstoy's novels. *Reds* (B) is Warren Beatty's film about the Russian Revolution.

5. **(C)** Francois Truffaut's 1966 film *Fahrenheit-451* was adapted from the Ray Bradbury novel, in which a repressive future world employs firemen not to stop fires, but to burn books. *A Clockwork Orange* (A) is Stanley Kubrick's version of Anthony Burgess's book set in an anarchistic future England, while *1984* (B) was based on George Orwell's prophetic novel of the same name. *Brazil* (D), by director Terry Gilliam, is a futuristic fantasy with a heavy debt to Orwell.

6. **(D)** Dmitri Shostakovich (1906–1975) was the Russian composer whose mature career coincided with the Stalinist regime in the Soviet

Union, and whose works were often circumscribed by the Soviet party line. He was never a member of the musical/theatrical avant garde in 1920s Paris, where composer Igor Stravinsky (A) and dancer Vaslav Nijinsky (C) were all associated with the *Ballet Russe*. Eric Satie (B) was the irreverent leader of the *Les Six*.

7.   **(C)**   John Wayne starred as the Ringo Kid in John Ford's *Stagecoach*, the 1939 film shot in Monument Valley which featured spectacular scenery as a major element in the action, and which set the tone for decades of Westerns to come. Humphrey Bogart (A) created an image of the cynical, laconic American male in such films as *The Treasure of the Sierra Madre*, while Gary Cooper (B) developed a similar persona in *High Noon*. David Wayne (D) portrayed more intellectualized heroes.

8.   **(A)**   Abel Gance (1889–1981) was the French film director of the 1920s, whose masterpiece was *Napoleon* (1927), a grand, sweeping epic which used such devices as a triple screen and early color to mythologize the French dictator. All of the other directors listed were members of the generation which reached maturity in post World War II France, and whose films explored new levels of social, political, and psychological complexity.

9.   **(D)**   *Pippin*, the fictionalized story of the youngest son of Charlemagne, was composed by the young American Stephen Schwarz. All of the other musicals were hits written by Stephen Sondheim.

10.   **(B)**   Wagner's 1865 opera *Tristan and Isolde*, his most fully developed treatment of romantic love and passion, is drawn from a medieval legend of Celtic origin, and tells the story of two people fated to die because of their love. *Parsifal* (A) is Wagner's version of the Holy Grail legend, *Siegfried* (C) is a section of Wagner's enormous Ring cycle, and *Die Meistersinger* (D) tells of a medieval German guild of singers.

11.   **(D)**   Giacomo Puccini (1858–1924) wrote *Madama Butterfly* in 1904; in it he dramatized the tale of a young Japanese bride first wooed and then abandoned by an American naval lieutenant. *La Bohème* (A) is Puccini's opera about a colony of poor artists, and *Tosca* (B), also by Puccini, is about a nineteenth-century singer in Rome. *Aida* (C) is Verdi's lavish opera about an African princess in Egypt.

12.   **(D)**   *Opera buffa* was the Italian comic opera of the early eighteenth century which, with its emphasis on humor, farcical plots, frivolity,

and catch musical numbers, closely parallels modern musical comedy. "Tragedy" (A) and "melodrama" (C) would best describe Wagner's Romantic works, while "serial" (B) would define a work such as Alban Berg's 12-tone *Wozzeck*.

13. **(B)** Nicholas Ray's 1955 film *Rebel Without a Cause* cast the young James Dean as a searching, alienated youth who rejects both the hypocritical values of his middle-class parents and the competitive violence of his peers. *East of Eden* (A) and *Giant* (D) were films which reinforced Dean's star status, while *The Wild One* (C) featured Marlon Brando as a cynical, rebellious youth.

14. **(D)** *Romeo and Juliet* provided the source for *West Side Story*, which was written by Jerome Robbins, Arthur Laurents, Leonard Bernstein, and Stephen Sondheim, and which opened on Broadway in 1957. Shakespeare's story of the doomed young lovers from feuding families was updated as the tale of New York City teenagers Tony and Maria.

15. **(D)** Performance art is a broad ranging term which includes environments and happenings, staged by such artists as Jim Dine, Claes Oldenberg, and Yves Klein in order to bombard the spectator with sensations and experiences which were extreme, bewildering, and often, subversive, of the social status quo. Pop art (A) was a predecessor of performance; minimalism (B) is a non-objective style; and video sculpture (C) exploits the kinetic imagery of television sets.

16. **(D)** Black choreographer Alvin Ailey (1931–1989) formed his own dance company in 1958, and drew a whole new kind of audience to modern dance with works such as *Revelations*, which used Negro spiritual music or blues and jazz to express the experience of the American black. Each of the other figures listed is also a prominent contemporary choreographer.

CHAPTER 4
MATHEMATICS REVIEW

Chapter 4

MATHEMATICS REVIEW

The following Mathematics Review is divided into eight sections, as follows:

By thoroughly studying this course review, you will be well-prepared for the material on the CLEP General Examination in Mathematics.

I. DESCRIPTION OF THE CLEP GENERAL EXAM IN COLLEGE MATHEMATICS

In the CLEP General Examination in College Mathematics there are approximately 65 multiple-choice questions, each with five possible answer choices, to be answered in two separately timed 45-minute sections.

The approximate breakdown of topics is as follows:

Sets	10%
Logic	10%
Real Number Systems	30%
Functions and their Graphs	20%
Probability and Statistics	15%
Miscellaneous Topics	15%

The questions are calculator-independent. However, the use of a scientific calculator (nongraphing, nonprogrammable) is permitted on the test. The question format for all questions is multiple-choice with special directions given for Quantitative Comparison type questions and Data Interpretation type questions.

TYPES OF QUESTIONS AND EXAMPLES

QUANTITATIVE COMPARISONS

This type of question will require you to compare two quantities in Column A and Column B and to choose your answers from four choices, (A), (B), (C), and (D). See examples which follow.

DIRECTIONS: The following question consists of two quantities, one in Column A and the other in Column B. Compare the two quantities and choose the best answer below:

(A)   if the quantity in Column A is greater

(B)   if the quantity in Column B is greater

(C)   if the two quantities are equal

(D)   if the relationship cannot be determined from the information given

● **EXAMPLE**

Column A	Column B
$-25 + 3 \times 7$	$-|5-9|$

The correct answer choice is (C) because both quantities are equal. Using the order of operations in arithmetic and algebra, $-25 + 3 \times 7$ is evaluated by multiplying 3 times 7 first, then adding -25. The result is -4. Recalling that the vertical lines around the $5 - 9$ represent the absolute value (positive) of $5 - 9$, we would take the positive value of -4, which is $+4$, but then the negative in front of the absolute value sign makes the answer -4 again. Therefore, the number in Column A and the number in Column B are equal to each other.

DATA INTERPRETATION

This type of question will ask you to take information presented in the form of tables, charts, graphs, circle/pie graphs, line graphs, and pictographs. The questions will present the table or graph and then have a series of related questions following the graphic information. The questions can come either before or after the table or chart.

● **EXAMPLE**

1. Using the information in the bar charts on the following page, find the total number of women over 40 years of age who perform in both movies and television?

    (A) 68%   (B) 17%   (C) 32%   (D) 1%

    The correct answer is (B), 17%. Looking at the graphs we see that 8% of women over 40 are given parts in movies and 9% of women over 40 are given parts in television. Adding 8% to 9% gives us a total of 17%.

MOVIES

TELEVISION

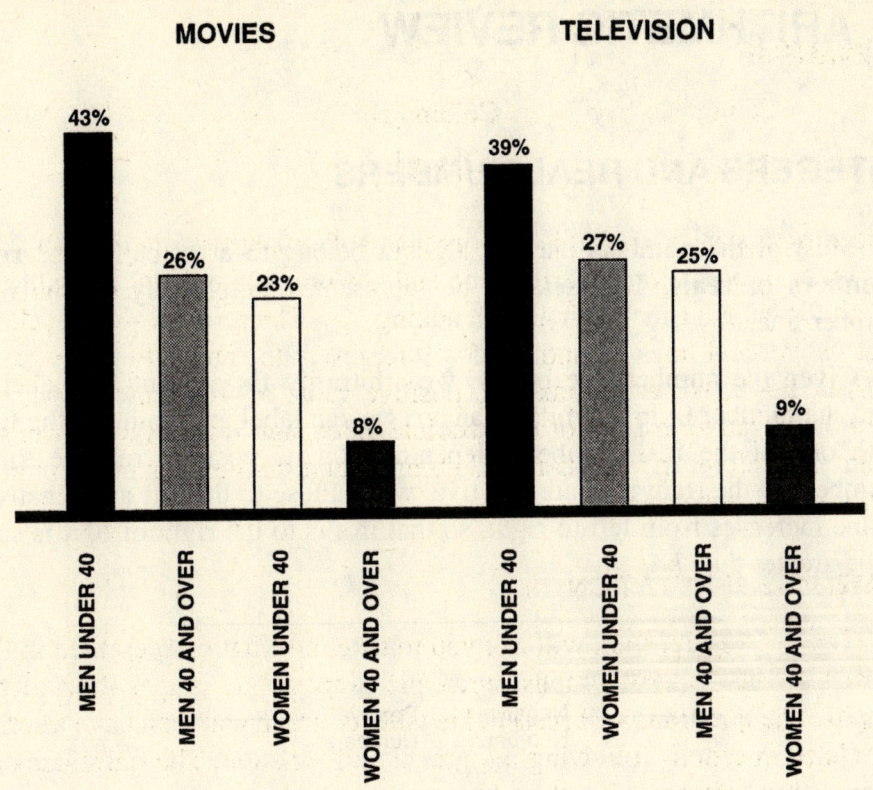

II. ARITHMETIC REVIEW

INTEGERS AND REAL NUMBERS

Most of the numbers used in algebra belong to a set called the **real numbers** or **reals**. This set can be represented graphically by the real number line.

Given the number line below, we arbitrarily fix a point and label it with the number 0. In a similar manner, we can label any point on the line with one of the real numbers, depending on its position relative to 0. Numbers to the right of 0 are positive, while those to the left are negative. Value increases from left to right, so that if a is to the right of b, it is said to be greater than b.

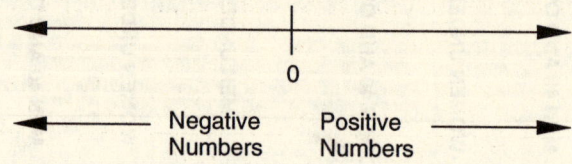

If we now divide the number line into equal segments, we can label the points on this line with real numbers. For example, the point 2 lengths to the left of 0 is -2, while the point 3 lengths to the right of 0 is $+3$ (the $+$ sign is usually assumed, so $+3$ is written simply as 3). The number line now looks like this:

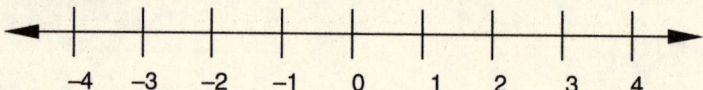

These boundary points represent the subset of the reals known as the **integers**. The set of integers is made up of both the positive and negative whole numbers:

$$\{\ldots, -4, -3, -2, -1, 0, 1, 2, 3, 4, \ldots\}.$$

Some subsets of integers are:

Natural Numbers or Positive Integers—the set of integers starting with 1 and increasing:

$$N = \{1, 2, 3, 4, \ldots\}.$$

Whole Numbers—the set of integers starting with 0 and increasing:

$$W = \{0, 1, 2, 3, \ldots\}.$$

Negative Integers—the set of integers starting with – 1 and decreasing:

$$Z = \{-1, -2, -3, \ldots\}.$$

Even Integers—the set of integers divisible by 2:

$$\{\ldots, -4, -2, 0, 2, 4, 6, \ldots\}.$$

Odd Integers—the set of integers not divisible by 2:

$$\{\ldots, -3, -1, 1, 3, 5, 7, \ldots\}.$$

Consecutive Integers—the set of integers that differ by 1:

$$\{n, n+1, n+2, \ldots\} \ (n = \text{an integer}).$$

Prime Numbers—the set of positive integers greater than 1 that are divisible only by 1 and themselves:

$$\{2, 3, 5, 7, 11, \ldots\}.$$

Composite—the set of integers, other than 0 and ± 1, which are not prime.

PROBLEM

Classify each of the following numbers into as many different sets as possible. Example: real, integer …

(1) 0   (3) $\sqrt{6}$ (5) $\dfrac{2}{3}$ (7) 11

(2) 9   (4) $\dfrac{1}{2}$ (6) 1.5

SOLUTION

(1) 0 is a real number, an integer, and a whole number.

(2) 9 is a real number, an odd number, and a natural number.

(3) $\sqrt{6}$ is a real number.

(4) $\dfrac{1}{2}$ is a real number.

(5) $\dfrac{2}{3}$ is a real number.

(6) 1.5 is a real number and a decimal.

(7) 11 is a prime number, an odd number, a real number, and a natural number.

ABSOLUTE VALUE

The **absolute value** of a number is represented by two vertical lines around the number, and is equal to the given number, regardless of sign.

The absolute value of a real number A is defined as follows:

$$|A| = \begin{cases} A \text{ if } A \geq 0 \\ -A \text{ if } A < 0 \end{cases}$$

● **EXAMPLE**

$$|5| = 5, |-8| = -(-8) = 8$$

Absolute values follow the given rules:

(A) $\quad |-A| = |A|$

(B) $\quad |A| \geq 0$, equality holding only if $A = 0$

(C) $\quad \left|\dfrac{A}{B}\right| = \dfrac{|A|}{|B|}, B \neq 0$

(D) $\quad |AB| = |A| \times |B|$

(E) $\quad |A|^2 = A^2$

PROBLEM

Calculate the value of each of the following expressions:

(1) $\quad ||2 - 5| + 6 - 14|$

(2) $\quad |-5| \times |4| + \dfrac{|-12|}{4}$

SOLUTION

Before solving this problem, one must remember the order of operations: parenthesis, multiplication and division, addition and subtraction.

(1) $\quad ||-3| + 6 - 14| = |3 + 6 - 14| = |9 - 14| = |-5| = 5$

(2) $\quad (5 \times 4) + \dfrac{12}{4} = 20 + 3 = 23$

POSITIVE AND NEGATIVE NUMBERS

A) **To add two numbers with like signs,** add their absolute values and write the sum with the common sign. So,

$$6 + 2 = 8, (-6) + (-2) = -8$$

B) **To add two numbers with unlike signs,** find the difference between their absolute values, and write the result with the sign of the number with the greater absolute value. So,

$$(-4) + 6 = 2, 15 + (-19) = -4$$

C) **To subtract a number *b* from another number *a*,** change the sign of *b* and add to *a*. Examples:

$$10 - (3) = 10 + (-3) = 7 \qquad\qquad (1)$$

$$2 - (-6) = 2 + 6 = 8 \qquad\qquad (2)$$

$$(-5) - (-2) = -5 + 2 = -3 \qquad\qquad (3)$$

D) **To multiply (or divide) two numbers having like signs**, multiply (or divide) their absolute values and write the result with a positive sign. Examples:

$$(5)(3) = 15 \qquad\qquad (1)$$

$$(-6) \div (-3) = 2 \qquad\qquad (2)$$

E) **To multiply (or divide) two numbers having unlike signs,** multiply (or divide) their absolute values and write the result with a negative sign. Examples:

$$(-2)(8) = -16 \qquad\qquad (1)$$

$$9 \div (-3) = -3 \qquad\qquad (2)$$

According to the law of signs for real numbers, the square of a positive or negative number is always positive. This means that it is impossible to take the square root of a negative number in the real number system.

PROBLEM

Calculate the value of each of the following expressions:

(1) $||2 - 5| + 6 - 14|$ (2) $|-8| \times 2 + \dfrac{|-12|}{4}$

SOLUTION

Before solving this problem, one must use the rules for the **order of operations.** Always work within the parentheses or with absolute values first while keeping in mind that multiplication and division are carried out before addition and subtraction.

$$(1) \quad ||-3|+6-14| = |3+6-14|$$
$$= |9-14|$$
$$= |-5|$$
$$= 5$$

$$(2) \quad (8 \times 2) + \frac{12}{4} = 16 + 3$$
$$= 19$$

ORDER OF OPERATIONS

To simplify an expression containing parentheses, multiplication, powers, addition, etc., use the rules for the **order of operations**, as follows:

1. parentheses or absolute value

2. powers

3. multiplication or division

4. addition or subtraction

PROBLEM

Calculate the value of each of the following expressions:

(1) $||2-5|+6-14|$

(2) $|-5| \times |4| + \dfrac{|-12|}{4}$

SOLUTION

$$(1) \quad ||-3|+6-14| = |3+6-14|$$
$$= |9-14|$$
$$= |-5|$$
$$= 5$$

(2) $(5 \times 4) + \dfrac{12}{4} = 20 + 3$

$$= 23$$

ODD AND EVEN NUMBERS

When dealing with odd and even numbers keep in mind the following:

Adding:

even + even = even

odd + odd = even

even + odd = odd

Multiplying:

even × even = even

even × odd = even

odd × odd = odd

☞ Drill: Integers and Real Numbers

Addition

1. Simplify $4 + (-7) + 2 + (-5)$.

   (A) -6 (B) -4 (C) 0 (D) 6

2. Simplify $144 + (-317) + 213$.

   (A) -357 (B) -40 (C) 40 (D) 357

Subtraction

3. Simplify $319 - 428$.

   (A) -111 (B) -109 (C) -99 (D) 109

4. Simplify $91,203 - 37,904 + 1,073$.

   (A) $54,372$ (B) $64,701$ (C) $128,034$ (D) $129,107$

Multiplication

5. Simplify $(-3) \times (-18) \times (-1)$.

    (A) -108 (B) -54 (C) -48 (D) 48

6. Simplify $|-42| \times |-7|$.

    (A) -294 (B) -49 (C) -35 (D) 294

Division

7. Simplify $(-24) \div 8$.

    (A) -4 (B) -3 (C) -2 (D) 3

8. Simplify $(-180) \div (-12)$.

    (A) -30 (B) -15 (C) 1.5 (D) 15

Order of Operations

9. Simplify $\dfrac{4+8\times 2}{5-1}$.

    (A) 4 (B) 5 (C) 6 (D) 8

10. $96 \div 3 \div 4 \div 2 =$

    (A) 65 (B) 64 (C) 16 (D) 4

11. $3 + 4 \times 2 - 6 \div 3 =$

    (A) -1 (B) $\dfrac{2}{3}$ (C) $\dfrac{8}{3}$ (D) 9

12. $[(4+8) \times 3] \div 9 =$

    (A) 4 (B) 8 (C) 12 (D) 24

13. $18 + 3 \times 4 \div 3 =$

    (A) 3 (B) 5 (C) 10 (D) 22

FRACTIONS

The fraction, *a/b*, where the **numerator** is *a* and the **denominator** is *b*, implies that *a* is being divided by *b*. The denominator of a fraction can never be zero since a number divided by zero is not defined. If the numerator is greater than the denominator, the fraction is called an **improper fraction**. A **mixed number** is the sum of a whole number and a fraction, i.e.,

$$4\frac{3}{8} = 4 + \frac{3}{8}.$$

OPERATIONS WITH FRACTIONS

A) **To change a mixed number to an improper fraction**, simply multiply the whole number by the denominator of the fraction and add the numerator. This product becomes the numerator of the result and the denominator remains the same, e.g.,

$$5\frac{2}{3} = \frac{(5 \times 3) + 2}{3} = \frac{15 + 2}{3} = \frac{17}{3}$$

To change an improper fraction to a mixed number, simply divide the numerator by the denominator. The remainder becomes the numerator of the fractional part of the mixed number, and the denominator remains the same, e.g.,

$$\frac{35}{4} = 35 \div 4 = 8\frac{3}{4}$$

To check your work, change your result back to an improper fraction to see if it matches the original fraction.

B) **To find the sum of fractions having a common denominator**, simply add together the numerators of the given fractions and put this sum over the common denominator.

$$\frac{11}{3} + \frac{5}{3} = \frac{11 + 5}{3} = \frac{16}{3}$$

Similarly for subtraction,

$$\frac{11}{3} - \frac{5}{3} = \frac{11 - 5}{3} = \frac{6}{3} = 2$$

C) **To find the sum of two fractions having different denominators**, it is necessary to find the **lowest common denominator** (**LCD**) of the different denominators using a process called **factoring**.

To **factor** a number means to find numbers that when multiplied together have a product equal to the original number. These numbers are then said to be **factors** of the original number; e.g., the factors of 6 are:

(1) 1 and 6 since $1 \times 6 = 6$.

(2) 2 and 3 since $2 \times 3 = 6$.

Every number is the product of itself and 1. A **prime factor** is a number that does not have any factors besides itself and 1. This is important when finding the LCD of two fractions having different denominators.

To find the LCD of $\dfrac{11}{6}$ and $\dfrac{5}{16}$, we must first find the prime factors of each of the two denominators.

$6 = 2 \times 3$

$16 = 2 \times 2 \times 2 \times 2$

$LCD = 2 \times 2 \times 2 \times 2 \times 3 = 48$

Note that we do not need to repeat the 2 that appears in both the factors of 6 and 16.

Once we have determined the LCD of the denominators, each of the fractions must be converted into equivalent fractions having the LCD as a denominator.

Rewrite $\dfrac{11}{6}$ and $\dfrac{5}{16}$ to have 48 as their denominators.

$6 \times ? = 48 \qquad\qquad\qquad 16 \times ? = 48$

$6 \times 8 = 48 \qquad\qquad\qquad 16 \times 3 = 48$

If the numerator and denominator of each fraction is multiplied (or divided) by the same number, the value of the fraction will not change. This is because a fraction b/b, b being any number, is equal to the multiplicative identity, 1.

Therefore,

$$\frac{11}{6} \times \frac{8}{8} = \frac{88}{48}, \; \frac{5}{16} \times \frac{3}{3} = \frac{15}{48}$$

We may now find

$$\frac{11}{6} + \frac{5}{16} = \frac{88}{48} + \frac{15}{48} = \frac{103}{48}$$

Similarly for subtraction,

$$\frac{11}{6} - \frac{5}{16} = \frac{88}{48} - \frac{15}{48} = \frac{73}{48}$$

D) **To find the product of two or more fractions,** simply multiply the numerators of the given fractions to find the numerator of the product and multiply the denominators of the given fractions to find the denominator of the product, e.g.,

$$\frac{2}{3} \times \frac{1}{5} \times \frac{4}{7} = \frac{2 \times 1 \times 4}{3 \times 5 \times 7} = \frac{8}{105}$$

E) **To find the quotient of two fractions,** simply invert (or flip-over) the divisor and multiply, e.g.,

$$\frac{8}{9} \div \frac{1}{3} = \frac{8}{9} \times \frac{3}{1} = \frac{24}{9} = \frac{8}{3}$$

F) **To simplify a fraction** is to convert it into a form in which the numerator and denominator have no common factor other than 1, e.g.,

$$\frac{12}{18} = \frac{12 \div 6}{18 \div 6} = \frac{2}{3}$$

G) A **complex fraction** is a fraction whose numerator and/or denominator is made up of fractions. To simplify the fraction, find the LCD of all the fractions. Multiply both the numerator and denominator by this number and simplify.

PROBLEM

If $a = 4$ and $b = 7$, find the value of $\dfrac{a + \frac{a}{b}}{a - \frac{a}{b}}$.

SOLUTION

By substitution,

$$\frac{a + \frac{a}{b}}{a - \frac{a}{b}} = \frac{4 + \frac{4}{7}}{4 - \frac{4}{7}}$$

In order to combine the terms, we must find the LCD of 1 and 7. Since both are prime factors, the LCD = $1 \times 7 = 7$.

Multiplying both the numerator and denominator by 7, we get

$$\frac{7\left(4+\frac{4}{7}\right)}{7\left(4-\frac{4}{7}\right)} = \frac{28+4}{28-4} = \frac{32}{24}$$

By dividing both the numerator and denominator by 8, $\frac{32}{24}$ can be reduced to $\frac{4}{3}$.

☞ Drill: Fractions

Changing an Improper Fraction to a Mixed Number

> **DIRECTIONS**: Write each improper fraction as a mixed number in simplest form.

1. $\frac{50}{4}$

   (A) $10\frac{1}{4}$ (B) $11\frac{1}{2}$ (C) $12\frac{1}{4}$ (D) $12\frac{1}{2}$

2. $\frac{17}{5}$

   (A) $3\frac{2}{5}$ (B) $3\frac{3}{5}$ (C) $3\frac{4}{5}$ (D) $4\frac{1}{5}$

3. $\frac{42}{3}$

   (A) $10\frac{2}{3}$ (B) 12 (C) $13\frac{1}{3}$ (D) 14

Changing a Mixed Number to an Improper Fraction

DIRECTIONS: Change each mixed number to an improper fraction in simplest form.

4. $2\dfrac{3}{5}$

   (A) $\dfrac{4}{5}$ (B) $\dfrac{6}{5}$ (C) $\dfrac{11}{5}$ (D) $\dfrac{13}{5}$

5. $4\dfrac{3}{4}$

   (A) $\dfrac{7}{4}$ (B) $\dfrac{13}{4}$ (C) $\dfrac{16}{3}$ (D) $\dfrac{19}{4}$

6. $6\dfrac{7}{6}$

   (A) $\dfrac{13}{6}$ (B) $\dfrac{43}{6}$ (C) $\dfrac{19}{36}$ (D) $\dfrac{42}{36}$

Adding Fractions with the Same Denominator

DIRECTIONS: Add and write the answer in simplest form.

7. $\dfrac{5}{12} + \dfrac{3}{12} =$

   (A) $\dfrac{5}{24}$ (B) $\dfrac{1}{3}$ (C) $\dfrac{8}{12}$ (D) $\dfrac{2}{3}$

8. $\dfrac{5}{8} + \dfrac{7}{8} + \dfrac{3}{8} =$

   (A) $\dfrac{15}{24}$ (B) $\dfrac{3}{4}$ (C) $\dfrac{5}{6}$ (D) $1\dfrac{7}{8}$

Subtracting Fractions with the Same Denominator

DIRECTIONS: Subtract and write the answer in simplest form.

9. $4\dfrac{7}{8} - 3\dfrac{1}{8} =$

   (A) $1\dfrac{1}{4}$ (B) $1\dfrac{3}{4}$ (C) $1\dfrac{12}{16}$ (D) $1\dfrac{7}{8}$

10. $132\dfrac{5}{12} - 37\dfrac{3}{12} =$

   (A) $94\dfrac{1}{6}$ (B) $95\dfrac{1}{12}$ (C) $95\dfrac{1}{6}$ (D) $105\dfrac{1}{6}$

Finding the LCD

DIRECTIONS: Find the lowest common denominator of each group of fractions.

11. $\dfrac{2}{3}, \dfrac{5}{9},$ and $\dfrac{1}{6}$

   (A) 9   (B) 18   (C) 27   (D) 54

12. $\dfrac{1}{2}, \dfrac{5}{6},$ and $\dfrac{3}{4}$

   (A) 2   (B) 4   (C) 6   (D) 12

13. $\dfrac{7}{16}, \dfrac{5}{6},$ and $\dfrac{2}{3}$

   (A) 3   (B) 6   (C) 12   (D) 48

14. $\dfrac{8}{15}, \dfrac{2}{5},$ and $\dfrac{12}{25}$

   (A) 5   (B) 15   (C) 25   (D) 75

15. $\dfrac{2}{3}, \dfrac{1}{5},$ and $\dfrac{5}{6}$

    (A) 15   (B) 30   (C) 48   (D) 90

Adding Fractions with Different Denominators

> **DIRECTIONS**: Add and write the answer in simplest form.

16. $\dfrac{1}{3} + \dfrac{5}{12} =$

    (A) $\dfrac{2}{5}$ (B) $\dfrac{1}{2}$ (C) $\dfrac{9}{12}$ (D) $\dfrac{3}{4}$

17. $3\dfrac{5}{9} + 2\dfrac{1}{3} =$

    (A) $5\dfrac{1}{2}$ (B) $5\dfrac{2}{3}$ (C) $5\dfrac{8}{9}$ (D) $6\dfrac{1}{9}$

18. $12\dfrac{9}{16} + 17\dfrac{3}{4} + 8\dfrac{1}{8} =$

    (A) $37\dfrac{7}{16}$ (B) $38\dfrac{7}{16}$ (C) $38\dfrac{1}{2}$ (D) $38\dfrac{2}{3}$

Subtracting Fractions with Different Denominators

> **DIRECTIONS**: Subtract and write the answer in simplest form.

19. $8\dfrac{9}{12} - 2\dfrac{2}{3} =$

    (A) $6\dfrac{1}{12}$ (B) $6\dfrac{1}{6}$ (C) $6\dfrac{1}{3}$ (D) $6\dfrac{7}{12}$

20. $185\dfrac{11}{15} - 107\dfrac{2}{5} =$

    (A) $77\dfrac{2}{15}$ (B) $78\dfrac{1}{5}$ (C) $78\dfrac{3}{10}$ (D) $78\dfrac{1}{3}$

21. $34\frac{2}{3} - 16\frac{5}{6} =$

    (A) 16   (B) $16\frac{1}{3}$ (C) $17\frac{1}{2}$ (D) $17\frac{5}{6}$

Multiplying Fractions

DIRECTIONS: Multiply and reduce the answer.

22. $\frac{2}{3} \times \frac{4}{5} =$

    (A) $\frac{6}{8}$ (B) $\frac{3}{4}$ (C) $\frac{8}{15}$ (D) $\frac{10}{12}$

23. $\frac{7}{10} \times \frac{4}{21} =$

    (A) $\frac{2}{15}$ (B) $\frac{11}{31}$ (C) $\frac{28}{210}$ (D) $\frac{1}{6}$

24. $5\frac{1}{3} \times \frac{3}{8} =$

    (A) $\frac{4}{11}$ (B) 2   (C) $\frac{8}{5}$ (D) $5\frac{1}{8}$

Dividing Fractions

DIRECTIONS: Divide and reduce the answer.

25. $\frac{3}{16} \div \frac{3}{4} =$

    (A) $\frac{9}{64}$ (B) $\frac{1}{4}$ (C) $\frac{6}{16}$ (D) $\frac{9}{16}$

26. $\frac{4}{9} \div \frac{2}{3} =$

    (A) $\frac{1}{3}$ (B) $\frac{1}{2}$ (C) $\frac{2}{3}$ (D) $\frac{7}{11}$

27. $5\dfrac{1}{4} \div \dfrac{7}{10} =$

(A) $2\dfrac{4}{7}$ (B) $3\dfrac{27}{40}$ (C) $5\dfrac{19}{20}$ (D) $7\dfrac{1}{2}$

DECIMALS

When we divide the denominator of a fraction into its numerator, the result is a **decimal**. The decimal is based upon a fraction with a denominator of 10, 100, 1,000, ... and is written with a **decimal point**. Whole numbers are placed to the left of the decimal point where the first place to the left is the units place; the second to the left is the tens; the third to the left is the hundreds, etc. The fractions are placed on the right where the first place to the right is the tenths; the second to the right is the hundredths, etc.

● EXAMPLES

$$12\,\dfrac{3}{10} = 12.3 \qquad 4\,\dfrac{17}{100} = 4.17 \qquad \dfrac{3}{100} = .03$$

Since a **rational number** is of the form a/b, $b \neq 0$, then all rational numbers can be expressed as decimals by dividing b into a. The result is either a **terminating decimal**, meaning that b divides a with a remainder of 0 after a certain point; or **repeating decimal**, meaning that b continues to divide a so that the decimal has a repeating pattern of integers.

● EXAMPLES

(A) $\dfrac{1}{5} = .2$

(B) $\dfrac{1}{3} = .333...$

(C) $\dfrac{11}{16} = .6875$

(D) $\dfrac{4}{7} = .5714285714...$

(A) and (C) are terminating decimals; (B) and (D) are repeating decimals. This explanation allows us to define **irrational numbers** as numbers whose decimal form is non-terminating and non-repeating, e.g.,

$$\sqrt{2} = 1.414\ldots$$
$$\sqrt{3} = 1.732\ldots$$

PROBLEM

Write $\dfrac{2}{7}$ as a repeating decimal.

SOLUTION

To write a fraction as a repeating decimal divide the numerator by the denominator until a pattern of repeated digits appears.

$$2 \div 7 = .285714285714\ldots$$

Identify the entire portion of the decimal which is repeated. A bar over a decimal means it is a repeating decimal. The repeating decimal can then be written in the shortened form:

$$\frac{2}{7} = .\overline{285714}$$

OPERATIONS WITH DECIMALS

A) **To add numbers containing decimals,** write the numbers in a column making sure the decimal points are lined up, one beneath the other. Add the numbers as usual, placing the decimal point in the sum so that it is still in line with the others.

● **EXAMPLES**

2.558 + 6.391	57.51 + 6.2

$$\begin{array}{r} 2.558 \\ +\ 6.391 \\ \hline 8.949 \end{array} \qquad \begin{array}{r} 57.51 \\ +\ \ 6.20 \\ \hline 63.71 \end{array}$$

Similarly with subtraction,

78.54 − 21.33	7.11 − 4.2

$$\begin{array}{r} 78.54 \\ -\ 21.33 \\ \hline 57.21 \end{array} \qquad \begin{array}{r} 7.11 \\ -\ 4.20 \\ \hline 2.91 \end{array}$$

Note that if two numbers differ according to the number of digits to the right of the decimal point, zeros must be added.

.63 – .214   15.224 – 3.6891

$$\begin{array}{r} .630 \\ -\ .214 \\ \hline .416 \end{array}$$ $$\begin{array}{r} 15.2240 \\ -\ 3.6891 \\ \hline 11.5349 \end{array}$$

B) **To multiply numbers with decimals**, simply multiply as usual. Then, to figure out the number of decimal places that belong in the product, find the total number of decimal places in the numbers being multiplied.

● **EXAMPLES**

$$\begin{array}{r} 6.555 \\ \times\ \ \ 4.5 \\ \hline 32775 \\ 26220 \\ \hline 29.4975 \end{array}$$
(3 decimal places)
(1 decimal place)

(4 decimal places)

$$\begin{array}{r} 5.32 \\ \times\ \ .04 \\ \hline 2128 \\ 000 \\ \hline .2128 \end{array}$$
(2 decimal places)
(2 decimal places)

(4 decimal places)

C) **To divide numbers with decimals**, you must first make the divisor a whole number by moving the decimal point the appropriate number of places to the right. The decimal point of the dividend should also be moved the same number of places. Place a decimal point in the quotient directly in line with the decimal point in the dividend.

● **EXAMPLES**

12.92 ÷ 3.4   40.376 ÷ 7.21

$$\begin{array}{r} 3.8 \\ 3.4\overline{)12.9.2} \\ -102 \\ \hline 272 \\ -272 \\ \hline 0 \end{array}$$ $$\begin{array}{r} 5.6 \\ 7.21\overline{)40.37.6} \\ -3605 \\ \hline 4326 \\ -4326 \\ \hline 0 \end{array}$$

If the question asks you to find the correct answer to two decimal places, simply divide until you have three decimal places and then round off. If the third decimal place is a 5 or larger, the number in the second decimal place is increased by 1. If the third decimal place is less than 5, that number is simply dropped.

PROBLEM

Find the answer to the following to two decimal places:

(1) 44.3 ÷ 3   (2) 56.99 ÷ 6

SOLUTION

(1)
$$
\begin{array}{r}
14.766 \\
3\overline{)44.300} \\
-3 \\
\hline
14 \\
-12 \\
\hline
23 \\
-21 \\
\hline
20 \\
-18 \\
\hline
20 \\
-18 \\
\hline
2
\end{array}
$$

(2)
$$
\begin{array}{r}
9.498 \\
6\overline{)56.990} \\
-54 \\
\hline
29 \\
-24 \\
\hline
59 \\
-54 \\
\hline
50 \\
-48 \\
\hline
2
\end{array}
$$

14.766 can be rounded off to 14.77.

9.498 can be rounded off to 9.50.

D) **When comparing two numbers which begin with a decimal point to see which is the larger,** first look at the tenths place. The larger digit in this place represents the larger number. If the two digits are the same, however, take a look at the digits in the hundredths place, and so on.

● **EXAMPLES**

.518 and .216
5 is larger than 2, therefore, .518 is larger than .216.

.723 and .726
6 is larger than 3, therefore, .726 is larger than .723.

☞ **Drill: Decimals**

Addition and Subtraction

DIRECTIONS: Solve the following equations.

1. 1.032 + 0.987 + 3.07 =

(A) 4.089   (B) 5.089   (C) 5.189   (D) 6.189

2. 132.03 + 97.1483 =

    (A) 98.4686   (B) 110.3513   (C) 209.1783   (D) 229.1783

3. 7.1 + 0.62 + 4.03827 + 5.183 =

    (A) 0.2315127   (B) 16.45433   (C) 16.94127   (D) 18.561

4. 3.972 – 2.04 =

    (A) 1.932   (B) 1.942   (C) 1.976   (D) 2.013

5. 16.047 – 13.06 =

    (A) 2.887   (B) 2.987   (C) 3.041   (D) 3.141

Multiplication and Division

> **DIRECTIONS**: Solve the following equations.

6. $1.03 \times 2.6 =$

    (A) 2.18   (B) 2.678   (C) 2.78   (D) 3.38

7. $93 \times 4.2 =$

    (A) 39.06   (B) 97.2   (C) 223.2   (D) 390.6

8. $123.39 \div 3 =$

    (A) 31.12   (B) 41.13   (C) 401.13   (D) 411.3

9. $1,428.6 \div 6 =$

    (A) 0.2381   (B) 2.381   (C) 23.81   (D) 238.1

10. $25.2 \div 0.3 =$

    (A) 0.84   (B) 8.04   (C) 8.4   (D) 84

Comparing

> **DIRECTIONS**: Solve the following equations.

11. Which is the **largest** number in this set—{0.8, 0.823, 0.089, 0.807, 0.852}?

    (A) 0.8   (B) 0.823   (C) 0.089   (D) 0.852

12. Which is the **smallest** number in this set—{32.98, 32.099, 32.047, 32.5, 32.304}?

    (A) 32.98   (B) 32.099   (C) 32.047   (D) 32.5

13. In which set below are the numbers arranged correctly from smallest to largest?

    (A) {0.98, 0.9, 0.993}   (C) {7.04, 7.26, 7.2}

    (B) {0.113, 0.3, 0.31}   (D) {0.006, 0.061, 0.06}

Changing a Fraction to a Decimal

> **DIRECTIONS**: Solve the following equations.

14. What is $\frac{1}{4}$ written as a decimal?

    (A) 1.4   (B) 0.14   (C) 0.2   (D) 0.25

15. What is $\frac{3}{5}$ written as a decimal?

    (A) 0.3   (B) 0.35   (C) 0.6   (D) 0.65

PERCENTAGES

A **percent** is a way of expressing the relationship between part and whole, where whole is defined as 100%. A percent can be defined by a fraction with a denominator of 100. Decimals can also represent a percent. For instance,

$$56\% = 0.56 = \frac{56}{100}$$

PROBLEM

Compute the value of

(1)   90% of 400   (2)   180% of 400

SOLUTION

The symbol % means per hundred, therefore, $5\% = \dfrac{5}{100}$.

(1) 90% of $400 = 90 \div 100 \times 400 = 90 \times 4 = 360$

(2) 180% of $400 = 180 \div 100 \times 400 = 180 \times 4 = 720$

PROBLEM

What percent of

(1)   100 is 99.5   (2)   200 is 4

SOLUTION

(1) $99.5 = x \times 100$

$99.5 = 100x$

$.995 = x;$ but this is the value of x per hundred. Therefore,

$99.5\% = x$

(2) $4 = x \times 200$

$4 = 200x$

$.02 = x.$ Again, this must be changed to percent, so

$2\% = x$

EQUIVALENT FORMS OF A NUMBER

Some problems may call for converting numbers into an equivalent or simplified form in order to make the solution more convenient.

A)   **Converting a fraction to a decimal:**

$\dfrac{1}{2} = 0.50$

Divide the numerator by the denominator:

$$2 \overline{\smash{)}\begin{array}{r} .50 \\ 1.00 \\ -10 \\ \hline 00 \end{array}}$$

B) Converting a number to a percent:

$0.50 = 50\%$

Multiply by 100:

$0.50 = (0.50 \times 100)\% = 50\%$

C) Converting a percent to a decimal:

$30\% = 0.30$

Divide by 100:

$30\% = 30 \div 100 = 0.30$

D) Converting a decimal to a fraction:

$0.500 = \dfrac{1}{2}$

Convert .500 to $\dfrac{500}{1000}$ and then simplify the fraction by dividing the numerator and denominator by common factors:

$$\frac{\cancel{2} \times \cancel{2} \times \cancel{5} \times \cancel{5} \times \cancel{5}}{\cancel{2} \times \cancel{2} \times 2 \times \cancel{5} \times \cancel{5} \times \cancel{5}}$$

and then cancel out the common numbers to get ½.

PROBLEM

Express

(1)   1.65 as a percent

(2)   0.7 as a fraction

(3) $-\dfrac{10}{20}$ as a decimal

(4) $\dfrac{4}{2}$ as an integer

SOLUTION

(1) $1.65 \times 100 = 165\%$

(2) $0.7 = \dfrac{7}{10}$

(3) $-\dfrac{10}{20} = -0.5$ (4) $\dfrac{4}{2} = 2$

☞ Drill: Percentages

Finding Percents

> **DIRECTIONS**: Solve to find the correct percentages.

1. Find 3% of 80.

   (A) 0.24   (B) 2.4   (C) 24   (D) 240

2. Find 50% of 182.

   (A) 9   (B) 90   (C) 91   (D) 910

3. Find 83% of 166.

   (A) 0.137   (B) 1.377   (C) 13.778   (D) 137.78

4. Find 125% of 400.

   (A) 425   (B) 500   (C) 525   (D) 600

5. Find 300% of 4.

   (A) 12   (B) 120   (C) 1,200   (D) 12,000

Changing Percents to Fractions

> **DIRECTIONS**: Solve to find the correct fractions.

6. What is 25% written as a fraction?

   (A) $\dfrac{1}{25}$ (B) $\dfrac{1}{5}$ (C) $\dfrac{1}{4}$ (D) $\dfrac{1}{3}$

7. What is $33\dfrac{1}{3}\%$ written as a fraction?

   (A) $\dfrac{1}{4}$ (B) $\dfrac{1}{3}$ (C) $\dfrac{1}{2}$ (D) $\dfrac{2}{3}$

8. What is 200% written as a fraction?

    (A) $\dfrac{1}{2}$ (B) $\dfrac{2}{1}$ (C) $\dfrac{20}{1}$ (D) $\dfrac{200}{1}$

Changing Fractions to Percents

DIRECTIONS: Solve to find the following percentages.

9. What is $\dfrac{2}{3}$ written as a percent?

    (A) 23%   (B) 32%   (C) $33\dfrac{1}{3}\%$ (D) $66\dfrac{2}{3}\%$

10. What is $\dfrac{3}{5}$ written as a percent?

    (A) 30%   (B) 35%   (C) 53%   (D) 60%

Changing Percents to Decimals

DIRECTIONS: Convert the percentages to decimals.

11. What is 42% written as a decimal?

    (A) 0.42   (B) 4.2   (C) 42   (D) 420

12. What is 0.3% written as a decimal?

    (A) 0.0003   (B) 0.003   (C) 0.03   (D) 0.3

13. What is 8% written as a decimal?

    (A) 0.0008   (B) 0.008   (C) 0.08   (D) 0.80

Changing Decimals to Percents

DIRECTIONS: Convert the following decimals to percents.

14. What is 0.43 written as a percent?

    (A) 0.0043%   (B) 0.043%   (C) 4.3%   (D) 43%

15. What is 1 written as a percent?

    (A) 1%   (B) 10%   (C) 100%   (D) 111%

RADICALS

The **square root** of a number is a number that when multiplied by itself results in the original number. Thus, the square root of 81 is 9 since $9 \times 9 = 81$. However, -9 is also a root of 81 since $(-9)(-9) = 81$. Every positive number will have two roots. The principal root is the positive one. Zero has only one square root, while negative numbers do not have real numbers as their roots.

A **radical sign** indicates that the root of a number or expression will be taken. The **radicand** is the number of which the root will be taken. The **index** tells how many times the root needs to be multiplied by itself to equal the radicand, e.g.,

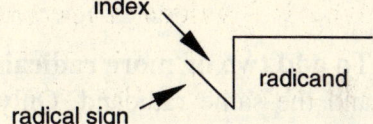

(1) $\sqrt[3]{64}$;

     3 is the index and 64 is the radicand. Since $4 \times 4 \times 4 = 64$, then $\sqrt[3]{64} = 4$.

(2) $\sqrt[5]{32}$;

     5 is the index and 32 is the radicand. Since $2 \times 2 \times 2 \times 2 \times 2 = 32$, then $\sqrt[5]{32} = 2$.

OPERATIONS WITH RADICALS

A) **To multiply two or more radicals**, we utilize the law that states

$$\sqrt{a} \times \sqrt{b} = \sqrt{ab}$$

Simply multiply the whole numbers as usual. Then, multiply the radicands and put the product under the radical sign and simplify, e.g.,

    (1) $\sqrt{12} \times \sqrt{5} = \sqrt{60} = 2\sqrt{15}$

    (2) $3\sqrt{2} \times 4\sqrt{8} = 12\sqrt{16} = 48$

    (3) $2\sqrt{10} \times 6\sqrt{5} = 12\sqrt{50} = 60\sqrt{2}$

B) **To divide radicals**, simplify both the numerator and the denominator. By multiplying the radical in the denominator by itself, you can make the denominator a rational number. The numerator, however, must also be multiplied by this radical so that the value of the expression does not change. You must choose as many factors as necessary to rationalize the denominator, e.g.,

$$(1) \quad \frac{\sqrt{128}}{\sqrt{2}} = \frac{\sqrt{64} \times \sqrt{2}}{\sqrt{2}} = \frac{8\sqrt{2}}{\sqrt{2}} = 8$$

$$(2) \quad \frac{\sqrt{10}}{\sqrt{3}} = \frac{\sqrt{10} \times \sqrt{3}}{\sqrt{3} \times \sqrt{3}} = \frac{\sqrt{30}}{3}$$

$$(3) \quad \frac{\sqrt{8}}{2\sqrt{3}} = \frac{\sqrt{8} \times \sqrt{3}}{2\sqrt{3} \times \sqrt{3}} = \frac{\sqrt{24}}{2 \times 3} = \frac{2\sqrt{6}}{6} = \frac{\sqrt{6}}{3}$$

C) **To add two or more radicals**, the radicals must have the same index and the same radicand. Only where the radicals are simplified can these similarities be determined.

● **EXAMPLES**

(1) $6\sqrt{2} + 2\sqrt{2} = (6+2)\sqrt{2} = 8\sqrt{2}$

(2) $\sqrt{27} + 5\sqrt{3} = \sqrt{9}\sqrt{3} + 5\sqrt{3} = 3\sqrt{3} + 5\sqrt{3} = 8\sqrt{3}$

(3) $7\sqrt{3} + 8\sqrt{2} + 5\sqrt{3} = 12\sqrt{3} + 8\sqrt{2}$

Similarly, to subtract,

(1) $12\sqrt{3} - 7\sqrt{3} = (12-7)\sqrt{3} = 5\sqrt{3}$

(2) $\sqrt{80} - \sqrt{20} = \sqrt{16}\sqrt{5} - \sqrt{4}\sqrt{5} = 4\sqrt{5} - 2\sqrt{5} = 2\sqrt{5}$

(3) $\sqrt{50} - \sqrt{3} = 5\sqrt{2} - \sqrt{3}$

☞ **Drill: Radicals**

Multiplication

DIRECTIONS: Multiply and simplify each answer.

1. $\sqrt{6} \times \sqrt{5} =$

   (A) $\sqrt{11}$ (B) $\sqrt{30}$ (C) $2\sqrt{5}$ (D) $3\sqrt{10}$

2. $\sqrt{3} \times \sqrt{12} =$

    (A) 3   (B) $\sqrt{15}$ (C) $\sqrt{36}$ (D) 6

3. $\sqrt{7} \times \sqrt{7} =$

    (A) 7   (B) 49   (C) $\sqrt{14}$ (D) $2\sqrt{7}$

Division

> **DIRECTIONS**: Divide and simplify the answer.

4. $\sqrt{10} \div \sqrt{2} =$

    (A) $\sqrt{8}$ (B) $2\sqrt{2}$ (C) $\sqrt{5}$ (D) $2\sqrt{5}$

5. $\sqrt{30} \div \sqrt{15} =$

    (A) $\sqrt{2}$ (B) $\sqrt{45}$ (C) $3\sqrt{5}$ (D) $\sqrt{15}$

6. $\sqrt{100} \div \sqrt{25} =$

    (A) $\sqrt{4}$ (B) $5\sqrt{5}$ (C) $5\sqrt{3}$ (D) 2

Addition

> **DIRECTIONS**: Simplify each radical and add.

7. $\sqrt{7} + 3\sqrt{7} =$

    (A) $3\sqrt{7}$ (B) $4\sqrt{7}$ (C) $3\sqrt{14}$ (D) $4\sqrt{14}$

8. $\sqrt{5} + 6\sqrt{5} + 3\sqrt{5} =$

    (A) $9\sqrt{5}$ (B) $9\sqrt{15}$ (C) $5\sqrt{10}$ (D) $10\sqrt{5}$

9. $3\sqrt{32} + 2\sqrt{2} =$

    (A) $5\sqrt{2}$ (B) $\sqrt{34}$ (C) $14\sqrt{2}$ (D) $5\sqrt{34}$

Subtraction

DIRECTIONS: Simplify each radical and subtract.

---

10. $8\sqrt{5} - 6\sqrt{5} =$

    (A) $2\sqrt{5}$ (B) $3\sqrt{5}$ (C) $4\sqrt{5}$ (D) $14\sqrt{5}$

11. $16\sqrt{33} - 5\sqrt{33} =$

    (A) $3\sqrt{33}$ (B) $33\sqrt{11}$ (C) $11\sqrt{33}$ (D) $11\sqrt{0}$

EXPONENTS

When a number is multiplied by itself a specific number of times, it is said to be **raised to a power**. The way this is written is $a^n = b$ where a is the number or **base**, n is the **exponent** or **power** that indicates the number of times the base is to be multiplied by itself, and b is the product of this multiplication.

In the expression 3^2, 3 is the base and 2 is the exponent. This means that 3 is multiplied by itself 2 times and the product is 9.

An exponent can be either positive or negative. A negative exponent implies a fraction such that if n is a negative integer

$$a^{-n} = \frac{1}{a^n}, a \neq 0. \quad \text{So, } 2^{-4} = \frac{1}{2^4} = \frac{1}{16}.$$

An exponent that is 0 gives a result of 1, assuming that the base is not equal to 0.

$$a^0 = 1, a \neq 0.$$

An exponent can also be a fraction. If m and n are positive integers,

$$a^{\frac{m}{n}} = \sqrt[n]{a^m}$$

The numerator remains the exponent of a, but the denominator tells what root to take. For example,

(1) $4^{\frac{3}{2}} = \sqrt[2]{4^3} = \sqrt{64} = 8$ (2) $3^{\frac{4}{2}} = \sqrt[2]{3^4} = \sqrt{81} = 9$

If a fractional exponent were negative, the same operation would take place, but the result would be a fraction. For example,

(1) $27^{-\frac{3}{2}} = \frac{1}{27^{2/3}} = \frac{1}{\sqrt[3]{27^2}} = \frac{1}{\sqrt[3]{729}} = \frac{1}{9}$

PROBLEM

Simplify the following expressions:

(1) -3^{-2}

(3) $\dfrac{-3}{4^{-1}}$

(2) $(-3)^{-2}$

SOLUTION

(1) Here the exponent applies only to 3. Since

$$x^{-y} = \frac{1}{x^y}, -3^{-2} = -(3)^{-2} = -\left(\frac{1}{3^2}\right) = -\frac{1}{9}$$

(2) In this case the exponent applies to the negative base. Thus,

$$(-3)^{-2} = \frac{1}{(-3)^2} = \frac{1}{(-3)(-3)} = \frac{1}{9}$$

(3) $\dfrac{-3}{4^{-1}} = \dfrac{-3}{\left(\dfrac{1}{4}\right)^1} = \dfrac{-3}{\dfrac{1^1}{4^1}} = \dfrac{-3}{\dfrac{1}{4}}$

Division by a fraction is equivalent to multiplication by that fraction's reciprocal; thus,

$$\frac{-3}{\frac{1}{4}} = 3 \times \frac{4}{1} = -12 \quad \text{and} \quad \frac{-3}{4^{-1}} = -12$$

GENERAL LAWS OF EXPONENTS

A) $a^p a^q = a^{p+q}$

$4^2 4^3 = 4^{2+3} = 1{,}024$

B) $(a^p)^q = a^{pq}$

$(2^3)^2 = 2^6 = 64$

C) $\dfrac{a^p}{a^q} = a^{p-q}$

$\dfrac{3^6}{3^2} = 3^4 = 81$

D) $(ab)^p = a^p b^p$

$$(3 \times 2)^2 = 3^2 \times 2^2 = (9)(4) = 36$$

E) $\left(\dfrac{a}{b}\right)^p = \dfrac{a^p}{b^p}, \ b \neq 0$

$$\left(\dfrac{4}{5}\right)^2 = \dfrac{4^2}{5^2} = \dfrac{16}{25}$$

☞ Drill: Exponents

Multiplication and Division

> **DIRECTIONS:** Simplify.

1. $4^6 \times 4^2 =$

   (A) 4^4 (B) 4^8 (C) 4^{12} (D) 16^8

2. $2^2 \times 2^5 \times 2^3 =$

   (A) 2^{10} (B) 4^{10} (C) 8^{10} (D) 2^{30}

3. $6^6 \times 6^2 \times 6^4 =$

   (A) 18^8 (B) 18^{12} (C) 6^{12} (D) 6^{48}

4. $6^5 \div 6^3 =$

   (A) 0 (B) 1 (C) 6 (D) 36

5. $11^8 \div 11^5 =$

   (A) 1^3 (B) 11^3 (C) 11^{13} (D) 11^{40}

Power to a Power

> **DIRECTIONS:** Simplify.

6. $(3^6)^2 =$

   (A) 3^4 (B) 3^8 (C) 3^{12} (D) 9^6

7. $(4^3)^5 =$

   (A) 4^2 (B) 2^{15} (C) 4^8 (D) 4^{15}

8. $(a^4b^3)^2 =$

   (A) $(ab)^9$ (B) a^8b^6 (C) $(ab)^{24}$ (D) a^6b^5

AVERAGES

MEAN

The mean is the arithmetic average. It is the sum of the variables divided by the total number of variables. For example, the mean of 4, 3, and 8 is

$$\frac{4+3+8}{3} = \frac{15}{3} = 5$$

PROBLEM

Find the mean salary for four company employees who make $5/hr., $8/hr., $12/hr., and $15/hr.

SOLUTION

The mean salary is the average.

$$\frac{\$5+\$8+\$12+\$15}{4} = \frac{\$40}{4} = \$10/hr$$

MEDIAN

The median is the middle value in a set when there is an odd number of values. The set of numbers needs to be ordered. There is an equal number of values larger and smaller than the median. When the set is an even number of values, the average of the two middle values is the median. For example:

The median of (2, 3, 5, 8, 9) is 5.

The median of (2, 3, 5, 9, 10, 11) is $\dfrac{5+9}{2} = 7$.

MODE

The mode is the most frequently occurring value in the set of values. For example, the mode of 4, 5, 8, 3, 8, 2 would be 8, since it occurs twice while the other values occur only once.

PROBLEM

For this series of observations, find the mean, median, and mode.

500, 600, 800, 800, 900, 900, 900, 900, 900, 1,000, 1,100

SOLUTION

The mean is the value obtained by adding all the measurements and dividing by the number of measurements.

$$\frac{500 + 600 + 800 + 800 + 900 + 900 + 900 + 900 + 900 + 1,000 + 1,100}{11}$$

$$= \frac{9,300}{11} = 845.45$$

The median is the value appearing in the middle. We have 11 values, so here the sixth, 900, is the median.

The mode is the value that appears most frequently. That is also 900, which has five appearances.

All three of these numbers are measures of central tendency. They describe the "middle" or "center" of the data.

☞ Drill: Averages

Mean

DIRECTIONS: Find the mean of each set of numbers.

1. 18, 25, and 32

    (A) 3   (B) 25   (C) 50   (D) 75

2. $\frac{4}{9}, \frac{2}{3},$ and $\frac{5}{6}$

    (A) $\frac{11}{18}$ (B) $\frac{35}{54}$ (C) $\frac{41}{54}$ (D) $\frac{35}{18}$

3. 97, 102, 116, and 137

    (A) 40   (B) 102   (C) 109   (D) 113

Median

DIRECTIONS: Find the median value of each set of numbers.

---

4. 3, 8, and 6

    (A) 3   (B) 6   (C) 8   (D) 17

5. 19, 15, 21, 27, and 12

    (A) 19   (B) 15   (C) 21   (D) 27

6. $1\frac{2}{3}, 1\frac{7}{8}, 1\frac{3}{4}$, and $1\frac{5}{6}$

    (A) $1\frac{30}{48}$ (B) $1\frac{2}{3}$ (C) $1\frac{3}{4}$ (D) $1\frac{19}{24}$

Mode

DIRECTIONS: Find the mode(s) of each set of numbers.

---

7. 1, 3, 7, 4, 3, and 8

    (A) 1   (B) 3   (C) 7   (D) None

8. 12, 19, 25, and 42

    (A) 12   (B) 19   (C) 25   (D) None

9. 16, 14, 12, 16, 30, and 28

    (A) 6   (B) 14   (C) 16   (D) None

ARITHMETIC REVIEW

ANSWER KEY

Drill: Integers and Real Numbers

1.	(A)	5.	(B)	8.	(D)	11.	(D)
2.	(C)	6.	(D)	9.	(C)	12.	(A)
3.	(B)	7.	(B)	10.	(D)	13.	(D)
4.	(A)						

Drill: Fractions

1.	(D)	8.	(D)	15.	(B)	22.	(C)
2.	(A)	9.	(B)	16.	(D)	23.	(A)
3.	(D)	10.	(C)	17.	(C)	24.	(B)
4.	(D)	11.	(B)	18.	(B)	25.	(B)
5.	(D)	12.	(D)	19.	(A)	26.	(C)
6.	(B)	13.	(D)	20.	(D)	27.	(D)
7.	(D)	14.	(D)	21.	(D)		

Drill: Decimals

1.	(B)	5.	(B)	9.	(D)	13.	(B)
2.	(D)	6.	(B)	10.	(D)	14.	(D)
3.	(C)	7.	(D)	11.	(D)	15.	(C)
4.	(A)	8.	(B)	12.	(C)		

Drill: Percentages

1.	(B)	5.	(A)	9.	(D)	13.	(C)
2.	(C)	6.	(C)	10.	(D)	14.	(D)
3.	(D)	7.	(B)	11.	(A)	15.	(C)
4.	(B)	8.	(B)	12.	(B)		

Drill: Radicals

1.	(B)	4.	(C)	7.	(B)	10.	(A)
2.	(D)	5.	(A)	8.	(D)	11.	(C)
3.	(A)	6.	(D)	9.	(C)		

Drill: Exponents

1.	(B)	3.	(C)	5.	(B)	7.	(D)
2.	(A)	4.	(D)	6.	(C)	8.	(B)

Drill: Averages

1.	(B)	4.	(B)	6.	(D)	8.	(D)
2.	(B)	5.	(A)	7.	(B)	9.	(C)
3.	(D)						

DETAILED EXPLANATIONS OF ANSWERS

Drill: Integers and Real Numbers

1. **(A)**
$$4 + (-7) + 2 + (-5) = \underbrace{4-7}_{-3} + \underbrace{2-5}_{-3}$$
$$= -3 \quad -3$$
$$= -6$$

2. **(C)**
$$144 + (-317) + 213 = \underbrace{144-317}_{-173} + 213$$
$$= -173 \quad +213$$
$$= 40$$

3. **(B)**
$$319 - 428 = -(428 - 319)$$
$$= -109$$

4. **(A)**
$$91{,}203 - 37{,}904 + 1{,}073 = 53{,}299 + 1{,}073$$
$$= 54{,}372$$

5. **(B)**
$$(-3) \times (-18) \times (-1) = (3) \times (18) \times (-1)$$
$$= 54 \times (-1)$$
$$= -54$$

6. **(D)**
$$|-42| \times |-7| = 42 \times 7$$
$$= 294$$

7. **(B)**
$$(-24) \div 8 = -3$$

8. **(D)**
$$(-180) \div (-12) = 180 \div 12$$
$$= 15$$

9. **(C)**
$$\frac{4 + 8 \times 2}{5 - 1} = \frac{4 + 16}{4} = \frac{20}{4} = 5$$

10. **(D)** $96 \div 3 \div 4 \div 2 = \dfrac{96}{3} \div 4 \div 2$

$$= (32 \div 4) \div 2$$
$$= 8 \div 2$$
$$= 4$$

11. **(D)** $3 + 4 \times 2 - 6 \div 3 = 3 + (4 \times 2) - (6 \div 3)$

$$= 3 + 8 - 2$$
$$= 9$$

12. **(A)** $[(4 + 8) \times 3] \div 9 = [12 \times 3] \div 9$

$$= 36 \div 9$$
$$= 4$$

13. **(D)** $18 + 3 \times 4 \div 3 = 18 + \dfrac{3 \times 4}{3}$

$$= 18 + 4$$
$$= 22$$

Drill: Fractions

1. **(D)** $\dfrac{50}{4} = 4\overline{)50} \;^{12} = 12\dfrac{2}{4} = 12\dfrac{1}{2}$

$$\begin{array}{r} \underline{4} \\ 10 \\ \underline{8} \\ 2 \end{array}$$

2. **(A)** $\dfrac{17}{5} = 5\overline{)17} \;^{3} = 3\dfrac{2}{5}$

$$\begin{array}{r} -\underline{15} \\ 2 \end{array}$$

3. **(D)** $\dfrac{42}{3} \qquad 3\overline{)42} \;^{14}$

$$\begin{array}{r} \underline{3} \\ 12 \\ \underline{12} \\ 0 \end{array}$$

4. **(D)** $2\dfrac{3}{5} = \dfrac{(5\times 2)+3}{5} = \dfrac{10+3}{5} = \dfrac{13}{5}$

5. **(D)** $4\dfrac{3}{4} = \dfrac{(4\times 4)+3}{4} = \dfrac{16+3}{4} = \dfrac{19}{4}$

6. **(B)** $6\dfrac{7}{6} = \dfrac{(6\times 6)+7}{6} = \dfrac{36+7}{6} = \dfrac{43}{6}$

7. **(D)** $\dfrac{5}{12} + \dfrac{3}{12} = \dfrac{5+3}{12} = \dfrac{8}{12} = \dfrac{2}{3}$

   $$(\text{GCF} = 4)$$

8. **(D)** $\dfrac{5}{8} + \dfrac{7}{8} + \dfrac{3}{8} = \dfrac{5+7+3}{8} = \dfrac{15}{8} = 1\dfrac{7}{8}$

9. **(B)** $4\dfrac{7}{8} - 3\dfrac{1}{8} = (4-3) + \left(\dfrac{7}{8} - \dfrac{1}{8}\right)$

   $$= 1 + \dfrac{7-1}{8}$$

   $$= 1 + \dfrac{6}{8} = 1\dfrac{3}{4}$$

   $$(\text{GCF} = 2)$$

10. **(C)** $132\dfrac{5}{12} - 37\dfrac{3}{12} = (132-37) + \left(\dfrac{5}{12} - \dfrac{3}{12}\right)$

    $$= 95 + \dfrac{5-3}{12}$$

    $$= 95\dfrac{2}{12} = 95\dfrac{1}{6}$$

    $$(\text{GCF} = 2)$$

11. **(B)** $3 = 3$
    $9 = 3 \times 3$
    $6 = 2 \times 3$ $\qquad$ $\text{LCD} = 3 \times 3 \times 2 = 18$

12. **(D)** $2 = 2$
$6 = 2 \times 3$
$4 = 2 \times 2 \qquad LCD = 2 \times 2 \times 3 = 12$

13. **(D)** $16 = 2 \times 2 \times 2 \times 2$
$6 = 2 \times 3$
$3 = 3 \qquad LCD = 2 \times 2 \times 2 \times 2 \times 3 = 48$

14. **(D)** $15 = 3 \times 5$
$5 = 5$
$25 = 5 \times 5 \qquad LCD = 3 \times 5 \times 5 = 75$

15. **(B)** $3 = 3$
$5 = 5$
$6 = 2 \times 3 \qquad LCD = 2 \times 3 \times 5 = 30$

16. **(D)** $\dfrac{1}{3} + \dfrac{5}{12} = \dfrac{4}{12} + \dfrac{5}{12} = \dfrac{4+5}{12} = \dfrac{9}{12} = \dfrac{3}{4}$
$$(GCF = 3)$$

17. **(C)** $3\dfrac{5}{9} + 2\dfrac{1}{3} = (3+2) + \left(\dfrac{5}{9} + \dfrac{1}{3}\right)$

$$= 5 + \left(\dfrac{5}{9} + \dfrac{3}{9}\right)$$

$$= 5 + \dfrac{5+3}{9} = 5\dfrac{8}{9}$$

18. **(B)** $12\dfrac{9}{16} + 17\dfrac{3}{4} + 8\dfrac{1}{8} = (12+17+8) + \left(\dfrac{9}{16} + \dfrac{3}{4} + \dfrac{1}{8}\right)$

$$= 37 + \left(\dfrac{9}{16} + \dfrac{12}{16} + \dfrac{2}{16}\right)$$

$$= 37 + \left(\dfrac{9+12+2}{16}\right)$$

$$= 37 + \dfrac{23}{16} = 38\dfrac{7}{16}$$

19. **(A)** $8\dfrac{9}{12} - 2\dfrac{2}{3} = (8-2) + \left(\dfrac{9}{12} - \dfrac{2}{3}\right)$

$$= 6 + \left(\dfrac{9}{12} - \dfrac{8}{12}\right)$$

$$= 6 + \dfrac{9-8}{12} = 6\dfrac{1}{12}$$

20. **(D)** $185\dfrac{11}{15} - 107\dfrac{2}{5} = (185 - 107) + \left(\dfrac{11}{15} - \dfrac{2}{5}\right)$

$$= 78 + \left(\dfrac{11}{15} - \dfrac{6}{15}\right)$$

$$= 78 + \left(\dfrac{5}{15}\right) = 78\dfrac{5}{15} = 78\dfrac{1}{3}$$

21. **(D)** $34\dfrac{2}{3} - 16\dfrac{5}{6} = (33 - 16) + \left(\dfrac{5}{3} - \dfrac{5}{6}\right)$

$$= (17) + \left(\dfrac{10}{6} - \dfrac{5}{6}\right)$$

$$= 17 + \left(\dfrac{10-5}{6}\right)$$

$$= 17 + \dfrac{5}{6} = 17\dfrac{5}{6}$$

22. **(C)** $\dfrac{2}{3} \times \dfrac{4}{5} = \dfrac{2 \times 4}{3 \times 5} = \dfrac{8}{15}$

23. **(A)** $\dfrac{7}{10} \times \dfrac{4}{21} = \dfrac{7 \times 4}{10 \times 21} = \dfrac{28}{210} = \dfrac{\cancel{2} \times 2 \times \cancel{7}}{\cancel{2} \times 5 \times 3 \times \cancel{7}} = \dfrac{2}{15}$

24. **(B)** $5\dfrac{1}{3} \times \dfrac{3}{8} = \dfrac{(15+1)}{\cancel{3}} \times \dfrac{\cancel{3}}{8} = \dfrac{16}{8} = 2$

25. **(B)** $\dfrac{3}{16} \div \dfrac{3}{4} = \dfrac{\cancel{3}}{\cancel{16}_4} \times \dfrac{\cancel{4}}{\cancel{3}} = \dfrac{1}{4}$

26. **(C)** $\dfrac{4}{9} \div \dfrac{2}{3} = \dfrac{^2\cancel{4}}{\cancel{9}_3} \times \dfrac{\cancel{3}}{\cancel{2}} = \dfrac{2}{3}$

27. **(D)** $5\dfrac{1}{4} \div \dfrac{7}{10} = \dfrac{^3\cancel{21}}{\cancel{4}_2} \times \dfrac{\cancel{10}^5}{\cancel{7}} = \dfrac{15}{2} = 7\dfrac{1}{2}$

Drill: Decimals

1. **(B)** $1.032 + 0.987 + 3.07 = $

$$
\begin{array}{r}
^{1\ 1}1.032 \\
0.987 \\
+\ 3.070 \\
\hline
5.089
\end{array}
$$

2. **(D)** $132.03 + 97.1483 = $

$$
\begin{array}{r}
^{1}132.0300 \\
+\ \ \ 97.1483 \\
\hline
229.1783
\end{array}
$$

3. **(C)** $7.1 + 0.62 + 4.03827 + 5.183 = $

$$
\begin{array}{r}
^{1\ 1}7.10000 \\
0.62000 \\
4.03827 \\
5.18300 \\
\hline
16.94127
\end{array}
$$

4. **(A)** $3.972 - 2.04 = $

$$
\begin{array}{r}
3.972 \\
-\ 2.040 \\
\hline
1.932
\end{array}
$$

5. **(B)** $16.047 - 13.06 = $

$$
\begin{array}{r}
^{5\ 9\ 1\ 4}1\cancel{6}.\cancel{0}47 \\
-\ 13.060 \\
\hline
2.987
\end{array}
$$

6. **(B)** $1.03 \times 2.6 = $
$$
\begin{array}{r}
1.03 \\
\times\ 2.6 \\
\hline
618 \\
2\ 06 \\
\hline
2.678
\end{array}
$$

7. **(D)** $93 \times 4.2 = $
$$
\begin{array}{r}
93 \\
\times\ 4.2 \\
\hline
186 \\
372 \\
\hline
390.6
\end{array}
$$

8. **(B)** $123.39 \div 3 = $
$$
\begin{array}{r}
41.13 \\
3\overline{)123.39} \\
\underline{12} \\
03 \\
\underline{\ 3} \\
03 \\
\underline{\ 3} \\
09 \\
\underline{\ 9} \\
0
\end{array}
$$

9. **(D)** $1,428.6 \div 6 = $
$$
\begin{array}{r}
238.1 \\
6\overline{)1428.6} \\
\underline{12} \\
22 \\
\underline{18} \\
48 \\
\underline{48} \\
06
\end{array}
$$

10. **(D)** $25.2 \div 0.3 = $
$$
\begin{array}{r}
84. \\
0.3\overline{)25.2} \\
\underline{24} \\
12 \\
\underline{12} \\
0
\end{array}
$$

11. **(D)** {0.82, 0.823, 0.089, 0.807, <u>0.852</u>}

12. **(C)** {32.98, 32.099, <u>32.047</u>, 32.5, 32.304}

13. **(B)** Choice (A) is incorrect, because 0.98 is larger than 0.9. Choice (C) is incorrect, because 7.26 is larger than 7.2. Choice (D) is incorrect because 0.061 is larger than 0.06.

14. **(D)**
$$\frac{1}{4} = 4\overline{)1.00} \quad \begin{array}{r} 0.25 \\ \hline \underline{8} \\ 20 \\ \underline{20} \\ 0 \end{array}$$

15. **(C)**
$$\frac{3}{5} = 5\overline{)3.00} \quad \begin{array}{r} 0.6 \\ \hline \underline{3.0} \\ 0 \end{array}$$

Drill: Percentages

1. **(B)**
$$0.03 \times 80 = \begin{array}{r} 80 \\ \times .03 \\ \hline 2.40 \end{array} = 2.4$$

2. **(C)**
$$\frac{50}{100} \times 182 = \begin{array}{r} \overset{1}{182} \\ \times .50 \\ \hline 91 \end{array}$$

3. **(D)**
$$\frac{83}{100} \times 166 = .83 \times 166 = \begin{array}{r} 166 \\ \times .83 \\ \hline 498 \\ 1328 \\ \hline 137.78 \end{array}$$

4. **(B)**
$$\frac{125}{100} \times 400 = 1.25 \times 400 = \begin{array}{r} 400 \\ 1.25 \\ \hline 2000 \\ 800 \\ 400 \\ \hline 500.00 \end{array}$$

5. **(A)** $\dfrac{300}{100} \times 4 = 3 \times 4 = 12$

6. **(C)** $\dfrac{25}{100}$ (GCF = 25) $= \dfrac{1}{4}$

7. **(B)** $\dfrac{33\frac{1}{3}}{100} = \dfrac{3(33\frac{1}{3})}{3(100)} = \dfrac{100}{300} = \dfrac{1}{3}$

8. **(B)** $\dfrac{200}{100} = \dfrac{2}{1}$

9. **(D)** $\dfrac{2}{3} \times 100 = \dfrac{200}{3} = 3\overline{)200}$
$$
\begin{array}{r}
66\frac{2}{3} \\
3\overline{)200} \\
\underline{18} \\
20 \\
\underline{18} \\
2
\end{array}
$$

10. **(D)** $\dfrac{3}{5} \times 100 = \dfrac{300}{5} = 5\overline{)300}$
$$
\begin{array}{r}
60 \\
5\overline{)300} \\
\underline{30} \\
00
\end{array}
$$

11. **(A)** $42\% = \dfrac{42}{100} = .42$

12. **(B)** $0.3\% = \dfrac{0.3}{100} = 0.003$

13. **(C)** $8\% = \dfrac{8}{100} = 0.08$

14. **(D)** $0.43 \times 100 = 43\%$

15. **(C)** $1 \times 100 = 100\%$

Drill: Radicals

1. **(B)** $\sqrt{6} \times \sqrt{5} = \sqrt{6 \times 5} = \sqrt{30}$

2. **(D)** $\sqrt{3} \times \sqrt{12} = \sqrt{3 \times 12} = \sqrt{36} = 6$

3. **(A)** $\sqrt{7} \times \sqrt{7} = \sqrt{7 \times 7} = \sqrt{49} = 7$

4. **(C)** $\sqrt{10} \div \sqrt{2} = \dfrac{\sqrt{10}}{\sqrt{2}} = \sqrt{\dfrac{10}{2}} = \sqrt{5}$

5. **(A)** $\sqrt{30} \div \sqrt{15} = \dfrac{\sqrt{30}}{\sqrt{15}} = \sqrt{\dfrac{30}{15}} = \sqrt{2}$

6. **(D)** $\sqrt{100} \div \sqrt{25} = \dfrac{\sqrt{100}}{\sqrt{25}} = \sqrt{\dfrac{100}{25}} = \sqrt{4} = 2$

7. **(B)** $\sqrt{7} + 3\sqrt{7} = (1+3)\sqrt{7} = 4\sqrt{7}$

8. **(D)** $\sqrt{5} + 6\sqrt{5} + 3\sqrt{5} = (1+6+3)\sqrt{5} = 10\sqrt{5}$

9. **(C)** $\begin{aligned} 3\sqrt{32} + 2\sqrt{2} &= 3\sqrt{16 \times 2} + 2\sqrt{2} \\ &= 3\sqrt{16} \times \sqrt{2} + 2\sqrt{2} \\ &= 3 \times 4 \times \sqrt{2} + 2\sqrt{2} \\ &= 12\sqrt{2} + 2\sqrt{2} \\ &= (12+2)\sqrt{2} = 14\sqrt{2} \end{aligned}$

10. **(A)** $8\sqrt{5} - 6\sqrt{5} = (8-6)\sqrt{5} = 2\sqrt{5}$

11. **(C)** $16\sqrt{33} - 5\sqrt{33} = (16-5)\sqrt{33} = 11\sqrt{33}$

Drill: Exponents

1. **(B)** $4^6 \times 4^2 = 4^{(6+2)}$

2. **(A)** $2^2 \times 2^5 \times 2^3 = 2^{(2+5+3)} = 2^{10}$

3. **(C)** $6^6 \times 6^2 \times 6^4 = 6^{(6+2+4)} = 6^{12}$

4. **(D)** $6^5 \div 6^3 = 6^{(5-3)} = 6^2 = 36$

5. **(B)** $11^8 \div 11^5 = 11^{(8-5)} = 11^3$

6. **(C)** $(3^6)^2 = 3^{(6)(2)} = 3^{12}$

7. **(D)** $(4^3)^5 = 4^{(3)(5)} = 4^{15}$

8. **(B)** $(a^4b^3)^2 = (a^4)^2(b^3)^2 = (a^{(4)(2)})(b^{(3)(2)}) = a^8b^6$

Drill: Averages

1. **(B)** $\dfrac{18+25+32}{3} = \dfrac{75}{3} = 25$

2. **(B)** $\dfrac{\frac{4}{9}+\frac{2}{3}+\frac{5}{6}}{3}$ (LCD = 18) $= \dfrac{\frac{8}{18}+\frac{12}{18}+\frac{15}{18}}{3}$

    $= \dfrac{\frac{8+12+15}{18}}{3} = \left(\dfrac{1}{3}\right)\left(\dfrac{35}{18}\right) = \dfrac{35}{54}$

3. **(D)** $\dfrac{97+102+116+137}{4} = \dfrac{452}{4} = 113$

4. **(B)** $\{\cancel{3}, 6, \cancel{8}\}$ 6 is the median

5. **(A)** $\{\cancel{12}, \cancel{15}, 19, \cancel{21}, \cancel{27}\}$ 19 is the median

6. **(D)** $\left\{1\dfrac{2}{3},\ 1\dfrac{3}{4},\ 1\dfrac{5}{6},\ 1\dfrac{7}{8}\right\}$

$$\dfrac{1\dfrac{3}{4}+1\dfrac{5}{6}}{2}=\dfrac{\dfrac{7}{4}+\dfrac{11}{6}}{2}\quad(\text{LCD}=12)\quad =\dfrac{\dfrac{21}{12}+\dfrac{22}{12}}{2}=\dfrac{\dfrac{43}{12}}{2}$$

$$=\dfrac{43}{12}\times\dfrac{1}{2}=\dfrac{43}{24}=1\dfrac{19}{24}$$

7. **(B)** $\{1, \mathbf{3}, 7, 4, \mathbf{3}, 8\}$ 3 is the Mode

8. **(D)** $\{12, 19, 25, 42\}$ No Mode

9. **(C)** $\{\mathbf{16}, 14, 12, \mathbf{16}, 30, 28\}$ 16 is the Mode

III. ALGEBRA REVIEW

In algebra, letters or variables are used to represent numbers. A **variable** is defined as a placeholder, which can take on any of several values at a given time. A **constant**, on the other hand, is a symbol which takes on only one value at a given time. A **term** is a constant, a variable, or a combination of constants and variables. For example: 7.76, $3x$, xyz, $\dfrac{5z}{x}$, $(0.99)x^2$ are terms. If a term is a combination of constants and variables, the constant part of the term is referred to as the **coefficient** of the variable. If a variable is written without a coefficient, the coefficient is assumed to be 1.

● **EXAMPLES**

$3x^2$
coefficient: 3
variable: x

y^3
coefficient: 1
variable: y

An **expression** is a collection of one or more terms. If the number of terms is greater than 1, the expression is said to be the sum of the terms.

● **EXAMPLES**

$9, 9xy, 6x + \dfrac{x}{3}, 8yz - 2x$

An algebraic expression consisting of only one term is called a **monomial**; of two terms is called a **binomial**; of three terms is called a **trinomial**. In general, an algebraic expression consisting of two or more terms is called a **polynomial**.

OPERATIONS WITH POLYNOMIALS

A) **Addition of polynomials** is achieved by combining like terms, terms which differ only in their numerical coefficients, e.g.,

$P(x) = (x^2 - 3x + 5) + (4x^2 + 6x - 3)$

Note that the parentheses are used to distinguish the polynomials.

By using the commutative and associative laws, we can rewrite $P(x)$ as:

$P(x) = (x^2 + 4x^2) + (6x - 3x) + (5 - 3)$

Using the distributive law, $ab + ac = a(b + c)$, yields:

$(1 + 4)x^2 + (6 - 3)x + (5 - 3)$

$= 5x^2 + 3x + 2$

B) **Subtraction of two polynomials** is achieved by first changing the sign of all terms in the expression which are being subtracted and then adding this result to the other expression, e.g.,

$$(5x^2 + 4y^2 + 3z^2) - (4xy + 7y^2 - 3z^2 + 1)$$

$$= 5x^2 + 4y^2 + 3z^2 - 4xy - 7y^2 + 3z^2 - 1$$

$$= 5x^2 + (4y^2 - 7y^2) + (3z^2 + 3z^2) - 4xy - 1$$

$$= 5x^2 + (-3y^2) + 6z^2 - 4xy - 1$$

C) **Multiplication of two or more polynomials** is achieved by using the laws of exponents, the rules of signs, and the commutative and associative laws of multiplication. Begin by multiplying the coefficients and then multiply the variables according to the laws of exponents, e.g.,

$$(y^2)\ (5)\ (6y^2)\ (yz)\ (2z^2)$$

$$= (1)\ (5)\ (6)\ (1)\ (2)\ (y^2)\ (y^2)\ (yz)\ (z^2)$$

$$= 60[(y^2)\ (y^2)\ (y)]\ [(z)\ (z^2)]$$

$$= 60(y^5)\ (z^3)$$

$$= 60y^5z^3$$

D) **Multiplication of a polynomial by a monomial** is achieved by multiplying each term of the polynomial by the monomial and combining the results, e.g.,

$$(4x^2 + 3y)\ (6xz^2)$$

$$= (4x^2)\ (6xz^2) + (3y)\ (6xz^2)$$

$$= 24x^3z^2 + 18xyz^2$$

E) **Multiplication of a polynomial by a polynomial** is achieved by multiplying each of the terms of one polynomial by each of the terms of the other polynomial and combining the result, e.g.,

$$(5y + z + 1)\ (y^2 + 2y)$$

$$[(5y)\ (y^2) + (5y)\ (2y)] + [(z)\ (y^2) + (z)\ (2y)] + [(1)\ (y^2) + (1)\ (2y)]$$

$$= (5y^3 + 10y^2) + (y^2z + 2yz) + (y^2 + 2y)$$

$$= (5y^3) + (10y^2 + y^2) + (y^2z) + (2yz) + (2y)$$

$$= 5y^3 + 11y^2 + y^2z + 2yz + 2y$$

F) **Division of a monomial by a monomial** is achieved by first dividing the constant coefficients and the variable factors separately, and then multiplying these quotients, e.g.,

$$6xyz^2 \div 2y^2z$$

$$= \left(\frac{6}{2}\right)\left(\frac{x}{1}\right)\left(\frac{y}{y^2}\right)\left(\frac{z^2}{z}\right)$$

$$= 3xy^{-1}z$$

$$= \frac{3xz}{y}$$

G) **Division of a polynomial by a polynomial** is achieved by following the given procedure, called long division.

Step 1: The terms of both the polynomials are arranged in order of ascending or descending powers of one variable.

Step 2: The first term of the dividend is divided by the first term of the divisor which gives the first term of the quotient.

Step 3: This first term of the quotient is multiplied by the entire divisor and the result is subtracted from the dividend.

Step 4: Using the remainder obtained from Step 3 as the new dividend, Steps 2 and 3 are repeated until the remainder is zero or the degree of the remainder is less than the degree of the divisor.

Step 5: The result is written as follows:

$$\frac{\text{dividend}}{\text{divisor}} = \text{quotient} + \frac{\text{remainder}}{\text{divisor}}$$

divisor $\neq 0$

e.g., $(2x^2 + x + 6) \div (x + 1)$

$$
\begin{array}{r}
2x - 1 \\
(x+1)\overline{)2x^2 + x + 6} \\
-(2x^2 + 2x) \\
\hline
-x + 6 \\
-(-x - 1) \\
\hline
7
\end{array}
$$

The result is $(2x^2 + x + 6) \div (x + 1) = 2x - 1 + \dfrac{7}{x+1}$.

☞ Drill: Operations with Polynomials

Addition

> **DIRECTIONS**: Add the following polynomials.

1. $9a^2b + 3c + 2a^2b + 5c =$

   (A) $19a^2bc$ (C) $11a^4b^2 + 8c^2$

   (B) $11a^2b + 8c$ (D) $19a^4b^2c^2$

2. $14m^2n^3 + 6m^2n^3 + 3m^2n^3 =$

   (A) $20m^2n^3$ (C) $23m^2n^3$

   (B) $23m^6n^9$ (D) $32m^6n^9$

3. $3x + 2y + 16x + 3z + 6y =$

   (A) $19x + 8y$ (C) $19x + 8y + 3z$

   (B) $19x + 11yz$ (D) $11xy + 19xz$

4. $(4d^2 + 7e^3 + 12f) + (3d^2 + 6e^3 + 2f) =$

   (A) $23d^2e^3f$ (C) $33d^4e^6f^2$

   (B) $33d^2e^2f$ (D) $7d^2 + 13e^3 + 14f$

5. $3ac^2 + 2b^2c + 7ac^2 + 2ac^2 + b^2c =$

   (A) $12ac^2 + 3b^2c$ (C) $11ac^2 + 4ab^2c$

   (B) $14ab^2c^2$ (D) $15ab^2c^2$

Subtraction

> **DIRECTIONS**: Subtract the following polynomials.

6. $14m^2n - 6m^2n =$

   (A) $20m^2n$ (C) $8m$

   (B) $8m^2n$ (D) 8

7. $3x^3y^2 - 4xz - 6x^3y^2 =$

   (A) $-7x^2y^2z$ (C) $-3x^3y^2 - 4xz$

   (B) $3x^3y^2 - 10x^4y^2z$ (D) $-x^2y^2z - 6x^3y^2$

8. $9g^2 + 6h - 2g^2 - 5h =$

   (A) $15g^2h - 7g^2h$ (C) $11g^2 + 7h$

   (B) $7g^4h^2$ (D) $7g^2 + h$

9. $7b^3 - 4c^2 - 6b^3 + 3c^2 =$

   (A) $b^3 - c^2$ (C) $13b^3 - c$

   (B) $-11b^2 - 3c^2$ (D) $7b - c$

10. $11q^2r - 4q^2r - 8q^2r =$

   (A) $22q^2r$ (C) $-2q^2r$

   (B) q^2r (D) $-q^2r$

Multiplication

> **DIRECTIONS**: Multiply the following polynomials.

11. $5p^2t \times 3p^2t =$

   (A) $15p^2t$ (C) $15p^4t^2$

   (B) $15p^4t$ (D) $8p^2t$

12. $(2r + s)\,14r =$

   (A) $28rs$ (C) $16r^2 + 14rs$

   (B) $28r^2 + 14sr$ (D) $28r + 14sr$

13. $(4m + p)(3m - 2p) =$

   (A) $12m^2 + 5mp + 2p^2$ (C) $7m - p$

   (B) $12m^2 - 2mp + 2p^2$ (D) $12m^2 - 5mp - 2p^2$

14. $(2a + b)(3a^2 + ab + b^2) =$

   (A) $6a^3 + 5a^2b + 3ab^2 + b^3$ (C) $6a^3 + 2a^2b + 2ab^2$

   (B) $5a^3 + 3ab + b^3$ (D) $3a^2 + 2a + ab + b + b^2$

15. $(6t^2 + 2t + 1)\,3t =$

    (A) $9t^2 + 5t + 3$ (C) $9t^3 + 6t^2 + 3t$

    (B) $18t^2 + 6t + 3$ (D) $18t^3 + 6t^2 + 3t$

Division

DIRECTIONS: Divide the following polynomials.

---

16. $(x^2 + x - 6) \div (x - 2) =$

    (A) $x - 3$ (C) $x + 3$

    (B) $x + 2$ (D) $x - 2$

17. $24b^4c^3 \div 6b^2c =$

    (A) $3b^2c^2$ (C) $4b^3c^2$

    (B) $4b^4c^3$ (D) $4b^2c^2$

18. $(3p^2 + pq - 2q^2) \div (p + q) =$

    (A) $3p + 2q$ (C) $3p - q$

    (B) $2q - 3p$ (D) $3p - 2q$

19. $(y^3 - 2y^2 - y + 2) \div (y - 2) =$

    (A) $(y - 1)^2$ (C) $(y + 2)\,(y - 1)$

    (B) $y^2 - 1$ (D) $(y + 1)^2$

20. $(m^2 + m - 14) \div (m + 4) =$

    (A) $m - 2$ (C) $m - 3 + \dfrac{4}{m + 4}$

    (B) $m - 3 + \dfrac{-2}{m + 4}$ (D) $m - 3$

SIMPLIFYING ALGEBRAIC EXPRESSIONS

    To factor a polynomial completely is to find the prime factors of the polynomial with respect to a specified set of numbers.

The following concepts are important while factoring or simplifying expressions.

A) The factors of an algebraic expression consist of two or more algebraic expressions which, when multiplied together, produce the given algebraic expression.

B) A **prime factor** is a polynomial with no factors other than itself and 1. The **least common multiple (LCM)** for a set of numbers is the smallest quantity divisible by every number of the set. For algebraic expressions, the least common numerical coefficients for each of the given expressions will be a factor.

C) The **greatest common factor (GCF)** for a set of numbers is the largest factor that is common to all members of the set.

D) For algebraic expressions, the greatest common factor is the polynomial of highest degree and the largest numerical coefficient which is a factor of all the given expressions.

Some important formulas, useful for the factoring of polynomials, are listed below.

$$a(c + d) = ac + ad$$

$$(a + b)(a - b) = a^2 - b^2$$

$$(a + b)(a + b) = (a + b)^2 = a^2 + 2ab + b^2$$

$$(a - b)(a - b) = (a - b)^2 = a^2 - 2ab + b^2$$

$$(x + a)(x + b) = x^2 + (a + b)x + ab$$

$$(ax + b)(cx + d) = acx^2 + (ad + bc)x + bd$$

$$(a + b)(c + d) = ac + bc + ad + bd$$

$$(a + b)(a + b)(a + b) = (a + b)^3 = a^3 + 3a^2b + 3ab^2 + b^3$$

$$(a - b)(a - b)(a - b) = (a - b)^3 = a^3 - 3a^2b + 3ab^2 - b^3$$

$$(a - b)(a^2 + ab + b^2) = a^3 - b^3$$

$$(a + b)(a^2 - ab + b^2) = a^3 + b^3$$

$$(a + b + c)^2 = a^2 + b^2 + c^2 + 2ab + 2ac + 2bc$$

$$(a - b)(a^3 + a^2b + ab^2 + b^3) = a^4 - b^4$$

$$(a - b)(a^4 + a^3b + a^2b^2 + ab^3 + b^4) = a^5 - b^5$$

$$(a - b)(a^5 + a^4b + a^3b^2 + a^2b^3 + ab^4 + b^5) = a^6 - b^6$$

$$(a - b)(a^{n-1} + a^{n-2}b + a^{n-3}b^2 + \ldots + ab^{n-2} + b^{n-1}) = a^n - b^n$$

where n is any positive integer $(1, 2, 3, 4, \ldots)$.

$$(a + b)(a^{n-1} - a^{n-2}b + a^{n-3}b^2 - \ldots - ab^{n-2} + b^{n-1}) = a^n + b^n$$

where n is any positive odd integer $(1, 3, 5, 7, \ldots)$.

The procedure for factoring an algebraic expression completely is as follows:

Step 1: First find the greatest common factor if there is any. Then examine each factor remaining for greatest common factors.

Step 2: Continue factoring the factors obtained in Step 1 until all factors other than monomial factors are prime.

● **EXAMPLE**

Factoring $4 - 16x^2$,

$$4 - 16x^2 = 4(1 - 4x^2) = 4(1 + 2x)(1 - 2x)$$

PROBLEM

Express each of the following as a single term.

(1) $3x^2 + 2x^2 - 4x^2$ 　　　　　　(2) $5axy^2 - 7axy^2 - 3xy^2$

SOLUTION

(1) Factor x^2 in the expression.

$$3x^2 + 2x^2 - 4x^2 = (3 + 2 - 4)x^2 = 1x^2 = x^2$$

(2) Factor xy^2 in the expression and then factor a.

$$5axy^2 - 7axy^2 - 3xy^2 = (5a - 7a - 3)xy^2$$
$$= [(5 - 7)a - 3]xy^2$$
$$= (-2a - 3)xy^2$$

PROBLEM

Simplify $\dfrac{\dfrac{1}{x-1} - \dfrac{1}{x-2}}{\dfrac{1}{x-2} - \dfrac{1}{x-3}}$.

SOLUTION

Simplify the expression in the numerator by using the addition rule:

$$\frac{a}{b} + \frac{c}{d} = \frac{ad + bc}{bd}$$

Notice bd is the Least Common Denominator, LCD. We obtain

$$\frac{x - 2 - (x - 1)}{(x - 1)(x - 2)} = \frac{-1}{(x - 1)(x - 2)}$$

in the numerator.

Repeat this procedure for the expression in the denominator:

$$\frac{x - 3 - (x - 2)}{(x - 2)(x - 3)} = \frac{-1}{(x - 2)(x - 3)}$$

We now have

$$\frac{\dfrac{-1}{(x - 1)(x - 2)}}{\dfrac{-1}{(x - 2)(x - 3)}}$$

which is simplified by inverting the fraction in the denominator and multiplying it by the numerator and cancelling like terms

$$\frac{-1}{(x - 1)(x - 2)} \times \frac{(x - 2)(x - 3)}{-1} = \frac{x - 3}{x - 1}.$$

☞ Drill: Simplifying Algebraic Expressions

> **DIRECTIONS**: Simplify the following expressions.

1. $16b^2 - 25z^2 =$

    (A) $(4b - 5z)^2$ (C) $(4b - 5z)(4b + 5z)$

    (B) $(4b + 5z)^2$ (D) $(16b - 25z)^2$

2. $x^2 - 2x - 8 =$

    (A) $(x - 4)^2$ (C) $(x + 4)(x - 2)$

    (B) $(x - 6)(x - 2)$ (D) $(x - 4)(x + 2)$

3. $2c^2 + 5cd - 3d^2 =$

   (A) $(c - 3d)(c + 2d)$ (C) $(c - d)(2c + 3d)$

   (B) $(2c - d)(c + 3d)$ (D) $(2c + d)(c + 3d)$

4. $4t^3 - 20t =$

   (A) $4t(t^2 - 5)$ (C) $4t(t + 4)(t - 5)$

   (B) $4t^2(t - 20)$ (D) $2t(2t^2 - 10)$

5. $x^2 + xy - 2y^2 =$

   (A) $(x - 2y)(x + y)$ (C) $(x + 2y)(x + y)$

   (B) $(x - 2y)(x - y)$ (D) $(x + 2y)(x - y)$

EQUATIONS AND LINEAR EQUATIONS

An **equation** is defined as a statement that two separate expressions are equal. A **solution** to an equation containing a single variable is a number that makes the equation true when it is substituted for the variable. For example, in the equation $3x = 18$, 6 is the solution since $3(6) = 18$. Depending on the equation, there can be more than one solution. Equations with the same solutions are said to be **equivalent equations**. An equation without a solution is said to have a solution set that is the **empty** or **null** set and is represented by ϕ.

Replacing an expression within an equation by an equivalent expression will result in a new equation with solutions equivalent to the original equation. Suppose we are given the equation

$$3x + y + x + 2y = 15.$$

By combining like terms we get

$$3x + y + x + 2y = 4x + 3y.$$

Since these two expressions are equivalent, we can substitute the simpler form into the equation to get

$$4x + 3y = 15$$

Performing the same operation to both sides of an equation by the same expression will result in a new equation that is equivalent to the original equation.

A) **Addition or subtraction**

$$y + 6 = 10$$

We can add (-6) to both sides

$$y + 6 + (-6) = 10 + (-6)$$

to get $y + 0 = 10 - 6$ $y = 4$

B) **Multiplication or division**

$$3x = 6$$
$$\frac{3x}{3} = \frac{6}{3}$$
$$x = 2$$

$3x = 6$ is equivalent to $x = 2$.

C) **Raising to a power**

$$a = x^2 y$$
$$a^2 = (x^2 y)^2$$
$$a^2 = x^4 y^2$$

This can be applied to negative and fractional powers as well, e.g.,

$$x^2 = 3y^4$$

If we raise both sides to the -2 power, we get

$$(x^2)^{-2} = (3y^4)^{-2}$$
$$\frac{1}{(x^2)^2} = \frac{1}{(3y^4)^2}$$
$$\frac{1}{x^4} = \frac{1}{9y^8}$$

If we raise both sides to the $\frac{1}{2}$ power, which is the same as taking the square root, we get

$$(x^2)^{1/2} = (3y^4)^{1/2}$$
$$x = \pm\sqrt{3}y^2$$

D) The **reciprocal** of both sides of an equation are equivalent to the original equation. Note: The reciprocal of zero is undefined.

$$\frac{2x+y}{z} = \frac{5}{2} \qquad \frac{z}{2x+y} = \frac{2}{5}$$

PROBLEM

Solve for x, justifying each step.

$$3x - 8 = 7x + 8$$

SOLUTION

$$3x - 8 = 7x + 8$$

Add 8 to both sides: $\quad 3x - 8 + 8 = 7x + 8 + 8$

Additive inverse property: $\quad 3x + 0 = 7x + 16$

Additive identity property: $\quad 3x = 7x + 16$

Add $(-7x)$ to both sides: $\quad 3x - 7x = 7x + 16 - 7x$

Commute: $\quad -4x = 7x - 7x + 16$

Additive inverse property: $\quad -4x = 0 + 16$

Additive identity property: $\quad -4x = 16$

Divide both sides by -4: $\quad x = \dfrac{16}{-4}$

$$x = -4$$

Check: Replacing x with -4 in the original equation:

$$3x - 8 = 7x + 8$$
$$3(-4) - 8 = 7(-4) + 8$$
$$-12 - 8 = -28 + 8$$
$$-20 = -20$$

LINEAR EQUATIONS

A linear equation with one unknown is one that can be put into the form $ax + b = 0$, where a and b are constants, $a \neq 0$.

To solve a linear equation means to transform it in the form $x = \dfrac{-b}{a}$.

A) If the equation has unknowns on both sides of the equality, it is convenient to put similar terms on the same sides. Refer to the following example.

$$4x + 3 = 2x + 9$$
$$4x + 3 - 2x = 2x + 9 - 2x$$
$$(4x - 2x) + 3 = (2x - 2x) + 9$$
$$2x + 3 = 0 + 9$$
$$2x + 3 - 3 = 0 + 9 - 3$$

383

$$2x = 6$$

$$\frac{2x}{2} = \frac{6}{2}$$

$$x = 3$$

B) If the equation appears in fractional form, it is necessary to transform it, using cross-multiplication, and then repeat the same procedure as in A. We obtain:

$$\frac{3x+4}{3} \diagup\hspace{-1.5em}\diagdown \frac{7x+2}{5}$$

By using cross-multiplication we would obtain:

$$3(7x + 2) = 5(3x + 4).$$

This is equivalent to:

$$21x + 6 = 15x + 20,$$

which can be solved as in A.

$$21x + 6 = 15x + 20$$
$$21x - 15x + 6 = 15x - 15x + 20$$
$$6x + 6 - 6 = 20 - 6$$
$$6x = 14$$
$$x = \frac{14}{6}$$
$$x = \frac{7}{3}$$

C) If there are radicals in the equation, it is necessary to square both sides and then apply A.

$$\sqrt{3x+1} = 5$$

$$(\sqrt{3x+1})^2 = 5^2$$

$$3x + 1 = 25$$

$$3x + 1 - 1 = 25 - 1$$

$$3x = 24$$

$$x = \frac{24}{3}$$

$$x = 8$$

☞ Drill: Equations

DIRECTIONS: Solve for *x*.

1. $4x - 2 = 10$

   (A) -1 (B) 2 (C) 3 (D) 4

2. $7z + 1 - z = 2z - 7$

   (A) -2 (B) 0 (C) 1 (D) 2

3. $\frac{1}{3}b + 3 = \frac{1}{2}b$

   (A) $\frac{1}{2}$ (B) 2 (C) $3\frac{3}{5}$ (D) 18

4. $0.4p + 1 = 0.7p - 2$

   (A) 0.1 (B) 2 (C) 5 (D) 10

5. $4(3x + 2) - 11 = 3(3x - 2)$

   (A) -3 (B) -1 (C) 2 (D) 3

TWO LINEAR EQUATIONS

Equations of the form $ax + by = c$, where a, b, c are constants and a, b $\neq 0$ are called **linear equations** with two unknown variables.

There are several ways to solve systems of linear equations with two variables.

Method 1: **Addition or subtraction**—If necessary, multiply the equations by numbers that will make the coefficients of one unknown in the resulting equations numerically equal. If the signs of equal coefficients are the same, subtract the equation, otherwise add.

The result is one equation with one unknown; we solve it and substitute the value into the other equations to find the unknown that we first eliminated.

Method 2: **Substitution**—Find the value of one unknown in terms of the other. Substitute this value in the other equation and solve.

Method 3: **Graph**—Graph both equations. The point of intersection of the drawn lines is a simultaneous solution for the equations, and its coordinates correspond to the answer that would be found analytically.

If the lines are parallel they have no simultaneous solution.

Dependent equations are equations that represent the same line; therefore, every point on the line of a dependent equation represents a solution. Since there is an infinite number of points on a line, there is an infinite number of simultaneous solutions. For example,

$$\begin{cases} 2x + y = 8 \\ 4x + 2y = 16 \end{cases}$$

These equations are dependent. Since they represent the same line, all points that satisfy either of the equations are solutions of the system.

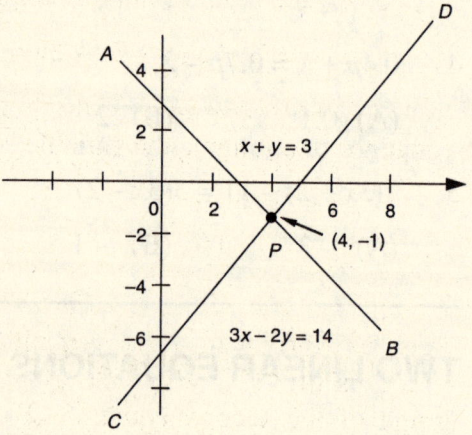

A system of linear equations is consistent if there is only one solution for the system.

A system of linear equations is inconsistent if it does not have any solutions.

● **EXAMPLE**

Find the point of intersection of the graphs of the equations as shown in the previous figure.

$$x + y = 3$$

$$3x - 2y = 14$$

To solve these linear equations, solve for y in terms of x. The equations will be in the form $y = mx + b$, where m is the slope and b is the intercept on the y-axis.

$$x + y = 3$$

Subtract x from both sides: $\qquad\qquad y = 3 - x$

Subtract $3x$ from both sides: $3x - 2y = 14$

Divide by -2: $-2y = 14 - 3x$

$$y = -7 + \frac{3}{2}x$$

The graphs of the linear functions, $y = 3 - x$ and $y = 7 + \frac{3}{2}x$ can be determined by plotting only two points. For example, for $y = 3 - x$, let $x = 0$, then $y = 3$. Let $x = 1$, then $y = 2$. The two points on this first line are

$(0, 3)$ and $(1, 2)$. For $y = -7 + \frac{3}{2}x$, let $x = 0$, then $y = -7$. Let $x = 1$, then

$y = -5\frac{1}{2}$. The two points on this second line are $(0, -7)$ and $(1, -5\frac{1}{2})$.

To find the point of intersection P of

$$x + y = 3 \quad \text{and} \quad 3x - 2y = 14,$$

solve them algebraically. Multiply the first equation by 2. Add these two equations to eliminate the variable y.

$$\begin{array}{rl} 2x + 2y = & 6 \\ 3x - 2y = & 14 \\ \hline 5x \quad\quad = & 20 \end{array}$$

Solve for x to obtain $x = 4$. Substitute this into $y = 3 - x$ to get $y = 3 - 4 = -1$. P is $(4, -1)$. AB is the graph of the first equation, and CD is the graph of the second equation. The point of intersection P of the two graphs is the only point on both lines. The coordinates of P satisfy both equations and represent the desired solution of the problem. From the graph, P seems to be the point $(4, -1)$. These coordinates satisfy both equations, and hence are the exact coordinates of the point of intersection of the two lines.

To show that $(4, -1)$ satisfies both equations, substitute this point into both equations.

$x + y = 3$	$3x - 2y = 14$
$4 + (-1) = 3$	$3(4) - 2(-1) = 14$
$4 - 1 = 3$	$12 + 2 = 14$
$3 = 3$	$14 = 14$

● **EXAMPLE**

Solve the equations $2x + 3y = 6$ and $4x + 6y = 7$ simultaneously.

We have two equations and two unknowns,

$$2x + 3y = 6 \quad (1)$$

and

$$4x + 6y = 7 \quad (2)$$

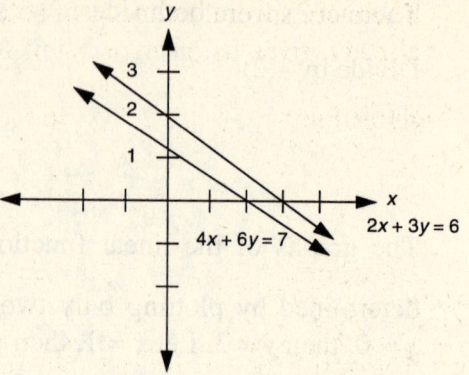

There are several methods to solve this problem. We have chosen to multiply each equation by a different number so that when the two equations are added, one of the variables drops out. Thus,

Multiply equation (1) by 2:	$4x + 6y = 12$	(3)
Multiply equation (2) by – 1:	$-4x - 6y = -7$	(4)
Add equations (3) and (4):	$0 = 5$	

We obtain a peculiar result!

Actually, what we have shown in this case is that if there were a simultaneous solution to the given equations, then 0 would equal 5. But the conclusion is impossible; therefore, there can be no simultaneous solution to these two equations, hence no point satisfying both.

The straight lines which are the graphs of these equations must be parallel if they never intersect, but not identical, which can be seen from the graph of these equations (see the accompanying diagram).

● **EXAMPLE**

Solve the equations $2x + 3y = 6$ and $y = -\left(\dfrac{2x}{3}\right) + 2$ simultaneously.

We have two equations and two unknowns.

$$2x + 3y = 6 \quad (1)$$

and

$$y = -\left(\frac{2x}{3}\right) + 2 \quad (2)$$

There are several methods of solution for this problem. Since equation (2) already gives us an expression for y, we use the method of substitution.

Substitute $-\left(\dfrac{2x}{3}\right) + 2$ for y in the first equation:

$$2x + 3(-\frac{2x}{3} + 2) = 6$$

Distribute: $$2x - 2x + 6 = 6$$
$$6 = 6$$

The result $6 = 6$ is true, but indicates no solution. Actually, our work shows that no matter what real number x is, if y is determined by the second equation, then the first equation will always be satisfied.

The reason for this peculiarity may be seen if we take a closer look at the

equation $y = -\left(\dfrac{2x}{3}\right) + 2$. It is equivalent to $3y = -2x + 6$, or $2x + 3y = 6$.

In other words, the two equations are equivalent. Any pair of values of x and y which satisfies one satisfies the other.

It is hardly necessary to verify that in this case the graphs of the given equations are identical lines, and that there are an infinite number of simultaneous solutions to these equations.

A system of three linear equations in three unknowns is solved by eliminating one unknown from any two of the three equations and solving them. After finding two unknowns substitute them in any of the equations to find the third unknown.

PROBLEM

Solve the system

$2x + 3y - 4z = -8$	(1)
$x + y - 2z = -5$	(2)
$7x - 2y + 5z = 4$	(3)

SOLUTION

We cannot eliminate any variable from two pairs of equations by a single multiplication. However, both x and z may be eliminated from equations (1) and (2) by multiplying equation (2) by -2. Then

$2x + 3y - 4z = -8$	(1)
$-2x - 2y + 4z = 10$	(4)

By addition, we have $y = 2$. Although we may now eliminate either x or z from another pair of equations, we can more conveniently substitute $y = 2$ in equations (2) and (3) to get two equations in two variables. Thus, making the substitution $y = 2$ in equations (2) and (3), we have

$$x - 2z = -7 \qquad\qquad (5)$$

$$7x + 5z = 8 \qquad\qquad (6)$$

Multiply equation (5) by 5 and multiply (6) by 2. Then add the two new equations. Then $x = -1$. Substitute x in either equation (5) or (6) to find z.

The solution of the system is $x = -1$, $y = 2$, and $z = 3$. Check by substitution.

A system of equations, as shown below, that has all constant terms $b_1, b_2, \ldots, b_n$ equal to zero is said to be a homogeneous system.

$$\begin{cases} a_{11}x_1 + a_{12}x_2 + \ldots + a_{1n}x_m = b_1 \\ a_{21}x_1 + a_{22}x_2 + \ldots + a_{2n}x_m = b_2 \\ \quad\vdots \qquad\quad \vdots \qquad\qquad \vdots \qquad \vdots \\ a_{n1}x_1 + a_{n2}x_2 + \ldots + a_{nn}x_m = b_n \end{cases}$$

A homogeneous system (one in which each variable can be replaced by a constant and the constant can be factored out) always has at least one solution which is called the trivial solution that is $x_1 = 0$, $x_2 = 0$, $\ldots$, $x_m = 0$.

For any given homogeneous system of equations, in which the number of variables is greater than or equal to the number of equations, there are non-trivial solutions.

Two systems of linear equations are said to be equivalent if and only if they have the same solution set.

☞ Drill: Two Linear Equations

> **DIRECTIONS**: Find the solution set for each pair of equations.

1. $3x + 4y = -2$

   $x - 6y = -8$

   (A) $(2, -1)$ (B) $(1, -2)$ (C) $(-2, -1)$ (D) $(-2, 1)$

2. $2x + y = -10$
       $-2x - 4y = 4$

    (A) $(6, -2)$ (B) $(-6, 2)$ (C) $(-2, 6)$ (D) $(2, 6)$

3. $6x + 5y = -4$
       $3x - 3y = 9$

    (A) $(1, -2)$ (B) $(1, 2)$ (C) $(2, -1)$ (D) $(-2, 1)$

4. $4x + 3y = 9$
       $2x - 2y = 8$

    (A) $(-3, 1)$ (B) $(1, -3)$ (C) $(3, 1)$ (D) $(3, -1)$

5. $x + y = 7$
       $x = y - 3$

    (A) $(5, 2)$ (B) $(-5, 2)$ (C) $(2, 5)$ (D) $(-2, 5)$

QUADRATIC EQUATIONS

A second degree equation in x of the type $ax^2 + bx + c = 0$, $a \neq 0$, a, b, and c are real numbers, is called a **quadratic equation.**

To solve a quadratic equation is to find values of x which satisfy $ax^2 + bx + c = 0$. These values of x are called **solutions**, or **roots**, of the equation.

A quadratic equation has a maximum of two roots. Methods of solving quadratic equations:

A) **Direct solution**: Given $x^2 - 9 = 0$.

    We can solve directly by isolating the variable x.

    $x^2 = 9$

    $x = \pm 3$

B) **Factoring**: Given a quadratic equation $ax^2 + bx + c = 0$, a, b, $c \neq 0$, to factor means to express it as the product $a(x - r_1)(x - r_2) = 0$, where r_1 and r_2 are the two roots.

Some helpful hints to remember are:

a) $r_1 + r_2 = -\dfrac{b}{a}$.

b) $r_1 r_2 = \dfrac{c}{a}$.

Given $x^2 - 5x + 4 = 0$.

Since

$$r_1 + r_2 = -\frac{b}{a} = -\frac{(-5)}{1} = 5,$$

the possible solutions are $(3, 2)$, $(4, 1)$, and $(5, 0)$. Also

$$r_1 r_2 = \frac{c}{a} = \frac{4}{1} = 4;$$

this equation is satisfied only by the second pair, so $r_1 = 4$, $r_2 = 1$, and the factored form is $(x - 4)(x - 1) = 0$.

If the coefficient of x^2 is not 1, it is necessary to divide the equation by this coefficient and then factor.

Given $2x^2 - 12x + 16 = 0$.

Dividing by 2, we obtain

$$x^2 - 6x + 8 = 0.$$

Since

$$r_1 + r_2 = -\frac{b}{a} = 6,$$

the possible solutions are $(6, 0)$, $(5, 1)$, $(4, 2)$, and $(3, 3)$. Also $r_1 r_2 = 8$, so the only possible answer is $(4, 2)$ and the expression $x^2 - 6x + 8 = 0$ can be factored as $(x - 4)(x - 2)$.

C) **Completing the square**: If it is difficult to factor the quadratic equation using the previous method, we can complete the square.

Given $x^2 - 12x + 8 = 0$.

We know that the two roots added up should be 12 because

$$r_1 + r_2 = -\frac{b}{a} = \frac{-(-12)}{1} = 12.$$

The possible roots are (12, 0), (11, 1), (10, 2), (9, 3), (8, 4), (7, 5), and (6, 6).

But none of these satisfy $r_1 r_2 = 8$, so we cannot use (B).

To complete the square, it is necessary to isolate the constant term,

$$x^2 - 12x = -8.$$

Then take $\frac{1}{2}$ of the coefficient of x, square it and add to both sides.

$$x^2 - 12x + \left(\frac{-12}{2}\right)^2 = -8 + \left(\frac{-12}{2}\right)^2$$
$$x^2 - 12x + 36 = -8 + 36 = 28$$

Now we can use the previous method to factor the left side.

$$r_1 + r_2 = 12, \ r_1 r_2 = 36$$

is satisfied by the pair (6, 6), so we have

$$(x - 6)^2 = 28.$$

Now extract the root of both sides and solve for x.

$$(x - 6) = \pm\sqrt{28} = \pm 2\sqrt{7}$$
$$x = \pm 2\sqrt{7} + 6$$

So the roots are

$$x = 2\sqrt{7} + 6, \ x = -2\sqrt{7} + 6.$$

PROBLEM

Solve the equation $x^2 + 8x + 15 = 0$.

SOLUTION

Since

$$(x + a)(x + b) = x^2 + bx + ax + ab$$
$$= x^2 + (a + b)x + ab,$$

we may factor the given equation,

$$0 = x^2 + 8x + 15,$$

replacing $a + b$ by 8 and ab by 15. Thus,

$$a + b = 8, \quad \text{and} \quad ab = 15.$$

We want the two numbers a and b whose sum is 8 and whose product is 15. We check all pairs of numbers whose product is 15.

(a) $1 \times 15 = 15$; thus, $a = 1$, $b = 15$, and $ab = 15$.

$1 + 15 = 16$; therefore, we reject these values because $a + b \neq 8$.

(b) $3 \times 5 = 15$; thus, $a = 3$, $b = 5$, and $ab = 15$.

$3 + 5 = 8$; therefore, $a + b = 8$, and we accept these values.

Hence, $x^2 + 8x + 15 = 0$ is equivalent to

$$0 = x^2 + (3 + 5)x + 3 \times 5 = (x + 3)(x + 5)$$

Hence, $x + 5 = 0$ or $x + 3 = 0$.

Since the product of these two numbers is zero, one of the numbers must be zero. Hence, $x = -5$, or $x = -3$, and the solution set is $x = \{-5, -3\}$.

Note that $x = -5$ or $x = -3$. We are certainly not making the statement that $x = -5$ and $x = -3$. Also, check that both these numbers do actually satisfy the given equations and hence are solutions.

Check: Replacing x by (-5) in the original equation:

$$x^2 + 8x + 15 = 0$$
$$(-5)^2 + 8(-5) + 15 = 0$$
$$25 - 40 + 15 = 0$$
$$-15 + 15 = 0$$
$$0 = 0$$

Replacing x by (-3) in the original equation:

$$x^2 + 8x + 15 = 0$$
$$(-3)^2 + 8(-3) + 15 = 0$$
$$9 - 24 + 15 = 0$$
$$-15 + 15 = 0$$
$$0 = 0$$

PROBLEM

Solve the following equations by factoring.

(1) $2x^2 + 3x = 0$

(2) $y^2 - 2y - 3 = y - 3$

(3) $z^2 - 2z - 3 = 0$

(4) $2m^2 - 11m - 6 = 0$

SOLUTION

(1) $2x^2 + 3x = 0$. Factor out the common factor of x from the left side of the given equation.

$$x(2x + 3) = 0$$

Whenever a product $ab = 0$, where a and b are any two numbers, either $a = 0$ or $b = 0$. Then, either

$$x = 0 \quad \text{or} \quad 2x + 3 = 0$$
$$2x = -3$$
$$x = -\frac{3}{2}$$

Hence, the solution set to the original equation $2x^2 + 3x = 0$ is: $\{-\frac{3}{2}, 0\}$.

(2) $y^2 - 2y - 3 = y - 3$. Subtract $(y - 3)$ from both sides of the given equation.

$$y^2 - 2y - 3 - (y - 3) = y - 3 - (y - 3)$$
$$y^2 - 2y - 3 - y + 3 = y - 3 - y + 3$$
$$y^2 - 2y - \cancel{3} - y + \cancel{3} = \cancel{y} - \cancel{3} - \cancel{y} + \cancel{3}$$
$$y^2 - 3y = 0$$

Factor out a common factor of y from the left side of this equation:

$$y(y - 3) = 0$$

Thus, $y = 0$ or $y - 3 = 0$, $y = 3$.

Therefore, the solution set to the original equation $y^2 - 2y - 3 = y - 3$ is $\{0, 3\}$.

(3) $z^2 - 2z - 3 = 0$. Factor the original equation into a product of two polynomials.

$$z^2 - 2z - 3 = (z - 3)(z + 1) = 0$$

Hence,

$$(z - 3)(z + 1) = 0; \text{ and } z - 3 = 0 \quad \text{or} \quad z + 1 = 0$$
$$z = 3 \qquad\qquad z = -1$$

Therefore, the solution set to the original equation $z^2 - 2z - 3 = 0$ is $\{-1, 3\}$.

(4) $2m^2 - 11m - 6 = 0$. Factor the original equation into a product of two polynomials.

$$2m^2 - 11m - 6 = (2m + 1)(m - 6) = 0$$

Thus,

$$2m + 1 = 0 \quad \text{or} \quad m - 6 = 0$$
$$2m = -1 \qquad\qquad m = 6$$
$$m = -\frac{1}{2}$$

Therefore, the solution set to the original equation $2m^2 - 11m - 6 = 0$ is $\left\{-\frac{1}{2}, 6\right\}$.

☞ Drill: Quadratic Equations

DIRECTIONS: Solve for all values of x.

1. $x^2 - 2x - 8 = 0$

    (A) 4 and –2   (B) 4 and 8   (C) 4   (D) –2 and 8

2. $x^2 + 2x - 3 = 0$

    (A) –3 and 2   (B) 2 and 1   (C) 3 and 1   (D) –3 and 1

3. $x^2 - 7x = -10$

    (A) –3 and 5   (B) 2 and 5   (C) 2   (D) –2 and –5

4. $x^2 - 8x + 16 = 0$

    (A) 8 and 2   (B) 1 and 16   (C) 4   (D) –2 and 4

5. $3x^2 + 3x = 6$

    (A) 3 and –6   (B) 2 and 3   (C) –3 and 2   (D) 1 and –2

ABSOLUTE VALUE EQUATIONS

The absolute value of a, $|a|$, is defined as

$|a| = a$ when $a > 0$,

$|a| = -a$ when $a < 0$,

$|a| = 0$ when $a = 0$.

When the definition of absolute value is applied to an equation, the quantity within the absolute value symbol is considered to have two values. This value can be either positive or negative before the absolute value is taken. As a result, each absolute value equation actually contains two separate equations.

When evaluating equations containing absolute values, proceed as follows:

● **EXAMPLE**

$|5 - 3x| = 7$ is valid if either

$$5 - 3x = 7 \qquad \text{or} \qquad 5 - 3x = -7$$

$$-3x = 2 \qquad\qquad\qquad -3x = -12$$

$$x = -\frac{2}{3} \qquad\qquad\qquad x = 4$$

The solution set is therefore $x = \left(-\dfrac{2}{3}, 4\right)$.

Remember, the absolute value of a number cannot be negative. So, for the equation $|5x + 4| = -3$, there would be no solution.

☞ Drill: Absolute Value Equations

DIRECTIONS: Find the appropriate solutions.

1. $|4x - 2| = 6$

   (A) -2 and -1 (C) 2

   (B) -1 and 2   (D) No solution

2. $\left|3 - \dfrac{1}{2}y\right| = -7$

   (A) -8 and 20   (C) 2 and -5

   (B) 8 and -20 (D) No solution

3. $2|x+7| = 12$

    (A) -13 and -1 (C) -1 and 13

    (B) -6 and 6 (D) No solution

4. $|5x| - 7 = 3$

    (A) 2 and 4 (C) -2 and 2

    (B) $\dfrac{4}{5}$ and 3 (D) No solution

5. $\left|\dfrac{3}{4}m\right| = 9$

    (A) 24 and -16 (C) -12 and 12

    (B) $\dfrac{4}{27}$ and $-\dfrac{4}{3}$ (D) No solution

INEQUALITIES

An inequality is a statement where the value of one quantity or expression is greater than ($>$), less than ($<$), greater than or equal to ($\geq$), less than or equal to ($\leq$), or not equal to ($\neq$) that of another.

● **EXAMPLE**

    $5 > 4$

The expression above means that the value of 5 is greater than the value of 4.

A **conditional inequality** is an inequality whose validity depends on the values of the variables in the sentence. That is, certain values of the variables will make the sentence true, and others will make it false.

    $3 - y > 3 + y$

is a conditional inequality for the set of real numbers, since it is true for any replacement less than zero and false for all others.

    $x + 5 > x + 2$

is an **absolute inequality** for the set of real numbers, meaning that for any real value x, the expression on the left is greater than the expression on the right.

$$5y < 2y + y$$

is inconsistent for the set of non-negative real numbers. For any y greater than 0 the sentence is always false. A sentence is inconsistent if it is always false when its variables assume allowable values.

The solution of a given inequality in one variable x consists of all values of x for which the inequality is true.

The graph of an inequality in one variable is represented by either a ray or a line segment on the real number line.

The endpoint is not a solution if the variable is strictly less than or greater than a particular value.

● **EXAMPLE**

$x > 2$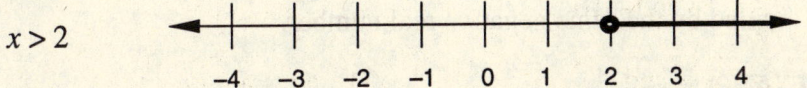

2 is not a solution and should be represented as shown.

The endpoint is a solution if the variable is either (1) less than or equal to or (2) greater than or equal to a particular value.

● **EXAMPLE**

$5 > x \geq 2$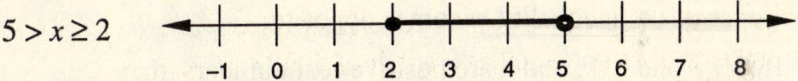

In this case 2 is the solution and should be represented as shown.

PROPERTIES OF INEQUALITIES

If x and y are real numbers, then one and only one of the following statements is true.

$x > y$, $x = y$, or $x < y$.

This is the order property of real numbers.

If a, b, and c are real numbers, the following statements are true:

A) If $a < b$ and $b < c$ then $a < c$.

B) If $a > b$ and $b > c$ then $a > c$.

This is the transitive property of inequalities.

If a, b, and c are real numbers and $a > b$, then $a + c > b + c$ and $a - c > b - c$. This is the **addition property of inequality**.

Two inequalities are said to have the same **sense** if their signs of inequality point in the same direction.

The sense of an inequality remains the same if both sides are multiplied or divided by the same positive real number.

● **EXAMPLE**

$4 > 3$

If we multiply both sides by 5, we will obtain

$4 \times 5 > 3 \times 5$

$20 > 15$

The sense of the inequality does not change.

The sense of an inequality becomes opposite if each side is multiplied or divided by the same negative real number.

● **EXAMPLE**

$4 > 3$

If we multiply both sides by -5, we would obtain

$4 \times -5 < 3 \times -5$

$-20 < -15$

The sense of the inequality becomes opposite.

If $a > b$ and a, b, and n are positive real numbers, then

$a^n > b^n$ and $a^{-n} < b^{-n}$

If $x > y$ and $q > p$, then $x + q > y + p$.

If $x > y > 0$ and $q > p > 0$, then $xq > yp$.

Inequalities that have the same solution set are called **equivalent inequalities**.

PROBLEM

Solve the inequality $2x + 5 > 9$.

SOLUTION

Add -5 to both sides:	$2x + 5 + (-5) > 9 + (-5)$
Additive inverse property:	$2x + 0 > 9 + (-5)$
Additive identity property:	$2x > 9 + (-5)$
Combine terms:	$2x > 4$

Multiply both sides by $\frac{1}{2}$: $\qquad \frac{1}{2}(2x) > \frac{1}{2} \times 4$

$$x > 2$$

The solution set is

$$X = \{x \mid 2x + 5 > 9\}$$
$$= \{x \mid x > 2\}$$

(that is all x, such that x is greater than 2).

☞ Drill: Inequalities

DIRECTIONS: Find the solution set for each inequality.

1. $3m + 2 < 7$

   (A) $m \geq \dfrac{5}{3}$ (B) $m > 2$ (C) $m < 2$ (D) $m < \dfrac{5}{3}$

2. $\dfrac{1}{2}x - 3 \leq 1$

   (A) $-4 \leq x \leq 8$ (B) $x \geq -8$ (C) $x \leq 8$ (D) $2 \leq x \leq 8$

3. $-3p + 1 \geq 16$

   (A) $p \geq -5$ (B) $p \geq \dfrac{-17}{3}$ (C) $p \leq \dfrac{-17}{3}$ (D) $p \leq -5$

4. $-6 < \dfrac{2}{3}r + 6 \leq 2$

   (A) $-6 < r \leq -3$ (C) $r \geq -6$

   (B) $-18 < r \leq -6$ (D) $-2 < r \leq -\dfrac{4}{3}$

5. $0 < 2 - y < 6$

   (A) $-4 < y < 2$ (C) $-4 < y < -2$

   (B) $-4 < y < 0$ (D) $-2 < y < 4$

RATIOS AND PROPORTIONS

The ratio of two numbers x and y written $x : y$ is the fraction $\dfrac{x}{y}$ where $y \neq 0$. A ratio compares x to y by dividing one by the other. Therefore, in order to compare ratios, simply compare the fractions.

A proportion is an equality of two ratios. The laws of proportion are listed below.

If $\dfrac{a}{b} = \dfrac{c}{d}$, then

    (A) $ad = bc$

    (B) $\dfrac{b}{a} = \dfrac{d}{c}$

    (C) $\dfrac{a}{c} = \dfrac{b}{d}$

    (D) $\dfrac{a+b}{b} = \dfrac{c+d}{d}$

    (E) $\dfrac{a-b}{b} = \dfrac{c-d}{d}$

Given a proportion $a : b = c : d$, then a and d are called **extremes**, b and c are called the **means**, and d is called the fourth proportion to a, b, and c.

PROBLEM

Solve the proportion $\dfrac{x+1}{4} = \dfrac{15}{12}$.

SOLUTION

Cross-multiply to determine x; that is, multiply the numerator of the first fraction by the denominator of the second, and equate this to the product of the numerator of the second and the denominator of the first.

$$(x + 1)\,12 = 4 \times 15$$

$$12x + 12 = 60$$

$$x = 4$$

☞ Drill: Ratios and Proportions

DIRECTIONS: Find the appropriate solutions.

---

1. Solve for n: $\dfrac{4}{n} = \dfrac{8}{5}$.

   (A) 10   (B) 8   (C) 6   (D) 2.5

2. Solve for n: $\dfrac{2}{3} = \dfrac{n}{72}$.

   (A) 12   (B) 48   (C) 64   (D) 56

3. Solve for n: $n : 12 = 3 : 4$.

   (A) 8   (B) 1   (C) 9   (D) 4

4. Four out of every five students at West High take a mathematics course. If the enrollment at West is 785, how many students take mathematics?

   (A) 628   (B) 157   (C) 705   (D) 655

5. At a factory, three out of every 1,000 parts produced are defective. In a day, the factory can produce 25,000 parts. How many of these parts would be defective?

   (A) 7   (B) 75   (C) 750   (D) 7,500

6. A summer league softball team won 28 out of the 32 games they played. What is the ratio of games won to games played?

   (A) 4 : 5   (B) 3 : 4   (C) 7 : 8   (D) 2 : 3

ALGEBRA REVIEW

ANSWER KEY

Drill: Operations with Polynomials

1.	(B)	6.	(B)	11.	(C)	16.	(C)
2.	(C)	7.	(C)	12.	(B)	17.	(D)
3.	(C)	8.	(D)	13.	(D)	18.	(D)
4.	(D)	9.	(A)	14.	(A)	19.	(B)
5.	(A)	10.	(D)	15.	(D)	20.	(B)

Drill: Simplifying Algebraic Expressions

1.	(C)	3.	(B)	4.	(A)	5.	(D)
2.	(D)						

Drill: Equations and Linear Equations

1.	(C)	3.	(D)	4.	(D)	5.	(B)
2.	(A)						

Drill: Two Linear Equations

1.	(D)	3.	(A)	4.	(D)	5.	(C)
2.	(B)						

Drill: Quadratic Equations

1.	(A)	3.	(B)	4.	(C)	5.	(D)
2.	(D)						

Drill: Absolute Value Equations

1.	(B)	3.	(A)	4.	(C)	5.	(C)
2.	(D)						

Drill: Inequalities

1. (D)   3. (D)   4. (B)   5. (A)
2. (C)

Drill: Ratios and Proportions

1. (D)   3. (C)   5. (B)   6. (C)
2. (B)   4. (A)

DETAILED EXPLANATIONS OF ANSWERS

Drill: Operations with Polynomials

1. **(B)** $9a^2b + 3c + 2a^2b + 5c = (9a^2b + 2a^2b) + (3c + 5c)$
$$= 11a^2b + 8c$$

2. **(C)** $14m^2n^3 + 6m^2n^3 + 3m^2n^3 = 23m^2n^3$

3. **(C)** $3x + 2y + 16x + 3z + 6y = (3x + 16x) + (2y + 6y) + 3z$
$$= 19x + 8y + 3z$$

4. **(D)** $(4d^2 + 7e^3 + 12f) + (3d^2 + 6e^3 + 2f) =$
$$(4d^2 + 3d^2) + (7e^3 + 6e^3) + (12f + 2f) =$$
$$7d^2 + 13e^3 + 14f$$

5. **(A)** $3ac^2 = +2b^2c + 7ac^2 + 2ac^2 + b^2c =$
$$(3ac^2 + 7ac^2 + 2ac^2) + (2b^2c + b^2c) =$$
$$12ac^2 + 3b^2c$$

6. **(B)** $14m^2n - 6m^2n = 8m^2n$

7. **(C)** $3x^3y^2 - 4xz - 6x^3y^2 = (3x^3y^2 - 6x^3y^2) - 4xz$
$$= -3x^3y^2 - 4xz$$

8. **(D)** $9g^2 + 6h - 2g^2 - 5h = (9g^2 - 2g^2) + (6h - 5h)$
$$= 7g^2 + h$$

9. **(A)** $7b^3 - 4c^2 - 6b^3 + 3c^2 = (7b^3 - 6b^3) + (-4c^2 + 3c^2)$
$$= b^3 - c^2$$

10. **(D)** $11q^2r - 4q^2r - 8q^2r = (11q^2r - 4q^2r) - 8q^2r$
$$= 7q^2r - 8q^2r$$
$$= -q^2r$$

11. **(C)** $5p^2t \times 3p^2t = (5 \times 3)(p^2 \times p^2)(t \times t)$
$$= 15p^4t^2$$

12. **(B)** $(2r + s)14r = (2r)(14r) + (s)(14r)$
$$= 28r^2 + 14sr$$

13. **(D)**
$(4m + p)(3m - 2p) = (4m)(3m) + (4m)(-2p) + (p)(3m) + (p)(-2p)$
$$= 12m^2 + [(-8mp) + 3mp] + (-2p^2)$$
$$= 12m^2 - 5mp - 2p^2$$

14. **(A)**
$(2a + b)(3a^2 + ab + b^2) = (2a)(3a^2) + (2a)(ab) + (2a)(b^2) + (b)(3a^2) +$
$(b)(ab) + (b)(b^2) = 6a^3 + 2a^2b + 2ab^2 + 3a^2b + ab^2 + b^3$
$$= 6a^3 + 5a^2b + 3ab^2 + b^3$$

15. **(D)** $(6t^2 + 2t + 1)(3t) = (6t^2)(3t) + (2t)(3t) + (1)(3t)$
$$= 18t^3 + 6t^2 + 3t$$

16. **(C)** $(x^2 + x - 6) \div (x - 2) = \dfrac{x^2 + x - 6}{(x - 2)} = \dfrac{(x + 3)(x - 2)}{(x - 2)} = x + 3$

17. **(D)** $24b^4c^3 \div 6b^2c = \dfrac{\overset{4}{\cancel{24}} \, \overset{b^2}{\cancel{b^4}} \, \overset{c^2}{\cancel{c^3}}}{\underset{}{\cancel{6}} \, \cancel{b^2} \, \cancel{c}} = 4b^2c^2$

18. **(D)** $(3p^2 + pq - 2q^2) \div (p+q) = \dfrac{3p^2 + pq - 2q^2}{(p+q)}$

$$= \frac{(3p - 2q)\cancel{(p+q)}}{\cancel{(p+q)}}$$

$$= 3p - 2q$$

19. **(B)** $(y^3 - 2y^2 - y + 2) \div (y - 2) = y - 2 \overline{\smash{\big)}\ \begin{array}{l} y^2 - 1 \\ y^3 - 2y^2 - y + 2 \end{array}}$

$$\underline{- \ (y^3 - 2y^2)}$$

$$0 - y + 2$$

$$\underline{- (-y + 2)}$$

$$0$$

20. **(B)**

$$(m^2 + m - 14) \div (m + 4) = m + 4 \overline{\smash{\big)}\ \begin{array}{l} m - 3 \\ m^2 + m - 14 \end{array}}$$

$$\underline{- \ (m^2 + 4m)}$$

$$-3m - 14$$

$$\underline{- (-3m - 12)}$$

$$-2 \qquad = \dfrac{-2}{m+4}$$

$$m - 3 + \frac{-2}{m + 4}$$

Drill: Simplifying Algebraic Expressions

1. **(C)** $16b^2 - 25z^2 = (4b + 5z)(4b - 5z)$

2. **(D)** $x^2 - 2x - 8 = (x - 4)(x + 2)$

3. **(B)** $2c^2 + 5cd - 3d^2 = (2c - d)(c + 3d)$

4. **(A)** $4t^3 - 20t = 4t(t^2 - 5)$

5. **(D)** $x^2 + xy - 2y^2 = (x - y)(x + 2y)$

Drill: Equations and Linear Equations

1. **(C)** $4x - 2 = 10$

$$\underline{+2 = +2}$$

$$\frac{4x}{4} = \frac{12}{4}$$

$$x = 3$$

2. **(A)** $7z + 1 - z = 2z - 7$

$$6z + 1 = 2z - 7$$

$$\underline{-1 \qquad -1}$$

$$6z = 2z - 8$$

$$-2z \quad -2z - 8$$

$$\frac{4z}{4} = \frac{-8}{4}$$

$$x = -2$$

3. **(D)** $\frac{1}{3}b + 3 = \frac{1}{2}b$

$$\underline{-\frac{1}{3}b \qquad -\frac{1}{3}b}$$

$$3 = \frac{1}{2}b - \frac{1}{3}b$$

$$6(3) = 6\left(\frac{1}{2}b - \frac{1}{3}b\right)$$

$$18 = 3b - 2b$$

$$18 = b$$

4. **(D)**
$$0.4p + 1 = 0.7p - 2$$
$$\underline{+2 = +2}$$
$$0.4p + 3 = 0.7p$$
$$\underline{-0.4p -0.4p}$$
$$3 = 0.3p$$
$$10(3) = 0.3p(10)$$
$$\frac{30}{3} = \frac{3p}{3}$$
$$10 = p$$

5. **(B)**
$$12x - 3 = 9x - 6$$
$$\underline{-\ 9x -9x}$$
$$3x - 3 = -6$$
$$\underline{+3 +3}$$
$$\frac{3x}{3} = \frac{-3}{3}$$
$$x = -1$$

Drill: Two Linear Equations

1. **(D)**
$$3x + 4y = -2 \quad = \quad 3x + 4y = -2$$
$$-3(\ x - 6y = -8) \quad = \quad +-3x + 18y = \ 24$$
$$0 + 22y = 22$$
$$y = 1$$

Substitute $y = 1$ in $x - 6y = -8$ to get
$$x - 6 = -8$$
$$\underline{+6 +6}$$
$$x = 2$$

$$(-2, 1)$$

2. **(B)**

$$2x + y = -10$$
$$\underline{-2x - 4y = 4}$$
$$0 - 3y = -6$$
$$\frac{-3y}{-3} = \frac{-6}{-3}$$
$$y = 2$$

$y = 2$ substitute in first equation to get

$$2x + 2 = -10$$
$$\underline{-2 = -2}$$
$$\frac{2x}{2} = \frac{-12}{2}$$

$$(-6, 2)$$

3. **(A)**

$$6x + 5y = -4 \qquad = \qquad 6x + 5y = -4$$
$$(3x - 3y = 9)(-2) \quad = \quad \underline{-6x + 6y = -18}$$
$$0 + 11y = -22$$
$$\frac{11y}{11} = \frac{-22}{11}$$
$$y = -2$$

substitute in the second equation to get

$$3x - 3(-2) = 9$$
$$3x + 6 = 9$$
$$\underline{-6 \quad -6}$$
$$\frac{3x}{3} = \frac{3}{3}$$
$$x = 1$$

$$(1, -2)$$

4. **(D)**

$$4x + 3y = 9 \qquad = \qquad 4x + 3y = 9$$
$$(2x - 2y = 8)(-2) \qquad = \qquad -4x + 4y = -16$$
$$0 + 7y = -7$$
$$\underline{y = -1}$$

substitute in the first equation to get
$$4x + 3(-1) = 9$$
$$4x - 3 = 9$$
$$\underline{+3 \ = +3}$$
$$\frac{4x}{4} = \frac{12}{4}$$
$$x = 3$$

$$(3, -1)$$

5. **(C)**

$$x + y = 7 \qquad = \qquad x + y = 7$$
$$(+y) + x = y - 3(-y) \qquad = \qquad x - y = -3$$
$$\frac{1}{2}(2x + 0 = 4)$$
$$\underline{y = 2}$$

substitute in the first equation
$$(-2x)2 + y = 7(-2)$$
$$\underline{y = 5}$$

$$(2, 5)$$

Drill: Quadratic Equations

1. **(A)**
$$(x^2 - 2x - 8) = 0$$
$$(x - 4)(x + 2) = 0$$
The values of x are 4 and –2.

2. **(D)**
$$x^2 + 2x - 3 = 0$$
$$(x + 3)(x - 1) = 0$$
The values of x are 3 and –1.

3. **(B)** $$x^2 - 7x = -10$$
$$x^2 - 7x + 10 = 0$$
$$(x - 5)(x - 2) = 0$$

The values of x are 5 and 2.

4. **(C)** $$x^2 - 8x + 16 = 0$$
$$(x - 4)(x - 4) = 0$$
$$(x - 4)^2 = 0$$

The value of x is 4.

5. **(D)** $$3x^2 + 3x = 6$$
$$3x^2 + 3x - 6 = 0$$
$$3(x^2 + x - 2) = 0$$
$$3(x + 2)(x - 1) = 0$$

The values of x are –2 and 1.

Drill: Absolute Value Equations

1. **(B)** $|4x - 2| = 6$ $4x - 2 = 6$ or $4x - 2 = -6$
$4x = 8$ $4x = -4$
$\underline{x = 2}$ or $\underline{x = -1}$

2. **(D)** $|3 - \frac{1}{2}y| = -7$

No solution. Absolute value must equal a positive number

3. **(A)** $2|x + 7| = 12$
$|x + 7| = 6$ $x + 7 = 6$ or $x + 7 = -6$
$x = -2$ or $x = -13$

4. **(C)** $|5x| - 7 = 3$
$|5x| = 10$ $5x = 10$ or $5x = -10$
500.00 or $x = -2$

5. **(C)** $\left|\dfrac{3}{4}m\right| = 9$

$$\dfrac{3}{4}m = 9$$
$$\dfrac{4}{3}\left(\dfrac{3}{4}m\right) = 9\left(\dfrac{4}{3}\right)$$
$$m = 12$$

$$\dfrac{3}{4}m = -9$$
$$\dfrac{4}{3}\left(\dfrac{3}{4}m\right) = (-9)\left(\dfrac{4}{3}\right)$$
$$m = -12$$

Drill: Inequalities

1. **(D)**
$$3m + 2 < 7$$
$$\underline{-2 \quad -2}$$
$$\left(\dfrac{1}{3}\right)3m < 5\left(\dfrac{1}{3}\right)$$
$$m < \dfrac{5}{3}$$

2. **(C)**
$$\dfrac{1}{2}x - 3 \leq 1$$
$$\underline{+3 \quad +3}$$
$$\dfrac{1}{2}x \leq 4$$
$$(2)\dfrac{1}{2}x \leq 4(2)$$
$$x \leq 8$$

3. **(D)**
$$-3p + 1 \geq 16$$
$$\underline{-1 \quad -1}$$
$$-3p \geq 15$$
$$\left(-\dfrac{1}{3}\right)-3p \geq 15\left(-\dfrac{1}{3}\right)$$
$$p \leq 5$$

4.　**(B)**　$-6 < \dfrac{2}{3}r + 6 \le 2$

$\underline{-6 \qquad\quad -6 \quad -6}$

$-12 < \dfrac{2}{3}r \le -4$

$\dfrac{3}{2}\left(-12 < \dfrac{2}{3}r \le -4\right)$

$-18 < r \le -6$

5.　**(A)**　$0 < 2 - y < 6$

$\underline{-2 - 2 \qquad -2}$

$-2 < \quad y < 4$

$-1(-2 < -y < 4)$

$-4 < y < 2$

Drill: Ratios and Proportions

1.　**(D)**　$\dfrac{4}{n} = \dfrac{8}{5}$　　　$5(4) = 8n$

$\left(\dfrac{1}{8}\right)20 = 8n\left(\dfrac{1}{8}\right)$

$\dfrac{20}{8} = n \Rightarrow 2.5 = n$

2.　**(B)**　$\dfrac{2}{3} = \dfrac{n}{72}$　　　$2(72) = 3n$

$\dfrac{1}{3}(144) = (3n)\dfrac{1}{3}$

$(2)(24) = n$

$48 = n$

3.　**(C)**　$n:12 = 3:4 \Rightarrow \dfrac{n}{12} = \dfrac{3}{4}$

$$4n = (12)(3)$$
$$4n = 36$$
$$n = 9$$

4.　**(A)**　$4:5 = x:785 \Rightarrow$　$\dfrac{4}{5} = \dfrac{x}{785}$

$$(785)(4) = 5x$$
$$\left(\dfrac{1}{5}\right)(785)(4) = (5x)\dfrac{1}{5}$$
$$(157)(4) = x$$
$$628 = x$$

5.　**(B)**　$3:1000 = y:25000 \Rightarrow$　$\dfrac{3}{1000} = \dfrac{y}{25000}$

$$(3)(25,000) = y(1000)$$
$$\dfrac{(3)(25,000)}{1000} = y$$
$$75 = y$$

6.　**(C)**　$28:32 \Rightarrow \dfrac{28}{32} = \dfrac{7}{8} \Rightarrow 7:8$

IV. GEOMETRY AND TRIGONOMETRY REVIEW

POINTS, LINES, AND ANGLES

Geometry is built upon a series of undefined terms. These terms are those which we accept as known in order to define other undefined terms.

A) **Point**: Although we represent points on paper with small dots, a point has no size, thickness, or width.

B) **Line**: A line is a series of adjacent points which extends indefinitely. A line can be either curved or straight; however, unless otherwise stated, the term "line" refers to a straight line.

C) **Plane**: A plane is a collection of points lying on a flat surface, which extends indefinitely in all directions.

If A and B are two points on a line, then the **line segment** $\overline{AB}$ is the set of points on that line between A and B and including A and B, which are endpoints. The line segment is referred to as $\overline{AB}$.

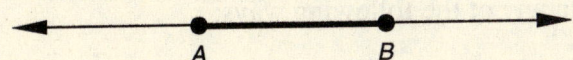

A **ray** is a series of points that lie to one side of a single endpoint.

PROBLEM

How many lines can be found that contain (a) one given point, (b) two given points, (c) three given points?

(figures labeled (a), (b), (c) with lines l_1 through l_8 and points A, B, C, D, E, F, G, H, I)

417

SOLUTION

(a)   *Given one point A*, there are an infinite number of distinct lines that contain the given point. To see this, consider line l_1 passing through point A. By rotating l_1 around A like the hands of a clock, we obtain different lines l_2, l_3, etc. Since we can rotate l_1 an infinite amount of ways, there are an infinite amount of lines containing A.

(b)   *Given two distinct points B and C*, there is one and only one straight line passing through both. To see this, consider all the lines containing point B: l_5, l_6, l_7, and l_8. Only l_5 contains both points B and C. Thus, there is only one line containing both points B and C. Since there is always at least one line containing two distinct points and never more than one, the line passing through the two points is said to be determined by the two points.

(c)   *Given three distinct points*, there may be one line or none. If a line exists that contains the three points, such as D, E, and F, then the points are said to be **colinear**. If no such line exists (as in the case of points G, H, and I), then the points are said to be **noncolinear**.

INTERSECTION LINES AND ANGLES

An **angle** is a collection of points which is the union of two rays having the same endpoint. An angle such as the one illustrated below can be referred to in any of the following ways:

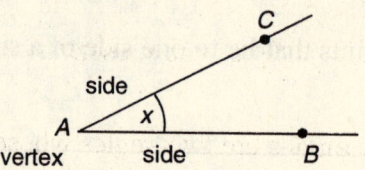

A)   by a capital letter which names its vertex, i.e., $\angle A$;

B)   by a lowercase letter or number placed inside the angle, i.e., $\angle x$;

C)   by three capital letters, where the middle letter is the vertex and the other two letters are not on the same ray, i.e., $\angle CAB$ or $\angle BAC$, both of which represent the angle illustrated in the figure.

TYPES OF ANGLES

A)   **Vertical angles** are formed when two lines intersect. These angles are equal.

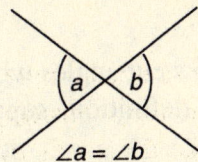

$\angle a = \angle b$

B) **Adjacent angles** are two angles with a common vertex and a common side, but no common interior points. In the following figure, $\angle DAC$ and $\angle BAC$ are adjacent angles. $\angle DAB$ and $\angle BAC$ are not.

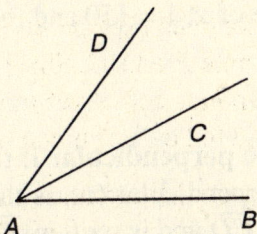

C) A **right angle** is an angle whose measure is 90°.

D) An **acute angle** is an angle whose measure is larger than 0° but less than 90°.

E) An **obtuse angle** is an angle whose measure is larger than 90° but less than 180°.

F) A **straight angle** is an angle whose measure is 180°. Such an angle is, in fact, a straight line.

G) A **reflex angle** is an angle whose measure is greater than 180° but less than 360°.

H) **Complementary angles** are two angles whose measures total 90°.

I) **Supplementary angles** are two angles whose measures total 180°.

J) **Congruent angles** are angles of equal measure.

PROBLEM

In the figure, we are given $\overline{AB}$ and triangle ABC. We are told that the measure of $\angle 1$ is five times the measure of $\angle 2$. Determine the measures of $\angle 1$ and $\angle 2$.

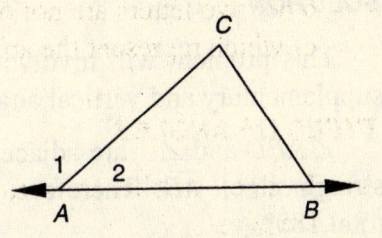

SOLUTION

Since ∠ 1 and ∠ 2 are adjacent angles whose non-common sides lie on a straight line, they are, by definition, supplementary. As supplements, their measures must total 180°.

If we let x = the measure of ∠ 2, then $5x$ = the measure of ∠ 1.

To determine the respective angle measures, set $x + 5x = 180$ and solve for x. $6x = 180$. Therefore, $x = 30$ and $5x = 150$.

Therefore, the measure of ∠ 1 = 150 and the measure of ∠ 2 = 30.

PERPENDICULAR LINES

Two lines are said to be **perpendicular** if they intersect and form right angles. The symbol for perpendicular (or, is therefore perpendicular to) is ⊥; $\overleftrightarrow{AB}$ is perpendicular to $\overleftrightarrow{CD}$ and is written $\overleftrightarrow{AB} \perp \overleftrightarrow{CD}$.

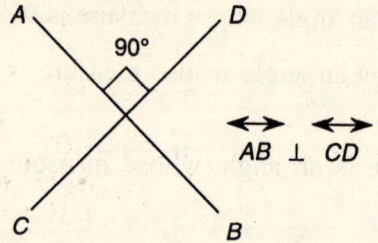

PROBLEM

We are given straight lines $\overleftrightarrow{AB}$ and $\overleftrightarrow{CD}$ intersecting at point P. $\overline{PR} \perp \overline{AB}$ and the measure of ∠ APD is 170°. Find the measures of ∠ 1, ∠ 2, ∠ 3, and ∠4.

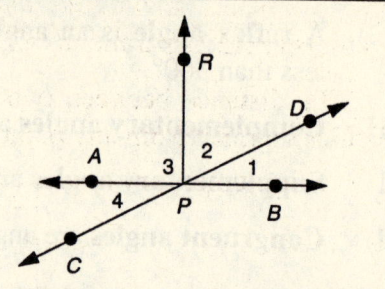

SOLUTION

This problem will involve making use of several of the properties of supplementary and vertical angles, as well as perpendicular lines.

∠ APD and ∠ 1 are adjacent angles whose non-common sides lie on a straight line, $\overline{AB}$. Therefore, they are supplements and their measures total 180°.

$$m \angle APD + m \angle 1 = 180°.$$

We know $m \angle APD = 170°$. Therefore, by substitution, $170° + m \angle 1 = 180°$. This implies $m \angle 1 = 10°$.

$\angle 1$ and $\angle 4$ are vertical angles because they are formed by the intersection of two straight lines, $\overline{CD}$ and $\overline{AB}$, and their sides form two pairs of opposite rays. As vertical angles, they are, by theorem, of equal measure. Since $m \angle 1 = 10°$, then $m \angle 4 = 10°$.

Since $\overline{PR} \perp \overline{CD}$, at their intersection the angles formed must be right angles. Therefore, $\angle 3$ is a right angle and its measure is $90°$. $m \angle 3 = 90°$.

The figure shows us that $\angle APD$ is composed of $\angle 3$ and $\angle 2$. Since the measure of the whole must be equal to the sum of the measures of its parts, $m \angle APD = m \angle 3 + m \angle 2$. We know the $m \angle APD = 170°$ and $m \angle 3 = 90°$, therefore, by substitution, we can solve for $m \angle 2$, our last unknown.

$$170° = 90° + m \angle 2$$

$$80° = m \angle 2$$

Therefore, $m \angle 1 = 10°$, $m \angle 2 = 80°$,

$m \angle 3 = 90°$, $m \angle 4 = 10°$

PARALLEL LINES

Two lines are called **parallel lines** if, and only if, they are in the same plane (coplanar) and do not intersect. The symbol for parallel, or is parallel to, is ‖; $\overline{AB}$ is parallel to $\overline{CD}$ is written $\overline{AB} \parallel \overline{CD}$.

The distance between two parallel lines is the length of the perpendicular segment from any point on one line to the other line.

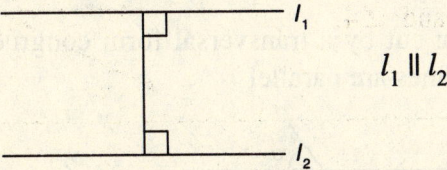

$l_1 \parallel l_2$

Given a line l and a point P not on line l, there is one and only one line through point P that is parallel to line l.

Two coplanar lines are either intersecting lines or parallel lines.

If two (or more) lines are perpendicular to the same line, then they are parallel to each other.

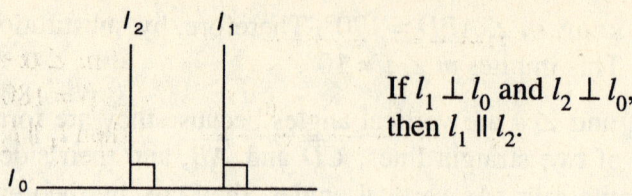

If $l_1 \perp l_0$ and $l_2 \perp l_0$, then $l_1 \parallel l_2$.

If two lines are cut by a transversal (a line intersecting two or more other lines) so that alternate interior angles are equal, the lines are parallel.

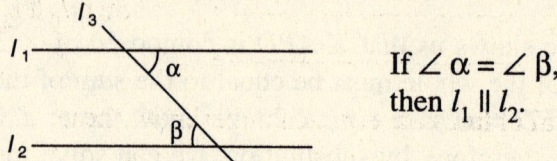

If $\angle \alpha = \angle \beta$, then $l_1 \parallel l_2$.

If two lines are parallel to the same line, then they are parallel to each other.

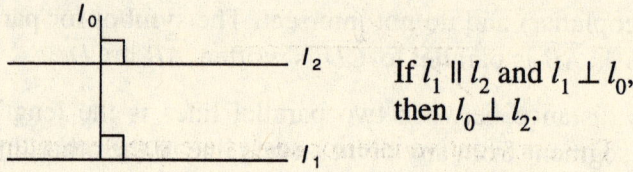

If $l_1 \parallel l_0$ and $l_2 \parallel l_0$, then $l_1 \parallel l_2$.

If a line is perpendicular to one of two parallel lines, then it is perpendicular to the other line, too.

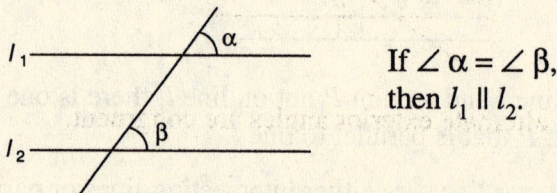

If $l_1 \parallel l_2$ and $l_1 \perp l_0$, then $l_0 \perp l_2$.

If two lines being cut by a transversal form congruent corresponding angles, then the two lines are parallel.

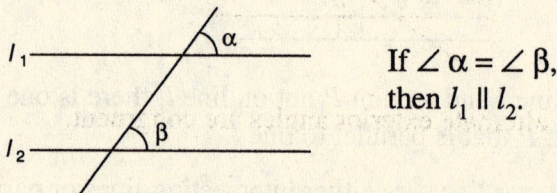

If $\angle \alpha = \angle \beta$, then $l_1 \parallel l_2$.

If two lines being cut by a transversal form interior angles on the same side of the transversal that are supplementary, then the two lines are parallel.

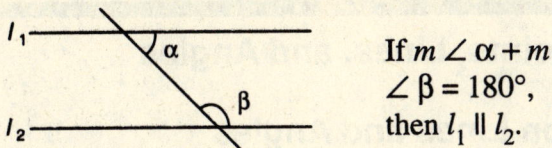

If $m \angle \alpha + m$
$\angle \beta = 180°$,
then $l_1 \parallel l_2$.

If a line is parallel to one of two parallel lines, it is also parallel to the other line.

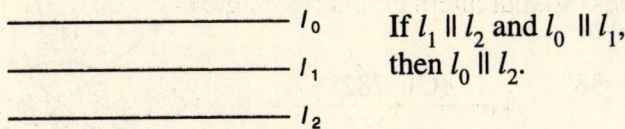

If $l_1 \parallel l_2$ and $l_0 \parallel l_1$,
then $l_0 \parallel l_2$.

If two parallel lines are cut by a transversal, then:

A)   The alternate interior angles are congruent.

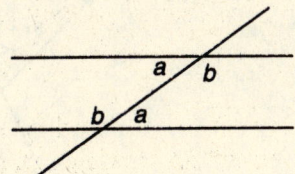

B)   The corresponding angles are congruent.

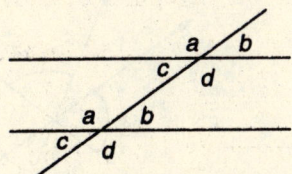

C)   The consecutive interior angles are supplementary.

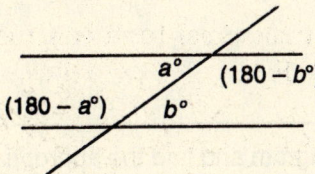

D)   The alternate exterior angles are congruent.

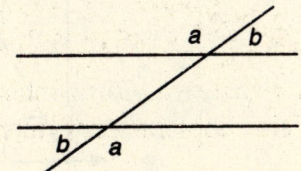

☞ Drill: Points, Lines, and Angles

Intersection Lines and Angles

1. Find a.

    (A) 38°   (C) 782°

    (B) 68°   (D) 90°

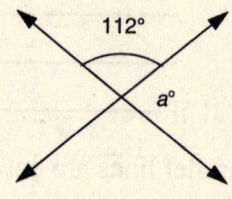

2. Find x.

    (A) 8   (C) 21

    (B) 11.75   (D) 23

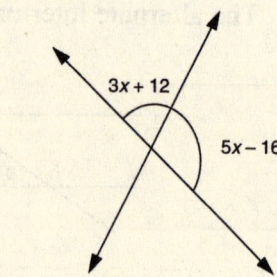

3. Find z.

    (A) 29°   (C) 61°

    (B) 54°   (D) 88°

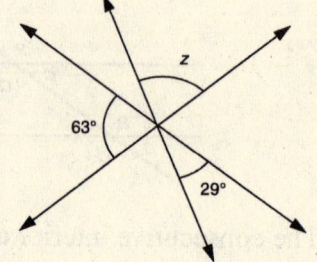

Perpendicular Lines

4. $\overline{BA} \perp \overline{BC}$ and $m \angle DBC = 53°$.
    Find $m \angle ABD$.

    (A) 27°   (C) 37°

    (B) 33°   (D) 53°

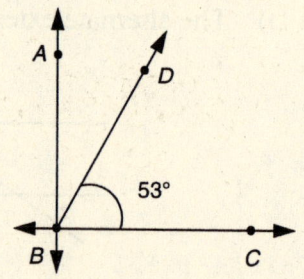

5. $m \angle 1 = 90°$. Find $m \angle 2$.

(A) 80°   (C) 100°

(B) 90°   (D) 135°

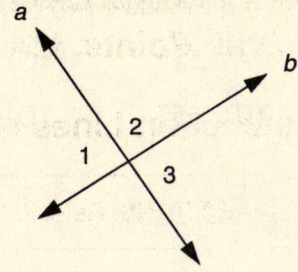

6. $\overline{CD} \perp \overline{EF}$. If $m \angle 1 = 2x$, $m \angle 2 = 30°$, and $m \angle 3 = x$, find x.

(A) 5°   (C) 12°

(B) 10°   (D) 20°

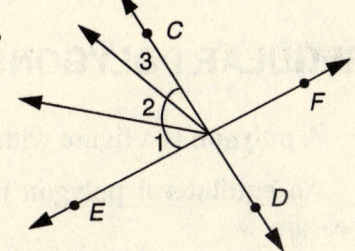

Parallel Lines

DIRECTIONS: Refer to the diagram and find the appropriate solution.

7. If $a \parallel b$, find z.

(A) 26°   (C) 64°

(B) 32°   (D) 86°

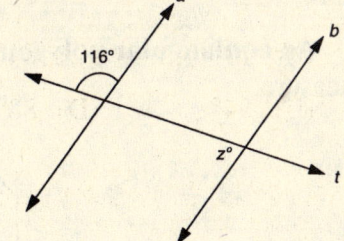

8. In the figure, $p \parallel q \parallel r$. Find $m \angle 7$.

(A) 27°   (C) 47°

(B) 33°   (D) 57°

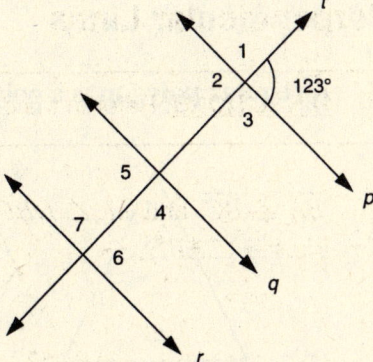

9. If $a \parallel b$ and $c \parallel d$, find $m \angle 5$.

   (A) 55°   (C) 75°

   (B) 65°   (D) 95°

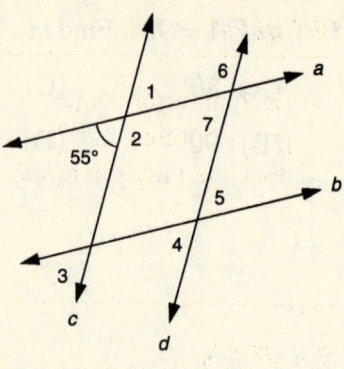

REGULAR POLYGONS (CONVEX)

A **polygon** is a figure with the same number of sides as angles.

An **equilateral polygon** is a polygon all of whose sides are of equal measure.

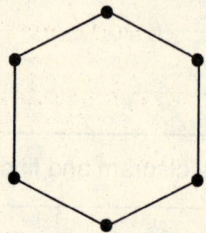

An **equiangular polygon** is a polygon all of whose angles are of equal measure.

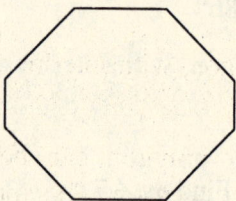

A **regular polygon** is a polygon that is both equilateral and equiangular.

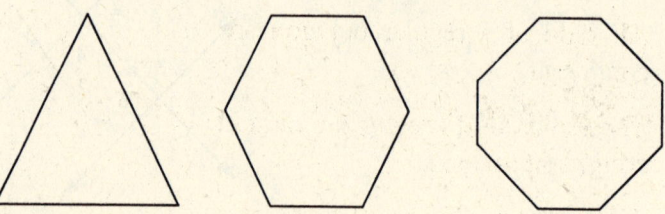

PROBLEM

Each interior angle of a regular poly-gon contains 120°. How many sides does the polygon have?

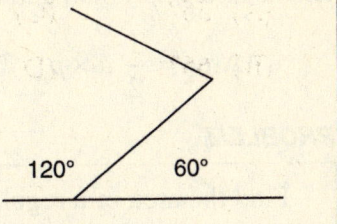

120°　　60°

SOLUTION

At each vertex of a polygon, the exterior angle is supplementary to the interior angle, as shown in the diagram.

Since we are told that the interior angles measure 120°, we can deduce that the exterior angle measures 60°.

Each exterior angle of a regular polygon of n sides measure $\dfrac{360°}{n}$ degrees. We know that each exterior angle measures 60°, and, therefore, by setting $\dfrac{360°}{n}$ equal to 60°, we can determine the number of sides in the polygon. The calculation is as follows:

$$\frac{360°}{n} = 60°$$

$$60°n = 360°$$

$$n = 6$$

Therefore, the regular polygon, with interior angles of 120°, has six sides and is called a hexagon.

The area of a regular polygon can be determined by using the **apothem** and **radius** of the polygon. The apothem (a) of a regular poly-gon is the segment from the center of the polygon perpendicular to a side of the polygon. The radius (r) of a regular polygon is the segment joining any vertex of a regular polygon with the center of that polygon.

(1)　All radii of a regular polygon are congruent.

(2)　The radius of a regular polygon is congruent to a side.

(3)　All apothems of a regular polygon are congruent.

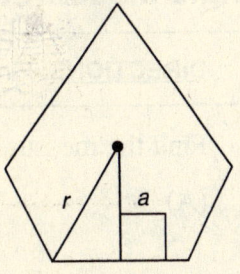

The **area** of a regular polygon equals one-half the product of the length of the apothem and the perimeter.

$$\text{Area} = \frac{1}{2}\, a \times p$$

PROBLEM

Find the area of a regular hexagon if one side has length 6.

SOLUTION

Since the length of a side equals 6, the radius also equals 6 and the perimeter equals 36. The base of the right triangle, formed by the radius and apothem, is half the length of a side, or 3. You can find the length of the apothem by using what is known as the Pythagorean theorem (discussed further in the next section).

$$a^2 + b^2 = c^2$$
$$a^2 + (3)^2 = (6)^2$$
$$a^2 = 36 - 9$$
$$a^2 = 27$$
$$a = 3\sqrt{3}$$

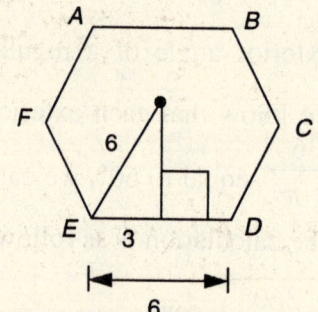

The apothem equals $3\sqrt{3}$. Therefore, the area of the hexagon

$$= \frac{1}{2}\, a \times p$$
$$= \frac{1}{2}\, (3\sqrt{3})\, (36)$$
$$= 54\sqrt{3}$$

☞ Drill: Regular Polygons (Convex)

Angle Measures

DIRECTIONS: Find the appropriate solution.

1. Find the measure of an interior angle of a regular pentagon.

    (A) 55°   (B) 72°   (C) 90°   (D) 108°

2. Find the sum of the measures of the exterior angles of a regular triangle.

   (A) 90°   (B) 115°   (C) 180°   (D) 360°

Area(s) and Perimeter(s)

<u>DIRECTIONS</u>: Find the appropriate solution.

3. A regular triangle has sides of 24 mm. If the apothem is $4\sqrt{3}$ mm, find the area of the triangle.

   (A) 72 mm²   (C) 144 mm²

   (B) $96\sqrt{3}$ mm²   (D) $144\sqrt{3}$ mm²

4. Find the area of a regular hexagon with sides of 4 cm.

   (A) $12\sqrt{3}$ cm²   (B) 24 cm²   (C) $24\sqrt{3}$ cm²   (D) 48 cm²

5. Find the area of a regular decagon with sides of length 6 cm and an apothem of length 9.2 cm.

   (A) 55.2 cm²   (B) 60 cm²   (C) 138 cm²   (D) 276 cm²

TRIANGLES

A closed three-sided geometric figure is called a **triangle**. The points of the intersection of the sides of a triangle are called the **vertices** of the triangle.

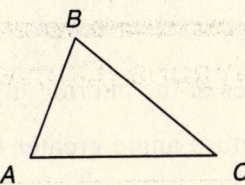

The **perimeter** of a triangle is the sum of the measures of the sides of the triangle.

A triangle with no equal sides is called a **scalene triangle**.

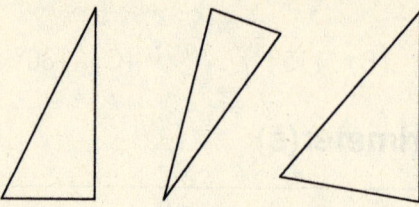

A triangle having at least two equal sides is called an **isosceles triangle**. The third side is called the **base** of the triangle.

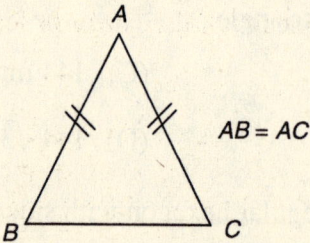

A side of a triangle is a line segment whose endpoints are the vertices of two angles of the triangle.

An **interior angle** of a triangle is an angle formed by two sides and includes the third side within its collection of points.

An **equilateral triangle** is a triangle having three equal sides. $\overline{AB} = \overline{AC} = \overline{BC}$.

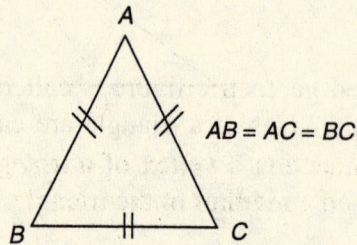

The sum of the measures of the interior angles of a triangle is 180°.

A triangle with one obtuse angle greater than 90° is called an **obtuse triangle**.

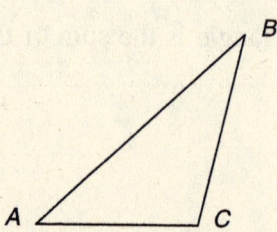

An **acute triangle** is a triangle with three acute angles (less than 90°).

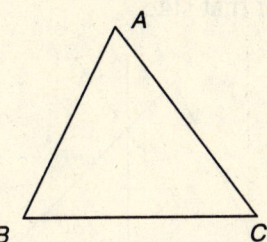

A triangle with a right angle is called a **right triangle**. The side opposite the right angle in a right triangle is called the hypotenuse of the right triangle. The other two sides are called arms or legs of the right triangle.

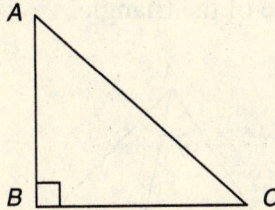

An **altitude** of a triangle is a line segment from a vertex of the triangle perpendicular to the opposite side.

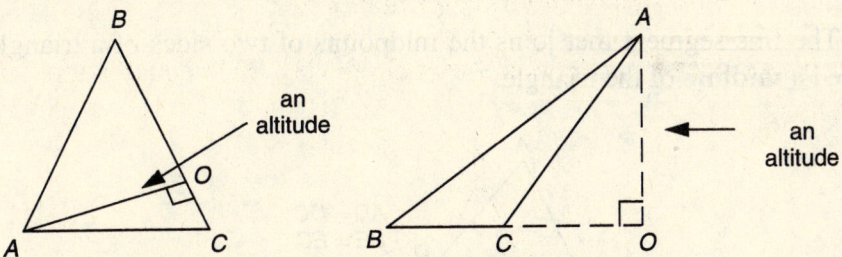

A line segment connecting a vertex of a triangle and the midpoint of the opposite side is called a **median** of the triangle.

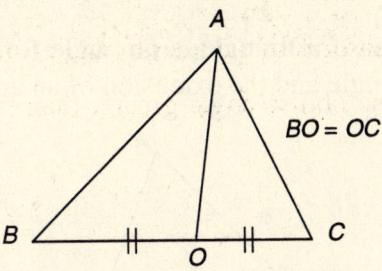

A line that bisects and is perpendicular to a side of a triangle is called a **perpendicular bisector** of that side.

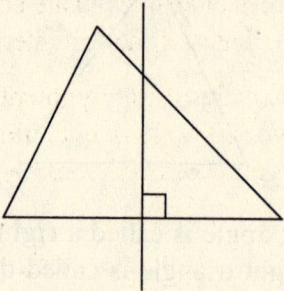

An **angle bisector** of a triangle is a line that bisects an angle and extends to the opposite side of the triangle.

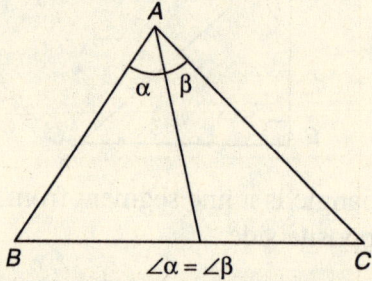

The line segment that joins the midpoints of two sides of a triangle is called a **midline** of the triangle.

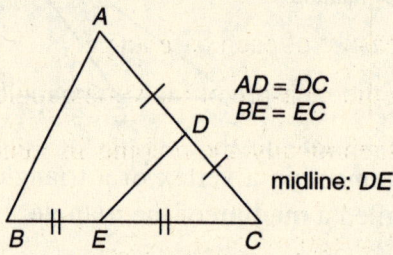

An **exterior angle** of a triangle is an angle formed outside a triangle by one side of the triangle and the extension of an adjacent side.

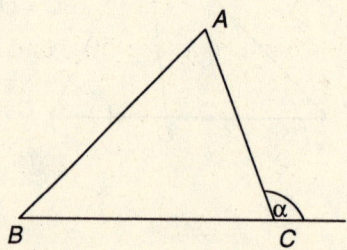

A triangle whose three interior angles have equal measure (60° each) is said to be **equiangular**.

Three or more lines (or rays or segments) are concurrent if there exists one point common to all of them, that is, if they all intersect at the same point.

In a right triangle, the square of the hypotenuse is equal to the sum of the squares of the other two sides. This is commonly known as the theorem of Pythagoras or the Pythagorean Theorem.

PROBLEM

The measure of the vertex angle of an isosceles triangle exceeds the measurement of each base angle by 30°. Find the value of each angle of the triangle.

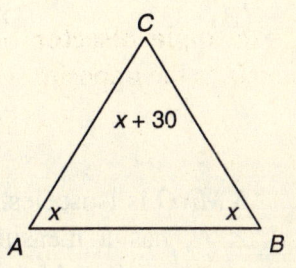

SOLUTION

We know that the sum of the values of the angles of a triangle is 180°. In an isosceles triangle, the angles opposite the congruent sides (the base angles) are, themselves, congruent and of equal value.

Therefore,

(1) Let x = the measure of each base angle.

(2) Then $x + 30$ = the measure of the vertex angle.

We can solve for x algebraically by keeping in mind the sum of all the measures will be 180°.

$$x + x + (x + 30) = 180$$
$$3x + 30 = 180$$
$$3x = 150$$
$$x = 50$$

Therefore, the base angles each measure 50°, and the vertex angle measures 80°.

☞ Drill: Triangles

Angle Measures

DIRECTIONS: Refer to the diagram and find the appropriate solution.
---

1. In $\triangle PQR$, $\angle Q$ is a right angle. Find $m \angle R$.

    (A) 27°   (C) 54°

    (B) 33°   (D) 67°

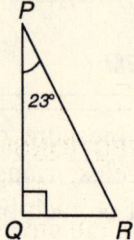

2. $\triangle MNO$ is isosceles. If the vertex angle, $\angle N$, has a measure of 96°, find the measure of $\angle M$.

    (A) 21°   (C) 64°

    (B) 42°   (D) 84°

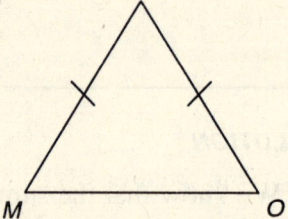

3. Find x.

    (A) 15°   (C) 30°

    (B) 25°   (D) 45°

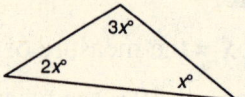

Similar Triangles

DIRECTIONS: Refer to the diagram and find the appropriate solution.
---

4. The two triangles shown are similar. Find b.

    (A) $2\frac{2}{3}$ (C) 4

    (B) 3   (D) 16

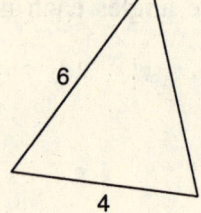 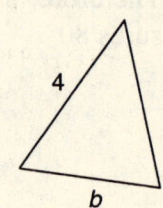

5. The two triangles shown are similar. Find *a* and *b*.

(A) 5 and 10

(C) $4\frac{2}{3}$ and $7\frac{1}{3}$

(B) 4 and 8

(D) $5\frac{1}{3}$ and 8

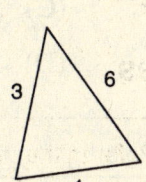
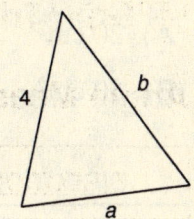

Area

> **DIRECTIONS**: Refer to the diagram and find the appropriate solution.

6. Find the area of Δ *MNO*.

(A) 22   (C) 56

(B) 49   (D) 84

7. Find the area of Δ *PQR*.

(A) 31.5   (C) 53

(B) 38.5   (D) 77

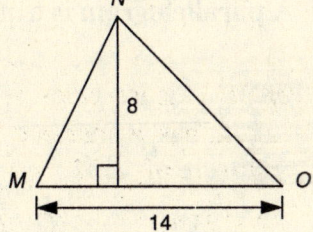

8. Find the area of Δ *STU*.

(A) $4\sqrt{2}$ (C) $12\sqrt{2}$

(B) $8\sqrt{2}$ (D) $16\sqrt{2}$

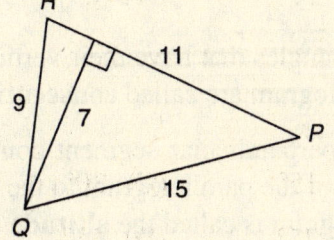

9. Find the area of Δ *ABC*.

(A) 54 cm²   (C) 108 cm²

(B) 81 cm²   (D) 135 cm²

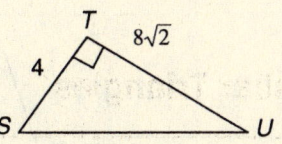
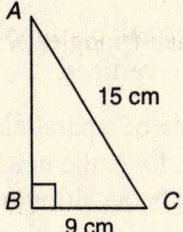

10. Find the area of $\triangle XYZ$.

(A) 20 cm^2

(B) 50 cm^2

(C) 50$\sqrt{2}$ cm^2

(D) 100 cm^2

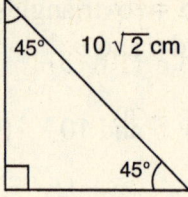

QUADRILATERALS

A **quadrilateral** is a polygon with four sides.

PARALLELOGRAMS

A **parallelogram** is a quadrilateral whose opposite sides are parallel.

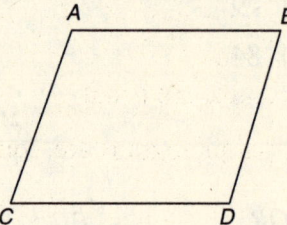

Two angles that have their vertices at the endpoints of the same side of a parallelogram are called **consecutive angles**.

The perpendicular segment connecting any point of a line containing one side of the parallelogram to the line containing the opposite side of the parallelogram is called the **altitude** of the parallelogram.

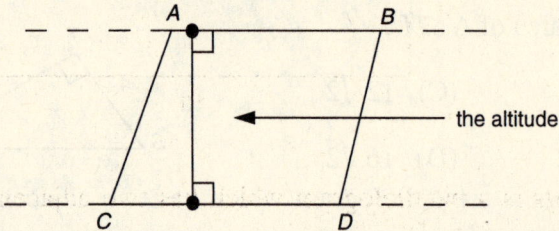

the altitude

A diagonal of a polygon is a line segment joining any two non-consecutive vertices.

The area of a parallelogram is given by the formula $A = bh$, where b is the base and h is the height drawn perpendicular to that base. Note that the height equals the altitude of the parallelogram.

$A = bh$

$A = (10)\,(3)$

$A = 30$

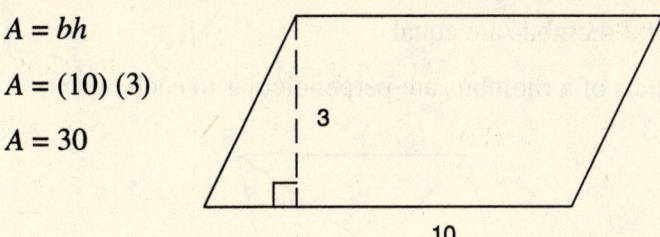

RECTANGLES

A **rectangle** is a parallelogram with right angles.

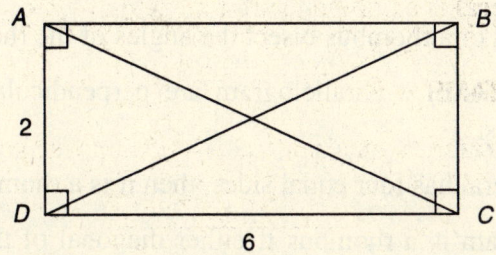

The diagonals of a rectangle are equal.

If the diagonals of a parallelogram are equal, the parallelogram is a rectangle.

If a quadrilateral has four right angles, then it is a rectangle.

The area of a rectangle is given by the formula $A = lw$, where l is the length and w is the width.

$A = lw$

$A = (3)\,(10)$

$A = 30$

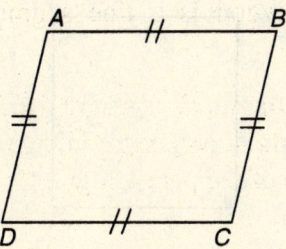

RHOMBI

A **rhombus** is a parallelogram which has two adjacent sides that are equal.

All sides of a rhombus are equal.

The diagonals of a rhombus are perpendicular to each other.

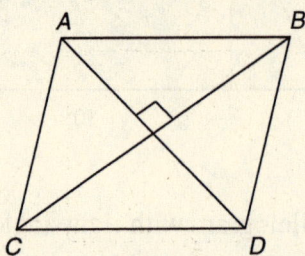

The diagonals of a rhombus bisect the angles of the rhombus.

If the diagonals of a parallelogram are perpendicular, the parallelogram is a rhombus.

If a quadrilateral has four equal sides, then it is a rhombus.

A parallelogram is a rhombus if either diagonal of the parallelogram bisects the angles of the vertices it joins.

SQUARES

A **square** is a rhombus with a right angle.

A square is an equilateral quadrilateral.

A square has all the properties of parallelograms and rectangles.

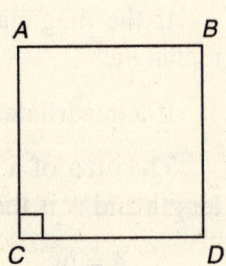

A rhombus is a square if one of its interior angles is a right angle.

In a square, the measure of either diagonal can be calculated by multiplying the length of any side by the square root of 2.

The area of a square is given by the formula $A = s^2$, where s is the side of the square. Since all sides of a square are equal, it does not matter which side is used.

$A = s^2$

$A = 6^2$

$A = 36$

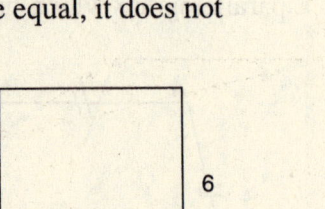

The area of a square can also be found by taking $\frac{1}{2}$ the product of the length of the diagonal squared.

$$A = \frac{1}{2}d^2$$

$$A = \frac{1}{2}(8)^2$$

$$A = 32$$

TRAPEZOIDS

A **trapezoid** is a quadrilateral with two and only two sides parallel. The parallel sides of a trapezoid are called **bases**.

The **median** of a trapezoid is the line joining the midpoints of the non-parallel sides.

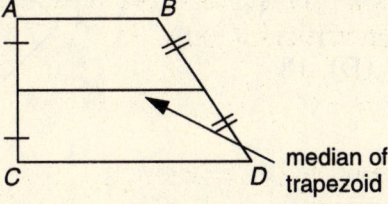

The perpendicular segment connecting any point in the line containing one base of the trapezoid to the line containing the other base is the **altitude** of the trapezoid.

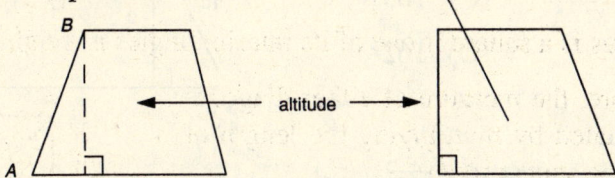

An **isosceles trapezoid** is a trapezoid whose non-parallel sides are equal. A pair of angles including only one of the parallel sides is called **a pair of base angles**.

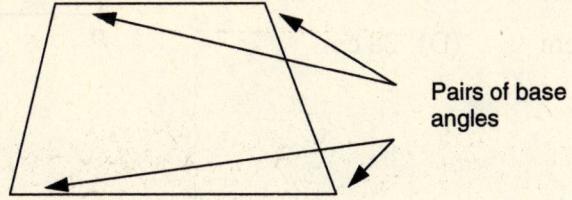

The median of a trapezoid is parallel to the bases and equal to one-half their sum.

The base angles of an isosceles trapezoid are equal.

The diagonals of an isosceles trapezoid are equal.

The opposite angles of an isosceles trapezoid are supplementary.

☞ Drill: Quadrilaterals

> **DIRECTIONS**: Refer to the diagram and find the appropriate solution.

1. Quadrilateral *ABCD* is a parallelogram. If $m \angle B = 6x + 2$ and $m \angle D = 98$, find *x*.

   (A) 12   (C) $16\frac{2}{3}$

   (B) 16   (D) 18

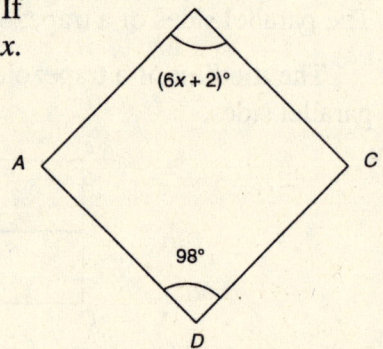

2. Find the area of parallelogram *STUV*.

   (A) 56   (C) 108

   (B) 90   (D) 162

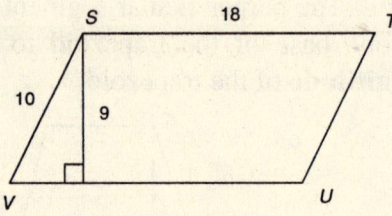

3. In rectangle *ABCD*, $\overline{AD} = 6$ cm and $\overline{DC} = 8$ cm. Find the length of the diagonal $\overline{AC}$.

   (A) 10 cm   (C) 20 cm

   (B) 12 cm   (D) 28 cm

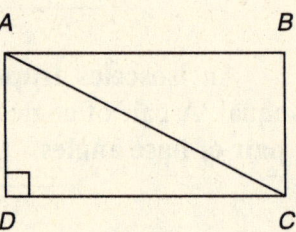

4. Find the area of rectangle *UVXY*.

    (A) 17 cm²   (C) 35 cm²

    (B) 34 cm²   (D) 70 cm²

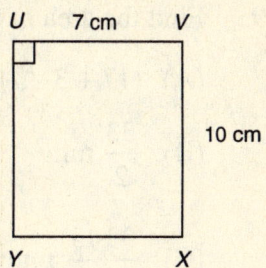

5. Find the length of $\overline{BO}$ in rectangle *BCDE* if the diagonal $\overline{EC}$ is 17 mm.

    (A) 6.55 mm   (C) 8.5 mm

    (B) 8 mm   (D) 17 mm

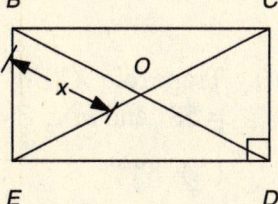

6. In rhombus *GHIJ*, $\overline{GI}$ = 6 cm and $\overline{HJ}$ = 8 cm. Find the length of $\overline{GH}$.

    (A) 3 cm   (C) 5 cm

    (B) 4 cm   (D) $4\sqrt{3}$ cm

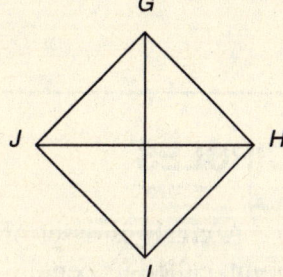

7. Find the area of the isosceles trapezoid *RSTU*.

    (A) 80 cm²   (C) 140 cm²

    (B) 87.5 cm²   (D) 175 cm²

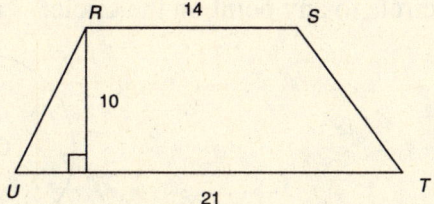

8. *ABCD* is an isosceles trapezoid. Find the perimeter.

    (A) 21 cm   (C) 30 cm

    (B) 27 cm   (D) 50 cm

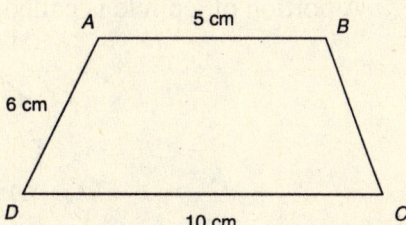

9. Find the area of trapezoid *MNOP*.

(A) $(17 + 3\sqrt{3})$ mm²

(B) $\dfrac{33}{2}$ mm²

(C) $\dfrac{33\sqrt{3}}{2}$ mm²

(D) 33 mm²

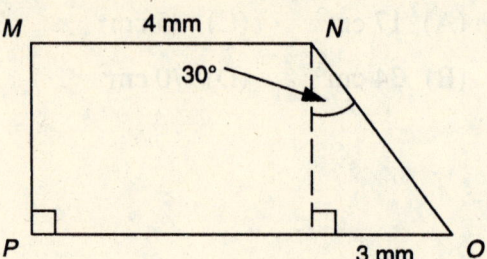

10. Trapezoid *XYZW* is isosceles. If $m \angle W = 58°$ and $m \angle Z = (4x - 6)$, find $x°$.

(A) 8°   (C) 13°

(B) 12°   (D) 16°

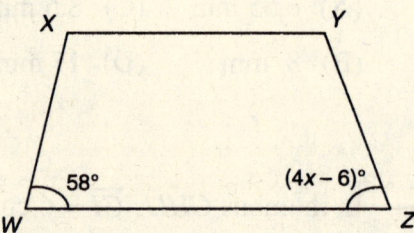

CIRCLES

A **circle** is a set of points in the same plane equidistant from a fixed point, called its center.

A **radius** of a circle is a line segment drawn from the center of the circle to any point on the circle.

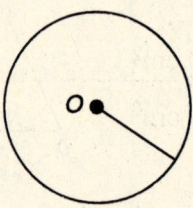

A portion of a circle is called an **arc** of the circle.

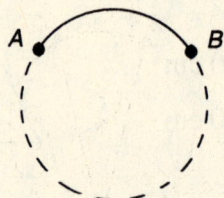

A line that intersects a circle in two points is called a **secant**.

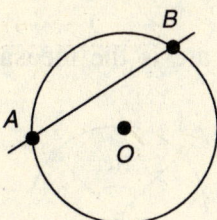

A line segment joining two points on a circle is called a **chord** of the circle.

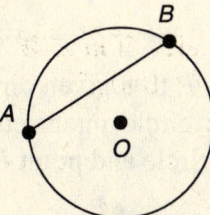

A chord that passes through the center of the circle is called a **diameter** of the circle.

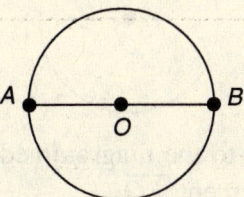

The line passing through the centers of two (or more) circles is called the **line of centers**.

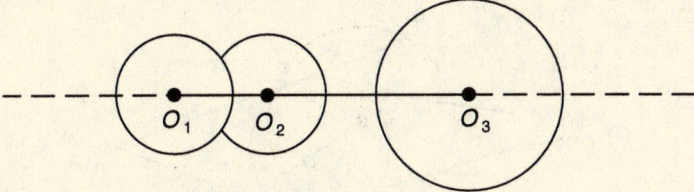

An angle whose vertex is on the circle and whose sides are chords of the circle is called an **inscribed angle**.

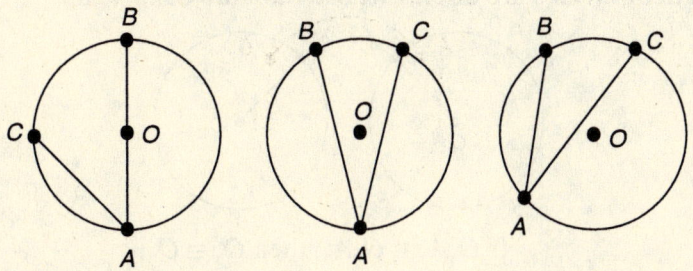

An angle whose vertex is at the center of a circle and whose sides are radii is called a **central angle.**

The measure of a minor arc is the measure of the central angle that intercepts that arc.

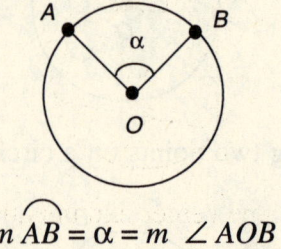

$$m \overset{\frown}{AB} = \alpha = m \angle AOB$$

The distance from a point P to a given circle is the distance from that point to the point where the circle intersects with a line segment with endpoints at the center of the circle and point P.

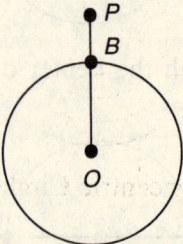

The distance of point P to the diagrammed circle with center O is the line segment $\overline{PB}$ of line segment $\overline{PO}$.

A line that has one and only one point of intersection with a circle is called a tangent to that circle, while their common point is called a **point of tangency**.

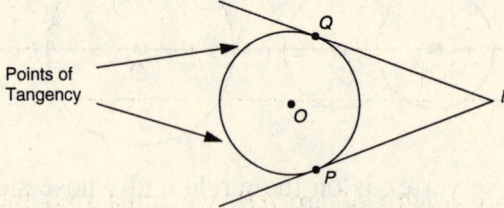

Congruent circles are circles whose radii are congruent.

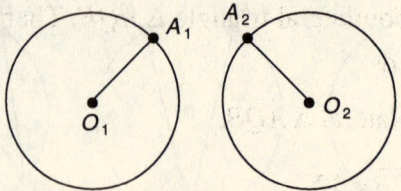

If $O_1A_1 \cong O_2A_2$, then $O_1 \cong O_2$.

The measure of a semicircle is 180°.

A **circumscribed circle** is a circle passing through all the vertices of a polygon.

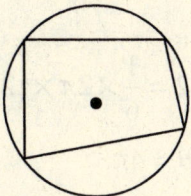

Circles that have the same center and unequal radii are called **concentric circles**.

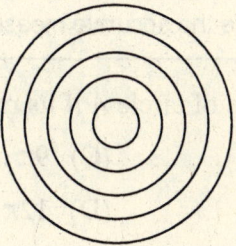

Concentric Circles

PROBLEM

A and B are points on circle Q such that △ AQB is equilateral. If the length of side $\overline{AB} = 12$, find the length of arc AB.

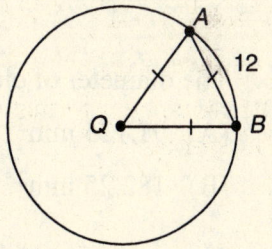

SOLUTION

To find the arc length of arc AB, we must find the measure of the central angle ∠ AQB and the measure of the radius $\overline{QA}$. ∠ AQB is an interior angle of the equilateral triangle △ AQB. Therefore,

$$m \angle AQB = 60°.$$

Similarly, in the equilateral △ AQB,

$$\overline{AQ} = \overline{AB} = \overline{QB} = 12.$$

Given the radius, r, and the central angle, n, the arc length is given by

$$\frac{n}{360} \times 2\pi r.$$

Therefore, by substitution,

$$\angle AQB = \frac{60}{360} \times 2\pi \times 12 = \frac{1}{6} \times 2\pi \times 12 = 4\pi.$$

Therefore, the length of arc $AB = 4\pi$.

☞ Drill: Circles

> **DIRECTIONS**: Determine the accurate measure.

1. Find the circumference of circle A if its radius is 3 mm.

   (A) 3π mm   (C) 9π mm

   (B) 6π mm   (D) 12π mm

2. Find the area of circle I.

   (A) 22 mm^2 (C) 121p mm^2

   (B) 121 mm^2 (D) 132 mm^2

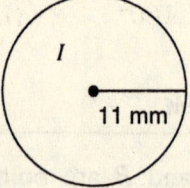

3. The diameter of circle Z is 27 mm. Find the area of the circle.

   (A) 91.125 mm^2 (C) 191.5p mm^2

   (B) 182.25 mm^2 (D) 182.25p mm^2

4. The area of circle B is 225π cm^2. Find the length of the diameter of the circle.

   (A) 15 cm   (C) 30 cm

   (B) 20 cm   (D) 20π cm

5. The area of circle X is 144π mm^2 while the area of circle Y is 81π mm^2. Write the ratio of the radius of circle X to that of circle Y.

   (A) $3:4$ (C) $9:12$

   (B) $4:3$ (D) $27:12$

6. The radius of the smaller of two concentric circles is 5 cm while the radius of the larger circle is 7 cm. Determine the area of the shaded region.

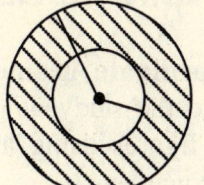

    (A) 7π cm²   (C) 25π cm²

    (B) 24π cm²   (D) 36π cm²

7. Find the measure of arc MN if $m \angle MON = 62°$.

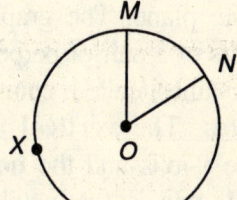

    (A) 16°   (C) 59°

    (B) 32°   (D) 62°

8. Find the measure of arc AXC.

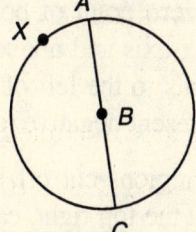

    (A) 150°   (C) 180°

    (B) 160°   (D) 270°

9. Find the measure of arc XY in circle W.

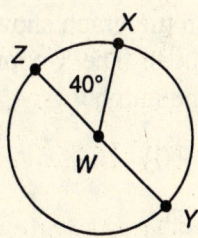

    (A) 40°   (C) 140°

    (B) 120°   (D) 180°

10. Find the area of the sector shown.

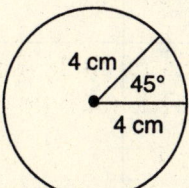

    (A) 4 cm²   (C) 16 cm²

    (B) 2π cm²   (D) 8π cm²

COORDINATE GEOMETRY

Coordinate geometry refers to the study of geometric figures using algebraic principles.

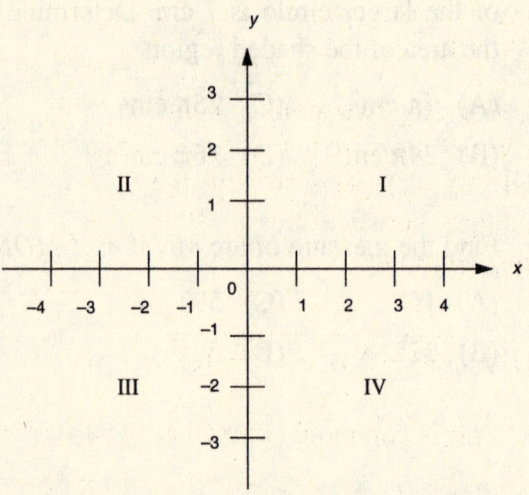

The graph shown is called the Cartesian coordinate plane. The graph consists of a pair of perpendicular lines called **coordinate axes**. The **vertical axis** is the *y*-axis and the **horizontal axis** is the *x*-axis. The point of intersection of these two axes is called the **origin**; it is the zero point of both axes. Furthermore, points to the right of the origin on the *x*-axis and above the origin on the *y*-axis represent positive real numbers. Points to the left of the origin on the *x*-axis or below the origin on the *y*-axis represent negative real numbers.

The four regions cut off by the coordinate axes are, in counterclockwise direction from the top right, called the first, second, third, and fourth quadrant, respectively. The first quadrant contains all points with two positive coordinates.

In the graph shown, two points are identified by the ordered pair, (x, y) of numbers. The *x*-coordinate is the first number and the *y*-coordinate is the second number.

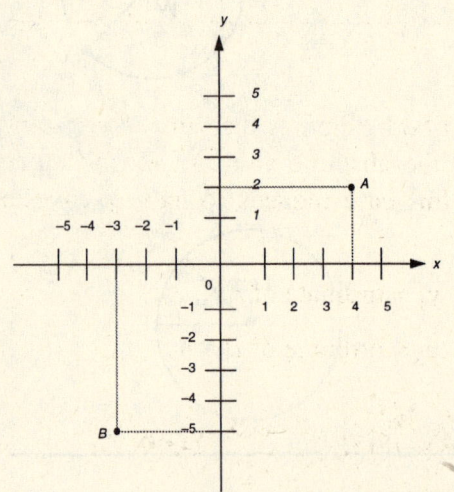

To plot a point on the graph when given the coordinates, draw perpendicular lines from the number-line coordinates to the point where the two lines intersect.

To find the coordinates of a given point on the graph, draw perpendicular lines from the point to the coordinates on the number line. The *x*-coordinate is written before the *y*-coordinate and a comma is used to separate the two.

In this case, point *A* has the coordinates (4, 2) and the coordinates of point *B* are (−3, −5).

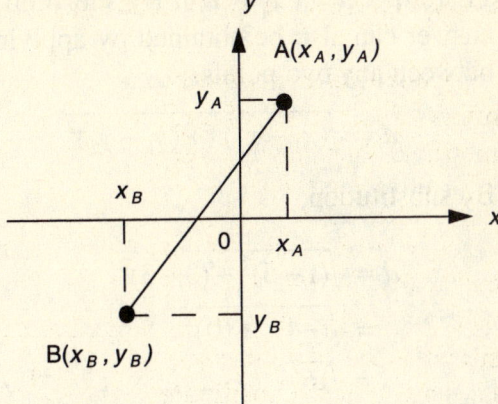

For any two points *A* and *B* with coordinates (X_A, Y_A) and (X_B, Y_B), respectively, the distance between *A* and *B* is represented by:

$$AB = \sqrt{(X_A - X_B)^2 + (Y_A - Y_B)^2}$$

This is commonly known as the distance formula.

PROBLEM

Find the distance between the point *A*(1, 3) and *B*(5, 3).

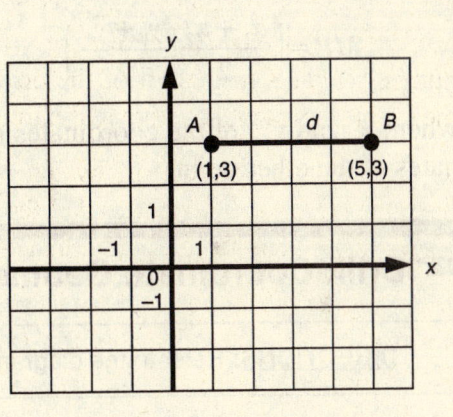

SOLUTION

In this case, where the ordinate of both points is the same, the distance between the two points is given by the absolute value of the difference between the two abscissas. In fact, this case reduces to merely counting boxes as the figure shows.

Let, x_1 = abscissa of *A* y_1 = ordinate of *A*

        x_2 = abscissa of *B* y_2 = ordinate of *B*

        d = the distance

Therefore, $d = |\, x_1 - x_2\,|$. By substitution, $d = |\, 1 - 5\,| = |-4| = 4$. This answer can also be obtained by applying the general formula for distance between any two points.

$$d = \sqrt{(x_1 - x_2)^2 + (y_1 - y_2)^2}$$

By substitution,

$$\begin{aligned} d &= \sqrt{(1-5)^2 + (3-3)^2} \\ &= \sqrt{(-4)^2 + (0)^2} \\ &= \sqrt{16} \\ &= 4 \end{aligned}$$

The distance is 4.

To find the midpoint of a segment between the two given endpoints, use the formula

$$MP = \left(\frac{x_1 + x_2}{2}, \frac{y_1 + y_2}{2} \right)$$

where x_1 and y_1 are the coordinates of one point; x_2 and y_2 are the coordinates of the other point.

☞ Drill: Coordinate Geometry

DIRECTIONS: Refer to the diagram and find the appropriate solution.

1. Which point shown has the coordinates $(-3, 2)$?

   (A) A   (C) C

   (B) B   (D) D

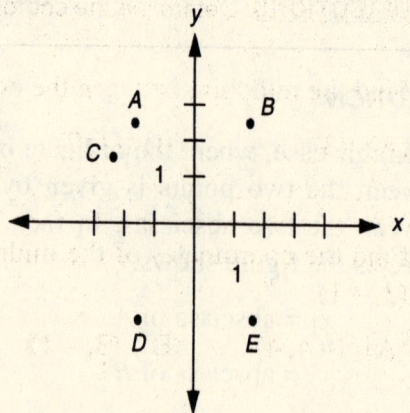

2. The correct *y*-coordinate for point *R* is what number?

   (A) − 7   (C) − 2

   (B) 2   (D) 7

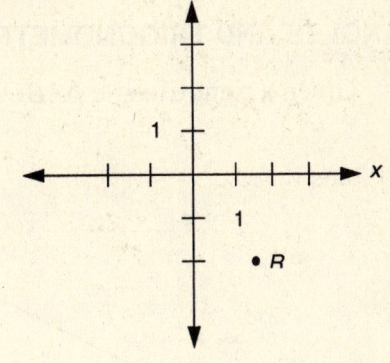

Distance

> **DIRECTIONS**: Determine the distance or value as appropriate.

3. Find the distance between (4, − 7) and (− 2, − 7).

   (A) 4   (B) 6   (C) 7   (D) 14

4. Find the distance between (3, 8) and (5, 11).

   (A) 2   (B) 3   (C) $\sqrt{13}$ (D) $\sqrt{15}$

Midpoints and Endpoints

> **DIRECTIONS**: Determine the coordinates or value as appropriate.

5. Find the midpoint between the points (− 2, 6) and (4, 8).

   (A) (3, 7)   (B) (1, 7)   (C) (3, 1)   (D) (1, 1)

6. Find the coordinates of the midpoint between the points (− 5, 7) and (3, − 1).

   (A) (− 4, 4)   (B) (3, − 1)   (C) (1, − 3)   (D) (− 1, 3)

TRIGONOMETRY

ANGLES AND TRIGONOMETRIC FUNCTIONS

Given a right triangle $\triangle ABC$ as shown in the figure below:

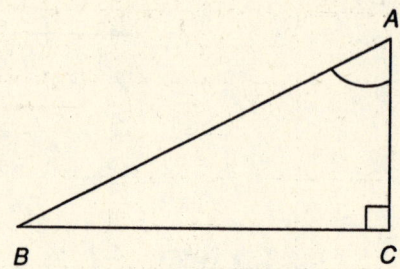

Definition 1:
$$\sin \angle A = \frac{BC}{AB}$$
$$= \frac{\text{measure of side opposite } \angle A}{\text{measure of hypotenuse}}$$

Definition 2:
$$\cos \angle A = \frac{AC}{AB}$$
$$= \frac{\text{measure of side adjacent to } \angle A}{\text{measure of hypotenuse}}$$

Definition 3:
$$\tan \angle A = \frac{BC}{AC}$$
$$= \frac{\text{measure of side opposite } \angle A}{\text{measure of side adjacent to } \angle A}$$

Definition 4:
$$\cot \angle A = \frac{AC}{BC}$$
$$= \frac{\text{measure of side adjacent to } \angle A}{\text{measure of side opposite } \angle A}$$

Definition 5:
$$\sec \angle A = \frac{AB}{AC}$$
$$= \frac{\text{measure of hypotenuse}}{\text{measure of side adjacent to } \angle A}$$

Definition 6:
$$\csc \angle A = \frac{AB}{BC}$$
$$= \frac{\text{measure of hypotenuse}}{\text{measure of side opposite } \angle A}$$

The following table gives the values of sine, cosine, tangent, and cotangent for some special angles. The angles are given in radians and in degrees.

α	Sin α	Cos α	Tan α	Cot α
$0°$	0	1	0	∞
$\dfrac{\pi}{6} = 30°$	$\dfrac{1}{2}$	$\dfrac{\sqrt{3}}{2}$	$\dfrac{1}{\sqrt{3}}$	$\sqrt{3}$
$\dfrac{\pi}{4} = 45°$	$\dfrac{1}{\sqrt{2}}$	$\dfrac{1}{\sqrt{2}}$	1	1
$\dfrac{\pi}{3} = 60°$	$\dfrac{\sqrt{3}}{2}$	$\dfrac{1}{2}$	$\sqrt{3}$	$\dfrac{1}{\sqrt{3}}$
$\dfrac{\pi}{2} = 90°$	1	0	∞	0

A circle with center located at the origin of the rectangular coordinate axes and radius equal to one unit length is called a unit circle.

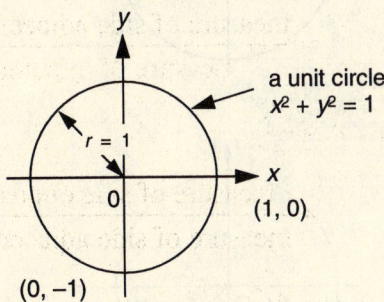

An angle whose vertex is at the origin of a rectangular coordinate system and whose initial side coincides with the positive x-axis is said to be in standard position with respect to the coordinate system.

An angle in standard position with respect to a Cartesian coordinate system whose terminal side lies in the first (or second or third or fourth) quadrant is called a first (or second or third or fourth) quadrant angle.

A quadrant angle is an angle in standard position whose terminal side lies on one of the axes of a Cartesian coordinate system.

If θ is a non-quadrantal angle in standard position and $P(x, y)$ is any point, distinct from the origin, on the terminal side of θ, then the six trigonometric functions of θ are defined in terms of the abscissa (x-coordinate), ordinate (y-coordinate), and distance $\overline{OP}$ as follows:

$$\text{sine } \theta = \sin \theta = \frac{\text{ordinate}}{\text{distance}} = \frac{y}{r}$$

$$\text{cosine } \theta = \cos \theta = \frac{\text{abscissa}}{\text{distance}} = \frac{x}{r}$$

$$\text{tangent } \theta = \tan \theta = \frac{\text{ordinate}}{\text{abscissa}} = \frac{y}{x}$$

$$\text{cotangent } \theta = \cot \theta = \frac{\text{abscissa}}{\text{ordinate}} = \frac{x}{y}$$

$$\text{secant } \theta = \sec \theta = \frac{\text{distance}}{\text{abscissa}} = \frac{r}{x}$$

$$\text{cosecant } \theta = \csc \theta = \frac{\text{distance}}{\text{ordinate}} = \frac{r}{y}$$

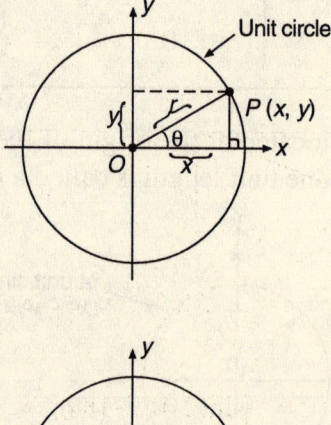

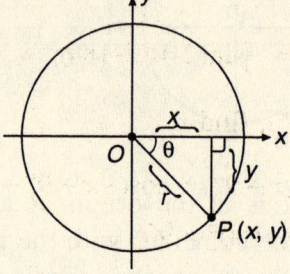

The value of trigonometric functions of quadrantal angles are given in the table on the next page.

θ	sin θ	cos θ	tan θ	cot θ	sec θ	csc θ
0°	0	1	0	±∞	1	±∞
90°	1	0	±∞	0	±∞	1
180°	0	−1	0	±∞	−1	±∞
270°	−1	0	±∞	0	±∞	−1

● EXAMPLES

1. Find $\sin \theta$ given $A = 30°$.

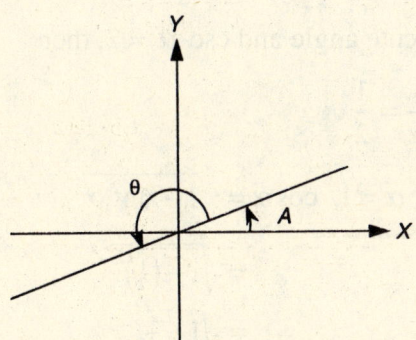

Obviously, $\theta = 180° + A = 210°$. Since sine is negative in the third quadrant, we have

$$\sin \theta = \sin 210° = -\left|\sin(210° - 180°)\right| = -\sin 30° = -\frac{1}{2}.$$

2. If $\sin 2x = -\cos(-x + 9°)$, find x.

$$\sin 2x = -\cos(-x + 9°) = \cos(-x + 9° + 180°)$$
$$\text{But } 2x + x + 9° + 180° = 90°$$
$$x = -99°$$

BASIC IDENTITIES

$$\sin^2 \alpha + \cos^2 \alpha = 1$$
$$\tan \alpha = \frac{\sin \alpha}{\cos \alpha}$$
$$\cot \alpha = \frac{\cos \alpha}{\sin \alpha} = \frac{1}{\tan \alpha}$$

$$\csc \alpha = \frac{1}{\sin \alpha}$$

$$\sec \alpha = \frac{1}{\cos \alpha}$$

$$1 + \tan^2 \alpha = \sec^2 \alpha$$

$$1 + \cot^2 \alpha = \csc^2 \alpha$$

One can find all the trigonometric functions of an acute angle when the value of any one of them is known.

● **EXAMPLE**

Given α is an acute angle and $\csc \alpha = 2$, then

$$\sin \alpha = \frac{1}{\csc \alpha} = \frac{1}{2}$$

$$\cos^2 \alpha + \sin^2 \alpha = 1, \quad \cos \alpha = \sqrt{1 - \sin^2 \alpha}$$

$$= \sqrt{1 - \left(\tfrac{1}{2}\right)^2}$$

$$= \sqrt{1 - \tfrac{1}{4}}$$

$$= \frac{\sqrt{3}}{2}$$

$$\tan \alpha = \frac{\sin \alpha}{\cos \alpha} = \frac{\frac{1}{2}}{\frac{\sqrt{3}}{2}} = \frac{1}{\sqrt{3}} = \frac{\sqrt{3}}{3}$$

$$\cot \alpha = \frac{1}{\tan \alpha} = \sqrt{3}$$

$$\sec \alpha = \frac{1}{\cos \alpha} = \frac{1}{\frac{\sqrt{3}}{2}} = \frac{2}{\sqrt{3}} = \frac{2\sqrt{3}}{3}$$

i) If θ is a first quadrant angle, then

   a) $\sin \theta \;=\; \sin \phi$ d) $\cot \theta \;=\; \cot \phi$

   b) $\cos \theta \;=\; \cos \phi$ e) $\sec \theta \;=\; \sec \phi$

   c) $\tan \theta \;=\; \tan \phi$ f) $\csc \theta \;=\; \csc \phi$

ii) If θ is a second quadrant angle:

a) $\sin\theta = \sin\phi$
b) $\cos\theta = -\cos\phi$
c) $\tan\theta = -\tan\phi$
d) $\cot\theta = -\cot\phi$
e) $\sec\theta = -\sec\phi$
f) $\csc\theta = \csc\phi$

iii) If θ is a third quadrant angle, then

a) $\sin\theta = -\sin\phi$
b) $\cos\theta = -\cos\phi$
c) $\tan\theta = \tan\phi$
d) $\cot\theta = \cot\phi$
e) $\sec\theta = -\sec\phi$
f) $\csc\theta = -\csc\phi$

iv) If θ is a fourth quadrant angle, then

a) $\sin\theta = -\sin\phi$
b) $\cos\theta = \cos\phi$
c) $\tan\theta = -\tan\phi$
d) $\cot\theta = -\cot\phi$
e) $\sec\theta = \sec\phi$
f) $\csc\theta = -\csc\phi$

ADDITION AND SUBTRACTION FORMULAS

$$\sin(A \pm B) = \sin A \cos B \pm \cos A \sin B$$
$$\cos(A \pm B) = \cos A \cos B \pm \sin A \sin B$$
$$\tan(A \pm B) = \frac{\tan A \pm \tan B}{1 \pm \tan A \tan B}$$
$$\cot(A \pm B) = \frac{\cot A \cot B \pm 1}{\cot B \pm \cot A}$$

DOUBLE-ANGLE FORMULAS

$$\sin 2A = 2\sin A \cos A$$
$$\cos 2A = \cos^2 A - 1$$
$$= 1 - 2\sin^2 A$$
$$= \cos^2 A - \sin^2 A$$
$$\tan 2A = \frac{2\tan A}{1 - \tan^2 A}$$

HALF-ANGLE FORMULAS

$$\sin\frac{A}{2} = \pm\frac{\sqrt{1-\cos A}}{2}$$

$$\cos\frac{A}{2} = \pm\frac{\sqrt{1+\cos A}}{2}$$

$$\tan\frac{A}{2} = \pm\frac{\sqrt{1-\cos A}}{1+\cos A}$$

$$= \frac{1-\cos A}{\sin A}$$

$$= \frac{\sin A}{1+\cos A}$$

$$\cot\frac{A}{2} = \pm\frac{\sqrt{1+\cos A}}{1-\cos A} = \frac{1+\cos A}{\sin A} = \frac{\sin A}{1-\cos A}$$

SUM AND DIFFERENCE FORMULAS

$$\sin\alpha + \sin\beta = 2\sin\left(\frac{\alpha+\beta}{2}\right)\cos\left(\frac{\alpha-\beta}{2}\right)$$

$$\sin\alpha - \sin\beta = 2\cos\left(\frac{\alpha+\beta}{2}\right)\sin\left(\frac{\alpha-\beta}{2}\right)$$

$$\cos\alpha + \cos\beta = 2\cos\left(\frac{\alpha+\beta}{2}\right)\cos\left(\frac{\alpha-\beta}{2}\right)$$

$$\cos\alpha - \cos\beta = -2\sin\left(\frac{\alpha+\beta}{2}\right)\sin\left(\frac{\alpha-\beta}{2}\right)$$

$$\cos\alpha - \cos\beta = -2\sin\left(\frac{\alpha+\beta}{2}\right)\sin\left(\frac{\alpha-\beta}{2}\right)$$

$$\tan\alpha + \tan\beta = \frac{\sin(\alpha+\beta)}{\cos\alpha\cos\beta}$$

$$\tan\alpha \times \tan\beta = \frac{\sin(\alpha-\beta)}{\cos\alpha\cos\beta}$$

PRODUCT FORMULAS OF SINES AND COSINES

$$\sin A \sin B = \frac{1}{2}[\cos(A - B) - \cos(A + B)]$$

$$\cos A \cos B = \frac{1}{2}[\cos(A + B) + \cos(A - B)]$$

$$\sin A \cos B = \frac{1}{2}[\sin(A + B) + \sin(A - B)]$$

$$\cos A \sin B = \frac{1}{2}[\sin(A + B) - \sin(A - B)]$$

● **EXAMPLE**

If $\sin \alpha = \dfrac{3}{5}$ and $\cos \beta = \dfrac{3}{5}$, find $\cos(\alpha + \beta)$.

Since $\cos(\alpha + \beta) = \cos \alpha \cos \beta - \sin \alpha \sin \beta$, we need to find $\cos \alpha$ and $\sin \beta$. But,

$$\cos \alpha = \sqrt{1 - \sin^2 \alpha} = \sqrt{1 - \tfrac{9}{25}} = \sqrt{\tfrac{16}{25}} = \tfrac{4}{5}$$

$$\sin \beta = \sqrt{1 - \cos^2 \beta} = \sqrt{1 - \tfrac{9}{25}} = \sqrt{\tfrac{16}{25}} = \tfrac{4}{5}$$

So,

$$\cos(\alpha + \beta) = \frac{4}{5} \times \frac{3}{5} - \frac{3}{5} \times \frac{4}{5} = 0$$

PROPERTIES AND GRAPHS OF TRIGONOMETRIC FUNCTIONS

The **sine function** is the graph of $y = \sin x$. Other trigonometric functions are defined similarly.

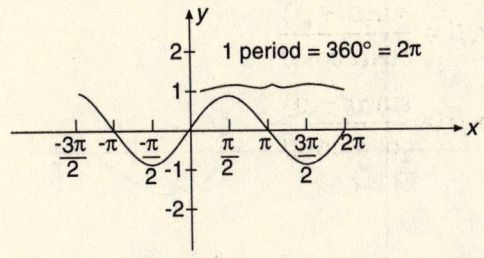

Sine Function

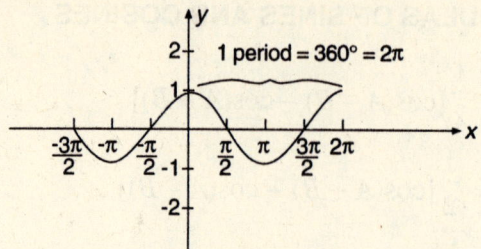

Cosine Function

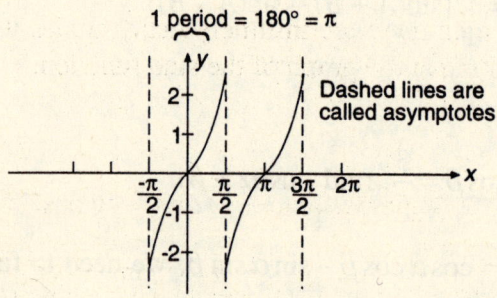

Tangent Function

● EXAMPLE

Draw one period of the graph for the function $y = 0.5 \sin(4x + \frac{\pi}{6})$ and indicate its amplitude, period, and phase shift.

$$x = 0, \; y = 0.5\sin\frac{\pi}{6}$$

$$x = \frac{\pi}{4}, \; y = 0.5\sin(\pi + \frac{\pi}{6}) = -0.5\sin\frac{\pi}{6}$$

$$x = \frac{\pi}{2}, \; y = 0.5\sin(2\pi + \frac{\pi}{6}) = 0.5\sin\frac{\pi}{6}$$

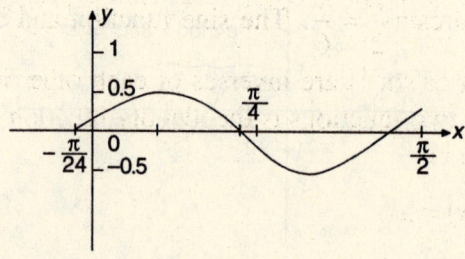

So, amplitude $= \dfrac{1}{2}$

period $= \dfrac{\pi}{2}$

phase shift $= -\dfrac{\pi}{24}$

INVERSE TRIGONOMETRIC FUNCTIONS

If $-1 < x < 1$, then there are infinitely many angles whose sine is x, as we can see by looking at the graph of the sine function.

Definition:

$\arcsin x =$ the angle between $-\dfrac{\pi}{2}$ and $\dfrac{\pi}{2}$ whose sine is x.

$\operatorname{arccsc} x =$ the angle between $-\dfrac{\pi}{2}$ and $\dfrac{\pi}{2}$ whose cosecant is x.

$\arctan x =$ the angle between $-\dfrac{\pi}{2}$ and $\dfrac{\pi}{2}$ whose cotangent is x.

$\arccos x =$ the angle between θ and π whose cosine is x.

$\operatorname{arcsec} x =$ the angle between θ and π whose secant is x.

$\arctan x =$ the angle between θ and π whose tangent is x.

PROBLEM

Evaluate $\arcsin \dfrac{1}{2}$.

SOLUTION

Since $\sin \dfrac{\pi}{6} = \dfrac{1}{2}$, $\arcsin \dfrac{1}{2} = \dfrac{\pi}{6}$. The sine function and the arcsine function (abbreviated arcsin or $\sin^{-1}$) are inverses of each other in the sense that the composition of the two functions is the identity function (that is the function that takes x back to x).

$\sin(\arcsin x) = x$

$\arcsin (\sin x) = x$

PERIODICITY

The **period** of a (repeating) function, f, is the smallest positive number p such that $f(x) = f(x + p)$ for all x.

The period of the tangent and cotangent function is π. This fact is clear from the graphs of the tangent and cotangent functions. Pick any angle, x, on the x-axis, and notice $x + \pi$ has the same tangent as x. The period of the other trigonometric functions is 2π.

If the period of a function f is p, and $g(x) = f(nx)$, then the period of g is p/n.

PROBLEM

What is the period of sin $3x$?

SOLUTION

Since the period of sin x is 2π, the period of sin $3x$ is $\dfrac{2\pi}{3}$.

☞ Drill: Trigonometry

1. $\tan^{-1}(-\sqrt{3}) =$

    (A) $-60°$ (B) $60°$ (C) $30°$ (D) $-30°$

2. Calculate $\dfrac{\sin^{-1}\frac{1}{2}}{\tan^{-1}1}$.

    (A) $\dfrac{1}{2}$ (B) $30°$ (C) $45°$ (D) $\dfrac{2}{3}$

3. Find $\cos[\arcsin(-1)]$.

    (A) $\dfrac{1}{2}$ (B) $\dfrac{\sqrt{3}}{2}$ (C) 0 (D) $-\dfrac{\sqrt{3}}{2}$

4. If x is inside $[0, 2\pi]$, one solution for the equation

    $\sqrt{1 + \sin^2 x} = \sqrt{2}\sin x$ is

    (A) $\dfrac{5}{2}\pi$.   (B) $\dfrac{\pi}{6}$.   (C) $\dfrac{3}{2}\pi$.   (D) $\dfrac{\pi}{2}$.

5. $\sec^2\theta - \tan^2\theta =$

   (A) $\dfrac{4}{5}$ (B) $\dfrac{1}{2}$ (C) -1 (D) 1

6. $\dfrac{\sin(45° + x) + \sin(45° - x)}{\cos x} =$

   (A) $\sqrt{2}$ (B) $\tan x$ (C) $\dfrac{\sqrt{2}}{2}$ (D) $\dfrac{\sqrt{2}}{2}\cos x$

7. The amplitude of $y = \dfrac{\sqrt{3}}{3}\sin x + \cos x$ is

   (A) $\dfrac{\sqrt{3}}{2}$.   (B) $\dfrac{\sqrt{2}}{2}$.   (C) $\dfrac{\sqrt{3}}{4}$.   (D) $\dfrac{2}{\sqrt{3}}$.

8. $\dfrac{\csc x}{2\cos x} =$

   (A) $\cos 3x$ (B) $\tan 2x$ (C) $\sin 2x$ (D) $\csc 2x$

GEOMETRY AND TRIGONOMETRY REVIEW

ANSWER KEY

Drill: Points, Lines, and Angles

1.	(B)	4.	(C)	6.	(D)	8.	(D)
2.	(D)	5.	(B)	7.	(C)	9.	(A)
3.	(D)						

Drill: Regular Polygons (Convex)

1.	(D)	3.	(D)	4.	(C)	5.	(D)
2.	(D)						

Drill: Triangles

1.	(D)	4.	(A)	7.	(B)	9.	(A)
2.	(B)	5.	(D)	8.	(D)	10.	(B)
3.	(C)	6.	(C)				

Drill: Quadrilaterals

1.	(B)	4.	(D)	7.	(D)	9.	(C)
2.	(D)	5.	(C)	8.	(B)	10.	(D)
3.	(A)	6.	(C)				

Drill: Circles

1.	(B)	4.	(C)	7.	(D)	9.	(C)
2.	(C)	5.	(B)	8.	(C)	10.	(B)
3.	(D)	6.	(B)				

Drill: Coordinate Geometry

1.	(C)	3.	(B)	5.	(B)	6.	(D)
2.	(A)	4.	(C)				

Drill: Trigonometry

1.	(A)	3.	(C)	5.	(D)	7.	(D)
2.	(D)	4.	(D)	6.	(A)	8.	(D)

DETAILED EXPLANATIONS OF ANSWERS

Drill: Points, Lines, and Angles

1. **(B)** A straight line, or straight angle is 180°. Therefore,
$a = 180 - 112 = 68$

2. **(D)** The equation with x is on a straight line, which is 180°.
Therefore, $3x + 12 + 5x - 16 = 180$
$$8x - 4 = 180$$
$$8x = 184$$
$$x = 23$$

3. **(D)** $29 + 63 + z = 180$
$$92 + z = 180$$
$$= 88$$

4. **(C)** $\angle ABC = 90°$ because $\overline{BA}$ and $\overline{BC}$ are perpendicular and form right angles. The $\angle ABD = 90 - 53 = 37$

5. **(B)** Since line b is a straight line, 180°, $\angle 2 = 180 - 90 = 90$

6. **(D)** Since $\overline{CD} \perp \overline{EF}$, we know the sum of 1, 2, and 3 will be 90°.
$$2x + 30 + x = 90$$
$$3x + 30 = 90$$
$$3x = 60$$
$$x = 20$$

7. **(C)** Since $a \parallel b$, $\angle z = 180 - 116 = 64$

8. **(D)** Since line $p \parallel r$, $\angle 7 = \angle 1 = 180 - 123 = 57$

9. **(A)** $m\angle 5 = m\angle 3 = 55°$

Drill: Regular Polygons (Convex)

1.   **(D)**   A regular pentagon is both equiangular and equilateral. A pentagon is five sided. Therefore,

$$360 \div 5 = 72 \qquad 180 - 72 = 108$$

2.   **(D)** $(3 \times 180) - 180 = 360$

3.   **(D)** $a = 4\sqrt{3} \quad h = 8\sqrt{3} + 4\sqrt{3} = 12\sqrt{3}$

$$A = \frac{1}{2}Bh = \frac{1}{2}(24)(12\sqrt{3}) = 144\sqrt{3} \text{ mm}^2$$

4.   **(C)** $s = 4$ therefore, radius = 4 too, which makes the apothem

$$\sqrt{(4)^2 - (2)^2} = 2\sqrt{3}$$

$$A = \frac{1}{2}(a)p = \frac{1}{2}\left(2\sqrt{3}\right)(6)(4) = 24\sqrt{3} \text{ cm}^2$$

5.   **(D)** $A = \frac{1}{2}ap = \frac{1}{2}a(s)(1) = \frac{1}{2}(9.2)(6)(10) = 276 \text{ cm}^2$

Drill: Triangles

1.   **(D)**   Since $\angle Q$ is a right angle, $\angle Q = 90°$. Therefore,
       $90 - 23 = 67°$

2.   **(B)** $\dfrac{180 - 96}{2} = \dfrac{84}{2} = 42$

3.   **(C)** $3x + 2x + x = 180$
       $$6x = 180$$
       $$x = 30$$

4.   **(A)** $6 : 4 = 4 : b \Rightarrow \dfrac{6}{4} = \dfrac{4}{b} \Rightarrow 6b = 16$

$$b = \frac{16}{6} = 2\frac{4}{6} = 2\frac{2}{3}$$

5.   **(D)** $3 : 6 = 4 : b$ $b = 8$

   $3 : 4 = 4 : a$

   $\dfrac{3}{4} = \dfrac{4}{a}$

   $3a = 16 \quad a = 16\left(\dfrac{1}{3}\right) = 5\dfrac{1}{3}$

6.   **(C)** $A = \dfrac{1}{2}bh = \dfrac{1}{2}(14)(8) = 56$

7.   **(B)** $A = \dfrac{1}{2}bh = \dfrac{1}{2}(11)(7) = 38\dfrac{1}{2}$ or 38.5

8.   **(D)** $A = \dfrac{1}{2}bh = \dfrac{1}{2}(4)\left(8\sqrt{2}\right) = 16\sqrt{2}$

9.   **(A)**   Using the Pythagorean theorem,

   $$\overline{AB} = \sqrt{\left(\overline{AC}\right)^2 - \left(\overline{BC}\right)^2} = \sqrt{(15)^2 - (9)^2} = \sqrt{144} = 12$$

   or

   then $A = \dfrac{1}{2}bh = \dfrac{1}{2}(9)(12) = 54\,\text{cm}^2$

10.   **(B)**   45-45-90Δ sides are 1-1-$\sqrt{2}$
   so the sides are 10 cm each

   $A = \dfrac{1}{2}bh = \dfrac{1}{2}(10)(10) = 50\,\text{cm}^2$

Drill: Quadrilaterals

1.   **(B)** $\angle B$ and $\angle D$ are opposite angles and are equal. Therefore,

   $6x + 2 = 98$

   $6x = 96$

   $x = 16$

2.   **(D)** $A = bh = (18)(9) = 162$

3.   **(A)**

$$\overline{AC} = \sqrt{\left(\overline{AD}\right)^2 + (DC)^2}$$
$$= \sqrt{(6)^2 + (8)^2}$$
$$= \sqrt{36 + 64}$$
$$= \sqrt{100}$$
$$= 10 \text{ cm}$$

4.   **(D)** $A = bh = (7)(10) = 70 \text{ cm}^2$

5.   **(C)** $EC = BD = 17$

$$BO = \frac{1}{2}BD = \frac{1}{2}(17) = 8.5$$

6.   **(C)**   Using the Pythagorean theorem,

$$\overline{GH} = \sqrt{\left(\frac{1}{2}GI\right)^2 + \left(\frac{1}{2}HJ\right)^2}$$
$$= \sqrt{\left[\left(\frac{1}{2}\right)(6)\right]^2 + \left[\left(\frac{1}{2}\right)(8)\right]^2}$$
$$= \sqrt{(3)^2 + (4)^2}$$
$$= \sqrt{25} = 5$$

7.   **(D)**

$$A = \frac{1}{2}(b_1 + b_2)h$$
$$= \frac{1}{2}(14 + 21)(10)$$
$$= \frac{1}{2}(35)(10)$$
$$= 175$$

8.   **(B)** $\overline{BC} = \overline{AD} = 6$

$P = 6 + 6 + 5 + 10 = 27$

9. **(C)** Since the triangular area is a 30-60-90 triangle the height is $3\sqrt{3}$, so the area is

$$A = \underset{\text{rectangle}}{bh} + \underset{\text{triangle}}{\frac{1}{2}bh} = (4)(3\sqrt{3}) + \frac{1}{2}(3\sqrt{3})(3)$$

$$= 12\sqrt{3} + \frac{9}{2}\sqrt{3} = \frac{33}{2}\sqrt{3}$$

10. **(D)** The base angles of an isosceles trapezoid are equal.

Therefore, $\angle W = \angle Z$ so

$$58 = 4x - 6$$
$$64 = 4x$$
$$16 = x$$

Drill: Circles

1. **(B)** $C = 2\pi r = 2(\pi)(3) = 6\pi$

2. **(C)** $A = \pi r^2 = \pi(11)^2 = 121\pi$

3. **(D)** $A = \pi r^2 \quad r = \frac{1}{2}d = \frac{1}{2}(27) = 13.5$

$$A = \pi(13.5)^2 = 182.25\pi$$

4. **(C)** $A = 225\pi = \pi r^2$ so $r = \sqrt{225} = 15$

$$d = 2r = 2(15) = 30$$

5. **(B)** $C_x = \pi r^2 = 144\pi \quad r_x = 12$

$C_y = \pi r^2 = 81\pi \quad r_y = 9$

$r_x : r_y = 12 : 9 = 4 : 3$

6. **(B)** Shaded Area = Larger − Smaller Area

$$= \pi r_1^2 - \pi r_2^2$$
$$= \pi(7)^2 - \pi(5)^5$$
$$= 49\pi - 25\pi$$
$$= 24\pi$$

7. **(D)** Measure of arc = measure of $\angle$

8. **(C)** The measure of a semicircle is 180°. Therefore, arc *AXC* = 180°.

9. **(C)** Since *XYZ* is semicircle, 180° – 40° = 140°

10. **(B)** $\dfrac{45}{360}\pi r^2 = \dfrac{1}{8}\pi(4)^2 = \dfrac{16}{8}\pi = 2\pi$

Drill: Coordinate Geometry

1. **(C)** To find the coordinates (–3, 2) on the graph, draw perpendicular lines from the point to the coordinates on the number line, as shown. *C* represents the coordinates (–3, 2).

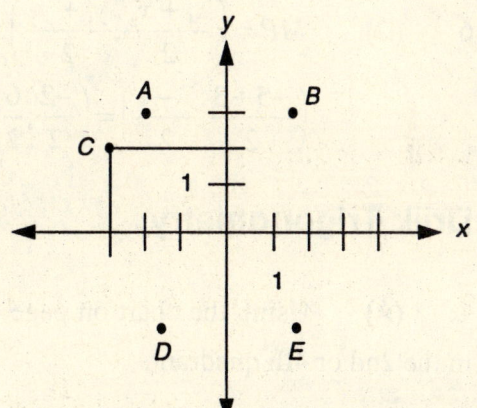

2. **(A)** To find the correct *y*-coordinate for point *R*, draw a vertical line through point *R*. –2 is the correct *y*-coordinate.

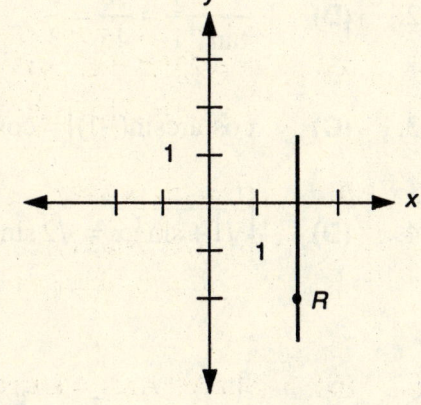

3. **(B)** $d = \sqrt{(x_1 - x_2) + (y_1 - y_2)^2}$

$d = \sqrt{(-2-4)^2 + (-7+7)^2} = \sqrt{(-6)^2 + (0)^2} = 6$

4. **(C)** $d = \sqrt{(x_1 - x_2) + (y_1 - y_2)^2}$

$d = \sqrt{(5-3)^2 + (11-8)^2} = \sqrt{(2)^2 + (3)^2} = \sqrt{4+9} = \sqrt{13}$

5. **(B)** $MP = \left(\dfrac{x_1 + x_2}{2}, \dfrac{y_1 + y_2}{2}\right)$

$\left(\dfrac{4-2}{2}, \dfrac{8+6}{2}\right) = \left(\dfrac{2}{2}, \dfrac{14}{2}\right) = (1,7)$

6. **(D)** $MP = \left(\dfrac{x_1 + x_2}{2}, \dfrac{y_1 + y_2}{2}\right)$

$\left(\dfrac{-5+3}{2}, \dfrac{7-1}{2}\right) = \left(\dfrac{-2}{2}, \dfrac{6}{2}\right) = (-1,3)$

Drill: Trigonometry

1. **(A)** Using the chart on page 453, you will find $\tan^{-1}\left(-\sqrt{3}\right) = 60°$ in the 2nd or 4th quadrant.

2. **(D)** $\dfrac{\sin^{-1}\dfrac{1}{2}}{\tan^{-1}1} = \dfrac{30}{45} = \dfrac{2}{3}$

3. **(C)** $\cos[\arcsin(-1)] = \cos(-90) = 0$

4. **(D)** $\left[\sqrt{1 + \sin^2 x} = \sqrt{2}\sin x\right]^2 \Rightarrow$

$$\begin{array}{rcl} 1 + \sin^2 x &=& 2\sin^2 x \\ -2\sin^2 x & & -2\sin^2 x \\ \hline 1 - \sin^2 x &=& 0 \\ \cos^2 x &=& 0 \end{array}$$

$\cos x = 0$ at $\dfrac{\pi}{2}$ or $\dfrac{3}{2}\pi$

$\dfrac{3}{2}\pi$ won't satisfy the original equation

So $\dfrac{\pi}{2}$ is the answer.

5. **(D)** $\sec^2\theta - \tan^2\theta = (\tan^2\theta + 1) - \tan^2\theta$

   $= 1$

6. **(A)** $\dfrac{\sin(45° + x) + \sin(45° - x)}{\cos x}$

   $= \dfrac{\sin 45 \cos x + \cos 45 \sin x + \sin 45 \cos x - \cos 45 \sin x}{\cos x}$

   $= \dfrac{2 \sin 45 \cos x}{\cos x}$

   $= 2 \sin 45$

   $= 2\left(\dfrac{\sqrt{2}}{2}\right)$

   $= \sqrt{2}$

7. **(D)** $y = \dfrac{\sqrt{3}}{3} \sin x + \cos x$

Testing reference angles 0, 30, 45, 60, and 90 we determine that 30 is the greatest

$$\dfrac{\sqrt{3}}{3}\sin(3) + \cos(30) = \dfrac{\sqrt{3}}{3}\left(\dfrac{1}{2}\right) + \left(\dfrac{\sqrt{3}}{2}\right)$$

$$= \dfrac{\sqrt{3}}{6} + \dfrac{\sqrt{3}}{2}$$

$$= \dfrac{\sqrt{3}}{6} + \dfrac{3\sqrt{3}}{6}$$

$$= \dfrac{4\sqrt{3}}{6}$$

$$= \dfrac{2\sqrt{3}}{3}$$

$$= \dfrac{2}{\sqrt{3}}$$

8. **(D)** $\dfrac{\csc x}{2\cos x} = \dfrac{\dfrac{1}{\sin x}}{2\cos x} = \dfrac{1}{2\sin x \cos x} = \dfrac{1}{\sin 2x} = \csc 2x$

V. SETS AND LOGIC REVIEW

SETS

A set is defined as a collection of items. Each individual item belonging to a set is called an element or member of that set. Sets are usually represented by capital letters, elements by lowercase letters. If an item k belongs to a set A, we write $k \in A$ ("k is an element of A"). If k is not in A, we write $k \notin A$ ("k is not an element of A"). The order of the elements in a set does not matter:

$$\{1, 2, 3\} = \{3, 2, 1\} = \{1, 3, 2\}, \text{ etc.}$$

A set can be described in two ways:

1)   it can be listed element by element, or

2)   a rule characterizing the elements in a set can be formulated.

For example, given the set A of the whole numbers starting with 1 and ending with 9, we can describe it either as $A = \{1,2,3,4,5,6,7,8,9\}$ or as {the set of whole numbers greater than 0 and less than 10}. In both methods, the description is enclosed in brackets. A kind of shorthand is often used for the second method of set description; instead of writing out a complete sentence in between the brackets, we write instead

$$A = \{k \mid 0 < k < 10, k \text{ a whole number}\}$$

This is read as "the set of all elements k such that k is greater than 0 and less than 10, where k is a whole number."

A set not containing any members is called the **empty** or **null** set. It is written either as ø or { }.

SUBSETS

Given two sets A and B, A is said to be a subset of B if every member of set A is also a member of set B. A is a *proper* subset of B if B contains at least one element not in A. We write $A \subseteq B$ if A is a subset of B, and $A \subset B$ if A is a proper subset of B.

Two sets are equal if they have exactly the same elements; in addition, if $A = B$ then $A \subseteq B$ and $B \subseteq A$.

e.g., Let $A = \{1,2,3,4,5\}$

$B = \{1,2\}$

$C = \{1,4,2,3,5\}$

Then 1) A equals C, and A and C are subsets of each other, but not proper subsets and 2) $B \subseteq A$, $B \subseteq C$, $B \subset A$, $B \subset C$ (B is a subset of both A and C. In particular, B is a proper subset of A and C).

A universal set U is a set from which other sets draw their members. If A is a subset of U then the complement of A, denoted A', is the set of all elements in the universal set that are not elements of A.

e.g., If $U = \{1,2,3,4,5,6,\ldots\}$ and $A = \{1,2,3\}$, then $A' = \{4,5,6,\ldots\}$.

Figure 1 illustrates this concept through the use of a *Venn diagram*.

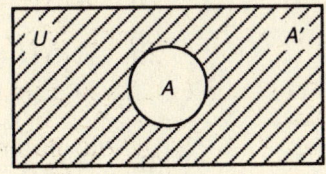

Figure 1

UNION AND INTERSECTION OF SETS

The union of two sets A and B, denoted $A \cup B$, is the set of all elements that are either in A or B or both.

The intersection of two sets A and B, denoted $A \cap B$, is the set of all elements that belong to both A and B.

If $A = \{1,2,3,4,5\}$ and $B = \{2,3,4,5,6\}$ then $A \cup B = \{1,2,3,4,5,6\}$ and $A \cap B = \{2,3,4,5\}$.

If $A \cap B = \emptyset$, A and B are *disjoint*. Figures 2 and 3 are Venn diagrams for union and intersection. The shaded areas represent the given operation.

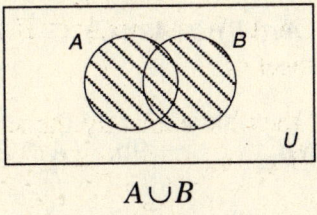

$A \cup B$

Figure 2

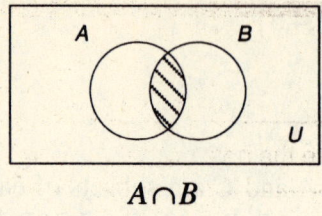

$$A \cap B$$

Figure 3

LAWS OF SET OPERATIONS

If U is the universal set and A is any subset of U, then the following hold for union, intersection, and complement:

Identity Laws

1a. $A \cup \phi = A$ 1b. $A \cap \phi = \phi$

2a. $A \cup U = U$ 2b. $A \cap U = A$

Idempotent Laws

3a. $A \cup A = A$ 3b. $A \cap A = A$

Complement Laws

4a. $A \cup A' = U$ 4b. $A \cap A' = \phi$

5a. $A \cup A' = U$ 5b. $\phi' = U;\ U' = \phi$

Commutative Laws

6a. $A \cup B = B \cup A$ 6b. $A \cap B = B \cap A$

Associative Laws

7a. $(A \cup B) \cup C = A \cup (B \cup C)$

7b. $(A \cap B) \cap C = A \cap (B \cap C)$

Distributive Laws

8a. $A \cup (B \cap C) = (A \cup B) \cap (A \cup C)$

8b. $A \cap (B \cup C) = (A \cap B) \cup (A \cap C)$

De Morgan's Laws

9a. $(A \cup B)' = A' \cap B'$ 9b. $(A \cap B)' = A' \cup B'$

☞ Drill: Sets

DIRECTIONS: Choose the best answer.

1. If a = {1, 2, 3, 4, 5} and b = {2, 3, 4, 5, 6}, find $a \cup b$.

   (A) {2, 3, 4, 5}   (C) {1, 2, 3, 4, 5, 6}

   (B) {2, 3, 4, 5, 6}   (D) {1, 2, 3, 4, 5}

2. If a = {1, 2, 3, 4, 5} and b = {2, 3, 4, 5, 6}, find $a \cap b$.

   (A) {2, 3, 4, 5}   (C) {2, 3, 4, 5, 6}

   (B) {1, 2, 3, 4, 5, 6}   (D) {1, 2, 3, 4, 5}

3.

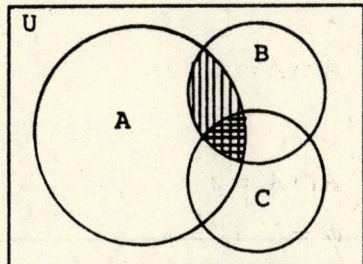   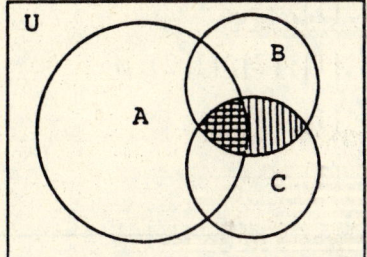

Fig. 1 (A∩B)∩C   Fig. 2 A∩(B∩C)

What do Figure 1 and 2 represent?

   (A) $A \cap (B \cap C)$

   (B) $(A \cap B) \cap C = A \cap (B \cap C)$

   (C) $(A \cap B) \cap C$

   (D) $(A \cap B)$

4. If U = {1, 2, 3, 4, 5, 6, 7, 8, 9, 10}, P = {2, 4, 6, 8, 10}, Q = {1, 2, 3, 4, 5}, what is $\overline{P}$?

   (A) {6, 7, 8, 9, 10}   (C) {3, 5, 7, 9}

   (B) {1, 2, 3, 4, 5}   (D) {1, 3, 5, 7, 9}

5. If $a = \{1, 2, 3\}$ and $b = \{5, 6\}$, find $a \times b$.

    (A) $\{(5, 1), (5, 2), (5, 3), (6, 1)\}$

    (B) $\{(1, 2), (2, 3), (5, 6)\}$

    (C) $\{(6, 2), (6, 3)\}$

    (D) $\{(1, 5), (1, 6), (2, 5), (2, 6), (3, 5), (3, 6)\}$

6. Let $M = \{1, 2\}$ and $N = \{p, q\}$. Find $M \times N$.

    (A) $\{(1, p), (1, q), (2, p), (2, q)\}$

    (B) $\{(p, 1)\}, (q, 1), (p, 2), (q, 2)\}$

    (C) $\{(1, 1), (1, 2), (2, 1), (2, 2)\}$

    (D) $\{(p, 1), (q, 1), (2, 1), (2, 2)\}$

7. List all the subsets of $C = \{1, 2\}$.

    (A) $\{1\}, \emptyset$

    (B) $\{1\}, \{2\}, \{1, 2\}, \emptyset$

    (C) $\{1\}, \{2\}$

    (D) $\{2\}, \emptyset$

LOGIC

FUNDAMENTAL CONCEPTS OF LOGIC

Sentential calculus is the "calculus of sentences," a field in which the truth or falseness of assertions is examined by using algebraic tools.

Sentence

A sentence is any expression that can be labeled either true or false.

Examples: Expressions to which the terms "true" or "false" can be assigned include the following:

1) "It is raining where I am standing."

2) "My name is George."

3) "$1 + 2 = 3$"

Examples: Expressions to which the terms "true" or "false" cannot be assigned include the following:

1) "I will probably be healthier if I exercise."

2) "It will rain on this day, one year from now."

3) "What I am saying at this instant is a lie."

Sentential Calculus

Sentential calculus is the "calculus of sentences," in which tools of algebra are used to examine whether sentences are true or false (when possible). Sentential calculus is also referred to as propositional calculus or algebra of logic.

Sentences can be combined to form new sentences using the connectives, AND, OR, NOT, and IF-THEN.

Examples: The sentences

1) "John is tired."

2) "Mary is cooking."

can be combined to form

1) "John is tired AND Mary is cooking."

2) "John is tired OR Mary is cooking."

3) "John is NOT tired."

4) "IF John is tired THEN Mary is cooking."

Literals

In any context, there is a collection of basic or fundamental sentences which, when linked together via the connectives NOT, AND, OR, and IF-THEN, can serve to express the content of any other sentence. These sentences, together with their negations, are referred to as the fundamental sentences, literals, or atoms of sentential calculus.

In the following we will use capital letters X, Y, Z, ... to represent sentences, and develop algebraic tools to represent new sentences formed by linking them with the above connectives. Our connectives may be regarded as operations transforming one or more sentences into a new sentence. To describe them in greater detail, we introduce symbols to represent them. You will find that different symbols representing the same idea may appear in different references.

Logical Value

The logical value of a sentence X is TRUE (or T) if X is true, and FALSE (or F) if X is false.

TRUTH TABLES AND BASIC LOGICAL OPERATIONS
Truth Table

The truth table for a sentence X is the exhaustive list of possible logical values of X.

Negation

If X is a sentence, then $\sim X$ represents the negation, the opposite, or the contradiction of X. Thus, the logical values of $\sim X$ are as shown in the following truth table:

X	$\sim X$
T	F
F	T

Table 1–Truth table for negation.

$\sim$ is called the negation operation on sentences.

Example: For

X = "Jane is eating an apple."

$\sim X$ = "Jane is NOT eating an apple."

Negation Is a "Unary" Operation

The negation operation is called unary, since it transforms a sentence into a unique image sentence.

IFF

We use the word IFF to represent the expression "if and only if."

AND

For sentences X and Y, "X AND Y," represented by X & Y, is the sentence which is true IFF both X and Y are true. The truth table for & is as follows:

X	Y	X & Y
T	T	T
T	F	F
F	T	F
F	F	F

Table 2–Truth Table for AND.

& is called the conjunction operator.

Conjunction Is a Binary Operation

The conjunction & is a binary operation since it transforms a pair of sentences into a unique image sentence.

Example: For

X = "Jane is eating an apple,"

and

Y = "All apples are sweet,"

X & Y = "Jane is eating an apple AND all apples are sweet."

AND/OR

For sentences X and Y, "X AND/OR Y," represented by X ∨ Y, denotes the sentence that is true if either or both X and Y are true. The truth table for ∨ is as follows:

X	Y	X ∨ Y
T	T	T
T	F	T
F	T	T
F	F	F

Table 3–Truth table for AND/OR.

∨ is called the disjunction operator.

Disjunction Is a Binary Operation

As with the conjunction operator, the disjunction is a binary operation, transforming the pair of sentences X, Y into a unique image sentence $X \vee Y$.

Example: For

X = "Jane is eating the apple,"

and

Y = "Marvin is running,"

$X \vee Y$ = "Jane is eating the apple AND/OR Marvin is running."

IF-THEN-

For sentences X and Y, $X \rightarrow Y$ represents the statement "IF X THEN Y." $X \rightarrow Y$ is false IFF X is true and Y is false; otherwise, it is true. The truth table for $\rightarrow$ is as follows:

X	Y	$X \rightarrow Y$
T	T	T
T	F	F
F	T	T
F	F	T

Table 4–Truth Table for IF-THEN-.

$\rightarrow$ is referred to as the implication operator.

Implication $\rightarrow$ Is a Binary Operation

$\rightarrow$ is a binary operator on pairs of sentences X, Y.

X IFF Y

For sentences X and Y, $X \leftrightarrow Y$ is true IFF X and Y have the same truth value; otherwise, it is false. The truth table for $\leftrightarrow$ is as follows:

X	Y	X ↔ Y
T	T	T
T	F	F
F	T	F
F	F	T

Table 5–Truth table for equivalence.

↔ represents logical equivalence, "IFF."

Example: For

X = "Jane eats apples,"

and

Y = "apples are sweet,"

$X ↔ Y$ = "Jane is eats apples IFF apples are sweet."

Equivalence ↔ Is a Binary Operation

↔ is again a binary operation on pairs of sentences.

LOGICAL EQUIVALENCE
Logically Equivalent Sentences

Two sentences, X, Y for which $X ↔ Y$ are said to be logically equivalent.

Logical Equivalence and Meaning the Same

Logical equivalence ↔ is not the same as equivalence of meanings. Thus, if Jane is eating an apple and Barbara is frightened of mice, then for X = "Jane is eating an apple" and Y = "Barbara is frightened of mice," X and Y are logically equivalent, since both are correct. However, they do not have the same meaning. Statements having the same meaning are, for example, the double negative ~~X (not-not) and X itself.

If Sentences Have the Same Meaning

If X AND Y have the same meaning, then we write

X EQ Y.

There is no truth table for EQ, since having the same meaning is far stronger than simply being simultaneously true or false.

Sentential Calculus and Equivalence

Sentential calculus is concerned only with logical equivalence, and ignores the meaning of the sentences considered.

THEOREM 1 — Double Negation Equals Identity

For any sentence X,

$$\sim\sim X \leftrightarrow X.$$

FUNDAMENTAL PROPERTIES OF OPERATIONS

THEOREM 2 — Properties of Conjunction Operation

For any sentences X, Y, Z, the following properties hold:

1) Commutativity: $X \& Y \leftrightarrow Y \& X$

2) Associativity: $X \& (Y \& Z) \leftrightarrow (X \& Y) \& Z$

THEOREM 3 — Properties of Disjunction Operation

For any sentences X, Y, Z, the following properties hold:

1) Commutativity: $X \vee Y \leftrightarrow Y \vee X$

2) Associativity: $X \vee (Y \vee Z) \leftrightarrow (X \vee Y) \vee Z$

THEOREM 4 — Distributive Laws

For any sentences X, Y, Z, the following laws hold:

1) $X \vee (Y \& Z) \leftrightarrow (X \vee Y) \& (X \vee Z)$

2) $X \& (Y \vee Z) \leftrightarrow (X \& Y) \vee (X \& Z)$

THEOREM 5 — DeMorgan's Laws for Sentences

For any sentences X, Y, the following laws hold:

1) $\sim (X \& Y) \leftrightarrow (\sim X) \vee (\sim Y)$.

2) $\sim (X \vee Y) \leftrightarrow (\sim X) \& (\sim Y)$.

Proof of A): Assertion A) can be proved by developing a truth table over all possible combinations of X and Y and observing that all values assumed by the sentences are the same. To this end, we first evaluate the expression $\sim (X \& Y)$:

X	Y	X & Y	~(X & Y)
T	T	T	F
T	F	F	T
F	T	F	T
F	F	F	T

Table 6a–Truth table for negation of conjunction.

Now we evaluate $(\sim X) \vee (\sim Y)$:

X	Y	~X	~Y	(~X) ∨ (~Y)
T	T	F	F	F
T	F	F	T	T
F	T	T	F	T
F	F	T	T	T

Table 6b–Truth table for disjunction of negation.

The last columns of the truth tables coincide, proving our assertion.

THEOREM 6 — Two Logical Identities

For any sentences X, Y, the sentences X and $(X \,\&\, Y) \vee (X \,\&\, \sim Y)$ are logically equivalent, i.e.,

$$(X \,\&\, Y) \vee (X \,\&\, \sim Y) \leftrightarrow X$$

This is proven in the following truth table:

X	Y	~Y	X & Y	X & ~Y	(X & Y) ∨ (X & ~Y)
T	T	F	T	F	T
T	F	T	F	T	T
F	T	F	F	F	F
F	F	T	F	F	F

Table 7a–Truth table for $(X \,\&\, Y) \vee (X \,\&\, \sim Y) \leftrightarrow X$.

For any sentences X, Y, the sentences X and $X \vee (Y \mathbin{\&} {\sim}Y)$ are logically equivalent, i.e.,

$$X \vee (Y \mathbin{\&} {\sim}Y) \leftrightarrow X$$

This is proven in the following truth table:

X	Y	${\sim}Y$	$Y \mathbin{\&} {\sim}Y$	$X \vee (Y \mathbin{\&} {\sim}Y)$
T	T	F	F	T
T	F	T	F	T
F	T	F	F	F
F	F	T	F	F

Table 7b–Truth table for $X \vee (Y \mathbin{\&} {\sim}Y) \leftrightarrow X$.

THEOREM 7 — Proof by Contradiction

For any sentences X, Y, the following holds:

$$X \to Y \leftrightarrow {\sim}Y \to {\sim}X .$$

To prove this, we consider the following truth table:

X	Y	$X \to Y$	${\sim}Y$	${\sim}X$	${\sim}Y \to {\sim}X$
T	T	T	F	F	T
T	F	F	T	F	F
F	T	T	F	T	T
F	F	T	T	T	T

Table 8–Truth table for proof by contradiction.

SENTENCES, LITERALS, AND FUNDAMENTAL CONJUNCTIONS

We have seen that logically equivalent sentences may be expressed in different ways, the simplest examples being that a sentence is equal to its double negation,

$${\sim}{\sim}X \leftrightarrow X,$$

while by DeMorgan's theorem,

$$X \vee Y \leftrightarrow {\sim}({\sim}X \mathbin{\&} {\sim}Y)$$

The significance of sentential calculus and the algebra of logic is that it provides us with a method of producing a "standard" form for representing a statement in terms of the literals. This is indeed unique and, while not usually the simplest representation, it does serve as a standard form for comparison and evaluation of sentences. This standard form is the disjunctive normal form introduced in the following lines.

Subsentences

Suppose that a sentence X is formed as the result of operating on sentences A, B, C, ..., by means of the operators &, $\vee$, $\sim$, $\rightarrow$, and $\leftrightarrow$. For example, $X = (A \vee B)$ & $((\sim C) \rightarrow D))$. Then the sentences A, B, C, ..., are referred to as subsentences of X.

Fundamental Conjunction

A sentence is a fundamental conjunction if it is either a literal or conjunction X & Y of at least two literals in which each literal only appears once.

Examples: If A, B, C, ..., are literals, then the sentences

$$X = A, \ X = A \ \& \ B, \ X = A \ \& \ B \ \& \ D$$

are fundamental conjunctions, while the sentence

$$X = (A \ \& \ B) \ \& \ A$$

is not.

Subjunction

A fundamental subjunction X is a subjunction of the fundamental conjunction Y if every literal appearing in X is a literal of Y.

Example: The fundamental conjunction

$$X = A \ \& \ B$$

is a subjunction of the fundamental conjunction

$$Y = A \ \& \ C \ \& \ B$$

Disjunctive Normal Form

A sentence X is in disjunctive normal form (DNF) if it is a fundamental conjunction or it is a disjunction of at least two disjuncts, or fundamental conjunctions, none of which is a subconjunction of any of the others.

Examples: Let A, B, C, D, ... be literals. Then the following sentences are in disjunctive normal form:

$$X = A, \quad Y = A \,\&\, B, \quad Z = A \lor (A \,\&\, C)$$

$$X = (A \,\&\, B \,\&\, C) \lor (D \,\&\, C) \lor (A \,\&\, D)$$

The following sentences are not in disjunctive normal form:

$$X = A \,\&\, (B \lor C), \quad Y = (A \,\&\, B) \lor (C \,\&\, A \,\&\, B)$$

THEOREM 8 — Fundamental Theorem of Sentences

Every sentence which is not a contradiction is logically equivalent to a sentence which is in disjunctive normal form.

Examples: Consider the sentence

$$X = \{[(A \lor {\sim}B) \lor C] \,\&\, [A \lor ({\sim}{\sim}B)]\} \,\&\, {\sim}A$$

We can reduce this sentence to disjunctive normal form as follows. Firstly, ${\sim}{\sim}B = B$. Similarly, the parentheses around the disjunction $A \lor {\sim}B$ may be removed using the associative law for disjunction. Thus, we find

$$X = [A \lor {\sim}B \lor C] \,\&\, [A \lor B] \,\&\, {\sim}A$$

Now by distributivity and Theorem 6,

$$[A \lor {\sim}B] \,\&\, {\sim}A = (A \,\&\, {\sim}A) \lor (B \,\&\, {\sim}A)$$

$$= B \,\&\, {\sim}A,$$

so that

$$X = (A \lor {\sim}B \lor C) \,\&\, (B \,\&\, {\sim}A)$$

By distributivity, this becomes

$$X = C \,\&\, B \,\&\, {\sim}A,$$

which is the disjunctive normal form consisting only of a single fundamental conjunction.

Full Disjunctive Normal Form

A sentence X is in full disjunctive normal form with respect to the set of literals $A_1, A_2, A_3, ..., A_N$ if the only literals appearing in X are chosen from among the A_2 and any disjunct in X contains all of the literals $A_1, A_2, A_3, ..., A_N$.

Example: In the system with literals A and B, B may be represented in the full disjunctive normal form as

$$B \Leftrightarrow (A \,\&\, B) \lor ({\sim}A \,\&\, B)$$

ADEQUATE SYSTEMS OF CONNECTIVES AND DUALITY

Are the connectives in our logic system independent, or are some of them redundant, that is, expressible in terms of the others? For example, the implication connective $\rightarrow$ may be expressed in terms of the negation and disjunction connectives

$$X \rightarrow Y \Leftrightarrow Y \vee {\sim}X,$$

as we see in Table 9:

X	Y	$X \rightarrow Y$	${\sim}X$	$Y \vee {\sim}X$
T	T	T	F	T
T	F	F	F	F
F	T	T	T	T
F	F	T	T	T

Table 9–Truth table for $X \rightarrow Y \Leftrightarrow Y \vee {\sim}X$.

Adequate System of Connectives

An adequate system of connectives is a set of connectives that can be used to represent every logical sentence in terms of their operation on its literals.

THEOREM 9 — Some Adequate Systems of Connectives

Each of the following systems of connectives constitutes an adequate system:

$$\{{\sim}, \&, \vee\}, \{{\sim}, \&\}, \{{\sim}, \vee\}, \{{\sim}, \rightarrow\}$$

Dependence of Connectives

The operation $X \& Y$ may be presented in terms of $\sim$ and $\vee$ by the negation of DeMorgan's theorem

$$X \& Y \leftrightarrow {\sim}({\sim}X \vee {\sim}Y)$$

Similarly,

$$X \vee Y \leftrightarrow {\sim}({\sim}X \& {\sim}Y)$$

Sheffer Stroke

The Sheffer stroke (|) is a connective defined by the truth table:

X	Y	X	Y
T	T	F
T	F	T
F	T	T
F	F	T

Table 10–Definition of Sheffer stroke.

Joint Denial

We define the joint denial connective (JD) by the truth table:

X	Y	X JD Y
T	T	F
T	F	F
F	T	F
F	F	T

Table 11–Truth table for joint denial operation.

THEOREM 10 — Adequate Systems of One Connective

The Sheffer stroke and joint denial operations are each adequate systems of connectives consisting of exactly one operation.

Proof: For the Sheffer stroke and any sentences X, Y,

$$\sim X \leftrightarrow X \mid X$$

$$X \vee Y \leftrightarrow (X \mid X) \mid (Y \mid Y) \, ;$$

similarly, $X \,\&\, Y$ can be expressed via DeMorgan's theorem in terms of $\sim$ and $\vee$, and so, in terms of $|$.

Theorem 11 — *Other Adequate Systems Do Not Exist*

The joint denial and Sheffer stroke operations are the only adequate connective systems consisting of a single connective.

We have seen earlier that

$$\sim(X \ \& \ Y) \Leftrightarrow \sim X \vee \sim Y,$$

while

$$\sim(X \vee Y) \Leftrightarrow \sim X \ \& \ \sim Y$$

These duality results can be extended to the general principle of duality for sentences.

Theorem 12 — *Duality Principle*

Given a sentence formed from literals and their negations by means of conjunctions and disjunctions only, the negation of the sentence is found by interchanging the symbols & and $\vee$ of conjunction and disjunction, and replacing every literal by its negation.

LOGICAL EQUIVALENCE CLASSES

It is 12 noon and Mary is eating sweets. The two statements

X = "It is 12 noon."

Y = "Mary is eating sweets."

are both true, and hence are logically equivalent:

$$X \leftrightarrow Y$$

However, they do not have the same meaning. Therefore, from the viewpoint of logical equivalence, these two totally different and unrelated statements are the same: in the collection of all literals and sentences of our universe, X and Y, while not saying the same thing, are equivalent. We may make their equivalence more rigorous by introducing the idea of equivalence classes over the sentences of our logical universe.

Statement Bundle

Let X be any sentence. Then $\{X\}$ denotes the collection of all sentences which are logically equivalent to X, that is, the set of all sentences Y for which

$$Y \leftrightarrow X$$

The collection {X} is referred to as the equivalence class or statement bundle corresponding to X.

Null Logical Equivalence Class

The null logical equivalence class ø is the equivalence class of the false sentence X & ~X for any sentence X:

$$ø = \{X \& {\sim}X\}$$

Null Equivalence Class and False Sentences

The null logical equivalence class ø is the class of all false sentences.

Unit Logical Equivalence Class

The unit logical equivalence class 1 is the equivalence of the true sentence X ∨ ~X for any sentence X:

$$ø = \{X \vee {\sim}X\}$$

Unit Equivalence Class

The unit logical equivalence class 1 is the class of all true sentences.

☞ Drill: Logic

> **DIRECTIONS**: Select the best answer.

1. Determine the truth value of the following conjunction. Is the conjunction true or false?

    Nine is an odd number less than four.

    (A) True   (B) False

2. Evaluate the truth values of the following disjunction. Is the disjunction true or false?

    Five can be divided by one or five.

    (A) True   (B) False

3. What is the negation of the following statement?

    France is not in Europe.

(A) Europe is in France.

(B) Europe is not in France

(C) France is not in Europe.

(D) France is in Europe.

4. Rewrite the following statement in the if – then form:

    We'll pay the postage, if you buy our products.

    (A) If you buy postage, then we will buy the products.

    (B) If you buy our products, we will pay the postage.

    (C) If you buy our products, then we will pay the postage.

    (D) If we buy our products, then you will pay the postage.

5. Rewrite the following statement in the if – then form:

    A grade point average of 4.0 is necessary for a student to receive this scholarship.

    (A) If a student receives this scholarship, then he has a grade point average of 4.0.

    (B) If a student does not receive this scholarship, then he has a grade point average of 4.0.

    (C) If a student receives this scholarship, then he has a grade point average of below a 4.0.

    (D) If a student receives this scholarship, he has a grade point average of 4.0.

SETS AND LOGIC REVIEW

ANSWER KEY

Drill: Sets

1.	(C)	3.	(B)	5.	(D)	7.	(B)
2.	(A)	4.	(D)	6.	(A)		

Drill: Logic

1.	(B)	3.	(D)	4.	(C)	5.	(A)
2.	(A)						

DETAILED EXPLANATIONS OF ANSWERS

Drill: Sets

1. **(C)** Choice (C) is correct. The symbol $\cup$ is used to denote the union of sets. Thus $a \cup b$ (which is read "the union of a and b") is the set of all elements that are in either a or b or both. In this problem, if,

$$a = \{1, 2, 3, 4, 5\} \text{ and } b = \{2, 3, 4, 5, 6\},$$

then

$$a \cup b = \{1, 2, 3, 4, 5, 6\}.$$

2. **(A)** Choice (A) is correct. The intersection of two sets a and b is the set of all elements that belong to both a and b; that is, all elements common to a and b. In this problem, if

$$a = \{1, 2, 3, 4, 5\} \text{ and } b = \{2, 3, 4, 5, 6\},$$

then

$$a \cap b = \{2, 3, 4, 5\}.$$

3. **(B)** Choice (B) is the correct answer. In Figure 1, the vertically shaded area represents $A \cap B$, and the horizontally shaded area represents the points common to the set $(A \cap B)$ and the set C, that is $(A \cap B) \cap C$. Similarly, in Figure 2, the vertically shaded area represents $B \cap C$, and the horizontally shaded area represents the points common to the set $(B \cap C)$ and the set A, that is $A \cap (B \cap C)$. Since the two horizontally shaded areas in the two figures are the same,

$$(A \cap B) \cap C = A \cap (B \cap C).$$

4. **(D)** Choice (D) is the correct answer. $\overline{P}$ and $\overline{Q}$ are the complements of P and Q respectively. That is, $\overline{P}$ is the set of all elements in the universal set, U, that are not elements of P, and $\overline{Q}$ is the set of elements in U that are not in Q. Therefore,

$$\overline{P} = \{1, 3, 5, 7, 9\}$$

5. **(D)** Choice (D) is the correct answer. The Cartesian product of two sets a and b, denoted by $a \times b$, is the set of all ordered pairs (x, y) such

that $x \varepsilon a$ and $y \varepsilon b$. In this problem, if $a = \{1, 2, 3\}$ and $b = \{5, 6\}$, then the Cartesian product $a \times b$ is:

$$a \times b = \{(1, 5), (1, 6), (2, 5), (2, 6), (3, 5), (3, 6)\}.$$

6.　**(A)**　Choice (A) is the correct answer. $M \times N$ is the set of all ordered pairs in which the first component is a member of M and the second component is a member of N. Thus,

$$M \times N = \{(1, p), (1, q), (2, p), (2, q)\}.$$

Note that the number of elements in M is 2,

the number of elements in N is 2,

and the number of elements in $M \times N = 2 \times 2 = 4$.

7.　**(B)**　Choice (B) is the correct answer. $\{1\}$, $\{2\}$, $\{1, 2\}$, ø, where ø is the empty set. Each set listed in the solution contains at least one element of the set C. The set $\{2, 1\}$ is identical to $\{1, 2\}$ and therefore is not listed. ø is included in the solution because ø is a subset of every set.

Drill: Logic

1.　**(B)**　The correct answer is (B). The conjunction can be rewritten as "Nine is an odd number and nine is less than four." It is false since the second simple statement is false.

2.　**(A)**　The correct answer is (A). This disjunction is true since both simple statements are true.

3.　**(D)**　The correct answer is (D). France is in Europe. Note that negations can be stated alternately in the following form: "It is not the case that p." For instance, the negation may be stated as "It is not the case that France is not in Europe." Finally, one must be careful in forming the negations of some statements. For example, the negation of "Four plus six is not twenty" is not "Four plus six is ten." The correct negation is "Four plus six is twenty."

4.　**(C)**　The correct answer is (C). If you buy our products, then we will pay the postage.

5.　**(A)**　The correct answer is (A). If a student receives this scholarship, then he has a grade point average of 4.0.

VI. REAL AND COMPLEX NUMBERS REVIEW

REAL NUMBERS AND THEIR COMPONENTS

Real numbers provide the basis for most precalculus mathematics topics. The set of all real numbers has various components. These components are the set of all natural numbers, N, the set of all whole numbers, W, the set of all integers, I, the set of all rational numbers, Q, and the set of all irrational numbers, S. Then,

$$N = \{1, 2, 3, \ldots\},$$

$$W = \{0, 1, 2, 3, \ldots\},$$

$$I = \{\ldots, -3, -2, -1, 0, 1, 2, 3, \ldots\},$$

$$Q = \left\{ \frac{a}{b} \,\middle|\, a, b \in I \text{ and } b \neq 0 \right\},$$

and $S = \{x \mid x$ has a decimal name which is nonterminating and does not have a repeating block$\}$.

It is obvious that $N \subseteq W$, $W \subseteq I$, and $I \subseteq Q$, but a similar relationship does not hold between Q and S. More specifically, the decimal names for elements of Q are

(1)   terminating or

(2)   nonterminating with a repeating block.

For example, $\frac{1}{2} = .5$ and $\frac{1}{3} = .333\ldots$. This means that Q and S have no common elements. Examples of irrational numbers include $.101001000\ldots$, π, and $\sqrt{2}$.

All real numbers are normally represented by R and $R = Q \cup S$. This means that every real number is either rational or irrational. A nice way to visualize real numbers geometrically is that real numbers can be put in a one-to-one correspondence with the set of all points on a line.

REAL NUMBER PROPERTIES OF EQUALITY

The standard properties of equality involving real numbers are:

REFLEXIVE PROPERTY OF EQUALITY

For each real number a,

$a = a$

SYMMETRIC PROPERTY OF EQUALITY

For each real number a, for each real number b,

if $a = b$, then $b = a$

TRANSITIVE PROPERTY OF EQUALITY

For each real number a, for each real number b, for each real number c,

if $a = b$ and $b = c$, then $a = c$

REAL NUMBER OPERATIONS AND THEIR PROPERTIES

The operations of addition and multiplication are of particular importance. As a result many properties concerning those operations have been determined and named. Here is a list of the most important of these properties.

CLOSURE PROPERTY OF ADDITION

For every real number a, for every real number b,

$a + b$

is a real number.

CLOSURE PROPERTY OF MULTIPLICATION

For every real number a, for every real number b,

ab

is a real number.

COMMUTATIVE PROPERTY OF ADDITION

For every real number a, for every real number b,

$a + b = b + a$.

COMMUTATIVE PROPERTY OF MULTIPLICATION

For every real number a, for every real number b,

$ab = ba$.

ASSOCIATIVE PROPERTY OF ADDITION

For every real number a, for every real number b, for every real number c,

$$(a + b) + c = a + (b + c).$$

ASSOCIATIVE PROPERTY OF MULTIPLICATION

For every real number a, for every real number b, for every real number c,

$$(ab)c = a(bc).$$

IDENTITY PROPERTY OF ADDITION

For every real number a,

$$a + 0 = 0 + a = a.$$

IDENTITY PROPERTY OF MULTIPLICATION

For every real number a,

$$a \times 1 = 1 \times a = a.$$

INVERSE PROPERTY OF ADDITION

For every real number a, there is a real number $-a$ such that

$$a + -a = -a + a = 0.$$

INVERSE PROPERTY OF MULTIPLICATION

For every real number a, $a \neq 0$, there is a real number a^{-1} such that

$$a \times a^{-1} = a^{-1} \times a = 1.$$

DISTRIBUTIVE PROPERTY

For every real number a, for every real number b, for every real number c,

$$a(b + c) = ab + ac.$$

The operations of subtraction and division are also important, but less important than addition and multiplication. Here are the definitions for these operations.

For every real number a, for every real number b, for every real number c,

$$a - b = c \text{ if and only if } b + c = a.$$

For every real number a, for every real number b, for every real number c,

$a \div b = c$ if and only if c is the unique real number such that $bc = a$.

The definition of division eliminates division *by* 0. Thus, for example, $4 \div 0$ is undefined, $0 \div 0$ is undefined, but $0 \div 4 = 0$.

In many instances, it is possible to perform subtraction by first converting a subtraction statement to an addition statement. This is illustrated below.

For every real number a, for every real number b,

$a - b = a + (-b)$.

In a similar way, every division statement can be converted to a multiplication statement. Use the following model:

For every real number a, for every real number b, $b \neq 0$,

$a \div b = a \times b^{-1}$

COMPLEX NUMBERS

As indicated above, real numbers provide the basis for most precalculus mathematics topics. However, on occasion there are situations in which real numbers by themselves are not enough to explain what is happening. As a result, complex numbers developed.

A **complex number** is a number that can be written in the form $a + bi$, where a and b are real numbers and $i = \sqrt{-1}$. The number a is the **real part**, and the number b is the **imaginary part** of the complex number.

Returning momentarily to real numbers, the square of a real number cannot be negative. More specifically, the square of a positive real number is positive, the square of a negative real number is positive, and the square of 0 is 0. Then i is defined to be a number with a property that

$i^2 = -1$.

Obviously i is not a real number. C is then used to represent the set of all complex numbers and

$C = \{a + bi \mid a \text{ and } b \text{ are real numbers}\}$.

Here are the definitions of addition, subtraction, and multiplication of complex numbers.

Suppose $x + yi$ and $z + wi$ are complex numbers. Then

$$(x + yi) + (z + wi) = (x + z) + (y + w)i$$

$$(x + yi) - (z + wi) = (x - z) + (y - w)i$$

$$(x + yi) \times (z + wi) = (xz - y) + (xw + yz)i.$$

To add, subtract, or multiply complex numbers, compute in the usual way, replace i^2 with -1, and simplify.

$$(a + bi) + (c + di) = (a + c) + (b + d)i$$

$$(a + bi) - (c + di) = (a - c) + (b - d)i$$

$$(a + bi)(c + di) = ac + adi + bci + bdi^2 = ac - bd + (ad + bc)i$$

PROBLEM

Simplify the following $(3 + i)(2 + i)$.

SOLUTION

$$
\begin{aligned}
(3 + i)(2 + i) &= 3(2 + i) + i(2 + i) \\
&= 6 + 3i + 2i + i^2 \\
&= 6 + (3 + 2)i + (-1) \\
&= 5 + 5i
\end{aligned}
$$

Complex numbers, $a + bi$, may be obtained when using the quadratic formula to solve quadratic equations.

PROBLEM

Solve the equation $x^2 - x + 1 = 0$.

SOLUTION

In this equation, $a = 1$, $b = -1$, and $c = 1$. Substitute into the quadratic formula.

$$
\begin{aligned}
x &= \frac{-(-1) \pm \sqrt{(-1)^2 - 4(1)(1)}}{2(1)} \\
&= \frac{1 \pm \sqrt{1 - 4}}{2}
\end{aligned}
$$

$$= \frac{1 \pm \sqrt{-3}}{2}$$

$$= \frac{1 \pm \sqrt{3}i}{2}$$

$$x = \frac{1 + \sqrt{3}i}{2} \quad \text{or} \quad x = \frac{1 - \sqrt{3}i}{2}$$

Division of two complex numbers is usually accomplished with a special procedure that involves the conjugate of a complex number. The conjugate of $a + bi$ is denoted by

$$\overline{a + bi} \quad \text{and} \quad \overline{a + bi} = a - bi.$$

Also, $(a + bi)(a - bi) = a^2 + b^2$.

The usual procedure for division is illustrated below.

$$\frac{x + yi}{z + wi} = \frac{x + yi}{z + wi} \times \frac{z - wi}{z - wi}$$

$$= \frac{(xz + yw) + (-xw + yz)i}{z^2 + w^2}$$

$$= \frac{xz + yw}{z^2 + w^2} + \frac{-xw + yz}{z^2 + w^2}i$$

All the properties of real numbers described in the previous section carry over to complex numbers, however, those properties will not be stated again.

If a is a real number, then a can be expressed in the form $a = a + oi$. Hence, every real number is a complex number and $R \subseteq C$.

☞ Drill: Real and Complex Numbers

DIRECTIONS: Solve the following equations.

1. $3i^3 =$

    (A) $-3i$ (B) $3i$ (C) $9i$ (D) $-i$

2. $2i^7 =$

    (A) $-128i$ (B) $2i$ (C) $14i$ (D) $-2i$

3. $-4i^4 =$

    (A) 4 (B) -4 (C) $4i$ (D) $-4i$

4. $-5i^6 =$

    (A) -5 (B) $-5i$ (C) $-i$ (D) 5

5. $(3 + 2i)(2 + 3i) =$

    (A) $12 + 13i$ (B) $-12 - 13i$ (C) $13i$ (D) $-13i$

6. $(2 - i)(2 + i) =$

    (A) -5 (B) $5i$ (C) $-5i$ (D) 5

7. $(5 - 4i)^2 =$

    (A) $9 - 40i$ (B) $-9 - 40i$ (C) $41 - 40i$ (D) $9 + 40i$

DIRECTIONS: Solve the following equations.

---

8. $x^2 + 16 = 0$

    (A) ± 4 (B) $\pm 4i$ (C) $4 \pm i$ (D) $-4 \pm i$

9. $4y^2 + 1 = 0$

    (A) $\pm \dfrac{1}{2}$ (B) $i \pm \dfrac{1}{2}$ (C) $-i \pm \dfrac{1}{2}$ (D) $\pm \dfrac{1}{2}i$

10. $x^2 - 4x + 13 = 0$

    (A) $3 \pm 2i$ (B) $\pm 6i$ (C) $\pm 5i$ (D) $2 \pm 3i$

REAL AND COMPLEX NUMBERS REVIEW

ANSWER KEY

Drill: Real and Complex Numbers

1.	(A)	4.	(D)	7.	(A)	9.	(D)
2.	(D)	5.	(C)	8.	(B)	10.	(D)
3.	(B)	6.	(D)				

DETAILED EXPLANATIONS OF ANSWERS

Drill: Real and Complex Numbers

1. **(A)** $3i^3 = 3i(i)^2 = 3i(-1) = -3i$

2. **(D)** $2i^7 = 2i(i^2)(i^2)(i^2) = 2i(-1)(-1)(-1) = -2i$

3. **(B)** $-4i^4 = -4(i^2)(i^2) = -4(-1)(-1) = -4$

4. **(D)** $-5i^6 = -5(i^2)(i^2)(i^2) = -5(-1)(-1)(-1) = 5$

5. **(C)**
$$(3+2i)(2+3i) = 6 + \underbrace{9i + 4i}_{} + 6i^2$$
$$= 6 + \quad 13i \quad -6$$
$$= 13i$$

6. **(D)**
$$(2-i)(2+i) = 4 + 2i - 2i - i^2$$
$$= 4 + 0 - (-1)$$
$$= 5$$

7. **(A)**
$$(5-4i)^2 = (5-4i)(5-4i)$$
$$= (25 - 20i - 20i + 16i^2)$$
$$= 25 - 40i + 16(-1)$$
$$= 9 - 40i$$

8. **(B)**
$$x^2 + 16 = 0$$
$$x^2 = -16$$
$$x^2 = (16)(-1)$$
$$x = \pm 4i$$

9. **(D)** $4y^2 + 1 = 0$

$$4y^2 = -1 \Rightarrow y^2 = -\frac{1}{4} \quad y = \pm\frac{1}{2}i$$

10. **(D)** $x^2 - 4x + 13 = 0$
by the quadratic formula

$$\frac{-b \pm \sqrt{b^2 - 4ac}}{2a} = \frac{4 \pm \sqrt{16 - 4(1)(13)}}{2}$$

$$= \frac{4 \pm \sqrt{16 - 52}}{2}$$

$$= \frac{4 \pm \sqrt{-36}}{2}$$

$$= \frac{4 \pm 6i}{2}$$

$$= 2 \pm 3i$$

VII. FUNCTIONS REVIEW

ELEMENTARY FUNCTIONS

A **function** is any process that assigns a single value of y to each number of x. Because the value of x determines the value of y, y is called the **dependent variable** and x is called the **independent variable**. The set of all the values of x which the function is defined is called the **domain** of the function. The set of corresponding values of y is called the **range** of the function.

PROBLEM

Is $y^2 = x$ a function?

SOLUTION

Graph the equation. Note that x can have two values of y. Therefore, $y^2 = x$ is not a function.

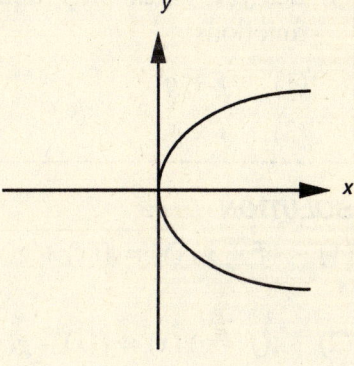

PROBLEM

Find the domain and range for $y = 5 - x^2$.

SOLUTION

First determine if there are any values that would make the function undefined (i.e., dividing by 0). There are none. The domain is the set of real numbers. The range can be found by putting some values in for x.

x	2	1	0	-1	-2
y	1	4	5	4	1

The range is the set of real numbers less than or equal to 5.

PROBLEM

Evaluate $f(1)$ for $y = f(x) = 5x + 2$.

SOLUTION

$$f(x) = 5x + 2$$
$$f(1) = 5(1) + 2$$
$$= 5 + 2$$
$$= 7$$

Functions can be added, subtracted, multiplied, or divided to form new functions.

a. $(f + g)(x) = f(x) + g(x)$
b. $(f - g)(x) = f(x) - g(x)$
c. $(f \times g)(x) = f(x) g(x)$
d. $(f / g)(x) = f(x) / g(x)$

PROBLEM

Let $f(x) = 2x^2 - 1$ and $g(x) = 5x + 3$. Determine the following functions:

(1) $f + g$ (2) $f - g$

(3) $f \times g$ (4) f / g

SOLUTION

(1) $(f + g)(x) = f(x) + g(x) = 2x^2 - 1 + 5x + 3$
$$= 2x^2 + 5x + 2$$

(2) $(f - g)(x) = f(x) - g(x) = 2x^2 - 1 - (5x + 3)$
$$= 2x^2 - 1 - 5x - 3$$
$$= 2x^2 - 5x - 4$$

(3) $(f \times g)(x) = f(x) g(x) = (2x^2 - 1)(5x + 3)$
$$= 10x^3 + 6x^2 - 5x - 3$$

(4) $(f / g)(x) = f(x) / g(x) = (2x^2 - 1) / (5x + 3)$

Note the domain of (4) is for all real numbers except $-\dfrac{3}{5}$

The **composite function** $f \circ g$ is defined $(f \circ g)(x) = f(g(x))$.

PROBLEM

Given $f(x) = 3x$ and $g(x) = 4x + 2$.

Find $(f \times g)(x)$ and $(g \times f)(x)$.

SOLUTION

$$(f \times g)\,(x) = f(g(x)) = 3(4x + 2)$$
$$= 12x + 6$$
$$(g \times f)\,(x) = g(f(x)) = 4(3x) + 2$$
$$= 12x + 2$$

Note that $(f \times g)\,(x) \neq (g \times f)\,(x)$.

PROBLEM

Find $(f \times g)\,(2)$ if

$f(x) = x^2 - 3$ and $g(x) = 3x + 1$

SOLUTION

$$(f \times g)\,(2) = f(g(2))$$
$$g(x) = 3x + 1$$

Substitute the value of x.

$$g(2) = 3(2) + 1$$
$$= 7$$
$$f(x) = x^2 - 3$$

Substitute the value of $g(2)$ in $f(x)$.

$$f(7) = (7)^2 - 3$$
$$= 49 - 3$$
$$= 46$$

The **inverse** of a function, f^{-1}, is obtained from f by interchanging the x and y and then solving for y.

Two functions f and g are inverses of one another if $g \times f = x$ and $f \times g = x$. To find g when f is given, interchange x and g in the equation $y = f(x)$ and solve for $y = g(x)$.

PROBLEM

Find the inverse of the functions

(1) $f(x) = 3x + 2$ (2) $f(x) = x^2 - 3$

SOLUTION

(1) $f(x) = y = 3x + 2$

To find $f^{-1}(x)$, interchange x and y.

$$x = 3y + 2$$
$$3y = x - 2$$

Solve for y.

$$y = \frac{x - 2}{3}$$

(2) $f(x) = y = x^2 - 3.$

To find $f^{-1}(x)$, interchange x and y.

$$x = y^2 - 3$$
$$y^2 = x + 3$$

Solve for y.

$$y = \sqrt{x + 3}$$

LOGARITHMS AND EXPONENTIAL FUNCTIONS AND EQUATIONS

An equation

$$y = b^x$$

(with $b > 0$ and $b \neq 1$) is called an **exponential function**. The exponential function with base b can be written as

$$y = f(x) = b^x.$$

The inverse of an exponential function is the **logarithmic function**,

$$f^{-1}(x) = \log_b x.$$

PROBLEM

Write the following equations in logarithmic form:

$3^4 = 81$ and $M^k = 5.$

SOLUTION

The expression $y = b^x$ is equivalent to the logarithmic expression $\log_b y = x$. Therefore, $3^4 = 81$ is equivalent to the logarithmic expression

$$\log_3 81 = 4$$

and $M^k = 5$ is equivalent to the logarithmic expression

$$\log_M 5 = k.$$

PROBLEM

Find the value of $\log_5 25$ and $\log_4 x = 2$.

SOLUTION

$\log_5 25$ is equivalent to $5^x = 25$. Thus $x = 2$, since $5^2 = 25$.

$\log_4 x = 2$ is equivalent to $4^2 = x \times x = 16$.

LOGARITHM PROPERTIES

If M, N, p, and b are positive numbers and $b = 1$, then

a. $\log_b 1 = 0$

b. $\log_b b = 1$

c. $\log_b b^x = x$

d. $\log_b M N = \log_b M + \log_b N$

e. $\log_b M / N = \log_b M - \log_b N$

f. $\log_b M^p = p \log_b M$

PROBLEM

If $\log_{10} 3 = .4771$ and $\log_{10} 4 = .6021$, find $\log_{10} 12$.

SOLUTION

Since $\quad\quad 12 = 4(3)$, $\log_{10} 12 = \log_{10}(4)\,(3)$

Remember

$$\log_b M N = \log_b M + \log_b N.$$

Therefore,

$$\begin{aligned}
\log_{10} 12 &= \log_{10} 4 + \log_{10} 3 \\
&= .6021 + .4771 \\
&= 1.0792
\end{aligned}$$

☞ Drill: Elementary Functions

DIRECTIONS: Find the value of x.

1. $\log_7 1 = x$

   (A) 1   (B) 7   (C) $\dfrac{1}{7}$ (D) 0

2. $\log_2 8 = x$

(A) 2   (B) 3   (C) 4   (D) 16

3. $\log_x 16 = 4$

(A) 2   (B) 4   (C) $\dfrac{1}{4}$ (D) 16

4. $\log_3 x = 2$

(A) $\dfrac{2}{3}$ (B) $\dfrac{3}{2}$ (C) 6   (D) 9

5. Given $\log_{10} 2 = 0.3010$ and $\log_{10} 3 = 0.4771$, find $\log_{10} 6 = x$.

(A) 0.1761   (B) 0.1436   (C) 0.6020   (D) 0.7781

DIRECTIONS: Evaluate each expression when $f(x) = 2x + 1$ and $g(x) = x^2 - 1$.

---

6. $(f \times g)(2)$

(A) 7   (B) 8   (C) 10   (D) 15

7. $(g \times f)(-3)$

(A) -40 (B) 3   (C) 13   (D) 24

8. $(g + f)(2)$

(A) -2 (B) 2   (C) 7   (D) 8

9. $f^{-1}(x)$

(A) $1 - 2x$ (B) $\dfrac{(x-1)}{2}$ (C) $x - \dfrac{1}{2}$ (D) x^2

10. $g^{-1}(x)$

(A) $\sqrt{x}$ (B) $1 - x^2$ (C) $x + 1$ (D) $(x + 1)^{1/2}$

FUNCTIONS REVIEW

ANSWER KEY

Drill: Elementary Functions

1. (D)
2. (B)
3. (A)

4. (D)
5. (D)
6. (A)

7. (D)
8. (D)

9. (B)
10. (D)

DETAILED EXPLANATIONS OF ANSWERS

Drill: Elementary Functions

1. **(D)** $\log_7 1 = x \Rightarrow 1 = 7^x \quad x = 0$

2. **(B)** $\log_2 8 = x \Rightarrow 8 = 2^x \quad x = 3$

3. **(A)** $\log_x 16 = 4 \Rightarrow 16 = x^4 = (2)(2)(2)(2) = 2^4$

4. **(D)** $\log_3 x = 2 \Rightarrow 16 = x = 3^2 = 9$

5. **(D)** $\log_{10} 2 = 0.3010 \quad \text{and} \quad \log_{10} 2 = 0.4771$
    $\log_{10} 6 = x$
    $\log_{10} 6 = \log_{10}(2)(3)$
    $\qquad = \log_{10} 2 + \log_{10} 3$
    $\qquad = 0.3010 + 0.4771$
    $\qquad = 0.7781$

6. **(A)** $(f \times g)2 = f(g(2))$
    $\qquad = f\big((2)^2 - 1\big)$
    $\qquad = f(3)$
    $\qquad = 2(3) + 1$
    $\qquad = 7$

7. **(D)** $(g \times f)(-3) = g(f(-3))$
    $\qquad = g(2(-3) + 1)$
    $\qquad = g(-5)$
    $\qquad = (-5)^2 - 1$
    $\qquad = 25 - 1$
    $\qquad = 24$

8. **(D)** $(g+f) = g(2) + f(2)$

$$= \left[(2)^2 - 1\right] + \left[2(2) + 1\right]$$
$$= 4 - 1 + 4 - 1$$
$$= 8$$

9. **(B)** $f^{-1}(x); \quad f(x) = 2x + 1$

$$f(x) - 1 = 2x$$
$$\frac{f(x) - 1}{2} = x \Rightarrow f^{-1}(x) = \frac{x - 1}{2}$$

10. **(D)** $g^{-1}(x); \quad g(x) = x^2 - 1$

$$g(x) + 1 = x^2$$
$$\left(g(x) + 1\right)^{1/2} = x \Rightarrow g^{-1}(x) = (x + 1)^{1/2}$$

VIII. PROBABILITY AND STATISTICS REVIEW

GRAPHS

The information requested from reading the graph and performing a calculation or two will be limited to obtaining:

A.   sums and differences of frequencies;

B.   a percent of the whole; and

C.   a frequency from a percent.

● **EXAMPLE**

Examine the bar graph below.

Number of bushels (to the nearest 5 bushels) of wheat and corn produced by farm RQS from 1975–1985

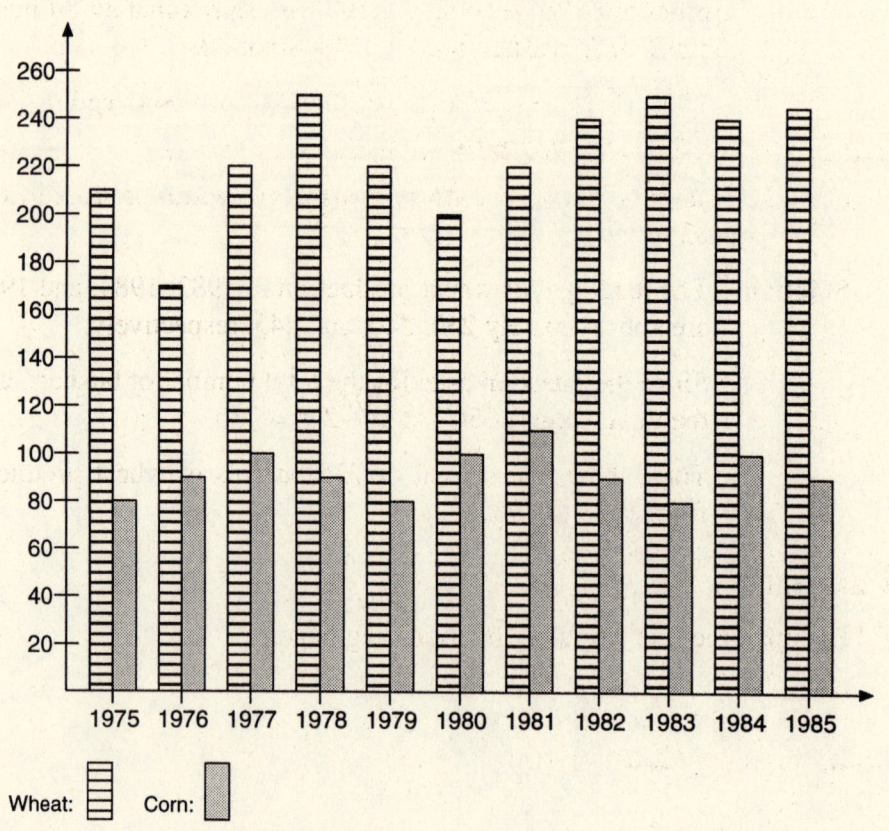

Question 1: In which year was the least number of bushels of wheat produced?

Solution: The number of bushels of wheat produced is represented by the vertical columns, as indicated in the legend below the graph.

By inspection of the graph, we find that the shortest bar representing wheat production is the one for 1976.

Thus, the least number of bushels of wheat was produced in 1976.

Question 2: How many more bushels of corn were produced in 1981 than in 1975?

Solution: The number of bushels of corn produced is represented by the dotted vertical columns, as indicated by the legend under the graph.

By reading the height of the vertical column for corn for the year 1981, we see that approximately 110 bushels were produced. The reading for 1975 is approximately 80 bushels. This is a difference of 110 − 80 or 30.

Thus, there were 30 more bushels of corn produced in 1981 than in 1975.

Question 3: What was the total number of bushels of wheat produced from 1983 to 1985?

Solution: The readings for wheat production in 1983, 1984, and 1985 are approximately 250, 240, and 245, respectively.

Since the question asks for the total number of bushels, add the three values: 250 + 240 + 245 = 735.

Thus, there was a total of 735 bushels of wheat produced from 1983 to 1985.

● **EXAMPLE**

Examine the line graph on the following page.

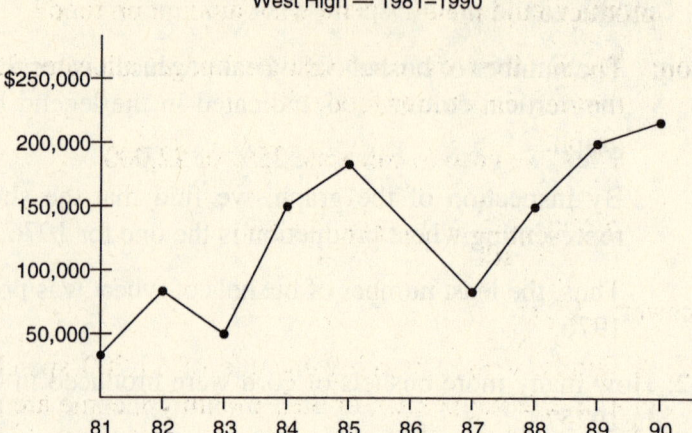

Amount of Scholarship Money Awarded to Graduating Seniors
West High — 1981–1990

Question 1: Between what two years did scholarship money increase the most?

Solution: With a visual inspection, one can see that the greatest increase occurred between the years of 1983 and 1984.

Question 2: In what year(s) did scholarship money actually decrease from the year before?

Solution: A decrease would be indicated by a data point for a particular year below the data point for the previous year. Through visual inspection, we see that scholarship money decreased in 1983, again in 1986, and again in 1987.

- **EXAMPLE**

Examine the pie chart below.

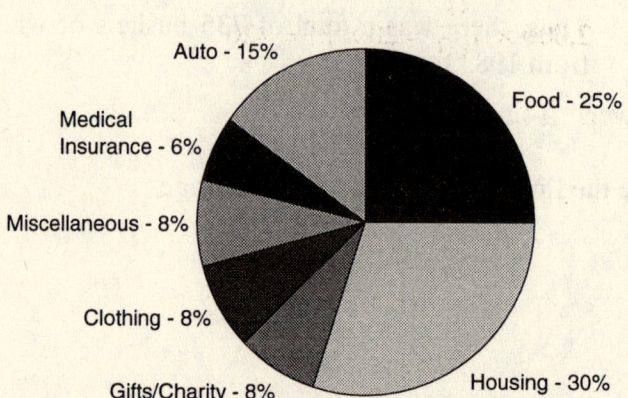

Sample Family Budget

Question 1: Using the budget shown, a family with an income of $2,000 a month would plan to spend what amount on food?

Solution: We see from the chart that the budget allocates 25% of the monthly income to food.

Thus, we need to calculate 25% of $2,000.

$$2,000 \times \frac{25}{100} = 2,000 \times \frac{1}{4} = 500$$

Answer: $500

Question 2: A family with a monthly income of $1,200 spends $72 on clothing. What percent of their monthly income are they actually spending on clothing?

Solution: To calculate the percentage, we will set up a proportion as covered in a previous skill area.

$$\frac{72}{1,200} = \frac{P}{100}$$

$$
\begin{array}{ll}
72 \times 100 = 1,200 \times P & \text{Cross multiply.} \\
7,200 = 1,200 \times P & \text{Simplify.} \\
6 = P &
\end{array}
$$

Answer: 6%

Question 3: Using the budget shown, a family with an income of $2,000 a month would plan to spend what amount on medical insurance or auto?

Solution: The combined percentage allocated to medical insurance and auto is 6% + 15% or 21%.

Thus, we need to calculate 21% of $2,000.

$$2,000 \times \frac{21}{100} = 20 \times 21 = 420$$

Answer: $420

☞ Drill: Graphs

> **DIRECTIONS:** Select the best answer.

Questions 1–3 refer to the bar graph on the following page.

Changes in Average Mileage

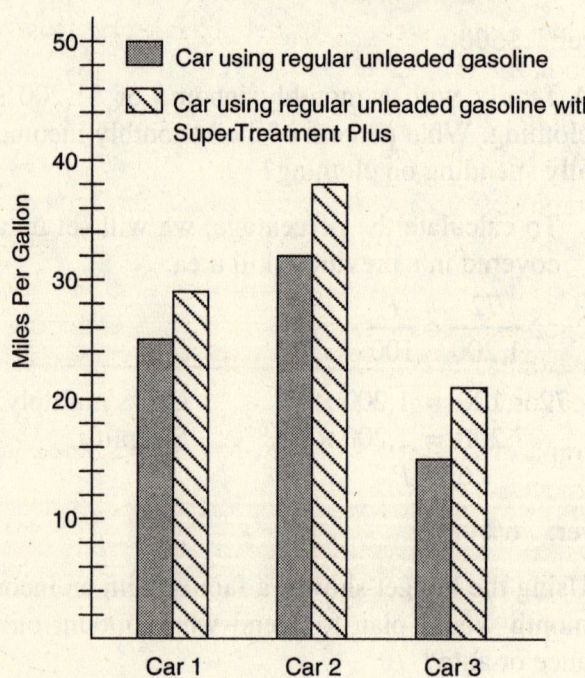

1. By how much did the mileage increase for Car 2 when the new product was used?

   (A) 5 mpg   (B) 6 mpg   (C) 7 mpg   (D) 10 mpg

2. The mileage of which cars increased the most in this test?

   (A) Car 2   (B) Car 3   (C) Cars 1 and 2   (D) Cars 2 and 3

3. According to the bar graph, if your car averages 25 mpg, what mileage might you expect with the new product?

   (A) 21 mpg   (B) 29 mpg   (C) 31 mpg   (D) 35 mpg

COMPARING THE MEAN, MEDIAN, AND MODE IN A VARIETY OF DISTRIBUTIONS

Mean, median, and mode were discussed earlier in terms of how to calculate each; however, in this skill area, you will be asked to make comparisons about the relative values of each without being able to calculate the exact values.

In order to make these comparisons, proceed as follows:

(1) If a bar graph is not provided, sketch one from the information given in the problem.

The graph will either be skewed to the left, skewed to the right, or approximately normal.

A graph skewed to the left will look like Figure 1 and the order of the three terms will be mean < median < mode (alphabetical order).

A graph skewed to the right will look like Figure 2 and the order of the three terms will be mode < median < mean (reverse alphabetical order).

A graph that is approximately normal will look like Figure 3 and the mean = median = mode.

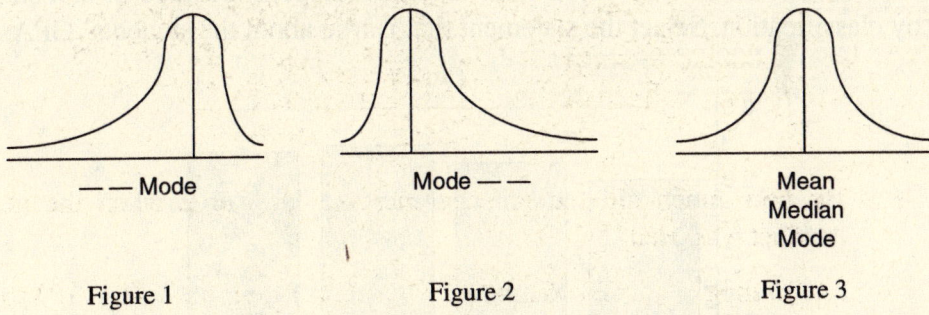

—— Mode	Mode ——	Mean Median Mode
Figure 1	Figure 2	Figure 3

(2) Write the word mode under the highest column of the bar graph, because the mode is the most frequent. If the graph is skewed right or left the positioning of the mode established the order for the remaining two terms according to the information provided above. If the graph is approximately symmetrical, the value of all three terms are approximately equivalent.

● **EXAMPLE**

On a trip to the Everglades, students tested the pH of the water at different areas. Most of the pH tests were at 6. A few read 7, and one read 8. Select the statement that is true about the distribution of the pH test results.

(A) The mode and the mean are the same.

(B) The mode is less than the mean.

(C) The mode is greater than the median.

(D) The median is less than the mode.

Solution: Sketch a bar graph.
The graph is skewed to the right.
The mode is furthest left.
Thus, mode < median < mean.

Choices (A), (C), and (D) do not coincide with what has been established in terms of relative order. (B) is the only choice which does follow from our conclusions. Thus, (B) is the correct response.

● **EXAMPLE**

The graph below represents the mean grade point average of students by classification. Select the statement that is true about the students' GPAs.

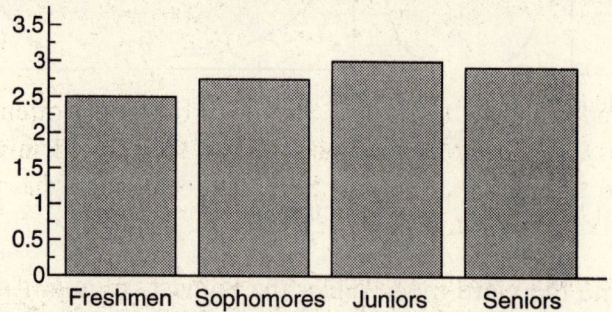

(A) The mode and median are equal.

(B) The mode is less than the median.

(C) The mean is greater than the mode.

(D) The mean is less than the median.

Solution: The graph is skewed to the left.
Thus, mean < median < mode.

Choices (A), (B), and (C) do not coincide with what has been established in terms of relative order. (D) is the only choice which does follow from our conclusions. Thus, (D) is the correct response.

☞ Drill: Comparing the Mean, Median, and Mode in a Variety of Distributions

DIRECTIONS: Select the best answer.

1. What is the mean of the data in the following sample?
   12, 15, 18, 24, 31

   (A) 18   (B) 19.3   (C) 20   (D) 25

2. What is the median of the data in the following sample?
   19, 15, 21, 27, 12

   (A) 19   (B) 15   (C) 21   (D) 27

3. What is the mode of the data in the following sample?
   16, 14, 12, 16, 30, 28

   (A) 6   (B) 14   (C) 16   (D) $19.\overline{3}$

4. Mrs. Brandish cans tomatoes. She finds that most often she gets 10 tomatoes in each jar. Sometimes she can squeeze 11 in and once she managed to get 12 in one jar. Select the statement that is true about the number of tomatoes in each jar.

   (A) The mode equals the mean.

   (B) The mean is less than the mode.

   (C) The median is greater than the mean.

   (D) The mode is less than the median.

THE FUNDAMENTAL COUNTING PRINCIPLE

The fundamental counting principle deals with identifying the number of outcomes of a given experiment and can be broken down into the following three areas.

THE COUNTING RULE

If one experiment can be performed in m ways, and a second experiment can be performed in n ways, then there are $m \times n$ distinct ways both experiments can be performed in this specified order. The counting principle can be applied to more than two experiments.

● EXAMPLE

A new line of children's clothing is color-coordinated. Niki's mother bought her five tops, three shorts, and two pairs of shoes for the summer. How many different outfits can Niki choose from?

Solution: How many choices are there for a top? 5
How many choices are there for shorts? 3
How many choices are there for shoes? 2

Apply the counting principle: $5 \times 3 \times 2$ or 30.

Thus, Niki has 30 different outfits.

PERMUTATIONS

A permutation is an arrangement of specific objects where order is of particular importance. To determine the number of possible permutations, the following formula can be used:

$$n^P r = \frac{n!}{(n-r)!}$$

(where n is the number of objects in the given set, r is the number of objects being chosen, and ! is the notation used for factorial)

or, more simply, use the counting rule described above.

● EXAMPLE

Ten children in Ms. Berea's fifth grade class competed in the school's science fair. First, second, and third place trophies will go to the top three projects. In how many ways can the trophies be awarded?

Solution: Order is of definite importance here.

How many children have a chance at the first place trophy?
10
How many children have a chance at the second place trophy? 9
How many children have a chance at the third place trophy? 8

Apply the counting principle: $10 \times 9 \times 8 = 720$.

Thus, there are 720 ways these 10 children could finish first, second, or third.

COMBINATIONS

A combination is an arrangement of specific objects where order is NOT of particular importance. To determine the number of possible combinations, use the following formula:

$$n^c r = \frac{n!}{r!(n-r)!}$$

(where n is the number of objects in the given set, r is the number of objects being ordered, and ! is the notation used for factorial)

$$3! = 3 \times 2 \times 1$$
$$12! = 12 \times 11 \times 10 \times ... \times 3 \times 2 \times 1$$
$$n! = n \times (n-1) \times (n-2) \times ... \times 3 \times 2 \times 1$$

● **EXAMPLE**

Simon has 10 compact discs and his player holds three discs at a time. How many combinations of three discs are possible?

Solution: $10^c 3 = \dfrac{10!}{3!(10-3)!}$

$$= \frac{10!}{3! \times 7!}$$

$$= \frac{10 \times 9 \times 8 \times 7 \times 6 \times 5 \times 4 \times 3 \times 2 \times 1}{(3 \times 2 \times 1) \times (7 \times 6 \times 5 \times 4 \times 3 \times 2 \times 1)}$$

$$= \frac{720}{6}$$

$$= 120$$

Thus, there are 120 combinations of discs taken three at a time.

☞ Drill: The Fundamental Counting Principle

DIRECTIONS: Select the best answer.

1. A local developer has five different floor plans, and each plan has two different elevations. How many different homes are available?

   (A) 5   (B) 7   (C) 10   (D) 25

2. A radio station is running a contest. They have eight phone lines, all of which light up instantly when the word "PYRAMID" is broadcast. The first caller will win $1,000, the second caller will win $250, and the third caller will win $25. In how many different ways can the callers be selected to win the prizes?

   (A) 21   (B) 56   (C) 336   (D) 40,320

3. From six sections of college algebra and four sections of calculus, a researcher will choose two college algebra sections and two calculus sections to be the subjects of a research study. How many different groupings can be selected?

   (A) 6   (B) 24   (C) 90   (D) 360

SELECTING AN UNBIASED SAMPLE

If a subset of a population is chosen such that every member had an equal and likely chance of being selected, then we would say that this subset is an unbiased or random sample.

To choose the most appropriate procedure for selecting a random sample,

(1) make sure that the sample is coming from the target population, and

(2) make sure that each member of the target population has an equal and likely chance of being selected.

● **EXAMPLE**

Two homeowners in a 250 home development are interested in starting an association. They decide to conduct a survey to find out if the other homeowners are interested. Which procedure would be the most appropriate for obtaining a statistically unbiased sample?

(A) Poll the homes directly adjacent to their own homes.

(B) Poll shoppers at the local supermarket on Saturday morning.

(C) Poll a random sample of homeowners within the development.

(D) Poll the parents of the children at the local playground.

Solution: Are there any choices which do not sample the target population? Yes, choices (B) and (D), so eliminate these.

Are there choices which do not allow for every member to have an equal and likely chance of being selected? Yes, choice (A), so eliminate this one.

Choice (C) remains and the sample is taken from the target population and every member has an equal and likely chance of being selected.

● EXAMPLE

A local health agency wishes to conduct a survey of the type and amount of health insurance carried on elementary school children. Which procedure would be the most appropriate for obtaining a statistically unbiased sample?

(A) Randomly select an elementary school in the district and send a questionnaire to the parents of every third grader.

(B) Survey the elementary school closest to the health agency and send a questionnaire home with every child whose last name begins with the letter A.

(C) Survey a random sample of homeowners in the area.

(D) Randomly select an elementary school in the district and then survey the parents of a random sample of children attending that school.

Solution: Are there any choices which do not sample the target population? Yes, choice (C). Eliminate it.

Are there choices which do not allow for every member to have an equal and likely chance of being selected? Yes, choices (A) and (B), so eliminate these.

Choice (D) remains and the sample is taken from the target population and every member has an equal and likely chance of being selected.

☞ Drill: Selecting an Unbiased Sample

1. A college librarian wants to determine if students are being fully served by the current library hours. She decides to conduct a survey. Which procedure would be the most appropriate for obtaining a statistically unbiased sample?

    (A) Get a list from the registrar of students enrolled at the college and select a random sample.

    (B) Place a questionnaire at the check-out desk.

    (C) Survey the first 50 students entering the library Tuesday morning.

    (D) Survey students at the student union building.

2. The Student Council at a local high school wants to raise money for a field day in the spring. They have five possible fund-raisers and decide to conduct a survey to see which would be most supported by the student body. Which procedure would be the most appropriate for obtaining a statistically unbiased sample?

    (A) Survey the advanced English classes from each grade level.

    (B) Survey a random sample of students from a list of all registered students.

    (C) Survey the first 100 students entering the cafeteria for lunch.

    (D) Survey all seniors.

PROBABILITY

Before discussing the actual calculation of a probability, examine the following probability facts:

(1) Probabilities are values ranging from 0 to 1 inclusive: $0 \leq P(E) \leq$

a. Probabilities cannot be negative or greater than 1.

b. A probability of 0 means that the event cannot or did not occur.

c. A probability of 1 means that the event must occur or always occurred.

(2) The sum of the probabilities of all possible events in any given experiment is 1.

(3) The notation used for the probability of an event E not happening is: $P(E')$, where E' is read E complement.

(4) Combining facts (2) and (3), we then see that: $P(E) + P(E') = 1$. That is, the probability of an event happening or its complement happening is 1. This formula may also be applied in the following form: $1 - P(E) = P(E')$, depending on the context of the problem.

● **EXAMPLE**

Past records indicate that 25% of the students drop college algebra. What is the probability that a student does not drop college algebra?

Solution: 25% means $\dfrac{25}{100}$ or $\dfrac{1}{4}$ of the students drop algebra.

Those who do drop algebra and those who do not drop it constitute the entire universal set.

Apply the formula: $1 - P(E) = P(E')$.

$$1 - \frac{1}{4} = \frac{3}{4}$$

Thus, $\dfrac{3}{4}$ or .75 is the probability that a student does not drop college algebra.

The mathematical formula associated with the probability of a simple event is: $P(E) = {}^{m}\!/\!_{n}$, where m is the number of favorable outcomes relative to event E, and n is the total number of possible outcomes.

● **EXAMPLE**

Given that Jeffrey gets two hits out of three times at bat at every T-ball game, what is the probability that Jeffrey will get a hit his next time up to bat?

Solution: The number of favorable outcomes, i.e., the number of hits, is two. The number of possible outcomes is three. Thus, the probability of a hit is $\dfrac{2}{3}$.

The mathematical formula which allows us to find the probability of obtaining either event A or event B is:

$P(A \text{ or } B) = P(A) + P(B) - P(A \text{ and } B)$.

Note: If events A and B are mutually exclusive, $P(A \text{ and } B) = 0$, then the formula above simplifies to $P(A \text{ or } B) = P(A) + P(B)$.

● **EXAMPLE**

On a field trip, the teachers counted the orders for a snack and sent the information in with a few people. The orders were for 94 colas and 56 fries. If there were 133 orders, what was the probability of an order for a cola and fries?

Solution: Before using the formula presented above, we must determine $P(\text{cola})$, $P(\text{fries})$, and $P(\text{cola or fries})$.

$$P(\text{cola}) = \frac{94}{133}$$

$$P(\text{fries}) = \frac{56}{133}$$

$$P(\text{cola or fries}) = \frac{133}{133}$$

$$P(A \text{ or } B) = P(A) + P(B) - P(A \text{ and } B)$$

$$\frac{133}{133} = \frac{94}{133} + \frac{56}{133} - P(\text{cola and fries})$$

$$\frac{133}{133} = \frac{150}{133} - P(\text{cola and fries})$$

$$P(\text{cola and fries}) = \frac{150}{133} - \frac{133}{133}$$

$$P(\text{cola and fries}) = \frac{17}{133}$$

From the conditional probability formula: $P(A \mid B) = \dfrac{P(A \text{ and } B)}{P(B)}$, we can derive the multiplication rule: $P(A \text{ and } B) = P(A \mid B) \times P(B)$. It is not necessary to fully understand what conditional probability is as long as you are able to apply the counting rules discussed earlier.

● **EXAMPLE**

If Kyle has eight pairs of socks (four white, two black, one blue, and one red,) what is the probability that he randomly chooses two pairs of white socks to wear on consecutive days?

Solution: What is the probability of selecting one pair of white socks? $\frac{4}{8}$

Given that Kyle already chose a pair of white socks, what is the probability that he chooses another pair of white socks? $\frac{3}{7}$ Why?

How many pairs of white socks are left to choose? 3

How many total pairs of socks are left? 7

Thus, the probability of drawing two pairs of white socks is: $\frac{4}{8} \times \frac{3}{7}$ or $\frac{3}{14}$.

If the occurrence of event A in no way effects the occurrence or non-occurrence of event B, then events A and B are said to be independent.

If events A and B are independent, then $P(A \text{ and } B) = P(A) \times P(B)$.

● **EXAMPLE**

The probability that a child born is male is 0.5. What is the probability that the next three children born at Memorial Hospital to unrelated parents are all boys?

Solution: The birth of three children to unrelated parents would be considered independent events.

$$P(3 \text{ males}) = (0.5)(0.5)(0.5)$$
$$= 0.125$$

Thus, the probability of three males is 0.125 which is 12.5%.

PROBABILITY WORD PROBLEMS

As with all prior real-world problems, the context of the problems is vast. A table or graph will provide the necessary information to calculate a single outcome, multiple outcomes, or conditional probability or an expected value.

● **EXAMPLE**

The students at a local college voted for a new student body president. The following table is a breakdown of the vote for the student who won the election.

	Freshman	Sophomore	Junior	Senior
Male	9%	17%	10%	9%
Female	16%	13%	15%	11%

Question 1: If a student who voted for the winner is selected at random, what is the probability that that person is a sophomore and a male?

   Solution: By locating the correct cell in the table, we see that 17% of votes were from sophomore males. This gives a probability of 0.17.

Question 2: What is the probability of a randomly selected student not being a senior?

   Solution: Locate the senior cells.

   9% males + 11% females = 20% seniors

   Nonseniors: 100% − 20% = 80%

   Thus, the probability of not being a senior is 0.80.

Question 3: Knowing that a selected person is a junior, what is the probability that the person is a female?

   Solution: This is a conditional probability problem.

   To solve such a problem, we need to identify how many are in the given category, in this case juniors.

   Locate the junior cells.

   10% males + 15% females = 25% juniors

   The numerical value associated with the given, the person is a junior, is the denominator for the fraction.

   Of the juniors, identify the percent that are females: 15%. This is the numerator.

   Thus, the probability that the person is female given that the person is a junior is $\dfrac{15}{25}$ or 0.60.

Question 4: If in this election there were 500 votes for the winner, how many females cast votes for the winner?

   Solution: Total number of females: 16% + 13% + 15% + 11% = 55%

   55% of 500 is $\dfrac{15}{25} \times 500 = 275$

   Thus, 275 females cast votes for the winner.

☞ Drill: Probability

DIRECTIONS: Select the best answer.

1. A note card manufacturer discovered that the packaging machine was sometimes inserting nine cards into a box which was to contain eight cards. The company opened 10 boxes and discovered that three contained the additional card. What is the probability that a randomly selected box would have nine cards?

    (A) $\dfrac{1}{10}$ (B) $\dfrac{3}{10}$ (C) $\dfrac{8}{10}$ (D) $\dfrac{9}{10}$

2. Refer back to problem 1. If 30% of the boxes contain nine cards, what is the probability of selecting two boxes with nine cards from a shipping crate containing 100 boxes?

    (A) $\dfrac{29}{330}$ (B) $\dfrac{9}{100}$ (C) $\dfrac{1}{15}$ (D) $\dfrac{9}{50}$

3. If the probability that a student is selected to be a National Merit Scholar is 0.02 and that the student is a female is 0.40, what is the probability that a female is selected to be a National Merit Scholar?

    (A) 0.42   (B) 0.008   (C) 0.38   (D) 0.20

DIRECTIONS: Questions 4–6 refer to the following information.

Mr. Bennett's 6th grade mathematics class is collecting data on eye color and gender. They organize the data they collected into the following table.

	Brown	Blue	Green
Male	22%	18%	10%
Female	18%	20%	12%

4. If a student is chosen at random, what is the probability that the student is a female with brown eyes?

    (A) 0.18   (B) 0.40   (C) 0.45   (D) 0.50

5. What is the probability of a randomly selected student not having green eyes?

    (A) 0.22   (B) 0.78   (C) 0.88   (D) 0.90

6. Given that the student selected has blue eyes, what is the probability that the student is a male?

    (A) 0.18   (B) 0.20   (C) 0.47   (D) 0.53

PREDICTIONS FROM STATISTICAL DATA

In this skill area, a table, histogram, broken line graph, scatter diagram, or line graph will be given. From this information, you will be asked to infer relationships and/or make predictions. More precisely, the types of questions which may be asked include:

(A) commenting on the relationship between two variables;

    A most critical concept to remember is that just because two variables appear to be related, there is no justification in presuming that one variable *causes* the other.

(B) commenting on the trend of a single variable;

(C) interpolating; and

(D) extrapolating.

● EXAMPLE

Tuition and average textbook price are given in the following table. Which statement best describes the relationship between tuition and average textbook price?

Year	Tuition	Average Textbook Price
1985	$3,000	$32.50
1986	$3,200	$31.75
1987	$3,800	$39.62
1988	$3,800	$41.94
1989	$4,500	$40.79
1990	$4,700	$45.21
1991	$5,000	$44.97
1992	$5,700	$49.52
1993	$6,100	$53.10

(A) An increase in the tuition caused an increase in textbook price.

(B) An increase in textbook price caused an increase in tuition.

(C) There appears to be a positive association between tuition and textbook price.

(D) There appears to be a negative association between tuition and textbook price.

Solution: Be cautious of cause-and-effect relationships. Unless there is a direct link between two variables, the relationship can be coincidental. Eliminate choices (A) and (B).

Examine the tuition column and the textbook price column. Both columns are effectively increasing over time. If two variables change in the same direction, both increase or both decrease, we say this is a positive relationship. If one increases while the other decreases, we say this is a negative relationship. Thus, we can eliminate (D) and realize that (C) is the correct choice.

● **EXAMPLE**

Consider the following line graph. Which of the following best describes the trend in pledge money?

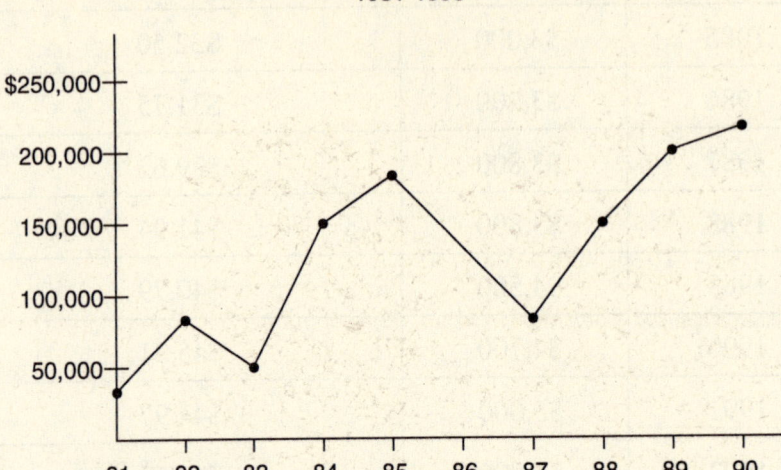

Amount of Money Pledged to Public Television during Telethons
1981-1990

(A) Pledge money has fluctuated but has in general increased over time.

(B) There is no trend in pledge money for any time.

(C) Pledge money actually decreased from 1987 to 1990.

(D) There was more pledge money available in the early 1980s than in the latter part of the decade.

Solution: Visually, we can see that pledge money has in general increased over time. Thus, we can eliminate (B).

Choice (C) is incorrect because pledge money increased from 1987 to 1990.

Choice (D) is incorrect because there was more money in the later 1980s than in the earlier 1980s.

This leaves choice (A). Even though pledge money has not consistently increased, it has in general over time.

● **EXAMPLE**

Using the same line graph from the previous example, between what two years was the increase in pledge money the most significant?

(A) 1981 – 1982   (C) 1985 – 1986

(B) 1983 – 1984   (D) 1987 – 1988

Solution: To determine the greatest increase, we must compare the differences between each two-year period.

1981 – 1982   80,000 – 40,000 = 40,000
1983 – 1984   150,000 – 50,000 = 100,000
1985 – 1986   120,000 – 175,000 = –55,000
1987 – 1988   150,000 – 70,000 = 80,000

We can see that the greatest increase came between 1983 – 1984, and this is choice (B).

☞ Drill: Predictions from Statistical Data

DIRECTIONS: Select the best answer.

1. Family income and food cost are given in the following table. Which statement best describes the relationship between family income and food cost?

Year	Family Income	Food Cost as a Percent of Income
1985	$23,000	25%
1986	$25,200	23%
1987	$28,800	20%
1988	$30,800	19%
1989	$34,500	17%
1990	$34,700	17%
1991	$35,000	16%
1992	$35,700	16%
1993	$38,100	15%

(A) As a family's income increases, they spend less money on food.

(B) An increase in income causes a decrease in the percent of that income spent on food.

(C) There appears to be a positive association between a family's income and the percent spent on food.

(D) There appears to be a negative association between a family's income and the percent spent on food.

2. Refer to the table in problem 1. Which of the following best describes the percent of income spent on food beyond 1993?

(A) Provided the family continues in the same trend, the percent of income spent on food will continue to decrease slightly.

(B) The percent spent on food will never drop below 15%.

(C) It is not possible to predict what will happen beyond 1993 because the trends represented here are unstable.

(D) Since 15% is such a small percent to pay for food, one would expect the percent to begin increasing independent of income.

3. Refer to the following scatter diagram showing students' scores on the math and science sections of a test. If a student scored 550 on the math section, what would you estimate the science score to be?

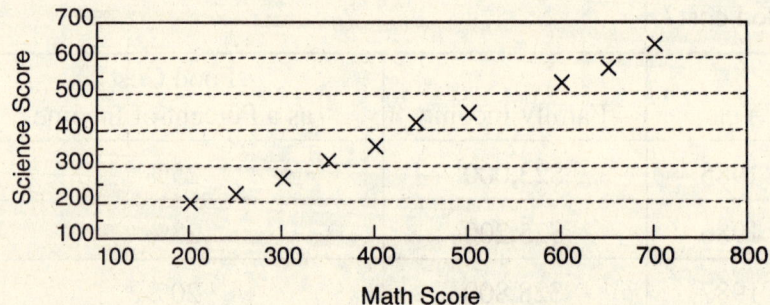

(A) Around 200   (C) Around 480

(B) Around 340   (D) Impossible to predict

4. Using the same scatter diagram in problem 3, if a student scored 600 on the math section, what would you expect that same student to score on the verbal section?

(A) Around 400   (C) Around 700

(B) Around 550   (D) Impossible to predict

INTERPRETING DATA FREQUENCY AND CUMULATIVE FREQUENCY TABLES

In this skill area, a frequency table or cumulative frequency table will be given. The questions in the following example represent the types of questions which may be asked.

● **EXAMPLE**

The following table represents the distribution of the homes in a given area by the total square footage of the home.

Square Footage	Proportion of Homes
1,000 – 1,200	0.02
1,200 – 1,400	0.08
1,400 – 1,600	0.15
1,600 – 1,800	0.18
1,800 – 2,000	0.22
2,000 – 2,200	0.25
2,200 – 2,400	0.10

Question 1: What is the mode of the distribution?

Solution: The mode is the most frequent.

Thus, the mode would be homes in the 2,000 – 2,200 square foot range because 25% of the homes fall within this range, more than any other frequency.

Question 2: What is the median of the distribution?

Solution: The median is the middle term. We will need to find the point at which half of the homes are above and half of the homes are below. To do this begin adding the decimal values until you reach .50 or just above.

$$0.02 + 0.08 = 0.10$$
$$+ 0.15 = 0.25$$
$$+ 0.18 = 0.43$$
$$+ 0.22 = 0.65$$

Since the value which put us over the 0.50 mark was 0.22, which represented the 1,800 – 2,000 square foot homes, this range is the median. In a case such as this, it is sometimes customary to use the midpoint of the range, 1,900 square feet, as the median.

Question 3: What is the mean of the distribution?

Solution: The mean is the arithmetic average.

To find the mean of this distribution, we must find the class mark, the middle value of each range, and multiply that value by the respective proportion.

$$
\begin{array}{rcr}
1,100 \times 0.02 = & 22 \\
1,300 \times 0.08 = & 104 \\
1,500 \times 0.15 = & 225 \\
1,700 \times 0.18 = & 306 \\
1,900 \times 0.22 = & 418 \\
2,100 \times 0.25 = & 525 \\
2,300 \times 0.10 = & \underline{230} \\
& 1,830
\end{array}
$$

Thus, the mean is 1,830 square feet.

Question 4: What proportion of the homes have more than 2,000 square feet?

Solution: Homes with more than 2,000 square feet would be the:

2,000 – 2,200 with a proportion of 0.25 and
2,200 – 2,400 with a proportion of 0.10.

This means that 0.25 + 0.10 or 0.35 or 35% of the homes have more than 2,000 square feet.

Question 5: What proportion of the homes have between 1,200 and 1,800 square feet?

Solution: Homes in this range are:

$$
\begin{array}{lr}
1,200 - 1,400 & 0.08 \\
1,400 - 1,600 & 0.15 \\
1,600 - 1,800 & \underline{0.18} \\
& 0.41
\end{array}
$$

Thus, 0.41 or 41% of the homes have between 1,200 and 1,800 square feet.

☞ Drill: Interpreting Data Frequency and Cumulative Frequency Tables

DIRECTIONS: Questions 1–5 refer to the following information.

The following table represents the number of presidents by age at the time of inauguration.

Age	Frequency
40 – 44	2
45 – 49	5
50 – 54	12
55 – 59	11
60 – 64	7
65 – 69	3

1. What is the mean of the distribution?

    (A) 52   (B) 55   (C) 57   (D) 67

2. What is the median of the distribution?

    (A) 52   (B) 55   (C) 57   (D) 67

3. What is the mode of the distribution?

    (A) 52   (B) 55   (C) 57   (D) 67

4. What proportion of the presidents was under 55 years of age when inaugurated?

    (A) 0.175   (B) 0.475   (C) 0.525   (D) 0.75

PROBABILITY AND STATISTICS REVIEW

ANSWER KEY

Drill: Graphs

1. (B)   2. (D)   3. (B)

Drill: Comparing the Mean, Median, and Mode in a Variety of Distributions

1. (C)   2. (A)   3. (C)   4. (D)

Drill: The Fundamental Counting Principle

1. (C)   2. (C)   3. (C)

Drill: Selecting an Unbiased Sample

1. (A)   2. (B)

Drill: Probability

1. (B)   3. (B)   5. (B)   6. (C)
2. (A)   4. (A)

Drill: Predictions from Statistical Data

1. (B)   2. (A)   3. (C)   4. (D)

Drill: Interpreting Data Frequency and Cumulative Frequency Tables

1. (B)   2. (C)   3. (A)   4. (B)

DETAILED EXPLANATIONS OF ANSWERS

Drill: Graphs

1. **(B)** The average mileage of Car 2 using regular unleaded gas was 32 gallons. When the new product was used, the mileage increased to 38 gallons. The increase of mileage was 6 gallons.

2. **(D)** The mileage for Cars 2 and 3 increased the most, six more miles per gallon.

3. **(B)** To answer this question, find Car 1 on the graph. Car 1 averaged 25 mpg. After using the new product, Car 1 averaged 29 mpg.

Drill: Comparing Mean, Median, Mode in a Variety of Distributions

1. **(C)** $\dfrac{12+15+18+24+31}{5} = \dfrac{100}{5} = 20$

2. **(A)** 12, 15, $\underline{19}$, 21, 27

3. **(C)** $\underline{16}$, 14, 12, $\underline{16}$, 30, 28. 16 repeats

4. **(D)** Sketch a bar graph. The graph is skewed to the right. The mode is furthest left. Thus, mode < median < mean. Choices (A), (B), and (C) do not coincide with what has been established in terms of relative order. (D) is the only choice which does follow from our conclusions. Therefore, (D) is correct.

Drill: The Fundamental Counting Principle

1. **(C)** Using the Counting Rule, $5 \times 2 = 10$

2. **(C)** $8 \times 7 \times 6$ 8 choices for the first caller, 7 then 6

3. **(C)** $n^c r = \dfrac{n!}{r!(n-r)!}$

$$\binom{6}{2} = \frac{6!}{2!(6-2)!} = \frac{6\cdot5\cdot4\cdot3\cdot2\cdot1}{(2\cdot1)(4\cdot3\cdot2\cdot1)} = 15$$

$$\binom{4}{2} = \frac{4!}{2!(4-2)!} = \frac{4\cdot3\cdot2\cdot1}{(2\cdot1)(2\cdot1)} = 6$$

There are 15 possible combinations of Algebra and 5 combinations of Calculus so the total possible combinations are $15 \times 6 = 90$.

Drill: Selecting an Unbiased Sample

1. **(A)** Choice (A) is the most unbiased and random. The survey would be taken from the target population and every student has an equal and likely chance of being selected.

2. **(B)** Choice (B) is the most unbiased and random. Choices (A), (C), and (D) can be eliminated because these choices do not allow for every member of the student body to have an equal or likely chance of being selected.

Drill: Probability

1. **(B)** Three out of ten boxes contained the additional card. Therefore, the probability a randomly selected box would have nine cards is $\dfrac{3}{10}$.

2. **(A)** The probability of selecting one box with nine cards from a shipping crate containing 100 boxes is $\dfrac{30}{100}$. Given that a person chooses a box the probability of choosing a second box is $\dfrac{29}{99}$. The probability of choosing two boxes is: $\dfrac{30}{100} \times \dfrac{29}{99} = \dfrac{870}{9900} = \dfrac{29}{330}$.

3. **(B)** $(0.02)(0.40) = 0.008$

4. **(A)**   18% from chart $= .18$

5. **(B)**   10% of the males have green eyes. 12% of the females have green eyes. 10% males + 12% females = 22% with green eyes. 100% − 22% = 78% = .78.

6. **(C)**   38 students have blue eyes. 18 are male. $\dfrac{18}{38} = .47$

Drill: Predictions from Statistical Data

1. **(B)**   According to the chart, as family incomes increases, the amount they spend on food decreases. In 1985, family income was at its lowest, $23,000, and food cost was at it highest, 25%. By 1993, family income was at its highest, $38,100, and food cost was at its lowest, 15%.

2. **(A)**   Family income has increased and food cost decreased every year since 1985, according to the chart. If this trend continues, the percent of income spent on food will continue to decrease slightly.

3. **(C)**   It is not impossible to predict the score (D). According to the graph, math scores increase as science scores increase. Therefore, choices (A) and (B) are eliminated.

4. **(D)**   There is no mention of a verbal score. Therefore, it is impossible to predict what a student will score on the verbal section.

Drill: Interpreting Data Frequency and Cumulative Frequency Tables

1. **(B)**   The mean is the arithmetic average. To find the mean of this distribution, we must find the class mark, the middle value of each range, and multiply the value by the respective frequency.

$$42 \times 2 = 84$$
$$47 \times 5 = 235$$
$$52 \times 12 = 624$$
$$57 \times 11 = 627$$
$$62 \times 7 = 434$$
$$67 \times 3 = 201$$
$$\overline{40 \quad 2205}$$

We divide 2205 by 40, which equals 55.125, or approximately 55. Note: we need to divide because this problem deals with frequencies, not proportions.

2.   **(C)**   The median is the middle term. We will need to find the point at which half of the number of presidents are below and half of the presidents are above the number 20, the midpoint of the total frequency, 40. To do so, begin adding the frequency values until you reach 20 or just above.

$$2+5=7$$
$$12=19$$
$$11=30$$

Since the value which put us over 20 was 11, which represented the ages ranging from 55–59, this range is the median. In a case such as this, it is sometimes customary to use the midpoint of the range, 57, as the median.

3.   **(A)**   The mode is the most frequent. Thus, the mode would be the presidents between the ages of 50–54 because 12 presidents were between the ages of 50–54, more than any other frequency. In a case such as this, it is sometimes customary to use the midpoint of the range, 52, as the mode.

4.   **(B)**   The range of presidents who were under 55 years of age when inaugurated are:

40–44	2
45–49	5
50–54	12
	19

19 out of 40 presidents were under 55 years of age when inaugurated. Therefore, $\frac{19}{40} = .475$. Thus .475 or 47.5% of presidents inaugurated have been under 55 years of age.

CHAPTER 5
NATURAL SCIENCES REVIEW

Chapter 5

NATURAL SCIENCES REVIEW

The following Natural Sciences Review is divided into eight sections, as follows:

I. **Description of the CLEP General Examination in Natural Sciences**

II. **Biology Review**

III. **Chemistry Review**

IV. **Physics Review**

V. **Earth Science Review**

VI. **Geology Review**

VII. **Astronomy Review**

VIII. **Meteorology Review**

By thoroughly studying this course review, you will be well-prepared for the material on the CLEP General Examination in Natural Sciences.

I. DESCRIPTION OF THE CLEP GENERAL EXAMINATION IN NATURAL SCIENCES

The CLEP General Examination in Natural Sciences is designed to give candidates an opportunity to show knowledge and understanding of topics frequently taught in first- or second-year college natural and physical science courses. The topics on this exam are taught in classes for non-science (liberal arts) majors. The CLEP Natural Sciences is a 120-question examination consisting of two sections of multiple-choice questions—one covering biological science, the other covering physical science—each 45 minutes in length. The percent distribution of topics is as follows:

Biological Science	**50%**
Origin and Evolution of Life; Classification of Organisms	10%
Cell Organization and Division; Genes; Bioenergetics; Biosynthesis	10%
Structure, Function, and Development of Organisms; Patterns of Heredity	20%
Concepts of Population Biology; Ecology	10%
Physical Science	**50%**
Atomic Structure and Properties; Particles; Nuclear Reactions	7%
Chemical Elements, Compounds, and Reactions; Molecular Structure and Bonding	10%
Heat; Thermodynamics; Classical Mechanics; States of Matter; Relativity	12%
Electricity and Magnetism; Waves; Light and Sound	4%
The Universe (galaxies, stars, planets)	7%
The Earth (atmosphere, hydrosphere, properties, surface features, geology, structure, history)	10%

To measure your knowledge of the above topics, the examination uses three main types of questions: 1) knowledge of fundamental facts, theories, and principles 2) understanding information presented in graphs, diagrams, tables, equations, charts, or written passages and 3) application of scientific principles (both qualitative and quantitative) from all disciplines of science.

TYPES OF QUESTIONS AND EXAMPLES
KNOWLEDGE OF FUNDAMENTAL FACTS

These questions test your background of sound scientific facts, concepts, and principles. Questions of this type will require you to recall specific terms and definitions from all disciplines of science.

● **EXAMPLE**

1.　Fungi have all of the following characteristics EXCEPT:

　　(A)　can undergo photosynthesis

　　(B)　have cell walls

　　(C)　live on dead organic matter

　　(D)　produce spores

　　(E)　secrete digestive enzymes

The correct answer choice is (A). This question asks about the characteristics of fungi. Fungi are eukaryotes. They are multicellular and multinucleate. Structurally, they have cell walls that are composed mainly of chitin, a derivative polysaccharide containing nitrogen. Mushrooms reproduce by spore production. They are not capable of undergoing photosynthesis, but instead feed on dead organic matter by secreting digestive enzymes into their environment, and breaking down food extracellularly. The products of digestion are then absorbed through the cell wall and cell membranes by structures called haustoria.

UNDERSTANDING AND INTERPRETING GRAPHIC INFORMATION

These type of questions will require you to read and understand the information as it is presented and answer the question, or series of questions, that follow. You will encounter several types of graphic information: graphs and charts; tables; figures; mathematical expressions; equations; and reading passages.

Graphs and charts will come in many forms. These will include line graphs, pie charts, and bar charts. Other types of graphs include line diagrams and scatter diagrams. In scatter diagrams the points are not connected together while in line diagrams the points are connected.

Sometimes data is represented in table form. Tables are easy to read, because you do not have to estimate data from a line or read contours. There are an infinite variety of tables that may be encountered on the examination.

Graphic information may also be presented in figures with non-numeric data. These figures will include flow diagrams, geology charts, and process diagrams. A flow diagram shows how a substrate is transformed, such as how glucose is metabolized by the mitochondria. Geology charts can show the change in soil composition through erosion or the evaporation of water through the water cycle. Finally, process diagrams display a series of chemical or physical changes. One example of a process diagram is showing the steps of fermenting beer.

Equations, either chemical or mathematical, contain several components describing a series of values or abbreviating objects. Carefully read through all of the components and try to understand what the equation is describing. Deciphering abbreviations and symbols is very important. Equations are usually only short-hand notation for a complex process or activity.

The final type of data you may be asked to interpret will be in the form of text, either a description of a system or experiment. Carefully read through the sentences, paying special attention to the first sentence as this will often contain the main idea of the passage.

● **EXAMPLE**

1. Which of the following serves as a catalyst in the following reaction?

$$CH_2 = CH_2 + H_2 + Pt \rightarrow CH_3CH_3 + Pt$$

(A) C

(B) $CH_2 = CH_2$

(C) H_2

(D) Pt

(E) CH_3CH_3

The correct answer choice is (D). One characteristic of a catalyst is that it remains unchanged by the reaction process. It is clear that after the reaction ($\rightarrow$) the only component that has not changed is Pt, so (D) is the correct choice.

APPLICATION OF SCIENTIFIC PRINCIPLES

These types of questions will contain the same presentations of data as you saw in the previous section. The only difference between Understanding and Interpreting Graphic Information questions and the Application of Scientific Principles questions is that the latter will ask you to go one step further and make a conclusion based on data presented, instead of merely reading the chart of graph. These question types may ask you to draw conclusions, estimate trends, or predict increases or decreases. You will not be asked to directly calculate quantities or formulas.

● **EXAMPLE**

1. A graph of distance vs. time for an object moving in a straight line is shown below. The acceleration of the object must be

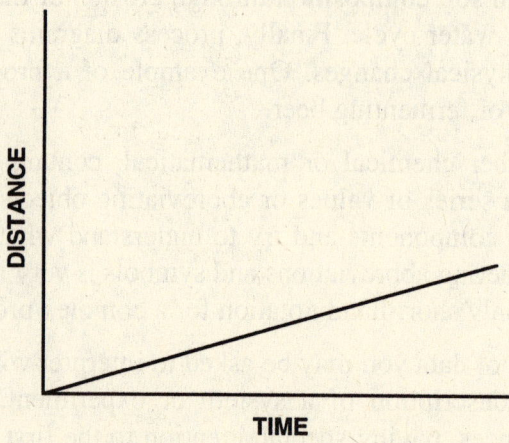

(A) zero.

(B) increasing.

(C) decreasing.

(D) constant and greater than zero.

(E) equal to *g*.

The correct answer choice is (A). The slope of the line is constant, indicating that the distance covered per time is constant. An object traveling in a straight line must be traveling at a constant velocity to cover the same distance in the same time. Acceleration is a measure of the change in velocity per time. No change in velocity results in zero acceleration.

COMMON TERMS

Below is a list of common terms that you should know. These terms all appear in boldface type in the following review sections.

absorption	allele
acceleration	allergy
acid	alveoli
activation energy	amino acid
adenoid	anaerobic
aerobic	anaphase

anatomy

animalae kingdom

Archimedes' Principle

assimilation

asteroid

astronomy

atmosphere

atom

atomic number

ATP

axosphere

bacteriology

basal body

base

behavior

binomial nomenclature

biology

biosphere

boiling point

botany

carbon cycle

cardiac muscle

cell

cell membrane

cell wall

Cenozoic era

centriole

chemical equation

chemical kinetics

chemical property

chemistry

chloroplast

chromosome

circulatory system

classification

climate

colloid

comet

compound

conductor

conservation

constellation

continental drift

continental shelf

corrosion

covalent bond

cytology

cytoplasm

density

dermis

digestion

digestive system

diurnal tide

DNA

earthquake

ecology

eddy

electrical circuit

electrical current

electricity

electrolytic reaction

electron

element

embryology

endothermic reaction

energy

energy cycle

enzyme

epidermis

equilibrium

erosion

eukaryote

excretion

exothermic reaction

flooding

fog

force
formula
freezing point
frequency
friction
fungi kingdom
galaxy
gas
gene
genetics
genotype
genus
Golgi apparatus
gravity
habitat
Hardy-Weinberg Law
heat
heterozygous trait
high water
histology
homeostasis
homologous chromosome
homozygous trait
hormone
Hot Big Bang Theory
hot spring
hurricane
hybrid
hypothesis
igneous rock
illumination
inertia
ingestion
insulator
interphase
ionic bond
ionosphere
irritability

kinetic energy
kingdom
laser
Law of Conservation of Matter and Energy
Law of Conservation of Momentum
Law of Constant Acceleration
Law of Dominance
Law of Independent Assortment
Law of Inertia
Law of Reflection
Law of Refraction
Law of Segregation and Recombination
Lenz's Law
lethal
light
liquid
low water
lysosome
machine
magnetic field
magnetism
mass
matter
meiosis
Mendel's Law of Genetics
mesosphere
mesozoic era
messenger RNA
metallic bond
metamorphic rock
metaphase
meteoroid
migration
mineral
mitochondria
mitosis

mixture
molecule
momentum
moneran kingdom
Moon
motion
movement
muscular system
mutation
neuron
nucleolus
nucleus
ocean
Ohm's Law
oogenesis
ore
organic chemistry
osmosis
oxidation
oxidation number
Periodic Table
peroxisome
pH
phenotype
photosynthesis
physical property
physics
physiology
planet
plantae kingdom
plasma
plastid
polarization
polyploidy
potential energy
power
Precambrian era
pressure

prokaryote
protein
protistae kingdom
Punnett Square
quantum
rate of reaction
reaction
reflection
refraction
regulation
reproduction
respiration
ribosomal RNA
RNA
rough endoplasmic reticulum
secretion
sedimentary rock
semidiurnal tide
skeletal muscle
skeletal system
smooth endoplasmic reticulum
smooth muscle
solar system
solid
solute
solution
solvent
sound
species
speed
static electricity
stratosphere
substance
suspension
Sutton Law
synthesis
telophase
temperature

Theory of Evolution
Theory of Natural Selection
Theory of Relativity
thymus
tide
tonsil
transfer RNA
transportation
transverse
troposphere
typhoon

vacuole
velocity
volcano
volume
water cycle
wave
weathering
weight
work
x-rays
zoology

II. BIOLOGY REVIEW

THEMES AND GENERAL VOCABULARY

Biology is an independent set of explanatory concepts. Thus, we describe biology as the study of living organisms/things.

A **hypothesis** is very tentative and is something to be proven; it is only tentatively held and must be checked out fully and possibly proven. A hypothesis is an educated guess.

There are many fields of study in the biological sciences. **Zoology**, for example, is the study of animal life. **Botany** is the study of plant life; **ecology** is the study of the relationship of living things to their environment; **embryology** is the study of embryos; **anatomy** is the study of structures of the body; **physiology** is the study of the function of the body; **genetics** is the study of heredity; **cytology** is the study of the cell; **histology** is the study of tissues; and **bacteriology** is the study of bacteria and/or one-celled plant life.

THE CELL

The **cell** is the basic structure of all living things. This is the foundation of the cell theory. Some cells are total living organisms while other cells are the basic units of structure of other living things. All cells reproduce from identical cells by reproduction. Sex cells reproduce by meiosis while somatic cells (autosomes or body cells) reproduce by mitosis.

Cells are of two types: **prokaryotic** or **eukaryotic**. Prokaryotes are cells that do not have a nuclear membrane or a membrane surrounding its organelles. Bacteria and blue-green bacteria are examples of prokaryotes. Eukaryote refers to most cells making up all other living organisms.

A generalized cell will contain:

1. a **cell membrane** which is a double layer of lipids that surrounds the cell, thus acting as a "gatekeeper," controlling what moves into and out of the cell.

2. a **nucleus** which is separated from the cytoplasm by a thickened membrane that is more selective than the cell membrane.

3. **cytoplasm**, the gel-like material that surrounds and protects by cushioning the organelles. It also contains all the chemicals for that particular cell to carry out its living activities.

Depending upon the kind of cell and the function of the cell, any cell can contain any number of the following organelles:

1. **Mitochondria:** the powerhouse of the cell. It is the site where energy is obtained from food consumed and made available for the cell's use.

2. **Chloroplast:** the site of photosynthesis.

3. **Plastids:** store chlorophyll for use by the chloroplasts.

4. **Lysosomes:** carry out digestive functions and store digestive enzymes as needed by the cell.

5. **Smooth endoplasmic reticulum:** does not have ribosomes attached and is the transportation system of the cell.

6. **Rough endoplasmic reticulum:** has ribosomes attached and also carries out cell transportation but mainly of necessary protein materials needed by the cell.

7. **Golgi apparatus:** manufacture, synthesize, store, and distribute hormone and enzyme materials needed by the cell.

8. **Peroxisomes:** manufacture, store, and secrete oxidation enzymes needed by the cell.

9. **Vacuoles:** spaces that act as a vacuum cleaner to rid the cell of wastes and water. Also, when not cleaning the cell, the vacuole will act as a storehouse for chemicals and compounds needed by the cell.

10. **Basal bodies:** structures that clean the cell.

11. **Cell wall:** a tough outer membrane that supports and protects the plant cell.

12. **Centrioles:** rod-shaped structures responsible for animal cell reproduction.

13. **Nucleolus:** the center of the nucleus that resembles a golf ball and houses the genes, chromosomes, and their needed materials.

14. **Chromosomes:** hereditary structures that contain the genes which determine the hereditary information contained in the cell.

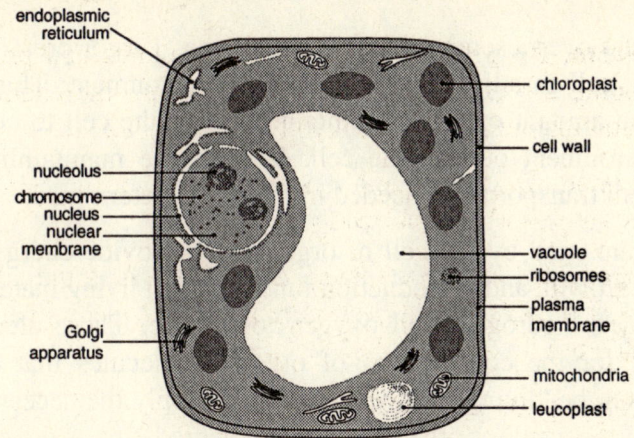

Typical Plant Cell

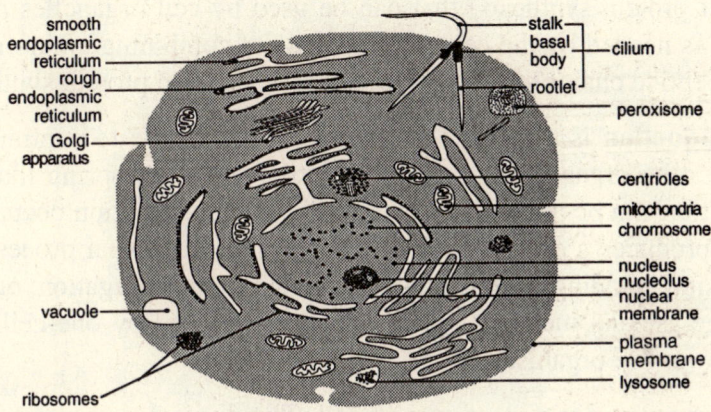

Typical Animal Cell

Cells maintain a balance or working equilibrium that is optimum for their needs. This balance, obtained by internal control, is called **homeostasis**, and accounts for all movement into and out of the cell. Though the cell can adjust to a wide range of environmental needs and amounts, there is a limit to how much and how often it can adjust.

To understand homeostasis, one must understand how molecules move by osmosis and diffusion. When molecular movement has met needed concentrations of materials on either side of the cell membrane, the state of equilibrium exists. It is in this state that the cell operates most efficiently.

Materials move into and out of the cell either by active transport, passive transport, endocytosis, phagocytosis, or exocytosis. The exact method used depends on the type, function, and environment of the cell. A cell exists in a constantly changing environment and has constantly changing needs which must be met in order to stay alive and function. All transport occurs over a semipermeable membrane. Turgor pressure is necessary for the cell to adjust to its needs and environment. This pressure determines the amount of water maintained inside the cell to counterbalance the environment outside the cell. It is by the maintaining of this pressure that all transportation needed in the cell is determined.

Proteins are used by the cell or organism to provide energy, general maintenance, growth, and reproduction functions. All living material needs carbon, nitrogen, hydrogen, and oxygen to survive. These elements are also essential for the construction of organic molecules that constitute what it means to be "living." Only protein will supply the necessary nitrogen for life within a cell or organism. Protein degradation is the process by which proteins are broken down into the smallest units, called **amino acids**. The amino acids are then reconstructed into peptide chains (by the process of protein synthesis) that can be used by cell organelles or other materials as needed by the cell. This process of combining amino acids to produce peptide chains to reconstruct proteins is called protein synthesis.

Reproduction is a process that is necessary for life to continue. It is the process the organism or cell utilizes to create an offspring like itself. Reproduction can be asexual or sexual. Asexual reproduction occurs when one split produces a carbon-copy of the cell itself. Asexual processes are called fission, budding, fragmentation, regeneration, conjugation, or sporulation. The asexual methods of reproduction are used by one-cell organisms or lower life organisms.

Mitosis is the division of a body cell. The division or reproduction is for the purpose of maintaining life as a productive and efficient organism. **Meiosis** is the division of sex cells, namely, production of the egg or the sperm.

CELL DIVISION
Mitosis
Mitosis is a form of cell division whereby each of two daughter nuclei receives the same chromosome complement as the parent nucleus. All kinds of asexual reproduction are carried out by mitosis; it is also responsible for growth, regeneration, and cell replacement in multicellular organisms.

Interphase – Interphase is no longer called the resting phase because a great deal of activity occurs during this phase. In the cytoplasm, oxidation and synthesis reactions take place. In the nucleus, DNA replicates itself and forms messenger RNA, transfer RNA, and ribosomal RNA.

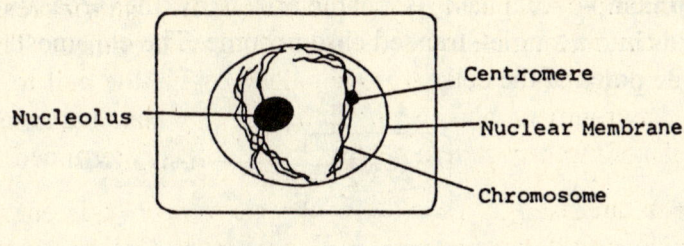

Interphase

Prophase – Chromatids shorten and thicken during this stage of mitosis. The nucleoli disappear and the nuclear membrane breaks down and disappears as well. Spindle fibers begin to form. In an animal cell, there is also division of the centrosome and centrioles.

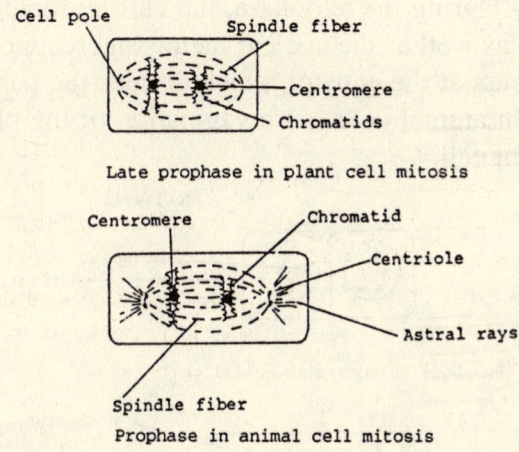

Late prophase in plant cell mitosis

Prophase in animal cell mitosis

Metaphase – During this phase, each chromosome moves to the equator, or middle, of the spindle. The paired chromosomes attach to the spindle at the centromere.

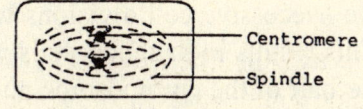

Metaphase in plant cell mitosis

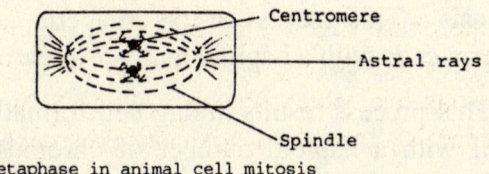

Metaphase in animal cell mitosis

Anaphase – Anaphase is characterized by the separation of sister chromatids into a single-stranded chromosome. The chromosomes migrate to opposite poles of the cell.

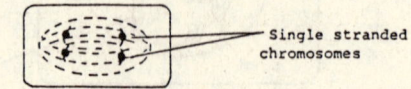

Anaphase in plant cell mitosis

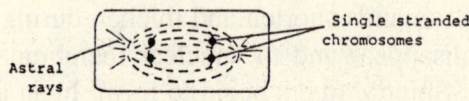

Anaphase in animal cell mitosis

Telophase – During the telophase, the chromosomes begin to uncoil and the nucleoli as well as the nuclear membrane reappear. In plant cells, a cell plate appears at the equator which divides the parent cell into two daughter cells. In animal cells, an invagination of the plasma membrane divides the parent cell.

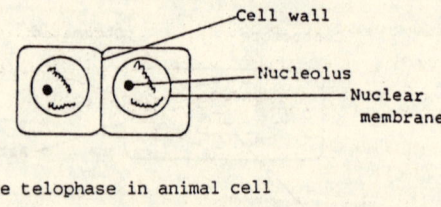

Late telophase in animal cell

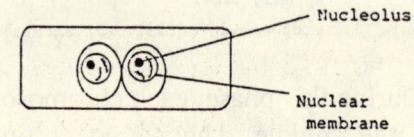

Late telophase in plant cell

Meiosis

Meiosis consists of two successive cell divisions with only one duplication of chromosomes. This results in daughter cells with a haploid number of chromosomes or one-half of the chromosome number in the original cell. This process occurs during the formation of gametes and in spore formation in plants.

Spermatogenesis – This process results in sperm cell formation with four immature sperm cells with a haploid number of chromosomes.

Oogenesis – This process results in egg cell formation with only one immature egg cell with a haploid number of chromosomes, which becomes mature and larger as yolk forms within the cell.

The first meiotic division consists of the following steps:

Interphase I – Chromosome duplication begins to occur during this phase.

Prophase I – During this phase, the chromosomes shorten and thicken and synapsis occurs with pairing of homologous chromosomes. Crossing-over between non-sister chromatids will also occur. The centrioles will migrate to opposite poles and the nucleolus and nuclear membrane begin to dissolve.

Metaphase I – The tetrads, composed of two doubled homologous chromosomes, migrate to the equatorial plane during Metaphase I.

Anaphase I – During this stage, the paired homologous chromosomes separate and move to opposite poles of the cell. Thus, the number of chromosome types in each resultant cell is reduced to the haploid number.

Telophase I – Cytoplasmic division occurs during telophase I. The formation of two new nuclei with half the chromosomes of the original cell occurs.

Prophase II – The centrioles that had migrated to each pole of the parental cell, now incorporated in each haploid daughter cell, divide, and a new spindle forms in each cell. The chromosomes move to the equator.

Metaphase II – The chromosomes are lined up at the equator of the new spindle, which is at right angles to the old spindle.

Anaphase II – The centromeres divide and the daughter chromatids, now chromosomes, separate and move to opposite poles.

Telophase II – Cytoplasmic division occurs. The chromosomes gradually return to the dispersed form and a nuclear membrane forms.

A living organism could be called a chemical factory. More chemical activity is carried on inside the cell or inside the living organism than any other place. Chemical bonds are broken, constructed, and reconstructed in a continuous operation. Chemical reactions occur simultaneously throughout the organism so that life will be an ongoing process. Carbohydrates, starches, lipids, proteins, water, and nucleic acids are the chemicals (organic molecules) and compounds that are basic to all life.

DNA was discovered in 1869. It was not until the development of the electron microscope in the mid-1940s that scientists gained a true realization of the functioning of DNA.

DNA (deoxyribonucleic acid) is the basic chemical of life. It is a giant molecule made of four different nitrogenous bases (adenine, guanine, cytosine, thymine), phosphate groups, and 5-carbon sugars that collectively are called a nucleotide. It is a self-duplicating molecule that is in a double helix (spiral staircase appearance). It is found inside the nucleus of the cell and contains the directions, or "blueprints," for the making of all the proteins that a cell needs. Proteins play a major role in cell metabolism and are the basic building blocks of a cell. DNA is the controller of heredity and all life activities of the cell. Its function is linked to the functioning of a companion chemical called **RNA** (ribonucleic acid).

The Chemical Composition of DNA

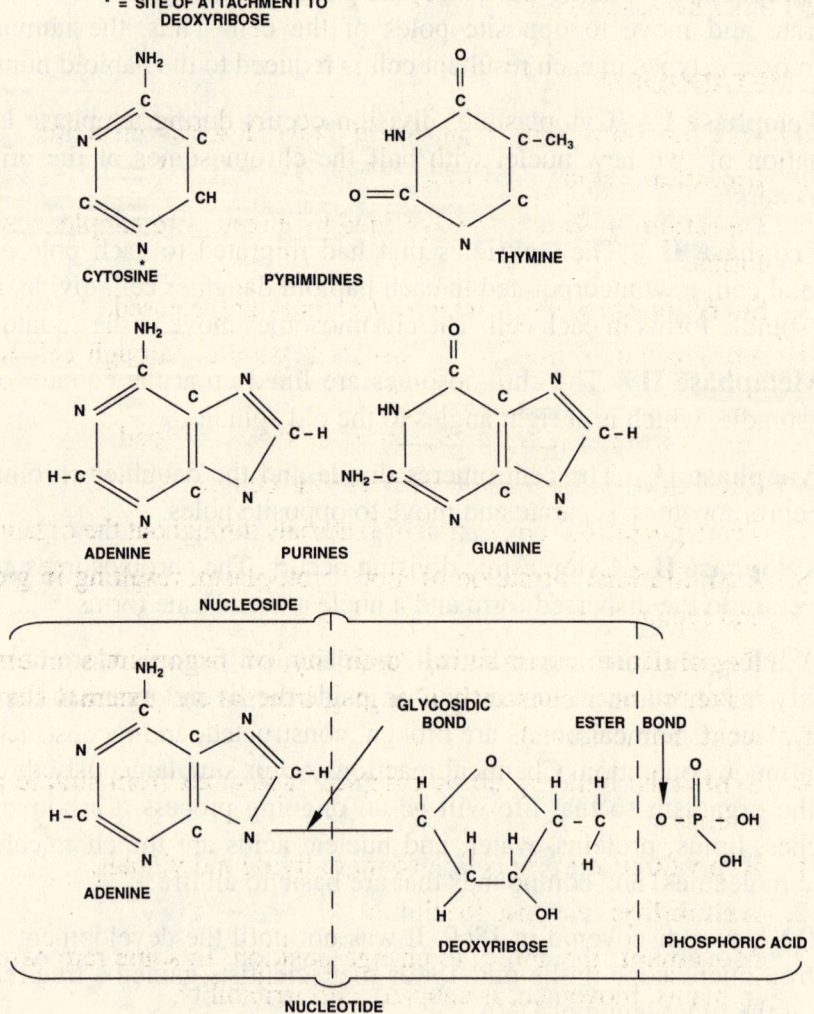

STRUCTURAL FORMULAS OF PURINES (ADENINE AND QUANINE),
PYRIMIDINES (THYMINE AND CYTOSINE), AND A NUCLEOTIDE

Ribonucleic acid differs from DNA in that uracil replaces thymine as nitrogenous base, and the sugar bond used by RNA has one less oxygen present. Also, RNA is a straight chain. The genetic information in DNA is carried out of the nucleus by what is called **messenger RNA** (mRNA). Protein synthesis is carried out in the cytoplasm of the cell by **transfer RNA** (tRNA) using ribosomes comprised of **ribosomal RNA** and proteins.

The DNA acts as an interpreter or decoder for the many chemical messages that are carried through the cell as a part of the life activities. The DNA cannot leave the nucleus and, therefore, must have a messenger and translator working directly with it. In addition, the **tRNA** picks up and delivers necessary amino acids to complete the needed activity. This process enables the cell to carry out digestion, oxidation, assimilation, synthesis, and other necessary cell activities.

CELL METABOLISM

The basic functions of life comprising total cell metabolism are:

1. **Ingestion:** taking in of food.
2. **Digestion:** breaking down of food by enzymes to simpler, soluble forms.
3. **Secretion:** process by which substances are released.
4. **Absorption:** diffusion of dissolved material through cell membranes.
5. **Respiration:** release of energy by oxidation of food.
6. **Excretion:** getting rid of wastes of the cells.
7. **Transportation:** circulation of materials throughout the organism.
8. **Assimilation:** formation of more protoplasm, resulting in growth and repair.
9. **Regulation:** maintaining stability of organism's chemical makeup under constantly changing internal and external environment (homeostasis).
10. **Synthesis:** building up of complex molecules from simple compounds.
11. **Reproduction:** production of more living individuals.
12. **Irritability:** response to stimuli.
13. **Movement:** the ability to change position. In some rare cases, as in plants, movement is coupled with irritability.
14. **Bioluminescence:** production of internal light within some organisms.

Photosynthesis is a process that occurs within all plant cells which supply all of the carbohydrates used by both plants and animals. Not only are essential organic compounds formed, but needed water and oxygen are given off as by-products in this autotrophic nutrition process.

Chloroplasts absorb light energy from the sun. Carbon dioxide and water are present as raw materials at the chloroplast manufacturing site.

An overall chemical description of photosynthesis is the equation

$$6\ CO_2 + 6\ H_2O \xrightarrow[\text{CHLOROPHYLL}]{\text{LIGHT}} C_6 H_{12} O_6 + 6\ O_2$$

Photosynthesis is a two-step process involving light reactions and dark reactions. In the light reaction process, light must be present along with chlorophyll to start the chemical reaction. Carbon dioxide and water are broken down into free atoms. Then the dark reaction can happen. Light is not necessary for this chemical reaction to occur. Carbon, acting as a centerpiece, joins with oxygen and hydrogen to form carbohydrates. Water and unused oxygen are given off as waste products.

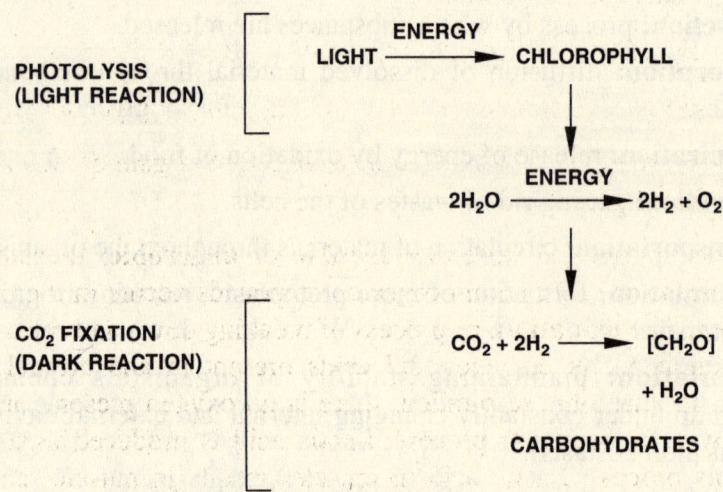

PHOTOLYSIS AND CO_2 FIXATION

Cellular respiration is the process by which the cell or organism gets energy for all of its activities. It is through this respiration process that chemical energy is released. This process occurs in the mitochondria through a series of steps.

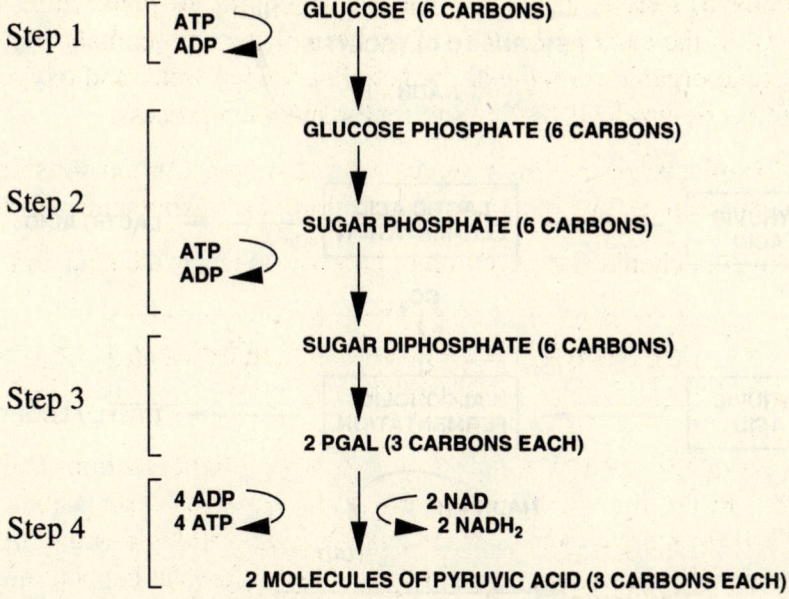

The steps are summarized as follows:

Step 1 – Activation of glucose

Step 2 – Formation of sugar diphosphate

Step 3 – Formation and oxidation of PGAL, phosphoglyceraldehyde

Step 4 – Formation of pyruvic acid ($C_3H_4O_3$). Net gain of two ATP molecules

Cellular respiration can be either **aerobic** or **anaerobic**. In aerobic respiration, release of energy from organic compounds occurs in the presence of oxygen. The **oxidation**, or process of breaking down and releasing energy, is stimulated by enzymes and acids present in and around the mitochondria. In anaerobic respiration, there is no oxygen present, and it must occur by a fermentation process. Lactic acid is produced as a by-product of this process. Lactic acid in muscles results in muscle fatigue and soreness.

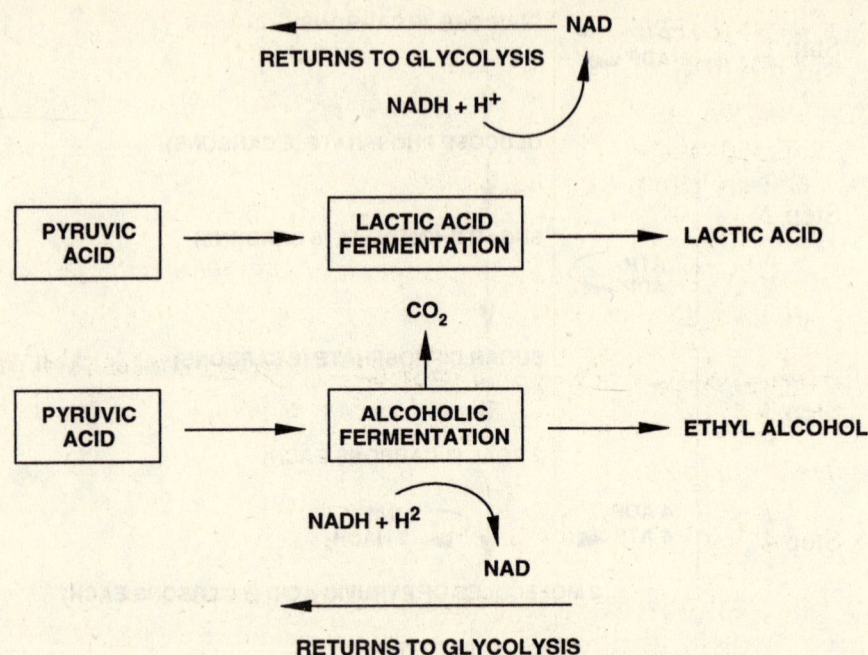

GENETICS

Usually, offspring will resemble their parents. Yet, the offspring may have traits that are not present in either parent. In 1857, Gregor Mendel developed his Laws of Genetics after seven years of studying the garden green pea. **Mendel's Laws of Genetics** are:

1. **Law of Dominance:** Every organism receives a trait from the mother and a trait from the father. One trait may have dominance over the other and mask the recessive trait to keep it from showing in the offspring. Dominant traits are normally the darker, heavier, or larger of the two traits.

2. **Law of Segregation and Recombinant:** Genes separate into single units at the time the egg and sperm unite. Each character links with a like character to form a gene. It is segregation that assures each parent contributes equally to the offspring.

3. **Law of Independent Assortment:** Each unit or character for a trait is independently distributed to link with a like gene to form another pair. There is no pattern to their separation and rejoining to form the genes for the potential offspring. Genes on separate chromosomes are inherited independently.

In 1900, Walter Sutton began further studies based on Mendel's studies. Sutton compared the behavior of the chromosomes to the principles of inheritance. He confirmed all that Gregor Mendel had formulated. Sutton learned that the "factors" Mendel referred to were units located in the **chromosomes**. Sutton named these factors "genes." The chromosomal theory of inheritance, established by Sutton, states that genes are located on chromosomes and forms the basis for the study of genetics.

The **Sutton Law** was followed by the **Hardy-Weinberg Law**, which was based on population studies. The law states that in a population at equilibrium, both genes and genotypic frequencies remain constant from generation to generation. Each trait, whether dominant or recessive, has an equal chance to exert its influence.

Basic Language of Genetics:

1. A **gene** is the part of a chromosome that codes for a certain hereditary trait.

2. A **chromosome** is a rod-shaped body formed from the genes found in the cell nucleus.

3. A **genotype** is the genetic makeup of an organism or the set of genes that it possesses. This is always expressed in capital letters to express dominant traits or small letters to express recessive traits.

4. The **phenotype** is the outward visible appearance or expression of gene action. It is the hereditary makeup of an organism that we see or measure.

5. **Homologous chromosomes** are chromosomes bearing genes for the same characters.

6. A **homozygous trait** is an identical pair of alleles on homologous chromosomes for any given trait.

7. A **heterozygous trait** is a mixed pair of alleles on homologous chromosomes for any given trait.

8. **Hybrid** refers to an organism carrying unlike genes for certain traits. This is a preferred trait when breeding for the "best of both" traits.

9. **Mutation** is a sudden appearance of a new trait or variation which is inherited.

10. **Lethal** means deadly. This trait will cause the death of the organism.

Each gene has a particular location on a chromosome (**allele**). Genes carried on the X chromosome are called sex-linked genes. Males carrying a recessive allele on their single X chromosome express a recessive phenotype. Females must carry recessive alleles on both X chromosomes to express a recessive phenotype.

Mutations can affect other chromosomes or individual genes. Chromosomal aberrations like mutations occur in reproductive cells and may be passed on to the offspring. Nondisjunction of the chromosomes results in gametes that have too few or too many chromosomes. In **polyploidy**, organisms have an extra set of chromosomes. In the disease called trisomy 21 or Down's Syndrome, a person has an extra twenty-first chromosome. Gene mutations occur due to a change in the DNA sequence for that particular gene at that particular time. A mutated gene does not give correct directions for protein synthesis and normally harms the organism. There are a few mutations that have proven to be beneficial, however.

The **Punnett Square** is a method used to predict the probable outcome of a particular genetic cross. This testcross will help determine information about an organism or potential organism. Study the basic crosses worked out below.

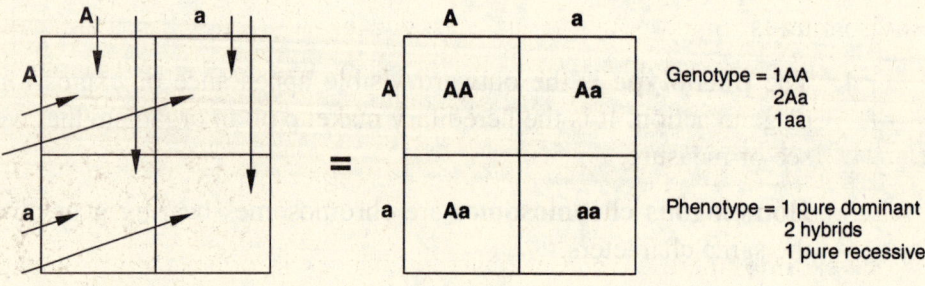

BREAKING THE CODE OF LIFE

More is being learned about the code of life that is locked into the DNA of every cell. Every living organism has its own unique pattern of DNA that accounts for the individualism in each organism. This is why DNA replication must occur prior to mitosis or meiosis in order for organisms to grow, develop, and reproduce. In this process, DNA unspirals, unzips, and separates, and new strands of DNA are constructed from nucleotides present in the nucleus. Then the process of cell division may occur. This occurrence is what holds the code of life. Never is the code altered in any replication that totally alters the organism. Although this may be the key to answering questions about cancer and other life-threatening diseases that affect certain organisms, much research still needs to be done.

EVOLUTION OF ORGANISMS

Several theories have been formulated on how life evolves. One such theory was proposed by Jean Lamarck in 1809 when he proposed that an organism evolves in response to its environment by acquiring a trait which would adapt it to life in its changing environment. For instance, if a giraffe's neck were too short, by the constant stretching during the parent's life, offspring would be born with longer necks.

In 1859, Darwin formulated his theory in his book called *The Origin of Species*. The book supported the **theory of evolution** but gave a completely different twist to the evolution idea. After studying many plants and animals, Darwin concluded that no two organisms are exactly alike, but instead differ in size, shape, color, etc., and that these traits are inherited from the parents to the offspring and not acquired. Individuals who inherit adaptive traits have a greater chance for survival; thus, Darwin's **theory of natural selection**.

Evidence that supports evolutionary theories includes adaptation to the environment, homologous organs, vestigial organs, similarity of embryonic development, similarity of nucleic acids, and similar protein structure. With the groundwork laid by Lamarck and Darwin, modern evolutionists include speciation, adaptive radiation, convergent evolution, divergent evolution, and population genetics as phenomena that support evolutionary theory.

Over time, there have been marked changes in atmospheric content, climate, and environment. If a species did not have the necessary adaptive traits to change with the external changes, the species became extinct.

Fossils are evidence of living things that existed long ago. The most common fossils are found in sedimentary rock that can be dated by using radioactive isotopes to measure the amount of carbon in the remains. This amount determines a close approximation to the exact age of the fossil remains.

It is proposed by evolutionary theory that each era is briefly marked by rapid adaptive radiation normally followed by mass extinction that ended each era. Stanley Miller provided evidence that life-supporting molecules arose under abiotic conditions. He produced the exact atmosphere that was thought to have first existed and showed how heterotrophs used the available organic substances for food.

Geological evolution is as follows:

Precambrian Era	unicellular organisms originated
Paleozoic Era	multicellular animals and fern-like plants originated
Mesozoic Era	birds, mammals, reptiles, and flowering plants originated
Cenozoic Era	radiation of birds, mammals, reptiles, and flowering plants occurred

CLASSIFICATION

Classification is a method of organizing information based on similarities. Aristotle was the first scientist to attempt to classify living things by grouping them into two major groups—plants or animals. Then they were divided into three major sub-groups as to their habitat—land, water, or air. Since Aristotle's first attempt at classification, man has used various systems of classifying living things in an effort to identify them. With so many languages and word meanings, a standard language had to be developed so that the use of common names in each language could be avoided. Thus, scientists began to use the genus and species names as this would be a consistent language in any nation. This classification system is called **binomial nomenclature**.

The levels of classification from largest to smallest are kingdom, phylum class, order, family, genus, and species. All living organisms are classified into one of five **kingdoms** to start the identifying procedure. Then the organism will be studied, compared to specific requirements, and placed in an appropriate level until a species is finally established. The biological name would be the **genus** and **species**.

A classification key can be used as an aid to identify organisms. It uses an organism's general characteristics and special features to find its appropriate placement. (Study the mini-key on the following page.)

Often, as seen throughout time, organisms change in order to survive. Natural selection causes all species to adapt to changing environmental conditions. This change is called adaptation. The organisms change to adapt to their new environments and through time they evolve into entirely different organisms. This is called speciation.

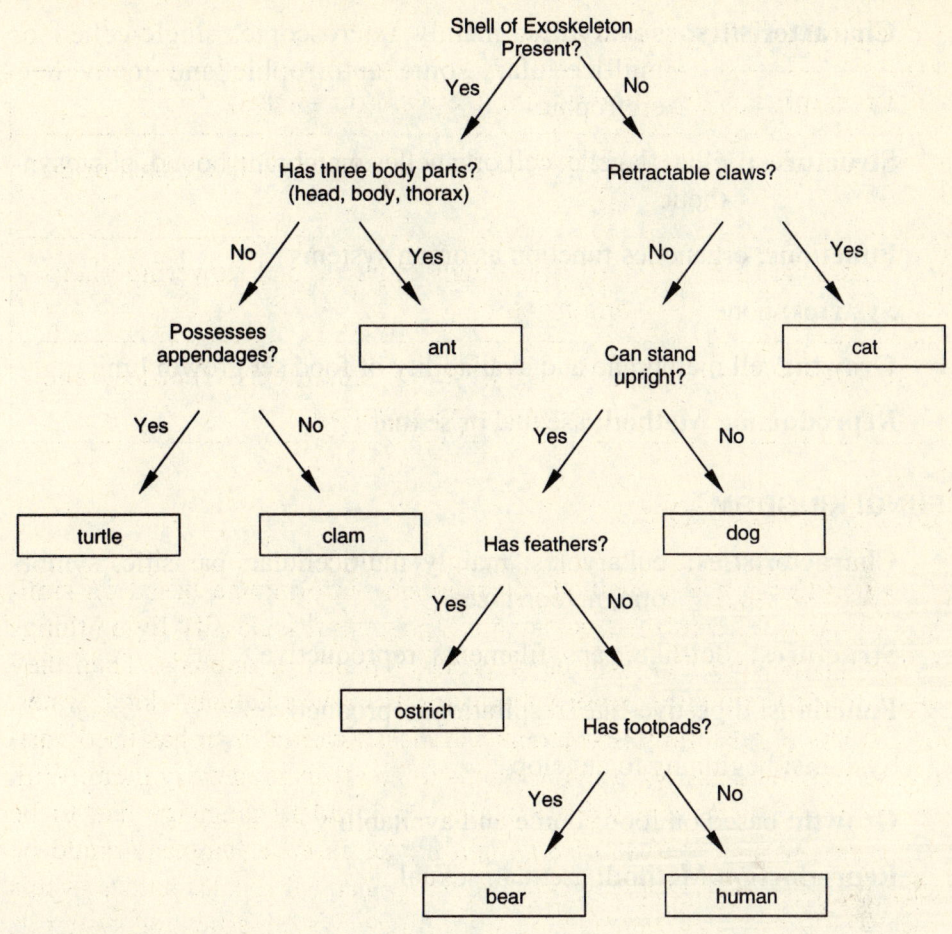

MONERAN KINGDOM

Bacteria and blue-green bacteria

Characteristics: prokaryotes, microscopic, lives as a single cell or in colonies in water, autotrophic, few heterotrophic

Structures: flagella capsules

Functions: food getting, respiration, reproduction

Systems: none

Growth: cell membrane and availability of food set growth limit

Reproduction Method: binary fission

PROTISTAE KINGDOM

Animal-like organism, distinguished by method of locomotion

Characteristics: eukaryotes, mainly microscopic, single-celled or multicellular; some autotrophic and many heterotrophic

Structures: cilia, flagella, cell organelles membrane bound, photosynthetic

Functions: organelles function as organ systems

Systems: none

Growth: cell membrane and availability of food set growth limit

Reproduction Method: asexual or sexual

FUNGI KINGDOM

Characteristics: eukaryotes, mainly multicellular, parasitic, symbiotic, mycorrhizae

Structures: root-like, caps, filaments, reproductive

Functions: digestive-like, respiration, reproductive

Systems: beginning to develop

Growth: based on food source and availability

Reproduction Method: asexual, sexual

PLANT KINGDOM

Characteristics: eukaryotes, multicellular, nonmotile, autotrophic

Structures: cellulose cell walls

Functions: based on cell and tissue chemistry

Systems: all present and functioning

Growth: based on hormone action

Reproduction Method: asexual, sexual by spores, seeds, flowers, and cones

ANIMAL KINGDOM

Characteristics: eukaryotes, multicellular, heterotrophic, most are motile at some point in lifetime

Structures: all present and unique to organism

Functions: based on nutrition, cell and tissue chemistry, and individual demands

Systems: all present and functioning

Growth: based on hormone action and nutrition

Reproduction Method: asexual, sexual

HUMAN SYSTEMS BIOLOGY
DIGESTIVE SYSTEM

The digestive system is responsible for both mechanical and chemical digestion that break down food into molecules so they can move into the cell and be used for the living process. The mouth, teeth, and tongue begin the chemical digestion by mechanically breaking down the food through the chewing process and the addition of saliva. The enzyme amylase breaks down carbohydrates and starts the breakdown of starches. Food moves from the mouth to the stomach by way of the esophagus. In the stomach, other digestive enzymes and hydrochloric acid begin the breakdown of proteins. The stomach churns and mixes the food. Food, now in a liquid-like state, moves from the stomach into the small intestine, where it is absorbed through the villa into the bloodstream where it is delivered and assimilated by the cells of the body. Waste materials and used food are carried back to the large intestine where they mix with roughage and water. The undigested materials are excreted from the body.

CIRCULATORY SYSTEM

The circulatory system is composed of the heart, arteries, veins, red blood cells, white blood cells, antibodies, thrombin, water, and plasma. A four-chambered heart, controlled by the pacemaker, rhythmically controls the pumping action by alternating contractions of the atria and ventricles. Blood circulates through the body in two loops—arteries carrying oxygenated blood away from the heart to all parts of the body, and veins returning deoxygenated blood to the heart and lungs to be reoxygenated. An auxiliary portion is the lymphatic system, which drains excess tissue fluids back into the circulatory system along with white blood cells that destroy harmful microorganisms.

SKELETAL SYSTEM

The skeleton is the basic framework of the human body and is made of connective tissue—bones and cartilage. Bone is living tissue with vitamins, collagen, and minerals to give it strength and hardness. The process by which the bones harden is called ossification. Bones are joined by cartilage at joints. Joints are classified as to the amount of movement they allow: stationary (skull), hinge (elbow), or ball and socket (hip).

MUSCULAR SYSTEM

Three human muscle types are **skeletal**, **cardiac**, and **smooth**. All muscle tissue exerts force when it contracts; therefore, muscles are responsible for all movement of the body, voluntary or involuntary. Energy for all movement is derived from an ample supply of mitochondria in the muscle cell. **ATP**, a high level energy carrier, is produced by the mitochondria for use by other cells and tissue parts during movement or exercise. Muscles are paired to accomplish full movement. Each contracting muscle will be paired with an antagonistic muscle, and tendons attach paired muscle groups to bones to complete the movement action. The skeletal muscles make up this grouping of muscles and are mainly voluntary.

Cardiac muscle is found only in the heart. The heart is the strongest muscle of the body. It is responsible for keeping the blood flowing through the circulatory system at a given pressure. The cardiac muscle is an involuntary muscle.

Smooth muscles are found in the linings of the body such as the digestive system and internal organs. They are generally involuntary muscles.

NERVOUS SYSTEM

The basic unit of the nervous system is the **neuron** (nerve cell). Its structure allows electrochemical signals to travel across synapses to activate muscles, glands, or organ tissue. The nervous system is divided into two parts. One part, the central nervous system, includes the brain, spinal cord, and the peripheral nervous system, which is a vast network of nerves that totally connect all parts of the body. Receptors located in sense organs and in the skin send information along the sensory neurons to the spinal cord and then to the brain where the information is chemically interpreted, causing a motor response.

RESPIRATORY SYSTEM

Respiration involves actions started by nerves stimulating muscles and bones to mechanically enlarge the respiratory cavity of the body. The breathing rate is controlled by nerves originating in the brain based on carbon dioxide content. The human nasal passages are adapted to clean, moisten, and warm the air before it enters the lungs by way of the trachea and bronchi. The lungs are made up of many tiny air sacs called alveoli that are found at the end of the bronchiole in clusters. The exchange of gases between the lungs and circulatory system occurs in the **alveoli**.

EXCRETORY SYSTEM

The excretory system is made up of the kidney, bladder, connecting tubes, and capillaries joined to the kidney. Urine is collected by structures in the kidney called nephrons. From the nephrons, the liquid wastes are collected and stored in the bladder. Urine leaves the body through the urethra.

ENDOCRINE SYSTEM

The endocrine system produces **hormones** which travel by way of the bloodstream to specific target cells. The manner in which the hormone acts on the target cells depends on whether it is a protein or steroid. Each will cause a feedback, which is one way to regulate hormones secreted into the body. Homeostasis depends on the actions of the nervous and endocrine systems. Organs, like the kidney, function based on endocrine stimulation.

INTEGUMENTARY SYSTEM

The integumentary covering of the body is called the skin. Skin consists of two layers, the **epidermis** and the **dermis**. Skin protects the body, rids the body of mineral salts and wastes, regulates body temperature, and picks up environmental signals. The skin is the bonding or holding agent that keeps the body intact and functioning. Also part of the integumentary system are the hair and nails.

IMMUNITY AND DISEASES

Important Lymphatic Organs – A defense against pathogens

Adenoids and Tonsils – Organs that filter out antigens (substances, such as viruses, which stimulate antibody synthesis) that enter the body via the upper-respiratory and gastrointestinal tracts.

Thymus – Produces cells that eventually become what are called peripheral T cells, which possess surface receptors for antigens.

Bone Marrow – Produces blood-forming stem cells.

Spleen – Has three functions:

(1) Can mount an immune response to antigens in the blood stream.

(2) Scavenges old red blood cells.

(3) Reserve site for making blood forming stem cells.

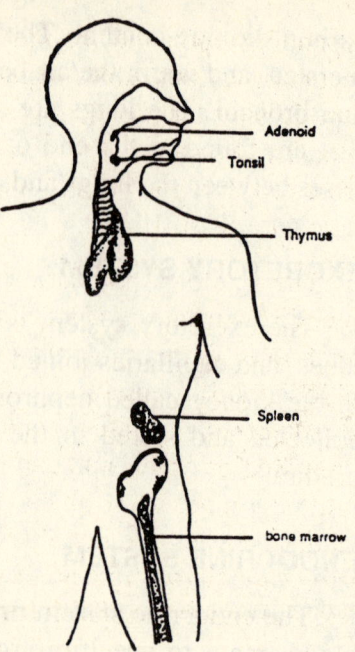

Disorders of the Immune System

Lupus – People develop immune reactions to their own nucleic acids.

Allergies – People become hypersensitive to environmental substances, called allergens.

AIDS (Acquired Immune Deficiency Syndrome) –

(1) People have reduced numbers of helper T cells.

(2) People may not be able to form antibodies against diseases like pneumonia.

ECOLOGY

Ecology can be defined as the study of interactions between groups of organisms and their environment. Groups are referred to as populations. Ecology is the basis of all life and all support systems of life. It is made up of chains—the food chain, carbon/oxygen chain, energy chain, and water chain. It is through the linking of the chains that life continues. Each organism has a specific **habitat** in an ecosystem carrying out a specific role (niche).

Ecology and **behavior** are closely linked. It is because of learned and innate behaviors that organisms are equipped to meet the ever-changing environmental demands and the interactions with other living organisms.

Life on earth exists in a thin layer known as the **biosphere**. The land, air, and water that make up the biosphere each have their own areas where life exists. The land, or terrestrial, biomes are determined mainly by climate. Water, or aquatic, biomes are classified as freshwater or marine, depending upon the amount of salt (salinity) in the water. Marine life occurs in various zones depending on depth, temperature, and light intensity. Freshwater abiotic factors are depth, turbidity, temperature, and light intensity. Estuaries are mixtures of salt and fresh water. They are more protected than the ocean, but more nutrient-rich than rivers and support a wide variety of species.

The size of a population at a given time is determined by its growth rate. Growth rate is determined by the factors of birth rate, immigration, death rate, and emigration. Other factors like natural disasters, availability of food, and disease also independently affect population. Environmental resistance to increased population often depends on population density. Crowding of organisms can reduce nutrients, spread disease, and interfere with reproduction. Competition for an environment's limited resources occurs between members of a population (intraspecific competition) and between different species in an area (interspecific competition). Competition also limits population size.

Humans are unique in their ability to modify the carrying capacity of their environment to be favorable for population growth. Most scientists agree that it is only a matter of time before humans will be unable to increase the earth's carrying capacity any further. At that time, the birth rate must decrease and the death rate must increase to balance population growth.

Natural resources are necessary for human survival and the making of necessary products. The natural resources are water, soil, air, wildlife, and forests. Problems that are now being faced are related to erosion, soil depletion, species extinction, deforestation, desertification, and water shortages. Efforts to reverse these problems and their environmental damages are found in the planned programs of reforestation, captive breeding, biological harvesting, or planned farming through efficient plowing and planting procedures.

Pollution is damaging both the ecosystems and living organisms. Air, water, soil, and food resources are being affected by pollution. Pollutants include automobile exhaust, fertilizers, pesticides, industrial wastes, radioactive wastes, and most of all, household wastes. The growing population and modern conveniences greatly contribute to this insurmountable problem. Government regulations, community efforts, and changes in the habits of industries and individuals are necessary to solve pollution problems.

☞ Drill: Biology

1. A hypothesis explains and relates
    (A) conclusions.   (C) theories.
    (B) facts.   (D) guesses.

2. Body cells, such as muscle or bone cells, reproduce by
    (A) osmosis.   (C) diffusion.
    (B) mitosis.   (D) meiosis.

3. According to the cell theory,
    (A) all living things are composed of cells.
    (B) the number of cells in an organism is set before birth.
    (C) cell activity is controlled by the nucleus.
    (D) eukaryotic cells have a cell wall for protection.

4. Which cellular component is responsible for the regulation of exchanges of substances between a cell and its environment?
    (A) The endoplasmic reticulum
    (B) The cell nucleus
    (C) The cytoplasm
    (D) The cell membrane

5. Maintaining a balanced internal control is called
    (A) homeostasis.   (C) diffusion.
    (B) osmosis.   (D) pump balance.

6. An organic molecule is any molecule
    (A) containing carbon.   (C) found in dead organisms.
    (B) containing phosphorus.   (D) that is naturally grown.

7. Mitosis results in
    (A) offspring cells exactly like the parent cell.
    (B) offspring cells different from the parent cell.
    (C) new combinations of mother cells.
    (D) a smaller number of cells.

8. Meiosis produces

    (A) gametes

    (B) body cells.

    (C) sex cells.

    (D) Both (A) and (C).

9. The RNA molecule that transcribes (receives information) from DNA and carries the information to code for a particular protein chain is called

    (A) hRNA.

    (B) mRNA.

    (C) tRNA.

    (D) sRNA.

10. The structural unit of photosynthesis is the

    (A) chloroplast.

    (B) stroma.

    (C) cristae.

    (D) mitochondrian.

11. The phenotype of an organism

    (A) represents its genetic composition.

    (B) is all the traits that are actually expressed.

    (C) cannot be observed.

    (D) is equivalent to the genotype.

12. The process by which DNA copies itself is called

    (A) transcription.

    (B) replication.

    (C) nucleotide.

    (D) translation.

13. The type of evolution that explains the differences between the polar bear and the brown bear is called

    (A) divergent evolution.

    (B) convergent evolution.

    (C) directional evolution.

    (D) disruptive evolution.

14. Monerans do not have a true nucleus or membrane-bound organelles; therefore they are called

    (A) eukaryotes.

    (B) cokaryotes.

    (C) prokaryotes.

    (D) nokaryotes.

15. An example of a fungus is

    (A) mushroom.   (C) penicillin.

    (B) bread mold.   (D) All of the above.

16. The circulatory system is responsible for all of the following except

    (A) the distribution of oxygen.

    (B) carrying nutrients.

    (C) removing urea from the body.

    (D) stopping the flow of blood after an injury.

17. The type of muscle tissue found in the walls of many internal organs is identified as

    (A) striated.   (C) skeletal.

    (B) smooth.   (D) cardiac.

18. The junction where an impulse travels from one neuron to another is called the

    (A) synapse.   (C) nerve message.

    (B) stimuli.   (D) affector node.

19. Infectious diseases are caused by

    (A) bacteria, fungi, and protozoans.

    (B) bacteria only.

    (C) fungi only.

    (D) protozoans only.

20. The biotic potential of a population is

    (A) the rate at which a population would reproduce if every individual lived.

    (B) the rate at which a population would die.

    (C) the rate at which a population would over-populate.

    (D) All of the above.

BIOLOGY REVIEW

ANSWER KEY

Drill: Biology

1.	(B)	6.	(A)	11.	(B)	16.	(C)
2.	(B)	7.	(A)	12.	(B)	17.	(B)
3.	(A)	8.	(D)	13.	(A)	18.	(A)
4.	(D)	9.	(B)	14.	(C)	19.	(A)
5.	(A)	10.	(A)	15.	(D)	20.	(A)

DETAILED EXPLANATIONS OF ANSWERS

Drill: Biology

1.   **(B)**   By definition a hypothesis is an educated guess based upon a set of facts. Further experiments, or more facts, are used to determine whether the hypothesis is true or false.

2.   **(B)**   Body cells reproduce by mitosis. Mitosis is a form of cell division whereby each of two daughter cells receives the same genetic material as the parent cell. Mitosis is responsible for growth, regeneration, and cell replacement in multicellular organisms.

3.   **(A)**   According to cell theory, all living things are composed of cells. Some cells are total living organisms, while other cells are the basic units of structure of other living things, such as tissues and organs.

4.   **(D)**   The cell membrane is the cellular component responsible for the regulation of exchanges of substances between a cell and its environment. The cell membrane is a double layer of lipids which surrounds the cell, and thus acts as a "gatekeeper." It controls what moves into and out of the cell.

5.   **(A)**   The definition of homeostasis is the ability to maintain the balance of internal control. Homeostasis accounts for all the movement into and out of the cell. While the cell can adjust to a wide range of environmental needs and wants, there is a limit to the extent of adjustment.

6.   **(A)**   By definition any molecule that contains carbon is organic. Molecules which do not contain carbon are referred to as inorganic.

7.   **(A)**   Mitosis is the process of cell division by which each of the two daughter nuclei receive the same chromosome, and thus genetic material, as the parent nucleus. Therefore, in mitosis the offspring cells are exactly like the parent cell.

8.   **(D)**   Meiosis consists of two successive cell divisions with only one duplication of chromosomes. Meiosis results in daughter cells with a

haploid number of chromosomes. This process occurs during the formation of gametes, or sex cells, and in spore formation.

9. **(B)** By definition, RNA that is transcribed from DNA and is carried out into the nucleus is called messenger RNA, or mRNA. Messenger RNA carries the information to code for a particular protein chain.

10. **(A)** Plant cells use a process called photosynthesis to absorb light energy from the sun, along with carbon dioxide and water, to manufacture carbohydrates. The chloroplast is the structural unit of the plant cell where photosynthesis process occurs.

11. **(B)** The phenotype is the outward appearance or expression of gene action. It is the hereditary makeup of an organism that we see or measure. The genetic makeup of the organism is defined as its genotype.

12. **(B)** When DNA unspirals, unzips, and separates, and two new strands of DNA are produced, it has copied itself, or in other words, it has replicated. Thus, this process is known as replication. When an RNA molecule copies the DNA template, the process is called transcription.

13. **(A)** Both the brown bear and the polar bear developed different traits to adapt to their environments. While the two are still bears, these traits separate them, such that a brown bear cannot survive in the same climate as the polar bear. The same species developing different traits in order to survive in different environments is an example of divergent evolution.

14. **(C)** Prokaryotes are cells that do not have a nuclear membrane or a membrane surrounding its organelles. Since monerans do not have a true nucleus or membrane-bound organelles, they are therefore prokaryotes.

15. **(D)** A fungus is a eukaryote, mainly multicellular and has structures that are rootlike, caps, of filaments and reproductive. They reproduce by asexual and sexual methods. The functions of the structures are digestive-like, respiration, and reproductive. Examples of fungus include mushrooms, bread mold, and penicillin, which is a specific type of bread mold.

16. **(C)** The main function of the circulatory system is to distribute oxygen and nutrients to all the organs. An auxiliary portion of the circulatory system, the lymphatic system, drains excess tissue fluids back into the circulatory system and carries white blood cells which destroy harmful

microorganisms. The circulatory system does not remove urea from the blood, the renal system does.

17. **(B)**   Of the three human muscles, striated, smooth, and cardiac, the smooth muscle is found in the linings of the body such as the digestive system and internal organs. Smooth muscles are generally involuntary muscles.

18. **(A)**   The basic unit of the nervous system in the neuron. The neuron allows electrochemical signals to travel across synapses to activate other neurons, muscles, glands, or organ tissue. Thus the junction where an electrochemical impulse travels from one neuron to another is called the synapse.

19. **(A)**   By definition, an infectious disease can be caused by bacteria, fungi, or protozoans. Infectious diseases are spread from one person to another.

20. **(A)**   The biotic potential of the population is the rate at which a population would reproduce if every individual lived. This is the maximum rate of reproduction. Factors such as natural disasters, availability of food, and disease reduce the reproduction rate.

III. CHEMISTRY REVIEW

INTRODUCTION TO CHEMISTRY

Chemistry is one of the oldest branches of science. The study of chemistry can be traced back as far as the Babylonian period. The field of chemistry seeks to transform one molecule into another to tailor or refine such chemicals as plastics, drugs, food technology, fuels, and dyes. Out of these raw materials, countless products required to meet our needs of daily living can be manufactured. Chemistry is defined as the study of the composition and behavior of elements in combination with each other.

Chemistry began to grow as knowledge spread about the atomic theory proposed by Thomas Dalton in 1807. He advocated that all matter is composed of small indivisible particles which he named **"atoms"** and described as little round balls. He believed these particles could combine with one another in many forms to produce all possible substances. It was remarkable how close his theory was to being correct considering the lack of experimental techniques available at that time. He was correct in stating that atoms join together to form complex substances. Dalton was incorrect in his assumption that all atoms are alike.

A great growth was experienced in the field of chemistry after the discovery of the group-forming pattern by D. L. Mendeleev in 1896. With the newly acquired information, a listing of all of the known chemical elements was placed on a chart in the order of their increasing atomic weights and number of energy levels. This charted information was the first periodic table.

As information in the field of chemistry grew, studies branched into the areas of organic chemistry and inorganic chemistry. **Organic chemistry** deals with the carbon compounds while inorganic chemistry deals with all the other elements and compounds.

The field of chemistry has vastly expanded based on the study of the atomic structure of **elements** and their behavior. Atomic structure is related to the properties and arrangement of elements in the periodic chart. The elements are classified into groups, periods, and families. It is from these groupings that matter is classified and its behavior is studied based on the ability of an element to combine or react with other elements. The study of the behavior of matter is based on properties of the elements and their ability to combine through the transfer and sharing of **electrons** to form compounds and other matter. This is commonly referred to as the process of bonding.

Every element has its own letter symbol. With these letter symbols and atomic numbers used together correctly, one can construct a formula. The formulas can be combined to show the composition of compounds, reactions between elements, chemical equilibrium, and oxidation and reaction rates. This is accomplished by the process of balancing equations.

It is necessary that everyone understands the basics of chemistry since our lives are centered around this subject. Also, how far we can progress is based on our ability to understand chemical concepts and apply them to our everyday life.

STRUCTURE OF MATTER

Matter is anything that occupies space and has mass. Matter resists changes in motion. It takes force to accelerate matter. There are four states of matter — **solid, liquid, gas**, and a fourth state called the **plasma** state. This state only exists at extremely high temperatures, such as those found on the sun. Plasma consists of high-energy, electrically charged particles. Plasma is created when a fluorescent lamp is turned on. Most of the matter in the universe is in the plasma state.

The structure of matter depends on the number and types of atoms that combine or react to form the matter. Matter is measured by the force with which gravity pulls on the mass toward the center of the earth. Matter can also be measured by its capacity for doing work, or the energy that it contains. This energy can be either activation, potential, or kinetic energy. **Activation energy** is that energy necessary to start a reaction. **Potential energy** is stored energy, while **kinetic energy** is the energy that matter possesses due to motion.

It can be shown experimentally that potential energy can be transformed into kinetic energy without any energy loss. This is an illustration of the **Law of Conservation of Matter or Energy**, which states that under ordinary conditions, matter or energy can neither be created nor destroyed but can be converted from one form to another.

One method of classifying matter is to find out if it is a substance or a **mixture** of substances. If a substance is composed of only one kind of atom, it is an element. If the substance is composed of two or more kinds of atoms, the matter can be a mixture or a compound, depending on how the atoms are joined as well as, how they react to each other under normal conditions.

Mixtures do not follow the law of definite proportions, which means that the two substances can be mixed in almost any proportion. Thus, the properties of a mixture vary with composition. If the substances in a mixture are spread out evenly, it is considered to be a homogeneous mixture. If the substances in a mixture are not spread out evenly, it is considered to be a heterogeneous mixture. Vinegar is a homogeneous mixture as the substances are spread evenly throughout. A homogenous mixture can be called a **solution**. Other solutions include seawater, soft drinks, tea, and milk.

A **suspension** is a heterogeneous mixture in which the particles are large enough to be seen by a microscope or the eye. These particles are affected by gravity and may settle out of the mixture. The particles can be temporarily suspended again by shaking. The mixing of water and pepper is an example of a suspension. Stirring up the bottom of a river will produce a suspension. With time, the action of gravity on the sand and soil will cause the particles to settle back to the bottom of the river.

If particles of a mixture are larger than those found in a solution, yet smaller than particles found in a suspension, the mixture is referred to as a **colloid**. Colloidal particles appear to be evenly distributed, and they will not settle out. The small size of the particles causes gravity to have less of an effect. Thus, there is less possibility of settling out caused by gravity.

All matter can be identified as having either **physical** or **chemical properties**. A **physical property** is a characteristic of matter that can be observed without changing the makeup of the substance. Boiling points and freezing points are examples of physical properties. Other physical properties are color, odor, hardness, density, and the ability to conduct heat or electricity. Physical properties can be used to separate mixtures. A mixture of iron and sand can be separated by a magnet. Iron is magnetic; sand is not. Thus, they can be separated with ease.

A physical change occurs when matter changes in size, shape, color, or state. A physical change does not change the chemical composition of a substance. When a glass breaks, the size and shape of the glass change, but the chemical makeup remains the same no matter in how many pieces the glass might exist.

A **chemical property** is a characteristic that determines how a substance reacts to form other substances. Chemical properties are determined by chemical changes. When a chemical change occurs, the substance seldom will, if ever, return to its original state. For example, iron will rust in the presence of water and oxygen. Rusting is an example of the chemical property known as corrosion. **Corrosion** occurs when metals are destroyed as they combine chemically with other substances.

In a chemical change, a substance is changed to a new substance which has different properties. Chemical changes may release thermal energy, light, or electricity. Some chemical changes need energy. All changes, chemical and physical, involve an energy change of some kind. Many compounds are formed from elements by chemical changes. In the same respect, many compounds are broken down by a chemical change.

When wood burns, heat is given off and a small amount of ashes is left. The substance of the wood has changed. Wood is made of carbon, hydrogen, and oxygen. When wood burns, the elements unite with atmospheric oxygen resulting in the formation of carbon dioxide and water. Also, carbon is the element of the ash substance that remains. This is a chemical change as energy is used to bring about the change and heat (an energy form) is given off; other compounds have been formed and the elements can never return to the state of wood (unless they again become integrated into the growth of a tree).

SIMPLE EQUATIONS SHOWING STRUCTURE OF MATTER

Matter can be identified not only by name, but by the way the element fits together with other elements to form matter. It is important for one to know if the proposed combination actually exists. For example, no chemist has ever been able to prepare hydrogen nitrate. Additionally, in making combinations, one must have a positive and a negative component. Generally speaking, metals are positive components, while nonmetals are negative components (with the exception of ammonia and radicals). When elements combine in varying proportions, prefixes are used for the naming of the compound and for formula writing. Mono- means one, bi- or di- means two, tri- means three, tetra- means four, pent- means five, and so on. Common suffixes and meanings are -ide (for naming monatomic anions), -ous (for the ion with the lower charge), and -ic (for the ion with the higher charge).

PERIODICITY OF ELEMENTS

The latter half of the 19th century brought about the updating of the **Periodic Law**: the properties of the elements are periodic functions of their atomic numbers. **Atomic numbers** represent the number of protons and also the number of electrons in a neutral atom. The electron structures of the atoms provide information showing the properties of the elements. Vertical columns represent the chemical families while horizontal columns represent the period or row. Proceeding across a row, the ability to hold electrons decreases. For example, lithium is the most metallic while fluorine is the least metallic. Study the **Periodic Table** which appears in the appendix of this book.

Some atoms tend to join with other atoms, while others will show no tendency to join with like atoms or like elements. The results of this tendency or attraction of the atoms involved in joining is called a chemical bond. When atoms combine to form new molecules, there is a shifting or transfer of valence electrons found in the outer shell of each atom. This usually results in the completing of outer shells by each atom. A more stable compound or form is achieved by the gaining, losing, or sharing of pairs of electrons. In forming chemical bonds, there is a release of energy or an absorption of energy. The bonds can be **ionic**, **covalent**, or **metallic**.

The kinetic model explains the forces between molecules and the energy they possess in three basic assumptions:

1. All matter is composed of extremely small particles.

2. The particles making up all matter are in constant motion.

3. When these particles collide with each other or with the walls of the container, there is no loss of energy.

BEHAVIOR OF MATTER

The behavior and classification of matter is dependent upon the electron attraction and interaction of electrons forming the matter. When atoms react with one another, it is the electrons that are involved in bonding, whether it be ionic or covalent.

All **reactions** need to receive a certain amount of energy before they can start. The amount of energy needed or received to start the chemical reaction is called activation energy. Some reactions require so little energy that it can be absorbed from the surroundings. This is called a spontaneous reaction which takes place with so little energy that it seems as if no energy was needed. A reaction that gives off energy is called an **exothermic reaction**. A reaction that absorbs energy is called an **endothermic reaction**. Combustion is a decomposition reaction. A catalyst can be added to a chemical reaction to control the reaction rate.

ACIDS

Acid properties are:

1. Water solutions of acids conduct electricity.

2. Acids will react actively with metals.

3. Acids will change blue litmus to pink.

4. Acids will react with bases resulting in both a loss of water and leaving a salt (neutralization).

5. Weak acid solutions taste sour.

6. Acids react with carbonates to release carbon dioxide.

BASES

Base properties are:

1. Bases are conductors of electricity in strong solutions.

2. Bases change red litmus paper blue.

3. Bases react with acids to neutralize each other and to form a salt and water.

4. Bases react with fats to form a class of compounds called soaps.

5. Bases feel slippery and strong solutions are caustic to the skin.

SALTS

A salt is an ionic compound containing positive ions other than hydrogen and a negative ion other than hydroxide ions. It is usually formed by neutralization when certain acids and bases are combined and form water and salt as the products.

A **formula** is a sort of road map, or a detailed description, of how something is organized or produced. A formula will not reveal the hidden structures of substances. In some reactions, no product is formed at completion, or reactants and products may react both ways. The reaction is said to have reached **equilibrium** when the rate of the forward reaction is equal to the rate of the reverse reaction. Factors that affect chemical equilibrium are changing concentration, temperature, and pressure.

Reactions that do not occur spontaneously can be forced by an external supply of energy. This is called an **electrolytic reaction**. Many chemicals and useful products are produced in this manner. Electroplating, electrolysis of water or salts, and the cathode functioning of a battery all are examples of electro-chemistry.

Simple electrochemical cells, in which electrons produced by the oxidation of zinc atoms are transferred through an external circuit into a copper solution, are called galvanic cells or voltaic cells. All electrochemical cells have the same general components: an oxidation half-cell, a reduction half-cell, and a means of separation so that the electrons produced by the oxidation reaction can be supplied through an external circuit into the reduction reaction. The voltage of the cell is the net voltage or potential voltage of two half-cell reactions. Lead storage cells contain a series of lead grids separated by an insulating material. The grids are alternately filled with spongy lead and lead dioxide that compose what are called dry cells. As long as the grids remain intact, the cell will deliver about two volts of electric current.

SOLUTIONS

Forces of attraction between particles produce a solution. One must mix a **solute** and a **solvent** to produce a solution. The particles making up each have certain forces of attraction that produce bonds. The bonds produced by these forces of attraction will determine the solubility of the solute. **Temperature** also affects the solubility of a solution. If the solution is made of gases, the solubility will be affected by **pressure**. Pressure does not affect the solubility of solids and liquids. If no more solute can be dissolved in the solvent, the solution is said to be saturated. In an unsaturated solution, more solute can be added to the solvent, while in a supersaturated solution, the solution is holding more dissolved solute than normal at that given temperature.

Matter exists as a substance or a mixture. If a substance is made of only one kind of atom, it is an element. If it is made of two or more kinds of atoms in a definite grouping, it is a compound. A compound always occurs in a definite composition based on the **Law of Definite Composition**, which states, "A compound is composed of two or more elements chemically combined in a definite ratio by weight." Compounds always have a fixed composition and will be classified as ionic or covalent depending on the type of bonding that occurs when the atoms are combined. The ability to combine is dependent upon the valence of the atom or element. An ionic compound contains ionic bonds—a force of attraction between oppositely charged ions. A covalent compound is a compound that is composed of covalent bonds—a bond in which the electrons are shared between atoms. When a compound is formed, the elements or atoms making up the compound lose their properties and take on the properties of the compound formed.

It is important to remember that the gain of electrons is reduction, and the loss of electrons is oxidation. The **oxidation number** of a bonded atom is the number of electrons gained, lost, or shared in a chemical reaction. The metal elements that lose electrons easily and become positive ions are placed high in the electromotive series.

The metal elements that lose electrons with greater difficulty are placed lower on the periodic chart. The energy required to remove electrons from metallic atoms can be assigned numeric values called electrode potentials. Binary compounds are named by changing the name of the element that has the negative oxidation number to end in "ide."

The **rate of the reaction** is defined as the quantity of product formed in some stated interval or the rate at which the reaction will take place. The rate of the chemical reaction can be defined in terms of the change in concentration of any species in the reaction with respect to time. The rate of the reaction can be determined by measuring how fast the product is formed after the reactants are mixed, or how many moles are formed per second. Also, an increase in temperature will increase frequency of molecular collision and increase rate of reaction. Activation energy is necessary to produce enough energy to break or weaken bonds before new bonds can be formed. Some reactions produce energy in the formation of new compounds or the products have more energy than the reactants (exothermic reactions) while other reactants need a greater amount of energy than the activation energy (endothermic reactions). The study of reaction rate factors is called **chemical kinetics**.

☞ Drill: Chemistry

1. The atomic theory states that all matter is composed of

   (A) carbon.   (B) atoms.   (C) molecules.   (D) compounds.

2. An element near the bottom of the periodic table would have

   (A) electrons in low energy levels only and low atomic weight.

   (B) electrons in high energy levels and low atomic weight.

   (C) electrons in high energy levels and high atomic weight.

   (D) one energy level and high atomic weight.

3. The sharing of electrons or transfer of electrons is called

    (A) bonding.   (C) boiling.

    (B) transference.   (D) kinetic flow.

4. Equilibrium can be expressed as the point at which

    (A) all the chemicals present stop reacting.

    (B) the chemical reactants are used up.

    (C) the products react together at the same rate as the reactants.

    (D) the reactants are chemically reacting at maximum velocity.

5. Mendeleev discovered there was a pattern when one started to ar-
    range elements based on their

    (A) name.   (C) particulate composition.

    (B) atomic weights.   (D) melting point.

6. Activation energy is

    (A) the energy necessary to cause motion.

    (B) the energy that measures an activity.

    (C) the energy necessary to start a reaction.

    (D) the energy needed to keep a reaction under control.

7. The Law of Conservation of Energy states

    (A) either energy or mass may be destroyed.

    (B) energy may neither be created nor destroyed.

    (C) energy can be converted to only one form.

    (D) energy may either be created or destroyed.

8. Chemical action may involve all of the following except

    (A) combining of atoms of the elements to form a molecule.

    (B) separation of the molecules in a mixture.

    (C) breaking down compounds into elements.

    (D) reacting a compound and an element to form an element and a
        new compound.

9. All chemical changes involve

   (A) a decreased stability in a solution.

   (B) an increased stability in a solution.

   (C) breaking of bonds and forming new ones.

   (D) formation of ion reactants.

10. Which of the following involves a chemical change?

    (A) The rusting of iron

    (B) The evaporation of water

    (C) The melting of ice

    (D) An ice cube floating in a glass of water

11. According to the kinetic model, matter is NOT made of

    (A) atoms.

    (B) atoms in constant motion.

    (C) particles moving without collisions.

    (D) atoms that do not lose energy during rebounding.

12. Under ideal gas circumstances, when atoms collide together

    (A) there is no energy loss.

    (B) there is an energy gain.

    (C) there is energy exchanged.

    (D) there is no source of comparison.

13. In a(n) _____ reaction, the products are lower in energy than the reactants.

    (A) exothermic   (C) isothermic

    (B) endothermic   (D) chemothermic

14. Combustion is a(n)

    (A) reaction where things are broken down to products with less potential energy.

    (B) reaction where things are combined together to form a more complex product.

    (C) endothermic reaction.

    (D) exothermic reaction.

15. A formula will

    (A) describe the organization and composition of a substance.

    (B) tell the rate of the chemical reaction.

    (C) show when equilibrium is reached.

    (D) describe the physical properties of each element involved.

16. In a chemical reaction at equilibrium, which of the following changes would always increase the concentration of the product?

    (A) Add a catalyst

    (B) Increase pressure

    (C) Increase temperature

    (D) Increase concentration of reactant

17. Which one of the following metals does not undergo corrosion and thus does not need to be electroplated?

    (A) Iron   (B) Copper   (C) Nickel   (D) Gold

18. A galvanic cell has a porous barrier between the half-cell on the left and the half-cell on the right in order to

    (A) halt the movement of ions.

    (B) preserve the strong acid nature of the solutions.

    (C) allow movement of ions for preserving neutrality.

    (D) measure the quantity of current.

19. The Law of Definite Composition is based on definite composition by

    (A) volume.   (C) specific weight.

    (B) density.   (D) temperature.

20. Chemical action may involve all of the following EXCEPT

    (A) combining of atoms of elements to form a molecule.

    (B) separation of the molecules in a mixture.

    (C) reacting a compound and an element to form a new compound and a new element.

    (D) combusting a compound to form a new substance.

CHEMISTRY REVIEW

ANSWER KEY

Drill: Chemistry

1.	(B)	6.	(C)	11.	(C)	16.	(D)
2.	(C)	7.	(B)	12.	(A)	17.	(D)
3.	(A)	8.	(B)	13.	(A)	18.	(C)
4.	(C)	9.	(C)	14.	(A)	19.	(C)
5.	(B)	10.	(A)	15.	(A)	20.	(B)

DETAILED EXPLANATIONS OF ANSWERS

Drill: Chemistry

1. **(B)** According to the atomic theory, proposed by Thomas Dalton, all matter is composed of small indivisible particles, or atoms.

2. **(C)** The periodic table is arranged so that the vertical columns represent the chemical families. Proceeding down a column, the atomic weight increases. The horizontal columns represent the period or row. Proceeding across a row, the ability to hold electrons decreases. Therefore, an element near the bottom of the periodic table would have electrons in high energy levels and high atomic weight.

3. **(A)** Bonding is defined as the sharing of electrons or transfer of electrons. Bonds can be ionic, covalent, or metallic.

4. **(C)** The equilibrium of a reaction occurs when the rate of forward reaction is equal to the rate of reverse reaction. Or stated in another way, the products react as the same rate as the reactants.

5. **(B)** The periodic table is based upon the observation of Mendeleev that a pattern develops when elements are arranged by their atomic weight.

6. **(C)** Reactions that do not occur spontaneously require an input of energy, referred to as activation energy. Activation energy is the energy necessary to start the reaction.

7. **(B)** The Law of Conservation of Energy states that energy may neither be created nor destroyed. Energy may be converted into many different forms. A separate law is used to describe mass. These laws hold under normal conditions.

8. **(B)** By definition, in a chemical action, a substance is changed to a new substance which has different properties. The act of separating molecules in a mixture is a physical change. The separated molecules do not have different properties.

9. **(C)** All chemical changes involve the breaking of bonds and formation of new ones. Changes that do not break bonds are known as physical changes.

10. **(A)** During the rusting of iron, the iron metal is changed to iron oxide. In the other examples, the water in the beginning of the process is still water at the end of the process, although it may be in a different state of matter, i.e., liquid or vapor.

11. **(C)** According to the kinetic model, matter is made of atoms. The atoms are in constant motion and the moving atoms do not lose energy during collisions. Thus, the particles must collide, so choice (C) does not fit the kinetic model.

12. **(A)** Under ideal conditions, gas particles collide together without any energy loss. This is an ideal situation that holds under most normal conditions of low pressure and temperature when the particles are far apart.

13. **(A)** When energy is released during a chemical reaction, the reaction is called exothermic. After an exothermic reaction, the products have a lower energy level than the reactants.

14. **(A)** Combustion is a reaction in which things are broken down into products with less potential energy than the reactants. An example of combustion is the burning of wood. A combustion reaction may be exothermic or endothermic.

15. **(A)** A chemical formula is a detailed description of how the elements are organized in the compound. The formula will not reveal the hidden structure of the substance, or tell how the substance will react.

16. **(D)** In a chemical reaction at equilibrium, changing the temperature, pressure, or amount of catalyst will result in a new equilibrium state, but may not increase the amount of product. The only way to increase the amount of product is to increase the concentration of reactants.

17. **(D)** Several metals do corrode; however, a few do not. Gold and platinum do not corrode. Therefore gold does not need to be electroplated.

18. **(C)** A galvanic cell, or battery, has a barrier between the half-cell on the right and the half-cell on the left, to allow the movement of ions for preserving neutrality. Sometimes this barrier is a salt bridge.

19. **(C)**   By definition, the Law of Definite Composition, is based on definite composition by specific weight. The Law of Definite Composition is used when describing solutions.

20. **(B)**   By definition, in a chemical action, a substance is changed to a new substance which has different properties. The act of separating molecules in a mixture is a physical change. The separated molecules do not have different properties.

IV. PHYSICS REVIEW

BASIC CONCEPTS OF PHYSICS

Physics is the study of matter, energy, and the relationships between the two phenomenal areas of study. Relationships between matter and energy have existed as long as the universe has existed, though man has not totally understood all relationships. Every time you lift a baby, push a wheelbarrow, or physically work out you are demonstrating or applying the principles of physics. Basic principles or concepts of physics may be divided into eight general areas: **mechanics** (motion and force), **energy**, **magnetism**, **sound**, **light**, **heat**, **waves**, and **electricity**.

A scientific law is usually constructed after a limited number of experiments or observations have been tried. It summarizes the order that is believed to exist within certain prescribed conditions and can only occasionally be modified or extended to fit new situations. A scientific law is a statement that (1) fits new facts, (2) uses inductive and deductive reasoning, and (3) successfully predicts what is found in nature.

LAW OF ACCELERATION

The amount of **acceleration** is directly proportional to the acting force and inversely proportional to mass:

$$F = ma$$

Drop a rock and it falls to the ground. The rock starts its fall from a resting position and gains speed as it falls. This gain in speed indicates the acceleration of the rock as it falls. **Gravity** (acting force) causes the rock to fall downward once it moves from its resting position. Remember, acceleration is equal to the change in speed divided by the time interval.

ARCHIMEDES' LAW OF BUOYANCY OR ARCHIMEDES' PRINCIPLE

The relationship between buoyancy and displaced liquid was discovered in ancient times by the Greek philosopher Archimedes in the third century B.C. It states that "an immersed object is pushed up by a force equal to the weight of the fluid it displaces." When an object is suspended in water, the pressures on opposite sides cancel each other. The pressure increases with depth, and the upward force on the bottom of the object will be greater than the downward forces on the top. Thus, an object is lighter in water than in air. This relationship, called **Archimedes' Principle**, is found to be true of both liquids and gases.

BERNOULLI'S LAW

"A moving stream of gas or liquid appears to exert less sideways pressure than if it were at rest." Bernoulli studied the relationship of fluid speed and pressure, and wondered how the fluid got the energy for extra speed. He discovered that the pressure in a fluid decreases as the speed of the fluid increases. This principle is a consequence of the conservation of energy and supports the concept of steady flow. If the flow speed is too great, then it becomes turbulent and follows changing, curling paths known as **eddies**. This same principle application also accounts for the flight of birds and aircraft abilities.

BOYLE'S LAW

If the temperature of a gas remains constant,

$$V = P$$

where P and V are the pressure and volume, respectively. When the density of the gas increases in a given space, the pressure is increased. The density of the gas also can be doubled by simply compressing the air to half its volume. This law is applied when one inflates a tire, balloon, or any other such object.

CHARLES' LAW

"The volume of gas increases as its temperature increases if the pressure stays the same." Charles' measurements suggested that the volume of a gas would become zero at a temperature of $-273°C$. Thus, this temperature is called absolute zero. This law applies only to gases. Scientists have found all gases become liquids or solids before they are cooled to the temperature of $-273°C$. Charles' Law is used to explain the kinetic theory as four factors are needed to describe a gas—the mass, the volume, the pressure, and the temperature. Charles' Law explains the increase in volume within tires after traveling long distances or traveling on hot days.

HOOKE'S LAW

The amount of stretch or compression, x, is directly proportional to the applied force F:

$$(x = F)$$

This law is used to explain the property of elasticity. Elasticity is the ability of a body to change shape when a force is applied and then return to its original shape when that force is removed. Steel is an example of an elastic material. It can be stretched and it can be compressed. Because of its strength and elastic properties, it is used to make springs for construction girders. Spring construction and functioning is also based on Hooke's Law.

NEWTON'S LAWS

Sir Isaac Newton's laws describe how forces change the motion of an object and are stated in the Three Laws of Motion.

The First Law (Law of Inertia) states that every body remains in a state of rest or uniform motion unless acted upon by forces from the outside.

The Second Law (Law of Constant Acceleration) states that the acceleration of an object increases as the amount of net force applied from outside the object increases. The formula of this law is:

Force = mass × acceleration

Force = mass × meter divided by seconds squared $\left(\dfrac{m}{s^2}\right) \dfrac{kg \times m}{s^2}$

Therefore, applying the formula to determine one newton is the force needed to give a mass of one kilogram an acceleration of one meter per second squared, or:

Force (1 newton) = mass 1(kg) × acceleration $\left(\dfrac{1m}{s^2}\right) 1\,N = 1\,kg \times 1\dfrac{m}{s^2}$

Newton's Third Law (Law of Conservation of Momentum) states that forces always come in pairs: to every action there is an equal and opposite reaction. When one object exerts a force on a second object, the second object exerts a force that would be equal to and opposite the force of the first object. Mass is a measure of the amount of inertia of a body. The product of mass and velocity is the amount of momentum an object possesses. A quantity that is not changed is said to be conserved. In a collision the total momentum of the colliding bodies is not changed. This is the Law of Conservation of Momentum or Newton's Third Law. Momentum is conserved provided there are no outside forces acting on a set of objects.

LAW OF CONSERVATION OF ENERGY

Energy cannot be created or destroyed; it changes form but does not cease to exist. This law explains how energy can change from one form to another. As energy can never be created or destroyed, the total energy of the universe remains the same.

LAW OF CONSERVATION OF MECHANICAL ENERGY

In the absence of friction, energy stored in a machine remains constant and work done by the machine is equal to the work done on it. The energy of an object enables it to do work. Mechanical energy is due to the position of something (potential energy) or the movement of something (kinetic energy). Mechanical energy is produced by a machine that is a device for multiplying forces or changing the directions of forces.

LAW OF GRAVITATION

Any two bodies in the universe attract each other with a force that is directly proportional to their masses and inversely proportional to the square of their distance apart:

$$F = Gm\frac{m}{d}$$

Forces are always applied at several different places under normal circumstances, not just at one point. This force on objects found on the Earth is what we call gravity.

LENZ'S LAW

The direction of an induced current is always such that its magnetic field opposes the operation that causes it. This law is the basis for the design of a generator and its ability to function by converting mechanical energy into electrical energy. A changing magnetic field induces an electric field. A generator uses the electromagnetic induction to convert mechanical energy into electrical energy.

OHM'S LAW

The current in a wire is proportional to the potential difference between the ends of the wire:

V (voltage) = I (current) × R (resistance)

Ohm's Law determines the strength of the current that flows into the circuit and the basis for the concept of electrical current. Any path along which electrons can flow is a circuit. A complete circuit is needed to maintain a continuous electron flow.

LAW OF REFLECTION

The angle of the incidence equals the angle of reflection. This law explains how a wave changes its direction or how it is reflected back. When light is reflected from a flat surface or plane such as a mirror, the incoming light ray (incident ray) and the reflected ray of light (reflected ray) are measured with respect to a line perpendicular to the flat surface. When a light ray strikes a flat surface, the angle of incidence always equals the angle of reflection. Sunlight is an example showing this law.

LAW OF REFRACTION

Light rays passing through a transparent substance are bent, or refracted; the thicker the substance is, the farther apart its actual and apparent locations will be. The law also states that the incident ray and the refracted ray both lie on one plane.

A theory applies to a broad range of phenomena and is applied to a small aspect of nature. A theory attempts to explain the "how's" and "why's" of science. It is in the establishing and testing of theories that discoveries are made. The primary purpose of a theory is to enable us to see a natural phenomenon as a part of a simple, unified whole as it,

1. correlates many facts in a single concept or reasonable assumption;

2. suggests or accommodates new ideas;

3. stimulates research;

4. is useful in solving long-range problems; and

5. makes predictions.

Albert Einstein developed the **Theory of Relativity**, which is often referred to as Einstein's Theory. The relativity theory is based on mathematical formulas and calculations dealing with gravitation, mass, motion, space, and time. Basic principles of this theory are:

1. Motion in a straight line will have constant velocity. All other motion is judged from this frame of reference.

2.   The speed of light in empty space will always have the same value regardless of the motion of the source or the motion of the observer.

Before a hypothesis can be scientific, it must conform to the scientific rule of being testable. Then, one must test by following the scientific method:

1.   recognize the problem;

2.   formulate your hypothesis;

3.   complete related research;

4.   perform test-to-test prediction;

5.   collect data while performing the test;

6.   summarize research and test results in an orderly manner; and

7.   draw conclusions.

MATTER, MASS, AND DENSITY

Matter is found in everything. Everything is made of atoms. All matter, living or nonliving, is a combination of elements (atoms). Matter is anything that has mass and occupies space. Matter can exist in four states dependent upon its Brownian Motion: (1) solid, (2) liquid, (3) gas, or (4) plasma, which makes up the greatest quantity of matter.

Mass is the quantity of matter in a body that exhibits a response to any effort (energy or movement) made to start it, stop it, or change in any way its state of motion. Mass is measured by the amount of inertia an object has. The greater the mass, the greater the force necessary to change its state of motion. Mass is often confused with weight. Weight is a specific numerical measurement or unit, while mass is anything that takes up space and has weight.

Density is the measure of compactness of a material. It being as light as a feather or heavy as a rock is dependent upon its density. Density is not mass nor is it volume. Density cannot be equated to size in all cases; rather, it is the compactness of the mass per unit of volume. Both the mass of the atoms making up the substance or material and the spacing between the atoms determine the density of materials or state of materials.

MOTION

Motion is all around us. Our bodies, no matter how still we think we are, are in a constant state of motion. Motion is easy to see but almost impossible to describe or define. Therefore, when speaking of motion, one must address it as relative to an object rate.

VELOCITY

Velocity is the speed in a given direction. Speed and velocity can be used interchangeably if the description is asking for how fast a movement occurs in a certain direction. Velocity can be described as constant or changing. A constant velocity requires that both the speed stay the same and direction not be changed or altered. Motion at constant velocity is motion in a straight line at a constant speed. A body may be moving at a constant speed along a curved path or the speed may vary along a constant path. The latter is referred to as changing velocity.

ACCELERATION

Acceleration is a rate that applies to a decreasing speed (deceleration) as well as an increasing speed (acceleration). Acceleration applies to a change in direction as well as the change in speed. Pressing the gas pedal of a car will accelerate the speed of the car; pressing the brakes will retard the speed, or decelerate the car. Like velocity, acceleration is directional.

MOMENTUM

Momentum is the mass of an object multiplied by its velocity

$$\text{momentum} = \text{mass} \times \text{velocity} = m \times v.$$

If the momentum of an object changes, either the mass or the velocity or both change. Thus, acceleration occurs.

Gravity causes a rock to fall downward once it has been dropped. This action on movement is referred to as gravitational motion. If there were no gravitational action, the motion would be called free fall. The time that it takes an object to fall from the beginning of the fall to the point of rest is called elapsed time. The concept of gravity effects was first credited to Isaac Newton after he was hit on the head with an apple that fell from a tree he was sitting beneath.

SPEED

Speed is a measure of how fast something is moving or the rate at which a distance is being covered. Speed is calculated as the distance covered divided by the unit of time. Speed is the rate of change of the position of an object. The average speed describes the motion of objects even if they are not moving at a constant speed. This average speed can be calculated by the total distance traveled divided by the total time taken for travel.

INERTIA

Inertia is the resistance an object has to a change in its state of motion. Inertia can be measured by its mass depending upon the amount and type of matter in it. The idea of inertia while in motion is called momentum in reference to moving objects.

FORCE

Force is the push or pull one body exerts on another body. "For every action, there is an equal and opposite reaction" is another way of describing force. Force is the product of acceleration. The combination of all the forces that act on an object is called the net force. When a body is at rest, a force is at work. The fact that the body is at rest rather than accelerating shows another force at work. Force is necessary to maintain balance and reach net force zero. For a book to be at rest on a table, the sum of the forces acting upon the book must equal zero.

The process of determining the components of a vector is called resolution. A person pushes a lawn mower. This in turn applies force against the ground causing the lawn mower to roll forward. In this example, the vector is a combination of two components. Any vector can be represented by a pair of components that are at right angles to each other.

Friction is the name given to the force that acts between materials that are moving past each other. Friction is a result that arises from irregularities in the surfaces of sliding objects. If no friction were present, a moving object would need no force whatever for its motion to continue. Even for a surface that appears to be smooth, there are microscopic irregularities causing friction to occur.

PARALLEL

When the forces on two opposite sides are equal, this is said to be a parallel force. Thus, this produces, considering all forces are equal, an action-reaction situation.

ENERGY

Energy is the ability of an object to cause change; energy is the ability to do work. Energy is produced when forces are at work. Objects in motion cause change. The greater the speed, the greater the change that occurs. If you experience an energy surge, then you can work more or move faster. Objects as well as people can have energy. Energy can exist in various forms and can change from one form to another form. This energy and its changes can be measured. The unit of measurement of energy is called a joule.

Energy exists in three states: potential, kinetic, and activation energies. An object possessing energy because of its motion has kinetic energy. The energy that an object has as the result of its position or condition is called potential energy. The energy necessary to transfer or convert potential energy into kinetic energy is called activation energy.

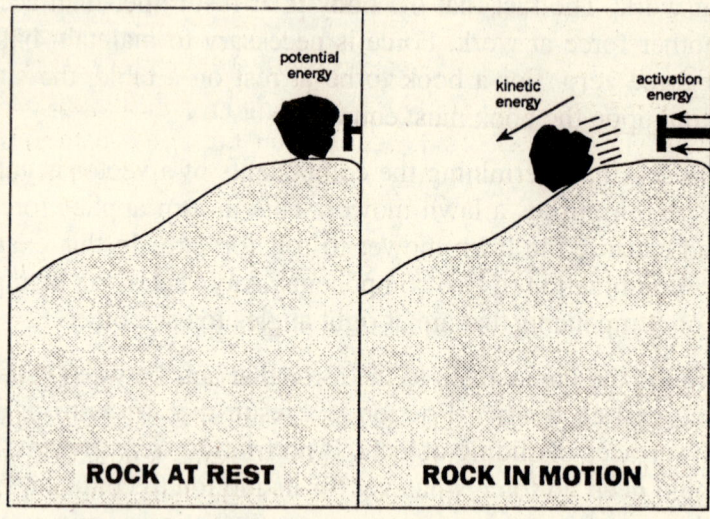

ROCK AT REST   ROCK IN MOTION

Study the diagram to see that a rock at rest is considered to be potential energy. If a force is used to set that rock in motion, that force would be the activation energy. The rock rolling down the hill until it reaches a point of rest (potential energy) is considered kinetic energy.

Other forms of energy are a result of conditions or combinations of the states of energy. When kinetic and potential energy of lifting, bending, and stretching are grouped together, they are called mechanical energy. The total energy of the particles that make up an object or body is thermal energy. A raised weight possesses potential energy called gravitational potential energy. When it is released, it will return to its former level. This is the principle applied to the functioning of a spring or the stretching of an object.

Work is the transfer of energy as the result of motion. Most people think of work as an amount of effort exerted. However, if you attempted to move a boulder without any success, you expended energy but no work was accomplished. Work is a derived unit; it may be expressed as any force unit times any distance unit. The only thing that matters in calculating work is the distance moved in the direction of the force.

A **machine** is any device by which energy can be transferred from one place to another or one form to another. Think back to the diagram of the rock rolling down the hill. This is an example of a machine. Often, when we think of a machine or using a machine, some outside agent—a motor, a battery, your muscles—does the work on the machine. The machine then delivers work to something on which it acts.

The principle of conservation of mechanical energy deals with the functioning of a machine. This principle dictates how two kinds of work are related. "In the absence of other forces that dissipate energy, the total mechanical energy of a system remains constant." So long as any energy that is stored within a machine remains constant, and in the absence of friction, the work done by the machine is exactly equal to the work done on it.

Power is the rate of doing work per unit of time. This is calculated by:

P (power) $= W$ (work) divided by t (time).

Suppose two workers are pushing identical boxes up an inclined plane. One pushes his box up the plane in 20 seconds while the other pushes his box up the plane in 40 seconds. Both do the same amount of work. The difference is the rate of time in which the work is done. The unit for power is watt. One watt is one joule of work per second.

HEAT

Heat is a necessity of life. It is also a very valuable tool that cooks our food, frees metals from ores, and creates usable products (to mention a few of its uses). Heat is a form of energy and that energy is created by the motion of the molecules making up an object. Heat is the transfer of energy from an object of high temperature to one of lower temperature.

Heat has several properties: it is a conductor, it can be measured, it can be transferred or radiated, and it can travel by convection. Nearly all materials will either expand or contract when heat is added or taken away. When the amount of heat within an object or around an object varies, that object will vary. There is an exact point at which the variation will occur. We call this the specific heat. The specific heat of any substance is defined as the quantity of heat required to raise the temperature of a unit of mass of that substance by one degree. For instance, a gram of water requires one calorie of energy to raise the temperature 1°C.

Heat is commonly measured in calories or kilocalories, although scientifically the SI or joule is preferred. SI is the abbreviation of Le Système International d'Unites (French), which is the international system of measurement. The term applied here would be the degree. The degree is a measure of temperature. Temperature is a measure of the average kinetic energy of the particles in a body. The degree might be stated in terms of Fahrenheit (F), Kelvin (K), or Celsius (C).

Fahrenheit is based on the freezing temperature of a body or substance being zero degrees. To totally remove all possible internal heat within a body or substance, one must reduce the temperature to −273 degrees. This point is considered to be zero on the Kelvin scale and is called absolute zero. The Fahrenheit scale measures the freezing point at 32°F. To convert from the Fahrenheit scale to the Celsius scale use the formula:

$$(degrees) \ F = 9/5 \ (degrees) \ C + 32$$

unless the temperature is below zero on either scale. In that case, you must place a minus sign in front of its number in the equation.

Heat and work are similar when discussing the transfer of energy. Heat is transferred by convection, conduction, or radiation. As work is accomplished, heat is transferred. One way that heat passes from one object to another is by conduction. Not all objects will conduct heat at the same rate; therefore, they are considered poor heat conductors. A very poor conductor of heat is called an **insulator**.

Most gases and liquids are poor **conductors**. They can transfer heat by convection, the mass movement of the heated gas or liquid. This is accomplished by spurring, or sporadic movement of molecules in the mass that pass heat when they bump together. Another method of heat transfer is called radiation. Unlike conduction and convection, radiation does not require direct contact between bodies or masses. Almost all of the energy that comes to Earth is by radiation from the sun. The amount of heat that a body can radiate depends not only on its temperature but on the nature of its surface. Dark, rough surfaces tend to send out more heat than smooth, light-colored surfaces.

THERMODYNAMICS

The first law of thermodynamics states that there is a constant amount of energy in the universe. If heat is added to a system, and work is done, then the change in energy of that particular system is equal to the heat added to the system, q, minus the work done by the system, w. Mathematically, this is

$$\Delta E = q - w.$$

The international unit of energy (and hence, heat and work) is the Joule, defined as the force of one Newton acting through the distance of one meter. Energy, potential or kinetic, can be measured in Joules. This can be energy stored by position, chemical bonds, or locked in the nucleus of an atom. It can also be energy due to motion, heat, or electromagnetic radiation. Other units of energy are listed in the table below:

UNIT	1 JOULE = _____ of these units
erg	10^7
foot–pound	0.73756
foot–poundal	23.730
calorie (*very* outdated)	0.2388
electron volt	6.2419×10^{18}

Temperature scales have been mentioned in an earlier section. As a quick review, the two main scales in use are Celsius (formerly centigrade) and Kelvin. On the Celsius scale, water freezes at 0° and boils at 100°. The Kelvin scale starts at absolute zero; hence, it has no negative temperatures. Water freezes at 273 on this scale and boils at 373. When a temperature is given followed by the degree symbol but the scale is not shown, it is presumed to be Celsius (e.g., 25°). Temperature in Celsius can be converted to Kelvin by adding 273.

Thermal energy (heat) can be transferred from one body to another in three ways:

1) **Conduction** — This occurs when one body is placed in direct contact with another, and heat flows from one to the other. An example of conduction might be a block of metal at 85° placed on top of another block of metal at 0°. The heat will flow by conduction from the warmer block to the colder one.

2) **Convection** — This occurs when a warm body heats the air surrounding it, and the air currents carry the heat to other bodies. A hot stove warms a room chiefly by convection.

3) **Radiation** — A warm body can emit photons of infrared wavelengths. These can travel through space and warm the bodies they strike. Heat travels from the sun through space to the earth by radiation.

When a substance is heated, its molecules move further apart, causing the material to expand. This is quite obvious with gases, as has been covered in an earlier section, and occurs to a much smaller extent in liquids and solids. The increase in volume can be calculated using the coefficient of volume expansion, ex_V, which is unique for each substance. For example, the ex_V for ethyl alcohol is 11×10^{-4} / °C. If 40.0 liters of ethyl alcohol are at 0°, and heated to 55°, what will its new volume be? First the change in temperature must be determined; $55 - 0 = 55°$. This is multipled by the ex_V and the original volume;

$$55 \times (11 \times 10^{-4}) \times 40.0 = 2.42 \text{ liters.}$$

This is added to the original volume to give the new volume of 42.4 liters. This is a change of only 6%, compared to a change of 20% had this been 40 liters of gas going from 0 to 55°. For solids, the change in volume is even less with temperature. The ex_V for ice is

$$0.5 \times 10^{-4} \text{ / °C.}$$

If 4,000 cm³ of ice are at −12° and cooled to −190°, what is its new volume? First, the temperature change is determined;

$$(-12) - (-190) = 178°.$$

The change in temperature is again multiplied by the ex_V and original volume;

$$(178) \times (0.5 \times 10^{-4}) \times (4,000) = 35.6 \text{ cm}^3.$$

This is subtracted from the original volume to give a new volume of 3,964.4 cm³. If the solids are greatly larger by one axis than any of the others (e.g., a wire), then a coefficient of linear expansion, ex_1, is used in the same manner as the ex_V to determine the change in length, rather than volume. The ex_1 for silver is 2.0×10^{-5}. If a silver needle is 15.0 cm long at 25°, how long will it be at 125°? The change in temperature is $125 - 25 = 100°$. We multiply the change in temperature by the ex_1 and the original length;

$$(100) \times (2.0 \times 10^{-5}) \times (15) = 0.03 \text{ cm.}$$

Adding this to the original length gives a new length of 15.03 cm.

Recall in a previous section, it was shown that energy must be absorbed by a substance to convert it from a solid to a liquid, and a liquid to a solid. There was an absorption of energy, but no change in temperature, only a change of state. The heat of fusion is the energy required to convert a certain amount of substance from the solid to the liquid state. For example, the heat of fusion for water is 6.03 kJ / mole. How much energy is required to melt 25.0 moles of ice at 0° to water at 0°? A simple multiplication tells us $6.03 \times 25.0 = 151$kJ, or 151,000 Joules are needed to do this.

Note that the units were in kJoules / mole. Sometimes they can be given in kJ / gram, kJ /kg, etc. Be on the watch for this. The energy required to convert a certain amount of a substance from the liquid to the gaseous state is the heat of vaporization. For example, the heat of vaporization of water is 40.6 kJ / mole. How much energy is required to change 29.9 grams of water at 100° to steam at 100°? First, we must convert grams to moles; $29.9 / 18 = 1.66$ moles.

$$1.66 \times 40.6 = 67.4 \text{ kJ,}$$

or 67,400 Joules are required.

PROBLEM

a) If 28.7 liters of mercury are heated from −15° to 25°, what is its new volume? The ex_V for mercury is 1.8×10^{-4} / °C.

b) An iron nail is 15.0000 cm long at 35°. How long will it be at −200°? The ex_1 for iron is 1.2×10^{-5}.

c) How much energy is required to melt 29.8 *grams* of mercury? The heat of fusion is 2.34 kJ / mole, and the atomic weight is 200 Daltons.

d) How much energy must be lost by 56.0 *moles* of mercury vapor to condense to liquid mercury? The heat of vaporization is 56.5 kJ / mole.

SOLUTION

a) 28.9 liters   c) 348 Joules

b) 14.9577 cm   d) 3,160 kJoules

WAVES

A British physicist, Edward Victor Appleton, received a Nobel Prize in 1947 for his work dealing with waves. His discoveries led to defining an important region of the atmosphere called the "**ionosphere**." It was established that there were definite layers that would reflect and absorb various radio waves, and thus, the Appleton layers were established. These layers reflect and absorb only the long radio waves used in ordinary radio broadcasts. The shorter waves, used for television broadcasting, pass through, and that is why televisions have a limited range and must use satellite relay stations. The ionosphere is the strongest at the end of the day, after the day-long effect of the sun's radiation, and weakens by dawn because many ions and electrons have recombined. Storms on the sun, intensifying the streams of particles and high-energy radiation sent to the Earth, cause the ionized layers to strengthen and thicken. The regions above the ionosphere also flare up into aurora displays.

A **wave** is a wiggle in space and time that can extend from one place to another. Light and sound are both forms of energy that move through space as waves. If this wiggle only occurs in time, it is called a vibration. A wave is measured in wavelengths. The high points are called the crests, the low points the troughs, and the distance from the midpoint to the crest is the amplitude. How frequently a vibration occurs is described by its frequency. The time necessary for the wave to complete one cycle is called a period.

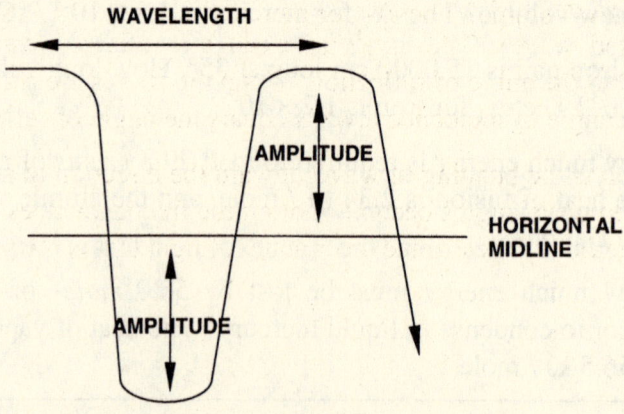

MICROWAVES

Microwaves, having wavelengths shorter than radio waves, are used in communications and to cook food.

LIGHT

The only thing that we can really see is light. Most objects are made visible by the light they reflect from such light sources. Scientists agree that light has a dual nature—part particle and part wave. The particles may be measured as photons. The waves are measured by the distance the light travels in one year. This is called a light year. Light is defined as the only visible portion of the electromagnetic spectrum and is produced by vibrating electrically charged atoms that have the ability to absorb energy and emit it as light. The transfer of energy by electromagnetic waves is called radiation.

PROPERTIES

The properties of light are reflection, refraction, diffraction, and interference. The amount of the property being demonstrated depends on the amount of light, angle of the light ray, object composition, and density. Material that allows all the light to pass through is called transparent. Material that blocks the light is called opaque.

Quantum is an elemental unit that describes the smallest amount of anything. One quantum of light energy is called a photon. In the micro-world, one quantum of anything is an atom. The Quantum Theory is the study of the behavior of the basic elemental form of anything. This can be adapted to all branches of science to explain behavior of matter.

Reflection occurs when a wave bounces off an object. Waves that strike the object are called incident waves, while waves that bounce off are called reflected waves. The angle between the reflected wave and the normal is called the angle of reflection. When the waves are reflected from a surface, the angle of incidence always equals the angle of reflection.

Refraction is the bending of waves toward the direction of slower wave velocity. When wavelengths become shorter, the frequency does not change. Thus, the material will determine the amount of light that is refracted.

DIFFRACTION

The bending of light around the edge of the object blocking its path is called diffraction. The effects of diffraction occur when waves pass either through an opening or around an object that blocks their path.

Light travels in waves that are **transverse**. This is called **polarization**. Other waves are longitudinal as they travel. Polarized light waves are waves that travel on one plane. Light vibrating parallel to a molecule is absorbed. The light vibrating at right angles to the rows passes through. This concept is used in the sunglass industry—sunglass lenses are designed to reduce glare.

Illumination is the process of making an object bright by increasing the amount of light per unit of area of a surface.

X-rays are electromagnetic waves with the shortest wavelength and the highest amount of energy. Electrically charged particles are filled with kinetic energy that is changed to radiation when these rays crash into other matter.

Lasers are a source of light that produces a bright and narrow beam of light of one color length that is coherent. Coherent light has the troughs and crests of the light lined up together. Lasers convert one form of energy into light energy. The laser is very bright but extremely inefficient as a light source. They are used extensively by surveyors, welders, surgeons, and by code interpreters for barcoding, as a method of ringing up sales at the supermarket.

SOUND

Sound travels about four and one-half times faster in seawater than in air. Its speed is affected by temperature, salinity, and pressure; an increase in any of these results in an increase in the speed of sound.

Sound energy does not travel in straight lines in the ocean because of density differences in water. It is refracted, or bent, differently at different depths, scattered by suspended material or marine organisms, reflected and scattered by the surface and bottom, and attenuated by the water through which it travels.

Ambient noise refers to any noise or sound produced by the environment or living creatures or organisms.

There are many varieties of sounds that are produced to be captured by the ear and interpreted by the brain. The brain easily distinguishes one sound from another, yet sound is only a longitudinal wave, a rhythmic disturbance of the air that carries energy. Sound waves are compression waves produced by vibrating matter. Ultrasound is used extensively in medical treatment. One way is through picturing a fetus in the womb without any danger to the fetus or the mother.

When any **frequency** of forced vibrations on an object matches the natural frequency of the object, the measure of the sound increases. The use of tuning forks adjusted to the same frequency and spaced a meter apart is the most common way to demonstrate resonance.

ELECTRICITY

An electrical charge resting on an object is called **static electricity**. If this static electricity is placed in motion, it becomes an **electrical current**. It is the electrical current that we use in most electrical appliances. This same static electricity can be produced by rubbing a hard rubber rod or sealing wax with a piece of fur or flannel. The same result can also be accomplished by rubbing a glass rod with a piece of silk.

Electricity can be carried by matter that is a conductor. Sometimes this is accomplished by a spark, which is a static discharge, or a transfer of static electricity. Materials that are poor conductors, such as wood, plastic, rubber, or glass, are used as insulators or grounds which allow an object to lose its charge in a given direction.

A flow of electrons or charged particles through a conductor is called an electric current. This is demonstrated by use of an electroscope.

Electrical circuits function very efficiently within homes. Most circuits are either alternating current (AC) or direct current (DC). Electricity can be supplied to a water heater to heat water, or through wiring and a bulb to produce artificial light. The energy is carried by means of electrical current from a power plant. One common **electrical circuit** is the series circuit. A path is formed by electric conductors in the form of wire to carry the current. The series circuit has only one path for the current so the current will be the same through every part.

Another circuit is the parallel circuit, in which there are two or more separate branches for the current to flow. This is the type of circuit used in string lights for a Christmas tree such that when one light goes out, the rest of the lights will stay on. Also, this type of wiring pattern is used for the outlets in our homes. It is not necessary for all the outlets to be in use at all times for electricity to be available at the flip of a switch.

One electronic device that is commonly used is the battery. A battery acts like a pump forcing electrons through a conductor. There are two types of batteries: wet cell battery and dry cell battery. A wet cell battery contains two different metals in a solution containing an electrode. The car battery is an example of the wet cell battery. The dry cell battery contains a carbon rod set in the middle of a zinc holder. A moist paste sets up a chemical reaction that causes electrons to be released.

MAGNETISM

Magnetism is the ability to attract iron and certain other metals that have a molecular structure similar to iron. Magnetism is related to electricity in that it travels in currents. Magnets exert a force on other magnets just like an electrical charge. They can attract or repel each other without touching because of their electrical charges. The strength of their interaction depends on the distance of separation of the two magnets.

Magnetism was explained by Albert Einstein in 1905 in his theory of special relativity when he showed that a magnetic field is a by-product of the electric field. Charges in motion have associated with them both an electric and a magnetic field. A **magnetic field** is produced by the motion of the electric charge.

A **voltmeter** is a calibrated device used to measure the electric potential. This electrical current produces a magnetic field. The same principal construction is used in the making of an electric motor. The principal difference is that the current is made to change direction every time the coil makes a half revolution.

Speakers used in car radios, home stereos, and loudspeaker systems belong in the grouping of electromagnets. A speaker consists of a coil of thin wire that goes between the poles of a magnet. The coil is attached to a cone-shaped piece of stiff paper that converts the electrical current into sound.

☞ Drill: Physics

1. Acceleration is defined as the

    (A) change in position divided by the time needed to make that change.

    (B) change in velocity divided by the time needed to make that change.

(C) time it takes to move from one speed to another speed.

(D) time it takes to move from one place to another place.

2. Archimedes' Principle says that an object is buoyed up by a force that is equal to

(A) the weight of the fluid displaced.

(B) the volume of the fluid displaced.

(C) the mass of the fluid displaced.

(D) the mass of the object.

3. Bernoulli's Principle states that

(A) internal fluid pressure decreases as fluid speed increases.

(B) as the volume of a gas increases at constant temperature, the pressure decreases.

(C) an object in air is buoyed up by a force equal to the weight of the air displaced.

(D) internal fluid pressure increases as fluid speed increases.

4. The ability of a body to change shapes when a force is applied and then return to its original shape when that force is removed is

(A) elasticity.   (C) springforce.

(B) compression.   (D) girders.

5. Energy can

(A) not be created.   (C) be changed in form.

(B) not be destroyed.   (D) All of the above.

6. Friction acts parallel to the surfaces which are sliding over one another and in the

(A) same direction as the motion.

(B) opposite direction of the motion.

(C) contact line and circular motion.

(D) direction of the sliding force.

7. When refraction occurs, part of a wave

    (A) is bent more than another part.

    (B) slows down before another part.

    (C) is pushed to one side.

    (D) is closer together than it appears.

8. When light is refracted,

    (A) the rays all lie on different planes.

    (B) the rays lie on one plane.

    (C) the rays lie on one thickness.

    (D) the rays lie behind the plane.

9. The greater the mass of an object, the greater the force necessary

    (A) to change its position.

    (B) to change its force.

    (C) to change its state of motion.

    (D) to change its shape.

10. The idea of inertia while in motion is called

    (A) momentum in reference to moving objects.

    (B) inertia frame of reference.

    (C) measurement of momentum.

    (D) momentum in reference to nonmoving objects.

11. The idea of parallel force can be applied to circuits. A parallel circuit would

    (A) have equal currents.

    (B) have action-reaction forces producing static electricity.

    (C) have a constant supply of electricity.

    (D) have an on-off supply of electricity depending on all forces being constant.

12. The two factors which determine the amount of work done are

   (A) the magnitude of the force exerted and the weight of the object moved.

   (B) the distance of the object moved in the time required.

   (C) the displacement of the object and the magnitude of the force in the direction of the displacement.

   (D) the magnitude of the force in the direction of the displacement and the time required.

13. Machines may be used

   (A) to divide the force.

   (B) to multiply speed.

   (C) to divide force and speed simultaneously.

   (D) to keep the direction of the force constant.

14. The principle of conservation of mechanical energy dictates how two kinds of work are related. They are

   (A) friction and mechanical energy.

   (B) absence of friction and work by a machine.

   (C) speed and type of machine.

   (D) mass and speed of machine.

15. Heat transfer occurs

   (A) from an object of a lower temperature to one of higher temperature.

   (B) from an object of a higher temperature to one of a lower temperature.

   (C) when electrons bump into each other.

   (D) when the temperature rises.

16. Specific heat is related to the amount of heat

   (A) a specific object has.

   (B) one molecule contains.

(C) transferred by one molecule.

(D) needed to change the temperature of one gram of a substance by one degree Celsius.

17. The wiggle formed by a wave in time is called the

(A) amplitude.   (C) vibration.

(B) frequency   (D) interference.

18. Diffraction

(A) occurs only for radio waves.

(B) occurs only for light.

(C) occurs only for X-rays.

(D) can occur for any wave.

19. Light traveling in waves that are transverse and travel on one plane is called

(A) diffracted light.   (C) polarized light.

(B) refracted light.   (D) distracting light.

20. The use of the tuning forks demonstrates

(A) amplitude.   (C) resonance.

(B) frequency.   (D) pitch.

PHYSICS REVIEW

ANSWER KEY

Drill: Physics

1.	(B)	6.	(B)	11.	(C)	16.	(D)
2.	(A)	7.	(B)	12.	(C)	17.	(C)
3.	(A)	8.	(B)	13.	(B)	18.	(D)
4.	(A)	9.	(C)	14.	(B)	19.	(C)
5.	(D)	10.	(A)	15.	(B)	20.	(C)

DETAILED EXPLANATIONS OF ANSWERS

Drill: Physics

1.   **(B)**   Acceleration is equal to the change in speed, or velocity, divided by the time interval. Acceleration is directly proportional to the acting force and inversely proportional to mass.

2.   **(A)**   Archimedes' Principle says that an object is buoyed up by a force that is equal to the volume of the fluid displaced. Buoyancy is dependent upon both the density and the shape of the object.

3.   **(A)**   Bernoulli's Principle states the internal fluid pressure decreases as the fluid speed increases. "A moving stream of gas or liquid appears to exert less sideways pressure than if it were at rest." However, if the flow is too great, then it becomes turbulent and eddies form.

4.   **(A)**   The ability of a body to change shapes when a force is applied and then return to its original shape when the force is removed is the definition of elasticity. Objects that do not return to their original shapes are said to be inelastic.

5.   **(D)**   According to the Law of Conservation of Energy, energy can neither be created nor destroyed, but it may change form.

6.   **(B)**   Friction is a force that acts between materials that are moving past each other. Friction is a result of irregularities in the surfaces. When two surfaces are sliding over one another, the frictional force acts in the opposite direction of motion.

7.   **(B)**   Refraction is the bending of waves toward the direction of the slower wave velocity. Part of the wave slows down before the other part.

8.   **(B)**   When light is refracted, all the waves lie in one thickness. Depending upon the degree of refraction, the waves may or may not lie in different planes.

9.   **(C)**   The greater the mass of an object, the greater the force necessary to change its rate of motion or acceleration. This is stated in Newton's second law, $F = ma$. As m increases, F must increase if the acceleration, a, is to remain the same.

10.   **(A)**   Inertia is the resistance of an object to change. The idea of inertia while in motion is called the momentum in reference to moving objects.

11.   **(C)**   The idea of parallel force, when applied to circuits, states that a parallel circuit would have a constant supply of electricity. A parallel circuit has two or more branches for the current to flow. The parallel circuit is used in Christmas tree lights, each light can have a constant supply of current, but it is not necessary for all the lights to be on for others to light.

12.   **(C)**   Work is the distance an object has been moved multiplied by the force used to move the object. Time is not needed to determine the amount of work done.

13.   **(B)**   Machines are devices by which energy can be transferred from one place to another or one form to another. Machines can be used to multiply the speed at which the work is done.

14.   **(B)**   The principle of conservation of mechanical energy deals with the functioning of machines. "In absence of other forces that dissipate energy, the total mechanical energy of a system remains constant." The principle of conservation of mechanical energy relates work and the absence of friction.

15.   **(B)**   Heat is a form of energy that is created by the motion of molecules making up the object. Heat transfer always occurs from an object of high temperature to one of a lower temperature.

16.   **(D)**   Specific heat is defined as the quantity of heat required to raise the temperature of a unit of mass of a substance by one degree. Specific heat is dependent upon the chemical composition of the substance.

17.   **(C)**   A wave is a wiggle in space and time that can extend from one place to another. If this wiggle occurs only in time, it is called a vibration.

18. **(D)** Diffraction is the bending of light around the edge of an object that is blocking its path. All forms of electromagnetic waves, light, radio, and x-rays, can be diffracted.

19. **(C)** When light travels in transverse waves, it is called polarization. The polarized light waves only travel on one plane. Other light waves may travel in longitudinal waves, these are not polarized.

20. **(C)** When any frequency of forced vibrations on an object matches the natural frequency of the object, it is said to resonate. Tuning forks are often used to demonstrate resonance.

V. EARTH SCIENCE REVIEW

ASPECTS OF EARTH SCIENCE

An understanding of the beginnings of the **solar system** and the Earth's development within it is essential to environmental survival. This understanding is filled with curiosity, and may be the price of environmental survival. A lack of curiosity and understanding may signal the environment's demise.

Hipparchus, in 150 B.C., determined the distance of the moon, based on his calculations of the Earth's diameter. The Greeks added to the study of **astronomy** by determining that an eclipse was caused by the Earth passing between the sun and the moon, and that the sun was at the center of the solar system. These and other basic studies concerning the sun, moon, planets, galaxies, and solar system have led to questions like, Does the universe go on forever? Where does it all end? Is space infinite? It is because of such challenging questions that astronomy has developed into an exact science.

THEORIES

The theory developed by Sir Isaac Newton is in direct opposition to the theory developed by Albert Einstein. Newton stated that a planet moves around the sun because of the gravitational force exerted by the sun. This theory holds true if one is studying the velocities of small objects compared to light. Einstein's theory of relativity states that the planet chooses the shortest possible path throughout the four-dimensional world which is defined by the presence of the sun. According to this theory, if you left home and walked in a straight line, you would eventually return home. Both these theories were inventions by human minds and have been used to create many of our scientific explanations (theories). New theories will show weaknesses and limitations to each theory.

Most scientists tend to believe the theory stating the solar system probably developed as a nebula (cloud of gas and dust) that once swirled around the sun and slowly flattened out. Sections of the cloud began to spin like eddies in a stream, collecting gases and dust and causing the sections to grow and form planets. They slowly developed into spinning planets that now travel around the sun.

How did the Earth and the life on it come into existence? The most widely held scenario on this is known as the **Big Bang Theory**, which states that it was from a colossal explosion 10 to 14 billion years ago that a highly concentrated mass of gaseous matter formed and then radiated outward, creating the universe. It is widely believed that the life on Earth is a natural consequence of the events set in motion by the Big Bang. It is also generally thought that the universe continues to expand today. The Big Bang, however, is not universally accepted. Among the things that cause it to be called into question are observations (a) that some globular clusters appear to be older than the universe itself and (b) that galaxies exist in superclumps, with enormous voids between them.

In the early 1700s, Abraham Werner presented his theory that an ocean once covered the Earth. The chemicals in the water slowly settled to the bottom of the water where they formed granite and other forms of rock layers. The Earth was completely formed with the settling of the water and no other changes occurred. All life, according to Werner, began with the settling of the water and the formation of the Earth.

The **Hutton Theory** of 1785 claimed that the Earth was gradually changing and would continue to change in the same ways. According to Hutton, these changes could be used to explain the past. He died before he could get other scientists to accept his ideas, yet after his death and publication of his ideas, they became a leading guide for the geological thinkers.

The **Creation Theory** with which we are most familiar is that given in the first chapters of Genesis. Various attempts have been made to work out the date of the creation on the basis of the data given in the Bible and the date of creation has been set at circa 3760 B.C. The creation, as explained in Genesis, is accepted by some people as the formation of the Earth and the origin of life.

But creation remains a subject of controversy. Battle lines have been drawn. One theorist will research and develop a possible strategy for solving the age-old question, only to have another theorist come along and find a flaw in that research and then develop a new theory. Thus, new theories are constantly springing up. Each theory is viewed in a manner to gain an understanding of the information presented pertaining to the Earth's formation for the purpose of survival and the prosperity of the universe.

PHYSICS AND CHEMISTRY OF THE EARTH
PHYSICAL PROPERTIES

The Earth moves in three ways: it spins like a top (though not at a precisely constant speed) on its axis, travels around the sun, and moves through the Milky Way with the rest of the solar system. The Earth's axis is an imaginary line that connects the north and south poles at either end of the planet. The elliptical path the Earth follows around the sun is called its orbit.

The Earth has one moon, which, because of its close proximity influences the tides. The sun's gravity acts on both the Earth and the moon, causing the moon to travel in an oval-like orbit around the Earth. How the Earth's axis inclines, or tilts, in relation to the sun determines the four seasons. In the Northern Temperate Zone, spring starts at the vernal equinox, summer at the summer solstice, autumn at the autumnal equinox, and winter at the winter solstice. In the South Temperate Zone, everything runs in reverse.

CHEMICAL COMPOSITION

The Earth's surface is about 70 percent water, with most of the water being oceans with depths extending to 12,450 feet. The land surface makes up the remaining 30 percent and extends an average of 2,757 feet above the division of land and water. The highest peak is Asia's Mount Everest, which rises 29,028 feet above sea level. Oceans, lakes, rivers, and all other bodies of water and ice make up a part of the Earth called the hydrosphere. Land bodies surrounded by water make up the continents. Together, land and water surfaces that support life are called the biosphere.

The chemical composition of the Earth is 46.6 percent oxygen, 27.72 percent silicon, 8.13 percent aluminum, 5.0 percent iron, 3.60 percent calcium, 2.83 percent sodium, 2.59 percent potassium, 2.09 percent magnesium, 0.44 percent titanium, and all other elements total 1.0 percent. A geologist is a person who studies the Earth and its contents. It is through the work of geologists that the chemical composition of the Earth has been established.

ORES

Ores are deposits high enough in an element content that it would be economically feasible to be mined and sold for a profit. Ore deposits are located from geological knowledge about crustal movements and ore formations along with sophisticated instruments and a lot of luck. Once the ore has been located, the mining process is based on the most economical method to remove the highest amount of the mineral from the rock with the least amount of environmental damage. Processes include leaching or separating the mineral from the rock by heat, brine solutions, evaporation of seawater, or chemically removing the metal from the ore.

EARTH'S MAGNETISM

Imaginary lines curve from the north pole to the south pole, making up the Earth's **magnetic field**. The Earth acts as though its center is a large magnet. These imaginary lines aid the compass needle to determine directions based on the Earth's natural magnetic field. Scientists are not sure what produces the enormous currents that are deep within the Earth and responsible for the Earth's magnetic fields.

EVOLUTION AND CRUSTAL PROCESS
CHANGING OF THE EARTH

The moon's gravitational pull actually produces tides both in the oceans *and* in the Earth's solid crust. Throughout time, slow evolutionary changes have taken place and continue to take place. As shorelines shrink in one place, mud and silt build up in other areas, adding to the land surface.

CONTINENTAL DRIFTS

The **continental shelves** are zones of relatively shallow portions of the continent extending out under the oceans. The continental shelves, or edges, are a part of the continent they adjoin, and the edge of the shelf is the true boundary of the continent. The continental shelf is not small. In some areas, it may contain the same area as the size of the former Soviet Union under the waters of the ocean. The shelves were formed eighteen to twenty thousand years ago due to the melting of the glaciers, along with time, wave-cutting terraces, erosion, and sedimentation all part of the formation explanation. At the edge of the shelf, the continental slope leads downward to the deep ocean. At the bottom of the slope, an area of deposition called the continental rise may form a gentler slope. Other features included in the continental margin are trenches, ridges, and submarine canyons. A reef is a rocky or coral elevation dangerous to surface navigation; it may or may not be covered by water. A rocky reef is always detached from the shoreline; a coral reef may or may not be connected to the shoreline.

NATURE'S RECYCLING

Nature's method of recycling is seen in many processes, including the water cycle, carbon cycle, oxygen cycle, and energy cycle as demonstrated by prey and predators. These processes are illustrated in the following drawings.

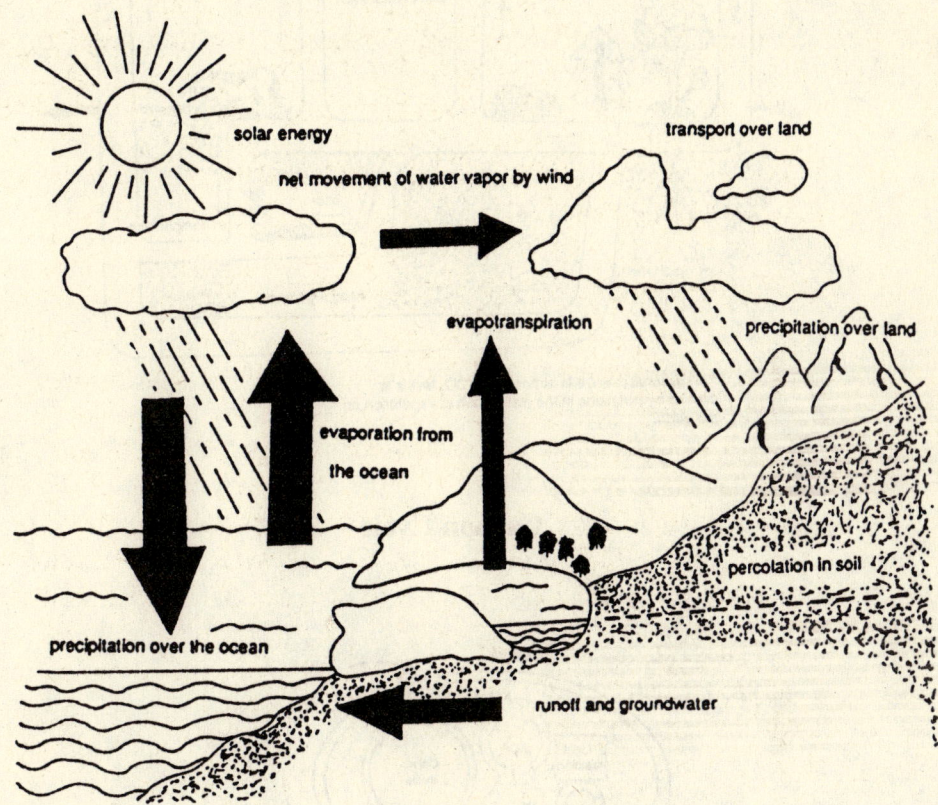

The Hydrologic (Water) Cycle

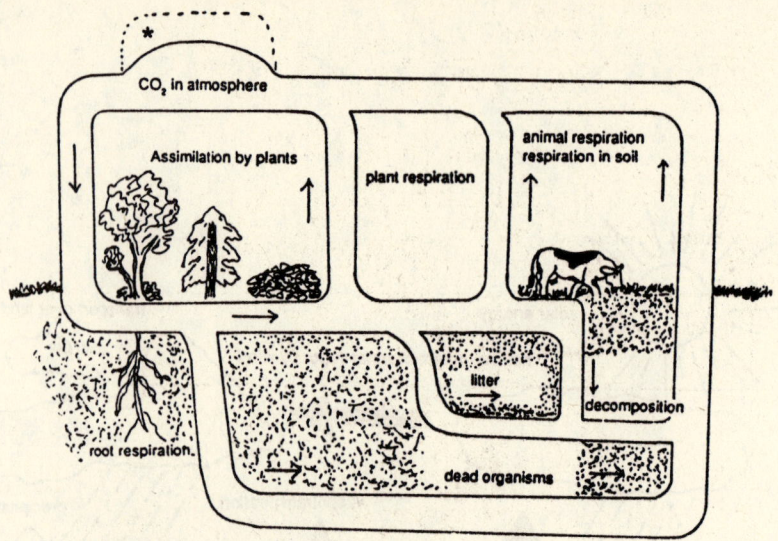

* A seasonal change in atmospheric CO₂ levels is caused by variations in the distribution of vegetation on the earth.

Carbon Cycle

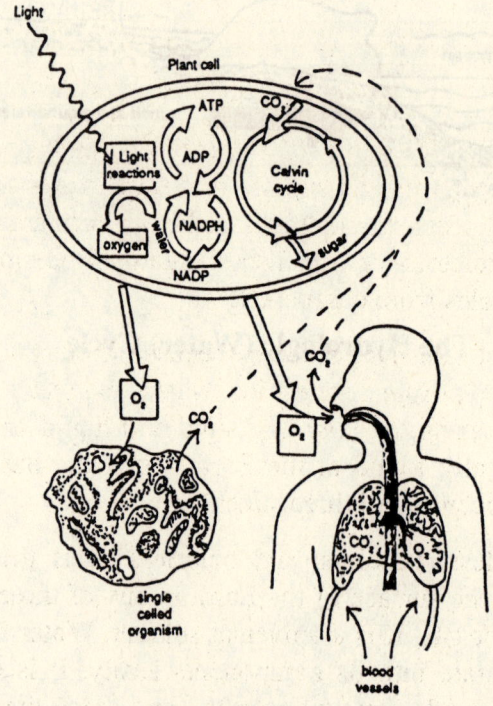

Oxygen Cycle

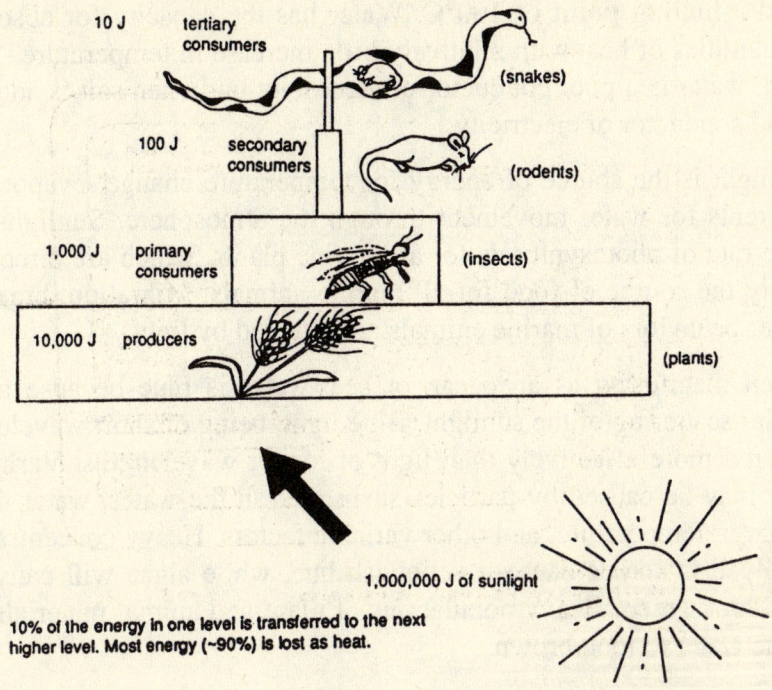

10 J   tertiary consumers   (snakes)

100 J   secondary consumers   (rodents)

1,000 J   primary consumers   (insects)

10,000 J   producers   (plants)

1,000,000 J of sunlight

10% of the energy in one level is transferred to the next higher level. Most energy (~90%) is lost as heat.

Energy Cycle

WATER

The most important source of sediment is earth and rock material carried to the sea by rivers and streams; the same materials may also have been transported by glaciers and winds. Other sources are volcanic ash and lava, shells and skeletons of organisms, chemical precipitates formed in seawater, and particles from outer space.

Water is a most unusual substance because it exists on the surface of the Earth in its three physical states: ice, water, and water vapor. There are other substances that might exist in a solid and liquid or gaseous state at temperatures normally found at the Earth's surface, but there are fewer substances which occur in all three states.

Water is odorless, tasteless, and colorless. It is the only substance known to exist on the surface of the Earth in any of three natural states—as a solid, liquid, or gas. It is a universal solvent. Water does not corrode, rust, burn, or separate into its components easily. It is chemically indestructible. It can corrode almost any metal and erode the most solid rock. A unique property of water is that, in its liquid state, it expands and floats on water that is in a frozen, or solid, state. Water has a **freezing point** of

0°C and a **boiling point** of 100°C. Water has the capacity for absorbing great quantities of heat with relatively little increase in temperature. When distilled, water is a poor conductor of electricity but when salt is added, it is a good conductor of electricity.

Sunlight is the source of energy for temperature change, evaporation, and currents for water movement through the atmosphere. Sunlight controls the rate of photosynthesis for all marine plants, which are directly or indirectly the source of food for all marine animals. Migration, breeding, and other behaviors of marine animals are affected by light.

When manifested as an ocean or sea, water is blue because of the molecular scattering of the sunlight. Blue light, being of short wavelength, is scattered more effectively than light of longer wavelengths. Variations in color may be caused by particles suspended in the water, water depth, cloud cover, temperature, and other variable factors. Heavy concentrations of dissolved materials cause a yellowish hue, while algae will cause the water to look green. Heavy populations of plant and animal materials will cause the water to look brown.

WEATHERING

Weathering is the natural wearing away of rock or soil due to chemical or physical actions on these Earth surfaces. This occurs very slowly over a long period of time. Through chemical weathering, rocks break down as oxygen, carbon dioxide, and water vapor react with rock until it is finally changed into soil. Physical weathering occurs in dry regions by the wind action constantly wearing away the surface of the rock.

EROSION

One of the most obvious forms of erosion is the natural weathering that led to the formation of mountains and mountain chains. The main causes of this type of natural erosion are air and/or water movement across rock or soil, changes in the temperature, or any combination of these factors. Chemical erosion can occur as carbon dioxide and water vapor are removed from dead organic matter. There are man-made causes of erosion as well, including poor crop-planting procedures, lack of crop rotation, and the cutting of trees without proper planning or replacement.

TEMPERATURE

Temperature is controlled by the position of the earth on its axis and its distance from the sun at rotation. At the equator, the air would be warmest and always pushing upward while cold air would be flowing in to be warmed. The constant changing of air will cause changes in the temperature.

PRESSURE

Air pressure also plays an important role in the movement of air and the changing of air temperatures and weather changes. Next to the equator, a low pressure cell is formed because the air is warmer, lighter, and moving upward. The low pressure is a result of the molecules of air being further apart. The colder air has closer air molecules; thus, a high pressure cell is formed. Extreme weather conditions, such as flooding, may result when both low cells and high cells occupy the same air space.

CLIMATE

Climate is the usual weather that occurs in a general area over a period of time. The study of climate is called climatology. When referring to climate, one takes into consideration air temperature, wind speed, sunshine, humidity, amount of precipitation, air pressure, and general geographic conditions. Climate has a direct effect upon living organisms and the type(s) of life that can exist in the region being considered. Climate also affects our method of transportation, outdoor activities, choices for employment, type of clothing, type of housing, and food naturally available or that can be grown.

ALTERNATE ENERGY FORMS

About 90 percent of today's energy is supplied from fossil fuels as crude oil, natural gas, and coal. These materials are a result of nature providing such supplies for man's use. Thus, these are considered nonrenewable resources as they cannot be replaced after they have been used. With conservation and suitable alternate energy sources, natural resources will last longer and these fossil fuels can be usable for many more years. Alternate energy sources include methanol, ethanol, wood and wood wastes, garbage and plant material, corn, other grains, solar energy, photovoltaic cells, hydroelectricity, nuclear power, wind energy (windmills), tidal energy, geothermal energy (geysers), and fusion using nuclear waste materials.

EARTH'S HAZARDS AND RESOURCES

EARTHQUAKES

Earthquakes are vibrations due to the movements within and beneath the Earth's crust. They occur as a result of faulting or other structural processes happening as a result of a strain on the rocks at the edge of the crust. A long series of quakes with none being greater than the others is called an **Earth swarm** and occurs near volcanic regions. Imperial Valley, California, is known for having Earth swarms. Earth tremors are vibrations of low intensity and can be felt only by those located directly over the affected area.

Earthquake intensity is measured on a scale from 0 to 9, where each number represents an energy release ten times that of the number. This energy release is measured by the "Richter Scale" as it was introduced by Charles F. Richter in 1935. Richter was an American seismologist. About 80 percent of earthquake energy is released in the areas bordering the vast Pacific Ocean, with 15 percent released in an east-west band across the Mediterranean. The remaining 5 percent occur sporadically throughout the remaining parts of the world bordering large bodies of water.

VOLCANOES

Volcanoes are a natural phenomenon with their effects confined to a small area. About 500 volcanoes are known to have been active, with two-thirds of them in the Pacific Ocean area. Modern research into volcanoes and their role in forming much of the Earth's crust began with the French geologist Jean Etienne Guettard in the mid-eighteenth century.

Volcanoes discharge a large amount of carbon dioxide into the air; the weathering of rocks utilizes carbon dioxide. This presents a pair of mechanisms for possible long-term climatic changes. A period of greater than normal volcanic action might initiate a warming of the Earth. The mountains built by the volcanic ash might expose large areas of new and unweathered rock to the air, which will lower the carbon dioxide levels, thus, reducing the atmospheric temperature.

OCEANS

It is estimated the world's oceans extend over 328 million cubic miles with the greatest depth being 36,198 feet off the coast of Guam. The deepest of all oceans is the Pacific Ocean, averaging 14,048 feet, and the most shallow is the Baltic Sea at 180.4 feet deep. Sedimentary rock at the bottom of the oceans has been dated at 3 billion years old with the water dated at 4 billion years old.

The oceans supply man with a means of transportation, habitat for aquatic life that is used for food, a source of minerals, and a means of weather control. The ocean also offers various sources of energy for consumption and use in the future. Currently, oil and gas are being derived from the ocean as sources of energy. Research is being conducted as to the feasibility of waves or water of the ocean being used to produce power. The ocean is used to stimulate islands of lush plant growth to increase the photosynthesis process as a possible way to reduce the depletion of the ozone layer.

HOT SPRINGS

Hot springs are naturally occurring bodies of water that are warmer than surrounding air. Hot springs (thermal springs) occur in regions of faulted or folded rock due to volcanic action. The water that comes from underground where the rocks are hot will produce hot water that rises to the Earth's surface in the form of a spring. Not all hot springs are a direct result of volcanoes; some are produced by geysers.

MIGRATION

Migration is the movement of people or animals from one area to another area. Migration occurs for the purpose of survival because of seasonal changes, wars, famines, floods, volcanic eruptions, weather, and other natural disasters. Migration practices began with prehistoric man. Little is known about the pattern of movement or why migrations took place. It is believed the first migrations were to escape the spread of the great glaciers and ice sheets. The most common application of migration is that of birds and other animals moving to survive winters or for the purpose of reproduction as illustrated by the salmon moving into the colder waters.

FLOODING

Flooding is the natural occurrence of an extremely large amount of water flowing into a given area faster than it can leave the area. As a result, the stream, lake, or river will overflow its natural level. Estuary zones and sand dunes are natural flood control devices. Man-made devices like dams and sandbags are used to control flood waters. The control of flood waters is important to the survival of coastal habitats for wading marsh birds, birds of prey, migratory birds, water fowl, and other aquatic life, as well as man himself—flood waters still claim human lives even as we begin the twenty-first century.

WATER-BASED FORMATIONS

The commonly seen waves on the surface of water are caused principally by wind. When a breeze blows over calm water, it forms small ripples or capillary waves. As the wind speed increases, larger, more visible gravity waves are formed. When the wind reaches high speeds, whitecaps are formed. However, submarine earthquakes, volcanic eruptions, and tides also cause waves. Waves will always break parallel to the shoreline.

The **tide** is the continuous cycle of alternating rise and fall of the sea level observed along the coastlines and bodies of water connected to the sea. On most coastlines, the cycle occurs about every 12 hours. Along the gulf coastline, a tidal cycle can occur about every 24-25 hours. The rise and fall of sea level observed along coastlines is produced by waves of extreme length; high water is the crest of the wave; low water is the trough. Tides can be predicted once observations have been mathematically related to the positions of Earth, moon, and sun. Tides are caused by the gravitational interaction between the sun, moon, and Earth. The moon exercises the greatest influence on our tide; although its mass is much less than the sun's, it is closer to the earth and its tide-producing effect is more than twice as great.

The maximum height reached by a rising tide is called **high water**. This is due solely to the periodic tidal force, but at times, the meteorological effects of severe storms or strong winds may be superimposed on the normal tide to produce high water.

Low water is the minimum height reached by a falling tide. Often, this is due solely to the influence of a periodic tidal force, but sometimes the influence of severe storms or strong winds may be superimposed on the normal tide to produce low water.

Tides are classified as **semidiurnal**, **diurnal**, and **mixed**. Areas having semidiurnal tides have two high waters and two low waters each day; this is the most common type. Diurnal tides consist of one high water and one low water each day. Tides are classified as mixed when they are diurnal on some days and semidiurnal on others.

Hurricanes occur when the atmospheric conditions, tail movements, winds, and pressure change severely. Hurricanes begin with winds moving in a circular motion over bodies of water, picking up both speed and rainy weather conditions. When a hurricane approaches a coastline, the sea level will go 20 feet above normal tide level. The months of June through November are considered hurricane season. August, September, and October normally have more hurricanes documented than any other months with September having the greatest number of hurricanes. May and December, on rare occasions, have logged hurricanes. Hurricanes can cause both property damage and personal damage when they move from the water to land surfaces with a tornado resulting from its wind force as it moves further inland.

A **typhoon** is a severe tropical cyclone of the western Pacific Ocean and China seas. In the oceans of the Americas and in the western South Pacific, the same kind of storm is known as a hurricane.

Currents are water movements in horizontal or vertical flow occurring at differing depths of the water. Currents stabilize the climate of adjacent land areas, preventing extremes of temperatures. Currents are also influenced/affected by the moon and its position relative to the equator.

Density differences may produce both horizontal and vertical movement of water, causing modifications to the wind-driven surface currents. Water tends to flow from an area of low density to an area of high density. Water may tend to become of greater density as the temperature decreases.

Fog consists of a visible collection of minute water droplets suspended in the atmosphere near the Earth's surface. It interferes with the ability to see at a distance over the area that it covers. It is caused by atmospheric humidity and a warm temperature layer being transported over a cold body of water or land surface.

ECONOMICS OF EARTH'S RESOURCES

Conservation is the protection and wise management of Earth's resources or natural resources, for the benefit of not only man, but all living things. Without wise practices of conservation and concern for the quality of the environment, all natural resources necessary for life, such as air, animals, energy, minerals, plants, soil, water, and other elemental forms would be damaged, wasted, or destroyed. With greater conservation enforcement, the cost of living will be lower for everyone and more ideal surroundings will be present. The Earth not only has limited resources, but the demands are greater as populations increase, which means there must be a wiser use of Earth's resources if they are to last as long as man, or if man is to survive. The cost of man's poor resource management can be life itself.

☞ Drill: Earth Science

1. When the Earth passes between the sun and the moon, this causes the occurrence of (a)

    (A) lunar phase. (B) solar eclipse. (C) sun spots. (D) lunar eclipse.

2. Which factor best tends to support the Big Bang Theory?

    (A) The existence of massive superclusters with huge voids between them.

    (B) The fact that static-universe models seem to fit available data better than expanding-universe models.

    (C) Some globular clusters appear to be older than the universe itself.

    (D) An enormous release of energy in a very short period of time.

3. Hutton's theory stated

    (A) how the sun and moon were the same.

    (B) how the Earth was gradually changing and would cease the gradual changing.

    (C) how the Earth was gradually changing and would continue to change in the same ways.

    (D) that the Earth is not changing.

4. Which planet is the closest to the sun?

    (A) Earth   (B) Mars   (C) Mercury   (D) Pluto

5. Meteoroids are chunks of iron resulting from collisions between

    (A) asteroids.   (B) planetoids.   (C) stars.   (D) meteorites.

6. An axis is

    (A) a connecting line at the equator.

    (B) a connecting line between the poles.

    (C) a connecting line between orbits.

    (D) a pole.

7. The percentage of the Earth's surface that is water is

    (A) 30 percent.   (C) 70 percent.

    (B) 50 percent.   (D) 90 percent.

8. Igneous rock forms are commonly called

    (A) marble.   (B) limestone.   (C) cement.   (D) granite.

9. To be considered a mineral, the substance must never have been a part of a living organism and must be found in

    (A) rock.   (B) ore.   (C) nature.   (D) sand.

10. The cause of the Earth's magnetic field is

    (A) enormous currents.   (C) a lost secret.

    (B) space satellites.   (D) in the Earth's crust.

11. An odorless, colorless gas that surrounds the Earth is commonly called

    (A) nitrogen.   (C) carbon dioxide.

    (B) oxygen.   (D) air.

12. The source of evaporation is the

    (A) movement of air.   (C) sunlight.

    (B) atmosphere.   (D) currents.

13. Warmer air has molecules of air that are far apart. Therefore, it produces

    (A) a low pressure cell.   (C) rainy weather.

    (B) a high pressure cell.   (D) dry conditions.

14. Crude oil, natural gas, and coal are called

    (A) nuclear energy sources.   (C) natural sources.

    (B) alternate energy sources.   (D) None of the above.

15. The Richter Scale was introduced in

    (A) 1934.   (B) 1844.   (C) 1935.   (D) 1955.

16. Two-thirds of all known active volcanoes have occurred in the

    (A) Atlantic Ocean.   (C) Gulf of Mexico.

    (B) Pacific Ocean.   (D) Baltic Sea.

17. Migration occurs because of

    (A) famines.

    (B) the need for cold weather.

    (C) the need to develop a pattern of movement to be studied.

    (D) the need to escape floods.

18. The continuous cycle of alternating rise and fall of the sea level observed along the coastlines and bodies of water connected to the sea is called

    (A) the tide.   (C) sun exercises.

    (B) moon exercises.   (D) a tidal wave.

19. Hurricanes occur over

    (A) land.   (C) land during the day.

    (B) water.   (D) water and land.

20. Fog is

    (A) the same as smog.

    (B) caused when cold air moves over warm air.

    (C) a collection of minute water droplets.

    (D) associated with a tornado.

EARTH SCIENCE REVIEW

ANSWER KEY

Drill: Earth Science

1. (D)	6. (B)	11. (D)	16. (B)
2. (D)	7. (C)	12. (C)	17. (A)
3. (C)	8. (D)	13. (A)	18. (A)
4. (C)	9. (C)	14. (D)	19. (D)
5. (A)	10. (C)	15. (C)	20. (C)

DETAILED EXPLANATIONS OF ANSWERS

Drill: Earth Science

1. **(D)** Eclipses occur either when all or part of the moon passes through the Earth's shadow or when all or part of the Earth passes through the moon's shadow. The former is a lunar eclipse, the latter a solar eclipse.

2. **(D)** The Big Bang Theory states that the universe was created by a violent explosion 10 to 14 billion years ago. The universe expanded from the center of the explosion, a process that is widely believed to continue today. Data gathered by the Cosmic Background Explorer, launched in 1989, showed that 99.97% of the radiant energy of the universe was dispersed within the first year of a violent explosion. This would seem to confirm the Big Bang.

3. **(C)** According to Hutton, the Earth was gradually changing and would continue to change in the same ways. These changes could be used to explain the past.

4. **(C)** Mercury is the planet closest to the sun. It is followed by Venus and Earth. Pluto is the planet farthest from the sun.

5. **(A)** Meteoroids are chunks of iron resulting from collisions between asteroids. Asteroids are small irregularly-shaped objects orbiting between Jupiter and Mars.

6. **(B)** An axis is defined as a line connecting two poles. The Earth has an axis connecting the North Pole and the South Pole.

7. **(C)** The Earth's surface is about 70% water. Most of the water is in the oceans. The land makes up the remaining 30%.

8. **(D)** An example of igneous rock is granite. Marble is a metamorphic rock, while limestone and cement are sedimentary rocks.

9. **(C)** To be considered a mineral, the substance must never have been part of a living organism and must be found in nature. Minerals are the most common form of solid material found in the Earth's crust. Even soils contain bits of minerals.

10. **(C)**   The Earth acts through its center as a large magnet. Scientists are not sure what produces the enormous magnetic currents that are deep within the Earth and responsible for the Earth's magnetic field.

11. **(D)**   Air is the odorless, colorless gas that surrounds the Earth and extends approximately 1,000 miles above the surface. Air is made up of 78% nitrogen, 21% oxygen, and argon, water vapor, dust particles, and other gases make up the remaining 1%.

12. **(C)**   Sunlight is the source of energy for temperature change, evaporation and currents for water movement through the atmosphere.

13. **(A)**   Warmer air has molecules of air that are far apart. Therefore, it produces a low-pressure cell, found next to the equator. Colder air has closer air molecules and, therefore, forms a high-pressure cell.

14. **(D)**   Most of today's energy is supplied from fossil fuels, such as crude oil, natural gas, and coal. Fossil fuels are from natural sources.

15. **(C)**   The Richter Scale measures the energy release of an earthquake. This scale was introduced by Charles Richter in 1935.

16. **(B)**   About 500 volcanoes are known to have been active, with two-thirds of them in the Pacific Ocean.

17. **(A)**   Migration is the movement of people or animals from one area to another area. Migration occurs because of seasonal changes, wars, famines, floods, volcanic eruptions, weather, and other natural disasters.

18. **(A)**   The tide is the continuous cycle of an alternately rising and falling sea level along the coastlines and in bodies of water connected to the sea. The moon is the single greatest influence on the tides.

19. **(D)**   Hurricanes occur when the atmospheric conditions, tail movements, winds, and pressure change severely. Hurricanes can move from water to land; a tornado results from the wind force when the hurricane moves further inland.

20. **(C)**   Fog consists of a visible collection of minute water droplets suspended in the atmosphere near the Earth's surface. It occurs when atmospheric humidity combines with a warm layer of air that is transported over a cold body of water or land surface.

VI. GEOLOGY REVIEW

Geology is the study of the earth. Several different aspects of geology exist: nature appreciation, environmental protection, hazard reduction, material resources, and scientific research. Geologists study from the history of the earth and its continents, rivers, and oceans, and the impacts of man on the planet. Geologists are also involved in the study of the planets, or **planetology**.

HISTORY OF THE EARTH

Several theories of creation have been proposed over the centuries. The **nebular hypothesis** was proposed by Immanuel Kant, and it states that the earth evolved from a rotating cloud of gases, or **nebula**. The **collision hypothesis** says that giant pieces of material broke away from the sun and became the planets. The recent theories involve the collapse of a nebula to form the sun and the planets, triggered by a **supernova**.

The earth was extremely hot, at temperatures high enough to melt iron. The composition was probably uniform, or homogeneous, throughout. As the earth cooled, an early ocean of molten rock, the **magma ocean**, was lighter than the solid material and floated to the surface, forming the earth's **crust**. This formation of the crust was the first step in the **differentiation** process. Gases may then have escaped from the interior and formed the atmosphere. As the earth continued to cool and further evolve, several layers formed. These are shown in the figure below.

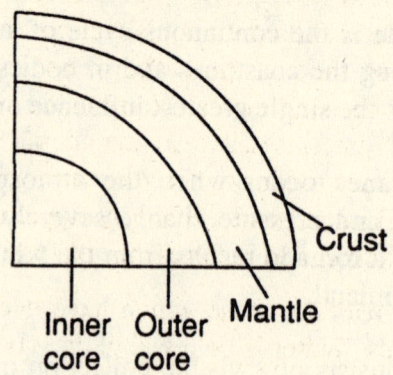

Inner core Outer core Mantle Crust

ROCKS

Geologists can determine the history of the earth's events by examining the rocks in the crust. Rock and soil particles settle and form layers. These layers are known as **stratification**, and are the basis for the **stratigraphic time scale** which is used as the first measure of the time and date of events. These time scales can cover thousands, even millions, of years. The next method for determining time is to examine **fossils**. Fossils are the remains of ancient plants and animals that have been preserved in the rocks. Sedimentary rocks such as limestone, shale, and sandstone are all good sources of fossils. A fossil's age can be determined by the layer of rock in which it was found. Another dating technique is to look at the amount of radioactive decay of the carbon-14 isotope found in the sample. Carbon-14 dating is used for samples 80,000 years old or younger.

Rocks are classified into three major groups: igneous, metamorphic, and sedimentary. **Igneous rocks** were solidified or hardened from the cooling of molten material, either magma or lava. Magma is molten rock plus dissolved gases and is found underground. Lava is just molten rock, and flows above the earth's surface. **Volcanic** rocks are fine-grained, and coarse-grained ones are called **plutonic** after the Greek god Pluto. Igneous rocks are further classified by texture: **phaneritic** or **aphanitic**. Some examples of igneous rocks are granite, rhyolite, pumice, obsidian, gabbro, basalt, scoria, and diorite.

Sedimentary rocks are formed at normal earth temperatures and pressure from the accumulation (or sedimentation) of weathered debris. This debris is composed of silt and small rock and soil particles found at the bottom of rivers, lakes, and oceans. These rocks are composed of clay (as found in shale), silica (sandstone), or calcium carbonate (limestone), or a combination of any three. **Clastic** rock is composed of particulate material of various sizes, from sand grains to boulders. In clastic rock the individual particles can be seen easily. **Non-clastic** rocks are composed of organic or inorganic material that has been chemically precipitated. Some examples of sedimentary rocks are breccia, sandstone, siltstone, shale, and limestone. These rocks can be identified by ripple marks, stratification (or layering), graded bedding, and the presence of fossils.

Metamorphic rocks are those which have been transformed by heat, pressure, or chemicals. Water is believed to dissolve and then transport the chemicals. The transformation may occur over hundreds or thousands of years. The alterations that occur during the metamorphosis may be categorized into reorientation, recrystallization, and the growth of new and stable minerals. **Reorientation** changes the random orientation normally found in the rock to a preferred orientation. Many times the rock will contain flat and elongated regions. **Recrystallization** occurs under high pressure. The rock's original grains lose their individual identity and the pores will appear smaller than those on the original rock. Under high heat and pressure, the chemical and physical properties of the rock can be altered to yield new minerals. Examples of minerals that are formed by the new and stable growth are garnet, graphite, tourmaline, and serpentine. Other common metamorphic rocks are marble from transformed limestone, slate from shale, gneiss from granite, and anthracite coal from bituminous coal.

MINERALS

To further understand rocks, which are defined as aggregates or collections of **minerals**, the structure of minerals will be outlined. Minerals exist in solid form, as opposed to liquids or gases, the other states of matter. Solids are found in one of three states: crystal, crystalline, or amorphous substances. A **crystal** has an orderly arrangement of atoms known as a **lattice**. Lattices are three-dimensional arrays which have length, width, and depth. The lattices may not be perfect, but may have defects which include missing ions, displaced ions, ordered substitutions, random substitutions, and interstitial substitutions. These defects ultimately affect the density of the crystal. The crystal lattice results in a regular external geometric form, or **symmetry**. Some shapes that crystals occur in are cubes, prisms, and pyramids among others. A **crystalline substance** also has an orderly arrangement of atoms, but it does not possess the external geometric form. Thus, it does not have symmetry. Most everyday substances are crystalline. The last type of substance, **amorphous**, does not have an orderly arrangement of atoms, nor does it have an external geometric form. The atoms are arranged randomly. Sometimes minerals are found in two or three forms but still maintain the same chemical composition; this is known as **polymorphism**. The polymorphism of carbon are diamond, oil, and graphite. Another example of polymorphism is quartz.

Minerals are often identified by their **physical properties**. The simplest property is its color. However, the color may not always be accurate since some colors may be due to impurities or lattice defects, as opposed to the true chemical composition. The next physical property is **luster**, or the way a mineral reflects light off of its surface. **Metallic** and **non-metallic** are the two major types of luster. Metallic luster is shiny like the surface of metals. Some types of non-metallic luster include: vitreous—glassy in appearance; pearly—looking like a pearl; earthy—dull and looking like clay; and finally adamantine—brilliant like a diamond. A mineral may cleave in one or more directions; this is referred to as **cleavage**. Cleavage is dependent upon the crystal structure of the mineral. **Fracture** is the random or haphazard breakage that occurs under one of two conditions. The atom structure may be too complex to give an even break (or cleave). The lattice may also have been poorly developed, and have many defects, or may even be amorphous. Some types of fracture are **conchoidal**—the breaks are with smooth curved surfaces (an example is glass); **splintering**—which shows fibers and long slices (asbestos); and **hackly**—which has a rough surface and many sharp points (metals). The mineral may be tested for its ability to resist scratching. This is known as a **hardness** test. The hardness scale is a relative scale that ranges from 1 for talc, the softest mineral, to 10 for diamond, the hardest naturally occurring mineral. The final physical property used for identification is streak. **Streak** is the color of the powdered mineral. The streak will always be the same for the same mineral, regardless of the crystal structure previous to pulverizing, and streak is thus a more accurate measure than the simple color. Other minor physical properties are sometimes used on select minerals. Examples are magnetism, taste, odor, feel, the ability to transmit light, and double refraction.

ROCK DEFORMATION

The two common ways that rocks deform are by folding and fracturing. Rocks can be either brittle or ductile. **Brittle** rocks break suddenly when forced beyond a critical limit. **Ductile** rocks will deform in a smooth, continuous way before they break. **Basement** rocks, sometimes called the bedrock, are found underneath the soil layer in the earth's crust. Basement rocks are crystalline and are usually more brittle than the sedimentary rocks that cover them. **Folded** rock was originally planar, or flat like a sheet. Folds are the result of either horizontal or vertical forces. The folds are often found in young mountains. The folds can be gentle slopes or steep breaks. They are classified as either asymmetrical shapes, overturned, or recumbent folds. Domes and basins are the results of folds.

Fractures are breaks in the rocks and are found in brittle rocks, whereas folds are usually in the more ductile rocks. Fractures are divided into two categories: joints and faults. A **joint** is a crack along a rock where no movement has occurred. If the rocks on both sides of the fracture have moved, then it is called a **fault**. If the movement is only vertical, then a **dip-slip fault** has been made. Horizontal movement leads to a **strike-slip fault**. If both horizontal and vertical movement has occurred, then the fault is classified as an **oblique-slip fault**. When two breaks result in the formation of a valley or trough, it is called a **graben**. Conversely, if a ridge is formed, it is a **horst**. When the folding and faulting happen, the igneous rocks in the structures are subjected to different forces and sometimes high pressure leading to metamorphism. The metamorphic rocks found in the folds and faults are used by geologists to understand the history of the rock deformation.

WEATHERING OF ROCK

Weathering is the wearing away of the rocks. It is a twofold process which is a combination of both **mechanical forces**, or fragmentation of the rock, and **chemical processes**, or decay. The weathering process results in the formation of sands and soils. Three major soils groups exist. The first is the **pedalfer** group which are high in aluminum and iron and cover the eastern half of the United States. Pedalfers are the result of the silicates in the soil being transformed to clays by the humid climate. The drier western half of the United States has soils that are high in calcium carbonate pellets and that contain less clay and more unaltered silicates. These soils are **pedocals**. The third type of soil is the **laterite** or the deep red soil found in the tropics. This soil has aluminum and iron oxides which give it its red color. All of the silicates have been chemically altered, and the calcium carbonate has been leached from it. The process of soil formation can occur very quickly—within a few years—or very slowly—over thousands of years.

The chemical reactions of weathering, the oxidation of iron to rust or the decay of organic material, will vary with the climate and composition of the rock. Chemical weathering is most active in warm and humid climates and least active in cold and dry ones. In different climates different types of clays—kaolinite, smectite, and illite—are formed. Physical weathering results in the formation of rock fragments from pebbles to boulders. The size of the fragment is largely due to the crystalline structure of the original rock.

EROSION AND LANDSCAPE

The **landscape** is the result of a combination of rock being uplifted from the earth's surface and the erosion of this rock. Mass movements are rock fall, landslides, and soil creep which are all induced by gravity. They occur when the slope of the land has been steepened by erosion. The study of the earth's surface and its heights and depths is called **topography**. All heights are compared to the reference height of the **mean sea level**. Vertical distances are called **altitudes** or **elevations**. On maps, lines that connect points of equal elevation are **contour lines**.

The landscape of the Grand Canyon was developed by erosion of the series of flat sediments. These sediments are seen as layers in the canyon's walls. The valley of the Grand Canyon is referred to as **V-shaped**. Another landscape, the Ozark Mountains, have much gentler shapes. Granite was initially uplifted and then eroded for a long time. Mountains, especially high and steep mountains, are eroded most quickly. On the other hand, low and flat areas usually are eroded the slowest. Similar to weathering, erosion is also dependent upon the climate of the region. The different chemical compositions of the rock also contribute to the erosion patterns.

MAPS AND TOPOGRAPHY

The geologist uses maps constantly for his work. A **map** is a graphic representation of the earth's surface. **Location** on a map is designated by the longitude and latitude. **Longitude** lines run from the North Pole to the South Pole, and they are used to measure the distances west or east of a reference. The reference point (or line) for longitude is the **Prime Meridian**. The **latitude** lines are used to measure distance north or south. The **equator** is used as the point of reference for the latitude lines.

Since a map is a portrayal of an area, the total area must be scaled to the sheet of paper that has the map. A **scale** is the proportion or ratio of distance on the map to the distance in reality, i.e., 1 inch = 10 miles. Sometimes a bar scale is used. Directions on a map are usually from **true north** (TN). This is sometimes called the **geographic north**. This north is different from the **magnetic north** to which compasses point. The true north and magnetic north are not the same; the magnetic north is located 900 miles south of the geographic north pole. The angle between the true north and magnetic north is called **declination**. The **Agonic line** is the location where the two poles appear to be in the same line. This line is where the declination is zero. **Elevations** are measured from the **mean sea level**. Elevations are shown on maps in many different ways: sometimes different colors are used, sometimes different designs. As mentioned before, in contour maps, the areas of equal elevation are connected by contour lines. The spacing of the contour lines indicate the steepness of the slope that is being presented. Occasionally, a **depression**, or decrease in elevation such as a sinkhole or volcanic crater, must be shown. The depression contours often have small tick marks or little hashures around the inside of the lines.

GROUNDWATER

Groundwater is the water that is found underground in the cracks and openings in rocks and sometimes in glaciated sands. It is a renewable resource. The branch of geology that studies groundwater is known as **hydrogeology**. The groundwater is surface water that has seeped downwards into the bedrock, which is also porous. Eventually, the rock is non-porous and the water can no longer migrate downward, but instead it collects in the underground spaces. The water will start to fill all spaces and completely saturate the rock. The region of rock which is completely saturated is known as the **zone of saturation**. Rock that is only partially filled with water is known as the **capillary fringe**. The top of the zone of saturation is defined as the **groundwater table**. The water in the zone of saturation, like the surface water, is always in motion. In most cases they both move in the same direction. The **porosity** of the rock is the amount of empty space in the rock which can be filled with water. **Permeability** is the measure of how the pores are interconnected and thus how well the water can move through the rock. The flow rate of water through the rock is dependent upon the permeability.

The major effect of groundwater movement is the dissolving of certain minerals and rocks. Limestone can be dissolved by acidic rain water into calcium and bicarbonate ions. The dissolved limestone will eventually be precipitated at another location. This is how **stalactites** and **stalagmites** are formed. Groundwater can also physically erode underground surfaces, increasing the likelihood of landslides. Groundwater has many useful purposes. It is used for drinking, irrigating crops, and watering livestock. It can come out of the ground naturally or be pumped out with a well. When a well is drilled, the water table is affected, and the water table around the well is changed into the shape of a cone called the **cone of depression**.

RIVERS

Water flow can be classified as either laminar or turbulent. In **laminar flow**, particles move in parallel layers and do not mix with one another. In **turbulent flow**, which is faster, water flows in confused patterns and particles are mixed. When a fast moving turbulent stream suddenly steepens and starts to move even faster, the water may appear to flow in a very smooth straight pattern. The flow is so fast that it is called **shooting flow**. Turbulent flow at slower velocities is referred to as **streaming flow**.

Particles can be moved in all of these flows. Laminar flows are the gentlest and carry only the smallest particles. Turbulent flows can carry much larger particles, up to the size of pebbles, thus eroding the streams and rivers. This debris is eventually deposited as sediment, or **alluvium**. The current in rivers can erode both the soil material and the hard rock, although the hard rock is eroded at a much slower rate.

Rivers are dynamic systems. Input to the river is all the water that reaches it from surface run-off, groundwater, plus the erosional debris from the entire area drained by the river. The output is the water and sediment that are carried to the ocean. Changes in the river occur when an imbalance exists between the output and input. **Floods** are an example of an imbalance when the river is not able to carry away extra water and sediment. Instead, the river overflows and invents new channels to carry the water.

The **continental divide** is located near Denver. It is a crest more than 11,000 feet above the sea level. This structure divides the water flow patterns in the United States. All water west of the continental divide eventually flows into the Pacific Ocean, and all water east flows into the Atlantic Ocean. **Drainage basins** are areas which funnel all their water into streams. These drainage networks show patterns in their branches—dendritic, rectangular, trellis, or radial. The patterns depend upon the topography, rock type, and structure of the area.

☞ Drill: Geology

1. One accepted theory for the formation of our solar system from a rotating cloud of gas and dust

    (A) has been proven to be true.

    (B) was proposed by many scientists, including Immanuel Kant.

    (C) is called the nebular hypothesis.

    (D) Both (B) and (C).

2. The names for the layers of the earth include all of the following EXCEPT

    (A) asthenosphere.   (C) differentiation.

    (B) lithosphere.   (D) solid iron core.

3. Which is the best term to describe the remains of ancient plants and animals that have been preserved in solid rock?

(A) Stratification

(C) Coproliths

(B) Fossils

(D) None of the above.

4. Sedimentary rocks are formed from the accumulation of silt, rock, and soil particles on the surface of the Earth. Of the following, which is NOT identified as a sedimentary rock type?

(A) Limestone

(C) Shale

(B) Diorite

(D) Both (B) and (C).

5. Rocks are classified into three main groups. Which major rock classi-fication consists of rock that forms from molten material that has solidified?

(A) Igneous

(C) Volcanic

(B) Sedimentary

(D) Metamorphic

6. Which of the following are characteristic of metamorphic rocks?

(A) Shows evidence of recrystallization

(B) Evidence of fossils of animals and plants

(C) Reorientation of crystals within rock

(D) Both (A) and (C).

7. The crust of the earth is composed of a thin layer of rocks covering the surface. Rocks are defined as aggregates or collections of

(A) symmetry.

(C) minerals.

(B) fossils.

(D) clastics.

8. Of the following, which types of fracture are associated with faults and earthquakes?

(A) Horsts

(C) Grabens

(B) Oblique-slip

(D) All of the above.

9. As a study of the surface of the earth, topography consists of an understanding of

(A) altitudes.

(C) mean sea level.

(B) elevations.

(D) All of the above.

10. Weathering is the wearing away of rocks, and is a neverending process. Chemical weathering, which is more active in warm and humid climates, consists of

    (A) the oxidation of iron in the rocks.

    (B) decay, alteration, and leaching.

    (C) the faulting and fracture of rocks.

    (D) Both (A) and (B).

11. Many geologists use maps as model representations of the surface of the earth. These maps consist of

    (A) latitude and longitude.   (C) All of the above.

    (B) declination and hashures.   (D) None of the above.

12. The proportion or ratio of distance on a map to the distance in reality is called

    (A) meridian.   (C) scale.

    (B) topography.   (D) agonic line.

13. Of the following, which is NOT a term that would directly be associated with hydrogeology?

    (A) Zone of saturation   (C) Groundwater table

    (B) Capillary fringe   (D) Aphanitic plutons

14. Laminar and turbulent water flow are SIMILAR in that

    (A) both have parallel layers that do mix.

    (B) both have parallel layers that do not mix.

    (C) both can carry large particles within their water flow.

    (D) None of the above.

15. Laminar and turbulent water flow are DIFFERENT in that

    (A) laminar water flow mixes, turbulent does not.

    (B) laminar water flows parallel, turbulent does not.

    (C) Both (A) and (B).

    (D) Neither (A) or (B).

16. Input into a river drainage system consists of all of the following EXCEPT

    (A) groundwater.   (C) floods.

    (B) surface run-off.   (D) rain.

17. Drainage basins funnel all water input into streams within the basin. The streams show patterns that form dependent upon topography, rock type, and geologic structure. All of the following are examples of drainage patterns EXCEPT

    (A) trellis.   (C) dendritic.

    (B) continental.   (D) radial.

18. Minerals can be found in two or more forms while still maintaining the same chemical composition. This property is called polymorphism. Examples of this property include

    (A) quartz.   (C) carbon.

    (B) conchoidal.   (D) Both (A) and (C).

19. Sedimentary rocks include samples that include non-clastic and clastic properties. Which of the following properties will NOT be found in sedimentary rocks?

    (A) Graded bedding   (C) Recrystallization

    (B) Stratification   (D) Ripple marks

20. Which is a type of fracture that is associated with mineral identification?

    (A) Streak   (C) Cleavage

    (B) Hackly   (D) Metallic

GEOLOGY REVIEW

ANSWER KEY

Drill: Geology

1.	(D)	6.	(D)	11.	(C)	16.	(C)
2.	(C)	7.	(C)	12.	(C)	17.	(B)
3.	(B)	8.	(D)	13.	(D)	18.	(D)
4.	(B)	9.	(D)	14.	(D)	19.	(C)
5.	(A)	10.	(D)	15.	(B)	20.	(B)

DETAILED EXPLANATIONS OF ANSWERS

Drill: Geology

1. **(D)** Choice (D) is the best answer. The name of this theory is the nebular hypothesis (C), and was proposed by Kant (B) as a possible explanation. At this time, choice (A) has not proven to be true.

2. **(C)** The process of differentiation (C) is not recognized as a layer of the earth, but is a step in the separation of the internal layers of earth. Choices (A), (B), and (D) do fit as recognized layers of the earth but are NOT correct answers for this question as the exception is the answer requested.

3. **(B)** Fossils are the remains of plants and animals found in rock, hence choice (B) is correct. Stratification (A) is the layering of sedimentary rock but does not refer directly to fossils. Choice (C) is incorrect. Coproliths are the fossilized remains of animal droppings or feces, and are considered animal trace fossils and not plant fossils. Choice (D) is incorrect because there is an acceptable answer for this question in choice (B).

4. **(B)** Diorite (B) is recognized and accepted as igneous in origin. Limestone (A) and shale (C) are both sedimentary in origin and thus do not fit the criteria of the question. Choice (D) is not correct since choice (C) is sedimentary and the question is directed to point out the non-sedimentary selection (B).

5. **(A)** Underground magma or above ground lava will cool and solidify to form igneous rocks (A) from molten material. Sedimentary rock (B) does not form directly from molten material. Volcanic (C) rock would seem to be an acceptable answer but both magma and lava are considered to be igneous, thus, choice (A) is the best possible answer, and the word volcanic is at best a partial answer. Metamorphic rock (D) is rock that has been pressurized and heated to create change, but has not been melted to create metamorphic changes.

6. **(D)** Choice (D) is the best possible answer since both recrystallization (A) and crystal reorientation (C) are recognized traits of metamorphic rocks. Due to the destructive nature of metamorphic change, fossils (B) are very rare in this rock group, thus, are not characteristic of metamorphic rocks.

7.   **(C)**   All rocks are made up of minerals (C), which are the building blocks of the crust of the earth. Symmetry (A) is the geometric shape of the crystal lattice of a mineral. Choices (B) and (D) do not apply as they are terms associated with sedimentary rock and do not universally apply to all types of rock.

8.   **(D)**   (D) is the best possible answer because (A), (B), and (C) are all tectonic features associated with ground movement. Horsts are blocks of earth that are forced upward due to compressional forces. Grabens are down-faulted blocks caused by tension; they create valley-like structures. Oblique-slip faults are caused by shearing forces.

9.   **(D)**   Choice (D) is the best possible answer because (A), (B), and (C) are some of the many topographic features that need to be studied and understood in order to have a complete grasp of landforms, their formation, and the topography of Earth.

10.   **(D)**   Chemical weathering is a complex process consisting of many factors. Choice (D) is most inclusive of the various parts (A) and (B), of the chemical weathering process. Faulting and fracturing (C) are mechanical forms of weathering, and though they may assist in speeding up the chemical cycle, they are still grouped in the mechanical process.

11.   **(C)**   (C) is the best selection for this question as latitude and longitude (A), as well as declination and hashures (B), are important aspects of map interpretation and understanding. (D) is an incorrect response as several selections are correct.

12.   **(C)**   The best answer is choice (C). Scale is defined as the ratio of distance on a map to the distance in the real world. Meridians (A) are lines of longitude. Topography (B) is a description of the structure of the landscape of a given area. Agonic line (D) is an indication of zero magnetic declination with reference to magnetic north.

13.   **(D)**   The excluded term for this question is choice (D) because aphanitic plutons are igneous rock masses. Choices (A) zone of saturation, (B) capillary fringe, and (C) groundwater table, are all terms that a person researching hydrogeology would need to understand and would also use often.

14.   **(D)**   Choice (D) is the best possible answer. Choices (A), (B), and (C) do not represent combinations of laminar and turbulent water flow that are correct in their description. If it were assumed that BOTH had (A) parallel layers that do mix, (B) parallel layers that do not mix, or (C) carry

large particles, then they may be similar enough in characteristics to be classified under the same name.

15. **(B)** Choice (B) is the choice that points out the difference in the types of water flow that is characteristic of laminar and turbulent. Choice (A) is incorrect because turbulent water is described as water that swirls and mixes, and laminar flow is calm and non-mixed. Selections (C) and (D) are incorrect in that they request the selection or exclusion of items that will not correctly help answer the question.

16. **(C)** The exception choice in this case is (C) floods. River floods are an output of overflow that occur when drainage systems cannot handle the input of water. Choices (A), (B), and (D) are all considered to be standard drainage input and thus are not correct selections for this question.

17. **(B)** Continental drainage (B) may be confused with a drainage pattern but in the case of a continental divide a drainage area is described, not a pattern to be identified in a geologic area. Thus, continental is not a type of stream drainage pattern. Choices (A) trellis, (C) dendritic, and (D) radial are all types of river drainage that help to identify the underlying geology of an area.

18. **(D)** Choice (D) is the best possible answer because it is inclusive of quartz (A) and carbon (C) which are well-known polymorphs. Quartz can be found in nature in many various colors and can take on several natural shapes though the basic chemical composition is the same. The same can be said for carbon in the form of graphite and diamond. Conchoidal (B) is a specific property of minerals that refers to a type of fracture or breaking in the silicates and thus is not a correct selection.

19. **(C)** Recrystallization (C) is a process that occurs in igneous and metamorphic rocks and will not be found in true sedimentary layers. Graded beds (A) and stratification (B) are the result of sediment precipitation in water and are very common in sedimentary rock. Ripple marks (D) are also found in sedimentary rock that forms in shallow to medium depth water.

20. **(B)** Hackly (B) is the best answer for this question. It is a type of fracture used to identify metallic minerals. Streak (A) is the color of powder that a mineral makes when crushed and is used to identify minerals. Cleavage (C) is described as the way a mineral splits according to its internal crystal structure. Each mineral will cleave in very specific patterns governed by the chemical composition of the mineral. Metallic (D) is described as a luster or shine that a mineral has.

VII. ASTRONOMY REVIEW

THE CELESTIAL SPHERE

Astronomy is the scientific study of the Universe and its contents beyond Earth's atmosphere. Earth is swimming in extraterrestrial space which can be thought of as a **celestial sphere**.

The celestial sphere is an imaginary sphere centered on and surrounding Earth, and upon which the background stars are projected. The Sun, Moon, planets, and other celestial bodies appear to move against this backdrop of fixed stars. In reality, the stars are at varying distances from Earth, and the celestial sphere is simply a model used in describing positions and motions of astronomical bodies. Earth's eastward rotation makes the celestial sphere appear to rotate westward. The projection of Earth's equator onto the celestial sphere is known as the **celestial equator**, and the **north** and **south celestial poles** are extensions of Earth's **north** and **south geographic poles**.

The apparent annual path of the Sun along the celestial sphere defines the **ecliptic**, and eclipses can only occur when the Moon's orbit crosses the ecliptic. A **solar eclipse** occurs when the new moon lies between the Sun and the Earth. A **lunar eclipse** occurs when the Earth lies between the Sun and the full moon.

There are two opposite points on the celestial sphere where the ecliptic crosses the celestial equator; they are called the **spring** and **autumnal equinoxes**. Similarly, there are two opposite points where the Sun reaches its highest declination north (+23.5°) or south (−23.5°) of the celestial equator, and these are known as the **summer** and **winter solstices**, respectively. Along the celestial sphere, distances between objects are measured in angular units of degrees, minutes, and seconds.

It is possible to define an ecliptic coordinate system to specify positions of celestial objects in the sky using angular coordinates called **celestial longitude** and **celestial latitude**. Celestial longitude is measured eastward along the ecliptic (from 0° to 360°) starting at the vernal equinox. Celestial latitude measures positions in degrees north (+) and south (−) from the ecliptic (at 0°) to the ecliptic poles (at + and − 90°).

Another widely used system is the **equatorial coordinate** system. This system specifies positions in the sky using time and angular coordinates called **right ascension** and **declination**. Right ascension measures angular direction in units of time (0 to 24 hours) eastward along the celestial equator from the vernal equinox. It is convenient to use time because it relates the position of a star to its apparent motion across the sky. Declination measures angular direction in degrees north (+) and south (–) from the celestial equator (0°) to the celestial poles (+ and –90°).

Another important element in the celestial sphere is the **celestial meridian**. This is an imaginary half-great circle that connects the north and south points on your horizon while passing through your **zenith** (point directly overhead). An hour angle is the angular measurement in units of time of how far westward an object is from your celestial meridian. One hour corresponds to 15° of arc.

MEASURING DISTANCES FROM EARTH

In order to measure distances from Earth to objects in the real sky, astronomers use the following units: The **astronomical unit** (AU); this is the average distance between Earth and the Sun—approximately 93 million miles. The **light year** (LY), which is the distance light travels through a vacuum in one year—approximately six trillion miles. The **parsec** (pc) is the distance at which an object would have a parallax of one arcsecond and is equal to 3.26 LY.

Stellar trigonometric parallax is the apparent displacement of a nearby star, relative to a background of far more distant stars, which results from the motion of the Earth around the Sun in half a year. The distance in parsecs equals the inverse of the parallax in arcseconds.

THE SOLAR SYSTEM

The nearest star is the Sun, and it is at the center of our solar system, which is comprised of nine major planets, natural planetary satellites, asteroids, meteoroids, comets, and the interplanetary medium. The Sun holds all members of the solar system captive within its gravitational field, and they orbit around it at various speeds and distances. The Sun is a hot glowing body of ionized gas (**plasma**). It is a star of medium size and brightness in comparison to other stars in our galaxy. It generates energy by nuclear fusion. The Sun's surface, known as the **photosphere**, is responsible for emitting the sunlight that we see and exhibits other activities such as sunspots and solar flares.

Planets are astronomical bodies which orbit a star (such as the Sun) and cannot produce their own light. Therefore, they shine by reflecting starlight. In the solar system, planets that orbit closer to the Sun than Earth are called "inferior" planets—these are Mercury and Venus. Those that orbit farther away than Earth are called "superior" planets—Mars, Jupiter, Saturn, Uranus, Neptune, and Pluto.

The distances and speeds at which planets orbit the Sun are not arbitrary; they are governed by three fundamental laws known as **Kepler's Laws of Planetary Motion**. Kepler's First Law states that all planets revolve along closed orbits called **ellipses**. The Second Law states that the rotating vector connecting the Sun to the planet moves across equal areas of its orbit in equal intervals of time. The Third Law states that the square of a planet's orbital period is directly proportional to the cube of its semi-major axis.

With respect to their increasing distance from the Sun, Mercury, Venus, Earth, and Mars are the innermost planets of the Solar System and are known as the **terrestrial planets**. All are rocky in nature and have a similar fundamental structure. Jupiter, Saturn, Uranus, and Neptune represent four of the five outermost planets and are known as the **Jovian planets**. They are gaseous giants with ring systems. Pluto is normally the farthest planet from the Sun, but its highly eccentric orbit causes it to pass inside of Neptune's orbit for 20 years of Pluto's 248-year orbit around the Sun. It is much smaller than the Jovian planets and is much like the terrestrial planets.

Except for Mercury and Venus, all planets have natural satellites. The Moon is Earth's natural satellite; it exhibits different phases depending on where it is in its orbit around the Earth, and it, along with the Sun, is responsible for ocean tides. The Jovian planets have eight or more natural satellites each, and also have ring systems. Other constituents of the solar system are **asteroids**, **meteoroids**, and **comets**. Asteroids can be thought of as minor planets, and they are concentrated in an orbital region between Mars and Jupiter known as the asteroid belt. Meteoroids are small celestial objects which pass through Earth's atmosphere, heat up, and glow (**meteors**). A **meteorite** is a meteor that actually falls on Earth. Comets are icy bodies a few kilometers across normally orbiting in the outer Solar System. They partially vaporize and form a diffuse envelope of gas around the nucleus (**coma**). The passage of Earth through the debris of comets is what causes **meteor showers**.

STARS

The most obvious feature of the night sky is the presence of stars. All of the stars seen with the unaided eye are part of our galaxy, the Milky

Way. They are always in the sky, but the brightness of the Sun during the day makes it impossible to see them. They appear to rise and set as the Earth rotates eastward, and their twinkling is due to turbulence in the Earth's atmosphere. We obtain information about stars by analyzing their light using a method called **spectroscopy**. Starlight is passed through a spectroscope and the resulting spectrum reveals information that includes temperature, composition, and relative motion. It is found that stars vary widely in mass, diameter, brightness, temperature, and spectral properties.

The brightness of stars and all other celestial objects is measured in **magnitudes**. Magnitudes follow a reverse logarithmic scale where a decrease of one unit corresponds to an increase of brightness by a factor of 2.5. On this scale, the lowest numbers correspond to the brightest objects. The Sun at magnitude –27 is the brightest star in the entire sky, while Sirius (the "dog" star) at magnitude 1.5 is the brightest in the night sky. The faintest magnitude detectable by the unaided human eye is +6. Note that these magnitudes refer to apparent brightness as seen from Earth, which depends on how distant the object is from us. **Apparent magnitude** increases as the distance to the object increases, resulting in the object appearing fainter. The **absolute magnitude** of an object, which is a measure of its intrinsic brightness or **luminosity**, is defined as its apparent magnitude as measured from a reference distance of 10 parsecs. In order to determine the absolute magnitude of a star from its apparent magnitude, you must know its distance. Trigonometric parallax is the only direct method of determining distance to stars, but this method only works for those stars that are nearby. Since the vast majority of stars are too distant to have their parallaxes measured, indirect or statistical methods are used.

A striking feature in the classification of stars appears when we plot their absolute magnitude versus their temperature. On this diagram, known as the **Hertzsprung-Russell (H-R) diagram**, approximately 90 percent of all stars (the Sun included) fall within a narrow region called the **main sequence**. Since absolute magnitude is a measure of a star's luminosity, and its temperature is a measure of its spectral type, the H-R diagram is also referred to as the luminosity-temperature diagram.

An example of an indirect method of determining a star's distance is the use of its known temperature or spectral type to determine its absolute magnitude (if it is a main sequence star), which is then combined with its apparent magnitude to give the distance.

Besides their apparent westward motion due to Earth's rotation, stars undergo their own true motion in space. The apparent angular shift of a star across the sky over a period of time is known as its **proper motion**.

The motion of a star in a direction across the line-of-sight is known as its **radial motion**. Its radial velocity can be determined from a shift in its spectral lines known as the **Doppler shift**; it is positive if the star is moving away from the Sun, and negative if it is approaching.

Stars have lives of their own and are not eternal. They are born from huge interstellar clouds of gas and dust known as star-forming regions, or **nebulae**. A star's life expectancy depends on how massive it is. The more massive the star, the shorter its lifetime and the more violent its death. The Sun will spend 10 billion years of its life on the main sequence, and then will expand and cool down to become a **red giant**. Finally, it will contract to a very dense Earth-size star called a **white dwarf** and then ultimately dim out to become a **black dwarf**. More massive stars live out their lives in more extreme states such as a **neutron star** or a **black hole**.

Another important feature of the night sky is the presence of **constellations**, which are star groupings that appear to connect stars in a certain pattern. Examples are Ursa Major (Big Bear) in the northern hemisphere; and the Southern Cross, seen from the southern hemisphere. These constellations are imaginary star patterns, and the stars in them are at varying distances from the Sun.

GALAXIES

Perhaps the most striking feature of the night sky is a band of diffuse light that stretches across the celestial sphere on a clear and moonless night. This is understood to be the giant disk of the Milky Way. It measures 100,000 LY across and is composed of 100 billion stars and their unseen planets, and interstellar gas and dust, as well as a central bulge of about 10,000 LY in diameter made up of densely packed older stars. The total mass of our galaxy, including the disk and the bulge is estimated at 200 billion solar masses. The disk and bulge are surrounded by a halo of matter on each side of the galaxy's central plane, perhaps adding ten times as much mass of unseen dark matter.

This system is arranged in a pinwheel pattern of spiral arms that revolve around the galactic center. Speeding along at about 200 kilometers per second, the Sun takes 230 million years to circle the galaxy once in a galactic year.

In addition, white spots with a cloudlike appearance, called nebulae, are visible in certain parts of the sky. Some of these bodies were proven to be so distant as to be far outside the Milky Way and were then resolved into galaxies in their own right. An example is the Andromeda Galaxy, which is two million light years away. Galaxies come in three basic shapes: **disk spiral**, **elliptical**, and **irregular**. An example of the latter is the Magellanic Clouds seen in the southern hemisphere. Distant galaxies appear to be receding from Earth at speeds increasing in proportion to their distance from Earth. This is observed as a Doppler red shift in their light spectra. Certain celestial objects resembling stars can be observed at distances greater than that of the farthest galaxy, yet are identifiable and seem to emit more energy than our own galaxy. They are characterized by a large red shift and are called **quasars** because of their quasi-stellar appearance.

The observable universe appears to be expanding as a result of the other galaxies receding. This expansion is the basis of the theory that the universe originated in a "Big Bang," occurring between 8 and 20 billion years ago. Additional support for this theory is provided by the cosmic microwave background radiation and the abundance of light chemical elements in the observable universe.

☞ Drill: Astronomy

1. This review treats astronomy as

   (A) a set of observations.

   (B) a systematic and scientific way of exploring and understanding what is observed in the sky.

   (C) the casting of horoscopes.

   (D) the study of the solar system.

2. The projection of the Earth's axis on the sky is the

   (A) celestial equator.   (C) celestial poles.

   (B) zenith.   (D) ecliptic.

3. The path of the Sun across the celestial sphere is called the

   (A) ecliptic.   (C) equinox.

   (B) celestial equator.   (D) solstice.

4. The Sun crosses the celestial equator going north on March 21. This is known as the

(A) solstice.   (C) solar eclipse.

(B) lunar eclipse.   (D) spring equinox.

5. If the Moon completely covers the Sun as seen by an earthbound observer, there is a

(A) total lunar eclipse.   (C) partial lunar eclipse.

(B) total solar eclipse.   (D) partial solar eclipse.

6. Declination is from what coordinate system?

(A) Ecliptic   (C) Equatorial

(B) Galactic   (D) Metric

7. The coordinate right ascension is usually measured in

(A) degrees, minutes, and seconds.

(B) radians.

(C) meters.

(D) hours, minutes, and seconds.

8. The parallax of a star is

(A) its temperature divided by its mass.

(B) its mass divided by its temperature.

(C) the angle through which the star appears to move in the course of half a year.

(D) the angle through which the star appears to move in the course of a year.

9. If a star has a parallax of 0.1 second of arc, its distance is how many parsecs?

(A)   2   (B)   1   (C)   ½   (D)   10

10. Astronomers call the visible surface of the sun the

(A) photosphere.   (C) sunspot.

(B) plasma.   (D) flare.

11. Which of the following planets is closer to the Sun than Earth is?

    (A) Mars   (B) Saturn   (C) Venus   (D) Jupiter

12. The AU is

    (A) the radius of the Moon.

    (B) the average distance of the earth from the Sun.

    (C) the force that the Sun exerts on a planet.

    (D) a recently discovered satellite of Jupiter.

13. Kepler's Second Law says, essentially, that

    (A) force equals mass times acceleration.

    (B) the square of the period is proportional to the cube of the semi-major axis.

    (C) the orbits of the planets are ellipses with the Sun at one focus.

    (D) the line from the Sun to a planet sweeps equal areas in equal times.

14. In order of increasing distance from the Sun, the terrestrial planets are

    (A) Mars, Venus, Earth, and Mercury.

    (B) Mercury, Venus, Earth, and Mars.

    (C) Jupiter, Saturn, Uranus, Neptune, and Pluto.

    (D) Mercury, Venus, Mars, and Earth.

15. Which of the following planets has no natural satellites?

    (A) Mars   (B) Earth   (C) Jupiter   (D) Venus

16. Icy worlds with a size of a few kilometers across are

    (A) meteoroids.   (C) comets.

    (B) meteors.   (D) asteroids.

17. If Star X appears to be 2.5 times as bright as Star Y, then the two stars differ in magnitude by

    (A) 0.   (B) 1.   (C) 2.5.   (D) 0.5.

18. We can get the temperature for a star by

    (A) measuring its spectrum.

    (B) measuring the Doppler shift of its spectral lines.

    (C) measuring its distance and apparent magnitude.

    (D) obtaining its chemical composition.

19. The Sun's galactic motion in the Milky Way can be described as

    (A) radial motion towards the center of the galaxy.

    (B) radial motion away from the center of the galaxy.

    (C) motion along a very elongated ellipse.

    (D) motion in a circular orbit.

20. The theory of an expanding universe is supported by which one of the following observations?

    (A) A cosmic explosion known as the Big Bang occurred 15 billion years ago.

    (B) The Doppler red shift of distant galaxies

    (C) The cosmic microwave background radiation

    (D) The observed abundances of light chemical elements

ASTRONOMY REVIEW

ANSWER KEY

Drill: Astronomy

1.	(B)	6.	(C)	11.	(C)	16.	(C)
2.	(C)	7.	(D)	12.	(B)	17.	(B)
3.	(A)	8.	(C)	13.	(D)	18.	(A)
4.	(D)	9.	(D)	14.	(B)	19.	(D)
5.	(B)	10.	(A)	15.	(D)	20.	(B)

DETAILED EXPLANATIONS OF ANSWERS

Drill: Astronomy

1. **(B)** Choice (B) is the correct answer. Astronomy is more than just a set of observations (A), but also an interpretation of these observations and their systematic organization in a system of inquiry and understanding of all phenomena in the sky, and not just the solar system (D). Astrology (C) is not really a science.

2. **(C)** The correct answer is celestial poles (C). The text states that "the north and south celestial poles are extensions of Earth's north and south geographic poles." Earth's rotation axis is the line that joins the geographic poles. Choice (A) identifies the projection of the Earth's equator. The zenith (B) is the point directly overhead an observer. The ecliptic (D) is the line that describes the Sun's orbit across the celestial sphere.

3. **(A)** Choice (A) is the correct response. The ecliptic is the apparent annual path through the stars that the Sun follows.

4. **(D)** Choice (D) is the correct answer. The text describes equinoxes as the two points on the celestial sphere where the ecliptic crosses the celestial equator, and since this crossing occurs on March 21, it is the spring equinox. Choice (A) is incorrect because solstices occur in the summer and winter, and correspond to the ecliptic being farthest from the celestial equator. Choices (B) and (C) should not be chosen because, in general, when this crossing occurs on March 21, the Moon is not necessarily aligned with the Earth and the Sun.

5. **(B)** The correct answer choice is (B), because the question describes an eclipse, and the eclipse must be a solar eclipse because the Moon is between the Earth and the Sun. Choices (A) and (C) are wrong answers since they do not refer to an eclipse. Choice (D) is incorrect; the solar eclipse is total because the Moon's disk covers the sun from our view completely.

6. **(C)** In the text, it is stated that "declination measures angular direction in degrees north (+) and south (–) from the celestial equator." Choices (A) and (D) are incorrect since neither is a coordinate system. Choice (B) should not be chosen, since it is not discussed in the text.

7.   **(D)**   The coordinate right ascension is usually measured in hours, minutes, and seconds; (D) is the correct answer. The coordinate is not measured in radians (B) or (C) meters. Choice (A) mixes units of measure, and should not be chosen.

8.   **(C)**   Choices (A) and (B) have no relevance to the concept of parallax. Choice (D) should not be chosen, since it does not refer to the proper time-frame. Therefore, the correct answer is choice (C), the angle through which a star appears to move in one half a year.

9.   **(D)**   The distance in parsecs is equal to the inverse of a star's parallax in arcseconds, therefore, choice (D) is correct. Choices (A), (B), and (C) all refer to the wrong distance.

10.   **(A)**   The correct answer is (A). The photosphere is what we observe of the Sun's surface. Plasma (B) is the state of the Sun's interior. Choices (C) and (D) are local phenomena on the Sun's surface, but not the whole surface; they should not be chosen.

11.   **(C)**   In the text, it is stated that Mercury and Venus are closer to the Sun than Earth, and are inferior planets. Therefore, choice (C) is the only correct answer out of the four choices. Choices (A), (B), and (D) all refer to superior planets, and are incorrect.

12.   **(B)**   The AU is defined in the text as the average distance of the earth from the Sun. Choices (A), (C), and (D) have no support in the text, and are therefore incorrect.

13.   **(D)**   Kepler's Second Law states that the line from the Sun to a planet sweeps equal areas in equal lines (D). Choice (A) is Newton's second law, choice (B) is Kepler's Third Law, and choice (C) is Kepler's First Law which are incorrect choices.

14.   **(B)**   Choice (B) is the correct choice. Choice (A) is wrong because it transposes the order of Mercury and Mars. Choice (C) incorrectly lists the Jovian planets. Choice (D) transposes the order of Mars and Earth, and should not be selected.

15.   **(D)**   It is stated in the text that "except for Mercury and Venus, all planets have natural satellites"; therefore, choice (D) should be selected. Mars (A), Earth (B), and Jupiter (C), are all incorrect choices.

16. **(C)** The correct choice is (C) comets. Meteoroids (A) and meteors (B) are generally smaller and not icy, and asteroids (D) are generally larger and rocky.

17. **(B)** It is stated in the text that "a decrease of one unit corresponds to an increase of brightness by a factor of 2.5." You can determine from that statement that the magnitude of the two stars differ by 1 (B). Choices (A), (C), and (D) are all incorrect.

18. **(A)** The temperature of a star is determined from measuring its spectrum, therefore choice (A) is correct. The text states the spectrum reveals information about the temperature, composition (D), and relative motion (B). Choice (C) is incorrect because it refers to absolute magnitude (intrinsic brightness), which is another property of the star and not directly related to its temperature.

19. **(D)** The correct choice is (D), since the Sun's orbit in the Milky Way galaxy is nearly circular. This can be inferred from the statement that "the Sun takes 230 million years to circle the galaxy once in a galactic year." The choices referring to radial motion towards the center of the galaxy (A) and radial motion away from the center of the galaxy (B) describe linear motion and are incorrect. Choice (C) refers to an extreme type of orbit which doesn't really agree with the statement given in the text.

20. **(B)** The Doppler red shift of distant galaxies (B), which is interpreted as recessional motion of the galaxies, and therefore an expansion of the universe, is the correct answer. Choice (A) is not an observation but rather a hypothesis drawn from choices (B), (C), and (D). Choices (C) and (D) directly support choice (A), but do not imply an expanding universe.

VIII. METEOROLOGY REVIEW

THE ATMOSPHERE

Our **atmosphere** is composed of several distinct layers which contain the necessary gases to support biological life on Earth. By volume, the atmosphere is 78.08 percent nitrogen and 20.95 percent oxygen. Other trace gases constitute the remaining 0.97 percent. Two of the most important trace gases vary in amount throughout the atmosphere. Carbon dioxide usually occupies 0.03 percent and water vapor takes up anywhere from near 0 percent to as much as 4 percent of the atmosphere. Gravitational compression of the gases creates a higher concentration of matter near the surface with decreasing amounts at higher elevations. Because of this, both air pressure and density decrease with height.

The atmosphere is divided into four primary layers. In ascending order, they are the **troposphere**, **stratosphere**, **mesosphere**, and the **thermosphere**. Each layer has different characteristics from any adjacent layer which makes layer identification possible. The troposphere is sometimes referred to as the "weather sphere" because it is in this layer where all significant weather phenomena take place. This layer contains nearly all of the water vapor and carbon dioxide found in the atmosphere and has a decrease in temperature with height. The stratosphere has a high concentration of ozone which is often referred to as the ozone layer. Because ozone is a strong absorber of the sun's ultraviolet rays, temperatures increase with height throughout the stratosphere (this is known as a temperature inversion). Though important in their own right, the mesosphere and thermosphere have only an indirect impact on daily weather events.

As radiant energy from the sun travels through the atmosphere, it is scattered, transmitted, reflected, and absorbed by all matter it comes into contact with. The energy left over is available to heat the surface of the Earth. Due to the 23.5° tilt of the Earth's rotational axis, equatorial regions annually receive more solar energy than they radiate back to space. Conversely, polar regions lose more energy than they receive. This is why the poles are ice-capped while lush rain forests can thrive in the tropics. However, without a mechanism to distribute the Earth's heat more evenly, the poles would grow colder every year while tropical areas got warmer. This redistribution of heat is the responsibility of global air's circulation and large scale storm systems.

THE SEASONS

How the Earth's axis inclines, or tilts, with respect to the Sun gives temperate zones four seasons: winter, spring, summer, and fall. Winter begins in the northern hemisphere on December 22nd (June 22nd in the southern hemisphere), the time of the **winter solstice**. On this date, the northern half of the Earth is tilted furthest from the Sun. Minimum winter temperatures are normally reached sometime after this date because of the time it takes for the mass of the Earth to radiate its stored heat. Summer begins on June 22nd in the northern hemisphere (December 22nd in the southern hemisphere), the time of the **summer solstice**. Now the northern half of the Earth is tilted closest to the Sun. Maximum summer temperatures occur at a later date due to the lag involved in heating large quantities of mass.

March 21st and September 23rd are the dates of the **vernal** (spring) and **autumnal** (fall) **equinoxes**, respectively. The dates are reversed for the southern hemisphere. At these times, the tilt of the Earth is perpendicular to the plane of the Earth and Sun. This puts the Earth at a neutral tilt relative to the sun and gives all locations in both hemispheres equal amounts of daylight and darkness. This is in contrast to summer and winter when the respective poles experience either 24 hours of daylight or 24 hours of darkness.

WEATHER TYPES

The amount of heat energy available to the Earth and atmosphere is also important on a daily basis. It is possible to estimate this amount of energy by using **radiosondes** to measure temperature, pressure, water vapor, and wind velocity vertically through the atmosphere. This estimate is represented in the concept of stability. Since hot air is less dense than cold air, isolated pockets of hot air that form near the surface will begin to rise. If the atmosphere is unstable, these isolated pockets of hot air, or **parcels**, will continue to rise without any additional forcing from below. The more energy available to the parcel, the faster it will rise. A stable atmosphere will act to force a rising parcel back to the surface and is thought of as having less energy available to the parcel. When a condition of neutral stability exists, a parcel will rise as long as it encounters an upward force. Once the force is removed and the parcel comes to rest, it will remain where it stops. Upward motion imparted to a parcel of air due to differential heating of the Earth's atmosphere is called convection.

By plotting data from a radiosonde on a skew-*t* diagram, a meteorologist can calculate how fast the temperature changes with height. This is called the **lapse rate** of the atmosphere. Since both pressure and density decrease with height in the troposphere, we know from the equation of state that a rising parcel will expand and therefore cool. A process which results in cooling or warming due to expansion or compression with no loss or gain of heat is called an **adiabatic process**. A standard atmosphere has been established for use in comparing daily values of meteorological parameters. Its dry adiabatic lapse rate has been set at 5.5°F per 1,000 feet (i.e., for every 1,000 ft. of elevation, the air will expand and cool 5.5°F). Saturation of a parcel complicates lapse rate computation and necessitates a second lapse rate for the standard atmosphere. Thus, its moist adiabatic lapse rate has been determined to be 3.3°F per 1,000 feet. It should now be obvious that stability computations can become quite involved. The main point is that if as a parcel rises it cools more slowly than the surrounding atmosphere, it will stay warmer and continue to rise.

Upward motion is very important to the production of precipitation. Convection, as well as **orographic lift**, **frontal lift**, and **convergence** all result in rising motion in the atmosphere. Orographic lift refers to air that is being forced up and over terrain features such as mountains. Frontal lift is created by warm and cold fronts. Since a cold front normally has a steep frontal surface with cold, dense air behind it, it forces the warmer and less dense air ahead of the front abruptly upward, resulting in convective-type weather. A warm front is normally not as steep and has warm air behind it. This less dense warm air will overrun the colder, denser air ahead of the front and cause **stratiform-type** weather. **Convergence** refers to air which flows together as in toward the center of a surface low pressure circulation. When the air converges at the center, it must either go up or down. The ground prohibits downward motion so the air is forced upward.

The two previously mentioned weather types, convective and stratiform, both originate from upward motion, yet produce distinctly different weather. The rapidly rising air involved with convection produces cumuliform clouds, which make up the group of clouds with vertical development. When these clouds are short, they are called cumulus (when very short, "fair-weather" cumulus may be used), and may resemble stalks of cauliflower. When these clouds grow to extreme heights and develop ice crystals at their tops, they are called cumulonimbus. Extensive convective activity will usually produce rain showers and thunderstorms. Cumulonimbus clouds, or cells, are sometimes called "thunderheads" and can produce lightning, heavy rain, and possibly hail. When the top of the cumulonimbus encounters stable air and strong winds aloft, the ice crystals spread out and get blown into the familiar anvil shape associated with thunderstorms.

A thunderstorm actually goes through a three-stage life cycle: the **cumulus stage**, the **mature stage**, and the **dissipating stage**. During the cumulus stage, the cell is composed only of rising air which is called the **updraft**. At this stage, the initial cumulus cloud forms and begins to tower skyward. A general rule of thumb is that the tallest thunderstorms are usually the strongest. As droplets within the cloud grow by the process of collision and coalescence, they eventually become too heavy to be supported by the updraft and fall out of the cloud as precipitation. Once precipitation begins, friction caused by precipitation drag will pull surrounding air down with it. This creates the **downdraft** and marks the start of the mature stage. As the downdraft descends, drier air from the surrounding atmosphere may mix in, causing evaporative cooling. Since cold air is more dense than warm air, this cooling strengthens the downdraft by allowing it to descend faster. Very strong downdrafts can cause damaging straight-line winds as they hit the ground and spread out radially.

After some time, the descending air will choke off the updraft producing downdraft throughout the cell. This begins the dissipating stage. With no more rising motion available, precipitation comes to an end and the cloud begins to evaporate. This entire life cycle can be completed in less than one hour. However, when atmospheric conditions are right, a supercell thunderstorm can develop. In a supercell, once the initial updraft is extinguished, a new updraft will form allowing the storm to sustain itself for several hours. Storms such as these produce severe weather such as large hail, damaging winds, flash floods, and tornadoes during their mature stage.

Stratiform weather is caused by a more gradual ascent of air and produces clouds of great horizontal extent. These clouds do not grow very tall and usually exhibit flat tops. The clouds often appear as a continuous layer which can stretch from horizon to horizon. Stratiform clouds are found in the low, middle, and high cloud groups. Stratiform weather is generally characterized by persistent light rain, drizzle, and fog. Fog, by definition, is a stratus cloud with its base at the surface.

It should be noted that these weather types are not mutually exclusive. It is not uncommon for stratiform areas to contain embedded convective cells. Likewise, it is not uncommon for cumulus clouds to spread out, merge bases, and form an extensive stratocumulus cloud deck. Some of the most challenging forecasts meteorologists face are caused by just such interactive situations.

Wind is the mechanism responsible for transporting weather phenomena around the world to balance the global energy budget. The pressure gradient force is what moves the air in a direction from higher pressure to lower pressure. On a weather map, wind speeds will be greatest where the isobars (lines connecting points of equal pressure) are packed closest together. An area such as this is said to have a steep pressure gradient. However, careful observation shows that the wind does not blow directly across the isobars. Further inspection reveals that wind is the vector sum of several forces acting on the air simultaneously.

THE CORIOLIS EFFECT

The **Coriolis force** is caused by the rotation of the Earth. It is strongest near the poles and weakest near the equator. Its strength is also related to wind velocity since stronger winds produce a stronger Coriolis force. Relative to the direction of wind flow, the Coriolis force acts to deflect the wind to the right in the northern hemisphere and to the left in the southern hemisphere. Thus, strong winds at high latitudes experience the greatest amount of deflection. The Coriolis force and pressure gradient force are equal and opposite for parallel isobaric fields in the upper atmosphere. Together, their net force causes the air to flow parallel to the isobars. However, if the isobaric field curves, centripetal acceleration causes an imbalance between the Coriolis and pressure gradient forces. The net force is now in the direction of the pressure gradient force and allows the wind to parallel a curved isobaric field.

Closer to the ground, air encounters friction due to the roughness of the Earth's surface. This slows the wind speed and causes a decrease in the Coriolis force. The result is an imbalance which leaves the net force in the direction of the pressure gradient force. This causes the wind to cross the isobars at an angle. The angle of crossing is dependent upon the amount of friction, and hence upon the roughness of the surface. Over the entire surface of the Earth, this angle averages about 30°. Putting all of this together, we can now see that in the northern hemisphere, wind will flow counter-clockwise around a low pressure circulation and converge to its center but will flow clockwise around a high pressure circulation and diverge from its center.

☞ Drill: Meteorology

1. Why is stratospheric ozone depletion (destruction of the ozone layer) a serious concern?

    (A) It is a major cause of the "greenhouse effect."

(B)   It will increase the amount of ultraviolet radiation reaching the ground.

(C)   It causes acid rain.

(D)   It is really nothing to worry about.

2.   Land and sea (or lake) breezes form because of

(A)   uneven heating of coastal environments.

(B)   the pressure gradient force.

(C)   the difference in temperature between land and water surfaces.

(D)   All of the above.

3.   Mountain and valley breezes form because of

(A)   gravity and the pressure gradient force.

(B)   the pressure gradient force and heating.

(C)   gravity and heating.

(D)   the pressure gradient force and the Coriolis force.

4.   Which of the following pictures represents a possible aerial view of tree damage caused by thunderstorm downdraft winds? (The arrows represent the trees with the arrow head being the top of the tree.)

(A)   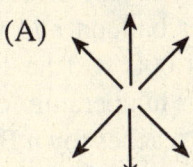   (C)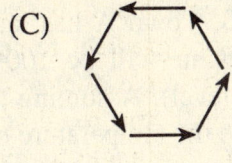

(B)   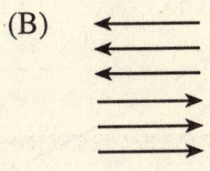   (D)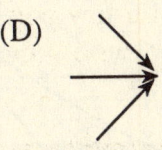

5.   How is the relative strength of a thunderstorm updraft estimated?

(A)   By the intensity of the lightning

(B)   By the height of the cloud base

(C) By the speed of the wind gusts measured at the surface

(D) By the size of the precipitation particles (raindrops or hail-stones)

6. Why does saturation of a rising parcel lead to a slower adiabatic lapse rate?

(A) Because of the release of latent heat by condensing water vapor

(B) Because of the release of latent heat by evaporating water droplets

(C) Because cloud droplets add frictional drag to the rising parcel and slow it down

(D) Because temperature decreases with height

7. What happens to descending air?

(A) It becomes more humid.

(B) It expands.

(C) It warms.

(D) It becomes less dense.

8. Mt. Adiabatic, a 3,000-ft. mountain, separates towns A and B. Air is being forced up on the side facing town A but downslope on the side facing town B. Town A has launched a weather balloon and found that the rising air will be 100% saturated at 1,000 ft. (the lifting condensation level). Assuming town A has an air temperature of 70° F, what will be the temperature of the air when it reaches town B?

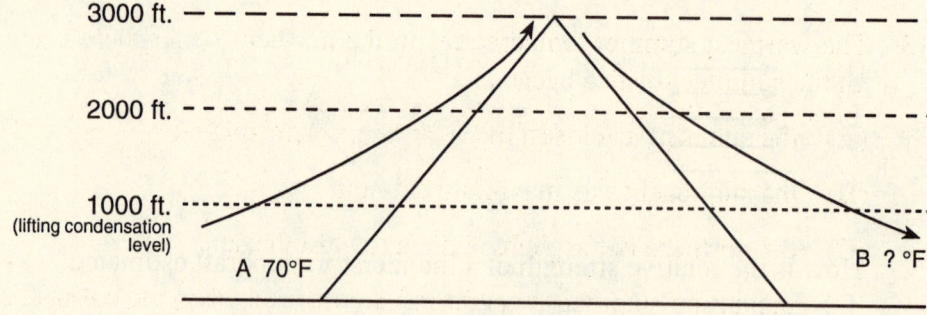

3000 ft.
2000 ft.
1000 ft.
(lifting condensation level)
A 70°F
B ? °F

(A) 70.0°F

(B) 67.8° F

(C) 74.4° F

(D) 70.2° F

9. An inversion is
    (A) unstable.
    (B) stable.
    (C) neutrally stable.
    (D) None of the above.

10. Why do we see lightning before we hear thunder?
    (A) Because the lightning occurred closer than the thunder
    (B) Because lightning is composed of multiple strokes
    (C) Because thunder occurs higher in the cloud
    (D) Because of the difference between the speeds of light and sound

11. Why is radiation the only method of heat transfer capable of bringing the sun's energy to the Earth?
    (A) Because space is a vacuum
    (B) Because other methods are too slow and lose too much energy by the time they reach Earth
    (C) Because blockage by stellar debris inhibits other methods
    (D) Because solar convection is propelled away from the Earth

12. Why does evaporation lead to cooling?
    (A) Because of the change in state involved as water evaporates
    (B) Because of the absorption of latent heat by water droplets
    (C) Because of the release of latent heat by water droplets
    (D) (A) and (B) only

13. The warmest summer temperatures in the northern hemisphere occur on the summer solstice because
    (A) the sun is at its closest to the northern hemisphere.
    (B) the sun reaches its maximum azimuth.
    (C) the northern hemisphere is tilted toward the sun.
    (D) maximum summer temperatures aren't reached on the solstice.

14. The sky is blue because
    (A) outer space is blue.

(B)   it is a reflection of the blue bodies of water at the surface.

(C)   sunlight is scattered by the atmosphere before it reaches the Earth.

(D)   the sun emits most of its light in the blue portion of the spectrum.

15.   Assume that the Earth does not rotate, has a homogeneous surface, and that the sun always shines on the equator. Which sort of global circulation pattern would you expect?

(A) 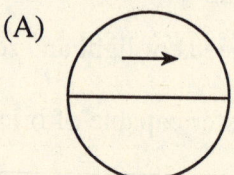   (C)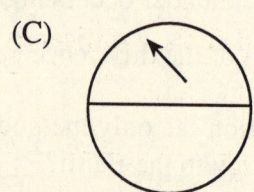

(B) 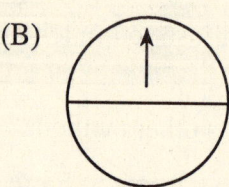   (D)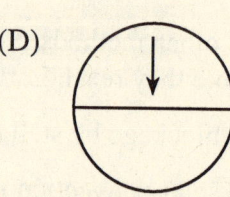

16.   You would expect higher surface pressure over land masses with lower surface pressure over bodies of water during

(A) winter.   (C) summer.

(B) spring.   (D) fall.

17.   It can rain when the temperature is

(A) 32°F.   (C) 33°F.

(B) 25°F.   (D) All of the above.

18.   Water can remain a liquid at

(A) 60°F.   (C) 0°F.

(B) 40°F.   (D) All of the above.

19.   Why does your body perspire when you get hot?

(A) Water vapor condenses on your skin.

(B) It is your body's biological method to cool itself.

(C) Your body temperature slowly increases and approaches the dew point of the surrounding air.

(D) None of the above.

20. It is possible for snow to fall in tropical regions because

(A) hurricanes can be very cold.

(B) of elevation considerations.

(C) the land cools significantly at night.

(D) All of the above.

METEOROLOGY REVIEW

ANSWER KEY

Drill: Meteorology

1.	(B)	6.	(A)	11.	(A)	16.	(A)
2.	(D)	7.	(C)	12.	(D)	17.	(D)
3.	(C)	8.	(C)	13.	(D)	18.	(D)
4.	(A)	9.	(B)	14.	(C)	19.	(B)
5.	(D)	10.	(D)	15.	(B)	20.	(B)

DETAILED EXPLANATIONS OF ANSWERS

Drill: Meteorology

1.   **(B)**   The "greenhouse effect" is caused mainly by other atmospheric gases such as water vapor and carbon dioxide, so choice (A) is incorrect. Acid rain is caused by oxides of sulfur and nitrogen, so choice (C) is incorrect. Photochemical reactions involving oxides of nitrogen and chlorofluorocarbons play a major role in ozone destruction. These chemicals react with ozone and lead to a net decrease in ozone concentration in the stratosphere. Since ozone is a strong absorber of incoming ultraviolet (uv) radiation, any decrease in ozone concentration will increase the amount of uv radiation reaching the surface. This will increase the risk of skin cancer from contact with the sun significantly. With this in mind, it is easy to see that choice (D) is incorrect, leaving choice (B) as the correct answer.

2.   **(D)**   Due to the high specific heat capacity of water, land surfaces will heat up more rapidly than water surfaces. Since warmer air is less dense than cooler air, this uneven heating along coastal areas causes vertical expansion of the isobaric field over the land and compression of the field over the water. This forms an elevated area of high pressure over the land and an elevated area of low pressure over the water. The pressure gradient force acts on the air and moves it from higher pressure to lower pressure. The net movement of air toward the low pressure aloft induces an area of high pressure on the water surface while the net movement of air away from the high pressure aloft induces an area of low pressure on the land surface. The pressure gradient force now begins to move the surface air from the higher pressure on the water surface towards the lower pressure on the land surface. It is this surface flow of air which is the sea (or lake) breeze. The greater the contrast between water temperature and land temperature, the stronger the breeze. At night, the land will cool faster than the adjacent water, reversing the process and forming a land breeze from the land towards the water.

3.   **(C)**   The pressure gradient force plays no significant role in vertical air circulations. This fact effectively eliminates choices (A), (B), and (D), leaving choice (C) as the correct answer. Since temperature decreases with height, as the valley air warms during the day, it becomes less dense

than the air along the adjacent hillsides and begins to flow up the surrounding slopes. At night, air in the hills cools faster than the air in the valleys. Gravity pulls the cooler, more dense air down the hillsides and into the valleys.

4.   **(A)**   Since a downdraft spreads out radially along the ground, any pattern showing divergence (i.e., resembling spokes on a wagon wheel) is correct. Choice (B) requires winds from two different directions to occur which would not normally happen during a downdraft. Choice (C) implies a rotating wind which is also not associated with downdrafts. Choice (D) would need several different wind directions. Of the sketches given, only choice (A) shows the necessary divergent pattern often associated with downdrafts. In this sketch, the downdraft would have impacted the ground at the center and spread out from there.

5.   **(D)**   The intensity of the lightning is determined by complex processes which electrify the cloud. The updraft is only indirectly associated with this, so choice (A) is not a good answer. The height of the cloud base is determined by the vertical temperature and dew point lapse rates in the atmosphere. This height can be estimated well before a thunderstorm ever forms and is not dependent on the updraft. This eliminates choice (B). Wind gusts at the surface are mainly caused by the downdraft, so choice (C) is also incorrect. Choice (D) is the correct answer. It is the strength of the updraft which determines how large individual precipitation elements will grow before they can no longer remain suspended in the cloud. Thus, stronger updrafts produce larger raindrops (or hailstones) than do weaker ones.

6.   **(A)**   Evaporation is an endothermic process which requires the input of additional energy to take place. When this energy is taken from the environment, evaporative cooling takes place. This would ultimately lead to an increase in the lapse rate, so choice (B) is incorrect. Choice (C) is a physical process which does not apply in any way to lapse rates because they involve thermodynamic processes. Thus, choice (C) is incorrect. Although choice (D) is correct, it offers no explanation as to why the lapse rate slows after parcel saturation. This eliminates choice (D), leaving choice (A) as the correct answer. As a parcel rises, it expands and cools. Eventually, it cools to its dew point temperature—the temperature at which the parcel is 100% saturated. Any further cooling will lead to condensation. Since condensation is an exothermic process, it releases the latent heat of condensation stored in the water vapor. This latent heat partially offsets the adiabatic cooling of a rising parcel.

7.   **(C)**   Descending air will compress, warm, become more dense, and dry out. This eliminates all choices except choice (C). The drying out refers to a decrease in relative humidity. Since warmer air can hold more water vapor than cooler air, an increase in temperature with no change in water vapor content will create drier air. This process is what causes the "rainshadow" on the leeward side of many mountains.

8.   **(C)**   Since the air is not saturated until it reaches 1,000 ft., we can use the dry adiabatic lapse rate of 5.5°F per 1,000 ft. from the surface up to 1,000 ft. At 1,000 ft., the air temperature is 64.5°F. From here to the top of the mountain, the air will be 100 percent saturated and cool at the moist adiabatic lapse rate of 3.3°F per 1,000 ft. So after rising the next 2,000 ft., the air is 57.9°F at the peak. Once the air begins to descend and warm, it will no longer be 100 percent saturated. This means it will warm at the dry adiabatic lapse rate of 5.5°F per 1,000 ft. This gives us an air temperature at Town B of 74.4°F.

9.   **(B)**   Since temperature will increase with height through an inversion, any rising air will be cooler than its surroundings and be forced back down. This represents stability. Instability (the condition where a parcel cools slower than its environment) and neutral stability (the condition where a parcel cools slower than its environment only after it is saturated) are never found in an inversion.

10.   **(D)**   Lightning heats the air to several thousand degrees in only a fraction of a second. This causes the air to expand rapidly. Surrounding air rushes in to fill the space left by the expanding heated air. It is the air rushing in which creates the sonic boom we know as thunder. By now, it should be evident that lightning and thunder originate at essentially the same location, making choices (A) and (C) incorrect. Choice (B) is also incorrect but can explain why some thunder rumbles for a very long time. We see the lightning before we hear the thunder because the speed of light is much faster than the speed of sound, choice (D). Since sound travels approximately one mile in five seconds, if we saw lightning and heard the thunder ten seconds later, the lightning struck two miles away.

11.   **(A)**   While other methods can be somewhat slower than radiation and may lose some energy in molecular transfer, this is not why they cannot function in space. Stellar debris is present in such small quantities, it has little effect on anything. And since the sun emits energy in essentially every direction, we have eliminated choices (B), (C), and (D), leaving choice (A) as the correct answer. Conduction relies on molecular

contact to transfer heat. Since space is nearly a perfect vacuum, not enough molecules are present to allow conduction to take place. Meteorologists refer to convection as the vertical component of heat transfer by mass movement of a fluid and advection as the horizontal component. Both methods require the presence of a fluid and cannot function in space for the same reason as conduction. Radiation transfers energy via electromagnetic waves which do not require a medium to propagate. This property makes radiation the only means possible to transfer energy through space.

12. **(D)** The change in state from liquid water to water vapor is an endothermic process which requires the addition of additional heat energy to take place. This heat is taken from the surrounding air, causing the air to cool. The amount of energy needed is called the latent heat of vaporization. Since choice (C) represents an exothermic process, choice (C) is incorrect. Thus, choice (B) is correct because it is endothermic and choice (A) is correct because it is directly related to choice (B). This makes the best choice (D).

13. **(D)** Choices (A), (B), and (C) are all generally correct statements but none of them lead to maximum summer temperatures on the date of the summer solstice. Warmest summer temperatures occur somewhat after the summer solstice due to the temperature lag associated with heating the mass of the earth. This leaves choice (D) as the correct answer.

14. **(C)** The sun emits energy throughout the entire electromagnetic spectrum, including all wavelengths of visible light. This eliminates choice (D). Bodies of water only appear to be reflected by the sky under certain conditions when a mirage forms. Since not every day meets these conditions but the sky is usually blue, choice (B) can be eliminated. And since very little light reaches our eyes from stars other than our sun, outer space appears black. This eliminates choice (A) and leaves choice (C) as the correct answer. Air molecules scatter the sun's light in all directions. However, air is a selective scatterer which scatters shorter wavelengths much more than longer ones. This causes more light from the shorter wavelength of the blue portion of the spectrum to be scattered to the earth. This gives the sky its bluish appearance. At sunrise and sunset, though, the light must travel through much more of the atmosphere due to its low angle of elevation. This causes most of the shorter wavelength blue portion of the spectrum to be scattered out before reaching the earth, leaving the longer wavelength red portion to be seen. This is what gives both sunrise and sunset a reddish appearance.

15. **(B)**   Since we assume the Earth is not rotating, airflow will be dictated by differential heating of the Earth. Heating at the equator will cause rising motion and form an area of surface low pressure. Cooling at the poles will cause sinking motion and form a surface area of high pressure. The pressure gradient force will now drive the air from the poles towards the equator, causing a return flow aloft from the equator towards the poles. No Coriolis force is available to deflect the winds so choices (A) and (C) are incorrect. Knowing that the poles are cooler than the equator, choice (D) is obviously wrong. This leaves (B) as the correct choice. This circulation would help even out the global heat distribution. The theoretical circulation is called the Hadley cell and would be the same for both northern and southern hemispheres. Since the earth does rotate, the Coriolis force breaks the circulation into three different cells per hemisphere. Surface convergence and divergence leads to the formation of surface high pressure and low pressure areas as shown in the diagram. The airflow around these surface pressure systems creates prevailing wind patterns such as the trade winds found in the tropics. Choice (B) is illustrated on the following page.

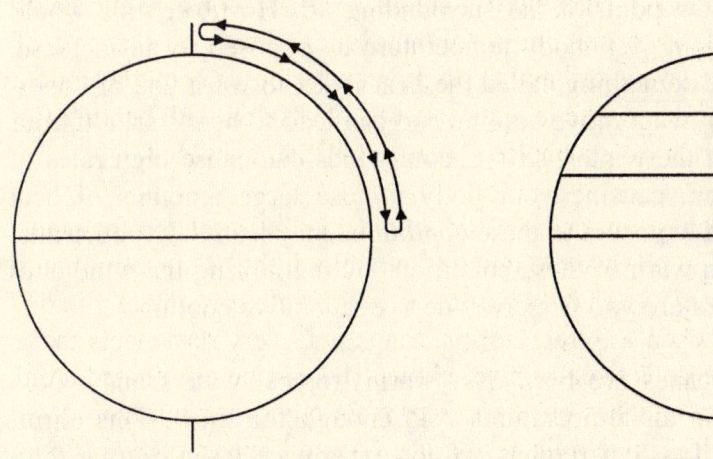

Hadley Cell: Non-rotating Earth   Three Cells: Rotating Earth

16.   **(A)**   In winter, the continents are cooler than the oceans, creating rising motion over the water and sinking motion over the land. This leads to surface high pressure over the land and surface low pressure over the water, so the correct answer is (A). The situation is reversed for summer with surface high pressure over the water and surface low pressure over the land. Spring and fall are transition seasons which typically find widely varied surface pressure patterns.

17. **(D)**   If a layer of cold air at the surface is shallow, rain will not have time to freeze before it reaches the ground. However, once it does hit the cold ground, it will freeze quickly. This is known as freezing rain. When large ice accumulations are observed, this type of event is often referred to as an ice storm. If the layer of cold air at the surface is thick, the rain may freeze before reaching the ground and fall as sleet (ice pellets). Although both are formed of ice, sleet (ice pellets) is not the same as hail. Hail only forms by a complex cyclical process high within a thunderstorm.

18. **(D)**   Very pure, very small water droplets can remain liquid at temperatures approaching –40°F. At these temperatures, the droplets are said to be supercooled.

19. **(B)**   Perspiration is the biological method of cooling your body. As the perspiration evaporates, you are cooled by evaporative cooling. The process is slowed by humid air, which makes it difficult to keep cool on hot and humid summer days. Choices (A) and (C) are related, but are both incorrect. In order for water vapor to condense on your skin, it would have to approach the dew point of the surrounding air. However, this would involve a decrease in your body temperature as opposed to an increase. Meteorologists use something called the heat index to warn you of conditions which inhibit evaporative cooling and can lead to heat stroke if your body overheats. In the winter, strong, cold winds can cause high rates of evaporative cooling, causing your body to lose large amounts of heat quickly. Prolonged exposure to these conditions may lead to hypothermia. Meteorologists can warn of these conditions by monitoring the wind chill factor—the temperature you perceive due to evaporative cooling.

20. **(B)**   Hurricanes are born over warm tropical waters and would quickly dissipate in air temperatures cold enough for snow. This eliminates choice (A). Tropical regions do not experience large diurnal temperature changes due to the dense vegetation cover and high moisture content of the tropical atmosphere. This eliminates choice (C). The fact that temperature decreases with height has profound effects on climate zones on a mountain. It is possible for lush vegetation to thrive at the base of a tall mountain while snow and ice cap its peak. This allows high mountains in the tropics to routinely experience snowfall at their higher elevations.

CHAPTER 6
SOCIAL SCIENCES AND HISTORY REVIEW

Chapter 6

SOCIAL SCIENCES AND HISTORY REVIEW

The following History and Social Sciences Review is divided into nine sections, as follows:

I. **Description of the CLEP General Examination in Social Sciences and History**

II. **Political Science Review**

III. **Sociology Review**

IV. **Economics Review**

V. **Psychology Review**

VI. **Geography Review**

VII. **Anthropology Review**

VIII. **Western and World Civilizations Review**

IX. **United States History Review**

By thoroughly studying this course review, you will be well-prepared for the material on the CLEP General Examination in Social Sciences and History.

I. DESCRIPTION OF THE CLEP GENERAL EXAMINATION IN SOCIAL SCIENCES AND HISTORY

The CLEP Social Sciences and History covers a broad range of material, focusing on the theories, terminology, and methods of the Social Sciences, as well as historical events and trends. It gives you an opportunity to demonstrate your knowledge and understanding of anthropology, geography, sociology, economics, political science, and psychology. It also assesses your knowledge and understanding of the history of the United States, Europe, Asia, and Africa. The emphasis is on the general principles and skills of these fields rather than mere facts. You will be asked not only to demonstrate your knowledge, but also to apply that knowledge. The material approximates what you would learn in introductory college courses in these areas.

The examination contains 125 multiple-choice questions that you will be asked to answer in two 45-minute periods. For some questions, you will be asked to choose the best answer, or to select the best phrase that completes a sentence. In other cases, questions will ask you to interpret visual material, such as a graph.

The questions on the test will be distributed roughly as follows:

History	**40%**
United States History	17%
Western Civilization	15%
World Civilization	8%
Social Sciences	**60%**
Government/Political Science	13%
Sociology	11%
Economics	10%
Psychology	10%
Geography	10%
Anthropology	6%

History occupies roughly a third of the test. Some of the questions in the history portion of the test will assess your knowledge of historical events or "facts," while others will test your knowledge of trends, movements, or concepts in history. Almost equal amounts of material will be taken from United States history and Western Civilization. For United States history, you will be tested on your knowledge of issues and events in U.S. history from colonial times to the present. The questions on Western Civilization are basically questions about European history, in the ancient, medieval, and modern periods. The ancient period may tend to emphasize areas which influenced the later development of Europe, such as ancient Egypt, Greece, or Rome. A smaller amount of material on the test will deal with World Civilization from prehistory through ancient history (500 B.C.) to present day. World Civilization covers all cultures not covered in the United States and Western Civilization headings, such as Asian, African, and Central/South American. There may be one or more questions about the role of Europeans in these areas.

For the social sciences section, the largest number of questions will come from the area of Government/Political Science (covering topics such as methods, constitutional government, voting and political behavior, international relations, and comparative government). The next largest number of questions will come from the area of Sociology (covering topics such as sociological methods, demography, ecology, stratification, statistics, interaction, and social change). The test will have roughly the same number of questions from the next three areas: Economics, Psychology, and Geography. Economics covers topics like cost, comparative advantage, competitive markets, monetary and fiscal policy, international trade, and measurement concepts. You may be expected to demonstrate an understanding of the methods of social psychology, plus theories of human behavior in groups, the formation of social groups, and particular behavior patterns such as conformity, socialization, or aggression for the Psychology area of the test. Geography covers topics such as weather and climate, cultural geography, and ecology. Finally, the Anthropology area will have the smallest number of questions. This area will cover subjects such as cultural anthropology, physical anthropology, demography, family, and anthropological methods.

TYPES OF QUESTIONS AND EXAMPLES

There are several significant points to keep in mind. Although there are only two basic types of questions—best answer/best phrase questions and questions requiring you to interpret a visual aid, such as graph—there are a large number of variations on these types.

Many questions will assess your knowledge of terminology. You may be asked to select the statement that best defines a Social Science term such as "socialization," or the question may present you with a real-life situation and ask you to select the term (the name of a theory or a principle) that best describes that situation. A question may cite a law or principle of economics and ask you to choose the answer that best describes how that law would operate in a given economic situation.

There will be questions testing your ability to understand, interpret, and analyze graphic material such as charts and tables. These questions will sometimes ask a question first and present the graphic information after, or the chart or table may be presented first and a series of questions relating to that information will follow.

Finally, you will be expected to apply abstractions to specific items, and also link hypotheses or concepts to data that is provided. The theories or hypotheses may span the entire spectrum of topics described above, often inter-relating diverse or opposite concepts.

Here are examples of the three types of questions you can expect to find on the CLEP Social Sciences and History examination.

QUESTIONS THAT TEST YOUR FAMILIARITY WITH TERMINOLOGY, FACTS, CONVENTIONS, CONCEPTS, AND PRINCIPLES

1. A social science project which makes a detailed study of a small group of people is called a

   (A) case study   (D) experimental group

   (B) select group   (E) random sample

   (C) control group

The correct answer is (A). This question tests your knowledge and understanding of terminology common to most of the Social Sciences. It also asks you to make fine distinctions, since some of the answers are similar. A case study concentrates on a distinct group of people, who are assumed to be representative of a larger group. A "select group" (answer B) is not a term usually used in the Social Sciences; it is, in effect, a decoy answer. A random sample (answer E) is a survey in which each member of a group has an equal chance to be questioned. Control groups and experimental groups (answers C and D) are two comparative groups studied at the same time, but under different conditions.

QUESTIONS THAT TEST ABILITY TO APPLY ABSTRACTIONS TO SPECIFIC PRINCIPLES, AND TO APPLY DIVERSE HYPOTHESES TO GIVEN DATA

2. The European political writer who most influenced the Founding Fathers of the United States was

   (A) Bentham   (D) Robespierre

   (B) Mill   (E) Rousseau

   (C) Locke

The correct answer is (C). John Locke's writings on the Glorious Revolution of 1688 in England were very influential with early American leaders, because he emphasized the idea that each individual possesses rights that government should not be allowed to overrun. Jeremy Bentham (answer A) was a nineteenth-century British social reformer. John Stuart Mill (answer B) was a nineteenth-century British liberal and political writer. The easiest answers to eliminate should be Maximilien de Robespierre (answer D)—the leading figure during the most violent period of the French Revolution of 1789, the Reign of Terror—and Jean Jacques Rousseau (answer E), an eighteenth-century French philosopher and political writer.

QUESTIONS THAT TEST ABILITY TO UNDERSTAND AND INTERPRET GRAPHIC INFORMATION

Curve AS represents total United States production of oil.
Curve TS represents total world production of oil.
Line Dd represents demand for oil.

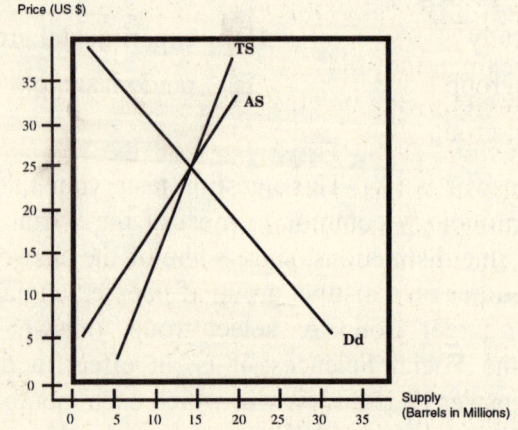

3.   What will the price of oil be if sufficient oil is produced to meet demand?

(A) $5

(B) $10

(C) $20

(D) $25

(E)   the price cannot be determined from the graph

The correct answer is (D). You will probably have one or more graph questions, and they may be in the form of a Social Science question—perhaps an Economics questions, like this one—or they may even relate to history. Possibly, the graph may be more complicated than this one. In this case, the answer may be found where the demand line (Dd) intersects with the total supply curve. Find that point, and then look to the price scale at the bottom of the graph.

II. POLITICAL SCIENCE REVIEW

INTRODUCTION TO POLITICAL SCIENCE
WHAT IS POLITICAL SCIENCE?

Political Science is the organized study of government and politics. It borrows from the related disciplines of history, philosophy, sociology, economics, and law. **Political scientists** explore such fundamental questions as: What are the philosophical foundations of modern political systems? What makes a government legitimate? What are the duties and responsibilities of those who govern? Who participates in the political process and why? What is the nature of relations among nations?

PRINCIPAL SUBFIELDS OF POLITICAL SCIENCE

At the present time, the study of political science in the United States is concerned with the following broad subtopics or subfields:

Political Theory is an historical exploration of the major contributions to political thought from the ancient Greeks to the contemporary theorists. These theorists raise fundamental questions about the individual's existence and his relationship to the political community. **Political theory** also involves the philosophical and speculative consideration of the political world.

American Government and Politics is a survey of the origins and development of the political system in the United States from the colonial days to modern times with an emphasis on the Constitution, various political structures such as the legislative, executive, and judicial branches, the federal system, political parties, voter behavior, and fundamental freedoms.

Comparative Government is a systematic study of the structures of two or more political systems (such as those of Britain and the People's Republic of China) to achieve an understanding of how different societies manage the realities of governing. Also considered are political processes and behavior and the ideological foundations of various systems.

International Relations is a consideration of how nations interact with each other within the frameworks of law, diplomacy, and international organizations such as the United Nations.

THE DEVELOPMENT OF THE DISCIPLINE OF POLITICAL SCIENCE
Early History

Political science as a systematic study of government developed in the United States and in Western Europe during the nineteenth century as new political institutions evolved. Prior to 1850, during its classical phase, political science relied heavily on philosophy and utilized the deductive method of research.

Post–Civil War Period

The political science curriculum was formalized in the United States by faculty at Columbia and Johns Hopkins, who were deeply influenced by German scholarship on the nation state and the formation of democratic institutions. Historical and comparative approaches to analysis of institutions were predominant. Emphasis was on constitutional and legal issues, and political institutions were widely regarded as factors in motivating the actions of individuals.

Twentieth Century Trends

Political scientists worked to strengthen their research base, to integrate quantitative data, and to incorporate comparative studies of governmental structures in developing countries into the discipline.

American Political Science Association (APSA)

The APSA was founded in 1903 to promote the organized study of politics and to distinguish it as a field separate from history.

The Behavioral Period

From the early 1920s to the present, political science has focused on psychological interpretations and the analysis of the behavior of individuals and groups in a political context. Research has been theory based, values neutral, and concerned with predicting and explaining political behavior.

Contemporary Developments

Since the 1960s, interest has focused on such subtopics as African-American politics, public policy, urban and ethnic politics, and women in politics. Influenced by the leadership of Harold Lasswell, political scientists showed greater concern for using their discipline to solve social problems.

THE SCIENTIFIC METHOD OF RESEARCH IN POLITICAL SCIENCE

The modern method of scientific inquiry in the field aims to compile a body of data based on direct observation (**empirical knowledge**) that can be utilized both to explain what has been observed and to form valid generalizations. The scientific method in political science has resulted in three types of statements: **observational/evidential**, which describe the principal characteristics of what has been studied; **observational laws**, which are hypotheses based on what has been observed; and **theories**, which analyze the data that has been collected and offer plausible general principles that can be drawn from what has been observed.

Examples of Statements Based on the Scientific Method

* **Observational/evidential:** In 1992, 518 out of 535 members of the U.S. Congress were males. In the British Parliament, 550 of the 635 members were males. Eighteen of France's 20 cabinet ministers were males.

* **Observational law (hypothesis):** Legislative and executive bodies in modern democracies tend to be dominated by males.

* **Theory:** Political power in modern democracies is in male hands.

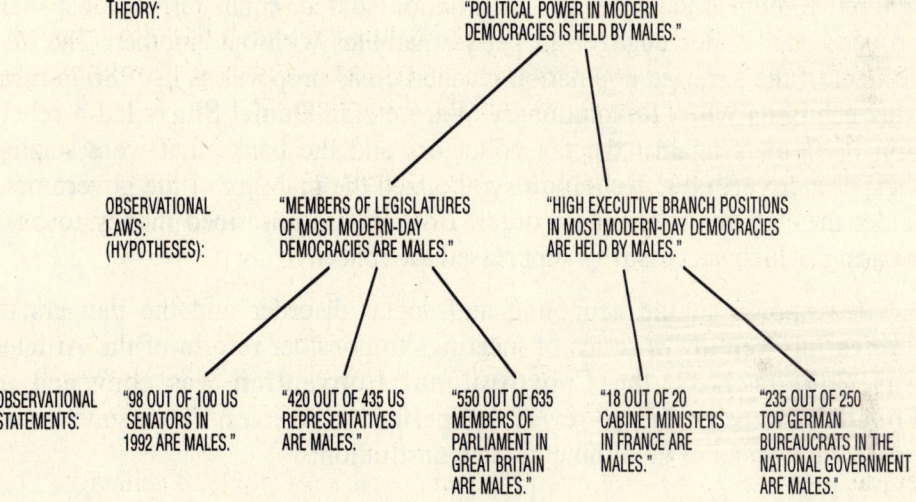

UNITED STATES GOVERNMENT AND POLITICS

CONSTITUTIONAL FOUNDATIONS

The government of the United States rests on a written framework created in an attempt to strengthen a loose confederation that was in crisis in the 1780s. The **Constitution** is a basic plan that outlines the structure and functions of the national government. Clearly rooted in Western political thought, it sets limits and protects both property and individual rights.

Historical Background

Following the successful revolt of the British colonies in North America against imperial rule, a plan of government was implemented that was consciously weak and ultimately ineffective, the **Articles of Confederation**.

The Articles served as the national government from 1781–1787. The government under the Articles consisted of a **unicameral** (one house) legislature which was clearly subordinate to the states. Representatives to the Congress were appointed and paid by their respective state legislatures, and their mission was to protect the interests of their home states. Each state, regardless of size, had one vote in Congress, which could request but not require states to provide financial and military support. **Key weaknesses of the Articles** included: its inability to regulate interstate and foreign trade, its lack of a chief executive and a national court system, and its rule that amendments must be approved by unanimous consent.

Dubbed the "**critical period**," the 1780s was a decade in the United States marked by internal conflict. The economy deteriorated as individual states printed their own currencies, taxed the products of their neighbors, and ignored foreign trade agreements. Inflation soared, small farmers lost their property, and states engaged in petty squabbles with one another. The discontent of the agrarian population reached crisis proportions in 1786 in rural Massachusetts when Revolutionary War veteran **Daniel Shays** led a rebellion of farmers against the tax collectors and the banks that were seizing their property. **Shays' Rebellion** symbolized the inability of the government under the Articles to maintain order. Bostonians subscribed money to raise an army, which successfully suppressed the rebels.

In response to the economic and social disorder and the dangers of foreign intervention, a series of meetings to consider reform of the Articles was held. In 1787, the **Constitutional Convention** was convened in **Philadelphia** ostensibly to revise the ineffective Articles. The result was an entirely new plan of government, the Constitution.

Philosophy and Ideology of the Founding Fathers

Among the distinguished men assembled at the Constitutional Convention in 1787 were **James Madison**, who recorded the debate proceedings; **George Washington**, president of the body; **Gouverneur Morris**, who wrote the final version of the document; and **Alexander Hamilton**, one of the authors of the *Federalist Papers* (1787–1788). This collection of essays, to which **Madison** and **John Jay** also contributed, expresses the political philosophy of the Founders and was instrumental in bringing about the ratification of the Constitution.

Clearly the framers of the Constitution were influenced by the ideological heritage of the seventeenth and eighteenth century Enlightenment in Western Europe. From Hobbes and Locke came the concept of the social contract. The latter had a marked influence upon **Thomas Jefferson**, who incorporated Locke's doctrines with respect to equality; government's responsibility to protect the life, liberty, and property of its constituency; and the right of revolution in his **Declaration of Independence** (1776). The Constitution itself includes Montesquieu's separation of powers and checks and balances. British documents, such as the **Magna Carta** (1215), the **Petition of Right** (1628), and the **Bill of Rights** (1689), all promoting the principle of limited government, were influential in shaping the final form of the Constitution.

Basic Principles of the Constitution

The authors of the Constitution sought to establish a government free from the tyrannies of both monarchs and mobs. Two of the critical principles embedded in the final document, **federalism** and **separation of powers**, address this concern.

The federal system established by the Founders divides the powers of government between the states and the national government. Local matters are handled on a local level, and those issues that affect the general populace are the responsibility of the federal government. Such a system is a natural outgrowth of the colonial relationship between the Americans and the mother country of England. American federalism is defined in the **Tenth Amendment** which declares: "those powers not delegated to the United States by the Constitution, nor prohibited by it to the States, are reserved to the States respectively, or to the people." In practice, the system may be confusing in that powers overlap (i.e., welfare). In cases where they conflict, the federal government is supreme.

The principle of separation of powers is codified in **Articles I, II**, and **III** of the main body of the Constitution. The national government is divided into three branches which have separate functions (**legislative, executive**, and **judicial**). Not entirely independent, each of these branches can check or limit in some way the power of one or both of the others (**checks and balances**). This system of dividing and checking powers is a vehicle for guarding against the extremes the Founders feared. Following are some examples of checks and balances:

- The legislative branch can check the executive by refusing to confirm appointments.

- The executive can check the legislative by vetoing its bills.

- The judicial can check both the legislative and the executive by declaring laws unconstitutional.

Additional basic principles embodied in the Constitution include:

- The establishment of a representative government (**republic**).

- **Popular sovereignty** or the idea that government derives its power from the people. This concept is expressed in the **Preamble** which opens with the words, "**We the People**."

- The enforcement of government with limits ("**rule of law**").

STRUCTURE AND FUNCTIONS OF THE NATIONAL GOVERNMENT

The national government consists of the three branches outlined in the Constitution as well as a huge bureaucracy comprised of departments, agencies, and commissions.

The Legislative Branch

Legislative power is vested in a **bicameral** (two-house) Congress which is the subject of Article I of the Constitution. The bicameral structure was the result of a compromise at the Constitutional Convention between the large states, led by Virginia, which presented a plan calling for a strong national government with representation favoring the larger states (**Virginia Plan**) and the smaller states, which countered with the **New Jersey Plan**. The latter would have retained much of the structure of the Articles of Confederation including equal representation of the states in Congress. Connecticut offered a solution in the form of the **Great Compromise**. It called for a two-house legislature with equal representation in the **Senate** and representation in the **House of Representatives** based on population.

The **expressed** or **delegated powers** of Congress are set forth in **Section 8** of Article I. They can be divided into several broad categories including economic, judicial, war, and general peace powers. **Economic powers** include:

- to lay and collect taxes

- to borrow money

- to regulate foreign and interstate commerce

- to coin money and regulate its value

- to establish rules concerning bankruptcy

Judicial powers include:

- to establish courts inferior to the Supreme Court

- to provide punishment for counterfeiting

- to define and punish piracies and felonies committed on the high seas

War powers include:

- to declare war

- to raise and support armies

- to provide and maintain a navy

- to provide for organizing, arming, and calling forth the militia

Peace powers include:

- to establish rules on naturalization

- to establish post offices and post roads

- to promote science and the arts by granting patents and copyrights

- to exercise jurisdiction over the seat of the federal government (**District of Columbia**)

The Constitution includes the so-called "**elastic clause**" which grants Congress **implied powers** to implement the delegated powers.

In addition, Congress maintains the power to discipline federal officials through **impeachment** (formal accusation of wrongdoing) and removal from office.

Article V empowers Congress to propose **amendments** (changes or additions) to the Constitution. A two-thirds majority in both houses is necessary for passage. An alternate method is to have amendments proposed by the legislatures of two-thirds of the states. In order for an amendment to become part of the Constitution, it must be **ratified** (formally approved) by three-fourths of the states (through their legislatures or by way of special conventions as in the case of the repeal of Prohibition).

Article I, Section 9 specifically denies certain powers to the national legislature. Congress is prohibited from suspending the right of **habeas corpus** (writ calling for a party under arrest to be brought before the court where authorities must show cause for detainment) except during war or rebellion. Other prohibitions include: the passage of export taxes, the withdrawal of funds from the treasury without an appropriations law, the passage of **ex post facto** laws (make past actions punishable that were legal when they occurred), and favored treatment of one state over another with respect to commerce.

The work of the Congress is organized around a committee system. The **standing committees** are permanent and deal with such matters as agriculture, the armed services, the budget, energy, finance, and foreign policy. Special or **select committees** are established to deal with specific issues and usually have a limited duration. **Conference committees** iron out differences between House and Senate versions of a bill before it is sent on to the President.

One committee unique to the House of Representatives is the powerful **Rules Committee**. Thousands of bills are introduced each term, and the Rules Committee acts as a clearing house to weed out those that are unworthy of consideration before the full House. Constitutionally, all revenue-raising bills must originate in the House of Representatives. They are scrutinized by the powerful House **Ways and Means Committee**.

Committee membership is organized on party lines with **seniority** being a key factor, although in recent years, length of service has diminished in importance in the determination of chairmanships. The composition of each committee is largely based on the ratio of each party in the Congress as a whole. The party that has a **majority** is allotted a greater number of members on each committee. The chairman of the standing committees are selected by the leaders of the majority party.

The legislative process is at once cumbersome and time consuming (see chart **How a Bill Becomes a Law**). A **bill** (proposed law) can be introduced in either house (with the exception of **revenue bills**, which must originate in the House of Representatives). It is referred to the appropriate **committee** and then to a **subcommittee**, which will hold **hearings** if the members agree that it has merit. The bill is reported back to the **full committee**, which must decide whether or not to send it to the **full chamber** to be debated. If the bill passes in the full chamber, it is then sent to the **other chamber** to begin the process all over again. Any differences between the House and Senate versions of the bill must be resolved in a **conference committee** before it is sent to the **President** for consideration. Most of the thousands of bills introduced in Congress die in committee with only a small percentage becoming law.

Debate on major bills is a key step in the legislative process because of the tradition of attaching **amendments** at this stage. In the House, the rules of debate are designed to enforce limits necessitated by the size of the body (435 members). In the smaller Senate (100 members), unlimited debate (**filibuster**) is allowed. Filibustering is a delaying tactic that can postpone action indefinitely. **Cloture** is a parliamentary procedure that can limit debate and bring a filibuster to an end.

Constitutional qualifications for the House of Representatives state that members must be at least **25** years of age, must have been **U.S. citizens for at least seven years**, and must be **residents of the state** that sends them to Congress. According to the **Reapportionment Act of 1929**, the size of the House is fixed at **435** members. They serve terms of **two years** in length.

HOW A BILL BECOMES A LAW

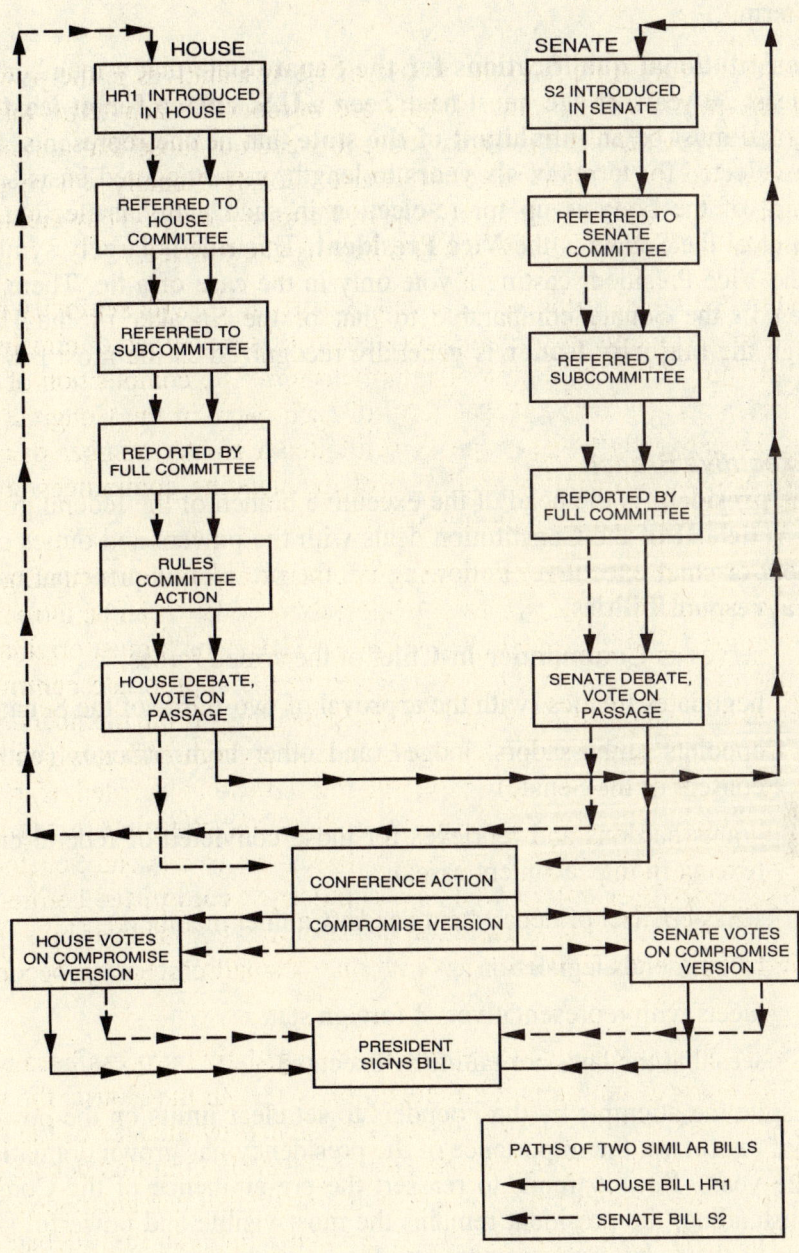

HOUSE

HR1 INTRODUCED
IN HOUSE

REFERRED TO
HOUSE
COMMITTEE

REFERRED TO
SUBCOMMITTEE

REPORTED BY
FULL COMMITTEE

RULES
COMMITTEE
ACTION

HOUSE DEBATE,
VOTE ON
PASSAGE

SENATE

S2 INTRODUCED
IN SENATE

REFERRED TO
SENATE
COMMITTEE

REFERRED TO
SUBCOMMITTEE

REPORTED BY
FULL COMMITTEE

SENATE DEBATE,
VOTE ON
PASSAGE

CONFERENCE ACTION

COMPROMISE VERSION

HOUSE VOTES
ON COMPROMISE
VERSION

SENATE VOTES
ON COMPROMISE
VERSION

PRESIDENT
SIGNS BILL

PATHS OF TWO SIMILAR BILLS

HOUSE BILL HR1

SENATE BILL S2

The presiding officer and generally the most powerful member is the **Speaker of the House**, who is the leader of the political party that has a majority in a given term.

Constitutional qualifications for the Senate state that a member must be at least **30** years of age, must have been a **U.S. citizen for at least nine years**, and must be an **inhabitant of the state** that he/she represents. Senators are elected for terms of **six years** in length on a staggered basis so that one-third of the body is up for re-election in each national election. The president of the Senate is the **Vice President**. This role is largely symbolic, with the Vice President casting a vote only in the case of a tie. There is no position in the Senate comparable to that of the Speaker of the House, although the **majority leader** is generally recognized as the most powerful member.

The Executive Branch

The **president** is the head of the executive branch of the federal government. **Article II** of the Constitution deals with the powers and duties of the President or chief executive. Following are the president's principal **constitutional responsibilities**:

- serves as **Commander-in-Chief** of the armed forces
- negotiates treaties (with the approval of two-thirds of the Senate)
- appoints ambassadors, judges, and other high officials (with the consent of the Senate)
- grants pardons and reprieves for those convicted of federal crimes (except in impeachment cases)
- seeks counsel of department heads (Cabinet members)
- recommends legislation
- meets with representatives of foreign states
- sees that the laws are faithfully executed

Despite the attempts by the Founders to set clear limits on the power of the chief executive, the importance of the presidency has grown dramatically over the years. Recent trends to reassert the pre-eminence of the Congress notwithstanding, the president remains the most visible and powerful single member of the federal government and the only one (with the exception of the vice president) elected to represent all the people. He shapes foreign policy with his diplomatic and treaty-making powers and largely determines domestic policy. Presidents also possess the power to **veto** legislation. A presidential veto may be overridden by a two-thirds vote in both houses, but such a majority is not easy to build, particularly in the face of the chief executive's opposition. A **pocket veto** occurs when the president neither signs nor rejects a bill, and the Congress adjourns within ten days of his receipt of the legislation. The fact that the president is the head of a vast federal bureaucracy is another indication of the power of the office.

Although the Constitution makes no mention of a formal **Cabinet** as such, since the days of George Washington, chief executives have relied on department heads to aid in the decision-making process. Washington's Cabinet was comprised of the secretaries of **state, war, treasury,** and an **attorney general**. Today there are 14 Cabinet departments, with **veterans' affairs** the most recently created post. Efforts to trim the federal government in the 1990s have resulted in suggestions to streamline and eliminate some Cabinet posts.

The **Executive Office of the President** is made up of agencies that supervise the daily work of the government. The **White House Staff** manages the President's schedule and is usually headed by a powerful **chief of staff**. Arguably the most critical agency of the Executive Office is the **Office of Management and Budget**, which controls the budget process for the national government. Other key executive agencies include the **Council of Economic Advisors** and the **National Security Council**, which advises the President on matters that threaten the safety of the nation and directs the **Central Intelligence Agency**.

The **Constitutional Requirements** for the office of president and vice president are as follows: a candidate must be at least **35** years of age, must be a **natural-born** citizen, and must have **resided in the United States for a minimum of 14 years**. Article II provides for an **Electoral College** to elect the president and vice president. Each state has as many votes in the Electoral College as it has members of Congress plus three additional electors from the District of Columbia—making a grand total of 538 electors. The Founding Fathers established the Electoral College to provide an **indirect** method of choosing the chief executive, but over time the body has become ceremonial due to the control the major political parties have over the election process.

The question of **presidential succession** has been addressed by both legislation and amendment. The Constitution states that if the President dies or cannot perform his duties, the "powers and duties" of the office shall "devolve" on the Vice President. The **Presidential Succession Act** (1947) placed the **speaker of the house** next in line if both the president and the vice president were unable to serve. Until recently, when the vice president assumed the office of President, his former position was left vacant. The **Twenty-Fifth Amendment** (1967) gives the president the power to appoint a new vice president (with the approval of a majority of both houses of Congress). It also provides for the vice president to serve as **Acting President** if the chief executive is disabled or otherwise unable to carry out the duties of the office. The **Twenty-Second Amendment** (1951) says "No person shall be elected to the office of the President more than twice...." In addition, anyone who has served more than two years while filling out another person's term may not be elected to the presidency more than once.

The Judicial Branch

Article III of the Constitution establishes the **Supreme Court** but does not define the role of this branch as clearly as it does the legislative and executive branches. Yet our contemporary judicial branch consists of thousands of courts and is in essence a dual system with each state having its own judiciary functioning simultaneously with a complete set of federal courts. The most significant piece of legislation with respect to establishing a network of federal courts was the **Judiciary Act of 1789**. This law organized the Supreme Court and set up the 13 **federal district courts**. The district courts have **original jurisdiction** (to hear cases in the first instance) for federal cases involving both civil and criminal law. Federal cases on appeal are heard in the **Courts of Appeal**. The decisions of these courts are final, except for those cases that are accepted for review by the Supreme Court.

The **Supreme Court** today is made of a **Chief Justice** and eight **Associate Justices**. They are appointed for life by the President with the approval of the Senate.

In the early history of the United States, the Supreme Court was largely preoccupied with the relationship between the federal government and those of the states. In 1803, the process of **judicial review** (power to determine the constitutionality of laws and actions of the legislative and executive branches) was established under **Chief Justice John Marshall** in the case of **Marbury v. Madison**. This power has become the foundation of the American judicial system and underscores the deep significance of the courts in determining the course of United States history.

The Supreme Court chooses cases for review based on whether or not they address substantial federal issues. If four of the nine justices vote to consider a case, then it will be added to the agenda. In such cases, **writs of certiorari** (orders calling up the records from a lower court) are issued. The justices are given detailed briefs and hear oral arguments. Reaching a decision is a complicated process. The justices scrutinize the case with reference to the Constitution and also consider previous decisions in similar cases (**precedent**). When all of the justices agree, the opinion issued is **unanimous**. In the case of a split decision, a **majority opinion** is written by one of the justices in agreement. Sometimes a justice will agree with the majority but for a different principle, in which case he/she can write a **concurring opinion** explaining the different point of view. Justices who do not vote with the majority may choose to write **dissenting opinions** to air their conflicting arguments.

In addition to the Supreme Court, the federal District Courts, and the Courts of Appeal, several special courts at the federal level have been created by Congress. The **U.S. Tax Court** handles conflicts between citizens and the Internal Revenue Service. The **Court of Claims** was designed to hear cases in which citizens bring suit against the U.S. government. Other special courts include the **Court of International Trade**, the **Court of Customs**, and the **Court of Military Appeals**.

The Federal Bureaucracy

In addition to the President's Cabinet and the Executive Office, a series of independent agencies makes up the federal bureaucracy, the so-called "**fourth branch**" of the national government. Most of these agencies were established to protect consumers and to regulate industries engaged in interstate trade. Others were set up to oversee government programs. From the time of the establishment of the Interstate Commerce Commission in 1887, these departments grew in number and influence. Late in the 1970s, the trend began to reverse, as some agencies were cut back and others eliminated altogether.

Among the most important of these powerful agencies are the **regulatory commissions**. The President appoints their administrators with the approval of the Senate. Unlike Cabinet secretaries and other high appointees, they cannot be dismissed by the chief executive. This system protects the independent status of the agencies. Following are examples of some of the major regulatory agencies and their functions.

Agency	Regulatory Functions
Interstate Commerce Commission	Monitors surface transportation and some pipelines
Federal Reserve Board	Supervises the banking system, sets interest rates, and controls the money supply
Federal Trade Commission	Protects consumers by looking into false advertising and antitrust violations
Federal Communications Commission	Polices the airwaves by licensing radio and television stations and regulating cable and telephone companies
Securities and Exchange Commission	Protects investors by monitoring the sale of stocks and bonds
National Labor Relations Board	Oversees labor and management practices

| Consumer Product Safety Commission | Sets standards of safety for manufactured products |
| Nuclear Regulatory Commission | Licenses and inspects nuclear power plants |

Another category of the "fourth branch" of government is made up of the **independent executive agencies**. These were created by Congress and resemble Cabinet departments, but they do not enjoy Cabinet status. Nonetheless they are powerful entities. Some of the key executive agencies include the Civil Rights Commission, the Environmental Protection Agency, and the National Aeronautics and Space Administration. Their names are indicative of their functions. The top level executives of these agencies are appointed by the President with the approval of the Senate.

Some of the independent agencies are actually **government corporations**. These are commercial enterprises created by Congress to perform a variety of necessary services. Their roots can be traced back to the **First Bank of the United States** established in 1791 by Secretary of the Treasury **Alexander Hamilton**. The **Federal Deposit Insurance Corporation** (FDIC), which insures bank deposits, is a more recent example. Under **Franklin Roosevelt's New Deal**, the **Tennessee Valley Authority** (TVA) was authorized to revive a depressed region of the nation. Today it oversees the generation of electric power throughout a vast region and maintains flood control programs as well. The largest of the government corporations and the most familiar to the general public is the **United States Postal Service**. The original Post Office Department was established in 1775 by the Second Continental Congress, and it enjoyed Cabinet status. It was reorganized in 1970 in hopes that it would eventually become self-supporting.

The large and powerful federal bureaucracy shapes and administers government policy. It is inherently political despite sporadic efforts throughout the years to maintain the integrity of the bureaucratic staff. Dating back to the administrations of **Andrew Jackson**, the practice of handing out government jobs in return for political favors (**spoils system**) had been the rule. The **Civil Service Act** (the **Pendleton Act**) was passed in 1883 in an attempt to reform the spoils system. Federal workers were to be recruited on the basis of merit determined by a competitive examination. Veterans were given preferential status. The Civil Service system was reorganized in the 1970s with the creation of the **Office of Personnel Management**. The OPM is charged with recruiting, training, and promoting government workers. Merit is the stated objective when hiring federal employees. A controversial policy of the OPM is affirmative action, a program to help groups discriminated against in the job market to find employment.

POLITICAL BELIEFS AND CHARACTERISTICS OF CITIZENS

The population of the United States, with its diverse components, is difficult to characterize with respect to political beliefs and attitudes. The process by which individuals form their political allegiances is called **political socialization**. Several factors (**cleavages**) are relevant to the formation of political opinions including family, race, gender, class, religion, education, and region. Following are some generalizations as to the impact of these cleavages on an individual's political identification and activity.

Family – affiliation with a political party is commonly passed from one generation to another.

Race – African Americans tend to be more liberal than whites on economic, social, and public policy issues.

Gender – women tend to be more liberal than men.

Class – citizens from the middle and upper classes tend to be more politically active than those from the lower socioeconomic brackets. Low income voters tend to identify more with the liberal agenda.

Religion – Protestants tend to be more conservative than Catholics and Jews. Evangelical Protestants seem to be most conservative on ethical and moral issues.

Education – higher education seems to have a liberalizing effect that remains potent after schooling is completed.

Region – Southerners tend to be most conservative, mid-westerners more liberal, and those living on the East and West coasts the most liberal of all.

Despite the categorization of Americans as either **liberals** or **conservatives**, most studies indicate that they do not follow clearly delineated **ideologies** (firm and consistent beliefs with respect to political, economic, and social issues). The terms liberal and conservative with reference to the political beliefs of Americans are difficult to define in precise terms. Liberals tend to favor change and to view government as a tool for improving the quality of life. Conservatives, on the other hand, are more inclined to view both change and government with suspicion. They emphasize individual initiative and local solutions to problems. A puzzling reversal is seen in the attitudes of liberals and conservatives when confronting moral issues such as abortion and school prayer. Here conservatives see a role for government in ensuring the moral climate of the nation while liberals stress the importance of individual choice.

POLITICAL INSTITUTIONS AND SPECIAL INTERESTS

Civic culture in the United States is dominated by the two major political parties and is heavily influenced by the activities of interest groups and the mass media. These latter forces, both directly and indirectly, are largely responsible for molding and swaying public opinion.

Political Parties

A **political party** is an organization that seeks to influence government by electing candidates to public office. The party provides a label for candidates, recruits and campaigns, and tries to organize and control the legislative and executive branches of government through a set of leaders.

The Constitution does not mention political parties, and the Founders in general were opposed to them. Yet they developed simultaneously with the organization of the new government in 1789. It was the initial conflict over the interpretation of the powers assigned to the new government by the Constitution that gave rise to the first organized American political parties.

The **Federalist Party** evolved around the policies of Washington's Secretary of the Treasury, **Alexander Hamilton**. He and his supporters favored a "**loose construction**" approach to the interpretation of the Constitution. They advocated a strong federal government with the power to assume any duties and responsibilities not prohibited to it by the text of the document. They generally supported programs designed to benefit banking and commercial interests, and in foreign policy, the Federalists were **pro-British**.

The **Democratic** or **Jeffersonian Republicans** formed in opposition to the Federalists. They rallied around Washington's Secretary of State, **Thomas Jefferson**. The Jeffersonians took a "**strict constructionist**" approach, interpreting the Constitution in a narrow, limited sense. Sympathetic to the needs of the "common man," the Democratic-Republicans were mistrustful of powerful centralized government. They saw the small farmers, shopkeepers, and laborers as the backbone of the nation. In the area of foreign affairs, the Democratic-Republicans were **pro-French**. The present day Democratic Party traces its roots to the Jeffersonians.

By the 1820s, the Democrats had splintered into factions led by **Andrew Jackson** (the Democrats) and **John Quincy Adams** (National Republicans). The Jacksonians continued with Jefferson's tradition of supporting policies designed to enhance the power of the common man. Their support was largely agrarian. The National Republicans, like their Federalist predecessors, represented the interests of bankers, merchants, and some large planters. Eventually a new party, the **Whigs**, was organized from the remnants of the old Federalists and the National Republicans. The Whigs were prominent during the 1840s, but like their Democratic rivals, they fragmented during the 1850s over the divisive slavery issue. The modern **Republican Party** was born in 1854 as Whigs and anti-slavery Democrats came together to halt the spread of slavery. The Republicans built a constituency around the interests of business, farmers, workers, and the newly emancipated slaves in the post-Civil War era.

Political parties exert a variety of functions essential to the democratic tradition in the United States. Nominating candidates, local, state, and national office is their most visible activity. At the national level, this function has been diluted somewhat by the popularity of **primary elections** allowing voters to express their preference for candidates. Raucous conventions where party bosses chose obscure "**dark horse**" candidates in "smoke filled rooms" are largely a thing of the past.

Political parties stimulate interest in public issues by highlighting their own strengths and maximizing the flaws of the opposition. They also provide a framework for keeping the machinery of government operating, most notably in their control of Congress and its organization, which is strictly along party lines.

American political parties appear in theory to be highly organized. The geographic size of the country coupled with the federal system of government keep the parties in a state of relative decentralization. At the local level, the fundamental unit of organization is the **precinct**. At this level, there is usually a captain or committee to handle such routine chores as registering voters, distributing party literature, organizing "**grass-roots**" meetings, and getting out the vote on election day.

State central committees are critical to the parties' fund raising activities. They also organize the state party conventions. There is great variety from state to state regarding the composition and selection of the state committees, which often formulate policies independent from those of the national committee.

In presidential election years, the **national party committees** are most visible. They plan the **national nominating convention**, write the party **platforms** (summaries of positions on major issues), raise money to finance political activities, and carry out the election campaigns. Representatives from each state serve on the national committees, and the **presidential nominee** chooses the individual to serve as the **party chairperson**.

Although the two-party system is firmly established in the United States, over the years, "**third parties**" have left their marks. The national nominating conventions were introduced in the 1830s by the **Anti-Masonic Party** and were soon adopted by the Democrats and the Whigs. The **Prohibition Party** opposed the use of alcohol and worked for the adoption of the **Eighteenth Amendment**. In the 1890s, the **Populist Party** championed the causes of the farmers and workers and impacted the mainstream parties with its reform agenda. Among the Populist innovations were the **initiative petition** (a mechanism allowing voters to put proposed legislation on the ballot) and the **referendum** (allowing voters to approve or reject laws passed by their legislatures). The **Progressive** or **Bull Moose Party** was a **splinter party** (one that breaks away from an established party, in this case the Republican Party) built around the personality of Theodore Roosevelt. Another party formed around the personality of a forceful individual was the 1992 **Reform Party** of **H. Ross Perot**. Perot did not capture any electoral votes but garnered 19 percent of the popular tally.

Elections

In comparison to citizens in other democratic systems, Americans elect a large number of public officials. Elections in the United States are largely regulated by **state** law. The Constitution does assign to Congress the responsibility for determining "the times, places, and manner of holding elections for Senators and Representatives." Article II establishes the Electoral College for presidential elections and specifies that they shall be held on the same day throughout the nation. Several of the Amendments deal with election procedures, voter qualifications, and **suffrage** (the right to vote) for target groups (former slaves, women, and those 18 years of age and older). Nonetheless, the principal responsibility for arranging and supervising elections rests with the states.

The actual election process consists of two phases: nominating the candidates and choosing the final officials. **Primary elections** screen and select the final party candidates. **Closed primaries** allow voters **registered** (legal procedure that must be completed before an individual can vote) in one of the political parties to express their preferences for the final candidate from among the field of hopefuls in that party. **Open primaries** allow voters to select their party affiliations on site. Some states allow "**crossover**" voting which permits voters registered in one party to vote for candidates in the other party. This practice can lead to the tactic of voting for the weakest choice in the opposition party to give an advantage in the final election to the candidate and the party the voter actually supports.

In **national elections** (those held in November of each even-numbered year to choose national officeholders), the **campaign** traditionally begins after Labor Day. **Off-year elections** are those in which only members of Congress are chosen and no presidential contest is held. In both presidential and off-year elections, candidates follow exhausting schedules and spend huge sums on media advertising. Their activities usually dominate the national and local news coverage, and debates are common forums for airing their differences. Funding for political campaigns comes from a variety of sources including the candidates own resources, private supporters, **Political Action Committees** (PACs), and the federal government. In the election reform drive of the 1970s, the **Federal Election Commission** was created to ensure that laws concerning campaign financing are followed.

The cost of the elections themselves is borne by the state and local governments which must prepare ballots, designate polling places, and pay workers who participate in administering the elections. **Registrars of voters** oversee the preparation of ballots, the establishment of polling places, and the tallying of the votes. In a close election, the loser may request a **recount**. Some states require them in closely contested races.

Voter Behavior

In recent years, attention has focused on the problem of voter apathy. Despite efforts to extend suffrage to all segments of the adult population, participation in the electoral process has been on the decline. Several theories have been advanced to explain this trend. There is widespread belief that Americans are dissatisfied with their government and mistrust all elected officials. Therefore, they refuse to participate in the electoral process. Some citizens do not vote in a given election, not because they are "turned-off" to the system, but because they are ill, homeless, away on business, or otherwise preoccupied on election day. College students and others away from their legal residences find registration and the use of **absentee ballots** cumbersome and inconvenient. Efforts have been made in the 1990s to streamline the registration process with such legislation as the **"motor-voter" bill** that makes it possible for citizens to register at their local registries of motor vehicles.

While most attempts to explain voter apathy focus on negatives such as citizen apathy, some analysts disagree. They see disinterest in the ballot as a sign that the majority of Americans are happy with the system and feel no sense of urgency to participate in the political process.

Political participation is not limited to voting in elections. Working for candidates, attending rallies, contacting elected officials and sharing opinions about issues, writing letters to newspapers, marching in protest, and joining in community activities are all forms of political participation. While voter turnout has decreased in recent years, other forms of participation seem to be on the increase.

Interest Groups

American officials and political leaders are continually subjected to pressure from a variety of **interest groups** seeking to influence their actions. Such groups arise from bonds among individuals who share common concerns. Interest groups may be loosely organized (**informal**), with no clear structure or regulations. A good example of such an informal or ad hoc interest group was the "March of the Poor" on Washington, D.C. in 1963 to focus Congress' attention on the needs of the "underclass" in America. A group of neighbors united in opposition to a new shopping mall that threatens a wetland is an example of this type of group. Other interest groups are much more **formal** and permanent in nature. They may have suites of offices and large numbers of employees. Their political objectives are usually clearly defined. Labor unions, professional and public-interest groups, and single issue organizations fall into this category. The National Rifle Association and the National Right to Life Organization are examples of **single issue** pressure groups.

Interest groups employ a variety of tactics to accomplish their goals. Most commonly, they **lobby** (influence the passage or defeat of legislation) elected officials, particularly members of Congress. Lobbyists provide legislators with reports and statistics to persuade them of the legitimacy of their respective positions. They may present expert testimony at public hearings and influence the media to portray their causes in a favorable light. Lobbyists are required to register in Washington and to make their positions public. They are barred from presenting false and misleading information and from bribing public officials. Regulatory legislation cannot, however, curb all the abuses inherent to a system of organized persuasion.

One particularly controversial brand of pressure group is the **Political Action Committee** (PAC). PACs were formed in the 1970s in an attempt to circumvent legislation limiting contributions to political campaigns. Critics see these interest groups as another means of diluting the influence individual voters may have on their elected officials. Some politicians refuse to accept PAC money.

Public Opinion

Public opinion refers to the attitudes and preferences expressed by a significant number of individuals about an issue that involves the government or the society at large. It does not necessarily represent the sentiments of all or even most of the citizenry. Nonetheless, it is an important component of a democratic society.

In today's technological society, the influence of the **mass media** on public opinion cannot be over-emphasized. The print and broadcast media can reach large numbers of people cheaply and efficiently, but the electronic media in particular have been criticized for over-simplifying complicated issues and reducing coverage of major events to brief sound bites. Both the print and broadcast media claim to present news in a fair and objective format, but both conservatives and liberals claim that coverage is slanted.

Paid political advertising is another vehicle for molding public opinion. In this case, objectivity is neither expected nor attempted, as candidates and interest groups employ "hard-sell" techniques to persuade voters to support their causes.

Measuring the effects of the media on public opinion is difficult, as is gauging where the public stands on a given issue at a particular point in time. **Public opinion polls** have been designed to these ends. Pollsters usually address a **random sample** and try to capture a **cross-section** of the population. Their questions are designed to elicit responses that do not mirror the biases of the interviewer or the polling organization. Results are tabulated and analyzed, and generalizations are presented to the media.

Although polls are more accurate today than in the past, they are still subject to criticism for oversimplifying complicated issues and encouraging pat answers to complex problems. Public opinion is constantly in a state of flux, and what may be a valid report today is passé tomorrow. Another criticism is that interviewees may not be entirely candid, particularly with respect to sensitive issues. They may answer as they think they should but not necessarily with full honesty.

A type of election poll that has been the target of sharp criticism is the **exit poll** in which interviewers question subjects about their votes as they leave the polling places. These polls may be accurate, but if the media present the results while voting is still in progress, the outcome may be affected. Predicting the winners before voters throughout the country have had the opportunity to cast their ballots in a national election robs a segment of the electorate of the sense that its participation is of any consequence. In recent presidential elections, broadcast outlets have shown more sensitivity to this problem.

CIVIL RIGHTS AND INDIVIDUAL LIBERTIES

Civil rights are those legal claims that individuals have to protect themselves from discrimination at the hands of both the government and other citizens. They include the right to vote, equality before the law, and access to public facilities. **Individual** or **civil liberties** protect the sanctity of the person from arbitrary governmental interference. In this category belong the fundamental freedoms of speech, religion, press, and rights such as **due process** (government must act fairly and follow established procedures, as in legal proceedings).

The origin of the concept of fundamental rights and freedoms can be traced to the British constitutional heritage and to the theorists of the Enlightenment. Jefferson's **Declaration of Independence** contains several references to the crown's failure to uphold the civil rights that British subjects had come to value and expect. When fashioning the Constitution, the Founding Fathers included passages regarding the protection of civil liberties, such as the provision in Article I for maintaining the right of *habeas corpus*. One of the criticisms of the Constitution lodged by its opponents was that it did not go far enough in safeguarding individual rights. During the first session of Congress in 1789, the first ten amendments (the **Bill of Rights**) were adopted and sent to the states for ratification. These amendments contain many of the protections that define the ideals of American life. The Bill of Rights was meant to limit the power of the federal government to restrict the freedom of individual citizens. The **Fourteenth Amendment** of 1868 prohibits **states** from denying civil rights and individual liberties to their residents. The Supreme Court is charged with interpreting the law, particularly as it applies to civil rights and individual liberties cases. Not until the **Gitlow Case** in 1925 did the Supreme Court begin to exercise this function with respect to state enforcement of the Bill of Rights. States are now expected to conform to the federal standard of civil rights.

The Amendment that is most closely identified with individual liberty in the United States is the **First Amendment**, which protects freedom of religion, speech, press, assembly, and petition. The First Amendment sets forth the principle of **separation of Church and State** with its **"free exercise"** and **"establishment"** clauses. These have led the Supreme Court to rule against such practices as school prayer (**Engle v. Vitale, 1962**) and Bible reading in public schools (**Abington Township v. Schempp, 1963**).

The **Fourth Amendment**, which outlawed **"unreasonable searches and seizures,"** mandates that warrants be granted only **"upon probable cause,"** and affirms the **"right of the people to be secure in their persons,"** is fundamental to the Court's interpretation of due process and the rights of the accused. The **Fifth Amendment**, which calls for a grand jury, outlawed **double jeopardy** (trying a person who has been acquitted of a charge for a second time) and states that a person may not be compelled to be a witness against himself, is also the basis for Supreme Court rulings that protect the accused. **"Cruel and unusual punishments"** are banned by the **Eighth Amendment**. This clause has been invoked by opponents of capital punishment to justify their position, but the Supreme Court has ruled that the death penalty can be applied if states are judicious and use equal standards in sentencing those convicted of capital crimes to death.

In the twentieth century, a major concern for litigation and review by the Supreme Court has been in the area of civil rights for minorities, particularly African Americans. When civil rights organizations such as the NAACP brought a series of cases before the courts under the **"equal protection clause"** of the **Fourteenth Amendment**, they began to enjoy some victories. Earlier when the Supreme Court enforced its **"separate but equal"** doctrine in the 1896 case **Plessy v. Ferguson**, it did not apply the equal protection standard and allowed segregation to be maintained. The Court reversed itself in 1954 in the landmark case **Brown v. Board of Education**, which ruled that separate but equal was unconstitutional. This ruling led to an end to most **de jure** (legally enforced) segregation, but **de facto** (exists in fact) segregation persisted, largely due to housing patterns and racial and ethnic enclaves in urban neighborhoods.

Landmark Supreme Court Cases

In addition to the previously cited Supreme Court rulings in civil rights and individual liberties cases, the following landmark decisions are notable for their relevance to the concepts of civil rights and individual freedoms.

- **Dred Scott v. Sanford** (1857) – ruled that as a slave Scott had no right to sue for his freedom, and further that Congressional prohibitions against slavery in U.S. territories were unlawful.

- **Near v. Minnesota** (1931) – states were barred from using the concept of prior restraint (outlawing something before it has taken place) to discourage the publication of objectionable material except during wartime or in the cases of obscenity or incitement to violence.

- **West Virginia Board of Education v. Barnette** (1943) – overturned an earlier decision and ruled that compulsory saluting of the flag was unconstitutional.

- **Korematsu v. United States** (1944) – upheld the legality of the forced evacuation of persons of Japanese ancestry during World War II as a wartime necessity.

- **Mapp v. Ohio** (1961) – extended the Supreme Court's exclusionary rule, which bars at trial the introduction of evidence that has not been legally obtained to states. The Court has modified this ruling, particularly with reference to drug cases, so that evidence that might not initially have been obtained legally, but which would eventually have turned up in lawful procedures, can be introduced.

- **Gideon v. Wainwright** (1963) – ruled that courts must provide legal counsel to poor defendants in all felony cases. A later ruling extended this right to all defendants facing possible prison sentences.

- **Escobedo v. Illinois** (1964) – extended the right to counsel to include consultation prior to interrogation by authorities.

- **Miranda v. Arizona** (1966) – mandated that all suspects be informed of their due process rights before questioning by police.

- **Tinker v. Des Moines School District** (1969) – defined the wearing of black armbands in school in protest against the Vietnam War as "symbolic speech" protected by the First Amendment.

- *New York Times* **v. United States** (1971) – allowed, under the First Amendment's freedom of the press protection, the publication of the controversial Pentagon Papers during the Vietnam War.

- **Roe v. Wade** (1973) – legalized abortion so long as a fetus is not viable (able to survive outside the womb).

- **Bakke v. Regents of the University of California** (1978) – declared the University's quota system to be unconstitutional while upholding the legitimacy of affirmative action policies in which institutions consider race and gender as factors when determining admissions.

- **Hazelwood School District v. Kuhlmeier** (1988) – ruled that freedom of the press does not extend to student publications that might be construed as sponsored by the school.

COMPARATIVE GOVERNMENT AND POLITICS

This subfield of government and politics includes two principal areas of scholarship and information: the theoretical frameworks for the government structures, functions, and political cultures of nations and a comparative analysis of the political systems of a series of targeted nations or societies.

THEORETICAL FRAMEWORKS FOR GOVERNMENT STRUCTURES, FUNCTIONS, AND POLITICAL CULTURE
Environmental Factors
In order to understand the political institutions and civic life of any nation, several environmental factors need to be considered. Such questions as the **size**, **location**, **geographic features**, **economic strength**, **level of industrialization**, and **cultural diversity** of a society must be explored. Both the **domestic** and **international** contexts need to be examined as well as the level of **dependence** on or **independence** from the world community. The location of the United States in the Western Hemisphere, separated from both Europe and Asia by vast expanses of ocean, is a critical component in the development of its relatively independent political culture. Conversely, the location of Eastern European countries in the shadow of the post-World War II Soviet Union led to political dependence. The cultural diversity and traditional hostilities of the Balkan peoples are key elements in the political and military volatility of the region. Industrialization and economic stability are conditions that are commonly conducive to a highly developed political system.

The **age** and **historical traditions** of a nation have great impact on its current political culture. France's contemporary unitary form of government can be viewed as an evolutionary manifestation of earlier traditions that centralized power in divine right monarchs and ambitious emperors. **Legitimacy** (acceptance by citizens) is quite another prospect in such places as Somalia and Haiti with their unstable political histories and economic vulnerability.

Government Structures and Functions

How a government is organized, its mechanisms for carrying out its mission, the scope of that mission, and how its structures and functions compare with other governments are prime considerations in comparative government.

The **geographic distribution of authority and responsibility** is a key variable. **Confederations**, such as the United States under the Articles of Confederation, have weak central governments and delegate principal authority to smaller units such as the states. **Federal systems**, on the other hand, divide sovereignty between a central government and those of their separate states. Brazil, India, and the United States are contemporary examples of federal republics. Highly centralized, **unitary** forms of government concentrate power and authority at the top, as in France and Japan.

Separation of governmental powers is another aspect of structure useful in comparing political systems. **Authoritarian** governments center power in a single or collective executive, with the legislative and judicial bodies having little input. The former Soviet Union is an example. Great Britain typifies the **parliamentary** form of government. Here legislative and executive combine, with a prime minister and cabinet selected from within the legislative body. They maintain power only so long as the legislative assembly supports their major policies. The **democratic presidential** system of the United States clearly separates the legislative, executive, and judicial structures. The branches, particularly the executive and the legislative, must cooperate, however, in order for policy to be consistent and for government operations to be carried out smoothly.

A third aspect of governmental structure and function involves the **limits** placed on the power to govern. This facet of politics closely reflects the theoretical and ideological roots of a system. **Constitutional** systems limit the powers of government through written and/or unwritten sources. Law, custom, and precedent combine to protect individuals from the unchecked power of a central authority. The United States and Great Britain have constitutional governments. **Authoritarian** regimes, such as those found in China and the former Soviet Union, do not limit the power of the central authority over the lives of individuals. Those in control impose their values and their will on the society at large regardless of popular sentiments. Authoritarianism is associated with **fascism**, **nazism**, and **totalitarianism** in general.

Political Culture, Parties, Participation, and Mechanisms for Change

Understanding a nation's **political culture** is key to analyzing the theoretical foundations, structure, and functions of its government. It can be defined as the aggregate values a society shares about how politics and government should operate. Some societies function from a **consensus** framework, while other political cultures are more **conflicted**. The Soviet Union's political culture after World War II, as contrasted with the situation there in the early 1990s, illustrates the difference between consensual and conflicted societies. The vehicles for transmitting the political culture and the social cleavages that characterize that culture will impact its system of governing and its legitimacy in the minds of its citizenry. Analysis of the extent to which citizens support their political systems is an important component of comparative government.

Questions regarding the methods citizens employ to impact their political systems and the ease of their access to the power structure need to be examined. Do elections offer a **choice** between candidates with diverse programs and contrasting agendas, as is often the case in the United States, or do they present citizens the opportunity to show their support for the government in a **one party** system such as in China? The number, nature, and power of political parties are additional factors for analysis with respect to how the demands and concerns of citizens in various nations are represented and met. The presence and proliferation of other interest groups such as labor unions and environmental activists provide additional clues as to the values and methods of a political culture.

Beyond voting in elections and joining and supporting political parties and interest groups, **citizen participation** can take other forms. Contacting politicians, lobbying for legislation, and demonstrating in the streets are common vehicles for involvement in the political life of a nation. The degree to which such expressions are encouraged and tolerated by government officials is another facet of political culture that varies from society to society.

Comparative politics and government as a field is concerned with **mechanisms for change** in different nations. Can citizens effect reform through ballots, protest, public opinion polls, or revolts? The underlying factors precipitating the need for change are relevant to an understanding of the overall process.

INTERNATIONAL RELATIONS
THE THEORETICAL FRAMEWORK

The study of how nations interact with one another can be approached from a variety of perspectives including the following:

- A **traditional analysis** uses the descriptive process and focuses on such topics as global issues, international institutions, and the foreign policies of individual nation states.

- The **strategists' approach** zeroes in on war and deterrence. Scholars in this camp may employ game theory to analyze negotiations, the effectiveness of weapons systems, and the likelihood of limited versus all-out war in a given crisis situation.

- The **middle range theorists** analyze specific components of international relations, such as the politics of arms races, the escalation of international crises, and the role of prejudice and attitudes toward other cultures in precipitating war and peace.

- A **world politics approach** takes into consideration such factors as economics, ethics, law, and trade agreements and stresses the significance of international organizations and the complexities of interactions among nations.

- The **grand theory** of international relations is presented by **Hans J. Morgenthau** in *Politics Among Nations* (1948). He argues for **realism** in the study of interactions on the international stage. Morgenthau suggests that an analysis of relations among nations reveals such recurring themes as "interest defined as power" and striving for equilibrium/balance of power as a means of maintaining peace.

- The **idealists** assume that human nature is essentially good; hence people and nations are capable of cooperation and avoiding armed conflict. They highlight global organizations, international law, disarmament, and the reform of institutions that lead to war.

An analysis of international politics can be conducted at various levels by looking at the actions of individual statesmen, the interests of individual nations, and/or the mechanics of a whole system of international players. In studying the rise of nazism and its role in precipitating WWII, the **individual** approach would focus on Hitler, the **state** approach would treat the German preoccupation with racial superiority and the need for expansion, and the **systemic** approach would highlight how German military campaigns upset the balance of power and triggered unlikely alliances, such as the linking of the democratic Britain and the United States with the totalitarian Soviet Union in a common effort to restore equilibrium.

FOREIGN POLICY PERSPECTIVES

International relations as a discipline is inextricably linked to the field of **foreign policy**. Foreign policy involves the objectives nations seek to gain with reference to other nations and the procedures in which they engage in order to achieve their objectives. The principal foreign policy goals of sovereign states or other political entities may include some or all of the following: independence, national security, economic advancement, encouraging their political values beyond their own borders, gaining respect and prestige, and promoting stability and international peace.

The **foreign policy process** involves the stages a government goes through in formulating policy and arriving at decisions with respect to courses of action. A variety of models have been identified in reference to the process of creating foreign policy. The **primary players** (nations, world organizations, multinational corporations, and non-state ethnic entities such as the Palestine Liberation Organization) are often referred to as **actors**.

The **unitary/rational actor model** assumes that all nations or primary players share similar goals and approach foreign policy issues in like fashion. The actions players take, according to this theory, are influenced by the actions of other players rather than by what may be taking place internally. The rational component in this model is based on the assumption that actors will respond on the world stage by making the best choice after measured consideration of possible alternatives. Maximizing goals and achieving specific objectives motivate the rational actor's course of action.

The **bureaucratic model** assumes that, due to the many large organizations involved in formulating foreign policy, particularly in powerful nation states, final decisions are the result of struggle among the bureaucratic actors. In the United States, the bureaucratic actors include the Departments of State and Defense, as well as the National Security Council, the Central Intelligence Agency, the Environmental Protection Agency, the Department of Commerce, and/or any other agencies and departments whose agendas might be impacted by a foreign policy decision. While the bureaucratic model is beneficial in that it assumes the consideration of multiple points of view, the downside is that inter-agency competition and compromise often drive the final decision.

A third model assumes that foreign policy results from the intermingling of a variety of political factors including national leaders, bureaucratic organizations, legislative bodies, political parties, interest groups, and public opinion.

The **implementation of foreign policy** depends upon the tools a nation or primary player has at its disposal. The major instruments of foreign policy include **diplomacy**, **military strength/actions**, and **economic initiatives**.

Diplomacy involves communicating with other primary players through official representatives. It might include attending conferences and summit meetings, negotiating treaties and settlements, and exchanging official communications. Diplomacy is an indispensable tool in the successful conduct of an entity's foreign policy.

The extent to which a player may rely on the **military** tool depends upon its technological strength, its readiness, and the support of both its domestic population and the international community. President Bush's decision to engage in a military conflict with Iraq's Saddam Hussein in 1991, after Iraq's invasion of Kuwait, largely rested on positive assessments of those factors. Sometimes the buildup of military capabilities is in itself a powerful foreign policy tool and thus a deterrent to armed conflict—as was the case in the Cold War between the United States and the Soviet Union.

Economic development and the ability to employ economic initiatives to achieve foreign policy objectives are effective means by which a principal player can interact on the international scene. The Marshall Plan, through which the United States provided economic aid to a ravaged Europe after World War II, could be viewed as a tool to block Soviet expansion as well as a humanitarian gesture. It was a tool to resurrect the devastated economies of Europe which had been major trading partners and purchasers of U.S. exports before the war. Membership in an economic community such as OPEC (Organization of Petroleum Exporting Countries) or the EC (European Community) can drive the foreign policy of both member nations and those impacted by their decisions.

THE MODERN GLOBAL SYSTEM

International systems today evidence many of the global forces and foreign policy mechanisms formulated in Western Europe in the eighteenth and nineteenth centuries. Largely due to the influence of Western imperialism and colonialism, the less developed countries of modern times have, to a great extent, embraced ideological and foreign policy values that originated in Europe during the formative centuries. Such concepts as political autonomy, nationalism, economic advancement through technology and industrialization, and gaining respect and prestige in the international community move the foreign policies of major powers and many less developed countries as well.

Historical Context of the Modern Global System

The modern global system or network of relationships among nations owes its origins to the emergence of the nation-state. It is generally recognized that the **Peace of Westphalia** (1648), which concluded the Thirty Years War in Europe and ended the authority of the Roman Catholic popes to exert their political dominance over secular leaders, gave birth to the concept of the modern nation-state. The old feudal order in Europe that allowed the Holy Roman Emperor to extend his influence over the territories governed by local princes was replaced by a new one in which distinct geographic and political entities interacted under a new set of principles. These allowed the nation-states to conduct business with each other, such as negotiating treaties and settling border disputes, without interference from a higher authority. Hence, the concept of sovereignty evolved.

The eighteenth century in Europe was notable for its relatively even distribution of power among the nation-states. With respect to military strength and international prestige, such nations as England, France, Austria, Prussia, and Russia were on the same scale. Some of the former major powers, such as Spain, the Netherlands, and Portugal, occupied a secondary status. Both the major and secondary players created alliances and competed with each other for control of territories beyond their borders. Alignments, based primarily on economic and colonial considerations, shifted without upsetting the global system. Royal families intermarried and professional soldiers worked for the states that gave them the best benefits without great regard for political allegiances.

Military conflicts in the eighteenth century tended to be conservative with the concept of the **balance of power** at play. Mercenaries and professionals controlled the action mindful of strategic maneuvers to bring about victory. Wiping out the enemy was not the principal goal. Major upheavals were avoided through the formation of alliances and a high regard for the authority of monarchs and the Christian Church. The eighteenth century has been dubbed the "**golden age of diplomacy**" because it was an era of relative stability where moderation and shared cultural values on the part of the decision-makers were the rule.

Structural changes in the process and implementation of international relations occurred in the nineteenth and twentieth centuries due to major political, technological, and ideological developments.

The nation-state of the eighteenth century was a relatively new phenomenon. Statesmen of the era traded territory with little consideration of ethnic loyalties. This style of diplomacy was irrevocably altered by the French Revolution and the Napoleonic Wars that saw **nationality** emerge as a rallying point for conducting wars and for raising the citizens' armies necessary to succeed in military conflicts. The trend was exacerbated in the mid-nineteenth century by the European drive for unification of distinct ethnic groups and the creation of the Italian and German nation-states. The twentieth century has seen a particularly impassioned link between nationalism and war.

The scientific and industrial revolutions of the eighteenth century gave rise to advancements in **military technology** in the nineteenth and twentieth centuries that dramatically altered the concept and the conduct of war. Replacing the eighteenth century conservative, play-by-the-rules approach was a new, fiercely violent brand of warfare that increasingly involved civilian casualties and aimed at utter destruction of the enemy. The World Wars of the twentieth century called for mass mobilization of civilians as well as of the military, prompting leaders to whip up nationalistic sentiments. The development of nuclear weapons in the mid-twentieth century rendered total war largely unfeasible. Nuclear arms build-ups, with the goal of **deterrent capabilities** (the means to retaliate so swiftly and effectively that an enemy will avoid conflict) was viewed by the super-powers as the only safety net.

Another factor molding the structural changes in international relations that surfaced in the nineteenth and twentieth centuries was the **ideological component**. Again the French Revolution, anchored in the ideology of "liberty, equality, and fraternity," is viewed as the harbinger of future trends. Those conservative forces valuing legitimacy and monarchy fought the forces of the Revolution and Napoleon to preserve tradition against the rising tide of republican nationalism. In the Twentieth Century, with its binding "isms"—Communism, democratic republicanism, liberalism, Nazism, socialism—competing for dominance, ideological conflicts have become more pronounced.

The Contemporary Global System

The values of the contemporary system are rooted in the currents of eighteenth and nineteenth century Europe, transplanted to the rest of the world through colonialism and imperialism. The forces of nationalism, belief in technological progress, and ideological motivations, as well as the desire for international respect and prestige, are evident worldwide. Principal players in Africa, Asia, Latin America, and the Middle East as often as not dominate the diplomatic arena.

The contemporary scene in international relations is comprised of a number of entities beyond the **nation-state**. These include: **non-state actors** or **principal players, nonterritorial transnational organizations**, and **nonterritorial intergovernmental** or **multinational organizations**.

Contemporary **nation-states** are legal entities occupying well-defined geographic areas and organized under a common set of governmental institutions. They are recognized by other members of the international community as sovereign and independent states.

Non-state actors or **principal players** are movements or parties that function as independent states. They lack sovereignty, but they may actually wield more power than some less developed nation-states. The **Palestine Liberation Organization (PLO)** is an example of a non-state actor that conducts its own foreign policy, purchases armaments, and has committed acts of terror with grave consequences for the contemporary international community. The **Irish Republican Army (IRA)** is another example of a non-state actor that has employed systematic acts of terror to achieve political ends.

Nonterritorial transnational organizations are institutions such as the Catholic Church that conduct activities throughout the world but whose aims are largely nonpolitical. A relatively new nonterritorial transnational organization is the **multi-national corporation (MNC)**, such as General Motors, Hitachi, or British Petroleum. These giant business entities have bases in a number of countries and exist primarily for economic profit. Despite their apparent nonpolitical agendas, multinational corporations can greatly impact foreign policy, as in the case of the United Fruit Company's suspect complicity in the overthrow of the government of Guatemala in the 1950s. Initially the MNC was largely an American innovation, but in recent years, Asian players, particularly the Japanese, have proliferated, changing the makeup of the scene.

An **intergovernmental organization**, such as the United Nations, NATO, or the European Community, is made up of nation-states and can wield significant power on the international scene. While NATO is primarily a military intergovernmental organization, and the EC is mainly economic, the UN is really a multipurpose entity. While its primary mission is to promote world peace, the UN engages in a variety of social, cultural, economic, health, and humanitarian activities.

The contemporary global system tends to classify nation-states based on power, wealth, and prestige in the international community. Such labels as **superpower, secondary power, middle power, small power**, and the like tend to be confusing because they are not based on a single set of criteria or a shared set of standards. Some countries may be strong militarily, as was Iraq prior to the Persian Gulf War, yet lack the wealth and prestige in the international community to classify them as super or secondary powers. Others like Japan may have little military capabilities, but wide influence due to economic preeminence.

The **structure** of the contemporary global system during the Cold War was distinctly **bipolar**, with the United States and the Soviet Union assuming diplomatic, ideological, and military leadership for the international community. With the breakup of the Soviet Union and the reorganization of the Eastern bloc countries has come the disintegration of the bipolar system. Since the 1970s, when tensions between the United States and the Soviet Union eased, a **multipolar system**, in which new alignments are flexible and more easily drawn, has been emerging. President Bush spoke of the **New World Order** at the end of the Cold War. This concept involves alliances that transcend the old bipolar scheme with its emphasis on ideology and military superiority and calls for multinational cooperation as seen in the Persian Gulf War. It also assumes greater non-military, transnational cooperation in scientific research and humanitarian projects. The multipolar system is less cohesive than the bipolar system of the recent past and the orders of the distant past, such as the **hierarchical system** (one unit dominates) of the Holy Roman Empire or the **diffuse system** (power and influence are distributed among a large number of units) of eighteenth-century Europe.

A set of fundamental rules has long governed international relations and, though often ignored, is still held as the standard today. These rules include **territorial integrity, sovereignty**, and the **legal equality of nation-states**. However, in an age of covert operations, mass media, multinational corporations, and shifting territorial boundaries, these traditional rules of international conduct are subject to both violation and revision.

INTERNATIONAL LAW

The present system of international law is rooted in the fundamental rules of global relations: territorial integrity, sovereignty, and legal equality of nation-states. It embodies a set of basic principles mandating what countries may or may not do and under what conditions the rules should be applied.

Historical Context

Despite evidence that the legal and ethical norms of modern international law may have guided interactions among political entities in non-Western pre-industrial systems, contemporary international law emanates from the Western legal traditions of Greece, Rome, and modern Europe. The development of the European nation-state gave rise to a system of legal rights and responsibilities in the international sphere that enlarged upon the religious-based code of the feudal era. In medieval Europe, the church's emphasis on hierarchical obligations, duty, and obedience to authority helped shape the notion of the "**just war**." **Hugo Grotius** (1583–1645), Dutch scholar and statesman, codified the laws of war and peace and has been called the "**father of international law**."

A new era was launched in 1648, with the Peace of Westphalia, that promulgated the idea of the treaty as the basis of international law. Multilateral treaties dominated the eighteenth century, while Britain, with its unparalleled sea power, established and enforced maritime law. By the nineteenth century, advances in military technology rendered the old standard of the "just war" obsolete. Deterrents, rather than legal and ethical principles, provided the means to a relatively stable world order. The concept of **neutrality** evolved during this period, defining the rights and responsibilities of both warring and neutral nations. These restraints helped prevent smaller conflicts from erupting into world wars.

Contemporary International Law

In the twentieth century, international law has retreated theoretically from the tradition of using force as a legitimate tool for settling international conflicts. The **Covenant of the League of Nations** (1920), the **Kellogg-Briand Pact** (1929), and the **United Nations Charter** (1945) all emphasize peaceful relations among nations, but the use of force continues to be employed to achieve political ends. The **International Court of Justice**, the judicial arm of the United Nations and its predecessor, the **Permanent Court of International Justice** represent concerted efforts to replace armed conflict with the rule of law. Unfortunately, the World Court has proven to be an ineffective organ. Nation-states are reluctant to submit vital questions to the Court, and there is a lack of consensus as to the norms to be applied. Members of the United Nations are members of the Court, but they are not compelled to submit their international disputes for consideration.

The UN Charter seeks to humanize the international scene in its admonition that all member nations assist victims of aggression. This approach negates the old idea of neutrality. It further dismisses the tradition of war as a legitimate tool for resolution of disputes between nation-states of equal legal status. Aggressive conflicts can be categorized as crimes against humanity, and individuals may be held personally accountable for launching them.

The concept of international law has been criticized on several fronts. The rise of **multiculturalism**, with its emphasis on multiple perspectives, has called into question the relevance of applying Western legal traditions to the global community. International law has been seen as an instrument of the powerful nations in pursuit of their aims at the expense of weaker nations. Strong nation-states are in a position to both enforce international law and to violate it without fear of reprisal. These observations have led some to conclude that international law is primarily an instrument to maintain the **status quo**.

International law can be effective if parties involved see some **mutual self-advantage** in compliance. **Fear of reprisal** is another factor influencing nations to observe the tenets of international law. **Diplomatic advantage** and **enhanced global prestige** may follow a nation's decisions to abide by international law. It can be argued that international law is valuable in that it seeks to impose **order** on a potentially chaotic system and sets expectations that, while not always met, are positive and affirming.

☞ Drill: Political Science

1. All of the following are major differences between the Congress of the United States and the parliaments of Western Europe EXCEPT

   (A) campaigns of parliament members are more personalistic.

   (B) members of parliament are more likely to support the party after election.

   (C) Congress functions more separately from the executive than does parliament.

   (D) party discipline is tighter within parliament.

2. During which time period was power in the House of Representatives most centralized in the leadership?

   (A) 1860s

   (B) Late 1800s and early 1900s

   (C) 1930s

   (D) Today

3. During which period in U.S. history was the House of Representatives more powerful than the Senate?

   (A) The early 1800s   (C) 1920s

   (B) 1870s   (D) 1970s

4. The seniority system of choosing committee chairmen

   (A) is less important today than it was a few years ago.

   (B) has never been particularly important in reality.

   (C) was often opposed openly by powerful Speakers.

   (D) has existed since the early 1800s.

5. The most powerful leader(s) in the Senate is (are) the

   (A) party whips.

   (B) Speaker.

   (C) president *pro tempore*.

   (D) majority and minority leaders.

6. Which of the following powers did the U.S. president lack until 1994?

    (A) Pocket veto

    (B) Executive privilege

    (C) Commander-in-chief of the armed forces

    (D) Line item veto

7. What is the maximum number of terms for which one may be elected president of the U.S.?

    (A) Three terms   (C) Three and a half terms

    (B) Two terms   (D) No limit

8. The number of bureaucrats in the U.S. government

    (A) has grown significantly since the end of World War II.

    (B) has not grown significantly, although the power of the bureaucracy has grown.

    (C) has not grown significantly, and the power of the bureaucracy has declined.

    (D) has grown significantly, as has the power of the bureaucracy.

9. The most important motivation for the limitation of civil liberties and civil rights early in this century was

    (A) national security.

    (B) violence caused by early civil rights leaders.

    (C) the lower percentages of minority groups within the U.S. population.

    (D) the need to control the inequalities caused by an industrialized society.

10. A recently organized country is MOST likely to have problems with

    (A) structures not matching functions.

    (B) survival in the international environment.

    (C) a high GNP.

    (D) establishing legitimacy.

11. The process whereby political culture is transmitted to the citizens is

    (A) political communication.   (C) political socialization.

    (B) domestic environment.   (D) political recruitment.

12. In a consensual political culture,

    (A) citizens always agree with political leaders.

    (B) citizens consent to give all power to a dictator.

    (C) there is usually only one political party.

    (D) citizens are in general agreement about the basics of government.

13. The ways in which a political system encourages individuals to serve in leadership roles is known as

    (A) political socialization.

    (B) political communication.

    (C) a democratic political structure.

    (D) recruitment of elites.

14. The theoretical point of view that focuses on building an understanding of deterrence in the nuclear age is

    (A) traditional analysis.

    (B) the strategists' perspective.

    (C) grand theory.

    (D) middle range theory.

15. A scholar who develops a theory of arms races would MOST likely be studying international relations from which theoretical perspective?

    (A) Traditional analysis

    (B) The strategists' perspective

    (C) Grand theory

    (D) Middle range theory

16. The major purpose of operational definitions in a research design is

    (A) to generate more data.

(B)   to establish criteria for judging reality on a more common basis.

(C)   to prove a theory to be correct.

(D)   to define the relationship between hypotheses and theories.

17. The level of measurement that provides ONLY discreet categories for data is

(A)   nominal.   (C)   operational.

(B)   ordinal.   (D)   integral.

18. Which of the following is an example of ordinal categorization?

(A)   Republican/Democrat

(B)   Liberal Democrat/Conservative Democrat/Liberal Republican/ Conservative Republican

(C)   Income levels per year: $10,000-$20,000; $20,000-$30,000; $30,000-$40,000; $40,000-$60,000

(D)   Democratic regime/totalitarian regime

19. Procedures that are repeatable and that yield similar readings on repeated applications are said to have

(A)   validity.   (C)   operationalism.

(B)   reliability.   (D)   empiricism.

20. A sample in which a random sample is selected from every sampling unit proportionate to the size of the sampling unit is called

(A)   cluster sampling.

(B)   systematic sampling.

(C)   stratified sampling.

(D)   multi-stage random sampling.

POLITICAL SCIENCE REVIEW

ANSWER KEY

Drill: Political Science

1.	(A)	6.	(D)	11.	(C)	16.	(B)
2.	(B)	7.	(B)	12.	(D)	17.	(A)
3.	(A)	8.	(B)	13.	(D)	18.	(B)
4.	(A)	9.	(A)	14.	(B)	19.	(B)
5.	(D)	10.	(D)	15.	(D)	20.	(C)

DETAILED EXPLANATIONS OF ANSWERS

Drill: Political Science

1. **(A)** Choice (A) is correct. Candidates can only be elected to parliament through the efforts of a political party, whereas Congressmen may have more personalistic campaigns that are only loosely supported by a party.

2. **(B)** Choice (B) is the correct answer. During the late 1800s and early 1900s, power in the House was centralized in the hands of Speakers Thomas B. Reed and Joseph Cannon.

3. **(A)** Choice (A) is the correct answer. In the early 1800s, the House of Representatives was more powerful than the Senate, and leadership was strongly centralized under House Speaker Henry Clay.

4. **(A)** Choice (A) is the correct answer. In the 1970s, a series of reforms weakened the seniority system, allowing election of chairmen by secret ballot, open committee meetings, and more authority to subcommittees and individual members.

5. **(D)** Choice (D) is the correct answer. The real leadership is in the hands of the majority and minority leaders.

6. **(D)** Choice (D) is correct. Congress granted the president the line item veto in 1994; however, it came under legal challenge by litigants who claim it upsets the balance of power between the Executive and Legislative branches.

7. **(B)** Choice (B) is the correct answer. The Twenty-Second Amendment, ratified in 1951, says "No person shall be elected to the office of the President more than twice...."

8. **(B)** Choice (B) is the correct answer. Although the number of bureaucrats has not grown significantly, the power of the bureaucracy has grown dramatically since the country's founding.

9. **(A)** Choice (A) is correct. Early in the twentieth century, the Supreme Court usually ruled to limit freedoms if national security was at stake.

10. **(D)** Choice (D) is the correct answer. A new country with a recently organized government may have trouble with legitimacy

(acceptance by the citizens) because no centralization of power has existed before.

11. **(C)** Choice (C) is correct. Political socialization is the way in which children and adults learn political values and attitudes. Some governments emphasize political socialization as an important basis for establishing the legitimacy of the government.

12. **(D)** Choice (D) is correct. In consensual political culture, citizens are in general agreement about the basics of government. In contrast, in a conflictual political culture, citizens have conflicting points of view about the way the government should be run.

13. **(D)** Choice (D) is correct. Political recruitment defines the way in which a government encourages citizens to participate in government (citizen recruitment), and the ways in which it encourages individuals to serve in leadership roles (recruitment of elites).

14. **(B)** Choice (B) is the correct answer. The strategists' perspective was particularly strong during the Cold War era. Their main concern has been to understand deterrence in the nuclear age, to analyze the importance of new weapon systems, and to maximize national security and minimize the possibility of nuclear war.

15. **(D)** Choice (D) is correct. Middle range theorists believe that international relations may be best understood by developing more specific explanations, such as a theory of arms races or crisis decision making. A number of middle range theories focus on the study of war and peace. These theories highlight some of the processes leading to escalation of violence, the relationship between prejudice and national hostility, the economic consequences of disarmament, and the sources of public attitudes toward foreign cultures.

16. **(B)** Choice (B) is correct. Operational definitions are required to set agreement on common meanings. Giving a concept an operational definition means providing a set of instructions to indicate how to measure, label, or otherwise designate a given concept.

17. **(A)** Choice (A) is the correct answer. The nominal level of measurement is the simplest measurement, providing only discreet categories for data. There is no metric order in nominal data. There are simply categories.

18. **(B)** Choice (B) is correct. The ordinal level of measurement categorizes *and* orders. For example, an ideological ordering may be attached to

the partisan categories of Democratic and Republican by using a liberal/conservative dimension. The ordinal level goes beyond mere categorization and is considered a higher and more meaningful level of measurement than is nominal categorization.

19. **(B)** Choice (B) is the correct answer. One way to assess the adequacy of a research design and its operational definitions and measurement procedures is to determine a measure's reliability. Procedures are deemed to have reliability if they are repeatable and if they yield similar readings on repeated applications.

20. **(C)** Choice (C) is correct. A stratified sample is drawn from different sub-groups of a theoretical population to insure the overall sample's representativeness.

III. SOCIOLOGY REVIEW

INTRODUCTION TO SOCIOLOGY
WHAT IS SOCIOLOGY

Sociology is the science or discipline that studies societies, social groups, and the relationships between people. The field encompasses both the formation and transformation of particular societies and social groups, including their continuation, dissolution, and demise, as well as the origins, structure, and functioning of social groups.

THE UNIT OF STUDY

Sociologists focus on a number of different levels of analysis in understanding social life. While some study the social interaction that occurs within groups (the social processes represented by behavior directed toward, affected by, or inspired by others in the group), other sociologists study the social structure of group life. Some are interested in the structure of societies. That is, the organization of populations living in the same area who participate in the same institutions and who share a common culture. Others in the field are concerned with the social system, a social group, or with society conceived as a whole unit distinct from the individuals that make it up.

Others concern themselves with social relationships, or relationships between people that are based upon common meaning, or with social action, defined as meaningful behavior that is oriented toward and influenced by others. But no matter what is designated to be the unit of study, the focus of the discipline is on social groups and society as a whole, rather than on the individual, which is the focus of psychology.

THE PERSPECTIVE: HUMANISTIC OR SCIENTIFIC

Some sociologists adopt a **humanistic** approach to their work, which means that they see sociology as a means to advance human welfare. They seek self-realization, the full development of a cultivated personality, or improvement of the human social condition.

On the other hand, some sociologists adopt the **scientific perspective**. They are primarily concerned with acquiring objective empirical knowledge (the actual knowledge derived from experience or observation that can be measured or counted) and not with the uses to which such knowledge is put.

They believe that in science one must be concerned with "what is" and not with "what should be." Some sociologists work to integrate both humanistic and scientific perspectives.

THE SOCIOLOGICAL IMAGINATION

According to C. Wright Mills, a certain quality of mind is required if we are to understand ourselves in relation to society. This quality of mind seeks to expand the role of freedom, choice, and conscious decision in history, by means of knowledge. Mills referred to this as "the **sociological imagination**."

The sociological imagination expresses both an understanding that personal troubles can and often do reflect broader social issues and problems and also faith in the capacity of human beings to alter the course of human history. The sociological imagination, therefore, expresses the humanistic aspect of the sociological perspective.

THE SCIENCE OF SOCIOLOGY

As in all other sciences, the sociologist assumes there is "order" in the universe and that with methods of science the order can be understood. The sociologist, however, cannot assume that human beings will always behave in predictable ways. There are times when we do and times when we don't.

Although most of us will think and act tomorrow as we did today, some of us won't. Unlike the rocks and molecules studied by natural scientists, we are capable of changing our minds and our behavior. Unlike the organisms studied by biologists, we are capable of treating each other as whole and complete beings. Hence, the explanations and predictions offered by sociology cannot be so precise as to express universal laws that are applicable to any thing or event under all circumstances.

THE SOCIAL SCIENCES

The social sciences are concerned with social life—psychology, with its emphasis on individual behavior and mental processes; economics, with its emphasis on the production, distribution, and consumption of goods and services; political science, with its emphasis on political philosophy and forms of government; and anthropology, with its current emphasis on both primitive and modern culture. What then distinguishes sociology from these other social sciences? In sociology the "social," however it is defined, is the immediate concern.

THE ORIGINS OF SOCIOLOGY

Compared to other academic disciplines (e.g., history, economics, and physics in particular), sociology is a discipline still in its prime. It was in 1838 that Auguste Comte coined the term from *socius* (the Latin word for "companion, with others") and *logos* (the Greek word for "study of") as a means of demarcating the field: its subject matter, society as distinct from the mere sum of individual actions, and its methods, prudent observation and impartial measurement based on the scientific method of comparison. Comte concluded that every science, beginning with astronomy and ending with sociology, follows the same regular pattern of development.

The first stage in this development is the **theological stage**. In the theological stage, scientists look toward the supernatural realm of ideas for an explanation of what they observed. In the second, or **metaphysical stage**, scientists begin to look to the real world for an explanation of what they have observed.

Finally, in the **positive stage**, which is defined as the definitive stage of all knowledge, scientists search for general ideas or laws. With such knowledge of society as how society is held together (social statics) and of how society changes (social dynamics), people can predict and, thereby, control their destiny. They can build a better and brighter future for themselves.

Was Comte's conception of a science of society ahead of its time, or was his conception of a science that would allow human beings control over lives timely? If one only considers the fast pace of technological and social change in Europe during the eighteenth century, the proliferation of factories, the spread of cities and of city life, and the loss of faith in "rule by divine right," then it would be timely. However, if one considers intellectual history, notwithstanding the accomplishments of Harriet Martineau (1802-1876) who was observing English social patterns at the same time that Comte was laying a foundation for sociology, Karl Marx (1818-1883) "the theoretical giant of communist thought" whose prophecies are still being hotly debated, and Herbert Spencer (1820-1903) whose idea that society follows a natural evolutionary progression toward something better, then Comte was clearly ahead of his time. More than 50 years passed before Emile Durkheim (1858-1917), in his statistical study of suicide, and Max Weber (1864-1920), in a series of studies in which he sought to explain the origins of capitalism, came along and tested Comte's ideas.

Under the influence of Lester Ward (1841-1913) and William Graham Sumner (1840-1910), American sociology experienced a loss of interest in the larger problems of social order and social change and began to concentrate on narrower and more specific social problems. Until 1940 attention in the discipline was focused on the University of Chicago where George Herbert

Mead was originating the field of social psychology. Robert Park and Ernest Burgess were concentrating on the city and on such social problems as crime, drug addiction, prostitution, and juvenile delinquency.

By the 1940s, attention began to shift away from reforming society toward developing abstract theories of how society works and standardizing the research methods that sociologists employ. Talcott Parsons (1902-1979), the famed functionalist, touched a generation of sociologists by advocating **grand theory**. This involved the building of a theory of society based on aspects of the real world and the organization of these concepts to form a conception of society as a stable system of interrelated parts.

Robert Merton (b. 1910) proposed building middle range theories from a limited number of assumptions from which hypotheses are derived. Merton also distinguished between manifest, or intended, and latent, or unintended, consequences of existing elements of social structure which are either functional or dysfunctional to the system's relative stability. This movement succeeded despite the efforts of C. Wright Mills to reverse the trend away from activism, as well as Dennis Wrong's attempt to end the "oversocialized," or too socially determined, conception of "man in sociology."

No single viewpoint or concern has dominated the thinking of sociologists since the 1970s. The questions of whether a sociologist can or should be detached and value-free, and how to deal with the individual remain controversial. Thus, sociologists have yet to agree on whether the goals of sociology are description, explanation, prediction, or control. More recently sociologists have begun to use sociological knowledge with the intent of applying it to human behavior and organizations. Such knowledge can be used to resolve a current social problem. For example, while some sociologists may study race relations and patterns of contact between minority and majority groups, applied sociologists may actually devise and implement strategies to improve race relations in the United States.

THE THEORETICAL APPROACH

Sociologists often use a theoretical approach or perspective to guide them in their work. In making certain general assumptions about social life, the perspective provides a point of view toward the study of specific social issues.

THE THEORY: INDUCTIVE OR DEDUCTIVE

A theory describes and/or explains the relationship between two or more observations. **Deductive theory** proceeds from general ideas, knowledge, or understanding of the social world from which specific hypotheses are logically

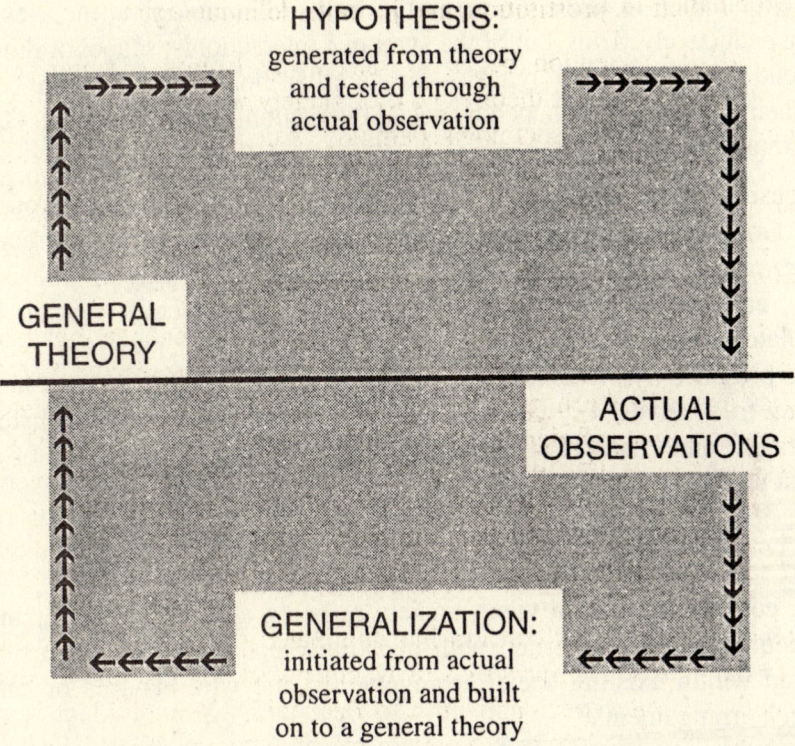

DEDUCTIVE PHASE

HYPOTHESIS:
generated from theory
and tested through
actual observation

**GENERAL
THEORY**

**ACTUAL
OBSERVATIONS**

GENERALIZATION:
initiated from actual
observation and built
on to a general theory

INDUCTIVE PHASE

deduced and tested. **Inductive theory** proceeds from concrete observations from which general conclusions are inferred through a process of reasoning.

More recent sociology includes three such approaches: **interpretative,** which includes the perspectives of symbolic interaction, dramaturgy, and ethnomethodology; **conflict theory**; and **structural functionalism**.

INTERPRETATIVE SOCIOLOGY

Interpretative sociology studies the processes whereby human beings attach meaning to their lives. Derived from the work of Mead and Blumer, symbolic interaction is focused on the process of social interaction and on the meanings that are constructed and reconstructed in that process. Human beings are viewed as shaping their actions based upon both the real and anticipated responses of others. Thus defined by an ongoing process of negotiation, social life is considered far from stable.

Actors are thought to be continually engaged in the process of interpreting, defining, and evaluating their own and others' actions, a process that defies explanation in lawlike terms or in terms of sociological theories proceeding deductively. Thus, out of the symbolic interactionist school of thought, the social construction of reality—the familiar notion that human beings shape their world and are shaped by social interaction—was conceived (Berger & Luckman, 1967).

Focused on the details of everyday life, the dramaturgical approach of Erving Goffman conceives social interaction as a series of episodes or human dramas in which we are more or less aware of playing roles and, thereby, engaging in impression management. We are actors seeking 1) to manipulate our audience, or control the reaction of other people in our immediate presence by presenting a certain image of ourselves; 2) to protect or hide our true selves, or who we really are offstage through "onstage," "frontstage," and "backstage" behavior; and 3) to amplify the rules of conduct that circumscribe our daily encounters.

CONFLICT THEORY

The **conflict paradigm** views society as being characterized by conflict and inequality. It is concerned with questions such as whose interests are expressed within existing social arrangements, and who benefits or suffers from such arrangements?

Sociologists viewing the social world from a conflict perspective question how factors such as race, sex, social class, and age are associated with an unequal distribution of socially valued goods and rewards (i.e., money, education, and power). Generally associated with the work of Coser, Dahrendorf, and Mills, modern conflict theory sees conflict between groups or within social organizations, and not merely class conflict (Marx), as a fact of life of any society. Conflict may have positive as well as disturbing effects (Coser). Conflict includes disagreement over who gets what, as well as tension, hostility, competition, and controversy within and between social groups over values and purposes.

FUNCTIONALISM

Inspired by the writings of Emile Durkheim and Herbert Spencer, functionalism (or structural functionalism) originally took as its logical starting point a society conceived as a social system of interrelated parts, and therefore analogous to a living organism where each part contributes to the overall stability of the whole. Society, then, is seen as a complex system whose components work with one another.

The components of a society are interdependent, with each one serving a function necessary for the survival of the system as a whole. Sociologists viewing the social world from a structural-functional perspective may identify components of society and explore the functions these structures may perform for the larger system.

THE METHODS OF RESEARCH

DEFINING RESEARCH METHODS

The term **research methods** refers both to a strategy or plan for carrying out research and the means of carrying out the strategy. Some sociologists favor **quantitative methods**. Following the example of the natural sciences, they make use of statistical and other mathematical techniques of quantification or measurement in their efforts to describe and interpret their observations. Others favor **qualitative methods**, relying on personal observation and description of social life in order to explain behavior. Conceding that their methods entail the loss of precision, they argue that their method achieves a deeper grasp of the texture of social life. Thus, Max Weber developed the method of *verstehen*.

Verstehen is understanding as a means of characterizing and interpreting or explaining. This is done through applying reason to the external and inner context of specific social situations, such as the origins of Western capitalism.

SURVEY RESEARCH

Sociologists most often use the **survey method** of observation in their research. Subjects are asked about their opinions, beliefs, or behavior, such as how they have behaved in the past or how they intend to behave in the future, in a series of questions. The information is collected from the respondents of the survey directly by means of an interview, or indirectly by means of a self-administered written form of a questionnaire that the respondents fill out themselves. Interviews may be conducted in person, by phone, or even by electronic means of communication.

The interview may be structured where respondents are asked a series of questions in which they are given a limited choice between several possible responses on each question, unstructured where respondents are asked questions to which they can respond freely in their own words, or may involve the use of a combination of both open-ended and close-ended questions. The researcher may be interested in determining or gauging the general characteristics of a population or in collecting information about some event from the persons involved.

A survey can be mainly **descriptive** or **explanatory**. In the latter case, researchers may be interested in understanding either causal or correlational relationships between variables. Variables can either be **independent** or **dependent**. An independent variable is one that influences another variable, while the dependent variable is the one being influenced by another variable (the cause and effect, respectively). In order to assess the relationship between two variables, controls may need to be applied. A control is a technique of differentiating between factors that may or may not influence the relationship between variables. Relationships between two variables can either be **correlational** or **causal**. A correlational relationship exists when a change in one variable coincides with, but doesn't cause a change in another. A causal relationship exists when a change in one variable causes or forces a change in the other.

How, then, is survey research carried out? First a population is selected. All members can be approached in the case of a relatively small population or in the case of an event that requires collecting information from certain key persons that were involved. If the population is relatively large, a sample will be selected for study from the entire population. A **representative sample** is one that accurately reflects the population from which it is drawn. A **random sample** is one where every member of the population has the same chance of being chosen for study, as in throwing the names of everyone in a hat, mixing them up, and selecting as many as are thought necessary to achieve representatives. **Systematic sampling** is a type of sample in which the nth unit in a list is selected for inclusion in the sample. For example, every fiftieth resident listed in a phone book of a given area will be selected. In this way, every member of the population is guaranteed the same chance of being selected for study.

Stratified sampling uses the differences that already exist in a population, such as between males and females, as the basis for selecting a sample. Knowing the percentage of the population that falls into a particular category, the researcher then randomly selects a number of persons to be studied from each category in the same proportion as exists in the population.

EXPERIMENTATION

Sociologists can and sometimes do conduct experiments. In the broadest sense, experimentation involves the observation, measurement, or calculation of the consequences of an action. Typically, the social science researcher selects a group of subjects to be studied (the **experimental group**), exposes them to a particular condition, and then measures the results. The researcher usually measures the results against that of a **control group** (a similar population upon which the action has not been performed). Experiments are used to test theories and the hypotheses drawn from them. In one type of experiment, researchers create a situation in which they test the extent of the relationship that presumably exists between an independent and a dependent variable, by means of controlling a third.

Experiments may be carried out in a laboratory or in the field. Field experiments are carried out in natural settings. One of the most famous field experiments of social science was conducted in the 1930s at the Hawthorne Plant of the Western Electric Company in Chicago. This research led Elton May to identify what has come to be known as the Hawthorne effect, which showed that the mere presence of a researcher affects the subject's behavior.

OBSERVATION

Observation is a technique that provides firsthand experience of real situations. **Unobtrusive observation** is observation from a distance, without being involved in the group or activity being studied. Unobtrusive observation may be observing subjects from afar (e.g., watching children play in a schoolyard) or observing subjects more closely (e.g., watching children play in a classroom from behind a one-way mirror).

Often referred to as field research, **participant observation** is observation by a researcher who is (or appears to be) a member of the group or a participant in the activity he/she is studying. Participant observers may or may not conceal their identities as researchers. They may conceal their identities as researchers so as not to influence their subjects who, not knowing they are being observed, will act naturally. On the other hand, they may disclose their identities as researchers and seek to minimize their influence by not allowing themselves to get too involved with subjects while they are establishing a rapport.

SECONDARY ANALYSIS

Secondary analysis refers to the analysis of existing sources of information. In the hope of discovering something new, the researcher examines old records and documents, including archives and official statistics provided by the government. Thus, by using available data, the researcher avoids having to gather information from scratch, and by analyzing old records and documents, the researcher can acquire an understanding of relations between people in the past.

Content analysis refers to the techniques employed to describe the contents of the materials. They may be quantitative—using such techniques as percentages, rates, or averages to describe how the contents vary, e.g., arithmetic means, modes, or medians, or qualitative—using concepts and employing reason to capture the contents of the materials observed.

THE STAGES OF RESEARCH

Research is a process that includes:

1. Defining the problem – the questions, issues, or topic with which one is concerned.

2. Identifying and reviewing the literature or relevant literature bearing upon the problem.

3. Formulating a hypothesis – a tentative statement about what one expects to observe, e.g., the prediction of a relationship between variables or the prediction that a certain relation between people will be obtained.

4. Selecting and implementing a research design to test one's hypothesis – the plan for collecting and analyzing information.

5. Drawing a conclusion – determining whether or not one's hypothesis is confirmed and presenting one's findings in an organized way that both describes and, wherever possible, explains what one has observed.

ETHICAL PROBLEMS IN CONDUCTING RESEARCH

Sociologists can and often do encounter ethical problems or dilemmas in conducting research. Some of the following are concerns of sociologists who conduct research:

1. What harm, if any, is the research likely to bring to participants? Does the knowledge gained justify the risks involved?

2. Is the privacy of subjects being invaded, and should the privacy of subjects be maintained under all circumstances?

3. Do subjects have a right to be informed that they are being studied? Is their consent necessary?

4. Does it matter how the research results will or can be applied? Should this affect the research design or the way in which the research is reported?

5. When, if at all, is deception in conducting research or in reporting the research results justified?

SOCIALIZATION

THE PROCESS OF SOCIALIZATION AND SELF-FORMATION

Socialization is the process through which we learn or are trained to be members of society, to take part in new social situations, or to participate in social groupings. In other words, it is the prescriptive term in sociology for the process of being "social."

Generally, sociologists consider the process of socialization to be based on social interaction, the ways in which we behave toward and respond to one another. Not all sociologists agree on what is formed by such reciprocal or mutual action. Does interaction imply society, social groups, social structure, or that human beings make the perpetuation and transformation of a particular culture possible? Sociologists tend to differ in their opinion of what is learned, produced, reproduced, or altered in the process of socialization: 1) in their orientation toward society, social groups, social structure, or man-made culture; and 2) in their conception of the part, if any, human biology and individual psychology play in socialization.

Primary and Secondary Forms of Socialization

Sociologists hold the view that the individual cannot develop in the absence of the social environment—the groups within which interaction takes place and socialization occurs. Within this context, **primary socialization** refers to the initial socialization that a child receives through which he or she becomes a member of society (i.e., learns and comes to share the social heritage or culture of a society through the groups into which he or she is born). **Secondary socialization** refers to the subsequent experience of socialization into new sectors of society by an already socialized person.

Personality

Focused on society, socialization is the process through which personality is acquired, marked by the fairly consistent patterns shown in the thoughts, feelings, and activities representative of the individual. Socialization is the essential link between the individual and the social realms, without which neither is thought to be capable of surviving.

Socialization not only makes it possible for society to reproduce itself, but for society's continuity to be assured across generations as well as within generations in the personalities that are its product. This is the biological and "historical" continuity of individual and social circumstances of the life course of birth, childhood, maturity, old age, and death, and in the cultural continuity in society up to the present.

Assuming that the content of socialization varies from one person to the next as a consequence of being subject to the influence of various cultures and subcultures including race, class, region, religion, and groups in society, then every person would be different. Most of the differences would be a product of socialization, with the remainder the result of the random impact of relatively different social and cultural environments.

The socialization process is thought to explain both the similarities in personality and social behavior of the members of society and the differences that exist in society between one person and the next. It does not matter then that the two factors of nature and nurture are intimately related and cannot be separated, which is the view of most social scientists. Hence, the part that human biology plays in socialization (i.e., of nature in nurture) cannot be accurately measured. Heredity represents a basic potential, the outlines and limits of which are biologically fixed, because the socialization process is thought to be all important to the development of personality, the uniqueness, the similarities, and the differences of which are relative to society and, thereby, to the groups to which people belong.

Consistent with a view held by modern psychologists, it is argued that any instincts (unlearned, inherited behavior patterns that human beings once had) have been lost in the course of human evolution. There is no human nature outside of what culture makes of us. Hence, the concern that children raised in isolation or in institutions, who have little or no opportunity to develop the sorts of emotional ties with adults that make socialization possible, will be devoid of personality and will lack the social skills necessary to face even the simplest of life's challenges.

The process of becoming human in the sense of being able to participate in society is understood to be the process of socialization. The self at the core of personality, the individual's conscious experience of having a separate unique identity, is thought to be a social product objectively created and transformed throughout a person's life by interaction with others.

AGENTS OF SOCIALIZATION

The various agents of socialization are the individuals, groups, and institutions that supply the structure through which socialization takes place in modern societies.

Family

Generally considered the most basic social institution, the **family** is a union that is sanctioned by the state and often by a religious institution such as a church. As such, the family provides continuity in such areas as language, personality traits, religion, and class. The family is generally believed to be the most important agent of socialization in a child's social world, until schooling begins. Although the school and peer group become central to social experience as the child grows older, the family remains central throughout the entire life course.

School

As the social unit devoted to providing an education, the school provides continuity both in cognitive skills and in the indoctrination of values. Many subject areas of knowledge that may or may not be available at home, or that the modern home is ill-equipped to provide, are also provided by the school. Unlike the family, which is based on personal relationships, in school the child's social experiences broaden to include people of a variety of different social backgrounds. It is here where children learn the importance society gives to race and gender.

Peer Groups

As a primary group whose members are roughly equal in status, **peer groups** (such as play groups) provide continuity in lifestyles. Although first peer groups generally consist of a young child's neighborhood playmates, as the child meets new people at school and becomes involved in other activities, his peer group expands. It is in the peer group where the child, free of direct supervision from adults, comes to define him or herself as independent from his family. During adolescence the peer group becomes particularly important to the child and sometimes proves to be a more influential agent of socialization than the family.

Mass Media

Instrumental in making communication with large numbers of people possible, mass media provides continuity as far as knowledge or public information about the people, the events, and changes occurring in society and the threat they sometimes pose to the existing social order. Among the various kinds of mass media are books, radio, television, and motion pictures.

RESOCIALIZATION AND THE ROLE OF TOTAL INSTITUTION

Resocialization refers to the process of discarding behavioral practices and adopting new ones as part of a transition in life. For example, when one becomes a parent for the first time, he or she may have to perform new duties. Resocialization such as this occurs throughout our lives. Resocialization, however, can be a much more dramatic process, especially when it takes place in a **total institution**, such as a place of residence to where persons are confined for a period of time and cut off from the rest of society. This type of resocialization involves a fundamental break with the past to allow for the rebuilding of personality and the learning of norms and values of a new, unfamiliar social environment. The environment of a total institution is deliberately controlled in order to achieve this end. Some examples of total institutions include mental hospitals, the military, and prisons.

MAJOR FIGURES IN SOCIOLOGY

SIGMUND FREUD

An Austrian physician and the founder of psychoanalysis, Sigmund Freud considered biological drives to be the primary source of human activity. Activated by the pleasure principle to demand immediate and complete gratification of biological needs, the id represents these unconscious strivings without specific direction or purpose, which must be repressed and subsequently channeled in socially acceptable directions. Otherwise, without socialization the human being would be a violent, amoral, predatory animal, and organized social life would be impossible. According to Freud it is through the processes or mechanisms of identification and repression (the holding back and the hiding of one's own feelings that the human personality is formed—which is comprised of the id, the ego, and the superego. The ego represents the most conscious aspect of personality. Defining opportunities, the goals one strives toward, and what is "real," the ego controls and checks the id. Operating according to the pleasure principle, the ego deals with the world in terms of what is possible, providing limits and direction.

CHARLES HORTON COOLEY

An economist turned social psychologist, Charles Horton Cooley (1864–1924) theorized that the self-concept, which is formed in childhood, is re-evaluated every time the person enters a new social situation. There are three stages in the process of self-formation, which Cooley referred to as "the **looking-glass self**": 1) we imagine how we appear to others; 2) we wonder whether others see us in the same way as we see ourselves, and in order to find out, we observe how others react to us; and 3) we develop a conception of ourselves that is based on the judgments of others. Thus, we acquire a conception of ourselves from the "looking glass" or mirror of the reactions of others.

GEORGE HERBERT MEAD

An American philosopher and social psychologist, George Herbert Mead (1863–1931) is best known for his evolutionary social theory of the genesis of the mind and self. Mead's basic thesis—that a single act can best be understood as a segment of a larger social act or communicative transaction between two or more persons—made social psychology central to his philosophical approach. To describe the process whereby mind and self evolve through a continuous adjustment of the individual to himself and to others, Mead used several concepts: the "Me" is the image one forms of one's self from the standpoint of a "generalized others" and the "I" is the individual's reaction to a situation as he sees it from his unique standpoint.

Mead pointed out that one outcome of socialization is the ability to anticipate the reactions of others and to adjust our behavior accordingly. We do this, Mead argues, by role taking or learning to model the behavior of significant others, such as our parents. For example, playing "house" allows children to view the world from their parents' perspective.

ERVING GOFFMAN

Like other sociologists, Erving Goffman (1922–1983) considered the self to be a reflection of others—the cluster of roles or expectations of the people with whom one is involved at that point in the life course. It is the product of a series of encounters in which we manage the impression that others receive to convince others that we are who we claim to be. In every role we undertake, there is a virtual self waiting to be carried out. Goffman used the term **role-distance** to describe the gap that exists between who we are and who we portray ourselves to be.

JEAN PIAGET

Based on experiments with children playing and responding to questions, Swiss psychologist Jean Piaget (1896–1980) proposed a theory of **cognitive development** that describes the changes that occur over time in the ways children think, understand, and evaluate a situation. Piaget not only stressed the part that social life plays in becoming conscious of one's own mind, but more broadly speaking, he also observed that cognitive development does not occur automatically. A given stage of cognitive development cannot be reached unless the individual is confronted with real life experiences that foster such development. In the **sensorimotor stage**, infants are unable to differentiate themselves from their environment. They are unaware that their actions produce results, and they lack the understanding that objects exist separate from the direct and immediate experience of touching, looking, sucking, and listening.

Through sensory experience and physical contact with their environment, the infant begins to experience his surroundings differently. The world becomes a relatively stable place, no longer simply the sifting chaos it is first perceived to be. In the **preoperational stage** the child begins to use language and other symbols. Not only do they begin to attach meaning to the world, they also are able to differentiate fantasy from reality.

In the **concrete operational stage**, children make great strides in their use of logic to understand the world and how it operates. They begin to think in logical terms, to make the connection between cause and effect, and are capable of attaching meaning or significance to a particular event. Although they cannot conceive of an idea beyond the concrete situation or event, they have begun to imagine themselves in the position of another and thus to grasp a situation from the other's point of view. In effect it is during this stage of cognitive development that the foundation for engaging in more complex activities with others (such as role taking) is laid. Finally, in the **formal operational stage** the child develops the capacity for thinking in highly abstract terms of metaphors and hypotheses which may or may not be based in reality.

ERIK ERIKSON

Departing from Freud's emphasis on childhood and instinct, Erik Erikson delineated eight stages of psychosocial development in which ego identity, that sense of continuity and sameness in the conception one has of one's self that does not change over time or situation, ego development, the potential for change and growth that exists over the course of a person's life, and the social environment are involved. They are:

Stage 1—the nurturing stage, in which a child's sense of either basic trust or mistrust are established.

Stage 2—there emerges the feeling of autonomy or feelings of doubt and shame from not being able to handle the situations one encounters in life.

Stage 3—the child develops either a sense of initiative and self-confidence or feelings of guilt depending on how successful they are in exploring their environment and in dealing with their peers.

Stage 4—the focus shifts from family to school where the child develops a conception of being either industrious or inferior.

Stage 5—failure to establish a clear and firm sense of one's self results in the person's becoming confused about their identity.

Stage 6—one meets or fails to meet the challenge presented by young adulthood of forming stable relationships, the outcome being "intimacy or isolation and loneliness."

Stage 7—a person's contribution to the well-being of others through citizenship, work, and family becomes self-generative, and hence, their fulfilling of the primary tasks of mature adulthood is complete.

Stage 8—the developmental challenge posed by the knowledge that one is reaching the end is to find a sense of continuity and meaning and hence, to break the sense of isolation and self-absorption that the thought of one's impending death produces, thereby yielding to despair.

LAWRENCE KOHLBERG

Inspired by the work of Piaget to conduct a series of longitudinal and cross-cultural studies extending over several decades, Lawrence Kohlberg has concluded that given the proper experience and stimulation, children go through a sequence of six stages of moral reasoning. At the earliest stage (between ages four and ten), a child's sense of good and bad is connected with the fear of being punished for disobeying those in positions of power. During adolescence, a child's conformity to the rules is connected with the belief that the existing social order must ultimately be the right and true order and therefore ought to be followed.

Finally, there are several factors that serve as a guide to action and self-judgment among older children and young adults. These individuals have reached the highest of two stages of moral development, and are able to consider the welfare of the community, the rights of the individual, and such universal ethical principles as justice, equality, and individual dignity. Kohlberg has been criticized for basing his model of human development on the male experience, having assumed that women and girls are incapable of reaching the higher stages of moral reasoning.

CAROL GILLIGAN

Taking Kohlberg to task on this point, Carol Gilligan found that women bring a different set of values to their judgments of right and wrong. For instance, males approached the moral problem of whether or not it is wrong to steal to save a life in terms of the ethic of ultimate ends. However, females approached the same problem from the standpoint of an ethic of responsibility by wondering what the consequences of the moral decision to steal or not to steal would be for the entire family—the goal being to find the best solution for everyone involved.

In effect, these different approaches to resolving the problem can be explained by the different roles women have in our society as compared with men. Thus, Gilligan concludes there is no essential difference between the inner workings of the psyches of boys and girls.

SOCIAL INTERACTION

DEFINING SOCIAL INTERACTION

Consistent with Weber's view of society, every culture has a structure that can be described and analyzed. This structure represents the multitude of shared values, shared beliefs, and common expectations of a particular culture around which people have organized their lives, and leads to a certain degree of predictability in human affairs.

SOCIAL STRUCTURE, SOCIETY, AND SOCIAL SYSTEMS

Consistent with a view of society as a continuing number of people living in the same region in a relatively permanent unit, **social structure** is the way in which people's relations in society are arranged to form a network. These networks are relatively organized in the sense that there is thought to be some degree of structure and system to the patterns of social interaction of which any society is composed.

Contrary then to the latter definition, "society" here does not represent a whole. The structure is thought to be composed of similar elements of statuses (position in a society or in a group), roles (the behavior of a person occupying a particular position), groups (a number of people interacting with one another in ways that form a pattern and who are united by the feeling of being bound together and by "a consciousness of kind"), and institutions (organized systems of social relationships that emerge in response to the basic problems or needs of every society).

In terms of society constituting more than one system, social structure consists of the patterns of interaction formed by the enactment of culture (the map for living in a society). The social structure is thought to be composed of multiple systems or institutions—each considered a total system unto itself—in addition to several other types of components. It is argued that there are certain elements that are necessary to both individual and collective survival. When these elements become organized into institutional spheres, they form a society's economic system, political structure, family system, educational processes, and belief system.

Besides being determined by the social context of statuses and roles, behavior is also thought to be largely determined by the definition of the situation (the process whereby we define, explain, and evaluate the social context of the situation we find ourselves in before deciding the behavior and attitudes that are appropriate). Each system forms an arrangement or structure of statuses and roles existing apart from their occupants.

STATUS

Status may refer to a position in society and/or in a group.

Ascribed Status

An **ascribed status** is automatically and involuntarily conferred on individuals without any effort or choice made on their part. Being a Native American, a woman, a son, or a widower are examples of ascribed statuses.

Achieved Status

The opposite status, one that is assumed largely through one's own doings or efforts, is referred to as **achieved status**. Examples of achieved statuses include being a husband, a rock star, an "A" student, and an engineering major.

Master Status

Master status is the status with which a person is most identified. It is the most important status that a person holds, not only because it affects almost every aspect of the person's life, but also because of its general symbolic value. People take for granted that a person holding the position possesses other traits associated with it.

Status Set

Status set consists of all the statuses that a person occupies. All of us occupy a number of statuses simultaneously. A woman may be a mother to her children, a wife to her husband, a professor to her students, and a colleague to her co-workers. The statuses of mother, wife, professor, and colleague together form the status set of this woman.

ROLES

Role refers to what a person does (i.e., the part they play or how one is expected to behave) by virtue of occupying a particular status or position.

Every status and role is accompanied by a set of norms or role expectations describing behavioral expectations, or the limits of what people occupying the position are expected to do and of how they are expected to do it. There are thought to be marked differences and, thus, extensive variations in how a particular role is played out, depending on differences in how those holding a particular position define their role. In effect, group differences and the conflicts they generate are thought to continually transform the system and structure.

Role Strain

Role strain refers to the situation where different and conflicting expectations exist with regard to a particular status. For example, a professor may enjoy his students and may socialize outside of class with them. At the same time, though, he is responsible for ascertaining that their performance is up to par and that they attend class regularly. To achieve this end, he may have to distance himself from his students.

Role Conflict

Role conflict occurs when a person occupies multiple statuses that contradict one another. For example, a single mother, who is the primary breadwinner, who plays on her church's softball team, and who is the den mother to her son's boy scout troop, may have conflicting roles corresponding to many of these statuses. This single mother may find that her volunteering duties conflict with her parenting and breadwinning duties.

GROUPS AND ORGANIZATIONS

SOCIAL GROUPS AND RELATIONSHIPS

Strictly speaking, a **group** is an assembly of people or things. However, not all people who are assembled together are thought to constitute human or social groupings. The members of a group are considered united generally through interaction, more specifically by the relationships they share, or in particular by the quality or specific character of the relationship between the individuals of which it is composed. In theory, any specific group represents no more than a relationship of "individual" persons.

ASSOCIATIONS AND COMMUNAL RELATIONSHIPS

An **association** is a type of relationship formed on the basis of an accommodation of interests or on the basis of an agreement. In either case, the basis of the rational judgment of common interest or of agreement is ultimate value or practical wisdom. A **communal relationship** is one formed on the basis of a subjective feeling of the parties "that they belong together" whether the feeling is personal or is linked with tradition. In practice, however, most actual associations and communities incorporate aspects of both types of relationships.

SOCIAL GROUPS

There are various types of social groups, from formally structured organizations to those that happen by chance. Sociologists have always been interested in types of social groups and the overall and individual characteristics of their members.

Peer Group

A peer group may be defined "as an association of self-selected equals" formed around common interests, sensibilities, preferences, and beliefs. By offering members friendship, a sense of belonging, and acceptance, peer groups compete with the family for the loyalty of their members. Peer groups serve to segregate their members from others on the basis of their age, sex, or generation. A peer group, as a type of social group, therefore consists of those whose ages, interests, and social positions or statuses are relatively equivalent and who are closely associated with one another.

Family

By contrast, the family serves to emotionally bind members of all ages, sexes, and various generations. As such, the family is plagued by issues surrounding succession. Particularly in a vacillating period of social change, the conflict between the family and peer group becomes more pronounced, caused by the widening of the cultural gap that separates different generations who may even speak a different language. For example, urbanism (which allowed for sustained contact between age-mates), paved the way not only toward age-grading (the sensitivity toward chronological age gradations characteristic of modern culture), but also toward the age-graded sociability that is characteristic of our times.

Aggregates and Social Categories

Unlike an **aggregate**, which consists of a number of people who happen to be in the same place at the same time, or a **social category**, which consists of a number of people with certain characteristics in common, a **social group** consists of a collection of people interacting with one another in an orderly fashion.

In a social group, there is an interdependence among the various members which forges a feeling of belonging and a sense that the behavior of each person is relevant to each other. Thus, whether or not the membership of a social group is stable or changing, all such group relationships are thought to have two elements in common: 1) members are mutually aware of one another, and 2) members are mutually responsive to one another, with actions therefore determined by or shaped in the group context.

Social groups have been classified in many different ways—according to the group's size; nature of the interaction or the quality of the relationship that exists; whether or not membership is voluntary; whether or not a person belongs to and identifies with the group; or according to the group's purpose or composition.

Primary and Secondary Groups

Charles Horton Cooley (1864–1924) distinguished between primary groups and secondary groups. In a **primary group**, the interaction is direct, the common bonds are close and intimate, and the relationships among members are warm, intimate, and personal. In **secondary groups**, the interaction is anonymous, the bonds are impersonal, the duration of time of the group is short, and the relationships involve few emotional ties.

CHARACTERISTICS OF GROUPS

Through the years, sociologists have developed various theories about groups. The following sections offer a sampling of these theories.

Gemeinschaft and Gesellschaft

Ferdinand Tonnies (1853–1936) distinguished between *gemeinschaft* (community) and *gesellschaft* (society). By **gemeinschaft**, Tonnies was referring to those small communities characterized by tradition and united by the belief in common ancestry or by geographic proximity in relationships largely of the primary group sort. **Gesellschaft** refers to contractual relationships of a voluntary nature of limited duration and quality, based on rational self-interest, and formed for the explicit purpose of achieving a particular goal.

Dyad and Triad

Focused on discovering the various and relatively stable forms of social relationship within which interaction takes place, George Simmel (1858–1918) made the distinction between the **dyad** of two people in which either member's departure destroys the group, and the **triad** of three, the addition of a third person sometimes serving as a mediator or nonpartisan party. An example of a triad with a mediator to close the circle is parents who strengthen their mutual love and union by conceiving a child. A nonpartisan-based triad is typified by a mediator who seeks harmony among colliding parties or who, as an arbitrator, seeks to balance competing claims.

Group Size and Other General Structural Properties

Small groups, as the name suggests, have so few members as to allow them to relate as whole persons. The smallest group consists only of two persons. Robert Bales developed the technique of **interaction process analysis**, that is, a technique of observing and immediately classifying in predetermined ways the ongoing activity in small groups.

Also, J. L. Moreno developed the technique of **sociometry**, a technique focused on establishing the direction of the interaction in small groups. An example of this technique is assessing who is interacting with whom by asking such questions as "Who is your best friend in the group?" or "Who would you most like to work with on an important project?"

In addition to size, some of the other general structural properties and related social processes affecting the functioning of social groups are 1) the extent of association (for instance, it has been suggested that the more people associate, the more common values and norms they share and the greater the tendency to get along) and 2) the social network of persons that together comprises all the relationships in which they are involved and groups to which they belong.

Interaction Processes

Also involved in the interaction processes (the ways role partners agree on goals, negotiate reaching them, and distribute resources) are such factors as:

1) the differentiation between the characteristics of the role structure with task or instrumental roles. Instrumental roles are "oriented toward specific goals and expressive roles, which are instrumental in expressing and releasing group tension.

2) front stage (public) and backstage (free of public scrutiny) behavior.

3) principles of exchange (characteristic of market relationships in which people bargain for the goods and services they desire).

4) competition between individuals and groups over scarce resources in which the parties not only agree to adhere to certain rules of the game but also believe they are necessary or fair.

5) cooperation (an agreement to share resources for the purpose of achieving a common goal).

6) compromise (an agreement to relinquish certain claims in the interest of achieving more modest goals).

7) conflict (the attempt by one party to destroy, undermine, or harm another) and such related methods of reducing or temporarily eliminating conflict as coaptation (the case of dissenters being absorbed into the dominant group), mediation (the effort to resolve a conflict through the use of a third party), and the ritualized release of hostility under carefully controlled circumstances such as the Olympics games.

In-Group and Out-Group

Other types of social groups include **in-groups** which, unlike **out-groups** (those groups toward which a person feels a sense of competition or opposition), are those to which "we" belong.

Reference Group

Reference groups are social groups that provide the standards in terms of which we evaluate ourselves. For example, if a college student is worried about how her family will react to her grades, she is using her family as a reference group. Similarly, if a lawyer is worried about how the other partners of his firm will react to a recent case he lost, the lawyer is using his colleagues as a reference group.

Group Conformity and Groupthink

Research on groups has illustrated the power of group pressure to shape human behavior. **Group conformity** refers to individuals' compliance with group goals, in spite of the fact that group goals may be in conflict with individual goals. In an attempt to be accepted or "fit in," individuals may engage in behaviors they normally would not.

Groupthink, a related phenomenon, occurs when group members begin to think similarly and conform to one another's views. The danger in this is that decisions may be made from a narrow view. Rather than exploring various sides of an issue, group members seeking conformity may adopt a limited view.

GROUP LEADERSHIP

Leadership is an element of all groups. A leader is a person who initiates the behavior of others by directing, organizing, influencing, or controlling what members do and how they think.

Instrumental and Expressive Leaders

Group research has found two different types of leaders: instrumental (task-oriented leaders who organize the group in the pursuit of its goals) and expressive (social-emotional leaders who achieve harmony and solidarity among group members by offering emotional support).

Authoritarian, Democratic, and Laissez-faire Styles of Leadership

Among the various styles of leadership are the authoritarian leader who gives orders, the democratic leader who seeks a consensus on the course of action to be taken, and the laissez-faire leader who mainly lets the group be—doing little if anything to provide direction or organization.

ORGANIZATIONS

In the sense in which sociologists use the term, an **organization** represents a specific type of social relationship or arrangement between persons that is either closed to outsiders or that limits their admission. Regulations are enforced by a person or by a number of persons in authority active in enforcing the order governing the organization.

Formal Organization

In the latter sense, a **formal organization**, which represents a type of group or structural pattern within which behavior is carried out in a society, is characterized by 1) formality, 2) a hierarchy of ranked positions, 3) large size, 4) a rather complex division of labor, and 5) continuity beyond its membership.

BUREAUCRACY

A **bureaucracy** is a rationally designed organizational model whose goal it is to perform complex tasks as efficiently as possible.

Weber's Ideal Type

The basic organization of society may be found in its **characteristic institution**. In prehistoric times, the characteristic institution of most societies was the kin, clan, or sib. In modern times, particularly in the West, as cities became urban centers for trade and commerce, the characteristic institution became, and remains today, a bureaucracy.

A bureaucracy is a rational system of organization, administration, discipline, and control. Ideally, a bureaucracy has the following characteristics:

1) Paid officials on a fixed salary which is their primary source of income.

2) Officials who are accorded certain rights and privileges as a result of making a career out of holding office.

3) Regular salary increases, seniority rights, and promotions upon passing exams.

4) Officials who qualify to enter the organization by having advanced education or vocational training.

5) The rights, responsibilities, obligations, privileges, and work procedures of these officials are rigidly and formally defined by the organization.

6) Officials are responsible for meeting the obligations of the office and for keeping the funds and files of that office separate from their personal ones.

Bureaucracy in Real Life

Weber never meant for his ideal type conception of bureaucracy to be confused with reality. Rather he intended that it be used as a measuring rod against which to measure empirical reality (as grounded in perceived experience). In so doing Joseph Bensman and Bernard Rosenberg (1976) learned, for instance, that most modern bureaucrats are "people pushing" rather than "pencil pushing" types of white-collar employees. The advancement opportunities for these employees hinge as much on how well they are liked, trusted, and how easy they are to get along with as on how well they objectively qualify for a position.

Once alert to the cash value in terms of income-producing opportunities of having "personality" in an employee society, the official begins to see him/herself as a salable item to be marketed and packaged like all other merchandise.

Such a self-rationalization as described by Karl Mannheim (1940) shows systematic control of impulses as a first step in planning one's course in life. In accordance with the official's goals, he compares his assets, liabilities, and background to what the market will bear as a first step in the research process of determining how his personality must be altered to meet the market's fluctuating demand.

Although the standards one must conform to will vary from one organization to the next, bureaucrats share the inclination to look for external standards upon which to base one's interests, activities, and thoughts. Thus, the appearance of a warm and friendly atmosphere belies the reality of the tensions that exist but that cannot be aired in public. As a compromise, occasions where spontaneity and controlled warmth are deemed acceptable are planned.

In these ways, officials never really internalize their roles or parts. They have no commitment to the organization or to one another beyond the formal requirements of their positions. The bureaucrat's all-too-human quest for personal identification (to personally identify with and relate to people in genuine terms) makes true bureaucratic impersonality impossible to achieve.

Parkinson's Law

In this context, we can begin to understand two well-known criticisms of bureaucracy expressed in "Parkinson's Law." Named after its author, C. Northcote Parkinson, **Parkinson's Law** states that in any bureaucratic organization "work expands to fill the time available for its completion."

The Peter Principle

Named after Lawrence Peter, the **Peter Principle** states that "in any hierarchy every employee tends to rise to his level of incompetence."

Michels' Iron Law of Oligarchy

We can now also begin to understand the context within which Robert Michels formulated his famous **Iron Law of Oligarchy**. As observed by Bensman and Rosenberg, the speedy proliferation of bureaucracy "is connected with everything else that gives our culture its uniqueness," i.e., a money economy, machine production, and the creation of nation-states with large-scale bureaucratized armies.

Bureaucracy also spreads throughout the various branches of civil government following the widening of the political boundaries of the territory under the control of a single person. When workers organized for the purpose of protecting and of advancing their claims to having certain inalienable rights (whether to form trade unions or political parties), their leadership was bureaucratized.

Thus, Robert Michels had in mind the working-class movements in America and in Europe when he drafted the Iron Law of Oligarchy, claiming that a small number of specialists generally hold sway over any organization.

DEVIANCE

DEFINING DEVIANCE

Strictly speaking, **deviance** represents a departure from a norm. Although deviance is usually associated with criminal activity or mental illness, it also includes behavior that stands out as being more ambitious, industrious, heroic, or righteous than the rest—behavior which is generally not expected nor very frequently found.

However, sociologists have primarily concerned themselves with deviant behavior that violates or is contrary to the rules of acceptable and appropriate behavior of a group or society. This becomes evident in the strong negative reaction, or ridicule, generated by the members of the group.

Sociologists have tended to differ in their understanding of deviance. The question is whether or not deviance represents more than a violation of a norm and, if so, what this contrary behavior is thought to ultimately represent.

DEVIANCE AND STIGMA

Consistent with an orientation toward society as a whole, the one characteristic shared by those with a deviant reputation is stigma. A **stigma** is the mark of social disgrace that sets the deviant apart from other members of society who regard themselves as "normal." In most instances, people escape having their deviant behavior discovered. Because they are not stigmatized or marked deviant, they think of themselves as being relatively normal.

Deviance is seen as relative to the time, place, and context of a group or society in which it is observed. In addition, it is also relative to the social status of the person doing the defining, and to whether or not that person is in a position to label the behavior as "deviant."

CONFORMITY, SOCIAL ORDER, AND SOCIAL CONTROL

Even if most people have violated significant social norms at some point in their lives, the majority of people at any given moment are thought to be conforming to those norms that are important to a society's continued existence. It is because of this that social order exists.

It is believed that a social order depends on its members generally knowing and doing what is expected of them. They have common values and guidelines to which they generally adhere. These norms prescribe the behavior that is appropriate to a situation as it is given or commonly construed at the time. In other words, a social order presumably cannot exist without an effective system of social control. Social control is best defined as a series of measures that serve as a general guarantee of people conforming to norms.

Through the process of socialization, social control is achieved. The success of this process is demonstrated by the fact that most people usually do what is expected out of sheer habit, and without question. When socialization cannot guarantee sufficient conformity through the informal, as well as the formal and organized ways of rewarding conformity and punishing nonconformity, there becomes a need for negative sanctions. Negative sanctions indicate that social control has failed and that deviance has occurred.

Deviance represents a residual category of behavior unlike that which is generally found. This behavior, unless adequately checked, may threaten the effectiveness of the system of social control and the social order. Ultimately some deviance is necessary so that the boundaries of permissible behavior may be defined. The major function of deviance is to reassure people that the system of social control is working effectively.

DEVIANCE AND SOCIAL GROUPS

Consistent with an orientation to social groups and the process through which conformity to norms is structured or organized in them, deviance represents an unusual departure from an established group rule of acceptable conduct. These norms denote a negotiated world of meanings; these are rules that shape what individuals perceive and how they behave, thereby eliminating the uncertainty that exists in the absence of such behavior guidelines. The acknowledgment of such a departure assures members that they are "normal." Members can feel that their own behavior falls within the usual parameters of what is and what is not acceptable in the group, while ridiculing those whose observed behavior departs from the expected.

In this way, the social order, which depends upon people doing what others expect of them, is more or less guaranteed. Those who usually behave in socially approved ways are provided with a reason for continuing to do what is expected and are momentarily relieved of their anxiety about the unusual occurring too soon again. Those who have departed from a norm have a reason to avoid behaving in ways that are unacceptable to group members.

Given the many different groups that make up a society, and the competing values and the diversity of interests they represent, social order is never guaranteed or certain without there being value systems. These value systems enjoy such wide acceptance in society that even those groups that represent opposing interests find them to be consistent with, or suited to, their own concerns.

In the competition or struggle between groups, those with the most to lose or gain in terms of immediate self-interest, or those who feel most strongly about their cause, may succeed in defining and shaping the standards of right and wrong that become the group's norms. But they may never succeed in altering the meaning that represents the core values or culture of a society.

As previously noted, the latter are acquired during primary socialization and are thought to be a product of unique circumstances. Thus, deviant behavior is not essentially different from that of conformity.

Both roles are socially constructed relative to the culture of the society in which they thrive. Therefore, the processes and actions that are defined as deviant in our society are merely those that fall outside the canon of processes and actions that are defined as conformist.

These "deviant" actions are those that powerful people, those in a position to both define and enforce social norms, find threatening. Because this sector of society agrees with, supports, and serves to define the status quo, anything that threatens this sector is then labeled deviant. In this way, deviance is defined by its opposite rather than any inherent threat it may pose.

Particularly in complex societies, some norms are thought to be more important than others in that they involve behavior necessary to a group's continuity, survival, or well-being. This is evidenced by the severity of the sanctions associated with them. Whether or not norms are proscriptive ("thou shalt not") or prescriptive ("thou shalt"), they all are thought to be relatively arbitrary in principle. Their definition changes over time and from one society to the next but never so much as to be inconsistent with a society's core values.

FUNCTIONS OF DEVIANCE

In terms of the group, deviance serves several functions. Consistent with Durkheim's viewpoint, deviance serves to unify the group by identifying the limits of acceptable behavior and thus identifying who are insiders and who are outsiders. Deviance also serves as a safety valve that allows people to express discontent with existing norms without threatening the social order. Principled challenges to norms are possible.

Social control refers to the ways of getting people to conform to norms. Such techniques, which include persuasion, teaching, and force, may be planned or unplanned, and may be informal (involving the approval or disapproval of significant others) or formal (involving those in positions responsible for enforcing norms). In this context, **primary deviance** is the term used to refer to behavior violating a norm, while **secondary deviance** refers to the behavior that results from the social response to such deviance.

It is in connection with secondary deviance that stigma symbolizes a moral blemish or undesirable label that tends to be extended to other undesirable traits. Deviant subcultures represent peer groups that support deviance by providing social networks to deviants.

BIOLOGICAL EXPLANATIONS OF DEVIANCE

In 1875 Cesare Lombroso published the results of his work comparing the body measurements of institutionalized criminals, non-criminals, and primitive human beings. He had concluded that deviant behavior is inherited and that the body measurements of criminals bore a greater resemblance to apes than to non-criminals.

William Sheldon (1941) based his work on the earlier work of Ernst Kretschmer (1925). He classified people according to their body types. He concluded that a relationship exists between body type, psychological state, and criminal behavior (with short and fat endomorphs being prone to manic depression and alcoholism; thin and small ectomorphs being prone to schizophrenia; and muscular and large boned mesomorphs being prone to criminal behavior, alcoholism, and manic depression).

Such studies attempting to link criminal behavior and body type have not always produced consistent results. More recently efforts have been made to link deviant behavior with an "abnormal" (XYY) chromosomal pattern found among inmates of prisons and mental hospitals. This pattern is unlike the usual male XY pattern or female XX pattern. Researchers also have been studying the relationship between the brain and body chemistry, diet, and behavior.

PSYCHOLOGICAL EXPLANATIONS OF DEVIANCE

Psychologists have attributed antisocial or deviant behavior to the unconscious making itself known to a superego that lacks the strength to overcome the id. This way of thinking was influenced by Freud and others who sought to trace personality and behavior to early childhood learning experiences and the manner in which the repression of the powerful biological drives of the id takes place. The unconscious is that part of the mind where unpleasant, or perhaps even antisocial, memories of experience are stored.

Such research has supported the use of personality tests to identify trouble-makers and delinquents, to assess the guilt or innocence of those suspected of committing a crime, and to ferret out problems before they occur.

SOCIOLOGICAL EXPLANATIONS OF DEVIANCE

Sociological explanations of deviance fall into two categories. The first category includes those sociologists who assume that most people conform most of the time as a consequence of adequate socialization. They treat deviance as a special category of behavior and the deviant as deserving of special consideration. They ask why every society has known deviance. They want to know why people become deviant. They wonder why social control mechanisms are applied as a means of limiting and punishing clear violations of significant social norms.

Sociologists also tend to locate the source of deviance outside the individual person. They look within the social structure or in a social process of labeling. Labeling focuses on the process through which persons come to be defined as deviant. It also focuses on the means through which deviant behavior is created through the interaction taking place between those committing acts in violation of group's norms and those responding to such violations.

Robert Merton (1957) expanded upon Durkheim's understanding of deviance as the product of a structural circumstance of disorganization in the individual and in society. Both Merton and Durkheim saw this as a result of weak, inconsistent, or even nonexistent social norms. Merton concluded that in American society, for example, there is a disjunction between means and ends, such as the emphasis on wealth and success without many legitimate means to achieve them. Those individuals without such opportunities attempt to bridge this gap in a number of ways:

- The "conformist" seeks to continue the acceptance of the goals and means offered for their attainment.

- The "innovator" may continue to accept the goals while seeking new, and in many cases, illegitimate revenues for the attainment of these goals.

- The "ritualist" may make the means into an end by rejecting the culturally prescribed goals as being out of his reach. This person is in favor of an overemphasis upon the means of achieving these goals. An example of this would be the bureaucrat who is more concerned with adhering to the rules and with keeping his job, than with his own personal achievement.

- The "retreater" rejects both the means and ends offered by society by dropping into drug use, mental illness, alcoholism, and homelessness.

- The "rebel" rejects both the means and ends while seeking to replace both with alternatives, thereby changing the way society as a whole is structured.

In his theory of differential association, Edwin Sutherland (1939) concluded that criminal behavior is learned through social interaction in primary groups. His theory states that it is in the primary group where a person acquires knowledge of the techniques used in committing crimes. This primary group also provides reasons for conforming to or violating rules of permissive or not permissive behavior in a given situation, as well as an understanding of what motivates criminal activity. It is claimed that becoming a criminal means that the definitions favorably outweigh those unfavorable to violating the law. Moreover, the kinds of differential associations favoring criminal activity occur frequently, are long lasting and intense, and take place earlier rather than later in life.

SOCIAL STRATIFICATION

DEFINING SOCIAL STRATIFICATION

All sociologists agree that societies are stratified, or arranged along many levels. Where they begin to differ is on the question of what, if anything, the layers represent beyond the distinctions made among differing degrees of power, wealth, and social prestige.

Stratification and inequality are consistent with an orientation toward society; it is claimed that all societies make distinctions between people. There are some distinctions that always receive differential treatment—as between old and young, or male and female. There are other distinctions that may or may not receive differential treatment depending upon a given society's values. The usual result of a society treating people differently on the basis of their age, sex, race, religion, sexual orientation, or education is social inequality. This inequality can take the form of an unfair distribution of wealth, prestige, or power.

Social stratification represents the structured inequality characterized by groups of people with differential access to the rewards of society because of their relative position in the social hierarchy. Thus, a fundamental task of sociology is the determination of why stratified societies are so prevalent. Because almost the entire human population lives in stratified societies, sociologists must try to decide whether stratification is inevitable, and if so, what the effects of social inequality might be.

LIFE CHANCES

Sociologists have found that those in the same social stratum generally share the same life chances or opportunities. They seem to benefit or suffer equally from whatever advantages or disadvantages society has to offer.

STRATIFICATION AND SOCIAL STRUCTURE

Consistent with an orientation toward social structure, stratification systems serve to rank some people (whether individuals or groups) as more deserving of power, wealth, and prestige than others.

Social Hierarchy

The inevitable result of this stratification is a **social hierarchy** of ranked statuses in which people function. These statuses may be either ascribed or achieved. An ascribed social position is either received at birth or involuntarily placed upon an individual later in life. An achieved social position is usually assumed voluntarily, and generally reflects personal ability or effort. Individuals in a society are treated differently depending on where their social position stands in the overall social hierarchy.

Social Mobility

Social mobility refers to the ability of a given individual or group to move through the social strata. Structural mobility refers to factors at the societal level that affect mobility rates. For example, the number and types of available jobs, dependent on changes in the economic system, have a profound effect on social mobility. In addition, the number of people available to fill those jobs will fluctuate depending on current birthrates and the changing birthrates of previous generations.

Social mobility may be either relative or absolute. An example of relative mobility would be an entire occupational structure being upgraded so that only the content of the work changes, not relative position in the social hierarchy from one generation to the next. An example of absolute mobility would be when a son's education, occupational prestige, and income exceeds that of his father.

SYSTEMS OF STRATIFICATION

A system of stratification refers to the institutions and ideas that permit or limit the distribution of prestige, status, and opportunities in life. Based on the degree of significance attached to certain values in a particular society at a particular time, and the extent to which a particular group monopolizes the areas in which the values are available as evidenced by the development or decline of institutions, stratification may have several sources. These sources include race, ethnicity, gender, age, and sexual orientation—which at times have served as the basis for assigning inferior or superior status to an entire population.

Race and Ethnicity

As sociologists use the term, **race** is more than a biologically complex phenomenon in that it involves the attribution of hereditary differences to human populations that are genetically distinct. The more than 5 billion people living in the world today display an array of physical characteristics—hair color, skin color, eye color and shape, height, weight, facial features, etc. That we categorize people into "races" is a social phenomenon rather than a biological one. In fact, the biological term for race is meaningless. Society, not biology, categorizes people into "races."

Ethnicity refers to a population known and identified on the basis of their common language, national heritage, and/or biological inheritance. Although race primarily refers to differences in physical characteristics, ethnic differences are culturally learned and not genetically inherited.

Gender

Gender stratification refers to those differences between men and women that have been acquired or learned and, hence, to the different roles and positions assigned to males and females in a society. Gender encompasses differences in hairstyle, in the types and styles of clothing worn, and in family and occupational roles. Across societies women have been systematically denied certain rights and opportunities based on assumptions regarding their abilities. This inferior status of women has often been legitimized through a sexist ideology (a belief system assuming that innate characteristics translate into one gender being superior to another) which is passed on across generations via culture.

Age

Age stratification refers to the ways in which people are differentially treated depending on their age. This form of stratification is concerned with the attitudes and behavior we associate with age, and to the different roles and statuses we assign to people depending upon their age.

Sexual Orientation

Stratification on the basis of sexual orientation or affection refers to the ways in which individuals are differentially treated on the basis of their sexual preferences. In some societies, the results of this stratification are relatively benign. However, results of this stratification have also taken the form of criminalization of same sex unions, as well as discrimination in housing, employment, and social status. Many societies forbid homosexual marriages, thereby systematically excluding homosexual couples from the social and economic benefits of marriage. In addition, this exclusion from major social institutions has often translated into a perceived social condonation of discrimination against homosexuals.

DAVIS AND MOORE—A FUNCTIONALIST VIEW OF SOCIAL STRATIFICATION

In their classic presentation of the functionalist view of stratification, Kingsley Davis and Wilbert Moore (1945) argue that some stratification is necessary. Not everyone has the same abilities. At any given time, some members of a society will have more of the qualities that are needed and desired than others. Also some roles will be more essential to the society's functioning effectively than others. Thus, in order to attract the appropriate people with the requisite talents and skills to the more demanding, often stressful, roles that are not only essential to a society's functioning effectively but that also involve prolonged training and sacrifice, a society must offer greater rewards and higher status. In this way inequality (the unequal distribution of social rewards) is considered functional for society in that it guarantees that those most able will be in the most demanding positions. Social stratification, in other words, is inevitable.

MARX, WEBER, AND MODERN CONFLICT THEORY

Marx attributed inequalities of wealth, power, and prestige to the economic situation that class structures present. Thus, the elimination of classes would serve to put an end to inequality, to the exploitation of man by man, and to the basic conflict of interest between the haves and the have nots. According to Marx, the elimination of class structure would also enable men and women to regain their humanity through the creation of a genuine or true community "where individuals gain their freedom in and through their association."

By contrast, Weber distinguished between class, status situation, and parties as a step toward explaining the origins of the different economic, social, political, and religious situations of society that he saw in India, China, ancient Greece, and Rome, and in the West extending from Great Britain to Russia. By class he meant economic situation as defined by wealth, property, and other opportunities for income. A status situation consisted of every aspect of a person's situation in life that is caused by a positive or negative social assessment of status. Parties were groups oriented toward acquiring social power, i.e., opportunities to realize their common goals despite resistance.

Focused on the origins of man-made culture, Weber often found such differences to be a source of conflict and change that he could not foresee ending. He discovered various systems of stratification. Some were modes of organization based on caste, where social mobility is not permitted by religious sanctions. Others were based on class, including the feudal system of medieval society that was based on vassalage, or reciprocal obligations of loyalty and service between lord and knight or lord and serfs.

Modern conflict theory continues to struggle with the question of the bases of conflict. Believing that Marx placed too much emphasis on class, Ralf Dahrendorf (1959) focused on the struggle among such groups as unions and employers. Randall Collins continues to focus on the way that different groups seek to maintain their social position by acquiring educational credentials that they then use to secure jobs and other advantages. And still others see the conflict over ideological hegemony, including beliefs, attitudes, and ideals, as being the decisive element distinguishing the higher from the lower strata.

☞ Drill: Sociology

1. Sociology is best defined as the scientific study of

    (A) social problems.　　　(C) social interaction.

    (B) human personality.　　(D) human development.

2. Sociology developed as a separate discipline in the nineteenth century in response to

    (A) the growth of socialism.

    (B) the spread of colonialism.

    (C) a desire to promote greater equality.

    (D) the growth of industrial society.

3. Demographers study all of the following aspects of human populations EXCEPT

    (A) growth.　　　　　　(C) composition.

    (B) distribution.　　　　(D) socialization.

4. Each of the following is an important agent of socialization EXCEPT

    (A) television.   (C) parents.

    (B) bankers.   (D) peers.

5. Deviant behavior is the term used by sociologists to describe behaviors which a group defines as

    (A) violating basic norms.

    (B) uncommonly brave or heroic.

    (C) the standard for others to follow.

    (D) very rare or unusual.

6. Which of the following behaviors would NOT be considered an example of deviance in contemporary American society?

    (A) Eating spaghetti with one's fingers

    (B) Running naked down a main street of a city

    (C) A man regularly dressing in women's clothing

    (D) College students drinking beer on Saturday night

7. Which of the following is an achieved status?

    (A) Television game show host

    (B) Senior citizen

    (C) Japanese-American teenager

    (D) Accident victim

8. Which of the following terms would be most clearly linked with the kind of social life and social interaction found in cities rather than rural communities?

    (A) *Gemeinschaft*   (C) Groupthink

    (B) In-group   (D) *Gesellschaft*

9. Which of the following people is considered the founder of the field of sociology and is credited with first using the word "sociology"?

    (A) Emile Durkheim   (C) Karl Marx

    (B) Talcott Parsons   (D) Auguste Comte

10. If a sociologist wished to collect data from a random sample of 1,500 people spread across the United States, it would be most feasible to use which type of research method?

    (A) A survey   (C) Face-to-face interviews

    (B) Participant observation   (D) Unobtrusive measures

11. Regarding theories of deviance, the idea that an individual commits deviant acts because he "hangs out with the wrong crowd" follows what line of thinking?

    (A) Cultural association   (C) Labeling theory

    (B) Strain theory   (D) Control theory

12. Jane wants to survey all Jewish men who are registered Republican in the state of New Jersey. Because she cannot interview all of them, the desirable alternative is to

    (A) survey a few that live in her neighborhood.

    (B) survey those who attend a local synagogue.

    (C) survey a random sample of the total population.

    (D) interview Jewish male Republicans who agree to be questioned.

SOCIOLOGY REVIEW

ANSWER KEY

Drill: Sociology

1. (C)	4. (B)	7. (A)	10. (A)
2. (D)	5. (A)	8. (D)	11. (A)
3. (D)	6. (D)	9. (D)	12. (C)

DETAILED EXPLANATIONS OF ANSWERS

Drill: Sociology

1.   **(C)**   Sociology studies human interaction, both in small groups and in larger settings, and the results of that interaction, such as groups, organizations, institutions, and nations. Social problems (A) are only a part of the subject matter of sociology. Human personality (B) and human development (D) are more often studied by psychologists.

2.   **(D)**   The Industrial Revolution in Europe brought about the decline of traditional agricultural societies and the rapid growth of cities. The social dislocations that resulted from this change stimulated thinkers to consider the nature of social order and social change, and the outcome was the emergence of sociology as a separate discipline. Socialism (A) was another result of this change, but socialism as a movement for political change was separate from the discipline of sociology. Choice (B) is incorrect because early sociologists were little concerned about the spread of colonialism during this period. While the founders of sociology were interested in the study of social inequality, they did little to promote greater equality; therefore, choice (C) is incorrect.

3.   **(D)**   Demography is the study of the growth (A), distribution (B), and composition (C) of human populations. Socialization is not usually studied by demographers.

4.   **(B)**   Agents of socialization teach social norms and values to children and adults. Parents (C) and peers (D) impart social norms directly to young people. Television (A) is also an important medium for teaching norms and values. Occupations such as banking do not involve the teaching of norms and values as part of their primary responsibilities.

5.   **(A)**   Deviance refers to those behaviors that a group stigmatizes because they are seen as violating basic norms. Rape, child abuse, and incest are examples of behaviors which are seen as deviant by many groups in the United States. Acts that are rare or unusual (D) are not considered deviant if they involve praiseworthy or inoffensive behaviors.

6.   **(D)**   In American society, social norms require that people eat spaghetti with a fork (A) and wear gender appropriate clothing in public. Beer

drinking (D), however, is a normal activity among many American college students.

7. **(A)** An achieved status is one which an individual receives through his or her own efforts. Categories based on age (B) or ethnic group (C) are ascribed, not achieved. Similarly, one has no control over being an accident victim (D).

8. **(D)** *Gesellschaft* is the German word used by Ferdinand Tonnies to refer to the highly impersonal and individualistic social relationships that predominate in urban life. Choice (A) is wrong because *gemeinschaft* is the word Tonnies used to describe the opposite: the personal, more collectively oriented relationships found in small towns and rural communities. Choices (B) and (C) are terms unrelated to distinguishing between social relations in urban and rural areas: in-groups are groups people belong to and identify with; groupthink refers to a form of decision making in groups.

9. **(D)** Comte is considered the first to formulate the idea of a separate field of study that tried to understand society from a scientific vantage point. Choice (A) is wrong because Durkheim is better known for his functionalist approach to topics such as religion and suicide. Choice (B) is wrong because Parsons is a much later figure best known for his development of the functionalist perspective. Choice (C) is wrong because Marx was a little later than Comte and focused more on promoting political and economic change than on developing a scientific discipline.

10. **(A)** A survey could be done quickly and inexpensively over the phone or through the mail. Choice (B) is normally used when a group is small and in a confined geographic location. Choice (C) is wrong because it would be very expensive and time-consuming. Choice (D) is wrong because it would also require going to many locations to collect the data.

11. **(A)** Cultural association theory of deviance contends that deviance is learned through social interactions. By saying that one becomes deviant by "hanging out with the wrong crowd" implies that the individual learned deviant behaviors via social interaction with this "wrong" crowd. (B) Strain theory focuses on goals and means for achieving those goals. Individuals who deviate do so because their legitimate opportunities for success have been blocked. The phrase "hanging out with the wrong crowd" does not address the dynamics of an individual trying to achieve particular goals, but who has limited means. (C) Labeling theory focuses more on how an individual becomes labeled as deviant, in spite of the fact that another person committing the same deviant act may not become labeled. This theory does

not address why some people come to commit acts, only why they become labeled as deviant. (D) Control theory focuses not on why some individuals deviate, but why they conform. The question specifically asks why an individual may deviate, not conform.

12. **(C)** In order for her survey to have any validity and generalizability, Jane needs to administer a survey to randomly sampled respondents. Only choice (C) takes into consideration random sampling. Choices (A), (B), and (D) are all examples of convenience samples. In this case, the researcher is finding the most convenient group to survey. The problem with this is that such samples lack generalizability.

IV. ECONOMICS REVIEW

INTRODUCTION TO ECONOMICS
WHAT IS ECONOMICS?

Economics—"Economics is what economists do." This statement, attributed to the famous economist Jacob Viner, may in fact be the best description of the discipline available. What it says is that economics cannot be defined by a series of topics that all economists study. For example, contrary to widespread belief, economics is **not** the study of business. Topics in business certainly occupy the time of many economists, but there is much more to it. It is more accurate to say that economics is a particular way of looking at topics. **It is a methodology for analyzing situations where human beings have to make choices from limited options.** Consequently, it can be used to study such business-related issues as capital investment, pricing policy, and interest rates, but it can also be used to look at the "bigger" issues of inflation, unemployment, economic growth, and the "non-economic" issues of love, marriage, childbearing, and discrimination, to name but a few.

Macroeconomics is the study of the economy as a whole. Some of the topics considered include inflation, unemployment, and economic growth.

Microeconomics is the study of the individual parts that make up the economy. The parts include households, business firms, and government agencies, and particular emphasis is placed on how these units make decisions and the consequences of these decisions.

ECONOMIC ANALYSIS

Economic Theory—An economic theory is an explanation of why certain economic phenomena occur. For example, there are theories explaining the rate of inflation, how many hours people choose to work, and the amount of goods and services the U.S. will import. Stripped down to essentials, a theory is a set of statements about cause-and-effect relationships in the economy.

Models—A model is an abstract replica of reality and is the formal statement of a theory. The best models retain the essence of the reality, but do away with extraneous details. Virtually all economic analysis is done by first constructing a model of the situation the economist wants to analyze. The reason for this is because human beings are incapable of fully understanding reality. It is too complex for the human mind. Models, because they avoid many of the messier details of reality, can be comprehended, but good models are always "unrealistic."

It would not be inaccurate to say that economists do not analyze the economy, they analyze models of the economy. Almost every prediction that an economist makes, e.g., the impact of changes in the money supply on interest rates, the effect of the unemployment rate on the rate of inflation, the effect of increased competition in an industry on profits, is based on a model.

Models come in verbal, graphical, or mathematical form.

Empirical Analysis—All models yield predictions about the economy. For example, a widely held model predicts that increases in the rate of growth of the money supply will lead to higher inflation. In empirical analysis, economists compare predictions with the actual performance of the economy as measured by economic data. Good empirical analysis often requires mastery of sophisticated statistical and mathematical tools.

Positive Economics—Positive economics is the analysis of "what is." For example, positive economics tries to answer such questions as these: What will the effect be on the rate of inflation if the rate of growth of the money supply is raised by one percentage point? What will happen to hours of work of welfare recipients if welfare benefits are raised $500? What will the effect be on our trade balance if the exchange rate is devalued five percent? Many economists view positive economics as "objective" or "scientific," and believe their special training gives them the expertise to draw conclusions about these types of issues.

Normative Economics—Normative economics is the analysis of "what should be." For example, normative economics tries to answer such questions as these: What inflation rate should our economy strive for? Should welfare recipients be expected to work? Is reducing our trade deficit a desirable thing? Normative economics is clearly a subjective area. There is nothing in an economist's training that gives his or her opinions on these issues any more validity than anyone else's.

THE ECONOMIC WAY OF THINKING

Economics analysis is characterized by an emphasis on certain fundamental concepts.

Scarcity—Human wants and needs (for goods, services, leisure, etc.) exceed the ability of the economy to satisfy those wants and needs. This is true for the economy as a whole as well as each individual in the economy. In other words, there is never enough to go around. Individuals never have enough money to buy all they want. Business firms cannot pay completely satisfactory wages without cutting into profits, and vice versa. Government never has enough money to fund all worthwhile projects.

Opportunity Cost—The reality of scarcity implies that individuals, businesses, and governments must make choices, selecting some opportunities while foregoing others. Buying a car may mean foregoing a vacation; acquiring a new copy machine may mean canceling the company picnic; paying higher welfare benefits may require terminating a weapons system. The opportunity cost of a choice is the value of the best alternative choice sacrificed.

Individualism—Economic analysis emphasizes individual action. Most economic theories attempt to model the behavior of "typical" individuals. All groups, such as "society," business firms, or unions, are analyzed as a collection of individuals each acting in a particular way. In a sense, the preceding sentence represents an ideal. Not all economic theory achieves this goal.

Rational Behavior—Individuals are assumed to act rationally. This is the most misunderstood term in economics. It does not necessarily mean people are cold, calculating, and greedy. Rather, it means that given a person's goals and knowledge, people take actions likely to achieve those goals and avoid actions likely to detract from those goals. A greedy person acts rationally if she spends on herself and does not give to charity. She is irrational if she does the opposite. An altruistic person acts rationally if she gives her money to the needy and does not spend on herself. Irrational behavior is the opposite.

Marginal Analysis—Economists assume that people make choices by weighing the costs and benefits of particular actions.

IMPORTANT ECONOMIC CONCEPTS AND TERMS

Specialization and Division of Labor—This is a strategy for producing goods and services. Division of labor means that different members of a team of producers are given responsibility for different aspects of a production plan. Specialization means that producers become quite apt at those aspects of production they concentrate on. Specialization and division of labor is alleged to lead to efficiency which facilitates economic growth and development.

THE ECONOMIC PROBLEM

UNIVERSALITY OF THE PROBLEM OF SCARCITY

Goods and Services—Goods and Services refers to anything that satisfies human needs, wants, or desires. Goods are tangible items, such as food, cars, and clothing. Services are intangible items, such as education, health care, and leisure. The consumption of goods and services is a source of happiness, well-being, satisfaction, or utility.

Resources (Factors of Production)—Resources refers to anything that can be used to produce goods and services. A commonly used classification scheme places all resources into one of five categories:

Land—All natural resources, whether on the land, under the land, in the water, or in the air; e.g., fertile agricultural land, iron ore deposits, tuna fish, corn seeds, and quail.

Labor—The work effort of human beings.

Capital—Productive implements made by human beings; e.g., factories, machinery, and tools.

Entrepreneurship—A specialized form of labor. Entrepreneurship is creative labor. It refers to the ability to detect new business opportunities and bring them to fruition. Entrepreneurs also manage the other factors of production.

Technology—The practical application of scientific knowledge. Technology is typically combined with the other factors to make them more productive.

Scarcity—Economists assume that human wants and needs are virtually limitless while acknowledging that the resources to satisfy those needs are limited. Consequently, society is never able to produce enough goods and services to satisfy everybody, or most anyone, completely. Alternatively, resources are scarce relative to human needs and desires.

Scarcity is a problem of all societies, whether rich or poor. As a mental experiment, write down the amount of income you think a typical family needs to be "comfortable" in the United States today: $44,456. Now compare your figure with the median family income in the United States. In most instances, what students think is necessary to be comfortable far exceeds median family income, which loosely implies that the typical family in the U.S. is not comfortable, even though we are the richest nation in the history of the world. If your figure is less than median income, think again. Do you think you would really be "comfortable" at that level of income?

UNIVERSAL PROBLEMS CAUSED BY SCARCITY

A society without scarcity is a society without problems, and, consequently, one where there is no need to make decisions. In the real world, all societies must make three crucial decisions:

1. **What goods and services to produce and in what quantities.**

2. **How to produce the goods and services selected**—what resource combinations and production techniques to use.

3. **How to distribute the goods and services produced among people**—who gets how much of each good and service produced.

UNIVERSAL ECONOMIC GOALS

Allocative (Economic) Efficiency—A society achieves allocative efficiency if it produces the types and quantities of goods and services that most satisfies its people. Failure to do so wastes resources.

Technical Efficiency—A society achieves technical efficiency when it is producing the greatest quantity of goods and services possible from its resources. Failure to do so is also a waste of resources.

Equity—A society wants the distribution of goods and services to conform with its notions of "fairness."

Standards of Equity—Equity is not necessarily synonymous with equality. There is no objective standard of equity, and all societies have different notions of what constitutes equity. Three widely held standards are:

1. **Contributory standard**—Under a contributory standard, people are entitled to a share of goods and services based on what they contribute to society. Those making larger contributions receive correspondingly larger shares. The measurement of contribution and what to do about those who contribute very little or are unable to contribute (i.e., the disabled) are continuing issues.

2. **Needs standard**—Under a needs standard, a person's contribution to society is irrelevant. Goods and services are distributed based on the needs of different households. Measuring need and inducing people to contribute to society when goods and services are guaranteed are continuing issues.

3. **Equality Standard**—Under an equality standard, every person is entitled to an equal share of goods and services, simply because they are a human being. Some of the ongoing issues with this theory are how to allow for needs and how to induce individuals to maximize their productivity when the reward is the same for everyone.

Economists remain divided over whether the goals of equity and efficiency (allocative and technical) are complementary or in conflict.

PRODUCTION POSSIBILITIES CURVE

The Production Possibilities Curve is a model of the economy used to illustrate the problems associated with scarcity. It shows the maximum feasible combinations of two goods or services that society can produce, assuming all resources are used in their most productive manner.

Assumptions of the Model

1. Society is only capable of producing two goods (guns and butter).

2. At a given point in time, society has a fixed quantity of resources.

3. All resources are used in their most productive manner.

Table 1 shows selected combinations of the two goods that can be produced given the assumptions.

Point	Guns	Butter
A	0	16
B	4	14
C	7	12
D	9	9
E	10	5
F	11	0

Table 1–Selected Combinations of Guns and Butter

Figure 1 is a graphical depiction of the Production Possibilities Curve (curve FA).

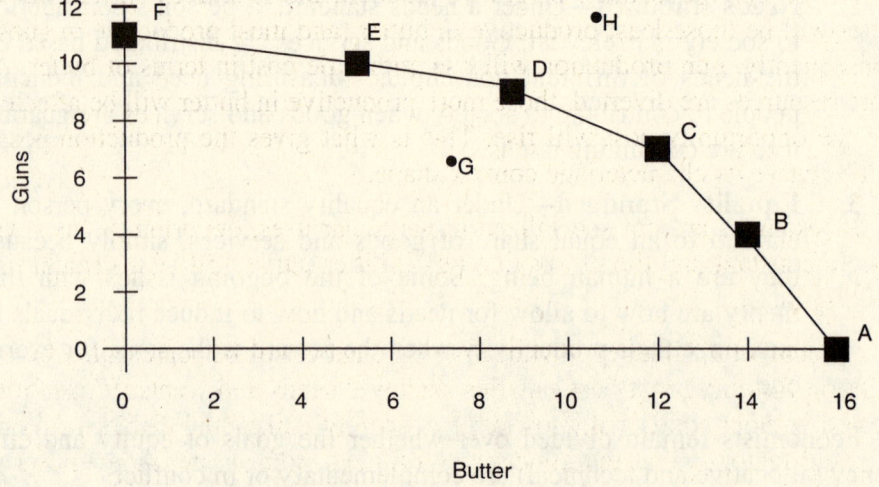

Figure 1–Production Possibilities Curve

Technical Efficiency—All points on the curve are points of technical efficiency. By definition, technical efficiency is achieved when more of one good cannot be produced without producing less of the other good. Find point D on the curve. Any move to a point with more guns (i.e., point E) will necessitate a reduction in butter production. Any move to a point with more butter (such as point C) will necessitate a reduction in guns production. Any point inside the curve (such as point G) represents technical inefficiency. Either inefficient production methods are being used or resources are not fully employed. A movement from G to the curve will allow more of one or both goods to be produced without any reduction in the quantity of the other good. Points outside the curve (such as H) are technically infeasible given society's current stock of resources and technological knowledge.

Opportunity Cost—Consider a move from D to E. Society gets one more unit of guns, but must sacrifice four units of butter. The four units of butter is the opportunity cost of the gun. One gun costs four butter.

Law of Increasing Costs—Starting from point A and moving up along the curve, note that the opportunity cost of guns increases. From point A to B, two butter are sacrificed to get four guns (one gun costs one half butter); from point B to C, two butter are sacrificed to get three guns (one gun costs two thirds butter); from C to D, three butter are sacrificed for two guns (one gun costs one and one half butter); from D to E, one gun costs four butter; and from E to F, one gun costs five butter.

The law of increasing costs says that as more of a good or service is produced, its opportunity cost will rise. It is a consequence of resources being specialized in particular uses. Some resources are particularly good in gun production and not so good for butter production, and vice versa.

At the commencement of gun production, the resources shifted out of butter will be those least productive in butter (and most productive in guns). Consequently, gun production will rise with little cost in terms of butter. As more resources are diverted, those more productive in butter will be affected, and the opportunity cost will rise. This is what gives the production possibilities curve its characteristic convex shape.

If resources are not specialized in particular uses, opportunity costs will remain constant and the production possibilities curve will be a straight line (see Figure 2).

Allocative Efficiency—Allocative efficiency will be represented by the point on the curve that best satisfies society's needs and wants. It cannot be located without additional knowledge of society's likes and dislikes. A complicating factor is that the allocatively efficient point is not independent of society's distribution of income and wealth.

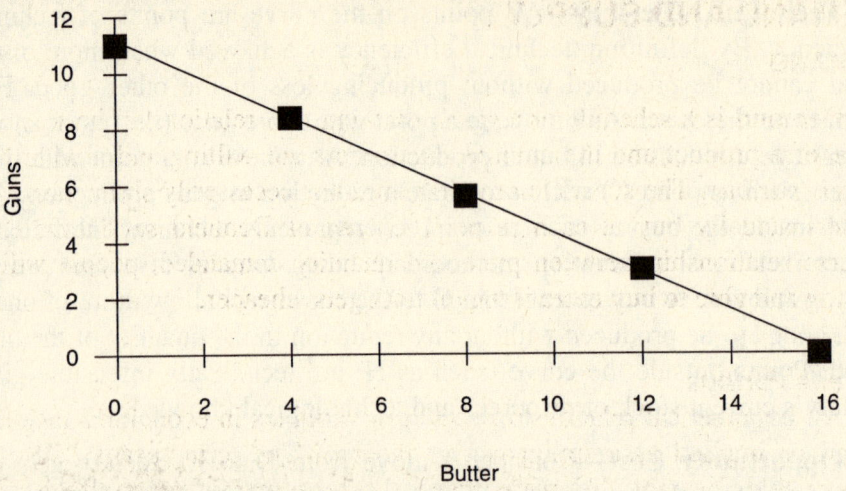

Figure 2–Production Possibilities Curve When Resources Not Specialized

Economic Growth—Society's production of goods and services is limited by its resources. Economic growth, then, requires that society increases the amount of resources it has or makes those resources more productive through the application of technology. Graphically, economic growth is represented by an outward shift of the curve to IJ (see Figure 3). Economic growth will make more combinations of goods and services feasible, but will not end the problem of scarcity.

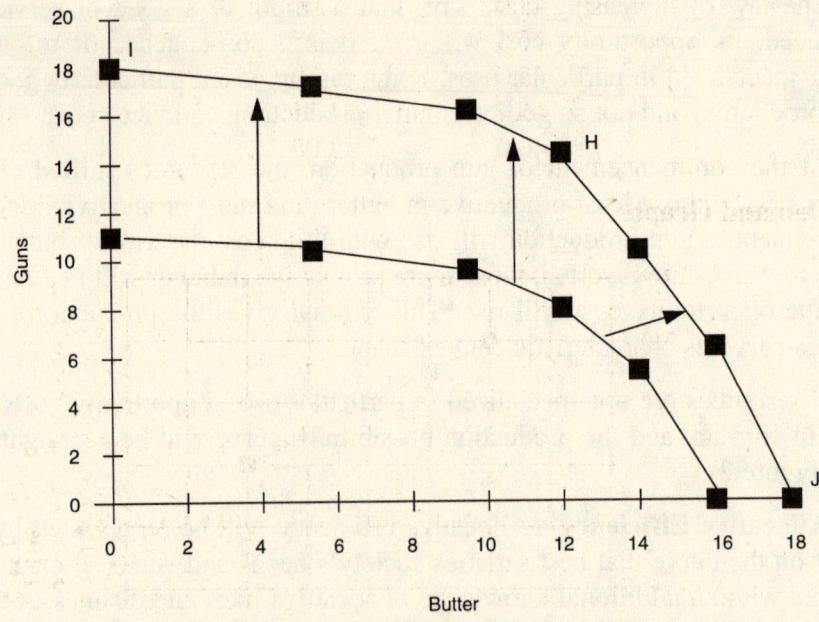

Figure 3–Production Possibilities Curve and Economic Growth

DEMAND AND SUPPLY

DEMAND

Demand is a schedule or a graph showing the relationship between the price of a product and the amount consumers are willing and able to buy, *ceteris paribus*. The schedule or graph does not necessarily show what consumers actually buy at each price. The Law of Demand says there is an inverse relationship between price and quantity demanded; people will be willing and able to buy more if the product gets cheaper.

Ceteris Paribus

All hypothetical relationships between variables in economics include a stated or implied assumption *ceteris paribus*. The term means "all other factors held constant." As we will see, there are many factors affecting the amount of a product people are willing and able to buy. The demand schedule shows the relationship between price and quantity demanded, holding all the other factors constant. This allows us to investigate the independent effect that price changes have on quantity demanded without worrying about the influence the other factors are having.

Demand Schedule—Assume the product is widgets. Let Qd be quantity demanded and P be price.

Qd	P
48.0	1.00
47.5	1.25
47.0	1.50
46.5	1.75
46.0	2.00

Demand Graph

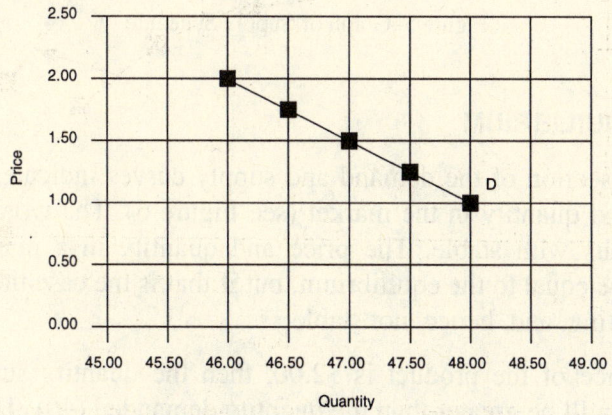

Figure 4–Graph of Demand Schedule

SUPPLY

Supply is a schedule or a graph showing the relationship between the price of a product and the amount producers are willing and able to supply, ceteris paribus. The schedule or graph does not necessarily show what producers actually sell at each price. There is generally a positive relationship between price and quantity supplied, reflecting higher costs associated with greater production.

Supply Schedule—Assume the product is widgets. Let Qs be quantity supplied.

Qs	P
46.0	1.00
46.5	1.25
47.0	1.50
47.5	1.75
48.0	2.00

Supply Graph—

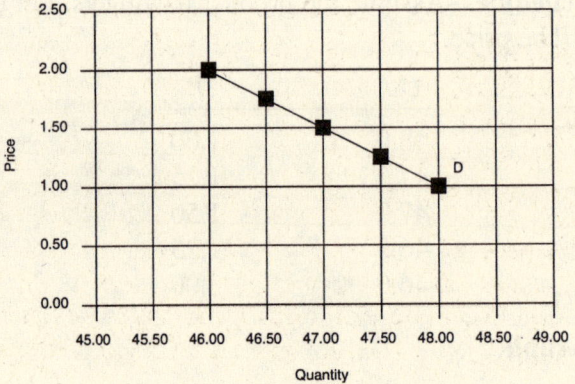

Figure 5–Graph of Supply Schedule

MARKET EQUILIBRIUM

The intersection of the demand and supply curves indicates the equilibrium price and quantity in the market (see Figure 6). The word equilibrium is synonymous with stable. The price and quantity in a market will frequently not be equal to the equilibrium, but if that is the case then the market will be adjusting, and, hence, not stable.

If the price of the product is $2.00, then the quantity supplied of the product (48) will be greater than the quantity demanded (46). There will be a surplus in the market of 48 – 46 = 2. The unsold product will force producers to lower their prices. A reduction in price will reduce the quantity supplied while increasing quantity demanded until the surplus disappears. Two dollars is not an equilibrium because the market is forced to adjust.

If the price of the product is $1.00, then the quantity supplied of the product (46) will be less than the quantity demanded (48). There will be a shortage in the market of 48 − 46 = 2. Unsatisfied customers will cause the price of the product to be bid up. The higher price will cause the quantity supplied to increase while decreasing the quantity demanded until the shortage disappears. One dollar is not an equilibrium because the market is forced to adjust.

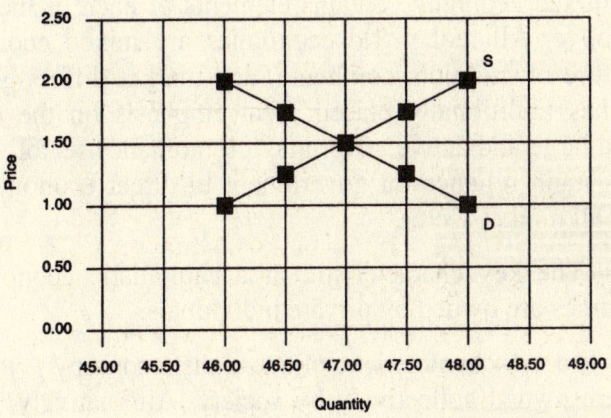

Figure 6–Market Equilibrium

If the price of the product is $1.50, then the quantity demanded (47) is just equal to the quantity supplied (47). Producers can sell all they want. Buyers can buy all they want. Since everyone is satisfied, there is no reason for the price to change. Hence, $1.50 is an equilibrium price and 47 is an equilibrium quantity.

ECONOMIC SYSTEMS

TYPES OF SYSTEMS

Every society must have some method for making the basic economic decisions.

Tradition—Traditional systems largely rely on custom to determine production and distribution questions. While not static, traditional systems are slow to change and are not well-equipped to propel a society into sustained growth. Traditional systems are found in many of the poorer Third World countries.

Command—Command economies rely on a central authority to make decisions. The central authority may be a dictator or a democratically constituted government.

Market—It is easier to describe what a market system is not than what it is. In a pure market system, there is no central authority and custom plays very little role. Every consumer makes buying decisions based on his or her own needs and desires and income. Individual self-interest rules. Every producer decides for him- or herself what goods or services to produce, what price to charge, what resources to employ, and what production methods to use. Producers are motivated solely by profit considerations. There is vigorous competition in every market.

Mixed—A mixed economy contains elements of each of the three systems defined above. All real world economies are mixed economies, although the mixture of tradition, command, and market differs greatly. The U.S. economy has traditionally placed great emphasis on the market, although there is a large and active government (command) sector. The Soviet economy places main reliance on government to direct economic activity, but there is a small market sector.

Capitalism—The key characteristic of a capitalistic economy is that productive resources are owned by private individuals.

Socialism—The key characteristic of a socialist economy is that productive resources are owned collectively by society. Alternatively, productive resources are under the control of government.

CIRCULAR FLOW

The Circular Flow is a model of economic relationships in a capitalistic market economy. Households, the owners of all productive resources, supply resources to firms through the resource markets, receiving monetary payments in return. Firms use the resources purchased (or rented, as the case may be) to produce goods and services, which are then sold to households and other businesses in the product markets. Household income not spent (consumed) may be saved in the Financial Markets. Firms may borrow from the financial markets to finance capital expansion (investment). Firm saving and household borrowing are not shown.

Circular Flow

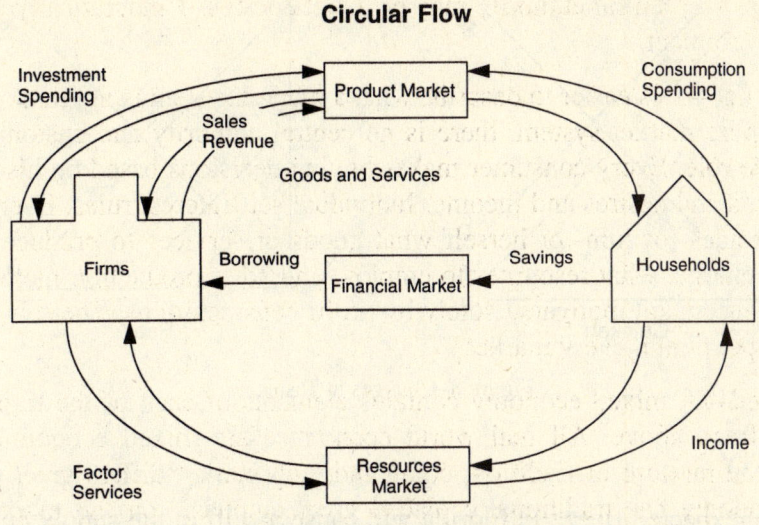

Figure 7–The Circular Flow

HOW A MARKET ECONOMY WORKS

Although the description of a market economy may suggest that chaos is the order of the day, economists believe that if certain conditions are met a market economy is easily capable of achieving the major economic goals.

How a Market Economy Achieves Allocation Efficiency—Market forces will lead firms to produce the mix of goods most desired. Unforeseen events can be responded to in a rational manner.

CHANGE IN TASTES

Assume a change in consumer tastes from beef to chicken (see Figure 8). An increase in demand in the chicken market will be accompanied by a decrease in demand in the beef market. The higher price of chicken will attract more resources into the market and lead to an increase in the quantity supplied. The lower price of beef will induce a reduction in the quantity supplied and exit of resources to other industries.

Note that the change in the level of output of both goods occurred because it was in the economic self-interest of firms to do so. Greater demand in the chicken market increased the profitability of chicken; lower demand in the beef market decreased the profitability of beef. Chicken and beef producers responded to society's desires not out of a sense of public spiritedness, but out of self-interest.

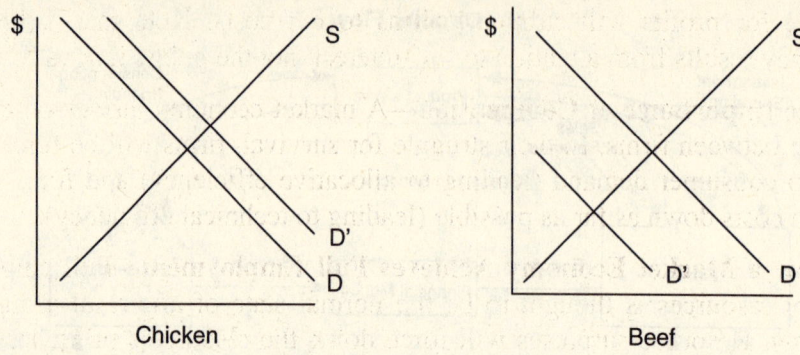

Figure 8–Changes in Tastes

SCARCITY

An unexpected freeze in Florida will cause a shift in the supply curve of orange juice, driving up its price, and causing consumers to cut back their purchases (see Figure 9). The higher price of orange juice will increase the demand for substitute products like apple juice, causing an increase in the quantity supplied of apple juice to take the place of orange juice.

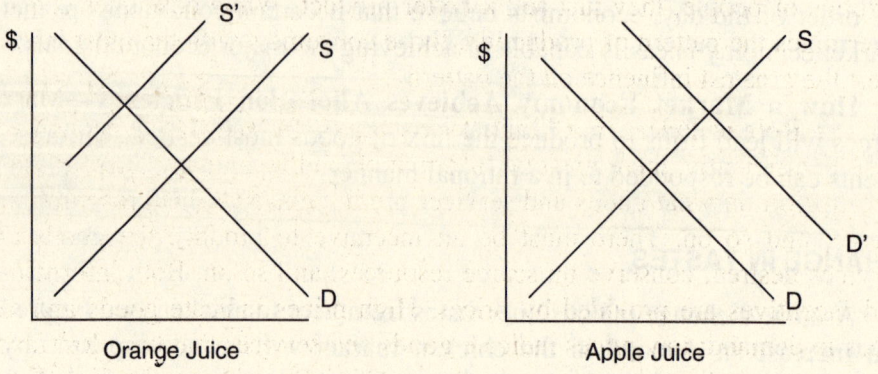

Figure 9–Freeze in Florida

As above, the reaction of market participants reflected their evaluation of their own self-interest. Consumers reduced their quantity demanded of orange juice because it was now more expensive. Apple juice producers expanded production because now it was more profitable.

Consumer Sovereignty—"The Consumer is King." Consumer sovereignty means that consumers determine what is produced in the economy. In a market economy, business must cater to the whims of consumer tastes or else go out of business.

How a Market Economy Achieves Technical Efficiency—Market forces will lead firms to produce output in the most efficient manner. The constant struggle for profits will stimulate firms to cut costs. Note that technical efficiency results from attention to self-interest, not the public interest.

The Importance of Competition—A market economy thrives on competition between firms. In their struggle for survival, firms will be forced to cater to consumer demand (leading to allocative efficiency) and force production costs down as far as possible (leading to technical efficiency).

How a Market Economy Achieves Full Employment—Full employment of resources is thought to be the normal state of affairs in a market economy. Resource surpluses will force down the resource's price, leading quickly to re-employment.

How a Market Economy Achieves Growth—Competition between firms for the consumer's dollar will force a constant search for better products and methods of production. The resulting technological change will lead to optimal growth.

The Market Economy and Equity—This is a problematic area for a market economy. Certainly there are financial rewards for those who produce the products that win consumer acceptance. There are losses for those who do not. Yet winners in a market economy are not necessarily the most virtuous of people, they just sell a better product. While consumer demand determines the pattern of production, those consumers with the most income exert the greatest influence on the pattern.

The Role of Prices in a Market Economy—In order for an economy to operate efficiently, there must be Information and Incentives. There must be information on what goods and services are in demand, which resources are scarce, and so on. There must be an incentive to produce the goods and services desired, conserve on scarce resources, and so on. Both information and incentives are provided by prices. High prices indicate goods and services in demand; low prices indicate goods and services that have lost favor. High prices indicate scarce resources; low prices indicate plentiful. Firms responding "properly" to high prices will earn profits; firms responding "properly" to low prices will avoid losses. Firms exploiting cheap resources will earn profits; firms conserving on expensive resources will avoid losses.

Prices always provide accurate information and appropriate incentives. Since traditional and command economies downplay the role of prices, they have a much more difficult time achieving allocational and technical efficiency.

ADAM SMITH AND *THE WEALTH OF NATIONS*

Adam Smith—Adam Smith (1723–1790) was a Scottish economist whose writing can be said to have inaugurated the modern era of economic analysis.

The Wealth of Nations—Published in 1776, *The Wealth of Nations* can be read as an analysis of a market economy. It was Smith's belief that a market economy was a superior form of organization from the standpoint of both economic progress and human liberty.

Invisible Hand—Smith acknowledged that self-interest was a dominant motivating force in a market economy, yet this self-interest was ultimately consistent with the public interest. Market participants were guided by an invisible hand to act in ways that promoted the public interest. Firms may only be concerned with profits, but profits are only earned by firms that satisfy consumer demand and keep costs down.

CONDITIONS THAT MUST BE MET FOR A MARKET ECONOMY TO ACHIEVE ALLOCATIVE AND TECHNICAL EFFICIENCY

A market economy will automatically produce the optimum quantity of every good or service at the lowest possible cost if four conditions are met:

Adequate Information—Consumers must be well-enough informed about prices, quality and availability of products, and other matters that they can make intelligent spending decisions. Workers must be well-enough informed about wages and working conditions that they can choose wisely among job opportunities. Other segments of the economy must be similarly well-informed.

Competition—There must be vigorous competition in every market. Monopolistic elements will reduce output, raise prices, and allow inefficiency in particular markets.

No Externalities—Externalities exist when a transaction between a buyer and seller affects an innocent third party. An example would be if *A* buys a product from *B* that *B* produced under conditions that polluted the air that others breathe. (Not all externalities result in damage to society. Some are beneficial.) Where externalities are present, there is the possibility of over- or under-production of particular goods and services.

No Public Goods—The market is unlikely to produce the appropriate quantity of public goods.

THE PUBLIC SECTOR IN THE AMERICAN ECONOMY

PUBLIC SECTOR

The Public Sector refers to the activities of government.

GOVERNMENT SPENDING

Government Expenditures on Goods and Services versus Transfer Payments—Government spending can be usefully broken down into two categories. One category is spending on goods and services. When government buys a battleship, typewriter, or the Space Shuttle, it is acquiring goods. When government pays the salary of a soldier, teacher or bureaucrat, it is getting a service in return. The second category is transfer payments. Transfers are money or in-kind items given to individuals or businesses for which the government receives no equivalent good or service in return. Examples would be social security payments, welfare, or unemployment compensation.

Functional Breakdown of Spending Side of Federal Budget—

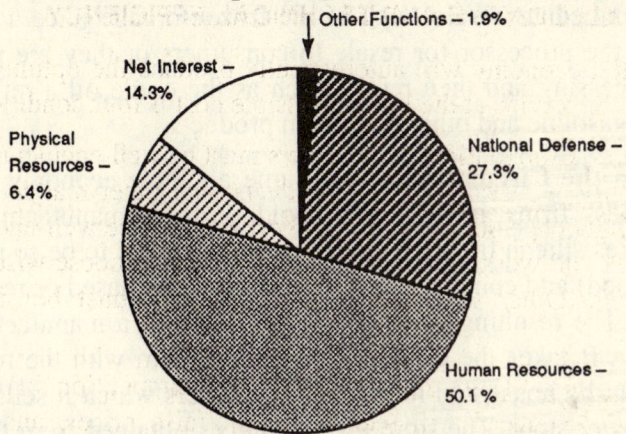

Figure 10–Federal Expenditures by Category, 1988

Functional Breakdown of Spending Side of State and Local Government Budgets—

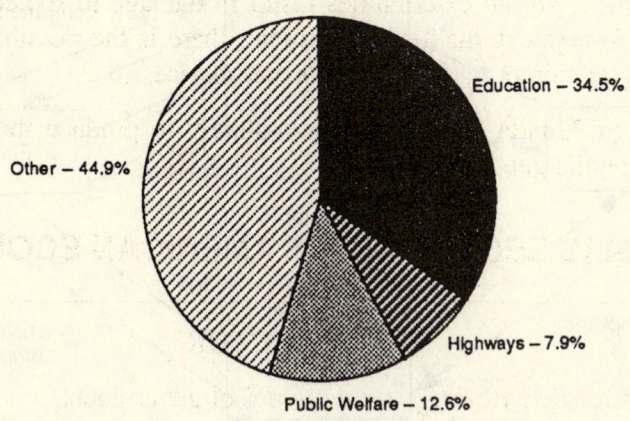

Figure 11–State and Local Government Spending by Category, 1988

GROSS NATIONAL PRODUCT
MEASURING GNP

Gross National Product—Gross National Product (or GNP) is a measure of the dollar value of final goods and services produced by the economy over a given period of time, usually one year. It is the most comprehensive indicator of the economy's health available, although it is not a measure of society's overall well-being.

Final Goods and Services—Final goods and services are those sold to their ultimate users.

Intermediate Goods and Services—Intermediate goods and services are those in an intermediate stage of processing. They are purchased by firms for immediate resale, such as the frozen orange juice a grocery store buys from the processor for resale to consumers or they are purchased for further processing and then resale, such as the crude oil a refinery buys to refine into gasoline and other petroleum products.

GNP in the Circular Flow—Assume a simple economy composed of three business firms and one household. Firm A manufactures computer chips. It takes silicon from the environment (assumed to be so plentiful as to be a free good) and combines it with resources purchased or rented from the household. The resulting chips are sold to Firm B, a manufacturer of computers. Firm B takes the chips and combines them with the resources purchased from the household to produce computers which it sells to firm C, a retail computer store. The store uses resources obtained from the household to resell the computers to the household, which is the ultimate user.

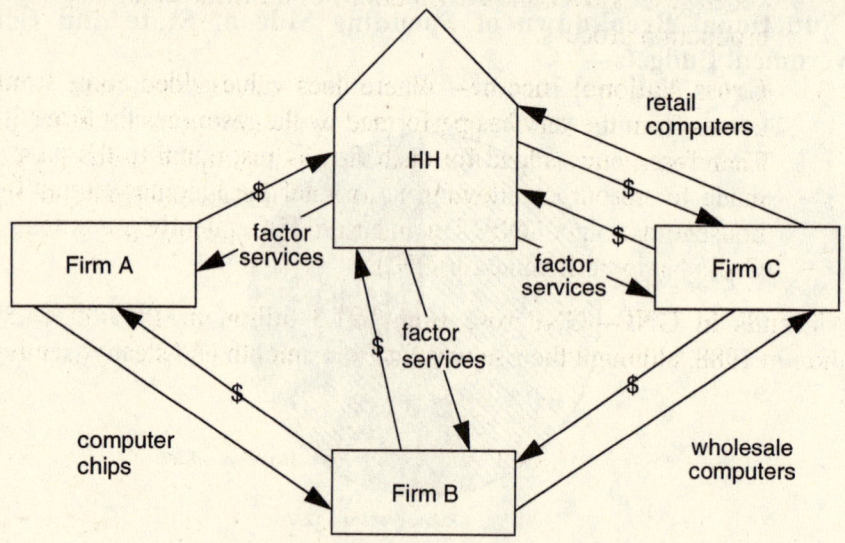

Figure 12–GNP in the Circular Flow

The table traces the transactions that take place in the economy during the course of a year.

Firm	Cost of Intermediate Goods Purchased	Resources Purchased	Cost of Goods Sold	Value-Added
A	0	50	50	50
B	50	75	125	75
C	125	40	165	40

There are three ways to measure GNP.

1. **Expenditures on Final Goods and Services**—In the example, computer chips and wholesale computers are intermediate goods while retail computers are a final good. Since the household spent $165 on retail computers, this is a direct measure of GNP.

2. **Sum of Value-Added for All Firms**—

> Value-Added (VA) = Cost of Goods Sold – Cost of
> Intermediate Goods Purchased

VA measures the value of the processing and resale activities that the firm performs on the intermediate goods and services it purchases. Adding value-added for all firms in the economy will give GNP. It follows because the value of final goods and services produced results from the contributions of all firms at all stages of the production process.

3. **Gross National Income**—Where does value-added come from? It comes from the services performed by the resources the firms hires. Therefore, value-added for each firm is just equal to the payments made for resources allowing us to total the incomes earned by all households to get GNP. This measure is frequently given the name Gross National Income (or GNI).

Trends in GNP—GNP rose from $91.3 billion in 1939 to $4,864.3 billion in 1988, although the rise was far from smooth and steady (see Figure 13).

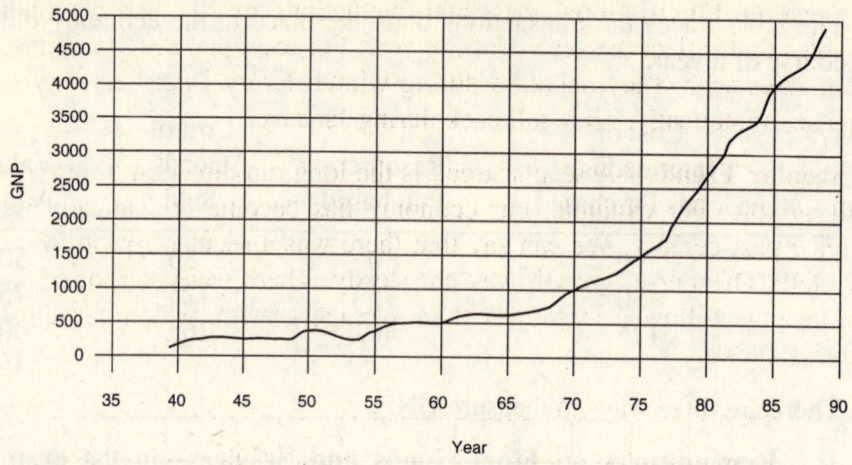

Figure 13–Trends in GNP

MACROECONOMIC PROBLEMS OF THE AMERICAN ECONOMY

THE BUSINESS CYCLE

Business Cycles—Business cycles are the alternating periods of prosperity and recession that seem to characterize all market-oriented economies.

Four Phases of the Cycle—Every business cycle consists of four phases. The peak is the high point of business activity. It occurs at a specific point of time. The contraction is a period of declining business activity. It occurs over a period of time. The trough is the low point in business activity. It, too, occurs at a specific point in time. The expansion is a period of growing business activity. It takes place over a period of time.

Although the word cycle implies a certain uniformity, that is misleading. Each business cycle differs from every other in terms of duration of contractions and expansions, and height of peak and depth of trough.

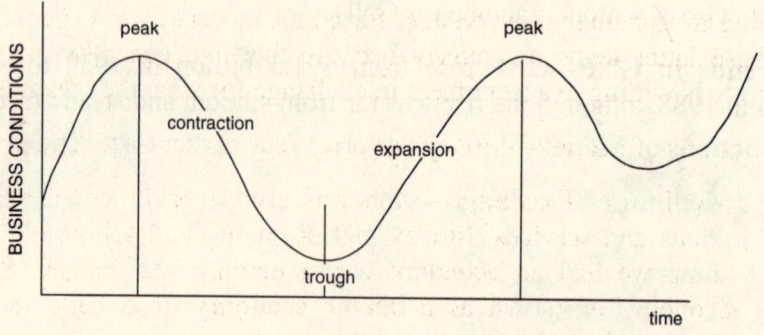

Figure 14–Phases of the Business Cycle

Seasonal Fluctuations—Seasonal fluctuations are changes in economic variables that reflect the season of the year. For example, every summer ice cream sales soar. They decrease during winter. Every December, toy sales increase dramatically. They fall back during January.

Secular Trends—A secular trend is the long run direction of movement of a variable. For example, our economy has become dramatically richer over the past century. We can say that there was a secular upward trend in real GNP. Of course, growth was not steady. There were periods of faster than average followed by slower than average growth, which accounts for business cycles.

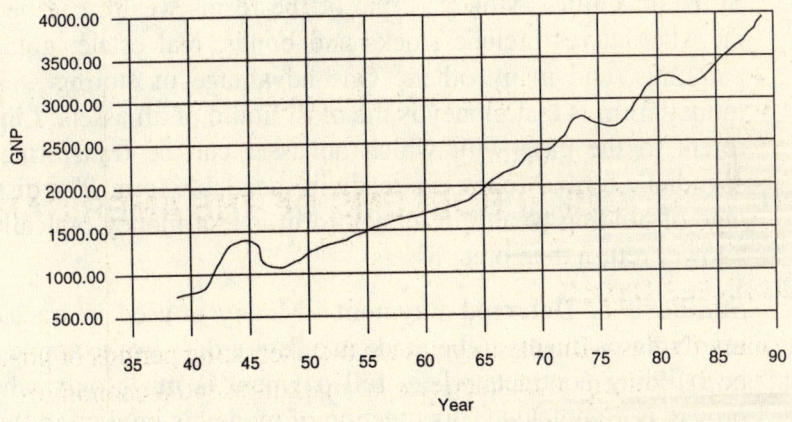

Figure 15–Secular Trend and Cycle in Real GNP, 1939–88

MONEY AND BANKING

WHAT MONEY IS AND DOES

Money is anything that is generally acceptable in exchange for goods and services and in payment of debts. Suppose you had something you wanted to sell. Few would be willing to part with their product for a commodity like a loaf of bread, a chicken, or an automobile hubcap. All would be willing to exchange their product for coins, currency, or a check. Therefore, these latter items are money because they are generally acceptable. Everybody is willing to accept them in exchange for what they want to sell.

Functions of Money—Money performs four particular functions:

1. **Medium of Exchange**—Money is used to facilitate exchanges of goods and services. Money makes buying and selling easier. Assume we had an economy where nothing was money. Such an economy is known as a **barter economy**. In a barter economy goods and services exchange directly for other goods and services.

If you want an axe that someone is selling, you must find an item that person wants to trade for it. Barter requires a **double coincidence of wants**, each party must want what the other party has. If that condition does not hold, then exchange cannot take place, and valuable resources can be wasted in putting together trades. With money this problem never arises because **everyone always wants money**. Consequently, the resources used to facilitate exchanges can be put to more productive use.

2. **Unit of Value**—We use our monetary unit as the standard measure of value. We say a shirt is worth $25.00, not 14 chickens.

3. **Store of Value**—Money is one of the forms wealth can be stored in. Alternatives include stocks and bonds, real estate, gold, great paintings, and many others. One advantage of storing wealth in money form is that money is the most liquid of all assets. **Liquidity** refers to the ease with which an asset can be transformed into spendable form. Money is already in spendable form. The disadvantage of holding wealth in money form is that money typically pays a lower return than other assets.

4. **Standard of Deferred Payment**—Money is used in transactions involving payments to be made at a future date. An example would be building contracts where full payment is made only when the project is completed. This function of money is implicit in the three already discussed.

What serves as money?—Virtually anything can and has served as money. Gold, silver, shells, boulders, cheap metal, paper, and electronic impulses stored in computers are examples of the varied forms money has taken. The only requirement is that the item be generally acceptable. Money does **not** have to have intrinsic value (see below). Typically the items that have served as money have had the following additional characteristics:

1. durability

2. divisibility

3. homogeneity (uniformity or standardization)

4. portability (high value-to-weight and value-to-volume)

5. relative stability of supply

6. optimal scarcity

What Makes Money Valuable?—Money is valuable if it can be used for or exchanged for something useful. Money's lack of intrinsic value means it cannot be used for anything useful. Why can it be exchanged for something useful? Sellers accept money because they know they can use it anywhere else in the country to buy goods and services and pay off debts. If they could not do that, they would not want it. What this means is that the substance that is used for money need not be valuable, and that money need not be backed by anything valuable. Such is the case. Our money is not backed by gold, silver, or anything else. It is just cheap metal, cheap paper, and electronic impulses stored in computers. Gold can be put to better use filling teeth!

THE UNITED STATES' MONEY SUPPLY

While there are many different definitions of the money supply available, the two most commonly used are M1 and M2.

M1—M1 consists of currency, demand deposits, other checkable deposits, and traveler's checks.

Currency—coins and paper money.

Demand deposits—These are checking accounts held in commercial banks. Funds can be transferred from person to person by means of a check. Demand deposits are considered money because checks are generally acceptable.

Other checkable deposits—This category, includes all other financial institution deposits upon which checks can be written. Among these are NOW accounts, ATS accounts, and credit union share drafts.

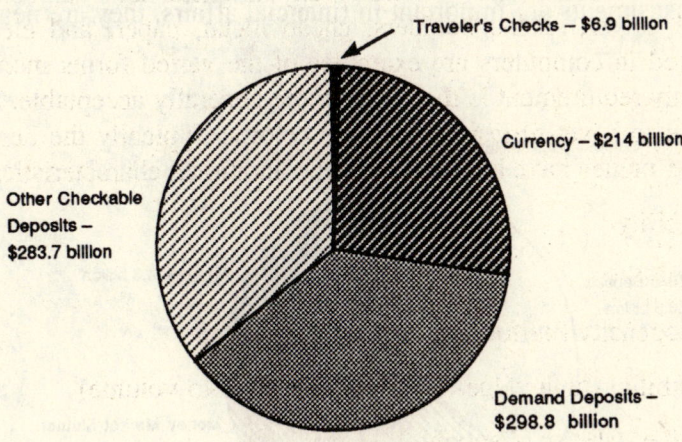

Figure 16–Composition of M1, December 1989

Traveler's checks—Most traveler's checks are generally acceptable throughout much of the world.

M2—M2 includes all of M1 plus savings deposits, small-denomination time deposits, money-market mutual funds and deposit accounts, overnight repurchase agreements (known as repos), and Eurodollars.

Savings Deposits—These are the common passbook savings accounts. They do not provide check-writing privileges.

Small Denomination time deposits—Better known as certificates of deposits, or CDs. They typically do not provide check-writing privileges.

Money market mutual funds and deposit accounts—Both mutual funds and deposit accounts are investment funds. Large numbers of people pool their money to allow for diversification and professional investment management. Mutual funds are managed by private financial companies. Deposit accounts are managed by commercial banks. Investors earn a return on their investment and have limited check-writing privileges. Mutual funds are not afforded protection by the government, as is the case with FDIC-insured bank accounts.

Overnight Repurchase Agreements and Eurodollars—Overnight repos essentially are short-term (literally, overnight) loans. A corporation with excess cash may arrange to purchase a security from a bank with the stipulation that the bank will buy the security back the next day at a slightly higher price. The corporation receives a return on its money, and the bank gets access to funds. Eurodollars are dollar-denominated demand deposits held in banks outside the United States (not just in Europe). From the standpoint of M2, deposits held in Caribbean branches of Federal Reserve member banks are relevant. These deposits are easily accessed by U.S. residents. While both instruments are important in financial affairs, they are negligible in the totality of M2.

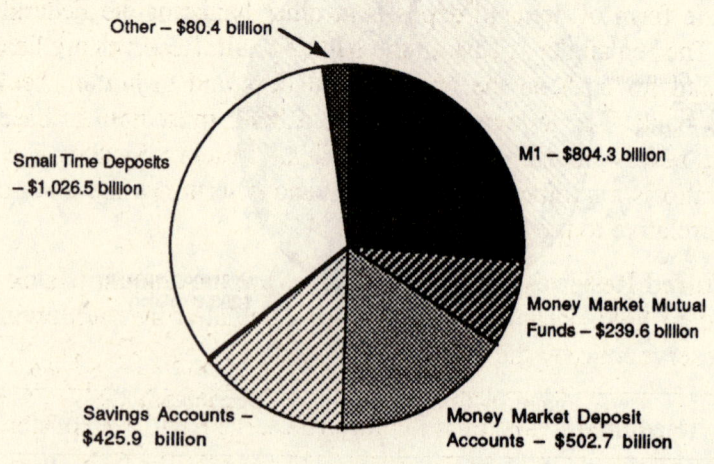

Figure 17–Composition of M2, December 1988

A significant proportion of M2 cannot be used as a medium of exchange. Why, then, are the items considered money? First, each of these items is highly liquid. Second, studies indicate that people's economic behavior is not very sensitive to their relative holdings of the various assets in question (see Figure 17).

THE FINANCIAL SYSTEM

Financial Intermediaries—Financial intermediaries are organizations such as commercial banks, savings and loan institutions, credit unions, and insurance companies. They play an important role in facilitating the saving and investment process which helps the economy grow. Savers typically look to place their money where the combination of return, liquidity, and safety is best. Through the various types of deposits they offer, financial intermediaries compete for the saved funds. The money so obtained is used to finance borrowing. Through their ability to obtain large pools of money from many depositors, intermediaries are able to service the needs of large borrowers.

Balance Sheet of Typical Bank

Assets	Liabilities
Reserves	Demand Deposits
Loans	Savings Deposits
Securities	Time Deposits
Property	Other Deposits
Other Assets	Net Worth

Reserves—Reserves are a bank's money holdings. Most reserves are held in the form of demand deposits at other banks or the Federal Reserve System. The remainder is cash in the bank's vault. Reserves are held to meet the demand for cash on the part of depositors and to honor checks drawn upon the bank. The amount of reserves a bank must hold is based on the **required reserve ratio**. Set by the Federal Reserve System, the required reserve ratio is a number from 0 to 1.00 and determines the level of reserve holdings relative to the bank's deposits.

Required Reserves—Required reserves are the amount a bank is legally obligated to hold. Required reserves are calculated by multiplying the required reserve ratio by the amount of deposits.

$$\text{Required Reserves} = \text{Required Reserve Ratio} \times \text{Deposits}$$

The required reserve ratio does not make banks safe. In the absence of a requirement, most banks would voluntarily hold adequate reserves to be "safe." In fact, the level of reserves banks are required to hold is probably higher than what they need to be safe. The main purpose of the requirement is to give the Federal Reserve System some control over the banks.

Excess Reserves—Excess reserves are the difference between the amount of reserves a bank holds and what it is required to hold.

All banks hold excess reserves at all times for reasons of financial prudence; however, greater excess reserves will be held during periods of financial uncertainty.

Excess Reserves = Reserves – Required Reserves

Why Can Banks Hold "Fractional" Reserves?—All banks constantly operate with reserve holdings only a fraction of deposit liabilities. This is known as **fractional reserve banking**. If all depositors tried to withdraw their money simultaneously, banks would not be able to honor the demands. Fortunately, this is unlikely to happen because people like to hold deposits because they are safe and convenient. On a normal business day, some withdrawals are made, but these are counterbalanced by new deposits. Reserve holdings need only be a small fraction of deposits for prudent operation.

MONETARY POLICY
THE FEDERAL RESERVE SYSTEM

The Federal Reserve System (known as the "Fed") is the central bank of the United States. Its responsibilities are to oversee the stability of the banking system and conduct monetary policy to the end of fighting inflation and unemployment and stimulating economic growth.

Structure—The Fed has an unusual structure. It consists of a Board of Governors, 12 regional banks, money subregional banks, and commercial banks that opt for membership in the system. Although created by an Act of Congress (in 1913), nominally the Fed is privately owned by the member banks. Members of the Board of Governors are appointed by the President and confirmed by the Senate for 14 year terms. The Chair of the Board is appointed by the President and confirmed by the Senate for a four year term. The Fed's budget is overseen by a committee of Congress, and it must report to Congress about its operations at least twice a year. To a large extent, the Fed can be considered an independent agency of the government.

The Fed's virtual independence has led to a continuing controversy. Is it wise to give the power to influence the state of the economy to an entity that is not directly accountable to the people? The "pro" side claims the Fed's independence puts it "above" politics and leads to decisions more in the "public interest." The "con" side says that in a democracy, the people should be given a voice in all decisions that affect them.

Functions—The major functions of the Fed are as follows:

1. **Bank Regulation**—The Fed has been given the responsibility of examining member banks to determine if they are financially strong and in conformity with the banking regulations. The Fed also approves mergers.

2. **Clearing Interbank Payments**—The Fed performs a service for member banks in operating the check clearing function. Banks receiving deposit checks drawn on other banks can present them to the Fed. The Fed will credit the receiving bank's reserve account, reduce the paying bank's reserve account, and send the check back to the paying bank. Banks do not universally avail themselves of this service. Local banks will frequently cooperate and establish their own check clearing process for local checks.

3. **Lender of Last Resort**—One of the original motivations for establishing the Fed was to have a bank that could act as a "lender of last resort."

Bank panics refer to situations where depositors lose faith in their bank and try to withdraw their money. Given the fractional reserve nature of modern banking, it is impossible for all depositors to withdraw their money simultaneously. Failure of depositors to withdraw their money from one bank has the potential of scaring other depositors and starting a "run on the banks." By standing ready to loan reserves to banks experiencing difficulties, the Fed helps reduce the danger of panics.

Federal Deposit Insurance was established during the New Deal era. Federal Deposit Insurance provides government guarantees for bank deposits should a bank fail. Both commercial banks and savings and loans are insured. Panics were much more common in the days before the Fed and the Federal Deposit Insurance Corporation, but are not unknown today. Witness the situations with savings and loan institutions in Ohio and Maryland (institutions which *lacked* federal insurance) within the last several years.

4. **Monetary Policy**—

   Open Market Operations—Open market operations refers to the Fed's buying or selling of U.S. Government bonds in the open market. The purpose is to influence the amount of reserves in the banking system, and, consequently, the banking system's ability to extend credit and create money.

a. **To expand the economy**—The Fed would buy bonds in the open market. If $50 million in bonds was purchased directly from commercial banks, the banks' balance sheet would change as follows:

All Commercial Banks

R	+ 50 million	
Bonds	− 50 million	

Banks are now holding an additional $50 million in excess reserves which they can use to extend additional credit. To induce borrowers, banks are likely to lower interest rates and credit standards. As loans are made, the money supply will expand. The additional credit will stimulate additional spending, primarily for investment goods.

The $50 million in bonds could be purchased directly from private individuals. The private individuals would then deposit the proceeds in their bank accounts. After the money was deposited, the balance sheet of all commercial banks would look as follows:

All Commercial Banks

R	+ 50 million	DD	+ 50 million

As above, the banks are now holding excess reserves which they can use to extend credit. Lower interest rates, a greater money supply, and a higher level of total expenditure will result.

b. **To contract the economy**—The Fed would sell bonds in the open market. If it sold $20 million in bonds directly to the commercial banks, the banks' balance sheet would change as follows:

All Commercial Banks

R	− 20 million	
Bonds	+ 20 million	

Banks are now deficient in reserves. They need to reduce their demand deposit liabilities, and will do so by calling in loans and making new credit more difficult to get. Interest rates will rise, credit requirements will be tightened, and the money supply will fall. Total spending in the economy will be reduced.

If the Fed sells the $20 million in bonds directly to private individuals, payment will be made with checks drawn against the private individuals' bank accounts. The banks' balance sheet will change as follows:

All Commercial Banks

R – 20 million	DD – 20 million

Again, banks are deficient in reserves. They are forced to reduce credit availability, which will raise interest rates, reduce the money supply, and lead to a drop in total spending.

Bonds are a financial instrument frequently used by government and business as a way to borrow money. Every bond comes with a par value (often $1,000), a date to maturity (ranging from 90 days to 30 years), a coupon (a promise to pay a certain amount of money each year to the bondholder until maturity), and a promise to repay the par value on the maturity date. The issuing government or business sells the bonds in the bond market for a price determined by supply and demand. The money received from the sale represents the principal of the loan, the annual coupon payment is the interest on the loan, and the principal is repaid at the date of maturity. There is also a secondary market in bonds.

Assume a bond carries a coupon of $100 and is sold for $1,000. Then the annual yield to the purchaser is roughly 10% ($100/$1,000). If the same bond was sold for $950, the yield would be roughly 10.5% ($100/$950). If the same bond was sold for $1,050, the yield would roughly be 9.5% ($100/$1,050). Note the inverse relationship between bond yield and price. Also note that the actual yield formulas are considerably more complicated than those used.

Reserve Ratio—The Fed can set the legal reserve ratio for both member and non-member banks. The purpose is to influence the level of excess reserves in the banking system, and consequently, the banking system's ability to extend credit and create money.

a. **To expand the economy**—The Fed would reduce the reserve requirement. Assume the reserve requirement is 8%, and all banks are "all loaned up."

   If the Fed reduces the reserve requirement to 6%, required reserves fall to $30 million, and there are immediately $10 million in excess reserves. Banks will lower the interest rates they charge and credit requirements in an attempt to make more loans. As the loans are granted, the economy's money supply and total spending will rise.

All Commercial Banks

R	40 million	DD	50 million

b. **To contract the economy**—The Fed would raise the reserve requirement. Assume the reserve requirement is 8%, and all banks are "all loaned up."

All Commercial Banks

R	40 million	DD	50 million

If the Fed raises the reserve requirement to 10%, required reserves rise to $50 million, and banks are immediately $10 million deficient in reserves. Banks will raise the interest rates they charge and credit requirements to reduce the amount of money borrowed. They may also call in loans. As the loans are reduced, the economy's money supply and total spending will fall.

Discount Rate—One of the responsibilities of the Fed is to act as a "lender of last resort." Member banks needing reserves can borrow from the Fed. The interest rate the Fed charges on these loans is called the **discount rate**. By changing the discount rate, the Fed can influence the amount member banks try to borrow, and, consequently, the banking system's ability to extend credit and create money.

a. **To expand the economy**—The Fed would lower the discount rate. A lower discount rate would make it less "painful" for member banks to borrow from the Fed. Consequently, they will be more willing to lend money and hold a low level of excess reserves. A lower discount rate would lead to lower interest rates and credit requirements, a higher money supply, and greater total spending in the economy.

b. **To contract the economy**—The Fed would raise the discount rate. A higher discount rate would make it more "painful" for member banks to borrow from the Fed. Consequently, they will be less willing to lend money and more likely to hold a high level of excess reserves. A higher discount rate would lead to higher interest rates and more stringent credit requirements, a lower money supply, and lower total spending in the economy.

Monetary Policy Summary Table

Tool	Action	Effect on Interest Rates	Effect on Money Supply	Effect on Total Spending	Effect on GNP
Open Market Operations	buy	lower	raise	raise	raise
	sell	raise	lower	lower	lower
Reserve Ratio	raise	raise	lower	lower	lower
	lower	lower	raise	raise	raise
Discount Rate	raise	raise	lower	lower	lower
	lower	lower	raise	raise	raise

☞ Drill: Economics

1. In *The Wealth of Nations*, Adam Smith attempted to demonstrate the following about international trade:

   (A) Tariffs and quotas should be used to protect domestic industries.

   (B) Countries should produce only those commodities for which they have an absolute advantage.

   (C) When countries specialize and trade, world wealth is enhanced.

   (D) Countries should be self-sufficient and produce all commodities they consume.

2. If the Treasury required the central bank to buy bonds in the amount of $10 million, the effect on the money supply would be the same as the effect of

   (A) the sale of $10 million in bonds by the central bank to commercial banks.

   (B) the purchase of $10 million in U.S. bonds by foreigners.

   (C) the purchase of $10 million in bonds by the central bank from commercial banks.

   (D) the Treasury printing $10 million in new money.

3. Which of the following is NOT a factor which enhances an economy's growth potential?

   (A) Increasing levels of investment

(B) Relatively high levels of training among the labor force

(C) A relatively high capital to output ratio

(D) New technologies

4. Conflicts between the goals of the Treasury and the Federal Reserve Bank exist when

(A) the GNP is increasing, thus causing tax revenues to increase.

(B) the Fed restrains money to reduce inflation and the Treasury needs to borrow.

(C) the Fed follows an easy money policy to reduce unemployment, and the Treasury needs to borrow.

(D) national debt and interest rates are decreasing due to fiscal restraint.

5. Which of the following represents monetary policy geared to increase the supply of money?

(A) The purchase of bonds by the Federal Reserve Bank

(B) The sale of bonds by the central bank

(C) An increase in reserve requirements

(D) An increase in the discount rate

6. Prices tend to be inflated during wartime because

(A) guns cost more than butter.

(B) there is competition for fully employed resources.

(C) the Consumer Price Index is calculated differently in wartime.

(D) the cost of government is not included in the CPI.

7. If people start eating more fish and chicken to reduce their intake of cholesterol, and the importation of Canadian pork is restricted due to a steroid problem, what will happen to meat prices in the U.S.?

(A) The prices of chicken, pork, and fish will go down.

(B) The prices of chicken, pork, fish, and beef will go up.

(C) There will be no substantial effect on prices.

(D) The price of pork will go down, while the prices of chicken and fish will go up.

8. Bank A and Bank B both are required to meet a 20% legal reserve requirement. Bank A has excess reserves of $20,000. Bank B has no excess reserves but receives a deposit of $20,000. Which of the following statements is correct?

    (A) Each bank can make a loan of $20,000.

    (B) Bank A can make a loan of $20,000, but Bank B can make a loan of only $16,000.

    (C) Bank B can make a loan of $20,000, but Bank A can make a loan of $16,000.

    (D) The most each bank can loan is $16,000.

9. If the Fed wants to create a situation of "tight" money, which of the following actions would be taken:

    (A) raise the discount rate, buy government securities, and lower the legal reserve requirement.

    (B) raise the discount rate, buy government securities, and raise the legal reserve requirement.

    (C) raise the discount rate, sell government securities, and raise the legal reserve requirement.

    (D) lower the discount rate, buy government securities, and raise the legal reserve requirement.

10. An economist's definition of investment in human capital would be represented by

    (A) labor costs in producing an intermediate good.

    (B) labor costs in producing a final good.

    (C) federal government's expenses for unemployment compensation.

    (D) the expenditure by an individual on college tuition and other college expenses.

ECONOMICS REVIEW

ANSWER KEY

Drill: Economics

1.	(C)	4.	(B)	7.	(B)	9.	(C)
2.	(D)	5.	(A)	8.	(B)	10.	(D)
3.	(C)	6.	(B)				

DETAILED EXPLANATIONS OF ANSWERS

Drill: Economics

1.   **(C)**   Choice (C) is correct. Adam Smith believed that each country producing what it does best, or relatively better, and trading for those commodities produced to advantage elsewhere, enhanced each nation's wealth and world wealth. Choices (A) and (D) would interfere with the types of specialization and trade described in choice (C). Smith stated that countries should produce those goods that they have an absolute and comparative advantage in, a comparative advantage being the least relative disadvantage.

2.   **(D)**   Choice (D) is the correct answer. If the central bank buys bonds in the amount of $10 million from the Treasury, it creates $10 million in "new money," the effect of which is identical to the Treasury printing this amount of money. Conversely, if the central bank buys $10 million in bonds from commercial banks, it creates less money because some must be used as reserves. Choices (A) and (B) reduce the supply of money.

3.   **(C)**   Choice (C) is correct. A growth formula derived from the Harrod-Domar model is:

$$\text{growth rate} = \frac{\text{average propensity to save}}{\text{capital/output ratio}}$$

It should be evident after inspection that as the capital to output ratio decreases, the growth rate increases. Choices (A), (B), and (D) enhance economic growth.

4.   **(B)**   Choice (B) is correct. The Treasury needs to borrow money to finance a debt and wants to do so at the lowest interest rates possible, but monetary restraint and tight money are inconsistent with this goal.

5.   **(A)**   Choice (A) is the correct answer. When the Fed purchases bonds, it pays for them with money which increases money supply. Choices (B), (C), and (D) are contractionary moves by the Fed.

6.   **(B)**   Choice (B) is correct. During wartime, the economy is working to produce more defense than in peacetime, which bids up prices. Choice (C) is false. Choice (D) is true, but if the government were included, it would probably cause more inflation.

7. **(B)** Choice (B) is the correct answer. The price of chicken and fish would be bid up by increased demand. The price of pork would go up due to controlled supply, and the price of beef would go up because it is a substitute for pork.

8. **(B)** Choice (B) is correct. A single commercial bank can make loans to the extent of its excess reserves. Therefore, Bank A can make loans of $20,000. Bank B, however, must hold 20% of the $20,000 deposit as federal reserve deposit. Therefore, Bank B can only make $16,000 of loans. The loans that banks make depend upon meeting the legal reserve requirements.

9. **(C)** Choice (C) is correct. Raising the discount rate raises the cost of commercial banks borrowing from the Fed. Selling government securities to commercial banks or the public takes money or potential money out of circulation. (Money becomes near money). Raising the legal reserve requirement wipes out excess reserves and lowers the value of the money multiplier. All three of the actions described in (C) are consistent in creating a "tight" money situation.

10. **(D)** Choice (D) is the correct answer. When an economist speaks of human capital, the emphasis is on capital theory which includes investment as a large component. Investment is performed to obtain a return. Investment in human capital consists of those expenditures which an individual makes to improve earning power. The concept is very specific and all other answers are not appropriate.

V. PSYCHOLOGY REVIEW

INTRODUCTION TO PSYCHOLOGY
WHAT IS PSYCHOLOGY?

Psychology is the science of behavior. Its goal is to measure, predict, and explain behavior. Some psychologists also describe psychology as the study of experience, or an organism's "internal" activities. Other psychologists believe that "experience" cannot be systematically studied. There are many varied approaches to the study of behavior, making psychology a rich and complex field.

Over time, psychology has acquired many definitions. Psychology was once considered to be the study of the mind. Researchers have come to agree that the mind is neither entirely open to study, nor very well defined. The mind can only be observed through the behavior it causes, but what this "mind" is and how it "causes" behavior has never been clearly defined. To make the discipline more objective and scientific, psychologists redefined psychology as the study of human behavior.

Behavior refers to any action or reaction of a living organism which can be observed. Psychologists study all levels of behavior. Some psychologists focus on the biology of behavior, such as the actions of nerve cells, genetics, or sweat glands. Other psychologists study higher level behaviors, such as aggression, prejudice, or problem solving.

The key to the definition of behavior is that behavior is observable. Behavior refers to overt movement, activity, or action. Some behaviors are more observable than others. For instance, any bystander can see aggressive behavior on a city street. However, more subtle behavior, such as the change in brain waves during sleep may require special equipment to be observed.

Psychologists do not want merely to describe behavior: they wish to predict and understand it. To do this, they have set forth four fundamental factors of behavior: the organism, motivation, knowledge, and competence.

The **organism** refers to the biological characteristics of a living biological entity, including the creature's nervous system, endocrine system, biological history, and heredity. **Motivation** entails the states which cause behavior. These are the immediate forces that act to energize, direct, sustain, and stop a behavior. The term is vague, but motivation generally includes the organism's internal state, e.g., tired, confused, and the behavior related to this state, e.g., searching for a warm den. Some psychologists include the goal of a behavior (rest) in their descriptions of motivation, though others deny that behavior has a goal. The term **cognition** refers to "knowledge," that is, what and how the organism thinks, knows, and remembers. For example, a contestant on a television game show who must choose which of three boxes she wants for a prize may base her decision on how big each box is, how much she trusts the game show host, and so on. Her guesses at the location of the prize, her reasoning about the estimation of the size of the boxes, and her memory of the host's past performance all make up her cognition. She does not know what is actually in the boxes. The contents of the boxes are not part of her cognition. **Competence** means the skills and abilities of an organism. How well can it perform a certain task? Does a rat have the physical ability to jump to the top of its cage? Does the sophomore have the skill at fast writing and the physical stamina to finish her term paper on time? These are questions of competence.

Psychology is not as simple as it may first appear. Psychologists today study many other scientific fields such as biology, physics, chemistry, and linguistics, as well as other social sciences like sociology, anthropology, economics, and political science. To evaluate behavior, a psychologist should be familiar with all of these areas.

HISTORY OF PSYCHOLOGY

Since the beginning of thought, humans have asked psychological questions, such as how do we experience the world around us? What is the relationship between the way we experience the world and how our bodies function, like the way food loses its taste when we are sick? How do we learn and what accounts for differences in behavior and temperament among people?

The science of psychology, like physics, chemistry, and biology, began in philosophy. Ancient Greek philosophers first observed and interpreted their environment, and organized their findings. Aristotle, in his *Poetics,* discussed the nature of sensory perception; in *The Republic,* Socrates and Plato explored the way government can influence individual behavior.

These philosophers were the first Europeans to reason that human beings have, in addition to a physical body, some kind of apparatus used for thinking. They called this thinking apparatus the psyche. Over the centuries, this word has meant such things as "soul," "form," and "function." The most popular equivalent evolved into "mind." The suffix "-ology" means "the study of." Thus, for many centuries psychology was considered to be the study of the mind.

The mind was an entity or structure with no physical substance. What, they asked, is the relationship between the mind and body? The French philosopher René Descartes (1596–1650) was very interested in this "mind-body" problem. He firmly believed in dualism, which states that humans have a dual nature—one part mental and the other physical. This is in contrast to "monism," which holds that only one type of nature exists.

In the eighteenth century, philosophers described the various functions of the mind as independent faculties. Every mental activity, such as loving, reading, or long division, was viewed as the work of a particular area of the mind. Any behavior could be explained by attributing it to the function of its respective faculty. This approach led to many explanations of behavior. It is easy to attribute a friend's hot temper to her "aggression faculty," but calling your friend's behavior a name does not explain it.

Certain scientists in the early nineteenth century tried to analyze the mind by examining the shape of the skull, a study called phrenology. (By this time, scientists commonly agreed that the mind was inside the head, as opposed to the heart or liver, two other popular spots.) Lumps in the skull were linked to faculties. For example, if a generous person had a very large lump on her head, that region of the skull would be labelled the "generosity" region of the mind.

By 1850, European laboratories were systematically experimenting with questions of perception, neural conduction, and other aspects of physiological psychology. Gustav Fechner (1801–1887) published a book titled *Elemente der Psychophysik* (Elements of Psychophysics), which detailed the measurement of sensory experiences. In 1879, Wilhelm Wundt (1832–1920) established the first laboratory solely devoted to psychology in Leipzig, Germany; the Johns Hopkins University started the first U.S. psychology lab in 1883.

MAJOR SCHOOLS OF THOUGHT

By the late 1800s, psychology had become empirical and left the realm of mere fanciful philosophy forever. In organizing and explaining their observations, psychologists created eight major schools of thought: structuralism, functionalism, gestalt, and biological, cognitive, humanistic, and psychodynamic theories. There are many other branches of psychological study: social, educational, developmental, and so on. These are merely the theories which have had the greatest impact on psychology as a whole.

Structuralism, the first theoretical school in psychology, derived from Wundt's work. Wundt believed that the science of psychology should study the conscious mind. Influenced by the physical scientists of his time, Wundt embraced the atomic theory of matter. This theory stated that all complex substances could be separated and analyzed into component elements. Wundt wished to divide the mind into mental elements. This approach came to be called structuralism.

To analyze mental elements, Wundt used an experimental method called introspection. Subjects reported the contents of their own minds as objectively as possible, usually in connection with stimuli such as light, sound, or odors. The subjects verbal reports were analyzed to see the number and types of "mental elements" they contained. Subjects were specially trained to give elaborate reports.

The major drawback of structuralism was that it focused on the internal structure and activity of the mind, rather than overt, objectively observable behavior. Subjective reports of the mind's activities are easily manipulated by both the subject and the experimenter, and they are unreliable. Psychologists today are still concerned with internal activities, but are primarily interested in how these activities influence behavior.

While structuralist psychologists were busy asking their subjects to describe mental images, **functionalists** examined behavior from a different point of view. While structuralists were concerned with what the mind is, functionalists were asking what the mind does, and why. Functionalists were inspired by Darwin's theory of evolution; they believed that all behavior and mental processes help organisms to adapt to a changing environment. They expanded their studies beyond perception to include questions of learning, motivation, and problem solving. Functionalist William James (1842–1910) coined the phrase "stream of consciousness" to describe the way the mind experiences perception and thought as a constant flow of sensation.

Functionalists did not reject the structuralists' introspection, but they preferred to observe both the stream of consciousness and behavior. The functionalists' most important contribution to psychology was the introduction of the concept of learning, and thus adaptation to the environment, to psychological study. The most influential proponents of functionalism were William James and John Dewey (1859–1952), a philosopher and educator who played a substantial role in the development of educational psychology.

Soon, psychologists tired of introspection's dainty ways. **Behaviorism**, as developed by John B. Watson (1878–1958), swept the United States at the turn of the century. Watson rejected the idea of the "mind," stating that this structure not only could not be objectively studied, but did not even exist! Instead, Watson presented behavior as consisting of the stimulus, a "black box" which processed the stimuli, and the response the "black box" produced. Nothing could be said about the "black box" apart from the behavior it regulated. Watson also disregarded introspection, asserting that only observations of outward behavior could provide valid psychological data. He stated that the major component of psychological study should be the identification of relationships between stimuli (environment) and responses (behavior).

While structuralists believed that the mind could be divided into mental/

experiential elements, behaviorists believed that all behavior could be broken down into a collection of conditioned responses. These conditioned responses (CRs) were simple learned responses to stimuli. All human behavior was supposed to be the result of learning. According to this theory, everyone could become lawyers, murderers, or trapeze artists, if only they were given the correct training.

Behaviorists have also studied animal behavior extensively. Many held that there was no difference between human and animal behavior, and several tried to formulate general theories of behavior based on animal experiments. Leaders of this school, prominent in the late 1930s and 1940s, include Edward C. Tolman (1886–1959), Clark L. Hull (1884–1952), and Edwin R. Guthrie (1886–1949).

Behaviorism is still an active, vibrant branch of psychology. Its rigorous experimentation and emphasis on actual behavior has proved useful, especially in treating difficult groups such as institutionalized and mentally retarded patients.

Gestalt psychology, though, survives only as a name for a collection of theories. Like functionalism and behaviorism, gestalt psychology was a reaction to structuralism. It was founded in Germany in 1912 by Max Wertheimer (1880–1943). The word "gestalt" has no exact equivalent in English, but its meaning is similar to "form," or "organization." Gestalt psychologists emphasized the organizational processes in behavior, rather than the content of behavior. Like the structuralists, gestalt psychologists mainly focused on problems of perception.

Unlike the reductionist structuralists and functionalists, gestaltists believed that behavior and experiences consisted of patterns and organized sets. Like many physical scientists, gestalt psychologists believed the whole is more than the sum of its parts. A series of lines shows a picture, jumbled notes become a song; the mind constantly organizes perception into unified wholes.

Gestalt psychologists stressed **phenomenology**, or the study of natural, unanalyzed perception, as the basis for behavior. They instructed untrained subjects to introspect without structuralist elaboration on their experience. However, they studied other problems as well, particularly those involving learning, thought, and problem solving. W. Kohler (1887–1967) argued that learning and problem solving were organizational processes like perception. He described the "moment of insight," when an individual realizes the solution to a problem suddenly crystallizes as a whole gestalt out of reasoning, intuition, etc.

Many of the gestaltists' observations about perception are still being explored. Current cognitive psychologists draw heavily on their ideas, particularly when dealing with questions of vision and information processing. How much information does a person need before she can figure out what she is seeing? What are the most important, salient parts of an object which let a person identify the whole? What kinds of information does a robot need to tell the difference between a rubber ball and an orange? These sorts of questions keep gestalt concerns alive.

Biological, cognitive, humanistic, and psychoanalytic psychologists are most active today. **Biological psychologists** explore the effect that changes in an organism's physical body or environment have on behavior, and the interaction between behavior and the brain. They do not study the mind, or soul, or most "internal" experiences. Biological psychologists concentrate on physical techniques, and hence find physical results.

The term biological psychology covers a wide range of study. Their topics include genetics, the nervous system, and the endocrine system. Biological psychologists' research may involve dissecting the brain of a human or animal who suffered a behavior disorder, experimenting with drug treatments for mental illness, measuring brain waves during sleep, or investigating the effects of biological factors on eating and drinking, sexual behavior, aggression, speech disorders, dyslexia, or learning.

Major contributors to biological psychology include Ivan Pavlov (1849–1936), who conditioned dogs to salivate when they heard a bell ring; Eric Kandel, who pioneered the use of the sea slug Aplysia to study motor neurons; and Norman Geschwind, who revolutionized studies of the neural basis of dyslexia.

Cognitive psychology is heir to the early experiential psychologists. It is concerned with the processes of thinking and memory, as well as attention, imagery, creativity, problem solving, and language use. In contrast to the behaviorists, cognitive psychologists discuss the mental processes which determine what humans can perceive, or communicate, as well as how they think. Cognitive psychologists also use animals, particularly in memory research.

In the 1950s, several events led to the rise of interest in the mind, after decades of neglect. Psychologists realized that behaviorism, while a useful approach, had taught them nothing about the "black box" of mental processing. Scientists like Norbert Wiener (1894–1964) began work on cybernetics, the study of automatic control systems like thermostats and computers, asking, "How does a thinking machine process information?" Noam Chomsky published his theories on language as a system with infinite, non-learned possibilities generated by rules. New technology and logic gave psychologists the power to explore realms that were considered too subjective by the dominant behaviorists. Many cognitive psychologists use computers to simulate human memory, language use, and visual perception.

Humanistic psychology also arose in the 1950s, with a completely different focus. According to the humanistic psychologists, behaviorism concentrated on scientific fact, to the exclusion of human experience, and psychoanalysis (described below) concentrated too much on human frailty. Humanistic psychologists sought to begin a psychology of mental health, not illness, by studying healthy, creative people.

Humanistic psychology grew out of two main influences: phenomenology, the idea that behavior is based on subjective perception, and **existentialism**, which states that humans' basic existential anxiety is fear of death. Both approaches concentrated on the individual's point of view. Humanistic psychologists had little use for statistics; the focus was to understand each person's struggle to exist.

Psychoanalytic theories have an important place in psychology. Sigmund Freud (1856–1939), the father of psychoanalysis, is perhaps the most famous psychologist in the world, as well as the most challenged. Though current psychodynamic theories of personality originated in his work, subsequent psychoanalysts have moved far beyond the scope of his theories.

In the nineteenth century, psychiatry did not offer either explanations of or treatment for mental illness. Freud developed his method of treatment and a theory of personality through empirical (observational) and experimental techniques. Freud developed a treatment called **psychoanalysis**, where patients work with a therapist to explore the sources of their illness in their own past, stressing early experience and unconscious, "repressed" memories. Freud's primary tool for investigation was the **case study**, which included both his commentary and a patient's autobiographical material, dream analysis, and free association.

Neo-Freudians revised Freud's theories to provide for more cogent views of women's development, learning throughout life, interpersonal influences on personality, and social interaction. Important writers included Eric Erikson, Karen Horney (1885–1952), C. G. Jung (1875–1961), and Alfred Adler (1870–1937).

Though psychoanalytic theory has its limitations, particularly with regard to biologically-based illnesses like schizophrenia, it is the most influential of psychological fields to date. Without it, clinical psychology as we know it would not exist.

METHODS OF STUDY
TYPES OF STUDIES

Psychology is a science, and many different research methods are used to study the behavior of subjects—the humans or animals who are observed.

Naturalistic observation is the systematic observation of an event or phenomenon in the environment as it occurs naturally. The researcher does not manipulate the phenomenon. Laboratory investigation often interferes with the natural occurrence of a phenomenon. Therefore, psychologists may prefer to witness it in its natural environment. For example, social behavior in monkeys may differ in a safe laboratory from that exhibited in the more perilous wild world.

When psychologists wish to manipulate conditions, they perform experiments. Some event, treatment, or condition is changed, controlled, or recorded by the psychologist: this factor is called the independent variable. The change in the organism—behavioral or biological—is recorded by the psychologist. This change is the dependent variable. By observing the change in the organism correlated with the change in conditions, the psychologist can infer the change in environment changed the organism's behavior. However, correlation is not causation. A social scientist must beware that the change in the dependent variable, behavior, is truly due to a change in the independent variable and not some other factor. Generally, psychologists perform their experiments in laboratories or other controlled settings, such as schools, prisons, or hospitals, where conditions are much the same for all subjects.

Surveys are another method of psychological investigation. Individuals are asked to reply to a series of questions or to rate items. The purpose is not to test abilities, but to discover beliefs, opinions, and attitudes. Psychologists may take answers to survey questions and see how they match with respondents' characteristics—age, gender, social class, and so on.

Three types of studies are typically used to examine human subjects: **longitudinal**, **cross-sectional**, and **case studies**. In longitudinal studies, psychologists study their subjects over a long period of time to observe changes in their behavior. Cross-sectional studies take a group of subjects and examine their behavior at one point in time. Case studies, or case histories, are commonly used in clinical psychology and medical research. A single individual is studied intensely to examine a problem or issue relevant to that person. Sigmund Freud favored case studies in his research.

RELIABILITY AND VALIDITY

To be applicable to the general population, any test a psychologist administers must be standardized. The results must be reproducible, and must measure what the psychologist wishes to measure. These concerns are termed **reliability** and **validity**.

In psychology, reliability refers to how consistently individuals score on a test. Reliability measures the extent to which differences between individuals' scores show true difference in characteristics, and not "error variance," or the proportion of the score due to errors in test construction. With a reliability value for a test, a psychologist can predict the range of error in a single individual's score. For example, Scholastic Assessment Tests generally have an error variance of 10 points: your score may vary 10 points in either direction from your "true score."

The question of validity is whether a test measures what the examiner wants it to measure. Specifically, **construct validity** is the extent to which a test measures something—a theoretical construct. **Criterion-related validity** refers to how effective a test is in predicting an individual's behavior in other, specified situations. For example, if a student does well on the SAT, does that student also have high grades now? Will that student do well in college? If that student's teacher hears that she did poorly on the math SAT, the teacher may expect that the student will do badly in math in school, and grade her more harshly. This is known as criterion contamination, when results on a test bias an individual's score on another test.

ETHICS IN PSYCHOLOGICAL RESEARCH

Since psychological research involves live, fragile humans and animals, psychologists must consider the ethical implications of their research. A careless experimenter can wreak havoc in a trusting subject's life. The United States government requires that every institution receiving federal support must set up review boards to decide the ethical implications of all research, and many other professional organizations have also set up ethical guidelines.

In general, experimenters must be honest, and practice **informed consent** (telling subjects all features of the experiment prior to the study), allow subjects to leave the experiment at any time, protect subjects from physical and mental harm, and protect all subjects' confidentiality.

STATISTICAL METHODS

Behavior is unbelievably complex. To scientifically study behavior, psychologists use statistics. Three terms psychologists use to refer to a set of scores are **population, sample**, and **distribution**. The population is the total set of possible scores, say, the weight of every person in the United States. Most statistics use a sample of a total population—the weights of 1,000 U.S. citizens, for example. A distribution is simply any set of scores taken from a population or population sample.

Inferential statistics, such as T-tests, chi-squares, and analyses of variance, test the differences between groups. They are used to measure sampling error, draw conclusions from data, and test hypotheses. They answer the question, "What does this data show?"

Descriptive statistics answer the question, "What is the data?" They include measures of **central tendency** (mean, median, and mode), or whether or not the data is clumped in the middle of a graph. Descriptive statistics also include measures of **variability**, or how the data spreads across a graph (i.e., standard deviation, range, and Z-scores), and measures of **correlation**, or the relationship between two sets of scores.

The **mean** is the average of a set of scores. The **median** is the score in the exact middle of the distribution: half the scores fall above the median, half fall below it. The **mode** is the most frequently occurring score. For example, in the series 3, 4, 4, 5, 6, 8, 100, the mode is 4—the number which occurs twice. The median is 5. The mean, though, is 65.

Variability is commonly measured by the **range**, or the distance between the highest and lowest score. In the example above, the range is (100 – 3), or 97. The **standard deviation** is an index of how much data generally varies from the mean. To find the standard deviation,

(i)   Find the mean of the distribution.

(ii)   Subtract each score from the mean.

(iii)   Square each result—the "deviations."

(iv)   Add the squared deviations from the mean.

(v)   Divide by the total number of scores; this result is called the **variance**.

(vi)   Find the square root of the variance; this is the standard deviation.

Many descriptive statistics involve the **normal distribution**. A distribution is a set of scores. A normal distribution is a bell-shaped curve which can be described completely by the mean and standard deviation. In a normal distribution, about 68 percent of the scores fall within plus or minus one standard deviation from the mean. Ninety-five percent of the scores fall within plus or minus two standard deviations from the mean. Ninety-nine point five percent of the scores fall within plus or minus three deviations from the mean.

Z-scores, or **standard scores**, are a way of expressing a score's distance from the mean in terms of the standard deviation. To find a Z-score for a number in a distribution, subtract the mean from that number and divide the result by the standard deviation. A positive Z-score shows that the number is higher than the mean; a negative Z-score, lower. Z-scores allow psychologists to compare distributions with different means and standard deviations.

Correlations show how closely related two sets of scores are to each other. Possible correlations range between +1.00 and –1.00. When a correlation is +1.00, high scores on one set are associated with high scores on the second set; in a correlation of −1.00, low scores are associated with high scores. There is a high positive correlation between children's age and height; there is a high negative correlation between driving competence and amount of alcohol drunk. A correlation of 0.00 shows that the two sets are not associated.

These statistics are all usually calculated on **samples**, not total populations. Using the sample, a psychologist can predict the intervals in which the mean and variance of the total population is likely to fall. To make this statement, the psychologist must know something about the populations of sample means and variances, i.e., their distributions.

CAREERS IN PSYCHOLOGY

In addition to being a science, psychology is also a profession. Psychologists can be either researchers or practitioners. They may work for colleges and universities, elementary or secondary schools, clinics, industry, government, or in private practice. Psychologists are generally employed in one of nine areas of psychology: experimental, biological, social, developmental, educational, personality, clinical, counseling, or industrial/organizational psychology.

Experimental psychologists conduct experiments in various areas of psychology, such as cognition or sensory perception, to further knowledge of the subject. **Biological** psychologists study the influence of biological factors on human and animal behavior. These factors include genetics, the nervous system, or the endocrine system. For example, they may study the effect of environmental lead contamination on intelligence in rats. **Social** psychologists use scientific research methods to study the behavior of individuals in groups; they are concerned with an organism's interaction with others. One topic social psychologists have studied is the effects of racial integration on school children. **Developmental** psychologists study individuals' behavioral development from conception through adulthood. They observe the acquisition of skills through the development of cognition, perception, language, motor abilities, and social behavior. A developmental psychologist might work with a dyslexic child, or a child who is unusually shy. Educational psychologists are concerned with the process of education. They engage in research to develop new ways of teaching and learning. They also implement new systems of education. **Educational** psychologists developed most of the "workbooks" American children use in school. **Personality** psychologists study individuals to discover the development of basic underlying dimensions of personality and how these dimensions or traits affect behavior. For example, personality psychologists could study what effect the trait of introversion might have on an individual's behavior in situations requiring confidence. **Clinical** psychologists assess abnormal behavior to diagnose and change it. They treat both patients whose disorders are so severe that they cannot cope with reality, and clients who may have less severe problems. Psychosis, substance abuse, and reactive depression (say, in response to a death) can be treated by clinical psychologists, though the line between medical and psychological illness grows more blurred each day. Other personnel working in clinical psychology include behavior analysts, psychological nurses, and music therapists. **Counseling** psychologists usually treat people whose disorders are not so serious. They offer advice on personal, educational, or vocational problems. Marriage counselors and school guidance counselors fall into this category.

Finally, **industrial/organizational** psychologists generally work for public and private businesses or the government. They apply psychological principles to areas such as personnel policies, consumerism, working conditions, production efficiency, and decision making. Two basic fields of industrial psychology are personnel psychology and consumer psychology.

Most researchers and college teachers of psychology have a Ph.D. (Doctor of Philosophy) degree, which requires four to five years of graduate study. Many of the other professions demand a master's degree, which requires one to two years of graduate study. Psychology offers endless possibilities to a person who is fascinated by human and animal behavior.

INTRODUCTION TO SOCIAL PSYCHOLOGY

Social psychology focuses on the psychology of the individual in society. Social psychologists may draw from sociology and cultural anthropology, though their primary interest is still the psychological level of thought and action. Using the scientific method and objective study, social psychologists have produced a body of knowledge about the underlying psychological processes in social interactions.

Within social psychology, there are two major schools of thought. **Cognitive theorists** concentrate on an individual's internal processes and thoughts. They believe that a human being organizes and processes experience, and that her "world view" greatly influences her social behavior. **Behaviorists**, on the other hand, put more emphasis on external events and tend to believe that people react to events that occur around them.

ATTITUDES AND ATTRIBUTIONS

An **attitude** is a person's beliefs about an object or a situation. An attitude both precedes behavior and causes behavior toward an object. The average adult probably has thousands of attitudes of which he is not aware. Attitudes usually occur in clusters or sets around a particular issue or situation—for example, taxes or abortion—supporting and reinforcing each other. A **value**, on the other hand, is a person's enduring belief about how she should act, and what goals are appropriate or desirable. Values direct behavior on a long-term basis. Examples of values (from Rokeach's Value Survey) are pleasure, wisdom, and a sense of accomplishment. A person generally holds many more attitudes than values.

Attitudes are generally formed through imitation, classical conditioning, or operant conditioning. Learning often occurs by imitation without obvious reinforcement. Hence, children often take on their parents' behavior and attitudes. In a study of Bennington College students, Theodore Newcomb found that incoming freshmen held conservative political attitudes, like those of their reference group—their parents. By graduation, though, they had acquired significantly more liberal attitudes, like those of their new reference group: classmates. One example of attitudes acquired by classical conditioning is the connotation of words. If you give a person a neutral word and immediately follow it with a word that evokes a strong negative or positive reaction, this will eventually cause the same type of reaction to the previously neutral word. In operant conditioning, a subject emits a behavior. If the behavior is reinforced, it will likely reoccur; if it is punished, it will not recur as often. If your child says, "I want to be a fireman!" and you respond with a smile and an assurance that she'll be just like Mommy then, the child will continue to have a positive attitude about firemen. If, on the other hand, you scowl and admonish her for even considering such a thing, you have punished her response, and the chances are that she will develop negative attitudes about the firefighting profession and all emergency-rescue careers.

Though it may seem that the principles of attitude acquisition are simple, the actual process is quite complex. An adult's attitudes are quite difficult to trace to their source. This is complicated by the fact that attitudes can change, even quite significantly, in the course of a person's lifetime. There is much yet to be learned about attitudes and their acquisition.

PERSUASION

Persuasion refers to a type of social influence that involves attitude change. Persuasion is not necessarily the result of conscious communication: a person can be persuaded that a street is dangerous if he sees a person being mugged there. In general, though, three factors affect how persuasive a particular communication is, i.e., how effective it is at changing attitudes. These factors are the source of the communication (who says it), the nature of the communication (how it is said), and the characteristics of the audience. All these factors can also be applied to print and broadcast media, not just face-to-face persuasion.

The first aspect of the source that the audience examines is credibility. People tend to believe people who appear to be experts or seem trustworthy. To the average person, it makes a lot of sense to be influenced by someone with these characteristics. Often, visual impressions are the only items a person can base impressions on, and these are what are used to infer credibility, whether of a TV news anchor, an auto mechanic, or a teacher. Trustworthiness, on the other hand, can be improved by arguing there is nothing to lose, arguing against one's (apparent) self-interest, and appearing not to be trying to influence people or change their minds.

The concern for the nature of communication is the emotional approach vs. the reasonable (or logical) approach. Research results generally indicate that a shocking (emotional-based) approach is usually more effective in communication and persuasion than the logical approach.

As for the audience, individuals with low self-esteem are quicker to be convinced if the speaker appears credible or takes an emotional approach, while high self-esteem listeners are in higher conflict when presented with less-than-reliable information from a medium-credibility speaker. The speaker's prior experience with the audience is another crucial factor, as are educational level and previous contact with the issue being discussed.

PREJUDICE

Prejudice is an attitude. It is generally a negative attitude held toward a particular group and any member of that group. Prejudice is translated into behavior through discrimination, which refers to any action that results from prejudiced points of view. **Ethnocentrism** is a special form of prejudice where a person holds positive prejudices about her own ethnic group and negative prejudices about all other ethnic groups.

It is possible for individuals to be quite prejudiced and still not discriminate. Civil rights laws, for example, have reduced a great deal of the more obvious discrimination. However, some evidence exists that the prejudicial attitudes of Americans have been influenced by civil rights law. For instance, in 1964, most Americans were opposed to the Civil Rights Act, but today over 75 percent of the public favors integration.

When discrimination decreases and prejudice remains, discrimination may begin to take more subtle forms, such as not being included in informal discussions with other managers at work, being assigned the more routine tasks of a project, and being listened to through the filter of prejudiced attitudes—"he's not too bright," "she's too emotional," and so forth.

Although prejudice is a complex topic and difficult to analyze on an individual level, psychologists hypothesize that there are four basic causes of prejudice. The first cause of prejudice is **economic** and **political competition**. This view states that when any resource is limited, majority groups will vie for resources and thus form prejudices against the competing group for their own personal gain and advantage. Research has demonstrated a clear link between the level of discrimination and prejudice against a certain group in an area and the scarcity of jobs in that area.

The second causal factor of prejudice is **personality needs**. After World War II, researchers began to search for a prejudiced personality type. The major piece of research in this area, by Adorno et al., is titled *The Authoritarian Personality*. Adorno developed the F (fascist) Scale for authoritarianism. These researchers established a relationship between the strictness of parental upbringing and authoritarianism and a correlational relationship between authoritarianism, prejudice, and ethnocentrism. Yet they did not determine what causes prejudice, only what personality traits accompany it.

The third cause of prejudice is the **displacement of aggression**. This is referred to as a "scapegoat" theory of prejudice. Here, aggression (described further below) that cannot be otherwise expressed is displaced onto socially acceptable victims.

The fourth cause of prejudice is **conformity to preexisting prejudices** within the society or subgroup. Researchers note that while there seems to be a large difference between the amount of anti-black prejudice in the North and the South, neither group is distinguishable on the basis of how they score on the Authoritarian test. The problem appears to be caused by socially acceptable beliefs in each region. As Elliot Aronson has noted, historical events in the South set the stage for greater prejudice against blacks, but it is conformity which keeps it going.

There are four other factors which contribute to the construction and continuation of prejudice. People tend to be prejudiced against the group which is directly under them on the socio-economic scale. The four additional contributions are 1) people need to feel superior to someone, 2) people most strongly feel competition for jobs from the next lower level, 3) people from the lower socio-economic levels are more frustrated and therefore more aggressive (see below), and 4) a lack of education increases the likelihood that they will simplify their world by the consistent use of stereotyping.

There are ways of reducing prejudice. One unsuccessful manner of reducing prejudice is to provide information contrary to people's beliefs. Unfortunately, people tend to pay attention only to information which agrees with their beliefs. However, if people of different backgrounds are brought together in **equal-status contact**, people tend to change their behavior and their attitudes towards other groups. Unfortunately, forced busing and desegregation efforts often bring people together in unequal status, defying their purpose. Finally, one very successful way to reduce prejudice is through **interdependence**, where all participants must work together with a mixed group. Social psychologists are currently trying to apply this method to educational settings.

ATTRIBUTES AND STEREOTYPES

An **attribute** is a perceived characteristic of some object or person. In attribution, people infer that some individual has certain characteristics. If a person infers that people possess certain characteristics because of their gender, race, or religion, that person is attributing a **stereotype** to that group. Stereotyping is not necessarily an intentional act of insult; very often it is merely used as a means of simplifying the complex world. However, if a stereotype narrows a person's views of actual interpersonal differences, prejudiced attitudes can result.

Attribution theory contends that individuals have a tendency to attribute a cause to any recently viewed behaviors. This attribution is essentially a specialized sort of stereotyping. When viewing an event, the observer uses the information available to her at the time to infer causality. Although there are many factors which affect what inference will be made, the major contributors are a person's beliefs, e.g., stereotypes or prejudices. The process of attribution based on a person's prejudices can be described as a "vicious circle." A person's prejudices affect her attributions, and her misdirected attributions then serve to reinforce and intensify her prejudice.

CONFORMITY AND OBEDIENCE

Conformity is a change in behavior or belief caused by real or imagined social pressure. For example, a teenager who goes to school in formal clothes will quickly observe that every other person her age is wearing blue jeans. No one may say a word about her dress, yet she observes that others are acting differently and may imagine that they are discussing her clothing. The next day, in blue jeans, she conforms. Conformity is generally divided into three subtypes: compliance, identification, and internalization.

Compliance is a change in external behavior, as opposed to a real attitude change, termed "private acceptance." Compliance is generally exhibited by individuals attempting to gain a reward or punishment. This behavior generally ceases once the reward or punishment is either not available or avoidable, respectively.

Identification results from the individual's desire to be like some other person, the person she is identifying with. Such behavior is self-satisfying, and does not require reward or threat of punishment. The individual loosely adopts the beliefs and opinions of the person she identifies with, a fact which differentiates identification from compliance.

Internalization occurs when the individual adopts the groups beliefs as his own. This process is a deeply rooted social response based on the desire to be right. The reward here is intrinsic. Identification is usually the method which introduces a belief to an individual, but once it is internalized it becomes an independent belief, and is highly resistant to change.

The most famous psychological demonstration of conformity was a series of experiments by Solomon Asch. Asch asked subjects to choose which of three lines on a card was the same length as line X, a line on a separate card. Each subject was on a panel with other "subjects" (Asch's confederates) who all initially gave the same wrong answer. Approximately 35 percent of the real subjects chose to give the obviously incorrect, but conforming, response. Since there were no explicit rewards or punishments, the reason for conformity could be that in the face of such "overwhelming" opposition the subjects doubted their own perceptions or agreed with the confederates to gain group acceptance (or avoid group rejection). Asch and his colleagues have repeated this study many times, varying the conditions in attempts to determine what variables play a causal role in decreasing or increasing conformity.

Obedience also involves conforming to others' expectations. Yet in obedience, an authority's demands are clearly expressed; the individual must consciously choose whether or not to obey. The study of obedience became especially important after World War II, when psychologists were eager to investigate just how and why the Nazis committed their death-camp atrocities.

While investigating obedience, Stanley Milgram discovered that the average middle-class American male would, under the direction of a legitimate authority figure, give severe shocks to other people in an experimental setting. Briefly, in his experiments two men were told that they would be taking part in an experiment on the effects of punishment on learning. One man was chosen as the learner (who was actually a confederate in the experiment), the other as the teacher. The learner was taken into an adjoining room and strapped into a chair. The experimenter read the instructions to the learner about a word list he was to learn so that the teacher-subject could hear. The teacher was placed in front of a generator which could administer shocks from 15 to 450 volts to the learner. Under the shock levels were descriptions of the effects of the shock from "slight shock" to "danger, severe shock." The learning session would begin: the first time the learner would give an incorrect answer, a mild shock was given, and with each subsequent wrong answer stronger and stronger shocks were administered. Even amidst cries from the learner of "Let me out, I've got a heart condition," the teacher would continue administering the shock, though more and more reluctantly.

Out of the 40 males who took part in the initial experiments, 26 or 65 percent went all the way to the maximum shock of 450 volts. This alarming finding has been replicated many times. It demonstrates how much ordinary people will comply with the orders of a legitimate authority even to the point of committing cruel and harmful actions. On a television interview, Milgram stated that he would have no trouble staffing a Nazi-style concentration camp with guards from any middle-sized American town. This is not due to American anti-Semitism, but because of the evidence of his experiments regarding the power of legitimate authorities to evoke obedience.

GROUP DYNAMICS

People tend to act differently when they are in a group. A few of the differences are outlined above in the Asch experiment. In general, a group's primary purpose is to achieve some definite goal. To accomplish the goal, the group establishes **positions**, or places, where people fit into a group's hierarchy. Individuals themselves choose to fill **roles**, the set of different behaviors an individual displays in connection with a given social position. There are certain behaviors associated with the role of mother, employer, student, secretary, and teacher, for example. Most people have many roles which must be filled each day. However, people who occupy the same type of position may play very different roles. Three different roles are possible in any given position in a group. The **task-oriented** role requires that a person be concerned directly with accomplishing the goal of the group. The **maintenance** role requires that the individual playing it be more concerned with the group morale. The final type of role is the **self-oriented** role; the person who takes this role cares mainly for herself, and may even attempt to undermine the group's goals if they interfere with her personal desires or needs.

If a group is large enough—say, the size of New York City—social influence may move the person away from socially acceptable behavior. **Deindividuation** is a state where a person feels a lessened sense of personal identity and a decreased concern about what people think of him. This state, which probably results from feelings of anonymity, lessened responsibility and arousal, can lead to anti-social behavior. Philip Zimbardo once left an apparently abandoned car with the license plates removed and the hood raised in two cities, New York and Palo Alto, CA (pop. 100,000). In New York, within 10 minutes a man, woman, and a nine-year-old child came by and immediately began to remove parts of the car. Within 24 hours, the car was completely ransacked. The vandals were not gangs, but most often well-dressed adults. In Palo Alto, the car remained untouched after 72 hours, except for one passerby who politely put the hood down when it began to rain. Zimbardo took this result as supporting the hypothesis that the anonymity of a large city gives rise to antisocial behavior. The chances of a person being recognized by someone in a city with a population of 8 million is much less than in a city with a population of 100,000.

Yet groups can also improve performance. In **social facilitation**, the mere presence of other people such as an audience or coworkers can increase individual performance. In the 1890s, Norman Triplett became interested in the fact that cyclists rode faster in groups than alone, while in the 1930s, John Dashiell discovered that though people respond more frequently in the presence of others, their rate of errors also increased. Robert Zajonc (1965) theorized that the presence of other people produces an increase in a person's arousal level and enhances strong responses. However, if responses are poorly learned or weak, responses will suffer. This theory helps explain why stage fright may paralyze young actors and galvanize more experienced thespians into grand performance.

ALTRUISM AND BYSTANDER INTERVENTION

Altruism and the "bystander effect" are two opposite responses to situations where another person needs help. In **altruism**, a person will risk his own health or well-being to help another. Yet if a large group of people witnesses an event where someone desperately needs assistance, each individual person is less likely to intervene than if she were alone. This phenomenon is called the **bystander effect**.

Latane and Darley produced the most famous experiments on bystander intervention. In their study, male subjects heard someone fall, apparently uninjured, in the room next door. Whether subjects tried to help and how long they took to do so were the main dependent variables in the experiment. Subjects were placed in one of four conditions: alone, with a friend, with another subject who was a stranger, and with a confederate in the experiment who had been instructed to remain passive at the sounds of injury. In the alone situation, subjects responded to the need for help 91 percent of the time, while with the passive confederate, subjects responded only 7 percent of the time. With pairs of strangers, at least one of the subjects responded in 40 percent of the pairs, while in the group of two friends, at least one person intervened in 70 percent of the pairs. This finding can be explained through **social influence** or **diffusion of responsibility**. The former option suggests that people are susceptible to the apparent reactions of other people present. The subject may not feel the situation is serious or merely be concerned and confused by the confederate's passivity. In diffusion of responsibility, when other people are present, each person's total sense of responsibility (and justification for responding to emergencies) may diminish.

AGGRESSION

In animals, many types of aggression are specific to certain species and are clearly controlled by brain structures and hormone levels, such as maternal aggression in rats. In humans, sex steroid hormones called **androgens** have been conclusively linked to an increase in aggressive behavior. However, it is not clear whether high levels of androgens produce aggression, or high levels of aggression result in the production of testosterone; there is evidence for both conclusions. Mazur and Lamb (1980) found that men who lost tennis matches had lower levels of testosterone (an androgen) an hour later, while the men who won had higher levels.

According to social psychologists, three different **distinctions** should be used when discussing aggressive behavior. The first distinction is between **harmful and nonharmful behavior**, which is judged by the outcome of the behavior. The second distinction involves the **intent of the aggressor**, as hitting a person accidentally is not considered aggressive. Finally, there is a distinction between aggression necessary to achieve a goal (as in professional boxing), called **instrumental aggression**, and aggression which is an end in itself (as in common street fighting), called **hostile aggression**. Interpersonal aggression occurs most often between friends, relatives, and acquaintances, and is much less often associated with crime than most people think.

Many social psychologists believe that aggression is a learned behavior, like other behaviors. Albert Bandura's work on modeling, or learning through imitation, was designed to explain aggressive tendencies in children. Aggression, like attitudes, may also be conditioned. The frustration-aggression hypothesis states that frustration toward the accomplishment of some goal produces aggression. For example, if you are trying to buy a soda in a convenience store, but the clerk will not serve you because he is busy talking on the telephone, that clerk is frustrating you with regard to buying the soda. If the source of frustration is available and unthreatening, the aggression will be displaced onto that person: you may yell at the talkative clerk. Otherwise, the aggression will be displaced onto someone or something else, called a "scapegoat."

However, some psychologists believe that aggression is an inborn tendency. The only reason, according to these theories, that we are not involved in more wars than we currently are is that humans use their intelligence to vent their aggression, and therefore do not always express aggression physically. Konrad Lorenz applied Darwin's "survival of the fittest" theory to aggression, arguing that aggression is necessary for the continued existence of the species. However, he based his argument on the observation of animals, not humans. Others, including Freud, believe the catharsis theory.

This theory states that aggression is a means of releasing inner tension. If this tension were to remain unreleased, mental illness would result. Research does not support this theory, though, and has actually shown the opposite to be true.

ORGANIZATIONAL PSYCHOLOGY

Organizational psychology studies human behavior in an industrial or organizational environment. It can be divided into two important subfields: **industrial psychology** and **human factors psychology**. Human factors psychology is concerned specifically with how people receive information through their senses, store this information, and process it when making decisions.

The differences in these two areas is best understood by examining the jobs of industrial psychologists and human factors engineers. The industrial psychologist helps to improve safety programs and works with engineers on the human aspects of equipment design. She assists the office of public relations in its interactions with consumers and the local community. Industrial psychologists also engage in programs dealing with workers' mental health, and assist management in finding ways to reduce absenteeism and grievances. The industrial psychologist may draw up a plan for the executive development of newly hired college graduates on one day and discuss problems of aging employees the next.

The role of a human factors engineer, on the other hand, is concerned with contriving, designing, and producing structures and machines useful to humans. He applies his knowledge of the mechanical, electrical, chemical, or other properties of matter to the task of creating all kinds of functional devices—safety pins and automobiles, mousetraps and missiles. Since the ultimate users of these machines are humans, human characteristics must be considered in their construction. Human muscular frailty dictated the need for and design of such devices as the lever, pulley, screw, and hand tools of all sorts (though these simple machines were not designed by human factors engineers). The L-shaped desk for the secretary was designed to bring an enlarged work space within easy reach. The task which confronts the human factors engineer is to describe humans' special abilities and limitations so that design engineers can effectively include the human operator in their man-made system. This requires knowledge about sensation and perception, psychomotor behavior, and cognitive processes as well as knowledge about the properties of the material world. It is because of the need for this special knowledge about human behavior that this type of engineer is also considered a psychologist.

☞ Drill: Psychology

1. In psychology, measurement devices must be

   (A) reliable.   (C) conclusive.

   (B) valid.   (D) both (A) and (B)

2. Deindividuation refers to

   (A) antisocial acts.

   (B) disinhibition.

   (C) anonymity in a group situation.

   (D) aggression.

3. A psychological theoretician in the process of developing a theory would be most interested in test measures in terms of their

   (A) construct validity.   (C) predictive validity.

   (B) face validity.   (D) concurrent validity.

4. Which is the most consistent measure of central tendency?

   (A) mean   (C) median

   (B) mode   (D) variance

5. Bandura's research on aggressive behavior mostly focused on aggression as

   (A) an innate, inherited trait.

   (B) a result of modeling.

   (C) an instinctual drive common to most everyone.

   (D) unrelated to rewards and punishments.

6. Which one of these psychologists thinks that aggression is an inborn tendency in all animals, including man?

   (A) Freud   (C) Bandura

   (B) Lorenz   (D) Both (A) and (B)

7. Which of the following is not a controlling factor of conformity?

   (A) Whether or not the opinion of the majority is unanimous

   (B) Self-esteem of the subjects

(C)   The desire to give the correct answer

(D)   Whether or not the group consists of people similar to the subject

8.   Social psychologists study _____ , while sociologists study _____ .

(A)   groups, individuals

(B)   group norms, national norms

(C)   individuals, groups

(D)   abnormal people, normal people

9.   Behavior deliberately intended to injure or destroy is the psychological definition of

(A)   sociopathy.   (C)   frustration.

(B)   hostility.   (D)   aggression.

10.   Which of the following is a technique used in psychoanalysis?

(A)   Client-centered therapy

(B)   Systematic desensitization

(C)   Dream analysis

(D)   Implosion therapy

PSYCHOLOGY REVIEW

ANSWER KEY

Drill: Psychology

1.	(D)	4.	(A)	7.	(C)	9.	(D)
2.	(C)	5.	(B)	8.	(C)	10.	(C)
3.	(A)	6.	(D)				

DETAILED EXPLANATIONS OF ANSWERS

Drill: Psychology

1. **(D)** Measuring devices must have two characteristics. First, they must be reliable. This means that an individual's score or rating should not vary with repeated testings. For example, an intelligence test which yields highly different scores each time the subject takes the test is useless. Second, a measuring device must be valid. This means that it should measure what it was designed to measure. An I.Q. test, for example, would not yield an accurate measure of anxiety, but it should be an accurate measure of intelligence.

2. **(C)** Deindividuation is a state in which a person feels a lessened sense of personal identity and responsibility. It is a state likely to be experienced by a person in a large group or crowd situation.

3. **(A)** When a test is designed to measure a theoretical idea or construct, its validity is judged by the extent to which it conforms to the requirements of the theory. Unlike predictive validity and concurrent validity, construct validity is a matter of logical analysis, not correlation.

4. **(A)** In comparison with other measures of central tendency, the mean is the most consistent measure. If you take large independent sets of data and analyze the measures of central tendency, the mean varies less from data set to set than do other measures of central tendency. Therefore, the mean is more consistent as a measure over many data sets and is the most commonly used of all the measures of central tendency.

5. **(B)** Most psychologists today believe that aggression is a learned behavior. Bandura, a social learning theorist, studied the effects of modeling on aggression. Modeling is simply a process whereby a person learns a new behavior by watching another person engage in it. He found that children exposed to aggressive models (either live, filmed, or cartoon) were significantly more likely to demonstrate aggressive behavior than those not exposed to aggressive models. He also found that reward contingencies played a very important role in the effectiveness of model learning.

6. **(D)** Freud originally introduced this idea in his psychoanalytic theory in the 1930s. Today this approach to aggressive behavior has been

most supported by the work of Lorenz. Lorenz is an ethologist—that is, one who studies the behavior of animals in their natural habitat. He believes that because humans use their intelligence to aggress, they have never developed natural controls on aggression against their own species.

7. **(C)** Controlling factors of conformity include whether or not the opinion of the majority is unanimous, whether or not the group consists of the subjects' friends or of experts or peers, and the self-esteem of the subjects. The desire to give the correct answer is not a factor since subjects will choose an obviously incorrect answer so as to avoid group rejection.

8. **(C)** Social psychologists study how the individual is affected by the group. They would be interested in how peer pressure influences the individual. Sociologists, on the other hand, are interested in group behavior.

9. **(D)** Aggression is defined as behavior intended to hurt living things for purposes other than survival, or the destruction of property. Instrumental aggression refers to cases where aggression is socially sanctioned, such as a fireman breaking down a door.

10. **(C)** In psychoanalysis, all problems stem from unresolved childhood conflicts and subconscious influences. Dreams are an avenue for the subconscious to manifest itself on the conscious mind. Choice (A) is the humanistic approach. The other choices are from the behavioral approach to therapy.

VI. GEOGRAPHY REVIEW

INTRODUCTION TO GEOGRAPHY

WHAT IS GEOGRAPHY?

Geography is the study of the earth's surface, including such aspects as its climate, topography, vegetation, and population. **Physical geography** is a branch of geography concerned with the natural features of the earth's surface. Physical geography concentrates on such areas as land formation, water, weather, and climate.

Population geography is a form of geography that deals with the relationships between geography and population patterns, including birth and death rates. **Political geography** deals with the effect of geography on politics, especially on national boundaries and relations between states. **Economic geography** is a study of the interaction between the earth's landscape and the economic activity of the human population.

UNITED STATES

San Diego, California	1,070,310
Omaha, Nebraska	353,170
Baltimore, Maryland	751,400
Houston, Texas	1,698,090
Boston, Massachusetts	577,830
New York, New York	7,352,700

Table 1 – U.S. City Populations

Year	Population	Year	Population
1860	31,443,321	1930	123,202,624
1870	38,558,371	1940	132,164,569
1880	50,189,209	1950	151,325,798
1890	62,979,766	1960	179,323,175
1900	76,212,168	1970	203,302,031
1910	92,228,496	1980	226,547,082
1920	106,021,537		

Table 2 – Population of the United States

There are many sources of energy in the United States that are being developed to lessen the country's dependence on foreign oil. Some of these sources are solar energy, nuclear energy, gasohol, fossil fuels, and others. With the development of these sources of energy, more jobs will be made available and our economy will not be afflicted by adverse situations in oil-rich countries.

The United States is a relatively young country made up of immigrants from all over the world. This country serves as a leader of the free world and has many allies around the world.

It has helped many countries that needed financial help to rebuild their countries and continues to play an important part in world affairs.

The Middle Atlantic states, which include New York, West Virginia, Delaware, Maryland, New Jersey, and Pennsylvania, are a hub of activity. This area is highly industrialized and includes a skilled work force. The financial center of the nation is found in New York and cultural activities of all kinds are found in this area.

The states of North Dakota, South Dakota, Nebraska, Kansas, Minnesota, Iowa, Missouri, Wisconsin, Illinois, Michigan, Indiana, and Ohio make up the Plains states. This area is also referred to as the Midwest Region of the United States. It is known as a great agricultural region. Some of the crops grown are wheat, corn, and oats.

The Plains states are highly industrialized. Their location near waterways and the close proximity to coal and iron deposits have made it relatively easy for industries to develop. Skilled laborers are available and are necessary to work in manufacturing plants.

The South includes the following states: Texas, Oklahoma, Louisiana, Arkansas, Mississippi, Alabama, Florida, Georgia, South Carolina, North Carolina, Tennessee, Kentucky, and Virginia. This area is known for its relatively mild weather and good, rich soil. Agriculture and oil are two of the most important industries in the South. Some of the crops grown are cotton, corn, tobacco, peanuts, and rice. Cattle raising is also very important in some of these states. Five of these states border on the Gulf of Mexico.

Texas is the second largest state. It is composed of 267,000 square miles and 254 counties. It is broken up into many large physical regions such as piney woods, post oak belt, plains, rolling prairie, high plains, valley, coastal prairie, and West Texas. The population of Texas as of the 1980 census was 14,225,513. Texas is, without a doubt, one of the most beautiful states in the United States.

The Pacific states include Washington, Oregon, and California. California has the largest population of any state in the United States. It is known for its agriculture and leads all other states in this regard. Oregon and Washington also are known for farming. All three states also have very developed industries.

Some of the major cities located in the Pacific states are Seattle, Spokane, Portland, Olympia, San Francisco, Los Angeles, Salem, and San Diego. There are many interesting places to visit in this area and thus tourism is a major industry.

The Mountain states are Montana, Idaho, Wyoming, Nevada, Utah, Colorado, Arizona, and New Mexico. These states are sparsely populated, even though the combined square mileage is over 800,000. The Rocky Mountains stretch through this area and most people feel they are a beautiful sight to behold.

The New England states include Maine, Massachusetts, New Hampshire, Vermont, Rhode Island, and Connecticut. Territorially, this is a very small region. The total size is about 67,000 square miles. The main industries in this area are fishing, shipping, manufacturing, and dairy farming.

MEXICO

Mexico borders the United States on the south and has about 88,000,000 people. The land area is about 762,000 square miles. The capital is Mexico City. Some of the chief crops are coffee, cotton, corn, sugar cane, and rice.

Mexico has an abundance of natural resources, such as oil, gold, silver, and natural gas. Textiles, steel production, tourism, and petroleum are the major industries in Mexico.

CANADA

Canada is the United States' neighbor to the north. It includes the second largest territory in the world. The current population is about 27 million people. The capital of Canada is Ottawa.

The United States and Canada are two sprawling countries that make up North America. Each country is an industrial giant and provides a very high standard of living for its population. The population of the United States is about nine or ten times larger than that of Canada.

The United States and Canada have large supplies of natural resources. In the United States, the minerals include coal, copper, gold, nickel, silver, zinc, and others. In Canada, the minerals found are nickel, gold, lead, silver, zinc, and others.

SOUTH AND CENTRAL AMERICA

Country	Population	Square Miles
Argentina	32,291,000	1,065,189
Brazil	153,771,000	3,286,470
Chile	13,000,000	292,257
Venezuela	29,753,000	352,143
Ecuador	10,506,000	109,483

Table 3 – Selected South American Countries

Central America is the connecting point between North and South America. The countries in Central America have an extremely long coastline. The main industry of this area is agriculture, and most people who live in this area are extremely poor. Bananas, coffee, and corn are some of their chief crops.

The seven nations that make up Central America are Belize, Guatemala, Honduras, El Salvador, Panama, Costa Rica, and Nicaragua.

CLIMATE AND WEATHER

Weather and climate conditions affect the way of life for people everywhere and in a variety of ways. A definition of weather refers to day-to-day conditions, such as how hot or cold it is or how dry or humid. Climate refers to the overall condition of the atmosphere over a period of time.

☞ Drill: Geography

Question 1 is based on Table 1 presented in the review.

1. Which city has the third largest population?

    (A) Houston   (B) Boston   (C) San Diego   (D) Baltimore

Questions 2 and 3 are based on Table 2 presented in this review.

2. How much did the population increase between 1970 and 1980?

    (A) By approximately 20,000

    (B) By approximately 200,000

    (C) By approximately 2,000,000

    (D) By approximately 20,000,000

3.   The population of the United States has
     (A)   steadily declined.   (C)   dropped markedly.
     (B)   remained about the same.   (D)   steadily increased.

4.   Two of the main industries of the South are
     (A)   oil and agriculture.   (C)   agriculture and fishing.
     (B)   oil and mining.   (D)   oil and cattle raising.

5.   The Pacific states have one thing in common. They are
     (A)   farming centers.
     (B)   extremely cold in the winter.
     (C)   located in the Southwest.
     (D)   not highly populated.

6.   Mexico has an abundance of
     (A)   oil and gold.   (C)   nickel and diamonds.
     (B)   natural gas and nickel.   (D)   diamonds and natural gas.

7.   Canada
     (A)   is the largest country in the world.
     (B)   is located to the south of the United States.
     (C)   includes the second largest territory in the world.
     (D)   is a part of the United States.

Question 8 is based on Table 3 presented in the review.

8.   Which country in South America is the largest in both population and square miles?
     (A) Ecuador   (B) Brazil   (C) Venezuela   (D) Argentina

9.   One of the chief crops in Central America is
     (A) wheat.   (B) bananas.   (C) barley.   (D) rice.

10. Which of the following is an example of climate?
     (A)   Changes in the temperature from time to time
     (B)   Long, extended periods of little or no rainfall in certain areas
     (C)   A forecast of sunshine
     (D)   An electrical storm

GEOGRAPHY REVIEW

ANSWER KEY

Drill: Geography

1. (C)	4. (A)	7. (C)	9. (B)
2. (D)	5. (A)	8. (B)	10. (B)
3. (D)	6. (A)		

DETAILED EXPLANATIONS OF ANSWERS

Drill: Geography

1. **(C)**   Choice (C) is the correct answer. San Diego has the third largest population, with approximately 1,070,310 people. New York City is first with 7,352,700; Houston is second with 1,698,090.

2. **(D)**   Choice (D) is the correct answer. Between 1970 and 1980, the population increased by 23,245,051.

3. **(D)**   Choice (D) is the correct answer. The population has increased every decade since 1860.

4. **(A)**   Choice (A) is the correct answer. Oil and agriculture are two of the main industries in the South. Some of the crops grown in the South are cotton, corn, tobacco, peanuts, and rice.

5. **(A)**   Choice (A) is the correct answer. Oregon and Washington are known for farming, and California leads all other states in agriculture.

6. **(A)**   Choice (A) is the correct answer. Mexico has an abundance of natural resources, such as oil, gold, silver, and natural gas.

7. **(C)**   Choice (C) is the correct answer. Choice (D) is incorrect because Canada is not part of the United States. Choice (B) is wrong because Canada is located north, not south, of the United States.

8. **(B)**   Choice (B) is the correct answer. The population of Brazil is 153,771,000 and 3,286,470 square miles.

9. **(B)**   Choice (B) is the correct answer. Some of Central America's chief crops are bananas, coffee, and corn.

10. **(B)**   Choice (B) is the correct answer. Choices (A), (C), and (D) are incorrect because they refer to day-to-day conditions, not an overall condition over a period of time.

VII. ANTHROPOLOGY REVIEW

INTRODUCTION TO ANTHROPOLOGY

WHAT IS ANTHROPOLOGY?

Anthropology is the study of human behavior in all places and at all times. It combines humanistic, scientific, biological, historical, psychological and social views of human behavior. Anthropology is divided into two broad subfields:

Physical Anthropology is the study of the biological, physiological, anatomical and genetic characteristics of both ancient and modern human populations. Physical anthropologists study the evolutionary development of the human species by a comparative analysis of both fossil and living primates. They study the mechanics of evolutionary change through an analysis of genetic variation in human populations.

Cultural Anthropology is the study of learned behavior in human societies. Most cultural anthropologists specialize in one or two geographic areas. They may also specialize in selected aspects of culture (e.g., politics, medicine, religion) in the context of the larger social whole. Cultural anthropology is further subdivided as follows:

1) **Archaeology** is the study of the cultures of prehistoric peoples. It also includes the study of modern societies, but from the evidence of their material remains rather than from direct interviews with or observations of the people under study.

2) **Ethnography** is the systematic description of a human society, usually based on first-hand fieldwork. All generalizations about human behavior are based on the descriptive evidence of ethnography.

3) **Ethnology** is the interpretive explanation of human behavior, based on ethnography.

4) **Social Anthropology** is the study of human groups, with a particular emphasis on social structure (social relations, family dynamics, social control mechanisms, economic exchange).

5) **Linguistics** is the study of how language works as a medium of communication among humans. Language is the vehicle through which all culture is learned and transmitted.

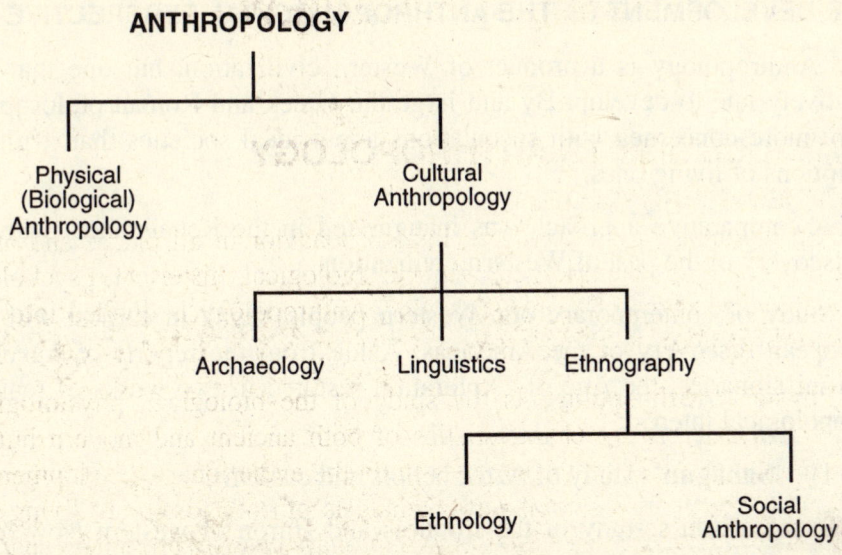

Figure 1 – The Subfields of Anthropology

DEFINING CHARACTERISTICS OF ANTHROPOLOGY

Holism is the belief that the experiences of a human group are unified and patterned. No one aspect of human behavior can be understood in isolation from all the rest.

Culture is the organized sum of everything a people produces, does, and thinks about—all of which they learn as members of a particular social group. A people's culture develops over time as they adapt to their environment.

Comparative Method is the belief that generalizations about human behavior can only be made on the basis of data collected from the widest possible range of cultures, both contemporary and historical.

Relativism is the belief that we cannot make value judgments about a culture based on standards appropriate to another culture. When such judgments are made on the basis of one's own culturally derived values, it is said that we are making **ethnocentric** judgments.

Fieldwork is the study of cultures in their natural settings, the communities in which people live, work, and interact on a regular basis.

Anthropologists attempt to live for an extended period of time among the people they study. They are both **participants** in and **observers** of the culture of the group.

THE DEVELOPMENT OF THE ANTHROPOLOGICAL PERSPECTIVE

Anthropology is a product of Western civilization, but one that was relatively late to develop. By and large the Greek and Roman philosophers were more concerned with speculations about ideal societies than with descriptions of living ones.

A comparative approach was inaugurated in the Renaissance, with the rediscovery of the past of Western civilization.

Study of contemporary non-Western people began in earnest with the European discovery of the Americas. Aside from the reports of travellers and missionaries, the Age of Exploration resulted in two works of real anthropological interest:

1) **Sahagun**'s study of Aztec beliefs and customs.

2) **Lafitau**'s study of the Iroquois and Huron of western New York State.

Scientific anthropology is based on several key assumptions:

1) Cultures evolve through time.

2) Peoples adapted to similar environments in distant parts of the world will establish roughly similar cultures.

3) Human behavior is shaped more by what we learn as members of a social group than by what we inherit genetically. There is no one interpretation or explanation of culture to which anthropologists subscribe. There are, however, several major orientations which guide the explanations of anthropologists.

Evolutionism is the belief that all cultures develop in a uniform and progressive manner. All societies pass through the same stages of development and reach a common end, since the basic problems which all humans have to face are fundamentally similar. This orientation, which is also known as **uni-lineal evolutionism**, flourished in the late nineteenth century. Key figures: Edward B. Tylor and Lewis Henry Morgan.

Diffusionism is the belief that cultures develop not so much by adapting themselves to specific environments as by borrowing traits from other people. This orientation flourished in the early twentieth century. Key figures: G. E. Smith, Fritz Graebner, and Clark Wissler.

Historical Particularism, which was founded on the objection to the evolutionist model, stresses the wide range of cultural variability. It is suspicious of "universal laws" of human development and advocates the study of the particular historical development of specific societies as a necessary prerequisite to the formulation of generalizations about cultural evolution.

This orientation was founded by Franz Boas early in the twentieth century and dominated anthropology in the United States until the 1960s.

Functionalism, which was another reaction to the extremes of evolutionism, is based on the analysis of specific traits of culture and the ways in which they serve the needs of individuals within the society. This orientation is associated with Bronislaw Malinowski who influenced anthropology in Britain from the period of World War I through the 1940s.

Structure-Functionalism, a variant of Malinowski's functionalism, advocated the analysis of specific traits and the ways in which they serve to maintain the equilibrium of the social structure (rather than the needs of the individuals). This point of view is associated with A. R. Radcliffe-Brown, who was a contemporary of Malinowski.

Psychological Anthropology is an attempt to analyze the interaction of cultural and psychological variables in the development of both culture and individual personality. This approach was stimulated by the translation of Freud's work into English in the 1920s. Key figures: Edward Sapir, Margaret Mead, Ruth Benedict, Ralph Linton, Abram Kardiner, and John Whiting.

Neo-evolutionism is the attempt to formulate scientifically testable propositions about cultural evolution, as distinct from the speculative generalizations of the early evolutionists.

Universal Evolutionism (general evolutionism) is the concern with the dynamics of culture as a general phenomenon, rather than with specific change within particular cultures. Key figure: Leslie White (1930s–1950s).

Multilineal Evolutionism (specific evolutionism) is concerned with patterns of interaction of culture and environment. It is sometimes also known as "cultural ecology." Key figure: Julian Steward (1940s–present).

Structuralism is the analysis of culture as represented in expressions such as art, ritual, and the patterns of daily life. These surface representations are reflections of underlying logical structures of the human mind. Key figure: Claude Levi-Strauss (contemporary).

Ethnoscience is the attempt to derive rules of culturally conditioned behavior by a detailed logical analysis of ethnographic data as seen strictly from the natives' point of view. Key figures: Ward Goodenough and Charles Frake (contemporary).

Sociobiology is the belief that human behavior, including social behavior, is basically the product of genetic and environmental influences. Key figures: Napoleon Chagnon and William Irons (contemporary).

THE FAMILY

When anthropologists study the relationships of marriage and family, they use a shorthand notation system whose symbols allow for the quick diagramming of relationships that would otherwise take extensive narrative description. The following symbols are used in kinship diagramming:

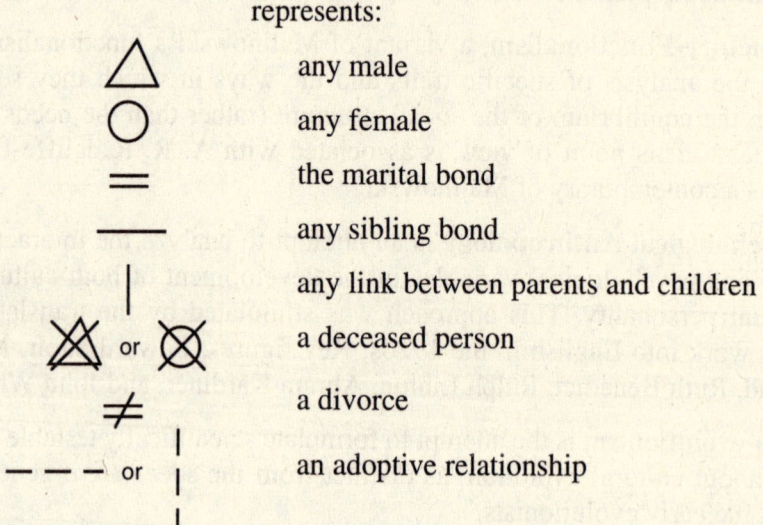

represents:

△	any male
○	any female
=	the marital bond
—	any sibling bond
│	any link between parents and children
⊠ or ⊗	a deceased person
≠	a divorce
– – – or ┊	an adoptive relationship

All kinship diagrams are drawn from the point of view of a single person at a time. This person, whether a male or a female, is known as **Ego**. Ego is usually shaded or marked in some other way to note his or her special place. All relationships on a kinship diagram are read in relation to Ego. For example,

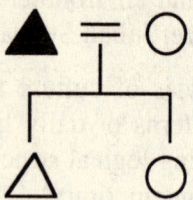

The woman married to Ego is called a "wife" in our kinship system. She is, of course, also a "mother" to the two children shown on the diagram, and she is probably also somebody else's daughter, sister, or aunt. But in terms of this diagram, we identify her relationship to Ego alone.

Marriage establishes the basic unit of family relationship—the nuclear family. The **nuclear family** serves four fundamental functions:

1) to regularize sexual relationships between certain men and women;

2) to bear and nurture new members of the community;

3) to organize and institutionalize a sexual division of labor and to regulate the transfer of property; and

4) to establish the members of the family within a larger network of kin.

Although the role of the family as a social institution has been somewhat de-emphasized in urban, industrial societies, it is still an institution of overwhelming importance.

1) There is no known human society lacking in a family organization.

2) There is no known human society in which the family is not the primary focus of socialization and the model for all later social relationships, no matter how widespread they may become.

Because the family is so basic to every person's social identity, it is the social institution most frequently seen in an ethnocentric light. We must keep in mind that although "the family" is universal, its structure and organization vary widely from culture to culture.

There are two types of nuclear family:

1) That into which a person is born is the **nuclear family of orientation**, in which Ego's statuses are those of child and sibling.

2) That which is established upon marriage is the **nuclear family of procreation**, in which Ego's statuses are those of spouse and parent.

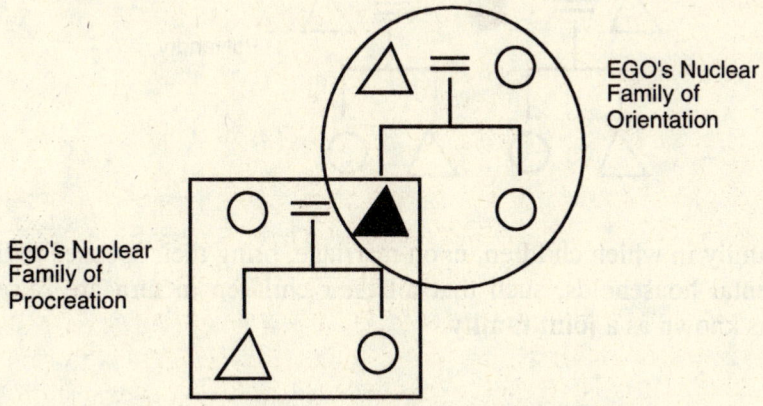

EGO's Nuclear Family of Orientation

Ego's Nuclear Family of Procreation

Our society is quite unusual in its emphasis on the nuclear family. It is much more common for social organization to be based on more extended family groups. One way to extend the family is by extending the marital bond (to create what are called **composite conjugal families**, or **polygamous** unions), which may occur in two ways:

1) **Polygyny**, the simultaneous marriage of one man to two or more women; if the women happen to be sisters, the union is technically called **sororal polygyny**.

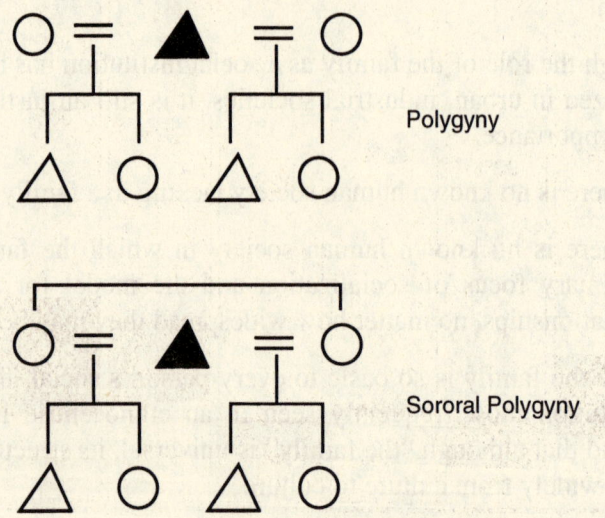

Polygyny

Sororal Polygyny

2) **Polyandry**, the simultaneous marriage of a woman to two or more men; this is a rare pattern, and only occurs when the men in question are brothers.

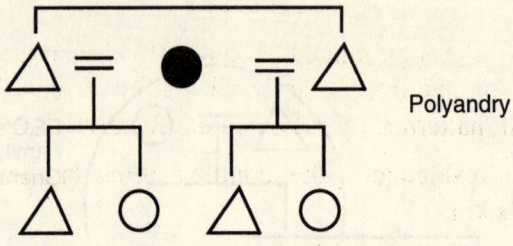

Polyandry

A family in which children, upon marriage, bring their spouses to live in the parental households, such that all their children in turn are raised together, is known as a **joint family**.

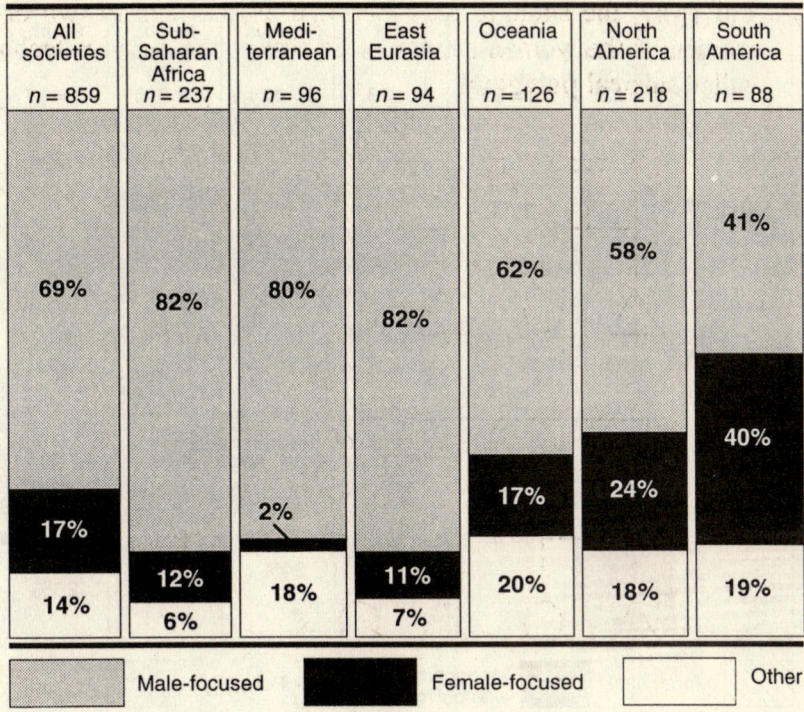

All societies $n = 859$	Sub-Saharan Africa $n = 237$	Medi-terranean $n = 96$	East Eurasia $n = 94$	Oceania $n = 126$	North America $n = 218$	South America $n = 88$
69%	82%	80%	82%	62%	58%	41%
17%		2%		17%	24%	40%
14%	12%	18%	11%	20%	18%	19%
	6%		7%			

Male-focused　　　Female-focused　　　Other

Adapted and reprinted from Hoebel, E. Adamson, and Thomas Weaver *Anthropology and the Human Experience,* 5th ed. (1979), page 430. Reprinted by permission of McGraw-Hill, Inc., New York.

Figure 2 – Relative frequency of male-focused and female-focused residence patterns, according to geographic areas. The male-focused pattern represents viri/patrilocal; the female-focused one, uxori/matrilocal, plus avunculocal.

After marriage, the most important question is where the newly joined couple will live. The decision is rarely allowed to be based on whim. It is, like marriage itself, patterned by rules and expectations:

1) **Virilocal** residence – the couple settles in the vicinity of the husband's kin.

2) **Patrilocal** residence – they settle in the actual household of the husband's father.

3) **Uxorilocal** residence – they settle in the vicinity of the bride's kin.

4) **Matrilocal** residence – they settle in the actual household of the bride's mother.

5) **Ambilocal** residence – they settle in the vicinity of either the husband's or the bride's kin.

6) **Avunculocal** residence – they settle in the household of the groom's mother's brother.

7) **Neolocal** residence – they settle in a new locale, without reference to the location of either family.

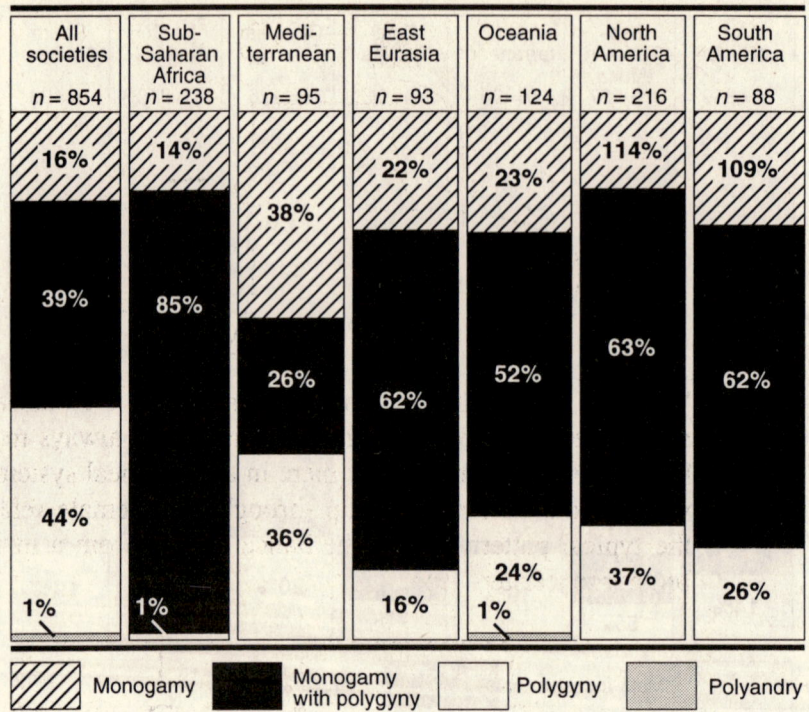

Adapted and reprinted from Hoebel, E. Adamson, and Thomas Weaver *Anthropology and the Human Experience*, 5th ed. (1979), page 431. Reprinted by permission of McGraw-Hill, Inc., New York.

Figure 3 – Relative frequency of monogamy, monogamy with polygyny, polygyny, and polyandry as expected marriage forms, according to geographic area. (Data adapted from E. Bourguignon and L. Greenbaum, *Diversity and Homogeneity*, table 26, p. 48.)

KINSHIP-BASED SOCIAL GROUPS

The family may also be extended through the extension of the lines of descent.

1) A **bilateral** kinship group reckons common descent through both parents (as in our system).

2) A **unilineal** kinship group does so through only one of the parents.

   a) When the line of descent passes through the father, it is known as **patrilineal** descent,

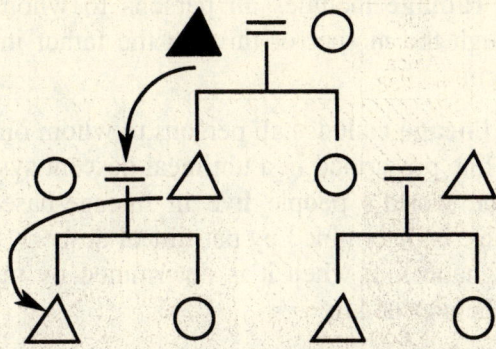

b) When it passes through the mother's line, it is known as **matrilineal** descent; even though it is almost always men inheriting property from other men, in a matrilineal system they will reckon their relationship through their female relations; the typical pattern is for inheritance to pass from a mother's brother to a sister's son.

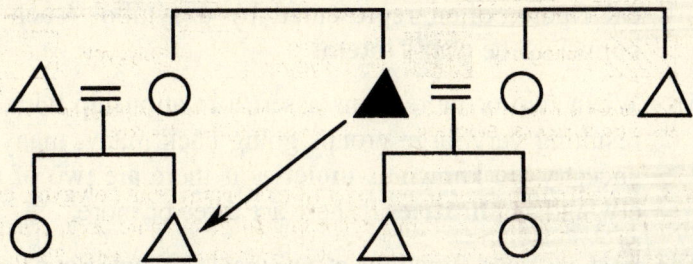

Note that in the preceding diagram, Ego's property passes to his sister's son, not to his own biological son. The latter will, rather, receive property from his mother's brother.

3) An **ambilineal** kinship group reckons common descent through *either* parental line (but not both, as in a bilateral system).

4) A **double descent** kinship group reckons descent from both parents, but for different purposes; for example, a boy might inherit only material property from his father's side, and only magical powers from his mother's side.

These principles of extended descent create several levels of kin organization:

1) The **kindred** includes all persons to whom one traces a bond, either through "blood" (a **consanguineal** relationship) or marriage (an **affinal** relationship); such persons are known as one's **cognates**. The kindred exists only in societies (such as ours) that practice bilateral descent.

2) The **ramage** includes all persons to whom one is related *either* through the mother or through the father in an ambilineal descent system.

3) The **lineage** includes all persons to whom one is related through the one line prescribed in a unilineal descent system. The vast majority of the world's people live in lineage-based societies. When the lineage is determined by patrilineal descent, the relatives are known as agnatic kin; when it is determined by matrilineal descent, they are the uterine kin.

   A lineage is an extended unilineal kinship group descended from a common, *known* ancestor, going back not more than five or six generations.

4) The **clan** is a group formed when two or more lineages assert a relationship with each other; their common ancestor, however, must have existed so far back in time that he or she is no longer known as a person. Therefore, that ancestor figure is replaced by a mythological figure, often represented by a symbol (such as an animal) known as the clan's **totem**.

5) When two or more clans assert a relationship with each other, the resulting very large groups going back many, many generations in ancestry are known as **moieties** if there are two of them in a society, and as **phratries** if there are three or more.

The most common functions of unilineal descent groups are

1) to broaden the base of the kinship group through mutual aid, protection, and support in disputes; and

2) to regulate and control marriage.

Other functions of unilineal descent groups are

1) to act as a governing or legal body, regulating disputes and setting or enforcing standards of behavior;

2) to administer common economic property; and

3) to regularize religious observances.

Kinship groups are determined by culture, not by biology. The kinship group represents the culture's fundamental beliefs about how people should behave toward one another. (Keep in mind that in most traditional societies, everyone one encounters is either a relative, or a stranger to be treated with distrust.) In any given kinship system, certain statuses are singled out as being of unique importance; they are given **descriptive** kinship terms — terms that apply to no other category of relative. For example, in our kinship system, mother, father, brother, sister, son, and daughter are all descriptive kin terms because they describe unique relationships. (We may, of course, have more than one brother or sister, but all of them are people who stand in the same unique "biological" or adoptive relationship to us. We may also use the terms "brother" and "sister" to address members of certain religious orders, or to refer to members of one's political party, but these are metaphoric usages outside the kinship system.) This practice emphasizes the special role of the nuclear family in our society.

1) All other terms, however, are formed by lumping people of various relationships together into a single category, and labelling them with **classificatory** terms. In English, for example, **cousin** is a classificatory term because it lumps people of both sexes, of all generations, and people related either through blood or marriage. Such a term is indicative of the social reality that, for most Americans, relatives outside the nuclear family are remote and do not need to be distinguished by special labels.

2) Kinship terms therefore designate categories of social status and suggest expected behaviors linking persons. It is for this reason that anthropologists have spent a great deal of effort in studying systems of **kinship terminology**.

Kinship terminology systems are based on one or more of the following principles:

1) differences in generational level (e.g., father/son),

2) differences in age level within the same generation (e.g., elder brother/younger brother),

3) differences between lineal (those in the direct line of descent) and collateral (those outside the direct line of descent) relations (e.g., father/uncle),

4) differences in sex of relations (e.g., brother/sister),

5) differences in sex of the speaker (e.g., male Ego's brother/female Ego's brother),

6) differences in sex of the person through whom relationship is established (e.g., father's brother/mother's brother),

7) differences between "blood" relatives and relatives through marriage (e.g., mother/mother-in-law), and

8) differences in status or life condition of the person through whom the relationship is established (e.g., son of a living sister/son of a deceased sister).

Kinship terminology systems based on classification of parental generation:

1) **Lineal system** – distinguishes lineal from collateral relations (our system) [on the following diagrams, letters stand for kin terms; figures with the same letter would be "lumped" into the same social category]:

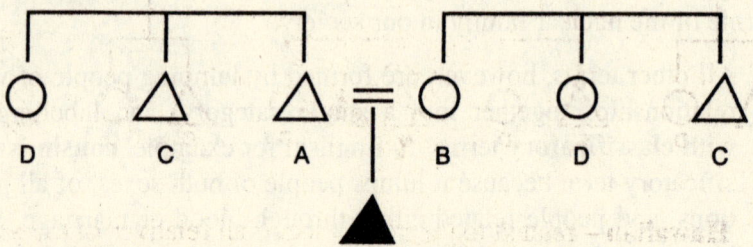

2) **Generational system** – all relatives of the same sex in a given generation are lumped together:

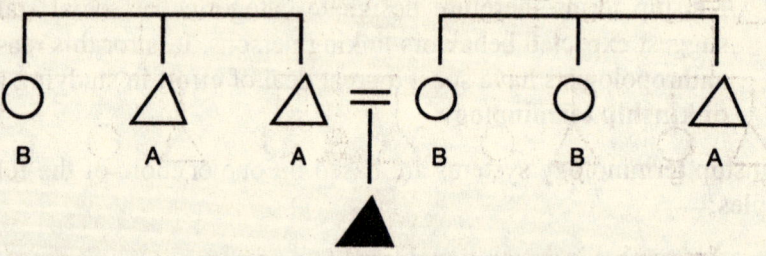

3) **Bifurcate Merging system** – siblings of the same sex are lumped with lineal relatives:

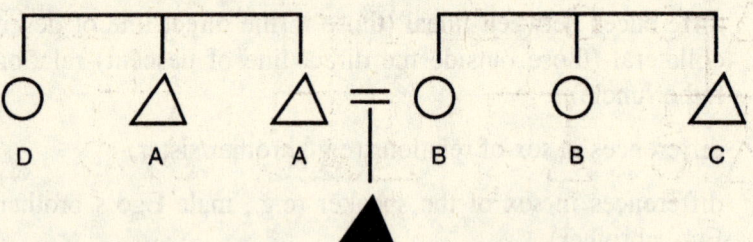

4) **Bifurcate Collateral system** – completely descriptive:

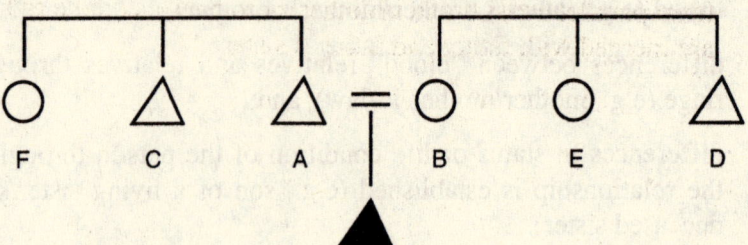

Kinship terminology systems based on classification of cousins:

1) **Eskimo** – related to the lineal; distinguishes lineal from collateral relatives (our system):

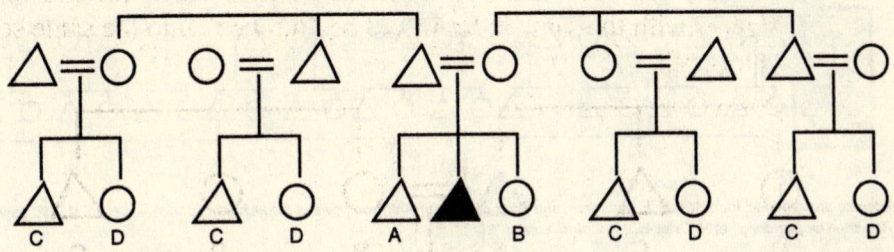

2) **Hawaiian** – related to the generational; all relatives of the same sex are lumped:

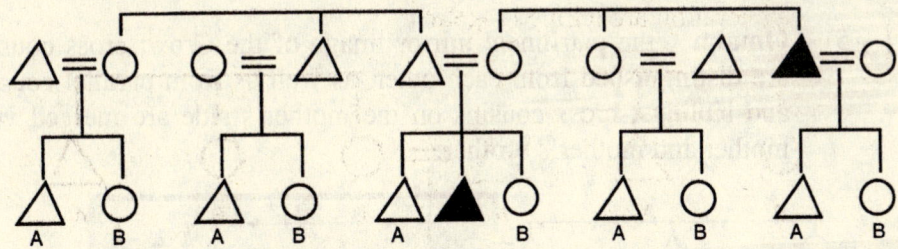

3) **Iroquois** – related to the bifurcate merging; children of siblings of the same sex are merged with lineal relatives;

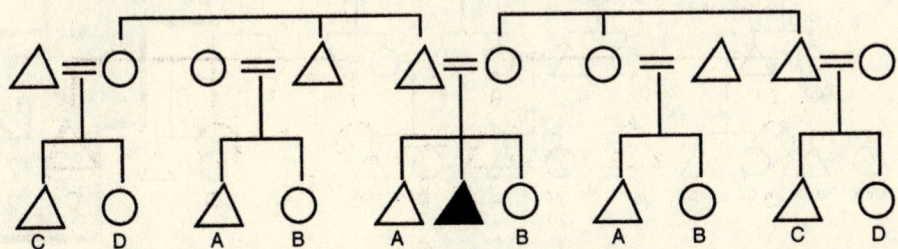

4) **Crow** – found in bifurcate merging systems in matrilineal descent groups; cross cousins are distinguished from each other as well as from parallel cousins and siblings; cross cousins on the father's side are merged with father and father's sister:

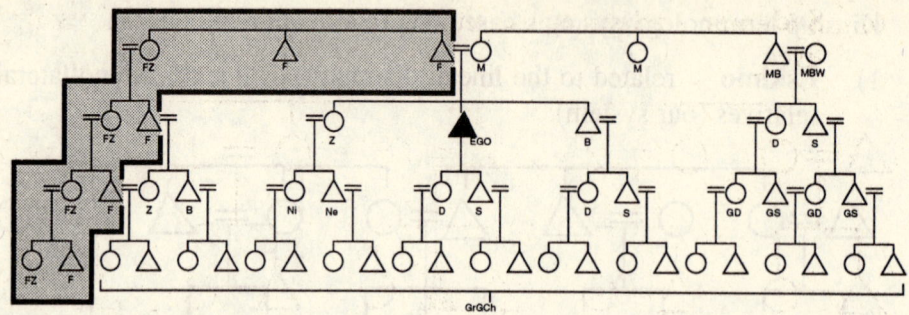

Figure 4 – Crow-type identifications. Note that the male patrilateral cross-cousin may marry ego's mother and is called by the same term as father. The female patrilateral cross-cousin is merged with father's sister. Since ego may marry his maternal uncle's wife, matrilateral cross-cousins are thereby called by the same term as son and daughter.

5) **Omaha** – the patrilineal mirror image of the Crow; cross cousins are distinguished from each other, as well as from parallel cousins and siblings; cross cousins on the mother's side are merged with mother and mother's brother:

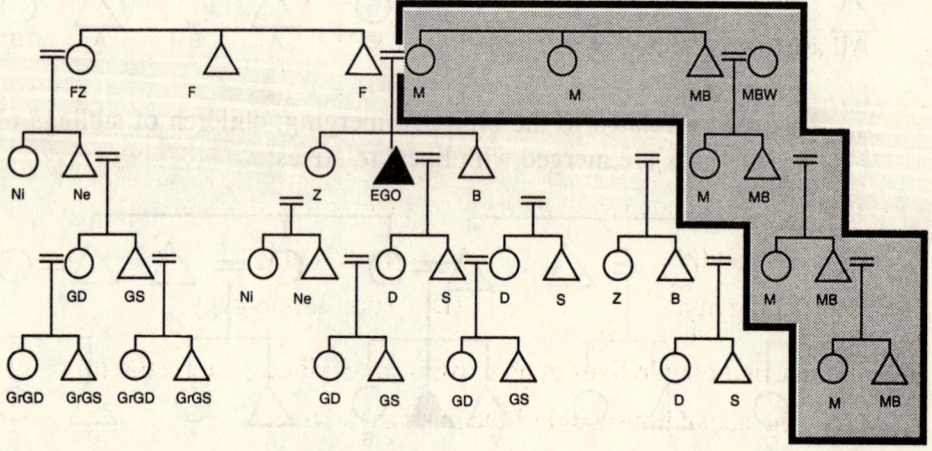

Figure 5 – Omaha-type kinship identifications. The relatives within the boxed area are members of Ego's mother's patrilineage. Females identified as "M" are all classified with "mother" under a term which means "female member of my mother's patrilineage." Note the differentiating terminologies on all generation levels.

6) **Sudanese** – related to the bifurcate collateral; completely descriptive:

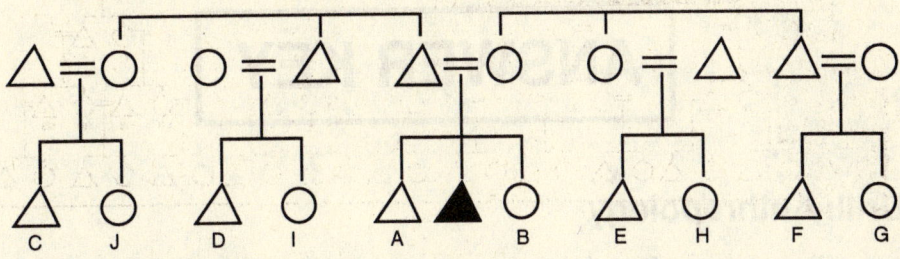

☞ Drill: Anthropology

1. Ethnography is

   (A) the study of the cultures of prehistoric peoples.

   (B) the systematic description of a human society.

   (C) the interpretive explanation of human behavior.

   (D) the study of human groups, with a particular emphasis on social culture.

2. All are key figures of diffusionism EXCEPT

   (A) G. E. Smith.   (C) Clark Wissler.

   (B) Fritz Groebner.   (D) Lewis Henry Morgan.

3. The simultaneous marriage of a woman to two or more men is

   (A) polyandry.   (C) joint family.

   (B) polygyny.   (D) sororal polygyny.

4. If a married couple lives in an uxorilocal residence, they settle in

   (A) the actual household of the husband's father.

   (B) the actual household of the bride's mother.

   (C) the vicinity of the bride's kin.

   (D) the household of the groom's mother's brother.

5. A married couple who settle in a new locale, without reference to the location of either family, live in a

   (A) neolocal residence.   (C) virilocal residence.

   (B) ambilocal residence.   (D) avunculocal residence.

ANTHROPOLOGY REVIEW

ANSWER KEY

Drill: Anthropology

1. (B)   3. (A)   4. (C)   5. (A)
2. (D)

DETAILED EXPLANATIONS OF ANSWERS

Drill: Anthropology

1. **(B)** Choice (B) is the correct answer. Ethnography is the systematic description of a human society, usually based on first-hand fieldwork. All generalizations about human behavior are based on the descriptive evidence of ethnography.

2. **(D)** Choice (D) is the correct answer. Lewis Henry Morgan was not a key figure of diffusionism. He was, however, a key figure of evolutionism.

3. **(A)** Choice (A) is correct. Polyandry is a rare pattern and only occurs when the men in question are brothers.

4. **(C)** Choice (C) is correct. If a married couple lives in an uxorilocal residence, they settle in the vicinity of the bride's family. It does not mean that couple lives with the bride's mother (B).

5. **(A)** Choice (A) is correct. If a couple settles in the vicinity of either the husband's or bride's family, they live in a ambilocal residence (B). If a couple settles in only the vicinity of their husband's family, it is a virilocal residence (C). If a couple lives in the household of the groom's mother's brother, it is an avunculocal residence (D).

VIII. WESTERN AND WORLD CIVILIZATIONS REVIEW

THE ANCIENT AND MEDIEVAL WORLDS

THE APPEARANCE OF CIVILIZATION

Between 6000 and 3000 B.C., humans invented the plow, utilized the wheel, harnessed the wind, discovered how to smelt copper ores, and began to develop accurate solar calendars. Small villages gradually grew into populous cities. The invention of writing in Mesopotamia around 3500 B.C., in combination with heightened refinement in sculpture, architecture, and metal working from about 3000 B.C., marks the beginning of civilization and divides prehistoric from historic times.

MESOPOTAMIA

Sumer (4000 to 2000 B.C.) included the city of Ur. The *Gilgamesh* is an epic Sumerian poem. The Sumerians constructed dikes and reservoirs and established a loose confederation of city-states. They probably invented writing (called "cuneiform" because of its wedge-shaped letters). The Amorites, or Old Babylonians (2000 to 1550 B.C.), established a new capital at Babylon, known for its famous Hanging Gardens. King Hammurabi (reigned 1792–1750 B.C.) promulgated a legal code that called for retributive punishment ("an eye for an eye") and provided that one's social class determined punishment for a crime.

The Assyrians (1100–612 B.C.) conquered Syria, Palestine, and much of Mesopotamia. They controlled a brutal, militaristic empire. The Chaldeans, or New Babylonians (612–538 B.C.), conquered the Assyrian territory, including Jerusalem. In 538 B.C., Cyrus, king of the southern Persians, defeated the Chaldeans. The Persians created a huge empire and constructed a road network. Their religion, Zoroastrianism, promoted worship of a supreme being in the context of a cosmic battle with the forces of evil. After 538 B.C., the peoples of Mesopotamia came under the rule of a series of different empires and dynasties.

EGYPT

During the end of the Archaic Period (5000–2685 B.C.), Menes, or Narmer, unified Upper and Lower Egypt around 3200 B.C. During the Old Kingdom (2685–2180 B.C.), the pharaohs came to be considered living gods. The capital moved to Memphis during the Third Dynasty (ca. 2650 B.C.). The pyramids at Giza were built during the Fourth Dynasty (ca. 2613–2494 B.C.).

After the Hyksos invasion (1785–1560 B.C.), the New Kingdom (1560–1085 B.C.) expanded into Nubia and invaded Palestine and Syria, enslaving the Jews. King Amenhotep IV or Akhenaton (reigned c. 1372–1362 B.C.) promulgated the idea of a single god, Aton, and closed the temples of all other Gods and Goddesses. His successor, Tutankhamen, reestablished pantheism in Egypt.

In the Post-Empire Period (1085–1030 B.C.), Egypt came under the successive control of the Assyrians, the Persians, Alexander the Great, and finally, in 30 B.C., the Roman Empire. The Egyptians developed papyrus and made many medical advances. Other peoples would elaborate their ideas of monotheism and the notion of an afterlife.

PALESTINE AND THE HEBREWS

Phoenicians settled along the present-day coast of Lebanon (Sidon, Tyre, Beirut, Byblos) and established colonies at Carthage and in Spain. They spread Mesopotamian culture through their trade networks.

The Hebrews probably moved to Egypt around 1700 B.C. and were enslaved about 1500 B.C. The Hebrews fled Egypt under Moses and around 1200 B.C. returned to Palestine. Under King David (reigned ca. 1012–972 B.C.), the Philistines were defeated and a capital established at Jerusalem. Ultimately Palestine divided into Israel (10 tribes) and Judah (two tribes). The 10 tribes of Israel—also known as the Lost Tribes—disappeared after Assyria conquered Israel in 722 B.C.

The poor and less attractive state of Judah continued until 586 B.C., when the Chaldeans transported the Jews to Chaldea as advisors and slaves (Babylonian captivity). When the Persians conquered Babylon in 539 B.C., the Jews were allowed to return to Palestine. Alexander the Great conquered Palestine in 325 B.C. During the Hellenistic period (323–63 B.C.) the Jews were allowed to govern themselves. Under Roman rule, Jewish autonomy was restricted. The Jews revolted in 70 B.C. The Jews also revolted in 132–135 A.D. These uprisings led to the Jews' loss of their holy lands. The Romans quashed the revolt and ordered the dispersion of the Jews. The Jews contributed the ideas of monotheism and humankind's convenant and responsibility to God to lead ethical lives.

GREECE

Homer's *Iliad* and *Odyssey* were poems that dramatized for Ancient Greek civilization ideas like excellence (*arete*), courage, honor, and heroism. Hesiod's *Works and Days* summarized everyday life. His *Theogony* recounted Greek myths. Greek religion was based on their writings.

In the Archaic Period (800–500 B.C.), Greek life was organized around the polis (city-state). Oligarchs controlled most of the poleis until the end of the sixth century, when individuals holding absolute power (tyrants) replaced them. By the end of the sixth century, democratic governments replaced many tyrants.

Sparta, however, developed into an armed camp. Sparta seized control of neighboring Messenia around 750 B.C. To prevent rebellions, every Spartan entered lifetime military service (as hoplites) beginning at age 7. Around 640 B.C., Lycurgus promulgated a constitution. Around 540 B.C., Sparta organized the Peloponnesian League.

Athens was the principal city of Attica. Draco (ca. 621 B.C.) first codified Athenian law. His Draconian Code was known for its harshness. Solon (ca. 630–560 B.C.) reformed the laws in 594 B.C. He enfranchised the lower classes and gave the state responsibility for administering justice. Growing indebtedness of small farmers and insufficient land strengthened the nobles. Peisistratus (ca. 605–527 B.C.) seized control and governed as a tyrant. In 527 B.C., Cleisthenes led a reform movement that established the basis of Athens's democratic government, including an annual assembly to identify and exile those considered dangerous to the state.

The Fifth Century (Classical Age)

The fifth century marked the high point of Greek civilization. It opened with the Persian Wars (490; 480–479 B.C.) after which Athens organized the Delian League. Pericles (ca. 495–429 B.C.) used League money to rebuild Athens, including construction of the Parthenon and other Acropolis buildings. Athens's dominance spurred war with Sparta.

The Peloponnesian War between Athens and Sparta (431–404 B.C.) ended with Athens's defeat, but weakened Sparta as well. Sparta fell victim to Thebes, and the other city-states warred amongst themselves until Alexander the Great's conquest. It was his conquest that unified the Greek city-states in fourth century B.C., the beginning of the Hellenistic Age.

A revolution in philosophy occurred in classical Athens. The Sophists emphasized the individual and his/her attainment of excellence through rhetoric, grammar, music, and mathematics. Socrates (ca. 470–399 B.C.) criticized the Sophists' emphasis on rhetoric and emphasized a process of questioning, or dialogues, with his students. Like Socrates, Plato (ca. 428–348 B.C.) emphasized ethics. His *Theory of Ideas or Forms* said that what we see is but a dim shadow of the eternal Forms or Ideas. Philosophy should seek to penetrate to the real nature of things. Plato's *Republic* described an ideal state ruled by a philosopher king.

Aristotle (ca. 384–322 B.C.) was Plato's pupil. He criticized Plato, arguing that ideas or forms did not exist outside of things. He contended that it was necessary to examine four factors in treating any object: its matter, its form, its cause of origin, and its end or purpose.

Greek art emphasized the individual. In architecture, the Greeks developed the Doric and Ionian forms. Euripides (484–406 B.C.) is often considered the most modern tragedian because he was so psychologically minded. In comedy, Aristophanes (ca. 450–388 B.C.) was a pioneer who used political themes. The New Comedy, exemplified by Menander (ca. 342–292 B.C.), concentrated on domestic and individual themes.

The Greeks were the first to develop the study of history. They were skeptical and critical and banished myth from their works. Herodotus (ca. 484–424 B.C.), called the "father of history," wrote *History of the Persian War*. Thucydides (ca. 460–400 B.C.) wrote *History of the Peloponnesian War*.

The Hellenistic Age and Macedonia

The Macedonians were a Greek people who were considered semibarbaric by their southern Greek relatives. They never developed a city-state system and had more territory and people than any of the polis.

In 359 B.C. Philip II (382–336 B.C.) became king. To finance his state and secure a seaport, he conquered several city-states. In 338 B.C., Athens fell. In 336 B.C., Philip was assassinated.

Philip's son, Alexander the Great (356–323 B.C.), killed or exiled rival claimants to his father's throne. He established an empire that included Syria and Persia and extended to the Indus River Valley. At the time of his death, Alexander had established 70 cities and created a vast trading network. With no succession plan, Alexander's realm was divided among three of his generals. By 30 B.C., all of the successor states had fallen to Rome.

ROME

The traditional founding date for Rome is 753 B.C. Between 800 and 500 B.C., Greek tribes colonized southern Italy, bringing their alphabet and religious practices to Roman tribes. In the sixth and seventh centuries, the Etruscans expanded southward and conquered Rome.

Late in the sixth century (the traditional date is 509 B.C.), the Romans expelled the Etruscans and established an aristocratically based republic in place of the monarchy. In the early Republic, power was in the hands of the patricians (wealthy landowners). A Senate composed of patricians governed. The Senate elected two consuls to serve one-year terms. Roman executives had great power (the imperium). They were assisted by two quaestors, who managed economic affairs.

Rome's expansion and contact with Greek culture disrupted the traditional agrarian basis of life. Tiberius Gracchus (163–133 B.C.) and Gaius Gracchus (153–121 B.C.) led the People's party (or *Populares*). They called for land reform and lower grain prices to help small farmers. They were opposed by the *Optimates* (best men). Tiberius was assassinated. Gaius continued his work, assisted by the *Equestrians*. After several years of struggle, Gaius committed suicide.

Power passed into the hands of military leaders for the next 80 years. During the 70s and 60s, Pompey (106–48 B.C.) and Julius Caesar (100–44 B.C.) emerged as the most powerful men. In 73 B.C., Spartacus led a slave rebellion, which General Crassus suppressed.

In 60 B.C., Caesar convinced Pompey and Crassus (ca. 115–53 B.C.) to form the First Triumvirate. When Crassus died, Caesar and Pompey fought for leadership. In 49 B.C., Caesar crossed the Rubicon, the stream separating his province from Italy, and a civil war followed. In 47 B.C., the Senate proclaimed Caesar as dictator, and later named him consul for life. Brutus and Cassius believed that Caesar had destroyed the Republic. They formed a conspiracy, and on March 15, 44 B.C. (the Ides of March), Caesar was assassinated in the Roman Forum. His 18-year-old nephew and adopted son, Octavian, succeeded him. Caesar reformed the tax code and eased burdens on debtors. He instituted the Julian calendar, in use until 1582. The Assembly under Caesar had little power.

In literature and philosophy, Plautus (254–184 B.C.) wrote Greek-style comedy. Terence, a slave (ca. 186–159 B.C.), wrote comedies in the tradition of Menander. Catullus (87–54 B.C.) was the most famous lyric poet. Lucretius's (ca. 94–54 B.C.) *Order of Things* described Epicurean atomic metaphysics, while arguing against the immortality of the soul. Cicero (106–43 B.C.), the great orator and stylist, defended the Stoic concept of natural law. He was an important advocate of the Roman Republic and an opponent of Caesar. His *Orations* described Roman life. Roman religion was family centered and more civic-minded than Greek religion.

The Roman Empire

After a period of struggle, Octavian (63 B.C.–14 A.D.), named as Caesar's heir, gained absolute control while maintaining the appearance of a republic. When he offered to relinquish his power in 27 B.C., the Senate gave him a vote of confidence and a new title, "Augustus." Augustus ruled for 44 years (31 B.C.–14 A.D.) He introduced many reforms, including new coinage, new tax collection, fire and police protection, and land for settlers in the provinces.

Between 27 B.C. and 180 A.D., Rome's greatest cultural achievements occurred under the Pax Romana. The period between 27 B.C. and 14 A.D. is called the **Augustan Age**. Vergil (70–19 B.C.) wrote the *Aeneid,* an account of Rome's rise. Horace (65–8 B.C.) wrote the lyric *Odes.* Ovid (43 B.C.–18 A.D.) published the *Ars Amatoria,* a guide to seduction, and the *Metamorphoses,* about Greek mythology. Livy (57 B.C.–17 A.D.) wrote a narrative history of Rome based on earlier accounts.

The Silver Age lasted from 14–180 A.D. Writings in this period were less optimistic. Seneca (5 B.C. to 65 A.D.) espoused Stoicism in his tragedies and satires. Juvenal (50–127 A.D.) wrote satire, Plutarch's (46–120 A.D.) *Parallel Lives* portrayed Greek and Roman leaders, and Tacitus (55–120 A.D.) criticized the follies of his era in his histories.

Stoicism was the dominant philosophy of the era. Epictetus (ca. 60–120 A.D.), a slave, and Emperor Marcus Aurelius were its chief exponents. In law, Rome made a lasting contribution. It distinguished three orders of law: civil law (*jus civile*), which applied to Rome's citizens, law of the people (*jus gentium*), which merged Roman law with the laws of other peoples of the Empire, and natural law (*jus naturale*), governed by reason.

After the Pax Romana, the third century was a period of great tumult for Rome. Civil war was nearly endemic in the third century. Between 235 and 284 A.D., 26 "barracks emperors" governed, taxing the population heavily to pay for the Empire's defense.

Rome's frontiers were attacked constantly by barbarians. Emperors Diocletian (reigned 285–305 A.D.) and Constantine (reigned 306–337 A.D.) tried to stem Rome's decline. Diocletian divided the Empire into four parts and moved the capital to Nicomedia in Asia Minor. Constantine moved the capital to Constantinople.

Some historians argue that the rise of Christianity was an important factor in Rome's decline. Jesus was born around 4 B.C., and began preaching and ministering to the poor and sick at the age of 30. The Gospels provide the fullest account of his life and teachings. Saul of Tarsus, or Paul (10–67 A.D.), transformed Christianity from a small sect of Jews who believed Jesus was the Messiah into a world religion. Paul won followers through his missionary work. He also shifted the focus from the early followers' belief in Jesus' imminent return to concentrate on personal salvation. His *Epistles* (letters to Christian communities) laid the basis for the religion's organization and sacraments.

The Pax Romana allowed Christians to move freely through the Empire. In the Age of Anxiety, many Romans felt confused and alienated, and thus drawn to the new religion. And unlike other mystery religions, Christianity included women. By the first century, the new religion had spread throughout the Empire.

Around 312 A.D., Emperor Constantine converted to Christianity and ordered toleration in the Edict of Milan (ca. 313 A.D.). In 391 A.D., Emperor Theodosius I (reigned 371–395 A.D.) proclaimed Christianity as the Empire's official religion. By the second century, the church hierarchy had developed. Eventually, the Bishop of Rome came to have preeminence, based on the interpretation that Jesus had chosen Peter as his successor.

THE BYZANTINE EMPIRE

Emperor Theodosius II (reigned 408–450 A.D.) divided his empire between his sons, one ruling the East, the other the West. After the Vandals sacked Rome in 455 A.D., Constantinople was the undisputed leading city of the Empire.

In 527 A.D., Justinian I (483–565 A.D.) became emperor in the East and reigned with his controversial wife Theodora until 565 A.D. The Nika revolt broke out in 532 A.D. and demolished the city. It was crushed by General Belisarius in 537 A.D., after 30,000 had died in the uprising.

The Crusaders further weakened the state. In 1204 A.D., Venice contracted to transport the Crusaders to the Near East in return for the Crusaders capturing and looting Constantinople. The Byzantines were defeated in 1204 A.D. Though they drove out the Crusaders in 1261 A.D., the empire never regained its former power. In 1453 A.D., Constantinople fell to the Ottoman Turks.

ISLAMIC CIVILIZATION IN THE MIDDLE AGES

Mohammed was born about 570 A.D. and received a revelation from the Angel Gabriel around 610 A.D. In 630 A.D., Mohammed marched into Mecca. The Sharia (code of law and theology) outlines five pillars of faith for Muslims to observe. First is the belief that there is one God and that Mohammed is his prophet. The faithful must pray five times a day, perform charitable acts, fast from sunrise to sunset during the holy month of Ramadan, and make a *haj*, or pilgrimage, to Mecca. The Koran, which consists of 114 *suras* (verses), contains Mohammed's teachings. *Mullahs* (teachers) occupy positions of authority, but Islam did not develop a hierarchical system comparable to that of Christianity.

A leadership struggle developed after Mohammed's death. His father-in-law, Abu Bakr (573–634 A.D.), succeeded as caliph (successor to the prophet) and governed for two years, until his death in 634 A.D. Omar succeeded him. Between 634 and 642 A.D., Omar established the Islamic Empire.

The Omayyad caliphs, based in Damascus, governed from 661–750 A.D. They called themselves Shiites and believed they were Mohammed's true successors. (Most Muslims were Sunnites, from *sunna*, oral traditions about the prophet.) They conquered Spain by 730 A.D. and advanced into France until they were stopped by Charles Martel (ca. 688–741 A.D.) in 732 A.D. at Poitiers and Tours. Muslim armies penetrated India and China. They transformed Damascus into a cultural center and were exposed to Hellenistic culture from the nearby Byzantine Empire.

The Abbasid caliphs ruled from 750–1258 A.D. They moved the capital to Baghdad and treated Arab and non-Arab Muslims as equals. Islam assumed a more Persian character under their reign. In the late tenth century, the empire began to disintegrate. In 1055 A.D., the Seljuk Turks captured Baghdad, allowing the Abbasids to rule as figureheads. Genghis Khan (ca. 1162–1227 A.D.) and his army invaded the Abbasids. In 1258 A.D., they seized Baghdad and murdered the last caliph.

FEUDALISM IN JAPAN

Feudalism in Japan began with the arrival of mounted nomadic warriors from throughout Asia during the Kofun Era (300–710). Some members of these nomadic groups formed an elite class and became part of the court aristocracy in the capital city of Kyoto, in western Japan. During the Heian Era (794–1185), a hereditary military aristocracy arose in the Japanese provinces, and by the late Heian Era, many of these formerly nomadic warriors had established themselves as independent land owners, or as managers of landed estates *(shoen)* owned by Kyoto aristocrats. These aristocrats depended on these warriors to defend their *shoen,* and in response to this need, the warriors organized into small groups called *bushidan.*

As the years passed, these warrior clans grew larger, and alliances formed among them, led by imperial descendants who moved from the capital to the provinces. After victory in the Taira-Minamoto War (1180–1105), Minamoto no Yorimoto forced the emperor to award him the title of *shogun,* which is short for "barbarian subduing generalissimo." He used this power to found the Kamakura Shogunate which survived for 148 years. Under the Kamakura Shogunate, many vassals were appointed to the position of *jitro* or land steward, or the position of provincial governors *(shugo)* to act as liasons between the Kamakura government and local vassals.

By the fourteenth century, the *shugo* had augmented their power enough to become a threat to the Kamakura, and in 1333 lead a rebellion that overthrew the shogunate. Under the Ashikaga Shogunate, the office of *shogu* was made hereditary, and its powers were greatly extended. These new *shogu* turned their vassals into aggressive local warriors called *kokujin,* or *jizamurai.* Following this move, the Ashikaga shoguns lost a great deal of their power to political fragmentation, which eventually lead to the Warring States Era (1467–1568).

By the middle of the sixteenth century, the feudal system had evolved considerably. At the center of this highly evolved system was the *daimyo,* a local feudal lord who ruled over one of the many autonomous domains.

Far reaching alliances of *daimyo* were forged under the Tokugawa Shogunate, the final and most unified of the three shogunates. Under the Tokugawa, the *daimyo* were considered direct vassals of the shoguns, and were kept under strict control. The warriors were gradually transformed into scholars and bureaucrats under the *bushido,* or code of chivalry, and the principles of Neo-Confucianism. A merchant class, or *chonin* gained wealth as the samurai class began to lose power, and the feudal system effectively ended when power was returned to the emperor under the Meji Restoration of 1868, when all special privileges of the samurai class were abolished.

CHINESE AND INDIAN EMPIRES

The Harappan or Indus civilization was confined to the Indus basin. Around 1500 B.C., during the so-called Vedic age, India came to be ruled by the Indo-Aryans, a mainly pastoral people with a speech closely related to the major languages of Europe.

The religion of the Harappan peoples revolved around the god Siva, the belief in reincarnation, in a condition of "liberation" beyond the cycle of birth and death, and in the technique of mental concentration which later came to be called *yoga.* The religion of the Indo-Aryans was based on a pantheon of gods of a rather worldly type, and sacrifices were offered to them. The traditional hymns that accompanied them were the Vedas, which form the basic scriptures for the religion of Hinduism. Indian society also came to be based on a *caste* system.

In the third century B.C., the Indian kingdoms fell under the Mauryan Empire. The grandson of the founder of this empire, named Asoka, opened a new era in the cultural history of India by introducing the Buddhist religion. Buddha had disregarded the Vedic gods and the institutions of caste and had preached a relatively simple ethical religion that had two levels of aspiration—a monastic life of renunciation of the world and a high, but not too difficult morality for the layman. The two religions of Hinduism and Buddhism flourished together for centuries in a tolerant rivalry, and in the end Buddhism virtually disappeared from India by the thirteenth century A.D.

Chinese civilization originated in the Yellow River Valley and gradually extended to the southern regions. Three dynasties ruled early China: the Xia or Hsia, the Shang (c. 1500 to 1122 B.C.), and the Zhou (c. 1122 to 211 B.C.). After the Zhous fell, China welcomed the teachings of Confucius, as warfare between states and philosophical speculation created circumstances ripe for such teachings. Confucius made the good order of society depend on an ethical ruler, who should be advised by scholar-moralists like Confucius himself.

In contrast to the Confucians, the Taoists professed a kind of anarchism; the best kind of government was none at all. The wise man did not concern himself with political affairs, but by means of mystical contemplation identified himself with the forces of nature.

SUB-SAHARAN KINGDOMS AND CULTURES

The Nok were a people that lived in the area now known as Nigeria. Artifacts indicate that they were peaceful farmers who built small communities consisting of houses of wattle and daub.

The people referred to as the Ghana lived about 500 miles from what we now call Ghana. The Ghana peoples traded with Berber merchants. The Ghana offered these traders gold from deposits found in the south of their territory. In the 1200s the Mali kingdom conquered Ghana and the civilization mysteriously disappeared.

The people known as the Mali lived in a huge kingdom that lay mostly on the savanna bordering the Sahara Desert. The city of Timbuktu, built in the thirteenth century, was a thriving city of culture where traders visited stone houses, shops, libraries, and mosques.

The Songhai lived near the Niger River and gained their independence from the Mali in the early 1400s. The major growth of the empire came after 1464 A.D. under the leadership of Sunni Ali, who devoted his reign to warfare and expansion of the empire.

The Bantu peoples, numbering about 100,000,000 lived across large sections of Africa. Bantu societies lived in tiny chiefdoms, starting in the third millennium B.C., and each group developed its own version of the original Bantu language.

CIVILIZATIONS OF THE AMERICAS

The great civilizations of early America were agricultural, and foremost of these was the Mayan, in Yucatan, Guatemala, and eastern Honduras.

Mayan history is divided into three parts, the Old Empire, Middle Period, and the New Empire. By the time the Spanish conquerors arrived, most of the Mayan religious centers had been abandoned and their civilization had deteriorated seriously, perhaps due to the wide gulf between the majority of the people, who were peasants, and the priests and nobles.

Farther north, in Mexico, there arose a series of advanced cultures that derived much of their substance from the Maya. Such peoples as the Zapotecs,

Totonacs, Almecs, and Toltecs evolved a high level of civilization. By 500 B.C. agricultural peoples had begun to use a ceremonial calendar and had built stone pyramids on which they performed religious observances.

The Aztecs then took over Mexican culture. A major feature of their culture was human sacrifice in repeated propitiation of their chief god. Aztec government was centralized, with an elective king and a large army. Like their predecessors, the Aztecs were skilled builders and engineers, accomplished astronomers and mathematicians.

Andean civilization was characterized by the evolution of beautifully made pottery, intricate fabrics, and flat-topped mounds called *huacas*.

The Incas, a tribe from the interior of South America who termed themselves "Children of the Sun," controlled an area stretching from Ecuador to central Chile. Sun worshippers, they believed themselves to be the viceregent on earth of the sun god; the Inca were all powerful; every person's place in society was fixed and immutable; the state and the army were supreme. They were at the apex of their power just before the Spanish conquest.

In the southwestern U.S. and northern Mexico, meanwhile, two ancient cultures are noteworthy. The Anasazi, who lived in the plateau region extending through today's northern Arizona and New Mexico, southern Utah and Colorado, developed adobe architecture, worked the land extensively, had a highly developed system of irrigation, and made cloth and baskets. Their time ran approximately from 100 to 1300 A.D. The Hohokam, roughly contemporaneous to the Anasazi, built separate stone and timber houses around central plazas in the desert Southwest.

EUROPE IN ANTIQUITY

Between 486 and 1050 A.D., Europe acquired a distinctive identity. In antiquity, much of Europe was occupied by Germanic tribes.

Nomadic tribes from the central Asian steppes invaded Europe and pushed Germanic tribes into conflict with the Roman Empire. Ultimately, in 410 A.D., the Visigoths sacked Rome, followed by the Vandals in 455 A.D. In 476 A.D., the Ostrogoth king forced the boy emperor Romulus Augustulus to abdicate, ending the empire in the West.

The Frankish Kingdom was the most important medieval Germanic state. Under Clovis I (reigned 481–511 A.D.), the Franks conquered France and the Gauls in 486 A.D. Clovis converted to Christianity and founded the Merovingian dynasty.

Pepin's son, known as Charles the Great or Charlemagne (reigned 768–814 A.D.), founded the Carolingian dynasty. In 800 A.D., Pope Leo III named Charlemagne Emperor of the Holy Roman Empire. In the Treaty of Aix-la-Chapelle (812 A.D.), the Byzantine emperor recognized Charles's authority in the West.

The Holy Roman Empire was intended to reestablish the Roman Empire in the West. Charles vested authority in 200 counts, who were each in charge of a county. Charles's son, Louis the Pious (reigned 814–840 A.D.), succeeded him. On Louis's death, his three sons vied for control of the Empire. The three eventually signed the Treaty of Verdun in 843 A.D. This gave Charles the Western Kingdom (France), Louis the Eastern Kingdom (Germany), and Lothair the Middle Kingdom, a narrow strip of land running from the North Sea to the Mediterranean.

In the ninth and tenth centuries, Europe was threatened by attacks from the Vikings in the north, the Muslims in the south, and the Magyars in the east. Under the leadership of William the Conqueror (reigned 1066–1087), the Normans conquered England in 1066 A.D. (Battle of Hastings).

Rome's collapse had ushered in the decline of cities, a reversion to a barter economy from a money economy, and a fall in agricultural productivity with a shift to subsistence agriculture.

Manorialism and feudalism developed in this period. Manorialism refers to the economic system in which large estates, granted by the king to nobles, strove for self-sufficiency. Large manors might incorporate several villages. The lands surrounding the villages were usually divided into long strips, with common land in-between. Ownership was divided among the lord and his serfs (also called villeins).

Feudalism describes the decentralized political system of personal ties and obligations that bound vassals to their lords. The nature of feudalism varied in different areas and changed over time. But at its base were serfs—peasants who were bound to the land. They worked on the demesne, or lord's property, three or four days a week in return for the right to work their own land. In difficult times, the nobles were supposed to provide for the serfs.

The church was the only institution to survive the Germanic invasions intact. The power of the popes grew in this period. Gregory I (reigned 590–604 A.D.) was the first member of a monastic order to rise to the papacy. He advanced the ideas of penance and purgatory. He centralized church administration and was the first pope to rule as the secular head of Rome. Monasteries preserved the few remnants of antiquity that survived the decline.

THE HIGH MIDDLE AGES (1050–1300)

1050 A.D. marked the beginning of the High Middle Ages. Europe was poised to emerge from five centuries of decline. Between 1000 and 1350 A.D., the population grew from 38 million to 75 million. Agricultural productivity grew, aided by new technologies, such as heavy plows, and a slight temperature rise, which produced a longer growing season. Horses were introduced into agriculture in this period, and the three-field system replaced the two-field system.

Enfranchisement, or freeing of serfs, grew in this period, and many other serfs simply fled their manors for the new lands.

THE HOLY ROMAN EMPIRE

Charlemagne's grandson, Louis the German, became Holy Roman Emperor under the Treaty of Verdun. Under the weak leadership of his descendants, the dukes in Saxony, Franconia, Swabia, Bavaria, and the Lorraine eroded Carolingian power. The last Carolingian died in 911 A.D. The German dukes elected the leader of Franconia to lead the German lands. He was replaced in 919 A.D. by the Saxon dynasty, which ruled until 1024 A.D. Otto became Holy Roman Emperor in 962 A.D. His descendants governed the Empire until 1024 A.D., when the Franconian dynasty assumed power, reigning until 1125 A.D.

When the Franconian line died out in 1125 A.D., the Hohenstaufen family (Conrad III, reigned 1138–1152 A.D.) won power over a contending family. The Hapsburg line gained control of the Empire in 1273 A.D.

The Romans abandoned their last outpost in England in the fourth century. Alfred the Great (ca. 849–899 A.D.) defeated the Danes who had begun invading during the previous century in 878 A.D. In 959 A.D., Edgar the Peacable (reigned 959–975 A.D.) became the first king of all England.

William (reigned 1066–1087 A.D.) stripped the Anglo-Saxon nobility of its privileges and instituted feudalism. He ordered a survey of all property of the realm, which was recorded in the Domesday Book (1086 A.D.).

In 1215 A.D., the English barons forced John I to sign the Magna Carta Libertatum, acknowledging their "ancient" privileges. The Magna Carta established the principle of a limited English monarchy. Henry III reigned from 1216–1272 A.D. In 1272 A.D., Edward I became king. His need for revenue led him to convene a parliament of English nobles, which would act as a check upon royal power.

In 710 A.D., the Muslims conquered Spain from the Visigoths. Under the Muslims, Spain enjoyed a stable, prosperous government. The caliphate of Córdoba became a center of scientific and intellectual activity. Internal dissent caused the collapse of Córdoba and the division of Spain into more than 20 Muslim states in 1031 A.D.

The Reconquista (1085–1340 A.D.), wrested control from the Muslims. Rodrigo Diaz de Bivar, known as El Cid (ca. 1043–1099 A.D.) was the most famous of its knights. The fall of Córdoba in 1234 A.D. completed the Reconquista, except for the small state of Granada.

Most of Russia and Eastern Europe was never under Rome's control, and it was cut off from Western influence by the Germanic invasions. Poland converted to Christianity in the tenth century, and after 1025 A.D. was dependent on the Holy Roman Empire. In the twelfth and thirteenth centuries, powerful nobles divided control of the country.

In Russia, Vladimir I converted to Orthodox Christianity in 988 A.D. He established the basis of Kievian Russia. After 1054 A.D., Russia broke into competing principalities. The Mongols (Tatars) invaded in 1221 A.D., completing their conquest in 1245 A.D., and cutting Russia's contact with the West for almost a century.

The Crusades were an attempt to liberate the Holy Land from infidels. There were seven major crusades between 1096 and 1300 A.D. Urban II called Christians to the First Crusade (1096–1099 A.D.) with the promise of a plenary indulgence (exemption from punishment in purgatory). Younger sons who would not inherit their fathers' lands were also attracted. The Crusades helped to renew interest in the ancient world. But thousands of Jews and Muslims were massacred as a result of the Crusades, and relations between Europe and the Byzantine Empire collapsed.

Charlemagne mandated that bishops open schools at each cathedral, and founded a school in his palace for his court. The expansion of trade and the need for clerks and officials who could read and write spurred an 1179 A.D. requirement that each cathedral set aside enough money to support one teacher.

Scholasticism was an effort to reconcile reason and faith and to instruct Christians on how to make sense of the pagan tradition.

Peter Abelard (ca. 1079–1144 A.D.) was a controversial proponent of Scholasticism. In *Sic et Non* (Yes and No), Abelard collected statements in the Bible and by church leaders that contradicted each other. Abelard believed that reason could resolve the apparent contradictions between the two authorities, but the church judged his views as heretical.

Thomas Aquinas (ca. 1225–1274 A.D.) believed that there were two orders of truth. The lower, reason, could demonstrate propositions such as the existence of God, but on a higher level, some of God's mysteries such as the nature of the Trinity must be accepted on faith. Aquinas viewed the universe as a great chain of being, with humans midway on the chain, between the material and the spiritual.

Latin was the language used in universities. But the most vibrant works were in the vernacular. The *chansons de geste* were long epic poems composed between 1050 and 1150 A.D. Among the most famous are the *Song of Roland,* the *Song of the Nibelungs,* the Icelandic *Eddas,* and *El Cid.*

The fabliaux were short stories, many of which ridiculed the clergy. Boccaccio (1313–1375 A.D.) and Chaucer (ca. 1342–1400 A.D.) belonged to this tradition. The work of Dante (1265–1321 A.D.), the greatest medieval poet, synthesized the pagan and Christian traditions.

In this period, polyphonic (more than one melody at a time) music was introduced. In architecture, Romanesque architecture (rounded arches, thick stone walls, tiny windows) flourished between 1000 and 1150 A.D. After 1150 A.D., Gothic architecture, which emphasized the use of light, came into vogue.

THE RENAISSANCE, REFORMATION, AND THE WARS OF RELIGION (1300–1648)
THE LATE MIDDLE AGES

The Middle Ages fell chronologically between the classical world of Greece and Rome and the modern world. The papacy and monarchs, after exercising much power and influence in the high Middle Ages, were in eclipse after 1300. During the late Middle Ages (1300–1500), all of Europe suffered from the Black Death. While England and France engaged in destructive warfare in northern Europe, in Italy the Renaissance had begun.

Toward the end of the period, monarchs began to assert their power and control. The major struggle, between England and France, was the Hundred Years' War (1337–1453).

The war was fought in France, though the Scots (with French encouragement) invaded northern England. A few major battles occurred—Crécy (1346), Poitiers (1356), Agincourt (1415)—although the fighting consisted largely of sieges and raids. Eventually, the war became one of attrition; the French slowly wore down the English. Technological changes during the war included the use of English longbows and the increasingly expensive plate armor of knights.

Joan of Arc (1412–1431), an illiterate peasant girl who said she heard voices of saints, rallied the French army for several victories. But she was captured by the Burgundians, allies of England, and sold to the English who tried her for heresy (witchcraft). She was burned at the stake at Rouen.

England lost all of its Continental possessions, except Calais. French farmland was devastated, with England and France both expending great sums of money. Population, especially in France, declined. In addition, both countries suffered internal disruption as soldiers plundered and local officials left to fight the war. Trade everywhere was disrupted and England's wool trade with the Low Countries slumped badly. To cover these financial burdens, heavy taxation was inflicted on the peasants.

Because of the war, nationalism grew. Literature also came to express nationalism, as it was written in the language of the people instead of in Latin. Geoffrey Chaucer portrayed a wide spectrum of English life in the *Canterbury Tales*, while François Villon (1431–1463), in his *Grand Testament*, emphasized the ordinary life of the French with humor and emotion.

THE NEW MONARCHS

The defeat of the English in the Hundred Years' War and of the duchy of Burgundy in 1477 removed major military threats. Trade was expanded, fostered by the merchant Jacques Coeur (1395–1456). Louis XI (1461–1483) demonstrated ruthlessness in dealing with his nobility as individuals and collectively in the Estates General.

The marriage of Isabella of Castile (reigned 1474–1504) and Ferdinand of Aragon (reigned 1474–1516) created a united Spain. The Moslems were defeated at Granada in 1492. Navarre was conquered in 1512.

THE BLACK DEATH AND SOCIAL PROBLEMS

The bubonic plague ("Black Death") is a disease affecting the lymph glands. It causes death quickly. Conditions in Europe encouraged the quick spread of disease. There was no urban sanitation, and streets were filled with refuse, excrement, and dead animals. Living conditions were overcrowded, with families often sleeping in one room or one bed. Poor nutrition was rampant. There was little personal cleanliness.

Carried by fleas on rats, the plague was brought from Asia by merchants, and arrived in Europe in 1347. The plague affected all of Europe by 1350 and killed perhaps 25 to 40 percent of the population, with cities suffering more than the countryside.

THE RENAISSANCE (1300–1600)

The Renaissance emphasized new learning, including the rediscovery of much classical material, and new art styles. Italian city-states, such as Venice, Milan, Padua, Pisa, and especially Florence, were the home to many Renaissance developments, which were limited to the rich elite.

LITERATURE, ART, AND SCHOLARSHIP

Humanists, as both orators and poets, were inspired by and imitated works of the classical past. The literature was more secular and wide-ranging than that of the Middle Ages.

Dante (1265–1321) was a Florentine writer whose *Divine Comedy*, describing a journey through hell, purgatory, and heaven, shows that reason can only take people so far and that God's grace and revelation must be used.

Petrarch (1304–1374) encouraged the study of ancient Rome, collected and preserved work of ancient writers, and produced much work in the classical literary style.

Boccaccio (1313–1375) wrote *The Decameron*, a collection of short stories in Italian, which were meant to amuse, not edify, the reader.

Artists also broke with the medieval past, in both technique and content. Renaissance art sometimes used religious topics, but often dealt with secular themes or portraits of individuals. Oil paints, chiaroscuro, and linear perspectives produced works of energy in three dimensions.

Leonardo da Vinci (1452–1519) produced numerous works, including *The Last Supper* and *Mona Lisa*. Raphael (1483–1520), a master of Renaissance grace and style, theory and technique, represented these skills in *The School of Athens*. Michelangelo (1475–1564) produced masterpieces in architecture, sculpture (*David*), and painting (the Sistine Chapel ceiling). His work was a bridge to a new, non-Renaissance style called Mannerism.

Renaissance scholars were more practical and secular than medieval ones. Manuscript collections enabled scholars to study the primary sources and to reject all traditions which had been built up since classical times. Also, scholars participated in the lives of their cities as active politicians.

Leonardo Bruni (1370–1444), a civic humanist, served as chancellor of Florence, where he used his rhetorical skills to rouse the citizens against external enemies.

Machiavelli (1469–1527) wrote *The Prince*, which analyzed politics from the standpoint of expedience. His work, amoral in tone, describes how a political leader could obtain and hold power by acting only in his own self-interest.

THE REFORMATION

The Reformation destroyed Western Europe's religious unity and introduced new ideas about the relationships between God, the individual, and society. Its course was greatly influenced by politics and led, in most areas, to the subjection of the church to the political rulers.

MARTIN LUTHER (1483–1546)

Martin Luther, to his personal distress, could not reconcile the problem of the sinfulness of the individual with the justice of God. How could a sinful person attain the righteousness necessary to obtain salvation? he wondered. During his studies of the Bible, especially of Romans 1:17, Luther came to believe that personal efforts—good works such as a Christian life and attention to the sacraments of the church—could not "earn" the sinner salvation, but that belief and faith were the only way to obtain grace. By 1515 Luther believed that "justification by faith alone" was the road to salvation.

On October 31, 1517, Luther nailed 95 theses, or statements, about indulgences, the cancellation of a sin in return for money, to the door of the Wittenberg church and challenged the practice of selling them. At this time he was seeking to reform the church, not divide it.

In 1519 Luther presented various criticisms of the church and was driven to say that only the Bible, not religious traditions or papal statements, could determine correct religious practices and beliefs. In 1521 Pope Leo X excommunicated Luther for his beliefs.

In 1521 Luther appeared in the city of Worms before a meeting (Diet) of the important figures of the Holy Roman Empire, including the Emperor, Charles V. He was again condemned. At the Diet of Worms Luther made his famous statement about his writings and the basis for them: "Here I stand. I can do no other." After this, Luther could not go back; the break with the pope was permanent.

Frederick III of Saxony, the ruler of the territory in which Luther resided, protected Luther in Wartburg Castle for a year. Frederick never accepted Luther's beliefs but protected him because Luther was his subject. The weak political control of the Holy Roman Emperor contributed to Luther's success in avoiding the pope's and the Emperor's penalties.

OTHER REFORMERS

Anabaptist (derived from a Greek word meaning to baptize again) is a name applied to people who rejected the validity of child baptism and believed that such children had to be rebaptized when they became adults. A prominent leader was Menno Simons (1496-1561).

Anabaptists sought to return to the practices of the early Christian church, which was a voluntary association of believers with no connection to the state. Anabaptists adopted pacifism and avoided involvement with the state whenever possible.

In 1536 John Calvin (1509–1564), a Frenchman, arrived in Geneva, a Swiss city-state which had adopted an anti-Catholic position. He left after his first efforts at reform failed. Upon his return in 1540, Geneva became the center of the Reformation. Calvin's *Institutes of the Christian Religion* (1536), a strictly logical analysis of Christianity, had a universal appeal.

Calvin emphasized the doctrine of predestination (God knew who would obtain salvation before those people were born) and believed that church and state should be united. Calvinism triumphed as the majority religion in Scotland, under the leadership of John Knox (ca. 1514–1572), and in the United Provinces of the Netherlands. Puritans in England and New England also accepted Calvinism.

REFORM IN ENGLAND

England underwent reforms in a pattern different from the rest of Europe. Personal and political decisions by the rulers determined much of the course of the Reformation there, when in 1533 Henry VIII defied the pope and turned to Archbishop Thomas Cranmer to dissolve his marriage to Catherine of Aragon.

Protestant beliefs and practices made little headway during Henry's reign, as he accepted transubstantiation, enforced celibacy among the clergy, and otherwise made the English church conform to most medieval practices.

Under Henry VIII's son, Edward VI (1547–1553), who succeeded to the throne at age 10, the English church adopted Calvinism. Clergy were allowed to marry, communion by the laity expanded, and images were removed from churches. Doctrine included justification by faith, the denial of transubstantiation, and only two sacraments.

Some reformers wanted to purify (hence "Puritans") the church of its remaining Catholic aspects. The resulting church, Protestant in doctrine and practice but retaining most of the physical possessions, such as buildings, and many of the powers, such as church courts, of the medieval church, was called Anglican.

THE COUNTER REFORMATION

The Counter Reformation brought changes to the portion of the Western church which retained its allegiance to the pope.

Ignatius of Loyola (1491–1556), a former soldier, founded the Society of Jesus in 1540 to lead the attack on Protestantism. Jesuits became the leaders of the Counter Reformation.

The Sack of Rome in 1527, when soldiers of the Holy Roman Emperor captured and looted Rome, was seen by many as a judgment of God against the lives of the Renaissance popes. In 1534 Paul III became pope and attacked abuses while reasserting papal leadership.

THE WARS OF RELIGION (1560–1648)

The period from approximately 1560 to 1648 witnessed continuing warfare, primarily between Protestants and Catholics. In the latter half of the sixteenth century, the fighting was along the Atlantic seaboard between Calvinists and Catholics; after 1600 the warfare spread to Germany, where Calvinists, Lutherans, and Catholics fought.

THE CATHOLIC CRUSADE

The territories of Charles V, the Holy Roman Emperor, were divided in 1556 between Ferdinand, Charles's brother, and Philip II (1556–1598), Charles's son. Ferdinand received Austria, Hungary, Bohemia, and the title of Holy Roman Emperor. Philip received Spain, Milan, Naples, the Netherlands, and the New World. It was Philip, not the pope, who led the Catholic attack on Protestants.

Spain dominated the Mediterranean following a series of wars led by Philip's half-brother, Don John, against Moslem (largely Turkish) forces. Don John secured the Mediterranean for Christian merchants with a naval victory over the Turks at Lepanto off the coast of Greece in 1571.

Portugal was annexed by Spain in 1580 following the death of the king without a clear successor. This gave Philip the only other large navy of the day as well as Portuguese territories around the globe.

ENGLAND AND SPAIN

England was ruled by two queens, Mary I (reigned 1553–1558), who married Philip II, and then Elizabeth I (reigned 1558–1603), while three successive kings of France from 1559 to 1589 were influenced by their mother, Catherine de' Medici (1519–1589).

Mary I sought to make England Catholic. She executed many Protestants, earning the name "Bloody Mary" from opponents. Mary married Philip II, king of Spain, and organized her foreign policy around Spanish interests. They had no children.

Elizabeth I, a Protestant, achieved a religious settlement between 1559 and 1563 which left England with a church governed by bishops and practicing Catholic rituals, but maintaining a Calvinist doctrine.

Catholics participated in several rebellions and plots. Mary, Queen of Scots, had fled to England from Scotland in 1568, after alienating the nobles there. In Catholic eyes, she was the legitimate queen of England. Several plots and rebellions to put Mary on the throne led to her execution in 1587. Elizabeth was formally excommunicated by the pope in 1570.

In 1588, as part of his crusade and to stop England from supporting the rebels in the Netherlands, Philip II sent the Armada, a fleet of more than 125 ships, to convey troops from the Netherlands to England as part of a plan to make England Catholic. The Armada was defeated by a combination of superior English naval tactics and a wind which made it impossible for the Spanish to accomplish their goal. A peace treaty between Spain and England was signed in 1604, but England remained an opponent of Spain.

THE THIRTY YEARS' WAR

Calvinism was spreading throughout Germany. The Peace of Augsburg (1555), which settled the disputes between Lutherans and Catholics, had no provision for Calvinists. Lutherans gained more territories through conversions and often took control of previous church-states—a violation of the Peace of Augsburg. A Protestant alliance under the leadership of the Calvinist ruler of the Palatinate opposed a Catholic League led by the ruler of Bavaria. Religious wars were common.

The war brought great destruction to Germany, leading to a decline in population of perhaps one-third, or more, in some areas. Germany remained divided and without a strong government until the nineteenth century.

After 1648, warfare, though often containing religious elements, would not be executed primarily for religious goals.

The Catholic crusade to reunite Europe failed, largely due to the efforts of the Calvinists. The religious distribution of Europe has not changed significantly since 1648.

Nobles, resisting the increasing power of the state, usually dominated the struggle. France, then Germany, fell apart due to the wars. France was reunited in the seventeenth century. Spain began a decline which ended its role as a great power of Europe.

THE GROWTH OF THE STATE AND THE AGE OF EXPLORATION

In the seventeenth century the political systems of the countries of Europe began dividing into two types, absolutist and constitutionalist. England, the United Provinces, and Sweden moved towards constitutionalism, while France was adopting absolutist ideas.

Overseas exploration, begun in the fifteenth century, expanded. Governments supported such activity in order to gain wealth and to preempt other countries.

ENGLAND

The English church was a compromise of Catholic practices and Protestant beliefs and was criticized by both groups. The monarchs, after 1620, gave leadership of the church to men with Arminian beliefs, a modified Calvinist creed that de-emphasized predestination.

Opponents to this shift in belief were called Puritans, a term that covered a wide range of beliefs and people. To escape the church in England, many Puritans began moving to the New World, especially Massachusetts.

In financial matters, inflation and Elizabeth's wars left the government short of money. Contemporaries blamed the shortage on the extravagance of the courts of James I and Charles I. The monarchs lacked any substantial source of income and had to obtain the consent of a Parliament to levy a tax.

Parliament met only when the monarch summoned it. Though Parliaments had existed since the Middle Ages, there were long periods of time between parliamentary meetings. Parliaments consisted of nobles and gentry, and a few merchants and lawyers. The men in a Parliament usually wanted the government to remedy grievances as part of the agreement to a tax.

Charles I inherited both the English and Scottish thrones at the death of his father, James I. He claimed a "divine right" theory of absolute authority for himself as king and sought to rule without Parliament. That rule also meant control of the Church of England.

Charles stumbled into wars with both Spain and France during the late 1620s. A series of efforts to raise money for the wars led to confrontations with his opponents in Parliament. A "forced loan" was collected from taxpayers with the promise it would be repaid when a tax was voted by a Parliament. Soldiers were billeted in subjects' houses during the wars. In 1628 Parliament passed the Petition of Right, which declared royal actions involving loans and billeting illegal. Charles ruled without calling a Parliament during the 1630s.

In August 1642 Charles abandoned all hope of negotiating with his opponents and instead declared war against them. Charles's supporters were called Royalists or Cavaliers. His opponents were called Parliamentarians or Roundheads, due to many who wore their hair cut short. This struggle is called the Puritan Revolution, the English Civil War, or the Great Rebellion.

Charles was defeated. His opponents had allied with the Scots who still had an army in England. Additionally, the New Model Army, with its general, Oliver Cromwell (1599–1658), was superior to Charles's army, and became a cauldron of radical ideas.

FRANCE

The regions of France had long had a large measure of independence, and local parliaments could refuse to enforce royal laws. The centralization of all government proceeded by replacing local authorities with intendants, civil servants who reported to the king.

Henry IV relied on the Duke of Sully (1560–1641), the first of a series of strong ministers in the seventeenth century. Sully and Henry increased the involvement of the state in the economy, acting on a theory known as mercantilism.

Louis XIII reigned from 1610 to 1643, but Cardinal Richelieu became the real power in France. The unique status of the Huguenots was reduced through warfare and the Peace of Alais (1629), when their separate armed cities were eliminated. The nobility was reduced in power through constant attention to the laws and the imprisonment of offenders.

Cardinal Mazarin governed while Louis XIV (reigned 1643–1715) was a minor. During the Fronde, from 1649 to 1652, the nobility controlled Paris, drove Louis XIV and Mazarin from the city, and attempted to run the government. Noble ineffectiveness, the memories of the chaos of the wars of religion, and the overall anarchy convinced most people that a strong king was preferable to a warring nobility.

Louis XIV saw the need to increase royal power and his own glory and dedicated his life to these goals. He steadily pursued a policy of "one king, one law, one faith."

EXPLORATIONS AND CONQUESTS

Portugal. Prince Henry the Navigator (1394–1460) supported exploration of the African coastline, largely in order to seek gold. Bartholomew Dias (1450–1500) rounded the southern tip of Africa in 1487. Vasco de Gama (1460–1524) reached India in 1498 and, after some fighting, soon established trading ports at Goa and Calicut. Albuquerque (1453–1515) helped establish an empire in the Spice Islands after 1510.

Spain. Christopher Columbus (1451–1506), seeking a new route to the (East) Indies, "discovered" the Americas in 1492. Ferdinand Magellan (1480–1521) circumnavigated the globe in 1521–1522. Conquests of the Aztecs by Hernando Cortes (1485–1547), and the Incas by Francisco Pizarro (ca. 1476–1541), enabled the Spanish to send much gold and silver back to Spain.

Other Countries. In the 1490s the Cabots, John (1450–1498) and Sebastian (ca. 1483–1557), explored North America, and after 1570, various Englishmen, including Francis Drake (ca. 1540–1596), fought the Spanish around the world. Jacques Cartier (1491–1557) explored parts of North America for France in 1534.

Samuel de Champlain (1567–1635) and the French explored the St. Lawrence River, seeking furs to trade. The Dutch established settlements at New Amsterdam and in the Hudson River Valley. The Dutch founded trading centers in the East Indies, the West Indies, and southern Africa. Swedes settled on the Delaware River in 1638.

BOURBON, BAROQUE, AND THE ENLIGHTENMENT

Through the Treaty of Paris (1763), France lost all possessions in North America to Britain. (In 1762 France had ceded to Spain all French claims west of the Mississippi River and New Orleans.)

France entered the French-American Alliance of 1778 in an effort to regain lost prestige in Europe and to weaken her British adversary. In 1779 Spain joined France in the war, hoping to recover Gibraltar and the Floridas.

With the Treaty of Paris (1783) Britain recognized the independence of the United States of America and retroceded the Floridas to Spain. Britain left France no territorial gains by signing a separate and territorially generous treaty with the United States.

ECONOMIC DEVELOPMENTS

There were several basic assumptions of mercantilism: 1) Wealth is measured in terms of commodities, especially gold and silver, rather than in terms of productivity and income-producing investments; 2) Economic activities should increase the power of the national government in the direction of state controls; 3) Since a favorable balance of trade was important, a nation should purchase as little as possible from nations regarded as enemies. The concept of the mutual advantage of trade was not widely accepted; 4) Colonies existed for the benefit of the mother country, not for any mutual benefit that would be gained by economic development.

Absentee landlords and commercial farms replaced feudal manors, especially in England. Urbanization, increased population, and improvements in trade stimulated the demand for agricultural products.

The steam engine, developed by James Watt between 1765 and 1769, became one of the most significant inventions in human history. It was no longer necessary to locate factories on mountain streams where water wheels were used to supply power. Its portability meant that both steamboats and railroad engines could be built to transport goods across continents. Ocean-going vessels were no longer dependent on winds to power them. At the same time, textile machines revolutionized that industry.

BOURBON FRANCE

Louis XIV (reigned 1643–1715) believed in absolute, unquestioned authority. Louis XIV deliberately chose his chief ministers from the middle class in order to keep the aristocracy out of government.

Council orders were transmitted to the provinces by intendants, who supervised all phases of local administration (especially courts, police, and the collection of taxes).

Louis XIV never called the Estates General. His intendants arrested the members of the three provincial estates who criticized royal policy, and the *parlements* were too intimidated by the lack of success of the *Frondes* to offer further resistance.

Control of the peasants, who comprised 95 percent of the French population, was accomplished by numerous means. Some peasants kept as little as 20 percent of their cash crops after paying the landlord, the government, and the Church. Peasants also were subject to the *corvée*, a month's forced labor on the roads. People not at work on the farm were conscripted into the French army or put into workhouses. Finally, rebels were hanged or forced to work as galley slaves.

Under Louis XV (reigned 1715–1774) French people of all classes desired greater popular participation in government and resented the special privileges of the aristocracy. All nobles were exempt from certain taxes. Many were subsidized with regular pensions from the government. The highest offices of government were reserved for aristocrats. Promotions were based on political connections rather than merit.

There was no uniform code of laws and little justice. The king had arbitrary powers of imprisonment. Government bureaucrats were often petty tyrants, many of them merely serving their own interests. The bureaucracy became virtually a closed class. Vestiges of the feudal and manorial systems taxed peasants excessively compared to other segments of society. The *philosophes* gave expression to these grievances and discontent grew.

Louis XVI (reigned 1774–1792) married Marie Antoinette (1770), daughter of the Austrian Empress Maria Theresa. Louis XVI was honest, conscientious, and sought genuine reforms, but he was indecisive and lacking in determination. One of his first acts was to restore judicial powers to the French parlements. When he sought to impose new taxes on the undertaxed aristocracy, the parlements refused to register the royal decrees. In 1787 he granted toleration and civil rights to French Huguenots (Protestants).

In 1787 the king summoned the Assembly of the Notables, a group of 144 representatives of the nobility and higher clergy. Louis XVI asked them to tax all lands, without regard to privilege of family; to establish provincial assemblies; to allow free trade in grain; and to abolish forced labor on the roads. The Notables refused to accept these reforms and demanded the replacement of certain of the king's ministers.

The climax of the crisis came in 1788 when the king was no longer able to achieve either fiscal reform or new loans. He could not even pay the salaries of government officials. By this time one-half of government revenues went to pay interest on the national debt.

For the first time in 175 years, the king called for a meeting of the Estates General (1789). The Estates General formed itself into the National Assembly, and the French Revolution was under way.

ENGLAND, SCOTLAND, AND IRELAND

One of the underlying issues in this conflict was the constitutional issue of the relationship between the king and Parliament. In short, the question was whether England was to have a limited constitutional monarchy, or an absolute monarchy as in France and Prussia.

The theological issue focused on the form of church government England was to have. The episcopal form meant that the king, the Archbishop of Canterbury, and the bishops of the church would determine policy, theology, and the form of worship and service in the presbyterian form. Each congregation would have a voice in the life of the church, and a regional group of ministers, or "presbytery," would attempt to ensure "doctrinal purity."

The political implications for representative democracy were present in both issues. That is why most Presbyterians, Puritans, and Congregationalists sided with Parliament and most Anglicans and Catholics sided with the king.

The Parliament in effect bribed the king by granting him a tax grant in exchange for his agreement to the Petition of Right in 1628. It stipulated that no one should pay any tax, gift, loan, or contribution except as provided by an act of Parliament; no one should be imprisoned or detained without due process of law; all were to have the right to the writ of *habeas corpus;* there should be no forced billeting of soldiers in the homes of private citizens; and martial law was not to be declared in England.

In 1629 Charles I dissolved Parliament—for 11 years. Puritan leaders and leaders of the opposition in the House of Commons were imprisoned by the king, some for several years.

The established Church of England was the only legal church under Charles I, a Catholic. Archbishop of Canterbury William Laud (1573–1645) sought to enforce the king's policies vigorously. Arminian clergymen were to be tolerated, but Puritan clergymen silenced. Criticism was brutally suppressed. Several dissenters were executed.

The king, however, had no money, no army, and no popular support. He summoned the Parliament to meet in November 1640. With mobs in the street and rumors of an army enroute to London to dissolve Parliament, a bare majority of an underattended House of Commons passed a bill of attainder to execute the Earl of Strafford, one of the king's principal ministers. Fearing mob violence as well as Parliament itself, the king signed the bill and Strafford was executed in 1641. Archbishop William Laud was also arrested and eventually tried and executed in 1645.

The House of Commons passed a series of laws to strengthen its position and protect civil and religious rights. The Triennial Act (1641) provided that no more than three years should pass between Parliaments. Another act provided that the current Parliament should not be dissolved without its own consent. Various hated laws, taxes, and institutions were abolished: the Star Chamber, the High Commission, and power of the Privy Council to deal with property rights.

Men began identifying themselves as Cavaliers if they supported the king, or Roundheads if they supported Parliament.

The king withdrew to Hampton Court and sent the queen to France for safety. In March 1642 Charles II went to York, and the English Civil War began. Charles put together a sizeable force with a strong cavalry and moved on London, winning several skirmishes.

Oliver Cromwell (1599–1658) led the parliamentary troops to victory, first with his cavalry, which eventually numbered 1,100, and then as lieutenant general in command of the well-disciplined and well-trained New Model Army. He eventually forced the king to flee.

During the Civil War, under the authority of Parliament, the Westminster Assembly convened to write a statement of faith for the Church of England that was Reformed or Presbyterian in content. Ministers and laymen from both England and Scotland participated for six years and wrote the *Westminster Confession of Faith*, still a vital part of Presbyterian theology.

The army tried Charles Stuart, formerly king of England, and sentenced him to death for treason. After the execution of the king, Parliament abolished the office of king and the House of Lords. The new form of government was to be a Commonwealth, or Free State, governed by the representatives of the people in Parliament. This commonwealth lasted four years, between 1649 and 1653.

Royalists and Presbyterians both opposed Parliament for its lack of broad representation and for regicide. The army was greatly dissatisfied that elections were not held, as one of the promises of the Civil War was popular representation. Surrounded by foreign enemies, the Commonwealth became a military state with a standing army of 44,000. The North American and West Indian colonies were forced to accept the government of the Commonwealth.

When it became clear that Parliament intended to stay in office permanently, Cromwell agreed to serve as Lord Protector from 1653–1659, with a Council of State and a Parliament. The new government permitted religious liberty, except for Catholics and Anglicans.

The new Parliament restored the monarchy from 1660–1688, but the Puritan Revolution clearly showed that the English constitutional system required a limited monarchy. Parliament in 1660 was in a far stronger position in its relationship to the king than it ever had been before.

Two events in 1688 goaded Parliament to action. In May, James reissued the Declaration of Indulgence with the command that it be read on two successive Sundays in every parish church. On June 10, 1688, a son was born to the king and his queen, Mary of Modena. As long as James was childless by his second wife, the throne would go to one of his Protestant daughters, Mary or Anne. The birth of a son, who would be raised Roman Catholic, changed the picture completely.

A group of Whig and Tory leaders, speaking for both houses of Parliament, invited William and Mary to assume the throne of England.

On November 5, 1688, William and his army landed at Torbay in Devon. King James offered many concessions, but it was too late. He finally fled to France. William assumed temporary control of the government and summoned a free Parliament. In February 1689 William and Mary were declared joint sovereigns, with the administration given to William.

The English Declaration of Rights (1689) declared the following:

1) The king could not be a Roman Catholic.

2) A standing army in time of peace was illegal without Parliamentary approval.

3) Taxation was illegal without Parliamentary consent.

4) Excessive bail and cruel and unusual punishments were prohibited.

5) Right to trial by jury was guaranteed.

6) Free elections to Parliament would be held.

The Toleration Act (1689) granted the right of public worship to Protestant Nonconformists, but did not permit them to hold office. The Act did not extend liberty to Catholics or Unitarians, but normally they were left alone. The Trials for Treason Act (1696) stated that a person accused of treason should be shown the accusations against him and should have the advice of counsel. They also could not be convicted except upon the testimony of two independent witnesses. Freedom of the press was permitted, but with very strict libel laws.

Control of finances was to be in the hands of the Commons, including military appropriations. There would no longer be uncontrolled grants to the king. Judges were made independent of the Crown. Thus, England declared itself a limited monarchy and a Protestant nation.

RUSSIA UNDER THE MUSCOVITES AND THE ROMANOVS

In 1480, Ivan III (1440–1505), "Ivan the Great," put an end to Mongol domination over Russia. Ivan took the title of Caesar (Tsar) as heir of the Eastern Roman Empire (Byzantine Empire). He encouraged the Eastern Orthodox Church and called Moscow the "Third Rome."

Ivan IV (1530–1584), "Ivan the Terrible," grandson of Ivan III, began westernizing Russia. A contemporary of Queen Elizabeth, he welcomed both the English and Dutch and opened new trade routes to Moscow and the Caspian Sea. English merchant adventurers opened Archangel on the White Sea and provided a link with the outer world free from Polish domination.

After a "Time of Troubles" following Ivan's death in 1584, stability returned to Russia in 1613 when the Zemsky Sobor (Estates General representing the Russian Orthodox church, landed gentry, townspeople, and a few peasants) elected Michael Romanov, who ruled as tsar from 1613 to 1645.

Under Michael Romanov, Russia extended its empire to the Pacific. Romanov continued westernization. By the end of the seventeenth century, 20,000 Europeans lived in Russia, developing trade and manufacturing, practicing medicine, and smoking tobacco, while Russians began trimming their beards and wearing western clothing.

In 1649 three monks were appointed to translate the Bible for the first time into Russian. The Raskolniki (Old Believers) refused to accept any Western innovations or liturgy in the Russian Orthodox church and were severely persecuted as a result.

Peter I (reigned 1682–1725) was one of the most extraordinary people in Russian history. The driving ambitions of Peter the Great's life were to modernize Russia and to compete with the great powers of Europe on equal terms. By the end of Peter's reign, Russia produced more iron than England.

Peter built up the army through conscription and a 25–year term of enlistment. He gave flintlocks and bayonets to his troops instead of the old muskets and pikes. Artillery was improved and discipline enforced. By the end of his reign, Russia had a standing army of 210,000, despite a population of only 13 million. The tsar ruled by decree (*ukase*). Government officials and nobles acted under government authority, but there was no representative body.

All landowners owed lifetime service to the state, either in the army, the civil service, or at court. In return for government service, they received land and serfs to work their fields. Conscription required each village to send recruits for the Russian army. By 1709 Russia manufactured most of its own weapons and had an effective artillery.

After a series of largely ineffective rulers, Catherine II "the Great," (reigned 1762–1796) continued the westernization process begun by Peter the Great. The three partitions of Poland, in 1772, 1793, and 1795 respectively, occurred under Catherine II's rule. Russia also annexed the Crimea and warred with Turkey during her reign.

ITALY AND THE PAPACY

Italy in the seventeenth and eighteenth centuries remained merely a geographic expression divided into small kingdoms, most of which were under foreign domination. Unification of Italy into a national state did not occur until the mid-nineteenth century.

THE SCIENTIFIC REVOLUTION AND SCIENTIFIC SOCIETIES

Science and religion were not in conflict in the seventeenth and eighteenth centuries. Scientists universally believed they were studying and analyzing God's creation, not an autonomous phenomenon known as "Nature." There was no attempt, as in the nineteenth and twentieth centuries, to secularize science.

For the first time in human history, the eighteenth century saw the appearance of a secular worldview. This became known as the age of the Enlightenment. In the past, some kind of a religious perspective had always been central to Western civilization. The philosophical starting point for the Enlightenment was the belief in the autonomy of man's intellect apart from God. The most basic assumption was faith in reason rather than faith in revelation.

The Enlightenment believed in the existence of God as a rational explanation of the universe and its form; "God" was a deistic Creator who made the universe and then was no longer involved in its mechanistic operation.

That mechanistic operation was governed by "natural law."

Rationalists stressed deductive reasoning or mathematical logic as the basis for their epistemology (source of knowledge). They started with "self-evident truths," or postulates, from which they constructed a coherent and logical system of thought.

René Descartes (1596–1650) sought a basis for logic and thought he found it in man's ability to think. "I think; therefore, I am" was his most famous statement.

Benedict de Spinoza (1632–1677) developed a rational pantheism in which he equated God and nature. He denied all free will and ended up with an impersonal, mechanical universe.

Gottfried Wilhelm Leibniz (1646–1716) worked on symbolic logic and calculus, and invented a calculating machine. He, too, had a mechanistic world- and life- view and thought of God as a hypothetical abstraction rather than a persona.

Empiricists stressed inductive observation—the "scientific method"—as the basis for their epistemology.

John Locke (1632–1704) pioneered in the empiricist approach to knowledge and stressed the importance of environment in human development. He classified knowledge as 1) according to reason, 2) contrary to reason or, 3) above reason. Locke thought reason and revelation were both complementary and from God.

David Hume (1711–1776) was a Scottish historian and philosopher who began by emphasizing the limitations of human reasoning and later became a dogmatic skeptic.

The Enlightenment believed in a closed system of the universe in which the supernatural was not involved in human life, in contrast to the traditional view of an open system in which God, angels, and devils were very much a part of human life on earth.

The "Counter-Enlightenment" is a comprehensive term encompassing diverse and disparate groups who disagreed with the fundamental assumptions of the Enlightenment and pointed out its weaknesses.

Roman Catholic Jansenism in France argued against the idea of an uninvolved or impersonal God. Hasidism in Eastern European Jewish communities, especially in the 1730s, stressed a joyous religious fervor in direct communion with God.

CULTURE OF THE BAROQUE AND ROCOCO

The Baroque emphasized grandeur, spaciousness, unity, and emotional impact. The splendor of Versailles typifies the baroque in architecture; gigantic frescoes unified around the emotional impact of a single theme is Baroque art; the glory of Bach's *Christmas Oratorio* expresses the baroque in music. Although the Baroque began in Catholic Counter-Reformation countries to teach in a concrete, emotional way, it soon spread to Protestant nations as well, and some of the greatest Baroque artists and composers were Protestant (e.g., Johann Sebastian Bach and George Frideric Handel).

Characteristics of the Rococo can be found in the compositions of both Franz Josef Haydn (1732–1809) and Wolfgang Amadeus Mozart (1756–1791).

REVOLUTION AND THE NEW WORLD ORDER (1789–1848)

THE FRENCH REVOLUTION I (1789–1799)

Radical ideas about society and government were developed during the eighteenth century in response to the success of the "scientific" and "intellectual" revolutions of the preceding two centuries. Armed with new scientific knowledge of the physical universe, as well as new views of the human capacity to detect "truth," social critics assailed existing modes of thought governing political, social, religious, and economic life. Ten years of upheaval in France (1789–1799) further shaped modern ideas and practices.

Napoleon Bonaparte spread some of the revolutionary ideas about the administration of government as he conquered much of Europe. The modern world that came of age in the eighteenth century was characterized by rapid, revolutionary changes which paved the way for economic modernization and political centralization throughout Europe.

Influence of the Enlightenment (c. 1700–1800)

While they came from virtually every country in Europe, most of the famous social activists were French, and France was the center of this intellectual revolution. Voltaire, Denis Diderot, Baron de Montesquieu, and Jean Jacques Rousseau were among the more famous philosophers.

The major assumptions of the Enlightenment were as follows:

Human progress was possible through changes in one's environment; in other words: better people, better societies, better standard of living.

Humans were free to use reason to reform the evils of society.

Material improvement would lead to moral improvement.

Natural science and human reason would discover the meaning of life.

Laws governing human society would be discovered through application of the scientific method of inquiry.

Inhuman practices and institutions would be removed from society in a spirit of humanitarianism.

Human liberty would ensue if individuals became free to choose what reason dictated was good.

The Enlightenment's Effect on Society:

Religion. Deism or "natural religion" rejected traditional Christianity by promoting an impersonal God who did not interfere in the daily lives of the people. The continued discussion of the role of God led to a general skepticism associated with Pierre Bayle (1647–1706), a type of religious skepticism pronounced by David Hume (1711–1776), and a theory of atheism or materialism advocated by Baron d'Holbach (1723–1789).

Political Theory. John Locke (1632–1704) and Jean Jacques Rousseau (1712–1778) believed that people were capable of governing themselves, either through a political (Locke) or social (Rousseau) contract forming the basis of society. However, most philosophes opposed democracy, preferring a limited monarchy that shared power with the nobility.

Economic Theory. The assault on mercantilist economic theory was begun by the physiocrats in France, who proposed a "laissez-faire" (nongovernmental interference) attitude toward land usage, and culminated in the theory of economic capitalism associated with Adam Smith (1723–1790) and his slogans of free trade, free enterprise, and the law of supply and demand.

Attempting to break away from the strict control of education by the church and state, Jean Jacques Rousseau advanced the idea of progressive education, where children learn by doing and where self-expression is encouraged. This idea was carried forward by Johann Pestalozzi, Johann Basedow, and Friedrich Fröbel, and influenced a new view of childhood.

Psychological Theory. In the *Essay Concerning Human Understanding* (1690), John Locke offered the theory that all human knowledge was the result of sensory experience, without any preconceived notions.

Causes of the French Revolution

The rising expectations of "enlightened" society were demonstrated by the increased criticism directed toward government inefficiency and corruption, and toward the privileged classes. The clergy (First Estate) and nobility (Second Estate), representing only two percent of the total population of 24 million, were the privileged classes and were essentially tax exempt. The remainder of the population (Third Estate) consisted of the middle class, urban workers, and the mass of peasants, who bore the entire burden of taxation and the imposition of feudal obligations. As economic conditions worsened in the eighteenth century, the French state became poorer, and totally dependent on the poorest and most depressed sections of the economy for support at the very time this tax base had become saturated.

Designed to represent the three estates of France, the Estates General had only met twice, once at its creation in 1302 and again in 1614. When the French parlements insisted that any new taxes must be approved by this body, King Louis XVI reluctantly ordered it to assemble at Versailles by May 1789.

Election fever swept over France for the very first time. The election campaign took place in the midst of the worst subsistence crisis in eighteenth-century France, with widespread grain shortages, poor harvests, and inflated bread prices. Finally, on May 5, 1789, the Estates General met and argued over whether to vote by estate or individual. Each estate was ordered to meet separately and vote as a unit. The Third Estate refused and insisted that the entire assembly stay together.

Phases of Revolution

The National Assembly (1789–1791): After a six-week deadlock over voting methods, representatives of the Third Estate declared themselves the true National Assembly of France (June 17). Defections from the First and Second Estates then caused the king to recognize the National Assembly (June 27) after dissolving the Estates General. At the same time, Louis XVI ordered troops to surround Versailles.

The "Parisian" revolution began at this point. Angry because of food shortages, unemployment, high prices, and fear of military repression, the workers and tradespeople began to arm themselves.

The Legislative Assembly (1791–1792): While the National Assembly had been rather homogeneous in its composition, the new government began to fragment into competing political factions. The most important political clubs were republican groups such as the Jacobins (radical urban) and Girondins (moderate rural), while the *Sans-culottes* (working-class, extremely radical) were a separate faction with an economic agenda.

The National Convention (1792–1795): Meeting for the first time in September 1792, the Convention abolished monarchy and installed republicanism. Louis XVI was charged with treason, found guilty, and executed on January 21, 1793. Later the same year, the queen, Marie Antoinette, met the same fate.

The most notorious event of the French Revolution was the famous "Reign of Terror" (1793–1794), the government's campaign against its internal enemies and counterrevolutionaries.

The Directory (1795–1799): The Constitution of 1795 restricted voting and office holding to property owners. The middle class was in control. It wanted peace in order to gain more wealth and to establish a society in which money and property would become the only requirements for prestige and power. Despite rising inflation and mass public dissatisfaction, the Directory government ignored a growing shift in public opinion. When elections in April 1797 produced a triumph for the royalist right, the results were annulled, and the Directory shed its last pretense of legitimacy.

But the weak and corrupt Directory government managed to hang on for two more years because of great military success. French armies annexed the Austrian Netherlands, the left bank of the Rhine, Nice, and Savoy. The Dutch republic was made a satellite state of France. The greatest military victories were won by Napoleon Bonaparte, who drove the Austrians out of northern Italy and forced them to sign the Treaty of Campo Formio (October 1797), in return for which the Directory government agreed to Bonaparte's scheme to conquer Egypt and threaten English interests in the East.

THE FRENCH REVOLUTION II: THE ERA OF NAPOLEON (1799–1815)

Consulate Period, 1799–1804 (Enlightened Reform): The new government was installed on December 25, 1799, with a constitution which concentrated supreme power in the hands of Napoleon. His aim was to govern France by demanding obedience, rewarding ability, and organizing everything in orderly hierarchical fashion. Napoleon's domestic reforms and policies affected every aspect of society.

Empire Period, 1804–1814 (War and Defeat): After being made Consul for Life (1801), Napoleon felt that only through an empire could France retain its strong position in Europe. On December 2, 1804, Napoleon crowned himself emperor of France in Notre Dame Cathedral.

Militarism and Empire Building: Beginning in 1805 Napoleon engaged in constant warfare that placed French troops in enemy capitals from Lisbon and Madrid to Berlin and Moscow, and temporarily gave Napoleon the largest empire since Roman times. Napoleon's Grand Empire consisted of an enlarged France, satellite kingdoms, and coerced allies.

French-ruled peoples viewed Napoleon as a tyrant who repressed and exploited them for France's glory and advantage. Enlightened reformers believed Napoleon had betrayed the ideals of the Revolution. The downfall of Napoleon resulted from his inability to conquer England, economic distress caused by the Continental System (boycott of British goods), the Peninsular War with Spain, the German War of Liberation, and the invasion of Russia. The actual defeat of Napoleon was the result of the Fourth Coalition and the Battle of Leipzig ("Battle of Nations"). Napoleon was exiled to the island of Elba as a sovereign with an income from France.

After learning of allied disharmony at the Vienna peace talks, Napoleon left Elba and began the Hundred Days by seizing power from the restored French king, Louis XVIII. Napoleon's gamble ended at Waterloo in June 1815. He was exiled as a prisoner of war to the South Atlantic island of St. Helena, where he died in 1821.

THE POST-WAR SETTLEMENT: THE CONGRESS OF VIENNA (1814–1815)

The Congress of Vienna met in 1814 and 1815 to redraw the map of Europe after the Napoleonic era, and to provide some way of preserving the future peace of Europe. Europe was spared a general war throughout the remainder of the nineteenth century. But the failure of the statesmen who shaped the future in 1814–1815 to recognize the forces, such as nationalism and liberalism, unleashed by the French Revolution, only postponed the ultimate confrontation between two views of the world—change and accommodation, or maintaining the status quo.

The Vienna settlement was the work of the representatives of the four nations that had done the most to defeat Napoleon: England (Lord Castlereagh), Austria (Prince Klemens Von Metternich), Russia (Tsar Alexander I), and Prussia (Karl Von Hardenberg).

Arrangements to guarantee the enforcement of the status quo as defined by the Vienna settlement included two provisions: The "Holy Alliance" of Tsar Alexander I of Russia, an idealistic and unpractical plan, existed only on paper. No one except Alexander took it seriously. But the "Quadruple Alliance" of Russia, Prussia, Austria, and England provided for concerted action to arrest any threat to the peace or balance of power.

From 1815 to 1822, European international relations were controlled by the series of meetings held by the great powers to monitor and defend the status quo: the Congress of Aix-la-Chapelle (1818), the Congress of Troppau (1820), the Congress of Laibach (1821), and the Congress of Verona (1822).

THE INDUSTRIAL REVOLUTION

Twentieth-century English historian Arnold Toynbee came to refer to the period since 1750 as "the Industrial Revolution." The term was intended to describe a time of transition when machines began to significantly displace human and animal power in methods of producing and distributing goods, and an agricultural and commercial society converted into an industrial one.

These changes began slowly, almost imperceptibly, gaining momentum with each decade, so that by the middle of the ninteenth century, industrialism had swept across Europe west to east, from England to Eastern Europe. Few countries purposely avoided industrialization, because of its promised material improvement and national wealth. The economic changes that constitute the Industrial Revolution have done more than any other movement in Western civilization to revolutionize Western life.

Roots of the Industrial Revolution could be found in the following: 1) the Commercial Revolution (1500–1700), which spurred the great economic growth of Europe and brought about the Age of Discovery and Exploration, which in turn helped to solidify the economic doctrines of mercantilism; 2) the effect of the Scientific Revolution, which produced the first wave of mechanical inventions and technological advances; 3) the increase in population in Europe from 140 million people in 1750, to 266 million people by the mid-part of the nineteenth century (more producers, more consumers); and 4) the political and social revolutions of the nineteenth century, which began the rise to power of the "middle class," and provided leadership for the economic revolution.

The revolution occurred first in the cotton and metallurgical industries, because those industries lent themselves to mechanization. A series of mechanical inventions (1733–1793) would enable the cotton industry to massproduce quality goods. The need to replace wood as an energy source led to the use of coal, which increased coal mining, and resulted ultimately in the invention of the steam engine and the locomotive. The development of steam power allowed the cotton industry to expand and transformed the iron industry. The factory system, which had been created in response to the new energy sources and machinery, was perfected to increase manufactured goods.

A transportation revolution ensued in order to distribute the productivity of machinery and deliver raw materials to the eager factories. This led to the growth of canal systems, the construction of hard-surfaced "macadam" roads, the commercial use of the steamboat (demonstrated by Robert Fulton, 1765–1815), and the railway locomotive (made commercially successful by George Stephenson, 1781–1848).

A subsequent revolution in agriculture made it possible for fewer people to feed the population, thus freeing people to work in factories, or in the new fields of communications, distribution of goods, or services like teaching, medicine, and entertainment.

The Industrial Revolution created a unique new category of people who were dependent on their job alone for income, a job from which they might be dismissed without cause. Until 1850 workers as a whole did not share in the general wealth produced by the Industrial Revolution. Conditions would improve as the century wore on, as union action combined with general prosperity and a developing social conscience to improve the working conditions, wages, and hours first of skilled labor, and later of unskilled labor.

The most important sociological result of industrialism was urbanization. The new factories acted as magnets, pulling people away from their rural roots and beginning the most massive population transfer in history. Cities made the working class a powerful force by raising consciousness and enabling people to unite for political action and to remedy economic dissatisfaction.

IMPACT OF THOUGHT SYSTEMS ("ISMS") ON THE EUROPEAN WORLD

Romanticism was a reaction against the rigid classicism, rationalism, and deism of the eighteenth century. Strongest between 1800 and 1850, the romantic movement differed from country to country and from romanticist to romanticist. Because it emphasized change, it was considered revolutionary in all aspects of life.

English literary Romantics like Wordsworth and Coleridge epitomized the romantic movement. Other romantics included Goethe of Germany, Hugo of France, and Pushin of Russia. Romanticism also affect music and the visual arts.

Romantic philosophy stimulated an interest in Idealism, the belief that reality consists of ideas, as opposed to materialism. This school of thought (Philosophical Idealism), founded by Plato, was developed through the writings of Immanuel Kant, Johann Gottlieb Fichte, and Georg Wilhelm Hegel, the greatest exponent of this school of thought. Hegel believed that an impersonal God rules the universe and guides humans along a progressive evolutionary course by means of a process called dialecticism; this is a historical process by which one thing is constantly reacting with its opposite (the thesis and antithesis), producing a result (synthesis) that automatically meets another opposite and continues the series of reactions.

Conservatism arose in reaction to liberalism and became a popular alternative for those who were frightened by the violence, terror, and social disorder unleashed by the French Revolution. Early conservatism was allied to the restored monarchical governments of Austria, Russia, France, and England. Support for conservatism came from the traditional ruling classes as well as the peasants who still formed the majority of the population. In essence, conservatives believed in order, society, and the state; faith and tradition.

The theory of liberalism was the first major theory in the history of Western thought to teach that the individual is a self-sufficient being whose freedom and well-being are the sole reasons for the existence of society. Liberalism was more closely connected to the spirit and outlook of the Enlightenment than to any of the other "isms" of the early nineteenth century. Liberalism was reformist and political rather than revolutionary in character.

Liberals also advocated economic individualism (i.e., laissez-faire capitalism), heralded by Adam Smith (1723–1790) in his 1776 economic masterpiece, *Wealth of Nations*.

The regenerative force of liberal thought in early nineteenth-century Europe was dramatically revealed in the explosive force of the power of nationalism. Raising the level of consciousness of people having a common language, soil, traditions, history, culture, and experience to seek political unity around an identity of what or who constitutes the nation, nationalism was aroused and made militant during the turbulent French Revolutionary era.

Nationalistic thinkers and writers examined the language, literature, and folkways of their people, thereby stimulating nationalist feelings. Emphasizing the history and culture of the various European peoples reinforced and glorified national sentiment.

SOCIALISM

The Utopian Socialists (from *Utopia*, Saint Thomas More's (1478–1535) book on a fictional ideal society) were the earliest writers to propose an equitable solution to improve the distribution of society's wealth. While they endorsed the productive capacity of industrialism, they denounced its mismanagement. Human society was to be organized as a community rather than a mixture of competing, selfish individuals. All the goods a person needed could be produced in one community.

The Anarchists rejected industrialism and the dominance of government.

"Scientific" Socialism, or Marxism, was the creation of Karl Marx (1818–1883), a German scholar who, with the help of Friedrich Engels (1820–1895), intended to replace utopian hopes and dreams with a militant blueprint for socialist working-class success. The principal works of this revolutionary school of socialism were *The Communist Manifesto* and *Das Kapital*.

The theory of dialectical materialism enabled Marx to explain the history of the world. By borrowing Hegel's dialectic, substituting materialism and realism in place of Hegel's idealism and inverting the methodological process, Marx was able to justify his theoretical conclusions. Marxism consisted of a number of key propositions: 1) An economic interpretation of history, i.e., all human history has been determined by economic factors (mainly who controls the means of production and distribution); 2) Class struggle, i.e., since the beginning of time there has been a class struggle between the rich and the poor or the exploiters and the exploited; 3) Theory of surplus value, i.e., the true value of a product was labor, and since the worker received a small portion of his just labor price, the difference was surplus value, "stolen" from him by the capitalist; and 4) Socialism was inevitable, i.e., capitalism contained the seeds of its own destruction (overproduction, unemployment, etc.); the rich would grow richer and the poor would grow poorer until the gap between each class (proletariat and bourgeoisie) is so great that the working classes would rise up in revolution and overthrow the elite bourgeoisie to install a "dictatorship of the proletariat." As modern capitalism was dismantled, the creation of a classless society guided by the principle "from each according to his abilities, to each according to his needs" would take place.

THE REVOLUTIONARY TRADITION

The year 1848 is considered the watershed of the nineteenth century. The revolutionary disturbances of the first half of the nineteenth century reached a climax in a new wave of revolutions that extended from Scandinavia to southern Italy, and from France to central Europe. Only England and Russia avoided violent upheaval.

The issues were substantially the same as they had been in 1789. What was new in 1848 was that these demands were far more widespread and irrepressible than ever. Whole classes and nations demanded to be fully included in society. Aggravated by rapid population growth and the social disruption caused by industrialism and urbanization, a massive tide of discontent swept across the Western world.

Generally speaking, the 1848 upheavals shared the strong influences of romanticism, nationalism, and liberalism, as well as a new factor of economic dislocation and instability.

Specifically, a number of similar conditions existed in several countries: 1) Severe food shortages caused by poor harvests of grain and potatoes (e.g., Irish potato famine); 2) Financial crises caused by a downturn in the commercial and industrial economy; 3) Business failures; 4) Widespread unemployment; 5) A sense of frustration and discontent among urban artisan and working classes as wages diminished; 6) A system of poor relief which became overburdened; 7) Living conditions, which deteriorated in the cities; 8) The power of nationalism in the Germanies, Italies and in Eastern Europe to inspire the overthrow of existing governments. Middle-class predominance within the unregulated economy continued to drive liberals to push for more government reform and civil liberty. They enlisted the help of the working classes to put more pressure on the government to change.

In France, working-class discontent and liberals' unhappiness with the corrupt regime of King Louis Philippe (reigned 1830–1848)—especially his minister Guizot (1787–1874)—erupted in street riots in Paris on February 22–23, 1848. With the workers in control of Paris, King Louis Philippe abdicated on February 24, and a provisional government proclaimed the Second French Republic.

The "June Days" revolt was provoked when the government closed the national workshop. This new revolution (June 23–26) was unlike previous uprisings in France. It marked the inauguration of genuine class warfare; it was a revolt against poverty and a cry for the redistribution of property. It foreshadowed the great social revolutions of the twentieth century. The revolt was extinguished after General Cavaignac was given dictatorial powers by the government. The June Days confirmed the political predominance of conservative property holders in French life.

The new Constitution of the Second French Republic provided for a unicameral legislature and executive power vested in a popularly elected president of the Republic. When the election returns were counted, the government's candidate was defeated by a "dark horse" candidate, Prince Louis Napoleon Bonaparte (1808–1873), a nephew of the great emperor. On December 20, 1848, Louis Napoleon was installed as president of the Republic. In December 1852 Louis Napoleon became Emperor Napoleon III (reigned 1852–1870), and France retreated from republicanism again.

Italian nationalists and liberals wanted to end Hapsburg (Austrian), Bourbon (Naples and Sicily), and papal domination and unite these disparate Italian regions into a unified liberal nation. A revolt by liberals in Sicily in January 1848 was followed by the granting of liberal constitutions in Naples, Tuscany, Piedmont, and the Papal States. Milan and Venice expelled their Austrian rulers. In March 1848 upon hearing the news of the revolution in Vienna, a fresh outburst of revolution against Austrian rule occurred in Lombardy and Venetia, with Sardinia-Piedmont declaring war on Austria. Simultaneously, Italian patriots attacked the Papal States, forcing the pope, Pius IX (1792–1878), to flee to Naples for refuge.

The temporary nature of these initial successes was illustrated by the speed with which the conservative forces regained control. In the north Austrian Field Marshal Radetzky (1766–1858) swept aside all opposition, regaining Lombardy and Venetia and crushing Sardinia-Piedmont. In the Papal States the establishment of the Roman Republic (February 1849) under the leadership of Giuseppe Mazzini and the protection of Giuseppe Garibaldi (1807–1882), would fail when French troops took Rome in July

1849 after a heroic defense by Garibaldi. Pope Pius IX returned to Rome cured of his liberal leanings. In the south and in Sicily the revolts were suppressed by the former rulers.

The immediate effect of the 1848 Revolution in France was a series of liberal and nationalistic demonstrations in the German states (March 1848), with the rulers promising liberal concessions. The liberals' demand for constitutional government was coupled with another demand—some kind of union or federation of the German states.

GREAT BRITAIN AND THE VICTORIAN COMPROMISE

The Victorian Age (1837–1901) is associated with the long reign of Queen Victoria, who succeeded her uncle King William IV at the age of 18, and married her cousin, Prince Albert. The early years of her reign coincided with the continuation of liberal reform of the British government, accomplished through an arrangement known as the "Victorian Compromise." The Compromise was a political alliance of the middle class and aristocracy to exclude the working class from political power. The middle class gained control of the House of Commons, the aristocracy controlled the government, the army, and the Church of England. This process of accommodation worked successfully.

Parliamentary reforms continued after passage of the 1832 Reform Bill. Laws were enacted abolishing slavery throughout the Empire (1833). The Factory Act (1831) forbade the employment of children under the age of nine. The New Poor Law (1834) required the needy who were able and unemployed to live in workhouses. The Municipal Reform Law (1835) gave control of the cities to the middle class. The last remnants of the mercantilistic age fell with the abolition of the Corn Laws (1846) and repeal of the old navigation acts (1849).

The revolutions of 1848 began with much promise, but all ended in defeat for a number of reasons. They were spontaneous movements which lost their popular support as people lost their enthusiasm. Initial successes by the revolutionaries were due less to their strength than to the hesitancy of governments to use their superior force. Once this hesitancy was overcome, the revolutions were smashed. They were essentially urban movements, and the conservative landowners and peasants tended, in time, to nullify the spontaneous actions of the urban classes. The middle class, who led the revolutions, came to fear the radicalism of their working-class allies. Divisions among national groups, and the willingness of one nationality to deny rights to other nationalities, helped to destroy the revolutionary movements in Central Europe.

However, the results of 1848–1849 were not entirely negative. Universal male suffrage was introduced in France; serfdom remained abolished in Austria and the German states; parliaments were established in Prussia and other German states, though dominated by princes and aristocrats; and Prussia and Sardinia-Piedmont emerged with new determination to succeed in their respective unification schemes.

A new age followed the revolutions of 1848–1849, as Otto von Bismarck (1815–1898), one of the dominant political figures of the second half of the nineteenth century, was quick to realize. If the mistake of these years was to believe that great decisions could be brought about by speeches and parliamentary majorities, the sequel showed that in an industrial era new techniques involving ruthless force were all too readily available. The period of *Realpolitik*—of realistic, iron-fisted politics and diplomacy—followed.

REALISIM AND MATERIALISM (1848–1914)
REALPOLITIK AND THE TRIUMPH OF NATIONALISM

After the collapse of the revolutionary movements of 1848, the leadership of Italian nationalism was transferred to Sardinian leaders Victor Emmanuel II (1820–1878), Camillo de Cavour (1810–1861), and Giuseppe Garibaldi (1807–1882). The new leaders did not entertain romantic illusions about the process of transforming Sardinia into a new Italian kingdom; they were practitioners of the politics of realism, *Realpolitik*.

In 1855, under Cavour's direction, Sardinia joined Britain and France in the Crimean War against Russia. At the Paris Peace Conference (1856), Cavour addressed the delegates on the need to eliminate the foreign (Austrian) presence in the Italian peninsula and attracted the attention and sympathy of the French Emperor, Napoleon III.

After being provoked, the Austrians declared war on Sardinia in 1859. French forces intervened and the Austrians were defeated in the battles of Magenta (June 4) and Solferino (June 24).

Napoleon III, without consulting Cavour, signed a secret peace (The Truce of Villafranca) on July 11, 1859. Sardinia received Lombardy but not Venetia; the other terms indicated that Sardinian influence would be restricted and that Austria would remain a power in Italian politics. The terms of Villafranca were clarified and finalized with the Treaty of Zurich (1859).

In 1860, Cavour arranged the annexation of Parma, Modena, Romagna, and Tuscany into Sardinia. These actions were recognized by the Treaty of Turin between Napoleon III and Victor Emmanuel II; Nice and Savoy were transferred to France.

Giuseppe Garibaldi and his Red Shirts landed in Sicily in May 1860 and extended the nationalist activity to the south. Within three months, Sicily was taken and by September 7, Garibaldi was in Naples and the Kingdom of the Two Sicilies had fallen under Sardinian influence. Cavour distrusted Garibaldi, but Victor Emmanuel II encouraged him.

In February 1861, in Turin, Victor Emmanuel was declared King of Italy and presided over an Italian Parliament which represented the entire Italian peninsula with the exception of Venetia and the Patrimony of St. Peter (Rome). Cavour died in June 1861.

Venetia was incorporated into the Italian Kingdom in 1866 as a result of an alliance between Bismarck's Prussia and the Kingdom of Italy which preceded the Austro-Prussian War between Austria and Prussia. In return for opening a southern front against Austria, Prussia, upon its victory, arranged for Venetia to be transferred to Italy.

Bismarck was again instrumental in the acquisition of Rome into the Italian Kingdom in 1870. In 1870, the Franco-Prussian War broke out and the French garrison, which had been in Rome providing protection for the Pope, was withdrawn to serve on the front against Prussia. Italian troops seized Rome, and in 1871, as a result of a plebiscite, Rome became the capital of the Kingdom of Italy.

BISMARCK AND THE UNIFICATION OF GERMANY

In the period after 1815, Prussia emerged as an alternative to a Hapsburg-based Germany.

Otto von Bismarck (1810–1898) entered the diplomatic service of Wilhelm I as the Revolutions of 1848 were being suppressed. By the early 1860s, Bismarck had emerged as the principal adviser and minister to the king. Bismarck was an advocate of a Prussian-based (Hohenzollern) Germany.

In 1863, the Schleswig-Holstein crisis broke. These provinces, which were occupied by Germans, were under the personal rule of Christian IX (1818–1906) of Denmark. The Danish government advanced a new constitution which specified that Schleswig and Holstein would be annexed into Denmark. German reaction was predictable and Bismarck arranged for joint Austro-Prussian military action. Denmark was defeated and agreed (Treaty of Vienna, 1864) to give up the provinces, and Schleswig and Holstein were to be jointly administered by Austria and Prussia.

In 1870, deteriorating relations between France and Germany collapsed over the Ems Dispatch. Wilhelm I was approached by representatives of the French government who requested a Prussian pledge not to interfere on the issue of the vacant Spanish throne. Wilhelm I refused to give such a pledge and informed Bismarck of these developments through a telegram from Ems.

Bismarck exploited the situation by initiating a propaganda campaign against the French. Subsequently, France declared war and the Franco-Prussian War (1870–1871) commenced. Prussian victories at Sedan and Metz proved decisive; Napoleon III and his leading general, Marshal MacMahon, were captured. Paris continued to resist but fell to the Prussians in January 1871. The Treaty of Frankfurt (May 1871) concluded the war and resulted in France ceding Alsace-Lorraine to Germany and a German occupation until an indemnity was paid.

The German Empire was proclaimed on January 18, 1871, with Wilhelm I becoming the Emperor of Germany. Bismarck became the Imperial Chancellor. Bavaria, Baden, Württemberg, and Saxony were incorporated into the new Germany.

THE CRIMEAN WAR

The Crimean War originated in the dispute between two differing groups of Christians and their protectors over privileges in the Holy Land. During the nineteenth century, Palestine was part of the Ottoman Turkish Empire. In 1852, the Turks negotiated an agreement with the French to provide enclaves in the Holy Land to Roman Catholic religious orders; this arrangement appeared to jeopardize already existing agreements which provided access to Greek Orthodox religious orders. Czar Nicholas I (reigned 1825–1855), unaware of the impact of his action, ordered Russian troops to occupy several Danubian principalities; his strategy was to withdraw from these areas once the Turks agreed to clarify and guarantee the rights of the Greek Orthodox orders. In October 1853, the Turks demanded that the Russians withdraw from the occupied principalities. The Russians failed to respond, and the Turks declared war. In February 1854, Nicholas advanced a draft for a settlement of the Russo-Turkish War; it was rejected and Great Britain and France joined the Ottoman Turks and declared war on Russia.

With the exception of some naval encounters in the Gulf of Finland off the Aaland Islands, the war was conducted on the Crimean Peninsula in the Black Sea. In September 1854, more than 50,000 British and French troops landed in the Crimea, determined to take the Russian port city of Sebastopol. In December 1854, Austria reluctantly became a co-signatory of the Four Points of Vienna, a statement of British and French war aims. In 1855, Piedmont joined Britain and France in the war. In March 1855, Czar Nicholas I died and was succeeded by Alexander II (reigned 1855–1881), who was opposed to continuing the war. In December 1855, the Austrians, under excessive pressure from the British, French, and Piedmontese, sent an ultimatum to Russia in which they threatened to renounce their neutrality. In response, Alexander II indicated that he would accept the Four Points.

The resulting Peace of Paris had the following major provisions: Russia had to acknowledge international commissions to regulate maritime traffic on the Danube, recognize Turkish control of the mouth of the Danube, renounce all claims to the Danubian Principalities of Moldavia and Wallachia (which later led to the establishment of Rumania), agree not to fortify the Aaland Islands, renounce its previously espoused position of protector of the Greek Orthodox residents of the Ottoman Empire, and return all occupied territories to the Ottoman Empire. The Straits Convention of 1841 was revised by neutralizing the Black Sea. The Declaration of Paris specified rules to regulate commerce during periods of war. Lastly, the independence and integrity of the Ottoman Empire were recognized and guaranteed by the signatories.

THE EASTERN QUESTION AND THE CONGRESS OF BERLIN

In 1876, Turkish forces under the leadership of Osman Pasha soundly defeated Serbian armies. In March 1878, the Russians and the Turks signed the Peace of San Stephano; implementation of its provisions would have resulted in Russian hegemony in the Balkans and dramatically altered the balance of power in the eastern Mediterranean.

Britain, under the leadership of Prime Minister Benjamin Disraeli (1804–1881), denounced the San Stephano Accord, dispatched a naval squadron to Turkish waters, and demanded that the San Stephano agreement be scrapped. The German Chancellor, Otto von Bismarck, intervened and offered his services as mediator.

The delegates of the major powers convened in Berlin in June and July 1878 to negotiate a settlement. Prior to the meeting, Disraeli had concluded a series of secret arrangements with Austria, Russia, and Turkey. The combined impact of these accommodations was to restrict Russian expansion in the region, reaffirm the independence of Turkey, and maintain British control of the Mediterranean.

The Russians, who had won the war against Turkey and had imposed the harsh terms of the San Stephano Treaty, found that they left the conference with very little (Kars, Batum, etc.) for their effort. Although Disraeli was the primary agent of this anti-Russian settlement, the Russians blamed Bismarck for their dismal results. Their hostility toward Germany led Bismarck (1879) to embark upon a new system of alliances which transformed European diplomacy and rendered any additional efforts of the Concert of Europe futile.

CAPITALISM AND THE EMERGENCE OF THE NEW LEFT (1848–1914)

During the nineteenth century, Europe experienced the full impact of the Industrial Revolution. The Industrial Revolution resulted in improving aspects of the physical lives of a greater number of Europeans; at the same time, it led to a factory system with undesirable working and living conditions and the abuses of child labor.

As the century progressed, the inequities of the system became increasingly evident. Trade-unionism and socialist political parties emerged which attempted to address these problems and improve the lives of the working class.

During the period from 1815 to 1848, Utopian Socialists such as Robert Owen (1771–1858), Saint Simon, and Charles Fourier advocated the establishment of a political-economic system which was based on romantic concepts of the ideal society. The failure of the Revolutions of 1848 and 1849 discredited the Utopian Socialists, and the new "Scientific Socialism" advanced by Karl Marx (1818–1883) became the primary ideology of protest and revolution. Marx stated that the history of humanity was the history of class struggle and that the process of the struggle (the dialectic) would continue until a classless society was realized. The Marxian dialectic was driven by the dynamics of materialism. The proletariat, or the industrial working class, needed to be educated and led towards a violent revolution which would destroy the institutions which perpetuated the struggle and the suppression of the majority. After the revolution, the people would experience the dictatorship of the proletariat, during which the Communist party would provide leadership. Marx advanced these concepts in a series of tracts and books including *The Communist Manifesto* (1848), *Critique of Political Economy* (1859), and *Capital* (1863–1864).

BRITAIN

In 1865, Palmerston died, and during the next two decades significant domestic developments occurred which expanded democracy in Great Britain. The dominant leaders of this period were William Gladstone (1809–1898) and Benjamin Disraeli (1804–1881). As the leader of the Liberal party (until 1895), Gladstone supported Irish Home Rule, fiscal responsibility, free trade, and the extension of democratic principles. He was opposed to imperialism, the involvement of Britain in European affairs, and the further centralization of the British government. Disraeli argued for an aggressive foreign policy, the expansion of the British Empire, and, after opposing democratic reforms, the extension of the franchise.

THE SECOND FRENCH REPUBLIC AND THE SECOND EMPIRE

Louis Napoleon became the president of the Second French Republic in December 1848. During the three-year life of the Second Republic, Louis Napoleon demonstrated his skills as a gifted politician through the manipulation of the various factions in French politics. His deployment of troops in Italy to rescue and restore Pope Pius IX was condemned by the republicans, but strongly supported by the monarchists and moderates.

Louis Napoleon minimized the importance of the Legislative Assembly, capitalized on the developing Napoleonic Legend, and courted the support of the army, the Catholic church, and a range of conservative political groups. The Falloux Law returned control of education to the church. Further, Louis Napoleon was confronted with Article 45 of the constitution, which stipulated that the president was limited to one four-year term; he had no intention of relinquishing power. With the assistance of a core of dedicated supporters, Louis Napoleon arranged for a coup d'état on the night of December 1–2, 1851. The Second Republic fell and was soon replaced by the Second French Empire.

Louis Napoleon drafted a new constitution which resulted in a highly centralized government. On December 2, 1852, he announced that he was Napoleon III, Emperor of the French.

The Second Empire collapsed after the capture of Napoleon III during the Franco-Prussian War (1870–1871). After a regrettable Parisian experience with a communist type of government, the Third French Republic was established; it would survive until 1940.

IMPERIAL RUSSIA

The autocracy of Nicholas I's (reigned 1825–1855) regime was not threatened by the revolutionary movements of 1848. In 1848 and 1849, Russian troops suppressed disorganized Polish attempts to reassert Polish nationalism.

Russian involvement in the Crimean War met with defeat. Russian ambitions in the eastern Mediterranean had been thwarted by a coalition of Western European states. In 1855 Nicholas I died and was succeeded by Alexander II (reigned 1855–1881).

Fearing the transformation of Russian society from below, Alexander II instituted a series of reforms which altered the nature of the social contract in Russia. In 1861, Alexander II declared that serfdom was abolished. Further, he issued the following reforms: 1) The serf (peasant) would no longer be dependent upon the lord; 2) all people were to have freedom of movement and were free to change their means of livelihood; and 3) the serf could enter into contracts and could own property.

The last years of the reign of Alexander II witnessed increased political opposition, manifested in demands for reforms from an ever more hostile group of intellectuals, the emergence of a Russian populist movement, and attempts to assassinate the czar. As the regime matured, greater importance was placed on traditional values. This attitude developed at the same time that nihilism, which rejected romantic illusions of the past in favor of a rugged realism, was being advanced by such writers as Ivan Turgenev in his *Fathers and Sons*.

The notion of the inevitability and desirability of a social and economic revolution was promoted through the Russian populist movement. Originally, the populists were interested in an agrarian utopian order. The populists had no national support. Government persecution of the populists resulted in the radicalization of the movement. In the late 1870s and early 1880s, leaders such as Andrei Zheleabov and Sophie Perovsky became obsessed with the need to assassinate Alexander II. In March 1881, the czar was killed in St. Petersburg when his carriage was bombed. He was succeeded by Alexander III (reigned 1881–1894), who advocated a national policy based on "Orthodoxy, Autocracy, and Nationalism." Alexander III died in 1894 and was succeeded by the last of the Romanovs to hold power, Nicholas II (reigned 1894–1917). Nicholas II displayed lack of intelligence, wit, political acumen, and the absence of a firm will throughout his reign. From his ministers to his wife, Alexandra, to Rasputin (1872–1916), Nicholas was influenced by stronger personalities.

The opposition to the Czarist government became more focused and thus, more threatening, with the emergence of the Russian Social Democrats and the Russian Social Revolutionaries. Both groups were Marxist. Vladimir Ilyich Ulyanov, also known as Lenin, became the leader of the Bolsheviks, a splinter group of the Social Democrats. By winter (1904–1905), the accumulated consequences of inept management of the economy and the prosecution of the Russo-Japanese War reached a critical stage. A group under the leadership of the radical priest Gapon marched on the Winter Palace in St. Petersburg (January 9, 1905) to submit a list of grievances to the czar. Troops fired on the demonstrators and many casualties resulted on this "Bloody Sunday." In June 1905, naval personnel on the battleship Potemkin mutinied while the ship was in Odessa. In October 1905, Nicholas II issued the October Manifesto calling for the convocation of a Duma, or assembly of state, which would serve as an advisory body to the czar, extending civil liberties to include freedom of speech, assembly, and press, and announcing that Nicholas II would reorganize his government.

The leading revolutionary forces differed in their responses to the manifesto. The Octobrists indicated that they were satisfied with the arrangements; the Constitutional Democrats, also known as the Kadets, demanded a more liberal representative system. The Duma convened in 1906 and, from its outset to the outbreak of the First World War, was paralyzed by factionalism which was exploited by the czar's ministers. By 1907, Nicholas II's ministers had recovered the real power of government. Russia experienced a general though fragile economic recovery by 1909, which lasted until the war.

ORIGINS, MOTIVES, AND IMPLICATIONS OF THE NEW IMPERIALISM (1870–1914)

By the 1870s, the European industrial economies required external markets to distribute products which could not be absorbed within their domestic economies. Further, excess capital was available and foreign investment, while risky, appeared to offer high returns. Finally, the need for additional sources of raw materials served as a rationale and stimulant for imperialism. Politicians were also influenced by the numerous missionary societies which sought government protection, in extending Christianity throughout the world. European statesmen, were also interested in asserting their national power overseas through the acquisition of strategic (and many not so strategic) colonies.

The focus of most of the European imperial activities during the late nineteenth century was Africa. Initially, European interest in these activities was romantic. With John Hanning Speke's discovery of Lake Victoria (1858), Livingstone's surveying of the Zambezi, and Stanley's work on the Congo River, Europeans became enraptured with the greatness and novelty of Africa south of the Sahara.

Disraeli was involved in the intrigue which would result in the British acquisition of the Suez Canal (1875), and during the 1870s and 1880s Britain was involved in a Zulu War and announced the annexation of the Transvaal, which the Boers regained after their great victory of Majuba Hill (1881). At about the same time, Belgium established its interest in the Congo; France, in addition to seizing Tunisia, extended its influence into French Equitorial Africa, and Italy established small colonies in East Africa. During the 1880s Germany acquired several African colonies including German East Africa, the Cameroons, Togoland, and German South West Africa. The Berlin Conference (1884–1885) resulted in an agreement which specified the following: 1) The Congo would be under the control of Belgium through an International Association; 2) More liberal use of the Niger and Congo river; 3) European powers could acquire African territory through first occupation and second notifying the other European states of their occupation and claim.

British movement north of the Cape of Good Hope involved Europeans fighting one another rather than a native African force. The Boers had lived in South Africa since the beginning of the nineteenth century. With the discovery of gold (1882) in the Transvaal, many English Cape settlers moved into the region. The Boers, under the leadership of Paul Kruger, restricted the political and economic rights of the British settlers and developed alternative railroads through Mozambique which would lessen the Boer dependency on the Cape colony. The crisis mounted and, in 1899, the Boer War began. Until 1902, the British and Boers fought a war which was costly to both sides. Britain prevailed and by 1909, the Transvaal, Orange Free State, Natal, and the Cape of Good Hope were united into the Union of South Africa.

Another area of increased imperialist activity was the Pacific. In 1890, the American naval Captain Alfred Mahan published *The Influence of Sea Power Upon History*; in this book he argued that history demonstrated that nations which controlled the seas prevailed. During the 1880s and 1890s naval ships required coaling stations. While Britain, the Netherlands, and France demonstrated that they were interested in Pacific islands, the most active states in this region during the last 20 years of the nineteenth century were Germany and the United States. The United States acquired the Philippines in 1898. Germany gained part of New Guinea, and the Marshall, Caroline, and Mariana island chains. The European powers were also interested in the Asian mainland. Most powers agreed with the American Open Door Policy which recognized the independence and integrity of China and provided economic access for all the powers. Rivalry over China (Manchuria) was a principal cause of the outbreak of the Russo-Japanese War in 1904.

THE AGE OF BISMARCK (1871–1890)

During the period from the establishment of the German Empire in January 1871 to his dismissal as chancellor of Germany in March 1890, Otto von Bismarck dominated European diplomacy and established an integrated political and economic structure for the new German state. Bismarck established a statist system which was reactionary in political philosophy and based upon industrialism, militarism, and innovative social legislation.

During the 1870s and 1880s, Bismarck's domestic policies were directed at the establishment of a strong united German state which would be capable of defending itself from a French war of revenge designed to restore Alsace-Lorraine to France. Laws were enacted which unified the monetary system, established an Imperial Bank and strengthened existing banks, developed universal German civil and criminal codes, and required compulsory military service. All of these measures contributed to the integration of the German state.

In order to develop public support for the government and to minimize the threat from the left, Bismarck instituted a protective tariff, to maintain domestic production, and introduced many social and economic laws to provide social security, regulate child labor, and improve working conditions for all Germans.

Bismarck's foreign policy was centered on maintaining the diplomatic isolation of France. In the crisis stemming from the Russo-Turkish War (1877–1878), Bismarck tried to serve as the "Honest Broker" at the Congress of Berlin. Russia did not succeed at the conference and incorrectly blamed Bismarck for its faiure. Early in the next year, a cholera epidemic affected Russian cattle herds, and Germany placed an embargo on the importation of Russian beef. The Russians were outraged by the German action and launched an anti-German propaganda campaign in the Russian press. Bismarck, desiring to maintain the peace and a predictable diplomatic environment, concluded a secret defensive treaty with Austria-Hungary in 1879. The Dual Alliance was very significant because it was the first "hard" diplomatic alliance of the era. A "hard" alliance involved the specific commitment of military support; traditional or "soft" alliances involved pledges of neutrality or to hold military conversations in the event of a war. The Dual Alliance, which had a five-year term and was renewable, directed that one signatory would assist the other in the event that one power was attacked by two or more states.

In 1882, another agreement, the Triple Alliance, was signed between Germany, Austria-Hungary, and Italy. In the 1880s, relations between Austria-Hungary and Russia became estranged over Balkan issues. Bismarck, fearing a war, intervened and by 1887, had negotiated the secret Reinsurance Treaty with Russia. This was a "hard" defensive alliance with a three-year term, that was renewable.

In 1888, Wilhelm I died and was succeeded by his son Friedrich III, who also died within a few months. Friedrich's son, Wilhelm II (reigned 1888–1918), came to power and soon found himself in conflict with Bismarck. Early in 1890, two issues developed which led ultimately to Bismarck's dismissal. First, Bismarck had evolved a scheme for a fabricated attempted coup by the Social Democratic Party; his intent was to use this situation to create a national hysteria through which he could restrict the SPD through legal action. Second, Bismarck intended to renew the Reinsurance Treaty with Russia to maintain his policy of French diplomatic isolation. Wilhelm II opposed both of these plans; in March 1890, Bismarck, who had used the threat of resignation so skillfully in the past, suggested that he would resign if Wilhelm II would not approve of these actions. Wilhelm II accepted his resignation; in fact, Bismarck was dismissed.

THE MOVEMENT TOWARD DEMOCRACY IN WESTERN EUROPE

Even after the reform measures of 1867 and 1884 to 1885, the movement toward democratic reforms in Great Britain continued unabated.

The most significant political reform of this long-lived Liberal government was the Parliament Act of 1911, which eliminated the powers of the House of Lords and resulted in the House of Commons becoming the unquestioned center of national power.

The most recurring and serious problem which Great Britain experienced during the period from 1890 to 1914 was the "Irish Question." The Irish situation became more complicated when the Protestant counties of the north started to enjoy remarkable economic growth from the mid-1890s; they were adamant in their rejection of all measures of Irish Home Rule. In 1914, an Irish Home Rule Act was passed by both the Commons and the Lords, but the Protestants refused to accept it. Implementation was deferred until after the war.

THE THIRD FRENCH REPUBLIC

In the fall of 1870, Napoleon III's Second Empire collapsed when it was defeated by the Prussian armies. Napoleon III and his principal aides were captured; later, he abdicated and fled to England. A National Assembly (1871–1875) was created and Adolphe Thiers was recognized as its chief executive. At the same time, a more radical political entity, the Paris Commune (1870–1871), came into existence and exercised extraordinary power during the siege of Paris. After the siege and the peace agreement with Prussia, the Commune refused to recognize the authority of the National Assembly. Led by radical Marxists, anarchists, and republicans, the Paris Commune repudiated the conservative and monarchist leadership of the National Assembly. From March to May 1871, the Commune fought a bloody struggle with the troops of the National Assembly. France began a program of recovery which led to the formulation of the Third French Republic in 1875. The National Assembly sought to 1) put the French political house in order; 2) establish a new constitutional government; 3) pay off an imposed indemnity and, in doing so, remove German troops from French territory; and 4) restore the honor and glory of France. In 1875 a constitution was adopted which provided for a republican government consisting of a president (with little power), a Senate, and a Chamber of Deputies, which was the center of political power. During the early years of the Republic, Leon Gambetta (1838–1882) led the republicans.

The most serious threat to the Republic came through the Dreyfus Affair. In 1894, Captain Alfred Dreyfus (1859–1935) was assigned to the French General Staff. A scandal broke when it was revealed that classified information had been provided to German spies. Dreyfus, a Jew, was charged, tried, and convicted. Later, it was determined that the actual spy was Commandant Marie Charles Esterhazy (1847–1923), who was acquitted in order to save the pride and reputation of the army. In 1906, the case was closed when Dreyfus was declared innocent and returned to the ranks. Rather than lead to the collapse of the Republic, the Dreyfus Affair demonstrated the intensity of anti-Semitism in French society, the level of corruption in the French army, and the willingness of the Catholic church and the monarchists to join in a conspiracy against an innocent man.

From 1905 to 1914 the socialists under Jean Jaurès gained seats in the Chamber of Deputies. The Third French Republic endured the crises which confronted it and, in 1914, enjoyed the support of the vast majority of French citizens.

INTERNATIONAL POLITICS AND THE COMING OF THE WAR (1890–1914)

During the late nineteenth century, the economically motivated "New Imperialism" resulted in further aggravating the relations among the European powers. The Fashoda Crisis (1898–1899), the Moroccan Crisis (1905–1906), the Balkan Crisis (1908), and the Agadir Crisis (1911) demonstrated the impact of imperialism in heightening tensions among European states and in creating an environment in which conflict became more acceptable.

In 1908, the decadent Ottoman Empire was experiencing domestic discord which attracted the attention of both the Austrians and the Russians. These two powers agreed that Austria would annex Bosnia and Herzegovina and Russia would be granted access to the Straits and thus the Mediterranean. Great Britain intervened and demanded that there be no change in the status quo in the Straits. Russia backed down from a confrontation, but Austria proceeded to annex Bosnia and Herzegovina.

On June 28, 1914, Archduke Franz Ferdinand (1863–1914), heir to the Austro-Hungarian throne, and his wife were assassinated while on a state visit to Sarajevo, the capital of Bosnia. The assassination resulted in a crisis between Austria-Hungary and Serbia. On July 23, Austria's foreign minister, Count Berchtold, sent a 10-point ultimatum to Serbia. Though the ultimatum was purposely drafted to inflame Serbia, the Serbians argued the validity of only one of its precepts.

German Chancellor Bethmann-Hollweg and British Foreign Secretary Sir Edward Grey attempted to mediate the conflict. It was too late. On July 28, Austria declared war on Serbia and by August 4, Britain, France, and Russia (The Allies) were at war with Germany and Austria-Hungary (The

Central Powers); later, other nations would join one of the two camps.

The initial military actions did not proceed as planned. The German Schlieffen Plan failed to succeed in the West as a result of German tactical adjustments and the French and British resistance in the First Battle of the Marne (September 1914). In the East, the Germans scored significant victories over the numerically superior Russians at the battles of Tannenberg and Masurian Lakes (August–September 1914).

WORLD WAR I AND EUROPE IN CRISIS (1914–1935)
THE ORIGINS OF WORLD WAR I

The long-range roots of the origins of World War I can be traced to numerous factors, beginning with the creation of modern Germany in 1871. Achieved through a series of wars, the emergence of this new German state completely destroyed Europe's traditional balance of power, and forced its diplomatic and military planners back to their drawing boards to rethink their collective strategies.

From 1871 to 1890, balance of power was maintained through the network of alliances created by the German Chancellor, Otto von Bismarck, and centered around his *Dreikaiserbund* (League of the Three Emperors) that isolated France, and the Dual (Germany, Austria) and Triple (Germany, Austria, Italy) Alliances. Bismarck's fall in 1890 resulted in new policies that saw Germany move closer to Austria, while England and France (Entente Cordiale, 1904), and later Russia (Triple Entente, 1907), drew closer.

Germany's dramatic defeat of France in 1870–1871 coupled with Kaiser William II's decision in 1890 to build up a navy comparable to that of Great Britain created a reactive arms race. This, blended with European efforts to carve out colonial empires in Africa and Asia—plus a new spirit of nationalism and the growing romanticization of war—helped create an unstable international environment in the years before the outbreak of World War I.

IMMEDIATE CAUSE OF WORLD WAR I

The Balkans, the area of Europe that now comprises Yugoslavia, Albania, Greece, Bulgaria, Macedonia, and Rumania, was Europe's most unstable area. Part of the rapidly decaying Ottoman (Turkish) Empire, it was torn by ethnic nationalism among the various small groups that lived there, and competition between Austria-Hungary and Russia over spheres of influence in the region. In 1912, with Russian encouragement, a Balkan League that included Serbia, Montenegro, Greece, and Bulgaria went to war with Turkey. Serbia, which wanted a spot on the Adriatic, was rebuffed when Austria created Albania in an attempt to deter Serbia. This intensified bitterness between both countries and prompted Russia to take a more protective attitude toward its southern Slavic cousins.

THE OUTBREAK OF THE WORLD WAR

On June 28, 1914, the Archduke Franz Ferdinand (1863–1914), heir to the Austrian throne, was assassinated by Gavrilo Princip, a young Serbian nationalist. Austria consulted with the German government on July 6 and received a "blank check" to take any steps necessary to punish Serbia. On July 23, 1914, the Austrian government presented Serbia with a 10-point ultimatum that required Serbia to suppress and punish all forms of anti-Austrian sentiment there with the help of Austrian officials. On July 25, 1914, three hours after mobilizing its army, the Serbians acceded to most of Austria's terms. In fact, they requested only that Austria's demand to participate in Serbian judicial proceedings be adjudicated by the International Tribunal at The Hague.

Austria immediately broke official relations with Serbia and mobilized its army. On July 28, 1914, Austria went to war against Serbia, and began to bombard Belgrade the following day. At the same time, Russia gradually prepared for war against Austria and Germany, declaring full mobilization on July 30.

German military strategy, based in part on the plan of the Chief of the General Staff Count Alfred von Schlieffen, viewed Russian mobilization as an act of war. The Schlieffen Plan was based on a two-front war with Russia and France. It was predicated on a swift, decisive blow against France while maintaining a defensive position against slowly mobilizing Russia, which would be dealt with after France.

Germany demanded that Russia demobilize in 12 hours and appealed to the Russian ambassador in Berlin. Russia's offer to negotiate the matter was rejected, and Germany declared war on Russia on August 1, 1914. On August 3, Germany declared war on France. Berlin asked Belgium for permission to send its troops through its territory to attack France, which Belgium refused. On August 4, England, which agreed in 1839 to protect Belgian neutrality, declared war on Germany; Belgium followed suit. Between 1914 and 1915, the alliance of the Central Powers (Germany, Austria-Hungary, Bulgaria, and Turkey) faced the Allied Powers of England, France, Russia, Japan, and in 1917, the United States. A number of smaller countries were also part of the Allied coalition.

THE WAR IN 1914

The Western Front: After entering Belgium, the Germans attacked France on five fronts in an effort to encircle Paris rapidly. However, the unexpected

Russian attack in East Prussia and Galicia from August 17 to 20 forced Germany to transfer important forces eastward to halt the Russian drive.

To halt a further German advance, the French army, aided by Belgian and English forces, counterattacked. In the Battle of the Marne (September 5–9), they stopped the German drive and forced small retreats. Mutual outflanking maneuvers by France and Germany created a battlefront that would determine the demarcation of the Western Front for the next four years. It ran, in uneven fashion, from the North Sea to Belgium and from northern France to Switzerland.

The Eastern Front: The Germans retreated after their assault against Warsaw in late September. Hindenburg's attack on Lodz, 10 days after he was appointed Commander-in-Chief of the Eastern Front (Nov. 1), was a more successful venture; by the end of 1914 this important textile center was in German hands.

THE WAR IN 1915

The Western Front: Wooed by both sides, Italy joined the Allies and declared war on the Central Powers on May 23 after signing the secret Treaty of London (April 26). This treaty gave Italy Austrian provinces in the north and some Turkish territory.

The Eastern Front: On January 23, 1915, Austro-German forces began a coordinated offensive in East Russia and in the Carpathians. The two-pronged German assault in the north was stopped on February 27, while Austrian efforts to relieve their besieged defensive network at Przemysl failed when it fell into Russian hands on March 22.

German forces, strengthened by troops from the Western Front under August von Mackensen, began a move on May 2 to strike at the heart of the Russian Front. By August 1915, much of Russian Poland was in German hands.

In an effort to provide direct access to the Turks defending Gallipoli, Germany and Austria invaded Serbia in the early fall, aided by their new ally, Bulgaria. On October 7, the defeated Serbian army retreated to Corfu.

THE EASTERN MEDITERRANEAN

Turkey entered the war on the Central Power side on October 28, 1914, which prevented the shipment of Anglo-French aid to Russians through the Straits.

THE WAR IN 1916

The Western Front: The Battle for Verdun lasted from February 21 to December 18, 1916. From February until June, German forces, aided by closely coordinated heavy artillery barrages, assaulted the forts around Verdun. The Germans suffered 281,000 casualties while the French, under Marshal Henri Pétain (1856–1951), lost 315,000 while successfully defending their position.

To take pressure off the French, an Anglo-French force mounted three attacks on the Germans to the left of Verdun in July, September, and November. After the Battle of the Somme (July 1–November 18), German pressure was reduced, but at great loss. Anglo-French casualties totaled 600,000.

The Eastern Front: Orchestrated by Aleksei Brusilov (1853–1926), The Brusilov Offensive (June 4–September 20) envisioned a series of unexpected attacks along a lengthy front to confuse the enemy. By late August, he had advanced into Galicia and the Carpathians.

Rumania entered the war on the Allied side as a result of Russian successes and the secret Treaty of Bucharest (August 17). The ensuing Rumanian thrust into Translyvania was pushed back, and on December 6, a German-Bulgarian army occupied Bucharest as well as the bulk of Rumania.

The death of Austrian Emperor Franz Joseph (reigned 1848–1916) on November 21 prompted his successor, Charles I (1887–1922), to discuss the prospect of peace terms with his allies. On December 12, the four Central Powers, strengthened by the fall of Bucharest, offered four separate peace proposals based on their recent military achievements. The Allies rejected them on December 30 because they felt them to be insincere.

By the end of 1914, Allied fleets had gained control of the high seas, which caused Germany to lose control of its colonial empire. Germany's failure in 1914 to weaken British naval strength prompted German naval leaders to begin using the submarine as an offensive weapon to weaken the British. On February 4, Germany announced a war zone around the British Isles, and advised neutral powers to sail there at their own risk. On May 7, 1915 a German submarine sank the *Lusitania*, a British passenger vessel, because it was secretly carrying arms.

NEW MILITARY TECHNOLOGY

Germany, Russia, and Great Britain all had submarines, but the German U-boats were the most effective. Designed principally for coastal protection, they increasingly used them to reduce British naval superiority through tactical and psychological means.

By the spring of 1915, British war planners finally awoke to the fact that the machine gun had become the mistress of defensive trench warfare. In a search for a weapon to counter trench defenses, the British developed tanks as an armored "land ship," and first used them on September 15, 1916, in the battle of the Somme.

Airplanes were initially used for observation purposes in the early months of the war. As their numbers grew, mid-air struggles using pistols and rifles took place, until the Germans devised a synchronized propeller and machine gun on its Fokker aircraft in May 1915. The Allies responded with similar equipment and new squadron tactics during the early days of the Verdun campaign in February 1916, and briefly gained control of the skies. They also began to use their aircraft for bombing raids against Zeppelin bases in Germany. Air supremacy shifted to the Germans in 1917.

During the first year of the war, the Germans began to use Zeppelin airships to bomb civilian targets in England. Though their significance was neutralized with the development of the explosive shell in 1916, Zeppelins played an important role as a psychological weapon in the first two years of the war.

In the constant search for methods to counter trench warfare, the Germans and the Allied forces experimented with various forms of internationally outlawed gas. On October 27, 1914, the Germans tried a nose/eye irritant gas at Neuve-Chapelle, and by the spring of 1915 had developed a poison chlorine gas at the Battle of Ypres. That fall, the British countered with a similar chemical at the battles of Champagne and Loos.

THE RUSSIAN REVOLUTIONS OF 1917
The February Revolution

The government's handling of the war prompted a new wave of civilian unrest. Estimates are that 1,140 riots and strikes swept Russia in January and February 1917. Military and police units ordered to move against the mobs either remained at their posts or joined them.

Though ordered by the czar not to meet until April, Duma leaders demanded dramatic solutions to the country's problems. Though dissolved on March 11, the Duma met in special session on March 13 and created a Provisional Committee of Elders to deal with the civil war. After two days of discussions, it decided that the czar must give up his throne, and on March 15, 1917, President Michael Rodzianko and Aleksandr Ivanovich Guchkov, leader of the Octobrist Party, convinced the czar to abdicate. He agreed, turning over the throne to this brother, the Grand Duke Michael, who himself abdicated the next day.

The Bolshevik October Revolution

On October 23–24, Lenin returned from Finland to meet with the party's Central Committee to plan the coup. Though he met with strong resistance, the Committee agreed to create a Political Bureau (Politburo) to oversee the revolution.

Leon Trotsky, head of the Petrograd Soviet and its Military Revolutionary Committee, convinced troops in Petrograd to support Bolshevik moves. While Trotsky gained control of important strategic points around the city, Kerensky, well-informed of Lenin's plans, finally decided on November 6 to move against the plotters. In response, Lenin and Trotsky ordered their supporters to seize the city's transportation and communication centers. The Winter Palace was captured later that evening, along with most of Kerensky's government.

The Second Congress opened at 11 p.m. on November 7, with Lev Kamenev (1883–1936), a member of Lenin's Politburo, as its head. Soon after it opened, many of the moderate socialists walked out in opposition to Lenin's coup, leaving the Bolsheviks and the Left Socialist Revolutionaries in control of the gathering.

At the Congress, it was announced that the government's new Cabinet, officially called the Council of People's Commissars (Sovnarkom), and responsible to a Central Executive Committee, would include Lenin as Chairman or head of government, Trotsky as Foreign Commissar, and Josef Stalin as Commissar of Nationalities. The Second Congress issued two decrees on peace and land. The first called for immediate peace without any consideration of indemnities or annexations, while the second adopted the Socialist Revolutionary land program that abolished private ownership of land and decreed that a peasant could only have as much land as he could farm. Village councils would oversee distribution.

The Constituent Assembly

The Constituent Assembly, long promised by the Provisional Government as the country's first legally elected legislature, presented serious problems for Lenin, since he knew the Bolsheviks could not win a majority of seats in it. Regardless, Lenin allowed elections for it to be held on November 25 under universal suffrage. When the assembly convened on January 18 in the Tauride Palace, it voted down Bolshevik proposals and elected Victor Chernov, a Socialist Revolutionary, as president, and declared the country a democratic federal republic. The Bolsheviks walked out. The next day, troops dissolved the Assembly.

WORLD WAR I: THE FINAL PHASE (1917–1918)
Russia Leaves the War

As order collapsed among Russian units along the Eastern Front, the Soviet government began to explore cease fire talks with the Central Powers. Leon Trotsky, the Commissar of Foreign Affairs, offered general negotiations to all sides, and signed an initial armistice as a prelude to peace discussions with Germany at Brest-Litovsk on December 5, 1917.

The Soviets accepted terms that were integrated into the Treaty of Brest-Litovsk of March 3, 1918. According to its terms, in return for peace, Soviet Russia lost its Baltic provinces, the Ukraine, Finland, Byelorussia, and part of Transcaucasia. The area lost totaled 1,300,000 square miles and included 62 million people.

The American Presence: Naval and Economic Support

The United States, which had originally hoped that it could simply supply the Allies with naval and economic support, made its naval presence known immediately and helped Great Britain mount an extremely effective blockade of Germany and, through a convoy system, strengthened the shipment of goods across the Atlantic.

An initial token group, the American Expeditionary Force under General John J. Pershing (1860–1948), arrived in France on June 25, 1917, while by the end of April 1918, 300,000 Americans a month were placed as complete divisions alongside British and French units.

Stirred by the successes on the Marne, the Allies began their offensive against the Germans at Amiens on August 8, 1918. By September 3, the Germans retreated to the Hindenburg Line. On September 26, Foch began his final offensive, and took the Hindenburg Line the following day. Two days later, Ludendorff advised his government to seek a peace settlement. Over the next month, the French took St. Quetin (October 1), while the British occupied Cambrai, Le Cateau, and Ostend.

On September 14, Allied forces attacked in the Salonika area of Macedonia and forced Bulgaria to sue for peace on September 29. On September 19, General Allenby began an attack on Turkish forces at Megiddo in Palestine and quickly defeated them. In a rapid collapse of Turkish resistance, the British took Damascus, Aleppo, and finally forced Turkey from the war at the end of October. On October 24, the Italians began an assault against Austria-Hungary at Vitto Veneto and forced Vienna to sign armistice terms on November 3. Kaiser Wilhelm II, pressured to abdicate, fled the country on November 9, and a republic was declared. On November 11, at 11 a.m., the war ended, with Germany accepting a harsh armistice.

THE PARIS PEACE CONFERENCE OF 1919–1920
Preliminary Discussions

To a very great extent, the direction and thrust of the discussions at the Paris Peace Conference were determined by the destructive nature of the war itself and the political responsibilities, ideals, and personalities of the principle architects of the settlements at Paris. The sudden, unexpected end of the war, combined with the growing threat of communist revolution throughout Europe created an unsettling atmosphere at the conference. The "Big Four" of Wilson (U.S.), Clemenceau (France), Lloyd-George (England), and Orlando (Italy) took over the peace discussions. The delays caused by uncertainty over direction at the beginning of the conference, Wilson's insistence that the League of Nations be included in the settlement, and fear of European-wide revolution resulted in a hastily prepared, dictated peace settlement.

THE TREATY OF VERSAILLES

The treaty's war guilt statements were the justification for its harsh penalties. The former German king, Wilhelm II, was accused of crimes against "international morality and the sanctity of treaties," while Germany took responsibility for itself and for its allies for all losses suffered by the Allied Powers and their supporters as a result of German and Central Power aggression.

Germany had to return Alsace and Lorraine to France and Eupen-Malmedy to Belgium. France got Germany's Saar coal mines as reparations, while the Saar Basin was to be occupied by the major powers for 15 years, after which a plebiscite would decide its ultimate fate. Poland got a number of German provinces and Danzig, now a free city, as its outlet to the sea. Additionally, Germany lost all of its colonies in Asia and Africa.

The German Army was limited to 100,000 men and officers with 12 year enlistments for the former and 25 for the latter. The General Staff was also abolished. The Navy lost its submarines and most offensive naval forces, and was limited to 15,000 men and officers with the same enlistment periods as the army. Aircraft and blimps were outlawed. A Reparations Commission was created to determine Germany's war debt to the Allies, which it figured in 1921 to be $32.4 billion, to be paid over an extended period of time. In the meantime, Germany was to begin immediate payments in goods and raw materials.

The Allies presented the treaty to the Germans on May 7, 1919, but the Germans stated that its terms were too much for the German people, and that it violated the spirit of Wilson's Fourteen Points. After some minor changes were made, the Germans were told to sign the document or face an Allied advance into Germany. The treaty was signed on June 28, 1919, at Versailles.

TREATIES WITH GERMANY'S ALLIES

The Allied treaty with Austria legitimized the breakup of the Austrian Empire in the latter days of the war and saw Austrian territory ceded to Italy and the new states of Czechoslovakia, Poland, and Yugoslavia. The agreement included military restrictions and debt payments.

WEIMAR GERMANY (1918–1929)

The dramatic collapse of the German war effort in the second half of 1918 ultimately created a political crisis that forced the abdication of the kaiser and the creation of a German Republic on November 9.

From the outset, the Provisional Government, formed by a coalition of Majority and Independent Social Democratic Socialists, was beset by divisions from within and threats of revolution throughout Germany.

Elections for the new National Constituent Assembly, which was to be based on proportional representation, gave no party a clear majority. A coalition of the Majority Socialists, the Catholic Center party, and the German Democratic party (DDP) dominated the new assembly. On February 11, 1919, the assembly met in the historic town of Weimar and selected Friedrich Ebert President of Germany. Two days later, Phillip Scheidemann (1865–1939) formed the first Weimar Cabinet and became its first Chancellor.

On August 11, 1919, a new constitution was promulgated, which provided for a bicameral legislature.

POLITICS AND PROBLEMS OF THE WEIMAR REPUBLIC (1919–1923)

The territorial, manpower, and economic losses suffered during and after the war, coupled with a $32.4 billion reparations debt, had a severe impact on the German economy and society, and severely handicapped the new government's efforts to establish a stable governing environment.

In an effort of good faith based on hopes of future reparation payment reductions, Germany borrowed heavily and made payments in kind to fulfill its early debt obligations. The result was a spiral of inflation. After the Allied Reparations Commission declared Germany in default on its debt, the French and the Belgians occupied the Ruhr on January 11, 1923.

Chancellor Wilhelm Cuno (1876–1933) encouraged the Ruhr's Germans passively to resist the occupation, and printed worthless marks. The occupation ended on September 26, and helped prompt stronger Allied sympathy to Germany's payment difficulties, though the inflationary spiral had severe economic, social, and political consequences.

Weimar Politics (1919–1923): Germany's economic and social difficulties deeply affected its infant democracy. From February 1919 to August 1923, the country had six chancellors.

Growing right-wing discontent with the Weimar Government resulted in the assassination of the gifted head of the Catholic Center Party, Matthias Erzberger (1875–1921), on August 29, 1921, and the murder of Foreign Minister Walter Rathenau (1867–1922) on June 24, 1922. These were two of the most serious of over 350 political murders in Germany since the end of the war.

Following the death of President Ebert on February 28, 1925, two ballots were held for a new president, since none of the candidates won a majority on the first vote. On the second ballot on April 26, the Reichsblock, a coalition of Conservative parties, was able to get its candidate elected. War hero Paul von Hindenburg was narrowly elected.

The elections of May 20, 1928, saw the Social Democrats get almost one-third of the popular vote which, blended with other moderate groups, created a stable, moderate majority in the Reichstag, which chose Hermann Müller (1876–1931) as chancellor.

ITALY (1919–1925)

Benito Mussolini, capitalizing on the sympathy of unfulfilled war veterans, disaffected nationalists, and those fearful of communism, formed the Fascio Italiano di Combattimento (Union of Combat) in Milan on March 23, 1919. Initially, Mussolini's movement had few followers, and it did badly in the November 1919 elections. However, Socialist strikes and unrest enabled him to convince Italians that he alone could bring stability and prosperity to their troubled country.

The resignation of the Bonomi Cabinet on February 9, 1922, underlined the government's inability to maintain stability. In the meantime, the Fascists seized control of Bologna in May, and Milan in August. In response, Socialist leaders called for a nationwide strike on August 1, 1922; it was stopped by Fascist street violence within 24 hours. On October 24, 1922, Mussolini told followers that if he was not given power, he would "March on Rome." Three days later, Fascists began to seize control of other cities, while 26,000 began to move towards the capital. On October 29, the king, Victor Emmanuel III (1869–1947), asked Mussolini to form a new government as Premier of Italy.

Beginning in 1925, Mussolini arrested opponents, closed newspapers, and eliminated civil liberties in a new reign of terror. On December 24, 1925, the legislature's powers were greatly limited, while those of Mussolini were increased as the new Head of State. Throughout 1926, Mussolini intensified his control over the country with legislation that outlawed strikes and created the syndicalist corporate system. A failed assassination attempt prompted the "Law for the Defense of the State" of November 25, 1926, that created a Special Court to deal with political crimes and introduced the death penalty for threats against the king, his family, or the Head of State.

Italian Foreign Policy

The nation's wish for post-war peace and stability saw Italy participate in all of the international developments in the 1920s aimed at securing normalcy in relations with its neighbors. Because Italy did not receive its desired portions of Dalmatia at the Paris Peace Conference, Italian nationalist Gabriele D'Annunzio seized Fiume on the Adriatic in the fall of 1919. D'Annunzio's daring gesture as well as his deep sense of Italian national pride deeply affected Mussolini. However, in the atmosphere of detente prevalent in Europe at the time, he agreed to settle the dispute with Yugoslavia in a treaty on January 27, 1924, which ceded most of the port to Italy, and the surrounding area to Yugoslavia.

In the fall of 1923, Mussolini used the assassination of Italian officials, who were working to resolve a Greek-Albanian border dispute, to seize the island of Corfu. Within a month, however, the British and the French convinced him to return the island for an indemnity.

SOVIET RUSSIA (1922–1932)

The Civil War and "War Communism" had brought economic disaster and social upheaval throughout the country. On March 1, 1921, as the Soviet leadership met to decide on policies to guide the country in peace, a naval rebellion broke out at the Kronstadt naval base. The Soviet leadership sent Trotsky to put down the rebellion, which he did brutally by March 18.

Vladimir Ilyich Lenin, the founder of the Soviet State, suffered a serious stroke on May 26, 1922 and a second in December of that year. Lenin died on January 21, 1924.

Iosef Vissarionovich Dzugashvili (Joseph Stalin, 1879–1953) took over numerous, and in some cases, seemingly unimportant party organizations after the Revolution and transformed them into important bases of power. Among them were Politburo (Political Bureau), which ran the country; the Orgburo (Organizational Bureau), which Stalin headed, and which appointed people to positions in groups that implemented Politiburo decisions, the Inspectorate (Rabkrin, Commissariat of the Workers' and Peasants' Inspectorate) which tried to eliminate party corruption, and the Secretariat, which worked with all party organs and set the Politburo's agenda. Stalin served as the party's General Secretary after 1921.

Lev Davidovich Bronstein (Trotsky, 1879–1940) was Chairman of the Petrograd Soviet, headed the early Brest-Litovsk negotiating team, served as Foreign Commissar, and was father of the Red Army. A brilliant organizer and theorist, Trotsky was also brusque and, some felt, overbearing.

In China the Soviets helped found a young Chinese Communist party

(CCP) in 1921. When it became apparent that Sun Yat-sen's (1866–1925) revolutionary Kuomintang (KMT) was more mature than the infant CCP, the Soviets encouraged an alliance between its party and this movement. Sun's successor, Chiang Kai-shek (1887–1975), was deeply suspicious of the Communists and made their destruction part of his effort to militarily unite China.

Founded in 1919, the Soviet-controlled Comintern (Third International or Communist International) sought to coordinate the revolutionary activities of Communist parties abroad, though it often conflicted with Soviet diplomatic interests. It became an effectively organized body by 1924, and was completely Stalinized by 1928.

EUROPE IN CRISIS: DEPRESSION AND DICTATORSHIP (1929–1935)

In Great Britain in 1929, Ramsay MacDonald formed a minority Labour government that would last until 1931. The most serious problem facing the country was the Depression, which caused unemployment to reach 1,700,000 by 1930 and over 3 million, or 25 percent of the labor force, by 1932. To meet growing budget deficits caused by heavy subsidies to the unemployed, a special government commission recommended budget cuts and tax increases. Cabinet and labor union opposition helped reduce the total for the cuts but this could not help restore confidence in the government, which fell on August 24, 1931.

THE "NATIONAL GOVERNMENT" (1931–1935)

The following day, King George VI (1895–1952) helped convince MacDonald to return to office as head of a National Coalition cabinet made up of four Conservatives, four Labourites, and two Liberals. MacDonald's coalition swept the November 1931 general elections winning 554 of 615 seats.

The British government abandoned the gold standard on September 21, 1931, and adopted a series of high tariffs on imports. Unemployment peaked at 3 million in 1932 and dropped to 2 million two years later.

MacDonald resigned his position in June 1935 because of ill health and was succeeded by Stanley Baldwin, whose conservative coalition won 428 seats in new elections in November.

FRANCE: RETURN OF THE CARTEL DES GAUCHES (1932–1934)

France remained plagued by differences over economic reform between the Radicals and the Socialists. The latter advocated nationalization of major factories, expanded social reforms, and public works programs for the unemployed, while the Radicals sought a reduction in government spending. This instability was also reflected in the fact that there were six Cabinets between June 1932 and February 1934. The government's inability to deal with the country's economic and political problems saw the emergence of a number of radical groups from across the political spectrum.

GERMANY: THE DEPRESSION

The Depression had a dramatic effect on the German economy and politics. The country's national income dropped 20 percent between 1928 and 1932, while unemployment rose from 1,320,000 in 1929 to 6 million by January 1932. This meant that 43 percent of the German work force were without jobs (compared to one-quarter of the work force in the U.S.).

In 1919, Adolf Hitler joined the German Workers party (DAP), which he soon took over and renamed the National Socialist German Workers party (NAZI). In 1920, the party adopted a 25–point program that included treaty revision, anti-Semitism, economic, and other social changes. They also created a defense cadre of the *Sturm-abteilung* (SA)—"Storm Troopers" or "brown shirts"—which was to help the party seize power.

The Beer Hall Putsch (1923): In the midst of the country's severe economic crisis in 1923, the party, which now had 55,000 members, tried to seize power, first by a march on Berlin, and then, when this seemed impossible, on Munich. The march was stopped by police, and Hitler and his supporters were arrested. Though sentenced to five years imprisonment, he was released after eight months. While incarcerated, he dictated *Mein Kampf* to Rudolf Hess.

Hitler's failed coup and imprisonment convinced him to seek power through legitimate political channels, which would require transforming the Nazi party. To do this, he reasserted singular control over the movement from 1924 to 1926. Party districts were set up throughout Germany, overseen by *gauleiters* personally appointed by Hitler.

Hindenburg's seven-year presidential term expired in 1932, and he was convinced to run for reelection to stop Hitler from becoming president in the first ballot of March 13. Hitler got only 30 percent of the vote (11.3 million) to Hindenburg's 49.45 percent (18.6 million).

On June 1, Chancellor Bruenig was replaced by Franz von Papen (1879–1969), who formed a government made up of aristocratic conservatives and others that he and Hindenburg hoped would keep Hitler from power.

Later in the year, Von Papen convinced Hindenburg to appoint Hitler as chancellor and head of a new coalition cabinet with three seats for the Nazis. Hitler dissolved the Reichstag and called for new elections on March 5.

Using presidential decree powers, he initiated a violent anti-Communist campaign that included the lifting of certain press and civil freedoms. On February 27, the Reichstag burned, which enabled Hitler to get Hindenburg to issue the "Ordinances for the Protection of the German State and Nation," that removed all civil and press liberties as part of a "revolution" against communism. In the Reichstag elections of March 5, the Nazis only got 43.9 percent of the vote and 288 Reichstag seats but, through an alliance with the Nationalists, got majority control of the legislature.

Once Hitler had full legislative power, he began a policy of *Gleichschaltung* (coordination) to bring all independent organizations and agencies throughout Germany under his control. All political parties were outlawed or forced to dissolve, and on July 14, 1933, the Nazi party became the only legal party in Germany. In addition, non-Aryans and Nazi opponents were removed from the civil service, the court system, and higher education. On May 2, 1933, the government declared strikes illegal, abolished labor unions, and later forced all workers to join the German Labor Front (DAF) under Robert Ley. In 1934 the Reichsrat was abolished and a special People's Court was created to handle cases of treason. Finally, the secret police or Gestapo (*Geheime Staatspolizei*) was created on April 24, 1933, under Hermann Göring to deal with opponents and operate concentration camps. The party had its own security branch, the SD (*Sicherheitsdienst*) under Reinhard Heydrich.

From the inception of the Nazi state in 1933, anti-Semitism was a constant theme and practice in all *Gleichschaltung* and nazification efforts. Illegal intimidation and harassment of Jews was coupled with rigid enforcement of civil service regulations that forbade employment of non-Aryans. This first wave of anti-Semitic activity culminated with the passage of the Nuremburg Laws on September 15, 1935, that deprived Jews of German citizenship and outlawed sexual or marital relations between Jews and other Germans, thus effectively isolating them from the mainstream of German society.

Hitler's international policies were closely linked to his rebuilding efforts to give him a strong economic and military base for an active, aggressive, independent foreign policy. The Reich simultaneously quit the League of Nations. On January 26, 1934, Germany signed a non-aggression pact with Poland, which ended Germany's traditional anti-Polish foreign policy and broke France's encirclement of Germany via the Little Entente. This was followed by the Saarland's overwhelming decision to return to Germany. The culmination of Hitler's foreign policy moves, though, came with his March 15, 1935, announcement that Germany would no longer be bound by the military restrictions of the Treaty of Versailles, that it had already created an air force (Luftwaffe), and that the Reich would institute a draft to create an army of 500,000 men.

ITALY (1926–1936)

Until Mussolini's accession to power, the pope had considered himself a prisoner in the Vatican. In 1926, Mussolini's government began talks to resolve this issue, which resulted in the Lateran Accords of February 11, 1929. Italy recognized the Vatican as an independent state, with the pope as its head, while the papacy recognized Italian independence. Catholicism was made the official state religion of Italy, and religious teaching was required in all secondary schools.

In an effort to counter the significance of France's Little Entente with Czechoslovakia, Yugoslavia, and Rumania, Mussolini concluded the Rome Protocols with Austria and Hungary which created a protective bond of friendship between the three countries.

In response to Hitler's announcement of German rearmament in violation of the Treaty of Versailles on March 16, 1935, France, England, and Italy met at Stresa in northern Italy on April 11–14, and concluded agreements that pledged joint military collaboration if Germany moved against Austria or along the Rhine.

Ethiopia (Abyssinia) became an area of strong Italian interest in the 1880s. The coastal region was slowly brought under Italian control until the Italian defeat at Ethiopian hands at Adowa in 1894. In 1906, the country's autonomy was recognized and in 1923 it joined the League of Nations. Mussolini, who had been preparing for war with Ethiopia since 1932, established a military base at Wal Wal in Ethiopian territory. Beginning in December 1934, a series of minor conflicts took place between the two countries, which gave Mussolini an excuse to plan for the full takeover of the country in the near future.

On October 2, 1935, Italy invaded Ethiopia, while the League of Nations, which had received four appeals from Ethiopia since January about Italian territorial transgressions, finally voted to adopt economic sanctions against Mussolini. Unfortunately, the League failed to stop shipments of oil to Italy and continued to allow it to use the Suez Canal. On May 9, 1936, Italy formally annexed the country and joined it to Somalia and Eritrea, which now became known as Italian East Africa.

SOVIET RUSSIA (1933–1938)

The Second Five Year Plan (1933–1937) was adopted by the Seventeenth Party Congress in early 1934. Its economic and production targets were less severe than the First Plan, and thus, more was achieved. By the end of the Second Plan, Soviet Russia had emerged as a leading world industrial power, though at great costs. It gave up quality for quantity, and created tremendous social and economic discord that ramifies in the nations of the former Soviet Union even today.

In the spring of 1935, the recently renamed and organized secret police, the NKVD, oversaw the beginnings of a new, violent Purge that eradicated 70 percent of the 1934 Central Committee, and a large percentage of the upper military ranks. Stalin sent between 8 and 9 million to camps and prisons, and caused untold deaths before the Purges ended in 1938.

The period from 1929 to 1933 saw the U.S.S.R. retreat inward as the bulk of its energies were put into domestic economic growth. Regardless, Stalin remained sensitive to growing aggression and ideological threats abroad such as the Japanese invasion of Manchuria in 1931 and Hitler's appointment as Chancellor in 1933. As a result, Russia left its cocoon in 1934, joined the League of Nations, and became an advocate of "collective security" while the Comintern adopted Popular Front tactics, allying with other parties against fascism, to strengthen the U.S.S.R.'s international posture. Diplomatically, in addition to League membership, the Soviet Union completed a military pact with France.

INTERNATIONAL DEVELOPMENTS (1918–1935)

Efforts to create an international body to arbitrate international conflicts gained credence with the creation of a Permanent Court of International Justice to handle such matters at the First Hague Conference (1899). But no major efforts towards this goal were initiated until 1915, when pro-League of Nations organizations arose in the United States and Great Britain. Support for such a body grew as the war lengthened, and creation of such an organization became the cornerstone of President Woodrow Wilson's postwar policy, enunciated in his "Fourteen Points" speech before Congress on January 8, 1918.

The Preamble of the League's Covenant defined the League's purposes, which were to work for international friendship, peace, and security. To attain this, its members agreed to avoid war, maintain peaceful relations with other countries, and honor international law and accords.

Headquartered in Geneva, the League came into existence as the result of an Allied resolution on January 25, 1919, and the signing of the Treaty of Versailles on June 28, 1919. The League had the right, according to Article 8 of the League Covenant, to seek ways to reduce arms strength, while Articles 10 through 17 gave it the authority to search for means to stop war. It could recommend ways to stop aggression, and could suggest economic sanctions and other tactics to enforce its decisions, though its military ability to enforce its decisions was vague.

THE LOCARNO PACT (1925)

Signed on October 16, 1925, by England, France, Italy, Germany, and Belgium, the Locarno Pact guaranteed Germany's western boundaries and accepted the Versailles settlement's demilitarized zones. Italy and Great Britain agreed militarily to defend these lines if flagrantly violated.

In the same spirit, Germany signed arbitration dispute accords that mirrored the Geneva Protocol with France, Belgium, Poland, and Czechoslovakia, and required acceptance of League-determined settlements. Since Germany would only agree to arbitration and not finalize its eastern border, France separately signed guarantees with Poland and Czechoslovakia to defend their frontiers.

The Locarno Pact went into force when Germany joined the League on September 10, 1926, acquiring, after some dispute, the U.S.'s permanent seat on the Council. France and Belgium began to withdraw from the Rhineland, though they left a token force there until 1930.

THE PACT OF PARIS (KELLOGG-BRIAND PACT)

The Locarno Pact heralded a new period in European relations known as the "Era of Locarno" that marked the end of post-war conflict and the beginning of a more normal period of diplomatic friendship and cooperation. It reached its peak, with the Franco-American effort in 1928 to seek an international statement to outlaw war. On August 27, 1928, 15 countries, including the U.S., Germany, France, Italy, and Japan, signed this accord with some minor limitations, which renounced war as a means of solving differences and as a tool of national policy. Within five years, 50 other countries signed the agreement.

LEAGUE AND ALLIED RESPONSE TO AGGRESSION

On September 19, 1931, the Japanese Kwantung Army, acting independently of the government in Tokyo, began the gradual conquest of Manchuria after fabricating an incident at Mukden to justify their actions. Ultimately, they created a puppet state, Manchukuo, under the last Chinese emperor, Henry P'u-i. China's League protest resulted in the creation of an investigatory commission under the Earl of Lytton that criticized Japan's actions and recommended a negotiated settlement that would have allowed Japan to retain most of its conquest. Japan responded by resigning from the League on January 24, 1933.

Hitler's announcement on March 15, 1935, of Germany's decisions to rearm and to introduce conscription in violation of the Treaty of Versailles prompted the leaders of England, France, and Italy to meet in Stresa, Italy

(April 11–14). They condemned Germany's actions, underlined their commitment to the Locarno Pact, and re-affirmed the support they collectively gave for Austria's independence in early 1934. Great Britain's decision, however, to separately protect its naval strength vis-à-vis a German buildup in the Anglo-German Naval Treaty of June 18, 1935, effectively compromised the significance of the Stresa Front.

FROM WORLD WAR II TO THE POST-COMMUNIST ERA (1935–1996)

THE COURSE OF EVENTS

Using a Franco-Soviet agreement of the preceding year as an excuse, Hitler, on March 7, 1936, repudiated the Locarno agreements and reoccupied the Rhineland (an area demilitarized by the Versailles Treaty). Neither France (which possessed military superiority at the time) nor Britain was willing to oppose these moves.

The Spanish Civil War (1936–1939) is usually seen as a rehearsal for World War II because of outside intervention. The government of the Spanish Republic (established in 1931) caused resentment among conservatives by its programs, including land reform and anti-clerical legislation aimed at the Catholic church. Following an election victory by a popular front of republican and radical parties, right-wing generals in July began a military insurrection. Francisco Franco, stationed at the time in Spanish Morocco, emerged as the leader of this revolt, which became a devastating civil war lasting nearly three years.

The democracies, including the United States, followed a course of neutrality. Nazi Germany, Italy, and the U.S.S.R. did intervene despite non-intervention agreements negotiated by Britain and France. Spain became a battlefield for fascist and anti-fascist forces with Franco winning by 1939 in what was seen as a serious defeat for anti-fascist forces everywhere.

The Spanish Civil War was a factor in bringing together Mussolini and Hitler in a Rome-Berlin Axis. Already Germany and Japan had signed the Anti-Comintern Pact in 1936. Ostensibly directed against international communism, this was the basis for a diplomatic alliance between those countries, and Italy soon adhered to this agreement, becoming Germany's ally in World War II.

In 1938 Hitler pressured the Austrian chancellor to make concessions and when this did not work, German troops annexed Austria (the *Anschluss*). Again Britain and France took no effective action, and about six million Austrians were added to Germany.

Hitler turned next to Czechoslovakia. Three million persons of German origin lived in the Sudetenland, a borderland between Germany and Czechoslovakia given to Czechoslovakia in order to provide it with a more defensible boundary. In 1938, after a series of demands from Hitler, a four-power conference was held in Munich with Hitler, Mussolini, Chamberlain, and Daladier in attendance, at which Hitler's terms were accepted. Britain and France, despite the French alliance with Czechoslovakia, put pressure on the Czech government to force it to comply with German demands. Hitler signed a treaty agreeing to this settlement as the limit of his ambitions. At the same time the Poles seized control of Teschen, and Hungary (with the support of Italy and Germany and over the protests of the British and French) seized 7,500 square miles of Slovakia. By the concessions forced on her at Munich, Czechoslovakia lost its frontier defenses and was totally unprotected against any further German encroachments.

In March 1939, Hitler annexed most of the rump Czech state while Hungary conquered Ruthenia. At almost the same time Germany annexed Memel from Lithuania. In April, Mussolini, taking advantage of distractions created by Germany, landed an army in Albania and seized that Balkan state in a campaign lasting about one week.

Disillusioned by these continued aggressions, Britain and France made military preparations. Guarantees were given to Poland, Rumania, and Greece. The two democracies also opened negotiations with the U.S.S.R. for an arrangement to obtain that country's aid against further German aggression. Hitler, with Poland next on his timetable, also began a cautious rapprochement with the U.S.S.R. On August 23, 1939, the world was stunned by the announcement of a Nazi-Soviet Treaty of friendship. A secret protocol provided that in the event of a "territorial rearrangement" in Eastern Europe the two powers would divide Poland. In addition, Russia would have the Baltic states (Latvia, Lithuania, and Estonia) and Bessarabia (lost to Rumania in 1918) as part of her sphere. Stalin agreed to remain neutral in any German war with Britain or France. World War II began with the German invasion of Poland on September 1, 1939, followed by British and French declarations of war against Germany on September 3.

WORLD WAR II

The German attack (known as the "blitzkrieg" or "lightning war") overwhelmed the poorly equipped Polish army, which could not resist German tanks and airplanes.

On September 17 the Russian armies attacked the Poles from the east. They met the Germans two days later. Stalin's share of Poland extended approximately to the Curzon Line. Russia also made demands on Finland. Later, in June 1940, while Germany was attacking France, Stalin occupied the Baltic states of Latvia, Lithuania, and Estonia.

The only military action of any consequence during the winter of 1939–1940 resulted from Russian demands made on Finland, especially for territory adjacent to Leningrad (then only 20 miles from the border). Finnish refusal led to a Russian attack in November 1939. The Finns resisted with considerable vigor, receiving some supplies from Sweden, Britain, and France, but eventually by March they had to give in to the superior Russian forces. Finland was forced to cede the Karelian Isthmus, Viipuri, and a naval base at Hangoe.

On May 10, the main German offensive was launched against France. Belgium and the Netherlands were simultaneously attacked. According to plan, British and French forces advanced to aid the Belgians. At this point the Germans departed from the World War I strategy by launching a surprise armored attack through Luxembourg and the Ardennes Forest (considered by the British and French to be impassable for tanks). The Dutch could offer no real resistance and collapsed in four days after the May 13 German bombing of Rotterdam.

Paris fell to the Germans in mid-June. The Pétain government quickly made peace with Hitler, who added to French humiliation by dictating the terms of the armistice to the French at Compiégne in the same railroad car used by Marshal Foch when he gave terms to the Germans at the end of the First World War. The complete collapse of France quickly came as a tremendous shock to the British and Americans.

Mussolini declared war on both France and Britain on June 10. Hitler's forces remained in occupation of the northern part of France, including Paris. He allowed the French to keep their fleet and overseas territories probably in the hope of making them reliable allies. Pétain and his chief minister Pierre Laval established their capital at Vichy and followed a policy of collaboration with their former enemies. A few Frenchmen, however, joined the Free French movement started in London by the then relatively unknown General Charles de Gaulle (1890–1970).

FROM THE FRENCH DEFEAT TO THE INVASION OF RUSSIA

By mid-summer 1940, Germany, together with its Italian ally, dominated most of Western and Central Europe. Germany began with no real plans for a long war, but continued resistance by the British made necessary the belated mobilization of German resources. Hitler's policy included exploiting areas Germany conquered. Collaborators were used to establish governments subservient to German policy. Germany began the policy of forcibly transporting large numbers of conquered Europeans to work in German war industries. Jews especially were forced into slave labor for the German war effort, and increasingly large numbers were rounded up and sent to concentration camps, where they were systematically murdered as the Nazis carried out Hitler's "final solution" of genocide against European Jewry. Although much was known about this during the war, the full horror of these atrocities was not revealed until Allied troops entered Germany in 1945.

With the fall of France, Britain remained the only power of consequence at war with the Axis. Hitler began preparations for invading Britain (Operation "Sea Lion"). Air control over the Channel was vital if an invasion force was to be transported safely to the English Coast. The German Air Force (Luftwaffe) under Herman Göring began its air offensive against the British in the summer of 1940. The Germans concentrated first on British air defenses, then on ports and shipping, and finally in early September they began the attack on London. The Battle of Britain was eventually a defeat for the Germans, who were unable to gain decisive superiority over the British, although they inflicted great damage on both British air defenses and major cities such as London. Despite the damage and loss of life, British morale remained high and necessary war production continued. German losses determined that bombing alone could not defeat Britain. "Operation Sea Lion" was postponed October 12 and never seriously taken up again, although the British did not know this and had to continue for some time to give priority to their coastal and air defenses.

During the winter of 1940–1941, having given up "Operation Sea Lion," Hitler began to shift his forces to the east for an invasion of Russia ("Operation Barbarossa"). Russian expansion towards the Balkans dismayed the Germans, who hoped for more influence there themselves.

The German invasion of Russia began June 22, 1941. The invasion force of three million included Finnish, Rumanian, Hungarian, and Italian contingents along with the Germans and advanced on a broad front of about 2,000 miles. They surrounded the city of Leningrad (although they never managed to actually capture it) and came within about 25 miles of Moscow. In November the enemy actually entered the suburbs, but then the long supply lines, early winter, and Russian resistance (strong despite heavy losses) brought the invasion to a halt. During the winter a Russian counterattack pushed the Germans back from Moscow and saved the capital.

With the coming of the Great Depression and severe economic difficulties, Japanese militarists gained more and more influence over the civilian government. On September 18, 1931, the Japanese occupied all of Manchuria. On July 7, 1937, a full-scale Sino-Japanese war began with a clash between Japanese and Chinese at the Marco Polo Bridge in Peking (now Beijing). An indication of ultimate Japanese aims came on November 3, 1938, when Prince Fumimaro Konoye's (1891–1946) government issued a statement on "A New Order in East Asia." This statement envisaged the integration of Japan, Manchuria (now the puppet state of Manchukuo), and China into one "Greater East Asia Co-Prosperity Sphere" under Japanese leadership. In July 1940, the Konoye government was re-formed with General Hideki Tojo (1884–1948) (Japan's principal leader in World War I) as minister of war.

All of these events led to worsening relations between Japan and the two states in a position to oppose her expansion—the Soviet Union and the United States. Despite border clashes with the Russians, Japan avoided any conflict with that state, and Stalin wanted no war with Japan after he became fully occupied with the German invasion. In the few weeks after attacking the U.S. at Pearl Harbor, Japanese forces were able to occupy strategically important islands (including the Philippines and Dutch East Indies) and territory on the Asian mainland (Malaya, with the British naval base at Singapore, and all of Burma to the border of India).

The Japanese attack brought the United States not only into war in the Pacific, but resulted in German and Italian declarations of war which meant the total involvement of the United States in World War II.

American involvement in the war was ultimately decisive, for it meant that the greatest industrial power of that time was now arrayed against the Axis powers. The United States became, as President Roosevelt put it, "the arsenal of democracy." American aid was crucial to the immense effort of the Soviet Union. Lend-Lease aid was extended to Russia. By 1943 supplies and equipment were reaching Russia in considerable quantities.

The German forces launched a second offensive in the summer of 1942. This attack concentrated on the southern part of the front, aiming at the Caucasus and vital oil fields around the Caspian Sea. At Stalingrad on the Volga River the Germans were stopped. With the onset of winter, Hitler refused to allow the strategic retreat urged by his generals. As a result, the Russian forces crossed the river north and south of the city and surrounded 22 German divisions. On January 31, 1943, following the failure of relief efforts, the German commander Friedrich Paulus (1890–1957) surrendered the remnants of his army. From then on the Russians were almost always on the offensive.

After entering the war in 1940, the Italians invaded British-held Egypt. In December 1940, the British General Archibald Wavell (1883–1950) launched a surprise attack. The Italian forces were driven back about 500 miles and 130,000 were captured. Then Hitler intervened, sending General Erwin Rommel with a small German force (the Afrika Korps) to reinforce the Italians. Rommel took command and launched a counter-offensive which put his forces on the border of Egypt. By mid-1942 Rommel had driven to El Alamein, only 70 miles from Alexandria.

A change in the British high command now placed General Harold Alexander (1891–1969) in charge of Middle Eastern forces, with General Bernard Montgomery (1887–1976) in immediate command of the British Eighth Army. Montgomery attacked at El Alamein, breaking Rommel's lines and starting a British advance which was not stopped until the armies reached the border of Tunisia.

Meanwhile, the British and American leaders decided that they could launch a second offensive in North Africa ("Operation Torch") which would clear the enemy from the entire coast and make the Mediterranean once again safe for Allied shipping.

The landings resulted in little conflict with the French, and the French forces soon joined the war against the Axis. It was only a matter of time before German troops were forced into northern Tunisia and surrendered. American forces, unused to combat, suffered some reverses at the Battle of the Kasserine Pass, but gained valuable experience. The final victory came in May 1943, about the same time as the Russian victory at Stalingrad.

Relatively safe shipping routes across the North Atlantic to Britain were essential to the survival of Britain and absolutely necessary if a force was to be assembled to invade France and strike at Germany proper. New types of aircraft, small aircraft carriers, more numerous and better-equipped escort vessels, new radar and sonar (for underwater detection), extremely efficient radio direction finding, decipherment of German signals plus the building of more ships turned the balance against the Germans despite their development of improved submarines by early 1943, and the Atlantic became increasingly dangerous for German submarines.

Success in these three campaigns—Stalingrad, North Africa, and the Battle of the Atlantic—gave new hope to the Allied cause and made certain that victory was attainable. With the beginning of an Allied offensive in late 1942 in the Solomon Islands against the Japanese, 1943 became the turning point of the war.

At their conference at Casablanca in January 1943, Roosevelt and Churchill developed a detailed strategy for the further conduct of the war. Sicily was to be invaded, then Italy proper. Rome was not captured by the Allied forces until June 4, 1944. With a new Italian government now supporting the Allied cause, Italian resistance movements in northern Italy became a major force in helping to liberate that area from the Germans.

At the Teheran Conference, held in November 1943 and attended by all three major Allied leaders, the final decision reached by Roosevelt and Churchill some six months earlier to invade France in May 1944 was communicated to the Russians. Stalin promised to open a simultaneous Russian offensive.

The Normandy invasion (Operation "Overlord") was the largest amphibious operation in history. The landings actually took place beginning June 6, 1944. The first day, 130,000 men were successfully landed. Strong German resistance hemmed in the Allied forces for about a month. Then the Allies, now numbering about 1,000,000, managed a spectacular breakthrough. By the end of 1944, all of France had been seized. A second invasion force landed on the Mediterranean coast in August, freed southern France, and linked up with Eisenhower's forces. By the end of 1944, the Allied armies stood on the borders of Germany ready to invade from both east and west.

Stalin's armies crossed into Poland July 23, 1944, and three days later the Russian dictator officially recognized a group of Polish Communists (the so-called Lublin Committee) as the government of Poland. As the Russian armies drew near the eastern suburbs of Warsaw, the London Poles, a resistance group, launched an attack. Stalin's forces waited outside the city while the Germans brought in reinforcements and slowly wiped out the Polish underground army in several weeks of heavy street fighting. The offensive then resumed and the city was liberated by the Red Army, but the influence of the London Poles was now virtually nil. Needless to say, this incident aroused considerable suspicion concerning Stalin's motives and led both Churchill and Roosevelt to begin to think through the political implications of their alliance with Stalin.

By late summer of 1944, the German position in the Balkans began to collapse. The Red Army crossed the border into Rumania leading King Michael (1921–) to seize the opportunity to take his country out of its alliance with Germany and to open the way to the advancing Russians. German troops were forced to make a hasty retreat. At this point Bulgaria changed sides. The German forces in Greece withdrew in October.

From October 9–18, Winston Churchill visited Moscow to try to work out a political arrangement regarding the Balkans and Eastern Europe. Dealing from a position of weakness, he simply wrote out some figures on a sheet of paper: Russia to have the preponderance of influence in countries like Bulgaria and Rumania, Britain to have the major say in Greece, and a fifty-fifty division in Yugoslavia and Hungary. Stalin agreed. The Americans refused to have anything to do with this "spheres of influence" arrangement.

In Greece, Stalin maintained a hands-off policy when the British used military force to suppress the Communist resistance movement and install a regent for the exiled government.

In early spring of 1945 the Allied armies crossed the Rhine. As the

Americans and British and other Allied forces advanced into Germany, the Russians attacked from the east. While the Russian armies were fighting their way into Berlin, Hitler committed suicide in the ruins of the bunker where he had spent the last days of the war. Power was handed over to a government headed by Admiral Karl Dönitz (1891–1980). On May 7, General Alfred Jodl (1890–1946), acting for the German government, made the final unconditional surrender at General Eisenhower's headquarters near Reims.

The future treatment of Germany, and Europe in general, was determined by decisions of the "Big Three" (Churchill, Stalin, and Roosevelt).

The first major conference convened at Teheran on November 28, 1943, and lasted until December 1st. Here the two Western allies told Stalin of the May 1944 date for the planned invasion of Normandy. In turn, Stalin confirmed a pledge made earlier that Russia would enter the war against Japan after the war with Germany was concluded. The Yalta Conference was the second attended personally by Stalin, Churchill, and Roosevelt. It lasted from the 4th to the 11th of February 1945. A plan to divide Germany into zones of occupation, which had been devised in 1943 by a committee under British Deputy Prime Minister Clement Attlee, was formally accepted with the addition of a fourth zone taken from the British and American zones for the French to occupy. Berlin, which lay within the Russian Zone, was divided into four zones of occupation also.

The third summit meeting of the Big Three took place at Potsdam outside Berlin after the end of the European war but while the Pacific war was still going on. The conference began July 17, 1945, with Stalin, Churchill, and the new American President Harry Truman attending. A Potsdam Declaration, aimed at Japan, called for immediate Japanese surrender and hinted at the consequences that would ensue if it were not forthcoming. While at the conference, American leaders received the news of the successful testing of the first atomic bomb in the New Mexico desert, but the Japanese were given no clear warning that such a destructive weapon might be used against them.

On August 6, 1945, the bomb was dropped by a single plane on Hiroshima and an entire city disappeared, with the instantaneous loss of 70,000 lives. In time many other persons died from radiation poisoning and other effects. Since no surrender was received, a second bomb was dropped on Nagasaki, obliterating that city. Even the most fanatical of the Japanese leaders saw what was happening and surrender came quickly. The only departure from unconditional surrender was to allow the Japanese to retain their emperor (Hirohito, 1901–1989), but only with the proviso that he would be subject in every respect to the orders of the occupation commander. The formal surrender took place September 2, 1945, in Tokyo Bay on the deck of the battle-ship *Missouri*, and the occupation of Japan began under the immediate control of the American commander General Douglas MacArthur (1880–1964).

EUROPE AFTER WORLD WAR II: 1945 TO 1953

Anglo-American ideas about what the postwar world should be like were expressed by Roosevelt and Churchill at their meeting off the coast of Newfoundland in August 1941. The Atlantic Charter was a general statement of goals: restoration of the sovereignty and self-government of nations conquered by Hitler, free access to world trade and resources, cooperation to improve living standards and economic security, and a peace that would ensure freedom from fear and want and stop the use of force and aggression as instruments of national policy.

At the Casablanca Conference, the policy of requiring unconditional surrender by the Axis powers was announced. This ensured that at the end of the war, all responsibility for government of the defeated nations would fall on the victors, and they would have a free hand in rebuilding government in those countries. No real planning was done in detail before the time arrived to meet this responsibility. It was done for the most part as the need arose.

At Teheran, the Big Three did discuss in a general way the occupation and demilitarization of Germany. They also laid the foundation for a postwar organization—the United Nations Organization—which like the earlier League of Nations was supposed to help regulate international relations and keep the peace and ensure friendly cooperation between the nations of the world.

At Potsdam, agreement was reached to sign peace treaties as soon as possible with former German allies. A Council of Foreign Ministers was established to draft the treaties. Several meetings were held in 1946 and 1947 and treaties were signed with Italy, Rumania, Hungary, Bulgaria, and Finland. These states paid reparations and agreed to some territorial readjustments as a price for peace. No agreement could be reached on Japan or Germany. In 1951, the Western powers led by the U.S. concluded a treaty with Japan without Russian participation. The latter made their own treaty in 1956. A final meeting of the Council of Foreign Ministers broke up in 1947 over Germany, and no peace treaty was ever signed with that country. The division of Germany for purposes of occupation and military government became permanent, with the three Western zones joining and eventually becoming the Federal Republic of Germany and the Russian zone becoming the German Democratic Republic.

Arrangements for the United Nations were confirmed at the Yalta Conference: the large powers would predominate in a Security Council, where they would have permanent seats together with several other powers elected from time to time from among the other members of the U.N. Consent of all the permanent members was necessary for any action to be taken by the Security Council (thus, giving the large powers a veto). The General Assembly was to include all members.

EASTERN EUROPE: 1945–1953

Much of European Russia had been devastated, and about 25 million people made homeless. In March 1946 a fourth five-year plan was adopted by the Supreme Soviet intended to increase industrial output to a level 50 percent higher than before the war. A bad harvest and food shortage in 1946 had been relieved by a good harvest in 1947, and in December 1947, the government announced the end of food rationing. At the same time a drastic currency devaluation was put through, which brought immediate hardship to many people but strengthened the Soviet economy in the long run. As a result of these and other forceful and energetic measures, the Soviet Union was able within a few years to make good most of the wartime damage and to surpass pre-war levels of production.

The fate of Eastern Europe (including Poland, Hungary, Rumania, Bulgaria, Czechoslovakia, and the Russian zone of Germany) from 1945 on was determined by the presence of Russian armies in that area.

Communization of Eastern Europe and the establishment of regimes in the satellite areas of the Soviet Union occurred in stages over a three-year period following the end of the war. The timetable of events varied in each country.

As relations broke down between the four occupying powers, the Soviet authorities gradually created a Communist state in their zone. On October 7, 1948, a German Democratic Republic was established. In June 1950, an agreement with Poland granted formal recognition of the Oder-Neisse Line as the boundary between the two states. Economic progress was unsatisfactory for most of the population, and on June 16–17, 1953, riots occurred in East Berlin which were suppressed by Soviet forces using tanks. In East Germany, a program of economic reform was announced which eventually brought some improvement.

In Yugoslavia, Marshal Tito (1892–1980) and his Communist partisan movement emerged from the war in a strong position because of their effective campaign against the German occupation. Tito was able to establish a Communist government in 1945 despite considerable pressure from Stalin, and pursue a course independent of the Soviet Union unique among the countries of Eastern Europe.

WESTERN EUROPE: 1945–1953

The monarchy which had governed Italy since the time of unification in the mid-nineteenth century was now discarded in favor of a republic. King Victor Emmanuel III (1869–1947), compromised by his association with Mussolini, resigned in favor of his son, but a referendum in June 1946 established a republic. In simultaneous elections for a constituent assembly, three parties predominated: the Social Democrats, the Communists, and the Christian Democrats.

In the last two years of the war, France recovered sufficiently under the leadership of General Charles de Gaulle to begin playing a significant military and political role once again. In July 1944, the United States recognized de Gaulle's Committee of National Liberation as the de facto government of areas liberated from the German occupation.

In foreign affairs, France occupied Germany. In addition, the Fourth Republic was faced with two major problems abroad when it attempted to assert its authority over Indochina and Algeria. The Indochina situation resulted in a long and costly war against nationalists and Communists under Ho Chi Minh (1890–1969). French involvement ended with the Geneva Accords of 1954 and French withdrawal. The Algerian struggle reached a crisis in 1958 resulting in General de Gaulle's return to power and the creation of a new Fifth Republic.

In May 1945, when Germany surrendered unconditionally, the country lay in ruins. About three-quarters of city houses had been gutted by air raids, industry was in a shambles, and the country was divided into zones of occupation ruled by foreign military governors. Economic chaos was the rule, currency was virtually worthless, food was in short supply, and the black market flourished for those who could afford to buy in it. By the Potsdam agreements, Germany lost about one-quarter of its pre-war territory. In addition, some 12 million people of German origin driven from their homes in countries like Poland and Czechoslovakia had to be fed, housed, and clothed along with the indigenous population.

Demilitarization, denazification, and democratization were the initial goals of the occupation forces in Germany. All four wartime allies agreed on the trial of leading Nazis for a variety of war crimes and "crimes against humanity." An International Military Tribunal was established at Nuremburg to try 22 major war criminals, and lesser courts tried many others. Most of the defendants were executed, although a few like Rudolf Hess were given life imprisonment.

As relations between the three Western powers and the Soviets gradually broke down in Germany, East and West became separate states. In the West, the British and American zones were fused into one in 1946, with the French joining in 1948. Political parties were gradually re-established.

In February 1948, a charter granted further powers of government to the Germans in the American and British zones. Later that year, the Russians and East Germans, in an effort to force the Western powers out of their zones in Berlin, began a blockade of the city which was located within the Russian zone. The response was an allied airlift to supply the city, and eventually, after some months, the blockade was called off.

In 1951 a Conservative majority was returned in Great Britain, and Winston Churchill, who had been defeated in 1945, became prime minister again. The new regime immediately reversed the nationalization of iron and steel. Other measures survived, however, especially the universal health care program which proved to be one of the most popular parts of the Labour achievement. In April 1955, Churchill resigned for reasons of age and health and turned over the prime minister's office to Anthony Eden (1897–1977).

THE MARSHALL PLAN

European recovery from the effects of the war was slow for the first two or three years after 1945. The European Recovery Program (Marshall Plan, named after the American secretary of state and World War II army chief of staff) began in 1948 and showed substantial results in all the Western European countries that took part. The most remarkable gains were in West Germany. The Plan aimed to strengthen Western Europe's resistance to communism.

NATO

The United States joined eleven other Atlantic regions in a mutual defense pact called the North American Treaty Organization (NATO) in 1949. NATO was a result of the Korean War.

BRITISH OVERSEAS WITHDRAWAL

Following World War II, there was a considerable migration of Jews who had survived the Nazi Holocaust to Palestine to join Jews who had settled there earlier. Conflicts broke out with the Arabs. The British occupying forces tried to suppress the violence and to negotiate a settlement between the factions. In 1948, after negotiations failed, the British, feeling they could no longer support the cost of occupation, announced their withdrawal. Zionist leaders then proclaimed the independent state of Israel and took up arms to fight the armies of Egypt, Syria, and other Arab states which invaded the Jewish-held area. The new Israeli state quickly proved its technological and military superiority by defeating the invaders.

The Jews of Israel created a modern parliamentary state on the European model with an economy and technology superior to their Arab neighbors. The new state was thought by many Arabs to be simply another manifestation of European imperialism made worse by religious antagonisms.

In 1967, Israel defeated Egypt, Syria, and Jordan in a six-day war, and the Israelis occupied additional territory including the Jordanian sector of the city of Jerusalem. An additional million Arabs came under Israeli rule as a result of this campaign.

Although defeated, the Arabs refused to sign any treaty or to come to terms with Israel. Palestinian refugees living in camps in states bordering Israel created grave problems. A Palestine Liberation Organization (PLO) was formed to fight for the establishment of an Arab Palestinian state on territory taken from Israel on the west bank of the Jordan River. The PLO resorted to terrorist tactics both against Israel and other states in support of their cause.

In October 1973, the Egyptians and Syrians launched an attack on Israel known as the Yom Kippur War. With some difficulty the attacks were repulsed. A settlement was mediated by American Secretary of State Henry Kissinger. The situation has remained unstable, however, with both sides resorting to border raids and other forms of violence short of full-scale war.

The British exercised control over Egypt from the end of the nineteenth century and declared it a British protectorate in December 1914. In 1922 Egypt became nominally independent.

The government under King Farouk I (1920–1965) did little to alleviate the overriding problem of poverty after the war. In 1952, a group of army officers, including Gamal Abdel Nasser (1918–1970) and Anwar Sadat (1918–1981), plotted against the government, and on July 23 the king was overthrown. Colonel Nasser became premier in April 1954. A treaty with Britain later that year resulted in the withdrawal of all British troops from the Canal Zone.

India under Jawaharlal Nehru (1889–1964) and the Congress Party became a parliamentary democracy. The country made economic progress, but gains were largely negated by a population increase to 600 million from 350 million.

THE FRENCH IN INDOCHINA AND ALGERIA

Following World War II, the French returned to Indochina and attempted to restore their rule there. The opposition nationalist movement was led by the veteran Communist Ho Chi Minh. War broke out between the nationalists and the French forces. In 1954 their army was surrounded at Dienbienphu and forced to surrender. This military disaster prompted a change of government in France.

This new government under Premier Pierre Mendès-France (1907–1982) negotiated French withdrawal at a conference held at Geneva, Switzerland in 1954. Cambodia and Laos became independent and Vietnam was partitioned at the 17th parallel. The North, with its capital at Hanoi, became a Communist state under Ho Chi Minh. The South remained non-Communist. Under the Geneva Accords, elections were to be held in the South to determine the fate of that area. However, the United States chose to intervene and support the regime of Ngo Dinh Diem (1901–1963), and elections were never held. Eventually a second Vietnamese war resulted, with the United States playing the role earlier played by France.

In a referendum, on January 8, 1961, the French people approved of eventual Algerian self-determination. In July 1962 French rule ended in Algeria. There was a mass exodus of Europeans from Algeria, but most Frenchmen were grateful to de Gaulle for ending the long Algerian conflict.

THE DUTCH AND INDONESIA

During World War II, the Japanese conquered the Dutch East Indies. At the end of the war, they recognized the independence of the area as Indonesia. When the Dutch attempted to return, four years of bloody fighting ensued against the nationalist forces of Achmed Sukarno (1901–1970). In 1949, the Dutch recognized Indonesian independence. In 1954, the Indonesians dissolved all ties with the Netherlands.

THE COLD WAR AFTER THE DEATH OF STALIN

Following Stalin's death 1953, Russian leaders appeared more willing than Stalin to be conciliatory and to consider peaceful coexistence.

In the U.S. the atmosphere also changed with the election of President Dwight Eisenhower and conciliatory gestures were not always automatically considered appeasement of the Communists. In 1955 a summit conference of Eisenhower, the British and French leaders, and Khrushchev (1894–1971) met at Geneva in an atmosphere more cordial than any since World War II. The "spirit of Geneva" did not last long, however.

After his return to power in France in 1958, General de Gaulle endeavored to make France a leader in European affairs with himself as spokesman for a Europe that he hoped would be a counter to the "dual hegemony" of the U.S. and U.S.S.R. His policies at times were anti-British or anti-American. Despite his prestige as the last great wartime leader, he did not have great success.

A NEW ERA BEGINS

Joseph Stalin died in March 1953. Eventually a little-known party functionary, Nikita Khrushchev, became Communist Party General Secretary in 1954. Khrushchev's policy of relaxing the regime of terror and oppression of the Stalin years became known as "The Thaw," after the title of a novel by Ilya Ehrenburg (1891–1967).

Change occurred in foreign affairs also. Khrushchev visited Belgrade and re-established relations with Tito, admitting that there was more than one road to socialism. He also visited the United States, met with President Eisenhower, and toured the country. Later, relations became more tense after the U-2 spy plane incident.

Following the loss of face sustained by Russia as a result of the Cuban Missile Crisis and the failure of Khrushchev's domestic agricultural policies, he was forced out of the party leadership and lived in retirement in Moscow until his death in 1971.

After Khrushchev's ouster, the leadership in the Central Committee divided power, making Leonid Brezhnev (1906–1982) party secretary and Aleksei Kosygin chairman of the council of ministers, or premier.

Stalin's successors rehabilitated many of Stalin's victims. They also permitted somewhat greater freedom in literary and artistic matters and even allowed some political criticism. Controls were maintained, however, and sometimes were tightened. Anti-semitism was also still present, and Soviet Jews were long denied permission to emigrate to Israel.

Brezhnev occupied the top position of power until his death in 1982. He was briefly succeeded by Yuri Andropov (1914–1984) (a former secret police chief) and then by Mikhail Gorbachev, who carried out a further relaxation of the internal regime. Gorbachev pushed disarmament and detente in foreign relations, and attempted a wide range of internal reforms known as *perestroika* ("restructuring"). Gorbachev resigned in 1991. Boris Yeltsin assumed control over the collapsing Soviet Union, which would later become known as the Commonwealth of Independent States, with Yeltsin as president.

Economic difficulties associated with a transition to a free economy, the mishandled repression of the Chechnya independence movement, and the forceful dispersal of Yeltsin's parliamentary opponents in 1993 gave ammunition to Yeltsin's opponents. In the 1996 elections, Yeltsin retained office as president, but the poor state of his health, despite successful heart bypass surgery in the fall of 1996, made his future leadership uncertain.

CHANGE IN EASTERN EUROPE

In the 1980s, the trade union movement known as Solidarity and its leader, Lech Walesa, emerged as a political force, organizing mass protests in 1980–1981 and maintaining almost continuous pressure on the government headed by General Wojciech Jaruzelski. Despite government efforts to maintain strong central control and suppress the opposition, the ruling Communists were forced to recognize the opposition and make concessions. In June 1989, after power had passed to the Polish Parliament, a national election gave Solidarity an overwhelming majority, and Walesa assumed the presidency. By 1993–94, economic problems resulted in a Communist majority and a change of administration, but there was no return to the old Communist dictatorship.

CHANGE IN WESTERN EUROPE

In March 1957, inspired chiefly by Belgian Foreign Minister Paul-Henri Spaak, two treaties were signed in Rome creating a European Atomic Energy Commission (Euratom) and a European Economic Community (the Common Market)—which eventually absorbed Euratom. The EEC was to be a customs union creating a free market area with a common external tariff for member nations. Toward the outside world, the EEC acted as a single bargaining agent for its members in commercial transactions, and it reached a number of agreements with other European and Third World states.

In 1973, the original six were joined by three new members: Britain, Ireland, and Denmark. The name was changed to "European Community." In 1979, there were three more applicants: Spain, Portugal, and Greece. These latter states were less well off and created problems of cheap labor, agricultural products, etc., which delayed their acceptance as members until 1986.

Relations with Northern Ireland proved a burden to successive British governments. The 1922 settlement had left Northern Ireland as a self-governing part of the United Kingdom. Of 1.5 million inhabitants, one-third were Roman Catholic and two-thirds were Protestant. Catholics claimed they were discriminated against and pressed for annexation by the Republic of Ireland. Activity by the Irish Republican Army brought retaliation by Protestant extremists. From 1969 on, there was considerable violence, causing the British to bring in troops to maintain order. Over 1,500 were killed in the next several years in sporadic outbreaks of violence.

Under Prime Minister Margaret Thatcher in the 1980s, the British economy improved somewhat. London regained some of its former power as a financial center. In recent years, an influx of people from former colonies in Asia, Africa, and the West Indies has caused some racial tensions.

Prime Minister Thatcher was a partisan of free enterprise. She fought inflation with austerity and let economic problems spur British employers and unions to change for greater efficiency. She received a boost in popularity when Britain fought a brief war with Argentina over the Falkland Islands and emerged victorious. She stressed close ties with the Republican administration of Ronald Reagan in the U.S. A Conservative victory in the 1987 elections made Thatcher the longest-serving prime minister in modern British history.

In 1990, having lost the support of Conservatives in Parliament, Thatcher resigned and was replaced by Chancellor of the Exchequer John Major. Under Major's leadership, Conservatives had to deal with slow economic growth, unemployment, and racial tensions caused by resentment over the influx of immigrants from other parts of the Commonwealth. And there remains the seemingly intractable religious strife in Northern Ireland, with its Protestant-Catholic animosities.

France under de Gaulle saw a new constitution drafted and approved establishing the Fifth Republic with a much strengthened executive in the form of a president with power to dissolve the legislature and call for elections, to submit important questions to popular referendum, and if necessary to assume emergency powers. De Gaulle used all these powers in his 11 years as president.

In domestic politics, de Gaulle strengthened the power of the president by often using the referendum and bypassing the Assembly. De Gaulle was re-elected in 1965, but people became restless with what amounted to a republican monarch. Labor became restive over inflation and housing while students objected to expenditures on nuclear forces rather than education. In May 1968, student grievances over conditions in the universities caused hundreds of thousands to revolt. They were soon joined by some 10 million workers, who paralyzed the economy. De Gaulle survived by promising educational reform and wage increases. New elections were held in June 1968, and de Gaulle was returned to power. Promised reforms were begun, but in April 1969, he resigned and died about a year later.

De Gaulle's immediate successors were Georges Pompidou (1969–1974) and Valéry Giscard d'Estaing (1974–1981). Both provided France with firm leadership, and continued to follow an independent foreign policy.

In 1981 François Mitterand succeeded Giscard d'Estaing. He inherited a troubled economy. During his first year Mitterand tried to revitalize economic growth, granted wage hikes, reduced the work week, expanded paid vacations, and nationalized 11 large private companies and banks. The aim was to stimulate the economy by expanding worker purchasing power and confiscating the profits of large corporations for public investment. Loans were made abroad to finance this program. When results were poor, these foreign investors were reluctant to grant more credit. Mitterand then reversed his policy and began to cut taxes and social expenditures. By 1984, this had brought down inflation but increased unemployment.

Mitterand lost his Socialist majority in Parliament in 1986, but regained it in 1988. In 1995, an ailing Mitterand indicated he would retire at the end of his term. He died in January 1996. Out of the election of April 1995 emerged a fractured right-of-center bloc that came to coalesce around Jacques Chirac, the major of Paris and former two-time prime minister. Following a second-round runoff, Chirac won 52 percent of the vote.

In Germany in November 1966, the Christian Democrats formed a so-called "great coalition" with the Social Democrats under Willy Brandt. Kurt Georg Kiesinger (1904–1988) became chancellor, and Brandt the Socialist took over as foreign minister. Brandt announced his intention to work step by step for better relations with East Germany, but found that in a coalition of two very dissimilar parties he could make no substantial progress.

Problems with the economy and the environment brought an end to Kiesinger's chancellorship and the rule of the Socialists in 1982. An organization called the Greens, which was a loosely organized coalition of environmentalists alienated from society, detracted from Socialist power. In 1982, the German voters turned to the more conservative Christian Democrats again, and Helmut Kohl became chancellor.

In Italy, the Christian Democrats, who were closely allied with the Roman Catholic Church, dominated the national scene. Their organization, though plagued by corruption, did provide some unity to Italian politics by supplying the prime ministers for numerous coalitions.

Italy advanced economically. Natural gas and some oil was discovered in the north and the Po valley area especially benefited. Unfortunately, business efficiency found no parallel in the government or civil service. Italy suffered from terrorism, kidnappings, and assassinations by extreme radical groups such as the Red Brigades. These agitators hoped to create conditions favorable to the overthrow of the democratic constitution. The most notorious terrorist act was the assassination in 1978 of Aldo Moro (1916–1978), a respected Christian Democratic leader.

In 1983, Bettino Craxi (Socialist) became prime minister at the head of an uneasy coalition that lasted four years—the longest single government in postwar Italian history. By the 1990s Italian industry and its economy generally had advanced to a point where Italy was a leading center in high-tech industry, fashion, design, and banking. But instability continued to mark Italian politics as it had since the end of World War II. Corruption within a system dominated by the Christian Democrats resulted in criminal trials in the 1990s that sent a number of high government officials to prison. In 1993 the electoral system for the Senate was changed from proportional representation to one that gives power to the majority vote-getting party. The 1994 elections for Parliament brought to power the charismatic, conservative Silvio Berlusconi and his *Forzia Italia* ("Let's go, Italy") movement.

In Portugal, Europe's longest right-wing dictatorship came to an end in September 1968, when a stroke incapacitated Antonio Salazar, who died two years later. A former collaborator, Marcelo Caetano (1906–1980), became prime minister, and an era of change began. Censorship was relaxed and some freedom was given to political parties.

In April 1974, the Caetano regime was overthrown and a "junta of national salvation" took over, headed by General Spinola, who later retired and went into exile. Portugal went through a succession of governments. Its African colonies of Mozambique and Angola were finally granted independence in 1975. Portugal joined the Common Market in 1986.

Spain's Francisco Franco, who had been ruler of a fascist regime since the end of the Civil War in 1939, held on until he was close to 70. He then designated the Bourbon prince, Juan Carlos, to be his successor. In 1975, Franco relinquished power and died three weeks later. Juan Carlos proved a popular and able leader and over the next several years took the country from dictatorship to constitutional monarchy. Basque and Catalan separatist movements, which had caused trouble for so long, were appeased by the granting of local autonomy. Spain also entered the European Community in 1986.

Under the Maastricht Treaties of 1991, all members of the EC began measured steps toward an economic and political union that would ultimately have its own common currency. In 1996, the 12 member nations of the EC accounted for one-fifth of world trade.

☞ Drill: Western and World Civilizations

> **Directions:** Each of the questions or incomplete statements below is followed by four answers or completions. Select the one that is best in each case.

1. Renaissance Humanism was a threat to the Church because it

   (A) espoused atheism.

   (B) denounced scholasticism.

(C) denounced neo-Platonism.

(D) emphasized a return to the original sources of Christianity.

2. *Defense of the Seven Sacraments* was a tract

   (A) written by Thomas More in which the Church is attacked because of its sacramental theology.

   (B) written by Zwingli which argued that the Eucharist was a symbolic reenactment of the Last Supper.

   (C) in which Luther called upon the German nobility to accept responsibility for cleansing Christianity of the abuses which had developed within the Church.

   (D) written by Henry VIII in which the Roman Catholic Church's position on sacramental theology was supported.

3. Erasmus of Rotterdam was the author of

   (A) *The Praise of Folly.*   (C) *Utopia.*

   (B) *The Birth of Venus.*   (D) *The Prince.*

4. The Henrician reaffirmation of Catholic theology was made in the

   (A) Ten Articles of Faith.

   (B) Six Articles of Faith.

   (C) Forty-two Articles of Faith.

   (D) Act of Supremacy.

5. The Peace of Augsburg

   (A) recognized that Lutheranism was the true interpretation of Christianity.

   (B) recognized the principle that the religion of the leader would determine the religion of the people.

   (C) denounced the Papacy and Charles V.

   (D) resulted in the recognition of Lutheranism, Calvinism, and Catholicism.

6. The Catholic Counter-Reformation included all of the following EXCEPT

   (A) the *Index of Prohibited Books.*

   (B) the Council of Trent.

(C)   a more assertive Papacy.

(D)   a willingness to negotiate non-doctrinal issues with reformers.

7.   Where did the Saint Bartholomew's Day Massacre occur?

(A)   France   (C)   Spain

(B)   England   (D)   The Netherlands

8.   The Price Revolution of the 16th century was caused by

(A)   the establishment of monopolies.

(B)   the importation of silver and gold into the European economy.

(C)   a shortage of labor.

(D)   the wars of religion caused by the Reformation.

9.   The Peace of Westphalia (1648)

(A)   transferred Louisiana from France to Britain.

(B)   recognized the independence of the Netherlands.

(C)   recognized the unity of the German Empire.

(D)   was a triumph of the Hapsburg polity to unity.

10.   Sir Isaac Newton's intellectual synthesis was advanced in

(A)   *Principia.*

(B)   *Discourse on Method.*

(C)   *Novum Organum.*

(D)   *Three Laws of Planetary Motion.*

11.   Richelieu served as "Prime Minister" to

(A)   Louis XII.   (C)   Louis XIV.

(B)   Henry IV.   (D)   Louis XIII.

12.   In the Edict of Fontainebleau, Louis XIV

(A)   abrogated the Edict of Nantes.

(B)   abrogated the Edict of Potsdam.

(C)   announced his divorce from Catherine de Medici.

(D) denounced Cardinal Mazarin.

13. In order to seize the Russian throne, Peter the Great had to overthrow his sister

    (A) Theodora.   (C) Sophia.

    (B) Natalia.   (D) Catherine.

14. Peter the Great's principal foreign policy achievement was

    (A) the acquisition of ports on the Black Sea.

    (B) the acquisition of ports on the Baltic Sea.

    (C) the Russian gains in the three partitions of Poland.

    (D) the defensive alliance with England.

Unemployment

(Numbers in thousands & percentage of appropriate work force)

	Germany		Great Britain	
1930	3,076	15.3	1,917	14.6
1932	5,575	30.1	2,745	22.5
1934	2,718	14.9	2,159	17.7
1936	2,151	11.6	1,755	14.3
1938	429	2.1	1,191	13.3

15. The chart above indicates

    (A) that Germany and Great Britain recovered from the Depression at about the same level and rate.

    (B) that Hitler's Germany reduced unemployment at a remarkable rate during the period from 1936 and 1938.

    (C) that Britain was complacent about its double-digit unemployment during the 1930s.

    (D) that the German economic system was superior to that of Great Britain.

16. A moderate proposal which called on France to adopt a political system similar to Great Britain was an element espoused by Montesquieu in

    (A) *The Social Contract.*

(B)   *The Spirit of the Laws.*

(C)   *The Encyclopedia.*

(D)   *The Declaration of the Rights of Man and the Citizen.*

17.   Which of the following chronological sequences on the French Revolution is correct?

(A)   Directory, Consulate, Legislative Assembly

(B)   Legislative Assembly, Convention, Directory

(C)   Convention, Consulate, Directory

(D)   National Assembly, Convention, Directory

18.   Thomas Hobbes' political philosophy can be most clearly identified with the thought of which of the following?

(A)   Rousseau   (C)   Quesnay

(B)   Voltaire   (D)   Montesquieu

19.   Who was the most important enlightened political ruler of the 18th century?

(A)   Catherine the Great   (C)   Maria Theresa

(B)   Louis XV   (D)   Frederick the Great

20.   The reaction to the Peterloo Massacre was characteristic of the conservative policies advanced by the British government under

(A)   George Canning.   (C)   Lord Melbourne.

(B)   Robert Peel.   (D)   Lord Liverpool.

21.   The Factory Act of 1833

(A)   established the five-day work week in Britain.

(B)   eliminated child labor in the mining of coal and iron.

(C)   required employers to provide comprehensive medical coverage for all employees.

(D)   alleviated some of the abuses of child labor in the textile industry.

22.   The Anglo-French Entente (also known as the Entente Cordiale)

(A)   was a defensive treaty directed at containing German expansion in Europe.

(B)   was a defensive treaty directed at containing German expansion overseas.

(C)   resolved Anglo-French colonial disputes in Egypt and Morocco.

(D)   was a 19th century agreement which ended the diplomatic isolation of Britain.

23. Who was the most prominent British advocate for the abolition of slavery during the early 19th century?

(A)   William Pitt the Younger

(B)   the Duke of Wellington

(C)   William Wilberforce

(D)   William Wordsworth

24. English Utilitarianism was identified with the phrase

(A)   all power to the people.

(B)   from each according to his labor, to each according to his need.

(C)   universal reason.

(D)   the greatest good for the greatest number.

25. An economic philosophy identified with "bullionism" and the need to maintain a favorable balance of trade was

(A)   Utopian Socialism.   (C)   Capitalism.

(B)   Marxism.   (D)   Mercantilism.

26. Which British Prime Minister was associated closely with the Irish Home Rule bill?

(A)   Benjamin Disraeli   (C)   Lord Salisbury

(B)   William Gladstone   (D)   Joseph Chamberlain

27. The Balfour Declaration (1917)

(A)   denounced the use of chemicals by the Germans on the Western Front.

(B)   was a pledge of British support for the future.

(C)   was a mediation effort to resolve the Anglo-Irish crisis.

(D)   was an attempt to persuade the United States to abandon its neutrality.

28. The Boulanger Crisis

    (A) was a left-wing attempt engineered by Leon Gambetta to over-throw the Third French Republic.

    (B) involved a financial scandal associated with raising funds to build the Panama Canal.

    (C) was caused by a right-wing scheme to overthrow the Third French Republic and install General Georges Boulanger as the political leader.

    (D) broke when the Dreyfus scandal became known to the French press.

29. All of the following were plots against Elizabeth I EXCEPT

    (A) the Babington Plot.

    (B) the Throckmorton Plot.

    (C) the Ridolfi Plot.

    (D) the Wisbech Stirs.

30. The map below indicates the partition of Africa in what year?

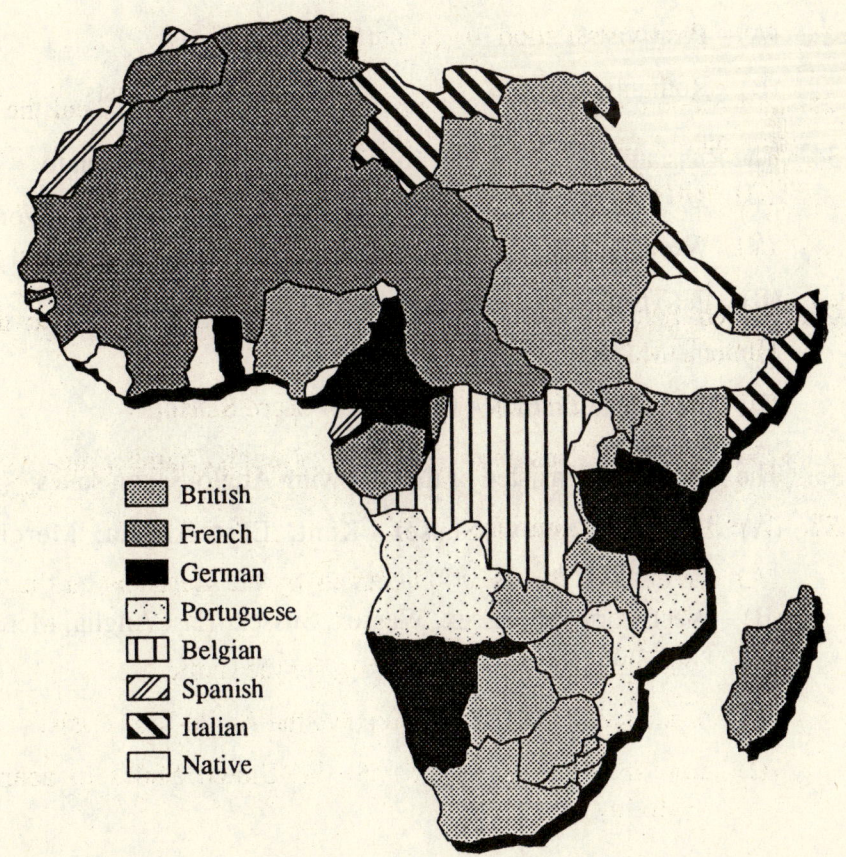

British
French
German
Portuguese
Belgian
Spanish
Italian
Native

(A) 1815   (C) 1870

(B) 1914   (D) 1960

31. The French essayist Montaigne was representative of which intellectual movement?

(A) Enlightenment   (C) Positivism

(B) Baroque   (D) Utopian Socialism

32. The Hundred Days was

(A) the label given to the reactionary period which followed the Manchester riots in Britain.

(B) an unsuccessful attempt by Napoleon to restore himself as a credible European leader.

(C) the worst phase of the Reign of Terror.

(D) a period which witnessed British defeats in Africa and the Low Countries.

33. Jeremy Bentham, James Mill and John Stuart Mill were

(A) Positivists.   (C) Utilitarians.

(B) Romantic Idealists.   (D) Utopian Socialists.

34. The Russian blockade of Berlin in 1948–49 was a reaction to

(A) the unification of the British, French, and American zones into West Germany.

(B) the Truman Doctrine.

(C) the Marshall Plan.

(D) the formation of NATO.

35. The Heptarchy consisted of the following Anglo-Saxon states:

(A) Essex, Wessex, Sussex, Kent, East Anglia, Mercia, and Northumbria

(B) West Cornwall, Essex, Wessex, Sussex, East Anglia, Mercia, and Northumbria

(C)   Wales, West Anglia, Kent, Essex, Wessex, Sussex, and Mercia

(D)   The Danelaw, Cumbria, Essex, Wessex, Sussex, Kent, and East Anglia

36.   All of the following were contributors in the Realist-Nominalist Controversy EXCEPT

(A)   Peter Abelard.   (C)   Albertus Magnus.

(B)   Peter Lombard.   (D)   Hildebrand.

37.   The reasons for the formation of the Delian League included

I.   the Greek victory over Xerxes.

II.   the Athenian intent to develop a defensive and offensive alliance against Persia.

III.   Athenian strategy to control all of the eastern Mediterranean.

IV.   an imminent Spartan threat to Athens.

V.   more than twenty years of crisis caused by Persian aggression.

(A)   I and II only   (C)   II and III only

(B)   I, II, and III only   (D)   I, II, and V only

38.   "Peasant" or "public" uprisings broke out in all of the following places on the dates listed EXCEPT

(A)   France in 1358.   (C)   Flanders in 1302.

(B)   Sicily in 1282.   (D)   Holy Roman Empire in 1190.

39.   During the late 2nd century B.C., Roman political life was dominated by the

(A)   First Triumvirate.

(B)   prevailing political parties; *Populares, Optimates*, and *Equites*.

(C)   Gracchi.

(D)   end of the Punic Wars.

40. After the death of Alexander, which of the following Hellenistic kingdoms emerged?

I. Antigonid Macedonia   IV. Bactria

II. Seleucid Asia   V. India

III. Ptolemaic Egypt

(A) I and II only   (C) I, II, III, and IV only

(B) I, II, and III only   (D) I, III, and IV only

WESTERN AND WORLD CIVILIZATIONS REVIEW

ANSWER KEY

Drill: Western and World Civilizations

1.	(D)	11.	(D)	21.	(D)	31.	(B)
2.	(D)	12.	(A)	22.	(C)	32.	(B)
3.	(A)	13.	(C)	23.	(C)	33.	(C)
4.	(B)	14.	(B)	24.	(D)	34.	(A)
5.	(B)	15.	(B)	25.	(D)	35.	(A)
6.	(D)	16.	(B)	26.	(B)	36.	(D)
7.	(A)	17.	(B)	27.	(B)	37.	(D)
8.	(B)	18.	(B)	28.	(C)	38.	(D)
9.	(B)	19.	(D)	29.	(D)	39.	(B)
10.	(A)	20.	(D)	30.	(B)	40.	(B)

DETAILED EXPLANATIONS OF ANSWERS

Drill: Western and World Civilizations

1.   **(D)**   Renaissance Humanism was a threat to the Church because it (D) emphasized a return to the original sources of Christianity — the Bible and the writings of the Fathers of Church. In that light, the humanists tended to ignore or denounce the proceedings of Church councils and pontiffs during the Middle Ages. While many Renaissance humanists denounced scholasticism, there was no inherent opposition to it and many retained support of the late Medieval philosophy. Renaissance humanism did not espouse atheism nor did it advance an amoral philosophy; it tended to advance a neo-Platonism through the writings of such individuals as Pico Della Mirandola and Marsiglio.

2.   **(D)**   The *Defense of the Seven Sacraments* was a tract (D) written by Henry VIII in which the Roman Catholic Church's position on sacramental theology was supported. This 1521 publication repudiated Luther's views on the sacraments which were advanced in pamphlets during the preceding year. While some earlier authorities have asserted that the real author of the tract was Thomas More (A), contemporary scholarship has affirmed that, while More no doubt provided assistance, authorship should be attributed to Henry VIII. Zwingli (B) did maintain that the Eucharist was a symbolic reenactment of the Last Supper but he did not write this tract. Obviously, Luther (C), to whom it was directed, was not the author.

3.   **(A)**   Erasmus of Rotterdam was the author of (A) *The Praise of Folly* which was a criticism of the ambitions of the clergy. *The Birth of Venus* (B) was not a literary work. Thomas More was the author of *Utopia* (C); Niccolo Machiavelli wrote (D) *The Prince*.

4.   **(B)**   The Henrican reaffirmation of the Catholic Theology was made in the (B) Six Articles of Faith of 1539. In response to mounting criticism and the vague (A) Ten Articles of Faith (1536) and the dissolution of the monasteries, Henry VIII retreated from the movement toward Protestantism. The (D) Act of Supremacy was passed by the Reformation Parliament to decree and enforce Henry VIII's authority over the Church in England. The Forty-Two Articles of Faith (E) was a statement of Protestant doctrines developed by Thomas Cranmer during the early 1550s.

5. **(B)** The Peace of Augsburg (1555) (B) recognized the principle that the religion of the leader would determine the religion of the people; it was a major victory for Lutheranism and a defeat of the Hapsburg aspirations to effectively control the Holy Roman Empire. Lutheranism (A) was not recognized as the true interpretation of Christianity. Calvinism (D) was not recognized until the Peace of Westphalia in 1648; (C) Charles V and the Papacy were negotiators in formulating the Peace of Augsburg.

6. **(D)** The Catholic Counter-Reformation did not include (E) a willingness to negotiate non-doctrinal issues with reformers; indeed, the Catholic Church considered all confrontational issues to be doctrinal. The Council of Trent (B) was convened in three sessions from 1545 to 1564 and reaffirmed traditional Catholic doctrines; the papacy (C) became more assertive as can be seen in the issuing of the *Index of Prohibited Books* in 1558-59.

7. **(A)** The St. Batholomew's Day Massacre occurred in 1572 in (A) France; it was the work of Queen Catherine De Medici and involved the execution of thousands of French Huguenots during the subsequent months. Obviously, this event did not transpire in (B) England, (C) Spain, or (D) the Netherlands.

8. **(B)** The Price Revolution of the 16th century was caused by (B) the importation of silver and gold into the European economy; the influx of specie from Latin America resulted in eliminating the scarcity of money — the result was a general fourfold increase in prices. The establishment of monopolies (A) was an important element in 17th century mercantilism. While there were occasional labor shortages (C) and the wars of religion (D) did not disrupt economic activities, these developments did not have any substantive impact on the price revolution.

9. **(B)** The Peace of Westphalia (1648) (B) recognized the independence of the Netherlands and Switzerland. Louisiana (A) was not transferred to Britain, and the Hapsburg plan (D) and (C) for a unified central Europe was destroyed.

10. **(A)** Sir Isaac Newton's intellectual synthesis was advanced in (A) *Principia* in 1687; he established scientism as a credible alternative to preceding intellectual approaches and methods. *Discourse on Method* (B) was written by René Descartes in 1637; *Novum Organum* (C) was a work by Francis Bacon which addressed the issue of empiricism; Kepler developed the Three Laws of Planetary Motion (D).

11. **(D)** Richelieu served as "Prime Minister" to (D) Louis XIII. For

over two decades during the turbulence of the Thirty Years' War and the LaRochelle crisis with the Huguenots, Cardinal Richelieu administered France for Louis XIII. Henry IV (B) was Louis XIII's father; Louis XIV (C) was his son. Louis XII (A) was an earlier French monarch.

12. **(A)** In the Edict of Fontainebleau (1685), Louis XIV (A) abrogated the Edict of Nantes of 1598 in which Henry IV had to extend some religious liberties to French Protestants. Fontainebleau directed that all Frenchmen would conform to Catholicism. The Edict of Potsdam (1686) (B) was issued by Elector Frederick William of Brandenburg-Prussia; it invited French Protestants to migrate to Brandenburg. The Fontainebleau decree was not related to (C) Catherine De Medici or (D) Cardinal Mazarin.

13. **(C)** In order to seize the Russian throne, Peter the Great had to overthrow (1689) his sister (C) Sophia. His mother, (B) served as regent until 1694 when Peter took over the government. Catherine (D) was a Russian leader in the 18th century. (A) Theodora was not a Romanov ruler.

14. **(B)** Peter the Great's principal foreign policy achievement was (B) the acquisition of ports on the Baltic Sea. His efforts to acquire ports on the Black Sea (A) were not realized; later Catherine the Great would expand in this area at the expense of the Ottoman Turks. The partitions of Poland (C) occurred after Peter's death; Russia did not enter into any alliance with England (D) during this period.

15. **(B)** This chart indicates (B) that Hitler's Germany reduced unemployment at a remarkable rate during the period from 1936 to 1938; the fascist economic controls facilitated this development. (A), (C), (D) are incorrect; the German economy was not "superior" to Britain's nor was Britain content with excessive unemployment — while there is much to criticize about the manner in which the Labour and Conservative parties handled economic recovery, one must remember that free economies are naturally more difficult to direct than state controlled economic systems.

16. **(B)** A moderate proposal which called on France to adopt a political system similar to that of Great Britain was an element espoused by Montesquieu in (B) *The Spirit of the Laws*. *The Social Contract* (A) was written by Jean Jacques Rousseau; *The Encyclopedia* (C) was by Denis Diderot; *The Declaration of the Rights of Man and the Citizen* (D) was produced by the National Assembly in August, 1789.

17. **(B)** The correct chronological sequence is (B) Legislative Assembly (1791–92), Convention (1792–95), and Directory (1795–99). The Na-

tional Assembly existed from 1789 to 1791; the Consulate from 1799 to 1804; and the Empire from 1804 to 1814.

18. **(B)**   Thomas Hobbes' political philosophy can be most clearly identified with the thought of (B) Voltaire. Voltaire maintained that Enlightened Despotism would be the best form of government for France; this position concurs with the Hobbesian view that people need to be governed, not government by the people; (C) Quesnay's program was similar though not as directly related. (A) Rousseau and (D) Montesquieu entertained political theories which were more revolutionary in the context of sovereign power and the exercise of that power.

19. **(D)**   The most prominent enlightened political ruler of the 18th century was (D) Frederick the Great of Prussia. He had a genuine interest in enlightened government and introduced a wide range of reforms. Catherine the Great (A) of Russia considered herself enlightened but her barbarism did not support that claim. Louis XV (C) and Maria Theresa (C) were opposed to the thought of the enlightenment.

20. **(D)**   The reaction to the Peterloo Massacre was characteristic of the conservative policies advanced by the British government under (D) Lord Liverpool. While George Canning (A) and Robert Peel (B) were involved in the government, they were not very influential at this time. Melbourne (C) became Prime Minister during the 1830s.

21. **(D)**   The Factory Act of 1833 (D) alleviated some of the abuses of child labor in the textile industry. The five-day work week (A) did not become a reality until the 20th century; reforms in the use of children in mining and heavy industry (B) were not implemented until later in the 19th century; employers were never required (C) to provide comprehensive medical coverage for all employees.

22. **(C)**   The Anglo-French Entente (also known as the Entente Cordiale) (C) resolved Anglo-French colonial disputes in Egypt and Morocco; northeast Africa (Egypt and the Sudan) was recognized as a British sphere of influence, northwest Africa (Morocco and Algeria) was recognized as a French sphere of influence. This arrangement was not (A) directed at German expansion in Europe or (B) overseas; it was signed in 1904 and therefore was not (D) a 19th century agreement.

23. **(C)**   The most prominent British advocate for the abolition of slavery during the early 19th century was (C) William Wilberforce. While Wordsworth (D) was sympathetic to abolitionism, he was not in the forefront

of opposition to slavery. William Pitt the Younger (A) and Wellington (B) were preoccupied with the Napoleonic Wars.

24. **(D)** English Utilitarianism was identified with the phrase (D) "the greatest good for the greatest number." Jeremy Bentham, James Mill, and John Stuart Mill were prominent Utilitarians. "All power to the people" and "From each according to his labor, to each according to his need" (B) were elements in Lenin's rhetoric. "Universal reason" (C) is identified with Georg Wilhelm Hegel.

25. **(D)** Mercantilism was an economic philosophy identified with "bullionism" and the need to maintain a favorable balance of trade. Utopian Socialism (A) was an early 19th century philosophy which emphasized the need for a more equitable distribution of wealth; (B) Marxism was a leftist approach to economics and politics. (C) Capitalism was the developing condition in which mercantilism operated.

26. **(B)** The British Prime Minister who was associated closely with Irish Home Rule was (B) William Gladstone. Gladstone maintained through his four ministries that one of his principal tasks was "to pacify Ireland." Benjamin Disraeli (A), Lord Salisbury (B), and Joseph Chamberlain (D) were not particularly interested or sympathetic to the Irish.

27. **(B)** The Balfour Declaration (1917) (B) was a pledge of British support for the future establishment of a Jewish state. It was not related to (A) the German use of chemicals, (C) the Anglo-Irish crisis stemming from the Easter Rebellion, or (D) American neutrality.

28. **(C)** The Boulanger Crisis (C) was caused by a right-wing scheme to overthrow the Third French Republic and install General Georges Boulanger as the political leader; it was supported by monarchists and other rightist enemies of the republic. It was not (A) a left-wing scheme, nor was it related to the (B) Panama Canal or (D) the Dreyfus Affair.

29. **(D)** While the (A) Babington Plot, (B) the Throckmorton Plot, and (C) the Ridolfi Plot were attempts to overthrow Elizabeth I, the Wisbech Stirs of the late 1590s was a controversy among Catholics over control of the outlawed English Catholic Church.

30. **(B)** The map indicates the partition of Africa in (B) 1914 after most of the European powers had participated in establishing colonial empires.

31. **(B)** The French essayist Montaigne was representative of an

intellectual movement known as (B) Baroque which was an intellectual quest for a new synthesis; it was caused by the chaos of the Reformation/Counter-Reformation era. The Enlightenment (A) developed in the 18th century and constituted an elaboration on the new scientific snythesis which emerged during the 17th century. (C) Positivism and (D) Utopian Socialism were 19th century intellectual movements.

32. **(B)**   The Hundred Days (1815) was (B) an unsuccessful attempt by Napoleon to restore himself as a credible European leader. The Hundred Days concluded in June, 1815 at the Battle of Waterloo when Wellington's army defeated Napoleon. Obviously, the Hundred Days did not relate to (A) the reactionary period in Britain following the Manchester riots, (C) the Reign of Terror, (D) British defeats in Africa and the Low Countries.

33. **(C)**   Jeremy Bentham, James Mill and John Stuart Mill were (C) Utilitarians who argued the case "the greatest good for the greatest number." Auguste Comte established (A) Positivism; Fichte and Hegel were German Romantic Idealists (B); Robert Owen and Charles Fourier were Utopian Socialists (D).

34. **(A)**   The Russian blockade of Berlin in 1948–49 was a reaction to (A) the unification of the British, French, and American zones into West Germany. While the (B) Truman Doctrine was directed at preventing communist victories in Greece and Turkey, and the Marshall Plan (C) was designed to assist in accelerating the economic recovery of Europe, they were not the direct causes of the blockade. NATO (D) was formed after the blockade began.

35. **(A)**   During the 6th century, the Heptarchy of Anglo-Saxon England included Essex, Wessex, Sussex, Kent, East Anglia, Mercia, and Northumbria. By the end of the 6th century Kent emerged as the primary power in Britain. West Cornwall (B), Wales (C), the Danelaw, and Cumbria (D) were not organized political entities during the 6th century and so were not part of the Heptarchy.

36. **(D)**   Hildebrand (D) was a medieval church reformer who became pope. Peter Abelard (A) (*Sic at Non*), Peter Lombard (B) (*Four Books of Sentences*) and Albertus Magnus (C) were all significant contributors to the Realist-Nominalist Controversy. While this controversy was initiated over Plato's Doctrine of Ideas, it was transformed into a discussion of whether truth obtained through reason was reconcilable with truth obtained through revelation.

37. **(D)** The Delian League was established in 477 B.C. after more than two decades of war (V) with Persian armies led by Darius and Xerxes (I). Under Athenian leadership, the Delian League was intended to provide a defensive and offensive alliance directed against Persia. Not until later was the Delian League interpreted as an Athenian attempt to dominate the Greek, not Mediterranean, world (III) for its own gain. The Spartan threat to Athens (IV) did not materialize until the early years of the Peloponnesian War in the late 430s.

38. **(D)** In 1190, the Holy Roman Empire (D) was preoccupied with the Third Crusade and did not experience any peasant uprisings. A popular uprising known as the Jacquerie broke out in France in 1358 (A). The "Sicilian Vespers" took place in Sicily in 1282 (B) when the people rebelled against French rule, and the peasants and laborers in Flanders in 1302 (C) followed the Sicilian example and expelled French rulers from Flanders.

39. **(B)** During the late 2nd century B.C., Roman political life was dominated by the prevailing political parties: Populares, the so-called "people's party"; Optimates, the "best men"; and the Equites, rich knights (B). The First Triumvirate (A) did not appear until the next century. The Gracchi (C), Tiberius and Gaius Gracchus, were significant public figures but did not hold substantive power. The Punic Wars (D) concluded in 146 BC; they did not dominate Roman political life.

40. **(B)** After Alexander the Great's death in 323 B.C., his empire was divided into three major units: Antigonid Macedonia (I), with a monarchy limited by an armed population; Seleucid Asia (II), with a monarchy restricted by autonomous cities; and Ptolemaic Egypt (III), with an unrestricted monarchy. As the Seleucid Empire later disintegrated, Bactria (IV) emerged as a buffer against the barbarians of the East. Most of India (V) was not included in Alexander's empire, although he did penetrate northwest India during his campaigns.

IX. UNITED STATES HISTORY REVIEW

AMERICAN HISTORY: THE COLONIAL PERIOD (1500–1763)

THE AGE OF EXPLORATION

The Treaty of Tordesillas (1493) drew a line dividing the land in the New World between Spain and Portugal. Lands east of the line were Portuguese. As a result, Brazil eventually became a Portuguese colony, while Spain maintained claims to the rest of the Americas.

To conquer the Americas, the Spanish monarchs used their powerful army, led by independent Spanish adventurers known as conquistadores. The European diseases they unwittingly carried with them devastated the local Native American populations, who had no immunities against such diseases.

Spain administered its new holdings as an autocratic, rigidly controlled empire in which everything was to benefit the parent country. The Spaniards developed a system of large manors or estates (encomiendas), with Indian slaves ruthlessly managed for the benefit of the conquistadores. The encomienda system was later replaced by the similar but somewhat milder hacienda system. As the Indian population died from overwork and European diseases, Spaniards began importing African slaves to supply their labor needs.

ENGLISH AND FRENCH BEGINNINGS

In 1497, the Italian John Cabot (Giovanni Caboto, ca. 1450–1499), sailing under the sponsorship of the king of England in search of a Northwest Passage (a water route to the Orient through or around the North American continent), became the first European since the Vikings more than four centuries earlier to reach the mainland of North America, which he claimed for England. Beginning in 1534, Jacques Cartier (1491–1557), authorized by the king of France, mounted three expeditions to the area of the St. Lawrence River, which he believed might be the hoped for Northwest Passage. He explored up the river as far as the site of Montreal.

When the English finally began colonization, commercial capitalism in England had advanced to the point that the English efforts were supported by private rather than government funds, allowing English colonists to enjoy greater freedom from government interference.

THE BEGINNINGS OF COLONIZATION

Two groups of merchants gained charters from James I, Queen Elizabeth's successor. One group of merchants was based in London and received a charter to North America between what are now the Hudson and the Cape Fear rivers. The other was based in Plymouth and was granted the right to colonize in North America from the Potomac to the northern border of present-day Maine. They were called the Virginia Company of London and the Virginia Company of Plymouth, respectively. They were joint-stock companies that raised their capital by the sale of shares of stock.

The Virginia Company of London settled Jamestown in 1607. It became the first permanent English settlement in North America. During the early years of Jamestown, the majority of the settlers died of starvation, various diseases, or hostile actions by Native Americans. The colony's survival remained in doubt for a number of years.

Impressed by the potential profits from tobacco growing, King James I was determined to have Virginia for himself. In 1624, he revoked the London Company's charter and made Virginia a royal colony. This pattern was followed throughout colonial history; both company colonies and proprietary colonies tended eventually to become royal colonies.

The French opened a lucrative trade in fur with the Native Americans. In 1608, Samuel de Champlain established a trading post in Quebec, from which the rest of what became New France eventually spread. French exploration and settlement spread through the Great Lakes region and the valleys of the Mississippi and Ohio rivers. French settlements in the Midwest were generally forts and trading posts serving the fur trade.

In 1609, Holland sent an Englishman named Henry Hudson (d. 1611) to search for a Northwest Passage. In this endeavor, Hudson discovered the river that bears his name. Arrangements were made to trade with the Iroquois for furs. In 1624, Dutch trading outposts were established on Manhattan Island (New Amsterdam) and at the site of present-day Albany (Fort Orange).

Many Englishmen came from England for religious reasons. For the most part, these fell into two groups, Puritans and Separatists. Though similar in many respects to the Puritans, the Separatists believed the Church of England was beyond saving and so felt they must separate from it.

Led by William Bradford (1590–1657), a group of Separatists departed in 1620, having obtained from the London Company a charter to settle just south of the Hudson River. Driven by storms, their ship, the *Mayflower*, made landfall at Cape Cod in Massachusetts. This, however, put them outside the jurisdiction of any established government; and so before going ashore they drew up and signed the Mayflower Compact, establishing a foundation for orderly government based on the consent of the governed. After a number of years of hard work, they were able to buy out the investors who had originally financed their voyage, and thus gain greater autonomy.

The Puritans were far more numerous than the Separatists. Charles I determined in 1629 to persecute the Puritans aggressively and to rule without the Puritan-dominated Parliament. In 1629, they chartered a joint-stock company called the Massachusetts Bay Company. The charter neglected to specify where the company's headquarters should be located. Taking advantage of this unusual omission, the Puritans determined to make their headquarters in the colony itself, 3,000 miles from meddlesome royal officials.

Puritans saw their colony not as a place to do whatever might strike one's fancy, but as a place to serve God and build His kingdom. Dissidents would only be tolerated insofar as they did not interfere with the colony's mission.

One such dissident was Roger Williams (ca. 1603–1683). When his activities became disruptive he was asked to leave the colony. He fled to the wilderness around Narragansett Bay, bought land from the Indians, and founded the settlement of Providence (1636).

Another dissident was Anne Hutchinson (1591–1643), who openly taught things contrary to Puritan doctrine. She was banished from the colony. She also migrated to the area around Narragansett Bay and with her followers founded Portsmouth (1638).

In 1663, Charles II, having recently been restored to the throne moved to reward eight of the noblemen who had helped him regain the crown by granting them a charter for all the lands lying south of Virginia and north of Spanish Florida. The new colony was called Carolina, after the king.

In 1664, Charles gave his brother James, Duke of York, title to all the Dutch lands in America, provided James conquered them first. New Amsterdam fell almost without a shot and became New York.

THE COLONIAL WORLD

New England enjoyed a much more stable and well-ordered society than did the Chesapeake colonies. Puritans placed great importance on the family, which in their society was highly patriarchal. Puritans also placed great importance on the ability to read, since they believed everyone should be able to read the Bible. As a result, New England was ahead of the other colonies educationally and enjoyed extremely widespread literacy. Since New England's climate and soil were unsuited to large-scale farming, the region developed a prosperous economy based on small farming, home industry, fishing, and especially trade and a large shipbuilding industry. Boston became a major international port.

On the bottom rung of Southern society were the black slaves. During the first half of the 17th century, blacks in the Chesapeake made up only a small percentage of the population, and were treated more or less as indentured servants. Between 1640 and 1670 this gradually changed, and blacks came to be seen and treated as life-long chattel slaves whose status would be inherited by their children. By 1750, they composed 30 to 40 percent of the Chesapeake population.

While North Carolina tended to follow Virginia in its economic and social development (although with fewer great planters and more small farmers), South Carolina developed a society even more dominated by large plantations and chattel slavery.

Beginning around 1650, British authorities began to take more interest in regulating American trade for the benefit of the mother country. A key idea that underlay this policy was the concept of mercantilism. Each nation's goal was to export more than it imported (i.e., to have a "favorable balance of trade"). To achieve their goals, mercantilists believed economic activity should be regulated by the government. Colonies could fit into England's mercantilist scheme by providing staple crops, such as rice, tobacco, sugar, and indigo, and raw materials, such as timber, that England would otherwise have been forced to import from other countries. Parliament passed a series of Navigation Acts (1651, 1660, 1663, and 1673) to help accomplish these goals.

Pennsylvania was founded as a refuge for Quakers. One of a number of radical religious sects that had sprung up about the time of the English Civil War, the Quakers held many controversial beliefs. They believed all persons had an "inner light" which allowed them to commune directly with God, and therefore they placed little importance on the Bible. They were also pacifists and declined to show customary deference to those who were considered to be their social superiors.

Delaware, though at first part of Pennsylvania, was granted a separate legislature by Penn, but until the American Revolution, Pennsylvania's proprietary governors also functioned as governors of Delaware.

THE EIGHTEENTH CENTURY

America's population continued to grow rapidly, both from natural increases due to prosperity and a healthy environment and from large-scale immigration, not only of English but also of other groups such as Scots-Irish and Germans.

It was decided to found a colony as a buffer between South Carolina and Spanish-held Florida. In 1732, a group of British philanthropists, led by General James Oglethorpe (1696–1785), obtained a charter for such a colony which was named Georgia.

England and France continued on a collision course, as France determined to take complete control of the Ohio Valley and western Pennsylvania. British authorities ordered colonial governors to resist this. George Washington (1732–1799), a young major of the Virginia militia, was sent to western Pennsylvania but was forced by superior numbers to fall back on his hastily built Fort Necessity and then to surrender.

While Washington skirmished with the French, delegates of seven colonies met in Albany, New York, to discuss common plans for defense. Delegate Benjamin Franklin proposed a plan for an intercolonial government. While the other colonies showed no support for the idea, it was an important precedent for the concept of uniting in the face of a common enemy.

Between 1756 and 1763 Britain and France fought the Seven years War (also known as the French and Indian War). By the Treaty of Paris of 1763, Britain gained all of Canada and all of what is now the United States east of the Mississippi River. France lost all of its North American holdings.

THE AMERICAN REVOLUTION (1763–1787)
THE COMING OF THE AMERICAN REVOLUTION

In 1763, George Grenville (1712–1770) became prime minister and set out to solve some of the empire's more pressing problems. Chief among these was the large national debt incurred in the recent war.

In 1764, Grenville pushed through Parliament the Sugar Act (also known as the Revenue Act), which aimed at raising revenue by taxing goods imported by the Americans.

The Stamp Act (1765) imposed a direct tax on Americans for the first time. It required Americans to purchase revenue stamps on everything from newspapers to legal documents, and would have created an impossible drain on hard currency in the colonies. Americans reacted first with restrained and respectful petitions and pamphlets in which they pointed out that "taxation without representation is tyranny." From there, resistance progressed to stronger protests that eventually became violent.

In October 1765, delegates from nine colonies met as the Stamp Act Congress, and passed moderate resolutions against the act, asserting that Americans could not be taxed without the consent of their representatives. The Stamp Act Congress showed that representatives of the colonies could work together, and gave political leaders in the various colonies a chance to become acquainted with each other.

Colonial merchants' boycott of British goods spread throughout the colonies and had a powerful effect on British merchants and manufacturers, who began clamoring for the act's repeal.

Meanwhile, the fickle King George III had dismissed Grenville over an unrelated disagreement and replaced him with a cabinet headed by Charles Lord Rockingham (1730–1782). In March 1766 Parliament repealed the Stamp Act. At the same time, however, it passed the Declaratory Act, which claimed the power to tax or make laws for the Americans "in all cases whatsoever."

The Rockingham ministry was replaced with a cabinet dominated by Chancellor of the Exchequer Charles Townshend (1725–1767). In 1766, Parliament passed his program of taxes on items imported into the colonies. These taxes came to be known as the Townshend duties.

American reaction was at first slow, but the sending of troops, aroused them to resistance. Nonimportation was again instituted, and soon British merchants were calling on Parliament to repeal the acts. In March 1770, Parliament, under the new prime minister, Frederick Lord North (1737–1792), repealed all of the taxes except that on tea, which was retained to prove Parliament had the right to tax the colonies if it so desired.

A relative peace was brought to an end by the Tea Act of 1773. In desperate financial condition—partially because the Americans were buying smuggled Dutch tea rather than the taxed British product—the British East India Company sought and obtained from Parliament concessions that allowed it to ship tea directly to the colonies rather than only by way of Britain. The result would be that East India Company tea, even with the tax, would be cheaper than smuggled Dutch tea. The colonists would thus, it was hoped, buy the tea, tax and all. The East India Company would be saved, and the Americans would be tacitly accepting Parliament's right to tax them.

The Americans, however, proved resistant to this approach; rather than seem to admit Parliament's right to tax, they vigorously resisted the cheaper tea. Various methods, including tar and feathers, were used to prevent the collection of the tax on tea. In most ports, Americans did not allow the tea to be landed.

In Boston, however, pro-British Governor Thomas Hutchinson (1711–1780) forced a confrontation by ordering Royal Navy vessels to prevent the tea ships from leaving the harbor. After 20 days, this would, by law, result in the cargoes being sold at auction and the tax paid. The night before the time was to expire, December 16, 1773, Bostonians thinly disguised as Native Americans boarded the ships and threw the tea into the harbor.

The British responded with four acts collectively titled the Coercive Acts. First, the Boston Port Act closed the port of Boston to all trade until local citizens would agree to pay for the lost tea (they would not). Secondly, the Massachusetts Government Act greatly increased the power of Massachusetts's royal governor at the expense of the legislature. Thirdly, the Administration of Justice Act provided that royal officials accused of crimes in Massachusetts could be tried elsewhere, where chances of acquittal might be greater. Finally, a strengthened Quartering Act allowed the new governor, General Thomas Gage (1721–1787), to quarter his troops anywhere, including unoccupied private homes.

THE WAR FOR INDEPENDENCE

The British government paid little attention to the First Continental Congress, having decided to teach the Americans a military lesson. More troops were sent to Massachusetts, which was officially declared to be in a state of rebellion. Orders were sent to General Gage to arrest the leaders of the resistance, or failing that, to provoke any sort of confrontation that would allow him to turn British military might loose on the Americans.

Gage decided on a reconnaissance-in-force to find and destroy a reported stockpile of colonial arms and ammunition at Concord. Seven hundred British troops set out on this mission on the night of April 18, 1775, which resulted in skirmishes with the colonists at Lexington and Concord.

Open warfare had begun, and the myth of British invincibility was destroyed. Militia came in large numbers from all the New England colonies to join the force besieging Gage and his army in Boston. The following month the Americans tightened the noose around Boston by fortifying Breed's Hill (a spur of Bunker Hill).

The British determined to remove them by a frontal attack. Twice the British were thrown back, but they finally succeeded when the Americans ran out of ammunition. Over a thousand British soldiers were killed or wounded in what turned out to be the bloodiest battle of the war (June 17, 1775). Yet the British had gained very little and remained bottled up in Boston.

Meanwhile in May 1775, American forces under Ethan Allen (1738–1789) and Benedict Arnold (1741–1801) took Fort Ticonderoga on Lake Champlain.

While these events were taking place in New England and Canada, the Second Continental Congress met in Philadelphia in May 1775. Congress was divided into two main factions. One was composed mostly of New Englanders and leaned toward declaring independence from Britain. The other drew its strength primarily from the Middle Colonies and was not yet ready to go that far.

The Declaration of Independence was primarily the work of Thomas Jefferson (1743–1826) of Virginia. It was a restatement of political ideas by then commonplace in America and showed why the former colonists felt justified in separating from Great Britain. It was formally adopted by Congress on July 4, 1776.

The British landed that summer at New York City, where they hoped to find many loyalists. Washington narrowly avoided being trapped there (an escape partially due to the Howes' slowness). Defeated again at the Battle of Washington Heights (August 29–30, 1776) in Manhattan, Washington was forced to retreat across New Jersey with the aggressive British General Lord Charles Cornwallis (1738–1805) in pursuit.

With his victory almost complete, General Howe decided to wait till spring to finish annihilating Washington's army. Scattering his troops in small detachments so as to hold all of New Jersey, he went into winter quarters.

Washington, with his small army melting away as demoralized soldiers deserted, decided on a bold stroke. On Christmas night 1776, his army crossed the Delaware River and struck the Hessians at Trenton. The Hessians, still groggy from their hard-drinking Christmas party, were easily defeated. A few days later, Washington defeated a British force at Princeton (January 3, 1777). Much of New Jersey was regained, and Washington's army was saved from disintegration.

Hoping to weaken Britain, France began making covert shipments of arms to the Americans early in the war. Shipments from France were vital for the Americans. The American victory at Saratoga convinced the French to join openly in the war against England. Eventually the Spanish (1779) and the Dutch (1780) joined as well.

Howe was replaced by General Henry Clinton (1738–1795), who was ordered to abandon Philadelphia and march to New York. Clinton maintained New York as Britain's main base. In November 1778, the British easily conquered Georgia. Late the following year, Clinton moved on South Carolina and in May 1780 Charleston surrendered. Clinton then returned to New York, leaving Cornwallis to continue the Southern campaign.

In the west, George Rogers Clark (1752–1818), led an expedition down the Ohio River and into the area of present-day Illinois and Indiana, defeating a British force at Vincennes, Indiana, and securing the area north of the Ohio River for the United States.

In the south, Cornwallis began to move northward toward North Carolina, but on October 7, 1780, a detachment of his force was defeated by American frontiersmen at the Battle of Kings Mountain in northern South Carolina. Cornwallis unwisely moved north without bothering to secure South Carolina first. The result was that the British would no sooner leave an area than American militia or guerilla bands, such as that under Francis Marion "the Swamp Fox" (ca. 1732–1795), were once again in control.

American commander Nathaniel Greene's (1742–1786) brilliant southern strategy led to a crushing victory at Cowpens, South Carolina (January 17, 1781), by troops under Greene's subordinate, General Daniel Morgan (1736–1802) of Virginia. It also led to a near victory by Greene's own force at Guilford Court House, North Carolina (March 15, 1781).

The frustrated and impetuous Cornwallis now abandoned the southern strategy and moved north into Virginia, taking a defensive position at Yorktown. With the aid of a French fleet which took control of Chesapeake Bay and a French army which joined him in sealing off the land approaches to Yorktown, Washington succeeded in trapping Cornwallis. After three weeks of siege, Cornwallis surrendered (October 17, 1781).

News of the debacle at Yorktown brought the collapse of Lord North's ministry, and the new cabinet opened peace negotiations.

The final agreement became known as the Treaty of Paris of 1783. Its terms stipulated the following: 1) The United States was recognized as an independent nation by the major European powers, including Britain 2) Its western boundary was set at the Mississippi River 3) Its southern boundary was set at 31° north latitude (the northern boundary of Florida) 4) Britain retained Canada, but had to surrender Florida to Spain 5) Private British creditors would be free to collect any debts owed by United States citizens and 6) Congress was to recommend that the states restore confiscated loyalist property.

THE CREATION OF NEW GOVERNMENTS

After the collapse of British authority in 1775, it became necessary to form new state governments. By the end of 1777, ten new state constitutions had been formed. Most state constitutions included bills of rights—lists of things the government was not supposed to do to the people.

In the summer of 1776, Congress appointed a committee to begin devising a framework for a national government. The end result preserved the sovereignty of the states and creating a very weak national government.

The Articles of Confederation provided for a unicameral Congress in which each state would have one vote, as had been the case in the Continental

Congress. Executive authority under the articles would be vested in a committee of 13, with one member from each state. In order to amend the articles, the unanimous consent of all the states was required.

The Articles of Confederation government was empowered to make war, make treaties, determine the amount of troops and money each state should contribute to the war effort, settle disputes between states, admit new states to the Union, and borrow money. But it was not empowered to levy taxes, raise troops, or regulate commerce.

Ratification of the Articles of Confederation was delayed by disagreements over the future status of the lands that lay to the west of the original 13 states. Maryland, which had no such claim, withheld ratification until, in 1781, Virginia agreed to surrender its western claims to the new national government.

THE UNITED STATES CONSTITUTION (1787–1789)
DEVELOPMENT AND RATIFICATION

As time went on, the inadequacy of the Articles of Confederation became increasingly apparent. It was decided in 1787 to call for a convention of all the states to meet in Philadelphia for the purpose of revising the Articles of Confederation.

The men who met in Philadelphia in 1787 were remarkably able, highly educated, and exceptionally accomplished. For the most part they were lawyers, merchants, and planters. Though representing individual states, most thought in national terms.

George Washington was unanimously elected to preside, and the enormous respect that he commanded helped hold the convention together through difficult times.

The delegates shared a basic belief in the innate selfishness of man, which must somehow be kept from abusing the power of government. For this purpose, the document that they finally produced contained many checks and balances, designed to prevent the government, or any one branch of the government, from gaining too much power.

Benjamin Franklin played an important role in reconciling the often heated delegates and in making various suggestions that eventually helped the convention arrive at the "Great Compromise," proposed by Roger Sherman (1721–1793) and Oliver Ellsworth (1745–1807). The Great (or Connecticut) Compromise provided for a presidency, a Senate with all states represented equally (by two senators each), and a House of Representatives with representation according to population.

Another crisis involved North-South disagreement over the issue of slavery. Here also a compromise was reached. Slavery was neither endorsed nor condemned by the Constitution. Each slave was to count as three-fifths of a person for purposes of apportioning representation and direct taxation on the states (the Three-Fifths Compromise). The federal government was prohibited from stopping the importation of slaves prior to 1808.

The third major area of compromise was the nature of the presidency. The result was a strong presidency with control of foreign policy and the power to veto Congress's legislation. Should the president commit an actual crime, Congress would have the power to impeach him. Otherwise, the president would serve for a term of four years and be reelectable without limit. As a check to the possible excesses of democracy, the president was to be elected by an electoral college, in which each state would have the same number of electors as it did senators and representatives combined. The person with the second highest total in the electoral college would be vice president. If no one gained a majority in the electoral college, the president would be chosen by the House of Representatives.

The new Constitution was to take effect when nine states, through special state conventions, had ratified it. As the struggle over ratification got under way, those favoring the Constitution astutely named themselves Federalists (i.e., advocates of centralized power) and labeled their opponents Antifederalists.

By June 21, 1788, the required nine states had ratified, but the crucial states of New York and Virginia still held out. Ultimately, the promise of the addition of a bill of rights helped win the final states. In March 1789, George Washington was inaugurated as the nation's first president.

THE NEW NATION (1789–1824)
THE FEDERALIST ERA

Few Antifederalists were elected to Congress, and many of the new legislators had served as delegates to the Philadelphia Convention two years before.

George Washington received virtually all the votes of the presidential electors, and John Adams received the next highest number, thus becoming the vice-president. After a triumphant journey from Mount Vernon, Washington was inaugurated in New York City, the temporary seat of government (April 30, 1789).

Ten amendments were ratified by the states by the end of 1791 and became the Bill of Rights. The first nine spelled out specific guarantees of personal freedoms, and the Tenth Amendment reserved to the states all those powers not specifically withheld or granted to the federal government.

The Judiciary Act of 1789 provided for a Supreme Court with six justices, and invested it with the power to rule on the constitutional validity of state laws. It was to be the interpreter of the "supreme law of the land." A system of district courts was set up to serve as courts of original jurisdiction, and three courts of appeal were established.

Congress established three departments of the executive branch—state, treasury, and war—as well as the offices of attorney general and postmaster general.

WASHINGTON'S ADMINISTRATION (1789–1797)

Treasury Secretary Alexander Hamilton, in his "Report on the Public Credit," proposed the funding of the national debt at face value, federal assumption of state debts, and the establishment of a national bank. In his "Report on Manufactures," Hamilton proposed an extensive program for federal stimulation of industrial development through subsidies and tax incentives. The money needed to fund these programs would come from an excise tax on distillers and from tariffs on imports.

Thomas Jefferson, Secretary of State, and others objected to the funding proposal because they believed it would enrich a small elite group at the expense of the more worthy common citizen.

Hamilton interpreted the Constitution as having vested extensive powers in the federal government. This "implied powers" stance claimed that the government was given all powers that were not expressly denied to it. This is the "broad" interpretation.

Jefferson and Madison held the view that any action not specifically permitted in the Constitution was thereby prohibited. This is the "strict" interpretation, and the Republicans opposed the establishment of Hamilton's national bank based on this view of government. The Jeffersonian supporters, primarily under the guidance of James Madison, began to organize political groups in opposition to the Federalist program. They called themselves Republicans.

The Federalists, as Hamilton's supporters were called, received their strongest support from the business and financial groups in the commercial centers of the Northeast and from the port cities of the South. The strength of the Republicans lay primarily in the rural and frontier areas of the South and West.

FOREIGN AND FRONTIER AFFAIRS

The U.S. proclaimed neutrality when France went to war with Europe in 1792, and American merchants traded with both sides. In retaliation, the British began to seize American merchant ships and force their crews into service with the British navy.

John Jay negotiated a treaty with the British that attempted to settle the conflict at sea, as well as to curtail English agitation of their Native American allies on the western borders in 1794.

In the Pinckney Treaty, ratified by the Senate in 1796, the Spanish opened the Mississippi River to American traffic and recognized the 31st parallel as the northern boundary of Florida.

INTERNAL PROBLEMS

In 1794, western farmers refused to pay the excise tax on whiskey which formed the backbone of Hamilton's revenue program. When a group of Pennsylvania farmers terrorized the tax collectors, President Washington sent out a federalized militia force of some 15,000 men and the rebellion evaporated, thus strengthening the credibility of the young government.

JOHN ADAMS' ADMINISTRATION (1797–1801)

In the Election of 1796 John Adams was the Federalist candidate, and Thomas Jefferson the Republican. Jefferson received the second highest number of electoral votes and became vice president.

REPRESSION AND PROTEST

The elections in 1798 increased the Federalist's majorities in both houses of Congress and they used their "mandate" to enact legislation to stifle foreign influences. The Alien Act raised new hurdles in the path of immigrants trying to obtain citizenship, and the Sedition Act widened the powers of the Adams administration to muzzle its newspaper critics.

Republican leaders were convinced that the Alien and Sedition Acts were unconstitutional, but the process of deciding on the constitutionality of federal laws was as yet undefined. Jefferson and James Madison decided that state legislatures should have that power, and they drew up a series of resolutions which were presented to the Kentucky and Virginia legislatures. They proposed that state bodies could "nullify" federal laws within those states. These resolutions were adopted only in these two states, and so the issue died, but the principle of states' rights would have great force in later years.

THE REVOLUTION OF 1800

Thomas Jefferson and Aaron Burr (1756–1836) ran on the Republican ticket against John Adams and Charles Pinckney (1746–1825) for the Federalists. The Republican candidates won handily, but both received the same number of electoral votes, thus throwing the selection of the president into the House of Representatives. After a lengthy deadlock, Alexander Hamilton threw his support to Jefferson and Burr had to accept the vice-presidency, the result obviously intended by the electorate. Jefferson appointed James Madison as secretary of state and Albert Gallatin (1761–1849) to the treasury.

The Federalist Congress passed a new Judiciary Act early in 1801, and President Adams filled the newly created vacancies with party supporters, many of them with last-minute commissions. John Marshall (1755–1835) was then appointed chief justice of the United States Supreme Court, thus guaranteeing continuation of Federalist policies from the bench of the high court.

THE JEFFERSONIAN ERA

Thomas Jefferson and his Republican followers envisioned a nation of independent farmers living under a central government that exercised a minimum of control and served merely to protect the individual liberties guaranteed by the Constitution. This agrarian paradise would be free from the industrial smoke and urban blight of Europe, and would serve as a beacon light of Enlightenment rationalism to a world searching for direction. But Jefferson presided over a nation that was growing more industrialized and urban, and which seemed to need an ever-stronger president.

DOMESTIC AFFAIRS

The Twelfth Amendment was adopted and ratified in 1804, ensuring that a tie vote between candidates of the same party could not again cause the confusion of the Jefferson-Burr affair.

Following the Constitutional mandate, the importation of slaves was stopped by law in 1808.

The Louisiana Purchase: An American delegation purchased the trans-Mississippi territory from Napoleon for $15 million in April 1803, even though they had no authority to buy more than the city of New Orleans.

Exploring the West: Meriwether Lewis (1774–1809) and William Clark's (1770–1838) group left St. Louis in 1804 and returned two years later with a wealth of scientific and anthropological information. At the same time,

Zebulon Pike and others had been traversing the middle parts of Louisiana and mapping the land.

MADISON'S ADMINISTRATION (1809–1817)

The Election of 1808: Republican James Madison won the election over Federalist Charles Pinckney, but the Federalists gained seats in both houses of the Congress.

The Native American tribes of the Northwest and the Mississippi Valley were resentful of the government's policy of pressured removal to the West, and the British authorities in Canada exploited their discontent by encouraging border raids against the American settlements.

At the same time, the British interfered with American transatlantic shipping, including impressing sailors and capturing ships.

The Congress in 1811 contained a strong pro-war group called the War Hawks led by Henry Clay (1777–1852) and John C. Calhoun (1782–1850). They gained control of both houses and began agitating for war with the British. On June 1, 1812, President Madison asked for a declaration of war and Congress complied.

After three years of inconclusive war, in 1815 the Treaty of Ghent provided for the acceptance of the status quo that had existed at the beginning of hostilities, and both sides restored their wartime conquests to the other.

The Federalists had increasingly become a minority party. They vehemently opposed the war, and Daniel Webster (1782–1852) and other New England congressmen consistently blocked the Administration's efforts to prosecute the war effort. On December 15, 1814, delegates from the New England states met in Hartford, Connecticut, and drafted a set of resolutions suggesting nullification—and even secession—if their interests were not protected against the growing influence of the South and the West.

Soon after the convention adjourned, the news of Andrew Jackson's victory over the British on January 8, 1815 at New Orleans was announced and their actions were discredited. The Federalist party ceased to be a political force from this point on.

POSTWAR DEVELOPMENTS

Protective Tariff (1816): The first protective tariff in the nation's history was passed in 1816 to slow the flood of cheap British manufactures into the country.

Rush-Bagot Treaty (1817): An agreement was reached in 1817 between Britain and the United States to stop maintaining armed fleets on the Great Lakes. This first "disarmament" agreement is still in effect.

The Adams-Onis Treaty (1819): Spain had decided to sell the remainder of the Florida territory to the Americans before they took it anyway. Under this agreement, the Spanish surrendered all their claims to Florida. The United States agreed to assume $5 million in debts owed to American merchants.

THE MONROE DOCTRINE

As Latin American nations began declaring independence, British and American leaders feared that European governments would try to restore the former New World colonies to their erstwhile royal owners.

In December 1823, President James Monroe (1758–1831) included in his annual message to Congress a statement that the peoples of the American hemisphere were "henceforth not to be considered as subjects for future colonization by any European powers."

INTERNAL DEVELOPMENT (1820–1830)

The years following the War of 1812 were years of rapid economic and social development, followed by a severe depression in 1819. But this slump was temporary, and it became obvious that the country was moving rapidly from its agrarian origins toward an industrial, urban future.

The Monroe Presidency (1817–1823): James Monroe, the last of the "Virginia dynasty," had been handpicked by the retiring Madison and he was elected with only one electoral vote opposed—a symbol of national unity.

THE MARSHALL COURT

John Marshall delivered the majority opinions in a number of critical decisions in these formative years, all of which served to strengthen the power of the federal government and restrict the powers of state governments.

Marbury vs. Madison (1803): This case established the precedent of the Supreme Court's power to rule on the constitutionality of federal laws.

Gibbons vs. Ogden (1824): In a case involving competing steamboat companies, Marshall ruled that commerce included navigation, and that only Congress has the right to regulate commerce among states. Thus, the state-granted monopoly was voided.

NATIONAL EXPANSION

The Missouri Compromise (1820): The Missouri Territory, the first to be organized from the Louisiana Purchase, applied for statehood in 1819. Since the Senate membership was evenly divided between slaveholding and free states at that time, the admission of a new state would give the voting advantage either to the North or to the South.

As the debate dragged on, the northern territory of Massachusetts applied for admission as the state of Maine. The two admission bills were combined, with Maine coming in free and Missouri coming in as a slave state. To make the package palatable for the House, a provision was added that prohibited slavery in the remainder of the Louisiana Territory north of the southern boundary of Missouri (latitude 36 degrees 30').

JACKSONIAN DEMOCRACY AND WESTWARD EXPANSION (1824–1850)

THE ELECTION OF 1824

Although John Quincy Adams, through the controversial action of the House of Representatives, became president in the 1824 election, Andrew Jackson instigated a campaign for the presidency immediately. He won the election of 1828.

Jackson was popular with the common man. He seemed to be the prototype of the self-made westerner: rough-hewn, violent, vindictive, with few ideas but strong convictions. He ignored his appointed cabinet officers and relied instead on the counsel of his "Kitchen Cabinet," a group of partisan supporters.

Jackson expressed the conviction that government operations could be performed by untrained, common folk, and he threatened to dismiss large numbers of government employees and replace them with his supporters.

He exercised his veto power more than any other president before him.

THE WAR ON THE BANK

The Bank of the United States had operated under the direction of Nicholas Biddle (1786–1844) since 1823. He was a cautious man, and his conservative economic policy enforced conservatism among the state and private banks—which many bankers resented. In 1832 Jackson vetoed the Bank's renewal, and it ceased being a federal institution in 1836.

Jackson had handpicked his Democratic successor, Martin Van Buren (1782–1862) of New York. The opposition Whig party had emerged from the ruins of the National Republicans and other groups who opposed Jackson's policies.

Van Buren, inherited all the problems and resentments generated by his mentor. He spent most of his term in office dealing with the financial chaos left by the death of the Second Bank. The best he could do was to eventually persuade Congress to establish an Independent Treasury to handle government funds. It began functioning in 1840.

THE ELECTION OF 1840

The Whigs nominated William Henry Harrison, "Old Tippecanoe," a western fighter against the Native Americans. Their choice for vice-president was John Tyler (1790–1862), a former Democrat from Virginia. The Democrats put up Van Buren again.

Harrison won but died only a month after the inauguration, having served the shortest term in presidential history.

THE MEANING OF JACKSONIAN POLITICS

The Age of Jackson was the beginning of the modern two-party system. Popular politics, based on emotional appeal, became the accepted style. The practice of meeting in mass conventions to nominate national candidates for office was established during these years.

The Democrats opposed big government and the requirements of modernization: urbanization and industrialization. Their support came from the working classes, small merchants, and small farmers.

The Whigs promoted government participation in commercial and industrial development, the encouragement of banking and corporations, and a cautious approach to westward expansion. Their support came largely from northern business and manufacturing interests and large southern planters. Calhoun, Clay, and Webster dominated the Whig party during the early decades of the nineteenth century.

REMAKING SOCIETY: ORGANIZED REFORM

The early antislavery movement advocated only the purchase and colonization of slaves. The American Colonization Society was organized in 1817, and established the colony of Liberia in 1830, but by that time the movement had reached a dead end.

In 1831, William Lloyd Garrison (1805–1879) started his paper, *The Liberator*, and began to advocate total and immediate emancipation. He founded the New England Anti-slavery Society in 1832 and the American

Anti-slavery Society in 1833. Theodore Weld (1803–1895) pursued the same goals, but advocated more gradual means.

The movement split into two wings: Garrison's radical followers, and the moderates who favored "moral suasion" and petitions to Congress. In 1840, the Liberty party, the first national anti-slavery party, fielded a presidential candidate on the platform of "free soil" (nonexpansion of slavery into the new western territories).

DIVERGING SOCIETIES—LIFE IN THE NORTH

As the nineteenth century progressed, the states seemed to polarize more into the two sections we call the North and the South, with the expanding West becoming ever more identified with the North.

THE ROLE OF MINORITIES

The women's rights movement focused on social and legal discrimination, and women like Lucretia Mott (1793–1880) and Sojourner Truth (ca. 1797–1883) became well-known figures on the speakers' circuit.

By 1850, 200,000 free blacks lived in the North and West. Their lives were restricted everywhere by prejudice, and "Jim Crow" laws separated the races. Black citizens organized separate churches and fraternal orders. The economic security of the free blacks was constantly threatened by the newly arrived immigrants, who were willing to work at the least desirable jobs for lower wages. Racial violence was a daily threat.

THE GROWTH OF INDUSTRY

By 1850, the value of industrial output had surpassed that of agricultural production. The Northeast produced more than two-thirds of the manufactured goods. Between 1830 and 1850, the number of patents issued for industrial inventions almost doubled.

DIVERGING SOCIETIES—LIFE IN THE SOUTH

The southern states experienced dramatic growth in the second quarter of the nineteenth century. The economy grew more productive and more prosperous, but still the section called the South was basically agrarian, with few important cities and only scattered industry. The plantation system, with its cash-crop production driven by the use of slave labor, remained the dominant institution.

The most important economic phenomenon of the early decades of the nineteenth century was the shift in population and production from the old "upper South" of Virginia and the Carolinas to the "lower South" of the newly opened Gulf states of Alabama, Mississippi, and Louisiana. In the older Atlantic states, tobacco retained its importance, but shifted westward to the Piedmont. It was replaced in the East by food grains. The southern Atlantic coast continued to produce rice, and southern Louisiana and east Texas retained their emphasis on sugar cane. But the rich black soil of the new Gulf states proved ideal for the production of short-staple cotton, especially after the invention of the "gin." Cotton soon became the center of the southern economy.

CLASSES IN THE SOUTH

The large plantations growing cotton, sugar, or tobacco used the gang system, in which white overseers directed black drivers who supervised large groups of workers in the fields, all performing the same operation. In the culture of rice, and on the smaller farms, slaves were assigned specific tasks, and when those tasks were finished, the worker had the remainder of the day to himself.

House servants usually were considered the most favored since they were spared the hardest physical labor and enjoyed the most intimate relationship with the owner's family.

COMMERCE AND INDUSTRY

The lack of manufacturing and business development has frequently been blamed for the South's losing its bid for independence in 1861–1865. Actually, the South was highly industrialized for its day and compared favorably with most European nations in the development of manufacturing capacity. However, it trailed far behind the North, so much so that when war erupted in 1861, the northern states owned 81 percent of the factory capacity in the United States.

MANIFEST DESTINY AND WESTWARD EXPANSION

Although the term "Manifest Destiny" was not actually coined until 1844, the belief that the American nation was destined to eventually expand all the way to the Pacific Ocean, and to possibly embrace Canada and Mexico, had been voiced for years by many who believed that American liberty and ideals should be shared with everyone possible, by force if necessary. The rising sense of nationalism which followed the War of 1812 was fed by the rapidly expanding population, the reform impulse of the 1830s, and the desire to acquire new markets and resources for the burgeoning economy of "Young America."

The Adams-Onis Treaty of 1819 had set the northern boundary of Spanish possessions near the present northern border of California. The territory north of that line and west of the vague boundaries of the Louisiana Territory had been claimed over the years by Spain, England, Russia, France, and the United States. By the 1820s, all these claims had been yielded to Britain and the United States. The United States claimed all the way north to the 54°40' parallel. Unable to settle the dispute, they had agreed on a joint occupation of the disputed land.

In the 1830s, American missionaries followed the traders and trappers to the Oregon country. They began to publicize the richness and beauty of the land. The result was the "Oregon Fever" of the 1840s, as thousands of settlers trekked across the Great Plains and the Rocky Mountains to settle the new Shangri-la.

Texas had been a state in the Republic of Mexico since 1822, following the Mexican revolution against Spanish control. The new Mexican government invited immigration from the north by offering land grants to Stephen Austin (1793–1836) and other Americans. By 1835, approximately 35,000 "gringos" were homesteading on Texas land.

The Mexican officials saw their power base eroding as the foreigners flooded in, so they moved to tighten control through restrictions on immigration and through tax increases. The Texans responded in 1836 by proclaiming independence and establishing a new republic. The ensuing war was short-lived. The Mexican dictator, Antonio López de Santa Anna (1794–1876), advanced north and annihilated the Texan garrisons at the Alamo and at Goliad. On April 23, 1836, Sam Houston (1793–1863) defeated him at San Jacinto, and the Mexicans were forced to let Texas go its way.

Houston immediately asked the American government for recognition and annexation, but President Andrew Jackson feared the revival of the slavery issue. He also feared war with Mexico and so did nothing. When Van Buren followed suit, the new republic sought foreign recognition and support, which the European nations eagerly provided, hoping thereby to create a counterbalance to rising American power and influence in the Southwest. France and England both quickly concluded trade agreements with the Texans.

The district of New Mexico had, like Texas, encouraged American immigration. Soon that state was more American than Mexican. The Santa Fe Trail, running from Independence, Missouri, to the town of Santa Fe, created a prosperous trade in mules, gold, silver, and furs, which moved north in exchange for manufactured goods. American settlements sprung up all along the route.

TYLER, POLK, AND CONTINUED WESTWARD EXPANSION

A states' rights southerner and a strict constitutionalist who had been placed on the Whig ticket to draw Southern votes, John Tyler, who became president in 1841 upon Harrison's death, rejected the entire Whig program of a national bank, high protective tariffs, and federally funded internal improvements (roads, canals, etc.). In the resulting legislative confrontations, Tyler vetoed a number of Whig-sponsored bills.

The Whigs were furious. In opposition to Tyler over the next few years, the Whigs, under the leadership of Clay, transformed themselves from a loose grouping of diverse factions to a coherent political party with an elaborate organization.

Rejected by the Whigs and without ties to the Democrats, Tyler was a politician without a party. Hoping to gather a political following of his own, he sought an issue with powerful appeal and believed he had found it in the question of Texas annexation. Tyler's new secretary of state, John C. Calhoun, negotiated an annexation treaty with Texas. Calhoun's identification with extreme proslavery forces and his insertion in the treaty of proslavery statements caused the treaty's rejection by the Senate (1844).

THE ELECTION OF 1844

Democratic front-runner Martin Van Buren and Whig front-runner Henry Clay agreed privately that neither would endorse Texas annexation, and that it would not become a campaign issue, but expansionists at the Democratic convention succeeded in dumping Van Buren in favor of James K. Polk (1795–1849). Polk, called "Young Hickory" by his supporters, was a staunch Jacksonian who opposed protective tariffs and a national bank, but favored territorial expansion, including not only annexation of Texas but also occupation of all the Oregon country (up to latitude 54° 40') hitherto jointly occupied by the United States and Britain.

The Whigs nominated Clay, who continued to oppose Texas annexation. Later, sensing the mood of the country was against him, he began to equivocate.

The antislavery Liberty party nominated James G. Birney. Apparently because of Clay's wavering on the Texas issue, Birney was able to take enough votes away from Clay in New York to give that state, and thus the election, to Polk.

Tyler, as a lame-duck president, made one more attempt to achieve Texas annexation before leaving office. By means of a joint resolution, which unlike a treaty required only a simple majority rather than a two-thirds vote, he was successful in getting the measure through Congress. Texas was finally admitted to the Union in 1845.

As a good Jacksonian, Polk favored a low, revenue-only tariff rather than a high, protective tariff. This he obtained in the Walker Tariff (1846). He also opposed a national debt and a national bank and reestablished Van Buren's Independent Sub-Treasury system, which remained in effect until 1920.

By the terms of the Oregon Treaty (1846), a compromise with Great Britain was reached. The current United States-Canada boundary east of the Rockies (49°) was extended westward to the Pacific. Some northern Democrats were angered and felt betrayed by Polk's failure to insist on all of Oregon, but the Senate readily accepted the treaty.

Though Mexico broke diplomatic relations with the United States immediately upon Texas's admission to the Union, there was still hope of a peaceful settlement. In the fall of 1845, Polk sent John Slidell (1793–1871) to Mexico City with a proposal for a peaceful settlement.

Nothing came of these attempts at negotiation. Racked by coup and counter-coup, the Mexican government refused even to receive Slidell.

Polk thereupon sent United States troops into the disputed territory in southern Texas. A force under General Zachary Taylor (1784–1850) (who was nicknamed "Old Rough and Ready") took up a position just north of the Rio Grande. Eight days later, April 5, 1846, Mexican troops attacked an American patrol. When news of the clash reached Washington, Polk sought and received from Congress a declaration of war against Mexico on May 13, 1846.

Americans were sharply divided about the war. Some favored it because they felt Mexico had provoked the war, or because they felt it was the destiny of America to spread the blessings of freedom to oppressed peoples. Others, generally northern abolitionists, saw in the war the work of a vast conspiracy of southern slaveholders greedy for more slave territory.

Negotiated peace finally came about when the State Department clerk Nicholas Trist negotiated and signed the Treaty of Guadalupe-Hidalgo (February 2, 1848), ending the Mexican War. Under the terms of the treaty, Mexico ceded to the United States the southwestern territory from Texas to the California coast.

Although the Mexican War increased the nation's territory by one-third, it also brought to the surface serious political issues that threatened to divide the country, particularly the question of slavery in the new territories.

SECTIONAL CONFLICT AND THE CAUSES OF THE CIVIL WAR (1850–1860)

THE CRISIS OF 1850 AND AMERICA AT MID-CENTURY

The Mexican War had no more than started when, on August 8, 1846, freshman Democratic Congressman David Wilmot (1814–1868) of Pennsylvania introduced his Wilmot Proviso as a proposed amendment to a war appropriations bill. It stipulated that "neither slavery nor involuntary servitude shall ever exist" in any territory to be acquired from Mexico. It was passed by the House, and though rejected by the Senate, it was reintroduced again and again amid increasingly acrimonious debate.

The southern position was expressed by John C. Calhoun, now serving as senator from South Carolina. He argued that the territories were the property not of the United States federal government, but of all the states together, and therefore Congress had no right to prohibit in any territory any type of "property" (by which he meant slaves) that was legal in any of the states.

Antislavery northerners, pointing to the Northwest Ordinance of 1787 and the Missouri Compromise of 1820 as precedents, argued that Congress had the right to make what laws it saw fit for the territories, including, if it so chose, laws prohibiting slavery.

A compromise proposal favored by President Polk and many moderate southerners called for the extension of the 36° 30' line of the Missouri Compromise westward through the Mexican Cession to the Pacific, with territory north of the line to be closed to slavery.

Another compromise solution, favored by northern Democrats such as Lewis Cass (1782–1866) of Michigan and Stephen A. Douglas (1813–1861) of Illinois, was known as "squatter sovereignty" and later as "popular sovereignty." It held that the residents of each territory should be permitted to decide for themselves whether to allow slavery.

The Election of 1848: The Democrats nominated Lewis Cass, and their platform endorsed his middle-of-the-road popular sovereignty position with regard to slavery in the territories.

The Whigs dodged the issue even more effectively by nominating General Zachary Taylor, whose fame in the Mexican War made him a strong candidate. Taylor knew nothing of politics, had never voted, and liked to think of himself as above politics. He took no position at all with respect to slavery in the territories.

Some antislavery northern Whigs and Democrats, disgusted with their parties' failure to take a clear stand against the spread of slavery, deserted the party ranks to form an antislavery third party. Their party was called the Free Soil party, since it stood for keeping the soil of new western territories free of slavery. Its candidate was Martin Van Buren.

The election excited relatively little public interest. Taylor won a narrow victory.

The question of slavery's status in the western territories was made more immediate when, on January 24, 1848, gold was discovered not far from Sacramento, California. The next year, gold seekers from the eastern United States and from many foreign countries swelled California's population from 14,000 to 100,000.

In September 1849, having more than the requisite population and being in need of better government, California petitioned for admission to the Union as a free state.

Southerners were furious. Long outnumbered in the House of Representatives, the South would now find itself, should California be admitted as a free state, also outvoted in the Senate.

At this point, the aged Henry Clay proposed an eight-part package. For the North, California would be admitted as a free state; the land in dispute between Texas and New Mexico would go to New Mexico; the New Mexico and Utah territories (all of the Mexican Cession outside of California) would not be specifically reserved for slavery, the status there would be decided by popular sovereignty; and the slave trade would be abolished in the District of Columbia.

For the South, a tougher Fugitive Slave Law would be enacted; the federal government would pay Texas's $10,000,000 pre-annexation debt; Congress would declare that it did not have jurisdiction over the interstate slave trade and would promise not to abolish slavery itself in the District of Columbia.

President Taylor died (apparently of gastroenteritis) on July 9, 1850, and was succeeded by Vice-President Millard Fillmore (1800–1874). In Congress, the fight for the Compromise was taken up by Senator Stephen A. Douglas of Illinois who broke Clay's proposal into its component parts so that he could use varying coalitions to push each part through Congress. The Compromise was adopted.

The 1852 Democratic convention deadlocked between Cass and Douglas and so settled on dark horse Franklin Pierce (1804–1869) of New Hampshire. The Whigs chose General Winfield Scott, a war hero with no political background.

The result was an easy victory for Pierce, largely because the Whig party, badly divided along North-South lines as a result of the battle over the Compromise of 1850, was beginning to come apart.

President Pierce expressed the nation's hope that a new era of sectional peace was beginning. He sought to distract the nation's attention from the slavery issue to an aggressive program of foreign economic and territorial expansion known as "Young America."

In 1853, Commodore Matthew Perry (1794–1858) led a United States naval force into Tokyo Bay on a peaceful mission to open Japan—previously closed to the outside world—to American diplomacy and commerce.

By means of the Reciprocity Treaty (1854), Pierce succeeded in opening Canada to greater United States trade.

From Mexico he acquired in 1853 the Gadsden Purchase, a strip of land in what is now southern New Mexico and Arizona along the Gila River. The purpose of this purchase was to provide a good route for a transcontinental railroad across the southern part of the country.

The chief factor in the economic transformation of America during the 1840s and 1850s was the dynamic rise of the railroads. They helped link the Midwest to the Northeast rather than just the South, as would have been the case had only water transportation been available.

The 1850s was the heyday of the steamboat on inland rivers, and the clipper ship on the high seas. The period also saw rapid and sustained industrial growth, especially in the textile industry.

In the North, the main centers of agricultural production shifted from the Mid-Atlantic states to the more fertile lands of the Midwest. Mechanical reapers and threshers came into wide use.

America's second two-party system, which had developed during the 1830s, was in the process of breaking down. The Whig party was now in the process of complete disintegration. This was partially the result of the slavery issue, which divided the party along North-South lines, and partially the result of the nativist movement.

The collapse of a viable two-party system made it much more difficult for the nation's political process to contain the explosive issue of slavery.

THE RETURN OF SECTIONAL CONFLICT

The strengthened Fugitive Slave Law enraged northerners. So violent was northern feeling against the law that several riots erupted as a result of attempts to enforce it. Some northern states passed personal liberty laws in an attempt to prevent the enforcement of the Fugitive Slave Law.

One northerner who was outraged by the Fugitive Slave Act was Harriet Beecher Stowe. She wrote *Uncle Tom's Cabin*, a fictional book depicting what she perceived as the evils of slavery. Furiously denounced in the South, the book became an overnight bestseller in the North, where it turned many toward active opposition to slavery.

All illusion of sectional peace ended abruptly in 1854 when Senator Stephen A. Douglas of Illinois introduced a bill in Congress to organize the area west of Missouri and Iowa as the territories of Kansas and Nebraska on the basis of popular sovereignty.

The Kansas-Nebraska Act aroused a storm of outrage in the North, where its repeal of the Missouri Compromise was seen as the breaking of a solemn agreement. It hastened the disintegration of the Whig party and divided the Democratic party along North-South lines.

In the North, many Democrats left the party and were joined by former Whigs and Know-Nothings in the newly created Republican party. Springing to life almost overnight as a result of northern fury at the Kansas-Nebraska Act, the Republican party included diverse elements whose sole unifying principle was the firm belief that slavery should be banned from all the nation's territories, confined to the states where it already existed, and allowed to spread no further.

For the next several years Kansas was in chaos, including at various times armed conflict, voter fraud, two governments, and a questionable constitution.

In *Dred Scott vs. Sanford*, the Supreme Court attempted to finally settle the slavery question. The case involved a Missouri slave, Dred Scott (ca. 1795–1858), who had been encouraged by abolitionists to sue for his freedom on the basis that his owner had taken him for several years to a free state, Illinois, and then to a free territory, Wisconsin.

Under the domination of aging pro-southern Chief Justice Roger B. Taney of Maryland, the Court attempted to read the extreme southern position on slavery into the Constitution, ruling not only that Scott had no standing to sue in federal court, but also that temporary residence in a free state, even for several years, did not make a slave free, and that the Missouri Compromise (already a dead letter by that time) had been unconstitutional all along because Congress did not have the authority to exclude slavery from a territory. Nor did territorial governments have the right to prohibit slavery.

The 1858 Illinois senatorial campaign produced a series of debates that got to the heart of the issues that were threatening to divide the nation. Incumbent Democratic senator and front-runner for the 1860 presidential nomination Stephen A. Douglas was opposed by a Springfield lawyer, little known outside the state, by the name of Abraham Lincoln.

Lincoln, in a series of seven debates that the candidates agreed to hold during the course of the campaign, stressed that Douglas's doctrine of popular sovereignty failed to recognize slavery for the moral wrong it was.

Douglas, for his part, maintained that his guiding principle was democracy, not any moral standard of right or wrong with respect to slavery.

At the debate held in Freeport, Illinois, Lincoln pressed Douglas to reconcile the principle of popular sovereignty to the Supreme Court's decision in the Dred Scott case. How could the people "vote it up or vote it down," if, as the Supreme Court alleged, no territorial government could prohibit slavery? Douglas, in what came to be called his "Freeport Doctrine," replied that the people of any territory could exclude slavery simply by declining to pass any of the special laws that slave jurisdictions usually passed for their protection.

Douglas's answer was good enough to win him reelection to the Senate, although by the narrowest of margins, but hurt him in the coming presidential campaign.

For Lincoln, despite the failure to win the Senate seat, the debates were a major success, propelling him into the national spotlight, and strengthening the resolve of the Republican party to resist compromise on the free-soil issue.

THE COMING OF THE CIVIL WAR

On the night of October 16, 1859, John Brown, an abolitionist, led 18 followers in seizing the federal arsenal at Harpers Ferry, Virginia, taking hostages, and endeavoring to incite a slave uprising. Quickly cornered by Virginia militia, he was eventually captured by a force under the command of army Colonel Robert E. Lee (1807–1870).

Brown was quickly tried, convicted, sentenced, and on December 2, 1859, hanged. Many northerners looked upon Brown as a martyr.

Though responsible northerners such as Lincoln denounced Brown's raid as a criminal act which deserved to be punished by death, many southerners became convinced that the entire northern public approved of Brown's action and that the only safety for the South lay in a separate southern confederacy.

As the 1860 presidential election approached, two Democratic conventions failed to reach consensus, and the sundered halves of the party nominated separate candidates. The southern wing of the party nominated Buchanan's vice president, John C. Breckinridge of Kentucky, on a platform calling for a federal slave code in all the territories. What was left of the national Democratic party nominated Douglas on a platform of popular sovereignty.

A third presidential candidate was added by the Constitutional Union party, a collection of aging former Whigs and Know-Nothings from the southern and border states, plus a handful of moderate southern Democrats. It nominated John Bell of Tennessee on a platform that sidestepped the issues and called simply for the Constitution, the Union, and the enforcement of the laws.

The Republicans met in Chicago, confident of victory and determined to do nothing to jeopardize their favorable position. Accordingly, they rejected as too radical front-running New York Senator William H. Seward in favor of Illinois' favorite son Abraham Lincoln. The platform called for federal support of a transcontinental railroad and for the containment of slavery.

On election day, the voting went along strictly sectional lines. Breckinridge carried the Deep South; Bell, the border states; and Lincoln, the North. Douglas, although second in popular votes, carried only a single state and part of another. Lincoln led in popular votes, and though he was short of a majority in that category, he did have the needed majority in electoral votes and was elected.

THE SECESSION CRISIS

On December 20, 1860, South Carolina, by vote of a special convention, declared itself out of the Union. By February 1, 1861, six more states (Alabama, Georgia, Florida, Mississippi, Louisiana, and Texas) had followed suit.

Representatives of the seceded states met in Montgomery, Alabama, in February 1861 and declared themselves to be the Confederate States of America. They elected former Secretary of War and United States senator Jefferson Davis of Mississippi as president, and Alexander Stephens (1812–1883) of Georgia as vice president. They also adopted a constitution for the Confederate states which, while similar to the United States Constitution in many ways, contained several important differences:

1) Slavery was specifically recognized, and the right to move slaves from one state to another was guaranteed.

2) Protective tariffs were prohibited.

3) The president was to serve for a single nonrenewable six-year term.

4) The president was given the right to veto individual items within an appropriations bill.

5) State sovereignty was specifically recognized.

THE CIVIL WAR AND RECONSTRUCTION (1860–1877)
HOSTILITIES BEGIN

In his inaugural address, Lincoln urged southerners to reconsider their actions, but warned that the Union was perpetual, that states could not secede, and that he would therefore, hold the federal forts and installations in the South.

Only two remained in federal hands: Fort Pickens, off Pensacola, Florida; and Fort Sumter, in the harbor of Charleston, South Carolina. Lincoln soon received word from Major Robert Anderson, commander of the small garrison at Sumter, that supplies were running low. Desiring to send in the needed supplies, Lincoln informed the governor of South Carolina of his intention, but promised that no attempt would be made to send arms, ammunition, or reinforcements unless southerners initiated hostilities.

Confederate General P.G.T. Beauregard (1818–1893), acting on orders from President Davis, demanded Anderson's surrender. Anderson said he would surrender if not resupplied. Knowing supplies were on the way, the Confederates opened fire at 4:30 a.m. on April 12, 1861. The next day, the fort surrendered.

The day following Sumter's surrender, Lincoln declared an insurrection and called for the states to provide 75,000 volunteers to put it down. In response to this, Virginia, Tennessee, North Carolina, and Arkansas declared their secession.

The remaining slave states, Delaware, Kentucky, Maryland, and Missouri, wavered, but stayed with the Union.

The North enjoyed at least five major advantages over the South. It had overwhelming preponderance in wealth and was vastly superior in industry.

The North also had an advantage of almost three to one in manpower; and over one-third of the South's population was composed of slaves, whom Southerners would not use as soldiers. Unlike the South, the North received large numbers of immigrants during the war. The North retained control of the United States Navy, and thus, would command the sea and be able to blockade the South. Finally, the North enjoyed a much superior system of railroads.

The South did, however, have several advantages. It was vast in size, making it difficult to conquer. Its troops would be fighting on their own ground, a fact that would give them the advantage of familiarity with the terrain, as well as the added motivation of defending their homes and families. Its armies would often have the opportunity of fighting on the defensive, a major advantage in the warfare of that day.

Though Jefferson Davis had extensive military and political experience, Lincoln was much superior to Davis as a war leader, showing firmness, flexibility, mental toughness, great political skill, and, eventually an excellent grasp of strategy.

At a creek called Bull Run near the town of Manassas Junction, Virginia, just southwest of Washington, D.C., the Union Army met a Confederate force under generals P.G.T. Beauregard and Joseph E. Johnston, July 21, 1861. In the First Battle of Bull Run (called First Manassas in the South), the Union army was forced to retreat in confusion back to Washington.

THE UNION PRESERVED

To replace the discredited McDowell, Lincoln chose General George B. McClellan (1826–1885). McClellan was a good trainer and organizer and was loved by the troops, but he was unable to effectively use the powerful army (now called the Army of the Potomac) he had built up.

Lee summoned General Thomas J. "Stonewall" Jackson (1824–1863) and his army from the Shenandoah Valley (where Jackson had just finished defeating several superior federal forces), and with the combined forces attacked McClellan.

After two days of bloody but inconclusive fighting, McClellan lost his nerve and began to retreat. In the remainder of what came to be called the Battle of the Seven Days, Lee continued to attack McClellan, forcing him back to his base, though at great cost in lives. McClellan's army was loaded back onto its ships and taken back to Washington.

Before McClellan's army could reach Washington, Lee took the opportunity to thrash Union General John Pope (1822–1892), who was in northern Virginia with another northern army, at the Second Battle of Bull Run.

West of the Appalachian Mountains, matters were proceeding differently. The northern commanders there, Henry W. Halleck (1815–1872) and Don Carlos Buell (1818–1898), were no more enterprising than McClellan, but Halleck's subordinate, Ulysses S. Grant, was.

With permission from Halleck, Grant mounted a combined operation—army troops and navy gunboats—against two vital Confederate strongholds, forts Henry and Donelson, which guarded the Tennessee and Cumberland rivers in northern Tennessee. When Grant captured the forts in February 1862, Johnston was forced to retreat to Corinth in northern Mississippi.

Grant pursued, but ordered by Halleck to wait until all was in readiness before proceeding, halted his troops at Pittsburg Landing on the Tennessee River, 25 miles north of Corinth. On April 6, 1862 General Albert Sidney

Johnston, who had received reinforcements and been joined by General P.G.T. Beauregard, surprised Grant there, but in the two-day battle that followed (Shiloh) failed to defeat him. Johnston was among the many killed in what was, up to this point, the bloodiest battle in American history.

Grant was severely criticized in the North for having been taken by surprise. Yet with other Union victories and Farragut's capture of New Orleans, the North had taken all of the Mississippi River except for a 110–mile stretch between the Confederate fortresses of Vicksburg, Mississippi, and Port Hudson, Louisiana.

Many southerners believed Britain and France would rejoice in seeing a divided and weakened America. They also believed the two countries would likewise be driven by the need of their factories for cotton and thus intervene on the Confederacy's behalf.

This view proved mistaken. Britain already had a large supply of cotton, and had other sources besides the U.S. British leaders may also have weighed their country's need to import wheat from the northern United States against its desire for cotton from the southern states. Finally, British public opinion opposed slavery.

Skillful northern diplomacy had a great impact. In this, Lincoln had the extremely able assistance of Secretary of State William Seward, who took a hard line in warning Europeans not to interfere, and of ambassador to Great Britain Charles Francis Adams (1807–1886). Britain remained neutral, and other European countries, including France followed its lead.

Congress in 1862 passed two highly important acts dealing with domestic affairs in the North. The Homestead Act granted 160 acres of government land free of charge to any person who would farm it for at least five years. Much of the West was eventually settled under the provisions of this act. The Morrill Land Grant Act offered large amounts of the federal government's land to states that would establish "agricultural and mechanical" colleges. Many of the nation's large state universities were later founded under the provisions of this act.

THE EMANCIPATION PROCLAMATION

By mid-1862, Lincoln, under pressure from radical elements of his own party and hoping to create a favorable impression on foreign public opinion, determined to issue the Emancipation Proclamation, which declared free all slaves in areas still in rebellion as of January 1, 1863. At Seward's recommendation, Lincoln waited to announce the proclamation until the North should win some sort of victory. This was provided by the Battle of Antietam (September 17, 1863).

After his victory at the Second Battle of Bull Run, Lee moved north and crossed into Maryland, where he hoped to win a decisive victory that would force the North to recognize southern independence.

The armies finally met along Antietam Creek, just east of the town of Sharpsburg in western Maryland. In a bloody but inconclusive day-long battle, known as Antietam in the North and Sharpsburg in the South, McClellan's timidity led him to miss another excellent chance to destroy Lee's cornered and badly outnumbered army. After the battle, Lee retreated to Virginia, and Lincoln removed McClellan from command.

To replace him, Lincoln chose General Ambrose E. Burnside (1824–1881), who promptly demonstrated his unfitness by blundering into a lop-sided defeat at Fredericksburg, Virginia (December 13, 1862).

Lincoln then replaced Burnside with General Joseph "Fighting Joe" Hooker (1814–1879). He was soundly beaten at the Battle of Chancellorsville (May 5–6, 1863). At this battle, the brilliant Southern general "Stonewall" Jackson was accidentally shot by his own men and died several days later.

Lee received permission from President Davis to invade Pennsylvania. He was pursued by the Army of the Potomac, now under the command of General George G. Meade (1815–1872), who had replaced the discredited Hooker. They met at Gettysburg in a three-day battle (July 1–3, 1863) that was the bloodiest of the war. Lee, who sorely missed the services of Jackson and whose cavalry leader, the normally reliable J.E.B. Stuart (1833–1864), failed to provide him with timely reconnaissance, was defeated. However, he was allowed by the victorious Meade to retreat to Virginia with his army intact if battered, much to Lincoln's disgust.

Meanwhile, Grant moved on Vicksburg, one of the two last Confederate bastions on the Mississippi River. In a brilliant campaign, he bottled up the Confederate forces of General John C. Pemberton (1814–1881) inside the city and placed them under siege. After six weeks, the defenders surrendered on July 4, 1863. Five days later, Port Hudson surrendered, giving the Union complete control of the Mississippi River.

After Union forces under General William Rosecrans (1819–1898) suffered an embarrassing defeat at the Battle of Chickamauga in northwestern Georgia (September 19–20, 1863), Lincoln named Grant overall commander of Union forces in the West.

Grant went to Chattanooga, Tennessee, where Confederate forces under General Braxton Bragg (1817–1876) were virtually besieging Rosecrans, and immediately took control of the situation. Gathering Union forces from other portions of the western theater and combining them with reinforcements from the East, Grant won a resounding victory at the Battle of

Chattanooga (November 23–25, 1863), in which federal forces stormed seemingly impregnable Confederate positions on Lookout Mountain and Missionary Ridge. This victory put Union forces in position for a drive into Georgia, which began the following spring.

Early in 1864, Lincoln made Grant commander of all Union armies. Grant devised a coordinated plan for constant pressure on the Confederacy. General William T. Sherman would lead a drive toward Atlanta, Georgia, with the goal of destroying the Confederate army under General Joseph E. Johnston (who had replaced Bragg). Grant would accompany Meade and the Army of the Potomac in advancing toward Richmond with the goal of destroying Lee's Confederate army.

In a series of bloody battles (the Wilderness, Spotsylvania, Cold Harbor) in May and June of 1864, Grant drove Lee to the outskirts of Richmond. Still unable to take the city or get Lee at a disadvantage, Grant circled around, attacking Petersburg, Virginia, an important railroad junction just south of Richmond and the key to that city's—and Lee's—supply lines. Once again turned back by entrenched Confederate troops, Grant settled down to besiege Petersburg and Richmond in a stalemate that lasted some nine months.

Sherman had been advancing simultaneously in Georgia. He maneuvered Johnston back to the outskirts of Atlanta with relatively little fighting. At that point, Confederate President Davis lost patience with Johnston and replaced him with the aggressive General John B. Hood (1831–1879). Hood and Sherman fought three fierce but inconclusive battles around Atlanta in late July, and then settled down to a siege of their own during the month of August.

THE ELECTION OF 1864 AND NORTHERN VICTORY

Lincoln ran on the ticket of the National Union party, essentially the Republican party with loyal or "War" Democrats. His vice-presidential candidate was Andrew Johnson (1808–1875), a loyal Democrat from Tennessee.

The Democratic party's presidential candidate was General George B. McClellan, who ran on a platform labeling the war a failure, and calling for a negotiated peace settlement even if that meant southern independence.

In September 1864, word came that Sherman had taken Atlanta. The capture of this vital southern rail and manufacturing center brought an enormous boost to northern morale. Along with other northern victories that summer and fall, it ensured a resounding election victory for Lincoln and the continuation of the war to complete victory for the North.

To speed that victory, Sherman marched through Georgia from Atlanta to the sea, arriving at Savannah in December 1864 and turning north into the Carolinas, leaving behind a 60–mile-wide swath of destruction.

Lee abandoned Richmond (April 3, 1865) and attempted to escape with what was left of his army. Pursued by Grant, he was cornered and forced to surrender at Appomattox, Virginia (April 9, 1865). Other Confederate armies still holding out in various parts of the South surrendered over the next few weeks.

Lincoln did not live to receive news of the final surrenders. On April 14, 1865, he was shot in the back of the head while watching a play in Ford's Theater in Washington.

THE ORDEAL OF RECONSTRUCTION

Reconstruction began well before the fighting of the Civil War came to an end. It brought a time of difficult adjustments in the South.

Among those who faced such adjustments were the recently freed slaves. To ease the adjustment for these recently freed slaves, Congress in 1865 created the Freedman's Bureau to provide food, clothing, and education, and generally look after the interests of former slaves.

To restore legal governments in the seceded states, Lincoln developed a policy that made it relatively easy for southern states to enter the collateral process.

Tennessee, Arkansas, and Louisiana formed loyal governments under Lincoln's plan, but were refused recognition by a Congress dominated by Radical Republicans.

Radical Republicans such as Thaddeus Stevens (1792–1868) of Pennsylvania believed Lincoln's plan did not adequately punish the South, restructure southern society, or boost the political prospects of the Republican party.

Instead, the radicals in Congress drew up the more stringent Wade-Davis Bill which Lincoln killed with a "pocket veto," and the radicals were furious. When Lincoln was assassinated the radicals rejoiced, believing Vice President Andrew Johnson would be less generous to the South, or at least easier to control.

FOREIGN POLICY UNDER JOHNSON

In 1866, the Russian minister approached Seward with an offer to sell Alaska to the United States. In 1867, the sale went through and Alaska was purchased for $7,200,000.

CONGRESSIONAL RECONSTRUCTION

Determined to reconstruct the South as it saw fit, Congress passed a Civil Rights Act and extended the authority of the Freedman's Bureau, giving it both quasi-judicial and quasi-executive powers.

Johnson vetoed both bills, claiming they were unconstitutional; but Congress overrode the vetoes. Fearing that the Supreme Court would agree with Johnson and overturn the laws, Congress approved and sent on to the states for ratification (June 1866) the fourteenth Amendment, making constitutional the laws Congress had just passed. The fourteenth Amendment defined citizenship and forbade states to deny various rights to citizens, reduced the representation in Congress of states that did not allow blacks to vote, forbade the paying of the Confederate debt, and made former Confederates ineligible to hold public office.

To control the president, Congress passed the Army Act, reducing the president's control over the army. Congress also passed the Tenure of Office Act, forbidding Johnson to dismiss cabinet members without the Senate's permission.

Johnson obeyed the letter but not the spirit of the Reconstruction acts, and Congress, angry at his refusal to cooperate, sought in vain for grounds to impeach him, until in August 1867 Johnson violated the Tenure of Office Act in order to test its constitutionality. The matter was not tested in the courts, however, but in Congress, where Johnson was impeached by the House of Representatives and came within one vote of being removed by the Senate.

THE ELECTION OF 1868 AND THE 15TH AMENDMENT

In 1868, the Republicans nominated, for president, Ulysses S. Grant, who had no political record and whose views—if any—on national issues were unknown.

The narrow victory of even such a strong candidate as Grant prompted Republican leaders to decide that it would be politically expedient to give the vote to all blacks, North as well as South. For this purpose, the 15th Amendment was drawn up and submitted to the states. Ironically, the idea was so unpopular in the North that it won the necessary three-fourths approval only with its ratification by southern states required to do so by Congress.

Though personally of unquestioned integrity, Grant naively placed his faith in a number of thoroughly dishonest men. His administration was rocked by one scandalous revelation of government corruption after another.

Many of the economic difficulties the country faced during Grant's administration were caused by the necessary readjustments from a wartime economy back to a peacetime economy. The central economic question was deflation versus inflation, or more specifically, whether to retire the unbacked paper money, greenbacks, printed to meet the wartime emergency, or to print more.

Early in Grant's second term, the country was hit by an economic depression known as the Panic of 1873. Brought on by the overexpansive tendencies of railroad builders and businessmen during the immediate postwar boom, the Panic was triggered by economic downturns in Europe, and more immediately, by the failure of Jay Cooke and Company, a major American financial firm.

The Panic led to clamor for the printing of more greenbacks. In 1874, Congress authorized a small new issue of greenbacks, but it was vetoed by Grant. Pro-inflation forces were further enraged when Congress in 1873 demonetized silver, going to a straight gold standard. Silver was becoming more plentiful due to western mining and was seen by some as a potential source of inflation. Pro-inflation forces referred to the demonetization of silver as the "Crime of '73."

In the election of 1876, the Democrats campaigned against corruption and nominated New York Governor Samuel J. Tilden (1814–1886), who had broken the Tweed political machine of New York City.

The Republicans passed over Grant and turned to Governor Rutherford B. Hayes (1822–1893) of Ohio. Like Tilden, Hayes was decent, honest, in favor of hard money and civil service reform, and opposed to government regulation of the economy.

Tilden won the popular vote and led in the electoral vote 184 to 165. However, 185 electoral votes were needed for election, and 20 votes, from the three Southern states still occupied by federal troops and run by Republican governments, were disputed.

A deal was made whereby those 20 votes went to Hayes in return for removal of federal troops from the South. Reconstruction was over.

INDUSTRIALISM, WAR, AND THE PROGRESSIVE ERA (1877–1912)

POLITICS OF THE PERIOD (1877–1882)

The presidencies of Abraham Lincoln and Theodore Roosevelt (1858–1919) mark the boundaries of a half century of relatively weak executive leadership and legislative domination by Congress and the Republican party.

"Stalwarts," led by New York senator Roscoe Conkling (1829–1888) favored the old spoils system of political patronage. "Half-Breeds," headed by Maine senator James G. Blaine (1830–1893), pushed for civil service reform and merit appointments to government posts.

THE ECONOMY (1877–1882)

Between 1860 and 1894, the United States moved from the fourth largest manufacturing nation to the world's leader through capital accumulation, natural resources, especially in iron, oil, and coal, an abundance of labor helped by massive immigration, railway transportation, and communications and major technical innovations such as the development of the modern steel industry and electrical energy .

By 1880, northern capital erected the modern textile industry in the New South by bringing factories to the cotton fields.

SOCIAL AND CULTURAL DEVELOPMENTS (1877–1882)

In time, advocates of the "social gospel" such as Jane Addams (1860–1939) and Washington Gladden (1836–1918) urged the creation of settlement houses and better health and education services to accommodate the new immigrants. In 1881, Booker T. Washington (1856–1915) became president of Tuskegee Institute in Alabama, a school devoted to teaching and vocational education for African Americans.

THE ECONOMY (1882–1887)

Captains of industry such as John D. Rockefeller in oil, J. P. Morgan (1837–1919) in banking, Gustavus Swift (1839–1903) in meat processing, Andrew Carnegie in steel, and E. H. Harriman (1848–1909) in railroads, put together major industrial empires.

The concentration of wealth and power in the hands of a relatively small number of giant firms led to a monopoly capitalism that minimized competition. This led to a demand by smaller businessmen, farmers, and laborers for government regulation of the economy in order to promote competition.

The Interstate Commerce Act (1887): Popular resentment of railroad abuses such as price-fixing, kickbacks, and discriminatory freight rates created demands for state regulation of the railway industry. The Interstate Commerce Act was passed providing that a commission be established to oversee fair and just railway rates, prohibit rebates, end discriminatory practices, and require annual reports and financial statements.

American Federation of Labor (1886): Samuel Gompers (1850–1924) and Adolph Strasser put together a combination of national craft unions to represent labor's concerns with wages, hours, and safety conditions. Although militant in its use of the strike and in its demand for collective bargaining in labor contracts with large corporations, it did not promote violence or radicalism.

Frederick W. Taylor (1856–1915), an engineer credited as the father of scientific management, introduced modern concepts of industrial engineering, plant management, and time and motion studies. This gave rise to a separate class of managers in industrial manufacturing — efficiency experts.

THE EMERGENCE OF A REGIONAL EMPIRE (1887–1892)

Despite a protective tariff policy, the United States became increasingly international as it sought to export surplus manufactured and agricultural goods. Foreign markets were viewed as a safety valve for labor employment problems and agrarian unrest.

THE ECONOMY (1887–1892)

Corporate monopolies (trusts) which controlled whole industries were subject to federal prosecution if they were found to be combinations or conspiracies in restraint of trade. Although supported by smaller businesses, labor unions, and farm associations, the Sherman Antitrust Act of 1890 was in time interpreted by the Supreme Court to apply to labor unions and farmers' cooperatives as much as to large corporate combinations. Monopoly was still dominant over laissez-faire, free-enterprise economics during the 1890s.

FOREIGN RELATIONS (1887–1892)

As secretary of state, James G. Blaine was concerned with international trade, political stability, and excessive militarism in Latin America. His international Bureau of American Republics was designed to promote a Pan-American customs union and peaceful conflict resolution. To achieve his aims, Blaine opposed U.S. military intervention in the hemisphere.

ECONOMIC DEPRESSION AND SOCIAL CRISIS (1892–1897)

The economic depression that began in 1893 brought about a collective response from organized labor, militant agriculture, and the business community. Each group called for economic safeguards and a more humane free-enterprise system which would expand economic opportunities in an equitable manner.

POLITICS OF THE PERIOD (1892–1897)

The most marked development in American politics was the emergence of a viable third-party movement in the form of the essentially agrarian Populist party.

Democrat Grover Cleveland (New York) regained the White House by defeating Republican president Benjamin Harrison (Indiana). Cleveland's conservative economic stand in favor of the gold standard brought him the support of various business interests. The Democrats won control of both houses of Congress.

The People's party (Populist) nominated James Weaver (Iowa) for president in 1892. The party platform called for the enactment of a program espoused by agrarians, but also for a coalition with urban workers and the middle class. Specific goals were the coinage of silver to gold at a ratio of 16 to 1; federal loans to farmers; a graduated income tax; postal savings banks; public ownership of railroads and telephone and telegraph systems; prohibition of alien land ownership; immigration restriction; a ban on private armies used by corporations to break up strikes; an eight-hour working day; a single six-year term for president and direct election of senators; the right of initiative and referendum; and the use of the secret ballot.

In the election of 1896, the Republicans nominated William McKinley (Ohio) for president on a platform which promised to maintain the gold standard and protective tariffs. The Democratic party repudiated Cleveland's conservative economics and nominated William Jennings Bryan (1860–1925) (Nebraska) for president on a platform similar to the Populists. Bryan delivered one of the most famous speeches in American history when he declared that the people must not be "crucified upon a cross of gold."

The Populist party also nominated Bryan. Having been outmaneuvered by the Silver Democrats, the Populists lost the opportunity to become a permanent political force.

McKinley won a hard-fought election by only about one-half million votes, as Republicans succeeded in creating the fear among business groups and middle-class voters that Bryan represented a revolutionary challenge to the American system. The Republicans retained control over Congress, which they had gained in 1894.

THE ECONOMY (1892–1897)

Homestead Strike (1892): Iron and steel workers went on strike in Pennsylvania against the Carnegie Steel Company to protest salary reductions.

The primary causes for the depression of 1893 were dramatic growth of the federal deficit, withdrawal of British investments from the American market and the outward transfer of gold, and loss of business confidence. Twenty percent of the work force was eventually unemployed. The depression would last four years.

March of Unemployed (1894): The Populist businessman Jacob Coxey (1854–1951) led a march of hundreds of unemployed workers on Washington asking for a government work-relief program.

Pullman Strike (1894): Eugene Debs's (1855–1926) American Railway Union struck the Pullman Palace Car Co. in Chicago over wage cuts and job losses. The strikes were all ended by force.

Wilson-Gorman Tariff (1894): This protective tariff did little to promote overseas trade as a way to ease the depression.

Dingley Tariff (1897): The Dingley Tariff raised protection to new highs for certain commodities.

SOCIAL AND CULTURAL DEVELOPMENTS (1892–1897)

The Anti-Saloon League was formed in 1893. Women were especially concerned about the increase of drunkenness during the depression.

Immigration declined by almost 400,000 during the depression. Settlement houses helped poor immigrants. Such institutions also lobbied against sweatshop labor conditions, and for bans on child labor.

FOREIGN RELATIONS (1892–1897)

The Cuban revolt against Spain in 1895 threatened American business interests in Cuba. Sensational "yellow" journalism, and nationalistic statements from officials such as Assistant Secretary of the Navy Theodore Roosevelt (1858–1919), encouraged popular support for direct American military intervention on behalf of Cuban independence. President McKinley, however, proceeded cautiously through 1897.

THE SINO-JAPANESE WAR (1894–1895)

Japan's easy victory over China signaled to the United States and other nations trading in Asia that China's weakness might result in its colonization by industrial powers, and thus, in the closing of the China market. This concern led the United States to announce the Open Door policy with China, designed to protect equal opportunity of trade and China's political independence (1899 and 1900).

FOREIGN POLICY (1897–1902)

On March 27, President McKinley asked Spain to call an armistice, accept American mediation to end the war, and end the use of concentration camps in Cuba. Spain refused to comply. On April 21, Congress declared war on Spain with the objective of establishing Cuban independence (Teller Amendment). The first U.S. forces landed in Cuba on June 22, 1898 and by July 17 had defeated the Spanish forces.

On May 1, 1898, the Spanish fleet in the Philippines was destroyed, and Manila surrendered on August 13. Spain agreed to a peace conference to be held in Paris in October 1898, where it ceded the Philippines, Puerto Rico, and Guam to the United States, in return for a payment of $20 million to Spain for the Philippines. The Treaty of Paris was ratified by the Senate on February 6, 1900.

Filipino nationalists under Emilio Aguinaldo (1869–1964) rebelled against the United States (February 1899) when they learned the Philippines would not be given independence. The United States used 70,000 men to suppress the revolutionaries by June 1902. A special U.S. commission recommended eventual self-government for the Philippines.

During the war with Spain, the United States annexed Hawaii on July 7, 1898. In 1900, the United States claimed Wake Island, 2,000 miles west of Hawaii.

Although Cuba was granted its independence, the Platt Amendment of 1901 guaranteed that it would become a virtual protectorate of the United States. Cuba could not: 1) make a treaty with a foreign state impairing its independence, or 2) contract an excessive public debt. Cuba was required to: 1) allow the United States to preserve order on the island, and 2) lease a naval base for 99 years to the United States at Guantanamo Bay.

POLITICS OF THE PERIOD (1900–1902)

The unexpected death of Vice President Garrett Hobart led the Republican party to choose the war hero and reform governor of New York, Theodore Roosevelt, as President William McKinley's vice-presidential running mate. Riding the crest of victory against Spain, the G.O.P platform called for upholding the gold standard for full economic recovery, promoting economic expansion and power in the Caribbean and the Pacific, and building a canal in Central America. The Democrats once again nominated William Jennings Bryan on a platform condemning imperialism and the gold standard. McKinley easily won reelection and the Republicans retained control of both houses of Congress.

While attending the Pan American Exposition in Buffalo, New York, the president was shot on September 6 by Leon Czolgosz, an anarchist. The president died on September 14. Theodore Roosevelt became the nation's 25th president, and at age 42, its youngest to date.

THEODORE ROOSEVELT AND PROGRESSIVE REFORMS (1902–1907)

President Roosevelt did much to create a bipartisan coalition of liberal reformers whose objective was to restrain corporate monopoly and promote economic competition at home and abroad.

The president pledged strict enforcement of the Sherman Antitrust Act (1890), which was designed to break up illegal monopolies and regulate large corporations for the public good.

Hepburn Act (1906): Membership of the Interstate Commerce Commission was increased from five to seven. The I.C.C. could set its own fair freight rates, had its regulatory power extended over pipelines, bridges, and express companies, and was empowered to require a uniform system of accounting by regulated transportation companies.

Pure Food and Drug Act (1906): This prohibited the manufacture, sale, and transportation of adulterated or fraudulently labeled foods and drugs in accordance with consumer demands.

Meat Inspection Act (1906): This provided for federal and sanitary regulations and inspections in meat packing facilities. Wartime scandals in 1898 involving spoiled canned meats were a powerful force for reform.

THE ECONOMY (1902–1907)

Antitrust Policy (1902): Attorney General P. C. Knox (1853–1921) first brought suit against the Northern Securities Company, a railroad holding corporation put together by J. P. Morgan (1837–1913), and then moved against Rockefeller's Standard Oil Company. By the time he left office in 1909, Roosevelt had indictments against 25 monopolies.

Department of Commerce and Labor (1903): A new cabinet position was created to address the concerns of business and labor. Within the department, the Bureau of Corporations was empowered to investigate and report on the illegal activities of corporations.

Coal Strike (1902): Roosevelt interceded with government mediation to bring about negotiations between the United Mine Workers union and the anthracite mine owners after a bitter strike over wages, safety conditions, and union recognition. This was the first time that the government intervened in a labor dispute without automatically siding with management.

A brief economic recession and panic occurred in 1907 as a result, in part, of questionable bank speculations, a lack of flexible monetary and credit policies, and a conservative gold standard. This event called attention to the need for banking reform which would lead to the Federal Reserve System in 1913.

SOCIAL AND CULTURAL DEVELOPMENTS (1902–1907)

There was not one unified progressive movement, but a series of reform causes designed to address specific social, economic, and political problems. Progressive reforms might best be described as evolutionary change from above rather than revolutionary upheaval from below.

Muckrakers (a term coined by Roosevelt) were investigative journalists and authors who were often the publicity agents for reforms.

FOREIGN RELATIONS (1902–1907)

Panama Canal: Roosevelt engineered the separation of Panama from Colombia and the recognition of Panama as an independent country. The Hay-Bunau-Varilla Treaty of 1903 granted the United States control of the canal zone in Panama for $10 million and an annual fee of $250,000, beginning nine years after ratification of the treaty by both parties. Construction of the canal began in 1904 and was completed in 1914.

Roosevelt Corollary to the Monroe Doctrine: The United States reserved the right to intervene in the internal affairs of Latin American nations to keep European powers from using military force to collect debts in the Western Hemisphere. The United States by 1905, had intervened in the affairs of Venezuela, Haiti, the Dominican Republic, Nicaragua, and Cuba.

Taft-Katsura Memo (1905): The United States and Japan pledged to maintain the Open Door principles in China. Japan recognized American control over the Philippines, and the United States granted a Japanese protectorate over Korea.

Gentleman's Agreement with Japan (1907): After numerous incidents of racial discrimination against Japanese in California, Japan agreed to restrict the emigration of unskilled Japanese workers to the United States.

THE REGULATORY STATE AND THE ORDERED SOCIETY (1907–1912)

Deciding not to run for reelection, Theodore Roosevelt opened the way for William H. Taft (1857–1930) (Ohio) to run on a Republican platform calling for a continuation of antitrust enforcement, environmental conservation, and a lower tariff policy to promote international trade. The Democrats nominated William Jennings Bryan for a third time on an antimonopoly and low tariff platform. Taft easily won and the Republicans retained control of both houses of Congress. For the first time, the American Federation of Labor entered national politics officially with an endorsement of Bryan. This decision began a long alliance between organized labor and the Democratic party in the twentieth century.

Antitrust Policy: In pursuing anti-monopoly law enforcement, Taft chose as his attorney general George Wickersham (1858–1936), who brought 44 indictments in antitrust suits.

Taft was less successful in healing the Republican split between conservatives and progressives over such issues as tariff reform, conservation, and the almost dictatorial power held by the reactionary Republican Speaker of the House, Joseph Cannon (Illinois).

The 1912 election was one of the most dramatic in American history. President Taft's inability to maintain party harmony led Theodore Roosevelt to return to national politics. When denied the Republican nomination, Roosevelt and his supporters formed the Progressive (Bull Moose) party and nominated Roosevelt for president on a political platform nicknamed "The New Nationalism." It called for stricter regulation on large corporations, creation of a tariff commission, women's suffrage, minimum wages and benefits, direct election of senators, initiative, referendum and recall, presidential primaries, and prohibition of child labor. Roosevelt also called for a Federal Trade Commission to regulate the economy, a stronger executive, and more government planning. Theodore Roosevelt did not see big business as evil, but as a permanent development that was necessary in a modern economy.

The Republicans: President Taft and Vice President Sherman were nominated on a platform of "Quiet Confidence," which called for a continuation of the progressive programs pursued by Taft.

The Democrats: A compromise gave the nomination to New Jersey Governor Woodrow Wilson. Wilson, who had also served as president of Princeton University, called his campaign the "New Freedom"; it borrowed pieces from the Progressive and Republican platforms. Wilson called for breaking up large corporations rather than just regulating them. He differed from the other two party candidates by favoring independence for the Philippines, and by advocating the exemption from prosecution of labor unions under the Sherman Antitrust Act. Wilson also supported such measures as lower tariffs, a graduated income tax, banking reform, and direct election of senators.

The Republican split paved the way for Wilson's victory. Although a minority president, Wilson garnered the largest electoral majority in American history up to that time. Democrats won control of both houses of Congress.

THE WILSON PRESIDENCY

Before the outbreak of World War I in 1914, President Wilson, working with cooperative majorities in both houses of Congress, achieved much of the remaining progressive agenda, including lower tariff reform (Underwood-Simmons Act, 1913), the sixteenth Amendment (graduated income tax, 1913), the seventeenth Amendment (direct election of senators, 1913), the Federal Reserve banking system (which provided regulation and flexibility to monetary policy, 1913), the Federal Trade Commission (to investigate unfair business practices, 1914), and the Clayton Antitrust Act (improving the old Sherman act and protecting labor unions and farm cooperatives from prosecution, 1914).

Other goals such as the protection of children in the work force (Keating-Owen Act, 1916), credit reform for agriculture (Federal Farm Loan Act, 1916), and an independent tariff commission (1916) came later. By the end of Wilson's presidency, the New Freedom and the New Nationalism had merged into one government philosophy of regulation, order, and standardization in the interest of an increasingly diverse nation.

SOCIAL AND CULTURAL DEVELOPMENTS (1907–1912)

In 1905, the African-American intellectual militant W.E.B. DuBois (1868–1963) founded the Niagara Movement which called for federal legislation to protect racial equality and for full rights of citizenship. The National Association for the Advancement of Colored People was organized in 1909.

A radical labor organization called the Industrial Workers of the World (I.W.W., or Wobblies, 1905–1924) was active in promoting violence and revolution. The I.W.W. organized effective strikes in the textile industry in 1912, and among a few western miners groups, but had little appeal to the average American worker. After the Red Scare of 1919, the government worked to smash the I.W.W. and deported many of its immigrant leaders and members.

FOREIGN RELATIONS (1907–1915)

President Taft sought to avoid military intervention, especially in Latin America, by replacing "big stick" policies with "dollar diplomacy" in the expectation that American financial investments would encourage economic, social, and political stability. This idea proved an illusion.

Wilson urged Huerta to hold democratic elections and adopt a constitutional government. Huerta refused, and Wilson invaded Mexico with troops at Veracruz in 1914. A second U.S. invasion came in northern Mexico in 1916.

The United States kept a military presence in the Dominican Republic and Haiti, and intervened militarily in Nicaragua (1911) to quiet fears of revolution and help manage foreign financial problems.

WILSON AND WORLD WAR I (1912–1920)

THE EARLY YEARS OF THE WILSON ADMINISTRATION

Wilson was only the second Democrat (Cleveland was the first) elected president since the Civil War. Key appointments to the cabinet were William Jennings Bryan as secretary of state and William Gibbs McAdoo (1863–1941) as secretary of the treasury.

The Federal Reserve Act of 1913: The law divided the nation into 12 regions, with a Federal Reserve bank in each region. Federal Reserve banks loaned money to member banks at interest less than the public paid to the member banks, and the notes of indebtedness of businesses and farmers to the member banks were held as collateral. This allowed the Federal Reserve to control interest rates by raising or lowering the discount rate.

The money loaned to the member banks was in the form of a new currency, Federal Reserve notes, which was backed 60 percent by commercial paper and 40 percent by gold. This currency was designed to expand and contract with the volume of business activity and borrowing.

The Federal Reserve system serviced the financial needs of the federal government. The system was supervised and policy was set by a national Federal Reserve Board composed of the secretary of the treasury, the comptroller of the currency, and five other members appointed by the president of the United States.

The Clayton Antitrust Act of 1914: This law supplemented and interpreted the Sherman Antitrust Act of 1890. Under its provisions, stock ownership by a corporation in a competing corporation was prohibited, and the same persons were prohibited from managing competing corporations. Price discrimination (charging less in some regions than in others to undercut the competition) and exclusive contracts which reduced competition were prohibited.

THE ELECTION OF 1916

The Democrats, the minority party nationally in terms of voter registration, nominated Wilson and adopted his platform calling for continued progressive reforms and neutrality in the European war.

The Republican convention bypassed Theodore Roosevelt and chose Charles Evans Hughes (1862–1948), an associate justice of the Supreme Court and formerly a progressive Republican governor of New York.

Wilson won the election.

SOCIAL ISSUES IN THE FIRST WILSON ADMINISTRATION

In 1913, Treasury Secretary William G. McAdoo and Postmaster General Albert S. Burleson segregated workers in some parts of their departments with no objection from Wilson. Many northern blacks and whites protested, especially black leader W.E.B. DuBois (1868–1963), who had supported Wilson in 1912.

Wilson opposed immigration restrictions and vetoed a literacy test for immigrants in 1915, but in 1917, Congress overrode a similar veto.

WILSON'S FOREIGN POLICY AND THE ROAD TO WAR

Wilson's Basic Premise: Wilson promised a more moral foreign policy than that of his predecessors, denouncing imperialism and dollar diplomacy, and advocating the advancement of democratic capitalist governments throughout the world.

Wilson signaled his repudiation of Taft's dollar diplomacy by withdrawing American involvement from the six-power loan consortium of China.

In 1912, American marines had landed in Nicaragua to maintain order, and an American financial expert had taken control of the customs station. The Wilson administration kept the marines in Nicaragua and negotiated the Bryan-Chamorro Treaty of 1914, which gave the United States an option to build a canal through the country.

Claiming that political anarchy existed in Haiti, Wilson sent marines in 1915 and imposed a treaty making the country a protectorate, with American control of its finances and constabulary. The marines remained until 1934.

In 1916, Wilson sent marines to the Dominican Republic to stop a civil war and established a military government under an American naval commander.

Wilson feared in 1915 that Germany might annex Denmark and its Caribbean possession, the Danish West Indies or Virgin Islands. After extended negotiations, the United States purchased the islands from Denmark by treaty on August 4, 1916, for $25 million and took possession of them on March 31, 1917.

In 1913, Wilson refused to recognize the government of Mexican military dictator Victoriano Huerta, and offered unsuccessfully to mediate between Huerta and his Constitutionalist opponent, Venustiano Carranza. When the Huerta government arrested several American seamen in Tampico in April 1914, American forces occupied the port of Veracruz, an action condemned by both Mexican political factions. In July 1914, Huerta abdicated his power to Carranza, who was soon opposed by his former general Francisco

"Pancho" Villa (1878–1923). Seeking American intervention as a means of undermining Carranza, Villa shot 16 Americans on a train in northern Mexico in January 1916 and burned the border town of Columbus, New Mexico, in March 1916, killing 19 people. Carranza reluctantly consented to Wilson's request that the United States be allowed to pursue and capture Villa in Mexico, but did not expect the force of about 6,000 army troops under the command of General John J. Pershing which crossed the Rio Grande on March 18. The force advanced more than 300 miles into Mexico, failed to capture Villa, and became, in effect, an army of occupation. The Carranza government demanded an American withdrawal, and several clashes with Mexican troops occurred. War threatened, but in January 1917 Wilson removed the American forces.

THE ROAD TO WAR IN EUROPE

When World War I broke out in Europe, Wilson issued a proclamation of American neutrality on August 4, 1914. The value of American trade with the Central Powers fell from $169 million in 1914 to almost nothing in 1916, but trade with the Allies rose from $825 million to $3.2 billion during the same period. In addition, the British and French had borrowed about $3.25 billion from American sources by 1917. The United States had become a major supplier of Allied munitions, food, and raw materials.

The sinking of the British liner *Lusitania* off the coast of Ireland on May 7, 1915, with the loss of 1,198 lives, including 128 Americans, brought strong protests from Wilson. Secretary of State Bryan, who believed Americans should stay off belligerent ships, resigned rather than insist on questionable neutral rights and was replaced by Robert Lansing.

The House-Grey Memorandum: Early in 1915, Wilson sent his friend and adviser Colonel Edward M. House on an unsuccessful visit to Europe to offer American mediation in the war. Late in the year, House returned to London to propose that Wilson call a peace conference; if Germany refused to attend or was uncooperative at the conference, the United States could enter the war on the Allied side. An agreement to that effect, called the House-Grey memorandum, was signed by the British foreign secretary, Sir Edward Grey, on February 22, 1916.

In an address to Congress on January 22, 1917, Wilson made his last offer to serve as a neutral mediator. He proposed a "peace without victory," based not on a "balance of power" but on a "community of power."

Germany announced on January 31, 1917, that it would sink all ships, belligerent or neutral, without warning in a large war zone off the coasts of the Allied nations in the eastern Atlantic and the Mediterranean. Wilson broke diplomatic relations with Germany on February 3. During February and March several American merchant ships were sunk by submarines.

The British intercepted a secret message from the German foreign secretary, Arthur Zimmerman, to the German minister in Mexico, and turned it over to the United States on February 24, 1917. The Germans proposed that, in the event of a war between the United States and Germany, Mexico attack the United States. After the war, the "lost territories" of Texas, New Mexico, and Arizona would be returned to Mexico. When the telegram was released to the press on March 1, many Americans became convinced that war with Germany was necessary. A declaration of war against Germany was signed by Wilson on April 6.

WORLD WAR I: THE MILITARY CAMPAIGN

The American force of about 14,500, which had arrived in France by September 1917, was assigned a quiet section of the line near Verdun. When the Germans mounted a major drive toward Paris in the spring of 1918, the Americans experienced their first important engagements. In June, they prevented the Germans from crossing the Marne at Chateau-Thierry, and cleared the area of Belleau Woods. In July, eight American divisions aided French troops in attacking the German line between Reims and Soissons. The American First Army, with over half a million men under Pershing's immediate command, was assembled in August 1918, and began a major offensive at St. Mihiel on the southern part of the front on September 12. Following the successful operation, Pershing began a drive against the German defenses between Verdun and Sedan, an action called the Meuse-Argonne offensive. He reached Sedan on November 7. During the same period the English in the north and the French along the central front also broke through the German lines. The fighting ended with the armistice on November 11, 1918.

MOBILIZING THE HOME FRONT

A number of volunteer organizations sprang up around the country to search for draft dodgers, enforce the sale of bonds, and report any opinion or conversation considered suspicious. Such groups publicly humiliated people accused of not buying war bonds, and persecuted, beat, and sometimes killed people of German descent. The anti-German and antisubversive war hysteria in the United States far exceeded similar public moods in Britain and France during the war.

The Espionage Act of 1917 provided for fines and imprisonment for persons who made false statements which aided the enemy, incited rebellion in the military, or obstructed recruitment or the draft. Printed matter advocating treason or insurrection could be excluded from the mails. The Sedition Act of May 1918 forbade any criticism of the government, flag, or uniform, even if there were not detrimental consequences, and expanded the mail exclusion. The laws were applied in ways that trampled on civil liberties. The Espionage Act was upheld by the Supreme Court in the case of *Shenk v. United States* in 1919. The opinion, written by Justice Oliver Wendell Holmes, Jr. (1841–1935), stated that Congress could limit free speech when the words represented a "clear and present danger," and that a person cannot cry "fire" in a crowded theater. The Sedition Act was similarly upheld in *Abrams v. United States* a few months later. Ultimately 2,168 persons were prosecuted under the laws, and 1,055 were convicted, of whom only 10 were charged with actual sabotage.

WARTIME SOCIAL TRENDS

Large numbers of women, mostly white, were hired by factories and other enterprises in jobs never before open to them. When the war ended, almost all returned to traditional "women's jobs" or to homemaking. Returning veterans replaced them in the labor market.

The labor shortage opened industrial jobs to Mexican-Americans and to African-Americans. W.E.B. DuBois, the most prominent African-American leader of the time, supported the war effort in the hope that the war would make the world safe for democracy and bring a better life for African-Americans in the United States. About half a million rural southern African-Americans migrated to cities, mainly in the North and Midwest, to obtain employment in war and other industries, especially in steel and meatpacking. In 1917, there were race riots in 26 cities in the North and South, with the worst in East St. Louis, Illinois.

In December 1917, a constitutional amendment to prohibit the manufacture and sale of alcoholic beverages in the United States was passed by Congress and submitted to the states for ratification.

PEACEMAKING AND DOMESTIC PROBLEMS (1918–1920)

From the time of the American entry into the war, Wilson had maintained that the war would make the world safe for democracy. He insisted that there should be peace without victory, meaning that the victors would not be vindictive toward the losers, so that a fair and stable international situation in the postwar world would ensure lasting peace. In an address to Congress on January 8, 1918, he presented his specific peace plan in the form of the Fourteen Points. The first five points called for open rather than secret peace treaties, freedom of the seas, free trade, arms reduction, and a fair adjustment of colonial claims. The next eight points were concerned with the national aspirations of various European peoples and the adjustment of boundaries. The fourteenth point, which he considered the most important and had espoused as early as 1916, called for a "general association of nations" to preserve the peace.

Wilson decided that he would lead the American delegation to the peace conference which opened in Paris on January 12, 1919. In doing so he became the first president to leave the country during his term of office. In the negotiations, which continued until May 1919, Wilson found it necessary to make many compromises in forging the text of the treaty.

Following a protest by 39 senators in February 1919, Wilson obtained some changes in the League of Nations structure to exempt the Monroe Doctrine and domestic matters from League jurisdiction. Then, on July 26, 1919, he presented the treaty with the League within it to the Senate for ratification. Almost all of the 47 Democrats supported Wilson and the treaty, but the 49 Republicans were divided. About a dozen were "irreconcilables" who thought that the United States should not be a member of the League under any circumstances. The remainder included 25 "strong" and 12 "mild" reservationists who would accept the treaty with some changes. The main objection centered on Article X of the League Covenant, where the reservationists wanted it understood that the United States would not go to war to defend a League member without the approval of Congress.

On September 3, 1919, Wilson set out on a national speaking tour to appeal to the people to support the treaty and the League and to influence their senators. He collapsed after a speech in Pueblo, Colorado, on September 25, and returned to Washington, where he suffered a severe stroke on October 2 which paralyzed his left side. He was seriously ill for several months, and never fully recovered. The treaty failed to get a two-thirds majority either with or without the reservations.

Many people, including British and French leaders, urged Wilson to compromise on reservations, including the issue of Article X. Many historians think that Wilson's ill health impaired his judgment, and that he would have worked out a compromise had he not had the stroke. The Senate took up the treaty again in February 1920, and on March 19 it was again defeated both with and without the reservations. The United States officially ended the war with Germany by a resolution of Congress signed on July 2, 1921, and a separate peace treaty was ratified on July 25. The United States did not join the League.

DOMESTIC PROBLEMS AND THE END OF THE WILSON ADMINISTRATION

In January 1919, the eighteenth Amendment to the Constitution prohibiting the manufacture, sale, transportation, or importation of intoxicating liquors was ratified by the states, and it became effective in January 1920. The nineteenth Amendment providing for women's suffrage, which had been defeated in the Senate in 1918, was approved by Congress in 1919. It was ratified by the states in time for the election of 1920.

Americans feared the spread of the Russian Communist revolution to the United States, and many interpreted the widespread strikes of 1919 spurred by inflation, as Communist-inspired and the beginning of the revolution. Bombs sent through the mail to prominent government and business leaders in April 1919 seemed to confirm their fears, although the origin of the bombs has never been determined. The anti-German hysteria of the war years was transformed into the anti-Communist and antiforeign hysteria of 1919 and 1920, and continued in various forms through the 1920s.

Attorney General A. Mitchell Palmer, who aspired to the 1920 presidential nomination, was one of the targets of the anonymous bombers in the spring of 1919. In August 1919, he named J. Edgar Hoover (1895–1972) to head a new Intelligence Division in the Justice Department to collect information about radicals. After arresting nearly 5,000 people in late 1919 and early 1920, Palmer announced that huge Communist riots were planned for major cities on May Day (May 1, 1920). Police and troops were alerted, but the day passed with no radical activity. Palmer was discredited and the Red Scare subsided.

White hostility based on competition for lower-paid jobs and black encroachment into neighborhoods led to race riots in 25 cities, with hundreds killed or wounded and millions of dollars in property damage. The Chicago riot in July was the worst. Fear of returning African-American veterans in the South led to an increase of lynchings from 34 in 1917 to 60 in 1918 and 70 in 1919. Some of the victims were veterans still in uniform.

THE ROARING TWENTIES AND ECONOMIC COLLAPSE (1920–1929)
THE ELECTION OF 1920

The Republican Convention: Senator Warren G. Harding (1865–1923) of Ohio was nominated as a dark-horse candidate, and Governor Calvin Coolidge (1872–1933) of Massachusetts was chosen as the vice presidential nominee. The platform opposed the League and promised low taxes, high tariffs, immigration restriction, and aid to farmers.

The Democratic Convention: Governor James Cox was nominated on the 44th ballot, and Franklin D. Roosevelt (1882–1945), an assistant secretary of the Navy and distant cousin of Theodore, was selected as his running mate. The platform endorsed the League, but left the door open for reservations.

THE TWENTIES: ECONOMIC ADVANCES AND SOCIAL TENSIONS

The principal driving force of the economy of the 1920s was the automobile. Automobile manufacturing stimulated supporting industries such as steel, rubber, and glass, as well as gasoline refining and highway construction. During the 1920s, the United States became a nation of paved roads. The Federal Highway Act of 1916 started the federal highway system and gave matching funds to the states for construction.

Unlike earlier boom periods, which had involved large expenditures for capital investments such as railroads and factories, the prosperity of the 1920s depended heavily on the sale of consumer products. Purchases of "big ticket" items such as automobiles, refrigerators, and furniture were made possible by installment or time payment credit. The idea was not new, but the availability of consumer credit expanded tremendously during the 1920s. Consumer interest and demand was spurred by the great increase in professional advertising, which used newspapers, magazines, radio, billboards, and other media.

There was a trend toward corporate consolidation during the 1920s. In most fields, an oligopoly of two to four firms dominated. This is exemplified by the automobile industry, where Ford, General Motors, and Chrysler produced 83 percent of the vehicles in 1929. Government regulatory agencies such as the Federal Trade Commission and the Interstate Commerce Commission were passive and generally controlled by persons from the business world.

There was also a trend toward bank consolidation. Because corporations were raising much of their money through the sale of stocks and bonds, the demand for business loans declined. Commercial banks then put more of their funds into real estate loans, loans to brokers against stocks and bonds, and the purchase of stocks and bonds themselves.

AMERICAN SOCIETY IN THE 1920s

By 1920, for the first time, a majority of Americans (51 percent) lived in an urban area with a population of 2,500 or more. A new phenomenon of the 1920s was the tremendous growth of suburbs and satellite cities, which grew more rapidly than the central cities. Streetcars, commuter railroads, and automobiles contributed to the process, as well as the easy availability of financing for home construction. The suburbs had once been the domain of the wealthy, but the technology of the 1920s opened them to working-class families.

Traditional American moral standards regarding premarital sex and marital fidelity were widely questioned for the first time during the 1920s. The automobile, by giving people mobility and privacy, was generally considered to have contributed to sexual license. Birth control, though illegal, was promoted by Margaret Sanger (1883–1966) and others and was widely accepted.

When it became apparent that women did not vote as a block, political leaders gave little additional attention to the special concerns of women. Divorce laws were liberalized in many states at the insistence of women. Domestic service was the largest job category. Most other women workers were in traditional female occupations such as secretarial and clerical work, retail sales, teaching, and nursing. Rates of pay were below those for men. Most women still pursued the traditional role of housewife and mother, and society accepted that as the norm.

The migration of southern rural African-Americans to the cities continued, with about 1.5 million moving during the 1920s. By 1930, about 20 percent of American blacks lived in the North, with the largest concentrations in New York, Chicago, and Philadelphia. While they were generally better off economically in the cities than they had been as tenant farmers, they generally held low-paying jobs and were confined to segregated areas of the cities.

A native of Jamaica, Marcus Garvey (1887–1940) founded the Universal Negro Improvement Association, advocating African-American racial pride and separatism rather than integration, and called for a return of African-Americans to Africa. In 1921, he proclaimed himself the provisional president of an African empire, and sold stock in the Black Star Steamship Line which would take migrants to Africa. The line went bankrupt in 1923, and Garvey was convicted and imprisoned for mail fraud in the sale of the line's stock and then deported. His legacy was an emphasis on African-American pride and self-respect.

Many writers of the 1920s were disgusted with the hypocrisy and materialism of contemporary American society. Often called the "Lost Generation," many of them, such as novelists Ernest Hemingway (1899–1961) and F. Scott Fitzgerald (1896–1940) and poets Ezra Pound (1885–1972) and T. S. Eliot (1888–1965), moved to Europe.

SOCIAL CONFLICTS

Many white Protestant families saw their traditional values gravely threatened. The traditionalists were largely residents of rural areas and small towns, and the clash of farm values with the values of an industrial society of urban workers was evident. The traditionalist backlash against modern urban industrial society expressed itself primarily through intolerance.

On Thanksgiving Day in 1915, the Knights of the Ku Klux Klan, modeled on the organization of the same name in the 1860s and 1870s, was founded near Atlanta by William J. Simmons. Its purpose was to intimidate African-Americans, who were experiencing an apparent rise in status during World War I. By 1923, the Klan had about five million members throughout the nation. The largest concentrations of members were in the South, the Southwest, the Midwest, California, and Oregon.

There had been calls for immigration restriction since the late nineteenth century. Labor leaders believed that immigrants depressed wages and impeded unionization. Some progressives believed that they created social problems. In June 1917, Congress, over Wilson's veto, had imposed a literacy test for immigrants and excluded many Asian nationalists. In 1921, Congress passed the Emergency Quota Act. In practice, the law admitted about as many as wanted to come from such nations as Britain, Ireland, and Germany, while severely restricting Italians, Greeks, Poles, and east European Jews. It became effective in 1922 and reduced the number of immigrants annually to about 40 percent of the 1921 total. Congress then passed the National Origins Act of 1924, which further reduced the number of south and east Europeans, and cut the annual immigration to 20 percent of the 1921 figure. In 1927, the annual maximum was reduced to 150,000.

The Eighteenth Amendment, which prohibited the manufacture, sale, or transportation of intoxicating liquors, took effect in January 1920.

Fundamentalist Protestants, under the leadership of William Jennings Bryan, began a campaign in 1921 to prohibit the teaching of evolution in the schools, and thus protect belief in the literal biblical account of creation. The idea was especially well received in the South.

Sacco and Vanzetti: On April 15, 1920, two unidentified gunmen robbed a shoe factory and killed two men in South Braintree, Massachusetts. Nicola Sacco and Bartolomeo Vanzetti, Italian immigrants and admitted anarchists, were tried for the murders. After they were convicted and sentenced to death in July 1921, there was much protest in the United States and in Europe that they had not received a fair trial. After six years of delays, they were executed on August 23, 1927. Fifty years later, on July 19, 1977, the pair were vindicated by Governor Michael Dukakis.

GOVERNMENT AND POLITICS IN THE 1920s: THE HARDING ADMINISTRATION

Harding was a handsome and amiable man of limited intellectual and organizational abilities. He had spent much of his life as the publisher of a newspaper in the small city of Marion, Ohio. He recognized his limitations, but hoped to be a much-loved president.

Harding appointed some outstanding persons to his cabinet, including Secretary of State Charles Evans Hughes, a former Supreme Court justice and presidential candidate; Secretary of the Treasury Andrew Mellon (1855–1937), a Pittsburgh aluminum and banking magnate and reportedly the richest man in America; and Secretary of Commerce Herbert Hoover, a dynamic multimillionaire mine owner famous for his wartime relief efforts. Less impressive was his appointment of his cronies Albert B. Fall as secretary of the interior and Harry M. Daugherty as attorney general.

The Teapot Dome Scandal began when Secretary of the Interior Albert B. Fall in 1921 secured the transfer of several naval oil reserves to his jurisdiction. In 1922, he secretly leased reserves at Teapot Dome in Wyoming to Harry F. Sinclair of Monmouth Oil and at Elk Hills in California to Edward Doheny of Pan-American Petroleum. Sinclair and Doheny were acquitted in 1927 of charges of defrauding the government, but in 1929, Fall was convicted, fined, and imprisoned for bribery.

Vice President Calvin Coolidge became president upon Harding's death in 1923.

THE ELECTION OF 1924

The Republicans: Calvin Coolidge was nominated. The platform endorsed business development, low taxes, and rigid economy in government. The party stood on its record of economic growth and prosperity since 1922.

The Progressives: Robert M. LaFollette, after failing in a bid for the Republican nomination, formed a new Progressive party, with support from Midwest farm groups, socialists, and the American Federation of Labor. The platform attacked monopolies, and called for the nationalization of railroads, the direct election of the president, and other reforms.

The Democrats: John W. Davis was nominated and presented little contrast with the Republicans.

THE ELECTION OF 1928

The Republicans: Coolidge did not seek another term, and the convention quickly nominated Herbert Hoover, the secretary of commerce, for president. The platform endorsed the policies of the Harding and Coolidge administrations.

The Democrats: Governor Alfred E. Smith (1873–1944) of New York, a Catholic and an anti-prohibitionist, controlled most of the nonsouthern delegations. Southerners supported his nomination with the understanding that the platform would not advocate repeal of prohibition. The platform differed little from the Republican, except in advocating lower tariffs.

THE GREAT DEPRESSION: THE CRASH

Herbert Hoover, an Iowa farm boy and an orphan, graduated from Stanford University with a degree in mining engineering. He became a multimillionaire from mining and other investments around the world. After serving as the director of the Food Administration under Wilson, he became secretary of commerce under Harding and Coolidge. He believed that cooperation between business and government would enable the United States to abolish poverty through continued economic growth.

Stock prices increased throughout the decade. The boom in prices and volume of sales was especially active after 1925, and was intensive during 1928–29.

Careful investors, realizing that stocks were overpriced, began to sell to take their profits. During October 1929, prices declined as more stock was sold. On "Black Thursday," October 24, 1929, almost 13 million shares were traded, a large number for that time, and prices fell precipitously. Investment banks tried to boost the market by buying, but on October 29, "Black Tuesday," the market fell about 40 points, with 16.5 million shares traded.

THE GREAT DEPRESSION AND THE NEW DEAL (1929–1941)

REASONS FOR THE DEPRESSION

A stock-market crash does not mean that a depression must follow. In 1929, a complex interaction of many factors caused the decline of the economy.

Many people had bought stock on a margin of 10 percent, meaning that they had borrowed 90 percent of the purchase through a broker's loan and put up the stock as collateral. When the price of a stock fell more than 10 percent, the lender sold the stock for whatever it would bring and thus further depressed prices. The forced sales brought great losses to the banks and businesses that had financed the broker's loans, as well as to the investors.

There were already signs of recession before the market crash in 1929. The farm economy, which involved almost 25 percent of the population, had been depressed throughout the decade. Coal, railroads, and New England textiles had not been prosperous. After 1927, new construction declined and auto sales began to sag. Many workers had been laid off before the crash of 1929.

During the early months of the depression, most people thought it was just an adjustment in the business cycle which would soon be over. As time went on, the worst depression in American history set in, reaching its bottom point in early 1932.

HOOVER'S DEPRESSION POLICIES

The Agricultural Marketing Act: Passed in June 1929, before the market crash, this law, proposed by the president, created the Federal Farm Board. It had a revolving fund of $500 million to lend agricultural cooperatives to buy commodities, such as wheat and cotton, and hold them for higher prices.

The Hawley-Smoot Tariff: This law, passed in June 1930, raised duties on both agricultural and manufactured imports.

The Reconstruction Finance Corporation: Chartered by Congress in 1932, the RFC loaned money to railroads, banks, and other financial institutions. It prevented the failure of basic firms, on which many other elements of the economy depended, but was criticized by some as relief for the rich.

The Federal Home Loan Bank Act: This law, passed in July 1932, created home-loan banks, to make loans to building and loan associations, savings banks, and insurance companies to help them avoid foreclosures on homes.

ELECTION OF 1932

The Republicans renominated Hoover while the Democrats nominated Franklin D. Roosevelt, governor of New York. Although calling for a cut in spending, Roosevelt communicated optimism and easily defeated Hoover.

THE FIRST NEW DEAL

In February 1933, before Roosevelt took office, Congress passed the Twenty-First Amendment to repeal prohibition, and sent it to the states. In March, the new Congress legalized light beer. The amendment was ratified by the states and took effect in December 1933.

When Roosevelt was inaugurated on March 4, 1933, the American economic system seemed to be on the verge of collapse. Roosevelt assured the nation that "the only thing we have to fear is fear itself," called for a special session of Congress to convene on March 9, and asked for "broad executive powers to wage war against the emergency." Two days later, he closed all banks and forbade the export of gold or the redemption of currency in gold.

LEGISLATION OF THE FIRST NEW DEAL

The special session of Congress, from March 9 to June 16, 1933, passed a great body of legislation which has left a lasting mark on the nation. The period has been referred to ever since as the "Hundred Days." Historians have divided Roosevelt's legislation into the First New Deal (1933–1935) and a new wave of programs beginning in 1935 called the Second New Deal.

The Emergency Banking Relief Act was passed on March 9, the first day of the special session. The law provided additional funds for banks from the RFC and the Federal Reserve, allowed the Treasury to open sound banks after 10 days and to merge or liquidate unsound ones, and forbade the hoarding or export of gold. Roosevelt, on March 12, assured the public of the soundness of the banks in the first of many "fireside chats," or radio addresses. People believed him, and most banks were soon open with more deposits than withdrawals.

The Banking Act of 1933, or the Glass-Steagall Act, established the Federal Deposit Insurance Corporation (FDIC) to insure individual deposits in commercial banks, and separated commercial banking from the more speculative activity of investment banking.

The Truth-in-Securities Act required that full information about stocks and bonds be provided by brokers and others to potential purchasers.

The Home Owners Loan Corporation (HOLC) had authority to borrow money to refinance home mortgages and thus prevent foreclosures. Eventually, it lent more than three billion dollars to more than one million home owners.

Gold was taken out of circulation following the president's order of March 6, and the nation went off the gold standard. Eventually, on January 31, 1934, the value of the dollar was set at $35 per ounce of gold, 59 percent of its former value. The object of the devaluation was to raise prices and help American exports.

The Securities and Exchange Commission was created in 1934 to supervise stock exchanges and to punish fraud in securities trading.

The Federal Housing Administration (FHA) was created by Congress in 1934 to insure long-term, low-interest mortgages for home construction and repair.

These programs, intended to provide temporary relief for people in need, were to be disbanded when the economy improved.

The Federal Emergency Relief Act appropriated $500 million for aid to the poor to be distributed by state and local governments. It also established the Federal Emergency Relief Administration under Harry Hopkins (1890–1946).

The Civilian Conservation Corps enrolled 250,000 young men aged 18 to 24 from families on relief to go to camps where they worked on flood control, soil conservation, and forest projects under the direction of the War Department.

The Public Works Administration, under Secretary of the Interior Harold Ickes, had $3.3 billion to distribute to state and local governments for building projects such as schools, highways, and hospitals.

In November 1933, Roosevelt established the Civil Works Administration to hire four million unemployed workers. The temporary and makeshift nature of the jobs, such as sweeping streets, brought much criticism, and the experiment was terminated in April 1934.

The Agricultural Adjustment Act of 1933 created the Agricultural Adjustment Administration (AAA). Farmers agreed to reduce production of principal farm commodities and were paid a subsidy in return. The money came from a tax on the processing of the commodities. Farm prices increased, but tenants and sharecroppers were hurt when owners took land out of cultivation. The law was repealed in January 1936 on the grounds that the processing tax was not constitutional.

The Federal Farm Loan Act consolidated all farm credit programs into the Farm Credit Administration to make low-interest loans for farm mortgages and other agricultural purposes.

The Commodity Credit Corporation was established in October 1933 by the AAA to make loans to corn and cotton farmers against their crops so that they could hold them for higher prices.

The Frazier-Lemke Farm Bankruptcy Act of 1934 allowed farmers to defer foreclosure on their land while they obtained new financing, and helped them to recover property already lost through easy financing.

National Industrial Recovery Act: This law was viewed as the cornerstone of the recovery program. It sought to stabilize the economy by preventing extreme competition, labor-management conflicts, and overproduction. A board composed of industrial and labor leaders in each industry or business drew up a code for that industry which set minimum prices, minimum wages, maximum work hours, production limits, and quotas. The antitrust laws were temporarily suspended.

The TVA, a public corporation under a three-member board, was proposed by Roosevelt as the first major experiment in regional public planning. Starting from the nucleus of the government's Muscle Shoals property on the Tennessee River, the TVA built 20 dams in an area of 40,000 square miles to stop flooding and soil erosion, improve navigation, and generate hydroelectric power. It also manufactured nitrates for fertilizer, conducted demonstration projects for farmers, engaged in reforestation, and attempted to rehabilitate the whole area.

The economy improved but did not recover. The GNP, money supply, salaries, wages, and farm income rose. Unemployment dropped from about 25 percent of nonfarm workers in 1933 to about 20.1 percent, or 10.6 million, in 1935.

THE SECOND NEW DEAL: OPPOSITION

The Share Our Wealth Society was founded in 1934 by Senator Huey "The Kingfish" Long (1893–1935) of Louisiana. Long was a populist demagogue who was elected governor of Louisiana in 1928, established a practical dictatorship over the state, and moved to the United States Senate in 1930. He supported Roosevelt in 1932, but then broke with him, calling him a tool of Wall Street for not doing more to combat the depression. Long called for the confiscation of all fortunes over five million dollars and a tax of one hundred percent on annual incomes over one million. His society had more than five million members when he was assassinated on the steps of the Louisiana Capitol on September 8, 1935.

THE SECOND NEW DEAL BEGINS

The Works Progress Administration (WPA) was started in May 1935, following the passage of the Emergency Relief Appropriations Act of April 1935. The WPA employed people from the relief rolls for 30 hours of work a week at pay double the relief payment but less than private employment.

The National Youth Administration (NYA) was established as part of the WPA in June 1935, to provide part-time jobs for high school and college students to enable them to stay in school, and to help young adults not in school to find jobs.

The Rural Electrification Administration (REA) was created in May 1935, to provide loans and WPA labor to electric cooperatives so they could build lines into rural areas not served by private companies.

The Social Security Act was passed in August 1935. It established a retirement plan for persons over age 65, which was to be funded by a tax on wages paid equally by employee and employer. The first benefits, ranging from $10 to $85 per month, were paid in 1942. Another provision of the act had the effect of forcing the states to initiate unemployment insurance programs.

The Banking Act of 1935 created a strong central Board of Governors of the Federal Reserve system with broad powers over the operations of the regional banks.

THE ELECTION OF 1936

Roosevelt had put together a coalition of followers who made the Democratic party the majority party in the nation for the first time since the Civil War. While retaining the Democratic base in the South and among white ethnics in the big cities, Roosevelt also received strong support from midwestern farmers. Two groups that made a dramatic shift into the Democratic ranks were union workers and African-Americans.

THE LAST YEARS OF THE NEW DEAL

Frustrated by a conservative Supreme Court which had overturned much of his New Deal legislation, Roosevelt, in February 1937, proposed to Congress the Judicial Reorganization Bill, which would allow the president to name a new federal judge for each judge who did not retire by the age of $70^1/_2$. The appointments would be limited to a maximum of 50, with no more than six added to the Supreme Court. The president was astonished by the wave of opposition from Democrats and Republicans alike, but he uncharacteristically refused to compromise. In doing so, he not only lost the bill but control of the Democratic Congress, which he had dominated since 1933. Nonetheless, the Court changed its position, as Chief Justice Charles Evans Hughes and Justice Owen Roberts began to vote with the more liberal members.

Most economic indicators rose sharply between 1935 and 1937. Roosevelt decided that the recovery was sufficient to warrant a reduction in relief programs and a move toward a balanced budget. The budget for fiscal year 1938 was reduced from $8.5 billion to $6.8 billion, with the WPA experiencing the largest cut. During the winter of 1937–1938, the economy slipped rapidly and unemployment rose to 12.5 percent. In April 1938, Roosevelt requested and received from Congress an emergency appropriation of about $3 billion for the WPA, as well as increases for public works and other programs. In July 1938, the economy began to recover, and it regained the 1937 levels in 1939.

SOCIAL DIMENSIONS OF THE NEW DEAL ERA

Unemployment for African-Americans was much higher than for the general population, and before 1933 they were often excluded from state and local relief efforts. Roosevelt seems to have given little thought to the special problems of African-Americans, and he was afraid to endorse legislation such as an antilynching bill for fear of alienating the southern wing of the Democratic party. More African-Americans were appointed to government positions by Roosevelt than ever before, but the number was still small. Roosevelt issued an executive order on June 25, 1941, establishing the Fair

Employment Practices Committee to ensure consideration for minorities in defense employment.

John Collier, the commissioner of the Bureau of Indian Affairs, persuaded Congress to repeal the Dawes Act of 1887 by passing the Indian Reorganization Act of 1934. The law restored tribal ownership of lands, recognized tribal constitutions and government, and provided loans to tribes for economic development.

LABOR UNIONS

Labor unions lost members and influence during the 1920s and early 1930s. The National Industrial Recovery Act gave them new hope when it guaranteed the right to unionize, and during 1933 about 1.5 million new members joined unions.

The passage of the National Labor Relations or Wagner Act in 1935 resulted in a massive growth of union membership, but at the expense of bitter conflict within the labor movement. The American Federation of Labor was made up primarily of craft unions. Some leaders wanted to unionize the mass-production industries, such as automobiles and rubber, with industrial unions. In November 1935, John L. Lewis and others established the Committee for Industrial Organization to unionize basic industries, presumably within the AFL. President William Green of the AFL ordered the CIO to disband in January 1936. When the rebels refused, they were expelled by the AFL in March 1937. The insurgents then reorganized the CIO as the independent Congress of Industrial Organizations.

During its organizational period, the CIO sought to initiate several industrial unions, particularly in the steel, auto, rubber, and radio industries. In late 1936 and early 1937, it used a tactic called the sit-down strike, with the strikers occupying the workplace to prevent any production. By the end of 1941, the CIO was larger than the AFL. Union members comprised about 11.5 percent of the work force in 1933 and 28.2 percent in 1941.

NEW DEAL DIPLOMACY AND THE ROAD TO WAR

Roosevelt and Secretary of State Cordell Hull continued the policies of their predecessors by endeavoring to improve relations with Latin American nations, and formalized their position by calling it the Good Neighbor Policy.

At the Montevideo Conference of American Nations in December of 1933, the United States renounced the right of intervention in the internal affairs of Latin American countries. In 1936, in the Buenos Aires Convention, the United States agreed to submit all American disputes to arbitration.

UNITED STATES NEUTRALITY LEGISLATION

Belief that the United States should stay out of foreign wars and problems began in the 1920s and grew in the 1930s. Examinations of World War I profiteering and revisionist history that asserted Germany had not been responsible for World War I and that the United States had been misled were also influential during the 1930s. A Gallup poll in April 1937 showed that almost two-thirds of those responding thought that American entry into World War I had been a mistake.

The Johnson Act of 1934: This law prohibited any nation in default on World War I payments from selling securities to any American citizen or corporation.

The Neutrality Acts of 1935: On outbreak of war between foreign nations, all exports of American arms and munitions to them would be embargoed for six months. In addition, American ships were prohibited from carrying arms to any belligerent, and the president was to warn American citizens not to travel on belligerent ships.

The Neutrality Acts of 1936: The laws gave the president authority to determine when a state of war existed, and prohibited any loans or credits to belligerents.

The Neutrality Acts of 1937: The laws gave the president authority to determine if a civil war was a threat to world peace and if it was covered by the Neutrality Acts. It also prohibited all arms sales to belligerents, and allowed the cash-and-carry sale of nonmilitary goods to belligerents.

THE AMERICAN RESPONSE TO THE WAR IN EUROPE

In August 1939, Roosevelt created the War Resources Board to develop a plan for industrial mobilization in the event of war. The next month, he established the Office of Emergency Management in the White House to centralize mobilization activities.

The Neutrality Act of 1939: Roosevelt officially proclaimed the neutrality of the United States on September 5, 1939. The Democratic Congress, in a vote that followed party lines, passed a new Neutrality Act in November. It allowed the cash-and-carry sale of arms and short-term loans to belligerents, but forbade American ships to trade with belligerents or Americans to travel on belligerent ships.

Almost all Americans recognized Germany as a threat. They divided on whether to aid Britain or to concentrate on the defense of America. The Committee to Defend America by Aiding the Allies was formed in May 1940, and the America First Committee, which opposed involvement, was incorporated in September 1940.

In April 1940, Roosevelt declared that Greenland, a possession of conquered Denmark, was covered by the Monroe Doctrine, and he supplied military assistance to set up a coastal patrol there.

In May 1940, Roosevelt appointed a Council of National Defense, chaired by William S. Knudson (1879–1948), the president of General Motors, to direct defense production and to build 50,000 planes. The Office of Production Management was created to allocate scarce materials, and the Office of Price Administration was established to prevent inflation and protect consumers.

Congress approved the nation's first peacetime draft, the Selective Service and Training Act, in September 1940.

Roosevelt determined that to aid Britain in every way possible was the best way to avoid war with Germany. In September 1940, he signed an agreement to give Britain 50 American destroyers in return for a 99–year lease on air and naval bases in British territories in Newfoundland, Bermuda, and the Caribbean.

THE ELECTION OF 1940

The Republicans: The Republicans nominated Wendell L. Willkie (1892–1944) of Indiana, a dark-horse candidate. The platform supported a strong defense program, but severely criticized New Deal domestic policies.

The Democrats: Roosevelt was nominated for a third term, breaking a tradition which had existed since George Washington. The platform endorsed the foreign and domestic policies of the administration.

The Election: Roosevelt won by a much narrower margin than in 1936.

AMERICAN INVOLVEMENT WITH THE EUROPEAN WAR

The Lend-Lease Act: This let the United States provide supplies to Britain in exchange for goods and services after the war. It was signed on March 11, 1941.

In April 1941, Roosevelt started the American Neutrality Patrol. The American navy would search out but not attack German submarines in the western half of the Atlantic and warn British vessels of their location. Also in April, U.S. forces occupied Greenland, and in May, the president declared a state of unlimited national emergency.

American marines occupied Iceland, a Danish possession, in July 1941 to protect it from seizure by Germany. The American navy began to convoy American and Icelandic ships between the United States and Iceland.

On August 9, 1941 Roosevelt and Winston Churchill issued the Atlantic Charter.

Germany invaded Russia in June 1941, and in November the United States extended lend-lease assistance to the Russians.

The American destroyer *Greer* was attacked by a German submarine near Iceland on September 4, 1941. Roosevelt ordered the American military forces to shoot on sight any German or Italian vessel in the patrol zone. An undeclared naval war had begun. The American destroyer *Kearny* was attacked by a submarine on October 16, and the destroyer *Reuben James* was sunk on October 30, with 115 lives lost. In November, Congress authorized the arming of merchant ships.

THE ROAD TO PEARL HARBOR

In late July 1941, the United States placed an embargo on the export of aviation gasoline, lubricants, and scrap iron and steel to Japan, and granted an additional loan to China. In December, the embargo was extended to include iron ore and pig iron, some chemicals, machine tools, and other products.

In October 1941, a new military cabinet headed by General Hideki Tojo took control of Japan. The Japanese secretly decided to make a final effort to negotiate, and to go to war if no solution was found by November 25. A new round of talks followed in Washington, but neither side would make a substantive change in its position, and on November 26, Hull repeated the American demand that the Japanese remove all their forces from China and Indochina immediately. The Japanese gave final approval on December 1 for an attack on the United States.

The Japanese planned a major offensive to take the Dutch East Indies, Malaya, and the Philippines in order to obtain the oil, metals, and other raw materials they needed. At the same time, they would attack Pearl Harbor in Hawaii to destroy the American Pacific fleet to keep it from interfering with their plans.

The United States had broken the Japanese diplomatic codes and knew that trouble was imminent. Between December 1 and December 6, 1941, it became clear to administration leaders that Japanese task forces were being ordered into battle. American commanders in the Pacific were warned of possible aggressive action there, but not forcefully.

At 7:55 a.m. on Sunday, December 7, 1941, the first wave of Japanese carrier-based planes attacked the American fleet in Pearl Harbor. A second wave followed at 8:50 a.m. The United States suffered the loss of two battleships sunk, six damaged and out of action, three cruisers and three destroyers sunk or damaged, and a number of lesser vessels destroyed or damaged. All of the 150 aircraft at Pearl Harbor were destroyed on the ground. Worst of all, 2,323 American servicemen were killed and about 1,100 wounded. The Japanese lost 29 planes, five midget submarines, and one fleet submarine.

WORLD WAR II AND THE POSTWAR ERA (1941–1960)
DECLARED WAR BEGINS

On December 8, 1941, Congress declared war on Japan, with one dissenting vote. On December 11, Germany and Italy declared war on the United States. Great Britain and the United States then established the Combined Chiefs of Staff, headquartered in Washington, to direct Anglo-American military operations.

On January 1, 1942, representatives of 26 nations met in Washington, D.C., and signed the Declaration of the United Nations, pledging themselves to the principles of the Atlantic Charter and promising not to make a separate peace with their common enemies.

THE HOME FRONT

War Production Board: The WPD was established in 1942 by President Franklin D. Roosevelt for the purpose of regulating the use of raw materials.

Wage and Price Controls: In April 1942, the General Maximum Price Regulation Act froze prices and extended rationing. In April 1943, prices, wages, and salaries were frozen.

Revenue Act of 1942: The Revenue Act of 1942 extended the income tax to the majority of the population. Payroll deduction for the income tax began in 1944.

Social Changes: Rural areas lost population, while population in coastal areas increased rapidly. Women entered the work force in increasing numbers. African-Americans moved from the rural South to northern and western cities, with racial tensions often resulting, most notably in the June 1943 racial riot in Detroit.

Smith-Connolly Act: Passed in 1943, the Smith-Connolly Antistrike Act authorized government seizure of a plant or mine idled by a strike if the war effort was impeded. It expired in 1947.

Korematsu v. United States: In 1944, the Supreme Court upheld President Roosevelt's 1942 order that Issei (Japanese-Americans who had emigrated from Japan) and Nisei (native born Japanese-Americans) be relocated to concentration camps. The camps were closed in March 1946.

Presidential Election of 1944: President Franklin D. Roosevelt, together with new vice-presidential candidate Harry S. Truman (1884–1972) of Missouri, defeated his Republican opponent, Governor Thomas E. Dewey of New York.

Roosevelt died on April 12, 1945, at Warm Springs, Georgia. Harry S. Truman became president.

THE NORTH AFRICAN AND EUROPEAN THEATERS

The United States joined in the bombing of the European continent in July 1942. Bombing increased during 1943 and 1944 and lasted to the end of the war.

The Allied army under Dwight D. Eisenhower attacked French North Africa in November 1942. The Vichy French forces surrendered.

In the Battle of Kassarine Pass, North Africa, February 1943, the Allied army met General Erwin Rommel's Africa Korps. Although the battle is variously interpreted as a standoff or a defeat for the United States, Rommel's forces were soon trapped by the British moving in from Egypt. In May 1943, Rommel's Africa Korps surrendered.

Allied armies under George S. Patton (1885–1945) invaded Sicily from Africa in July 1943, and gained control by mid-August. Moving from Sicily, the Allied armies invaded the Italian mainland in September. The Germans, however, put up a stiff resistance, with the result that Rome did not fall until June 1944.

In March 1944, the Soviet Union began pushing into Eastern Europe.

On "D-Day," June 6, 1944, Allied armies under Dwight D. Eisenhower, now commander in chief of the Allied Expeditionary Forces, began an invasion of Normandy, France.

Allied armies liberated Paris in August. By mid-September, they had arrived at the Rhine, on the edge of Germany.

Beginning December 16, 1944, at the Battle of the Bulge, the Germans counterattacked, driving the Allies back about 50 miles into Belgium. By January, the Allies were once more advancing toward Germany. The Allies crossed the Rhine in March 1945. In the last week of April, Eisenhower's forces met the Soviet army at the Elbe. On May 7, 1945, Germany surrendered.

THE PACIFIC THEATER

By the end of December 1941, Guam, Wake Island, the Gilbert Islands, and Hong Kong had fallen to the Japanese. In January 1942, Raboul, New

Britain, fell, followed in February by Singapore and Java, and in March by Rangoon, Burma. U.S. forces surrendered at Corregidor, Philippines, on May 6, 1942.

The Battle of the Coral Sea, May 7–8, 1942, stopped the Japanese advance on Australia.

The Battle of Midway, June 4–7, 1942, proved to be the turning point in the Pacific.

A series of land, sea, and air battles took place around Guadalcanal in the Solomon Islands from August 1942 to February 1943, stopping the Japanese.

The Allied strategy of island hopping, begun in 1943, sought to neutralize Japanese strongholds with air and sea power and then move on.

U.S. forces advanced into the Gilberts (November 1943), the Marshalls (January 1944), and the Marianas (June 1944). After the American capture of the Marianas, General Tojo resigned as premier of Japan.

The Battle of Leyte Gulf, October 25, 1944, resulted in Japan's loss of most of its remaining naval power. Forces under General Douglas MacArthur (1880–1964) liberated Manila in March 1945.

Between April and June 1945, in the battle for Okinawa, nearly 50,000 American casualties resulted from the fierce fighting, but the battle virtually destroyed Japan's remaining defenses.

THE ATOMIC BOMB

The Manhattan Engineering District was established by the army engineers in August 1942 for the purpose of developing an atomic bomb (it eventually became known as the Manhattan Project). J. Robert Oppenheimer directed the design and construction of a transportable atomic bomb at Los Alamos, New Mexico.

On December 2, 1942, Enrico Fermi (1901–1954) and his colleagues at the University of Chicago produced the first atomic chain reaction.

On July 16, 1945, the first atomic bomb was exploded at Alamogordo, New Mexico.

The *Enola Gay* dropped an atomic bomb on Hiroshima, Japan, on August 6, 1945, killing about 78,000 persons and injuring 100,000 more. On August 9, a second bomb was dropped on Nagasaki, Japan.

On August 8, 1945, the Soviet Union entered the war against Japan.

Japan surrendered on August 14, 1945. The formal surrender was signed on September 2.

DIPLOMACY

Casablanca Conference: On January 14–25, 1943, Franklin D. Roosevelt and Winston Churchill, prime minister of Great Britain, declared a policy of unconditional surrender for "all enemies."

Moscow Conference: In October 1943, Secretary of State Cordell Hull obtained Soviet agreement to enter the war against Japan after Germany was defeated, and to participate in a world organization after the war was over.

Declaration of Cairo: Issued on December 1, 1943, after Roosevelt met with General Chiang Kai-shek in Cairo from November 22 to 26, the Declaration of Cairo called for Japan's unconditional surrender and stated that all Chinese territories occupied by Japan would be returned to China and that Korea would be free and independent.

THE EMERGENCE OF THE COLD WAR AND CONTAINMENT

In 1947, career diplomat and Soviet expert George F. Kennan wrote an anonymous article for *Foreign Affairs* in which he called for a counterforce to Soviet pressures, for the purpose of "containing" communism.

Truman Doctrine: In February 1947, Great Britain notified the United States that it could no longer aid the Greek government in its war against Communist insurgents. The next month President Harry S. Truman asked Congress for $400 million in military and economic aid for Greece and Turkey. In what became known as the "Truman Doctrine," he argued that the United States must support free peoples who were resisting Communist domination.

Marshall Plan: Secretary of State George C. Marshall (1880–1959) proposed in June 1947 that the United States provide economic aid to help rebuild Europe. The following March, Congress passed the European Recovery Program, popularly known as the Marshall Plan, which provided more than $12 billion in aid.

After the United States, France, and Great Britain announced plans to create a West German Republic out of their German zones, the Soviet Union in June 1948 blocked surface access to Berlin. The United States then instituted an airlift to transport supplies to the city until the Soviets lifted their blockade in May 1949.

NATO

In April 1949, the North Atlantic Treaty Organization was signed by the United States, Canada, Great Britain, and nine European nations. The signatories pledged that an attack against one would be considered an attack against all. The Soviets formed the Warsaw Treaty Organization in 1955 to counteract NATO.

INTERNATIONAL COOPERATION

Representatives from Europe and the United States, at a conference held July 1–22, 1944, signed agreements for an international bank and a world monetary fund to stabilize international currencies and rebuild the economies of war-torn nations.

From April to June 1945, representatives from 50 countries met in San Francisco to establish the United Nations. The U.N. charter created a General Assembly composed of all member nations which would act as the ultimate policy-making body. A Security Council, made up of 11 members, including the United States, Great Britain, France, the Soviet Union, and China as permanent members and six additional nations elected by the General Assembly for two-year terms, would be responsible for settling disputes among U.N. member nations.

CONTAINMENT IN ASIA

General Douglas MacArthur headed a four-power Allied Control Council which governed Japan, allowing it to develop economically and politically.

Between 1945 and 1948, the United States gave more than $2 billion in aid to the Nationalist Chinese under Chiang Kai-shek, and sent George C. Marshall to settle the conflict between Chiang's Nationalists and Mao Tsetung's Communists. In 1949, however, Mao defeated Chiang and forced the Nationalists to flee to Formosa (Taiwan). Mao established the People's Republic of China on the mainland.

KOREAN WAR

On June 25, 1950, North Korea invaded South Korea. President Truman committed U.S. forces commanded by General MacArthur, but under United Nations auspices. By October, the U.N. forces (mostly American) had driven north of the 38th parallel, which divided North and South Korea. Chinese troops attacked MacArthur's forces on November 26, pushing them south of the 38th parallel, but by spring 1951, the U.N. forces had recovered their offensive.

In June 1953, an armistice was signed, leaving Korea divided along virtually the same boundary that had existed prior to the war.

EISENHOWER-DULLES FOREIGN POLICY

Dwight D. Eisenhower, elected president in 1952, chose John Foster Dulles (1888–1959) as secretary of state. Dulles talked of a more aggressive foreign policy, calling for "massive retaliation" and "liberation" rather than containment. He wished to emphasize nuclear deterrents rather than conventional armed forces.

After several years of nationalist war against French occupation, France, Great Britain, the Soviet Union, and China signed the Geneva Accords in July 1954, dividing Vietnam along the 17th parallel. The North would be under Ho Chi Minh and the South under Emperor Bao Dai. Elections were scheduled for 1956 to unify the country, but Ngo Dinh Diem overthrew Bao Dai and prevented the elections from taking place. The United States supplied economic aid to South Vietnam.

Dulles attempted to establish a Southeast Asia Treaty Organization parallel to NATO, but was able to obtain only the Philippine Republic, Thailand, and Pakistan as signatories in September 1954.

President Eisenhower announced in January 1957 that the United States was prepared to use armed force in the Middle East against Communist aggression. Under this doctrine, U.S. marines entered Beirut, Lebanon, in July 1958 to promote political stability during a change of governments. The marines left in October.

The United States supported the overthrow of President Jacobo Arbenz Guzman of Guatemala in 1954 because he began accepting arms from the Soviet Union.

In January 1959, Fidel Castro overthrew Fulgencio Batista, dictator of Cuba. Castro soon began criticizing the United States and moved closer to the Soviet Union, signing a trade agreement with the Soviets in February 1960. The United States prohibited the importation of Cuban sugar in October 1960, and broke off diplomatic relations in January 1961.

THE POLITICS OF AFFLUENCE: DEMOBILIZATION AND DOMESTIC POLICY

Harry S. Truman, formerly a senator from Missouri and vice president of the United States, became president on April 12, 1945.

Congress created the Atomic Energy Commission in 1946, establishing civilian control over nuclear development and giving the president sole authority over the use of atomic weapons in warfare.

Taft-Hartley Act (1947): The Republicans, who had gained control of Congress in 1946, sought to control the power of the unions through the

Taft-Hartley Act. This act made the "closed-shop" illegal; labor unions could no longer force employers to hire only union members. The act slowed down efforts to unionize the South, and by 1954, 15 states had passed "right to work" laws, forbidding the "union-shop."

In 1948, the president banned racial discrimination in federal government hiring practices and ordered desegregation of the armed forces.

The Presidential Succession Act of 1947 placed the Speaker of the House and the president pro tempore of the Senate ahead of the secretary of state and after the vice president in the line of succession. The Twenty-Second Amendment to the Constitution, ratified in 1951, limited the president to election to two terms.

ELECTION OF 1948

Truman was the Democratic nominee, but the Democrats were split by the States' Rights Democratic party (Dixiecrats) which nominated Governor Strom Thurmond of South Carolina, and the Progressive party, which nominated former Vice President Henry Wallace. The Republicans nominated Governor Thomas E. Dewey of New York. After traveling widely, and attacking the "do-nothing Congress," Truman won a surprise victory.

ANTICOMMUNISM

In 1950, Julius and Ethel Rosenberg and Harry Gold were charged with giving atomic secrets to the Soviet Union. The Rosenbergs were convicted and executed in 1953.

On February 9, 1950, Senator Joseph R. McCarthy (1908–1957) of Wisconsin stated that he had a list of known Communists who were working in the State Department. He later expanded his attacks. After making charges against the army, he was censured by the Senate in 1954.

EISENHOWER'S DYNAMIC CONSERVATISM

The Republicans nominated Dwight D. Eisenhower, most recently NATO commander, for the presidency. The Democrats nominated Governor Adlai E. Stevenson (1900–1965) of Illinois for president. Eisenhower won by a landslide; for the first time since Reconstruction, the Republicans won some southern states.

Eisenhower sought to balance the budget and lower taxes but did not attempt to roll back existing social and economic legislation. Eisenhower first described his policy as "dynamic conservatism," and then as "progressive moderation." The administration abolished the Reconstruction Finance

Corporation, ended wage and price controls, and reduced farm price supports. It cut the budget and in 1954 lowered tax rates for corporations and individuals with high incomes; an economic slump, however, made balancing the budget difficult.

Social Security was extended in 1954 and 1956 to an additional 10 million people, including professionals, domestic and clerical workers, farm workers, and members of the armed services.

The Rural Electrification Administration announced in 1960 that 97 percent of American farms had electricity.

In 1954, Eisenhower obtained congressional approval for joint Canadian-U.S. construction of the St. Lawrence Seaway, which was to give ocean-going vessels access to the Great Lakes. In 1956, Congress authorized construction of the Interstate Highway System, with the federal government supplying 90 percent of the cost and the states 10 percent.

The launching of the Soviet space satellite *Sputnik* on October 4, 1957, created fear that America was falling behind technologically. Although the United States launched *Explorer I* on January 31, 1958, the concern continued. In 1958, Congress established the National Aeronautics and Space Administration (NASA) to coordinate research and development, and passed the National Defense Education Act to provide grants and loans for education.

On January 3, 1959, Alaska became the 49th state, and on August 21, 1959, Hawaii became the 50th.

CIVIL RIGHTS

Eisenhower completed the formal integration of the armed forces, desegregated public services in Washington, D.C., naval yards, and veteran's hospitals, and appointed a Civil Rights Commission.

Brown v. Board of Education of Topeka: In this 1954 case, NAACP lawyer Thurgood Marshall challenged the doctrine of "separate but equal" (*Plessy v. Ferguson*, 1896). The Court declared that separate educational facilities were inherently unequal. In 1955, the Court ordered states to integrate "with all deliberate speed."

Although he did not personally support the Supreme Court decision, Eisenhower sent 10,000 National Guardsmen and 1,000 paratroopers to Little Rock, Arkansas, to control mobs and enable African-Americans to enroll at Central High in September 1957.

On December 11, 1955, in Montgomery, Alabama, Rosa Parks, a black woman, refused to give up her seat on a city bus to a white and was arrested. Under the leadership of Martin Luther King (1929–1968), an African-American pastor, African-Americans of Montgomery organized a bus boycott that lasted for a year, until in December 1956, the Supreme Court refused to review a lower court ruling that stated that separate but equal was no longer legal.

In 1959, state and federal courts nullified Virginia laws that prevented state funds from going to integrated schools. This proved to be the beginning of the end for "massive resistance."

On February 1, 1960, upon being denied service, four African-American students staged a sit-in at a Woolworth lunch counter in Greensboro, North Carolina. This inspired sit-ins by thousands elsewhere in the South and led to the formation of the Student Nonviolent Coordinating Committee.

THE ELECTION OF 1960

Vice President Richard M. Nixon won the Republican presidential nomination, and the Democrats nominated Senator John F. Kennedy (1917–1963) for the presidency, with Lyndon B. Johnson (1908–1973), majority leader of the Senate, as his running mate.

Kennedy won the election by slightly more than 100,000 popular votes and 94 electoral votes, based on majorities in New England, the Middle Atlantic, and the South.

THE NEW FRONTIER, VIETNAM, AND SOCIAL UPHEAVAL (1960–1972)

KENNEDY'S "NEW FRONTIER" AND THE LIBERAL REVIVAL

Kennedy was unable to get much of his program through Congress because of an alliance of Republicans and southern Democrats.

Kennedy did gain congressional approval for raising the minimum wage from $1.00 to $1.25 an hour and extending it to 3 million more workers.

The 1961 Housing Act provided nearly $5 billion over four years for the preservation of open urban spaces, development of mass transit, and the construction of middle-class housing.

CIVIL RIGHTS

In May 1961, blacks and whites boarded buses in Washington, D.C., and traveled across the South to New Orleans to test federal enforcement of regulations prohibiting discrimination. They met violence in Alabama but continued to New Orleans.

The Justice Department, under Attorney General Robert F. Kennedy (1925–1968), began to push for civil rights, including desegregation of interstate transportation in the South, integration of schools, and supervision of elections.

In the fall of 1962, President Kennedy called the Mississippi National Guard to federal duty to enable an African-American, James Meredith, to enroll at the University of Mississippi.

Kennedy presented a comprehensive civil rights bill to Congress in 1963. With the bill held up in Congress, 200,000 people marched, demonstrating on its behalf on August 28, 1963, in Washington, D.C. Martin Luther King gave his "I Have a Dream" speech.

THE COLD WAR CONTINUES

Under Eisenhower, the Central Intelligence Agency had begun training some 2,000 men for an invasion of Cuba to overthrow Fidel Castro, the left-leaning revolutionary who had taken power in 1959. On April 19, 1961, this force invaded at the Bay of Pigs, but was pinned down and forced to surrender. Some 1,200 men were captured.

In August 1961, Khrushchev closed the border between East and West Berlin and ordered the erection of the Berlin Wall.

The Soviet Union began the testing of nuclear weapons in September 1961. Kennedy then authorized resumption of underground testing by the United States.

On October 14, 1962, a U-2 reconnaissance plane brought photographic evidence that missile sites were being built in Cuba. Kennedy, on October 22, announced a blockade of Cuba and called on Khrushchev to dismantle the missile bases and remove all weapons capable of attacking the United States from Cuba. Six days later, Khrushchev backed down, withdrew the missiles, and Kennedy lifted the blockade.

In July 1963, a treaty banning the atmospheric testing of nuclear weapons was signed by all the major powers except France and China.

In 1961, Kennedy announced the Alliance for Progress, which would provide $20 million in aid to Latin America.

JOHNSON AND THE GREAT SOCIETY

On November 22, 1963, Kennedy was assassinated by Lee Harvey Oswald in Dallas, Texas. Jack Ruby, a nightclub owner, killed Oswald two days later.

Succeeding Kennedy, Lyndon B. Johnson had extensive experience in both the House and Senate, and as a Texan, was the first southerner to serve as president since Woodrow Wilson.

A tax cut of more than $10 billion passed Congress in 1964, and an economic boom resulted.

The 1964 Civil Rights Act outlawed racial discrimination by employers and unions, created the Equal Employment Opportunity Commission to enforce the law, and eliminated the remaining restrictions on black voting.

Michael Harrington's *The Other America* (1962) showed that 20 to 25 percent of American families were living below the governmentally defined poverty line. The Economic Opportunity Act of 1964 sought to address the problem by establishing a Job Corps, community action programs, educational programs, work-study programs, job training, loans for small businesses and farmers, and Volunteers in Service to America (VISTA), a "domestic peace corps." The Office of Economic Opportunity administered many of these programs.

ELECTION OF 1964

Lyndon Johnson was nominated for president by the Democrats. The Republicans nominated Senator Barry Goldwater, a conservative from Arizona. Johnson won more than 61 percent of the popular vote and could now launch his own "Great Society" program.

The Medicare Act of 1965 combined hospital insurance for retired people with a voluntary plan to cover physician's bills. Medicaid provided grants to states to help the poor below retirement age.

EMERGENCE OF BLACK POWER

In 1965, Martin Luther King announced a voter registration drive. With help from the federal courts, he dramatized his effort by leading a march from Selma to Montgomery, Alabama, between March 21 and 25. The Voting Rights Act of 1965 authorized the attorney general to appoint officials to register voters.

Seventy percent of African-Americans lived in city ghettos. In 1966, New York and Chicago experienced riots, and the following year there were riots in Newark and Detroit. The Kerner Commission, appointed to investigate the riots, concluded that they were directed at a social system that prevented African-Americans from getting good jobs and crowded them into ghettos.

Stokely Carmichael, in 1966, called for the civil rights movements to be "black-staffed, black-controlled, and black-financed." Later, he moved on to the Black Panthers, self-styled urban revolutionaries based in Oakland, California. Other leaders such as H. Rap Brown also called for Black Power.

On April 4, 1968, Martin Luther King was assassinated in Memphis by James Earl Ray. Riots in more than 100 cities followed.

THE NEW LEFT

Students at the University of California at Berkeley staged sit-ins in 1964 to protest the prohibition of political canvassing on campus. In December, police broke up a sit-in; protests spread to other campuses across the country.

Student protests began focusing on the Vietnam War. In the spring of 1967, 500,000 gathered in Central Park in New York City to protest the war, many burning their draft cards. Students for a Democratic Society (SDS) became more militant and willing to use violence.

More than 200 large campus demonstrations took place in the spring, culminating in the occupation of buildings at Columbia University to protest the university's involvement in military research and its poor relations with minority groups. Police wielding billy clubs eventually broke up the demonstration. In August, thousands gathered in Chicago to protest the war during the Democratic convention.

Beginning in 1968, SDS began breaking up into rival factions. By the early 1970s, the New Left had lost political influence, having abandoned its original commitment to democracy and nonviolence.

WOMEN'S LIBERATION

In *The Feminine Mystique* (1963), Betty Friedan argued that middle-class society stifled women and did not allow them to use their individual talents. She attacked the cult of domesticity.

Friedan and other feminists founded the National Organization for Women (NOW) in 1966, calling for equal employment opportunities and equal pay.

VIETNAM

After the French defeat in 1954, the United States sent military advisors to South Vietnam to aid the government of Ngo Dinh Diem. The pro-Communist Vietcong forces gradually grew in strength, partly because Diem failed to follow through on promised reforms. They received support from North Vietnam, the Soviet Union, and China.

In August 1964—after claiming that North Vietnamese gunboats had fired on American destroyers in the Gulf of Tonkin—Lyndon Johnson pushed the Gulf of Tonkin resolution through Congress, authorizing him to use military force in Vietnam. After a February 1965 attack by the Vietcong on

Pleiku, Johnson ordered operation "Rolling Thunder," the first sustained bombing of North Vietnam. Johnson then sent combat troops to South Vietnam; under the leadership of General William C. Westmoreland, they conducted search and destroy operations. The number of troops increased to 184,000 in 1965, 385,000 in 1966, 485,000 in 1967, and 538,000 in 1968.

"Hawks" defended the president's policy and, drawing on containment theory, said that the nation had the responsibility to resist aggression. If Vietnam should fall, it was said, all Southeast Asia would eventually go. The administration stressed its willingness to negotiate the withdrawal of all "foreign" forces from the war.

Opposition began quickly, with "teach-ins" at the University of Michigan in 1965 and a 1966 congressional investigation led by Senator J. William Fulbright. Antiwar demonstrations were gaining large crowds by 1967. "Doves" argued that the war was a civil war in which the United States should not meddle.

On January 31, 1968, the first day of the Vietnamese new year (Tet), the Vietcong attacked numerous cities and towns, American bases, and even Saigon. Although they suffered large losses, the Vietcong won a psychological victory, as American opinion began turning against the war.

THE ELECTION OF 1968

In November 1967, Senator Eugene McCarthy of Minnesota announced his candidacy for the 1968 Democratic presidential nomination, running on the issue of opposition to the war.

In February, McCarthy won 42 percent of the Democratic vote in the New Hampshire primary, compared with Johnson's 48 percent. Robert F. Kennedy then announced his candidacy for the Democratic presidential nomination.

Lyndon Johnson withdrew his candidacy on March 31, 1968, and Vice President Hubert H. Humphrey took his place as a candidate for the Democratic nomination.

After winning the California primary over McCarthy, Robert Kennedy was assassinated by Sirhan Sirhan, a young Palestinian. This event assured Humphrey's nomination.

The Republicans nominated Richard M. Nixon. Governor George C. Wallace of Alabama ran for the presidency under the banner of the American Independent party, appealing to fears generated by protestors and big government.

Johnson suspended air attacks on North Vietnam shortly before the election. Nonetheless Nixon, who emphasized stability and order, defeated Humphrey by a margin of 1 percent. Wallace's 13.5 percent was the best showing by a third-party candidate since 1924.

THE NIXON CONSERVATIVE REACTION

The Nixon administration sought to block renewal of the Voting Rights Act and delay implementation of court-ordered school desegregation in Mississippi.

In 1969, Nixon appointed Warren E. Burger, a conservative, as chief justice. Although more conservative than the Warren court, the Burger court did declare the death penalty, as used at the time, unconstitutional in 1972, and struck down state antiabortion legislation in 1973.

VIETNAMIZATION

The president turned to "Vietnamization," the effort to build up South Vietnamese forces while withdrawing American troops. In 1969, Nixon reduced American troop strength by 60,000, but at the same time ordered the bombing of Cambodia, a neutral country.

In April 1970, Nixon announced that Vietnamization was succeeding but a few days later, he sent troops into Cambodia to clear out Vietcong sanctuaries and resumed bombing of North Vietnam.

Protests against escalation of the war were especially strong on college campuses. After several students were killed during protests, several hundred colleges were closed down by student strikes, as moderates joined the radicals. Congress repealed the Gulf of Tonkin Resolution.

The publication in 1971 of classified Defense Department documents, called "The Pentagon Papers," revealed that the government had misled the Congress and the American people regarding its intentions in Vietnam during the mid-1960s.

Nixon drew American forces back from Cambodia but increased bombing. In March 1972, after stepped-up aggression from the North, Nixon ordered the mining of Haiphong and other northern ports.

In the summer of 1972, negotiations between the United States and North Vietnam began in Paris. A few days before the 1972 presidential election, Henry Kissinger, the president's national security advisor, announced that "peace was at hand."

Nixon resumed bombing of North Vietnam in December 1972, claiming that the North Vietnamese were not bargaining in good faith. In January

1973, the opponents reached a settlement in which the North Vietnamese retained control over large areas of the South and agreed to release American prisoners of war within 60 days. Nearly 60,000 Americans had been killed and 300,000 more wounded and the war had cost Americans $109 billion. On March 29, 1973, the last American combat troops left South Vietnam.

FOREIGN POLICY

With his national security advisor, Henry Kissinger, Nixon took some bold diplomatic initiatives. In February 1972, Nixon and Kissinger went to China to meet with Mao Tse-tung and his associates. The United States agreed to support China's admission to the United Nations and to pursue economic and cultural exchanges.

Nixon and Kissinger called their policy *détente*, a French term meaning a relaxation in the tensions between two governments.

THE ELECTION OF 1972

Richard M. Nixon, who had been renominated by the Republicans, won a landslide victory over the Democratic nominee, Senator George McGovern.

WATERGATE, CARTER, AND THE NEW CONSERVATISM (1972–1999)
WATERGATE

What became known as the Watergate crisis began during the 1972 presidential campaign. Early on the morning of June 17, James McCord, a security officer for the Committee to Re-elect the President (sometimes known as CREEP), and four other men broke into Democratic headquarters at the Watergate apartment complex in Washington, D.C., and were caught while going through files and installing electronic eavesdropping devices.

In March 1974, a grand jury indicted Haldeman, Ehrlichman, former Attorney General John Mitchell, and four other White House aides and named Nixon an unindicted coconspirator.

Meanwhile, the House Judiciary Committee televised its debate over impeachment, adopting three articles of impeachment. It charged the president with obstructing justice, misusing presidential power, and failing to obey the committee's subpoenas.

Before the House began to debate impeachment, Nixon announced his resignation on August 8, 1974, to take effect at noon the following day. Gerald Ford then became president.

THE FORD PRESIDENCY

Gerald Ford was in many respects the opposite of Nixon. Although a partisan Republican, he was well liked and free from any hint of scandal. Ford almost immediately encountered controversy when in September 1974 he offered to pardon Nixon. Nixon accepted the offer, although he admitted no wrongdoing and had not yet been charged with a crime.

VIETNAM

As North Vietnamese forces pushed back the South Vietnamese, Ford asked Congress to provide more arms for the South. Congress rejected the request, and in April 1975 Saigon fell to the North Vietnamese.

CARTER'S MODERATE LIBERALISM

Ronald Reagan, a former movie actor and governor of California, opposed Ford for the Republican presidential nomination, but Ford won by a slim margin. The Democrats nominated James Earl Carter, formerly governor of Georgia, who ran on the basis of his integrity and lack of Washington connections. Carter narrowly defeated Ford in the election.

Carter offered amnesty to Americans who had fled the draft and gone to other countries during the Vietnam War. He established the Departments of Energy and Education and placed the civil service on a merit basis. He created a "superfund" for cleanup of chemical waste dumps, established controls over strip mining, and protected 100 million acres of Alaskan wilderness from development.

CARTER'S FOREIGN POLICY

Carter negotiated a controversial treaty with Panama, affirmed by the Senate in 1978, that provided for the transfer of ownership of the canal to Panama in 1999 and guaranteed its neutrality.

Carter ended official recognition of Taiwan and in 1979 recognized the People's Republic of China. Conservatives called the decision a "sell-out."

In 1978, Carter negotiated the Camp David Agreement between Israel and Egypt. Israel promised to return occupied land in the Sinai to Egypt in exchange for Egyptian recognition, a process completed in 1982. An agreement to negotiate the Palestinian refugee problem proved ineffective.

THE IRANIAN CRISIS

In 1978, a revolution forced the shah of Iran to flee the country, replacing him with a religious leader, Ayatollah Ruhollah Khomeini. Because the

United States had supported the shah with arms and money, the revolutionaries were strongly anti-American, calling the United States the "Great Satan."

After Carter allowed the exiled shah to come to the United States for medical treatment in October 1979, some 400 Iranians broke into the American embassy in Teheran on November 4, taking the occupants captive. They demanded that the shah be returned to Iran for trial and that his wealth be confiscated and given to Iran. Carter rejected these demands; instead, he froze Iranian assets in the United States and established a trade embargo against Iran.

THE ELECTION OF 1980

Republican Ronald Reagan defeated Carter by a large electoral majority, and the Republicans gained control of the Senate and increased their representation in the House.

After extensive negotiations with Iran, in which Algeria acted as an intermediary, American hostages were freed on January 20, 1981, the day of Reagan's inauguration.

THE REAGAN PRESIDENCY: ATTACKING BIG GOVERNMENT

An ideological though pragmatic conservative, Ronald Reagan acted quickly and forcefully to change the direction of government policy. He placed priority on cutting taxes. His approach was based on "supply-side" economics, the idea that if government left more money in the hands of the people, they would invest rather then spend the excess on consumer goods. The results would be greater production, more jobs, and greater prosperity, and thus more income for the government despite lower tax rates.

Reagan asked for a 30 percent tax cut, and despite fears of inflation on the part of Congress, in August 1983 obtained a 25 percent cut, spread over three years.

Congress passed the Budget Reconciliation Act in 1981, cutting $39 billion from domestic programs, including education, food stamps, public housing, and the National Endowments for the Arts and Humanities. While cutting domestic programs, Reagan increased the defense budget by $12 billion.

From a deficit of $59 billion in 1980, the federal budget was running $195 billion in the red by 1983.

Because of rising deficits, Reagan and Congress increased taxes in various ways. The 1982 Tax Equity and Fiscal Responsibility Act reversed some concessions made to business in 1981. Social Security benefits became taxable income in 1983. In 1984, the Deficit Reduction Act increased taxes by another $50 billion. But the deficit continued to increase.

Reagan ended ongoing antitrust suits against International Business Machines and American Telephone and Telegraph, thereby fulfilling his promise to reduce government interference with business.

ASSERTING AMERICAN POWER

Reagan took a hard line against the Soviet Union, calling it an "evil empire." He placed new cruise missiles in Europe, despite considerable opposition from Europeans.

Reagan also concentrated on obtaining funding for the development of a computer-controlled strategic defense initiative system (SDI), popularly called "Star Wars" after the widely seen movie, that would destroy enemy missiles from outerspace.

In Nicaragua, Reagan encouraged the opposition (*contras*) to the leftist Sandinista government with arms, tactical support, and intelligence, and supplied aid to the government of El Salvador in its struggles against left-wing rebels. In October 1983, the president also sent American troops into the Caribbean island of Grenada to overthrow a newly established Cuban-backed regime.

THE ELECTION OF 1984

Walter Mondale, a former senator from Minnesota and vice president under Carter, won the Democratic nomination. Mondale criticized Reagan for his budget deficits, high unemployment and interest rates, and reduction of spending on social services. However, Reagan was elected to a second term in a landslide.

SECOND-TERM FOREIGN CONCERNS

After Mikhail S. Gorbachev became the premier of the Soviet Union in March 1985 and took a more flexible approach toward both domestic and foreign affairs, Reagan softened his anti-Soviet stance.

Reagan and Gorbachev had difficulty in reaching an agreement on arms limitations at summit talks in 1985 and 1986. Finally, in December 1987, they signed an agreement eliminating medium-range missiles from Europe.

IRAN-CONTRA

In 1985 and 1986, several Reagan officials sold arms to the Iranians in hopes of encouraging them to use their influence in getting American hostages in Lebanon released. The profits from these sales were then diverted to the Nicaraguan *contras* in an attempt to get around congressional restrictions on funding the *contras*. The president was forced to appoint a special prosecutor, and Congress held hearings on the affair in May 1987.

SECOND-TERM DOMESTIC AFFAIRS: THE ECONOMY

The Tax Reform Act of 1986 lowered tax rates. At the same time, it removed many tax shelters and tax credits. The law did away with the concept of progressive taxation, the requirement that the percentage of income taxed increased as income increased.

The federal deficit reached $179 billion in 1985. At about the same time, the United States experienced trade deficits of more than $100 billion annually

Black Monday: On October 19, 1987, the Dow Jones Industrial Average dropped more than 500 points. Between August 25 and October 20, the market lost over a trillion dollars in paper value.

NASA: The explosion of the shuttle *Challenger* soon after take-off on January 28, 1986, damaged NASA's credibility and reinforced doubts about the complex technology required for the SDI program.

Supreme Court: Reagan reshaped the Court in 1986, replacing Chief Justice Warren C. Burger with Associate Justice William H. Rehnquist, probably the most conservative member of the Court. Although failing in his nomination of Robert Bork for associate justice, Reagan did appoint other conservatives to the Court: Sandra Day O'Connor, Antonin Scalia, and Anthony Kennedy.

THE ELECTION OF 1988

Vice President George Bush won the Republican nomination. Bush easily defeated Michael Dukakis, the Democratic nominee, but the Republicans were unable to make any inroads in Congress.

THE BUSH ADMINISTRATION

Soon after George Bush took office, the budget deficit for 1990 was estimated at $143 billion. In September, the administration and Congress agreed to increase taxes on gasoline, tobacco, and alcohol, establish an excise tax on luxury items, and raise Medicare taxes. Cuts were also to be made in medicare and other domestic programs. In a straight party vote, Republicans voting against and Democrats voting in favor, Congress in December transferred the power to decide whether new tax and spending proposals violated the deficit cutting agreement from the White House Office of Management and Budget to the Congressional Budget Office.

The Commission on Base Realignment and Closure proposed in December 1989 that 54 military bases be closed. In June 1990, Secretary of Defense Richard Cheney sent to Congress a plan to cut military spending by 10 percent and the armed forces by 25 percent over the next five years. The following April, Cheney recommended the closing of 43 domestic military bases, plus many more abroad.

With the savings and loan industry in financial trouble in 1989, largely because of bad real-estate loans, Bush signed a bill which created the Resolution Trust Corporation to oversee the closure and merging of savings and loans, and which provided $166 billion over 10 years to cover the bad debts. Estimates of the total costs of the debacle were over $300 billion.

BUSH'S ACTIVIST FOREIGN POLICY

Panama: Since coming to office, the Bush administration had been concerned with Panamanian dictator Manuel Noriega because he allegedly served as an important link in the drug traffic between South America and the United States. After economic sanctions, diplomatic efforts, and an October 1989 coup failed to oust Noriega, Bush ordered 12,000 troops into Panama on December 20. The Americans installed a new government headed by Guillermo Endara, who had earlier apparently won a presidential election that was promptly nullified by Noriega. On January 3, 1990, Noriega surrendered to the Americans and was taken to the United States to stand trial on drug trafficking charges; he was convicted and jailed for assisting the Medellín drug cartel. Twenty-three United States soldiers and three American civilians were killed in the operation. The Panamanians lost nearly 300 soldiers and more than 500 civilians.

Nicaragua: After years of civil war, Nicaragua held a presidential election in February 1990. Because of an economy largely destroyed by civil war and large financial debt to the United States, Violeta Barrios de Chamorro of the National Opposition Union defeated Daniel Ortega Saavedra of the Sandinistas, thereby fulfilling a long-standing American objective. The United States lifted its economic sanctions in March and put together an economic aid package for Nicaragua. In September 1991, the Bush administration forgave Nicaragua most of its debt to the United States.

China: After the death in April 1989 of reformer Hu Yaobang, formerly general secretary and chairman of the Chinese Communist party, students began pro-democracy marches in Beijing. By the middle of May, more than one million people were gathering on Beijing's Tiananmen Square, and other protestors elsewhere in China, calling for political reform. Martial law was imposed and in early June the army fired on the demonstrators. Estimates of the death toll in the wake of the nationwide crackdown on demonstrators ranged between 500 and 7,000. In July 1989, United States National Security Advisor Brent Scowcroft and Deputy Secretary of State Lawrence Eagleburger secretly met with Chinese leaders. When they again met the Chinese in December and revealed their earlier meeting, the Bush administration faced a storm of criticism for its policy of "constructive engagement" from opponents arguing that sanctions should be imposed. While establishing sanctions in 1991 on Chinese high-technology satellite-part exports, Bush continued to support renewal of Most Favored Nation trading status.

Africa: To rescue American citizens threatened by civil war, Bush sent 230 marines into Liberia in August 1990, evacuating 125 people. South Africa in 1990 freed Nelson Mandela, the most famous leader of the African National Congress, after 28 years of imprisonment. South Africa then began moving away from apartheid, and in 1991 Bush lifted economic sanctions imposed five years earlier. Mandela and his wife, Winnie, toured the U.S. in June 1990 to a tumultuous welcome, particularly from African-Americans. During their visit, they also addressed Congress.

COLLAPSE OF EAST EUROPEAN COMMUNISM

In August 1989 Hungary opened its borders with Austria. The following October, the Communists reorganized their party, calling it the Socialist party. Hungary then proclaimed itself a "Free Republic."

With thousands of East Germans passing through Hungary to Austria, after the opening of the borders in August 1989, Erich Honecker stepped down as head of state in October. On November 1, the government opened the border with Czechoslovakia and eight days later the Berlin Wall fell. On December 6, a non-Communist became head of state, followed on December 11 by large demonstrations demanding German reunification. Reunification took place in October 1990.

After anti-government demonstrations were forcibly broken up in Czechoslovakia in October 1989, changes took place in the Communist leadership the following month. Then, on December 8, the Communists agreed to relinquish power and Parliament elected Václav Havel, a playwright and anti-Communist leader, to the presidency on December 29.

When anti-government demonstrations in Romania were met by force in early December, portions of the military began joining the opposition which captured dictator Nicolae Ceauşescu and his wife, Elena, killing them on December 25, 1989. In May 1990 the National Salvation Front, made up of many former Communists, won the parliamentary elections.

In January 1990 the Bulgarian national assembly repealed the dominant role of the Communist party. A multi-party coalition government was formed the following December.

Albania opened its border with Greece and legalized religious worship in January 1990, and in July ousted hardliners from the government.

Amid the collapse of Communism in Eastern Europe, Bush met with Mikhail Gorbachev in Malta from December 1 through December 3, 1989; the two leaders appeared to agree that the Cold War was over. On May 30 and 31, 1990, Bush and Gorbachev met in Washington to discuss the possible reunification of Germany, and signed a trade treaty between the United States and the Soviet Union. The meeting of the two leaders in Helsinki on September 9 addressed strategies for the developing Persian Gulf crisis. At the meeting of the "Group of 7" nations (Canada, France, Germany, Italy, Japan, United Kingdom, and the United States) in July 1991, Gorbachev requested economic aid from the West. A short time later, on July 30 and 31, Bush met Gorbachev in Moscow where they signed the START treaty, which cut U.S. and Soviet nuclear arsenals by 30 percent, and pushed for Middle Eastern talks. With the collapse of the Soviet Union, the United States remained the lone world super-power.

PERSIAN GULF CRISIS

Saddam Hussein of Iraq charged that Kuwait had conspired with the United States to keep oil prices low and began massing troops at the Iraq-Kuwait border.

On August 2, Iraq invaded Kuwait, an act that Bush denounced as "naked aggression." One day later 100,000 Iraqi soldiers were poised south of Kuwait City near the Saudi Arabian border. The United States quickly banned most trade with Iraq, froze Iraq's and Kuwait's assets in the United States, and sent aircraft carriers to the Persian Gulf. After the United Nations Security Council condemned the invasion, on August 6 Bush ordered the deployment of air, sea, and land forces to Saudi Arabia, dubbing the operation "Desert Shield." At the end of August there were 100,000 American soldiers in Saudi Arabia.

Bush encouraged Egypt to support American policy by forgiving Egypt its debt to the United States and obtaining pledges of financial support from Saudi Arabia, Kuwait, and Japan, among other nations, to help pay for the operation. On October 29, the Security Council warned Saddam Hussein that further actions might be taken if he did not withdraw from Kuwait. In November Bush ordered that U.S. forces be increased to more than 400,000. On November 29, the United Nations set January 15, 1991, as the deadline for Iraqi withdrawal from Kuwait.

On January 9, Iraq's foreign-minister, Tariq Aziz, rejected a letter written by Bush to Hussein. Three days later, after an extensive debate, Congress authorized the use of force in the Gulf. On January 17, an international force including the United States, Great Britain, France, Italy, Saudi Arabia, and Kuwait launched an air and missile attack on Iraq and occupied Kuwait. The U.S. called the effort "Operation Desert Storm." Under the overall command of Army General H. Norman Schwarzkopf, the military effort emphasized high-technology weapons, including F-15 E fighter-bombers, F-117 A stealth fighters, Tomahawk cruise missiles, and Patriot anti-missile missiles. Beginning on January 17, Iraq fired SCUD missiles into Israel in an effort to draw that country into the war and splinter the U.S.-Arabian coalition. On January 22 and 23, Hussein's forces set Kuwaiti oil fields on fire and spilled oil into the Gulf.

On February 23, the allied ground assault began. Four days later Bush announced that Kuwait was liberated and ordered offensive operations to cease. The United Nations established the terms for the cease-fire: Iraqi annexation of Kuwait to be rescinded, Iraq to accept liability for damages and return Kuwaiti property, Iraq to end all military actions and identify mines and booby traps, and Iraq to release captives.

On April 3, the Security Council approved a resolution to establish a permanent cease-fire; Iraq accepted U.N. terms on April 6. The next day the United States began airlifting food to Kurdish refugees on the Iraq-Turkey border who were fleeing the Kurdish rebellion against Hussein, a rebellion that was seemingly encouraged by Bush, who nonetheless refused to become militarily involved. The United States estimated that 100,000 Iraqis had been killed during the war while the Americans had lost about 115 lives.

On February 6, 1991, the United States had set out its postwar goals for the Middle East. These included regional arms control and security arrangements, international aid for reconstruction of Iraq and Kuwait, and resolution of the Israeli-Palestinian conflict. Immediately after cessation of the conflict, Secretary of State James Baker toured the Middle East attempting to promote a conference to address the problems of the region. After several more negotiating sessions, Saudi Arabia, Syria, Jordan, and Lebanon had accepted the U.S. proposal for an Arab-Israeli peace conference by the middle of July; Israel conditionally accepted in early August. Despite continuing conflict with Iraq, including United Nations inspections of its nuclear capabilities, and new Israeli settlements in disputed territory—which kept the conference agreement tenuous—the nations met in Madrid, Spain, at the end of October. Bilateral talks in early November between Israel and the Arabs concentrated on procedural issues.

BREAKUP OF THE SOVIET UNION

Following the collapse of Communism in Eastern Europe, the Baltic republic of Lithuania, which had been taken over by the Soviet Union in 1939 through an agreement with Adolf Hitler, declared its independence from the Soviet Union on March 11, 1990.

Two days later, on March 13, the Soviet Union removed the Communist monopoly of political power, allowing non-Communists to run for office. The process of liberalization went haltingly forward in the Soviet Union. Perhaps the most significant event was the election of Boris Yeltsin, who had left the Communist party, as president of the Russian republic on June 12, 1991.

On August 19, Soviet hard-liners attempted a coup to oust Gorbachev, but a combination of their inability to control communication with the outside world, a failure to quickly establish military control, and the resistance of Yeltsin, members of the military, and people in the streets of cities such as Moscow and Leningrad, ended the coup on August 21, returning Gorbachev to power.

In the aftermath of the coup, much of the Communist structure came crashing down, setting the stage for opposition parties to emerge. The remaining Baltic republics of Latvia and Estonia declared their independence, which was recognized by the United States several days after other nations had done so. Most of the other Soviet republics then followed suit in declaring their independence. The Bush administration wanted some form of central authority to remain in the Soviet Union; hence, it did not seriously consider recognizing the independence of any republics except the Baltics. Bush also resisted offering economic aid to the Soviet Union until it presented a radical economic reform plan to move toward a free market. However, humanitarian aid such as food was pledged in order to preserve stability during the winter.

In September 1991, George Bush announced unilateral removal and destruction of ground-based tactical nuclear weapons in Europe and Asia, removal of nuclear-armed Tomahawk cruise missiles from surface ships and submarines, immediate destruction of intercontinental ballistic missiles covered by START, and an end to the 24-hour alert for strategic bombers that the U.S. had maintained for decades. Gorbachev responded the next month by announcing the immediate deactivation of intercontinental ballistic missiles covered by START, removal of all short-range missiles from Soviet ships, submarines, and aircraft, and destruction of all ground-based tactical nuclear weapons. He also said that the Soviet Union would reduce its forces by 700,000 troops, and he placed all long-range nuclear missiles under a single command. Gorbachev's hold on the presidency progressively weakened in the final months of 1991, with the reforms he had put in place taking on a life of their own. The dissolution of the U.S.S.R. led to his resignation in December, making way for Boris Yeltsin, who had headed popular resistance. The United States was now the world's only superpower.

THE DEMOCRATS RECLAIM THE WHITE HOUSE

William Jefferson Clinton, governor of Arkansas, overcame several rivals to win the Democratic presidential nomination in 1992 and with his running mate, Senator Albert Gore of Tennessee, went on to win the White House. During the campaign, Clinton and independent candidate H. Ross Perot, a wealthy Texas businessman, emphasized jobs and the economy, while attacking the mounting federal debt. The incumbent, Bush, stressed traditional values and his foreign policy accomplishments. In the 1992 election, Clinton won 43 percent of the popular vote and 370 electoral votes, defeating Bush and Perot. Perot took 19 percent of the popular vote, but was unable to garner any electoral votes.

Clinton came to be dogged by a number of controversies, ranging from alleged ill-gotten gains in a complex Arkansas land deal that came to be known as the Whitewater Affair to charges of sexual misconduct, brought by a former Arkansas state employee (with whom he would ultimately reach an out-of-court settlement), that dated to an incident she said had occurred when Clinton was governor. In December 1998 Clinton was impeached by the House on charges that stemmed from an adulterous affair with a White House intern, Monica Lewinsky. The affair had been uncovered by Independent Counsel Kenneth Starr in the course of a long-running investigation into alleged malfeasance by the president and his wife, Hillary, in the Whitewater land deal and other matters. Extraordinary detail about Clinton's encounters with Lewinsky was revealed in a voluminous report from Starr's office. Its release triggered the impeachment proceedings.

On the legislative front, Clinton was strongly rebuffed in an attempt during his first term to reform the nation's healthcare system. In the 1994 midterm elections, in what Clinton himself considered a repudiation of his administration, the Republicans took both houses of Congress from the Democrats and voted in Newt Gingrich of Georgia as Speaker of the House. Gingrich had helped craft the Republican congressional campaign strategy to dramatically shrink the federal government and give more power to the states.

Clinton, however, was not without his successes, both on the legislative and diplomatic fronts. He signed a bill establishing a five-day waiting period for handgun purchases, and he signed a Crime Bill emphasizing community policing. He signed the Family Leave Bill, which required large companies to provide up to 12 weeks' unpaid leave to workers for family and medical emergencies. He also championed welfare reform (a central theme of his campaign), but made it clear that the legislation he signed into law in August 1996 radically overhauling FDR's welfare system disturbed him on two counts—its exclusion of legal immigrants from getting most federal benefits and its deep cut in federal outlays for food stamps; Clinton said these flaws could be repaired with further legislation. In foreign economic affairs, Clinton debated the North American Free Trade Agreement (NAFTA), which lifted most trade barriers with Mexico and Canada as of 1994. Clinton sought to ease tensions between Israelis and Palestinians, and he helped bring together Itzhak Rabin, prime minister of Israel, and Yasir Arafat, chairman of the Palestine Liberation Organization, for a summit at the White House. Ultimately, the two Middle East leaders signed an accord in 1994 establishing Palestinian self-rule in the Gaza Strip and Jericho. In October 1994 Israel and Jordan signed a treaty to begin the process of establishing full diplomatic relations. Rabin was assassinated a year later by a radical, right-wing Israeli. The Clinton administration also played a central role in hammering out a peace agreement in 1995 in war-torn former Yugoslavia—where armed conflict had broken out in 1991 among Serbs, Croats, Bosnian Muslims, and other factions and groups.

Clinton recaptured the Democratic nomination without a serious challenge, while longtime GOP Senator Robert Dole of Kansas, the Senate majority leader, had to overcome several opponents, but orchestrated a harmonious nominating convention with running mate Jack Kemp, a former New York congressman and Cabinet member. In November 1996, with most voters citing a healthy economy and the lack of an enticing alternative in Dole or the Reform Party's Perot, Clinton received 49 percent of the vote, becoming the first Democrat to be re-elected since FDR, in 1936. The GOP retained control of both houses of Congress.

Clinton, intent on mirroring the diversity of America in his Cabinet appointments, chose Hispanics Henry Cisneros (Housing and Urban Development) and Federico Peña (Transportation and, later, Energy), African Americans Ron Brown (Commerce) and Mike Espy (Agriculture), and women, including the nation's first woman attorney general, Janet Reno, and Madeleine Albright, the first woman secretary of state in U.S. history (Albright succeeded Warren Christopher, who served through Clinton's first term). Brown and 34 others on a trade mission died when his Air Force plane crashed in Croatia in April 1996. Cisneros and Espy both resigned under ethics clouds.

LATE TWENTIETH CENTURY SOCIAL AND CULTURAL DEVELOPMENTS

AIDS: In 1981 scientists announced the discovery of Acquired Immune Deficiency Syndrome (AIDS), which was especially prevalent among homosexual males and intravenous drug users. Widespread fear resulted, including an upsurge in homophobia. The Centers for Disease Control and Prevention (CDC) and the National Cancer Institute, among others, pursued research on the disease. The Food and Drug Administration responded to calls for fast-tracking evaluation of drugs by approving the drug AZT in February 1991. With the revelation that a Florida dentist had infected three patients, there were calls for mandatory testing of healthcare workers. Supporters of testing argued before a House hearing in September 1991 that testing should be regarded as a public health, rather than a civil rights, issue. In early 1998, the CDC estimated that between 400,000 and 650,000 Americans were HIV-positive, meaning that they had the virus that causes AIDS. Public health officials expressed concern about the difficulties in tracking the spread of AIDS, as the HIV infection was being reported to health agencies only when patients developed symptoms, which could be years after infection. New drug therapies, meanwhile, were preventing AIDS symptoms from ever appearing, creating the specter of growing numbers of people going unseen by public-health agencies as they spread the virus. These developments came against the backdrop of a marked change in the demographic makeup of the epidemic's victims—from mostly white homosexual males to African-Americans, Hispanics, and women, particularly those who were poor, intravenous drug users, or the sex partners of drug users.

Families: More than half the married women in the United States continued to hold jobs outside the home. Nearly one out of every two marriages was ending in divorce, and there was an increase in the number of unmarried couples living together, which contributed to a growing number of illegitimate births. So-called family values became a major theme in presidential politics, powered in part by the publication of leading conservative William J. Bennett's best-selling anthology *The Book of Virtues: A Treasury of Great Moral Stories*. Bennett had served as Bush's secretary of education and, later, as director of the Office of National Drug Control Policy, which the press shortened to "drug czar."

Terrorism Hits Home: While terrorist attacks continued to be a grim reality overseas through the 1980s and early 1990s, with Americans frequently targeted, such incidents had come to be perceived as something the United States wouldn't have to face on its own soil—until February 26, 1993, when a terrorist bomb ripped through the underground parking garage of the World Trade Center in New York City, killing six people and injuring more than 1,000. The blast shattered America's "myth of invulnerability," wrote foreign policy analyst Jeffrey D. Simon in his book *The Terrorist Trap*. Convicted and sentenced to 240 years each were four Islamic militants. On April 19, 1995, in the deadliest act of domestic terrorism in U.S. history, the Oklahoma City federal building was bombed: 168 people were killed and 500 injured. Timothy James McVeigh, a gun enthusiast involved in the American militia movement who had often expressed hatred toward the U.S. federal government and was particularly aggrieved over the government's assault exactly two years earlier on a self-proclaimed prophet's compound in Waco, Texas, was convicted and sentenced to death in June 1997. A second defendant, Terry Nichols, was convicted of conspiracy.

Murder Trial a National Spectacle: In Los Angeles, former pro-football star, broadcaster, and actor O.J. Simpson was tried for the brutal murder in June 1994 of his ex-wife, Nicole Brown Simpson, and her friend Ronald Goldman. The nationally televised trial became a running spectacle for months, with the lengthy, tortuous courtroom proceedings transfixing the nation. Simpson was found not guilty, but would later, in a civil trial, be found responsible for the slaying of Goldman and for committing battery against Nicole. The civil judgment awarded the plaintiffs, Ronald's parents and Nicole's estate, $33.5 million in damages. (The Browns refrained from bringing a wrongful-death suit to spare the young Simpson children the agony of having to testify.)

Crime and Politics: George Bush had won the presidency in 1988 on a strong anti-crime message, crystallized in a controversial TV spot that demonized Willie Horton, an African-American inmate in the Massachusetts jail system who was released while then-presidential candidate Michael Dukakis was the Democratic governor. Bill Clinton co-opted the traditional Republican crime issue by pushing through legislation for more community policing, an approach that, together with aggressive central management, was credited for the plummeting crime rate in New York City, for example.

U.S. Prisoner Count Grows: Between 1987 and 1997, the period spanning the Bush administration and Clinton's first term, the number of Americans in prison doubled, soaring from 800,000 to 1.6 million.

Drug Abuse Continues: Drug abuse continued to be widespread, with cocaine becoming more readily available, particularly in a cheaper, stronger form called "crack."

Labor: Labor union strength continued to ebb in the 1990s (though some observers pointed to the success of the 1997 Teamsters strike against United Parcel Service, the giant shipper, as a sign that labor was rebounding), with the U.S. Department of Labor's Bureau of Labor Statistics reporting that union membership dropped to 14.5 percent of wage and salary employment in 1996, down from 14.9 percent in 1995. In 1983, union members made up 20.1 percent of the work force. Unions continued to be responsible for higher wages for their members: organized workers reported median weekly earnings of $615, as against a median of $462 for non-union workers, according to the bureau.

Abortion and the High Court: In a July 1989 decision, *Webster v. Reproductive Health Services*, the U.S. Supreme Court upheld a Missouri law prohibiting public employees from performing abortions, unless the mother's life is threatened. With this decision came a shift in focus on the abortion issue from the courts to the state legislatures. Pro-life (anti-abortion rights) forces moved in several states to restrict the availability of abortions, but their results were mixed. Florida rejected abortion restrictions in October 1989, the governor of Louisiana vetoed similar legislation nine months later, and in early 1991 Maryland adopted a liberal abortion law. In contrast, Utah and Pennsylvania enacted strict curbs on abortion during the same period. At the national level, Bush in October 1989 vetoed funding for Medicaid abortions. The conflict between pro-choice (pro-abortion) and pro-life forces gained national attention through such events as a pro-life demonstration held in Washington in April 1990, and blockage of access to abortion clinics by Operation Rescue, a militant anti-abortion group, in the summer of 1991. Abortion clinics around the country continued to be the targets of protests and violence through the mid-'90s.

Gap Between Rich and Poor Widens: Kevin Phillips's *The Politics of Rich and Poor* (1990) argued that 40 million Americans in the bottom fifth of the population experienced a 1 percent decline in income between 1973 and 1979 and a 10 percent decline between 1979 and 1987. Meanwhile, the top fifth saw a rise of 7 percent and 16 percent during the same periods. The number of single-parent families living below the poverty line (annual income of $11,611 for a family of four) rose by 46 percent between 1979 and 1987. Nearly one-quarter of American children under age six were counted among the poor, said Phillips.

Censorship: The conservative leaning of the electorate in recent years revealed its cultural dimension in a controversy that erupted over the National Endowment for the Arts in September 1989. Criticism of photographer Robert Mapplethorpe's homoerotic and masochistic pictures, among other artworks that had been funded by the Endowment, led Senator Jesse Helms of North Carolina to propose that grants for "obscene or indecent" projects, or those derogatory of religion, be cut off. Although the proposal ultimately failed, it raised questions about the government's role as a sponsor of art in an increasingly pluralistic society. The Mapplethorpe photographs also became an issue the following summer when Cincinnati's Contemporary Art Center was indicted on charges of obscenity when it exhibited the artist's work. A jury later struck down the charges. Meanwhile, in March 1990, the Recording Industry Association of America, in a move advocated by, among others, Tipper Gore, wife of Democratic Senator Al Gore of Tennessee (the man who would be elected vice-president in 1992), agreed to place new uniform warning labels on recordings that contained potentially offensive language.

Crisis in Education: The National Commission on Excellence in Education, appointed in 1981, argued in "A Nation at Risk" that a "rising tide of mediocrity" characterized the nation's schools. In the wake of the report, many states instituted reforms, including higher teacher salaries, competency tests for teachers, and an increase in required subjects for high school graduation. In September 1989 Bush met with the nation's governors in Charlottesville, Virginia, to work on a plan to improve the schools. The governors issued a call for the establishment of national performance goals to be measured by achievement tests. In February 1990 the National Governors' Association adopted specific performance goals, stating that achievement tests should be administered in grades four, eight, and twelve. As the new millenium approached, however, signs began to emerge that the tide might be turning: a major global comparison found in June 1997 that America's 9- and 10-year-olds were among the world's best in science and also scored well above average in math.

Literary Trends: The 1980s and 1990s saw the emergence of writers who concentrated on marginal or regional aspects of national life. William Kennedy wrote a series of novels about Albany, New York, most notably *Ironweed* (1983). The small-town West attracted attention from Larry McMurtry, whose *Lonesome Dove* (1985) used myth to explore the history of the region. The immigrant experience gave rise to Amy Tan's *The Joy-Luck Club* (1989) and Oscar Hijuelos's *The Mambo Kings Play Songs of Love* (1990). Tom Wolfe satirized greed, and class and racial tensions in New York City in *The Bonfire of the Vanities* (1987). Toni Morrison's *Beloved* (1987) dramatized the African-American slavery experience.

☞ Drill: United States History

> **DIRECTIONS:** Each of the questions or incomplete statements below is followed by four suggested answers or completions. Select the one that is best in each case.

1. Which of the following statements is true of the Kansas-Nebraska Act?

    (A) It led to the disintegration of the Democratic party.

    (B) It was a measure that the South had been demanding for decades.

    (C) It led directly to the formation of the Republican party.

    (D) By applying "popular sovereignty" to territories formerly closed to slavery by the Missouri Compromise, it succeeded in maintaining the tenuous sectional peace that had been created by the Compromise of 1850.

2. All of the following were steps taken by the United States to aid Great Britain prior to U.S. entry into World War II EXCEPT

(A) the sale of 50 destroyers to the British in exchange for 99-year leases on certain overseas naval bases.

(B) gradual assumption by the U.S. Navy of an increasing role in patrolling the Atlantic against German submarines.

(C) institution of the Lend-Lease Act for providing war supplies to Britain beyond its ability to pay.

(D) the stationing of U.S. Marines in Scotland to protect it against possible German invasion.

3. Thomas Nast achieved fame and influence as a

(A) radio commentator.   (C) photographer.

(B) newspaper publisher.   (D) political cartoonist.

4. Which of the following is true of the Stamp Act Congress?

(A) It was the first unified government for all the American colonies.

(B) It provided an important opportunity for colonial stamp agents to discuss methods of enforcing the act.

(C) It was attended only by Georgia, Virginia, and the Carolinas.

(D) It provided an important opportunity for colonial leaders to meet and establish ties with one another.

5. The map below depicts the United States immediately after which of the following events?

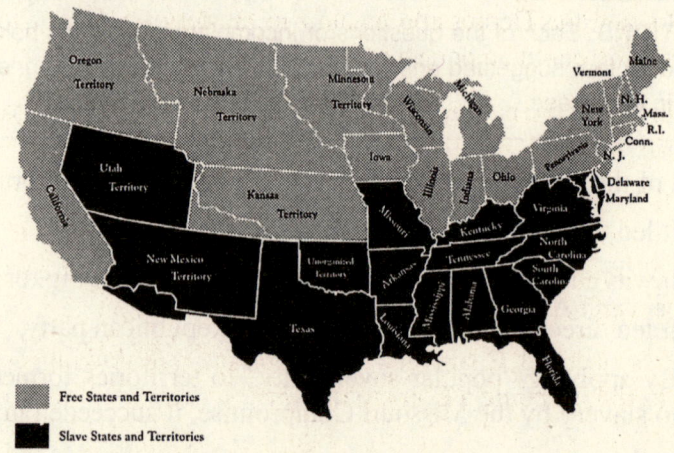

Free States and Territories

Slave States and Territories

(A) Passage of the Compromise of 1850

(B) Negotiation of the Webster-Ashburton Treaty

(C) Passage of the Northwest Ordinance

(D) Settlement of the Mexican War

6. The principle of "popular sovereignty" was

(A) first conceived by Senator Stephen A. Douglas.

(B) applied as part of the Missouri Compromise.

(C) a central feature of the Kansas-Nebraska Act.

(D) a policy favored by the Whig party during the late 1840s and early 1850s.

7. In issuing the Emancipation Proclamation, one of Lincoln's goals was to

(A) gain the active aid of Britain and France in restoring the Union.

(B) stir up enthusiasm for the war in such border states as Maryland and Kentucky.

(C) please the Radicals in the North by abolishing slavery in areas of the South already under the control of Union armies.

(D) keep Britain and France from intervening on the side of the Confederacy.

8. Which of the following was not one of Hoover's responses to the Great Depression?

(A) He at first stressed the desirability of localism and private initiative rather than government intervention.

(B) He saw the Depression as akin to an act of nature, about which nothing could be done except to ride it out.

(C) He urged the nation's business leaders to maintain wages and full employment.

(D) His strategy for ending the Depression was a failure.

9. Which of the following statements is correct about the case of Whitaker Chambers and Alger Hiss?

(A) Hiss accused Chambers, an important mid-ranking government official, of being a Communist spy.

(B) The case gained national attention through the involvement of Senator Joseph R. McCarthy.

(C) Hiss was convicted of perjury for denying under oath that he had been a Communist agent.

(D) The case marked the beginning of American concern about Communist subversion.

10. Which of the following best characterizes the methods of Martin Luther King, Jr.?

(A) Nonviolent defiance of segregation

(B) Armed violence against police and troops

(C) Patience while developing the skills that would make blacks economically successful and gain them the respect of whites

(D) A series of petitions to Congress calling for correction of racial abuses

11. Which of the following best describes the agreement that ended the 1962 Cuban Missile Crisis?

(A) The Soviet Union agreed not to station troops in Cuba, and the United States agreed not to invade Cuba.

(B) The Soviet Union agreed to withdraw its missiles from Cuba, and the United States agreed not to invade Cuba.

(C) The Soviet Union agreed not to invade Turkey, and the United States agreed not to invade Cuba.

(D) The Soviet Union agreed to withdraw its missiles from Cuba, and the United States agreed not to invade Turkey.

12. The most common form of resistance on the part of black American slaves prior to the Civil War was

(A) violent uprisings in which many persons were killed.

(B) attempts to escape and reach Canada by means of the "Underground Railroad."

(C) passive resistance, including breaking tools and slightly slowing the pace of work.

(D) arson of plantation buildings and cotton gins.

13. Which of the following best describes the attitudes of Southern whites toward slavery during the mid-nineteenth century (ca. 1835–1865)?

    (A) Slavery was a necessary evil.

    (B) Slavery should be immediately abolished.

    (C) Slavery was a benefit to both whites and blacks.

    (D) Slavery should gradually be phased out and the freed slaves colonized to some place outside the United States.

14. For farmers and planters in the South, the 1850s was a period of

    (A) low prices for agricultural products.

    (B) rapid and violent fluctuations in crop prices.

    (C) high crop prices due to repeated crop failures.

    (D) high crop prices and sustained prosperity.

15. Immigrants coming to America from Eastern and Southern Europe during the late nineteenth century were most likely to

    (A) settle in large cities in the Northeast or Midwest.

    (B) settle on farms in the upper Midwest.

    (C) seek to file on homesteads on the Great Plains.

    (D) migrate to the South and Southwest.

16. Which of the following had the greatest effect in moving the United States toward participation in the First World War?

    (A) The German disregard of treaty obligations in violating Belgian neutrality

    (B) Germany's declaration of its intent to wage unrestricted submarine warfare

    (C) A German offer to reward Mexico with U.S. territory should it join Germany in a war against the United States

    (D) The beginning of the Russian Revolution

17. The Berlin Airlift was America's response to

    (A) the Soviet blockade of West Berlin from land communication with the rest of the western zone.

    (B) the acute war-time destruction of roads and railroads, making land transport almost impossible.

(C)   the unusually severe winter of 1947.

(D)   a widespread work stoppage by German transportation workers in protest of the allied occupation of Germany.

18.   The economic theory of mercantilism would be consistent with which of the following statements?

(A)   Economies will prosper most when trade is restricted as little as possible.

(B)   A government should seek to direct the economy so as to maximize exports.

(C)   Colonies are of little economic importance to the mother country.

(D)   It is vital that a country imports more than it exports.

19.   The primary American objection to the Stamp Act was that

(A)   it was an internal tax, whereas Americans were prepared to accept only external taxes.

(B)   it was the first tax of any kind ever imposed by Britain on the colonies.

(C)   its proposed tax rates were so high that they would have crippled the colonial economy.

(D)   it was a measure for raising revenue from the colonies but it had not been approved by the colonists through their representatives.

20.   In seeking diplomatic recognition from foreign powers during the War for Independence, the American government found it necessary to

(A)   make large financial payments to the governments of France, Spain, and Holland.

(B)   promise to cede large tracts of American territory to France upon a victorious conclusion of the war.

(C)   demonstrate its financial stability and self-sufficiency.

(D)   demonstrate a determination and potential to win independence.

21.   William Lloyd Garrison in his publication *The Liberator* was outspoken in calling for

(A)   the gradual and compensated emancipation of slaves.

(B)   colonization of slaves to some place outside the boundaries of the United States.

Étiez

Social Sciences and History Review

(C) repeal of the congressional "gag rule."

(D) immediate and uncompensated emancipation of slaves.

22. The Congressional "gag rule" stipulated that

(A) no law could be passed prohibiting slavery in the territories.

(B) no member of Congress could make statements or speeches outside of Congress pertaining to slavery.

(C) no antislavery materials could be sent through the mail to addresses in Southern states.

(D) no antislavery petitions would be formally received by Congress.

23. The main idea of Theodore Roosevelt's proposed "New Nationalism" was to

(A) make the federal government an instrument of domestic reform.

(B) undertake an aggressive new foreign policy.

(C) increase economic competition by breaking up all trusts and large business combinations.

(D) seek to establish a large overseas empire.

24. Franklin D. Roosevelt's New Deal program contained all of the following EXCEPT

(A) the attempt to raise farm prices by paying farmers not to plant.

(B) the attempt to encourage cooperation within industries so as to raise prices generally.

(C) the attempt to invigorate the economy by lowering tariff barriers.

(D) effectively eliminating the gold standard as it had previously existed.

25. The Haymarket Incident involved

(A) a riot between striking workers and police.

(B) a scandal involving corruption within the Grant administration.

(C) allegations of corruption on the part of Republican presidential candidate James G. Blaine.

(D) a disastrous fire that pointed out the hazardous working conditions in some factories.

26. The "New Immigration" was made up primarily of

   (A) Europeans who came for economic rather than religious reasons.

   (B) Europeans who were better off financially than those of the "Old Immigration."

   (C) persons from Northern and Western Europe.

   (D) persons from Southern and Eastern Europe.

27. As a result of the Spanish-American War, the United States gained possession of Puerto Rico, Guam, and

   (A) the Philippines.   (C) Bermuda.

   (B) Cuba.   (D) the Panama Canal Zone.

28. The term "Long Hot Summers" refers to

   (A) major outdoor rock concerts during the late 1960s and early 1970s.

   (B) major Communist offensives against U.S. troops in Vietnam.

   (C) protests held in large American cities against the Vietnam War.

   (D) race riots in large American cities during the 1960s.

29. The immediate issue in dispute in Bacon's Rebellion was

   (A) the jailing of individuals or seizure of their property for failure to pay taxes during a time of economic hardship.

   (B) the under-representation of the backcountry in Virginia's legislature.

   (C) the refusal of large planters to honor the terms of their contracts with former indentured servants.

   (D) the perceived failure of Virginia's governor to protect the colony's frontier area from the depredations of raiding Indians.

30. The Newburgh Conspiracy was concerned with

   (A) betrayal of the plans for the vital fort at West Point, New York.

   (B) the use of the Continental Army to create a more centralized Union of the states.

   (C) resistance to the collection of federal excise taxes in western Pennsylvania.

(D)   New England's threat to secede should the War of 1812 continue.

31. The Wilmot Proviso stipulated that

(A)   slavery should be prohibited in the lands acquired as a result of the Mexican War.

(B)   no lands should be annexed to the United States as a result of the Mexican War.

(C)   California should be a free state while the rest of the Mexican Cession should be reserved for the formation of slave states.

(D)   the status of slavery in the Mexican Cession should be decided on the basis of "Popular Sovereignty."

32. Which of the following was a goal of the Populist movement?

(A)   Free coinage of silver

(B)   Reform of child labor laws

(C)   Using modern science to solve social problems

(D)   Eliminating the electoral college as a method of choosing the nation's president

33. The settlement-house movement drew its workers primarily from which of the following groups?

(A)   Young, affluent, college-educated women

(B)   Poor Eastern European immigrants

(C)   Disabled veterans of the Spanish-American War

(D)   Idealistic young men who came to the city largely from rural areas

34. In its decision in the case of *Dred Scott v. Sanford,* the Supreme Court held that

(A)   separate facilities for different races were inherently unequal and therefore unconstitutional.

(B)   no black slave could be a citizen of the United States.

(C)   separate but equal facilities for different races were constitutional.

(D)   Affirmative Action programs were acceptable only when it could be proven that specific previous cases of discrimination had occurred within the institution or business in question.

35. The Whig party turned against President John Tyler because

    (A) he was felt to be ineffective in pushing the Whig agenda through Congress.

    (B) he spoke out in favor of the annexation of Texas.

    (C) he opposed the entire Whig legislative program.

    (D) he criticized Henry Clay's handling of the Nullification Crisis.

36. In coining the phrase "Manifest Destiny," journalist John L. O'Sullivan meant that

    (A) the struggle for racial equality was the ultimate goal of America's existence.

    (B) America was certain to become an independent country sooner or later.

    (C) it was the destiny of America to overspread the continent.

    (D) America must eventually become either all slave or all free.

37. All of the following were causes of the Mexican War EXCEPT

    (A) American desire for California.

    (B) Mexican failure to pay debts and damages owed to the U.S.

    (C) U.S. annexation of the formerly Mexican-held Republic of Texas.

    (D) Mexican desire to annex Louisiana.

38. The primary motive of those who founded the British colony in Virginia during the seventeenth century was the

    (A) desire for economic gain.

    (B) desire for religious freedom.

    (C) desire to create a perfect religious commonwealth as an example to the rest of the world.

    (D) desire to recreate in the New World the story of feudalistic society that was fading in the Old.

39. Which of the following is true of the Gulf of Tonkin incident?

    (A) It involved a clash of U.S. and Soviet warships.

    (B) In it, two North Vietnamese fighter-bombers were shot down as they neared U.S. Navy ships.

(C)   It involved the seizure, by North Vietnam, of a U.S. Navy intelligence ship in international waters.

(D)   It led to major U.S. involvement in the Vietnam War.

40.   Which of the following statements is true of the SALT I treaty?

(A)   It brought sharp reductions in the number of ballistic missiles in both the U.S. and Soviet arsenals.

(B)   It was intended to encourage the deployment of defensive rather than offensive strategic weapons.

(C)   It indicated U.S. acceptance of the concept of Mutual Assured Destruction.

(D)   It was never ratified by the U.S. Senate.

UNITED STATES HISTORY REVIEW

ANSWER KEY

Drill: United States History

1.	(C)	11.	(B)	21.	(D)	31.	(A)
2.	(D)	12.	(C)	22.	(D)	32.	(A)
3.	(D)	13.	(C)	23.	(A)	33.	(A)
4.	(D)	14.	(D)	24.	(C)	34.	(B)
5.	(A)	15.	(A)	25.	(A)	35.	(C)
6.	(C)	16.	(B)	26.	(D)	36.	(C)
7.	(D)	17.	(A)	27.	(A)	37.	(D)
8.	(B)	18.	(B)	28.	(D)	38.	(A)
9.	(C)	19.	(D)	29.	(D)	39.	(D)
10.	(A)	20.	(D)	30.	(B)	40.	(C)

DETAILED EXPLANATIONS OF ANSWERS

Drill: United States History

1.   **(C)**   The Republican party came into being primarily out of the controversy stirred up by the Kansas-Nebraska Act. While this same controversy did cause a sizable splinter faction to leave the Democratic party and join the newly formed Republican party, it did not cause the disintegration of the Democratic party (A), which continued as a political force up to and beyond the Civil War. It is also true that the Kansas-Nebraska Act applied popular sovereignty to territory north of the Missouri Compromise line for the first time, but far from preserving the nation's fragile sectional harmony (D), it had quite the opposite effect. Although the South generally supported the Act, most Southerners had given the area little thought before Douglas introduced the issue (B).

2.   **(D)**   U.S. Marines were stationed in Iceland, not Scotland, to guard against possible German attack. Choice (C) may seem impossible, but the United States first instituted the Cash-and-Carry System and later began the Lend-Lease Act when British financial assets began to dwindle. The sale of destroyers to Britain (A) and the growing role of the U.S. Navy in the struggle to keep the Atlantic sea lanes open (B) were both steps taken by President Franklin D. Roosevelt prior to official U.S. entry into the war.

3.   **(D)**   Thomas Nast was a famous political cartoonist of the late nineteenth century.

4.   **(D)**   One of the most important aspects of the Stamp Act Congress was the opportunity it provided for colonial leaders to meet and establish acquaintances with one another. Nine colonies — not merely Georgia, Virginia, and the Carolinas (C) — were represented at it, but far from being a unified government for all the American colonies (A), it simply passed mild resolutions protesting the Stamp Act. It was not, therefore, either a vehicle for enforcing the act (B).

5.   **(A)**   The map depicts the United States after the Compromise of 1850. The states of Texas and California as well as the Utah and New Mexico Territories were not part of the United States at the time of the 1842 Webster-Ashburton Treaty (B), dealing with the Maine-New Brunswick boundary; and the 1787 Northwest Ordinance (C), organizing what was to

become the states of Ohio, Indiana, Illinois, Michigan, and Wisconsin. California and the two territories were gained as a result of the Mexican War (D), but California statehood, as well as territorial status for Utah and New Mexico, had to await the Compromise of 1850.

6.   **(C)**   The principle of popular sovereignty was a central feature of the Kansas-Nebraska Act. Though championed by Senator Stephen A. Douglas (A) it had previously been put forward by 1848 Democratic presidential candidate Lewis Cass. A favorite policy of Democrats — not Whigs (D) — during the late 1840s and early 1850s, it proved a failure in solving the impasse over the status of slavery in the territories. It differed from the system of congressionally specified free and slave areas used in the Missouri Compromise (B).

7.   **(D)**   One of Lincoln's reasons for issuing the Emancipation Proclamation was to keep Britain and France from intervening on the side of the Confederacy. Lincoln neither needed, wanted, nor could have obtained the active aid of these countries in restoring the Union (A). The Radicals in the North would indeed have been pleased had Lincoln freed the slaves in areas of the South already under the control of Union armies (C), but it was precisely that which the Emancipation Proclamation did not do, largely out of concern for the more-or-less loyal slaveholding border states such as Maryland and Kentucky, who were not at all enthused about Lincoln's action even as it was (B).

8.   **(B)**   Hoover did NOT see the Depression as akin to an act of nature, about which nothing could be done. He did stress the desirability of localism and private initiative (A) and urged the nation's business leaders to maintain wages and full employment (C), but his efforts ended in failure (D).

9.   **(C)**   Hiss, a mid-ranking government official, was convicted of perjury for denying under oath that he had been a Communist agent, after being accused as such by admitted former Communist Whitaker Chambers, not the other way around (A). The case gained national attention through the involvement of young Congressman Richard Nixon, not Senator Joseph R. McCarthy (B), and while it did increase American concern about Communist subversion, it was by no means the beginning of such concern (D).

10.   **(A)**   Martin Luther King's methods were characterized by nonviolent defiance of segregation. While King and/or his supporters might make speeches or send petitions (D), civil disobedience gave his movement its urgency. Patience while developing the skills that would make blacks economically successful and gain them the respect of whites was the advice of

late nineteenth century black leader Booker T. Washington, while armed violence was called for by King's more radical contemporaries of the 1960s.

11.   **(B)**   The agreement ending the Cuban Missile Crisis called for the Soviet Union to withdraw its missiles from Cuba while the United States agreed not to overthrow Castro's regime there. Turkey pertained to the matter involving the Soviet's objection to U.S. missiles there, but it was not included in the agreement (C) and (D). The agreement also said nothing with regard to Soviet troops in Cuba (A).

12.   **(C)**   Blacks most commonly resisted slavery passively, if at all. The Underground Railroad (B), though celebrated in popular history, involved a relatively minute number of slaves. Arson (D) and violent uprising (A), though they did sometimes occur and were the subject of much fear on the part of white Southerners, were also relatively rare.

13.   **(C)**   During the period from 1835-1865 Southerners generally defended slavery as a positive benefit to society and even to the slaves themselves. That slavery was a necessary evil (A) and should be gradually phased out as the slaves were colonized outside the United States (D) was the attitude of an earlier generation of white Southerners, including Thomas Jefferson. That slavery should be immediately abolished (B) was the view of the Abolitionists, a minority even in the North during this period.

14.   **(D)**   Farmers and planters in the South enjoyed high crop prices and sustained prosperity during the 1850s. Crops were large (C) and prices were high and steady (A) and (B).

15.   **(A)**   For whatever reasons, immigrants of the "New Immigration" tended to settle in the large cities of the Northeast and Midwest. Very few of them settled on farms (B), filed on homesteads (C), or migrated to the South and Southwest (D).

16.   **(B)**   Germany's 1917 declaration of its intent to wage unrestricted submarine warfare was the most important factor in bringing the United States into World War I. German violation of Belgian neutrality in 1914 (A) did nothing to aid Germany's cause in America, and revelation of Germany's suggestions to Mexico (C) was even more damaging, but neither of these had the impact of the U-boats. The fall of the Tsar and beginning of the Russian Revolution (D) may or may not have had an influence on President Woodrow Wilson.

17.   **(A)**   The Berlin Airlift was Truman's response to the Soviet block-

ade of Berlin. Neither wartime destruction (B) nor a severe winter (C) would have necessitated such a measure and no such work stoppage (D) occurred.

18. **(B)** Mercantilists believed the government should seek to direct the economy so as to maximize exports. Mercantilists DID, however, believe in government interference in the economy (A) and the possession of colonies (C). Exports, they asserted, must exceed imports, not the other way around (D).

19. **(D)** Americans' primary objection to the Stamp Act was its purpose of raising revenue from the Americans without the consent of their representatives. A few Americans and a future British prime minister mistook this for opposition to internal taxes only (A). The proposed tax rate was not ruinously high (C), and the British had previously imposed taxes on America (B).

20. **(D)** In order to gain foreign recognition during the War for Independence, it was necessary for the United States to demonstrate a determination and potential to win independence. The U.S. could not have demonstrated financial stability (C) at this time, nor could it have made financial payments (A). It did not prove necessary to make territorial (B) concessions to France.

21. **(D)** Garrison called for the immediate and uncompensated emancipation of all slaves. He definitely opposed either gradualism or compensation (A). He also opposed colonization (B). Though he opposed the congressional gag rule, its repeal was not his main issue of concern.

22. **(D)** The congressional "gag rule" held that no antislavery petitions would be formally received by Congress. It did not directly govern the laws that could be considered (A) nor did it limit what a member could say outside of Congress (B). Anti-slavery materials sent through the mail would not be delivered to Southern addresses (C), but this was a separate matter.

23. **(A)** Roosevelt's New Nationalism pertained to domestic reform. Unrelated was the fact that Roosevelt always favored an aggressive foreign policy (B) including the establishment of an overseas empire (D). Though he gained a reputation as a trust-buster, Roosevelt was by no means in favor of breaking up all trusts and large business combinations (C).

24. **(C)** Tariff reduction was generally left untried as a means of getting out of the Depression. Roosevelt did, however, attempt to raise prices by reducing farm production (A), encouraging cooperation within industries (B), and essentially altering the gold standard (D).

25. **(A)** The Haymarket Incident involved the throwing of a bomb at Chicago police and a subsequent riot involving police and striking workers. There were plenty of scandals within the Grant administration (B), but this was not one of them. Allegations of corruption on the part of Republican presidential candidate James G. Blaine (C) were contained in the Mulligan Letters. The disastrous fire that pointed out the hazardous working conditions in some factories (D) was New York's Triangle Factory fire.

26. **(D)** The "New Immigration" was made up primarily of persons from Southern and Eastern Europe. Some, such as persecuted Russian Jews, came for religious reasons (A). The great majority were financially less well off (B) than those of the "Old Immigration," who came from Northern and Western Europe (C). Persons from Asia, Africa, and the Americas would not generally be considered part of the "New Immigration."

27. **(A)** The U.S. gained possession of the Philippines through the Spanish-American War. Cuba (B), though originally the primary issue of contention between Spain and the United States, was not annexed but rather granted its independence under the terms of the Platte Amendment. The Panama Canal Zone (D) was acquired within a few years of the Spanish-American War but in unrelated incidents and not from Spain. Bermuda (C) has never been acquired by the United States.

28. **(D)** The "Long Hot Summers" were filled with race rioting in America's large cities during the 1960s. Major outdoor rock concerts (A), such as the 1969 Woodstock concert, did occur during these years. The large Communist offensives against U.S. troops in Vietnam (B) went by the name Tet. The protests (C), which were many, were called anti-war protests.

29. **(D)** Bacon's followers were disgruntled at what they saw as the governor's refusal to protect their frontier area from Indian raids. The jailing of individuals or seizure of their property for failure to pay taxes during a time of economic hardship (A) was the source of Shays' Rebellion in 1786. The under-representation of the backcountry areas in colonial legislatures (B) was an ongoing source of irritation in the colonial South. The mistreatment of former indentured servants by large planters (C) and the favoritism of Virginia's governor Berkeley to his clique of friends may have been underlying causes but were not the immediate issue in dispute in Bacon's Rebellion.

30. **(B)** The Newburgh Conspiracy was composed of army officers disgusted with a central government too weak to collect taxes to pay them and their troops. Betrayal of the plans for the fort at West Point (A) was Benedict

Arnold's treason. Resistance to the collection of federal excise taxes in western Pennsylvania (C) took the form of the Whiskey Rebellion of 1791. New England's threat to secede should the War of 1812 continue (D) was made at the 1814 Hartford Convention.

31. **(A)** The Wilmot Proviso was intended to prohibit slavery in the area acquired through the Mexican War. Congress generally agreed that the United States would acquire some territory from the war (B). That California should be a free state while the rest of the Mexican Cession was reserved for slavery (C), and that the status of slavery in the Mexican Cession should be decided on the basis of "Popular Sovereignty" (D), were suggestions for a compromise that might calm the furor aroused by the Wilmot Proviso.

32. **(A)** The Populists desired free coinage of silver. They also desired direct election of U.S. Senators, not necessarily an end to the electoral college (D). The Progressive movement, which followed Populism, favored the reform of child labor laws (B) and the use of modern science to solve social problems (C).

33. **(A)** The settlement-house workers were often young, affluent, college-educated women such as Jane Addams. Poor immigrants (B) and disabled veterans (C) would have had less opportunity for such things. Idealistic young men (D) were apparently drawn to such enterprises in smaller numbers.

34. **(B)** In the 1857 case *Dred Scott v. Sanford* the Supreme Court held that no black slave could be a citizen of the United States. It was in the 1954 case *Brown v. Topeka Board of Education* that the court held separate facilities for the races to be unconstitutional (A). The reverse (C) was the court's holding in the 1896 case *Plessy v. Ferguson*. Affirmative Action was limited (D) in the 1970s and '80s.

35. **(C)** The Whigs turned on Tyler because he opposed their entire legislative program. He did speak out in favor of Texas annexation (B), but this offense would have been relatively minor in Whig eyes by comparison.

36. **(C)** O'Sullivan spoke of America's "manifest destiny to overspread the continent." The idea that America must eventually become either all slave or all free (D) was expressed by Lincoln in his "House Divided" speech and was called by William H. Seward the "Irrepressible Conflict." Racial equality (A) was still not a popular idea when O'Sullivan wrote in the first half of the nineteenth century. By that time, of course, America was already an independent country (B).

37. **(D)** Mexico did expect to win the war, invade the U.S., and dictate a peace in Washington, but whatever desire, if any, the Mexicans may have had for the state of Louisiana was not a factor in the coming of the war. The U.S. did, however, desire to annex California (A) and did annex Texas (C); Mexico did refuse to pay its debts (B) and did claim Texas (C). All of these contributed to the coming of the war.

38. **(A)** The colony at Jamestown was founded primarily for economic gain. Desire for religious freedom in some form (B) was the motivation of the settlers of Plymouth and some of those who settled Maryland and Pennsylvania. Desire to create a perfect religious commonwealth as an example to the rest of the world (C) was the motive for the Massachusetts Bay colony; and desire to recreate in the New World the sort of feudalistic society that was fading in the Old (D) was probably a motive of some of the colonial proprietors such as those of the Carolinas.

39. **(D)** The Gulf of Tonkin Incident led to major U.S. involvement in the Vietnam War. In the Gulf of Sidra during the 1980s two clashes occurred involving the shooting down of Libyan, not Vietnamese, jets approaching U.S. ships (B). Off the coast of North Korea in 1968, Korean, not Vietnamese, forces seized the U.S. Navy intelligence ship *Pueblo* (C).

40. **(C)** The SALT I Treaty indicated U.S. acceptance of the concept of Mutual Assured Destruction. It was ratified by the U.S. Senate (D) — unlike the SALT II Treaty — but did not bring substantial reductions in the number of missiles on either side (A). It discouraged the deployment of defensive weapons (B).

THE PERIODIC TABLE

METALS — NONMETALS

KEY

Atomic Number →
Atomic Weight → ( ) indicates most stable or best known isotope
Group Classification

| 22 |
| Ti |
| 47.88 |

4
IVA
IVB

↑ Symbol

TRANSITIONAL METALS

Group→	1 IA	2 IIA	3 IIIB	4 IVB	5 VB	6 VIB	7 VIIB	8 VIIIA	9 VIIIA	10 VIIIA	11 IB	12 IIB	13 IIIB / IIIA	14 IVB / IVA	15 VB / VA	16 VIB / VIA	17 VIIB / VIIA	18 VIII / 0
	1 H 1.008																	2 He 4.003
	3 Li 6.941	4 Be 9.012											5 B 10.811	6 C 12.011	7 N 14.007	8 O 15.999	9 F 18.998	10 Ne 20.180
	11 Na 22.990	12 Mg 24.305											13 Al 26.982	14 Si 28.086	15 P 30.974	16 S 32.066	17 Cl 35.453	18 Ar 39.948
	19 K 39.098	20 Ca 40.078	21 Sc 44.956	22 Ti 47.88	23 V 50.942	24 Cr 51.996	25 Mn 54.938	26 Fe 55.847	27 Co 58.933	28 Ni 58.693	29 Cu 63.546	30 Zn 65.39	31 Ga 69.723	32 Ge 72.61	33 As 74.922	34 Se 78.96	35 Br 79.904	36 Kr 83.8
	37 Rb 85.468	38 Sr 87.62	39 Y 88.906	40 Zr 91.224	41 Nb 92.906	42 Mo 95.94	43 Tc (97.907)	44 Ru 101.07	45 Rh 102.906	46 Pd 106.4	47 Ag 107.868	48 Cd 112.411	49 In 114.818	50 Sn 118.710	51 Sb 121.757	52 Te 127.60	53 I 126.905	54 Xe 131.29
	55 Cs 132.905	56 Ba 137.327	57 La 138.906	72 Hf 178.49	73 Ta 180.948	74 W 183.84	75 Re 186.207	76 Os 190.23	77 Ir 192.22	78 Pt 195.08	79 Au 196.967	80 Hg 200.59	81 Tl 204.383	82 Pb 207.2	83 Bi 208.980	84 Po (208.982)	85 At (209.982)	86 Rn (222.018)
	87 Fr (223.020)	88 Ra (226.025)	89 Ac (227.028)	104 Unq (261.11)	105 Unp (262.114)	106 Unh (263.118)	107 Uns (262.12)	108 Uno (265)	109 Une (266)	110 Uun (272)								

Alkali Metals — 1 IA
Alkaline Earth Metals — 2 IIA
Halogens — 17 VIIB/VIIA
Noble Gases — 18 VIII/0

LANTHANIDE SERIES

58 Ce 140.115	59 Pr 140.908	60 Nd 144.24	61 Pm (144.913)	62 Sm 150.36	63 Eu 151.965	64 Gd 157.25	65 Tb 158.925	66 Dy 162.50	67 Ho 164.930	68 Er 167.26	69 Tm 168.934	70 Yb 173.04	71 Lu 174.967

ACTINIDE SERIES

90 Th 232.038	91 Pa 231.036	92 U 238.029	93 Np (237.048)	94 Pu (244.064)	95 Am (243.061)	96 Cm (247.070)	97 Bk (247.070)	98 Cf (251.080)	99 Es (252.083)	100 FM (257.095)	101 Md (258.1)	102 No (259.101)	103 Lr (262.11)

MAXnotes®

REA's Literature Study Guides

MAXnotes® are student-friendly. They offer a fresh look at masterpieces of literature, presented in a lively and interesting fashion. **MAXnotes®** offer the essentials of what you should know about the work, including outlines, explanations and discussions of the plot, character lists, analyses, and historical context. **MAXnotes®** are designed to help you think independently about literary works by raising various issues and thought-provoking ideas and questions. Written by literary experts who currently teach the subject, **MAXnotes®** enhance your understanding and enjoyment of the work.

Available **MAXnotes®** include the following:

Absalom, Absalom!	Henry IV, Part I	Othello
The Aeneid of Virgil	Henry V	Paradise
Animal Farm	The House on Mango Street	Paradise Lost
Antony and Cleopatra	Huckleberry Finn	A Passage to India
As I Lay Dying	I Know Why the Caged	Plato's Republic
As You Like It	Bird Sings	Portrait of a Lady
The Autobiography of	The Iliad	A Portrait of the Artist
Malcolm X	Invisible Man	as a Young Man
The Awakening	Jane Eyre	Pride and Prejudice
Beloved	Jazz	A Raisin in the Sun
Beowulf	The Joy Luck Club	Richard II
Billy Budd	Jude the Obscure	Romeo and Juliet
The Bluest Eye, A Novel	Julius Caesar	The Scarlet Letter
Brave New World	King Lear	Sir Gawain and the
The Canterbury Tales	Leaves of Grass	Green Knight
The Catcher in the Rye	Les Misérables	Slaughterhouse-Five
The Color Purple	Lord of the Flies	Song of Solomon
The Crucible	Macbeth	The Sound and the Fury
Death in Venice	The Merchant of Venice	The Stranger
Death of a Salesman	Metamorphoses of Ovid	Sula
The Divine Comedy I: Inferno	Metamorphosis	The Sun Also Rises
Dubliners	Middlemarch	A Tale of Two Cities
The Edible Woman	A Midsummer Night's Dream	The Taming of the Shrew
Emma	Moby-Dick	Tar Baby
Euripides' Medea & Electra	Moll Flanders	The Tempest
Frankenstein	Mrs. Dalloway	Tess of the D'Urbervilles
Gone with the Wind	Much Ado About Nothing	Their Eyes Were Watching God
The Grapes of Wrath	Mules and Men	Things Fall Apart
Great Expectations	My Antonia	To Kill a Mockingbird
The Great Gatsby	Native Son	To the Lighthouse
Gulliver's Travels	1984	Twelfth Night
Handmaid's Tale	The Odyssey	Uncle Tom's Cabin
Hamlet	Oedipus Trilogy	Waiting for Godot
Hard Times	Of Mice and Men	Wuthering Heights
Heart of Darkness	On the Road	Guide to Literary Terms

RESEARCH & EDUCATION ASSOCIATION
61 Ethel Road W. • Piscataway, New Jersey 08854
Phone: (732) 819-8880

Please send me more information about MAXnotes®.

Name _____

Address _____

City _____ State _____ Zip _____

REA's **Problem Solvers**

The "PROBLEM SOLVERS" are comprehensive supplemental textbooks designed to save time in finding solutions to problems. Each "PROBLEM SOLVER" is the first of its kind ever produced in its field. It is the product of a massive effort to illustrate almost any imaginable problem in exceptional depth, detail, and clarity. Each problem is worked out in detail with a step-by-step solution, and the problems are arranged in order of complexity from elementary to advanced. Each book is fully indexed for locating problems rapidly.

ACCOUNTING
ADVANCED CALCULUS
ALGEBRA & TRIGONOMETRY
AUTOMATIC CONTROL
   SYSTEMS/ROBOTICS
BIOLOGY
BUSINESS, ACCOUNTING, & FINANCE
CALCULUS
CHEMISTRY
COMPLEX VARIABLES
DIFFERENTIAL EQUATIONS
ECONOMICS
ELECTRICAL MACHINES
ELECTRIC CIRCUITS
ELECTROMAGNETICS
ELECTRONIC COMMUNICATIONS
ELECTRONICS
FINITE & DISCRETE MATH
FLUID MECHANICS/DYNAMICS
GENETICS
GEOMETRY
HEAT TRANSFER

LINEAR ALGEBRA
MACHINE DESIGN
MATHEMATICS for ENGINEERS
MECHANICS
NUMERICAL ANALYSIS
OPERATIONS RESEARCH
OPTICS
ORGANIC CHEMISTRY
PHYSICAL CHEMISTRY
PHYSICS
PRE-CALCULUS
PROBABILITY
PSYCHOLOGY
STATISTICS
STRENGTH OF MATERIALS &
   MECHANICS OF SOLIDS
TECHNICAL DESIGN GRAPHICS
THERMODYNAMICS
TOPOLOGY
TRANSPORT PHENOMENA
VECTOR ANALYSIS

If you would like more information about any of these books,
complete the coupon below and return it to us or visit your local bookstore.

REA's Test Preps
The Best in Test Preparation

- REA "Test Preps" are **far more** comprehensive than any other test preparation series
- Each book contains up to **eight** full-length practice exams based on the most recent exams
- **Every** type of question likely to be given on the exams is included
- Answers are accompanied by **full** and **detailed** explanations

REA has published over 60 Test Preparation volumes in several series. They include:

Advanced Placement Exams (APs)
Biology
Calculus AB & Calculus BC
Chemistry
Computer Science
English Language & Composition
English Literature & Composition
European History
Government & Politics
Physics
Psychology
Statistics
Spanish Language
United States History

College-Level Examination Program (CLEP)
Analyzing and Interpreting Literature
College Algebra
Freshman College Composition
General Examinations
General Examinations Review
History of the United States I
Human Growth and Development
Introductory Sociology
Principles of Marketing
Spanish

SAT II: Subject Tests
American History
Biology
Chemistry
English Language Proficiency Test
French
German

SAT II: Subject Tests (continued)
Literature
Mathematics Level IC, IIC
Physics
Spanish
Writing

Graduate Record Exams (GREs)
Biology
Chemistry
Computer Science
Economics
Engineering
General
History
Literature in English
Mathematics
Physics
Political Science
Psychology
Sociology

ACT - ACT Assessment

ASVAB - Armed Services Vocational Aptitude Battery

CBEST - California Basic Educational Skills Test

CDL - Commercial Driver License Exam

CLAST - College Level Academic Skills Test

ELM - Entry Level Mathematics

ExCET - Exam for the Certification of Educators in Texas

FE (EIT) - Fundamentals of Engineering Exam

FE Review - Fundamentals of Engineering Review

GED - High School Equivalency Diploma Exam (U.S. & Canadian editions)

GMAT - Graduate Management Admission Test

LSAT - Law School Admission Test

MAT - Miller Analogies Test

MCAT - Medical College Admission Test

MSAT - Multiple Subjects Assessment for Teachers

NJ HSPT- New Jersey High School Proficiency Test

PPST - Pre-Professional Skills Tests

PRAXIS II/NTE - Core Battery

PSAT - Preliminary Scholastic Assessment Test

SAT I - Reasoning Test

SAT I - Quick Study & Review

TASP - Texas Academic Skills Program

TOEFL - Test of English as a Foreign Language

TOEIC - Test of English for International Communication

REA's Test Prep Books Are The Best!
(a sample of the <u>hundreds of letters</u> REA receives each year)

" I am writing to congratulate you on preparing an exceptional study guide. In five years of teaching this course I have never encountered a more thorough, comprehensive, concise and realistic preparation for this examination. "
Teacher, Davie, FL

" I have found your publications, *The Best Test Preparation...*, to be exactly that. "
Teacher, Aptos, CA

" I used your *CLEP Introductory Sociology* book and rank it 99% — thank you! "
Student, Jerusalem, Israel

" Your GMAT book greatly helped me on the test. Thank you. "
Student, Oxford, OH

" I recently got the French SAT II Exam book from REA. I congratulate you on first-rate French practice tests. "
Instructor, Los Angeles, CA

" Your AP English Literature and Composition book is most impressive. "
Student, Montgomery, AL

" The REA LSAT Test Preparation guide is a winner! "
Instructor, Spartanburg, SC

(more on front page)